Human–Computer Interaction

IFIP – The International Federation for Information Processing

IFIP was founded in 1960 under the auspices of UNESCO, following the First World Computer Congress held in Paris the previous year. An umbrella organization for societies working in information processing, IFIP's aim is two-fold: to support information processing within its member countries and to encourage technology transfer to developing nations. As its mission statement clearly states,

> IFIP's mission is to be the leading, truly international, apolitical organization which encourages and assists in the development, exploitation and application of information technology for the benefit of all people.

IFIP is a non-profitmaking organization, run almost solely by 2500 volunteers. It operates through a number of technical committees, which organize events and publications. IFIP's events range from an international congress to local seminars, but the most important are:

- the IFIP World Computer Congress, held every second year;
- open conferences;
- working conferences.

The flagship event is the IFIP World Computer Congress, at which both invited and contributed papers are presented. Contributed papers are rigorously refereed and the rejection rate is high.

As with the Congress, participation in the open conferences is open to all and papers may be invited or submitted. Again, submitted papers are stringently refereed.

The working conferences are structured differently. They are usually run by a working group and attendance is small and by invitation only. Their purpose is to create an atmosphere conducive to innovation and development. Refereeing is less rigorous and papers are subjected to extensive group discussion.

Publications arising from IFIP events vary. The papers presented at the IFIP World Computer Congress and at open conferences are published as conference proceedings, while the results of the working conferences are often published as collections of selected and edited papers.

Any national society whose primary activity is in information may apply to become a full member of IFIP, although full membership is restricted to one society per country. Full members are entitled to vote at the annual General Assembly, National societies preferring a less committed involvement may apply for associate or corresponding membership. Associate members enjoy the same benefits as full members, but without voting rights. Corresponding members are not represented in IFIP bodies. Affiliated membership is open to non-national societies, and individual and honorary membership schemes are also offered.

Human–Computer Interaction

INTERACT '97

IFIP TC13 International Conference on Human–Computer Interaction, 14th–18th July 1997, Sydney, Australia

Edited by

Steve Howard
Swinburne University of Technology Australia

Judy Hammond
University of Technology, Sydney, Australia

and

Gitte Lindgaard
Gitte Lindgaard & Associates Australia

SPRINGER-SCIENCE+BUSINESS MEDIA, B.V.

First edition 1997

Originally published by Chapman & Hall in 1997
MyCopy version of the original edition 1997

DOI 10.1007/978-0-387-35175-9

A catalogue record for this book is available from the British Library

∞ Printed on permanent acid-free text paper, manufactured in accordance with ANSI/NISO Z39.48-1992 and ANSI/NISO Z39.48-1984 (Permanence of Paper).
www.springer.com/mycopy

CONTENTS

PREFACE

The theme of the 1997 INTERACT conference, 'Discovering New Worlds of HCI', signals major changes that are taking place with the expansion of new technologies into fresh areas of work and leisure throughout the world and new pervasive, powerful systems based on multimedia and the internet. HCI has a vital role to play in these new worlds, to ensure that people using the new technologies are empowered rather than subjugated to the technology that they increasingly have to use. In addition, outcomes from HCI research studies over the past 20 years are now finding their way into many organisations and helping to improve and enhance work practices. These factors have strongly influenced the INTERACT'97 Committee when creating the conference programme, with the result that, besides the more traditional HCI research and education focus found in previous INTERACT conferences, one strand of the 1997 conference has been devoted to industry and another to multimedia.

The growth in the IFIP TC13 committee itself reflects the expansion of HCI into new worlds. Membership of IFIP TC13 has risen to now include representatives of 24 IFIP member country societies from many parts of the world. In 1997, IFIP TC13 breaks new ground by holding its sixth INTERACT conference in the Asia-Pacific region. This is a significant departure from previous INTERACT conferences, that were all held in Europe, and is especially important for the Asia-Pacific region, as HCI expands beyond its traditional base.

In addition, IFIP TC13 is very pleased to welcome two HCI conferences, CHISIG and APCHI, held annually in the Asia-Pacific region, that have agreed to be incorporated into INTERACT'97.

OZCHI is the highly successful Australian annual conference of CHISIG (Computer Human Interaction Special Interest Group of the Ergonomics Society of Australia). This conference started in 1987 with 40 participants, created its unique conference name (OZCHI) in 1991 to reflect its Australian origins, and has become an internationally recognised conference drawing an audience of up to 200 participants each year. This year, CHISIG (Australia) celebrates its tenth annual conference by participating in INTERACT'97.

The APCHI conference is also incorporated into INTERACT'97. The first Asia-Pacific HCI conference was held last year in Singapore and attracted participants from many countries. This conference made its mark on the international community with a significant contribution to the cross-cultural HCI debate. With the globalisation of communication and the increase in interactions occurring in cyberspace, this discussion is expected to continue. IFIP TC13 co-sponsored the first APCHI conference and continues this support through its inclusion of APCHI into INTERACT'97 and its co-sponsorship of the 1998 APCHI conference to be held in Japan.

I wish to take this opportunity to formally record the thanks of IFIP TC13 to the Australian Computer Society for their invitation to host INTERACT'97. The ACS has provided the conference with a firm foundation for planning and organising this important event. Their

Human–Computer Interaction: INTERACT'97 S. Howard, J. Hammond & G. Lindgaard (editors)
Published by Chapman & Hall ©IFIP 1997

foresight and significant role in helping to disseminate knowledge about HCI in this region of the world is warmly acknowledged.

In addition, IFIP TC13 acknowledges and thanks the corporate sponsors who have so generously supported INTERACT'97 in tangible ways to enhance the organisation and facilities of the conference. Our thanks also go to the many professional societies from around the world that have aligned with INTERACT'97 and given encouragement and support to the work of IFIP TC13 by becoming INTERACT'97 Co-operating Societies. The active support of these groups is evidence of the importance of INTERACT in the international conference community.

A very special and warm thanks goes to CHISIG. Many of our committee members are members of CHISIG. Without the support of CHISIG and the energy, knowledge and hard work of its members, this conference would not have been possible.

The organisation of INTERACT'97 has been made possible by conducting much of the committee work electronically. With the International Conference Committee living in Europe, and Australian committee members residing in Melbourne, Canberra and New Zealand (Technical Committee), Sydney and Wollongong (Organising Committee) and Canberra (Professional Conference Organiser), email and list server facilities have been invaluable. Much has been discovered in the course of this new world of work, and clearly much still needs to be done to make this world a better, more efficient and effective way for humans to work together on shared tasks.

IFIP TC13 is deeply appreciative of all the efforts made by the members of the Australian Steering Committee, the Technical Committee and the Organising Committee and our Professional Conference Officers at the Australian Convention and Travel Services, who have worked so hard for so long on all aspects of planning and managing INTERACT'97, the largest HCI conference ever mounted in Australia.

We also thank the members of the International Conference Committee who have provided us with their vast knowledge of previous INTERACT conference organisation and have helped to ensure that Australia has carried on in a similar mode.

Emeritus Professor Brian Shackel, immediate past-Chairman of IFIP TC13 and a key person in the creation and conduct of the INTERACT series of conferences, deserves special mention for the critical role he has played as INTERACT'97 advisor. He has been a constant and tireless source of support and advice to the INTERACT'97 committees about all aspects of organisation. We are very much indebted to him for the inspiration and guidance he has given us while creating this conference.

Finally, all the authors who have given presentations at the Conference and who are included in this book of Proceedings deserve special thanks, as without their scientific work and writing there would be no sharing of information and advances in HCI knowledge. We are most grateful for the comments and advice of our International Programme Committee and the Additional Reviewers Panel, who worked hard to complete their reviews of full text submissions in the short time required, and so helped to ensure a high standard for the INTERACT'97 conference programme and this book.

Judy Hammond,
IFIP TC13 Chair and INTERACT'97 Conference Chair
University of Technology, Sydney
Australia

EDITORS' NOTE

Welcome to INTERACT'97, and to this volume containing the Proceedings of the conference.

INTERACT's theme this year, 'Discovering New Worlds of HCI', invites us to step outside the worlds we inhabit on a day to day basis and explore, appreciate and learn from the new worlds to be found in the INTERACT'97 event.

So, what new worlds are there to discover? We hope you will find three new worlds: the 'what-world', the 'who-world' and the 'where-world'.

The 'what-world' is inhabited by new ideas, new concerns, new ways of working and new sensibilities for how humans and technology interact. This volume contains reports on the very latest research and practice in relatively new areas of HCI, such as world-wide web, designing and evaluating multimedia systems, sound and speech based interfaces, accessing and browsing video databases, and groupware, as well as in more established and ongoing concerns, including cognitive modelling, usability case studies, graphical user interfaces, visual interfaces, evaluation, and task and interaction modelling.

The 'who-world' is inhabited by the presenters and delegates attending the INTERACT'97 event. We hope that you will meet old friends and acquaintances, build new relationships, learn about the concerns and values of others and extend and strengthen the INTERACT network.

The 'where-world' is inhabited by communities, possibly quite different from those with whom we normally interact; for example, different disciplinary communities, communities from different countries and cultures, even, dare we say, Australasians! INTERACT'97 can truly claim to be an international conference with presentations published in this volume coming from every inhabited continent on earth - Africa, the Americas, Asia, Australia and Europe. Many distinct disciplinary communities involved in research and practice are also represented, including multimedia, computer-supported cooperative work, design, psychology and computing.

By partaking in these new worlds, we hope that delegates attending INTERACT'97, and readers of this volume, will find something germane to their interests and inspiring for their future work.

The proceedings contain submissions that were accepted for presentation at INTERACT'97 following an open call for participation. Full submissions were blind reviewed by at least three referees drawn from an extensive International Programme Committee of 73 HCI experts and a large additional reviewing panel. The final conference technical programme, as represented in this volume, was selected on the basis of submission quality and programme balance.

The proceedings are structured to mirror the structure of the INTERACT'97 conference. In this volume, you will find addresses from our keynote and invited speakers and the full technical programme of scientific papers, including the highly interactive sessions (posters, panels), the visual sessions (videos), and sessions with a special focus (organisational and laboratory overviews, new technologies), as well the pre-conference sessions (tutorials, workshops) and the doctoral consortium.

Human–Computer Interaction: INTERACT'97 S. Howard, J. Hammond & G. Lindgaard (editors)
Published by Chapman & Hall

We hope that you find these proceedings to be a useful conference companion and a permanent record of the INTERACT'97 event, and that, together with the conference itself, they help you in discovering new ideas, new people, new communities- in 'Discovering New Worlds of HCI'.

Steve Howard,
Swinburne CHI Laboratory,
Swinburne University of Technology,
Australia

Judy Hammond,
School of Computing Sciences,
University of Technology,
Sydney,
Australia

Gitte Lindgaard,
Gitte Lindgaard & Associates,
Australia.

IFIP TC13

Since its inception as an International Federation for Information Processing Technical Committee on Human-Computer Interaction (IFIP TC13) in 1989, IFIP TC13's membership has grown to include representatives from 24 member national societies and has created four Working Groups.

IFIP TC13's principal aim is to encourage development towards a science and a technology of human-computer interaction. It is mainly oriented toward the users, especially the non-computer-professional users, and how to improve the human-computer relationship between them. Areas of study include: the problems people have with computers; the impact of computers on people in individual and organisational contexts; the determinants of utility, usability and acceptabilit; the appropriate allocation of tasks between computers and users; modelling the user as an aid to better system design; and harmonising the computer to the characteristics and needs of users.

While the scope is thus set wide, with a tendency towards general principles rather than particular systems, it is recognised that progress will only be achieved through both general studies to advance theoretical understanding and specific studies on practical issues (e.g. interface design standards, software system consistency, documentation, appropriateness of alternative communication media, human factors guidelines for dialogue design, the problems of integrating multi-media systems to match user needs and organisational practices, etc.)

IFIP TC13 organises conferences, publications and other activites itself, and also by stimulating and supervising smaller meetings and many other activities via its Working Groups. During the 1990s, the four Working Groups of IFIP TC13 have been active in expanding knowledge in particular areas. These are outlined below:

WG13.1 Education in HCI and HCI Curriculum aims to improve HCI education at all levels of higher education, coordinate and unite efforts to develop HCI curricula and to promote the teaching of HCI;
WG13.2 Methodology for User-Centred System Design aims to foster research, dissemination of information and good practice in the methodical application of HCI to software engineering;
WG13.3 HCI and People with Special Needs aims to make HCI designers aware of the special needs of disabled and elderly people, to recommend guidelines for the design of HCI to facilitate the use of computers by disabled people, and to encourage the development of systems equipped with hardware and software tools that permit the adaptation of the human interface to each specific user; and
WG2.7(13.4) User Interface Engineering aims to investigate the nature, concepts and construction of user interfaces for software systems.

Human–Computer Interaction: INTERACT'97 S. Howard, J. Hammond & G. Lindgaard (editors)
Published by Chapman & Hall

IFIP TC13 Members

Australia
Judy Hammond (IFIP TC13 Chair)
Australian Computer Society

Austria
Michael Tauber
Austrian Computer Society

Belgium
Monique Noirhomme-Fraiture
Federation des Associations Informatiques de Belgique Institut d'Informatique

Canada
Mary Frances Laughton
Canadian Information Processing Society

Chile
Jose A. Pino
Centro Latinoamericano de Estudios Informatica

China
Ming Lu
Chinese Institute of Electronics

Czech Republic
Vaclav Matousek
Czech Society for Cybernetics & Informatics

Denmark
Leif Loevborg
Danish Federation for Information Processing

Finland
Pekka Lehtio
Finnish Information Processing Association

France
Gerard Ligozat
Association Francaise des Sciences et Technologies de l'Information et des Systemes

Germany
Peter Gorny
Gesellschaft fur Informatik

Greece
John Darzentas
Greek Computer Society

India
P. K. Patwardhan
Computer Society of India

Italy
Fabio Paterno
Associazione Italiana per l'Informatica ed il Calcolo Automatico

Japan
Hisao Yamada
Information Processing Society of Japan

Netherlands
Gerrit van der Veer
Nederlands Genootschap voor Informatica

Norway
Svein A. Arnesen
Norwegian Computer Society

Portugal
Mario Rui Gome
Associacao Portuguesa de Informatica

Singapore
Liang Moung
Singapore Computer Society

Spain
Julio Gonzalez-Abascal
Federacion Espanola de Sociedades de Informatica

Sweden
Lars Oestreicher
Swedish International Federation for Information Processing

Switzerland
Matthias Rauterberg
Swiss Federation for Information Processing

U.K.
Brian Shackel
British Computer Society

U.S.A.
John Karat
Federation on Computing U.S. (FoCUS)

Affiliate Member
Andrew J. Westlake
International Association for Statistical Computing

Working Group Chairmen

WG 13.1 Peter Gorny
WG 13.2 Alistair Sutcliffe
WG 13.3 Julio Gonzalez-Abascal
WG 2.7(13.4) Len Bass

CO-OPERATING SOCIETIES

All IFIP Member Societies
Association Francaise des Sciences et Technologies de L'Information et des Systemes (AFCET)
Association for Artificial Intelligence of Russia (RAAI)
Australian Society for Computers in Learning in Tertiary Education (ASCILITE)
Australian Society for Technical Communications (NSW) (ASTC)
Australian Society of Educational Technology (ASET)
Australian Telecommunications User Group (ATUG)
British HCI Group (B-HCI-G,BCS)
Committee for Human Interface, The Society of Instrument and Control Engineers (SICE)
CHISIG, New Zealand
Ergonomics Society of Australia (ESA)
European Association of Cognitive Ergonomics (EACE)
Gesellschaft fuer Informatik, Fachgruppe Software-Ergonomie (GI)
HCI Special Interest Group of the Ergonomics Society of Australia, CHISIG
Institute of Chartered Accountants (IT Chapter)
International Association for Statistical Computing (IASC)
Schweitzer Informatiker Gesellschaft (SI)
Slovak Society for Cybernetics and Informatiks
Sociedad Chilena de Ciencia de Computacion (Chile)
Software Psychology Society, (Potomac Chapter)
Swedish Interdisciplinary Interest Group for Human-Computer Interaction (STIMDI)
Werkgroep Mens-Computer Interactie (MCI)

International Programme Committee

Additional Reviewers Panel

Abdul Hanan Abdullah, Malaysia
Austin Adams, Australia
Ghassan Al-Qaimari, Australia
Sandrine Balbo, Australia
Elizabeth Bednall, Australia
David Benyon, UK
Sarah Bloomer, Australia
Dan Boyarski, USA
Rachel Croft, Australia
Richard Davis, Australia
Dan Diaper, UK
Lone Dirckinck-Holmfeld, Denmark
Susan Dray, USA
Susan Dumas, USA
Jonathon Earthy, UK
John Fabre, Australia
Geraldine Fitzpatrick, Australia
Jim Foley, USA
John Grundy, New Zealand
Karen Gunn, Australia
Susan Harker, UK
Morten Harning, Denmark
Michael Harrison, UK
Helen Hasan, Australia
Ron Henderson, Australia
David Hill, Canada
Troy Innocent, Australia
Robert Jacob, USA
Lorraine Johnson, Australia
Steve Jones, New Zealand
Claire-Marie Karat, USA
Wendy Kellogg, USA Cliff McKnight, UK
Fiona Meighan, Australia
Naomi Miyake, Japan
Helen Kieboom, Australia
Andrew Monk, UK
Jane Mosier, USA
Kon Mouzakis, Australia
Dianne Murray, UK
Laurence Nigay, France
Brad Noakes, Australia
James Noble, Australia
Gary Olson, USA
Nadine Ozkan, Australia
Robert Pedlow, Australia
Robin Penner, USA
Chris Pilgrim, Australia
Greg Ralph, Australia
Penny Roberts, Australia
Toni Robertson, Australia
Mary Beth Rosson, USA
Angela Sasse, UK
Dominque Scapin, France
Andrew Sears, USA
Kirsty Spence, Australia
Robert Spence, UK
Tom Stewart, UK
Gerd Szwillus, Germany
John Tang, USA
John Thomas, UK
Mark Utting, New Zealand
Frank Vetere, Australia
Michael Wagner, Australia
Huaiquing Wang, Hong Kong
Jim Winkles, Australia
Terry Winograd, USA
William Wong, New Zealand
Larry Wood, UK

INTERACT'97 Committees

International Conference Committee

Conference Chair

Judy Hammond
University of Technology, Sydney
Australia

INTERACT Conference Advisor

Brian Shackel
HUSAT Research Institute
United Kingdom

Committee Members

David Gilmore
University of Nottingham
United Kingdom

Gerrit van der Veer
Vrije Universiteit & University of Twente
The Netherlands

Alistair Kilgour (INTERACT'99 Chair)
Herriott-Watt University
United Kingdom

National Steering Committee

Chair and International Liaison
Judy Hammond
University of Technology, Sydney

Treasurer
Steve Gillett
Ernst & Young

Industry Liaison
Sarah Bloomer
The Hiser Group

Conference Advisor
Roger Hall
University of New South Wales

Mark Apperley
University of Waikato, NZ

Steve Howard
Swinburne University of Technology

Clark Quinn
University of New South Wales

Professional Conference Organiser

Australian Convention and Travel Services Pty Ltd
Canberra, Australia

Technical Programme

Chair
Steve Howard
Swinburne University of Technology

Doctoral Consortium
Mark Apperley
University of Waikato

New Technologies
Kon Mouzakis
Swinburne University of Technology

Organisation and Laboratory Overviews
Fiona Meighan
Telstra Research Laboratories

Panels
Lorraine Johnson
University of Melbourne

Papers
Steve Howard and Ying Leung
Swinburne University of Technology

Tutorials
Gitte Lindgaard
Gitte Lindgaard & Associates

Videos
Chris Pilgrim
Swinburne University of Technology
Simon Oldfield
AMRL

Interactive Experience
Troy Innocent
The Hiser Group

Workshops
Penny Collings and Terry Webb,
University of Canberra *DSTO*

Organising Committee

Co-Chairs
Clark Quinn
University of New South Wales
and
Judy Hammond
University of Technology, Sydney

Treasurer
Steve Gillett
Ernst & Young

Electronic Communications
Sandrine Balbo and Ken Yap
CSIRO-MIS

Exhibition
Michael Bromham
The Hiser Group

Local Arrangements
Dana Anspal
Equity Systems

Publicity
Donald Day
University of New South Wales

Social Arrangements
Toni Robertson
University of New South Wales

Sponsorship
Sarah Bloomer
The Hiser Group

Student Volunteers,
Environmental Impact
Judy Kay,
University of Sydney

Venue Arrangements
Austin Adams and Roger Hall
University of New South Wales

Website Design
Helen Hasan
University of Wollongong

PART ONE

Keynote and Invited Speakers

1

From Interactions to Integrations

Lucy A. Suchman

Xerox Palo Alto Research Center
3333 Coyote Hill Road
Palo Alto, CA 94304
U.S.A.
suchman@parc.xerox.com

ABSTRACT This address offers a reflection on the aptness of the metaphor of interactive technologies, in light of developments over the past ten years. It argues for a shift from the focus on interaction narrowly defined, to a project of integration of artifacts into work environments and working practices.

KEYWORDS interaction, work practice, integration

1. SUMMARY

The growth of the Internet has brought with it a renewed interest in the idea of artificial "agents," "knowbots," and other computational artifacts attributed with a capacity for intelligent, interactive behavior. In "Plans and Situated Actions: The problem of human-machine communication" (1987) I proposed that the term "interaction" might best be reserved to describe what goes on between persons, rather than extended to encompass relations between people and machines. My argument was based on the observation that human interaction relies on interpretive resources not available to machines. The difference is one of an embodied user, on the one hand, present in specific, historically and culturally mediated circumstances of action, and what remains effectively an artifact, however dynamic its presentation. The language of interactivity and dynamics of computational machinery obscure this difference, but the user of the machine invariably rediscovers it in practice.

In this address I will re-examine this argument in light of reflections on the past ten years of developments in computing and HCI. I will suggest that while interesting developments have unquestionnably emerged during that time in terms of what Bruno Latour and others have characterized as non-human agency, critical issues remain. These issues have to do with the fundamental character of the problem of mutual intelligibility of action between people and machines, and the reliance of mutual intelligibility on participation in a social world not reducible to discrete abilities and skills.

The intractability of the problem of mutual intelligibility recommends a new research agenda for system design, aimed less at the creation of interactive machines than at an understanding of the distinctive dynamics of working with computational artifacts. Those dynamics, moreover, extend beyond the interface narrowly defined to the relations of people with each other and to the place of computing in their ongoing activities. The future of information systems, on this view, lies neither in the single, all encompassing workstation nor the universal, seamless web, but in an ecology of always partial information resources, assembled together through the skilled activities of their use. System design, it follows, must include not only the design of innovative artifacts, but their artful integration with the rest of the social and material world.

Human–Computer Interaction: INTERACT'97 S. Howard, J. Hammond & G. Lindgaard (editors)
Published by Chapman & Hall

2

The Mind As A Reliable Switch: Challenges Of Rapidly Controlling Devices Without Prior Learning

Ashley Craig,* Les Kirkup ** Paul McIsaac * and Andrew Searle **

*Department of Health Sciences, ** Department of Applied Physics
Faculty of Science, University of Technology, Sydney
a.craig@uts.edu.au; kirkup@phys.uts.edu.au; asearle@phys.uts.edu.au

ABSTRACT Activity within the brain causes electrical potentials to exist on the scalp. The study of these potentials is generally referred to as electroencephalography (EEG). EEG is widely used in medical diagnosis and in biofeedback studies in which a person can learn to control some element of their EEG spectrum, usually in response to some visual stimulus. This paper reports the control of the alpha component of the EEG spectrum which does not require the learning that biofeedback demands. We show that participants can achieve rapid and reliable remote control of electrical devices using increase in alpha wave activity associated with reduced visual input. The physiological basis, technical achievements and challenges, and applications will be discussed.

KEYWORDS Alpha wave, switch, electroencephalograph, environmental control, noise suppression

1. INTRODUCTION

Controlling the environment with our mind has always been a wish of humankind. Early attempts to achieve this using thoughts or 'willpower' alone has been called telekinesis. Though telekinesis is being investigated scientifically (McCrone, 1994), the raw electrical signal in the brain is just too small to have any direct influence over objects external to the brain. Nonetheless, 'mind control' remains a possibility for controlling electrical devices because neural activity is associated with signals called electroencephalograph waves (EEG; Fisch, 1991). 'Biofeedback' has been used to control electrical devices by providing visual or auditory feedback of the EEG signal to the person. The goal of EEG biofeedback would be to enhance the conscious manipulation of the EEG spectrum, such as increasing or decreasing alpha levels (which is in the frequency range of 8 to 12 Hz). For instance, using EEG signal feedback, people have been able to control a cursor on a computer screen, transmit Morse code messages, start a robot or model electric train by raising their alpha levels, or stop it by decreasing levels (Bozinovski, Sestakov & Bozinovska, 1988). People have also been able to communicate by varying their high and low EEG frequencies (Elder, Lashley, Kedouri, Regenbogen, Martyn, Roundtree, & Grenier, 1986). Unfortunately, biofeedback has slow response times and usually takes at least 8-12 hours to learn control over their physiological responses (Craig & Cleary, 1982). In the experience of the authors, few people have the ability to consistently and quickly control their EEG (alpha) levels, especially when stressed. These problems limit the usefulness of biofeedback in reliably controlling devices like a computer or lamp.

An alternative strategy for 'mind control' involves using increases in alpha EEG wave activity amplitude levels (synchronisation) associated with a reduction in visual input (eyes closed), and alpha level decreases

Human–Computer Interaction: INTERACT'97 S. Howard, J. Hammond & G. Lindgaard (editors)

(desynchronisation) associated with an increase in visual input (eyes opened). This paper reports work that builds upon the research of Dewan (1967) who published 30 years ago on environmental control and the conscious control of alpha levels using this strategy. Scientists in the Faculty of Science of the University of Technology, Sydney have recently made an advance in this area following detailed investigation of the response of 31 subjects' EEG to various stimuli. They observed that all subjects were producing reproducible and consistent EEG signal responses in the alpha range (8 to 11.5 Hz) linked with closure of eyes. This was unexpected as there are few reports of EEG being predicted or manipulated consistently and reliably. This led the scientists to believe that intentional and reliable control over the environment is a possibility. As an consequence of this research, technology has been developed which allows electrical devices or appliances to be immediately and remotely operated by a person through the conscious control of specific signals generated by the brain. With further research and development, a person will have a sophisticated environmental control device. It was labelled "the ultimate interface between man and machine" (Australian Financial Review, 1996).

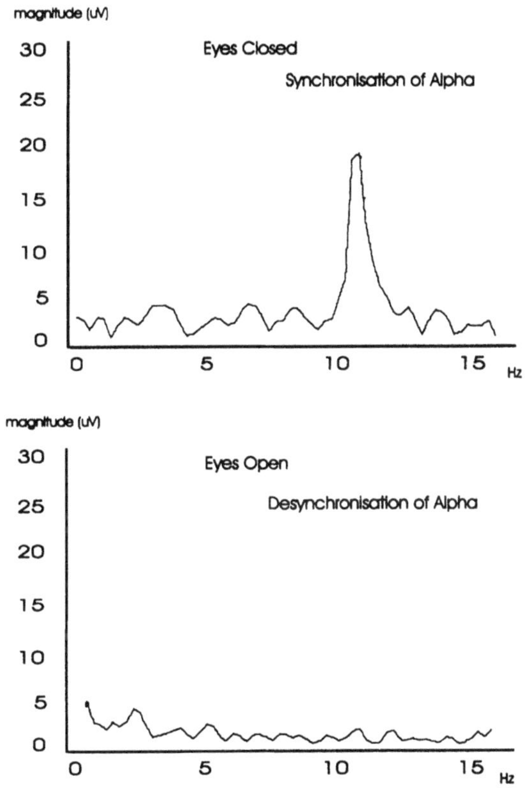

Figure 1 Showing spectral analyses of right hemisphere EEG up to 16 Hz from the visual cortex. Synchronisation and desynchronisation of alpha associated with reduced visual input (eyes closed) and increased visual input (eyes open) respectively is shown at 10.5 Hz for a subject assessed in our laboratories. The difference in alpha amplitude at 10.5 Hz between eyes closed and eyes open is the basis for the conscious control of devices.

The aim of this paper is to present the physiological background for the nature of the EEG phenomenon harnessed by the technology, to discuss the technical achievements and challenges, and to conclude with a brief description of possible applications.

2. PHYSIOLOGICAL BACKGROUND OF ALPHA EEG ACTIVITY

The physiological importance of the alpha EEG wave remains unknown (Shaw, 1992). While the alpha wave occurs all over the cortex, it is believed to be prominent in the posterior (visual or occipital cortex) and central/ parietal regions. It is also known that attentiveness, concentration, anxiety and visual fixation reduce the amplitude of alpha levels (called desynchronisation) (Mulholland, 1995). Alpha levels are increased (or synchronised) when one reduces visual input by closing the eyes, rolls the eyes upwards or when one relaxes (Craig, McIsaac, Kirkup, Searle & Moses, in press; Mulholland & Evans, 1966). It is

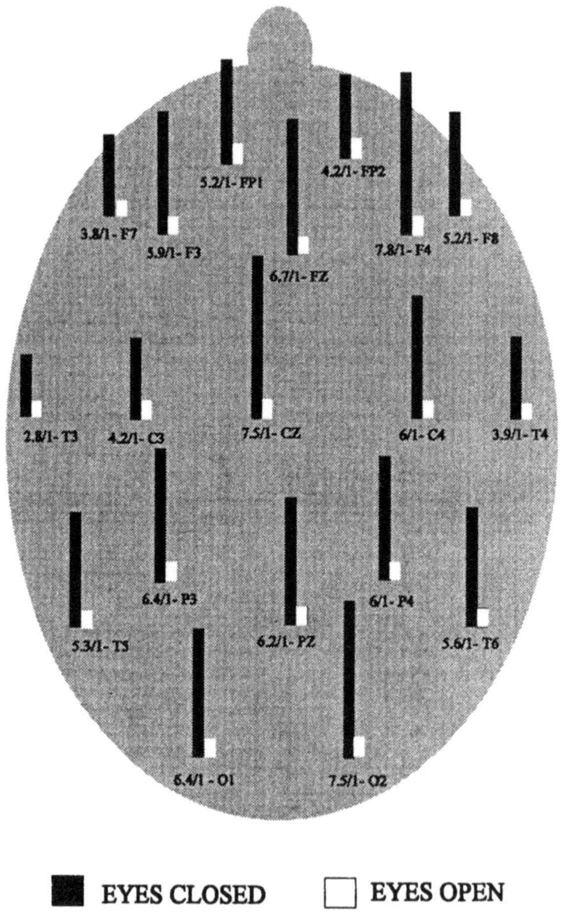

Figure 2 shows the ratio of alpha increases contingent with eye closure with alpha levels when eyes are open, for all the cortex (average responses for 21 participants).

possible that the alpha level increases seen during reduced visual input is a function of decreased activity in oculomotor control systems in the brain. With reduced visual input, scanning and visual attention decrease. Alpha wave amplitude reduction is associated with opening the eyes, increasing visual scanning activity and attentiveness and this is most likely the result of increased cortical oculomotor activity. Alpha levels decrease when cortical activation increases. In central cortical sites, alpha wave levels may also be decreased during high levels of mental attention and non-occipital alpha rhythm, called mu alpha (seen in central areas), is also decreased by cortical activation associated with the muscle movement (Mulholland, 1995).

The synchronisation of the alpha rhythm has been studied extensively in our laboratories in a number of male and female subjects of varied ages from children to older age persons (Craig et al., in press). A typical alpha wave synchronisation response is illustrated in Figure 1 which shows the alpha wave magnitude when eyes are closed for one participant. This response was recorded from the occipital cortex (right hemisphere) at 10.5 Hz. The sharp increase in alpha wave magnitude contingent with eye closure seen in this person generally occurs all over the cortex, and this increase, (calculated from "eyes open" alpha levels), is usually of the order of a 300 to 1000% increase. Substantial increases in alpha resulted contingent with eye closure and this occurred all over the cortex. Alpha wave level increases associated with eye closure were shown to be greatest in occipital (O_1, O_2), central (C_3, C_4, C_z), parietal (P_z, P_3, P_4), and frontal areas (F_z, F_3, F_4). Figure 2 further illustrates alpha level increases all over the cortex in contrast to alpha levels when eyes are open. The majority of subjects assessed in our laboratory show alpha synchronisation contingent with eye closure in the 9.5 to 11 Hertz range while a minority show eye closure alpha synchronisation in the 8.5 to 9.5 Hertz region.

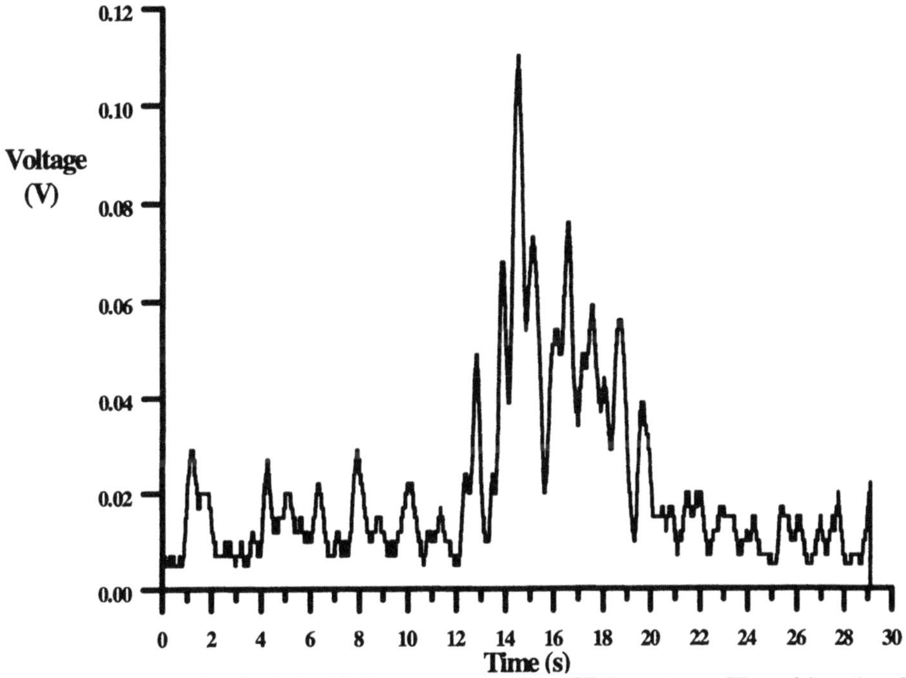

Figure 3 Variation in the amplitude of the 10 Hz component of the EEG spectrum. The subject closed his eyes at t = 12 s

There were no differences between the right and left hemispheres in synchronisation of alpha, nor were there any significant differences in the size of the alpha increases associated with eye closure in any of the cortical sites between males and females, or age within the age range for the subjects. Handedness was also not significantly related to alpha eye closure responses.

3. TECHNOLOGY DEVELOPMENT

For many individuals, the ratio of the (average) amplitude of the alpha component of the EEG spectrum between eye closed to eyes open is about 2 to 3 s (Craig et al. in press). Such a significant increase in this component upon eye closure facilitates the development of a system designed to detect and utilise the change.

Essential elements of the system are signal amplification, filtering and smoothing. The 'raw' EEG signal at ≈ 10 Hz is typically in the range 10 to 50 μV. Therefore in order to allow other operations to be reliably performed on the signal, such as comparison with a d.c reference, it is convenient to apply a gain to the signal of around 100 dB. A bandpass filter with centre frequency at 10 Hz and bandwidth of 2 Hz adequately spans the frequencies at which most subjects show a significant increase between eyes open and eyes closed.

Figure 3 shows the variation in the amplitude of the EEG signal over a period of 30 s. At t = 12 s the subject closed his eyes. At this point in time a marked increase in the signal amplitude can clearly be seen. However, due to this signal's large variation, any switching system based on this amplitude variation is likely to suffer from intermittent switching. In order to largely eliminate spurious switching, a simple averager with a time constant of about 2 s is applied to the amplified and filtered. signal.

Figure 4 shows the smoothed output of the signal averager. The smoothed signal can now be used as an input to a signal comparator which switches the state of the device (such as a lamp) once the EEG signal has exceeded some predetermined value. Further details of the system can be found elsewhere (Kirkup, Searle, Craig, McIsaac and Moses, in press). An attractive feature of the system is that it has a single adjustable parameter: the threshold voltage at which switching

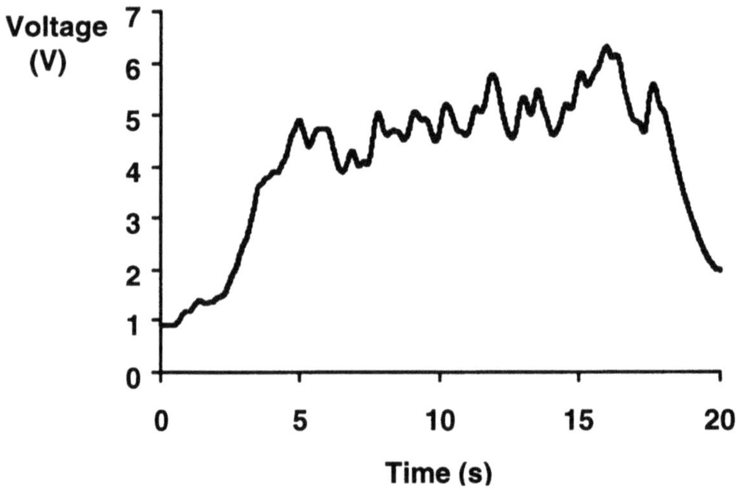

Figure 4 The smoothed output of the system. The subject closed his eyes at t = 2s. Between approximately 3 s and 5 s the voltage increases approximately proportionally with time.

occurs. It has been noted in a longitudinal study of one subject over 24 months that, once set, the threshold setting requires no further adjustment. The average time for switching after eye closure is around 2 to 3 s for the subjects tested. Figure 4 shows that the voltage increase after eye closure is approximately proportional with time, suggesting that proportional control or multilevel switching is possible. Indeed the basic system has been developed to the stage where two level switching has been demonstrated. By setting two switching levels, an alpha signal can control a toy slot car. The car may be started, stopped and its speed toggled high and low through control of the amplitude of the smoothed EEG signal. The time delay between eye closure and detection of the increase in the alpha signal is a matter of great importance as it affects the number of switching operations that may be performed in a given time. It is not known at this time whether repeated attempts to switch devices on and off results in a decrease in the mean switching time, though early indications do suggest a marginal decrease in the mean time with habituation. We are currently evaluating a number of other methods of detecting the change in the alpha signal level which may yield mean switching time between 1 and 2 s. Our studies show that the occurrence of the alpha change can differ significantly from person to person. Specifically, upon eye closure, some subject show 'bursts' of alpha which are sustained so long as the eyes remain closed, while others burst momentarily upon eye closure only to relax to the 'eyes open' level before bursting again. It seems likely that different methods of alpha detection will suit those who exhibit continuous or intermittent alpha enhancement.

4. TECHNOLOGICAL CHALLENGES

A major issue to be addressed is that of spurious switching which is not related to the natural variation in the alpha signal that exists with eyes open or closed, but is due to the large excursions in signal amplitude caused by other sources of electrical activity at 10 Hz. An example of such a source is due to head movement (e.g. nodding or rotation) which generates electrical signals due to muscle activity (often referred to as EMG). EMG generally has a wide frequency spectrum ranging from close to d.c. to beyond 100 Hz. Though much of the energy in the EMG spectrum lies beyond 15 Hz (Sadasivan and Dutt, 1995), enough normally exists at 10 Hz to swamp the true EEG signal. If a system, for example, is to be built that will be used to assist severely physically disabled, it is of paramount importance to address the issue of electrical noise. We have devised a simple method which relies on the fact that EMG signals have a recognisable electrical 'signature' (Kirkup et al. 1997). When the EMG sources are active this signature is detected and the output of the system is 'frozen' so that no spurious switching can occur. The system becomes 'live' again once the noise component has relaxed below some predetermined threshold. This approach has the attraction of simplicity and real time signal processing, but the disadvantage that the system is insensitive to real changes in EEG signal while the system is frozen. We are currently developing other methods of reducing the effect of noise signals which does not cause the output of the system to be disabled.

Perhaps more challenging than the suppression of noise is the issue of electrode design. Conventional electrodes are generally constructed from silver/silver chloride and require the use of conducting paste or gel in order to assure that good, low impedance electrical contact is established and maintained between electrode and scalp. In many clinical applications of EEG the scalp must be prepared by scraping with a blunt needle or similar in order that the impedance is 2 kΩ or less (Fisch, 1991). Though the requirements of our system are less exacting (impedance of less than 20 kΩ is quite adequate), the challenge of providing good electrical contact remains. 'Wet' electrodes using conducting gel dry out over time and in doing so tend to impair the quality of the electrical contact. Additionally, wet electrodes are not viewed favourably by users. We are pursuing the possibility of creating dry electrodes in which EEG signals are coupled capacitively between scalp and electrode (Taheri, Knight and Smith, 1994). These offer the advantages of no skin preparation nor the use of conducting gel, but introduce their own problems such as very high electrode impedances which are susceptible to electromagnetic interference. We believe that significant improvements in electrode design are demanded if this technology is to enjoy widespread application.

5. APPLICATIONS

There are many possible applications of environmental control using brain signals. For instance, disabled people who have limited control of devices with their arms and hands, would benefit greatly if they could remotely and quickly control a range of devices using their brain. Switches already exist that allow some control, for example, eye blinking and infra-red signals and breath activated switches. Voice activated systems especially offer a promising environmental control system. However, this strategy would not be useful for persons with voice disorders. There are significant problems when the voice is altered due to say the common cold. Additionally, the technology requires extensive training and it could not be used easily in a noisy environment. The issue is one of providing a range of switches that can be utilised by people who are disabled. Controlling the environment with alpha synchronisation provides another potentially versatile strategy for enhancing environmental control for those with disabilities such as spinal chord injury and cerebral palsy. The alpha wave switch would obviously require the person using the switch, to have a significant alpha synchronisation and to be able to close their eyes on demand.

Possible further applications are:

(a) basis of an environmental control system in the house of the future, or possibly for environmental control in space.
(b) hands free industrial applications.
(c) computing and multimedia purposes,
(d) communication purposes,
(e) recreational pastimes, such as interactive computer games

6. ACKNOWLEDGMENT

The authors would like to acknowledge the part funding of this work by the Motor Accident Authority of New South Wales, Australia

REFERENCES

Bozinovski, S., Sestakov, M., & Bozinovska, L. (1988). Using EEG alpha rhythm to control a mobile robot. *IEEE Engineering in Medicine & Biology Society, 10th Annual International Conference,* 1515 CH2566.

Craig, A. R., & Cleary, P. J. (1982). Reduction of stuttering by young male stutterers using EMG feedback. *Biofeedback and Self-Regulation* 7, 241-255.

Craig, A., McIsaac, P., Kirkup, L., Searle, A., & Moses, P. (in press). Brain signals and control of electrical devices. *Today's Life Science.*

Dewan, E. M. (1967). Occipital alpha rhythm eye position and lens accommodation. *Nature,* 214, 975-977.

Elder, S. T., Lashley, J. K., Kedouri, N., Regenbogen, D., Martyn, S., Roundtree, G. & Grenier, C. (1986). Can subjects be trained to communicate through the use of EEG biofeedback? *Clinical Biofeedback and Health,* 9, 42-47.

Fisch, B. (1991). *Spehlmann's EEG primer (2nd Ed).* Amsterdam: Elsevier.

Kirkup, L., Searle, A., Craig, A., McIsaac, P. & Moses, P. (in press). EEG based system for rapid on-off switching without prior learning. *Medical and Biological Engineering and Computing.*

McCrone, J. (1994) Psychic powers. What are the odds? *New Scientist, November 34-38.*

Mulholland, T. (1995). Human EEG, behavioral stillness and biofeedback. *International Journal of Psychophysiology,* 19, 263-279.

Mulholland, T., & Evans, C. R. (1966). Oculomotor function and the alpha activation cycle. *Nature,* 211, 1278-1279.

Sadasivan, P.K. and Dutt, D.N. (1995): Use of finite wordlength FIR digital filter structures with improved magnitude and phase characteristics for reduction of muscle noise in EEG signals. *Medical and Biological Engineering and Computing.* **33** pp. 306-312

Shaw, J. C. (1992). The ubiquitous alpha rhythm- a selective review. *Journal of Electrophysiology Technology,* 18, 5-27.

Taheri, B., Knight, R. and Smith, R. (1994) A Dry Electrode for EEG recording. *Electroencephalography and Clinical Neurophysiology,* 90, pp376-383.

3

Worker Expertise and New Worlds of HCI: Implications of Sociotechnical Systems Design

Bruce Wilson,

Union Research Centre on Organisations and Technology, Australia.

Over the last 40 years, Socio-Technical Systems Design (STSD) has provided extensive insights into the relationships between the technical and social processes in workplaces. Although STSD has been used most commonly in manufacturing environments, it has much to offer also in workplaces dependent on computers, especially as more complex forms of information technology become more prevalent in workplace life.

This paper presents a case study of the work of the Union Research Centre on Organisations and Technology (URCOT) which has drawn on Scandinavian experience with STSD to develop an applied participative approach which enables worker expertise to be contributed effectively in large-scale organisational and technological change projects. Some background to the formation of the Centre, the nature of the work being undertaken and its benefits will be provided, before concluding with an examination of the implications of URCOT's work for the 'new worlds' of HCI.

Human–Computer Interaction: INTERACT'97 S. Howard, J. Hammond & G. Lindgaard (editors)
Published by Chapman & Hall

PART TWO

Technical Sessions

4

Usability Engineering in Industrial Practice

Søren Lauesen

Copenhagen Business School, Howitzvej 60
DK-2000 Frederiksberg, Denmark
slauesen @ cbs.dk

ABSTRACT Do developers use proven usability techniques like user involvement, usability testing, and iterative design in industrial practice? Based on inside knowledge of many different types of projects, the author must conclude that these techniques are seldom used. There are several reasons for that. For instance:

(1) The market pressure is not there. Users ask primarily for functionality, and cannot formulate their usability requirements.

(2) Developers misunderstand the usability techniques. For instance they assume that usability testing is a kind of debugging, rather than a step in designing the interface. Or they believe that expensive labs have to be used, rather than a low-cost approach that can be learned in a day and carried out by developers.

(3) There is no proven way to make a good, first prototype. Since development in practice seems restricted to modifications of the first prototype, it is essential to make it good.

(4) There is no proven way to correct observed problems.

KEYWORDS usability engineering, software engineering, industry, iterative design, thinking-aloud

1. INTRODUCTION

Most system development is dealing with rather traditional systems for business, banking, government, technical purposes, embedded systems, etc. How are user interfaces designed in such systems? Do developers use proven techniques like user involvement, usability testing, and iterative design?

It is not easy to get a true picture of the situation through questionnaires because experience shows that developers often misunderstand terms like usability testing and iterative design. Also, they often say they do something, when observation shows that they do not.

This report is based on my own observations. I have inside knowledge of many development projects in Denmark. With a background as a developer, I am often consulted in usability issues, give courses in interface design, and talk a lot with people from industry. I have observed many kinds of projects like standard business administration (accounting, invoicing, etc.); shipyard administration; hospital support; teacher administration; TV broadcast planning; insurance applications; network software packages; process control systems; embedded systems, etc.

So what is the general picture? Do developers care about usability? Yes. Do they do something about it? Very little. Do they know what to do? Partially, but often they do it incorrectly, misunderstand the approaches, or give up after incomplete attempts.

In this paper I will explain what typically goes wrong and what seems to work. Basically, I will try to look at usability issues from the developer's perspective, comparing them with the technical side of development.

I will concentrate on the proven techniques: user in-

Human–Computer Interaction: INTERACT'97 S. Howard, J. Hammond & G. Lindgaard (editors)
Published by Chapman & Hall

volvement, usability testing, and iterative design. Other techniques are important but not yet available in a form ready for general industrial use. One example is task analysis which covers many things and overlaps with software engineering concepts like "use cases", "scenarios", and requirements specifications. See Lim (1996) for a discussion of the industrial applicability of task analysis.

2. USER INVOLVEMENT

It is a proven approach to involve users during the entire development process from analysis to deployment. Grudin (1991) discusses the many obstacles to user involvement, so I will just report how my Danish observations fit into his picture.

The degree of user involvement seems to depend on whether the project has a specific customer or aims at a particular market:

Specific customer

These projects can be in-house projects, for instance in banks and insurance companies; or they can be software house projects for a specific customer. In these cases we always find a great deal of user involvement during analysis and design. Particularly with in-house projects it is common to have users in the project team during these phases. However, the "Scandinavian Model" where users actually formulate the system objectives and do part of the design is very rare in Denmark.

The users involved are "expert users" with a good understanding of the application domain. Management gives their involvement in the new system a relatively high priority, but the pressure of many daily activities can make it somewhat difficult to find time for cooperation. However, the amount of user involvement seems somewhat better than what Grudin (1991) describes.

User involvement during usability testing, however, is not as successful; as will be discussed later.

Product for a market

Products can be business applications, technical systems, or embedded software. In these projects we see all the problems mentioned by Grudin: Marketing tries to represent the users, barriers are set up to prevent developers from contacting users, the international market is difficult to contact "face to face", etc.

3. USABILITY TESTING

Usability testing is probably the most important step in assuring usability. Without a usability test we can only make guesses at the level of usability. In order to understand why developers don't readily accept usability testing, it may be useful to compare usability testing with traditional program testing.

When a developer tests a program, he tests whether it works correctly with the hardware and other technical environment. Usability testing does not test the correctness of the program, but whether the user can work correctly and conveniently with it. During a usability test, the system - or a prototype of it - is used by typical users to carry out realistic tasks that the system was intended to support. The testers observe the users and write down any problems encountered by them. Next, developers try to repair the problems, and a new usability test is made to check whether the problems have disappeared. The process will typically have to be repeated several times, just as you have to repeat program testing.

Developers are confident with technical program testing. They have learnt to accept that they commit errors and that most errors can be identified through testing. They have also learnt how to locate the source of the error and how to correct it, and they know that repeated testing is necessary to make sure that the error actually disappeared. Their managers know that testing is costly and so provide good test equipment to save working hours.

Not so with usability testing. Developers are usually surprised that users can have problems with a program that is technically correct, and they doubt that it is the developer's responsibility to fix such problems. On several occasions I have heard product developers discuss what the market value of increased usability would be. They tend to conclude that sales wouldn't increase due to increased usability. In some cases users have complained about usability, and that seems to have some effect. Mostly, however, users complain about functionality and compare products based on functionality. So that is where efforts for the next release are directed.

Managers seem to share many of these beliefs and are reluctant to fund usability testing. The critical "test equipment" for usability testing is the users. Developers will normally have to find users themselves, sometimes fighting with marketing and managers to be allowed to contact users.

If developers try to correct the usability problems,

they soon realize that it is difficult to find ways to do it. The reason for this is that while they know how the technical environment works in painful detail, they don't know how the users "work" or think, and consequently they cannot find good solutions.

While a developer wouldn't dream of shipping a program without careful testing, most programs are actually shipped without any kind of usability testing.

In spite of all the motivational issues, some project teams try to do some usability testing. They encounter many procedural problems that may cause usability testing to fail. I will discuss some of them.

3.1 When to Test?

Ideally the usability tests should be made early in development, in order to allow a complete redesign. Early prototypes are suitable for that. In practice, however, this is almost never done. Usability testing is started late in the development cycle, almost as a kind of debugging or technical program testing. This issue is discussed further in Section 4.

3.2 Use Video and Usability Lab?

Many developers believe that usability testing requires a usability lab with video and computer log of the user's actions (Neal & Simons, 1984). Therefore they conclude that they cannot afford usability testing since they have no access to such a lab. This is a very unfortunate misunderstanding, since most usability testing can be done fast and efficiently without a lab. Even many usability experts believe that a lab is necessary. In Denmark this misunderstanding probably arose because a large software house invested in a lab and used it to market themselves as usability conscious. In many cases this seemed to override earlier attempts to promote a low-cost technique in Denmark (Jørgensen, 1990).

Large American companies also put much emphasis on usability labs, and often start with the lab as a promotional thing (Wiklund , 1994). I have even heard usability specialists complain that to management, the usability goal is "to utilize the lab 80% of the time".

In Section 5, I have outlined a low-cost technique used extensively by my colleagues and myself for usability testing. The main feature is to manually make a log of the problems as they occur during the test, and write a final problem list soon after the test, based on the log and memory. This is quite reliable in most cases and saves the expensive equipment and a lot of work viewing the video tapes.

Our technique finds ease-of-learning problems, and also *soft performance problems,* where the user finds the system too slow or requiring too many user actions.

Hard performance problems, where fast reactions or motoric aspects are the issue, require eye movement sensors and video to identify detailed task steps, fast and unconscious user reactions, etc. Examples are support systems for pilots or surgeons. However, there are few systems of this kind.

3.3 Thinking Aloud or Observe Only?

Some proponents of usability testing stress that it is important not to interfere with the user. They recommend a silent test where the user's actions are logged and video taped while he works in his normal fashion. Later the tester studies the actions in detail. This approach may be correct if we just want to observe the problems, but most usability testing deals with finding problems *and* correcting them.

To observe the usability problems is one thing, to find their cause and repair the problems is a different issue. In order to do that, it is essential to know what the users actually thought, and why they did not do this and that. This information is not available from the user's behavior or a video tape. The easiest way is to have the users think aloud during the test, or cautiously ask them what they are trying to do in case their behavior seems strange.

The very act of thinking aloud causes the users to proceed differently, for instance with a different performance, but do they encounter different problems? Henderson et al. (1995) and Hoc & Leplat (1983) have investigated this issue. They compared four techniques:

1. Thinking-aloud: The users think aloud while doing the task
2. Record and thinking-aloud: User actions are recorded and later replayed while the users explain why they did what they did.
3. Record and study: User actions are recorded and later studied by the testers.
4. Explain later: The users try to do the task and later comment on the problems they encountered.

Technique 1 and 2 seem to reveal the same problems, but technique 2 is much more time consuming. Techniques 3 and 4 don't reveal the correct problems. Technique 3 is also very time consuming.

I would add that techniques 1 and 2 reveal soft performance problems. Hard performance problems, where fast reactions or motoric aspects are the issue, can be revealed by technique 2 or 3.

The recommendation for all ordinary applications is to use only technique 1: Thinking aloud.

3.4 Which Test Tasks?

Developers initially have some difficulties defining good test tasks. Here is a typical badly defined task from a system that can measure and compare sounds and noises:

Task: Set sensor sensitivity

1. Open settings window
2. Select the sensor
3. Set the sensitivity to 10 mW

Testing with this task will not find out whether the user is able to perform a real-life task. One weakness is that the task description is a step-by-step instruction that tells the user how to perform the task. But we wanted to find out whether he could do it on his own. Another weakness is that the task is not closed and meaningful to the user. The user would never use the system just to set the sensor sensitivity. He wants to make a measurement, and setting the sensor sensitivity is a necessary step that he might not think of himself. We also want to test that he discovers this step.

A better task would be:

Task: Compare the noise at the top and bottom of the dishwasher

Equipment: Sensor supplied in a separate box. Dishwasher is a dummy during prototype testing (a small table will do)

This task is closed and meaningful, and we don't provide "hidden assistance". We also leave it to the user to find the proper sensitivity - just as in real life. My experience is that when developers have seen a few examples of good and bad tasks, they can define good tasks on their own.

3.5 Developer in the Test Team?

Some usability specialists make usability tests without developers on the test team. The developers get the report later and may see the video tape of the session. The reason is that the developer would interfere with the test, discuss issues with the users, or guide the users.

This is a realistic risk, but there is a serious drawback of the approach: It drastically reduces the chance of having the problems corrected. First of all, developers seem to distrust a report stating various problems that they have not experienced themselves and cannot reproduce. (The same pattern is seen when unrepeatable technical errors are reported to developers.) Second, they cannot see what the real problem is, why the user did not see what was at the bottom of the screen, etc. As a result they fail to make a proper correction of the system. If they had been present during the test, they could have asked such questions.

In my experience, many developers are very good participants in a usability experiment once they get the idea of the whole thing. With a bit of support during the first session, they find a good balance between inappropriate interference and important information gathering. Jørgensen (1990) reported similar success with test teams consisting of just one developer.

3.6 Rely On Standards and Heuristic Evaluation?

Some developers believe that adherence to standards or various kinds of heuristic evaluation (e.g. design inspection) will ensure usability. It would be nice if this were true, but at present these techniques cannot replace usability tests.

Standards (or style guides) improve learnability for users knowing other systems that follow this standard. However, domain-specific problems and many other problems cannot be covered by a standard. For instance, no standard can specify what terms to use for domain-specific concepts. Only a usability test can reveal whether the developer got it right. Several studies have shown that a check against standards only find about 25% of the problems users encounter, although they find a lot of standard violations that users don't notice (Cuomo & Bowen, 1994; Desurvire et al., 1992; Jeffries et al.,1991).

In some cases, we have observed usability problems caused by a standard. A good example is the use of modal dialogue boxes under MS-Windows. Many users complain that in order to enter the data needed in the dialogue box, they have to see the windows behind the dialogue box. But they cannot move windows around or bring other windows forward until they have closed the dialogue box.

Heuristic evaluation can be an expert's inspection of the design, or a check against guidelines. Surprisingly, heuristic evaluation finds only about half of the problems that users encounter (Cuomo & Bowen, 1994; Desurvire et al., 1992; Jeffries et al.,1991). Furthermore, about half of the problems reported with heuristic evaluation are "false" in the sense that real users do not notice these problems. Trying to remedy the false problems is a waste of development effort. Generally, heuristic evaluation should only be used to detect the most obvious problems. If a problem seems dubious or is difficult to repair, let the usability test reveal whether it is important.

In conclusion, standards and heuristic evaluation may help, but do not eliminate the need for a usability test.

3.7 Usability Test Or Demo?

Talking with developers, I often hear them say that they made a usability test of their latest product. Great, I say, how many problems did you find? None, they say, the users were very happy with the system. That surprises me a bit, since we usually find 20 to 30 problems during a one hour usability test. A closer discussion reveals that what the developers did was a demo of the system. They showed the system to the users, walking through typical cases. The users were invited to comment on the system, but did not noticc any problems.

In my experience, users can find a system very attractive when seeing a demo of it, yet be completely unable to perform anything with it on their own. The system is thus not easy to learn.

I have noticed several times that developers feel very uncomfortable with the thought of a real usability test, whereas they love to make demos. The reason may be their pride in their own work combined with the suspicion that the users will just mess up the whole thing. (This is what we actually expect users to do during the usability test. That is why we make it).

In early stages of development, a demo may be very useful for finding missing functionality, but that has little to do with usability factors like ease-of-learning.

3.8 How To Find Test Subjects?

Maybe the greatest obstacle in usability testing is to find test subjects. I have observed several times that this issue blocks serious thoughts about usability testing. The responsibility for finding test subjects is usually with the developers, but they hesitate and don't know how to go about it. They have few social contacts with users, and their attitude is far from approaching users or customers whom they don't know. In many product developing companies they are not even allowed to. Grudin (1991) discusses many other barriers between users and developers. Sales and marketing staff have much better potential for getting user contact. I strongly suggest that support in finding test users is planned early and provided from other parts of the company.

Since test subjects are difficult to find, the same test subjects are often used for testing successive system versions. The result is that the new version seems surprisingly much better than the old version. The reason may be that the users learned the concepts in the first version and successfully transferred the concepts to the next version. New users would likely encounter more problems.

A related mistake is to test the system with users who have been involved with analysis or design of the system. They also know too much to be representative users. However, as pointed out by Carlshamre & Karlsson (1996), expert users are very good at finding missing functionality as part of a usability test.

If we are to test the ease-of-learning aspect of the system, we should use new users for testing each new version. Testing for performance, however, assumes experienced users, and the same users may well test several versions if we allow them to gain experience with each version.

4. ITERATIVE DESIGN

As mentioned earlier, the first usability tests should be made on an early prototype in order to allow a complete redesign. In practice, however, this is almost never done. Usability testing comes in late, almost as a kind of debugging or technical program testing.

In order to understand why it is so, it is useful to compare the iterative design with traditional program development. Experienced developers proceed in this way:

Design: The overall structure of the system is developed. The process is highly iterative, particularly in the first part of design. The product of design can be inspected by fellow developers, but it is not in a form where it can be tested.

Programming: The different modules are programmed. It may happen that the design has to be modified, but a complete redesign is considered a disaster. Modifying what you have programmed is always the preferred solution.

Testing: The modules are tested individually and in combination. Many errors are detected, but mostly they can be repaired through simple program modifications. Reprogramming a module or redesigning a part is considered a sign of bad craftsmanship.

It is obvious that developers try to use the same pattern on the user interface. They assume that they can conceive a good design, inspect it (heuristic evaluation), implement it, and then correct the problems. But in reality, we cannot inspect whether or not the interface design is good, we have to test the design, as discussed under heuristic evaluation above.

Even when an early prototype is made, it turns out to be so difficult to conceive a new design that it is never done. What we have conceived seems so precious that we prefer to repair it, rather than start all over. Bailey (1993) has made the same observation in an experimental setting, and he concludes that the first prototype is *the* major factor in how usable the system can become.

4.1 Problem Correction

A late usability test is better than no usability test. When a test has been made and the problem list is available, it is time to remove the problems. But this is another point where the process often stops. There are several reasons for this:

1. The long list of problems was a surprise. Actually, the development team had expected that the test proved that the user interface was good. And they have no time to remove the problems or cannot see how they could remove them.
2. The developers have some time to remove problems, but cannot agree with the "customer" on what to remove.
3. The developers try to remove some problems, but the problems don't seem to disappear.

4.2 Problem Classification

Even if there is very little time available, some errors can be removed. The question is: which errors? Many development teams try to prioritize the problems, but cannot agree on the priorities. The problem is that they unconsciously mix up the importance to the user with the difficulty of removing the problem. Separating the two factors helps. I have good experience with this approach:

1. **User importance.** On the list of problems, note the number of users that encountered the problem. Also classify each problem according to its importance to the user. For instance, use a scale with these steps: **failure** (task failure), **slow** (performance problem), **inconvenient** (small performance problem), **difficult** (to learn), **minor** (fast to learn). When classifying the problems it is important not to worry about how to correct the problem, because it influences your judgment of the importance to the user.
2. **Difficulty.** Let the problem list rest in the mind at least one night. That often brings ideas for solution. Then classify each problem according to how difficult it is to repair. A simple scale could be: **small** effort (change of screen text, etc.), **medium** effort (several modules to be changed), **large** effort (new logic and data structure), **uncertain** how to repair.
3. **Cost/benefit.** Now prioritize according to user importance compared with difficulty of repair (cost/benefit). This can be formalized, but a discussion based on the two factors is usually sufficient.

4.3 Removing a Problem

In programming, it is usually obvious how to remove an error once we have found its cause. The repair may be more or less costly, but the solution is usually clear. In usability issues it is not that easy. We can roughly distinguish these classes of problems:

1. **Obvious solution.** It is easy to say what the proper solution should be, although the actual repair can be small, medium, or large. This is the frequent case in programming, but in my experience less than half of

the usability problems are of this kind.

2. **Wrong solution.** You believe you have a solution, but actually the solution does not work. This is frequent in usability, but rare in programming. Note that only a new usability test can reveal whether the problem was of class 1 or 2.
3. **Unknown solution.** We understand the problem and its cause, but don't have any idea how it could be overcome. This is frequent in usability, but extremely rare in programming.
4. **Unknown cause.** We can observe the problem, but cannot find its cause. The think-aloud approach in usability testing can almost eliminate this class of problems. In programming it often requires hard work to find the cause of the problem, but once found, the solution tends to be obvious.

Unfortunately the only thing to do about cases 2 and 3 above is to experiment with various solutions. In some teams I have worked in, we have had to realize that we could not find a solution within the existing framework. The problem could be, for instance, that the users did not have a consistent domain terminology, so whatever terms we used, some users misunderstood them. We had to rely on a written user introduction or personal instruction to overcome the problem. (This is of course better than not knowing the existence of the problem.)

It would be wonderful to have a usability handbook where you could look up various problems and find a set of possible solutions. However, this is an area for further research.

5. A LOW-COST USABILITY TEST TECHNIQUE

Below I have summarized a usability test technique used extensively by my colleagues and myself. It is easy to learn: we practice one session with developers and help them write the problem list. Then they seem able to do it on their own.

1. Test team: At least one developer and preferably another person knowing the system and the test technique. If the system is a prototype, the developer is the Wizard of Oz, simulating the system. If there is another person, he keeps a manual log during the test, focusing on the problems encountered by the users. If not, the developer keeps the log.
2. Preparation: Make sure that the system is in the right state, data base initialized, etc. Have copies available of windows with blank fields. Have a tape recorder and tapes ready (optional).
3. Start of test: Explain the test purpose to the user, the system purpose and the domain, but don't give more introduction to the system than would realistically be given in real life. (Many developers assume that users will have a course on how to use the system, but in real-life users rarely get such courses, or they get them only after having already used the system for some time.) Start the tape recording (optional).
4. Give the users exercises with real-life tasks. State the purpose of the task, but don't explain how to perform the task. Give them only one exercise at a time.
5. Ask the users to think aloud while trying to perform the tasks. If testing with two users at a time, encourage them to discuss what to do and why.
6. During the test, log the rough flow of the dialogue (menu points selected, windows brought up). When a user encounters a problem or makes a comment on the system, make a note in the log. If convenient, use blank copies of screens to sketch the situation. Log also the clock at various points of the session and the point where you change tapes.
7. If the users asks for help, encourage them to find the solution themselves.
8. If the users have searched for the solution for some time, help them out, but make sure that you have made a note of the problem. Such a problem is to be categorized as a Task Failure, i.e. that the users couldn't complete the task on their own. So make sure that the users had ample time to try on their own. By experience, the developer finds ten seconds a long time, while the users finds it a brief moment.
9. If you don't understand what the users are doing, ask cautiously.
10. End of test: Terminate the test itself after roughly one hour. Everybody will be tired at that time. Interview the users about what they liked and what they didn't like. To get an impression of their understanding of the system, ask them what they believe the system would do in some specific cases of your choice.
11. Within 24 hours, write a list of the problems detected. This list may include problems from two or more test sessions. Unless you have ample time, don't listen to the entire tape recording, but refer to

it in cases where you are not quite sure what happened. Classify the problems as described in Section 4.2.

A usability test session should last about 1.5 hours in total. Usually, we will run two or three sessions and then write a joint problem list. It takes about 2 hours to write the problem list. The report will generally contain 20 to 30 problems of various severity.

On a number of occasions, we have had two independent log keepers. Each log keeper wrote their own problem list. Later we compared them. The agreement was quite good: 90% of the problems were in both lists.

CONCLUSION

Observations show that proven usability techniques are used very little in industrial practice. We can summarize the causes in this way:

Barriers:

Developers are concerned about usability, but doubt that much can be done about it. They also doubt that it is worth doing anything, or that it is their responsibility.

The market pressure is not there. Users ask primarily for functionality, and cannot formulate their usability requirements.

Developers have difficulties finding users, particularly for usability testing. When seeing the results of a usability test, developers are surprised at the number of problems, and don't know how to correct them.

Misunderstandings:

Developers assume that usability testing is a kind of debugging, rather than a step in designing the interface. Or they assume that a demo of the system is a usability test.

Developers often believe that expensive labs have to be used, rather than a low-cost approach that can be learned in a day and carried out by developers.

Developers believe that standards and inspection/evaluation are sufficient.

Where HCI theory falls short:

There is no proven way to make a good, first prototype. Since development in practice seems restricted to modifications of the first prototype, it is essential to make it good.

There is no proven method for correcting observed problems.

REFERENCES

Bailey, G. (1993): Iterative methodology and designer training in human-computer interface design. Proceedings of InterCHI'93, pp. 198-205.

Carlshamre, P. & Karlsson, J. (1996): A usability-oriented approach to requirements engineering. Proceedings of ICRE'96, pp. 145-152.

Cuomo, D.L. & Bowen, C.D. (1994): Understanding usability issues addressed by three user-system interface evaluation techniques. Interacting with Computers, Vol.6, No.1, pp. 86-108.

Desurvire, H.W., Kondziela, J.M & Atwood, M.E. (1992): What is gained and lost when using evaluation methods other than empirical testing. Proceedings of HCI 92, pp. 89-102. Cambridge University Press.

Grudin, J. (1991): Systematic sources of suboptimal interface design in large product development organizations. Human-Computer Interaction, Vol.6, pp. 147-196.

Henderson, R. Podd, J., Smith. M. & Varela-Alvarez, H. (1995): An examination of four user-based software evaluation methods. Interacting with Computers, Vol.7, No.4, pp. 412-432.

Hoc, J.M. & Leplat, J. (1983): Evaluation of different modalities of verbalization in a sorting task. Int. J. Man-Machine Studies, Vol. 18, pp. 283-306.

Jeffries, R., Miller, J.R., Wharton, C., and Uyeda, K.M. (1991): User interface evaluation in the real world: A comparison of four techniques. CHI'91 Proceedings, pp. 119-124. ACM 0-89791-383-3/91/0004/0119..0124.

Jørgensen, A.H. (1990): Thinking-aloud in user interface design: a method promoting cognitive ergonomics. Ergonomics, 1990, Vol. 33, No.4, pp. 501-507.

Lim, K.Y. (1996): Structured task analysis: an instantiation of the MUSE method for usability engineering. Interacting with Computers, Vol.8, No.1, pp. 31-50.

Neal, A.S. & Simons, R.M. (1984): Playback: A method for evaluating the usability of software and its documentation. IBM Systems Journal, Vol 23, No 1, pp. 82-96.

Wiklund, M.E. (ed.): Usability in practice. AP Professional, 1994.

5

User-Centered GUI Standards Design: A Case Study

Barbee Teasley

Ameritech
Human Factors
2000 W. Ameritech Center Drive
Hoffman Estates, IL 60196 USA
01-847-248-1400
FAX 01-847-248-6043
e-mail: teasley@acm.com

Jean Scholtz[1]

National Institute of Standards and Technology (NIST)
Building 225, Room A216
Gaithersburg, MD 20899 USA
01-301-975-2520
FAX 01-301-840-1357
e-mail: jean.scholtz@nist.gov

ABSTRACT Many organizations are aware of the benefits of standardizing their GUIs and go to the effort of creating their own standards. However, oftentimes the standards languish on the desk of human factors specialists, and fail to impact those who actually design and develop software user interfaces. Best practice, as reported in the literature, includes involving the end user, understanding the user's needs, providing flexibility, and allowing for evolution. This case study describes how a project to create GUI standards at a large telecommunications corporation attempted to follow these guidelines, while working under a tight schedule.

KEY WORDS standards, GUI standards, user-centered design, case study

1. INTRODUCTION

The Ameritech human factors group has been in existence since 1989. Ameritech provides communications and information services, mainly to customers in the midwestern United States, with growth into national and international venues. Services include traditional telephony (local and long distance), cellular telephone service, cable television, home security, teleconferencing, business communications, etc. Ameritech was originally part of the AT&T Bell System, and was created when AT&T was divested in 1984.

The group's goal is to ensure that all products and services receive appropriate human factors support. Activities include participation in ideation; creating conceptual demonstrations; and iterative prototyping, testing and redesign throughout product/system development. Members of the group participate in development teams; work to resolve conflicts among requirements, usability and implementation constraints;

Human–Computer Interaction: INTERACT'97 S. Howard, J. Hammond & G. Lindgaard (editors)
Published by Chapman & Hall

and follow through with field testing. (See Lund, 1994, for a more detailed description of Ameritech's human factors department.)

Partly as a result of historical factors, including divestiture, Ameritech internal systems and software are very diverse across business units. As one example, in 1996, six different voice messaging systems were offered under the Ameritech brand. In Fall, 1995, the company created a corporate-wide umbrella organization, Technology Solutions (TS), to tackle the diversity problem. TS was formed to first develop and then communicate a unified standard across information systems, including environments, architecture and the software development lifecycle. In early 1996, Human Factors was invited to flesh out the usability-related portions of the software development standards and to otherwise become involved in the standardization program.

Under the banner of the Ameritech Look & Feel Initiative (ALFI), a group from human factors worked on three different efforts to launch the initiative. One was the creation and announcement of a Look & Feel Policy. The policy stated that the Human Factors group defines, publishes and maintains Ameritech's look and feel for all interactive systems. It also stated that all systems sponsored by the corporate Information Systems unit were required to use the Look & Feel process. The second effort was the enhancement of the existing software lifecycle process to include usability. The Look & Feel process document laid out usability efforts and signoffs that were to be part of any software development effort, whether internal or externally staffed. The final effort was directed toward supplementing the existing general graphical user interface guidelines with more platform- and application-specific standards. The guidelines had originally been published in 1992. They cover three different GUI environments - Apple, Motif and Windows 3.x - and discuss general principles of design. There was no attempt to focus the guidelines on typical communications software. They were and continue to be publicly available on Ameritech's web site (http://www.ameritech.com/news/testtown/library/standard).

It is the design and creation of the new GUI guidelines which is the focus of the current paper. One of our first steps was to review some of the existing literature on the development of style guides and standards, and on the role standards can play in the system development process.

Hopper, Hambrose and Kanevsky (1996) describe the development of a GUI interface to create a comprehensive, integrated computing environment for financial consultants and other professionals, most of whom were not computer literate. Aside from the design challenge itself, they were working with a big development team, a large portion of whom came from a mainframe environment with no GUI development experience. Faced with a demand for user interface standards, the group initially produced guidelines which "didn't go beyond the UI guidelines already available from software manufacturers and industry experts" (p. 491). Furthermore, the guidelines "...failed. Standards spoke of what a control was, but offered little assistance in how a control was to be used." (p. 492) A second standards document incorporated more corporate standards which promoted the company's look and feel. The team found, however, that the document needed amendments and updates on a relatively frequent basis.

Gale (1996) outlines what a style guide typically contains, and the benefits of using the guide from the perspective of end users, developers and business. He also lists a number of reasons why style guides fail. These include:

a. The document is difficult to use, often as a result of sheer length.
b. The document is never updated.
c. Little consideration is given to how the guide is introduced into the organization.
d. Often, the release of the guide is seen as solving usability problems, and no further action is needed.
e. The guide is perceived as moving the responsibility for usability out of the hands of the developers.
f. Developers and users are not involved in creating the content.
g. The guide does not explain how it is to be used in practice.

Gale goes on to describe a development approach used in his organization characterized as "collaborative". This approach involves engaging the potential end users of the guide in its creation, providing support materials and training when the document is introduced, educating the users on the rationale, and allowing evolution. In addition, the author suggests going beyond the document by providing such things as checklists for conformity, quick reference cards, interactive demonstrations, competitions to spot the deliberate mistakes in user interface designs, and source code, custom controls and property tables for sharing.

Miller (1996) also discusses pitfalls and successes related to standards. An initial attempt combined standards with information on the design and implementation of usability engineering within the organization. This approach appeared to overwhelm developers with information, was difficult to apply to specific situations, and did not map well with the realities of project development. A second approach involved the development of a prototypical model application which was used to show what an application would look like if the standards were implemented. Because the prototype did not apply well to the broad range of projects the group was involved with, it has since evolved to skeletal framework that a range of design options can be plugged into to create prototypes. Other activities including educating developers, and being closely involved with the developers during a project. Miller's group was working in an environment where conformity was enforced by budgeting. Key activities, including usability tasks, had to be completed in each stage before funding was approved for the next stage.

These reports paint a clear picture of an approach to developing and integrating standards into an organization that will maximize the probability of success. Not surprisingly, a key factor is involving the end user during development. Another key factor is getting to know the users' needs by working along with them to a common goal. It is also clear that standards and processes need to be flexible to meet the resource demands placed on projects, and that they need to evolve as projects become more varied and complex, and as technology and styles change.

Unfortunately, as often occurs, there was a gap between what best practice prescribes, and what was feasible within allotted resources and time. For this project, we were faced with a very short development time. The organization-wide standardization effort was well underway before the human factors group became involved. The older GUI standards were still being used, and were causing confusion. The time to impact upcoming projects was rapidly approaching. It was important to get a new version of the standards published quickly.

Our approach was to view the short development time as a "feature". Clearly, there was not enough time to involve end users to the extent we would have liked, nor to create an encompassing set of standards. We decided to publish a basic set of standards, and to encourage the end users to evolve and grow the standards with us. However, we were aware that it would be very detrimental to completely exclude end-user input during initial development.

2. METHODOLOGY

A consultant (the second author) was hired to facilitate development of the standards in conjunction with members of the human factors group. A group leader from the human factors group (the first author) was in charge of the project and acted as a liaison to the consultant. The liaison assigned human factors' members to help with various portions of the standards development as small blocks of time became available in their schedules. This helped to make standards development a group effort, at least within the human factors group.

Work was started in mid-May of 1996 with the goal of releasing the standards document around the end of August. The first step was for the consultant to become familiar with the types of applications and interfaces currently being used and developed at Ameritech. She looked at the multi-platform guidelines that were available on the Ameritech Web site. Decisions had recently been made at Ameritech concerning platform standards for future application development. Using this information, the consultant and the liaison formulated several possible approaches, based on prior experiences as well as information from the existing literature.

2.1 Collecting Initial Input

Early on, a meeting was set up with the human factors group and the consultant. During this meeting, the group was asked for thoughts on:

- the use of the guidelines
- tensions between the needs of various groups and the structure and content of the standards document
- ways to encourage development groups to use the guidelines
- barriers to developers using guidelines
- good structures of guidelines
- providing different ways to access guideline information
- electronic versus paper guidelines
- support for legacy systems
- evolution of guidelines
- evaluating the impact of guidelines
- what constitutes "look and feel".

The consultant and the liaison also interviewed some Ameritech software developers about their development process for interfaces. During the interview, the developers expressed their opinions about what would make a standards document useful for them. In return for this information, the consultant and liaison provided a heuristic review of their prototype. This also provided information as to the type of guidelines that were needed.

The heuristic evaluation revealed the following problems:

- redundant menu terminology
- lengthy menus containing seldom or never-used functionality
- inconsistent button order
- inefficient grouping of text entry boxes
- inconsistent use of button vs. menu vs. toolbar icon
- inconsistencies in placing results of searches (main windows vs. dialog window).

Based on this example, our discussion with the human factors group, and collective experience, we classified the types of guideline and heuristic information needed to provide solutions to GUI development problems as:

- general interface guidelines
- a user task analysis or early functionality testing
- platform-specific interface guidelines
- corporate "look and feel" guidelines.

Our specific goal, however, was to focus on platform-specific and corporate guidelines. We felt that general interface guidelines are readily available from any number of sources, and were perceived by developers, in general, as not pertinent to "getting the job done."

2.2 Requirements for the Standards

We collated the information collected from the developers and the human factors group into requirements that the standards document had to meet. They were:

- The main use of the standards will be for design with conformance support as a secondary use.
- The main users of the standards document will be developers and human factors professionals.
- The standards document should contain guidelines for signature (look and feel), platform and operating-system specific guidelines as well as more general interface guidelines .
- Users of the standards document should be able to quickly access needed information.
- The document must be easy to maintain.
- The document should provide for easy evolution.
- The document must be accessible by those without access to the Ameritech intranet, as well as to those with access.
- Developers and human factors professionals should be able to contribute "best practices" easily and quickly.
- The document must serve both internal users and, eventually, external users.

To meet the requirement for easy maintenance, we determined that there would be one version of the standards document that would be kept current. Any other formats would have to be produced from the maintained format. Given that all of the UI guidelines published by the human factors group are accessible on the Web, the Web was chosen as the primary publication site. An added advantage of a Web version is that it facilitates collecting feedback and input from users. However, because not all employees have access to the intranet, and because many prefer a paper version, a printed version needed to be produced as well. This necessitated finding a way for paper users to be kept up to date on changes made to the intranet version.

Because the initial version would include Ameritech signature, an edited version would need to be created for public release. Thus, an additional consideration was easy generation of an alternative, external version.

Developers do not want to spend time reading many pages of text in order to answer a simple question. However, we wanted to provide easy access to in-depth information if it was so desired. Thus, the document would contain guidelines at the control level (e.g., menu design), at the task level (e.g., searching for a keyed record in a database), and at the level of general principles (e.g., screen layout). Links would be provided to small portions of more detailed information, as well as links to other relevant portions. Current best practices were to be used as illustrations.

To provide developers with significant benefits at a low cost in effort, we decided to produce templates for them to use in producing interfaces. Because the corporation uses four different development languages, the ultimate goal is to produce multiple templates and allow all developers access to the associated reusable source code.

Based on the need for fast turnaround, we prioritized what would appear in the first deliverable. Because the design of a Web-based version posed hard design questions, initial attention was focused there. We concluded that it would be more profitable to do the Web design first, keeping in mind how the paper document could be generated from this, than the other way around. Although the eventual goal was to have reusable code along with the standards document, initially the document would include text and static examples. Dynamic examples would be added later, followed by reusable code for each of the different development environments.

2.3 Design and Implementation

At this point, the "to do" list looked about like this:
- Develop control guidelines
- Collect possible examples for "best practices"
- Evaluate the chosen examples
- Put together a "task" list based on current applications
- Design the look of the intranet document.

The control guidelines were written by a contractor who was working in the human factors group at Ameritech. She and the consultant worked together to decide upon a style that seemed easy to read and quickly locate information. They developed a template for control information and refined it by writing the guidelines and descriptions for several very different controls. The contractor then worked in the time blocks she had available producing the guidelines and descriptions for the rest of the controls. One member of the human factors group worked on collecting examples of "best practices". The human factors group was in the process of doing some evaluations on different products at the time and many of their redesigns also became examples. The consultant oversaw the work on controls and worked on developing a possible task list. The task list was produced by noting commonalties and frequently-used fields, buttons and menus from the examples collected by the human factors group. Using this information, a template was designed that could be used to describe tasks and guidelines for them. As with the controls, this template was developed iteratively.

The consultant brought in a programmer to help with the actual intranet development. They came up with several possible designs based on existing information, including guidelines published on the Web by Ameritech (Schumacher, 1996). The Ameritech requirements for the document and information from the consultant, based on Web evaluations that she had just completed were also factored into the initial designs. Several designs were prototyped and feedback was gathered from the human factors group.

A more advanced prototype was generated and an evaluation was done. Draft versions of guidelines about the controls were circulated at Ameritech for feedback. Example screens were also circulated to the human factors members. They were asked to comment on the layout of these screens and how they related to other implementations within the company.

A usability evaluation was conducted with potential users of the standards document. One part of the evaluation focused on collecting terminology appropriate to describe the tasks we were using. For the most part, developers discussed the tasks in terms of the end-user task being done, and not in terms of the controls used or the underlying program function. Participants were also asked to look for answers to six different types of questions using the prototype. Feedback was collected on navigation, expectations about where information would be found. We also noted how much instruction was necessary for them to use the Web version of the standards document. The basic design was refined based on the collected information. The sessions also served to get buy-in from potential users.

3. VERSION 1.0

The final format design made use of frames. Normally, Web usability guidelines suggest avoiding frames, due to variation in net browsers (e.g., Deitweiler and Omanson, 1996). However, because Ameritech standards direct the use of Netscape 3.0 or Explorer 3.0 (or higher) versions for employees, there was justification for assuming that frames would display properly on all users' screens. Furthermore, it appeared that their use would facilitate navigation. An example of the use of frames as done throughout the document is shown in Figure 1. Figure 1 shows the Introduction section, which describes the structure and use of the document. The main frame (the largest) contains the contents of the Web page currently being viewed. The frame on the left side contains the table of contents, which enables users to quickly navigate to another section. The table of contents lists the general sections, a task section and a control section. The task

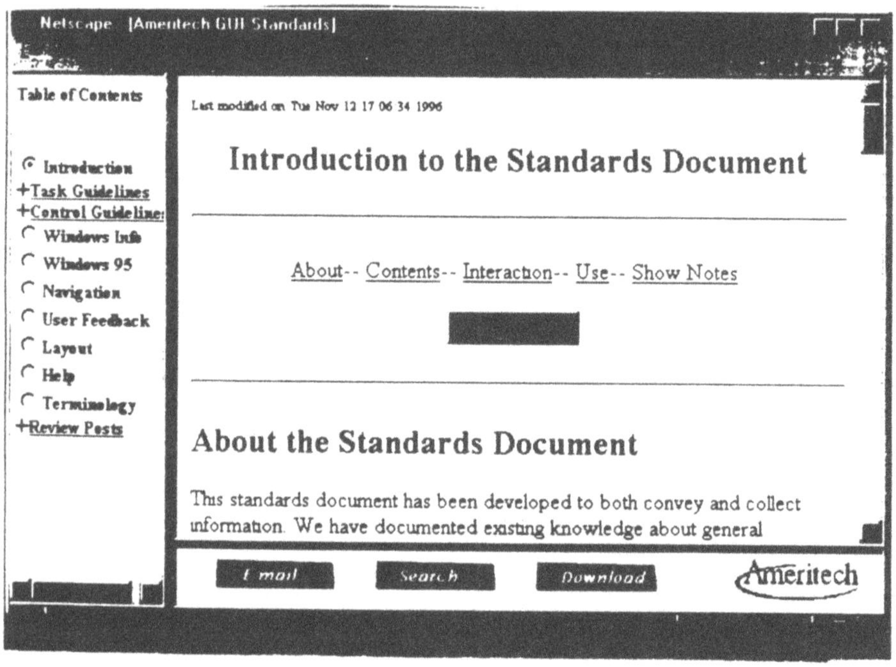

Figure 1: A Sample Screen from the Standards Document

and control sections can be expanded to list the individual sections, much like many present day file managers. Users can also view only the contributions by expanding the "show notes" section and selecting the individual entries to view.

The menu items are paired with "option buttons" that show what is currently selected and provide feedback about which section a user is viewing. The frame in the bottom of the screen contains functionality that exists on all pages on the Web site. Buttons for "print," "e-mail," "download" and "search" are displayed here. "Print" allows the user to print the entire document, rather than having to print each individual page separately. The "e-mail" button allows users to send an e-mail message to the standards maintainer. A "post notes" button appears at the top of each page and allows users to make contributions to individual pages in the form of comments that can be viewed by all future users. The notes area will also be used to post notices about revisions to individual sections. The first version included numerous graphics, as well as several executables in Visual Basic. The "download" button on the pages takes users to a page which serves as a menu of downloadable controls and tasks. The page contains a list of all controls and tasks available. The user can choose to see a screen "snapshot" of the item and/or download the executable file and, eventually, source code for the all executables. Individual executables can also be viewed and downloaded as they are encountered in the document.

To facilitate rapid access to information, a search function that returns a list of places where the entered term is found was included as a button in the lower frame. Because users are not always familiar with the "correct" terminology, a terminology cross-reference section was included. The section supplied other terms commonly used (synonyms). For example, what many interface designers refer to as a "radio button" is called an "option button" by Microsoft. By including this alternate term in the terminology section along with the common term, the reference appears when users search for "radio button."

The templates for the guidelines were designed so that users could quickly locate the desired type of infor-mation within each control, task, or general section. A standard set of links was provided at the top of each control or task. For example, every control contains "Proper Use", "Behavior", "Guidelines", "Used By", "Related Topics", and "Show Notes" as standard links at the beginning of the page. These links take the user directly to that section of the page. Rather than embed many links within each individual section for the first version, all external links were placed in the "used by" and "related to" sections. This was done for two reasons: 1) to avoid adding complexity, and 2) because the proportion of users who would access the document from paper as opposed to accessing it on-line was not clear. Keeping the links compacted in two sections helps users reading the paper document understand the links. The "used by" section will eventually link to all tasks in which the control is used to allow users to see examples incorporating the control.

Task pages had similar links, but contained a "Uses" link. This link allows users to access information about a component control and, if desired, view any particular control for more information. Using these links also makes it possible to limit the amount of scrolling users need to do to view a specific section of the controls and tasks. The sections on general guidelines contain direct jumps to specific information appropriate to the individual section.

Users need information about enhancements and updates. From the beginning , the developer created a "development page" to communicate what had been done. Because this technique proved so effective during development, we decided this was a good approach to incorporate into the final version. It was modified to say "what's new" and it is used by the maintainer of the document to note change information. In addition, each page was implemented so that the date it is posted on the Web server appears automatically on the top of the page. This allows users to see how recently a particular page had been revised.

The document was delivered less than one week later than planned, and was operational at Ameritech the next week.

4. CONCLUSIONS

The challenges we faced were, broadly speaking, threefold: 1) to produce GUI standards that would support designers and developers, be highly usable, and be easy to maintain and evolve, 2) to enhance usability and acceptance through user involvement, and 3) to do so in a short time frame. This required some hard decisions, prioritization of resources and some creativity.

To address challenge 1, the document was carefully designed and prototyped to ensure that it conveyed just the most essential information in an easy-to-find, easy-to-understand way. The use of hypertext on intranet facilitates this goal by allowing the user to unfold detail as needed, to search quickly through the document, to easily contribute content, and to always have the latest version available.

Challenge 2 was addressed by obtaining input from a wide variety of sources, including end-users and human factors specialists. Although these activities could not be done to the depth or breadth ideally desired, we used "fast and cheerful" methods that brought in much good information and raised awareness of the project.

At this time, two months following the publication of the standards, the word is spreading about their availability. A means of counting hits on the Web site was built into the standards document and will be used to monitor access. Although the organization does not enforce the use of standards, human factors members who are on projects involving GUIs are using the standards and working to educate others on the projects about the standards and their use.

5. REFERENCES

Deitweiler, M. C. and Omanson, R. C. (1996) Ameritech Web Page User Interface Standards and Design Guidelines. <http://www.ameritech.com/news/testtown/library/standard>

Gale, S. (1996) A collaborative approach to developing style guides. *Proceedings of CHI 96*, ACM Press, p. 362-367.

Hopper, S., Hambrose, H. and Kanevshy, P. (1996) Real world design in the corporate environment: Designing an interface for the technically challenged. *Proceedings of CHI 96*, ACM Press, p. 489-495.

Lund, A. (1994) The evolution of broad-band work in Ameritech's customer interface systems and human factors department. In M. E. Wiklund (ed.), *Usability in Practice: How Companies Develop User-Friendly Products*. Cambridge, MA: AP Professional.

Miller, A. (1996) Integrating human factors in customer support systems development using a multi-level organizational approach. *Proceedings of CHI 96*, ACM Press, p. 368-375.

Schumacher, R. (1992) Ameritech Graphical User Interface Standards and Design Guidelines. <http://www.ameritech.com/news/testtown/library/standard>

6. NOTES

[1] The second author, Jean Scholtz, was an independent consultant at the time this work was done.

7. ACKNOWLEDGEMENTS

The authors would like to thank Gavin Lew, Scott Lively, Kay Burnett, Cory Lebson and Yee Yin Choong for their extensive contributions to the work described in this paper,

6

Designing for Usability : A Case Study

Janet Wesson, Gideon de Kock and Peter Warren*

Department of Computer Science and Information Systems
University of Port Elizabeth, SOUTH AFRICA
* Department of Computer Science
University of Natal (Pietermaritzburg), SOUTH AFRICA
csajlw@upe.ac.za, csagdk@upe.ac.za, peterw@cs.unp.ac.za

ABSTRACT This paper is concerned with an investigation into a structured, user-centered design methodology using a case study approach. The case study selected was a new genealogical information system (GIS), to replace the University of Port Elizabeth's genealogical information system (UPEGIS), which exhibited a number of usability problems. The methodology selected was the Method for Usability Engineering (MUSE). This paper will show that the use of a user-centered design approach, coupled with a structured methodology, resulted in a useable design. Several limitations were, however, discovered in the use of the MUSE methodology. Specifically, MUSE was found to need extensions in the areas of object modelling and detailed user interface design.

KEYWORDS Design methodology, MUSE, object modelling, usability, user interface design.

1. INTRODUCTION

The current trend towards highly interactive systems has resulted in a shift in design emphasis from functionality to usability. Traditionally, the user interface (UI) design was left until relatively late in the system development lifecycle. With the advent of user-centered design, the focus has changed to addressing human factors issues much earlier in the design. Under design methods, two different approaches have evolved: *rapid prototyping* and structured analysis and design methods. Rapid prototyping is based on the premise that the design process will consist of an iterative process of prototype construction and testing. This activity normally involves little design analysis and specification and may result in numerous iterations. In addition, the resultant design may suffer from inherent design defects and a lack of adequate design documentation (Walsh, 1989), (Newman,1995), (Redmond-Pyle, 1995). Prototyping is considered, nevertheless, by some to be essential for producing good UI design. Our hypothesis is that structured methods, possibly incorporating iterative design, can also achieve a good UI design, without incurring the disadvantages of pure prototyping.

Structured analysis and design methods, on the other hand, are characterized by a stage-wise approach and have a definite set of deliverable design products for each stage. Specifically, design analysis is completed before design specification and implementation, although an iterative process may also be used. These methods have been developed in two main areas: Software Engineering (SE), and Human-Computer Interaction (HCI). SE methods have traditionally adopted a data or process-oriented approach to systems development, whereas HCI methods focus on user-centered design. The two main techniques proposed in SE were Structured Systems Analysis and Design

Human–Computer Interaction: INTERACT'97 S. Howard, J. Hammond & G. Lindgaard (editors)
Published by Chapman & Hall

(SSADM) (DeMarco, 1978), which concentrates on functional analysis, and Semantic Data Modelling (SDM) (Hull, 1987), which focuses on data analysis. These two different approaches were later combined and replaced with Object-Oriented Analysis and Design (OOAD), which encapsulates data and processes into objects. During the past few years, several structured HCI design methodologies have emerged. These include the Method for Usability Engineering or MUSE (Lim, 1994), the TRIDENT methodology (Bodart, 1995), and the Graphical User Interface and Design or GUIDE method (Redmond-Pyle, 1995). These methods are all based on task analysis but vary considerably in stages covered, notation used, and degree of formality.

The use of a case study to evaluate a structured method is motivated for several reasons. Few case studies have been published reporting on the use of structured methods and more empirical evidence is needed to fully evaluate these methods. The case study will be used to apply all the stages of the structured method, and an evaluation made at several stages, in order to evaluate not only the method, but also the final product. This approach has also been used by other authors to evaluate new design methods (Sullivan, 1996). The choice of the case study is important: the nature of the case study should be highly interactive if usability is to be seen as a critical factor. The case study selected was a new genealogical information system (GIS), to replace the University of Port Elizabeth's Genealogical Information System (UPEGIS). This system consists of a database of some 300 000 persons, representing the results of extensive genealogical research relating to a period of some 350 years of South African history. The system is highly interactive in nature, and exhibited many obvious usability problems, particularly in the area of UI design and task support.

2. COMPARISON OF STRUCTURED DESIGN METHODOLOGIES

Several different design methodologies, including both Software Engineering (SE), and Human-Computer Interaction (HCI) methods were compared and evaluated using a set of evaluation criteria. The purpose of this evaluation was to select the most suitable method for the analysis and design of the case study. The methodologies evaluated were Structured Systems Analysis and Design (SSADM), Semantic Data Modelling (SDM), the Object Modelling Technique (OMT) (Rumbaugh, 1991), the Methodology for Usability Engineering (MUSE) (Lim, 1994), the TRIDENT methodology (Bodart, 1995), and the GUIDE methodology (Redmond-Pyle, 1995). The criteria selected were the following: support for the entire software development lifecycle (SDLC), support for extant systems analysis, task analysis, data (or object) analysis, functional analysis, top-level UI design, detailed UI design, data (or object) design, functional design, and prototyping the UI design. The results of this evaluation are contained in Table 1 below.

The MUSE methodology was selected as the most suitable method, since it effectively covers the entire lifecycle from task analysis to implementation, and involves a detailed usability study of existing systems. A number of limitations were however noted. The conceptual model in MUSE is represented using a *semantic net*, which is inadequate for the detailed design of the database. No specific guidelines are given in MUSE as to the selection and placement of interaction objects on the screen. We suggest, however, that these limitations can be overcome by extending the data model to produce an *object model*, using techniques from OMT, and by including detailed UI guidelines from the TRIDENT methodology.

The next section will briefly review the MUSE methodology, before going on to illustrate how this method was used in the design and implementation of the new GIS.

Criteria	SSADM	SDM	OMT	MUSE	TRIDENT	GUIDE
1. Entire SDLC	√	×	√	√	×	×
2. Extant systems analysis	×	×	×	√	×	×
3. Task analysis	×	×	×	√	×	√
4. Data (object) analysis	×	√	√	√	√	√
5. Functional analysis	√	×	√	√	√	√
6. Top-level UI design	×	×	×	√	√	√
7. Detailed UI design	×	×	×	√	√	×
8. Data (object) design	×	√	√	×	×	×
9. Functional design	√	×	√	×	×	×
10. Prototyping UI design	×	×	×	√	√	√
TOTAL	**3**	**2**	**5**	**8**	**5**	**5**

Table 1 Evaluation of Structured Design Methodologies

3. METHOD FOR USABILITY ENGINEERING (MUSE)

The MUSE method defines the UI design process by specifying the design products to be generated and the procedures to be followed at each stage (Lim, 1994). The MUSE method is structured into three phases, each of which is divided into several distinct stages:

1) The Information Elicitation and Analysis Phase is concerned with capturing user requirements using techniques such as task analysis. Existing and related systems are analyzed to derive a high-level, device-independent task model. The stages included here are Extant Systems Analysis and the Generalized Task Model Stage.
2) The Design Synthesis Phase is concerned with deriving a conceptual design for the target system, based on the task models produced earlier. The stages involved here consist of the Statement of User Needs, the Composite Task Model and the System and User Task Model Stages.
3) The Design Specification Phase produces a device-dependent specification of the UI design, including descriptions of the screens, interaction objects and dialogue design. Its stages comprise the Interaction Task Model, Interface Model and Display Design Stages.

Each stage of the method is characterized by a set of design products, each with an associated set of procedures and documentation or notation. Part of the notation used has been adapted from existing SE methods, such as the Jackson structured diagram (JSD) notation (Jackson, 1983), and semantic nets. Integration with existing SE methods is supported through the existence of several *handshake* points, such as the Functions List produced during the Design Synthesis Phase. The basic focus of the method should be seen as *user-task oriented*, implying that a user model may be constructed or *synthesized* from the task model. The focus of the method remains, however, on the UI design, no explicit integration with a SE method is proposed.

4. CASE STUDY: A GENEALOGICAL INFORMATION SYSTEM

The MUSE method was used to analyze the detailed requirements for a new genealogical information system (GIS), to replace the University of Port Elizabeth's Genealogical Information System (UPEGIS). This method was supplemented in the Design Synthesis Phase with object modelling techniques from OMT (Rumbaugh, 1991). The object model derived using this process was then used, together with design guidelines from the TRIDENT methodology (Bodart, 1995), in the Design Specification Phase to produce the user interface (UI) specification. This process will be discussed briefly in the sections that follow.

4. 1 Information and Elicitation Phase

Two extant systems: UPEGIS, and a related system, Brother's Keeper for Windows (BKWIN), were analyzed to characterize the user needs and problems.

The products produced during this phase were those prescribed by the MUSE method. In particular, the Task Descriptions (TDs(ext)), and the summary of user problems and needs (SUN(ext)), served to identify the problems with both UPEGIS and BKWIN. The major problems identified were the following:

- The crucial task of locating a person in the GIS was not well supported. The search for a person was based only on name or Id number, and did not include any date or place information.
- The user view was limited to only two generations: the current person, the spouse and the parents.
- In the case of UPEGIS, entering a person required entering the Id numbers of both parents.
- In the case of UPEGIS, entering a marriage required re-entering the Id numbers of both spouses.
- UPEGIS only provided support for first-order events: namely birth, baptism and death dates only. Second-order events had to be encoded using special *field markers* in the Information field.
- References and images could not be linked to individual events as well as to persons.

The above problems are illustrated in the UPEGIS screen contained in Figure 1 below. The names of the father and mother are not displayed, only the Id numbers. Note also the use of the field markers (*, =, #, &, >), in the information field to denote birth, baptism, burial, other, and source information respectively.

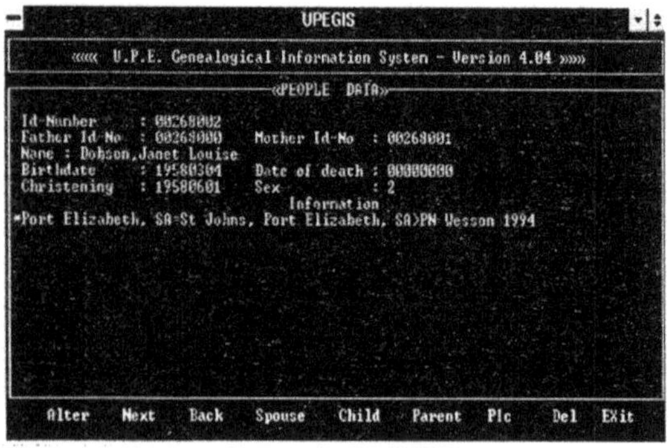

Figure 1 Browse Screen in UPEGIS

The Generalized Task Model (GTM(y)), developed during this phase provided a device-independent model of the tasks in the target system. This model was used to ultimately design the menu structure in the Design Specification Phase (see section 4.3).

4.2 Design Synthesis Phase

During this phase, the results of the extant systems analysis were summarized and extended to produce several products. The MUSE method does not, however, address the issue of a conceptual data model, other than from the perspective of the Domain of Design Discourse (DoDD(y)). The DoDD(y) summarizes the semantics of the target system by identifying explicit relationships among the various domain entities and is represented using a semantic net of nodes and relations. The DoDD(y) and the Actions/Objects List were thus extended to produce an *object model* using the Object Modelling Technique (OMT), as initially proposed by Rumbaugh (Rumbaugh, 1991) (see Figure 4).

The production of the object model was seen as essential, not only for the design of the database for the new GIS, but also for the detailed design of the user interface. We consider that the objects in the user interface (*user view*), should be based on the objects in the conceptual data model. This approach to object-oriented user interface (OOUI) design is supported by several other authors (Collins, 1995), (Redmond-Pyle, 1995), but is significantly missing from the MUSE methodology. The object model depicted in Figure 4 was used to decide both on the *presentation units* (PUs), and the selection and placement of the *abstract interaction objects* (AIOs). The actual method used to derive these was based on the TRIDENT methodology, and is discussed briefly in the next section.

4.3 Design Specification Phase

During this phase, the conceptual design was refined and decomposed to produce the UI specification. In addition to the products prescribed in the MUSE method, it was found necessary to draw an *UI Class Table* for the target system. The purpose of this table is to describe each of the screens in the System Task Model (STM(y)), in terms of the user view, the domain objects, and the user actions (tasks) supported in each view. This concept of views of user objects is similar to that used in the GUIDE methodology (Redmond-Pyle, 1995), and may be compared to the concept of presentation units (PUs), in the TRIDENT methodology (Bodart, 1995). Separate screens were not designed for each task: screens were designed for each visible UI class. The selection of the UI classes were based both on the task model, and the object model. This object-oriented approach resulted in significantly less screens than would have been produced by either the MUSE methodology, or TRIDENT.

The MUSE method does not give detailed guidelines as to the design and layout of the different screens. This may be considered as one of the major shortcomings of the MUSE method. Guidelines from the TRIDENT methodology were therefore used to derive the layout of these. These guidelines are the subject of several papers (Bodart, 1993), (Bodart, 1994a), (Bodart, 1994b) and (Bodart, 1995), and are summarized here as follows:

a) The selection of a suitable interaction style or UI environment (UIE). In the case of the new GIS, MS-Windows was selected as the target UIE.
b) The definition of screens (PUs), based on both the task and the object model.
c) The selection of applicable abstract interaction objects (AIOs), independent of the chosen UIE.
d) The translation of AIOs into suitable *concrete interaction objects* (CIOs), based on both the UIE selected, and the object and user model.
e) The placement of the CIOs on the screen, using a Right/Bottom strategy.

Examples of the screens produced for the new GIS are contained in Figures 2 and 3 below. The Browse screen depicted in Figure 2 displays information for three generations on one screen. The layout of this screen was based both on the task model, and the object model. Information for the current person, spouse, father, mother or child is edited using the Edit screen in Figure 3. The Edit screen is also used for searching for a person, the search process being based on *all* data entered. The design of this screen thus encapsulates the Person object, together with all the available operations on this object, and is therefore seen to be object-oriented. The use of object modelling as a basis for the UI design is supported by several authors (Collins, 1995), (Redmond-Pyle, 1995). Object-oriented UIs are seen as providing *isomorphism* between the conceptual model and the UI design. The main benefits of this are in the area of learnability, where the simplicity and consistency of the UI design can have significant usability advantages (see section 6).

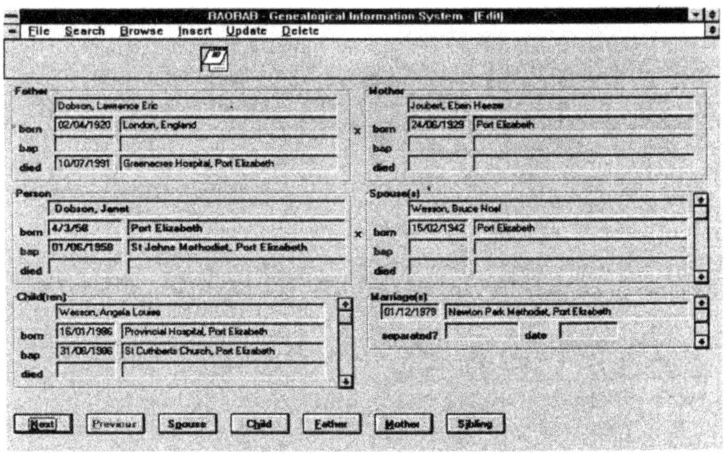

Figure 2 Browse Screen in the New Genealogical System

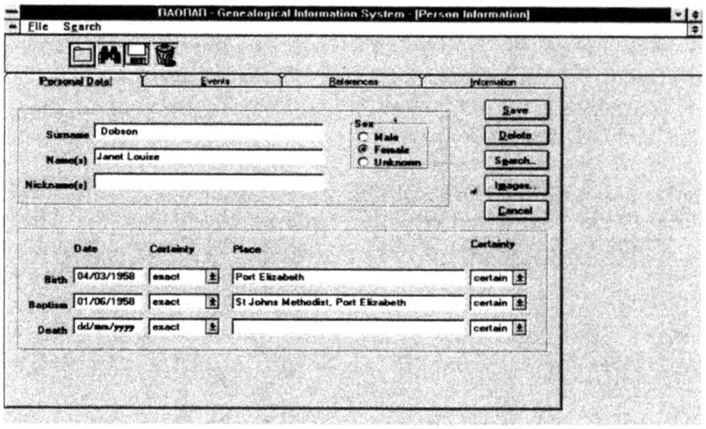

Figure 3 Edit Screen in the New Genealogical System

5. OBSERVATIONS

The use of the MUSE method to design the new GIS resulted in several observations. The major advantages of using the method are seen to be the following:

- The MUSE method is based on task analysis and adopts a user-centered approach. This was found to be particularly important when designing a highly interactive system, like a GIS.
- A single notation is used throughout the method, namely that of the structured diagram.
- MUSE is one of the few methodologies which prescribes an in-depth study of the usability of extant and partially related systems. This enabled us to identify the usability problems of both UPEGIS and BKWIN.

The above must, however, be seen in the light of several disadvantages which were encountered in the use of the method:

- The use of the structured diagram is inappropriate for describing device-level interaction in a Windows-based interface. As a result of this, difficulties were experienced in modelling the dialogue in both BKWIN and the new GIS.
- The method produces a large number of intermediate design products and is very time-consuming.
- The method does not currently have any computer-aided support tools. The structured diagrams and supporting tables had to be drawn with a word processor, and the screens were created using Visual Basic.
- The method needs to be explicitly integrated with an object-oriented analysis and design method (Booch, 1994), (Rumbaugh, 1991), (Yourdon, 1994). The object model for the new GIS was essential both for the presentation design, and for the database design.
- The presentation design stage does not provide any explicit human factors guidelines and fails to take into account the data model of the target system. This stage had to be supplemented with guidelines from the TRIDENT methodology.

6. DESIGN EVALUATION

A detailed usability analysis of the design of the new GIS, BAOBAB, was performed by conducting an analytical evaluation (Newman, 1995). This comprised a heuristic evaluation of the UI design, a comparative keystroke-level analysis of two critical tasks, and a cognitive walkthrough of the same two tasks. The heuristic evaluation revealed that the overall system usability was good. Minor design problems were identified in the areas of learnability and flexibility, but the area of robustness was found to be particularly strong (Dix, 1993), (Nielsen, 1993). The observability and recoverability of the systems were found to be good, and a high degree of task conformance was evident.

Keystroke-level analysis was used to compare the methods used in UPEGIS, BKWIN and the new GIS (BAOBAB), to perform the critical tasks of inserting and updating person information. BAOBAB was found to exhibit the lowest interaction time for the two tasks. This we attribute both to the object-oriented design of the UI, and the user-centered design approach of the MUSE methodology.

Cognitive Walkthroughs were used to assess the degree of user support provided in the UI design. The results obtained here corresponded closely with the heuristic evaluation: no user problems were encountered in the performance of either the two critical tasks.

7. CONCLUSIONS

Although the subject of this paper has discussed the design of only a single case study, yet several conclusions can be made. Firstly, since significant gains in usability have been achieved in the design of the new GIS, the use of structured methods to produce useable systems is supported. These gains are attributed to the broad lifecycle support provided by the MUSE methodology, and in particular, the study of extant systems. The problem had to be approached, however, from two sides: UI design and object modelling. More work is needed, therefore, to develop an integrated, user-centered design methodology which will seamlessly integrate UI design with an object-oriented design approach.

REFERENCES

Bodart, F., Hennebert, A., Leheureux, J., Sacre, I., and Vanderdonckt, J. (1993) *Architecture Elements for Highly-Interactive Business-Oriented Applications*, in Lecture Notes in Computer Science, vol. 753, L.Bass, J. Gornostaev and C. Unger (ed.), Springer-Verlag, Berlin, 83-104.

Bodart, F., Hennebert, A., Leheureux, J., and Vanderdonckt, J. (1994a) *Towards a Dynamic Strategy for Computer-aided Visual Placement*, in Proceedings of AVI'94. T.Catarci, M. Costaile, S. Levialdi and G. Santucci (ed.), ACM Press, 78-87.

Bodart, F. and Vanderdonckt, J. (1994b) *On the Problem of Selecting Interaction Objects*, in Proceedings of HCI'94. G. Cockton, S. Draper, G. Weir (ed.), Cambridge University Press, Cambridge, 25-39.

Bodart, F., Hennebert, A., Leheureux, J., Provot, I. Vanderdonckt, J., Zucchinetti, G. (1995) *Key Activities for a Development Methodology for Interactive Applications*. In D. Benyon and Ph. Palanque (ed.), Critical Issues in User Interface Systems Engineering, chapter 7. Springer-Verlag.

Booch, G. (1994) *Object-Oriented Analysis and Design, with Applications*. Benjamin/Cummings, 2nd Edition.

Collins, Dave. (1995) *Designing Object-Oriented User Interfaces*. Benjamin/Cummings.

DeMarco, Tom. (1987) *Structured Analysis and System Specification*. Yourdon Press.

Dix, A., Finlay, J., Abowd, G., Beale, R. (1993) *Human-Computer Interaction*. Prentice-Hall.

Hull, R. and King, R. (1987) *Semantic Database Modeling: Survey, Applications and Research Issues*. ACM Computing Surveys, **19(3)**.

Jackson, M. (1983) *Systems Development*. .Prentice-Hall.

Lim, K.Y. and Long, J. (1994) *The MUSE Method for Usability Engineering*. Cambridge series on Human-Computer Interaction. Cambridge University Press.

Newman, W.M. and Lamming, M.G. (1995) *Interactive Systems Design*. Addison-Wesley.

Nielsen, Jacob. (1993) *Usability Engineering*. Academic Press.

Redmond-Pyle, D. and Moore, A. (1995) *Graphical User Interface and Design (GUIDE): A practical process*. Prentice-Hall.

Rumbaugh, J., Blaha, M., Premerlani, W., Eddy, F., Lorensen, W. (1991) *Object-Oriented Modeling and Design*. Prentice-Hall.

Sullivan K.J., Kalet, I.J., and Notkin, D. (1996) *Evaluating the Mediator Method: Prism as a Case*

Study. IEEE Transactions on Software Engineering, **22(8)**, 563-569.

Walsh, P., Lim, K.Y., Long, J. and Carver, M.K. (1989) JSD and the Design of User Interface Software. In P. Barber and J. Laws, (ed.) *Ergonomics* (Special Issue on Methodological Issues in Cognitive Economics), **32(11)**, 1483-1498.

Yourdon, E. (1994) *Object-Oriented Systems Development: An Integrated Approach*. Prentice-Hall.

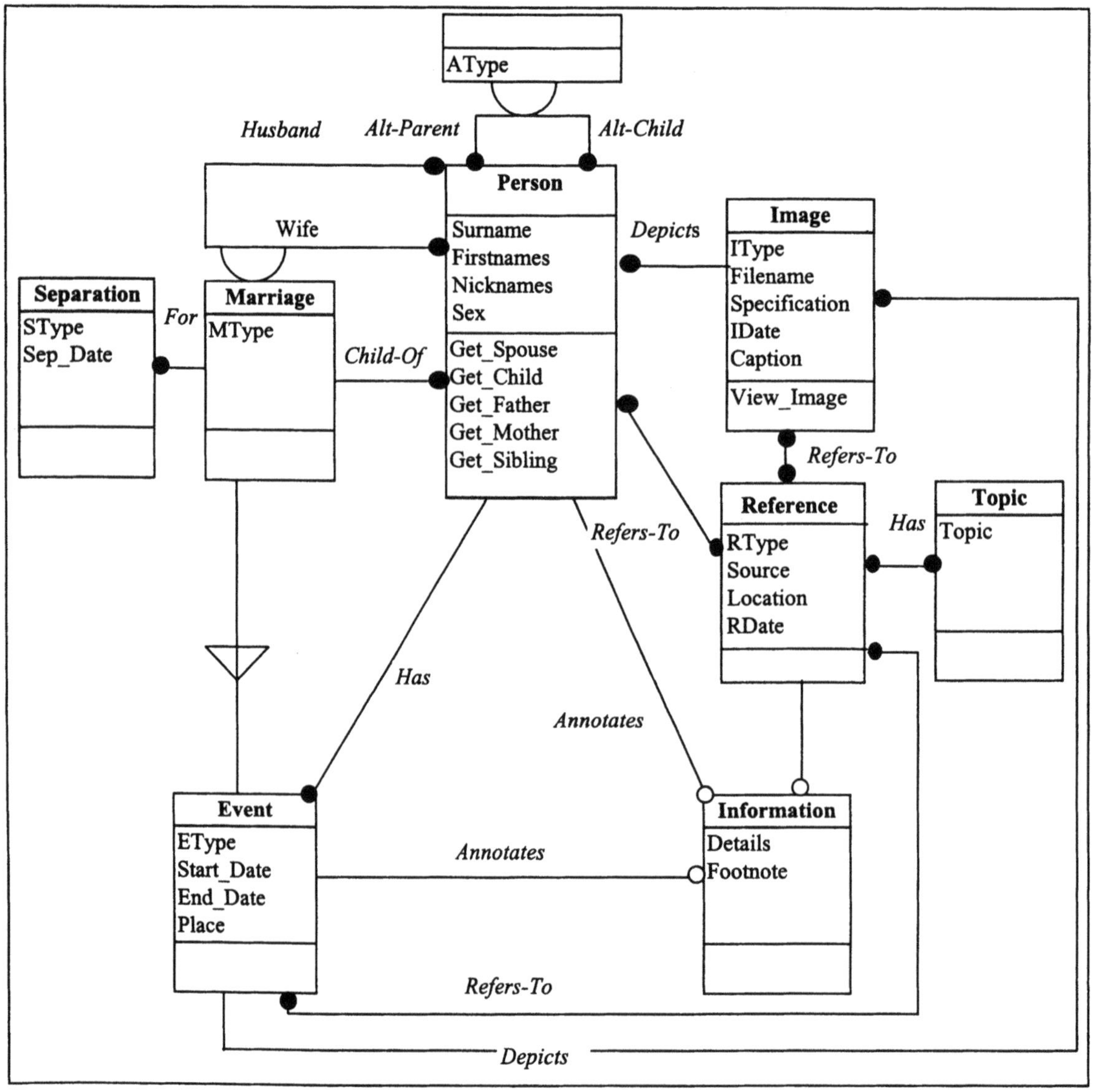

Figure 4 OMT Model for the Target Genealogical System

7

Navigation in Information Spaces: supporting the individual

David Benyon

Dept. Computer Studies
Napier University
219, Colinton road
Edinburgh
EH14 1JD, UK
D.Benyon@dcs.napier.ac.uk

Kristina Höök

SICS (Swedish Institute of Computer Science)
Box 1263
S-164 28 Kista, Sweden
kia@sics.se

ABSTRACT The issue of how users can navigate their way through large information spaces is one that is crucial to the ever expanding and interlinking of computer systems. There are many ways of dealing with the issue of navigation. The use of appropriate metaphors is one, virtual reality and 3D interfaces another. A third is to provide adaptive interfaces based on individual differences in users navigational ability. This paper takes a critical look at the alternatives for assisting users to navigate information spaces and concludes by outlining a research agenda for navigation support.

KEYWORDS Navigation, Wayfinding, Information Space, Individual Differences

1. INFORMATION SPACES

The concept of an 'information space' is one that is becoming increasingly important in the current era of large and/or networked computers. Information spaces are manifested in such areas as multiple interacting databases where 'data mining' is a major issue, and in large hypermedia systems such as the World Wide Web (WWW). Traditional information retrieval systems can be seen as information spaces as can more everyday media such as a CD-ROM or a one or two gigabyte disc.

The concept of an information space is best understood by appealing to the notion of an information system, or information artifact. An information artifact is 'any artifact whose purpose is to allow information to be stored, retrieved, and possibly transformed' (Green and Benyon, 1996). Interactive devices such as spreadsheets, word processors, and music notations are clearly examples of information artifacts, but so are non-interactive devices like tables, documents and musical scores. An information artifact consists of two levels of description; a conceptual level provides some abstraction of the experienced world and a perceptual level provides a view, or viewport onto that structure. Thus a paper train timetable is one information artifact providing information about train journeys and a talking timetable is another (Bental, Benyon and Green, in press).

All information artifacts employ various symbols, structured in some fashion, and provide functions to manipulate the symbols (whether conceptually or physically). From these symbols people are able to derive information. Thus every information artifact defines an information space - the symbols, structure and functions which allows information to be stored, retrieved and transformed.

Human–Computer Interaction: INTERACT'97 S. Howard, J. Hammond & G. Lindgaard (editors)
Published by Chapman & Hall

As humans we live, work and relax in information spaces. At one level of description all our multifarious interactions with the experienced world are effected through the discovery, exchange, organisation and manipulation of information. Information spaces are not the province of computers. They are central to our everyday experience. Finding your way through an airport, a hotel or a city involves travelling in an information space. Paper documents represent another type of information space. Users will get quite different information from books, from newspapers and from magazines. Similarly they will find various information in timetables, guides and maps.

In computer systems there is a range of information spaces which demonstrate different characteristics. Cyberspace is 'a three-dimensional domain in which cybernetic feedback and control occur' (Walker, 1990). Navigation in such spaces is relatively unconstrained. Hyperspace, typified by hypertext or hypermedia systems, provides a structure in which the information nodes are linked and functions provided which facilitate following these links.

Large software systems such as spreadsheets and word processors are information spaces in which the user navigates by clicking on icons or selecting from menus. In contrast to these spaces which have been designed by system developers, physical media such as discs and CDROMs are information spaces which are primarily user structured. Users are responsible for deciding how to organise their information, how to name things, when to duplicate items and where to store them. Where networks of computers are involved issues such as authorisation and access become more important. On a single machine the user is rarely too worried about where he or she is in the system. In contrast location is a vital piece of information on a network.

Issues concerning the number of types of object and their attributes, the range of manipulative functions and the organisation and distribution of the information characterise different sorts of computer-based information space. It is also important to recognise that these spaces exist within time. A well-structured information space can soon become a tangled mess if someone or something is not there to organise it. Authorisations change, passwords expire and computers are replaced. Information space/time may be a better conceptualisation.

2. MOVING AROUND IN INFORMATION SPACE

Humans spend their lives in spaces; whether social, geographical, personal or informational, so it is not surprising that the nature of spaces and the ways in which we move around spaces has been studied from a number of perspectives. City planners (e.g. Lynch, 1977), geographers, anthropologists and historians deal with spaces, though from a social rather than psychological perspective. Architectural design (Passini, 1992) has considered issues of navigation in relation to the construction of buildings, shopping malls and theatres. Post-modern analysis of spaces takes a critical view of the 'traditional' psychological approach to space and navigation. (See Liggett and Parry, 1995 for a variety of perspectives on spatial theory and urban studies). It is perhaps surprising that these disciplines have commented so little on information spaces *per se.* For example, in his thorough account of spaces, Lefebvre (1991) identifies many different types of space: geographical spaces, ethnographical space, demographic space, musical spaces, plastic spaces and so on. However he comments 'we know enough...to suspect the existence of a space peculiar to information science, but not enough to describe that space, mush less to claim acquaintance with it' (p. 86). Shields (1991) is quick to dismiss the objectivist view of traditional geography, preferring instead a semiotic, culturally-based approach. The importance of socially-constructed ideas and values is indeed important, but by emphasising that people derive meaning from such interactions, he shifts us from a geographical to an informational space. The issue of how to travel in that space remains (O'Day and Jeffries, 1993; Shum, 1990).

Psychologists have tended to focus their attentions on the topic of moving around in information spaces; navigation. Neisser (1976) deals with navigation in terms of cognitive maps; the mental representations which people have of their environment. However, these are not static models. Ecological considerations are important as people draw important cues from the immediate environment and develop knowledge of the space over time and through the experience of interacting with it. Issues of navigation are central to Hutchins recent discussion of distributed cognition (Hutchins, 1995) and cultural differences have been explored with respect to navigation (Hutchins, 1983). A considerable amount has been published on Polynesian navigators in particular (see Hutchins, 1995 p 65 - 93).

Much of the psychology of navigation is couched in terms of *wayfinding*. How do people work out how to reach their destination? The answers to this question are many and, often, unsurprising. People use maps and guides. They exploit landmarks in order to have something to aim for and to recognise a place when they arrive or use 'dead reckoning' at sea when there are no landmarks. Novel techniques can be provided to give the user different views of a real or virtual landscape - fish-eye views focus attention on one area but provide a wide angle to overall view. Three dimensional 'fly overs' of virtual spaces are made possible with computer technology.

Learning to find ones way in a new space is another aspect of navigation considered by psychologists (Kuipers, 1982, Gärling et al. 1982). First, we learn a "linked-list-of-items" – when we see the hedge we know that we should turn left. Then we get to know some landmarks and can start relating our position with regards to this landmark. We learn the relative position of landmarks and start building mental "maps" of parts of the space in-between these landmarks. These maps are not complete but rather like pages in an atlas. Some of the pages are detailed others are not, and more importantly, the relation between the pages are not perfect. Some may be distorted with respect to one-another. This process is fairly quick for a new city as shown by (Gärling et al. 1982). In a couple of weeks new students in a university city had formed their "atlas" over the city.

For the interests of developers of large scale computer-based information spaces, there may be much which can be learned from the psychological experiences of wayfinding in general. However, wayfinding is primarily concerned trying to reach a destination. Whilst trying to obtain some specific information is certainly one thing which users of computer systems do it is not the only thing. Users do not simply make plans and carry out appropriate actions. They browse, scan and wander through information space.

We might oppose the idea of wayfinding with the notion of *exploration*. With exploration, people are not trying to get anywhere, they are not trying to find their way. Instead they are just interested to have a look around. On many occasions they will not want to return to this particular space. Exploration is concerned with finding out about a local environment and perhaps how that environment relates to other environments. The user is interested in the nature of the terrain, with seeing new vistas. The recognition of place can be important, but much knowledge in exploration is knowledge in the world, and need not be made knowledge in the explorer's head.

A third activity which is undertaken in information space is *identifying objects*. Here the user is less interested in the location of objects, nor is the user interested in finding a path or reaching a goal. Although object identification is somewhat akin to exploration, the purpose of the activity is different. Exploration focuses on understand what exists in an environment and how the things are related. Object identification is concerned with finding categories and clusters of objects spread across environments, with finding interesting configurations of objects and finding out information about the objects.

3. INDIVIDUALS IN INFORMATION SPACES

One of the main problems with systems design is dealing with individuals. In the information spaces which we provide, we need to cater for users who have very different goals from other users. We need to accommodate users who have ill-formed goals, different experiences and different domain knowledge.

Users have different capabilities, preferences and different skills. There is now enough knowledge of individual differences and navigation to say that these differences are important and significant. In some experimental work (Benyon and Murray, 1993), found a clear influence of spatial ability on navigation in a database. Subjects used a command interface to a database system and were measured on experience of using command interfaces and spatial ability. The results showed that many limitations on subjects' performance on the command interface, which related to their spatial ability, could be overcome with experience. However, a scatter plot of subjects' spatial ability scores against their test session times shows clearly that not all the limitations of low spatial ability are overcome by high experience (Figure 1).

Vicente and colleagues (1987) also found that spatial ability affected users ability to navigate a large file structure. More recently Höök and her colleagues have found a similar result (Dahlbäck, et al., 1996). This study is particularly interesting as the researchers have tried to tease apart the nature of the cognitive ability which affects navigation in information as opposed to geographic space. The experiment demanded that users undertake real navigation problems in a hypermedia system. The strongest result showed a correlation (with a chance probability less than .005) between users abilities on tests involving the mental rotation of images and their task completion time (see Figure 2). Overall the distribution is similar distribution to that shown in Figure 1. The differences between the individuals overall shows just how important individual differences are in navigating information spaces. The fastest subject solved the tasks 19 times faster than the slowest

The tests of spatial ability used in the study by Dahlbäck et al (1996) showed that the tests which allowed subjects to rotate or manipulate blocks or draw figures did *not* correlate with navigation in hypermedia, but instead correlated with the subjects subjective estimating of their map-reading ability. The researchers conclude that there is a difference between spatial ability for solving problems in the world and the spatial ability for solving problems in the abstract world of information spacesubject.

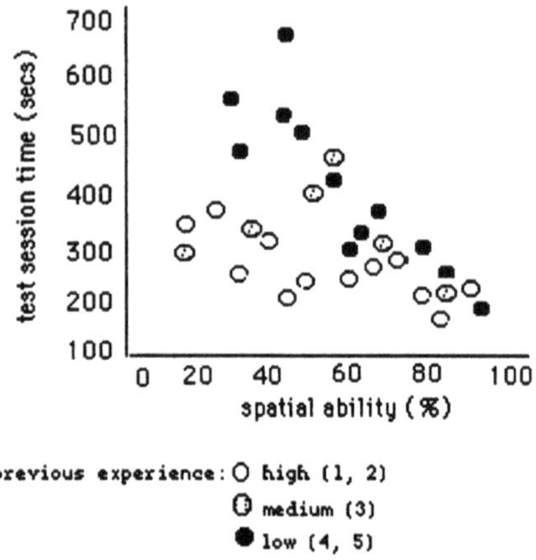

Figure 1 Subjects' test session times against their spatial ability scores, giving their command experience.

The fact that individual differences do have an impact on navigation seems incontrovertible. The spatial ability to rotate objects is certainly one factor which has been found to influence people's abilities to navigate. Experience is another, technical aptitude another (Borgman, 1989) and learning style appears to be another (Esichaikul et al., 1994). We also know that some individuals like using maps and others do not, preferring verbal instructions over graphical representations (Streeter et al., 1985, Streeter and Vitello, 1986) There are important novice vs. expert differences as demonstrated by studies of taxi drivers (Pailhous, 1970, Chase, 1983).

4. METAPHORS FOR INFORMATION SPACES

One solution which designers have is to exploit a metaphor in the design of their navigational aids. Vicente and Williges (1988) found that by introducing a visual, concrete metaphor, they were able to assist users in navigating their file system. However, metaphor needs using with care if it is to deal with the range of activities which users are engaged in, the nature of the information space and differences between individuals.

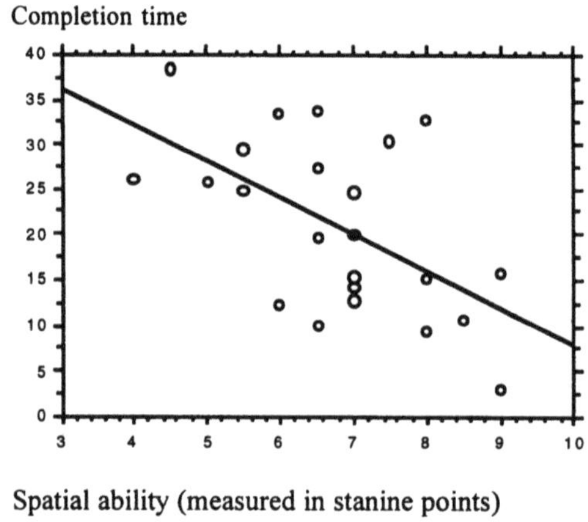

Figure 2. The correlation between completion time and spatial ability.

Alan Kay has criticised the use of metaphor as a design approach because the computer allows us to escape from the limitations of erstwhile devices and we do not want to import the restrictions inherent in a metaphor into novel systems (Kay, 1990). However the use of extended and complex metaphors continues to be popular with designers and there have been many examples of designers employing rich metaphors in their systems. For example, Card's Rooms metaphor (Card, et al., 1991), the Information City (Dieberger, 1994), Guides (Oren, et al., 1990) and so on. General advice on selecting a metaphor (such as considering the nature of the user population and the correspondence between the structure and functioning of the metaphor and the underlying system) has been published (e.g. Erickson, 1990; Carroll et al., 1988), but little has been said about metaphor and navigation in general. As we have seen, users will want to do different things in the information spaces, and metaphors will help or hinder them in those activities. The different types of information space will demand different types of metaphor.

One recent conference on spatial metaphors and hypertext (Dieberger, 1994) offers some useful ideas. For example, Benking and Judge (1994) identify types of metaphor: 'geometric forms (cube, sphere, polyhedra in general), artificial forms (townscapes, house, room), natural forms (landscape, trees, etc.), systemic structures (highway systems, pathways, flow systems), dynamic systems (atomic, molecular, planetary, galactic systems), traditional symbol systems (mandalas, sand paintings, etc.)'. Besides these overall metaphors, 3D style interfaces can be effective in helping users to visualise the information space, providing a simulated 'fly-over' effect. Given the right software (such as Hyper-G and the Harmony browser), the visualisation can be generated automatically with the attributes of the information objects being used to structure the display (Maurer, 1996 gives a full description of the Hyper-G server and its browsers).

Spatial metaphors come in a wide variety of forms. A city metaphor is one popular example. A city metaphor employs the familiar constructs of roads, subways, houses, shops and a variety of buildings. For example, Dieberger (1994) states 'We are used to navigate cities using very vague descriptions and using various navigational tools like maps, verbal descriptions, sketches, navigational infrastructure (signposts), personal inquiry, transport systems (taxis, subways) and collaboration. Cities are large structured spaces and they can easily be connected to systems containing several cities by using some simple transport systems between cities. Cities are dynamic spaces and people cope well with limited change in those spaces whereas they get quite confused when there is some change in the spatial structure of - say - a desktop. There is a rich body of knowledge about the organization of cities and navigation in cities that can provide a starting point how to make the city metaphor usable as organising principle in a virtual world.' He also points out that users can be transported quickly 'by magic' from one part of the city to another without feeling disorientated as the concept maps well onto using the subway (which counters some of Kay's criticism). There is no doubt that cities provide a rich metaphor, suitable for exploring and locating specific objects.

Other metaphors which might be useful for thinking about navigation include a wilderness (frightening, confusing, enchanting) or a desert (intimidating, beautiful, with no landmarks). Such metaphors might encourage forging a path, enjoying the scenery and getting out. Wilderness and desert can be included in an overall countryside metaphor where different types of terrain represent different types of information. These metaphors encourage exploration by the user; the system provides a high level metaphor, but the user provides a more detailed structure

The night sky offers a different sort of space. It represents objects, clusters, patterns and it is very big. It supports the activities of mapping and identifying objects. However, there are relatively few types of object in the night sky (galaxies, stars, planets). It is the configurations and sub-types of these objects which is of interest. Science fiction concepts such as warp drives and worm holes can be sued for quick and magic transportation to distant parts of the space.

The open sea is another metaphor. It encourages a distinction between the surface and depth. Thus it is natural to think of a lot of information as being hidden beneath the surface and only available for viewing if the user dives down. Currents can link continents and islands and take people to unexpected places. People can look for islands of information; archipelagos provide clusters. Waterworth (1996) combines an island metaphor with a personal 'vehicle' space.

A 3D or 4D object offers a different perspective. Here the user can see the whole of the space and can manipulate it, rotate it. It is suited to users who want to see the whole space and become orientated. A museum has been structured to allow free roaming, yet is also structured to facilitate learning. A library is suitable for finding information. It is well-organised and structured. The librarian has already organised the material with like subjects kept together. A breakfast bar (so popular in holiday hotels) offers another type of metaphor. Here a whole range of choices are laid out for the users. The user can see how far the space extends and can be offered choice. Users are encouraged to feed a need, to take what they want and to come back for more. It's a constrained, help yourself environment.

This is not intended to be an exhaustive list, nor even to provide an example of each possible type of metaphor. Metaphors work by providing correspondences between one domain and another (Lakoff, 1988). In using them as the basis of a physical design, it is important that these correspondences are consistent and meet with users expectations. Moreover, it is important that the metaphors support what users want to do in that space - to find a way, to identify, cluster and classify, or simply to wander around and explore.

5. A WAY FORWARD FOR NAVIGATION SUPPORT

We live in a world of information spaces. Increasingly these are very large computer-based information spaces. Whether the information space is an application, a hard disc, a CD-ROM, a local area network or the Internet, the problem of how to help the user to navigate, explore and identify the objects of interest is critical to the success of the system.

There is much that computer system designers can learn from other disciplines which deal with space. Lynch (1977) identifies techniques based on a number of characteristics such as; spatial form (different types of models, maps, etc.), temporal form (showing the history of development), sequencing to show paths through a space, visibility to show alternative vistas and ambient qualities of different parts of the space. Architecture (Passini, 1992) provides another perspective. However, we have, in addition, our own problems and our own opportunities.

The abstract nature of information space means that designers have to import the concrete from elsewhere. Metaphors for conceptualising information space can exploit common well-grounded experience from the users world. But care needs to be taken to provide consistency and completeness. We must be wary about importing from the concrete world to the abstract informational world what we *think* aids navigation. We must also be aware that it is important not simply to wander around an information space. Users usually want to obtain and remember some information and solutions which hide too much may aid navigation at the expense of reducing the amount of information obtained. Metaphors must also be chosen which allow the users to find their way, to wander, scan the space and identify what they want. Information spaces also make different demands on different users owing to their different cognitive capabilities - in particular some measure of their spatial ability.

Computer-based information spaces, however, have a great opportunity. They do not have to be single, stable spaces; they can be adaptive. In a review of adaptive hypermedia systems, (Brusilovsky, 1996) identifies the following types of navigational support which may benefit from some adaptiveness. Direct guidance systems decide which is the next most appropriate node for users. Adaptive ordering adjusts the order of links on a page - for example by making more relevant links nearer to the top of a display. Hiding constrains the size of the information space by automatically hiding pages from users and adaptive annotation adds additional information to links in the form of textual annotation, icons, colour and so on. To be effective these adaptations need knowledge of the individual user; the cognitive characteristics, purpose and domain knowledge which the individual has. Maes (1994) has shown that relevant knowledge about user preferences can be quickly inferred from their early choices and (Benyon and Murray, 1993) show how cognitive characteristics can be inferred from error rate.

Although we have a good understanding of the factors which affect navigation and we have a range of possible design solutions to these problems, the research has yet to demonstrate which problems can be solved by which solutions. For example, adaptive hypermedia systems that hide parts of the nodes can be used to reduce the information space. However, a low-spatial user may still have problems — not with the overview of the space, perhaps but with local decisions such as where to go next. If the adaptive system proposes where to go next it won't necessarily prevent the user from feeling lost.

Adaptive annotations and adaptive interfaces (for example changing a graphical map into a verbal set of instructions) can be of use if carefully designed and matched with individuals differences which have a real impact on the usability of the system. Appropriate metaphors and visualisations of the information space can aid object identification and object clustering.

A radical alternative to these approaches is to base navigation on a socially-based, rather than geographically-based footing. "Social navigation" could be one way forward to help users who cannot be helped by maps. Such users might prefer to converse with interface agents, to discuss their information needs rather than having to find their own way to the information. This notion can be extended to filtering agents (Maes, 1994) which organise and structure information, leaving the user to evaluate the relevance of the contents.

The use of narrative offers another solution as suggested by Laurel and others (Laurel, 1991). Through a mixture of stereotypical narratives learnt by everybody and ways of moving between scenes and lines of actions, film or theatre can seduce us to think that we know how to orient ourselves and also to look in certain directions for interesting things.

We see the issue of navigation in information space as one of the most important in interactive system design. From our research we can confidently predict that if designers create large information spaces without paying careful attention to navigational aids, then there will be significant differences in performance between individuals. These differences will include the time they take to retrieve information, the confidence which they have in the results which they obtain, their satisfaction in using the system and in their ability to learn the system. In short, the usability of the system will be radically different for different users.

To combat this lack of usability, we propose that designers should look at the use of metaphor, at employing adaptive techniques and at utilising social approaches to supporting navigation. We must also look at the experiences of navigational support provided by both the geographical view of space, by social alternatives to this view and by semiotic approaches (Gottdiener and Lagopoulos, 1986).

We as designers are involved in the production of information space. However, users of the space are equally involved in its production. It is they who attach meaning to the space. It is they who have to live in the space.

6. REFERENCES

Benking, H. and Judge, A. J. N. (1994) Design Considerations for Spatial Metaphors. Presentation at *ECHT'94 - the European Conference on Hypermedia technology*, Sept. 1994, Edinburgh. Available from http://www.lcc.gatech.edu/faculty/Dieberger/ECHT94.WS.toc.html

Bental, D. Benyon D. R. and Green, T. R. G. (in press) *Understanding and Building Entity-relationship Models of Information Artifacts.*

Benyon, D. R. and Murray, D. M. (1993) Adaptive Systems; from intelligent tutoring to autonomous agents. *Knowledge-based Systems,* 6 (3)

Borgman, C. L. (1989) All Users of Information Retrieval Systems are not Created Equal: an exploration into individual differences, *Information processing and management* vol. 25, no. 3, pp. 237-251.

Brusilovsky, P. (1996) Adaptive Hypermedia: An Attempt to Analyse and Generalise. In Brusilovsky, P., Kommers, P. and Streitz, N. (eds.) *Multimedia, Hypermedia and Virtual Reality* LNCS 1077 Springer Verlag

Card, S. K., Robertson, G. C. and Mackinlay, J. D. (1991) The Information Visualizer, an Information Workspace. In Proceedings of CHI '91 Conference on Human factors in Computing Systems, ACM publications, New York pp 181 - 188.

Carroll J.M., Mack R.L., and Kellogg W.A. (1988) Interface Metaphors and User Interface Design, in Helander M. (Ed.): *Handbook of Human-Computer Interaction*, Elsevier pp. 67-85

Chase, W.G. (1983) Spatial Representations of Taxi Drivers, In D. R. Rogers and J.A. Sloboda (eds.) *Acquisition of Symbolic Skills*, pp. 391-405, New York Plenum.

Dahlbäck, N., Höök, K., and Sjölinder, M. (1996) Spatial Cognition in the Mind and in the World - the case of hypermedia navigation, *The Eighteenth Annual Meeting of the Cognitive Science Society*, University of California, San Diego, July, 1996.

Dieberger, A. (1994) Spatial environments to organize and navigate information and to communicate about this organization, Presentation at *ECHT'94 - the European Conference on Hypermedia technology*, Sept. 1994, Edinburgh. Available from http://www.lcc.gatech.edu/faulty/Dieberger/ECHT94.WS.toc.html

Erickson, T. D. (1990) Working with Interface metaphors. In Laurel, B. (ed.) *The Art of Human-Computer Interface Design* Addison-Wesley, Cambridge, Ma.

Esichaikul, V., Smith,, R. D. and Madely, G. R. (1994) The impact of learning style on problem-solving performance in a hypertext environment *Hypermedia* 6 (2) 101 - 111

Gottdiener, M. and Lagopoulos, A. (1986) (eds.) *The City and the Sign* Columbia University Press, New York

Green, T. R. G. and Benyon, D. R. (1996) The skull beneath the skin; Entity-relationship modelling of Information Artefacts. *International Journal of Human-Computer Studies* 44(6) 801-828.

Gärling, T., Böök, A., and Ergesen, N. (1982) Memory for the Spatial Layout of the Evryday Physical Environment: Different Rates of Acquisition of Different Types of Information, *Scandinavian Journal of Psychology*, 23, pp. 23-35.

Hutchins, E. (1983) Understanding Micronesian Navigation. In Gentner, D. and Stevens, A. L. (eds) *Mental Models.* Erlbaum

Hutchins, E. (1995) *Cognition in the Wild* MIT press, Cambridge Ma.

Kay, A. (1990) User Interface: A Personal View. In Laurel, B. (ed.) *The Art of Human-Computer Interface Design* Addison-Wesley, Cambridge, Ma.

Kuipers, B. (1982) The 'Map in the Head' Metaphor, *Environment and Behaviour*, 14, pp. 202-220.

Lakoff, G. (1988) Cognitive Semantics. In Eco, U., Santambrogio, M. & Violi, P. (eds.). *Meaning and Mental Representations*. Indiana University Press.

Laurel, B. (1991) Computers as Theatre, Addison-Wesley Publ. Comp.

Lefebvre, H. (1991) *The Production of Space* Blackwell, Oxford

Liggett, H. and Parry, D. C. (eds.) (1995) *Spatial Practices* SAGE publications Thousand Oaks, Ca.

Lynch K (1977) *Managing the sense of a Region* MIT press, Cambridge, Ma.

Maes P. (1994) Learning Agents in *Communications of the ACM*. August

Maurer, H. (1996) *HyperWave. The next generation web solution* Addison-Wesley Longman, Harlow, UK

Neisser U. (1976) *Cognition and Reality* W. H. Freeman and Company, San Francisco.

O'Day, V. and Jeffries, R. (1993) Orienteering in an Information Landscape: How Information Seekers Get from Here to There, *Proc. ACM InterCHI'93*, pp. 438-445.

Oren, T. Salomon, G., Kreitman, K. and Don, A. (1990) Guides: Characterising the Interface. In Laurel, B. (ed.) *The Art of Human-Computer Interface Design* Addison-Wesley, Cambridge, Ma.

Pailhous, J. (1970) *La Représentation de l'Espace* Urbain, Paris: Presses Universitaires de France.

Passini, R. (1992) *Wayfinding in Architecture* Van Nostrand Reinhold

Shields, R. (1991) *Places on the Margin* Routledge, London, UK

Shum S.B. (1990) Real and Virtual Spaces: Mapping from spatial cognition to Hypertext, *Hypermedia*, Vol .2, No.2 pp. 133-158

Streeter, L., Vitello D., and Wonsiewicz, S. (1985) How to Tell People Where to Go: Comparing Navigational Aids, *International Journal of Man-Machine Studies*, 22, pp. 549-562.

Streeter, L. and Vitello, D. (1986) A Profile of Drivers' Map-Reading Abilities, *Human Factors*, 28(2).

Vicente, K.J., Hayes, B.C., and Williges, R.C. (1987) Assaying and Isolating Individual Differences in Searching a Hierarchical File System, *Human Factors*, 29(3), pp. 349-359.

Vicente, K.J., and Williges, R.C. (1988) Accomodating Individual Differences in Searching a Hierarchical Fiel System, *International Journal of Man-Machine Studies*, 29, pp. 647-668.

Vicente, K. and Williges, R.C., (1988) *Visual Momentum as a means of accommodating individual differences among users of a hierarchical file system.* In: J. Rasmussen and P. Zunde (Eds.), Proc. 5th Symposium EFISS, Risø National Laboratory, Denmark, November 1987 (New York: Plenum Publishing).

Walker, J. (1990) Through the Looking Glass In Laurel, B. (ed.) *The Art of Human-Computer Interface Design* Addison-Wesley, Cambridge, Ma.

Waterworth, J., (1996). A Pattern of Islands: Exploring Public information Space in a Private Vehicle. In Brusilovsky, P., Kommers, P. and Streitz, N. (eds.) *Multimedia, Hypermedia and Virtual Reality* LNCS 1077 Springer Verlag.

8

Constructing memorable asymmetric information diagrams in three dimensions

Brian Regan

University of Newcastle
Callaghan
NSW
Australia
mgbgr@newcastle.edu.au

ABSTRACT This paper presents a model for presenting relational information as a graph in three dimensions, where the emphasis is on the location of nodes by recognition of their locality in the drawing rather than the tracing of paths through the graph. The approach exploits the potential of 3D to present graphs with a high number of nodes specific to an individual user, such as a graph of web-page bookmarks. The key element is the creation of a memorable structure that contains a variety of sub-structures which act as reference points for the viewer as they manipulate their own viewpoint within the three dimensional virtual space of the graph layout. The layout algorithm used here challenges the need for an aesthetic of symmetry in graph drawing within 3D and exploits the user's ability to recall sub-structures within a drawing to replace edge-tracing as the means for locating nodes in the drawing.

KEY WORDS graph drawing, interaction models, World Wide Web; usability testing

1. INTRODUCTION

Graph drawing algorithms provide a mechanism for taking relational information and expressing this in a layout which can be displayed by a computer. With the increasing power of display technologies, graph drawing algorithms have moved from two to three dimensional presentations (Robertson, 1993). Three dimensions gives a new perspective on both the display space available for drawing a graph and the relationship of the users to the drawing of the graph on the display device.

The *Starship Algorithm* presented in this paper is a mechanism for displaying graphs with a large number of nodes (> 500) in three dimensions (*3D*) in an environment where the users can move their viewpoint around the graph layout within the 3D drawing space.

In such an environment, the users need: (i) to be able to maintain their orientation such that they can identify areas of interest in the drawing, and (ii) to be able to recognise the location of a given node even though the resolution of the display or their own vision will be insufficient to read individual labels on nodes in a display of the full graph. The *Starship Algorithm* is designed to create a graph layout which is *memorable*, so that the users can both orientate themselves as they move within the 3D space and recognise distinct structural features as a guide to the location of individual nodes. One of the keys to

Human–Computer Interaction: INTERACT'97 S. Howard, J. Hammond & G. Lindgaard (editors)
Published by Chapman & Hall

creating this memorable drawing is that the algorithm produces an *asymmetric* shape in the resulting drawing.

The algorithm takes an undirected graph, clusters the nodes to form a spanning tree over the graph which forms the basis for a structure based on a series of cone trees attached to a central spine. Of the many types of relational information that may be displayed - a user's collection of Web references and their inter-relationships are a candidate for representation by this algorithm. The result will be a distinctive and thus memorable shape, specific to a particular user.

2. MANAGING LARGE GRAPHS

In many applications, the size of graphs (in the number of nodes) to be presented to users is beyond the ability of a single display device to present all the nodes and their labels simultaneously on the screen such that individual items are discernable to the user. A number of strategies have been devised to present large complex graphs on displays of limited screen size.

2.1. Decomposition

Graph based software design techniques such as data flow diagrams (DFD) (Gane, 1979) have used a series of layers to present a large complex graph as a hierarchy of component diagrams. The component diagrams can be constrained so that they fit comfortably on a single display screen with enough space for each component to allow the user to read labelling information on both nodes and edges.

2.2. Windowing

Where the graph structure or the application is not amenable to decomposition, then the whole graph may be displayed as a single structure but with a scrolling window which highlights a section of the displayed graph drawing. The most common form of this can be seen in the tree structures displayed in file management software and software to manage bookmarks in web browsers, where the user has a scrollable window to scan a tree drawing of directories. Variations of this approach include the fish-eye lens and perspective wall (Furnas, 1986) (Mackinlay, 1991) (Robertson, 1993).

2.3. Three Dimensional Motion

With the improving performance of 3D graphics software, large graphs can be drawn in a three dimensional virtual space with the user's viewpoint able to move within the virtual space. The complete graph drawing may still be too large for the whole graph to be seen with all the node and edge labelling readable, however, the user can control the position of their viewpoint to place it close to areas of the graph drawing of particular interest. Once the motion controls have been mastered, movement around the virtual space of the drawing is more intuitive, than the previous two techniques. The 3D drawings produced by the Starship Algorithm are device independent, such that they can be applied to planar display screens or sophisticated virtual reality environments. This approach is similar in effect to the scrollable windowing techniques mentioned previously, however, the 3D environment provides a depth of view which allows elements of the graph drawing to appear within view but at a distance which prohibits the display of their detail (such as labelling) whilst other elements are still close to the viewpoint. An example of this approach are cone trees (Roberston, 1991) (Hemmje, 1993) (Koike, 1993). The illusion of the 3D environment provides a sense that all components of the graph are viewable by simple manipulation of the user's viewpoint. It is into this last category to which the Starship algorithm belongs.

3. A MEMORABLE STRUCTURE

For each of the above drawing conventions, the focus has been on the user gaining information by tracing a path through the graph drawing (Ware, 1996). The emphasis on path tracing by users has encouraged aesthetics for evaluating graph layouts which focus on minimum number of bends in edges, minimum number of crossings and minimum edge length (Sugiyama, 1981) (Supowit, 1983).

Barreau (Barreau, 1993) studied the usage of file systems and found a preference by users for browsing the displayed tree structure of the file system rather than waiting for the results of a search mechanism based on name. Even though the browsing time was often longer than the time taken by the search facility, subjects preferred to retain control of the searching process. In addition, the scanning of a graph drawing facilitates the identification of a node by 'recognition' of the pattern displayed by the graph drawing in the vicinity of the target node. On the other hand, specifying search criteria will require the 'recall' of the node's label and recognition memory has long been acknowledged as faster and larger in scope than human recall memory (Dix, 1993). Therefore a graph drawing and presentation environment which exploits 'recognition' of nodes or edges by their placement within shapes representing subgraphs within a drawing should facilitate convenient access to graph elements (nodes or edges).

The Starship algorithm creates a graph layout in three dimensions which forms a memorable shape for easier location of objects by recognition of their position. In a graph which must contain many nodes, the individual nodes will be difficult to identify individually, but the layout produced by the Starship algorithm creates a graph drawing with sub-structures which provide recognisable cues to locations.

4. THE NEED FOR ASYMMETRY

Many 2D graph layout algorithms, particularly those concerned with tree layout (Supowit, 1983), have sought to satisfy aesthetic criteria which include a requirement for a symmetrical layout. Symmetry can enhance the aesthetic 'beauty' of a planar 2D layout, but Purchase (Purchase, 1995) found inconclusive results as to whether symmetry was useful in following the displayed graph.

The Starship algorithm seeks to create an asymmetrical layout because in the mobile viewing space of a 3D layout, the user needs as many distinctive features as possible to orientate themselves as they move their viewpoint around the layout of the graph. The primary objective of the Starship algorithm is to produce a layout which aids the user in remembering the locations of nodes in the layout. Symmetrical structures only increase the number of possible similar regions where a node may be located and confuse the user's ability to locate the sub-structure to which they had previously visited.

5. EXAMPLE APPLICATION

In order to place the discussion of the Starship algorithm within the context of an application domain, we will consider the requirements for maintaining references to information resources on the World Wide Web (Bookmark references to URLs). With increased usage of the Web, browser software packages have incorporated the facility to record the URL for sites of interest to a user in a 'hotlist' or 'bookmark list'. As the amount of time spent on the web and the number of interesting sites increases then the user will accumulate a lengthening list of interesting sites and management of this list becomes a bottleneck in terms of gaining access to previously visited sites.

The problem is analogous to the problem arising with early disk file systems (Eg IBM DOS/360 file system) where linear lists of files were considered satisfactory while disk drives were of limited capacity, however it was soon necessary to create the system of sub-directories in a tree structured hierarchy used by most contemporary file systems.

Commercial solutions to displaying web bookmarks have followed the same evolution as file systems to 2D layouts of a bookmark hierarchy. Graph layout methods for displaying hierarchies to exploit the potential of 3D layouts have been developed (Robertson, 1993) but these have not attempted to exploit the users familiarity with the information layout over time or move into 3D presentations.

Just as related files can be linked in a graph structure, so the details of interesting Web sites can be linked into a graph structure according to some semantic knowledge of their contents. The key attributes of the graph so formed are that it will be a network, contain a large number of nodes and be specific to an individual user. The Starship graph layout uses all these attributes to create a memorable shape for the user to locate their Web page references, with the possibility that the pre-existing hypertext links for a new page reference may be used to automatically provide the edges for the graph.

6. STARSHIP ALGORITHM

6.1. Definitions

A **cluster** is a connected sub-graph of nodes and clusters with maximum path length of two.

The **significance** (s) of a node is a number representing the semantic importance of the node as a component of the information application by combining a weighting for the node and weightings for each edge attached to that node.

A **committed** node or cluster is one which has been assigned to a cluster.

A **core node** is the initial node in a given cluster.

A **major-edge** is an edge which is marked for inclusion in the spanning tree.

6.2. Algorithm Description

The Starship algorithm starts with an undirected graph over a set of nodes. In addition the algorithm may accept a weighting on a node or edge representing the semantic significance of some or all of the nodes or edges, which can be user defined and related to the semantics of the application domain. The algorithm goes through the following stages.

(1) Order the nodes: Each node is assigned a 'significance' derived by summing the weights of the edges attached to the node with the weight assigned to the node itself. The nodes are then sorted in order of decreasing significance.

(2) Cluster the nodes: Clusters of nodes are formed by scanning the node list, in a similar manner to the clustering used in (Tarjan, 1983). For each node a cluster is formed by grouping any node with an edge connected to the current node and which is not already committed to a cluster. Once every node is in a cluster, then the clustering continues by incorporating clusters into their neighbouring clusters. The choice of which cluster will incorporate the other is based on the cluster containing the node with the highest significance value. As each cluster is incorporated, the first edge identified as a link between the clusters is marked as a major edge. This process continues until all connected sub-graphs have been linked. Any uncommitted clusters apart from the first cluster created are linked by a created edge from their starting node to the starting node of a cluster connected to the first cluster. This pattern of clustering mimics the growth of bacterial cultures; with each node being drawn into the cluster representing the local centre of activity in the graph.

(3) Form Spanning Tree: A spanning tree is now formed from the edges used to identify the clustering relationships, which minimises the path between nodes of greater significance.

(4) Layout Nodes: The longest path in the spanning tree is found and used as the spine of the layout along the x-axis. Thus nodes on this path are located along the x-axis. The distance between these nodes is determined by the maximum diameter of the cone trees formed for each of the sub-trees of the spanning tree at that given node.

6.3. Algorithm

i. Let G{V,E} be a graph over the set of nodes V and the set of edges E, such that:

(a) For every $v_i \in V$ there is a weight w_{vi} and for every $e(i,j) \in E$ which connects v_i and v_j, there is a weight w_{eij}

(b) For every node v_p with degree(v_p) = j, there is a significance s_p,

where $s_p = w_{vp} + \sum_{i=1}^{j} w_{epq}$ and e(p,q) is an edge which connects with v_p and v_q.

ii. Sort the node set, V, in order of descending node significance.

iii. For node v_i in V (where v_1 is the node with the largest significance value and $s_i > s_{i+1}$), if v_i is committed then repeat **iii** for v_{i+1}, otherwise form a new cluster C_j with v_i as the core node. Include in C_j all nodes v_k, where v_k is not currently committed and $e(i,k) \in E$. Mark all the nodes in C_j as committed. Mark edge e(i,k) as a major edge.

iv. For each cluster C_i (where i=1..c and c = |C|), examine the nodes in order of their significance (s).

For each node v_j, in C_i, if ∃ node v_k in cluster C_p where e(j,k) ∃ E, and C_p is not committed (ie linked to another cluster), then mark C_p as committed, and mark e(j,k) as a major edge.

v. For any cluster C_i, apart from C_1, which is not committed; create a major edge from the core node of C_i to the core node of any other cluster.

vi. Form a spanning tree T{V,E'} by including every major edge in E .

vii. Determine the longest path SP in T.

viii. Assign coordinates for all the nodes in SP along the x-axis.

ix. For each node v_{sp} in SP, create a cone tree for the sub-tree in T for every descendent of v_{sp} in T, which is not in SP, orthogonal with the x-axis.

x. The graph is then drawn with every cone tree initially replaced by a single cone to create the 3D drawing of the graph.

7. USABILITY TESTING

The key premise behind this layout is that by providing users with an asymmetric shape they will be able to remember the location of a node by recognition of the nearby features in the layout and that the features will be recognisable as the user's viewpoint moves around in the three dimensional viewing space. To validate these claims for the graph layout algorithm and more generally for the principle of drawing graphs in 3D using memorable asymmetric layouts, sample drawings will be trialed with some test subjects. Some user testing of graph drawings has already been conducted, [Purchase95] however, those tests have been able to present the test subjects with a variety of graph drawings and measure the ease with which subjects can trace paths on the drawing or locate objects in the drawing. The Starship drawings are designed to be optimal for the location of graph objects after the user has become familiar with the overall shape of the drawing. Thus a key aspect of the test protocol will be the need for each test subject to become familiar with the location of information in the graph drawing which they may then be required to find again.

To ensure that all subjects understand the nature of the information contained in the graph drawing, yet also provide a large complex network graph, the test data is a graph structure based on movies, actors and directors. Each edge links either an actor or a director with a movie. The test procedure will consist of two phases:

(i) **Learning phase.** Subjects will be given a series of questions about movie actors and the system will highlight the location of the node containing the answer. The subject will then move their viewpoint to the node. In addition to training the subject on the location of information in the graph drawing, the time they take to navigate the user software to the highlighted node will be measured to provide a benchmark for that test subject's speed of manipulation.

(ii) **Testing phase.** The following procedure will be followed by subjects with either the Starship layout, a symmetric version of the Starship layout, or a linear alphabetical listing. The subjects will be given a series of questions, where each question contains either a request to find a node already visited in the learning phase or a new node which they had not previously visited but which is connected to a node visited in the learning phase. The software will measure:

(a) the time the user takes to locate the previously visited node - this will provide a measure of the memorability of the structure in the speed with which they return to the correct node.

(b) the distance along the axis of the regions where they hit in trying to find the given node - this will give some measure of locality to the subjects first positioning and so a measure of the memorability of the structure.

8. FURTHER DEVELOPMENTS

There are three main areas into which this

project is currently heading.

(i) The current area of activity is in implementing the software support required for the user testing. To be followed by the actual testing by users of the drawings produced by the algorithm.

(ii) The current version of the Starship algorithm creates a layout from input of a full graph theoretic structure. When slight variations occur in the input graph (for example, the addition of a single edge), the algorithm may generate a noticeably different layout. As an objective of the algorithm is to produce a layout wherein users will remember features of the resulting 3D drawing, it is important that the layout be stable under such minor change and thus an area of development is to find a relatively stable method for incremental change to the graph layout.

(iii) The other aspect of variability is in the user's viewpoint of the 3D structure being projected onto the plane of the screen or other viewing device. It is planned to include into the viewing software, an 'abridgement' procedure which will change some aspects of the drawing depending on the user's viewpoint. Thus when the viewpoint is distant from a sub-graph in the drawing, then the sub-graph may be replaced by a single shape.

9. CONCLUSION

The layout algorithm presented in this paper challenges the need for an aesthetic of symmetry in graph layout when we move into the realm of 3D and has proposed exploiting the user's ability to recall sub-structures within a drawing to replace edge-tracing as the means for locating information in a graph drawing. With the future movement toward 3D/VR presentations on the Web, it would seem appropriate to move the management of bookmark lists beyond the display formats of the first GUI's. Further work in this project is under-explored areas in graph drawing, such as, user testing of layouts, incremental graph drawing and abridgement of graph layouts.

REFERENCES

Barreau,Deborrah and Nardi,Bonnie. (1993) Finding and Reminding: File Organization from the Desktop. *SIGCHI Bulletin* 27(3):39-43.

Dix, A. Finlay, J. Abowd,G. and Beale,R. (1993) *Human-Compter Interaction.* Hemel Hempstead: Prentice Hall.

Furnas, G.W.(1986) Generalized fisheye views. *CHI'86 Proceedings*:16-23.

Gane,C and Sarson,T. (1979) *Structured Systems Analysis.* Englewood Cliffs, N.J.: Prentice Hall.

Hemmje,M.(1993) LyberWorld-A 3D-based User Interface for Computer-supported Information Retreival in Documented Sets. *GMD-Spiegel*(1):56-63.

Koike,H and Yoshihara,H. (1993) Fractal Approaches for Visualizing Huge Hierarchies. *IEEE* :55-60.

Mackinlay, J. Roberston,G. and Card,S. (1991) Perspective Wall:Detail and context smoothly integrated. *Proceedings of SIGCHI'91* .

Purchase,H. Cohen,R. and James,M. (1995) Validating Graph Drawing Aesthetics. Pp. 435-46 in *Graph Drawing*, (Ed) F. J. Brandenburg. Berlin: Springer.

Roberston,G. Mackinlay,J. and Card,S. (1991) Cone Trees: Animated 3D visualizations of hierarchical information. *Proceedings of SIGCHI'91* 189-94.

Robertson,G. Card,S. and Mackinlay,J. (1993) Information Visualization Using 3D Interactive Animation.*Comm of the ACM* 36(4):57-71.

Sugiyama,K. Tagawa,S. and Toda,M. (1981) Methods for Visual Understanding of Hierarchical System Structures. *IEEE Transactions on Systems, Man, and Cybernetics* SMC-11(2):109-25.

Supowit,K. and Reingold,E. (1983) The Complexity of Drawing Trees Nicely. *Acta Informatica* 18:377-92.

Tarjan,R. (1983) An Improved Algorithm for Hierarchical Clustering using Strong Components. *Information Processing Letters* 17(July):37-41.

Ware,C. and Franck,G. (1996) Evaluating Stereo and Motion Cues for Visualizing Information Nets in Three Dimensions. *ACM Transactions on Graphics* 15(April):121-140.

9

ViewNet - Conceptual Design and Modelling of Navigation

Jürgen E. Ziegler

Fraunhofer Institute IAO
Nobelstrasse 12, D-70569 Stuttgart
GERMANY
Juergen.Ziegler@iao.fhg.de

ABSTRACT This paper presents an approach to modelling navigation structures for complex, database-oriented applications. Navigation dialogues are first classified according to a number of underlying principles. The ViewNet technique is introduced for the conceptual design of the navigation structure of a system. ViewNets are diagrams composed of views and navigation links. Different view types are introduced on the basis of the mapping from conceptual objects to views and their role in the dialogue. These types are represented by specific graphical symbols which support the designer in getting a clear overview of the navigation structure and for optimizing dialogues according to the user's task.

KEYWORDS design methods, modelling techniques, navigation, dialogue structures, object-oriented user interfaces

1. INTRODUCTION

The main design issues in developing complex, database-oriented applications with graphical user interfaces are increasingly related to defining the dialogue structure of an application „in the large", i. e. to designing the overall structure of the user interface. Whereas design aids, e. g. in the form of styleguides are available for selecting and designing the standard interaction objects of a graphical user interface, the issue of designing suitable dialogue structures must usually be solved by the developer for each application specifically. In the best case, this process is currently supported by guidelines which are specific to an application or an organization. As yet, there is little methodological support for solving the complex design decisions involved. An appropriate conceptual design of the dialogue paths which make the functionality of a complex system accessible is , however, essential for the usability of the system, particularly as users are becoming more and more familiar with the basic handling of graphical user interfaces.

In order to better distinguish it from those parts of the dialogue which serve for manipulating the different interaction objects (like buttons, entry fields or lists), the term „navigation" shall be used here to describe the user's movement through the different views of a system. A „view" is defined here as a collection of elements which represent one or more underlying application objects or tasks in a coherent manner, e. g. in a window or screen form.

A number of techniques for modelling navigation sequences have been developed till now which basically aim at describing precisely the system's behaviour depending on the system's state and the user's input. Those techniques are typically based on state transition diagrams (see e. g. Denert 1977, Jacob 1986) or Petri nets (see e. g. Janssen 1993). Due to the detailed specification of trigger events, conditions and actions, however, they entail the danger of obstructing the view of the overall dialogue structure for the developer rather than making it transparent. Although some approaches have been proposed for designing the structure of the navigation e.g. in the field of hypermedia systems (see Nielsen 1990, Berk

Human–Computer Interaction: INTERACT'97 S. Howard, J. Hammond & G. Lindgaard (editors)
Published by Chapman & Hall

& Devlin 1991, they are not well suited to database-oriented applications where the dialogue design has to take the cardinalities of object classes (many instances of the same type) into account.

On the other hand, the existing dialogue modelling techniques say little about the type and the properties of the views of which the navigation structure is composed (they generally only indicate the views´names). That is why they can be described as being rich in transition information but poor in state information. Information concerning the meaning and role of a view, however, is pertinent to the design of efficient and consistent dialogues, arguably more important during the early conceptual design stages than a detailed behavioural specification. Till now, a method has been lacking which takes both aspects into account and which particularly make the type and meaning of the views evident from which the navigation structure is built. This paper presents the ViewNet method which takes these requirements into consideration and supports the conceptual design of the navigation structures through a graphical modelling technique.

2. PRINCIPLES OF NAVIGATION DESIGN

Navigation dialogues can be structured according to a number of different principles. These principles relate to the respective predominant aspect of the user's task, such as the function to be performed, the object to be manipulated, or the selection of a task step from a complete business process to be accomplished. These different goal components translate into different requirements with respect to how the user will access the functionality needed for performing the task and the corresponding dialogue paths required. In general, navigation structures may be based either on a functional decomposition of the system, on the objects of an application and their relations or on arbitrary associations between different pieces of information. In the following, we will discuss some of these principles and their implications for the usability of the system.

Function-oriented navigation: The selection of a specific function or operation represents the starting point for the navigation (e. g. in a conventional hierarchical menu system). The actual data view becomes visible and can only be manipulated after one or several consecutive steps. This type of navigation is particularly suited to well-defined and repetitive tasks with little variability but has major drawbacks if the operation component of the user's task is not well defined at the outset or changes during the interaction.

Process-oriented navigation can be seen as an extension of the function-oriented principle and provides support for a complete set of tasks belonging to a specific work or business process. The system can control the status of the process and according to the situation, enable or disable the access to the objects and functions needed. Whereas early systems of this type used to force the user to perform a fixed sequence of steps, today´s graphical interfaces allow a more flexible design , e. g. through visualizing the status of the process and currently available tasks in lists, task bars etc..

Object-oriented navigation represents the main paradigm in direct manipulation. It uses the objects of the application and of their semantic relations for the design of dialogue paths. Operations become only available when the object to be manipulated is selected and visible . Object-oriented navigation represents one of the basic principles of the graphical user interfaces and is particularly characterized by its high degree of consistency and flexibility.

Association-oriented navigation characterizes the typical navigation form in hypertext/hypermedia systems. The nodes of the navigation structure are represented by individual information units (in contrast to fixed object types with arbitrarily many instances in object-oriented navigation). The possible transitions are defined through the arbitrary associations between those information units.

These forms of navigation have different profiles concerning usability criteria such as efficiency, comprehensibility and flexibility. Combined forms are therefore frequently used in real applications.In the following section, we will focus on the different types of views which are involved in the composition of such navigation structures.

3. VIEW TYPES

In the ViewNet method, views are defined as logical collections of information elements, not as concrete visual representations. Views represent the underlying application objects, tasks or general information units wholly or in part and can be visualized in a coherent manner. Multiple views of an object are possible. Views can be composed of a hierarchy of subviews. In the following, we will introduce a classification of the different types of views relevant for user navigation and introduce a graphical notation for these types which forms the elements of a ViewNet representation.

Object views represent a single instance of a specific object class (e. g. 'customer') in different forms. Three types of object views can be distinguished: the object reference view, which is often in the form of an icon (*icon view*), the *attribute view*, which represents all or some attributes of an object, and the *graphical view* which shows an arbitrary graphical representation of an object instance (e.g. as a map, a business graphic etc.).

In order to structure object-oriented dialogues, **collection views** are required which either show a partial or a complete collection of instances of a certain object class (e.g. as a list of instances) or comprise objects of different types as e.g. the objects on a desktop *(inhomogenous collection*). A special case of collection views are filtered collections through which the user has access to pre- or self-defined subsets of the data (e. g. all payable bills). In many cases, it will be advantageous if users can set up and manage such filter objects themselves at the user interface in a flexible way.

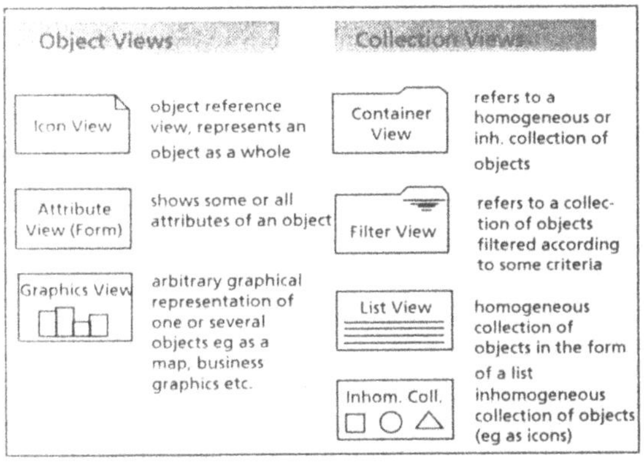

Figure 1: Object and collection views

Function views offer functionally oriented possibilities for navigation, as they are represented, for example, by menu screens or modal dialogue boxes (Figure 2). Object attributes may be shown in a function view but usually only as needed for the operation selected (e. g. search attributes in a search dialogue box). *Actor views* are a special form of a function view and represent the differente steps of a complex task or process the user needs to perform. Actor views help to guide the user through the steps of a complex process while maintaining application-specific dependencies and constraints. They can be realized in very different forms, e.g. as to-do lists, task lists or assistant windows which are becoming more and more popular in standard office products.

Information views, represented either as single nodes or clusters, can be used in association-oriented navigations. Examples for this can be found in hypertext-based help systems or generally in hypermedia systems. In contrast to the links between of object and collection views which represent 1:n or n:m relations in an underlying object model (or entity-relationship model), the relations involved in the navigation between information views are usually of a one-to-one type.

Figure 3 shows **composite views**. Typical aggregations which are often used in graphical interfaces like *master-detail views* or *notebooks*, are depicted with their own graphical symbol in order to get a comprehensive and intuitive overview of the dialogue structure. *Generic building blocks* allow to collapse the parts of a complete navigation substructure into a single element which can be parameterized with the object class accessed in this navigation. This way, for example, a search dialogue for instances of a class which consists of several views can be parameterized with the name of the class. Similar search dialogues for different classes (e. g. orders, customers, products) can then be represented by a single symbol with an additional indication of the respective class. This mechanims reduces the size of the diagram, improves clarity and supports a consistent development of the navigation structure.

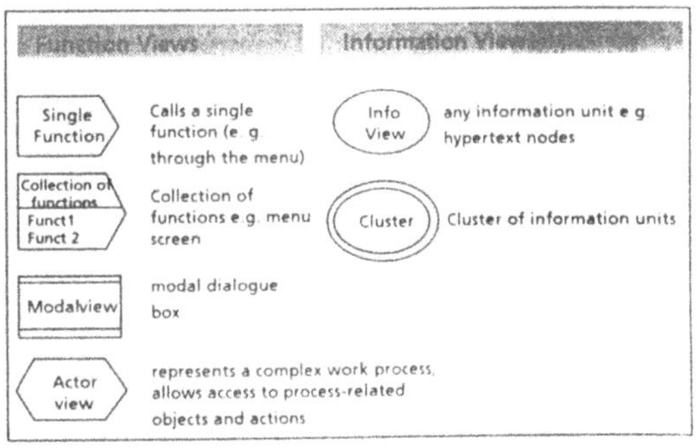

Figure 2: Dialogue and information views

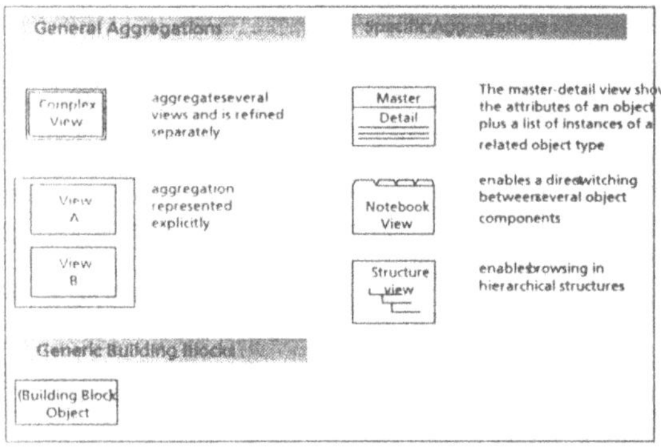

Figure 3: Composite views

4. MODELLING NAVIGATION WITH VIEWNETS

By using the view types defined and their graphical symbols, navigational structures can be conveniently represented in a diagrammatic form. In order to achieve a clear overview of the navigation, especially during the initial design steps, ViewNets in their simplest form model only whether a user can reach other views from a given node. Trigger events, conditions and actions are not represented at this stage. For a more detailed specification of the dynamic behaviour of the dialogue, however, the model can be extended in the form of dialogue nets, a specific Petri net representation for dialogues (Janssen, Weisbecker & Ziegler, 1993). For the purpose of designing the navigation at a conceptual level, it will in most cases be more appropriate to abstract from the details of the interaction.

Figure 4 shows a typical object-oriented navigation structure which might be used, for example, in the design of an order management system. The topmost level of the navigation (e.g. a graphical desktop) corresponds here to the drawing surface in order to simplify the model. Starting from an icon view of object collections (customers) on the desktop, the user can reach the attribute view of a particular object instance by opening a list of customers and selecting a specific instance or by a suitable search mechanism. Operations are made available locally in the attribute view e.g. as buttons or menu entries. The attribute view ‚Customer´ is represented here as a composite notebook view as we assume a larger number of attributes for each customer. At this stage, the details of this composite view are not yet specified. Semantic relations between different object classes (e.g. between ‚customer´and 'order') as modelled e.g. in typical domain object models are realized through corresponding navigation paths by normalizing the cardinalities of these relations through appropriate collection views (e.g. by a list of orders given by a particular customer).

Element (a) additionally shows the possibility to access objects through filters (e.g. Customers in Southern Germany) which can be defined by the developer or the user. By this mechanism, the interface can be adapted to recurring tasks and object collections needed for a particular purpose. The complete sub-structure of the search dialogue for customers can be defined as a generic building block and used in the same way for the class ‚Order´ or other object classes (b). Building blocks are defined in separate diagrams in order to make them reusable for different dialogues or systems. (c) shows a functional navigation path, which is provided in addition to the overall object-oriented navigation used in this example. This function provides a shortcut by means of an icon or a menu entry ‚New Customer´. Functional navigation paths may be added in order to achieve higher efficiency for repetitive tasks and can be super-imposed on an object-oriented structure which is used as a consistent and flexible basis of the overall system. On the basis of an initial ViewNet representation, dialogue sequences can be further optimized with respect to the users´ tasks which may lead to changing the type and contents of some of the views. In order to represent 'order data' and 'order items', for example, one could argue that a composed master-detail view showing both kinds of data simultaneously will be more transparent to the user and can save dialogue steps (Figure 5). A ViewNet model forms a useful basis for such optimizations, particularly for translating object relations with cardinalities 1:n or m:n into appropriate navigation sequences. The immediate visibility of the view types facilitates the conceptual design and supports the developer in providing dialogues which are adequate to the task.

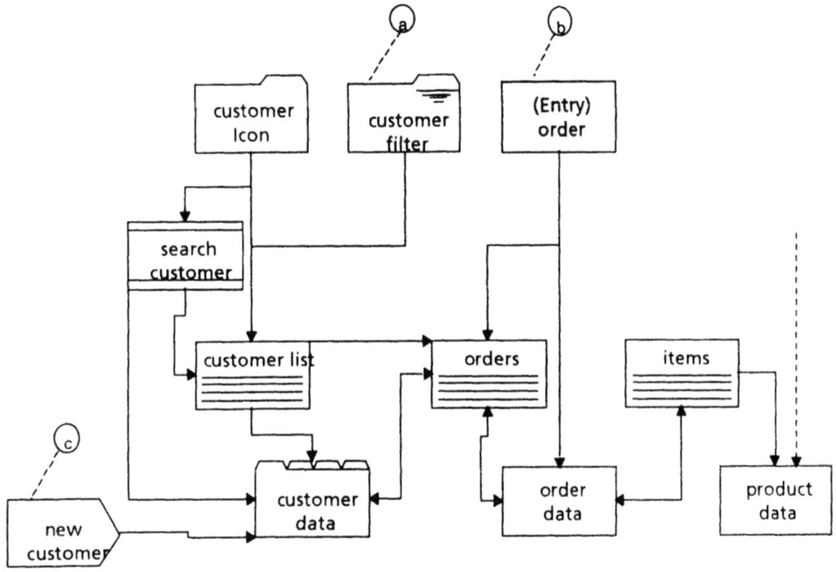

Figure 4: Example of a navigational structure modelled by a ViewNet (order management system).

ViewNets are not only useful for applications of the class-instance type in which more or less fixed views (e.g. screen forms) are filled with changing contents. They can also represent navigation between hypertext-like information units or mixed forms.

Figure 6 shows a part of an internet-based product information system which utilizes both database and hypertext components. If an appropriate clustering is used for the hypertext part of the system, a good overview representation can be maintained. The designer can quickly distinguish between the hypertext- and database-oriented parts of the system and optimize it according to the users´needs.

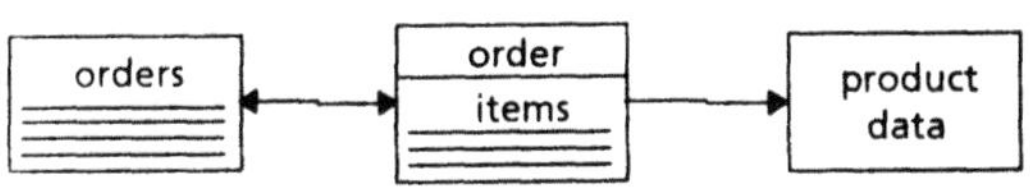

Figure 5: Optimized views and navigation steps for a part of the example in figure 4.

5 DISCUSSION

The ViewNet modelling technique presented here facilitates an understanding of the role and semantics of the different views involved in the navigation structure of a system. This contrasts with existing dialogue modelling techniques which focus on describing the dynamics of the dialogue in detail. The development of the conceptual structure of an application is supported by introducing different types of views. By using graphic pictograms to represent the different types of views, the designer as well as the users involved in the development process can more easily understand and modify the navigation structure. It is particularly important that the designers´ attention is directed to the principles underlying the design of the navigation structure such as object-oriented versus function-oriented navigation. The trade-offs between different approaches can be highlighted and usability issues arising from the design of the navigation structure be reflected in a systematic manner..

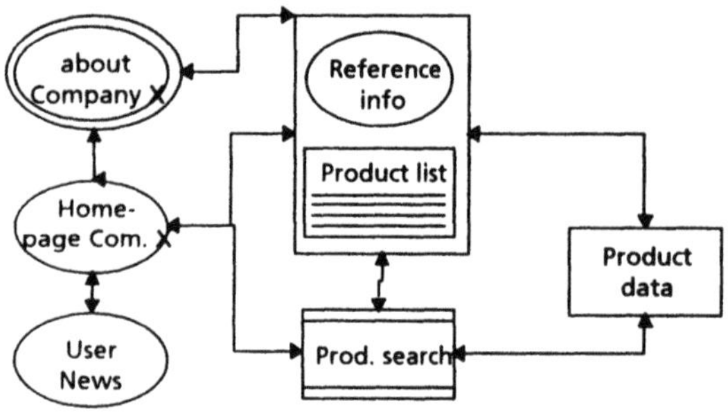

Figure 6: Example of a mixed hypertext/database-oriented navigation.

When applying the ViewNet approach, the problem of structuring the navigation for a large system can be more decomposed into several design steps. In many cases, it will be advantageous to develop first an object-oriented navigation structure as the basis of the application. Additional task- or process-related navigation paths can then be super-imposed on that structure in a second step.

The ViewNet technique can be consistently embedded in an overall software engineering process, especially in object-oriented development methods such as OMT (Object Modelling Technique, Rumbaugh et al. 1991). ViewNet forms part of a larger system development method which comprises the following steps and techniques and which is described in detail in (Ziegler 1997):

- Development of an object model of the application in OMT notation
- Specification of tasks and work processes using a statechart-like representation (Task-Object Charts, Ziegler 1997)
- Systematic, rule-driven derivation of the navigation structure from the object and task model using the ViewNet representation
- Specification of the dynamic behaviour of the dialogue by extending ViewNets into Petri-net based Dialogue Nets
- Visual design of the user interface
-

An initial ViewNet model can be easily extended by including a definition of the dynamics of the dialogue. This can be done by adding transition information, for instance, with the constructs used in dialogue nets. The further refinement of a ViewNet model, however, is beyond the scope of this paper. We claim that, especially in the early design phases, the development of the conceptual structure of the navigation is more important than the dynamic aspects of the interaction.

The ViewNet technique has as yet been applied in a number of development projects and assessed in a qualititative fashion. Its main value was seen in its informality and the intuitive graphical representation which was comprehensible for users participating in the development. The representation technique proved to be particularly useful in group discussions in which the requirements of an application and the initial dialogue strucures were developed. In such situations it is important that all participants can see the design on a large whiteboard or display. Currently, the technique is applied in a paper-based form or by using of a standard diagramming tool with predefined ViewNet symbols. Future work will focus on appropriate tool support, particularly for working in joint development sessions.

6. REFERENCES

Berk, E. & Devlin, J. (1991): Hypertext/Hypermedia Handbook. New York: McGraw-Hill.

Denert, E. (1977): Specification and design of dialog system with state transition diagrams. In Morlet, E. & Ribbens, D. (Eds.), Proc. Int. Computing Symposium. Amsterdam: Noth-Holland, 417-427.

Jacob, R.J.K. (1986): A specification language for direct manipulation user interfaces. ACM Transactions on Graphics, Vol. 5, 283-317.

Janssen, C.; Weisbecker, A. & Ziegler, J. (1993): Generating user interfaces from data models and dialogue net specifications. In Proceedings of INTERCHI (Amsterdam, 24-29 April), New York: ACM, 418-423.

Janssen, Chr. (1993): Dialognetze zur Beschreibung von Dialogabläufen in graphisch-interaktiven Systemen. In K.-H. Rödiger (Hrsg.): Software-Ergonomie '93. Stuttgart: Teubner, 67-76 (in German).

Nielsen, J. (1990): The art of navigating through hypertext. Communications of the ACM, March 1990, Vol. 33, No. 3, 296-310

Rumbaugh, J.; Blaha, M.; Premerlani, W.; Eddy, F. & Lorensen, W. (1991): Object-Oriented Modelling and Design. Englewood Cliffs N.J.: Prentice-Hall.

Ziegler, J. E. (1997): Eine Vorgehensweise zur objektorientierten Entwicklung graphisch-interaktiver Informationssysteme. Heidelberg: Springer-Verlag (in German).

10

Graphical Means of Directing Users' Attention in the Visual Interface

Shumin Zhai Julie Wright Ted Selker Sabra-Anne Kelin

IBM Almaden Research Center
650 Harry Road, MS NWE/B2
San Jose, CA 95120 USA
{zhai, amethyst, selker}@almaden.ibm.com, sakelin@mit.edu

ABSTRACT This paper presents two experiments in using "masks" to direct users' attention within a graphical user interface. Bleaching, darkening, blurring, and a solid-color pattern overlay (screening) are used to de-emphasize background material, causing the target to visually "pop-out" at the user. The tradeoff between effectively directing the user's attention and ensuring the readability of the background material is explored. Experimental results indicate that there is a wide range of darkening and screening levels that can create a pop-out effect without degrading the readability of the masked area.

KEYWORDS attention, pop-out effect, help systems, visual masking, user interface techniques

1. INTRODUCTION

Computers can present users with a seemingly endless variety of options and data. This complexity, which can easily overload users, has lead to the use of techniques such as 'wizards', simplified, step-by-step interfaces that break up tasks into small, easy-to-digest parts. This simplicity, however, is often gained at the expense of the flexibility and efficiency more traditional interfaces can provide. For instance, a wizard often locks the user into a particular sequence of choices that may not be suitable for a particular user. The tradeoff between simplicity and flexibility/ efficiency suggests a third interface approach that combines both the simplicity of wizards and the flexibility and efficiency of a more traditional interface. One such an approach is illustrated by the Cognitive Adaptive Help (COACH) agent system, which annotates traditional interfaces for inexperienced users (Selker, 1994). In COACH, dialogs are partially covered with a bitmap (mask). Only one step in the task remains uncovered at a time, in order to focus the user's attentions on this single step. At each step, COACH provides help and navigational control information in an external bubble.

Directing a user's attention by masking (de-emphasizing) parts of the visual display also has applications beyond help or tutor systems. Many examples exist in mainstream applications, such as Lotus Word Pro and Microsoft Windows95. When a user chooses to quit Microsoft Windows95, the desktop is covered with a pattern of black dots, making it appear darker than the confirmation dialog. In Word Pro, the brightness of colors on inactive icons or controls is reduced, causing them to look washed-out.

Masked objects may retain their readability so as to provide orientation, access to obscure or advanced options, or recall of previous settings. Yet by creating perceptual distance between the highlighted (unmasked) and de-emphasized (masked) areas, it is possible to direct the user's visual attention to the emphasized area.

The process of highlighting information is a significant part of traditional graphic design. Underlining, changing font, changing color, and changing the background are commonly used in printed

Human–Computer Interaction: INTERACT'97 S. Howard, J. Hammond & G. Lindgaard (editors)
Published by Chapman & Hall

media. Many such visual dimensions that can produce a "pop out" effect. One candidate dimension is color. However, a color's pop-out effect is complicated. For example, an orange dot will stand out amidst a mass of yellow dots. An orange dot will also stand out amidst many red dots, but the same orange dot will not stand out among a collection of both yellow and red dots (D'Zmura, 1991). Consider also a 460-nm (wavelength) spot. Such a spot will usually appear blue. But, if that same spot is made very small, it will look white. Brightness is also a factor. The perceived brightness of a region depends heavily on the brightness of the surrounding area. A lighter background tends to darken, while a darker background tends to lighten. Color, luminance, contrast, area, spatial frequency, and temporal considerations are among the factors that interact to determine visual perception (Rogowitz, 1983). Most importantly, color is also a dimension that application designers rely heavily upon. Using color to produce a pop out effect in a computer interface is likely to interfere with the application's use of color.

Groupings of many small elements can form textures that also have a pop-out effect. For example, a vertical bar will stand out in a field of horizontal bars (D'Zmura, 1991). Elements of different size or complexity, such as a group of plus signs ('+') randomly oriented in a field of randomly oriented minus signs ('-') will also pop-out, but the same phenomenon will not work using a 'T' and an 'L' (Julesz, *et al.*, 1983). Using texture to produce a 'pop-out' effect may also invade or restrict an application designer's visual design space.

Instead of using color or texture that invade an application designer's design space, the techniques explored in the following experiments manipulate brightness, contrast, and resolution to produce a perceptual difference between what is masked and what is unmasked. We were interested in testing if these approaches would produce effective pop-out effect without damaging the legibility of the masked objects.

2. EXPERIMENT 1

2.1 Design

Three masking techniques, namely darkening, bleaching, and blurring, were used in this experiment. Each has a metaphor grounded in everyday experience. Darkening creates the effect of a spotlight on a darkened stage. Bleaching makes the masked area look faded, possibly causing the bright, vivid colors in the unmasked area to stand out. Blurring was an attempt to mimic a person's vision system: only the area being focused on is received in high acuity, but the objects in the periphery are in low resolution. We hoped the user's attention would be automatically drawn to the unblurred object.

An experiment was designed to test if these techniques were indeed effective. Adobe Photoshop was used to produce the masked image. To darken the masked areas, the brightness was reduced (-100), while the contrast was increased (+35). Bleached masking was created by reducing the contrast (-60). A Gaussian filtering of 1.5 pixels was applied to create the blurred condition.

In the experimental task, a dialog was created containing over 40 common interface items (buttons, radio buttons, check-boxes, entry fields, and so forth, see Figure 1 and 2). For each mask condition, subjects

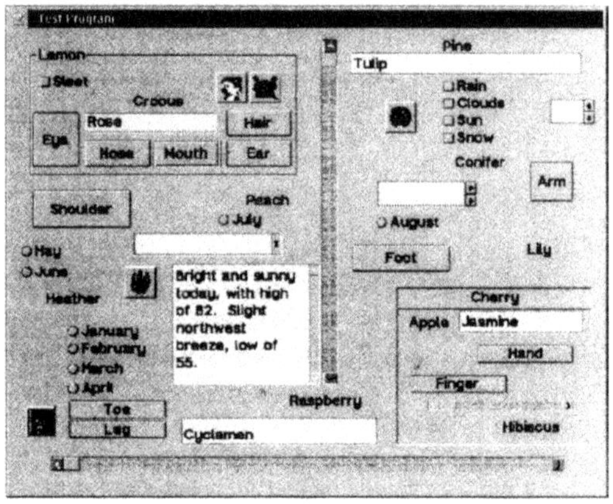

Figure 1: Dialog for Experiment 1 before masking

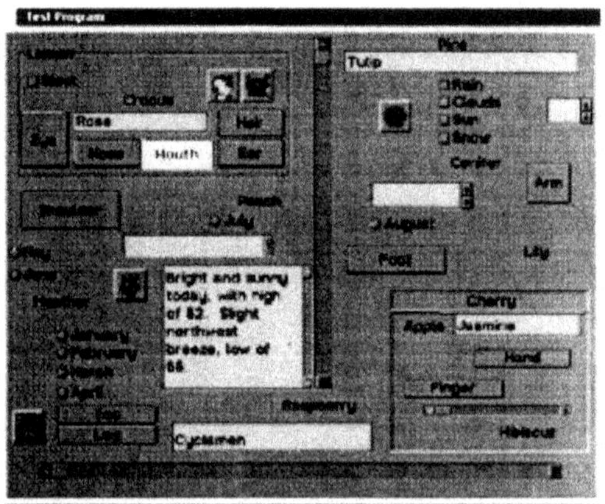

Figure 2: The same dialog after masking (by darkening) all objects but the button 'mouth'

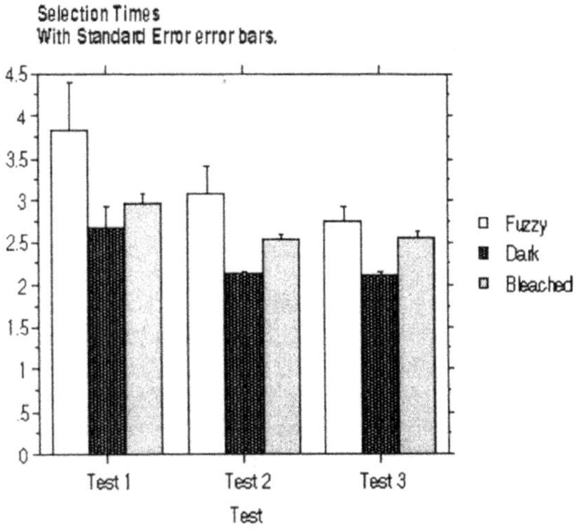

Figure 3: Response times (seconds) for experiment 1

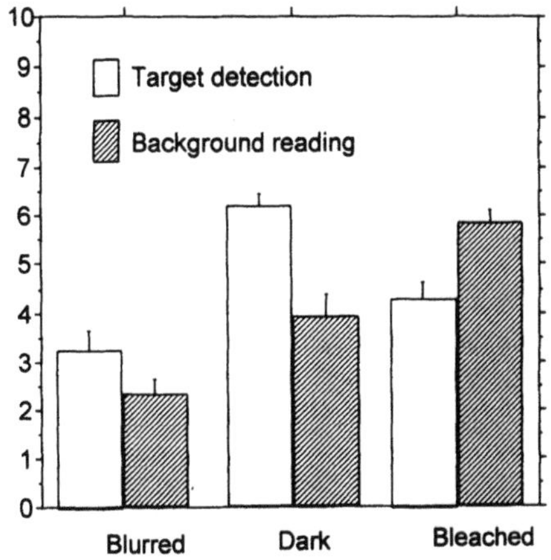

Figure 4: Subjective rating in Experiment 1
(10 = very easy, 0 = very difficult)

were shown the dialog with the mask applied everywhere but on the target item (Figure 2). Subjects were instructed to find the target that stood out and to click it as quickly as possible. The dialog would disappear, then reappear with a different target item unmasked. Three tests were conducted for each masking technique. Each test consisted of 20 target selections. The testing order of the three masking techniques was balanced in a Latin square pattern. A total of 18 subjects participated in the experiment. A questionnaire, filled out at the end of the experiment, asked subjects to rate the three masking techniques according to the ease of finding the target and the readability of the masked portion of the dialog.

2.2 Results

Repeated measure analysis of variance (ANOVA) on the selection time data showed that the blurring technique was significantly inferior to the darkening technique ($F_{1,\ 15}$ = 6.5. $p < 0.05$). Other pair comparisons were insignificant. Subjects' performance improved through practice (from early tests to later tests, see Figure 3) significantly ($F_{2,\ 130} = 7.3$. $p < 0.01$), but such a factor did not interact with the techniques. Neither experimental order, nor target type (pictures, words and others) nor any interaction was significant.

As measured by subjective rating data, all pairs of techniques were significantly different from each other, both for target selection ($p < 0.05$) and for readability of background information ($p < 0.001$) (see Figure 4).

Based upon the performance measurements and the subjective ratings, the blurring technique appeared to be inferior to the other two techniques, both for target selection and background readability. The difference between bleaching and darkening was less clear. Darkening appeared to be better for target pop-out effect; bleaching better for maintaining background readability (Figure 4).

This experiment indicated that the design of a mask could affect both performance and preference, and that an interesting design (such as the blurring technique) does not necessarily produce good results. It is also informative to note that the target type (either icon, words or others) did not change the masking effect.

There are a number of issues that were not resolved by this experiment. First, while the fact that the subjects were able to find the unmasked target (they were asked to click objects that stand out, no additional description of the targets was given) showed that all of the masking techniques effectively directed the user to the targets and two of the techniques were more effective than the other, it was unclear how strong such an effect was in comparison to searching for a target in the absence of a mask. Second, the experiment's assessment of the readability of the masked area was supported only by subjective data. Third, we suspected that the gain in making a target stand out might sacrifice the readability of the masked area. This would certainly be true if masking was taken to the extreme. Consider, for example, the most extreme level of the darkening technique. The background area would be darkened until it turned solid black. This would

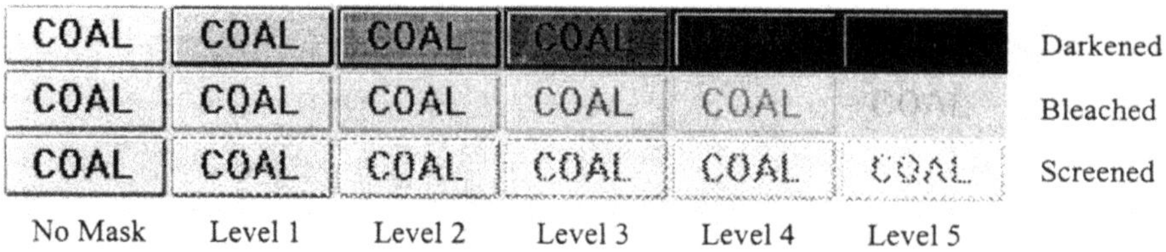

Figure 5: Sample buttons for each mask and density in Experiment 2

certainly cause the target item to stand out, but items in the masked area would be completely hidden. The tradeoff between the pop-out effect and the readability of the masked area might be a function of the masking density: the heavier the masking is, the stronger the pop-out effect might be, but the poorer the readability of the masked area could become (See Figure 5). Is this a linear tradeoff, or is there, as in the design of partially transparent menus (Harrison, et al., 1996), a range of masking density that provides both a pop-out effect and readability of the masked objects? A second experiment was designed to address these issues.

3. EXPERIMENT 2

3.1 Design

Four masking conditions were tested: bleaching, darkening, screening, and no-masking (see Figure 5 for the samples used). The bleaching and darkening masks were similar to those used in the first experiment. The addition of the screening technique, which overlaid a uniform, periodic, yellow pattern onto the masked areas, was motivated by its low cost of implementation: only a percentage of pixels have to be replaced with yellow color. The blurred mask was not tested because it did not perform well in the first experiment. The "no mask" condition was used as a control condition.

Experiment 1 only tested one level of masking for each technique. This experiment tested five levels (from 1 to 5) of masking with for each technique were tested. The five levels of bleaching were created by reducing the contrast (-30, -45, -60, -75, -95). The five levels of darkening were created by increasing the contrast (+50) and decreasing brightness (-20, -40, -60, -80, -100). The levels of screening were created by replacing a pattern of pixels with yellow pixels (RGB 255 255 85) such that a percentage of the pixels were blocked out (12%, 25%, 37%, 62%, 75%). Note that the intervals within each technique were not necessarily equal. The values were chosen and adjusted to cover as wide as possible a range of appearance (see Figure 5) according the authors' subjective experience and pilot testing. The lowest levels of masking appeared sufficiently close to no-mask condition and the highest levels of masking made the masked words nearly indistinguishable.

A target matching task was designed for this experiment. Subjects were instructed to select, as quickly as possible, the button that matches the target word at the top of the dialog as shown in Figure 6. The advantage of this experimental scenario, in comparison with Experiment 1 was that all three aspects of masking could be evaluated. First, subjects' performance of searching the target word when no mask was applied served as the normal, control condition. Such a normal condition can also be considered as Level 0 masking with any of the three technique. Second, when the target word was highlighted by various levels of masks applied to other words, the pop-out effect could be measured in comparison to the control condition. Third, when the target word was masked together with all other buttons, the readability of the masked area could be evaluated.

A total of 13 subjects performed the task under the normal control condition as well as all five levels of all three masking techniques. For each level in each masking technique, two sets of trials were run. In one set of trials, the target word was left unmasked (therefore highlighted) while the rest of the buttons

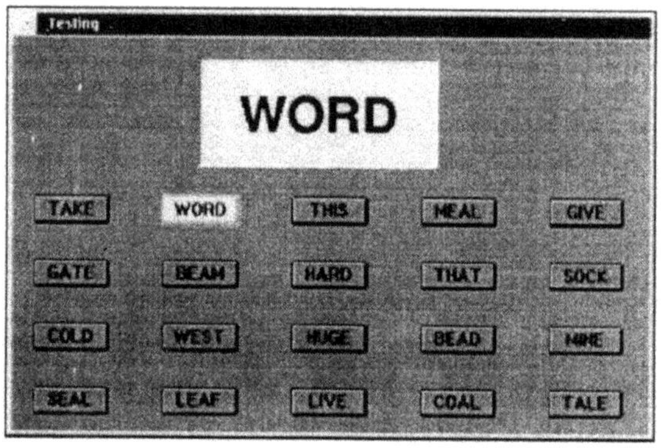

Figure 6: Test dialog for Experiment 2 (in darkening condition)

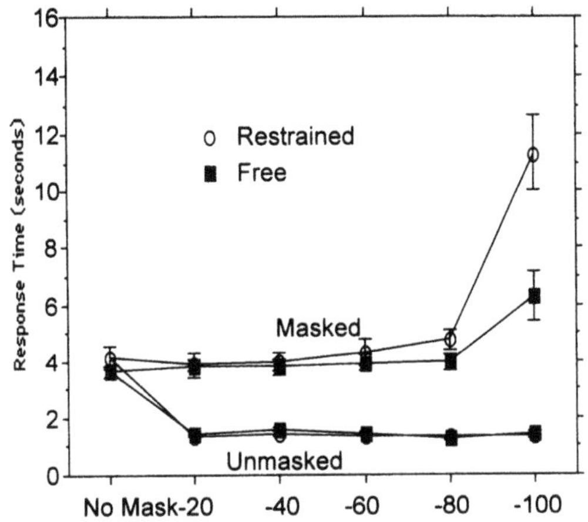

Figure 7: Mean task completion times and standard errors when the target was (top curves) masked or (bottom curves) highlighted / unmasked using the darkening technique.

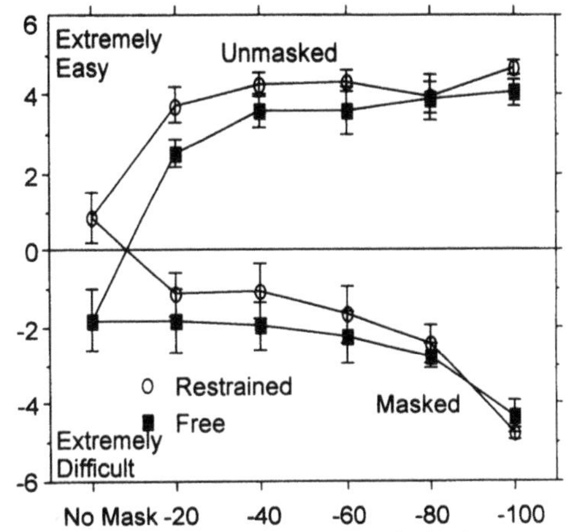

Figure 8: Subjective ratings with the darkening technique. +5 is extremely easy and -5 is extremely difficult.

were masked. In the second set, the entire dialog was masked, including the target word.

Each set of trials consisted of 5 practice trials followed by 20 test trials. Each of the test trials in a set corresponded to one of the 20 words (buttons) in the dialog (Figure 6), so all sets of trials encompassed the equal total travel distances. The order of the buttons was changed randomly between sets to avoid memorization of a button's placement.

The order of the masking conditions was determined by a Latin-square sequence of the darkening, bleaching, and screening techniques. The normal control condition was randomly inserted into the Latin-square sequence. For a given masking condition, the order in which the densities were tested was random.

During pilot testing, subjects tended to move closer to the computer screen under the more difficult conditions, presumably to compensate for increased difficulty. It seemed possible that subjects could maintain the same performance by exerting extra effort in more difficult conditions. A between-subject factor was introduced to explore this possibility. Six of the subjects were allowed to move their head position freely and seven subjects were prevented from moving closer than 1.5 feet by a string across the chest.

3.2 Results

Masking by Darkening

Figure 7 illustrates the performance results of the darkening technique. First, let us examine the pop-out effect when the target was the highlighted/unmasked word. The bottom curves showed that, in comparison to Level 0 (no masking), selection time was significantly reduced when the rest of window was masked (darkened) to each of the masked levels: $F_{5, 55} = 110.9$, $p < .0001$, once again showing that darkening is an effective means of creating a pop-out effect. Interestingly, even the slightest level of darkening tested appeared to make the unmasked object "pop out": mean selection time changed from 3.9 seconds at no darkening to 1.4 second at Level 1 (-20) darkening. It appeared that even the lowest level of masking enabled the subjects to be "cued" to, instead of searching for, the target. Further darkening did not make subjects perform much faster: mean selection time changed from 1.41 seconds at Level 1 to 1.36 second at Level 5. Such a difference was not statistically significant. Subjective rating data, however, appeared to be more sensitive to the darkening level increase (Figure 8). The higher levels of darkening appeared to make the unmasked target more distinguishable and were rated significantly easier than the lower levels of darkening. For example, a T-test showed $p < .0001$ significance between Level 1 (-20) and 5 (-100).

Second, as shown by the top curves in Figure 7, subjects' performance in reading the masked area was not significantly affected by darkening level except at the very extreme (Level 5). T-tests showed that selection in the masked area at the highest level (-100) was significantly slower than the other levels ($p < .0001$), but the differences among other levels tested were relatively small (from 3.9 seconds at Level 0 to 4.4 seconds at Level 4, statistically insignificant). It is remarkable that subjects maintained similar performance for such a wide range of apparent difficulty (See Figure 5). Subjective rating scores on selecting masked targets moved towards "extremely difficult" as darkening level increased (Figure 8). Not only was highest level (-100) rated significantly more difficult than other levels ($p < 0.0001$), but levels 3 and 4 were also rated more difficult than Level 0 (no darkening): $p < 0.05$.

Viewing condition (Restrained vs. Free moving) was weakly significant to selection time in masked area: $F_{1,11} = 4.4$, $p = 0.06$. By moving closer to the screen as one strategy to compensate the increasing difficulty, the free moving group had faster selection time only at the very dark levels. There was a strong interaction between viewing condition and darkening level ($F_{5,55} = 8.6$, $p < 0.0001$) in selecting masked targets. This was the only case in all performance and subjective data with all masking techniques where viewing condition made a statistically significant difference in the experiment.

To summarize, the results showed that except at the very extreme, a wide range of darkening levels can create a pop-out effect without significantly damaging the readability of the masked objects, although as the darkening level increases users may subjectively experience a slight increase in pop-out effect and a slight decrease in readability (compare Figure 7 and 8). Subjects tended to maintain the same level of performance by exerting additional effort, as indicated by the smaller time increase in selecting masked targets by the free moving group (Figure 7).

Masking by Bleaching

As shown in Figure 9 (bottom curves), the lowest level (-30) of bleaching tested did not appear to be effective enough to direct the subjects' attention. Although it caused significantly shorter selection time than without masking (mean time 3.89 vs. 3.33, $p < .005$), stronger bleaching produced still shorter selection time: $p < .0001$. This suggests that Level 1 bleaching used in the experiment did not produce the pop-out effect needed to fully utilize viewers' preattentive perception. For the rest of the bleaching levels, mean selection times were (from Level 2 to Level 5) 1.65, 1.33, 1.38, 1.39 seconds, no significant difference was found among these means. Subjective rating indicated that as bleaching level increased,

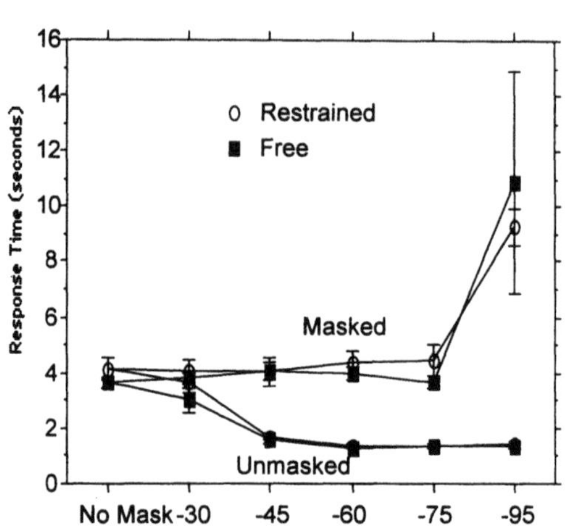

Figure 9: Task completion times when the target was (top curves) masked or (bottom curves) highlighted / unmasked using the bleaching technique.

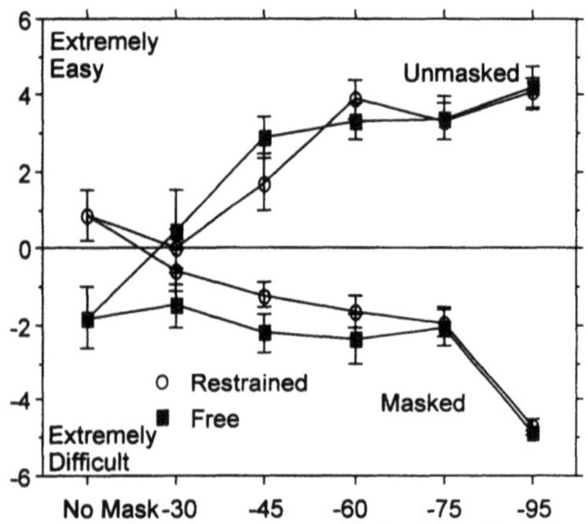

Figure 10: Subjective ratings with the bleaching technique. +5 is "extremely easy" and -5 is "extremely difficult".

selecting the unmasked target became significantly easier (see Figure 10).

The readability of the bleached area was similar to that of the area masked by darkening: selection time at the very extreme (-95) was significantly different from the rest ($p < 0.0001$). Differences among Level 0 (no mask) to Level 4 (-75) were not significant, although subjective rating indicated increased difficulty.

Overall, in comparison to the darkening technique, a much narrower range of bleaching levels can accommodate both the pop-out effect and readability (compare Figure 9 against 7, Figure 10 against 8), although the best performances achieved by the bleaching technique were similar to those achieved by the darkening technique (about 4 seconds for selection in masked area and 1.4 seconds for selecting unmasked target).

Masking by screening

As shown in Figure 11, even the slightest level of screening tested (Level 1, 12% pixels screened out) appeared to provide a strong cue: mean selection time of unmasked targets changed from 3.9 seconds at Level 0 screening to 1.5 second at Level 1 screening ($p < 0.0001$). Further screening did not appear to be much more effective; mean selection time changed from 1.5 seconds at Level 1 to 1.38 seconds at Level 5 (not statistically significant). Subjectively, even the lowest level of screening (level 1) made the task significantly easier ($p < 0.0001$). Further increase in screening level made the task seem even easier ($p < 0.05$) (Figure 12).

As the percentage of pixels masked out increased, the readability of the masked area was expected to decrease. Indeed, T-tests showed significantly different ratings from lower levels to higher levels (e.g. $p < 0.05$ from Level 2 to Level 4) (see Figure 12). However, the time of selecting the target word from the masked area remained flat except at the extreme Level 5 (Figure 11). From Level 0 to Level 4, mean selection time changed from 3.9 to 4.1 seconds (not statistically significant). Only Level 5 was significantly different from the rest ($p < 0.0001$). This once again showed users' ability to overcome increased difficulty without significantly reducing time performance.

Overall, a wide range of screening, from 12% of pixels to 62% pixels being masked out, produced the optimal performance (again 4 seconds for selection in masked area and 1.4 seconds for selecting unmasked target).

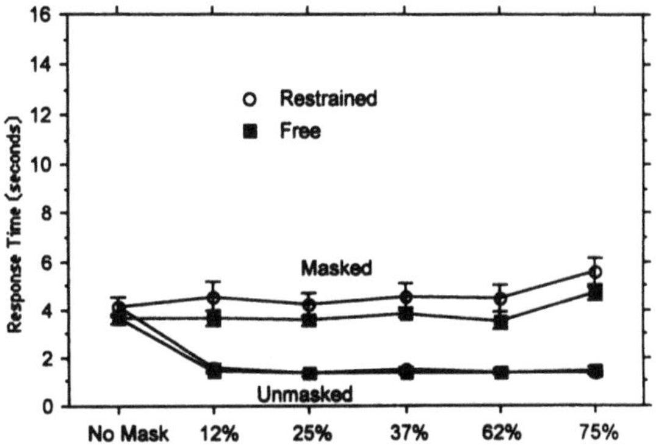

Figure 11: Task completion times when the target was (top curves) masked or (bottom curves) highlighted / unmasked using the screening technique.

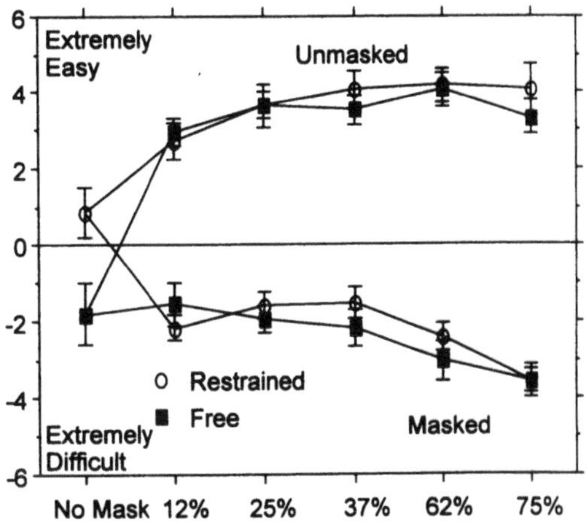

Figure 12: Subjective ratings with the screening technique. Horizontal axis is the degree of screening. +5 is "extremely easy" and -5 is "extremely difficult".

4. DISCUSSION

All three techniques used in the second experiment were effective when adequate levels of masking were selected. The highlighted target selection time at such levels was around 1.4 seconds for all three techniques, much faster than with no masking (around 4 seconds). Bear in mind that motor control (moving cursor to target) was involved in target selection. The visual difference between finding a pop-out target and searching for the same target without masking cues was much greater than 4.0:1.4, the ratio of response times for the two conditions. Furthermore, for several levels of each mask, the time to find an item in the masked area was similar to Level 0 (no mask), suggesting that the readability of the masked areas had been well preserved.

The range of such adequate masking levels that can provide strong cues to direct users' attention without readability loss in the masked area differed among the three techniques. The flat area of the performance curve where performance did not differ significantly in this experiment was -20 to -80 with the darkening technique, -45 to -75 with the bleaching technique, and 12% to 62 % for the screening condition. Bleaching provided a narrower optimal range than the other two techniques. Darkening and screening both worked well, although they offer very different masking appearances and require different implementation mechanisms.

Although subjective data tend to vary from individual to individual, the rating data collected in the experiments did offer information not revealed by the performance data. The rated difficulty changed faster than the performance measurement as masking level moved to the two extrema. It is interesting that this increase in subjective difficulty did not correspond to immediate performance loss. Subjects tended to compensate for the increased difficulty, perhaps by exerting extra effort. See (Wickens, 1992) for related theories of performance and resources.

Note also that the experimental scenario is simpler than a typical application where both the visual features and the user's cognitive activities are much more complex. A narrowed range of effective masking level is expected in more complex applications.

5. CONCLUSION

Two experiments were conducted to evaluate means of drawing user's attention to various parts of a computer dialog. Four masking techniques were studied. One of them, blurring, did not appear to be as effective as the rest. Two techniques, darkening and screening, can provide a wide range of masking levels that could produce strong pre-attentive visual cues to pop-out the targets and still allow the user to read the masked area. Masks with as little as 12 % pixels being screened out could produce a strong pop-out effect.

The studies presented here indicated that important information can be made to pop-out using darkening or screening masks. Darkening or screening the less relevant parts of the user interface provides strong attention cues to the important information. Yet the non-important information can still be accessed. Such a way of directing a user's attention by masking is a graceful human-machine communication method: telling the user what the user interface agent "thinks" is important, while allowing the user act according to his own will.

6. ACKNOWLEDGMENTS

We would like to thank Ron Barber, Paul Maglio and other members of the USER (User System Ergonomics Research) group at the IBM Almaden Research Center for their contributions to the development of this research.

REFERENCES

D'Zmura, M. Color in Visual Search. *Vision Research, 31, 6* (1991), 951-966.

Harrison, B., and Vicente, K. An Experimental Evaluation of Transparent Menu Usage. *Proceedings of CHI 96: Human Factors in Computing Systems* (1996), 391-398.

Julesz, B., and Bergen, J. R. Textons, the Fundamental Elements in Preattentive Vision and Perception of Textures. *The Bell System Technical Journal, 62, 6* (July-August, 1983), 1619-1645.

Rogowitz, B. E. The Human Visual System: A Guide for the Display Technologist. *Proceedings of the SID, 24, 3* (1983), 235-252.

Selker, T. COACH: A teaching agent that learns. *Communications of the ACM 37, 7* (1994), 92-99.

Wickens, C. D. *Engineering Psychology and Human Performance, Second Edition* (1992). HarperCollins Publishers, Inc.

11

An Adaptive Window Management System

Stefan Stille, Shailey Minocha and Rolf Ernst

Institut für Datenverarbeitungsanlagen
Technische Universität, Braunschweig
Hans–Sommer–Str. 66, D-38106 Braunschweig, Germany
stille@ida.ing.tu-bs.de

ABSTRACT Modern complex and information intensive computer applications involve multi-window operations. To simultaneously visualize all the necessary information for a task requires time–consuming window management operations by the user. Since these activities are not directly related to the user's task domain, time spent on window management results in loss of user's mental context and an increase in the actual task completion time. We propose an Adaptive Window Manager (AWM) which automates the layout of the windows on the display screen according to the current user and his current task domain and learns the user's layout requirements. In this paper, we shortly address what user model we used for building AWM.

KEYWORDS Adaptive Window Management, Adaptive User Interfaces, User Model

1. Introduction

With an ever–increasing rate of advances in computers, a user is burdened with a cluttered multi–window desktop and has to deal with rearranging the display layout (that is, positioning and sizing of windows) quite often to suit his current task or information requirement. In order to relieve the user from these activities, we are currently developing an Adaptive Window Manager (AWM), a realization of the idea of Adaptive Automatic Display Layout (A^2DL)[1].

In (Stille et al., 1996), we have treated the motivation, software ergonomic requirements, the architecture and working of the proposed AWM. AWM is an auto–adaptive layout system, which would be able to identify the user's current working context, on the basis of each working context's distinguishing software–tools and their states, and would be able to adapt the layout characteristics to suit the current user and his current working context. It is *auto–adaptive* in the sense that during the user–computer interaction, it *learns* about the user's layout preferences for his various working contexts from his layout actions, *updates* this 'learnt' information with the change in user's preferences, and uses this 'learnt' knowledge to *adapt* the layouts to suit the working contexts of the user in his future interactions. AWM maintains a profile that is specific to each user and contains the learnt contexts and layout features for each context as per the user's preferred layout characteristics for that context. During the user's work, AWM not only learns new contexts and the associated layout features but also updates the information for the previously learnt contexts through feedback (layout corrections or modifications made by the user) and thereby, presents layouts for the learnt contexts which are appropriate for the user and his tasks.

In order to be able to provide adaptivity, AWM needs to have a user model which represents general knowledge about user's layout whishes. The appropriateness of this model is crucial for user acceptance of the adaptive system as it represents the information that is the basis for adaptation.

[1]This research work is being supported by German Research Foundation under grant no. Er 168/7-2

Human–Computer Interaction: INTERACT'97 S. Howard, J. Hammond & G. Lindgaard (editors)
Published by Chapman & Hall

2. The User-Model of AWM

In research prototypes described in literature, a user model is built by classifying the user's expertise on the basis of his behavior and action patterns with the computer system for a *particular task*, or by querying the user. Since AWM's support should not be restricted to a particular user or task domain, a more general user model had to be developed.

Our user model has been derived from an analysis of user behavior with a UI in a multi–window setup. The model is non-specific as it does not pertain to each *individual* user or does not model a group of users with common characteristics. Rather it is a *single* user model for all users, describing how users perform their activities in a multi–window environment. We, first, performed a theoretical analysis of user behaviour and verified the results by an empirical study based on protocols of user's actual interaction with a computer system.

An observational study of user–computer interaction indicates that a user views his work as composed of tasks to achieve certain goals and a goal is the desired output from a performed task. Typical tasks of users could vary from writing a document to debugging a program. A user divides his job into several tasks and each task may constitute of several sub–tasks. For each sub–task, the user may choose a software tool from a tool group (a group of software tools of the same functionality) that supports him in the best possible manner. On a UI level, each tool constitutes of several graphical objects, like windows, menus, list boxes, combo boxes, etc. The task or sub–task–status can be determined by observing the states of the active software tool and the graphical objects of this tool.

It is obvious that a user manipulates the layout of windows on the screen to suit his current context and the current activity within the context. The layout characteristics may vary with the current activity within a task. We conclude that the layout whishes of a user are closely related to the set of graphical objects which he currently works with and also to their current states.

Our source of information for our empirical study has been protocols of user interaction while performing their *everyday work* under UNIX/X11 over the window manager fvwm. We took log–files of 17 users into account and could clearly verify the results of (Henderson and Card, 1986) in the sense that we could detect working sets of usually no more than 5 windows that users tend to use for accomplishing a task. An additional analysis of layout–activities (moving, resizing or iconifying of windows) showed that these are normally bound to a change of the working set. We thereby proved our theoretical analysis described above.

However, we also found out that the information we can get on the window manager level is not sufficient to explain the user's layout activities completely. This is due to the lack of information about the current state of tools. Hence, we decided to define a protocol for communication between applications and AWM so that they can supply information about their states. The decision which states are to be supplied can be made during the task analytic design of the application. This will be discussed in other communications.

3. Future Work

We are currently designing a UI for AWM which would enable the user to initiate or inhibit the layout actions performed by the system. It would also allow the user to specify a distinct task which he wants to perform. AWM will then start the appropriate applications in the desired state and arrange the appropriate layout on the screen. This will extend AWM to a session manager similar to xsm in X11R6.

A working prototype of AWM will be soon ready to evaluate the system by performing usability studies with actual users through questionnaires and interviews to discover whether the proposed system can really support users while working with a multi-window system aided by AWM. We will especially examine what kind of strategy for AWM's layout proposals users prefer and whether our approach to context recognition is appropriate.

References

Henderson, D. A. and Card, S. K. (1986). Rooms: The Use of Multiple Virtual Workspaces to Reduce Space Contention in a Window–Based Graphical User Interface. *ACM Transactions on Graphics*, 5(3):211–243.

Stille, S., Minocha, S., and Ernst, R. (1996). A^{2}DL–An Adaptive Automatic Display Layout System. In *Proceedings of the IEEE 3rd Annual Symposium on Human Interaction with Complex Systems (HICS 96)*, Dayton, OHIO, USA. IEEE Computer Society Press.

12

Elements of a Three-dimensional Graphical User Interface

Geoff Leach, Ghassan Al-Qaimari, Mark Grieve, Noel Jinks, Cameron McKay

Department of Computer Science, RMIT, Melbourne, Vic., 3000, Australia
{gl|ghassan}@cs.rmit.edu.au

ABSTRACT The graphical user interface (GUI) is now firmly established as the preferred user interface for end users in most situations. Just as decreasing hardware prices and increasing hardware capabilities made two-and-a-half dimensional ($2\frac{1}{2}$D) GUIs affordable in the early eighties and widespread in the ninetees, we believe declining hardware prices and increasing hardware capabilities will make three-dimensional (3D) GUIs possible and affordable in the near future. Three-dimensional GUIs raise many issues of design, metaphor and usability. In this paper we discuss elements of a prototype 3D GUI we are developing.

KEYWORDS 3D graphical user interface, 3D window manager, 3D cursor, prototyping, usability.

1. Introduction

The GUI was developed at Xerox PARC in the late seventies for the Star system (Shneiderman, 1992, Smith et al., 1982). It was first successfully commercialised by Apple with the Macintosh computer in the early eighties and has since become an integral part of every modern operating system for personal computers and graphics workstations. One reason for this growth is productivity: a number of studies have shown GUIs, with their direct manipulation style of interaction, enhance productivity (Rauterberg, 1992, Margono and Shneiderman, 1987). Another reason is subjective preference: people express a preference for GUI interfaces. Coupled with the rise of the GUI has been a general elevation of the importance of the user interface, which is now recognised as a key, and sometimes central, component of an interactive product or environment.

Today's GUI depended on declining hardware prices to make it affordable at the low-end of the computer market — personal computers. The same trend, a doubling of performance approximately every 18 months to two years (widely known as Moore's Law), now means personal computers are capable of performing interactive 3D graphics. In tandem with improving hardware performance, graphics libraries such as OpenGL (Neider et al., 1993) which were previously available only on workstations have now become available for personal computers.

We believe that **3D GUIs** — graphical user interfaces which utilise 3D graphics — offer significant potential for improvement over today's $2\frac{1}{2}$D GUIs, and furthermore, that it is now, or very shortly will be, possible to run such interfaces on personal computers. In this paper, we discuss elements of a prototype 3D GUI we are developing and discuss some early feedback from usability tests.

2. Background

The researchers and developers at Xerox PARC who produced the Star system were determined to produce a system far easier and more intuitive to use than the command-line interfaces which predominated at the time (Smith et al., 1982). A key part of achieving this was providing a metaphor to integrate the visual elements of a graphical user interface into a recognisable and comprehensible framework. In the **desktop metaphor** used for the Star, and for most commercial GUIs since, the interface is conceptualised and presented as a graphical version of a typical office. Its key elements are:

- **A desktop** or space on which **icons** or small pictographs which correspond to commonly found equipment in offices (bins, printers, documents and folders) are placed.

*A copy of the paper with colour figures is available at http://www.cs.rmit.edu.au/~gl/research/HCC/interact97.html

Human–Computer Interaction: INTERACT'97 S. Howard, J. Hammond & G. Lindgaard (editors)
Published by Chapman & Hall

- Overlapping rectangular **windows** which house applications and documents which correspond to working sheets of paper.
- **Folders** for storing other documents and folders.
- **Pull-down menus** to allow the user to make choices and provide instructions (which have no direct office analogue).

An example of the desktop metaphor GUI is shown in figure 1.

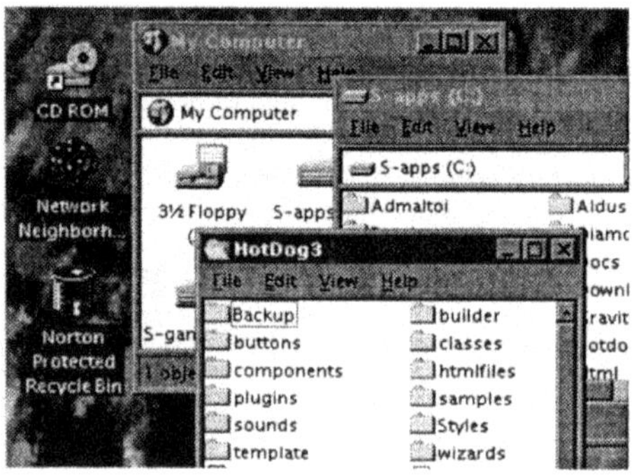

Figure 1: Desktop metaphor (Windows 95)

Another key aspect of the GUI, although not strictly part of the desktop metaphor, is the use of a pointing device, typically a mouse (Johnson et al., 1989, Shneiderman, 1992), to control the position of a 2D **cursor** on the screen. Operations may be invoked with the mouse in a variety of ways, with the user being provided with continuous visual feedback. For example, a **copy** operation may be invoked by **selecting** an object's icon with the cursor and then **dragging** it to another location, with the exact semantics of the copy operation depending on the selected object and the source and destination positions. For example, if the selected object is a document, the source position is a folder on one disk and the destination position is a second disk then a copy of the document is made on the second disk. The user is provided with continuous feedback through smooth animation of the movement of the document icon whilst it is being dragged from source to destination. In some cases, further feedback on the progress of the copy operation is provided by another visual element constantly displaying what proportion of the document has been copied.

The desktop metaphor GUI is described as a **direct manipulation** interface. Direct manipulation is a term introduced by Ben Shneiderman in 1982 (Shneiderman, 1982, Shneiderman, 1983) to describe interfaces exhibiting the following characteristics:

- Continuous visibility of objects of interest. For example, an object stays where it is until the operator moves it.
- Rapid, incremental reversible operations whose impact is immediately visible.
- Pointing, selecting and dragging techniques replacing the need to type complex syntax, such as command lines like MS-DOS or shell interfaces.

The copy operation described above, for example, exhibits these characteristics.

Advocates of direct manipulation maintain that systems designed with these principles in mind are easier to use than command-line oriented systems, because they allow the creation of a prefered mental model and because they reduce the mental workload by allowing recognition rather than recall (Hix and Hartson, 1993). For a person to complete a task, they must transform their mental goals ("I want to write a document") into physical ones ("Move the mouse to the word processor icon, and double-click to open it"). The process of constructing a task-action mental model (Young, 1983), visualising the desired outcome, and mapping this to physical actions can be measured by two gulfs: the gulf of execution and the gulf of evaluation (Hutchins et al., 1986). The gulf of execution refers to the distance between the goals of the user and the means of achieving them through the system, and the gulf of evaluation refers to the distance between the system's behaviour and the user's goals. These gulfs are reduced in GUIs where by directly manipulating objects and data visually users are given a sense of direct engagement and of control, both of which facilitate understanding of the nature of tasks (Johnson et al., 1989, Shneiderman, 1992, Carroll, 1987).

3. The 3D GUI

The desktop metaphor GUI is **$2\frac{1}{2}$D**. It is **2D** because its visual elements are two-dimensional: they lie in the xy plane, are defined in 2D coordinates, are flat and contain only planar regions (areas). It is **$2\frac{1}{2}$D** because where visual elements overlap they obscure each other according to their **priority**. In a 3D GUI the visual elements are genuinely three-dimensional: they are situated in xyz space, are defined in terms of 3D coordinates, need not be flat and may contain spatial regions (volumes).

The design considerations for a 3D GUI appear more complex than for a $2\frac{1}{2}$D GUI. To begin with, the issues of metaphor and elements arise afresh. The desktop metaphor with its windows, icons, menus and pointing device elements is firmly established for $2\frac{1}{2}$D GUIs. In contrast no clearly defined metaphor and set of elements for 3D GUIs are manifest — yet. 3D GUIs offer considerably more scope for metaphors than $2\frac{1}{2}$D GUIs; there are many metaphors which could be based on our physical 3D environment, including the obvious extension of the desktop metaphor into a 3D office metaphor. On the other hand, much more abstract metaphors are possible, such as one based "starmaps" where objects are simply placed somewhere in "cyberspace". Likewise the elements of a 3D GUI may resemble, or differ substantially from, the elements of the $2\frac{1}{2}$D GUI.

In our prototype we identify essentially the same elements in the 3D GUI as in the $2\frac{1}{2}$D desktop GUI: windows, icons, menus, a general space in which to arrange the visual elements, a cursor and an input device to manipulate the cursor. At this stage we are not proposing radical change to the GUI, in so far as we regard provision of an appropriate metaphor and the use of familiar elements as important design criteria — our 3D GUI is clearly recognisable as a GUI. It will be seen, however, that some of these elements are quite different from their $2\frac{1}{2}$D counterparts.

There are two main thrusts to our prototyping work. The first is a 3D window manager, which we call MaW^3. Currently it is a simulator rather than a working window system in that windows do not contain editable documents. The second thrust is the use of a 3D cursor, which we call the Magic Wand, controlled by a 3D (six degrees of freedom) input device (a Spacetec spaceball (Spacetec, 1996)).

3.1 Related Work

Today's desktop metaphor GUIs are largely unchanged from those of twenty years ago, which is testament to the strength of the original design. There have been, of course, efforts to improve it. Of specific relevance to our work are efforts utilising 3D graphics. Work in this area tends to be focussed on experimental systems directed at a particular application or application area — as is our system. The Information Visualizer developed at Xerox PARC is an experimental system which explores a 3D user interface paradigm suitable for applications to manipulate large amounts of information (Robertson et al., 1993). At Apple, as part of the meta content format (MCF) project (Apple, 1996), a 3D MCF browser called HotSauce has been developed. It allows the user to explore a hierarchical (branching) structure in 3D space. Another example is the WebForager for exploring the world wide web (Card et al., 1996). In the WebForager 3D WebBooks containing collections of web pages, and other objects, are placed in a 3D workspace.

An innovative 2D approach to the user interface is proposed in the Pad system (Perlin and Fox, 1993). There the workspace is an infinite 2D plane on which information can be placed at arbitrary places with arbitrary scale. The user can repeatedly zoom in on particular regions through **portals** which act as magnifying glasses. Our system shares some of these characteristics, although it has only finite scaling, rather than infinite scaling.

3.2 MaW^3: A 3D Window Manager

A task which occurs in the $2\frac{1}{2}$D desktop GUI is window management. Windows house applications and documents, and may overlap and obscure each other. A natural mode of human operation is **multitasking**, that is, to have a number of tasks or jobs underway concurrently. A consequence of this, and the small screen size (up to 21" maximum typically) dictated by today's CRT and LCD display technologies, is the need to manage the position and layout of windows. The **window manager** performs this task in response to user input.

A situation which arises in the use of windowing environments is the need to constantly arrange and rearrange windows to get access to the particular window which houses the task or information one needs at a given point in time — which has been described as **window thrashing** (Henderson and Card, 1986). A number of techniques have been proposed to facilitate efficient display usage and application switching to reduce or overcome window thrasing, including tiled layout, "virtual" desktops (Hines, 1996, Harch, 1996) and fisheye views (Furness, 1986). However, most of these approaches adhere to the $2\frac{1}{2}$D desktop model and whilst helping considerably still suffer residual problems: multiple overlapping windows are hard to identify, iconified windows more so, and one quickly runs out of space trying to group related applications. Alleviating the problem of window thrashing is one of the main design goals of our 3D window manager.

The metaphor we have used for the 3D space in which we arrange windows is that of a **tunnel**. The user is positioned in the middle of the mouth of the tunnel looking toward the other end. The tunnel, and windows in it, are displayed with a perspective projection, as shown in figure 2. Windows are essentially 2D, in that their "work area" is 2D, although they have 3D frames, decoration and buttons. At this stage we do not plan on changing the structure of documents, which are essentially 2D constructs, although there may be contexts in which some kind of 3D presentation may be advantageous — outlining for example.

Windows may be positioned at arbitrary depths in the

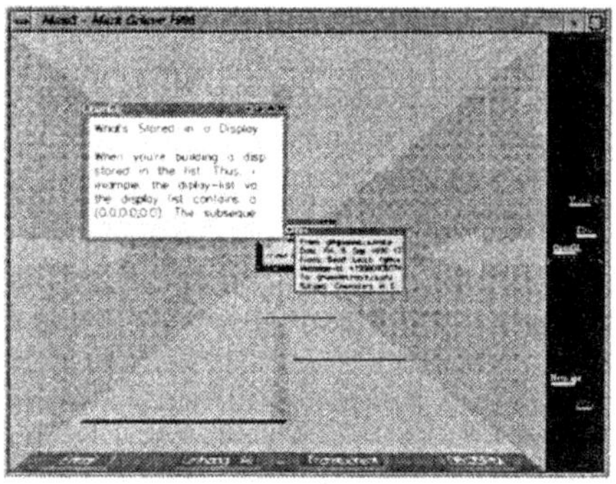

Figure 2: Tunnel

tunnel but are restricted in their orientation. The normal orientation is orthogonal to the longitudinal axis of the tunnel, or more simply, "front-on". As a user pushes a window further into the tunnel its size is diminished in the normal inverse size to distance relationship of perspective projection. Window positions are constrained so that at least a portion of a window always remains inside the tunnel, although, for example, a window can be moved downwards so that only its top part, or status bar, is visible.

In addition to the front-on window display mode there is a "hanging" mode where the windows are hung on the left or right walls of the tunnel, as shown in figure 3. Individual windows may be hung or all the windows may be hung at once. Hanging all the windows allows the user to quickly gain an overall idea of where the windows are in the tunnel.

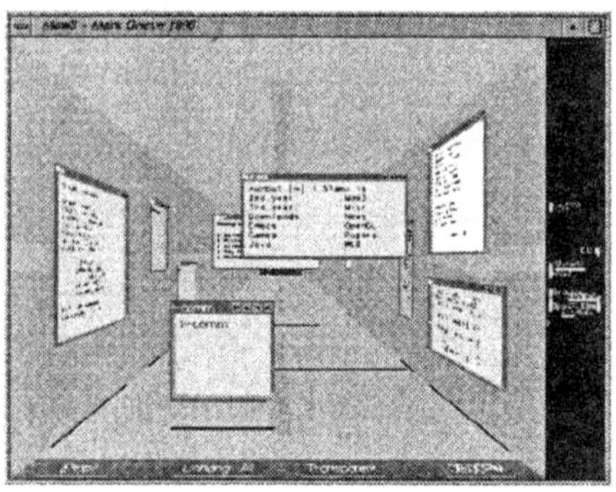

Figure 3: Window hanging

There are two further major components of our 3D window manager. The first is an **overview** area to the right of the tunnel which may be seen in figures 2 and 3. The overview area provides a plan or top view of the tunnel and is provided in addition to the main "down the tunnel" view. Windows may be selected and then moved up and down in the overview area, corresponding to back and forward in the tunnel. Windows' names are displayed in the overview area to aid identification of specific windows, although, due to the small font the names are hard to see in the diagrams.

The last major component of our window manager is a console, positioned at the bottom of the screen as shown in figures 2 and 3. Controls are provided on the console for changing global settings affecting windows. There is a button to hang all the windows at once, rather than hanging invididual windows. There is another button to toggle transparency: windows can be rendered partially see-through, so that windows may be seen through other windows. There are also mechanisms to control lighting, which provides enhanced visual cues about the position of windows in the tunnel, and options to set different rendering modes — solid, wireframe and invisible — for the walls to allow the user to customise their appearance. The console is attached to the user's viewpoint so that it moves through the tunnel with the user. Finally, a clock is provided on the console as an example of the more general functionality we envisage a working model to incorporate.

We now return to the issue of window thrashing. Our 3D window manager addresses it in four main ways:

1. Through window hanging. Hanging some or all of the windows allows the user to obtain a global view of window locations in a natural and easily invoked manner. It also allows better allocation of the available screen real estate.

2. Through the scaling of window size in inverse proportion to distance down the tunnel. Windows which are not in use may be pushed back down the tunnel where they will be small but visible.

3. By reducing mouse movement required to access windows. The centralising of windows in the screen via the tunnel, combined with the inverse size versus distance relationship, appears to reduce mouse movement required to access windows compared to the approaches to window thrashing adopted for $2\frac{1}{2}$D desktop GUIs (see section 5).

4. Through the use of transparency. If windows are made transparent, obscured windows are able to be seen (although selection becomes difficult).

3.3 The Magic Wand: A 3D Cursor

The second thrust of our 3D GUI prototyping work is exploring the design and usability of a 3D cursor controlled by a 3D input device. One of our 3D cursors is shown (at close range) in figure 4 where it is being used to select a chess piece.

Figure 4: 3D cursor

Most interactive 3D graphics applications employ a 2D cursor and 2D pointing device for interaction. Given that the user is manipulating 3D objects or worlds in these applications, this gives rise to a fundamental mismatch in dimensionality. In the context of a 3D application the cursor "floats" over the top of the objects rather than being part of the scene. We believe the use of a 3D cursor, introduced into the scene as an object in its own right, controlled by a 3D (six-degree-of-freedom input) device is a better approach for interactive 3D applications, including a 3D user interface, than the traditional approach. Recently, work in the area of 3D interaction has intensified (Bier, 1990, Herndon et al., 1994, Houde, 1992). We believe this to be a significant area for research in its own right, with the potential for many important practical outcomes.

In the $2\frac{1}{2}$D GUI there are different cursors — arrow, hourglass, cross-hair, etc. — for different contexts. Likewise we believe a 3D cursor should take on different characteristics and behaviours, to allow a better relationship to the particular type of interaction task being performed. However, we believe these cursor changes are better applied if the user is given more control over them. The user can be made aware, or reminded, of the particular characteristics and behaviours of a given cursor by the visual characteristics of the cursor — adhering to the principles of direct manipulation. By putting more control of the cursor in the user's hands the 3D cursor becomes a far more sophisticated tool than its 2D counterpart — a sort of "magic wand".

To provide a framework for comprehension of the different characteristics and behaviours of our 3D cursor we use different metaphors. These are shown in figure 5. The user may switch between the type of cursor displayed by pressing a button on the spaceball. The cursors are intended for different types of interaction:

(a) Arrow (b) Laser (c) Bar magnet

Figure 5: Cursor metaphors

- The arrow cursor is our general purpose cursor and is the 3D equivalent of the 2D arrow. It must be in contact with objects to select them. Once selected objects may be dragged.
- The laser cursor is used for precision selection of objects. It sends out a "light ray" which can be swept over objects. As objects fall in the path of the light ray they are highlighted to give the user continuous feedback consistent with the principles of direct manipulation. Unlike the general arrow cursor the laser cursor may select objects from a distance. When a particular object of interest is highlighted it may be selected by clicking a button. Once selected, objects may be dragged or **tractored**, that is, moved along the light ray's path towards (or away from) the cursor. At this stage the light ray does not penetrate objects, and thus only the first object intersected is highlighted. An example of the laser cursor being used to select an object is given in figure 7.
- The bar magnet cursor is used to select groups of objects within a certain distance of the cursor, that is, within its magnetic field. It is intended for interaction tasks where less accurate but faster gross selection is required rather than precise selection and tasks where multiple objects are to be selected and operated on at once.

3.4 The Spaceball: A 3D Input Device

In order to effectively control the 3D cursor we use a spaceball (Spacetec, 1996), as shown in figure 6. The

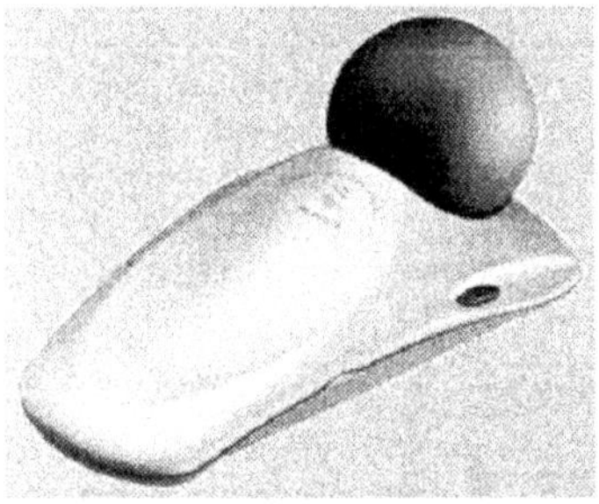

Figure 6: Spaceball

spaceball is a 3D input device with six-degrees-of-freedom to match those of the cursor. It consists of a **powersensor**, which is a ball slightly smaller than a tennis ball, mounted on a platform that rests on the top of the desk. Pushing, pulling and twisting actions on the powerball are mapped onto translations and rotations of the 3D cursor. For instance, by pushing forward on the powersensor whilst similtaneously twisting it around the vertical axis, the user is able to direct the cursor into the scene, (increase its z value) whilst similtaneously rotating it about the y axis.

4. Implementation

For our prototyping work we have used two 3D graphics libraries: OpenGL and Open Inventor. OpenGL (Neider et al., 1993) is a low level graphics library originally developed by Silicon Graphics but which is now available for most UNIX graphics workstations and personal computer operating systems. Open Inventor (Wernecke, 1994) is a higher level, object-oriented, 3D graphics, C++ class library from Silicon Graphics.

The 3D window manager is implemented in C and uses OpenGL. The 3D cursor is implemented in C++ and uses Open Inventor. We have used both the OpenGL and Open Inventor libraries to explore their suitability for our 3D GUI project. OpenGL, with its lower level facilities tends to give the programmer greater control and better performance, and its wide availability is obviously important. On the other hand, the object oriented approach of Open Inventor offers advantages for prototyping work.

Implementation of a working 3D GUI is a considerably larger and more complicated task than the building of a prototype. For instance, implementing "live" windows in a 3D GUI requires an inversion of the current GUI architecture in which 3D graphics are displayed in 2D windows in a $2\frac{1}{2}$D environment — and it appears that considerable low level programming is required to achieve this. Another major issue is performance. We have found that our 3D window manager and 3D cursor perform quite well on an Indy workstation and that the 3D window managers performs satisfactorily on a pentium based personal computer running Windows 95 (without a 3D graphics accelerator board). There are undoubtedly specialised approaches to improve the performance of both the 3D window manager and the 3D cursor, rather than using the traditional brute force redraw approach of 3D graphics (which we use), however, the performance of today's low-end architectures already appears to be adequate, or nearly adequate, to support at least simple 3D GUIs.

5. Usability Testing

The star life cycle approach to system development (Hix and Hartson, 1993) stresses rapid prototyping and incremental development of interactive systems. The star model is highly iterative and flexible enough to allow development to commence from the prototyping stage when the design specifications are not clear in the mind of the developer. This can be advantageous when novel design ideas are considered as it allows developers to better understand the limitations of technology and how these ideas should be implemented in order to match users needs. Advances in technology make possible imaginative and innovate approaches to both existing and new problems. Rapid prototyping offers designers an opportunity to test their novel ideas with representative users, and to set realistic requirements before committing time and effort to implement them.

In the case of our 3D cursor and 3D window manager prototypes, we conducted exploratory evaluations (Nielsen, 1993, Rubin, 1994) to help us test our high-level concepts, and to solicit users' ideas about how to improve confusing areas. Our emphasis during the exploratory test was on understanding users' mental models and why they perform as they do. Later, after implementing the prototypes, we conducted another assessment evaluation for the purpose of determining how effectively the high-level concepts were implemented. Rather than just exploring the intuitiveness of our 3D cursor and 3D window manager, we were interested in testing how well users can actually perform realistic tasks, and in identifying usability deficiencies. Some of the issues we aimed to investigate in our exploratory evaluation with the help of our representative users are:

- Subjective satisfaction with both the 3D window manager and the 3D cursor.
- Ease of navigation in the tunnel and how efficiently

windows could be managed.

- Whether users are cognizant that the 3D cursor is an object in its own right in the environment.
- The intuitiveness of the idea of associating different behaviours (metaphors) to the 3D cursor.
- Whether a 3D cursor controlled by the spaceball is a good approach for 3D interaction.

The results of our evaluation were very encouraging. A key result is users' subjective satisfaction where we found the attitude toward using the 3D window manager, the 3D cursor and the spaceball to be enthusiastic, to an extent which was surprising. We also sought quantative results, although space constraints preclude their detailed reporting here. An example of one of the tasks users performed as part of our usability testing is shown in figure 7. Here

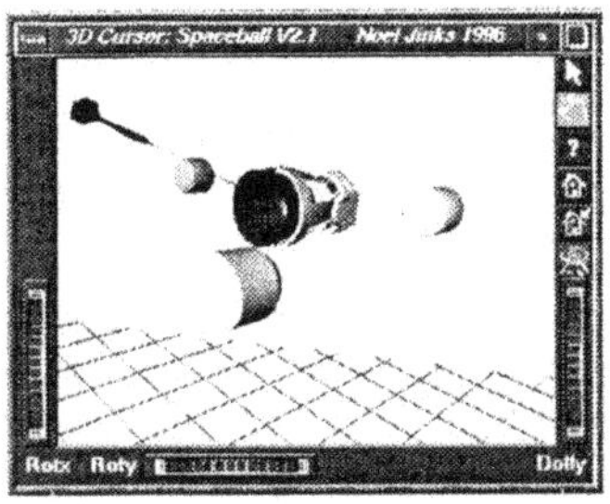

Figure 7: 3D interaction task

users were required to select the components of the object (an exhaust system for a jet engine) one-by-one and pull the object apart using the laser cursor. Users' performance in this task, and others, clearly indicated that: they were cognizant of the fact that the 3D cursor is an object in its own right in the scene, that assigning effective metaphors to the cursor improved its usability when performing selection, highlighting and movement operations, and that using a 3D pointing device reinforces the feeling of a direct engagement between the user and the environment. We also measured the speed of performance and the number of errors made: this task was one the users were able to complete more effectively using the 3D (laser) cursor and spaceball than using the 2D cursor and a mouse.

One of our aims with the 3D window manager was to reduce the amount of mouse movement required to find windows — as part of the goal of addressing the problem of window thrashing. The evaluations indicate that the 3D tunnel may facilitate better management of screen space. We have implemented a routine which tracks mouse movements in an effort to try and quantify the mouse movements performed. An example trace is shown in figure 8, which shows that most of the mouse movement occurs in the centre of the screen with occasional moves to the bottom and right of the screen. The trace was produced by performing operations a user would typically engage in: moving, grouping and hanging windows. As yet we have not performed comparisons based on this metric between our 3D window manager and any $2\frac{1}{2}$D window manager.

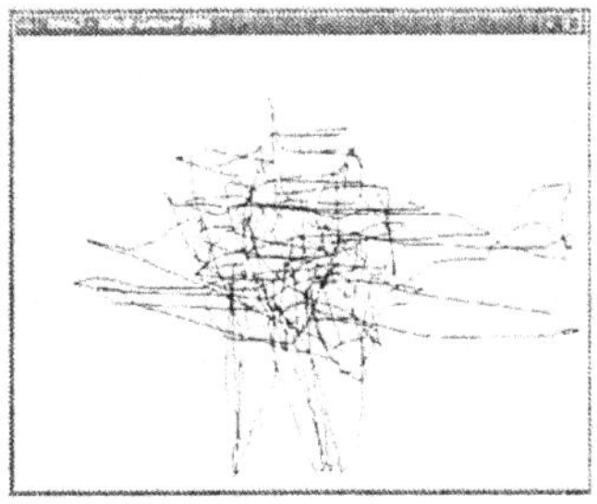

Figure 8: Mouse trace

We intend to conduct more rigorous evaluations to obtain statistically significant results following completion of a working 3D window manager. Further experiments are also needed to examine the issue of alternating between 2D and 3D cursors and 2D and 3D input devices.

6. Conclusions and Future Work

The elements of the 3D GUI prototype we have discussed have been well received by a sample group of users. Obvious further work is to integrate the 3D window manager and the 3D cursor in a working windowing system, and to provide other elements of a 3D GUI. There is also the issue of providing both 2D and 3D cursors and using both 2D and 3D input devices. For tasks which are inherently 2D, a 2D cursor controlled by a 2D input device is superior, whilst, we believe, for tasks which are inherently 3D, a 3D cursor controlled by a 3D input device is superior. Beyond these aspects there is the potential for incorporating intelligence into the interface and the cursor.

References

Apple (1996). Hotsauce. http://mcf.research.apple.com.

Bier, E. (1990). Snap-dragging in three dimensions. In

The Proceedings of the Symposium on Interactive 3D Graphics.

Card, S. K., Robertson, G. G., and York, W. (1996). The webbook and the web forager: An information workspace for the world-wide web. In *CHI 96*, pages 111–117.

Carroll, J. (1987). *Interfacing Thought.* MIT Press.

Furness, G. (1986). Generalized fisheye views. In *CHI '86 Conference on Human Factors in Computing Systems*, pages 16–23.

Harch, G. H. (1996). Impvwm 32bit virtual window manager for windows 95. http://www.kent.edu/ gharth.

Henderson, D. A. and Card, S. K. (1986). Rooms: The use of multiple virtual workspaces to reduce space contention in a window-based graphical user interface. *ACM Transactions on Graphics*, 5(3):211–243.

Herndon, K., van Dam, A., and Gleicher, M. (1994). The challenges of 3d interaction. *SIGCHI Bulletin*, 26(4):36–39.

Hines, C. (1996). Fvwm window manager. http://www3.hmc.edu/ tkelly/docs/proj/fvwm.html.

Hix, D. and Hartson, H. R. (1993). *Developing User Interfaces.* John Wiley and Sons.

Houde, S. (1992). Iterative design of an interface for easy 3d direct manipulation. In *The Proceedings of CHI '92 Workshop.*

Hutchins, E., Hollan, J. D., and Norman, D. A. (1986). Direct manipulation interfaces. In Norman, D. A. and Draper, S. W., editors, *User centered system design:New perspectives on human-computer interaction.* Erlbaum Associates.

Johnson, J., Roberts, T., Verplank, W., Smith, D., Irby, C., Beard, M., and Mackey, K. (1989). The xerox star: A retrospective. *Computer*, pages 11–26.

Margono, S. and Shneiderman, B. (1987). A study of file manipulation by novices using commands vs. direct manipulation. In *Proc. ACM D.C. Chapter 6th Annual Technical Symposium.*

Neider, J., Davis, T., and Woo, M. (1993). *OpenlGL Programming Guide.* Addison-Wesley.

Nielsen, J. (1993). *Usability Engineering.* Academic Press.

Perlin, K. and Fox, D. (1993). Pad: An alternative approach to the computer interface. In *SIGGRAPH Computer Graphics*, pages 57–64.

Rauterberg, M. (1992). An empirical comparison of menu-selection (cui) and desktop (gui) computer programs carried out by beginners and experts. *Behaviour and Information Technology*, 11(4):227–236.

Robertson, G. R., Card, S. K., and Mackinlay, J. D. (1993). Information visualisation using 3d interactive animation. *Communications of the ACM*, 36(4):57–71.

Rubin, J. (1994). *Handbook of Usability Testing.* Wiley.

Shneiderman, B. (1982). The future of interactive systems and the emergence of direct manipulation. *Behaviour and Information Technology*, 1(3):237–256.

Shneiderman, B. (1983). Direct manipulation: A step beyond programming languages. *IEEE Computer*, 16(8):57–69.

Shneiderman, B. (1992). *Designing the User Interface: Strategies for Effective Human-Computer Interaction, 2nd ed.* Addison-Wesley.

Smith, D., Irby, C., Kimball, R., and Verplank, B. (1982). Designing the star user interface. *Byte*, pages 242–282.

Spacetec (1996). Spacetec imc web site. http://www.spacetec.com/.

Wernecke, J. (1994). *The Inventor Mentor: Programming Object-Oriented 3D Graphics with Open Inventor, Release 2.* Addison Wesley.

Young, R. (1983). Surrogates and mappings: two kinds of conceptual models for interactive devices. In Gentner, D. and Stevens, A., editors, *Mental Models.* Lawrence Erlbaum Associates.

Automated Usability Testing

Elizabeth Chang and Tharam S. Dillon

School of Computer Science and Computer Engineering
La Trobe University, Bundoora, Melbourne, Australia
chang@latcs1.lat oz.au; tharam@latcs1.lat.oz.au

ABSTRACT: Currently Laboratory Testing for Usability evaluation requires external monitoring and recording devices such as video and audio, as well as evaluator observation of user and user actions. It then requires review of these recordings, a time consuming and tedious process. We describe an automatic Usability Testing and Evaluation tool that we have developed. This consists of a piece of software called AUS (Automatic Usability Software) running at the operating system level that collects all the information related to user actions when s/he is using a particular application. It then displays this information in various useful formats as well as calculates suitable measures of Usability. There is no need with this system for any external recording devices. Patent protection has been applied for in respect of the inventive aspects of this system.

KEY WORDS: Usability Testing, Usability Evaluation, Usability Measurement.

1. INTRODUCTION

A variety of techniques for carrying Usability Evaluation are explained in the literature and these include: (a) Empirical testing [Molich and Nielsen 1990], (b) Inspection [Nielsen and Philips 1993], (c) Comparative Usability measures [Dillon and Maquire 1993], (d) Formal complexity based measures [Thimbleby 1994], (e) The MUSIC methodology [Bevan & Macleod 1994]

Empirical testing consists of testing an implementation of the user interface and software in a fairly controlled situation so as to ascertain the problems that the user is experiencing with the user interface. It can be carried out using three different environments, and these are: (1) Fixed LaboratoryTesting, (2) Portable Usability Laboratory Testing, (3) Remote Usability Testing.

Fixed Laboratory Testing involves a test room and a separate observation room, which are linked together usually through a one way mirror. Drawbacks of the fixed laboratories include: (i) they are relatively expensive, costing typically around US$50,000 to $100,000. (ii) the test is performed away from the work environment and could be artificial. (iii) it is expensive to shift staff observation and test staff to test site.

Portable Laboratory Testing moves equipment to the user site so the testing can be carried out in the user's company close to or at the actual work site where the user is likely to be using the software [Dorward 1994, Rowley 1994]. Advantages of Portable useability testing include, (a) it is much cheaper costing about US$20,000 for a Portable Laboratory, (b) it involves less cost for the corporation as no people are moved to the test site, (c) the tests involved are carried out in a more realistic environment. This approach still relies on extensive video recording which has to be reviewed, a time consuming process. Further, there are only a limited number of things that are actually captured by

Human-Computer Interaction: INTERACT'97 S. Howard, J. Hammond & G. Lindgaard (editors)
Published by Chapman & Hall

the video camera. In addition it still has the problem that test personnel and test equipment have to be sent to the site where the test subjects, are in order to carryout the testing.

Remote Usability Testing. uses computer networks and modem connections to monitor what the user is doing, so, neither the Usability tester nor the test subjects have to travel. However the disadvantages are that the Usability tester cannot observe the test subject's reactions, nor does s/he have access to the dialogue that the user is encouraged to enter into to provide some feedback.

All these Usability laboratory tests have been found to be very effective in actually picking up specific useability problems that relate only to the designated tasks. There could still be Usability problems with the User Interface which are not covered by the designated tasks. Furthermore, these approaches do not give an overall figure of merit either to the whole user interface or to significant aspects of the user interface. Thus it might uncover a specific problem but it does not give you an overall measure of goodness of the Usability of the user interface.

These difficulties with Usability Testing have meant that whilst it might be utilised for some expensive projects, it is not in widespread use for a large proportion of the software that is being produced today. However, the need to make software user friendly is becoming greater as time passes. There is clearly, therefore, a need for a more convenient approach to Usability Testing that would lead to more widespread Usability Testing.

2. NEW PROPOSAL

In the proposed method, a piece of software know as the Automated Usability Testing System is installed in the user's computer together with the software that is actually tested.

This Usability Software is automatically linked into the operating system. it runs as part of operating system. It works quietly in the background of the users' application. The user will not notice that there is Automatic Usability Testing software running. It is like many other tools in Windows, such as Print Manager, because it works in the background. You can continue working with your applications while the Print Manager manages the printing queue to print many files frem many applications. AUS can run in several ways. ie: click the icon or automatically start with the StartUP program. The Usability software opens and closes when the Windows Operating System comes on and off. It always does an auto save data at every time interval (which can be specified) and protects the data when computer is turned off. AUS is only run and used by UI analysts or UI evaluators, not by the user. AUS automatically collects all data concerned with UI analysis and Usability evaluation.

This Usability software should be able to monitor all the user actions when s/he is carrying out the specified series of tasks. It should be able to store all the information that it has gathered allowing the test personal to gather various statistics, or frequencies. The Automated Usability Testing software should also permit test personal to replay user actions and hence be able to review a user's test session, at normal speed and fast speed. This Usability Testing software must also be able to generate the required Usability Metrics.

3. SPECIFICATION OF AUTOMATED USABILITY SOFTWARE (AUS)

The AUS should be capable of eventually capturing all user interactions with the system through any user interface device. The Automated Usability System needs to be able to:

- Monitor multiple applications that the user is interacting with at the same time;
  Monitor multiple windows rather than just current activated window.

For the purpose of the prototype system, the following function should provide:

(I) UI data collection needs to occur:

⇒ Keystrokes within application; within each window and within each time interval.

- Input and output from a port
- Help system use
- Delete (string, number..) function use
- Select, searching or find (a menu, submenu or a item in a multiple choice field) function use;
- Modification to what they have entered;
- Retrieve function use;
- Copy function use;

- Edit function use;
- Undo function use;
- Cancel function use;
- Resizing of windows;
- Move windows;
- Scroll button use;
- Network UI data transfer (Sound receiver, Video Recording)

⇒ Mouse movements within application; within each window and within each time interval

- Left mouse key down-up
- Right mouse key down-up
- Middle mouse key down-up
- Double click
- Drag and Drop
- Mouse travel distance

(II) The following information needs to stored for later retrieval by the AUS:

- Keystrokes with window number and timer
- Mouse location with window number and timer
- System Messages with timer

(III) The Automatic Usability Software (AUS) needs to carry out the following analysis :

⇒ Task time measurement data are collected as below:

- Total task finishing time;
- Total computer idle time (unproductive time or wasted time);
- Total computer user dialogue time;
- Total computer response time;
- Average operation time;

⇒ Error measurements determined include:

- Number of dialogue errors;
- Number of user requests from or to the system;
- Number of user requests that failed due to user error;
- Number of user requests that failed due to system error (eg not enough memory);
- Number of times the application was terminated by user (user control to quit the system);
- Number of times the application crashed (out of user control);

⇒ Statistical Data analysis of the following type is carried out:

- Fuzzy Logic Based Metric
- Standard deviation among 4-100 users
- Normal distribution fits to data
- Learning curve (Correlation and Regression)
- FFT and Spectral Analysis
- Best Case /Worst Case Analysis

(IV) The Usability Results Output should display:

- Historical keystrokes (virtual keys, extended keys, and system keys) within each predefined time interval;
- Total density of mouse clicks within each predefined time interval;
- Density of mouse clicks in each window opened within a selected time interval;
- Total number of application windows opened (created) (eg 20 WD opened);
- Times when each window is opened (activated or deactivated) (eg WD1 opened 10 times);
- Times when each menu (system menu, pop up menu) is selected;
- Times when each button is pressed (system button, speed button, dialogue button)
- Time of every user action
- Time of task completion
- User action playback with selected speed, pause, fast forward, backward, stop and continue. (This allows a complete playback of all user actions carried out on the system within a specified time interval automatically).
- Overall Usability figure of merit (Fuzzy Model)
- Statistical graph and metric displays
- A playback operation of all user interactions with the system at different speeds of display
- User action sequence diagram
- Mouse movement pattern
- Three categories of user file creation and choice (Novice, Intermediate, Expert)
- Up to 24 window partitions of the Screen for visual comparison of all outputs for up to 24 users.

The AUS has two main components and these are: (1) UI data Collection; (2) Usability analyser and UI metrics. For the purposes of the prototype system, the following implementation has been done:

- Collect the messages user sends to the application;
- Collect the messages the system sends to the user;
- Collect every user action for user performance playback;

- Collect historical keystrokes (virtual keys, extended keys, and system key) and time stamps;
- Collect density of mouse clicks and mouse click time stamps;
- Collect density of mouse clicks in each window (WD) opened and open time stamps;
- Calculate total number of windows opened (created) (eg 20 Windows opened);
- Calculate the number of times each window (WD) is opened (activated or deactivated) (eg WD1 opened 10 times);
- Calculate times of each menu (system menu, pop up menu) being selected;
- Calculate times of each button being pressed (system button, speed button, dialogue button);
- Compare Mouse density for up to 24 users
- Compare Key Strokes for up to 24 users using Bar and Line graphs
- Draw mouse movement diagram.
- Output overall figure of merit

4. SYSTEM DISPLAY AND RESULTS

This section presents some typical user input screens, results screens and displays obtained using the Automated Usability Testing prototype system. The program can be placed in any Window group. It can be executed by double clicking on the AUS icon. Figure 1 shows AUS running in a minimised fashion, like PrintManager in the background of any user's application software.

Figure 1. AUS is running in a minimised fashion.

The main control of the AUS Prototype is shown in Figure 2. It allows the evaluator to view (i) the Statistical Distribution of Keystrokes with timer; (ii) Mouse clicks with timer and each window opened and times of each window opened; (iii) Playback of user actions; (iv) overall figure of merit. It also allows the evaluator to pre-set the test time and data store time interval as well as transferring the UI data file across platforms. The File name is automatically assigned by a Date and Time and no user control is needed to run this program. The time is never duplicated. So when the user, for some reason reboots the system, AUS will continue working with a new time stamp on the file. The default recording time is 240 minutes (4 hours). This recording time can be reassigned by the evaluator for upto hundreds of hours. When the 4 hour limit is reached, AUS is closed automatically.

If the 4 hour limit is not reached, but the user wishes to take a break or simply to reboot the system, this poses no difficulties for AUS. It automatically saves the intermediate results gathered in every predefined time-interval, such as every 30 seconds or every 1 minute or 5 minutes. This time interval can be assigned by the evaluator. It depends on the type of the software you are testing. For a big system, there is no need to save every 30 seconds, but for some small software, it is necessary.

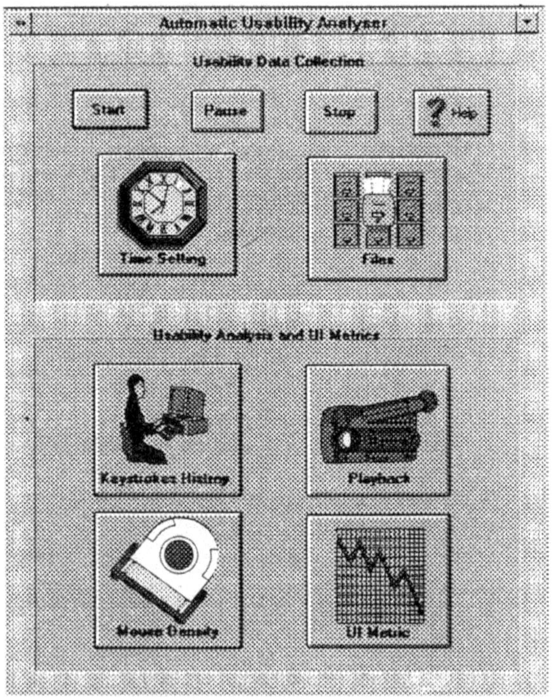

Figure 2. AUS main menu

Once the user finishes using the computer, the evaluator can either copy or transfer the data file to disk or other machine (Figure 3) and the test results at their own time or then can just directly run AUS on the user's machine. AUS has great potential to summarise the UI metric. We carried out some sample tests with the prototype. The following screen dumps from AUS are the results of testing Peter Coad OO Tools which are used for drawing OO conceptual models. The user had 3
to 4 hour of learning time with this tool before we started the recording. We asked the user to draw four different diagrams using this Tool from the projects: (i) Authors and Referee; (ii) Course Booking System;(iii) JCE Company Database; and (iv) HP Call Dispatcher.

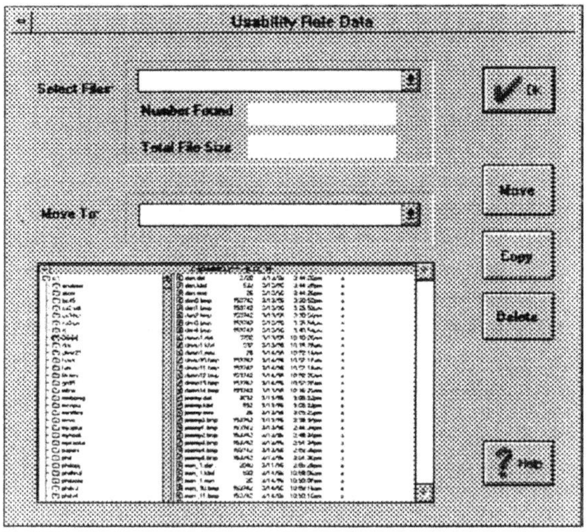

Figure 3 UI data transfer or backup window.

Figure 4 shows at the 30 minutes time, the user's finished a single task and the keystroke statistics and the mouse clicks. Again, the time interval can be set by evaluator. The Arrow buttons here are to switch the time forward and backward. As you can see, that there are not many different variety of keys that the user used. This is because the test software is an OO Diagramming Tool which is a piece of modern software, that should not need too much keyboard use, rather it should use the mouse.

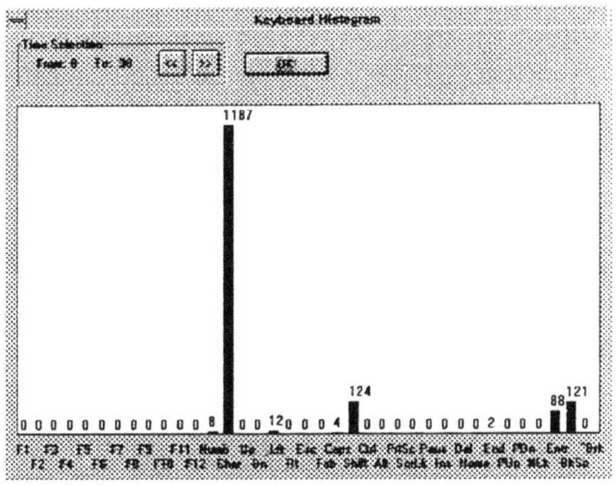

Figure 4. Keystrokes for a single task.

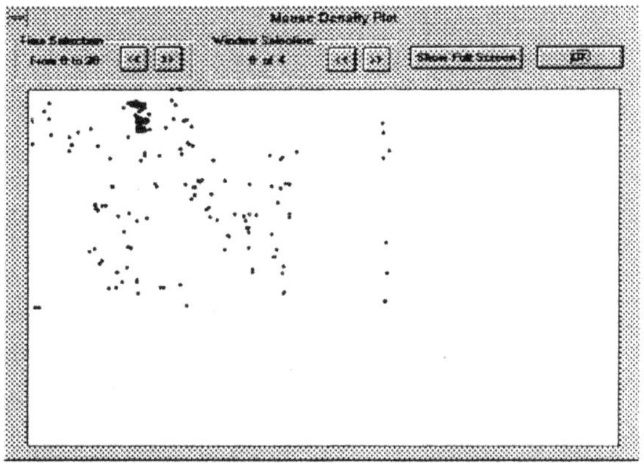

Figure 5. Mouse click density for a single task.

Figure 5 shows the total mouse clicks on doing one predefined task, and finishes within 30 minutes. From the mouse density, we look for regions where the number of clicks is largest, and search the relevant menus or buttons or any widgets which has caused the user difficulties. The Arrow buttons on Window selection allows the evaluator to switch several window images to match the mouse clicks.

A multiple comparison is shown in Figure 6. The user has to use the same package and enters the four diagrams during four different dates and times. The number of Ctrl, Shift and BackSpace ,keystrokes reduce as time goes on.

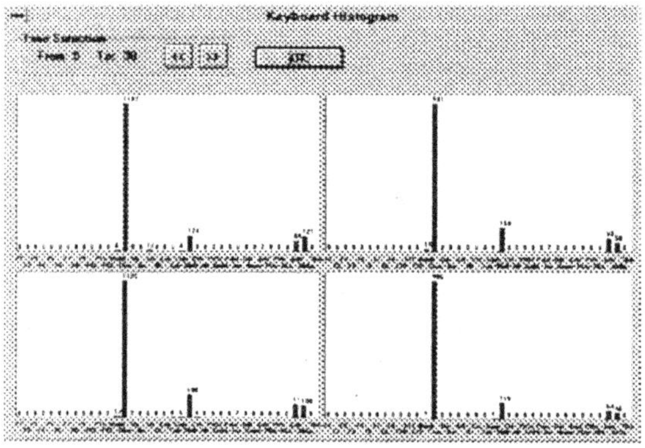

Figure 6. Multiple window comparison of keystrokes.

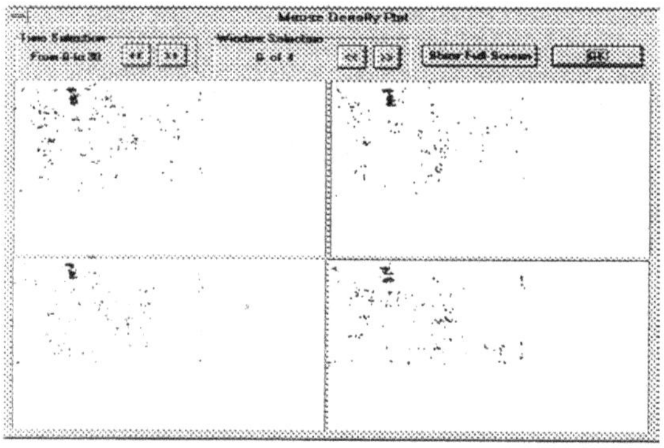

Figure 7. Multiple window comparison of mouse clicks

Figure 7, shows the user entered the four conceptual diagram using OO tools at different times. The mouse clicks show that the user's skills have improved and the mouse clicks density is getting lighter.

Because we capture each window opened. So we can match the mouse clicks with each particular window or menus or button. Figure 8 show that the OO Tool main window image is brought up. The database shows that there are 182 mouse clicks on menu called "Drawing". The database stored the exact number of clicks on a particular window, or a menu, or a button.

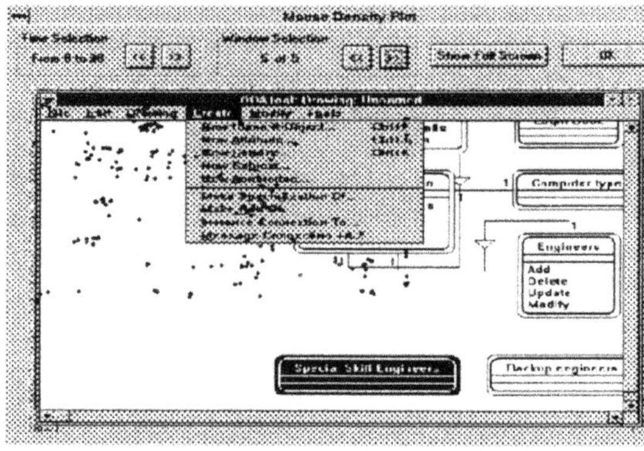

Figure 8. Match mouse clicks with menus/ sub-menus.

Figure 9 display the mouse travel pattern. Multiple windows can be shown comparing different users doing the same tasks, or one user doing one task on different software packages.

Figure 10 shows the menu used for playback users operation or actions. It is like a video recorder. The playback speed can be set to *fast mode*, which is usual if the user used software for two hours, the playback time in *fast* mode is about 10 minutes; the *slow mode*, is the speed at which the user actually worked on the computer and did the predefined tasks. This is a better option than with video, since one can exactly see what the user clicks on. This is not clear in a fast speed playback on video.

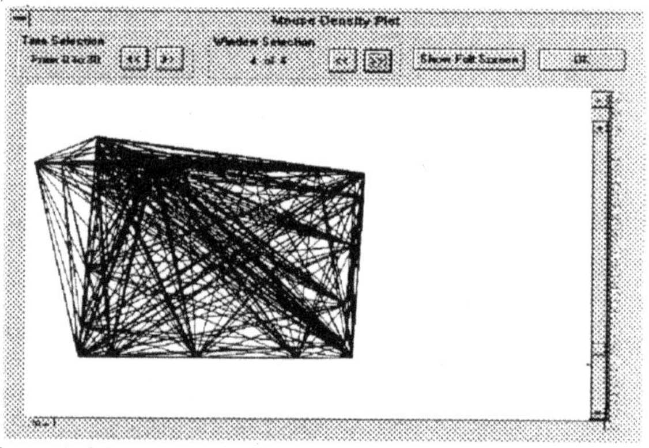

Figure 9, Mouse travel pattern.

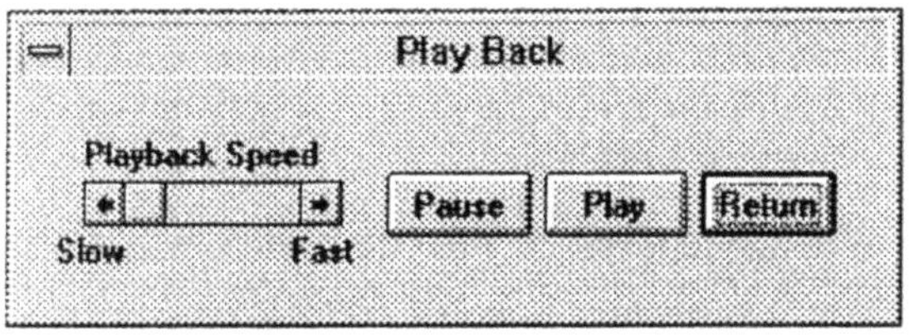

Figure10. User action playback.

Some software utilities such as Word Macro or Excel Macro or Macro-recorder allow a replay of keystrokes, but not the mouse clicks or movements, for a single window or a single application only [Sybex 1993] AUS does not have these restrictions and is capable of playback for multiple windows and multiple applications.

Figure 11, we show the overall figure of merit using fuzzy system approach [Chang, Dillon & Cook 1996].

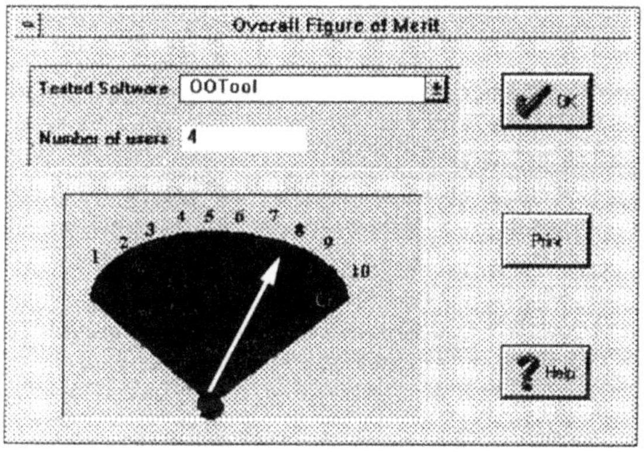

Figure 11. Overall figure of merit.

The ASCII database file for keystrokes can be viewed by any Word document The keystroke statistics for all the 256 virtual keys can be recorded in AUS. In the future, it is intended to include the extended keys, which is another 256 keys, such as Ctrl-Shift-A, etc. All statistical data are saved in ASCII format, which can be viewed in any Word document. Figure 12 shows the example in Figure 4 shows that in the first 30 minutes, there were 705 mouse clicks.

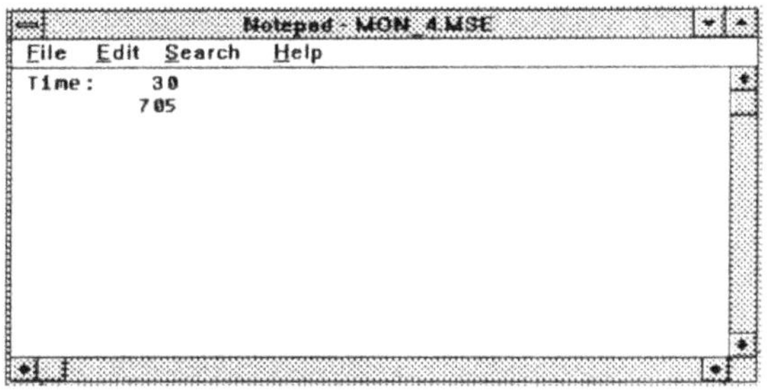

Figure 12. Total mouse click in a single task.

This prototype AUS can also record each window the user opened and number of keystrokes in this window. If this window is opened again and again, it calculates the number of times each window is opened. Tis is shown in Figure 13.

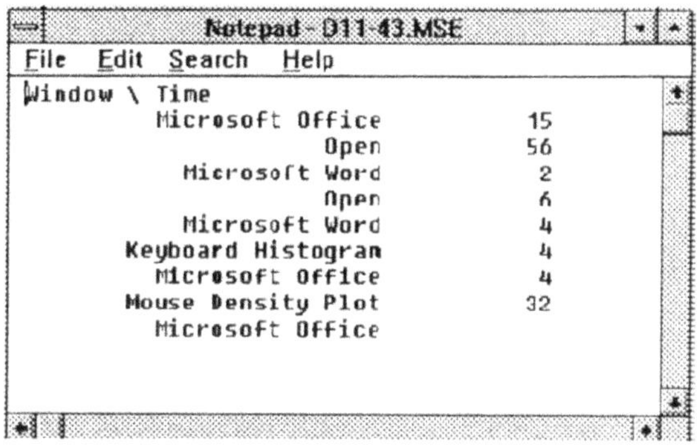

Figure 13. The number of times each window is opened.

The number of clicks is listed in 30 minute intervals. This time interval can be set. The size of the keystrokes database file is a 500 bytes ASCII file for a 30 minutes session and that of mouse density file is 20 bytes to 30 bytes, and mouse clicks and timer and window pop-up information is about 2k-3k bytes. The size of the executable code for the prototype of AUS is only 620K. The dynamic link library that we created which is used at run-time, and does all the major work, is only about 158K. This DLL is designed to be compatible across different platforms for C++, such as X window environment.

5. RECAPITULATION

In this paper, we presented a Computer Aided Usability Testing and Evaluation Software Tool. This overcomes a number of the difficulties associated with more manual methods of Usability Testing.

The AUS is able to permit replay of user actions such as mouse movements, screen opening and menu selection etc. for multiple screens and multiple applications. Some software utilities such as Word Macro or Excel Macro or Microsoft Macro-recorder allow a replay of keystrokes, but not the mouse clicks or movements, for a single window or a single application only. Also, there are many restrictions required when running such tools, such as closing all un-used windows, not moving or dragging a window around or re-sizing the window, not being able to use the mouse, etc [Sybex 1993]. AUS system should be capable of replaying for multiple window and multiple applications.

Note that, several tool developments [Eldh 1996] that are used for keeping track of keystrokes information are for: (1) debugging purposes and, (2) repeated tasks or demonstration

The debugging process uses the recorded key information to determine bugs or errors in the system. The Macro uses the key-in sequences for repeated tasks, such as automatic re-configuration of serial ports to specific settings for use with a variety of external hardware, or to change the screen colours from one set of saved colours to another, or the playback function can be used for demonstrate some flow of presentation. Most Macros are built into the application software to display a sequence that a user has pre-typed information within the software itself. Such tools are not capable of being used or run with any other commercial software. In her survey and evaluation [Eldh 1996], she pointed out that the Tool for use in Debugging and Software Testing is not mature and causes the difficulties for Industry Engineers in in-house software development. The software that we have developed has a totally different purpose and goal and can be used for User Interface Testing as well as Software Quality Testing. It runs with any software or application, tool and prototype, and is capable of analysing the interaction between multiple windows and multiple applications and between the user and the system at the same time for the purpose of Usability Testing and Evaluation.

REFERENCES

[1] Bevan, N. & Macleod, M (1994) "Usability measurement in context". *Behaviour and Inf. Tech.*,pp132-145

[2] Chang E, Dillon T.S., Cook D. "Measurement of Usability of Software Using a Fuzzy System Approach" Invited paper *Proc. of 8th Int. Conf. on Software Eng. and Knowledge Eng.*, pp69-76, Lake Tahoe, USA 1996.

[3] Dillon, A and Maquire, M. (1993) Usability Measurement- Its Practical Value to the Computer Industry. *Proc. of ACM/IFIP Human Factors in Comp. Sys., INTERCHI 4*,93 pp 145-148

[4] Dorward, F (1994) "The advantages of portable Usability Testing" Proc. of OZCHI'94 pp125-126

[5] Eldh, S. (1996) "*The Challenge of Test Automation- a Process Change*" Research report, Ericsson Hewlett-packard Telecommunications AB, Sweden.

[6] Molich, R and Nielsen, J. (1990) Heuristic evaluation of User Interfaces Proc. of *ACM Human Factors in Comp. Sys. CHI'90 4*, pp249-256

[7] Nielsen, J. and Philips, V. (1993) Estimating the relative Usability of Two Interfaces: Heuristic, Formal, and Empirical Methods Compared. *Proc. of ACM/IFIP Human Factors in Comp. Sys.*, 93 pp214-221

[8] Nielsen, J. (1993) Enhancing the Explanatory power of Usability Heuristics. Proc. of *ACM/IFIP Human Factors in Comp. Sys. INTERCHI'93* 4, 93 pp152-158

[9] Rowley, D.E., "Usability Testing in the Field: Bringing the Laboratory to the User" Proc. of ACM/SIGCHI Human Factors in Comp. Sys. CHI'94 pp252-257

[10] Thimbleby, H. (1994) Formulating Usability. *SIGCHI Bulletin* APRIL 94 pp59-64

[11] Treu, S. (1994)"*User Interface Evaluation -A Structured Approach*" pp 175-195

14

The Best among Six Strategies for Selecting a Minute Target and the Determination of the Minute Maximum Size of the Targets on a Pen-Based Computer

Xiangshi Ren and Shinji Moriya

Department of Information and Communication Engineering
Tokyo Denki University
2-2 Kanda-Nishikicho, Chiyoda-ku, Tokyo 101, JAPAN
+81-3-5280-3335
{ren, moriya}@c.dendai.ac.jp

ABSTRACT This study concentrates on finding the relationship between target-pointing strategies and target sizes. Concretely, an evaluation experiment was performed in which the experimental system used five kinds of targets (1, 3, 5, 7 and 9 dot diameter circles in respectively, 0.36 mm per dot), eight pen-movement-directions and six strategies of systematic election on a pen-based computer. The results showed that the "Land-on2" strategy was the best strategy for selecting a minute target, in terms of error rates, selection time and subjective preferences. "The minute maximum size" of 5 dots was also determined to be the largest size among the targets which had a significant main effect on the six strategies in terms of error rates.

KEYWORDS input devices, pen-based input, target-pointing strategies, minute targets, the minute maximum size.

1. INTRODUCTION

Pen-based computers operated only with pens are attracting attention in many fields. Yet, many problems remain. One of the main goals is to achieve an efficient pen input user interface. The pen-based user interface is very different from other user interfaces. In portable systems, it is much easier to do all the operations with a pen than with a keyboard or a mouse. In portable pen-based systems selection is used more often than data input. "Selection" means using a pen to select menus, data (one character of the text or graphic segment, etc.), and ranges, etc. In this paper, these are called "targets".

It is predicted that the target size on pen-based systems will decrease while the amount of information on the screen will increase. Up to now, there have been only a few leading studies on the selection of a small target (Sears and Shneiderman, 1991; Potter, Weldon and Shneiderman, 1988; McClintock and Hoiem, 1993). Sears and Shneiderman (1991) tested three selection devices; touch screen, touchscreen with stabilization and mouse. The task was the selection of rectangular targets of 1, 4, 16 and 32 pixels per side. Their results showed that a stabilized touchscreen was effective for reducing the error rates when selecting small targets. Potter, Weldon and Shneiderman (1988) compared three touchscreen strategies, *land-on*, *first-contact* and *take-off*. The results showed that the *take-off* strategy had the lowest error rate and highest satisfaction for users. However, experimental targets were limited to only one size (6.4 mm × 6.4 mm square). McClintock and Hoiem

Human–Computer Interaction: INTERACT'97 S. Howard, J. Hammond & G. Lindgaard (editors)
Published by Chapman & Hall

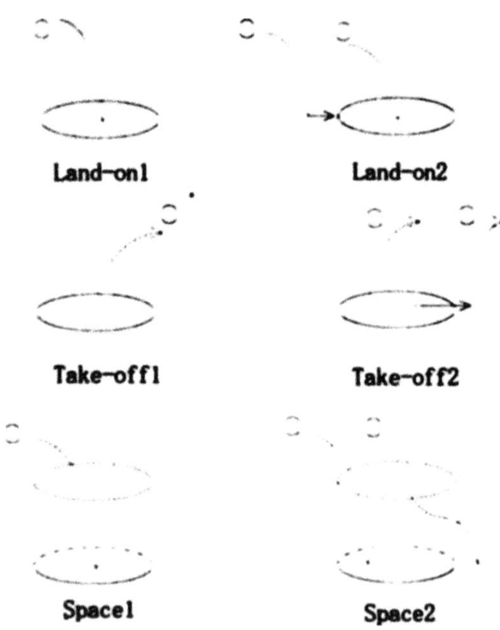

Figure 1. Six strategies used by the experiment.

(1993) conducted a study to determine the smallest optimal size for targets in a pen-based system. Eight kinds of targets were used but the study did not report on any target-pointing strategies. Some findings concerning the pointing strategies have been described elsewhere (see, for example, Sears, Plaisant and Shneiderman, 1992; Buxton, 1990). However, current target-pointing strategies on pen-based computers are mostly only imitations of selection techniques for mouse and touch-screen devices. Investigations have not been conducted which focus on strategies suitable for selecting minute targets in pen-input systems. Based upon our previous experiment (Ren and Moriya, 1995), this study focuses on the relationships between target-pointing strategies and target sizes.

2. THE SIX STRATEGIES AND THE REASON FOR USING THEM

2.1. The Six Strategies

The six strategies are illustrated in **Figure 1**. We used an electromagnetic tablet. When the pen-tip is within a given height above the tablet surface (1 cm), the coordinates (x, y) of the pen-tip are able to input data. Thus, even though the menu on the screen is 2 dimensional (2D), it can be highlighted or selected when the pen is above the tablet surface (within 1cm). This means that the menu can be expressed as a 3 dimensional (3D) target.

The oval and the cylinder shown in Figure 1 illustrate targets on the pen computer screen. The oval shows that the target is a 2D target. The cylinder shows that the target is a 3D target. That is, the circle with a solid line is at the bottom of the 3D target. Some responses will take place when the pen is in the cylinder. It is important to note that although the illustration (Figure 1) shows circular targets, the shape of the target has no definitive bearing on this discussion.

The arrow in Figure 1 shows the movement of the pen-tip. A dashed line arrow means the pen-tip is above the screen and a solid line arrow shows that the pen-tip is on the screen. ○ shows that the target is selected by the movement of the pen.

- Land-on1: the pen approaches from above. The target is selected only momentarily at the time the pen makes contact with the screen in the target area.
- Land-on2 is an extension of the Land-on1 strategy. Here also the target is selected when the pen touches it for the first time, but in this case the pen lands outside the target area before moving into it.
- Take-off1: the target is highlighted only while the pen is touching it. The selection is made at the moment the pen is taken off the target.
- Take-off2 is an extension of the Take-off1 strategy. The target is highlighted only while the pen is in contact with it, however the selection is made when the pen is removed from any point on the screen either inside or outside the target area.
- Space1: the pen approaches from above. The target is highlighted while the pen is within the 1 cm high cylinder above the target. Selection is made at the

moment the pen makes initial contact with the target area (i.e. inside the bottom circle).

- Space2 is an extension of the Space1 strategy. The target is highlighted while the pen is within the 1 cm high cylinder above the target. After highlighting, the selection is made when the pen makes contact with any point on the screen either inside or outside the target area.

Land-on1 and Take-off1 strategies are already in common use. The Land-on2 strategy corresponds to the *first-contact strategy* (Potter, Weldon and Shneiderman, 1988). However, the Take-off2, Space1 and Space2 strategies were new strategies designed for this experiment.

2.2. Characteristics of the Six Strategies and their Classification, and Reasons for the Determination of those Six Strategies

What characteristics do these various strategies have? What criteria were used to select the six strategies used here? Regarding the above questions, we concentrated on the six conditions created by the pen parameters. They are: contact with the screen, remove from the screen, contact inside the target, contact outside the target, target highlighted and target not highlighted.

Targets exist both as planes (2D) and as solid bodies (3D). Here, the 2D strategies are the Land-on1, Land-on2, Take-off1 and Take-off2 strategies. The 3D strategies are the Space1 and Space2 strategies.

Contact and removal of the pen were considered as movements between the 2D plane and 3D space. Pen contact involves a movement from 3D to 2D, while removal involves a movement from 2D to 3D. These changes were considered to be suitable conditions for the subject to recognize and confirm the moment of target selection. The strategies in which selection was made by contact with the screen (Land-on1, Land-on2, Space1 and Space2 strategies) were named On strategies. The strategies in which selection was made by removal from the screen (Take-off1 and Take-off2 strategies) were named Off strategies. Where the target existed on the 2D plane, both the On and Off strategies were deployed. Where the target existed in 3D space, only the On strategies were used, assuming that the pen was approaching the target from above.

We considered the movement of the pen into and out of the target from the perspective of the user's eyes and ears. When the pen moved into or out of the target, users could confirm whether or not the target was highlighted. Those strategies in which selection was made by contact within the target area were named In strategies (the Land-on1, Take-off1 and Space1 strategies). On the other hand, those strategies in which selection was made by contact either inside or outside the target were named In-Out strategies (Land-on2, Take-off2 and Space2 strategies).

Those strategies in which selection was made when the pen was removed from the surface of the target or from above the target after visual confirmation, were named 2Stage strategies (the Take-off1, Take-off2, Space1 and Space2 strategy). Those strategies in which visual confirmation was not possible were named 1Stage strategies (Land-on1 and Land-on2 strategies).

3. METHOD

3.1. Subjects

Nineteen subjects (14 male, 5 female; 18 right-handed, 1 left-handed), all university students, were tested for the experiment. Their ages ranged from twenty-one to twenty-three years old. Seven people had previous experience with pen-input systems, while the others had no experience.

3.2. Equipment

The hardware used in this experiment was: a tablet-cum-display (HD-640A, WACOM Co.), a stylus pen (SP-200A, WACOM Co.), and a personal computer (PC9801-DA, NEC Co.). The space resolution of the tablet input was 0.05 mm/point. The height of the liquid crystal screen was 144.0 mm and the width was 230.4 mm. The liquid crystal display resolution was 400 dots high and 640 dots wide. 1 dot was about 0.36 mm.

3.3. Procedure

First we explained the experiment to each subject and they each had 20 practice trials. A message "Select a target as quickly and accurately as possible using the strategy" was displayed on the screen of the experimental tool when the experiment started.

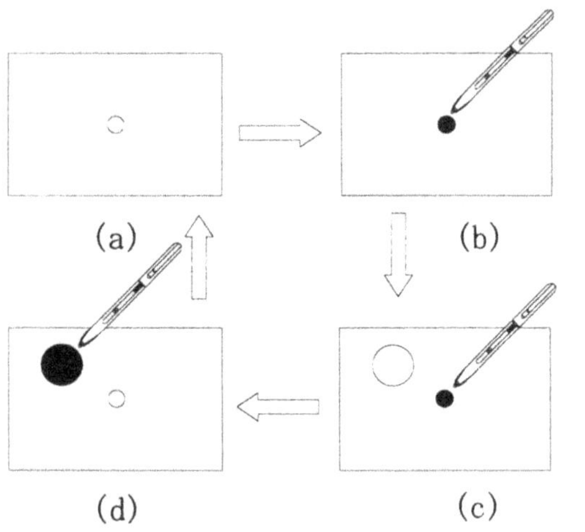

Figure 2. Steps in selecting a target.
(a) Initial position, (b) Pointing at the initial position, (c) Display of a target, (d) Target selection.

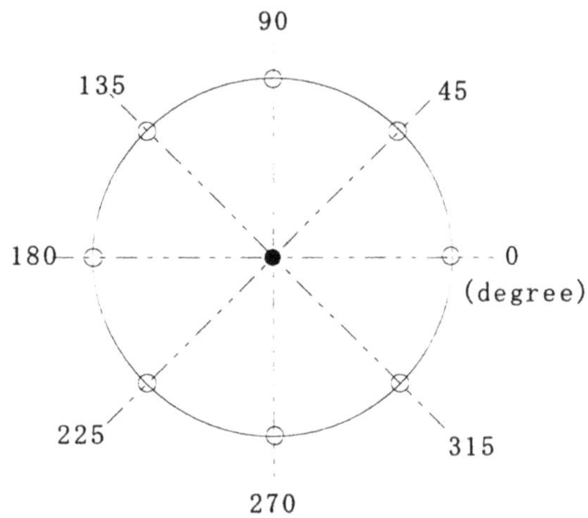

Figure 3. An example of arranging a target.
● : *Initial position,* ○: *Position of a target display.*

Figure 2 shows a typical display which would appear when a target was being selected using any one of the strategies. (a) initial position: a circular initial position was displayed at the center of the screen. The initial position was the place where the pen would be pointed immediately before beginning the selection procedure. The subject had been told which strategy he/she was to use and how many trails he/she had to do. (b) Pointing at the initial position: the subject pointed to the initial position with the pen. (c) Display of a target: the target was displayed with the size and direction changed at random (See 3.4.). The parameters of the target (position and size) were randomly selected by the computer. Targets of a particular size were never displayed in the same position twice. The distance between the initial position to the target was constant at 131 dots. (d) Target selection: the subject would receive a message on the screen to indicate whether he/she had made a successful selection or not. (e) The subject then repeated (a) and (d) above. (f) End of selection: a message indicating the end of the experiment was displayed when the subject had completed the task.

The strategies were not mixed. In a given trial each subject used only one strategy.

3.4. Design and Data Processing

Figure 3 shows the eight possible target positions.

Size of target: all the targets were circular. To examine the relationship between target size and the six strategies we used five target sizes in all trials (1, 3, 5, 7 and 9 dot diameter circles).

Distance to target: the distance to the target was the radius of a circle in which the center point was the initial position. The distance of 131 dots (4.70· cm) was determined by a preliminary experiment. This was the average distance that ten subjects could extend the pen to the target.

Pen-movement directions : eight directions were used. They were at 0, 45, 90, 135, 180, 225, 270 and 315 degrees from the initial position.

The subject had a total of 60 trials for each strategy. These consisted of 20 practice trials and 40 test trials (= 5 target sizes × 8 directions).

A break was taken at the end of each strategy trial. Whenever the subject felt tired he/she was allowed to take a rest. Each subject completed 240 test trials (= 6 strategies × 40). In each strategy 760 test trials (= 19 subjects × 40) were completed. The order for the six strategies was different for each of the nineteen subjects.

The data for each strategy were recorded automatically as follows:

(i) Presence or absence of error when a target was selected: one selection was a continuous operation from the approach of the pen to the target until the removal of the pen from the tablet surface. Feedback to the subject indicated whether the selection was successful or not. In either case, the subject could not cancel the selection.

(ii) Position and size of the target displayed.

(iii) The time lapsed between display of the target and the moment when the pen contacts the screen.

(iv) The time lapsed between contact with the target and removal from the screen.

(v) The time lapsed between contact with the screen and contact with the target.

These times were measured to an accuracy of 10 ms using a special program.

Data as defined in item (iii) was recorded for the Land-on1, Space1 and Space2 strategies. Data as defined in item (v) above was recorded for the Land-on2 strategy. Data as defined in item (iv) above was recorded for the Take-off1 and Take-off2 strategies.

3.5. Subjective Evaluation

The subjects were questioned about their preferences after they ended each trial. The first question was: "For the strategy tested just now, how do you rate P? Please answer on a 1-to-9 scale (123456789).". P consisted of six subquestions regarding selection accuracy, selection speed, selection ease, learning ease, satisfaction and desire to use. The second question was: "Which direction was most comfortable for selecting the target in the above strategies? ". The subject marked his/her preferences on Figure 3.

4. RESULTS

To determine the effect, in all six strategies, of target size and pen-movement-direction on error rates, selection times and subject preferences, an ANOVA with repeated measures was performed.

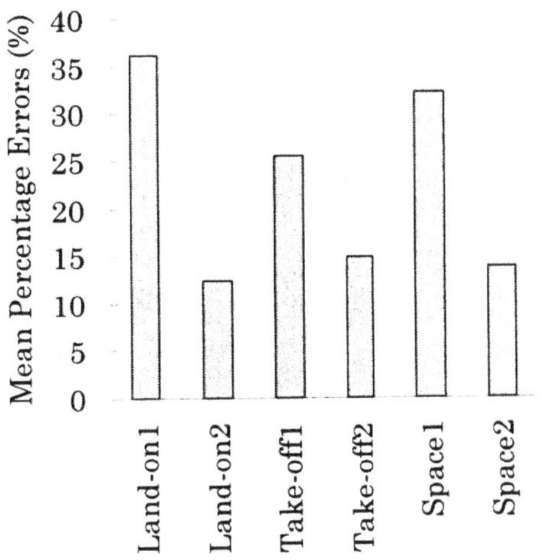

Figure 4. The error rates for each strategy.

Error rates were determined by dividing the number of errors by the total number of selection attempts. Selection time was the time required to select the target correctly.

4.1. Error Rates

The error rates for each of the six strategies is shown in **Figure 4**. There was a significant difference for the six strategies, $F(5,108) = 9.76$, $p < .01$. This means that the difference in error rates was due to the difference in the various strategy operations.

To investigate why there was a significant difference for the six strategies, analyses were conducted between each of four strategy groups. The results showed that there were no significant differences ($p < .05$) between the On and Off strategies, or between 2D and 3D strategies, or between 1Stage and 2Stage strategies.

However, there was a significant difference between the In and In-Out strategies, $F(1,36) = 18.1$, $p < .001$. When the average values of In and In-Out strategies were compared, the In strategies produced a 31% error rate and the In-out strategies produced a 14% error rate. **Figure 5** shows that the In-Out strategies had lower error rates than the In strategies in every target size (1, 3, 5, 7 and 9 dots). The error rates for the Land-on2 strategy

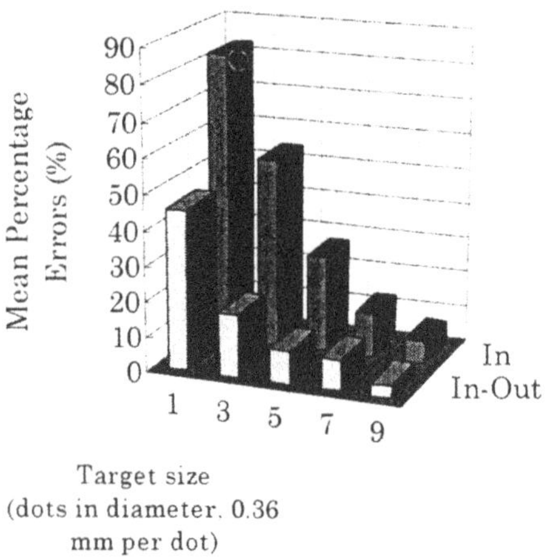

Figure 5. Error rates per target size for the In strategies and the In-Out strategies.

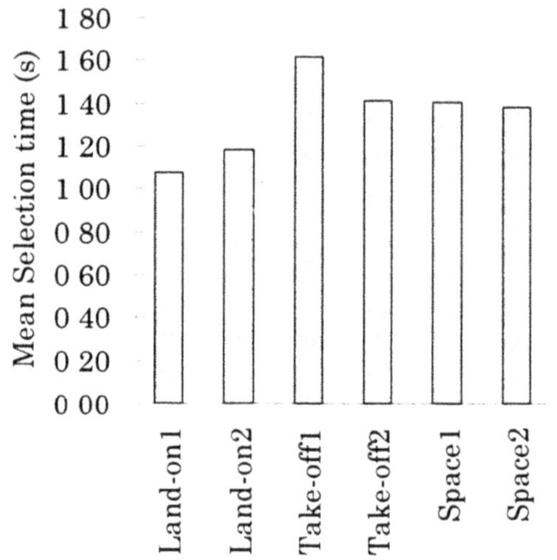

Figure 6. The selection time for each strategy.

were the lowest among the six strategies (see Figure 4). But there was no significant difference in the total numbers of errors for the five target sizes (1, 3, 5, 7 and 9 dots) for the Land-on2, Take-off2 and Space2 strategies in the In-Out strategy group, $F(2,54) = 0.19$. The error rates for these three strategies did not differ for target sizes of 1, 3 and 5 dots, $F(2, 54) = 0.07$.

However, when all six strategies were compared, there were significant differences in error rate, in terms of the target sizes of 1, 3 and 5 dots. On the other hand, there were no significant differences in 7 or 9 dots between the six strategies ($p <.05$).

Regarding the pen-movement directions, significant differences were seen in the six strategies for each direction ($p <.01$). This means even when pen-movement directions were different, there were no changes in error rates for the six strategies.

4.2. Selection Time

The selection time for each of the six strategies is shown in **Figure 6**. There was a significant difference between the six strategies, $F(5,108) = 3.17$, $p < .05$. This means selection times varied according to the strategy used. This indicates that the strategies influenced the selection times.

We investigated the cause of the significant differences in the six strategies. Comparisons between each of the four strategy groups showed there were significant differences between the On and Off strategies, $F(1,36) = 242.9$, $p < .0001$, and between the 1Stage and 2Stage strategies, $F(1,36) = 8.37$, $p < .01$. There were no significant differences between the 2D and 3D strategies, or between the In and In-Out strategies ($p < .05$). The average times of the On and Off strategies and the 1Stage and 2Stage strategies, showed that the On strategies (1.26 s) were faster than the Off strategies (2.41 s) and 1Stage strategies (1.13 s) were faster than 2Stage strategies (1.46 s).

There was a significant difference in selection time between the six strategies. There were significant differences for every target size (1 dot, $p <.05$; 3, 5, 7 and 9 dots, $p <.01$). The differences in selection times caused by variations in the target size were constant.

Regarding the pen-movement directions; there were significant differences for the six strategies in the pen-movement-directions 0, 45, 90, 135, 225 and 270 degrees ($p <.05$). On the other hand, there were no significant differences for the six strategies in the directions 180 or 315 degrees ($p <.05$).

4.3. Subject Preferences

The analysis of the questionnaire showed a significant main effect on subject preferences for each of the six strategies. $F(5,30) = 258.5$, $p < .0001$. In addition there was a significant difference in subject preferences between the In and In-Out groups of strategies. $F(1,10) = 803.1$, $p < .0001$. This agreed with the test results. Moreover, among three of the strategies (Land-on2, Take-off2 and Space2 strategies) there was also a significant difference in preferences. $F(2,15) = 7.90$, $p < .01$. Rated on a scale of 1-to-9 the Land-on2 strategy was the most preferred (mean = 8.0).

There was a significant difference in subject preferences regarding pen-movement directions. $F(7,40) = 17.5$, $p < .0001$, however, the preferences marked by the subjects in Figure 3 revealed that 225 degrees was the most preferred direction (mean = 10.5).

5. DISCUSSION

Of the six strategies, the Land-on1 and Take-off1 strategies are used most often. However, according to our results, we found the Land-on2 strategy was the most effective for selection of a minute target.

As for selection time, a significant difference appeared between 1Stage and 2Stage strategies, and between On and Off strategies. This difference did not depend on target size or pen-movement-direction (180 and 315 degrees were excluded). On strategies were selected faster than Off strategies. 1Stage strategies were selected faster than 2Stage strategies. It is believed that of the six strategies tested, Land-on1 and Land-on2 strategies were the fastest in selection times. This is because they are both On strategies and 1Stage strategies. In addition, the Land-on2 strategy had lower error rates. Thus we have determined that the Land-on2 strategy was the best strategy for selection of a minute target in terms of selection time and error rates. In addition, there was no significant difference in selection times between the Land-on1 and Land-on2 strategies. $F(1,36) = 0.53$. Furthermore the subjects also rated the Land-on2 strategy most highly.

Comparisons of each classified group revealed a significant difference in error rates between the In and the In-Out strategies. This implies that differences in error rates were independent of target size (1, 3 and 5 dots) and pen-movement-directions for these strategy groups. We concluded that the In-Out strategy group was the most effective for selecting a minute target.

Regarding error rates, there was no significant difference in the results when the targets were large (7 or 9 dot). On the other hand, there were significant differences for the six strategies when the target sizes were minute (1, 3 and 5 dots). The reason for this lies in the difference between the In and In-Out strategies. The In strategies were adequate when choosing large targets because there was no strain on the subject. When choosing a minute target, the selection was not accurate using the In strategies only, thus the In-Out strategies were more effective, for example, where targets could be selected by directly pressing the target with the pen. In the case of a minute target, it was necessary for the subjects to confirm visually whether or not the pen was inside the target area while either making contact or taking off. Using the In strategies, selection is completed at the moment of contact or take off. On the other hand, the In-Out strategies do not require visual confirmation of the pen position vis-a-vis the target. When selecting a minute target with the In-Out strategies, one can direct the pen from a point on the surface of the target after landing on the screen, even if it is impossible to place the pen directly inside the target (as in the Land-on2 strategy). In the case of the Take-off2 strategy, selection was achieved even if a parallax on hand-movement occurred. In the questionnaire subjects overwhelmingly preferred the In-Out strategies. From this it is clear that the In-Out group of strategies is superior.

We have observed the following concerning the strategies of selecting a minute target. When a minute target on the 2D tablet surface is used (e.g. a pressure perception type tablet like ZAURUS, SHARP Co.), it is possible to condude: if there are no other targets near a minute target (e.g. a point or width of a line with 1 to 5 dots on a graphic screen or a minute icon on a small pen-input system), the Land-on2 and Take-off2 strategies in the In-Out group are most effective for selecting the target. The Land-on2 strategy is especially effective when selection speed is considered.

When selecting target sizes of more than 5 dots, the selection performance became identical even when using different strategies. We concluded that 5 dots (1.80 mm circle in diameter) was the largest size among the targets.

in which there was a significant main effect on error rates for the six strategies. We called this "the minute maximum size". Therefore, 5 dots was the minute maximum value from the experimental results.

In Fitts' law (Fitts, 1954), ID=$\log_2(2D/W)$, ID is an abbreviation of *Index of Difficulty* of pointing, D is the distance, and W is the width of the target. If D is a constant, $ID_1=\log_2(2D/W_1)$, $ID_2=\log_2(2D/W_2)$,..., W_1, W_2,... > 5 dots, then, as far as our results are concerned, there are no significant differences among ID_1, ID_2, ..., ID_n. In other words, when selecting target sizes of more than 5 dots, differences in the ID (error rates) due to target size will disappear. Thus, we clarified the boundary value of the target size which controlled the difficulty of strategies. When a target is less than 5 dots, the strategy should be designed in line with our findings. This work defines values by which not only pen-based devices but also other devices may be researched.

In this experiment, circular targets were used so that the distance which the pen reaches to the edge of a target remained constant in all directions. In another experiment (Ren and Moriya, 1995), it was found that there were significant differences in terms of error rates and selection times when various distances were used; 39, 131 and 160 dots. By using only one of the three distances we were able to decrease the number of trials in this experiment. 131 dots was chosen as the distance because we had determined that it was the maximum finger-movement-distance when the wrist was in a fixed condition using a portable pen-input systems.

Regarding pen-movement-directions, a vector of 225 degrees was preferred by most of the subjects. We assumed that the reason was that this direction was a position from which right-handed subjects could see most. Moreover, a significant difference was not seen for the six strategies using directions180 and 315 degrees. Wrist angle and sight angle are factors to be considered. In future research we will consider the relationships between pen-movement-directions and target-pointing strategies.

In this experiment, we focused only on the selection of a single target. We will attempt to compare the six strategies in multi-targets environments in future studies. It has been reported elsewhere that differences in the target shapes influence the selection time (Sheikh and Hoffmann, 1994). It is necessary to examine other target shapes in order to compare them with the results pertaining to circular targets used in this experiment. It is also necessary to investigate the relationships between strategies and target shapes and to find strategies which are suitable for specific shapes. Attention should be given to whether or not those shapes change the minute maximum size of a target area.

6. REFERENCES

Ren X. and Moriya S. (1995). The concept of various pointing strategies on pen-based computers and their experimental evaluation, *Proceedings of the Eleventh Symposium on Human Interface* (Kyoto, Japan), pp.565-574.

Sears A. and Shneiderman B. (1991). High precision touchscreens: Design strategies and comparisons with a mouse, *International Journal of Man-Machine Studies*, Vol.34, No.4, pp.593-613.

Potter R., Weldon L. and Shneiderman B. (1988). Improving the accuracy of touch screens: An experimental evaluation of three strategies, *Proceedings of ACM the CHI'88 Conference on Human Factors in Computing Systems*, pp.27-32.

Buxton W.(1990). A three state model of graphical input. In D. Diaper et al. (Eds.), *Human-Computer Interaction --INTERACT '90*, pp.449-456.

Sheikh I. and Hoffmann E. (1994). Effect of target shape on movement time in a Fitts task. *Ergonomics*, Vol.37, No.9, pp.1533-1547.

Fitts P.M. (1954). The information capacity of the human motor system in controlling amplitude of movement, *Journal of Experimental Psychology*, Vol.47, No.6, pp.381-391.

McClintock M. and Hoiem D. (1993). Minimal target size in a pen-based system, *In Abridged Proceedings of 5th International Conference on Human-Computer Interaction*, Elsevier Science Publishers B.V., p.243.

Sears A., Plaisant C. and Shneiderman B. (1992). A new era for high precision touchscreens, *Advances in Human-Computer Interaction*, Vol.30, Ablex, Norwood, NJ, pp.1-33.

15

Evaluating User Performance to Experienced Level and Beyond

Jackie Moyes

Information Technology Institute
11 Science Park Road
Singapore Science Park II
SINGAPORE 117685
moyes@iti.gov.sg

ABSTRACT

Studies focusing on two iconic attributes, form and relative position, suggested subjects rely on form to recognise a particular icon when the form is representational. However, when form is abstract users switch from attempting to use form, to using position. Results had suggested that some degree of positional learning still occurred for subjects using representational form. However, a more in depth study of this suggestion was impossible since the standard performance measures of error rate and reaction time settled quickly into an optimal level of performance. To gain better insight into what was occurring, cursor movements were tracked, allowing pre-emptive move data to be captured. The showed that, irrespective of the type of form presented, subject learned and eventually switched to relying on position to identify the icon. More importantly, results suggest that this learning continued after the traditional measures of reaction time and error rate had reached what Jordan et al. (1991) termed experienced user performance level, or asymptote. The suggestion therefore is that traditional performance measures are perhaps not sensitive enough to measure learning at the experienced end of the learning curve, and that interface designers should thus consider ways in which to capture this potentially enlightening information which, as yet, remains unexamined.

KEYWORDS usability evaluation, icon design, quantitative measures, pre-emptive move data

1. INTRODUCTION

A series of experiments had been conducted with the aim of trying to predict which icon attributes users were likely to rely upon to associate a particular icon with a command (Moyes 1995). This study originated from the observation that most designers stressed the importance of the icon form in communicating the icon's meaning, while ignoring other potential attributes (e.g. position, colour, size, outline shape, etc.). The theory being tested, therefore, was that initially users will rely on the attribute which was the most representational, but, over time, may switch to identifying the icon using another attribute, if this attribute offered an increased performance advantage.

This was in line with the theory established by Kaptelinin (1993) who suggested that users focus on local attributes initially (e.g. icon form) but over time switch to identifying attributes that are global, or require the user to consider the interface as a whole into consideration (e.g. the icon's relative position amongst all other icons on the screen).

Human–Computer Interaction: INTERACT'97 S. Howard, J. Hammond & G. Lindgaard (editors)
Published by Chapman & Hall

Additionally, in an attempt to formally identify when users were likely to switch between attributes, a multi-component definition of usability, as established by Jordan et al., 1991), was adopted. This definition suggested that there were three identifiable stages in the learning curve (as illustrated in Figure 1); guessability, learnability and experienced user performance (EUP). Their definitions are as follows:

- Guessability - the measure of the cost to the user involved in using an interface to perform a new task for the first time. The lower the cost, the higher the guessability (cost can be measured either in terms of time, errors, or effort).
- Learnability - the measure of the cost to the user in reaching some reasonable level of performance on a task, but excluding the special difficulties of completing the task for the first time. A highly learnable interface would be one where a task was instantly memorable once the method had been shown to the user. Conversely, interfaces which cause 'interference' with user expectations are likely to be un-learnable.
- EUP - a measure of the ability of the user to perform a task when he or she has reached a relatively steady level of performance. Again, the lower the cost, the higher EUP

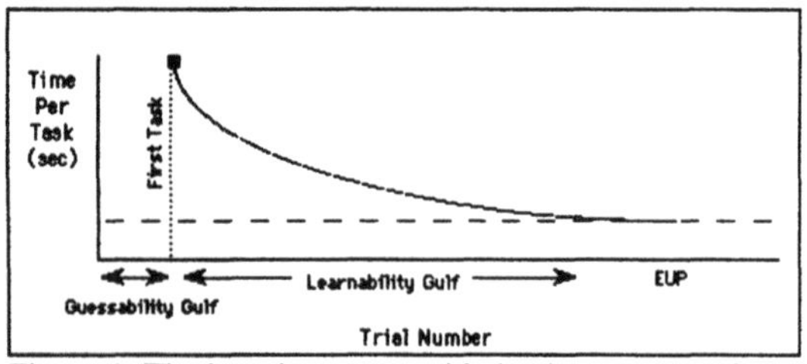

Figure 1. The learning curve with the three stages of usability illustrated.

The series of experiments conducted had focused on the attributes form and position, and had studied user performance, using these attributes, throughout the entire learning curve. It was predicted that if form was representational then users would ignore the icon's position and rely on form to identify the icon. However, if the icon form was abstract then users would initially attempt to use form to identify the icon, but since position offered a better performance advantage, in the learnability stage they would switch to position to identify the icon.

To test this theory 4 experimental conditions were created:

- Representational -> Blank
  In this condition subjects were trained to EUP using icons with representational form (see Figure 2) and fixed position. Once EUP had been achieved an unexpected change would take place and position would remain the same but icon form would be removed. The position of the icons would be marked by empty rectangles
- Abstract -> Blank
  Here subject were initially presented with icons in their abstract form (see Figure 2), and fixed position. At changeover the position of the icons would again remain the same, but the form would be removed.
- Representational -> Random
  For this condition users were presented with representational form throughout, but at changeover the position of the icons was be randomised.
- Abstract -> Random
  Users were presented with abstract form throughout, but at changeover the position of the icons was randomised.

It was predicted that if the theory was correct, subjects in conditions 1 and 4 would be affected by the changeover (indicated by significantly slower reaction times and increased errors) since the attribute that they had been relying on had been removed, thus requiring a degree of re-learning to occur. Subjects in conditions 2 and 3 should not show any significant disruption since the attribute they had been predicted to rely on had not changed.

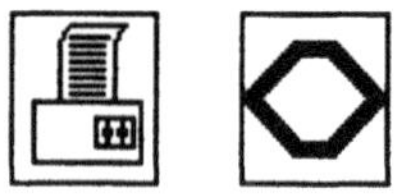

Figure 2: The print icon. One representational and one abstract version, as used in the experiment (actual size).

Results from previous experiments support this hypothesis. At changeover the biggest disruption in performance was found for the condition where representational form was removed (condition 1), followed closely by the condition where abstract form icons were randomised (condition 4). However, although there was a significant disruption, in each of these cases, recovery to performance levels similar to those achieved before changeover was extremely rapid. It was therefore unclear whether disruption at changeover was simply due to surprise rather than the need to relearn. In other words, perhaps the quick recovery rate was indicative of the fact that subjects in all conditions had actually learned both attributes to some degree. This may be acceptable for conditions 3 and 4 where subjects were expected to have initially attempted to learn icon form, but moved to using position later in the learning curve. However, it had been predicted that subjects using the representational form icons would remain using this attribute, therefore the question being posed was whether subjects in these conditions were indeed learning position.

The experiment presented here replicates the methodology used in previous experiments, but with two major differences. Firstly, the size of the icon set is increased from 2 to 16. In previous experiments only 2 icons had been presented on the interface. It was therefore assumed that perhaps an additional reason for the fast recovery rates was because subjects found learning the new attribute extremely easy when there was only a two way choice involved. Increasing the number of icons displayed to 16 was hoped to make the interface more complex, thus increasing the amount of learning time involved (assuming no learning of the attribute had taken place prior to the changeover).

The second, and more interesting change was that cursor movement was recorded. A standard trial consisted of presenting subjects with a screen showing only the command they were required to find the appropriate icon for, and an OK button. Subjects read the command and then clicked on the button to move onto the interface. It was possible therefore to record the movement of the cursor between the time when the user clicked the button until the time when the interface appeared. If the trajectory of the cursor appeared to be moving towards the position of the correct icon before the interface was actually visible, then this was marked as a correct pre-emptive move, and assumed to be indicative that the subject had learned that icon's position.

This new quantitative measure could then be compared between the 4 conditions to give a better idea of whether subjects in the representational conditions were indeed learning position, and if so, to the same extent as users in the abstract form conditions.

2. METHODOLOGY

2.1 Apparatus

The experimental sessions were performed using a Macintosh Quadra (system 7.1.2).

2.2 Design

The dependent variables were:

- Time taken in each trial
- Number of errors
- Number of pre-emptive moves

The independent variables were:

Icon form	**2 levels** Representational Abstract
Position	**2 levels** Consistent Random

Subjects were grouped into one of 4 possible conditions:

- representational -> blank
- abstract -> blank
- representational -> random
- abstract -> random

Sixteen icons were used for each set.

Changeover only occurred after users had been recognised as EUP; namely by the time reaction time and error rate had reached optimal, steady levels. For this experiment performance levels were predicted to level by block 20 (20 x 16 trials), therefore changeover occurred at block 21.

2.3 Subjects

Sixteen subjects were used (four per group). Thirteen subjects were male and three were female. The mean age was 26.

2.4 Procedure

Subjects were initially presented with a block of practice trials to familiarise themselves with the experimental task. Although the task itself was identical to that performed in the experiment a mock experimental interface was created where the icons in each of the positions were replaced by numbers (e.g. 1), and the commands were in textual format (e.g. Number One).

The trial commenced when the command screen, showing the command and OK button situated in the centre of the screen. Once the user clicked on the button the interface card opened, displaying an icon set. The icons were positioned in an equi-distant circular format. The subject was required to respond by clicking the mouse over the icon he or she considered to be appropriate for the command. If a correct response were made the set disappeared and approximately 0.5 seconds later the next trial commenced. An erroneous response was signalled by a high tone and a penalty was induced. A dialogue box appeared and subjects were informed that they had made an error and would be shown the correct icon. The subject clicked the OK button, the dialogue box disappeared and the correct icon was indicated, after which the next trial commenced.

2.4.1 Details Recorded

For every trial eight pieces of data were captured. These were:

1. The errors. Each icon had a number, and the number of the correct icon was stored, followed by the number(s) of any incorrect icons that were selected.
2. The time that the command and the OK button appeared.
3. The time that the subject clicked on the button to move to the interface.
4. The (x,y) position of the pointer on the screen as the screen closed. This showed whether or not the mouse was outside the button area, and in what direction it was travelling. This data was collected from experiment 2 onwards.
5. The time that the screen closed.
6. The (x,y) position of the cursor as the interface screen opened.
7. The time that the first icon was selected (and whether it was correct or incorrect).
8. The time that the interface screen closed.

A typical reaction time was measured from the time that the command appeared until the user had selected the correct icon, or been informed of its position, and the interface card had closed.

3. RESULTS

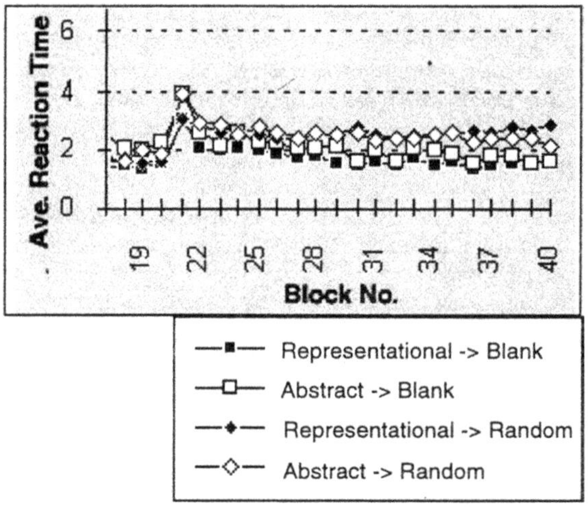

Figure 3. Graph of the mean reaction times across blocks 1 to 40.

The main aims of this experiment were:

- To evaluate whether the recorded disruption was due to surprise or learning.
- To discover when subjects began to learn position and whether subjects in all conditions learned it or just those using icons with abstract icon forms.

Interpreting the results from the traditional dependent variables, reaction time (Figure 3) and error rate (Figure 4), it would appear that the disruption not due to surprise, since in both cases, the disruption lasts beyond 1 or 2 blocks of trials. The results, however, do appear to indicate that some degree of position learning by subjects in the representational conditions, prior to the changeover, had indeed occurred. Even using larger icon sets, the disruption at changeover, in comparison with the performance levels at the start of the test is, for all conditions, minimal. Additionally, any evidence of disruption, after block 25 is almost imperceptible.

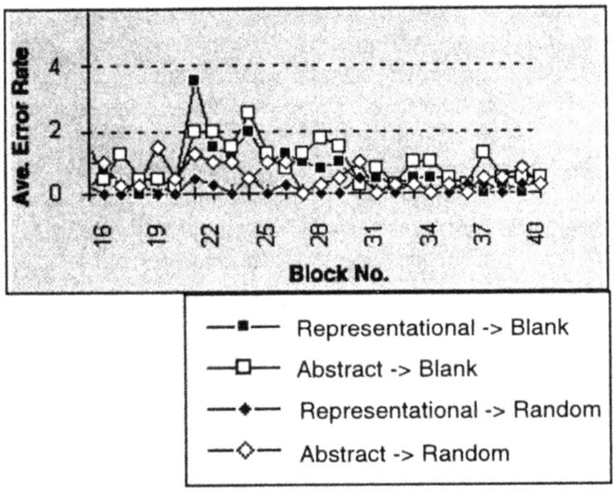

Figure 4. Graph of mean errors across 40 blocks of trials

Figure 5, displaying the graph of pre-emptive moves however tells a far more enlightening story. A pre-emptive move was recorded whenever the trajectory of the cursor from the OK button on the command screen to the correct icon on the interface card could be plotted as a direct line. If pre-emptive moves are indeed taken as evidence for position knowledge, then the graph

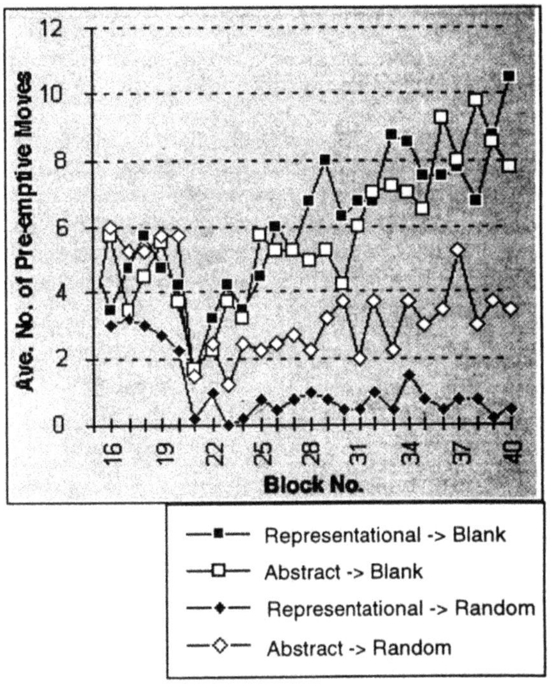

Figure 5. Graph of the mean number of correct pre-emptive moves made in each condition across 40 blocks of trials (16 being the maximum number of moves possible).

suggests that position is learned by subjects in all 4 conditions. There appears to be a gradual learning curve that commences at block 1 and increases steadily until the disruption at block 21. The 2 conditions where form is removed quickly recover to an almost identical learning curve shortly after the changeover. Where position is randomised there is a difference between the groups. In both cases there is a significant drop in the degree of pre-emptive moves made. However, the group using the representational form appear to give up on position almost entirely. However, there is an indication that some learning of position does occur in the abstract condition. This is likely to be an effect of the experimental design, since the position of each icon was randomised to appear in 1 of 2 possible positions. This result, therefore, suggests that people using abstract icons found it easier to try to learn both icon positions, and make a guess as to which one the icon would actually be located in, rather than rely upon the icon's form. In other words, they would rather learn 32 possible positions than 16 iconic forms.

By the end of 40 blocks of trials subjects in the conditions where position remains constant appear to be making pre-emptive moves for an average of 10 out of every 16 trials. This result is extremely important since it suggests that learning has not ended, even though the traditional measures of reaction time and error rate have reached optimal levels.

4. DISCUSSION

Therefore, results appear to suggest that it was not surprise that caused the disruption, since the disruption lasted longer than one or two trials. However, the disruption in almost all cases tended to be shorter than was predicted if the user was learning a completely new attribute. This suggests that subjects had learnt the attribute, considered in the initial hypothesis to be the recessive attribute, and so were able to return to a similar level of performance in a short period of time.

The pre-emptive move data convincingly supports the idea that position is learned by subjects in all conditions. The graph in Figure 4 suggests that there is a gradual learning curve commencing from block number one for all conditions. This confirms the assumption that people learn form first and then move on to learn position. However, the speed of learning position as opposed to form in this experiment could be influenced by the obvious performance advantage offered by knowing icon position. This is an extremely important point in interface design since it suggests that the interface context (e.g. the amount of information present on the interface) is going to have a strong influence on which attributes are used.

The graph also suggests that by block 40 users have not yet reached an optimal state in the number of pre-emptive moves they will make. It is possible that the curve will plateau only when the user is able to make pre-emptive moves for all icons in the set. Again this result is probably influenced by the high performance advantage offered by learning position. The interesting point to note, however, is that both reaction times and error rates have stabilised around block 30, yet the pre-emptive move data suggests that learning is still occurring. So, although learning appears to continue, reaction times and error rates fail to detect it. Therefore, other measures need to be considered if learning beyond what Jordan et. al (1992) define as EUP is to be detected and analysed.

5. CONCLUSION

This latter point is extremely important. It appears that an attribute considered to be important in the guessability stage of performance is not necessarily the attribute used throughout the rest of the usability curve. There is a distinct contrast between the "effort after meaning" made by the user in the guessability stage, and demand for a highly discriminable attribute with a small cognitive load in the learnability and EUP stages. Therefore as the experiments have suggested, icons which contain attributes which appear to offer no meaning to the user in the guessability stage perform as well as icons possessing these meaningful attributes at EUP. Although icon-oriented interfaces tend to be aimed at the computer novice, by restricting study of icon design to how to attain meaningful icons, researchers are ignoring the potential design issues apparent to the majority of the usability curve.

However results have shown that learning and fine tuning of procedures to recognise particular icons with minimum effort and cognitive load continue to occur after experienced user performance level has been achieved using the classical performance measures of time and error. This may suggest that Jordan et al.'s (1991) model of usability may be too simplistic. With the ability to capture continued learning through measures such as the number of pre-emptive moves a more detailed picture may be achieved.

There are also many questions raised by considering performance throughout the learning curve. As suggested, we could ask does EUP exist? Do users ever reach a plateau, or do they continue fine tuning their performance? Do users fine tune their performance to such an extent and then switch off to any changes in the environment, or do they continue to monitor change? How can we measure EUP beyond the stage where reaction time and error rates reach optimal performance levels? Pre-emptive move data may be an important step towards this, however, this methodology is limited to situations where learning of position is being measured. It does, however, indicate that more creative usability measures need to be developed, perhaps not only for icon design, but for screen design in general.

6. ACKNOWLEDGEMENTS

Thanks to Phil Gray, Steve Draper and Paddy O'Donnell for their advice, practical suggestions and encouragement during this period of research.

6. REFERENCES

Jordan, P W, Draper, S W, MacFarlane, K K & McNulty, S-A. (1991) Guessability, Learnability, and Experienced User Performance. In *People and Computers VI,* Diaper, D. & Hamond, N. (eds.), Cambridge University Press.

Jordan, P.W. & O'Donnell, P.J. (1992) Quantifying guessability, learnability and experienced user performance. *Contemporary Ergonomics 1992*, Lovesey, E.J. (ed.), London: Taylor & Francis, pp. 404-410.

Kaptelinin, V. (1993) Icon Recognition in Menu Selection: The Effect Of Practice. In *INTERCHI'93 Adjunct Proceedings*, Ashlund, S. et al. (eds.), ACM Press.

Moyes, J. (1995) Putting Icons in Context: The influence of Contextual Information on the Usability of Icons. *Ph.D. Thesis*, University Of Glasgow.

16

Zoom Star : a solution to complex statistical object representation

Monique Noirhomme-Fraiture, Manuel Rouard

Institute of Informatics - University of Namur (FUNDP)
Rue Grandgagnage, 21, B-5000 Namur
BELGIUM
mno@info.fundp.ac.be

ABSTRACT - In the statistical field, graphical representations are largely used in order to help users visualize large amounts of information. Symbolic Objects are a new type of statistical data that are characterized by their complexity. Therefore, it was necessary to design a corresponding representation that allows all the needed information to be visualized without overloading the graphic. The solution we propose, called Zoom Star, is described in this paper. We have created a prototype that displays on the screen the Zoom Star corresponding to data located in files. This prototype has been developed with a view to adding it to a more complete software. This software, designed as part of a European project, will handle Symbolic Objects.

KEY WORDS - Visualization, Statistical Data, Symbolic Objects, Multivariate Objects.

1. INTRODUCTION

Symbolic Objects are complex statistical data represented by a set of variables. Statisticians need a graphical representation that gives a synthetic image of the Symbolic Object and allows all available information to be displayed. Even if some variables can depend on others, a hierarchical representation, such as the cone trees (Robertson, 1991), is not relevant because few relations of this type actually exist. It is important that the representation gives a general image of the Symbolic Object in order to make easier the comparison of two objects. This is not the case for some representations even when all information is displayed (Turo, 1994).

2. THE SYMBOLIC OBJECTS

Symbolic Objects allow better statistical analyses to be performed in many application domains (biology, road statistics, Labor Force Survey, ...).

Symbolic Objects, studied by Diday (Diday, 1993), can be defined as a class of individuals described by a set of quantitative and/or categorical variables, that can be :

- *multivaluated*
- divided in *intervals*
- distributed according to *weighted values*
- *ordered* or not
- *dependent* on another variable
- organized in a *taxonomy*

3. ZOOM STAR

The graphical representation we propose, called Zoom Star, is based on the Kiviat Diagrams but each axis allows more complex data to be represented. We chose the following conventions :

- A quantitative variable is represented as is usual by a graduated axis, with a chosen unit.
- Categories of a categorical variable are represented by dots equally distributed on an axis.

Human–Computer Interaction: INTERACT'97 S. Howard, J. Hammond & G. Lindgaard (editors)
Published by Chapman & Hall

- When a variable is not applicable for a particular object, the corresponding axis is represented in gray.
- Values of each variable are joined to give the shape of the star (a surface represents an interval).

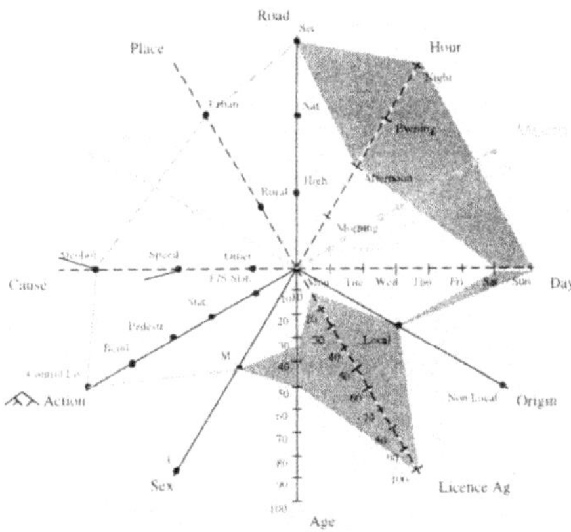

Figure 1 : Example of a 2D Zoom Star.

We provide a 2D and a 3D (see Figure 2) representation. On the 2D representation, distributions do not directly appear so that the representation is left as simple as possible but they are displayed in a separate window when the user selects an axis with his mouse. Axes of this type are characterized by a dashed line.

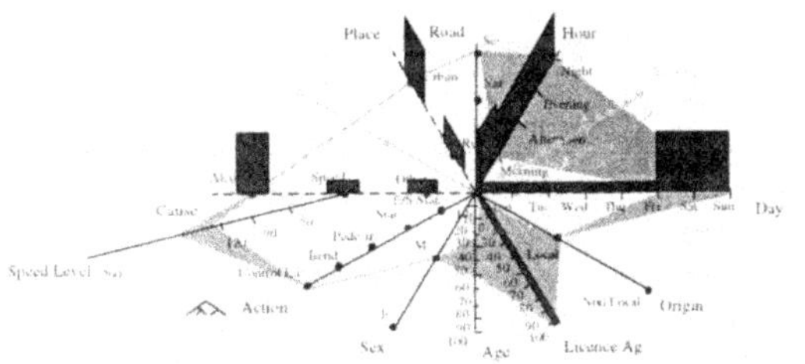

Figure 2 : Example of a 2D Zoom Star.

On both representations, users can request further information on dependencies and taxonomies. Small lines linked to a category are drawn to show that a variable depends on the value of this category (see Alcohol and Speed on the Cause axis of figure 1). If the user points to this line with the mouse, the dependent variable is added to the graphic as shown on figure 2 for the variable 'Speed level'. The presence of a taxonomy is indicated by a small icon representing a hierarchy beside the axis name (see Action axis on figures 1 and 2).

On the 3D representation, the point of view can be moved vertically or horizontally to enable the user to find the best angle to visualize the data needed.

A prototype of this system has been implemented under the Windows environment. It will be added to a more complete software for Symbolic Objects handling. This software is designed within the framework of a CEE project called SODAS.

4. FUTURE WORK

The next step consists in creating a Zoom Star editor in order to allow basic modifications to be performed on data by interacting with the graphical representation.

5. CONCLUSION

The Zoom Star gives a synthetic and hierarchical representation of complex multivariate objects. At present, users positively react to the demonstration of our prototype. A complete evaluation of the software will be done later.

6. REFERENCES

Diday, E. (1993) « *Quelques aspects de l'analyse des données symboliques* », Research report of the INRIA, N°1937.

Robertson G. , Mackinlay, J. , and Card, S. (1991) « *Cone Trees: Animated 3D Visualizations of Hierarchical Information* ». Proceedings of the ACM SIGCHI '91 Conference on Human Factors in Computing Systems, pages 121-135, New Orleans, April 1991.

Turo, D. (19694) « Hierarchical visualization with treemaps : making sense of probasketball data », CHI'94, ACM, Boston, Video, 1994.

Three Dimensional Animation for Performance Debugging Utilizing Human Cognitive Ability

Noritaka OSAWA and Toshitsugu YUBA

The University of Electro-Communications
1-5-1 Chofugaoka, Chofu-shi, Tokyo, JAPAN
{osawa,yuba}@is.uec.ac.jp

ABSTRACT Visualization is a useful first step for performance debugging, that is, performance tuning of a parallel program if it shows the balance between computation and communication. In visualizing performance data, it is important to exploit the human cognitive ability of recognizing slight differences in shapes, positions and velocities of familiar objects. We have proposed animation for performance debugging that utilizes this human cognitive ability. It animates performance data based on dynamic system modeling where the data is mapped to a dynamic system model, the model is simulated and the result of simulation is made visible in 3 dimensions.

KEYWORDS 3-D animation, performance debugging, parallel program, dynamic system, cognitive ability

1. INTRODUCTION

In parallel programming, not only are parallel algorithms very important but also distribution of data and computation because inappropriate processor scheduling and data placement make a parallel program slower. It is important to schedule distribution of computation and data appropriately in addition to using a suitable parallel algorithm in parallel programming. Generally speaking, performance debugging (performance tuning) is needed in addition to logical debugging.

The first step of performance debugging is to find locations of bad balance (performance bugs). Visualization is useful to help find performance bugs. Visualization of behavior and performance of parallel programs have been studied (Heath, 1995). They directly map state values or their statistical values, which represent states of a parallel program or a parallel computer, to *graphical attributes* like coordinates, shapes, color and brightness.

We propose animation of parallel processing states that exploits human cognitive ability (OSAWA, 1996). Our proposed animation does not directly map the states into graphical attributes but maps them to bodies and forces in a dynamic system model that is familiar to human beings.

2. ANIMATION BASED ON DYNAMIC SYSTEM MODELING

A goal of visualization of data is to present data in a form that a human being is familiar with and is easily understood. Utilizing human cognitive ability, the user can understand states that are represented by a lot of values.

A human being lives in a dynamic world macroscopically and is familiar with motion in a dynamic system. Thus we have considered utilizing or exploiting the human ability to easily recognize balanced states, unbalanced states and natural (unforced) movement in a dynamic system. We propose an animation method of state values where we map the values into quantities of states in a dynamic system model, then simulate the dynamic system, and

Human–Computer Interaction: INTERACT'97 S. Howard, J. Hammond & G. Lindgaard (editors)
Published by Chapman & Hall

make the result of simulation visible. This animation shows changes in balance between computation and communication as movement in a familiar dynamic system.

First, we need to determine the dynamic system to be used, and the mapping of elements and structures in a parallel computer to bodies and forces in the dynamic system. We can model a parallel computer based on its network topology. For example, processor elements (PEs), computational load of a PE, communication links and amounts of communication in a parallel computer can be mapped to bodies, mass of a body, springs among bodies and attractive forces among bodies respectively. Mapping to a dynamic system does not necessarily refer to precise mapping to the real world.

Next, we formulate equations of motion to simulate the dynamic system model. The motion in the system is simulated by solving the equations of motion (that is, an initial value problem of ordinary differential equations) numerically.

The simulation result can be visualized using usual visualization techniques. Not only visualization techniques for performance debugging but also techniques of scientific visualization can be used.

Let us consider a parallel computer that takes 3 x 3 x 3 computational nodes and communication links in 3-D mesh topology as shown in Figure 1 (a). Elastic force is exerted between neighbor nodes to maintain the structure. Communication between nodes applies attractive force to them. Weak repulsive forces are exerted among bodies. Frictional force is caused that is proportional to the velocity of a body.

Figure 1 shows snapshots of animation based on the above modeling and pseudo trace data. In Figure 1, a small cube and a thin cylinder represent a processor element and a communication link respectively. Whiskers represent tracks of movement of the cubes. Figure 1(a) shows the initial state. When communication load is balanced, the shapes of 3-D mesh structure is almost maintained as shown in Figure 1(b). We can see that the communication is imbalanced by looking at the distortion of the structure in Figure 1(c).

Spring model (Kamada, 1989) and other models have been studied in static planar graph drawing. They are similar to our method in relation to visualization by use of a dynamic model. Their drawings are based on a stable solution of the system however our animation is based on solving equations of motion. Furthermore, our proposed method changes external force and mass of objects depending on trace data of message transfer and computational load on nodes.

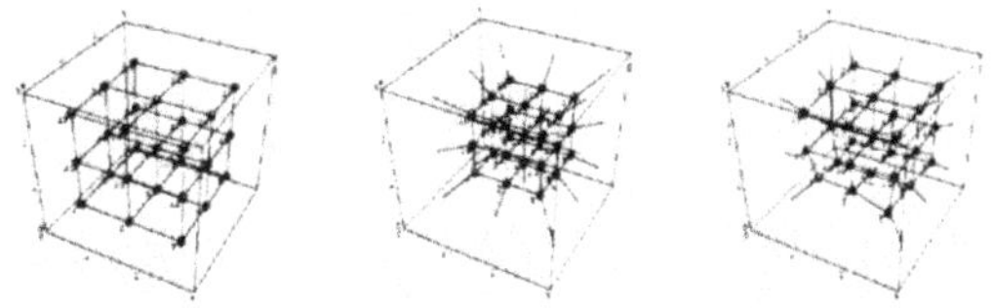

(a) Initial (b) Balanced (c) Imbalanced

Figure 1: Snapshots of Animation Based on Pseudo Trace Data on a Parallel Computer with 3-D Mesh Topology Network.

3. CONCLUDING REMARKS

This paper proposed 3-D animation for performance debugging of a parallel program that utilizes the human cognitive ability, and showed snapshots of animation examples for performance debugging and effectiveness of our proposed animation. Animation of the system is based on dynamic system modeling, simulation and visualization.

4. REFERENCES

Heath, Michael T., Allen D. Malony and Diane T. Rover (1995) Parallel Performance Visualization: From Practice to Theory. *IEEE Parallel & Distributed Technology*, Vol. 3, No. 4, pp. 44-60.

Kamada, T., and S. Kawai (1989) Algorithms for drawing general undirected graphs. *Information Processing Letters*, Vol.31, No.1, pp.7-15.

Osawa, Noritaka and Toshitsugu Yuba (1996) Animation of Parallel Computer Behavior Based on Dynamic System Modeling. *Fourth Workshop on Interactive Systems and Software*, pp.189-197, 1996 (in Japanese).

18

In Search for an Ideal Computer-Assisted Drawing System

†Takeo Igarashi, ‡Sachiko Kawachiya, †Satoshi Matsuoka, †Hidehiko Tanaka
†Dept. of Information Engineering, ‡Dept. of Information Science
The University of Tokyo
Hongo 7-3-1, Bunkyoku, Tokyo, Japan
+81-3-3812-2111 ext 7413
{takeo, tanaka}@mtl.t.u-tokyo.ac.jp, {sachiko, matsu}@is.s.u-tokyo.ac.jp

ABSTRACT Diagram drawing with conventional computer-assisted drawing(CAD) editors often tend to take considerable amount of time despite their seeming ease of use. We analyzed the problems of such systems focusing on the problem of cognitive overload, and observed that 1) the necessity of cognitive *planning* process in current CAD system causes the problems and that 2) reducing the overload can lead to fundamental improvement in overall drawing efficiency. We have conducted an experiment to verify these observations by comparing a typical drawing system and our prototype drawing system called *Interactive Beautification*, which combines the ease of freehand drawing and precision of traditional drawing editors by extracting various constraints in input strokes, and generating the desired diagrams automatically. Results show that significant amount of time is spent for cognitive *planning* process, and reduction of such planning time by *Interactive Beautification* can significantly improve the efficiency of CAD.

KEYWORDS CAD, Interaction technique, Cognitive workload, Constraint hierarchy, Beautification.

1 INTRODUCTION

Computer-assisted, Object-Oriented(OO) drawing editors are now used widely, allowing precise drawings not possible with traditional pen-on-paper drawing techniques. Furthermore considerable research and development have been conducted on creating new and innovative drawing systems resulting in those with abundance of functionalities. Despite such developments, drawing with such systems remains time-consuming and non-trivial, especially for novice or casual users.

The problem is that most research and development efforts on drawing systems have basically been 'feature wars', adding new drawing capabilities and interaction techniques, without deep, profound insights into their usability in practice. Instead we need studies to find "where does the fundamental problem exist" based on the close analysis of drawing processes on practical drawing systems.

Based on such a motivation, we propose an abstract model of drawing to explain the problems with computer-assisted drawing(CAD) systems focusing on the cognitive overload (Suchman, 87) (Norman, 86), and verify it through several experiments. In the model, we assume that the fundamental problem with CAD lies in considerable requirements imposed on the user's cognitive *planning* process. By *planning* we mean the cognitive process during drawing, where a user plans on the combination of the physical operations available in drawing editors to obtain the desired image. In addition, we confirm through an experiment with our prototype system that the reduction of such cognitive *planning* process can improve the efficiency of CAD.

Our prototype system frees the users of the cognitive *planning* process by automatically generating the desired diagram from freestrokes, but detailed descriptions of the salient technical features of the system itself is not the purpose of this paper; rather, we generalize on the effectiveness of the approaches to remove user's cognitive *planning* process from drawing editors.

This paper is organized as follows. First, we analyze the problems with CAD and propose an abstract model that captures the problems of excessive cognitive workload. Second, we conduct an experiment to quantify the workload. Third, we introduce a new drawing system where the objective is to reduce the workload, and conduct an experiment to quantify its effectiveness versus traditional OO-based

Human–Computer Interaction: INTERACT'97 S. Howard, J. Hammond & G. Lindgaard (editors)
Published by Chapman & Hall

drawing editors. Finally, we conclude with the future directions of our the research.

2 A TASK MODEL OF DIAGRAM DRAWING

In this section, the problems of excessive cognitive *planning* workload in current drawing systems are analyzed and a task model to explain the problems is proposed.

2.1 Problems with Current Drawing Systems

In some informal studies, the following problems have been observed for drawing on typical OO-based CAD systems.

Problem 1: it takes considerable amount of time to figure out how to combine the functions of editor to draw desired diagrams.

Problem 2: it takes considerable amount of time for users to realize that she has come to a "dead end" with the current drawing "plan", with which the desired diagram can never be obtained.

For example, to draw a line perpendicular to a slope, one can either a) count grids, b) duplicate the slope and rotate it 90 degrees, c) draw a horizontal and vertical lines and rotate them, etc. The user has to identify and select at least one of the strategies, requiring cognitive processing time. On the other hand, if the user fails to select an appropriate strategy (for instance, to draw a slope and a line separately and adjust the line with free rotation, which is often a wrong strategy because it is often difficult to obtain the exact desired angle with free rotation), a considerable amount of time is spent on 'wasteful operations'.

We explain these problems as the effect of the overhead of the cognitive *planning* process. By *planning*, we mean the translation of image in one's mind into physical operations, where image is the concrete visual image of a diagram to draw, and physical operations are the executions of various commands(draw lines, draw rectangles, copy, flip, rotate, etc.) or grid adjustment, etc. Problem 1 can be explained as the *planning* process causing additional overhead for each operation, and problem 2 can be explained as failure during the *planning* process resulting in wasteful operations.

2.2 An Abstract Model for Drawing Systems

To explain the problems and to clarify the structure of a drawing task, we propose a simple abstract model of diagram drawing with a typical OO-based editor(Figure 1). This model explains the interactions between the user's mental image of the desired result of drawing, and physical drawing operations the user performs during the drawing process.

Initially, the user has a visual image of the intended diagram in her mind. Then, to materialize the image on the editor, she must translate the visual image into a sequence of commands available on the editor(*planning* process)(A), and perform physical operations based on the planned command sequence. The operations are usually accompanied by direct manipulation of visual images on the display(C). Notice that the resulting diagram on the screen and the initial image in her mind has a visual representation, while the command sequence has a symbolic representation. That is, the user must go back and forth between the two representations.

For example, if a user tries to draw a tilted rectangle, the user first plans a series of operations such as creating a rectangle first, and then rotating it(A). Next, she executes the command operations physically, based on the *plan* by selecting the appropriate menu items(B). Then, she directly manipulates the drawn object to get the desired placement, size, and tilt(C). In this way, the drawing progresses repeating the sequence (A),(B), and (C). This model does not capture the entire aspects of diagram drawing, but is sufficient to explain the problems in CAD.

According to this abstract model, what we pointed out in the previous section are the problems pertaining to the *planning* process (A), i.e., the transition from visual representations to symbolic representations. However, many research activities in diagram drawing systems focused on the process (B) and (C), while the *planning* process has not been extensively explored. Our experiments show that large overhead is due to such a *planning* process, and imply that the removal of the commands and *planning* process dramatically improves drawing efficiency.

2.3 Expert Users and Casual Users

Recently, Bhavnani,S.K. and John,B. extensively studied the improvement of CAD productivity, focusing on the mental model of users (Bhavnani, 96). The main observation is that CAD experts are employing suboptimal strategies in drawing diagrams. Then, they identified a set of actual strategic knowledge for using CAD effectively and concluded that teaching these strategies to CAD users may improve the overall productivity.

On the other hand, the basis of their cost analysis is the number of operations expert users have to perform in the editor to complete a particular task, in a accordance with KLM (Card, 80) and GOMS

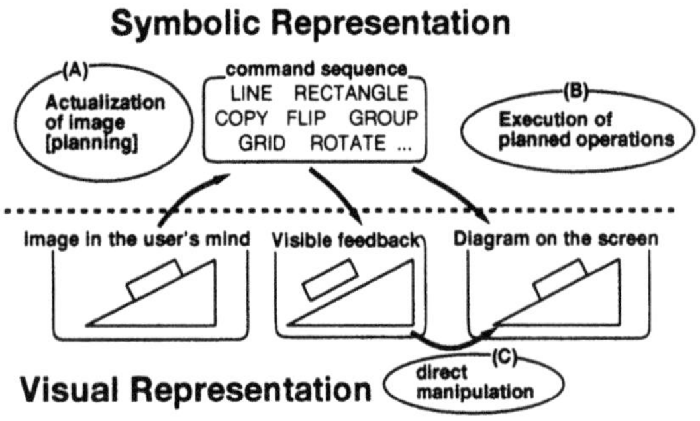

Figure 1: An abstract model of drawing editor

(Card, 83) (Olson, 90). As a result, they do not cover the task model where casual users may spend extra time to find out the appropriate operations, or time being wasted for making and recovering from erroneous operations. Furthermore, their proposal, i.e., to make strategic knowledge explicit and teach it to users, may not be applicable to casual users. We next describe an experiment to quantitatively determine the overhead of planning for casual users.

3 AN EXPERIMENT TO ESTIMATE THE AMOUNT OF COGNITIVE WORKLOAD

3.1 Experimental Set-Up

In this experiment, we observe and video-record the users drawing a given set of sample pictures using a typical OO-based drawing editor.

Systems. The machine used is an Apple Powerbook, and the drawing software is CANVAS 3.5 by Deneba Software.

Subjects. 14 casual CAD users who are accustomed to typical window-based GUI, and have used drawing tools occasionally. They vary in their proficiency in using CANVAS.

Task. Each user is first given a brief tutorial of CANVAS and conducts a series of short exercises several times. Then the users are instructed in the following manner:

- To draw as rapidly and clearly as possible,
- To draw in a natural way, as he would with drawing programs he is accustomed to.
- There is no need to reproduce perfectly the given diagram, if the task appears to be too difficult.

Then the users draw the two given diagrams(Figure 2), verbally speaking out the task he intends to perform. No time limits or feature restrictions are imposed so as to simulate standard drawing activities.

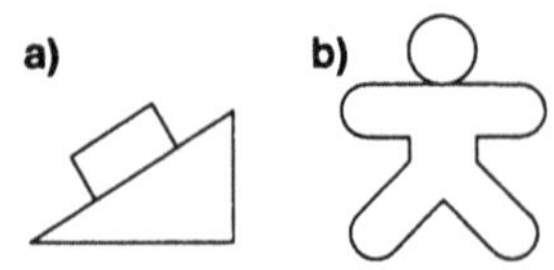

Figure 2: Diagrams used in the experiment

We analyze the video recording of each subject, dividing and categorizing time spent for the following behaviors into three categories: the time spent not pressing the mouse button(**NON**), the time spent during which the objects are directly operated upon with a mouse(OBJ), and the time during which the menus are selected with a mouse(**MENU**). Next, we add explanations of the user's activities to each unit by referring to the video recordings. For example, to draw a line, a user first moves the cursor to a tool menu (**NON**), and selects the 'line' palette(**MENU**), After the selection, the cursor moves to the starting point (**NON**), and then to the end point(OBJ).

3.2 Results

Based on the basic data collected as described above, we perform detailed analysis of the diagram drawing. The analysis consists of two parts. One is *local level analysis*, where the time consumed during each individual operation is calculated without considering its respective meaning or role in the total drawing sequence. From this analysis, we can examine detailed information on how quickly subjects performed each step. The other is *global level analysis*, where the underlying meaning of each step is analyzed with respect to its role in the total drawing sequence. This analysis is expected to reveal the nature of trial and error sequences during the drawing process.

Local Level Analysis

Figure 4 shows the histogram of the categorized operation steps classified by the time they required. First, we observe that some operation steps consume considerable amount of time. If each step consists of a simple physical operation which does not require cognitive processing, the time consumed during each step should stay relatively constant. However, the histogram shows that the time for each step varies widely, where there are some steps that exceed 6-8 seconds, indicating that extra time is consumed for cognitive processing.

We investigated such time-consuming steps by analyzing the videotaped verbal protocols and observed some common phenomena:

- A user fails to obtain his desired result because of inappropriate grid settings(Figure 3); and further-

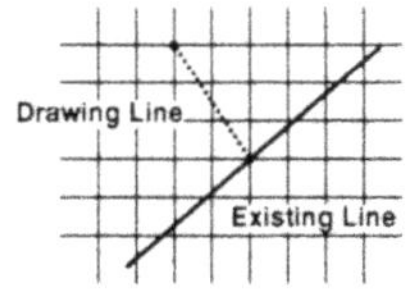

Figure 3: An example of time consuming operation: the user wants to draw a perpendicular line, but it is impossible in this grid setting. Further, it takes time for him/her to realize it.

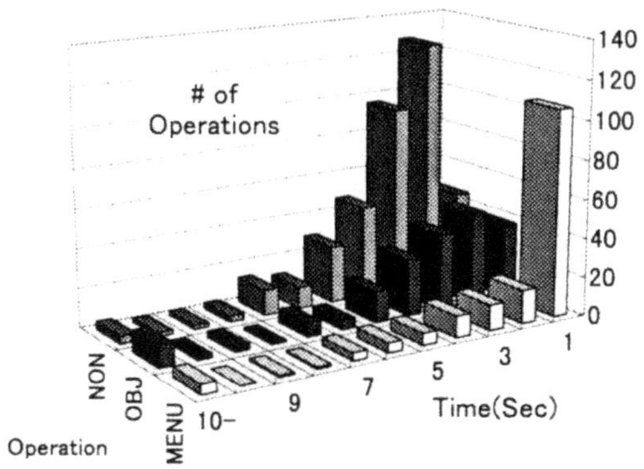

Figure 4: The number of operations categorized by the time they consumed: this figure shows that some operations are much more time consuming then others, which can be seen as the result of effect of cognitive processing.

more fails to realize this fact and repetitive futile attempts are made to draw.

- The mouse pointer makes aimless movements and/or momentarily pauses, failing to make any meaningful contributions to the intended drawing. Rather, time is seemingly spent on *planning*, e.g., wondering whether to draw the slope first or the box first in Figure 2a.

We regard these phenomena as the manifestation of cognitive workload because these time losses are not directly relevant to physical operations or the final result. In the following, we calculate an estimate of the percentage of the time spent on cognitive processing during the entire drawing process.

In order to obtain the basis of the estimate, we performed a series of experiments, where subjects are specifically instructed to perform a certain operation, such as to select a rectangle in the tool menu and draw a rectangle, or to select an object and 'flip' it along the x-axis by selecting the flip command in

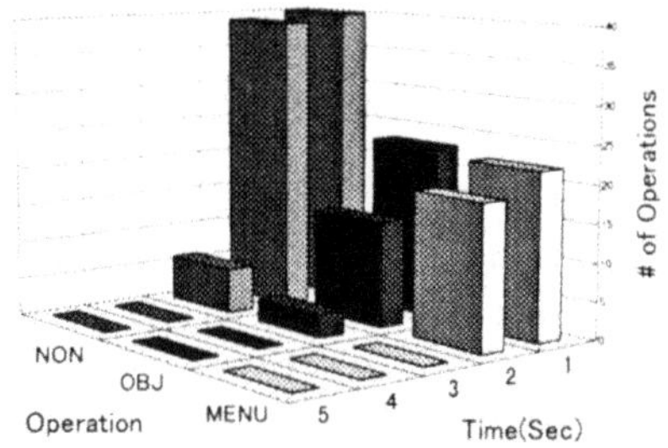

Figure 5: The number of operations categorized by the time they consumed in a task where no planning is necessary: all operations terminate within 2-3 seconds.

the menu bar, etc., thereby eliminating their cognitive planning workload. The results are shown in Figure 5, which show that time spent for such physical operations is short and uniform, taking approximately 2-3 seconds each. This result is in accordance with the results reported in previous work (Card, 83)(Olson, 90).

Based on this result, the time spent for cognitive planning process is calculated by basically subtracting the physical operation time from the total drawing time. The actual calculation is based on the following equation:

[Eq.1] cognitive processing time

$$= \sum(\max(0 , t(x) - \text{threshold})) \quad [x \in \text{all steps}],$$

where

$t(x)$ = time spent for step x,

threshold = assumed average time required for each physical operation.

In the equation, we make a simplification that the assumed average time for each physical operation remain constant. This is because with the current experiments, the distinction between the physical operation versus cognitive planning cannot be clearly determined. So instead, we assume a constant average threshold for physical operations, and any time spent for each operation exceeding this threshold is assumed to be spent for cognitive planning process. Based on the baseline experiments in Figure 5, we varied the threshold value between 2-4 seconds. The result is shown in Table 1 — here, we estimate that roughly 20% ~ 40% of the time is spent for cognitive planning process.

	Assumed threshold (Sec)		
	4.0	3.0	2.0
Figure 2a	22.50%	30.90%	45.10%
Figure 2b	17.6%	26.7%	41.5%

Table 1: The ratio of time required for cognitive processing to the total drawing time: this figure is the result of the calculation of cognitive processing time based on [Eq.1].

Global Level Analysis

In this analysis, the role of individual operations in the context of the entire drawing processes is examined. Then the 'wasteful' operations, whose effects are not reflected in the final results, are extracted, and the total time spent for such wasteful operations is calculated.

For example, a subject in the experiment tried to draw Figure 2a by drawing a rectangle and a triangle separately, and then rotating the rectangle so that its edge will be parallel to the slope of the triangle. However, he could not do so because it is not possible to specify a rotation angle explicitly in CANVAS other than integer values (e.g., if the necessary rotation angle was 35.5 degrees while it is only possible for the user to specify either 35 or 36 degrees.) We observed that it took considerable amount of time for the subject to become aware of the nature of the problem. After numerous futile attempts, the subject gave up and deleted the rectangle. Here the time used for the operations from the generation to the deletion of the rectangle is calculated as 'wasteful' time.

Figure 2b posed even more difficulties for most users. For example, it was difficult to draw the legs, and achieve proper symmetry; either the limbs would not properly join, the half-circle signifying the foot could not be merged, or the leg lines would end up not being parallel, depending on the user's initial plan. This seemed to surprise and frustrate the users, because of the apparent simplicity of the figure, plus the fact that minor local adjustments usually failed.

Figure 6 shows the results. The amount of wasteful time varies among subjects, but the existence of wasteful operations, and its effects are clearly observed. (One may notice that there is not a strong correlation between time for fig 2a and fig2b. This is because the amount of wasting time greatly changes depending on accidental failures rather than subject-specific reasons which are constantly observed.) Thus, we claim that, it is not only essential for the user interface of drawing systems to help in decreasing the

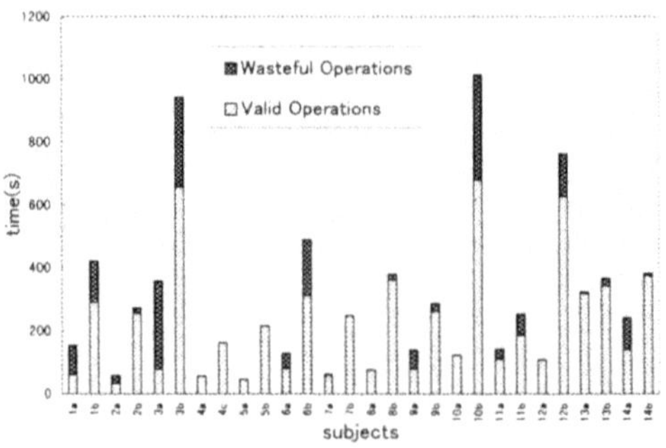

Figure 6: The time used in the wasteful operations: numbers 1a-14a indicate the drawing of Figure 2a by the 14 subjects and numbers 1b-14b that of Figure 2b accordingly: this figure shows that some subjects spend considerable time on wasteful operations.

amount of time required for an optimal drawing procedure, but also to prevent users from making a plan which would actually not lead to the desired results.

4 REQUIREMENTS FOR AN IDEAL DRAWING SYSTEMS

The experiments showed that considerable overhead is due to the cognitive *planning* process for casual users of OO-drawing systems. Thus, alleviating the overhead of *planning* process can fundamentally reduce the overhead. In other words, helping users to translate images to operations and freeing user of this translation are some of the most essential approach to improve drawing systems.

Based on the proposed abstract model of Figure 1, this means that improvement of the process (A) is critical for improvement of the overall drawing systems. However, most research focused mainly on process (B) and (C), whereas only few has explicitly intended to improve (A).

4.1 Previous Efforts on Improving the Drawing Systems

Previous constraint-based layout approaches such as (Bier, 86), (Bouma, 95), (Nelson, 85), (Borning, 81), (Sutherland, 63), etc. allow drawing precise diagrams without wasteful operations during (C), but most systems required the users to state necessary constraints explicitly, which can increase the user's cognitive burden during (A). Adding new features and functionalities, which are often the strategies with commercial editors, can decrease the number of required operation steps in (B) or possibility of mistakes in (C), but the added complexity also can increase the cognitive burden in (A). Programming-by-example approaches (Kurlander, 92) (Lieberman, 92) (Maulsby, 89) could be regarded as decreasing the burden of (B) and (C), but in practice could impose considerable overload when the user has to carefully plan what are the 'right' set of examples to present to the system. Gesture based systems (Apte, 93) (Zao, 93) (Rubine, 92) (Gross, 96) can free the users of menu selection in (B), but gestures in these systems correspond to the individual commands in OO-based systems, and the problem of planning remains. Beautification systems (Pavlidis, 85) intend to free users of fine placement of objects in (C), but the initial drawing process would be basically the same as in OO-based systems.

The work of Saund et al.(Saund, 94) can be viewed as helping the users during process (A). Their system, PerSketch, allows the system to understand the perceived image of the drawing in the user's mind and translate it into a system representation. However, it only handles the movement of sketch objects, and does not deal with precise drawings.

5 INTERACTIVE BEAUTIFICATION: an Experimental System to Reduce the Planning Overhead

We are currently developing an experimental drawing system called *Pegasus*, which assists the planning process (A) of user drawings. We call the interaction technique *Interactive Beautification*, which reduces the overload of the planning process by removing editing commands entirely from diagram drawing process. Here, we investigate how the system could improve the drawing task. [1]

We first give an overview of the interactive beautification in *Pegasus*. First, the user draws an approximate shape of his desired diagram with free stroke (Figure 7(A)) using a pen or a mouse. Then, the drawing system infers the desired precise diagram based on the *perceptual constraints* between the input stroke and surrounding context, and displays the multiple possible beautified candidates on the screen (Figure 7(B)). In this diagram generation, the system automatically detects higher level constraints such as similarity or symmetry. Among the several possible candidates, the system returns the most confident one as the primary candidate. If the user is satisfied with the candidate, he can proceed on to the next stroke without any additional operations(Figure 7(C)). Otherwise, the user can select the desirable one using a slider that appears near the cursor(Figure 8). During the selection, the system displays the constraints satisfied by the currently selected candidate visually, which makes rapid and precise interaction possible. Overall, users can draw a precise diagram without abstract manipulations such as gridding or rotation.

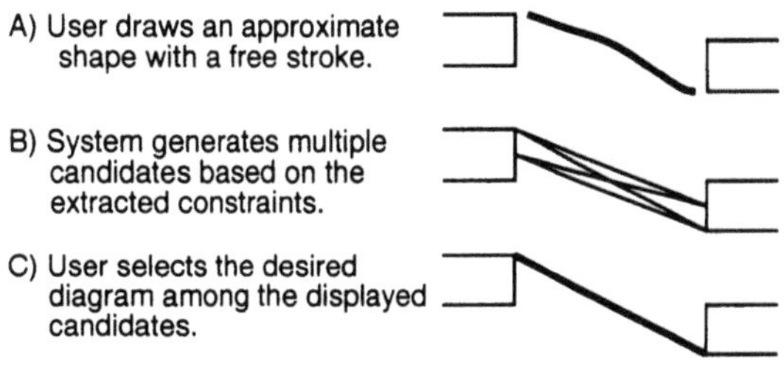

Figure 7: Interaction of the proposed system

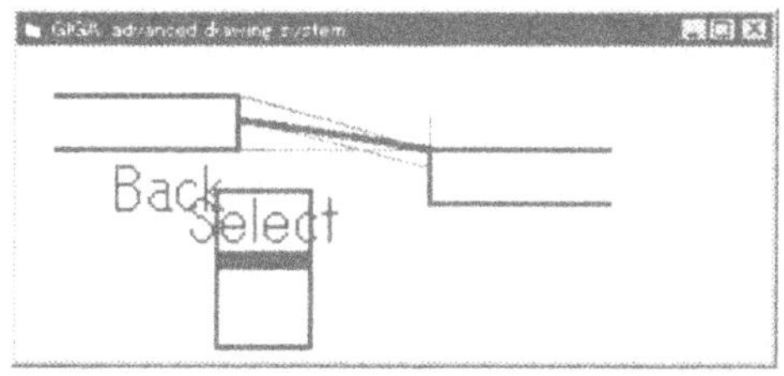

Figure 8: Sample image of the prototype system on Windows 95: the user is selecting a desired candidate using a slider.

Interactive Beautification resolves the ambiguity of input strokes and allows the usage of complex constraints that were not easily specifiable in previous OO-based drawing systems. We construct a constraint hierarchy consisting of a set of weighed constraints extracted from the input stroke and surrounding context. Multiple candidates are generated by changing the strength of the constraints in the constraint hierarchy (Sannella, 94). The use of a constraint hierarchy is superior to other ad hoc strategies in that it effectively generates plausible candidates by separating constraint solving and constraint abstraction. (Detailed description of this algorithm and prototype system will be given in another paper.)

At a glance, the system may seem similar to ex-

[1] As we have mentioned, the evaluation of the system itself is *not* the purpose of this section, but confirmation of the validity of our proposal is the current objective.

isting sketch-based interfaces including commercial ones such as Apple Newton, GO's Penpoint, and other freestroke mode in drawing softwares (SmartSkech, Corel Draw, etc.). These systems accept freestroke input and convert them into vector segments. They also automatically connect nearby segments, straighten lines, and recognize geometric primitives (circle, rectangle, etc.). However, *Pegasus* is different in that if handles complex, global constraints such as parallelism, symmetry, or similarity, which requires global analysis of the drawing, besides basic constraints such a connecting adjacent points. Considering such higher-level constraints is essential in freeing the users of the planning process. For example, if one wants to draw a symmetric diagram precisely in existing systems, he must draw one half of the desired diagram, and use explicit commands (copy, flip, and move) to complete the drawing. If any editing occurs, such command actions have to be repeated every time. In contrast, desired symmetry could be automatically accomplished in our system without little or no additional operations.

5.1 Implementation

The prototype system is being developed with Microsoft Visual Basic and Visual C++ on Windows 95. Sample drawings are shown in Figure 8. The currently implemented constraints are coincidence of edge points, horizontal / vertical alignment of edges, equivalence of segment length, parallelism / perpendicularity among segments, and horizontal and vertical symmetry. Time required for generating multiple candidates is about 100 msec (IBM PC/AT, Pentium 75MHz), sufficient for interactive drawing. Constraints for curves are currently being worked on.

5.2 Experiment

Using the prototype system described above, we performed an experiment to investigate whether reduction of *planning* process could really reduce the cognitive workload and improve efficiency of drawing processes.

In the experiment, the same 14 subjects as the previous experiment were instructed to draw the diagram shown in figure 1a, and the drawing processes were recorded and analyzed as had been with the previous experiment. Subjects were given a brief explanation of the prototype system, and practiced with the system for approximately one minute.

Figure 9 shows the time required for each subject to complete the drawings. On the average, drawing time for our prototype system was approximately 43% of that for the OO-based system. This indicates

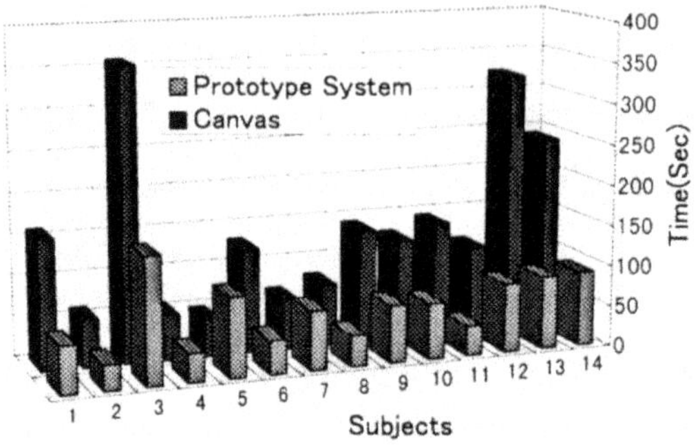

Figure 9: Time required to draw figure 2a in CANVAS and in the prototype system: per average, drawing in the prototype system requires only 43% of the drawing time in CANVAS.

	Assumed threshold (Sec)		
	4.0	3.0	2.0
Figure 2a	11.8%	19.3%	34.3%

Table 2: The ratio of time required for cognitive processing to the total drawing time in the prototype system.

that the time required in our system is shortened and more stable. The result of local level analysis is shown in Figure 10 and Table 2. The ratio of cognitive processing time is reduced to 12% ~ 34% compared with 17% ~ 45% for that of CANVAS. Investigation of Figure 10 shows that **SELECT** operations (selection of a candidate by a slider), is the sole operation that takes some time to complete, and other operations (**NON** and **STROKE**) finish quickly. Furthermore, future improvements of both the interface for **SELECT** and the associated constraint solving algorithm may improve the time for **SELECT**. Lastly, we observed that the wasteful operations due to the misunderstanding of the system behavior and wrong planning are greatly reduced. The quality of the drawings were not quantified in these experiments, but no conclusive differences in quality between the two experiments were observed.

The result shows that reduction of planning time achieved in the prototype system improved the efficiency of diagram drawing; it remains to be seen, however, whether our proposed *Interactive Beautification* is applicable to a wider range of applications.

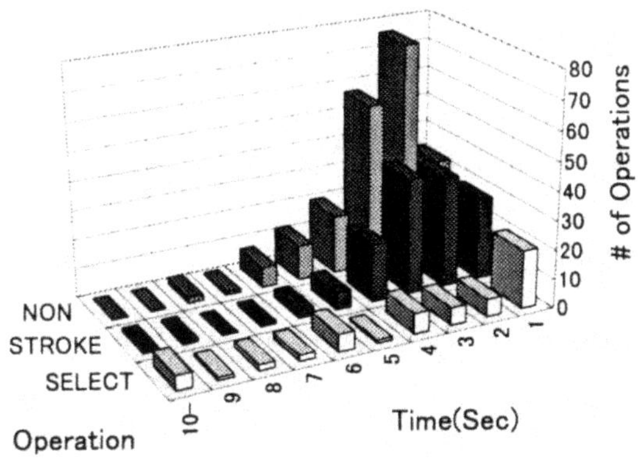

Figure 10: The number of operations categorized by the time they consumed in the prototype system: STROKE means the free stroke input, and SELECTION means the candidate selection by the slider.

6 CONCLUSION

We have conjectured that, for casual users, the necessity of cognitive planning process results in major overhead in current OO-based drawing systems, and interaction techniques to fundamentally reduce planning overhead improve the overall drawing process.

Our experiments to verify the conjecture showed that *planning* process consumed about 17% ~ 45% of the total drawing time, and that wasteful operations consumed up to 78% of total drawing time. By contrast, our prototype *Pegasus* drawing system with *Interactive Beautification*, exhibited significantly reduced *planning* process time, or approximately 12% ~ 34% of the total drawing time. Furthermore, due to the reduction of wasteful operations, the overall drawing time is reduced to 43% of the drawing time with conventional OO-based drawing system.

As a future work, we must perform a more detailed and comprehensive comparative studies among other types of drawing systems, using a more extensive set of drawing samples. We also need to make our drawing system more robust by incorporating other kinds of constraints and their solvers especially curves, and furthermore improve the SELECTion interface for multiple candidates.

References

Apte, A., Vo, V., and Kimura, T.D. (1993) "Recognizing Multistroke Geometric Shapes: An Experimental Evaluation," *Proc. of UIST'93*, pp. 121 - 128.

Bhavnani,S.K., John,B.E. (1996) "Exploring the Unrealized Potential of Computer-Aided Drafting", *Proc. of CHI'96*, pp. 332-339.

Bier,E.A., Stone,M.C. (1986) "Snap Dragging", Computer Graphics, Vol.20, No.4, pp. 233-240.

Borning,A. (1981) "The Programming Language Aspects of ThingLab, A constraint-Oriented Simulation Laboratory", ACM Trans. on Program. Lang. Syst., Vol.3, No.4, pp.353-387.

Bouma,W., Fudos,I., Hoffman,D., Cai,J., Paige,R. (1995) "Geometric constraint solver", Computer Aided Design, Vol.27, No.6, pp. 487-501.

Card, S.K., Moran, T.P. (1980) "The Keystroke-Level Model for User Performance Time with Interactive Systems", Communications of the ACM, Vol.23, No.7, pp. 396-410.

Card, S.K., Moran, T.P., Newell, A. (1983) "The Psychology of Human-Computer Interaction", Lawrence Erlbaum Associates, Inc. .

Gross,M.D., Do,E.Y. (1996) "Ambiguous Intentions: A Paper-like Interface for Creative Design", *Proc. of UIST'96*, pp. 183-192.

Kurlander,D., Geiner,S. (1992) "A History-Based Macro by Example System", *Proc. of UIST'92*, pp. 99-106.

Lieberman,H. (1992) "Dominoes and Storyboards: Beyond "Icons on Strings"", *Proc. of VL'92*, pp. 65-71.

Maulsby,D.L., Witten,I.H, Kittlitz,K.A. (1989) "Metamouse: Specifying Graphical Procedures by Example", Computer Graphics, Vol.23, No.3, pp.127-136.

Nelson,G. (1985) "Juno, A Constraint-based Graphics System", Computer Graphics, Vol.19, No.3, pp. 235-243.

Norman, D.A., S.W.Draper (1986) "User Centered System Design", Lawrence Erlbaum Associates, Inc. .

Olson, J.R., Olson G.M. (1990) "The Growth of Cognitive Modeling in Human-Computer Interaction Since GOMS", Human-Computer Interaction, Vol.5, pp. 221-265.

Pavlidis,T., VanWyk,C.J. (1985) "An Automatic Beautifier for Drawings and Illustrations", Computer Graphics, Vol.19, No.3, pp. 225-234.

Rubine,D. (1992) "Combining Gestures and Direct Manipulation", *Proc. of CHI'92*, pp.659-660.

Sannella, M. (1994) "Analyzing and Debugging Hierarchies of Multi-way Local Propagation Constraints", PPCP '94, pp. 63-77.

Saund,E., Moran,T.P. (1994) "A Perceptually Supported Sketch Editor", *Proc. of UIST'94*, pp. 175-184.

Suchman, S.A. (1987) "Plans and Situated Actions: The Problem of Human-Machine Communication", Cambridge Univ. Press.

Sutherland,I.E. (1963) "Sketchpad: A Man-Machine Graphical Communication System", *Proc. of Spring Joint Comp. Conf.*, No.23, pp.329-346.

Zao,R. (1993) "Incremental Recognition in Gesture-Based and Syntax-Directed Diagram Editors", *Proc. of InterCHI'93*, pp. 95-100.

19

The FRANK Video Navigation Interface

Bill Simpson-Young, Ken Yap, Jordi Robert-Ribes, Nadine Ozkan

Research Data Network Cooperative Research Centre/
CSIRO Mathematical and Information Sciences
Macquarie University Campus, North Ryde, Sydney, NSW 2113
Australia
bill.simpson-young@cmis.csiro.au

ABSTRACT We will demonstrate a tool which supports users in the navigation and searching of remote video archives. The tool features a tight coupling between navigation of the video and of the textual and image-based aids used to search and navigate through it.

KEYWORDS video navigation, media archives, distributed multimedia, multimedia synchronisation

1. BACKGROUND

Film researchers working in television studios or film archives spend a great deal of time in search of archival footage as part of the production process. Often descriptions of the footage, such as shotlists (ie textual descriptions of each sequence in some footage) and transcripts, are available and these can be used in the first stage of finding appropriate footage. When some potentially relevant footage has been identified, the tape can be retrieved and browsed to determine its usefulness. This is currently a very time-consuming process (Simpson-Young and Yap, 1995).

Now, with the availability of digital video technology and broadband networks, there is the opportunity of integrating the searching and browsing of textual or image-based representations of video with the navigation through the video itself. This integration allows more effective and more efficient searching and browsing mechanisms as well as providing the ability to perform such tasks over a network.

However, the availability of the multiple representations of the video material leads to a challenge with regard to the user interface. The challenge is to provide an interaction model that best facilitates the navigation through these different media while retaining the focus of the task as the discovery of appropriate footage from the video.

2. FRANK

FRANK (the Film Researcher's Archival Navigation Kit) is a prototype tool that has been created as part of the development of a distributed system for the searching and browsing of digital video over wide-area broadband networks. Although developed for use over networks between cities, there has been a lot of interest in FRANK for use across intranets and the system has undergone trials in this environment within the Australian Broadcasting Corporation (ABC) and other film and television archives and libraries.

Human–Computer Interaction: INTERACT'97 S. Howard, J. Hammond & G. Lindgaard (editors)
Published by Chapman & Hall

The FRANK user interface consists of a web browser component and a video player component. The functionality of the two is tightly coupled to provide linking and synchronisation of video with a selected navigation aid (such as a transcript). The synchronisation model supports synchronisation from text to video (i.e so that as a user browses through a transcript, the video remains synchronised with the current location in the transcript) and from video to text (i.e so that as the video plays, the transcript display will be kept aligned). Other aspects of the synchronisation model are described in Simpson-Young and Yap (1996).

3. DEMONSTRATION OVERVIEW

Several interfaces have been evaluated in usability tests with professional film researchers and cataloguers within the ABC Television Archive. This presentation will involve a demonstration of the FRANK system and a discussion of which interaction mechanisms have been found to be appropriate for this type of application and which mechanisms have not been so successful.

4. ACKNOWLEDGMENTS

The authors acknowledge the support provided by the Cooperative Research Centre for Research Data Networks established under the Australian Government's Cooperative Research Centre Program and the support of the Advanced Computational Systems CRC under which the work described in this paper is administered.

5. REFERENCES

Simpson-Young, B. and Yap K. (1995) Work Processes of Film and Television Researchers, *CSIRO Division of Information Technology Technical Report 95/11*.

Simpson-Young, B. and Yap K. (1996) FRANK: Trialing a system for remote navigation of film archives, *SPIE International Symposium on Voice, Video and Data Communications*, Boston, 18-22 November 1996.

Orbit - supporting social worlds

Tim Mansfield, Simon Kaplan[1], Ted Phelps, Mark Fitzpatrick, Winnie Qiu, Rik Taylor, Geraldine Fitzpatrick and Andrew Berry

wOrlds Project
CRC for Distributed Systems Technology
University of Queensland
St Lucia, Queensland
AUSTRALIA
timbomb@dstc.edu.au

ABSTRACT Orbit is a prototype collaboration-support system intended to demonstrate a vision of a distributed, computer-mediated work environment. The prototype is an attempt to articulate and test the ideas contained in the Locales Framework - a proposed set of patterns for successful collaborative systems based on the work of Anselm Strauss.

KEYWORDS computer-supported cooperative work, CSCW, collaboration systems

1. Orbit

Orbit is a prototype collaboration-support system intended to implement a vision of a distributed, computer-mediated work environment.

Rather than offering support for individual collaborative tasks such as collaborative web browsing, cooperative editing or real-time discussion around a whiteboard, Orbit is intended to become each user's everyday working environment.

The prototype serves as a framework for collaboration in which other collaborative tools can be embedded, a test-bed for useful collaborative components and a ubiquitous collaborative environment for members of several work-groups.

2. Locales Framework

Orbit is based on a set of ideas about collaboration we have dubbed the *Locales Framework.* The framework is based in part on the work of sociologist Anselm Strauss, in part on existing work in CSCW and in part on our own intuitions (from designing previous systems such as wOrlds (Kaplan et al 1997)). It is intended to provide both a way to understand the collaborative needs of a given workplace as well as a guide for designers of collaborative systems.

The framework hinges on the simple, but powerful idea of *social worlds* for which we owe a debt to Anselm Strauss (1993).

Social worlds have a shared purpose, some means of communication which allow them to do their work and

[1] Simon Kaplan is a professor at the School of Information Technology of the University of Queensland and an associate professor in the Computer Science Department at the University of Illinois at Urbana-Champaign.

Human–Computer Interaction: INTERACT'97 S. Howard, J. Hammond & G. Lindgaard (editors)
Published by Chapman & Hall

some sense of membership so it is usually possible to say who is a member and who isn't. Social worlds often use some kind of *locale* - a physical or virtual "place" which allows the group to communicate, collect its history, objects and information and carry out its work, whether that is simply a conversation or the organization of a country. A locale provides a "context for interaction" (Giddens 1984) for the members of a social world.

Social worlds may last for hours or centuries, they may have two members or hundreds, they may use completely physical locales or completely virtual ones.

They are bound, not by walls but by "the limits of effective communication" (Strauss, 1993). The purpose of our project and of the Orbit prototype is to build a software system to support social worlds by allowing their members to construct virtual locales of various kinds to support their work and extend the limits of effective communication.

The first version of the framework is described in detail by Fitzpatrick et al (1996), but in essence the framework describes five aspects of an adequate collaboration system:

1. **Locale Foundations** - a system must provide support for locales with adequate mechanisms for sharing objects and documents, supporting a group's notions of membership and controlling access and allowing privacy.
2. **Mutuality** - locales must provide a sense of shared place for users. Users should be mutually aware of each other's presence in a locale, of the objects in the locale and of actions and of activities which are going on.
3. **Individual Views** - individual users must be able to construct personalized, idiosyncratic views of the multiple locales of which they are members based on their current level of participation in the corresponding social worlds.
4. **Interaction Trajectories** - interaction happens over time so every social world has a past and projects one or more futures. An adequate collaboration system must allow the members of a social world to maintain their shared history (for example in the form of shared knowledge or stored records) and plan their collective future (workflow tools provide a highly prescriptive way to define the future of a group's interaction).
5. **Civic Structures** - locales (and their social worlds) are constantly forming and dissolving. An adequate collaboration system must provide support for these lifecycle processes and for some way of structuring the world of locales, defining the relationship of locales to each other in terms of their mutual visibility and access.

3. Orbit Technical Overview

Orbit is an implementation of some of the aspects of the Locales Framework. We believe it provides an interesting demonstration of techniques for the support of Foundations, Mutuality and Individual Views and some early ideas in support of Interaction Trajectories and Civic Structures.

The prototype is built in a combination of Java, Distributed Smalltalk and a variety of other languages. The user interface is accessible using standard web browsers such as Netscape, although the interface does not execute entirely within the browser.

Orbit allows users to access multiple locales simultaneously and swiftly adjust their intensity of participation in each locale. Participation can range from a vague awareness of the level of activity in a given locale to a high-intensity, real-time video-conference with shared documents.

The system provides a notification service and a variety of user notification agents which afford continuous awareness of the user's objects of interest and whichever locales are in view. This notification service is the backbone of Orbit's awareness mechanisms.

The Organizational Information Locator - OIL (Resource Discovery Unit 1997) - uses Orbit to provide context for searches launched from within locales. Orbit in turn uses OIL as a way of continuously updating locales with new, more relevant information.

4. Relevance

Orbit is unique among CSCW prototyping efforts because it unites

- a principled approach to design, exemplified in the Locales Framework,
- an attempt to exploit the strengths of computer-mediated communication rather than simply trying to simulate the physical,

- a realistic approach to supporting distributed collaboration using cutting-edge distributed technology and
- an approach that emphasizes both the primacy of groups in collaboration and the seamless way in which collaborative work is interleaved with individual work.

We intend that the Locales Framework should provide a logical approach to the design of collaborative systems. Part of the function of Orbit is to test the validity of the concepts in the framework.

5. Commercial Status

Orbit is a non-commercial research prototype produced by the CRC for Distributed Systems Technology under funding from various sources (see Acknowledgements below). We hope to arouse interest in our work so that Orbit or related prototypes could be licensed to a commercial partner.

Orbit is not subject to any patents.

6. Equipment Needed

We can supply all equipment needed to demonstrate Orbit, however a projector or projection panel would be useful to allow the workspace of one of the demonstrators to be enlarged for easier viewing.

7. Acknowledgments

This work has been supported by the Defense Advanced Research Projects Agency under grant F30603-94-C-0161, the US Army Corps of Engineers Research Laboratory, by Sun Microsystems and Hewlett-Packard and School of Information Technology at the University of Queensland. The work reported in this paper has also been funded in part by a Co-operative Research Centre Program through the Department of the Prime Minister and Cabinet of Australia. Geraldine Fitzpatrick has received additional support through an Australian Postgraduate Research Award and an Australian Telecommunications and Electronics Research Board scholarship.

The views and conclusions expressed in this document are those of the authors and should not be interpreted as representing the official policies, expressed or implied, of the Defense Advanced Research Projects Agency or the U.S. Government.

8. References

Arnold, D. et al (1997). *Hector: Distributed Objects in Python.* Doctor Dobb's Sourcebook - Emerging Trends in Software Technology, Jan-Feb 1997, vol 22, No. 13.

Fitzpatrick, G. et al. (1996). *Locales Framework: Exploring foundations for collaboration support,* IEEE Proceedings of OzCHI96, Hamilton, New Zealand.

Giddens, A. (1984). *The Consitution of Society.* University of California Press, Berkeley, 1984.

Kaplan, S. et al. (1997). *MUDdling Through* Proceedings Thirtieth Annual Hawaii International Conference on System Sciences (HICSS30), vol II, pp 539-548, IEEE Computer Society Press, Los Alamitos, CA, 1997.

Resource Discovery Unit (1997) http://www.dstc.edu.au/RDU

Strauss, A. (1993). *Continual Permutations of Action.* New York, Adeline De Gruyter.

21

Virtual Environments for Industrial Applications

Duncan Stevenson, Kevin Smith, Paul Veldkamp, John McLaughlin, Rochelle O'Hagan, Dione Smith, Chris Gunn

CSIRO Mathematical and Information Sciences
GPO Box 664 Canberra ACT 2601
Australia
duncan.stevenson@cmis.csiro.au

ABSTRACT A small-scale immersive virtual environment system (Virtual Workbench) and a haptic force-feedback device (PHANToM) are used to show direct 3-dimensional interaction with fully 3-dimensional data. Real scenarios are used to show the value of the fully 3-dimensional interaction using both haptic and non-haptic devices.

KEYWORDS virtual environment, haptic

1. INTRODUCTION

The use of Virtual Environment systems for the display of and interaction with industrial and scientific data is about to become widely accepted in many industries which previously relied on older technologies such as printed plans and sections or 2-dimensional display and interaction techniques on a computer screen. The systems demonstrated here are commercially available products, at prices that are becoming affordable, and the time is ripe for serious consideration of the HCI research and advanced development that will lead to marketable products.

These systems focus on enhancing direct human sensory perception in the data interaction process. The Virtual Workbench (Poston, 1994) allows the user to put his or her hands directly into the data. The user perceives that the data and the hand-held location tools are in the same place, and can therefore make use of the hand and arm muscle receptors to locate and operate on the data.

The light, hand-held locating devices are easily manipulated, with their representation as virtual tools in the virtual display being whatever is appropriate to the application situation. For example, in a medical situation they might be a scalpel or tweezers; in a mine modelling situation they might be a selector or a drawing tool.

The PHANToM (Massie, 1994) haptic device gives the user both a 3D locating device and also feedback on the "feel" of the data. This sensory feedback will apply to quite different metaphors. For instance, in simulating a medical application - say inserting a needle into human tissue - the PHANToM would provide the appropriate resistance as the needle penetrated various different layers of tissue, each with different type of resistance to penetration.

The work in progress on these two systems which is demonstrated here represents ongoing research in a range of projects. It will provide those who try out the demonstrations with the experience of feeling and seeing the possibilities of this new range of HCI technologies.

Human–Computer Interaction: INTERACT'97 S. Howard, J. Hammond & G. Lindgaard (editors)
Published by Chapman & Hall

2. DESCRIPTION

2.1 Virtual Workbench

The Virtual Workbench consists of a fibreglass frame with a footprint of 900mm x 600mm and a height of 700mm. A workstation monitor is mounted on top of the frame. The user sits at the frame looking at a tilted mirror which is at about shoulder height and which reflects the image on the monitor. The user's hands reach in under the mirror into the same space as the reflected monitor image appears to occupy. With shutter glasses this becomes a 3D image. Two radio-frequency hand held tracking devices let the user manipulate the displayed data.

The software which currently supports the Virtual Workbench runs on Silicon Graphics workstations, either an Indigo2 or Onyx. This demonstration system uses an Indigo2 with a "Maximum Impact" graphics subsystem.

2.2 PHANToM Haptic Device

The PHANToM is a robotic arm sitting on a 330mm x 250mm base. At the end of the arm is a pen-like tool which the user holds. The hardware can provide the XYZ location of the pen tip and the pitch, yaw and roll of the pen to the controlling software, and can respond to controlling instructions by providing in real time, a 3D force vector at the tip of the pen. The pen is equipped with one finger-operated button.

These features allow the PHANToM to act both as a 3D tracking/input device and as a 3D force-feedback device. With appropriate programming, the PHANToM can simulate things like a hard surface, a soft squishy surface, a rough surface and so forth. The nature of interaction with this haptic device is quite different to interactions with visual devices, and involves dynamic rather than static interaction.

3. INDUSTRIAL APPLICATIONS

The initial development work on the Virtual Workbench, by staff at the Institute of Systems Science at the National University of Singapore, focused on medical applications where the data sets were typically 3D reconstructions of body parts from CAT or MRI scans. The scale of the data is of the same order of magnitude as the scale of the virtual workspace in which the operator's hands sit. The nature of the data is primarily voxel, leading to very large data sets and demanding voxel resolution algorithms and texture mapping.

A second set of applications is being built around geological, mine and minerals exploration data. This data is characterised by lines (drillholes), surfaces (geological contacts, ore body boundaries, digital elevation models) and volumes (interpolated ore grade). The data items often have many different attribute sets - for example drillhole data records position, lithology, assay values for many minerals as well as geophysical measurements. A large industry already exists to handle these data sets, and it is facing major obstacles in displaying and interpreting the many data sets in the true 3-dimensional context. Developments using this virtual environment technology show great promise towards satisfying the needs of professionals in this area.

4. REFERENCES

Massie, T and Salisbury, J.K. (1994) The PHANToM Haptic Interface: A Device for Probing Virtual Objects *Proceedings of the ASME Winter Annual Meeting* 295-302

Poston, T and Serra, L. (1994) The Virtual Workbench: Dextrous VR. *Proceedings ACM VRST'94*, 111-122.

ACKNOWLEDGEMENT

The authors wish to acknowledge that this work was carried out within the Cooperative Research Centre for Advanced Computational Systems established under the Australian Government's Cooperative Research Centre Program.

22

Whose Actions are Interactions? From Interface to In-Your-Face

Moderator: **Leigh Snelling**

URCOT
Level 1, 171 La Trobe Street
Melbourne,
Australia, 3000.
zleigh@minyos.its.rmit.edu.au

Panellists

Lucy Suchman

Xerox Palo Alto Research Center
3333 Coyote Hill Road
Palo Alto
California 94304
USA
suchman@parc.xerox.com

Toni Robertson

University of Technology, Sydney
PO Box 123 Broadway
Sydney
New South Wales
Australia 2021
T.Robertson@unsw.edu.au

Joan Greenbaum

City University of New York
La Guardia College
31-10 Thompson Ave
Long Island City
New York 11101
joanbaum@ix.netcom.com

Patsy Segall

URCOT
Level 1, 171 La Trobe Street
Melbourne,
Australia, 3000.
zpatsy@minyos.its.rmit.edu.au

ABSTRACT The concept of Human Computer Interaction has been a useful one for getting designers and companies to focus on people sitting in front of computers. Much has happened however, in the almost 15 years since HCI concepts have taken root, and chief among these changes is the importance of the rich picture of how people use computers in their work and daily lives. The panellists will provide critical perspectives on HCI's foundational notions of action and interaction, and constructive proposals for new directions.

Human–Computer Interaction: INTERACT'97 S. Howard, J. Hammond & G. Lindgaard (editors)
Published by Chapman & Hall

KEYWORDS CSCW, HCI in organisations, participatory design, situated action, social and political issues

1. TOPIC OVERVIEW

This panel proposes that a critical challenge for workers in the field of HCI is to recognise already existing worlds of interaction at work and daily life and to engage with them in respectful and appropriate ways. To this end, the essential interface when designing computer applications is that between the user and their situation of use, not between an individual user and a computer. We share a concern that the concept of 'interface' has been progressively narrowed to the point where it now represents a set of concerns far removed from the reality of the workplace, the university and the home. Allied to these concerns is a recognition that most human activities are social. The contributions of the panellists are based in traditions that have recognised the sociality of work and the involvement of users in the design of their work and its technologies. These traditions have formed various and changing kinds of relations with HCI over time and include Participatory Design, situated cognition and action, and the efforts to understand and design for the sociality of work that have been defining of Computer Supported Cooperative Work (CSCW).

Participatory Design, an approach to the design of technology that is firmly tied to wider traditions of workplace democracy, has influenced the development of HCI by insisting that its focus on the design of the human computer interface includes the meaningful inclusion of workers at every stage in the design process. Both situated cognition and action emphasise the role of interaction and context in organising behaviour. It recognises the limitations of the symbol processing metaphor for cognition and insists, instead, on an understanding of human cognition as situated, embodied action that always occurs within a context of particular, concrete circumstances.

Finally, Computer Supported Cooperative Work (CSCW) represents a welcomed wider scope to the original HCI focus by expanding the focus of study to include the support of people working together. This shift has highlighted the collaborative and social nature of *all* work. As a result, insights from research disciplines devoted to understanding human action and social organisation, have been applied to the design of computer systems that aim to effectively support human interaction.

Viewed from each of these perspectives, the notion of human-computer interaction is problematic, as it implies that what happens when people use computers equates, in some way, with interactions between people. The equation of human-human and human-computer interactions has contributed to the development of discourses and practices that assume the computer to be some kind of surrogate other. The result is the attribution of interactional agency to computers, when their role is more appropriately conceptualised as mediating the interaction between people and their work, other people, their collective work and the environment within which that work is performed.

The concept of Human Computer Interaction has been a useful one for getting designers and companies to focus on people sitting in front of computers. Much has happened however, in the almost 15 years since HCI concepts have taken root, and chief among these changes is the importance of the rich picture of how people use computers in their work and daily lives

The panellists will argue, in various ways, that HCI needs to contribute to an understanding of computers as artefacts that mediate human action and interaction within specific contexts of use. Further, the panellists do not assume that work places are not comprised of groups of people with equal roles, responsibilities and power, but are constructed of layers of bureaucracy, of fine distinctions between decision makers and operators, and between those representing the interests of capital and those representing the interests of labor.

In sum, the panel will provide both critical perspectives on HCI's foundational notions of action and interaction as well as constructive proposals for new, politically and historically aware research and development directions.

2. PANELLISTS' PERSPECTIVES

Lucy Suchman

In his contribution to the volume Design at Work (1991), Liam Bannon proposed a shift for HCI 'from human factors to human actors.' In this concise phrase, Bannon points us away from a narrow construal of the user as a necessary element of interface design, to a view of system design as a multifaceted enterprise in support of persons engaged in ongoing activity.

In the years since Bannon's proposal, research in HCI has made significant moves out of the laboratory and into the workplace. Yet, for the most part, technologies continue to be evaluated with reference to feature sets and comparable offerings, rather than in terms of their fit with the environments and activities of their use. In my panel comments I'll sketch a vision of an alternative future for HCI in which design awards are given not for discrete, decontextualised devices but for the collective achievement of new, more productive connections among artifacts, and more powerful integrations between artifacts and the settings of their use.

Joan Greenbaum

I will bring the Participatory Design perspective to the debate. Participatory design has strong local traditions in Australia, Germany, Scandinavia and the U.S. where it has represented both a better way to design systems that fit use situations and a movement to gain more workplace rights through participation in technological decision-making. Joan Greenbaum has worked in the computer field for the last 30 years actively focusing on getting users involved in all stages of design. In this panel she will present the need for integrating HCI techniques such as usability labs with more active participation of users in design. In addition she argues that realistic design alternatives need to include labor issues as well as the direct participation of workers, customers and citizens in order to reframe design agendas. In-your-face design is more than just a pretty interface.

Toni Robertson

Because people are always situated in social contexts, all work can be considered as cooperative. What varies are the degree of reliance on other people at different stages in the work processes and the degree of control any individual has over both the definition of a particular process as well as the organisation of their own and others' contribution to that process. Negotiating and achieving cooperative work then, is itself part of that work and its success is determined by the skills and commitment of those involved. When work is mediated by the use of technology, the successful use of that technology is determined as much by the skills of the users in meshing the technology into the work process, as it is by any specific qualities of the technology itself. These skills are excluded from consideration when the concerns of technology designers are limited to whether users are novices or experts in the use of a particular software application.

HCI has traditionally relied on the cognitivist metaphor for human cognition that sets up an opposition between 'inside the head' and 'outside the head'. Cognition is reduced to input and output from an information processing brain. Based on empirical studies of cooperative design I will consider the inadequacies of the cognitivist metaphor, and related oppositions, to account for human cognition as it is lived and for cooperative work as it is achieved in practice.

The basic problem is that cognitivism ignores that human cognition is embodied cognition that is continually defined by, and defining of, both interaction and context. The result is that communicative work involved in achieving a cooperative process as well as the skills required to do this work remain unacknowledged and frequently unsupported in the design of technology that might be used in cooperative work.

Patsy Segall

Traditional, formal methods of systems development clearly identified the points at which 'user' input formed part of the development process. Typically, critical points identified in the waterfall model were in the requirements gathering phase and, much further down the track, the interface design phase. Testing an interface after the functional specification phase will ensure only that it is 'usable', not that it is 'really useful'. Contrasting approaches which attempt to solve this problem involve intensive joint participation of users and developers. For example, Tom Dayton has described the approach he and others developed at Bellcore as a 'whitewater' approach which encourages very rapid iteration of analysis, design and testing.

These kinds of approaches acknowledge that what is accessed (and how) on a screen is not readily separable from deep functionality. However they do not explicitly address the issue raised by Grudin: the terms 'user' and 'user interface', obscure the complexity and variability of the work different 'users' undertake and the environment within the work is carried out. Further, the screen and how it is manipulated is a product of the technical infrastructure which supports the presentation layer. In large organisations, this infrastructure consists of mixed resources laid down at different times for different purposes. Landscape gardening has been proposed by Mike Hales and others as a metaphor which may be a helpful way to conceptualize the tasks and processes needed to achieve durable improvements in work practices and the systems supporting the work, and I would like to explore this further.

23

Who Needs Usability Metrics?

Nigel Bevan and Ian Curson

National Physical Laboratory, Usability Services
Teddington, Middlesex, TW11 0LW, UK
Nigel.Bevan@npl.co.uk

ABSTRACT There is a great deal of debate about the relative value of usability evaluation techniques which produce metrics, versus techniques aimed at rapid problem diagnosis and feedback. Are metrics only of value to researchers, or do they provide real business benefits? Individual opinion tends to be polarised, and to generate champions for either concentrating on measuring usability, or on improving the product through identifying usability defects. The panel will discuss the following issues. When, if ever, is it useful to obtain metrics? Are metrics useful in a business context? What metrics are most useful? Are there inherent dangers in presenting metrics to a statistics-naive audience?

KEYWORDS usability, metrics, measures, evaluation, cost-effectiveness

"...when you can measure what you are speaking about, and express it in numbers, you know something about it; but when you cannot express it in numbers, your knowledge is of a meagre and unsatisfactory kind." (Lord Kelvin, addressing the Institute of Civil Engineers in 1883)

How can you tell whether a system is usable unless you have some way of measuring it? Without measurement, usability remains a matter of opinion. Usability metrics would allow usability to be assessed along with other software metrics. Numerical goals for usability could form part of the product specification and be tracked in a quality system.

But do we know how to measure usability? Do we even know what usability is? (Bevan et al 1991, Bevan 1995). Incomplete or incorrect measures of usability give a false sense of confidence.

One well established approach to usability measurement is the MUSiC method (Bevan and Mac'eod 1994) based on ISO 9241-11 (1997). To obtain these measures requires user testing in controlled conditions with 8 or more users. But is this approach an appropriate use of scarce usability resources during development, when we know that iterative evaluation with 3-5 users is more cost effective for improving usability? (Nielsen 1993).

With resource constraints there is a temptation to measure and quote usability metrics based on 3 or 4 users who may have been using a product in conditions which are far removed from the real world. The resulting figures quoted in reports sound convincing, but how many people have the expertise to judge whether they are meaningful?

Given the appalling usability of many systems in everyday usage, wouldn't we be better to concentrate all our efforts in working to remove the maximum number of usability defects before delivery?

Clare-Marie Karat

IBM TJ Watson Research Center, USA

Clare-Marie has worked for the last fifteen years in industry and government as a user interface designer and human factors engineer. She has published widely on the topic of human factors cost-benefit analysis.

Usability metrics are a key component of usability engineering in successful product development. To develop a successful product, it is critical to understand the goals of the product for the organization developing it and for the product's intended customers and target user populations. It has been my practical experience, that when the goals for a product and the associated

Human–Computer Interaction: INTERACT'97 S. Howard, J. Hammond & G. Lindgaard (editors)
Published by Chapman & Hall

metrics are defined, and the product team commits to them, success is more likely to be achieved. Product goals may address a number of areas (e.g., productivity, usability, professionalism of service delivery, security, customer satisfaction, profit). When the business decision is made to fund product development, the expected business impact of the goals is defined within the organization. A subset of the goals needs to address the usability of the system. Usability metrics to measure progress towards the usability goals may be based on quantitative and qualitative indicators, and the expected business value of achieving these goals is employed in making appropriate tradeoffs during product development. All of the product goals must be understood in terms of their relative importance and the time, money, and resource required to achieve them. It is the common language in which the multidisciplinary product team and senior management in an organization can communicate from the time of product concept to its release. As the product nears release. the financial business value of customer and end-user product goals is the common language in which marketing can communicate the benefits of the product to those who will purchase and use it.

The cost-benefit analysis of product goals and the amount of effort necessary to achieve them in development can be based on subjective judgement or on qualitative and quantitative data that can be shared and discussed amongst the team members and decision makers. For example, consider a situation where the business value of a product to customers (and its competitive advantage in the marketplace) is to be a productivity enhancement to customers' business workflows in meeting their clients requests, and a means of improving end user satisfaction with their work environments. How is the product team to achieve these goals during the development process without the definition of usability goals to address these business goals, the use of usability metrics to measure progress towards the goals, and the use of cost-benefit data based on these measures to make tradeoffs in time, money and resource for competing goals? I will present examples from development situations where usability goals and metrics were employed and situations where they were not part of the development process.

Ian Curson

National Physical laboratory, UK

Ian is an experienced usability consultant with a background in programming and systems design. He provides regular training courses in the MUSiC Performance Measurement Method

The goal for commercial systems developers is to meet an agreed specification. If usability targets are not included in that specification, then usability is nothing more than an optional extra - a bonus feature to be considered only in the unlikely event that development progresses ahead of schedule. This should be no great surprise: the specification forms part of the contract and dictates the criteria for success. For usability to be considered, it must be explicitly stated in those criteria. Statements like "usability must be considered" are not good enough, because usability can be considered without doing anything about it. So we need clear goals against which we can compare the system.

For me, the issue is not whether we need metrics - of course we do. Rather, it is to ensure that metrics are meaningful to developers and customers alike, and are quick and inexpensive to apply. Metrics must be meaningful to enable customers to specify reasonable targets, and to enable developers to work towards them. They must be quick and easy to apply because the system should be assessed at key stages throughout development, and not just as part of acceptance testing.

Metrics must also accurately reflect the goals of the system in use, so they must be obtained from a controlled study of real world use. This is best achieved by setting realistic goals for representative users in an appropriate environment and assessing the outcome against customer-supplied quality criteria. Such a scientific yet pragmatic approach often quells the scepticism of developers, who may be expecting what is to them an inconsequential and incomprehensible stream of psychobabble. The results are perceived as useful, and the evaluation method is straightforward enough to be applied by developer and customer alike.

Metrics are essential - but only if they are the right metrics.

Jon Mysel

The Hiser Group, Australia

Jon is a Principal Consultant with The Hiser Group, Jon brings with him 10 years of experience in the specification, design and evaluation of computer system user interfaces.

Usability metrics play a vital role in convincing a potential client of the benefits of usability and user centred design methods. Metrics can present a persuasive argument. For example, some work we recently did for an insurance company on the evaluation of an existing application led to a two thirds reduction in help desk calls. When attempting to secure funding for usability activities, the ability to show benefits which result in real cost savings go a long way in convincing organisations to invest in usability activities.

However, once the design has begun, the issue is not so much *measurement*, but rather *identification*. The focus of our analysis, design and evaluation activities is to identify potential usability issues and develop appropriate recommendations to resolve them. If one user has difficulty using a part of an application, we need to understand why. It is not necessary to wait for a *statistically significant* number of users to have a problem in order to obtain valuable design insights.

It is not whether you are for or against usability metrics, but when they are helpful. Metrics can illustrate real business benefits. Detailed statistics relating to usability testing is rarely valuable. Statistics tied to real business goals is. Measurement can demonstrate when the usability techniques have delivered real value. By tracking the improvements in real numbers such as reduced help desk calls, greater productivity, increased sales. In other instances it is more important to identify issues than it is to measure them. If you are trying to develop successful designs, you need to understand what the issues are and when users are having difficulty. By identifying these issues early in the design process, you can quickly, and effectively resolve them.

Jurek Kirakowski

Human Factors Research Group, Ireland

Jurek is Director of the Human Factors Research Group at University College, Cork, and originator of psychometric questionnaires, including SUMI, for assessing perceived usability.

Many 'metrics' and 'measures' of software quality, complexity, as well as of process and organisational characteristics have been proposed. By and large, most of these metrics and measures fail the two principal requirements that they should be reliable and valid.

A key question in the production of metrics is the kind of activity that is carried out in order to generate them:

Testing with end users This is the only way of finding out how end users will react to the software when it is released, and may reveal problems with the software that cannot be detected by inspections or appeal to the use of standards. But you have to deal with people in order to derive the metrics, which is often difficult for a technology-orientated company to take on board, and you have to understand a lot about the software in relation to its intended context of use in order to be able to test it in realistic conditions.

Testing with expert assessors These are often consultants, part of whose professional expertise is fitting in with the goals and the work practices of the employing organisation. The extent of an expert's knowledge base usually enables them to summarise comparative judgements about the software in metric-like data which is easily assimilated by management. But expert assessors are usually expensive, often committed to a particular approach or philosophy, and usually offer no index of how reliable their quantitative assessments are.

Testing against a theoretical model This kind of testing is usually supplied as a software suite which fits in with the testing practices of most organisations (ie validating against known good and bad input cases) and therefore fits in well with the work practices of most organisations developing software. But by definition such approaches are theory-driven, most tools to support such evaluations are time-consuming, and the output metrics may be difficult to relate to actual user experience with the software.

The biggest problem with most proposed metrics is that there are no standards regarding what one should expect a 'good' software product to score on the metric: no real baseline data.

Metrics emerging from the 'softest' kinds of activities (testing with end users) may hold the brightest ray of hope for the future. Such metrics can be validated and have their reliability assessed using psychometric models established by psychologists in a work effort that spans most of the 20th century.

REFERENCES

Bevan N (1995) Usability is quality of use. In: Anzai & Ogawa (eds) Proc. 6th International Conf. on Human Computer Interaction, July 1995. Elsevier.

Bevan N, Kirakowski J and Maissel J (1991) What is usability? In: Bullinger HJ (1991) Proc. 4th International Conf. on HCI, Stuttgart. Elsevier.

Bevan N, Macleod M (1994) Usability measurement in context. Behaviour and Information Technology, 13, 132-145.

ISO (1997) ISO DIS 9241-11 Guidance on Usability.

Nielsen J (1993) Usability Engineering. Academic Press.

24

Interacting with Haggis: Implementing Agent Based Specifications in a Functional Style

Meurig Sage and Chris Johnson

GIST,
Department of Computer Science,
University of Glasgow, Glasgow, United Kingdom, G12 8QQ.
{meurig, johnson}@dcs.gla.ac.uk

ABSTRACT Formal specifications, of interactive systems, provide a precise and concise means of representing and reasoning about interactive systems. Executing these specifications allows designers to conduct usability testing. This, in turn, provides the feedback necessary for an iterative approach to interface design. We argue that new developments in concurrent functional languages, make them ideally suited as tools for executing specifications. To demonstrate this, we make use of Haggis, a concurrent functional graphical toolkit. We describe the development of a highly interactive game, from specification to execution, using this system. This application is appropriate as it demonstrates the real-time interaction that previous approaches to the prototyping of formal specifications could not support.

KEYWORDS formal methods, executable specifications, prototyping, functional programming.

1. INTRODUCTION

Formal specification techniques allow designers to satisfy themselves that systems are functionally correct. When applied to interactive systems, they can be used to analyse interaction problems (Shum et al, 1996). A number of different formalisms have been used for this purpose, including temporal logics (Johnson and Harrison, 1992), state-based CSP (Abowd, 1990), and LOTOS (Paterno, 1993). Specifications, based around multiagent models, which treat a system as a group of interactors or "communicating interactive processes", have received a great deal of attention (Abowd, 1992; Duke et al, 1994). However, techniques for executing these specifications, to allow proper user testing of the interfaces, are lacking (Harrison and Duke, 1995)

1.1 Why executable specifications?

It has been claimed that making specification languages executable can restrict their expressiveness (Hayes and Jones, 1989). However, (Fuchs, 1992) has shown that this is not necessarily true. (Alexander, 1987) has shown that executable specifications allow rapid prototyping, and therefore iterative development. This enables designers to fully experiment with different ideas, to ensure systems really meet their users' needs. For instance, partial implementations may be evaluated within a user's working environment.

1.2 Functional programming

In this paper, we argue that Alexander's work, should be brought up to date with new developments in functional programming. We make use of Haggis (Finne and Peyton Jones, 1995b), a Graphical User Interface

Human–Computer Interaction: INTERACT'97 S. Howard, J. Hammond & G. Lindgaard (editors)
Published by Chapman & Hall

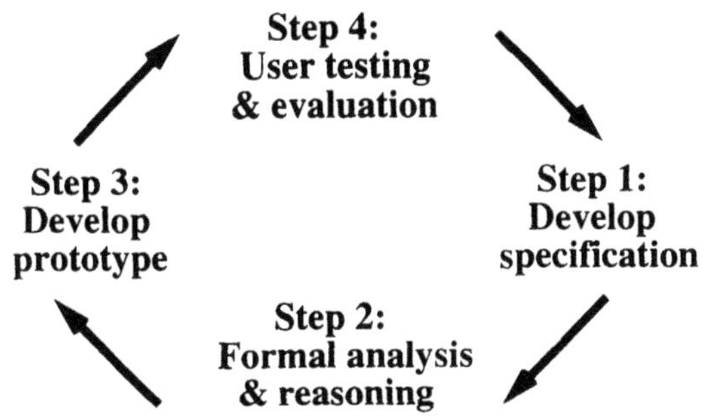

Figure 1: Iterative Development of Interactive Systems

development environment, for the lazy functional language Haskell (Peterson et al, 1996). To bridge the specification-execution gap, it provides a compositional, concurrent programming language. This makes it easy to transform a high level specification into Haggis code, and so to develop a prototype. This supports user testing and evaluation.

To show how this can be done, we use a highly interactive game, as an example. We specify it in LOTOS (Figure 1, step 1), and convert this into Haggis code (Figure 1, step 3). This demonstrates the power of the Haggis framework: we can represent the game at almost the same level of abstraction. We, however, still need the LOTOS specification to be able to clearly understand, and therefore reason about, the concurrent interaction (Figure 1, step 2). This is important because previous studies have shown that programmers frequently have great difficulty in exploiting the full potential of concurrent programming languages (Hoc et al, 1990). The example also serves to show that Haggis is capable of dealing with the kind of highly interactive systems that declarative languages are usually bad at.

2. FUNCTIONAL PROGRAMMING & EXECUTABLE SPECS

This paper uses 'leading edge' techniques from functional programming and formal specifications, to bring Heather Alexander's work into the 1990s.

This earlier work used eventCSP, a subset of the concurrent specification language CSP, to specify human-computer dialogues. For instance, we could specify part of an ATM (Alexander, 1990) - which accepts a card, and either ejects it, if it is invalid, or otherwise continues - as follows:

```
atm = (put-in-card ->
         (read-card -> ATM1
       [] cant-read -> eject-card ->
          take-card -> ATM))
```

Alexander argued that it is easy to understand, and reason about human-computer interaction using such a notation. Possible sequences could be built using the prefix (->) operator. Different paths of interaction could be described with the choice ([ ]) operator.

Alexander's approach was based around the specification of events, which had pre and post-conditions. These were defined using "me too". The me too system was used for executing VDM (Vienna Development Model) specifications, and was based within Lisp (Alexander and Jones, 1990). In common with her approach, we use a functional language as an execution tool. However, we exploit a number of developments in functional languages that make executing specifications more practical.

3. FUNCTIONAL PROGRAMMING & SPECIFICATION IN THE 1990s

3.1 Imperative Functional Programming

Though functional languages have been shown to be useful, they have had serious problems. One of the major difficulties has been supporting human-computer interaction. Older approaches were based around **stream based I/O**, which produce unnatural and confusing code. For instance, a simple program that copies it's standard input to its standard output (Gordon and Hammond, 1995), would be:

```
main ~(Str input: ~(Success : _)) =
  [ ReadChan stdin,
    AppendChan stdout input
  ]
```

The transfer of input from `ReadChan` to `AppendChan` is unclear, and counterintuitive.

Newer approaches based around **monadic I/O** allow a more imperative style of programming, that is familiar to most programmers (Gordon and Hammond, 1995; Peyton Jones and Wadler, 1993). The same program, with monadic I/O, is shown below.

```
main = do
         ch <- getChar
         putChar ch
         main
```

The sequencing of actions is clearer here. We can see that `putChar` uses the value (`ch`) returned by `getChar`.

3.2 Concurrency

Newer approaches to interactive system specification, make better use of concurrency than Alexander's work in the late 1980's. The interactor model, developed under the Amodeus project, treats a system as a number of interactors, each with a state, and the ability to communicate with users, other interactors and the underlying application. This allows for more modular and readable specifications. Systems can be built by relating tasks to interactors and so encouraging user centred design. For example, the York interactor model exploits various logics and the specification language Z. It is concerned with states, and displays and the relationships between the two (Duke et al, 1994). In contrast, the CNUCE interactor model uses LOTOS to specify interactors. It is more event based (Duke et al, 1994), making for a clearer dialogue structure.

A limitation with many of the previous approaches to interface specifications, is that they have not attempted to exploit concurrency in a specification, using a concurrent programming language. In contrast, this paper describes how concurrent specifications can be executed using concurrent functional languages. In particular, we use **Concurrent Haskell** (Peyton Jones et al, 1996), which provides for lightweight processes, and makes use of monadic IO. New child processes can be created with the `forkIO` function. Communication occurs in an asynchronous manner, through shared variables (`MVars`), that operate like semaphores. Unlike Alexander, we are able to turn our concurrent specification into concurrent code. We argue that this makes executing concurrent specifications easier.

To make the transformation from specification to execution simple, we have extended this underlying asynchronous communication, with a library of LOTOS like operators. These give programmers access to full synchronous communication through a `parallel` operator. We have also included separate asynchronous communication along channels. This provides, arguably a more elegant way, and certainly a more efficient way, of implementing the asynchronous communication, which is only simulated in LOTOS. Asynchronous and synchronous communication can be combined freely within this system (Sage and Johnson, 1997).

3.3 Virtual I/O device

Haggis, the graphical framework, is built on top of Concurrent Haskell. This approach offers a number of additional benefits for user interface design (Finne and Peyton Jones, 1995b). A common problem with many graphical user interface systems is the central role of an event loop. This style has well known problems (Myers, 1991). Instead Haggis treats the user interface as a virtual device, allowing the application to maintain control. The concurrent features of Haggis enable several virtual I/O devices to operate simultaneously. For instance, one process could wait for keyboard input, blocking if there wasn't any, while others did other necessary work.

3.4 Declarative structured graphics

A further problem for the development of graphical user interfaces is that conventional languages tend to be highly imperative. By this we mean that the resulting image might be completely ruined if one instruction were omitted or placed out of sequence. In contrast, all graphical output is described declaratively using a `Picture` type (Finne and Peyton Jones, 1995a). For instance, we could describe the simple picture in Figure 2 as follows:

```
picture = Overlay
            (ellipse (40,20))
            (ellipse (20,40))
```

The image in Figure 2 would remain the same irrespective of which ellipse was drawn first. Haggis takes care of converting pictures into calls to the window system drawing interface, with the `Glyph` output abstraction. This

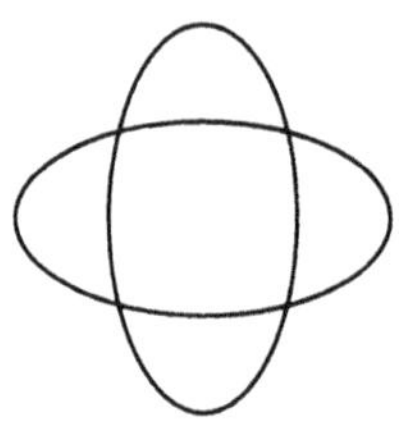

Figure 2: A simple Picture

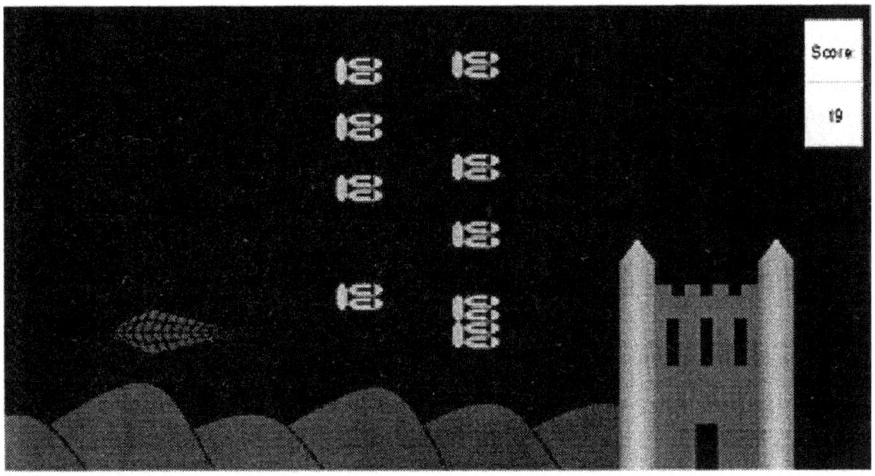

Figure 3: Game Display

declarative approach makes it easy to build, and manipulate, complicated images.

3.5 User interface, application separation

To separate the interface from its application, a user interface component is represented by two different parts. For instance, the glyph output abstraction returns a `Glyph` handle which the application can use, for instance, to update the picture displayed. It also returns a `DisplayHandle`, which is a reference to the interactive graphical surface.

```
glyph :: Picture
      -> Component
          (Glyph,
           DisplayHandle)
```

This separation helps programmers to develop more modular systems.

3.6 Compositional structure

Haggis provides layout combinators and encapsulating functions, that can combine the `Display Handles` mentioned above. This enables more complicated components to be built from simpler ones. For instance, an input device controller can be composed with a `Glyph` picture displayer, to produce an interactive widget.

```
widget =
  (gl,dh) <- glyph picture
  (kb,dh) <- catchKeyboardEv dh
```

The resulting widget would receive input and pass it on via the `kb` handle. It's image would be updatable via the `gl` handle.

4. THE EXAMPLE

In the past, these functional programming developments have been used to build very simple systems (Finne and Peyton Jones, 1995b). As a more complex example, we describe the development of a highly interactive, real-time user interface. It is a space ship game, as seen in Figure 3. Input commands occur via the keyboard. There are a number of enemy ships that move across the screen in waves. These will destroy the player's ship if they come into contact with it. The ship must also avoid hitting the hills at the bottom of the screen and the enemy base. The player's ship moves slowly forward until the enemy base becomes visible. The objective is to make it to as far as the enemy base and then shoot the base a given number of times. The current score will always be displayed on the screen. Though the graphics are fairly simple, the example does require real-time animation. The example also provides a highly concurrent system, with a number of different agents: lasers, enemies... The specification therefore concentrates on this concurrency.

5. LOTOS SPECIFICATION

In common with the CNUCE approach to interactors (Paterno, 1993), we specify our system in LOTOS. The game can be modelled as 4 different processes:

- a process for the lasers (`HandleLasers`);
- a process for enemy ships (`HandleEnemies`);
- an input process (`HandleInput`);
- a screen update process (`ScreenUpdate`).

These can then be synchronised over a number of events to allow the necessary communication. The `ScreenUpdate` process, discovers input events through the `Buffer` process.

```
process Game :=
   (ScreenUpdate
       ||
    HandleInput
       ||
    Buffer)
       ||
   (HandleEnemies
       ||
    HandleLasers)
endproc
```

In LOTOS, `a || b` means run process `a` in parallel with process `b`, synchronising over any common events. As an example of a process specification, consider the `HandleInput` process. It will continue to receive input events, and place them in the buffer until the `closeDown` event occurs. It interprets the input events before passing them on. For instance, it might change a press of the `"q"` key into the data `MoveUp`.

```
process HandleInput
             [sendChannel,closeDown,
              getKeyboardEv]
             (buffer:Buffer,
              kb:Keyboard) :=
  closeDown
  []
  getKeyboardEv!kb?inp:KeyboardEv;
  [valid inp] ->
    sendChannel!buffer!(interpret inp);
    HandleInput [sendChannel,closeDown,
                 getKeyboardEv]
                (buffer,kb)
  [not (valid inp)] ->
    HandleInput [sendChannel,closeDown,
                 getKeyboardEv]
                (buffer,kb)
endproc
```

In common with the interactor approach, we treat the system as a number of communicating interacting objects. We achieve a rendering of the state through presentation layer events, enacted by the `ScreenUpdate` process. Though we do not strictly adhere to the interactor model, we do model user level agents (`ScreenUpdate` and `HandleInput`) communicating with more application oriented agents (`HandleLasers` and `HandleEnemies`).

In common with Alexander (Alexander and Jones, 1990), we define the data manipulated by the processes in a functional style. This allows a more easily programmable notion of state, as data and operations can be packaged up, and combined with processes, in a modular style. This approach makes it easy to specify the behaviour of the lasers, enemies, ship and background. We therefore abandon the ACT ONE algebraic data specification language, normally used with LOTOS. ACT ONE lacks modularity and has been shown to be difficult to use and to implement. The new LOTOS standard, E-LOTOS, itself replaces ACT ONE with a functional approach because of these problems (Jeffrey and Leduc, 1996). Our approach overcomes some of the problems with a LOTOS style of specification. We now have both a behaviour (defined as a set of LOTOS processes) and internal state (manipulated by, and packaged up inside, each process), but with the behaviour still clearly visible on top.

Our approach gives us a clear, high level specification which designers may use to reason about a potential implementation. It is also possible to prove properties about the behaviour of the LOTOS specification using tools such as LITE (Eijk, 1991). This tool supports the automatic analysis and verification of concurrent specifications. Design errors may therefore be found prior to implementation, using this approach.

6. CONVERSION TO HAGGIS

We can convert LOTOS specifications into Haggis code as follows:

- events correspond to Haggis I/O actions (section 3.1); these IO actions may need to be defined. They can be input or output actions (presentation layer), usually predefined in Haggis, using the virtual I/O device concept, and structured graphics primitives (sections 3.3, 3.4.) They can also be communication actions, or can alter the state of the system (application layer);
- synchronous LOTOS communication can be implemented using our extended concurrency library (Sage and Johnson, 1997);
- data manipulation operations need not be altered, as they are already in a functional, executable form.

We can, for instance, implement the `HandleInput` process as:

```
handleInput :: Channel InputEvent
            -- an asynchronous channel
            -- (which is the buffer)

            -> Keyboard
            -- an asynchronous channel
            -- source of
            -- keyboard Events

            -> IO ()

handleInput buffer kb =
 do
   gate "closeDown"
   'choose'
   (inp <- getKeyboardEv kb
    if valid inp then
      sendChannel buffer (interpret inp)
      handleInput buffer kb
    else
      handleInput buffer kb)
```

The resulting code looks very similar to the earlier LOTOS specification. The `gate` action, provided by the LOTOS library, performs synchronisation on the given `"closeDown"` gate. The `Buffer` in the LOTOS specification, has become an asynchronous channel. The input is received via the asynchronous `kb` channel, using the predefined `getKeyboardEv` action.

We have now described what the system does. As a final step, we will show how to describe what the system looks like, and so build the full screen shown in Figure 3. Again, we are concerned with supporting full graphical interaction as easily as possible.

We build the screen with four types of operation. The `mkDC` operation creates a Display Context `dc`, which contains information about style values and the window that will be created. The `label` operation creates a label displaying the given string, which may be updated (using the `lbl` handle). The `glyph` operation creates a simple output area containing the specificed picture. The `catchKeyboardEv` operation makes the glyph interactive and able to receive keyboard events (via the `kb` channel). Finally the `realiseDH` operation renders the components on to a window using the `vbox` combinator to place Display Handles above one another, and using `hbox` to place Display Handles next to one other.

```
screen
 = do
    dc <- mkDC []
    (_,ldh) <- label "Score:" dc
    (lbl,ldh2) <- label "0" dc
    (gl,screendh) <- glyph screenImage dc
    (kb,sdh) <- catchKeyboardEv screendh
    realiseDH dc (hbox [sdh,vbox[ldh,ldh2]]
```

The resulting system can be run, and tested on users. At this stage, problems with the system can be discovered and used to reshape the initial specification. For example, early prototypes of the system did not provide on screen prompts about the current score. This was clearly necessary if users were to keep track of their interaction with the game.

7. CONCLUSIONS AND FURTHER WORK

Through our short example, we have shown that by using functional languages as an implementation tool, it is easy to convert from high-level specifications of concurrent user interfaces, into executable code. This work builds upon Alexander's work, but uses newer functional programming techniques, in particular concurrency and monadic I/O. This concurrency provides a number of benefits. For the programmer, it supports the development of highly modular, agent based systems. For the user, it supports highly interactive, real-time presentation techniques. The resulting interfaces can be subjected to rigorous user testing. It is important to emphasise, however, that high level specifications are still necessary. They make clear the behaviour of concurrent systems, and allow designers to reason about them. We could also use the specification to target areas for user testing.

We have shown, through our example, that Haggis is capable of implementing highly interactive, real-time interfaces, something most prototyping tools are incapable of. However, we need to try building systems with more complicated interaction, and therefore more interaction objects. We need to fully automate the translation between specification and executable Haggis code. This should be combined with some automatically generated graphical representation of the specification, which would make it easier for the designer to understand the interaction.

8. ACKNOWLEDGEMENTS

Thanks go to Simon Peyton Jones, and Sigbjorn Finne for providing Haggis for us to work with. Thanks also to Phil Gray and other members of the Glasgow Interactive Systems Group (GIST). This work was supported by UK EPSRC Grant No GR/K69148.

REFERENCES

Gregory D. Abowd (1990), Agents: Communicating Interactive Processes. In *Human Computer Interaction - INTERACT '90*, D. Diaper et al Eds. Elsevier Science Publishers, North-Holland, pp.143-148.

Heather Alexander (1987), Executable specifications as an aid to dialogue design. In *Human-Computer Interaction - INTERACT '87*, H. J. Bullinger and B. Shackel Eds. Elsevier Science Publishers, North-Holland, pp.739-744.

Heather Alexander (1990), Structuring dialogues using CSP,. In *Formal methods in Human computer interaction*, MD Harrison and H Thimbleby Eds, Cambridge University Press, Cambridge, pp.273-295.

Heather Alexander, Val Jones (1990), *Software design and prototyping using me too*, Prentice Hall.

David Duke, Giorgio Faconti, Michael Harrison, Fabio Paterno (1994), Unifying Views of Interactors. Technical Report WP18, ESPRIT BRA 7040 Amodeus-2, October 1994.

P.van Eijk (1991), The Lotosphere Integrated Tool Environment LITE. In *Proceedings 4th International Conference on Formal Description Techniques*, Sydney, November 1991, North-Holland, pp.473-476.

Sigbjorn Finne, Simon Peyton Jones (1995a), Pictures: A simple structured graphics model. In *Glasgow Functional Programming Workshop*, Ullapool, July 1995.

Sigbjorn Finne, Simon Peyton Jones (1995b), Composing Haggis. In *Proceedings of the fifth Eurographics workshop on Programming Paradigms in Graphics*, Maastricht, Sept 2-3 1995.

N.E. Fuchs (1992), Specifications are (preferably) executable. In *Software Engineering Journal*, September 1992, 7, (5), pp. 323-334

Andrew D. Gordon and Kevin Hammond (1995), Monadic I/O in Haskell 1.3. In Paul Hudak, editor, *Proceedings of the Haskell Workshop*, pp 50-69. La Jolla, California, June 25 1995.

M.D. Harrison and D.J. Duke (1995), The Specification of User Requirements in Interactive Systems. Technical Report WP60, ESPRIT BRA 7040 Amodeus-2, September 1995.

I.J. Hayes and C.B. Jones (1989), Specifications are not (necessarily) executable. In *Software Engineering Journal*, 1989, 4, (6), pp.330-338

J.M. Hoc, T.R.G. Green, R. Samurcay and D.J. Gilmore (eds) (1990), *Psychology of Programming*, Computers and People Series, Academic Press Ltd.

A. Jeffrey and G.Leduc (1996), E-LOTOS core language. Output of the Kansas City meeting, version 1996/09/20, (ISO-IEC/JTC1/SC21/WG7).

C.W. Johnson and M.D. Harrison (1992), Using temporal logic to support the specification of interactive control systems. In *International Journal of Man-Machine Studies*, 37, pp.357-385.

Brad A. Myers (1991) Separating application code from toolkits: Eliminating the spaghetti of callbacks. In *Proceedings of the ACM SIGCHI'91 Conference on User Interface Software Technology*. ACM Press. November 11-13 1991.

Fabio Paterno (1993), A methodology to design interactive systems based on Interactors. Technical Report WP7, ESPRIT BRA 7040 Amodeus-2. February 1993.

John Peterson et al (1996), Haskell 1.3: A non-strict, purely functional language. Technical Report YALEU/DCS/RR-1106: Department of Computing Science. Yale University. May 1996.

Simon Peyton Jones and Philip Wadler (1993). Imperative functional programming. In *ACM Conference on the Principles of Programming Languages*, pp 71-84. ACM Press, January 1993.

Simon Peyton Jones, Andrew Gordon, and Sigbjorn Finne (1996), Concurrent Haskell. In *ACM Symposium on the Principles of Programming Languages*, St. Petersburg Beach, Florida, January 1996.

Meurig Sage, Chris Johnson (1997), Executing LOTOS with Haggis. Technical Report, Department of Computing Science, University of Glasgow (in press).

Simon Buckingham Shum, Ann Blandford, David Duke, Jason Good, Jon May, Fabio Paterno, and Richard Young (1996), Multidisciplinary Modelling for User-Centred System Design: An Airtraffic Control Case Study. In *People and Computers XI: Proceedings of HCI '96*.

25

Abstract modelling of interactive systems

D. Goldson

Department of Computer Science,
Massey University,
New Zealand.
D.Goldson@massey.ac.nz

ABSTRACT One approach to modelling interactive systems uses abstract models to define system classes. A system can then be evaluated with respect to a model that captures some generic user interface criteria. This paper describes a case study in applying this methodology to the analysis of a text editor. Criteria of predictability, observability and reachability are postulated for the editor. The paper concludes that abstract modelling is a useful design methodology that can be effectively integrated with a methodology of prototyping.

KEYWORDS Prototyping, formal methods, interaction models, software engineering.

1. INTRODUCTION

One approach to modelling interactive systems uses abstract models to define classes of systems. A particular system can then be evaluated with respect to properties of a model thought of as generic interface design principles or as normative interface criteria. From a system development perspective, this methodology offers a framework for design and decision support in which properties of an interaction model are viewed as system requirements. From a completed system perspective, it can also be used as a framework for evaluation in which model properties are viewed as evaluation criteria.

A number of abstract interaction models are proposed by (Dix, 1991), including the PIE model used in this paper. Dix identifies three kinds of property relevant to PIE systems. These are

- *predictability*:what can you predict from what you see or can potentially see?
- *observability*: what can you potentially see?
- *reachability*: what can you reach from where you are?

These suggest themselves as being, in some general sense, desirable. Predictability and observability can be interpreted as asserting a user's mastery of a system (the user always knows what will appear next, they always know what the result will be, and so on) and, in a similar way, reachability can be interpreted as expressing general usability criteria (the user will never get stuck, will always be able to get back to a certain point, and so on). The difficulty of design, of course, lies in finding the right properties for the system of interest. These principles can be used to express necessary conditions for usability that are "able to stop interfaces being fundamentally unusable, but not ensure that they *are* usable" (Dix p14). No methodology can guarantee that.

The paper describes a case study in interface analysis. The motivation for this work is pragmatic. Given the potential benefits of using abstract models, (Dix, 1991) and (Runciman, 1990), it is important to test them on realistic problems since this is the only way that their potential can be assessed. The editor, while itself simple, is a realistic analysis task rather than a merely illustrative one. The main positive outcome of the case study is the support it lends to using modelling and prototyping as an integrated methodology.

Human–Computer Interaction: INTERACT'97 S. Howard, J. Hammond & G. Lindgaard (editors)
Published by Chapman & Hall

Subsequent sections describe the case study. The focus is on HCI design principles concerned with aspects of system *behaviour* as it effects the user. The evaluation of the interface in isolation is of no interest. §2 briefly reviews Dix's PIE and red-PIE models. The editor (Goldson, 1996) is prototyped in the functional programming language Haskell (Jones, 1996) and its main features are described in §3. §4 modifies the editor to fit these models and §5 then uses them to analyse the prototype. §6, the final section, draws some conclusions.

2. *P*ROGRAM *I*NTERPRETATION *E*FFECT MODELS

A PIE model is given by an *i*nterpretation function which maps *p*rograms (command sequences) onto *e*ffects. This is about as general as a model can get: input, process, output. An instance of the model is given by specifying the type of commands over which programs are defined, the type of their effects and the interpretation function that maps programs to effects.

An alternative definition uses a `doit` function defined over system states and commands. If the effect space is identified with the state space, with a distinguished intitial state `s0`, a function `pie` from programs to effect histories is defined so that

```
pie doit s0 [c1,c2,..]          =
[s0, doit s0 c1, doit (doit s0 c1) c2,..]

pie :: (e -> c -> e) -> e -> [c] -> [e]
pie = scanl
```

The interpretation function of this PIE is just some function of its effect history.

The red-PIE model adds extra structure by distinguishing the *r*esult and *d*isplay as two components of the effect. Following (Runciman, 1990) a red-PIE can be modelled as a function `red` which takes PIE `pi`, display `dp` and result `rt` functions and returns a pair consisting of the display history and the final result of the interaction.

```
red :: ([c] -> [e]) -> ([e] -> d)
          -> ([e] -> r) -> [c] -> (d,r)
red pi dp rt = (\es -> (dp es, rt es)) . pi
```

A PIE model of a text editor defined by a `doit` function is described in (Dix p161). The effect space is the cartesian product of edited objects and displays. Commands are applied to objects or displays using a pair of state transition functions $\texttt{doit}_{\texttt{object}}$ and $\texttt{doit}_{\texttt{display}}$ and an adjustment function `adjust` is used to maintain any invariants of the object-display relationship. This is basically the same as the model used by (Sufrin, 1982) and prototyped in (Goldson, 1996), except that changes to the display are there modelled as side effects of changes to the edited object so that all commands are applied to the edited object and no commands are directly applied to the display itself. There is no role for $\texttt{doit}_{\texttt{display}}$. §4 will apply this model to the editor but to follow the details it is first necessary to describe the editor's main features.

3. A PROTOTYPE TEXT EDITOR

A full specification of the prototype is given in (Goldson). This section summarises the main features. The edited and display objects are modelled as objects of type `EDSTATE` and `DPSTATE` and an editor is got by combining these components.

```
type EDITOR = (EDSTATE,DPSTATE)
```

3.1 Documents

The edited document is a component of the inner state. It is modelled as a pair of strings. For example, the document with text `"Beautiful Soup"` and the cursor to the left of `'S'` is

```
(" lufituaeB","Soup")
```

Storing the text on the left in reverse order simplifies the definition of commands. These are modelled as state to state transformations on `DOC`s.

```
type DOC = ([Char],[Char])
type DCOMMAND = DOC -> DOC
```

3.2 Editor states

The full inner state supports a modal command interface in which, for some commands, the user is required to switch mode before entering the command.

```
data EDMODE     = Edit | Command | Exit
type EDSTATE    = (DOC,DOC,EDMODE)
```

In `Edit` mode edit commands effect the document (the first component). In `Command` mode they effect a command buffer (the second component). Commands are now modelled as state to state transformations on `EDSTATE`s.

```
type ECOMMAND  = EDSTATE -> EDSTATE
```

There are only two. `basic` selects the right text for editing based on the mode.

```
basic :: DCOMMAND -> ECOMMAND
```

```
basic f (d,c,m) = case m of
                    Edit    -> (f d,c,m)
                    Command -> (d,f c,m)
```

edswitch defines the modal commands. switch switches mode. mcommand interprets the contents of the command buffer (ctext eds) as an ECOMMAND and applies it to the current state.

```
edswitch, switch, mcommand :: ECOMMAND

edswitch = mcommand . switch

switch (d,c,m) =
   case m of
      Edit    -> (d,emptydoc,Command)
      Command -> (d,c,Edit)

mcommand eds =
   (case ctext eds of
     "t"       -> basic lmdoc
     "b"       -> basic rmdoc
     "q"       -> exit
     otherwise -> basic docid) eds
```

The mode also effects the way the state is displayed. In Edit mode only the document is displayed. In Command mode both document and command text are displayed. This relationship is modelled by edisplayed.

```
edisplayed   :: EDSTATE  -> DISP
```

To give an example, the editor state

```
((" lufituaeB",
"Soup, so rich and green,\nWaiting in a hot
tureen!"), ("",""),Edit)
```

has an unbounded display with document cursor at (1,10)

```
(["Beautiful Soup, so rich and green,",
  "Waiting in a hot tureen!"], (1,10))
```

3.3 Displays

DISP is the type of an intermediate display defined by its contents and cursor. It represents an abstract view of the edited object through an 'elastic' or unbounded display.

```
type DISP     = (CONTENTS,CURSOR)
type CURSOR   = (Int,Int)
type LINE     = [Char]
type CONTENTS = [LINE]
```

The actual display is more complicated, being of fixed size with an origin onto the unbounded display. window defines its contents, given its size and origin and the contents of the unbounded display.

```
type ORIGIN = (Int,Int)

type DPSIZE = (Int,Int)

window :: ORIGIN -> DPSIZE ->
                    CONTENTS -> CONTENTS
```

The display cursor is got by projecting the document cursor onto the display, counting from the origin of the display rather than the origin of the document.

```
project :: ORIGIN -> CURSOR -> CURSOR
```

The display contents, its cursor, size and origin define the state of the display.

```
type DPSTATE  = (DISP,DPSIZE,ORIGIN)
```

To give an example, a display of size (2,40), origin at (1,8) and the unbounded display of §3.2 gives a display state with display cursor (1,2)

```
((["l Soup, so rich and green,",
   "in a hot tureen!"],
  (1,2)),(2,40),(1,8))
```

The relationship between the edited object EDSTATE and the display DPSTATE is determined by an invariant inview that keeps the document cursor in view. inview is kept invariant by a scrolling function scroll that derives a new origin for DPSTATE whenever EDSTATE is changed.

```
inview :: ORIGIN -> DPSIZE -> CURSOR
                 -> Bool
scroll :: ORIGIN -> DPSIZE -> CURSOR
                 -> ORIGIN
```

3.4 Interaction

The editor commands are shown in Table 1. To keep the prototype simple they were restricted to insertion, navigation and deletion commands. Quiting the editor is modal, top and bottom are both modal and non-modal, and the rest are non-modal. edswitch switches between the two modes.

A key event is interpreted as a character insertion command unless it is escaped by kbesc when it is interpreted as a navigation or deletion command. The function key interprets the event depending on the state of the bimodal keyboard.

```
data KBMODE     = Insert | Function

key :: KBMODE -> Char -> (KBMODE,ECOMMAND)
```

Keys	*Name*	*Description*
Any printable character or `nl`	`ins`	Insert character at the current cursor position
`kbesc` \`	`lmchar`	Move left one character
" 1	`lmword`	Move left to the beginning of a word
" 2	`lmline`	Move left to the beginning of a line
" 3	`lmdoc`	Move left to the beginning of the document
`kbesc` =	`rmchar`	Move right one character
" -	`rmword`	Move right to the beginning of a word
" 0	`rmline`	Move right to the beginning of a line
" 9	`rmdoc`	Move right to the end of the document
`kbesc` ~ or `delete`	`ldchar`	Delete left one character
`kbesc` !	`ldword`	Delete left to the beginning of a word
" @	`ldline`	Delete left to the beginning of a line
" #	`lddoc`	Delete left to the beginning of the document
`kbesc` +	`rdchar`	Delete right one character
" _	`rdword`	Delete right to the beginning of a word
")	`rdline`	Delete right to the beginning of a line
" (	`rddoc`	Delete right to the beginning of the document
`kbesc s`	`edswitch`	Switch editor mode
None	`lmdoc`	Move left to the `top` of the document
None	`rmdoc`	Move right to the bottom of the document
None	None	quit the editor
Any other key	`docid`	Do nothing

Table 1: Editor commands.

4. MODELLING THE EDITOR AS A PIE

The editor can be modelled as a simple two layer PIPE (Dix). This retains a surface view of the interaction while also taking into account that the user will interact with the editor at a deeper level than the purely surface level of the keyboard. The user *interprets* key sequences as *commands* on an *underlying* document.

The PIPE model in Figure 1 splits a system PIE `pies` into an outer PIE `piep` that maps user input at the keyboard into the commands of the inner PIE `pief`. In fact, all three are red-PIEs. The display and result of `pies` is identified with `pief` and the result of `piep` is the input to `pief`.

4.1 The functional PIE `pief`

The effect space is the editor state space. `doiteds` is the $\texttt{doit}_{\texttt{object}}$ function and defines the effect of commands on the edited object.

```
doiteds :: EDSTATE -> ECOMMAND -> EDSTATE
doiteds eds c = c eds
```

There is no $\texttt{doit}_{\texttt{display}}$ since none of the editor commands act directly on the display. There are no scroll commands for example. Of course, the display still requires adjustment to take account of changes to the edited object, so the doit function for the complete state `doitf` is defined

```
doitf :: EDITOR -> ECOMMAND -> EDITOR
doitf (eds,wns) c =
    let ceds = doiteds eds c in
        (ceds, adjust wns ceds)
```

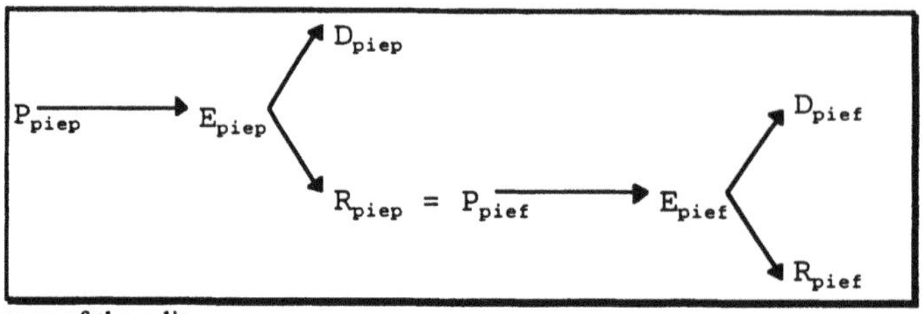

Figure 1: PIPE architecture of the editor.

```
adjust  :: DPSTATE -> EDSTATE -> DPSTATE
adjust (_,ws,o) eds =
   let (dp,dc)     = edisplayed eds
       or          = scroll o ws dc in
       ((window or ws dp,project or dc),
        ws,or)
```

The new display is got by `scrolling` to a new origin `or` on the unbounded display `dp` and then truncating this to fit the actual display at `or` and then projecting the document cursor `dc` onto this display.

The initial state is given with respect to a start up document `d`.

```
open :: RESULT -> EDITOR
ed0   = open d
```

If the quit command was non-modal the environment would signal termination to `pief` by terminating its input, and `pief` would be defined

```
pief :: [ECOMMAND] -> [EDITOR]
pief = pie doitf ed0
```

However, the quit command is modal and signals termination to the environment by changing the editor's mode to `Exit` (§3.1.2), thereby terminating output.

```
pief = takeWhile continue . pie doitf ed0
```

```
continue :: EDITOR -> Bool
continue = (/= Exit) . edmode
```

The display history and final result are projected from the effect space by a red-PIE.

```
redpief :: [ECOMMAND] -> ([DISPLAY],RESULT)
redpief = red pief displayf resultf
```

`resultf` returns the text of the edited document and forgets its cursor.

```
resultf  :: [EDITOR] -> RESULT
resultf es =
let (l,r) = eddoc (last es) in reverse l++r
```

`displayf` displays display states by inserting the cursor, filling out the contents with whitespace and framing the result.

```
displayf :: [EDITOR] -> [DISPLAY]
displayf = map (dpscreen . screen)
```

```
screen :: EDITOR -> CONTENTS
screen  = view . winst
```

```
view :: DPSTATE -> CONTENTS
view (dp,(h,w),_) =
   let ws = (h,w+1) in
   (frame ws . contents ws . dpcursor) dp
```

Here is the result of `viewing` the display state in §3.3 (`'^'` is the cursor)

```
["|-------------------------------------|",
 "|1 ^Soup, so rich and green,          |",
 "|in a hot tureen!                     |",
 "|-------------------------------------|"]
```

4.2 The surface PIE `piep`

`piep` models the keyboard interaction. The state space has type `(KBMODE,ECOMMAND)`, `p0` is the initial state before anything is typed and `doitp` defines the effect of a key on the current state.

```
p0 = (Insert,undef)
```

```
doitp :: (KBMODE,ECOMMAND) -> Char
                 -> (KBMODE,ECOMMAND)
doitp (m,_) c = key m c
```

The effect space is the `piep` state space and `piep` is defined

```
piep :: [Char] -> [(KBMODE,ECOMMAND)]
piep = tail . pie doitp p0
```

This is factored as a red-PIE with the mode and command histories giving the display and result.

```
redpiep  :: [Char] -> ([KBMODE],[ECOMMAND])
redpiep   = red piep displayp resultp
```

```
displayp :: [(KBMODE,ECOMMAND)] -> [KBMODE]
displayp  = fst . unzip
```

```
resultp  :: [(KBMODE,ECOMMAND)]->[ECOMMAND]
resultp   = snd . unzip
```

4.3 The system PIE **pies**

`pies` joins the two red-PIEs by making the result of `redpiep` the input of `redpief`.

```
pies :: [Char] -> ([DISPLAY],RESULT)
pies = redpief . resultp . redpiep
```

5. ANALYSIS OF THE EDITOR

This section shows how the editor's interface can be explored by postulating reachability, predictability and observability properties for it. Since the model is two level it is reasonable to examine each level for these characteristics. Starting with the inner level, let `if`, `rif` and `dif` define the effect, result and display of a `pief` interaction

```
if  = last . pief
dif = last . fst . redpief
rif = snd  . redpief
```

Every program `p` implicitly defines an effect `if p`, result `rif p` and display `dif p`.

5.1 Reachability

`pief` is reachable if and only if you can get from any state `p` to any state `q` using a strategy `s`.

```
∀p,q ∃s if (p++s) = if q                        (R)
```

`pief` is strong reachable if and only if reachable states are indistinguishable.

```
∀p,q,s,r (if (p++s) = if q ⇒
            if (p++s++r) = if (q++r))    (SR)
```

`pief` is both reachable and strong reachable. This is not surprising since the effect space is the entire system state. ((`SR`) is a consequence of (`R`) and (`EP`) below.) The concept of reachability is related to the concept of functional completeness of commands but it does *not* define it. Think of deleting to the end of a DOC

```
rddoc ("","Beautiful Soup") = ("","")
```

and then restoring the state with

```
[ins 'B',…,ins 'p']
```

This is no reason to leave undo out of the command set.

5.2 Predictability and observability

The easiest property to state is effect predictability or monotonicity. Two equal effects `p` and `q` are effect predictable if and only if future effects are unaffected by how `p` and `q` are reached.

```
∀p,q,r (if p = if q ⇒
              if (p++r) = if (q++r))  (EP)
```

`pief` *is* effect predictable but this is not interesting because the effect type is artificial. The user can observe the display and potentially observe the result but can not directly observe other important components of the effect, such as the display origin and the mode.

Only the display is directly observable so what can be predicted from this? Display predictability, along the lines of (`EP`), is out of the question, making equal displays imply equal documents. In fact, even mode predictability is too strong. Two displays that look the same may not have the same mode.

```
∃p,q (dif p = dif q &
       edmode (if p) ≠ edmode (if q))
```

Given the current display, we don't necessarily expect to know where we are, or what we've got, or even what mode we are in, but we do expect to be able to find these things out. Observability principles are needed to connect a display with other 'possible' displays, as well as other aspects of the effect, such as the mode and the current result. Since none of these are directly observable, strategies, such as document browsing, are needed.

An obvious strategy to reveal the mode from the behaviour of the display is to 'switch mode and see what happens'. Two displays that look the same after switching mode have the same mode.

```
∀p,q (dif (p++[edswitch]) =
       dif (q++[edswitch]) ⇒
       edmode (if p) = edmode (if q))  (MO)
```

For observing the result we are interested in all possible displays of `p`, defined by a characteristic function (`dreach p`).

$$
\begin{array}{l}
\forall \texttt{p::[ECOMMAND]}, \forall \texttt{d::DISPLAY} \\
\quad \texttt{(dreach p d} \Leftrightarrow \\
\quad \exists \texttt{s (dif (p++s) = d \& rpassive s))} \quad (\mathrm{DR}_{df})
\end{array}
$$

`d` is a possible display for `p` if and only if `d` is the display of a state that is reachable from `p` using some strategy `s`. The change to `p` must be passive and only alter 'allowable' aspects of its state. This gives a useful notion of display reachability. Two states `p` and `q` are display reachable if and only if `q`'s display is a possible display for `p`, `dreach p (dif q)`.

What is allowable may vary but the change must at least preserve the result and so `s` must at least be result passive. Changing `p`'s state to match `q`'s display does not alter `p`'s result.

```
∀p,s (rpassive s ⇔
        rif p = rif (p++s))                  (RPdf)
```

Result connectedness states that if two states yield the same result, whatever *is* observed of the one can be observed of the other. They should be display reachable.

```
∀p,q(rif p = rif q ⇒
                         dreach p (dif q))   (RC)
```

Of course, the converse is not true. Displays that can be made equal, by some strategy, do not imply equal results. This requires a stronger notion of display equivalence. Two states `p` and `q` are display equivalent if and only if they have the same displays.

```
∀p,q::[ECOMMAND],∀d::DISPLAY
  (dequiv p q ⇔
   dreach p d ⇔dreach q d)                  (DEdf)
```

Result observability states that observationally indistinguishable or display equivalent states yield the same result.

```
∀p,q (dequiv p q ⇒ rif p = rif q)       (RO)
```

In fact the equivalence follows from `(RC)` since if two states yield the same result, whatever *can* be observed of the one can be observed of the other.

```
∀p,q (rif p = rif q ⇒ dequiv p q)
```

Predicting future results based on observations requires a stronger notion of equivalence than `dequiv`. Intuitively, future results can only be predicted if both the mode and the *document* cursor can be worked out by observation. Any strategy to move from `p` to `q` must align document cursors with a resultant change to the display *only*. This is captured by a state equivalence `stequiv` that requires equality of the 'inner' state.

```
∀p,q(mequiv p q ⇔
      edmode (if p) = edmode (if q)) (MEdf)

∀p,q(docequiv p q ⇔
      eddoc (if p) = eddoc (if q))   (DEdf)

∀p,q(stequiv  p q ⇔
      mequiv p q & docequiv p q)      (SEdf)
```

We are interested in the reachability of `q` from `p`, via `s`, that makes the states internally the same without disturbing `p`'s result.

```
∀p,q,s (streach p q s ⇔
       rpassive s & stequiv (p++s) q) (PRdf)
```

Two state equivalent effects are result predictable if and only if future results are unaffected by how they are reached.

```
∀p,q,r,s (streach p q s ⇒
            rif (p++s++r) = rif (q++r)) (RP)
```

In other words, you can predict the effect on the result of a program on a state `p` if you have a strategy to work out `p`'s mode and where you are in the document.

5.3 piep and pies

Reachability at the `piep` level is about the users access to inner level commands. Any `pief` program `qf` should be available from any state `pf` of the `pief` you have reached. If you have got to `pf` using `piep` commands `pp` then there should exist `piep` commands `qp` that give you `qf`.

```
∀pf,qf::[ECOMMAND],∀pp::[Char],∃qp::[Char]
  (piep pp = pf ⇒ piep (pp++qp) = pf++qf)
```

At the `pies` level the keyboard mode is not directly observable from the `pies` display. However, it can be observed using a strategy analogous to `(MO)`: 'type a command key and see what happens'.

```
∀p,q (dis (p++['s']) = dis (q++['s']) ⇒
        dip p = dip q)                       (KO)
```

where `dis` and `dip` are the displays of `pies` and `piep`

```
dis = last . fst . pies
dip = last . fst . redpiep
```

The effect on the display of typing `'s'`

```
------------------------------------
Beautiful ^Soup, so rich and green,
Waiting in a hot tureen!


------------------------------------
```

depends on the mode of the keyboard. Either the mode of the editor is switched or the character is inserted.

```
------------------------------------
Beautiful
>
^
<
------------------------------------
------------------------------------
Beautiful s^Soup, so rich and green,
Waiting in a hot tureen!


------------------------------------
```

6. CONCLUSION

This section briefly assesses the PIE approach under the four headings of architecture, dynamics, prototyping and development.

The PIPE model makes the limitations of the prototype's architecture clear. Since all user interaction is directed at the edited object, and no component of the display is used to define it, the architecture is not suited to indicative input where the display is central to the interpretation of input. In the PIPE model commands are determined by their content rather than their position.

The ability to model system *behaviour* carries more positive benefits. This is *the* essential component of interface analysis and all three notions of reachability, predictability and observability are strongly behaviour oriented. Dix argues that system dynamics "are difficult to describe [but] often crucial to the feel and effectiveness of the system" (p271). Furthermore, if "the relation between the functional core [`pief`] and the system as a whole [`pies`] is *not* as a *component*, but as an *abstraction*" (p171) then the evaluation of an interface in *isolation* is a meaningless notion, since there is no interface to evaluate.

The case study supports a methodology that combines modelling and prototyping. Prototyping has a useful role in the validation process in bridging the formality gap and providing the user with an opportunity for involvement. It can also play a useful role in clarifying ideas during design (Henderson, 1986). The functional programming paradigm is well suited to the demand for rapid prototyping in the development cycle, (Henderson, 1986), (Hughes, 1989), (Runciman, 1990), and while the integration of prototyping and modelling is not without problems, creating a tension between the prototype as both specification and evaluation tool for example, the case study shows that their combination can be effective.

Finally, the use of abstract modelling gives the designer a useful framework for analysis. The methodology focuses on key abstractions, such as the effect, result and display spaces, and identifies relations between them that are important for the user. Although the red-PIE model is architecturally too general for direct manipulation systems, it can still give useful insights into behavioural properties that are relevant to all interactive systems.

The process of applying a model is likely to foster a deeper understanding of a system as the designer is forced to consider the implications of their decisions for the user. In analysing for reachability the designer is forced to consider functional completeness and the relations between different system layers. With predictability and observability, the focus is on aspects of state that effect the interaction (cursor position, mode and command buffer, window origin) and whether these can be observed.

Observability principles were given in terms of strategies, what the user would have to do to find out x, but, in all but the simplest cases, such as `(MO)` and `(KO)`, where a strategy is obvious, the strategies were left implicit. The principles say what would have to be true of a strategy for the principle to hold. For example, in `(RC)`, it must move the user from one display to another. As more is demanded of the observability of the system, in `(RO)` and `(RP)`, the requirements on these strategies become more stringent. The usefulness of the principles lie in the insights into the system that are gained in framing them but there is no expectation that the designer should *prove* them true.

Modelling the editor was done as an exercise in how modelling and prototyping can be integrated. The editor itself is perhaps too simple for the analysis to turn up any real insights, though the PIPE model did highlight a useful modularisation of the original program to give the two layer `piep` and `pief`. The model was found to be usable, useful and compatible with a prototyping methodology. Future work will look at modelling direct manipulation systems in the same way.

7. REFERENCES

Dix, A. (1991) Formal Methods for Interactive Systems, Academic Press.

Goldson, D. (1996) Functional Prototyping of Interactive Systems, Technical Report, Department of Computer Science, Massey University, New Zealand.

Henderson, P. (1986) Functional programming, formal specification, and rapid prototyping, in *IEEE Transactions on Software Engineering*, **12**, 2.

Hughes, J. (1989) Why Functional Programming Matters, in *The Computer Journal*, **32**, 2.

Jones, M. (1996) The Haskell User's Gofer System, available from `http://www.cs.nott.ac.uk/Department/Staff/mpj/hugs.html`.

Runciman, C. (1990) From Abstract Models to Functional Prototypes, in *Formal Methods in Human-Computer Interaction* (ed. M. Harrison, H. Thimbleby), CUP.

Sufrin, B. (1982) Formal Specification of a Display-Oriented Text Editor, in *Science of Computer Programming*, **1**.

26

NPL Usability Services

Nigel Bevan

National Physical Laboratory
Teddington, Middlesex, TW11 0LW, UK
Nigel.Bevan@npl.co.uk

KEYWORDS: Usability evaluation, metrics, usability engineering, standards.

NPL Usability Services is headed by Nigel Bevan, and currently has five other permanent staff with varied backgrounds in computing, psychology and HCI (Cathy Thomas, Ian Curson, Owen Daly-Jones, Richard Lakin and Andy Harry).

NPL Usability Services operates as a commercial consultancy within the Information Systems Engineering Branch at the National Physical Laboratory. The National Physical Laboratory is the UK's national standards laboratory, owned by the Department of Trade and Industry, and since 1995 operated by NPL Management Ltd, a wholly owned subsidiary of SERCO Ltd.

NPL Usability Services evolved from the HCI Group at NPL, a pioneering group formed in the 1960s by Chris Evans. Chris Evans, author of "The Mighty Micro", investigated how computers could be made easy enough for the public to use. One application used a Teletype connected to a time-sharing computer to interview patients in doctors' surgeries. Patients actually preferred interaction with a Teletype to a real doctor, and alcoholics were found to be considerably more honest when reporting their drinking habits to a computer!

Nigel Bevan joined the group at this time, and worked on a simple language for scripting medical interviews. This evolved into the popular Microtext authoring language, widely used by teachers in the UK to produce their own educational applications on the BBC Micro in the early 1980s.

MUSiC PROJECT

In 1990 NPL took the technical lead in the European ESPRIT MUSiC project: Measurement of Usability in Context. This was a three year project with the ambitious aim of turning usability from a broad aspiration into a quantifiable objective. The methods developed by MUSiC are still the only integrated approach to usability measurement. They operationalise ISO 9241-11: Guidance on Usability, which defines usability as the extent to which a product can be used by specified users to achieve specified goals with effectiveness, efficiency and satisfaction in a specified context of use.

The MUSiC methods provide a precisely specified and documented procedure for carrying out user-based usability evaluation providing both measures and design feedback. Usability Context Analysis (developed in conjunction with HUSAT) is a structured method for identifying the relevant characteristics of users, tasks and environments. The Performance Measurement Method specifies how effectiveness and efficiency can be measured in a valid and reliable way, and is supported by the DRUM software tool for annotating video tapes. SUMI (developed by University College Cork) provides metrics for user satisfaction.

A major advantage of the methods is that they are sufficiently well documented to allow NPL to train organisations without previous experience of usability in their use. Many organisations find that the ability to specify usability requirements and evaluate whether they have been met is an attractive starting point for introducing usability into design. NPL offers a package of training and assistance in the use of MUSiC methods leading to certification of competency in their use. NPL has provided usability tools, training and services based on MUSiC to over 40 organisations worldwide. Clients have included financial services, government departments and developers of multi-media kiosks.

The tools have been adapted to meet a wide variety of organisational requirements. The challenge is now to place them in the broader context of user-centred design, so that an organisation can select the methods best-suited to the skills, development environment, and individual project. The ability to set and evaluate usability goals provides an overall framework for this process.

TECHNOLOGY TRANSFER

The emphasis at NPL continues to be on technology transfer of state-of-the art tools. Achieving industrial uptake is as big a challenge as the original tool

Human–Computer Interaction: INTERACT'97 S. Howard, J. Hammond & G. Lindgaard (editors)
Published by Chapman & Hall

development. The two major contributions that NPL is making to this process are to incorporate usability into standards for ergonomics and software engineering, and to set up a network of European Usability Support Centres.

NPL is actively contributing to the new ISO 13407 Human Centred Design standard, and is incorporating the principles of MUSiC and ISO 9241-11 into ISO 14598-1: Software Product Evaluation, and ISO 9126-1: Software Quality Characteristics (the latter three standards are edited by Nigel). ISO 14598-1 identifies the quality of a product in use as the highest level objective of software product design. Quality in use, measured by effectiveness, efficiency and satisfaction, is a generalisation of the approach to usability in ISO 9241-11, thus making usability the prime design objective in software engineering!

The EC MAPI (MUSiC-Assisted Process Improvement) project (Sep 95 - Dec 96) applied and extended the methods developed in the MUSiC project to a range of trial applications across Europe. One of the outputs of the project was a cookbook of user-centred design methods produced in conjunction with the UK Inland Revenue for use in their software development process.

EUROPEAN USABILITY SUPPORT CENTRES

MAPI provided a useful contribution to the more ambitious INUSE project (Jan 96 - Dec 97, managed by NPL) which has set up a network of Usability Support Centres for the European information engineering industry. INUSE has produced an information pack which includes guides to: user-centred design, usability validation and an introduction to multi-media design (these can be down loaded from the INUSE web site). A co-ordinated service incorporating common core methods is being provided by centres including NPL, HUSAT (Loughborough), Lloyds Register (London), University College Cork, Fraunhofer IAO (Stuttgart), SINTEF (Oslo), Nomos Management (Stockholm), and other usability consultancies in Europe (see Figure 1).

INUSE is complemented by the RESPECT project (Requirements Engineering and Specification) which is also managed by NPL with the longer term objective of producing a co-ordinated set of methods for user-based requirements analysis. It has many of the same partners as INUSE, and the methods are expected to be exploited by INUSE. The challenge in RESPECT is to integrate HCI methods for user requirements with conventional requirements engineering methods.

NPL plans to continue the mix of research and consultancy, working together with other centres of expertise in usability to produce the most appropriate methods and tools to enable industry to develop products and systems which meet the needs of their users.

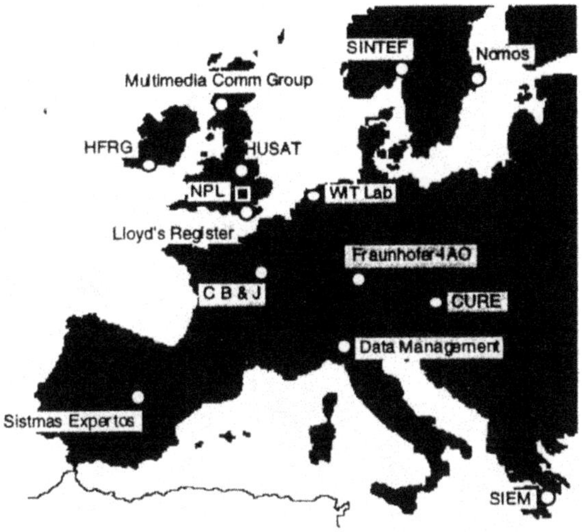

Figure 1. European Usability Support Centres

RECENT PUBLICATIONS

Bevan N (1995) Measuring usability as quality of use. Journal of Software Quality, 4, 115-130.

Bevan N (1995) Usability is quality of use. In: Anzai & Ogawa (eds) Proc. 6th International Conference on Human Computer Interaction, July 1995. Elsevier.

Bevan N (1995) Human-Computer Interaction standards. In: Anzai & Ogawa (eds) Proc. 6th International Conference on Human Computer Interaction, July 1995. Elsevier.

Bevan N and Macleod M (1994) Usability measurement in context. Behaviour and Information Technology, 13, 132-145.

INUSE (1996) see http://www.npl.co.uk/inuse

ISO (1996) ISO/IEC DIS 14598-1 Information Technology - Evaluation of Software Products - Part 1 General guide.

ISO (1997a) ISO DIS 9241-11 Ergonomic requirements for office work with visual display terminals (VDT)s - Part 11 Guidance on usability.

ISO (1997b) ISO DIS 13407 User centred design process for interactive systems.

ISO (1997c) ISO/IEC CD 9126-1 Software quality characteristics and metrics - Part 1: Quality characteristics and sub-characteristics.

Macleod M, Bowden R and Bevan N. (in press) The MUSiC Performance Measurement Method. Behaviour and Information Technology.

Thomas C and Bevan N, eds (1995) Usability Context Analysis Guide V 4. National Physical Laboratory, Teddington, UK.

27

Usability at Microsoft

Gayna Williams and Marshall McClintock

Microsoft Corporation
One Microsoft Way
Redmond, WA
98052-6399
Gaynaw@microsoft.com Marshalm@microsoft.com

1. INTRODUCTION

This paper outlines the work of usability engineers at Microsoft. It gives an overview of our organization, our goals, our usability work, and some of the challenges faced in software usability work.

2. USABILITY ORGANIZATION

There are five product usability groups at Microsoft, and one central group. At its inception in 1988, usability work at Microsoft was centralized in one group. However, by 1995 the group had significantly increased in size, and it was recognized that a closer relationship between usability and product development was necessary to better support the teams. Today there are 76 usability engineers, and 22 support staff working at Microsoft.

The usability groups support products within particular divisions. Each major product has a dedicated usability engineer, and we also support some of our minor products. The engineer reports to a usability manager but is also a member of the product team and is located with the team. Thus, the engineer has support both from a usability group and the advantage of being tightly integrated into a product team.

In addition to understanding HCI (human computer interaction) and test methodologies, usability engineers at Microsoft need excellent team skills. By working consistently with product teams, we can educate them in understanding what user issues need to be addressed and when in the product cycle. By getting the teams to ask the right questions maximizes the impact of our usability work.

The central usability group supports several smaller product teams and addresses cross-product issues in addition to supporting all the usability groups. On average our test coordinators schedule 70 tests a month, requiring around 650 participants.

3. OUR MISSION AND GOALS

Our mission is to provide empirical data about users to support the product design process. We want to develop good product designs as well as good design process, so product teams get the information they need about users at the right time. We also try to provide measures of how successful product designs are to make sure teams know how well users can work with their products. We constantly look for ways to integrate usability into the product cycle.

4. THE PRODUCTS WE SUPPORT

Microsoft produces a wide variety of software (business systems, networking, multimedia, platforms, hardware, financial, educational, games, children's products, etc.) and the usability groups attempt to support them all. Such a variety of products lead to engineers adopting slightly different strategies in evaluation methods and usability goals for their

Human–Computer Interaction: INTERACT'97 S. Howard, J. Hammond & G. Lindgaard (editors)
Published by Chapman & Hall

particular product. For example, the product goals, customers, and evaluation methods for setting up a network server are different from playing a golf game. Nonetheless, there are some general similarities that we describe below.

5. THE PRODUCT CYCLE

The first thing to understand is Microsoft creates generic software as opposed to software to support a specific business process. At the beginning of a cycle we use techniques such as contextual inquiry (Holtzblatz & Beyer, 1993) to understand what activities people are doing, field studies to focus on the use of a particular product, and remote data collection studies if a version of the product has been released. The remote data collection involves having users work with instrumented versions from which we can analyze the usage from the data collected. We can apply heuristics to early product specifications to assess potential usability problems. In addition, teams get data from market research, and for existing products, from our Product Support Services (help lines).

Because we are integrated into the product team, it is much easier to track the product schedule and better determine when a certain type of usability activity should be used, or what features are going to require extra usability attention. We strongly advocate low level testing with paper and Visual Basic prototypes before testing more fully developed code. Developers create daily builds of a product, the purpose of which is to test new code, but they are very useful for us to monitor the changes in the design.

We continue with rapid iterative lab testing until the code complete stage, after which time very few user interface changes are made. During the beta stages of a product more field studies, often longitudinal, may be conducted. Occasionally a usability 'show-stopper' occurs at beta, at which point more testing will take place, but generally by the beta stage we are starting to work with team members on the next version of the product.

After shipping a product we conduct benchmark tests to measure changes between product versions and competing products, and to allow us to set usability goals for the next version.

Occasionally we need to look at issues from a broader perspective, something more akin to HCI research. In addition we may conduct supportability usability tests for product support services. Here the goal is to discover how best to handle support calls.

6. TOOLS AND FACILITIES

At Microsoft we have 18 usability labs and two focus group rooms. Each room is divided by a one-way mirror creating a participant side, and a soundproof observer's side. There is plenty of room for team members to observe tests.

A number of tools have been developed in-house to support usability testing (Cordes et al, 1993). One tool allows us to track user actions and take notes which are time synchronized with the video of the session. Another tool is to quickly review videos. Usability issues are tracked in databases that are shared with product teams and assist in monitoring issues (Sullivan, 1996). Data from tests are shared more widely from our internal web site where all our usability reports are available.

We have completed a number of tests in Europe, and more recently in Japan. In 1996 a usability facility was established at Microsoft's Tokyo office (Aykin et al, 1996).

7. CHALLENGES

Products teams are much more aware today of the need to create easy to use products, they are receptive to usability activities. However the issue of time for usability work in the product cycle is constantly pressing. Our challenges include streamlining usability processes to integrate into the fast dynamic software product cycle. We are constantly trying to find ways to improve our efficiency of delivering usability findings and training product teams to understand user behavior.

8. REFERENCES

Aykin, N., Fernandes, T., Rojek, J., Uren, E. (1996). Usability: Think Global, Act local! *Proc. APCHI '96*, 296-301.

Cordes, R., Hammontree, M., Hoiem, D., & Thompson, M. (1993). Software for the usability lab: A sampling of current tools. *Proc. INTERCHI '93*, 55-60

Holtzblatt, K. & Beyer, H. (1993). "Making Customer-Centered Design Work for Teams" *Communications of the ACM*, October 1993.

Sullivan, K. (1996). The Windows 95 User Interface: A Case Study in Usability Engineering. *Proc CHI '96*. 473-480

28

Usability and the multimedia industry: the Australian Multimedia Testing Centre

Clark N. Quinn & Malcolm Raymond

Access Australia Cooperative Multimedia Centre
Australian Technology Park
Cornwallis Street
Eveleigh NSW 1430
Australia

clarkq@cmcaccess.com.au

ABSTRACT The Australian Multimedia Testing Centre performs usability evaluation to support the multimedia industry. The Centre is equipped with an industry-standard usability laboratory including a testing room, video recording and mixing, and an observation room. The Centre takes a client-centred approach, providing usability evaluation consulting services and a variety of options for testing. A free initial consultation is offered to establish an evaluation plan which meets the client's time frame, scope of project, and budget. In addition, the Centre is pro-actively sponsoring research to increase the understanding of the specific issues of usability for multimedia, including cognitive and affective issues.

KEY WORDS usability, evaluation, multimedia

1. INTRODUCTION

The Australian Multimedia Testing Centre (AMTC) was established in September 1996 by Access Australia Cooperative Multimedia Centre. Access Australia is one of six such centres established under an initiative of the Commonwealth government with a mission to support the multimedia industry through collaboration between industry partners and cultural and educational institutions. The AMTC is one of several avenues through which Access Australia is supporting multimedia development.

The AMTC offers a range of test services appropriate to the Australian multimedia industry. Initial services are centred in the areas of performance and usability testing, implemented through laboratory facilities dedicated to each. Performance testing of multimedia products includes evaluating whether specified functionality is met, how the product handles under stress conditions including low memory and storage, compatibility testing across vendor platforms, and testing for performance with different configurations.

In order to ensure provision of the complete suite of services required by the industry, the Centre is assessing the need for and viability of other testing services, including educational evaluation of learning products and marketability analysis. This report specifically addresses the usability activities of the AMTC.

2. THE LAB

The usability lab consists of one fixed and one portable facility. The fixed installation was designed to be practical yet at a very affordable price and was based on the recommendations made in a study commissioned by Access Australia.

The fixed lab uses a typical usability set-up with one room to contain the evaluator (typical end user) engaged in the task, and another room for observers who are making an assessment of usability issues occuring in the evaluation session. In addition, an operator controls the video mixing equipment to combine images of the screen and the user. The two rooms are separated by a one way mirror so that the evaluators are not immediately aware of the operator.

The practice of usability testing arises from the AMTC policies.

3. POLICY

The AMTC necessarily takes a broad view of what constitutes multimedia, including CDROM product as well as World Wide Web-based (WWW) projects. The AMTC is equipped through the performance laboratory with a vast array of different hardware and software on which to conduct testing. The AMTC is also provided with internet server capability for WWW tests.

The AMTC is committed to the utmost quality in practice, and is in the process of ISO 9000 certification

Human–Computer Interaction: INTERACT'97 S. Howard, J. Hammond & G. Lindgaard (editors)
Published by Chapman & Hall

to that end. Quality procedures ensure regular review of the methodology. The AMTC's partners play a major role in the quality of the usability evaluation method.

4. PARTNERS

In order to ensure practical services and to ensure that the results of research are applied in an appropriate manner, AMTC has established a relationship with Performance Technologies, a usability consultation firm. Performance Technologies provides the usability evaluation methodology used at the Centre.

The AMTC has also partnered with the Human Computer Interaction (HCI) Group of the Commonwealth Science and Industry Research Organisation's (CSIRO) Division of Information Technology. The HCI Group has a quality audit role ensuring that the services of the Centre are of the highest standard and that techniques and methodologies used are appropriate and reflect the latest understanding of usability testing for multimedia products. The HCI Group of CSIRO also plays a role with the AMTC to define new usability requirements.

Access Australia, in support of the multimedia industry also provides education and training. Access Australia and the AMTC are working with the Hiser Group, and the other partners, to develop usability training.

5. RESEARCH

Usability issues with multimedia products can be very different to those encountered in more traditional task oriented computer systems. In particular, there are a whole series of new usability issues to consider in Web-based environments. In order to provide a better understanding of usability issues of multimedia projects the AMTC has initiated an ongoing research program with the HCI Group of CSIRO.

A steering committee with representatives from Access Australia, the AMTC, CSIRO's HCI Group, and Performance Technologies, consults on the research directions. In collaborative research, the AMTC and the HCI Group seek to identify the ways in which usability is affected by multiple media, as well as the changes that occur when the goal of the product is education, entertainment, or both.

The results of multimedia usability research will also be disseminated through Access Australia education and training.

6. OUTCOMES

The consequences of this commitment to quality are already being seen. In its first few months the Centre has already successfully tested both CDROM and WWW products. The results of evaluation are not just provided to the client, but a subset of the projects are selected to be case studies to evaluate the process. Client satisfaction has been evidenced in both word of mouth recommendations and repeat business.

29

Assessing the usability and efficiency of Design Rationale

Alistair Sutcliffe and Michele Ryan

Centre for HCI Design,
School of Informatics, City University, Northampton Square,
London, EC1V OHB, UK.
Email: A.G.Sutcliffe@City.ac.uk

ABSTRACT Many positive claims have been made about the benefits of Design Rationale (DR). MacLean et al., (1991) argue that an explicit design rationale can be a useful tool in the design process in a variety of ways: from reasoning and reviewing to managing, documenting, and communicating. Design rationale is the notion that goes beyond merely accurate descriptions of artifacts, such as specifications, and articulates and represents the reasons and reasoning process behind the design and specification of artifacts (Moran & Carroll, 1996). QOC (Questions, Options, Criteria) is a straightforward notation for representing design rationale (MacLean et al., 1991). In this paper we present the results of a study investigating the usability and efficiency of DR/QOC as a design support tool, and provide an analysis of the designers' reflections on the role of DR/QOC in the design process.

KEY WORDS Design Rationale, QOC, Design Space Analysis, Empirical study, Design method.

1. INTRODUCTION

Design Rationale (DR) in its simplest form is the explicit listing of decisions made during a design process and the reasons why those decisions were made (Jarcyzyk et al., 1992). There are a number of different approaches to DR, for example, MacLean et al., (1989) see DR as a description of the design space, whereas Carroll & Rosson (1991) see design rationale as a set of psychological claims embodied in an artifact, that is, claims that would have to be true if the artifact is to be usable or claims about psychological consequences for the users of the artifact.

Design Space Analysis is a method for understanding design through analysis, thus a particular artifact is understood in terms of its relationship to plausible alternative designs (MacLean et al., 1991). The basic concepts of Design Space Analysis are expressed using QOC (Questions, Options and Criteria), a semi-formal notation. Design Space Analysis using QOC allows designers to record their choices with supportive criteria or non-functional requirements that either justify or detract from a design option. MacLean et al., (1991) believe that if designers used QOC to structure their deliberations, they could improve their reasoning by working with a structure more logically related to the design problem.

There are a number of reported DR empirical studies, e.g. Jorgensen and Aboulafia (1995) found their students were in general able to make good use of DR/QOC and considered the approach very useful for organisation and documentation purposes, but less useful for communication and reflection.

Human–Computer Interaction: INTERACT'97 S. Howard, J. Hammond & G. Lindgaard (editors)
Published by Chapman & Hall

Karsenty (1996) describes a study evaluating the usefulness of DR documents when re-using a previous design. DR documents describing the solution to a problem in mechanical engineering and the reasons for the design decisions, were made available to the designers. The results showed that 41% of the designers' questions were answered by the DR documents (*e.g.* they asked about the reasons for the design decisions, and the different possible choices). However, the DR documents were not sufficient to answer the remaining 59% of their questions (*e.g.* they asked questions about the properties of the interfaces and the way the artifact carries out its functionality). Buckingham Shum (1995) reports a study involving pairs of software designers, drawn from professionals and students. He concludes that QOC played both facilitatory and obstructive roles. Olson et al., (1995), researched problem solving during group design and found the structure of activity during ten design meetings was more similar than different.

Our work follows on from these reported studies and we attempt to investigate how DR/QOC can assist the reasoning and decision process, and to assess its usability as a practical method. However, we also wished to explore the utility of QOC for supporting early stages of design (*i.e.* requirements) and in safety critical domains. In this paper we report the results of a study of industrial designers who used DR/QOC collaboratively as a group to solve a safety critical problem. The study involved: (1) Teaching DR/QOC to a group of software designers, and, (2) Presenting the group with a design problem, their task being to work together and rough-out design choices using QOC.

The paper is organised in four sections. First the experimental study is described. This is followed by a section reporting the data analysis and results. Section four summarises the designers' feedback. The paper concludes with a discussion and ideas for future work.

2. THE STUDY METHOD

A group of (approximately) twelve software designers attended a seminar where they were taught DR using the QOC notation. The QOC notation was chosen in preference to other DR representations, *e.g.* IBIS (Kunz & Rittel, 1970), and DRL (Lee & Lai, 1991), because it is relatively simple and the trainer had previous experience of the technique. All of the designers were employed by the same company and many of them had worked together previously.

An example of DR using QOC was illustrated by considering the various options for designing house shelving. Options included 'open shelving' or 'glass fronted shelving', and criteria included 'items being accessible' and 'safe from climbing kids'. During the seminar the designers asked questions about QOC and how it could be used. Illustrating QOC and answering questions took approximately twenty minutes. The group were then presented with a 160 word narrative of a safety critical problem. They were asked to use QOC to rough-out the choices involved in designing a safety device for handling a gas jet, which must not lead to explosions. This task had initially been reviewed by a manager who considered it to be a realistic problem, within the designers' domain, but unlikely to be one they would have solved previously. The group were given fifteen minutes to work on the problem. One member of the group acted as a facilitator and wrote the options and criteria on a whiteboard, while the rest of group called out their ideas. This part of the seminar was audio taped and then transcribed.

The data obtained from the study consists of: (1) A transcript of the group discussion that took place while constructing the QOC, and, (2) A copy of the QOC diagram created by the group.

3. DATA ANALYSIS AND RESULTS

The QOC diagram produced by the group is shown in Figure 1. The numbers indicate the order in which the options, criteria and links were identified, showing a rather irregular development process. This supports Buckingham Shum's findings that externalising ideas as structured argumentation is not a smooth top down process (Buckingham Shum, 1995). Due to time constraints the criterion 'reliable' remained unconnected to options.

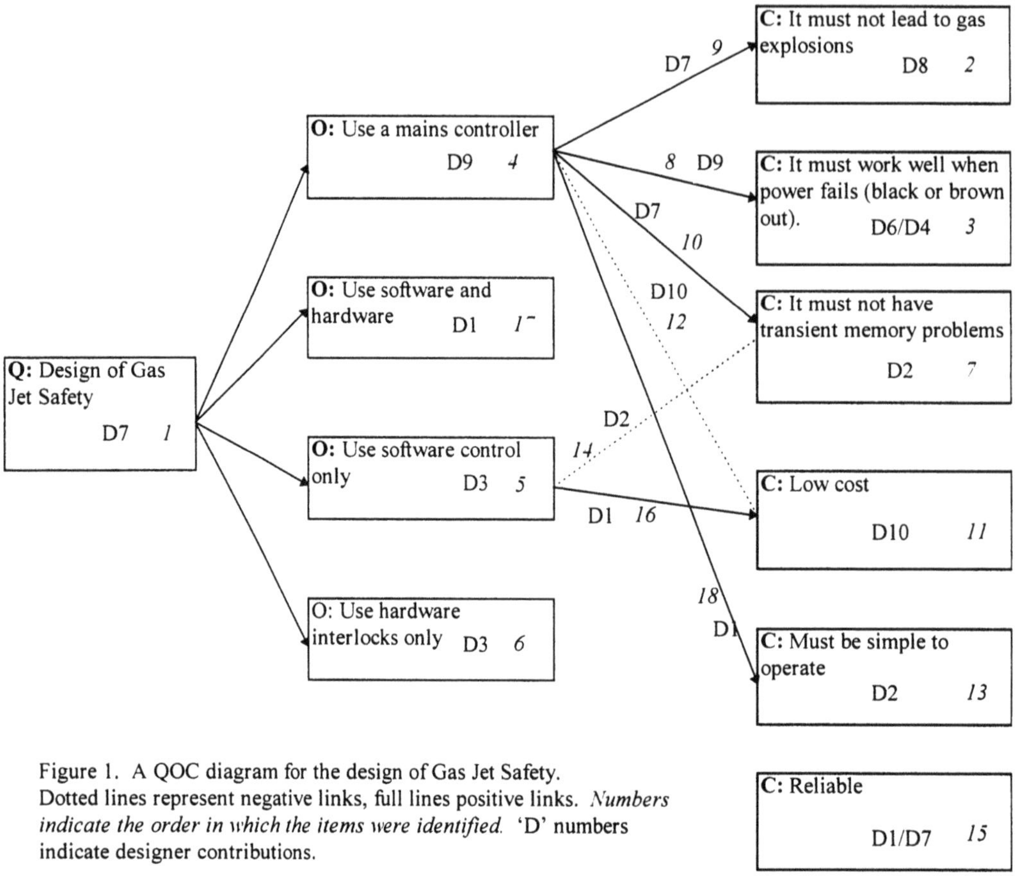

Figure 1. A QOC diagram for the design of Gas Jet Safety.
Dotted lines represent negative links, full lines positive links. *Numbers indicate the order in which the items were identified.* 'D' numbers indicate designer contributions.

The transcript was analysed three times. The first pass involved analysing the content topics (see 3.1), the second pass involved analysing how the designers applied and used the QOC technique (see 3.2), and the third pass analysed the designers' individual contributions (see 3.3).

3.1 Content Analysis - first pass

Speech segments in the transcripts were associated with topic categories. These are shown in Figure 2 and a timeline graph of topics discussed is shown in Figure 3.

Content cat.	Description
Problem requirements (2%)	Statements in the transcripts identifying the problem being addressed.
Non-functional requirements (29%)	Statements referring to non-functional requirements of the system (*e.g.* cost, reliability, safety, must be easy to understand).
QOC technique (31%)	Statements that refer to the QOC technique/notation (*e.g.* whether an item should be classified as an option or a criterion).

Design alternatives (24%)	Statements identifying alternative designs (*e.g.* implement the solution in hardware or software, or a mixture of both). Includes descriptions and comparison of design alternatives.
Other (8%)	Statements that do not fall into any of the above categories.
Design requirements (2%)	Statements referring to the requirements of the design (*e.g.* whether the solution had to be implemented in hardware or software).
Users (2%)	References to the knowledge of users who will use the system
Volume of work (2%)	References to how long it may take to implement a solution.

Figure 2. Topic categories discussed by the designers.

The topic the designers talked about most was the QOC technique (31% of speech segments). They experienced a number of difficulties with the method, (*e.g.* they often did not know whether to classify an item as an option or a criterion). Also, on a number of occasions the notation did not naturally reflect their thoughts. See section 3.2.2 for further analysis.

The next most discussed topic was non-functional requirements (29% of speech segments). These include: safety, cost (product and development), simple operation, easy to understand, reliability, robustness, prevention of gas explosions and handling power failure. Most of the requirements identified by the designers, which were represented as Criteria, are non-functional requirements. Discussing design alternatives was common (24% of speech segments), Options in the QOC diagram show the alternatives discussed. The designers made few references to users (2% of speech segments), and no reference to user interface design.

Design and problem requirements were only mentioned briefly (2% of speech segments for each category), and due to the time constraint, the discussion did not consider system functionality (*i.e.* the components of the system and how the system requirements would be fulfilled). Work required to implement a solution was referred to (2% of speech segments). Other statements not categorised accounted for 8% of speech segments. These consisted of interactions that did not refer to any specific topic (*e.g.* 'Nigel you were about to say something..').

Non-functional requirements, the QOC technique, and design alternatives were discussed throughout the session (see Figure 3).

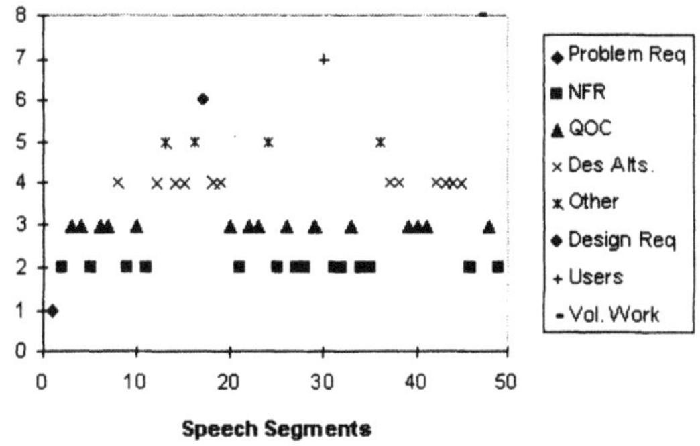

Figure 3. Timeline graph of topics discussed.

3.2. Using QOC - second pass

Speech segments in the transcript were classified into the following 2 categories:

1. Applying QOC to the problem - Utterances that specify questions, options and criteria and construct negative and positive links. Also, reasoning about the options and criteria chosen.
2. Reflections on the QOC technique - Utterances about QOC (*e.g.* statements expressing difficulty in using the notation). In fact, this essentially involved de-composing the content analysis 'QOC Technique' category in Figure 2.

The purpose of this analysis was to separate statements which simply involved the designers using the technique in a straightforward way, from statements expressing the designers' reflections about the method, (*e.g.* where the designers were puzzled or confused by the technique).

3.2.1 Applying QOC to the problem

70% of speech utterances in the transcripts involved the designers constructing questions, options and linking criteria. Of these, 3% of speech statements referred to Questions, 33% to Options, 40% to Criteria and 24% to linking Options to Criteria.

On the whole the designers did reason effectively about their choice of options and criteria, but they did not reason in any great depth. We investigated this by tracing their reasoning and decision process, to explain how each QOC item was produced (see Figure 4).

QOC Item	Prompted by narrative / Designers' reasoning.
Q: The design of the gas jet safety.	Problem narrative.
C: It must not lead to gas explosions.	Problem narrative.
O: Hardware or software.	Reasoning - considering *how* the solution should be implemented prompted hardware/software options.
C: It must handle power failure.	Just stated by designers.
C: It must work well when power fails (black or brown out).	Reasoning - a specialisation of criterion, 'It must handle power failure'.
O: Mains controller.	Reasoning - proposed to prevent black/brown out (as specified in the criterion, 'It must work well when power fails').
C: It must not have transient memory problems.	Reasoning - transient memory problems may result if the solution is implemented in software.
L: Negative link from transient memory to software.	As above.
L: Positive link from mains controller	Reasoning - because an instrument which does not have black or brown outs is safe.
C: Low cost	Reasoning - because it's a solution for the 3rd world (as per problem narrative).
C: Robust	Just stated by designers.
C: Reliable	Just stated by designers.
O: Mixture of hardware and software.	Reasoning - because the options hardware only and software only were identified, so an option is to have both together.
L: Software to low cost	Reasoning - because software is cheaper than hardware. Some designers disagreed with this.
L: Positive link from simple operation to mains controller	Reasoning - because it will be a 'dead simple' operation.
L: Negative link from robust to mains controller	Reasoning - because compared to other things, it was not considered particularly robust.

Figure 4. Reasoning in the creation of (Q)uestions, (O)ptions, (C)riteria and (L)inks.

On a number of occasions the designers did not appear satisfied with the populated QOC diagram. For example, one designer considered that the criterion 'It must not have transient memory problems', was 'not that obvious'. Another designer considered the software/hardware options had produced a 'woolly' statement, because one could then ask, 'which is software and which is hardware ... we're talking about extremes'. Further on, the designers claim it's a 'bit of a cop out saying use software .. and hardware .. it's a bit general'.

3.2.2 Reflections on the QOC technique

30% of transcript speech segments reflected the designers' concern in understanding the semantics of the QOC technique. These include the designers having difficulty specifying whether an item is an option or a criterion (*e.g.* 'What you are saying it's an option rather than a criterion), and feeling constrained by the notation, (*e.g.* 'You have to express that in a positive way').

The following observations summarise the designers' experience of using QOC.

- Early on they encountered problems working with QOC. Finding options to questions was difficult as one engineer noted, 'whatever option you put down, you do not have anything that's a possibility for the design of gas jet safety'.
- They experienced difficulty when attempting to classify ideas. The notation caused confusion between what might be an option and what might be a criterion (*e.g.* a discussion took place around whether, 'handling power failure', was an option or a criterion). The method distracted the

designers. Discussion within the group often focused on how to classify an issue rather than identifying the issues needed to solve the problem.

- The notation was constraining as the designers felt they had to express criteria in a positive way.
- Understanding the meaning of options was a problem. The group were not satisfied that options were really solutions to questions, as one designer pointed out the option, 'use a mains condition', is 'not really a sort of answer in itself. ... it's use of mains conditioner, but that's not a design for a gas jet safety'.
- The designers' expression of ideas was difficult (*e.g.* they didn't think they could represent, 'if it's going to take a year of software to do, it might not be worth doing it for the amount of the size of the contract'). Finally, they decided on 'low product' and 'low development costs' as criteria, but they had to change their natural way of thinking.

3.3. Individual Contributions - third pass

The facilitator D7 contributed most to the discussion, followed by D8, while D6 contributed least.

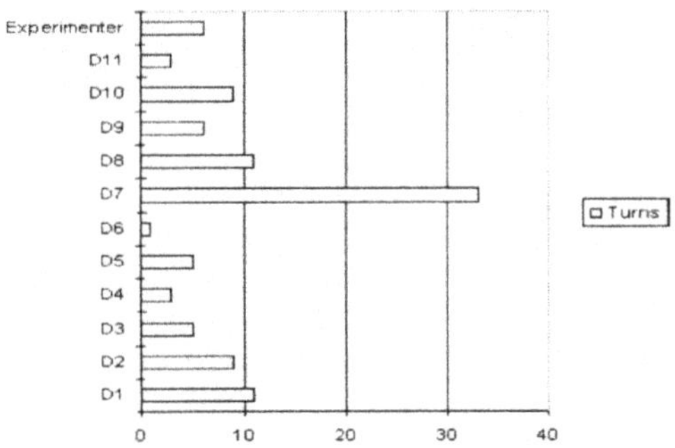

Figure 5. Designers' speech turns frequency.

The facilitator D7 consistently talked throughout the discussion. He did not dominate the group discussion, rather he held it together, where necessary passing an undecided point to the group for their opinion, encouraging speakers to articulate their thoughts and accepting overall agreement.

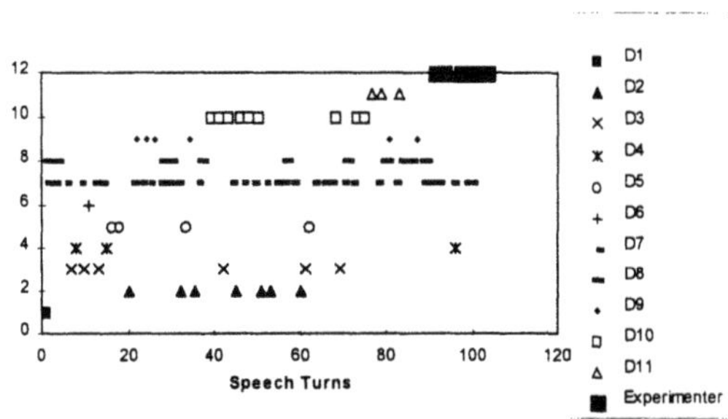

Figure 6. Designers' speech turns shown over time.

The QOC method facilitated participation. Most of the designers made contributions that were included in the final QOC, with exception to designers D5 and D6. See Figures 1 and 7.

Designer	1	2	3	4	5	6	7	8	9	10
Contribution	4	3	2	1	0	0	4	1	2	2

Figure 7. Designer QOC Contribution Frequency.

4. DESIGNERS' FEEDBACK

Only half of the designers who attended the seminar gave feedback anonymously at the end. They were asked to provide feedback on QOC using a Likert scale. Figure 8 shows their ratings on a 7 point scale, where 7 indicates that the condition has been fully satisfied and 1 indicates the reverse.

Condition	**D1**	**D2**	**D3**	**D4**	**D5**	**D6**	**Av.**
1. The extent the QOC diagram included relevant options and criteria.	1	5	2	2	2	1	2.2
2. How accurately the QOC diagram represented the options and criteria (regardless of how correct they were).	4	2	3	4	2	2	2.5
3. How clearly the QOC diagram represented the options and criteria.	3	5	2	5	2	1	3
4. The correctness of the options/criteria in the QOC.	2	2	3	4	2	3	3

5. How easy it is to learn the QOC notation.	6	6	2	6	5	5	5
6. How useful QOC is for representing design issues in your field.	4	3	2	5	1	3	3

Figure 8. Designers' initial feedback (1 low, 7 high).

Most of the designers considered that the QOC diagram they produced in the experiment did not include relevant options and criteria for this problem (see condition 1, Figure 8). This may reflect the experimental time constraint or their opinion that QOC was not a suitable way of representing the relevant issues for the problem. This is supported by their general low rating of the correctness of the options and criteria (see condition 4, Figure 8).

4.1 Feedback after 8 months

Eight months after the seminar the designers were asked to give further feedback on their use of QOC. None of the them had used QOC at all since the seminar eight months previously. However, there had been no management impetus to do so. Five of the seven designers gave lack of opportunity as the reason for not using QOC. The other two cited that QOC was inappropriate. Most of the designers' work involves producing new versions of existing software packages or adding new features. They explained that this does not often lend itself to producing new designs; they simply reuse existing designs. This may reflect the need to introduce DR via a library of rationales to promote a critical mass of useful documentation. Alternatively, they may have been an anti-method culture, but the designers did employ other design methods. Seven of the designers used methods from the following list; Object Oriented Design, Object Oriented Diagrams, OMT, Coad/Yourdon and State Tables. Only one of the designers reported that he did not use any other design notation or method.

4.1.1 Benefits of using QOC

Three of the seven software designers considered that there were no advantages in using QOC. Advantages given by the rest of the group follow:

- Helps to record our thought processes.
- Useful for small projects or sub-projects but not for large projects.
- QOC may be useful if starting a new project, but not for an existing project.
- Anything is an improvement on ad-hoc techniques.

4.1.2 Disadvantages of using QOC

Six of the seven designers considered that QOC was not very useful for representing design issues in their field. Two of the designers who did not cite any benefits, did not cite any disadvantages either. Other disadvantages included:

- Even very small areas of design generate massive QOC diagrams. Unwieldy for large problems.
- Learning curve required albeit short.
- Seems too theoretical.
- If you do not know what the questions are, it is not possible to design relevant criteria.

None of the designers thought they would use the technique again. They gave the following reasons.

- Too time consuming for the benefits.
- Projects are already satisfied by using existing tools. Quite risky to use new tools.
- Most of their work involves using existing designs
- No CASE support available. The various notations/methods used in the past have needed good CASE tools to cope with real problems.

5. DISCUSSION

Generally the QOC categories did not give significant problems. However, the designers did have difficulty in decomposition, but this could be because the trainer did not explain this aspect clearly. The confusion between options and criteria highlights the problem of how QOC elements change during the analytical process (*i.e.* the solution to a criteria becomes a lower level option). QOC does not guide decomposition as clearly as some top down methods (*e.g.* DeMarco, 1978).

The QOC notation tended to keep the focus on high level options (software vs. hardware) which seemed to inhibit detailed reasoning. The QOC framework may encourage a leap from questions to possible solutions, thereby missing the reasoning process in between. However, QOC did function effectively for trade-off analysis as illustrated in the final QOC diagram. This suggests the need to encourage QOC decomposition and annotations on diagrams for impact consequences. Using QOC with some other modeling technique may help more detailed reasoning.

Any new notation needs considerable training even if it is relatively simple. Our study showed that the designers spent much of their time discussing the method, rather than focusing on the problem, but this was probably an artifact of the method's novelty. The lack of long term take up is probably due to lack of management impetus, a factor necessary for adoption of structured methods, and the application domain which needed a critical mass of QOCs. The lack of CASE tools could have discouraged using the method.

QOC is supposed to be a general representation, so it should be applicable to any trade-off problem with design options and criteria. QOC may be sensitive to the scale of the problem, indeed previous reports have used it for small scale user interface design issues (MacLean et al, 1991) so our findings suggest that QOC may not scale to problems which are more open ended and complex in the requirements and early scope stages of design. The users were novices, no doubt we may have got better results with QOC experts, but the point of the study (and QOC) is to test a light weight, supposedly easily learned notation in industry. We found it didn't always work, as have others (Buckingham Shum, 1995).

Finally, the study did show evidence that QOC can help structure requirements agreeing with other studies (*e.g.* Sutcliffe, 1995) which demonstrated that DR is partially successful for requirements analysis. However, it also demonstrated that in-depth training is necessary for even a simple method and that other specification languages are necessary for use with DR to support more detailed reasoning.

Acknowledgments
This research was supported by the SERC/DTI Safety Critical programme in project GR H/89944 DATUM. Many thanks to Dr Gordon Rugg for collecting the data and to Liz Bromley for transcribing the tape.

REFERENCES

Buckingham Shum S. Analyzing the Usability of a Design Rationale Notation, 1995. In T. P. Moran & J. M. Carroll (Eds.), Design Rationale: Concepts, techniques, and use. Lawrence Erlbaum, 1996.

Carroll M J and Rosson B M. Deliberated Evolution: Stalking the View Matcher in Design Space, 1991. In T. P. Moran & J. M. Carroll (Eds.), Design Rationale: Concepts, techniques, and use. Lawrence Erlbaum Associates, 1996.

DeMarco T. Structured Analysis and System Specification. New York: Yourdon Press, 1978.

Jarczyk A, Loffler F, & Shipman M. Design Rationale for Software Engineers: A survey. IEEE, 1992.

Jorgensen A H and Aboulafia A. Perceptions of Design Rationale. Human-Computer Interaction, Interact, Eds. K Nordby et al, pp. 61-66, 1995.

Karsenty L. An Empirical Evaluation of Design Rationale Documents. In Proceedings of CHI-96, April 13-18th, Ed. M. J. Tauber, 1996.

Kunz W and Rittel H W J. Issues as elements of information systems (Working Paper No. 131). Berkeley: University of California, Berkeley, Center for Planning and Development Research, 1970.

Lee J and Lai K-Y. What's in Design Rationale?, 1991. In T. P. Moran & J. M. Carroll (Eds.), Design Rationale: Concepts, techniques, and use. Lawrence Erlbaum Associates, 1996.

MacLean A, Young R & Moran T. Design Rationale: The Argument Behind The Artifact, CHI, 1989.

MacLean A, Bellotti V, and Moran T. Questions, Options, and Criteria: Elements of design space analysis, 1991. In T P Moran & J M Carroll (Eds.), Design Rationale: Concepts, techniques, and use. Lawrence Erlbaum Associates, 1996.

Moran T P and Carroll J M. Design Rationale: Concepts, techniques, and use. Lawrence Erlbaum Associates, 1996.

Olson M G, Olson S J, Storrosten M, Carter M, Herbsleb J, and Rueter H. The Structure Of Activity During Design Meetings, 1995. In T. P. Moran & J. M. Carroll (Eds.), Design Rationale: Concepts, techniques, and use. Lawrence Erlbaum, 1996.

Sutcliffe A. Requirements Rationales: Integrating Approaches to Requirement Analysis. Symposium on Designing Interactive Systems: Processes, Practices, Methods & Techniques Conference Proceedings. Eds. G. M. Olson & S. Schuon, 1995.

30

Breaking the Rules of Direct Manipulation

David Golightly & David J. Gilmore

Psychology Dept
University of Nottingham
Nottingham, NG7 2RD, UK

dag@psyc.nott.ac.uk

Abstract: There is a clear conflict between making an interface easier to use and making computer-based problems easier to solve. Making the control of the problem-solving domain more complex helps users to reach their solutions in less steps. Previous explanations of this phenomena have been centred in how the interface impacts on learning or planning of the problem solving domain. This paper adds a new element to this work by drawing on observational analysis. Interface differences are closely related to the types of strategy a user employs. A more complex interface makes the user more sensitive to their problem solving situation. Explanations of the phenomena are reconsidered in the light of strategy analysis. The effect occurs in problem solving interfaces because the domain specific requirements of the interface cannot be divorced from the domain independent goals. The application of the effect to design is discussed in relation to several areas.

Keywords: Interaction design, task analysis, problem solving, cognitive load, direct manipulation.

1. INTRODUCTION

The interface is the access point to the computer. If the computer contains information we wish to manipulate, learn about and generally operate on in any way then we do so through the interface.

HCI is often a drive towards User Centred Design. Encompassed within this drive is the accepted notion that, if the interface is a window, it should not be opaque or distorted, but clear, smooth and seamless. This will allow manipulation of the data with the user almost unaware that they are communicating through the interface medium. This is exemplified in the Apple Interface Guidelines. Objects represented by the interface should be clearly understood by a user, should respond almost instantaneously to input with feedback and should represent as closely as possible the objects

Human–Computer Interaction: INTERACT'97 S. Howard, J. Hammond & G. Lindgaard (editors)
Published by Chapman & Hall

they refer to in the actual data being manipulated. Also, a user should be allowed to quickly reverse actions with the most minimal damage to their overall state. These are some of the key principles behind Direct Manipulation (Norman, 1986).

The benefits of Direct Manipulation are the rapid learning of functionality for novices coupled with ease-of-execution for experts with any given system. Implicit with these benefits is the idea that making an interface conform to Direct Manipulation reduces the mental workload necessary to operate any application. In other words, by making the interface neutral to the user they can concentrate less on interface goals and more on their domain goals.

Increasingly, the 'neutrality' of the interface is coming into question. This paper focuses on the concern that different tasks require qualitatively different interface requirements. Easier interaction is not always more effective interaction.

Many conclusions and guidelines about manipulation style have been drawn from the domains such as word processing or spreadsheet tasks. In such situations the domain knowledge is already known by the user. What is new to them is the interface. A group of studies have looked at how the interface affects domain learning (Svendsen(1991) , O'Hara & Payne (1994), Golightly, Gilmore & Churchill (1996)) where the domain, as well as the interface, is new to a user. These studies deal specifically with problem solving tasks.

The Svendsen study looked at the Tower of Hanoi task. Both the O'Hara & Payne and the Golightly et al task looked at sliding tile 8-puzzle (see figure 1). All three studies found that increasing the difficulty of manipulating these problem domains improved users performance. Making a move more difficult leads the user to take fewer moves to solve the puzzle.

Several explanations have been offered as to why this effect may occur. It may be the case that making control of the interface more difficult leads the user to develop a richer knowledge of the domain. This knowledge is explicit; it can be transferred from one task to another and is more easily open to verbal report. Svendsen argues that the standard direct manipulation interface promotes implicit learning. The knowledge is robust but is not open to conscious retrieval and adaptation. This makes it more difficult for the user to be aware of situations where knowledge about a domain is relevant.

For O'Hara and Payne, the more difficult interface leads the user to plan more. The cost of carrying out an action with a more difficult interface warrants the user to make a more efficient choice. In order to choose the optimum move the user may work several moves ahead mentally to assess its outcome. This enhanced planning is not necessary for a Direct Manipulation interface. In that situation it is much easier to perform trial-and-error action and asses the impact of a move by simply executing it.

What is clear from these studies is that an interface can have an influence on how a user performs in a domain. If the domain has a strong problem solving element then a more difficult interface will help the user to solve the problem more efficiently. The Golightly et al study found that only certain types of difficulty induced this improved performance. The execution had to be made *cognitively* more difficult. This was done by moving the control of the puzzle away from the puzzle itself and onto a separate set of buttons on the interface. This did not require any extra interface operations from the user to move a tile (though, as we shall see, it does involve extra cognitive activity). It is moving the point of input away from the point of action (and thus breaking one of the key rules of Direct Manipulation) that makes the difference.

These studies have all used gross measures of behaviour. They have taken dependent variables such as time per move, time per puzzle or number of errors and applied statistics to show the effect is valid. The results are then used to develop theory about what users are doing to exhibit these discrepancies between interfaces. This paper offers some observational analyses of the moves that users make in terms of their strategies, goals and subgoals. These observations clarify some of the explanations of the effect and point to where it will be of use in design.

Observing patterns of problem solving might be seen as a subjective process. There are two ways to give it rigour. The first is to use data collected from a conventional study. This can be analysed statistically to show it is a valid replication of the effect and

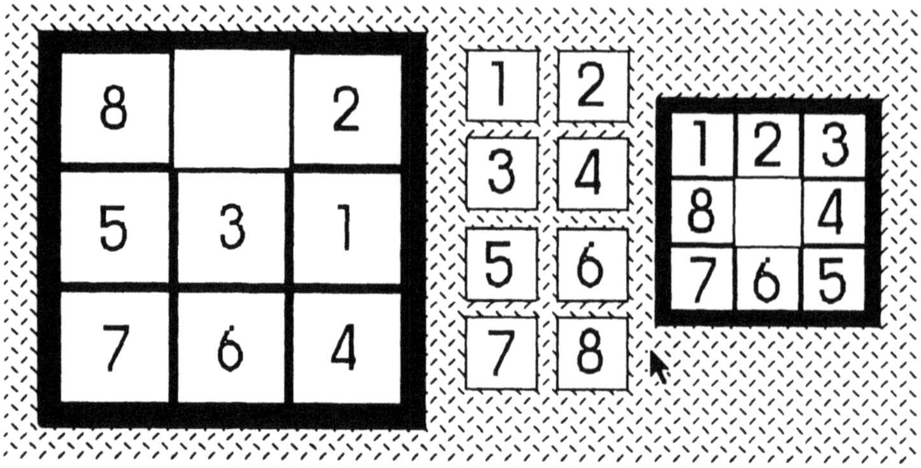

Figure 1. The IM interface. The actual puzzle is on the left, the goal state is shown on the right and the buttons used for moving the tiles (hidden on the DM interface) are in the middle.

eligible for more qualitative analysis. The second is to use a candidate strategy. The candidate is formally defined beforehand and then used as a comparison to see in which ways any observed strategy conforms or differs. These two features strengthen any conclusions that are drawn from the observation.

2. A STUDY

2.1 Method

The following is a brief description of the experiment used to elicit results for further analysis. Two groups of participants were given a set of 8-puzzles with various starting configurations. The puzzles were presented on an Apple Macintosh. Participants were asked to complete as many as possible in 15 minutes. Half of the participants were given an Indirect Manipulation (IM) interface (see figure. 1). In order to move a tile they had to click on the corresponding button in the middle of the display. The distance between the buttons and the display of the puzzles meant that it was not possible to see both at once. This was verified by the subject's observations after the experiment. For the DM interface, the participants had to click on the actual tile on the puzzle. For this interface the buttons were hidden.

Each group were given the same puzzles in the same order. The puzzles were ordered so that even those participants who only solved a few puzzles had both easy and harder starting configurations.

The following measures of performance were taken; average time to make a move (ln transformed), number of puzzles solved in the 15 minutes and average number of moves to solution.

2.2 Results

The two groups differed in the number of puzzles they solved in 15 minutes . The IM group completed significantly less puzzles (IM = 5.33, DM = 8.25)($F(1,22) = 26.165$, $p<0.01$). They also took longer over their moves (mean IM move time(ln) = 0.46) than the DM group (mean DM move time(ln) = -0.23) ($F(1,22) = 79.79$, p = $p<0.01$).

The IM group took fewer moves to solve their puzzles with a mean of 75 moves as opposed to the DM groups 104.8 ($F(1,22) = 11.64$, p = $p<0.01$).

A further dependent variable was taken, standard deviation of move times (ln). Briefly, with planned action, a problem solver will spend a long time at one particular point in the problem. This is when the planning occurs. Then the next few moves will occur in quick succession as the plan is executed. There will then be another long period while the next few moves are planned. The standard deviation of move times is a numerical measure of the range of move times that a participant exhibits. A higher standard deviation correlates with greater planning.* The IM group displayed a greater range of move times (SDev (ln) for IM = 0.65) than the DM group (SDev (ln) for DM = 0.55) ($F(1,22) = 5.96$, $p=0.023$).

3. ANALYSING STRATEGIES
3.1 Methodology

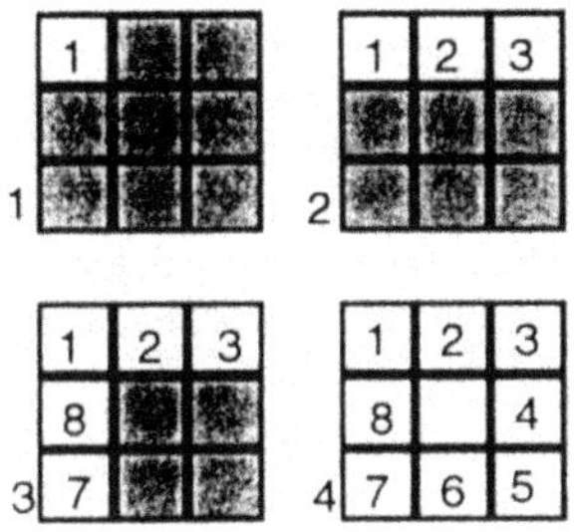

Figure 2. Subgoals and final goal state of the 8-puzzle when using the candidate 'Place' strategy (the greyed squares are not relevant to any given state.)

These results clearly replicate previous findings of Svendsen, O'Hara & Payne and Golightly et al. The DM interface allowed for the participants to make quicker moves and, as a result, allowed for them to complete more puzzles in the allotted period. The IM interface allowed the participants to complete the puzzles in fewer moves. They also displayed a higher range of move times suggesting planning activity.

The two interfaces do lead to different performance. Is it possible to define this in the nature of the participant's problem solving? The IM interface is promoting more efficient problem solving in that they take fewer moves to solution. They are making less errors in their selection of which tile to move and making choices which direct them more quickly to the goal state. Using observation to explore the nature of the interface reveals it also promotes *different* moves to solution.

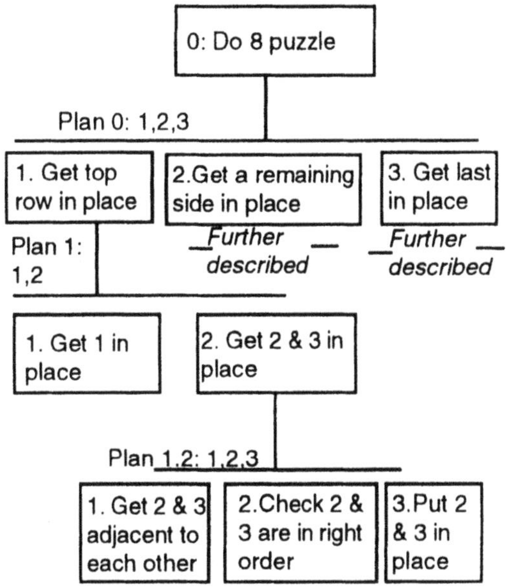

Figure 3. Heirarchical Task analysis of the candidate 'Place' strategy.

A candidate strategy was used as a comparison. One obvious strategy to employ can be described as a 'place' strategy. Here, the problem solving involves basic problem reduction. The aim of the strategy was to achieve a series of subgoals; first, place a corner then complete that side. A second side is then completed and finally the last 3 tiles are put in place (see figure 2.)

Though this is only a loose description of the strategy, further rigour can be added by describing it within a conventional formalism. In this case a Heirarchical Task Analysis (Shepherd, 1989) of the subgoal structure was used.

The HTA constrained the description of the strategy. By having a formalism of the subgoal structure it was possible to predict from the HTA which subgoal would be attempted next. However, it was not possible to start making predictions about the actual moves that would be made (e.g. below the level

* A complete explanation of the theory behind this measure is offered in Golightly et al.

of plan 1.2. The plans marked with '-further described-' had also been constructed at two more levels of complexity but no further). As a result, the analysis made no commitment to defining the moves taken to reach a subgoal.

A feature of having the constrained formalism was that it made clear how much a new strategy would deviate from the candidate strategy. Some participants could form the same subgoal structure but with other parts of the puzzle substituted in (e.g. tile 3 could have been placed first instead of tile 1). Some strategies would differ radically from the candidate to the point where they are qualitatively different. Alternatively it would be clear when no strategy was being used whatsoever.

The performances of the same 24 participants used for the statistical analysis were played back on a viewer application. Similarities and differences between the candidate strategy and the actual strategy were noted. Though problems of subjectivity have been discussed the strategic features of the two groups were striking enough to justify this approach.

Of the 12 DM participants 11 used either the candidate strategy or a derivative. These derivations involved slight substitutions e.g. doing the left-hand row instead of the top row. However the subgoal structure was in essence the same. What was clear was that the subgoals were solved in a trial-and-error manner sometimes taking hundreds on moves to complete a side or to position the remaining five tiles.

The difficulty in perceiving any structure to the solution of the subgoals was in line with the HTA. It was difficult to predict a very deep hierarchy of sub goals in the task analysis but it appears that DM participants do not hold a deep hierarchy of subgoals anyway. They appeared to be focusing on one quite high level subgoal and using trial-and-error performance to achieve it. Within participants the strategies were regimented; participants found the strategy within one or two moves and stuck with it.

The IM group was much more loose in their use of strategies. They seemed to be far less consistent in their choice of strategy. There was a strong tendency to get the tiles in the right order first before trying to position them. The candidate strategy might be used on one puzzle but not on the next. Quite often it was hard to see any deliberate strategy. In essence, the IM participants appeared much more sensitive to the particular state the problem was in at any given point. They were able to make choices about which move to make which that more relevant to the position they were in rather than attempting to follow a rigid structure. It is important to remember that both groups were given the same puzzles in the same order. So, it is not the case that each groups strategy selection was a result of the puzzles they were presented with.

4. INTERPRETATION

The problem solving of the DM group appears rigid to the IM groups fluid, state-sensitive problem solving. These strategic observations give extra weight to explanations offered by O'Hara & Payne and Svendsen, these being a) that the more complex interface improves planning b) that the more complex interface leads to richer, more explicit learning. We do not see these two explanations as conflicting. It is more likely the case that extra planning leads to more explicit understanding of the problem domain later on. The interpretation of the observational analysis makes this link.

We take the DM case first. When the problem solving can take place at the point of action the user does not need to build a deep cognitive representation of the problem. This is because the action can be based at the display which represents the problem for the user. A goal or sub goal can be held and the user can just try to get the display to match it using trial-and-error. This would explain the type of behaviour that the DM group exhibited.

If the point of action is moved away from the point of consequence then the user cannot use the display based representation. In order to reduce the effort of switching from the two points the user builds a cognitive representation of a small part of the problem state. They use the representation at the point of interaction (the buttons) for a few moves before checking against the actual puzzle display.

This would explain why the IM group show a higher range of move times. On some moves the representation will be being built from the display. Also there will be moves where the internal and external representations must be checked against each other. But on other moves the representation will already be internalised so the cognitive effort for these moves will be much less. On these moves the response times will be lower.

Building an internal representation explains the more fluid problem solving. The DM user needs only to focus on the particular tile to be moved (e.g. focusing on '1' to get it in the corner). The IM user has to internalise the surrounding tiles as well to build this representation. So, they become sensitive to more of the problem state. This results in the strategic behaviour that the IM group shows.

This broadly conforms to the O'Hara & Payne explanation of the effect. (The IM interface is not promoting planning in the strictest sense of the word. But it does promote the building and manipulation of an internal representation. However, it could be argued that the action is not planned but situated, albeit in an internal representation; this has been covered by Vera & Simon (1993). We acknowledge this debate but do not wish to make a commitment to either viewpoint at this time.)

Having to build this internal representation requires deeper processing of the problem domain. This would, in turn, lead to the learning benefits that have been predicted with a more difficult problem solving interface.

5. ANALYSING THE INTERFACE

So far, we have defined the differences in performance between the two interfaces. But the discussion has been based in the differences of problem solving style. There must be an element to interfaces which creates these effects in the problem solving case. What is it about the problem solving situation that makes it a special case of interaction?

Using task analysis of the two interfaces defines how they are different and how this relates to the problem solving behaviour we have described. Both interfaces have identical grammatical consistency. Both have an equivalent representation of the problem domain. What differs between them is the set of procedures for manipulating a tile i.e. the unit task (Card, Moran & Newell, 1983).

For the purposes of this discussion the analysis will be anchored in the N-GOMS-L notation (Kieras, 1989). This notation has a parsimony which is all that the current analysis requires. Also, his discussion draws a line between device specific goals, particular to the application that is being used, and device independent goals which are part of the domain that is being worked on.

This helps us to define the types of goal a user has to achieve in this problem solving case. One level of device independent goal in the 8-puzzle is to complete an 8-puzzle. The next level of device independent goal is moving a tile. That is, solving a puzzle and moving a tile are not related to the interface that is being used. They are general to the domain of solving 8-puzzles. What is specific to the interface is the methods for achieving that goal.

The action of moving a tile in the DM interface consists 3 steps.

Method 1. Accomplishing goal of move tile (DM)
Step 1. Select tile
Step 2. Move cursor to tile
Step 3. Click mouse

Moving with the IM interface is almost identical except for step 2.

Method 2. Accomplishing goal of move tile (IM)
Step 1. Select tile
Step 2. Locate corresponding button
Step 3. Move cursor to button
Step 4. Click mouse

The selection (step 1) in these analyses is not a selection of a method, as is normally the case in a GOMS type analysis. It is a marker under N-GOMS-L notation for a domain independent activity or a 'complex cognitive process' (Keiras, 1989, p.140) that is off-line from the analyses. The 'select tile' marker denotes the cognitive activity which is the domain related problem solving. It is at this point that the type of subgoaling we have observed occurs.

The domain specific component of these interfaces is the method for moving the tile once it has been selected (DM step 2 & 3; IM step 2, 3, 4). The difference between the two methods clearly illuminates the difference between the two interaction styles. The

IM method has the extra action of locating the button. The types of strategic differences we have described and the explanations for them are driven by users trying to minimise the effect of this extra step. (NB. Though there is an extra action it is still part of the overall operation of moving a tile. It is this increased complexity that forces the performance difference, not simply adding an extra operation of very low complexity as in the Golightly et al study. Such an extra operation can be easily executed by the user so that it does not induce any extra cognitive load.)

The centre of this effect is that a small difference results in a large in impact on step 1-selecting a tile. This is because it occurs in a problem solving interface. What is different about problem solving situations, as opposed to tasks such as text editing or spreadsheets, is that the off line marker 'select tile' is a vital part of the method.

The assumption with most task analysis methods is that expert performance exists both in carrying out the method and in carrying out the cognitive activity that the off-line markers encompass. If expert performance cannot be guaranteed for the domain independent cognition then it is presumed that this has occurred at some other point in time. So, in a GOMS analysis of word processing, it is assumed that the document is already marked up before the user starts text editing.

But how can domain related cognition be moved off-line in an interface that is designed to support on-line cognition? In the problem solving situation the domain independent cognition is an integral part of the task.

This can be summed up as follows. The method of operation is not neutral to a selection process when the selection of the item to be operated on, rather than the execution of that operation, is the purpose of the interaction. Not only is the method not neutral, but our evidence shows that making it more complex leads the user to make more on-target selections.

It is not necessary for all of the extra cognitive activity to temporally occur at step 1. But at some point a user reflects more on the domain independent act of selecting a tile because the method of executing that selection has been made more complex.

6. A PRINCIPLE FOR DESIGN

We now have some clear ideas about how, why and where more difficult interfaces should help problem solving. The observational data gives us the 'how'- the more difficult interface makes problem solving more efficient by making it more fluid and sensitive to the current problem state. From this we have enhanced existing theories of 'why'- moving the point of action away from the point of consequence encourages the problem solver to develop their own representation of the domain. This leads to deeper learning of the problem domain. The 'where' comes from considering the relationship between the device specific cognition and the device independent cognition- the more complex interface can help the user to make selections when their domain independent goal is problem solving.

There have been many discussions of how traditional cognitive approaches can trade with more holistic, situational studies to build more effective interactions while, at the same time, enhancing psychological theory (e.g. Landauer, 1987). The situation we have here is an excellent opportunity for this trade.

There are many research questions that can be further explored in the laboratory. For instance, this paper has considered how the interface impacts on learning. Much more work needs to be done into understanding how robust these effects are over time and in the face of transfer to other tasks. The laboratory would be an ideal place to study the effects of training regimes. A study is currently being analysed to explore these aspects of the effect.

This is only one side of the laboratory/ real world relationship. The time has come to really consider whether more complex interaction can be of use in actual interfaces. We can say with certainty that it is not a general design principle. When most users approach an application they are already aware of what they intend on doing. The key issue for a user is normally not 'what do I want to do?' but 'how do I do it?' Here the interface should be the common conception of a transparent window. Making the task user centred in such cases means making the 'how to do it' knowledge quick to learn, quick to execute and as engaging as possible.

But there is a second situation where making decisions about choosing what to do efficiently takes precedence over the ease of doing it. Consider safety critical systems. Infrequent, high-cost failures need additional contextual information (Johnson, 1995). A common occurrence in accident situations is that operators focus in on performing one subgoal. Their focus is such that they fail to see other factors which may be giving them additional or even conflicting information. In such situations, an interface which allows an operator to see a broader context and make decisions that are more sensitive to the overall problem state would be highly advantageous. This is exactly the sort of benefits a more complex interface could deliver.

These interfaces *are* harder to learn how to work. An operator would not want to be faced with a highly counterintuitive interface in a moment of crisis. The question of training users so that the interface does not completely throw them has to be addressed. Equally such interfaces do not make you any quicker at your task. If speed is an issue then a more complex interface will probably slow down the overall time taken to complete a task. But if the domain involves making as few decisions as possible and making them as accurately as possible then this type of interface may offer much.

The safety critical system is an extreme case. There are a whole other range of situations that may benefit, either in whole or in part, from an interface which supports problem solving. Direct manipulation interface in educational situations may not always be of benefit (Gilmore,1996). The direct manipulation interface is supposed to 'engage' the user. Maybe in a learning situation it engages the learner in the interface rather than the information he or she is manipulating. Making the interaction less direct would make a learner focus more on the domain they are working in.

Exploratory navigation, whether in hypertext environments or more literally in virtual environments, might be made more effective by interaction styles that force the user to be sensitive to the information they have available to them at any one time. There also may be smaller parts of larger applications where the problem solving interface may be appropriate. A user can be aware of the tasks they wish to perform but may occasionally come across sub tasks which they have make decisions about. At these points it may be advantageous to support this decision making process.

References

Card, S.K., Moran, P.T. & Newell, A. (1983) The Psychology of Human-Computer Interaction. Lawrence Erlbaum Associates, inc.

Gilmore, D. J. (1996) The relevance of HCI guidelines for educational interfaces. in Machine-Mediated Learning, 5(2): 119-133.

Golightly, D., Gilmore, D. J. & Churchill, E.F. (1996) Puzzling Interfaces: the relationship between manipulation and problem solving in Thimbleby, H. & Blandford, A. HCI '96: Adjunct proceedings

Johnson, C. W. (1995) Decision theory and safety critical interfaces in Nordby, K, Helmerson, P.H. Gilmore, D. J. & Arnesen, S. A. eds. Proceedings of Interact '95.

Kieras, D. (1988) Towards a practical GOMS model of methodology for user interface design. In Helander, M., ed Handbook of Human-Computer Interaction. Amsterdam: North-Holland.

Landauer, T. K. (1987) Relations between cognitive psychology and computer system design. in Carroll, J. M. Interfacing thought: cognitive aspects of Human-Computer Interaction. Cambridge, MA: MIT.

Norman, D.A. (1986) Cognitive Engineering. in Norman D.A. & Draper S.W. User Centred System Design: New Perspectives in Human-Computer Interaction. Lawrence Erlbaum Associates, inc.

O'Hara, K & Payne, S.J. (1994) Cost of Operation Affects Planfulness of Problem-Solving Behaviour. School of Psychology, University of Wales, College of Cardiff.

Shepherd, A. (1989) Analysis and training in information tasks. In Task Analysis for Human-Computer Interaction (Diaper, D. ed.) Chichester: Ellis-Harwood.

Svendsen, G.B. (1991) Influences of Interface Style on Problem Solving. International Journal of Man-Machine Studies, 35: 379-397.

Vera, A. H. & Simon, H. A. (1993) situated action: a symbolic interpretation. in Cognitive Science 17, 7-48.

31

Objectives, strategies and resources as design drivers

Bob Fields, Peter Wright and Michael Harrison

Human-Computer Interaction Group
Department of Computer Science
University of York, York, YO1 5DD, UK
{bob, pcw, mdh}@cs.york.ac.uk

ABSTRACT This paper builds on an existing model of human-computer interaction that focuses on the information structures employed as *distributed information resources* by users in deciding how to act. Such resources are not limited to internal mental constructs, but may be distributed between the single user and their environments, as representations in artefacts or the heads of other human actors. The concept of *interaction strategy* is introduced and used as a theoretical construct that generalises over a number of modelling perspectives in HCI. They are used to form a link between users' high-level objectives and resources and the way they're implemented. The usefulness in design of the general idea of distributed information resources and the concepts of strategies and objectives is illustrated by an example.

KEYWORDS Interaction design, interaction strategy, distributed cognition

1. INTRODUCTION

This paper uses a framework in which alternative theoretical perspectives on HCI modelling problems are integrated, and illustrates its applicability to designing interactive systems. An example is given from a particular domain: the construction of hypertext documents. The paper expands on the framework referred to as the *resources model* of human-computer interaction (Wright et al., 1996; Fields et al., 1996) by adding notions of "interaction strategy" and "objective", and showing their application in design.

The paper begins with the observation that there are a number of rather diverse ways of supporting apparently identical or similar tasks. In order to understand some of the similarities and differences between the various ways of supporting a task, the model presented here steps outside of the traditional task analytic explanations of work (for example, Kirwan and Ainsworth, 1992) and reflects the way designs support different ways of interacting or *interaction strategies*. The general architecture of strategy-based distributed cognition can be explained in terms of *information resources* and *objectives*. Resources include constructs traditionally considered as part of a human's internal cognitive processing (such as plans and goals); the difference is that resources may also be externally represented. Objectives correspond to the high-level purposes of users' work (for example, acquiring information about some subject could be an objective). In general, an abstract information resource can be represented or implemented by any of the (human or machine) agents in a cognitive system. Resources are treated as objects in a distributed cognitive system, rather than the controlling mechanisms of cognition.

Paradigms for modelling human-computer interaction such as situated action (Suchman, 1987), display-based interaction (Kitajima and Polson, 1995), and planning (John and Kieras, 1994) emerge as strategies in the resources view. Strategies and resources help the designer generate design concepts, thereby forming a bridge in the development process between a high-level view of users'

Human–Computer Interaction: INTERACT'97 S. Howard, J. Hammond & G. Lindgaard (editors)
Published by Chapman & Hall

objectives and the lower level goals and other resources that may be considered as design objects. The ideas are illustrated by an example using the relationship between objectives, strategies and resources: the design of a hypertext information system.

A perspective that will emerge in the paper is that designing interactive artefacts is a process of deciding how *information resources* are to be *implemented*; this involves understanding the *objectives* underlying a user's activity and the *interaction strategies* that are appropriate to those objectives.

2. DESIGN CHOICES

It is clear that numerous design possibilities exist for giving users access to a system's underlying functionality. Consider as examples, two tasks: following a procedure described in the online help system of a word processor (Figure 1), and producing a chart using a computer spreadsheet package such as Excel (Figure 2).

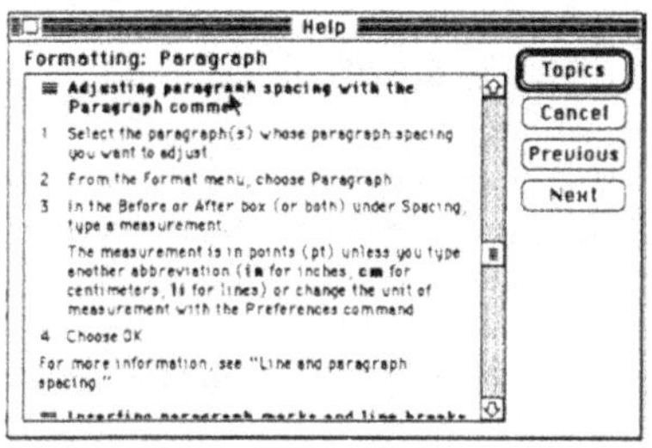

Figure 1: Word help screen

Besides the obvious superficial differences between these two interfaces and the tasks they support, what are the differences in terms of how the user's interaction is constructed? In the first case, the actions that the user should perform are very clearly defined and are displayed as a procedure by the online help. In addition, the steps of the procedure may be memorised by the user and recalled as necessary. This is an example of what Hutchins, 1995, Chapter 7) refers to as a "pre-computed plan". In the second case, however, the user need not have a very clearly defined goal about the kind of chart to be produced nor a clear plan for how to go about producing it. The interface presents possible goals (types of chart) and ways

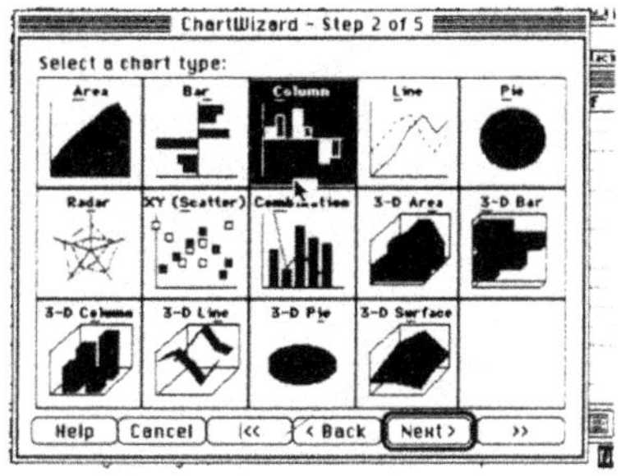

Figure 2: Chart type selection

the interaction may be moved forward (buttons and so on), obviating the need for the user to plan the course of the interaction in advance. This paper will argue that the difference between these two situations, and many others, can be captured by saying that each of the interfaces aims to provide support for a different *interaction strategy*. Different strategies require the presence of different information, and in the next section, we look at the information resources that allow users to follow strategies. The concept of information resources can be seen as laying out a space of possible design choices; objectives refer to the things a user will try to achieve using a design, and strategies, the means by which they go about doing so.

3. RESOURCES FOR ACTION

3.1 Resources

Instead of focusing on task knowledge the user may have, the resources model looks at the information, distributed *throughout* a system, that is needed to decide which actions to perform. A user may, in some situations, rely on knowing the current goal to select appropriate actions from those that are possible, while in others rely on knowing a pre-determined plan. The effects of actions in the current context or a record of past events can be similarly employed. Furthermore, there is no single place where all this information resides – some items are explicitly represented in external artefacts (the system interfaces, pieces of paper, and so on), some are external but implicit in the constraints of the dialogue, while others must necessarily be stored internally in the user's memory. A number of usability issues can be understood in terms of this assignment of *abstract information resources* to *concrete representational media*. A set of resources that play a role in shaping interaction is shown in Figure 3 and contains: *plans*, specifying actions to be performed; *goals* and sub-goals to be achieved; the *current state* of the world or interactive system; *historical information* about previous actions and what properties held of the state in the past; a model of the *effect* that actions have on the system; and the set of *actions* or "affordances" that the system currently supports (including constraints on the interaction arising from when it is legitimate to perform actions; for example, see (Zhang and Norman, 1994)).

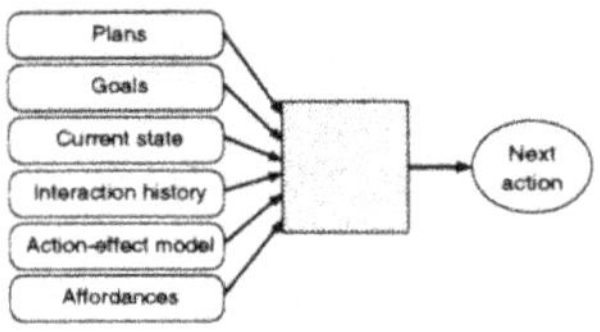

Figure 3: Information resources employed in interaction

Interactions consist of a number of steps, each being characterised by the set of resources that are available. In making a step, two processes are carried out by the joint human-machine system: determining a next action and doing it, and updating the required resources ready for the next step. Both are important from the perspective of design because the allocation of resources to representational media will affect how the processing is done. For instance, if a goal or a plan is implemented in the system's interface, then updating it can be performed by the system rather than the human.

In the early stages of understanding a task and designing to support it, no commitment need be made about where in the human-machine system the information resources and processing will reside. This is deliberate and allows us to talk about user activities early in the development process prior to the precise allocation of task information between user and system.

3.2 Implementation and distribution of resources

The resources described above are abstract specifications of the information required for a particular strategy of interacting. In any real situation, the resources must be represented or "implemented" in some physical medium. The expression of resources in media has a number of dimensions of variability: *distribution* (is the resource in the user's head or in the system interface?); *explicitness* (how is the resource expressed?); and *accessibility* (how much work is needed to "acquire" the resource in a form that can be used?).

Note that the relationship between these aspects of resources and the strategy that is employed is a complex one. The set of resources that are provided externally doesn't determine, in a simple way, the strategy that is adopted. The nature of the implementation is one crucial factor in this relationship.

A central part of the work of the designer is therefore to decide how the abstract information structures needed to support a strategy of interaction are to be implemented as concrete resources. The designer must decide whether a resource is to be represented externally (i.e., in the designed artefact), or whether the user must rely on their memory or that of another human agent. If the resource representation is to be external, the designer must decide whether it should be explicit (in that the user will be aware of it) or more implicitly (as is the case in plan-type structures embedded in Macintosh-style dialogues).

4. SUPPORTING STRATEGIES WITH INFORMATION RESOURCES

The concept of resources can go further than simply allowing us to describe particular interaction scenarios. The framework of resources allows a number of paradigms that have emerged in the HCI literature to emerge as what we refer to as *strategies*.

Plan following The "plan following" strategy requires the following two resources from the set identified in the previous section: a *plan* (with information about what actions are to be carried out, as well as an indication of which is the current item in the plan), and the *current state* of the work or the interactive system (which may be required in carrying out conditional parts of the plan). This is the kind of interaction described by the GOMS model (John and Kieras, 1994): plans correspond roughly to methods, and conditionals requiring a knowledge of system state are selection rules.

An example of support for this type in strategy is when a written procedure is followed, as in Figure 1, for example. This kind of implementation supplies the user with an external representation of the sequence of actions in a plan, though the "marker" showing the current item must be represented by the user. Halverson, 1994), however, describes a situation where the "marker" is separate from the actions of the plan and is externally represented.

Planning In contrast to plan following, the result of planning is to produce a plan (which can then be used in plan following). The input resources required are a *goal, system state* information, an *action-effect map* and *action affordances* for each stage of the interaction.

This strategy is often used in interactions with command line-based interfaces such as those found on unix systems: the goal resides only in the user's head; by default, very little resides in the interface, though actions' effects and status information (and some history) can be accessed by issuing commands.

Semantic matching In many situations, it is not plausible to claim that humans act by recalling and following previously formulated plans. Many of the studies of users of graphical user interfaces conclude that this is not how users act, and that they often have rather poor recall of the tasks being performed and the interfaces used (see, for example (O'Malley and Draper, 1992)). In the *semantic matching* strategy, the user decides what to do in a much more localised way by matching the effects of an action with the current goal, and checking to see if the resulting system state satisfies the goal. When the effects and availability of actions is represented externally in the interface, the strategy may be called *display-based interaction* (Kitajima and Polson, 1995). The information used to determine the next action can be a *goal*, the current *system state* information, an *action-effect map* and *action affordances*.

Many Macintosh style direct manipulation interfaces (like the one shown in Figure 2) provide support for this strategy by providing, in the interface, representations of the commands that are available and the effects that they have. Planning, however, is not so well supported because of the complexity of interactions and the contingency of action effects of the current state.

Goal-directed exploration In some situations the user may not be able to follow a plan or perform semantic matching of actions to goals. In such situations, users may, either through lack of information (about plans or actions), or in response to excessive cognitive demands, revert to an alternative strategy. A very simple sounding strategy is to act in an exploratory way by "trial and error". This involves selecting actions, possibly even at random, from those that are available, and checking to see if the resulting system state satisfies a goal. If not, then another action is tried.

Maximally, a trial and error strategy for selecting actions can require a goal and system state (to determine when the end-point of the interaction has been reached), the set of actions available at each point, a history of actions performed (to avoid going around in circles), and possibly a partial model of actions' effects (so as to rule out some actions as being unhelpful or dangerous).

Learning by exploring The above strategy, although it might seem rather inefficient, is one of the ways in which users can learn about their tasks and systems (Carroll and Mack, 1986). In addition to selecting next actions, the outputs of this strategy can be new plans. By reflecting on the history of a successful interaction, a plan can be developed and used in a future plan following interaction. Alternatively, exploration can help to enrich the user's model of actions' effects, which can be used in future semantic matching interactions.

This kind of exploration can be captured as a strategy in its own right, requiring a system state, actions' availability, and a history of which actions have already been performed. The product of such a strategy is an enriched model of actions and effects, as well as actions that are performed.

An example of learning or achieving goals by exploration is in complex, but highly structured, interactions such as with a mathematical theorem proving assistant system (e.g., the Jape system: Bornat and Sufrin, 1996)). The user can often learn, or even make progress by a trial and error exploration, which can move from an apparently hopeless state to one where another strategy will bear more fruit.

5. FROM OBJECTIVES TO DESIGNS

The previous sections have sketched out a framework for constructing "broad brush" models of human computer interaction. This section looks at one way these ideas may be used in design and the next one shows how the ideas are being used in the design of a hypertext document.

5.1 Objectives

A common starting point for interactive systems design is to understand the high-level objectives of the work being carried out. After deciding which aspects of this work are to be computerised, a process of task decomposition is used, eventually reaching a level where the sub-tasks can be supported by features of the interface.

A suggestion of this paper is that different high-level objectives of users may be best supported by different interaction strategies, and that design can progress from high-level objectives to lower level designs by way of a consideration of strategies and resources (see Figure 4).

To illustrate the importance of thinking about interface design in terms of user's objectives, strategies, and resources and their distribution through the cognitive system, consider the following three activities for which a user may make use of a hypertext system: getting an overall idea of the subject matter; secondly, answering a specific question; and learning about a highly structured collection of information. Each can be achieved most effectively by a different strategy: browsing and querying can both be thought of as goal directed, so appropriate strategies may be variants of semantic matching. Learning can be supported by a tutorial-style "tour" based on a plan embedded in the interface. Section 6 follows these ideas through in a little more detail.

5.2 Designing the external environment

As mentioned earlier, when viewed from the perspective of the resources model, part of the process of designing interactive systems involves making decisions about which strategies are to be supported, which resources are to be represented, and precisely how they will be represented. The process of doing design is therefore one of deciding which resources are to be embodied in system agents, and how they are to be implemented.

As we begin to move the ideas of the resources model towards a set of concepts that can be used in design, it is important to emphasise what the scope of design activity is in this context. In deciding how to provide resources to support an interaction strategy, the designer is engaged in designing the *external environment*; the designer cannot mandate what is represented internally by a user of the system. This fact might seem to limit the usefulness of the resources model (or indeed any similar activity) as a tool for thinking about design. However, two implications of the design of external artefacts rather than internal structures suggest ways in which the model can deliver benefits to the design process.

Firstly, although one cannot design the structure of users' knowledge, a resources model captures assumptions about what the user must know for a particular strategy to work. This has the effect of recording requirements that are placed upon a human agent in order to be able to carry out a particular strategy.

Secondly, we want to design not just an interface, but also an "ecology" for the development and evolution of strategies. In other words, a designer may anticipate the ways in which the strategies used may change over time, as a result of resources becoming internalised by the user. A simple example of this is where a resource represented in the interface (such as the "plan" in Figure 1) becomes, over a period of time, internalised by the user. The abstract information resources used to carry out a strategy may remain the same, but their physical location changes, with a consequent impact on performance (cf. Hutchins, 1995).

A more interesting example occurs when a plan is being followed. If the user interface provides sufficient information about the system state as it changes during the plan's execution. Over time, the user may internalise a model of the effects that actions have. On it's own, that may not be particularly useful, but if combined with a representation of which actions are available at any point in time, the user may be able to make a transition to a semantic matching strategy.

6. A DESIGN EXAMPLE

The ideas of strategy and information resource have been applied to the design (and implementation using the SuperCard authoring system) of a hypertext document describing certain aspects of the process of safety analysis for critical interactive systems. The target user population is composed of engineers who design and evaluate such systems. The hypertext is intended to provide support for a range of activities and objectives the users engage in, including:

1. *browsing* to find general information;

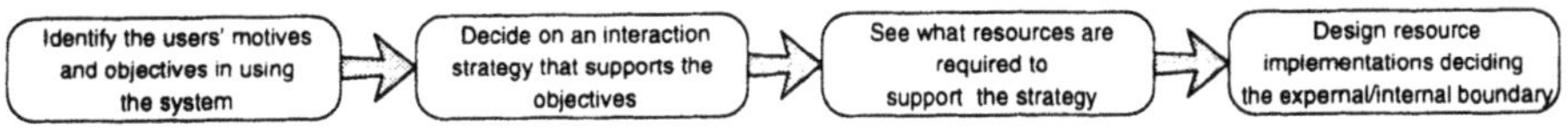

Figure 4: From high level objectives to designs via strategies and resources

2. *learning* in detail how the analysis process works;

3. *querying* to find particular information.

The view taken in this paper is that a single cognitive perspective provides a rather narrow basis for designing interactive technology and that the concept of strategy allows the modeller to generalise over a number of paradigms. In this section we aim to show how such a wide-ranging view can yield some benefits in design.

In HCI in general and hypertext design in particular, many authors have sought to provide advice to the designer in the form of principles and guidelines (e.g., Hardman and Sharratt, 1990). This often leads to principles that are general but rather abstract and hard to apply, or guidelines that tend to be numerous and address only low-level aspects of the design. The aim of this section is to show how the resources concepts might help to occupy some of the middle ground by being more constructive without focusing on the detail of interaction.

The need to support a number of cognitive styles is discussed by Hammond and Allinson, 1989), who suggest that a range of strategic options can be supported in an interface without undue increase in its complexity.

We shall see that for the three classes of objective, there are three corresponding interaction strategies, or cognitive styles, that are appropriate. This presents the interface designer with a number of choices for how to provide resources to support the strategies.

6.1 Supporting browsing

A user interacting with the hypertext may have an objective to acquire fairly general information about the process being described ("get an overview of the process", or to "look at the information on task analysis"). Since the objective in a specific situation can be articulated, a goal-oriented exploration strategy seems most appropriate. A plan-based strategy is likely to be less effective because the user with a browsing objective is unlikely to have a sufficiently good knowledge of the hypertext's structure, and the designer cannot be expected to anticipate all the browsing styles and possible user preferences a priori. The implications of this for design are twofold: the user should be able to see how their work-level objective can be re-expressed in terms of interaction-level goals, and that sufficient resources should be provided in the interface to support matching of actions to goals formed in this way.

These two issues together can be addressed by the design of the overall structure of the hypertext and the linking structure within it. The text can be organised so that there is a rich linking structure within a "domain" or logical group of information (such as the information on task analysis); the link labels can make it clear when selecting a link would leave one domain and enter another, thus providing support for browsing objectives like "see what's available on topic X".

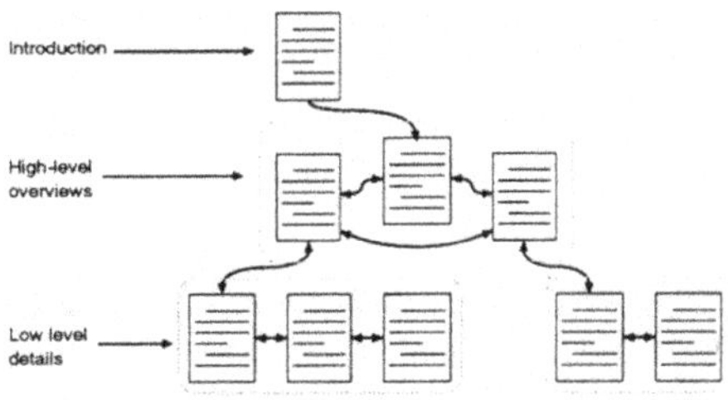

Feedback may be provided on where the user has been in the text, to help the user determine when a goal like "look at *all* the information on task analysis" has been accomplished.

6.2 Taking the user on a tour

Allowing the user to learn about the process in detail may seem very similar to browsing. There is, however, a difference: the process itself embodies a sequencing of sub-processes, and this may be reflected in a plan resource for the order in which the text is navigated. Learning can be supported by a tutorial-style presentation where the user is taken on a "guided tour" of the process. The design will accommodate a plan following strategy, and the plan will be located externally in the interface of the system, encouraging the user to see *all* the relevant material and to look at it in the *right order*. This still leaves a number of questions open, not least of which is the issue of how explicitly the plan should be implemented.

A fairly explicit way of representing a plan is to show a "map", either in a separate window, or integrated with the rest of the text. Boxes in the map represent sub-processes in the safety analysis method, and clicking on a box follows a link to an appropriate page. The current "marker" item is shown and items which have been seen previously can be indicated.

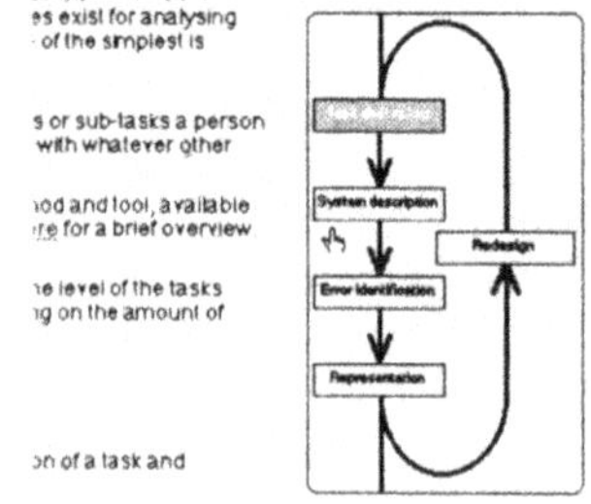

More implicit implementations of the plan structure are also possible by, for example, providing hypertext links or navigation buttons to move around the structure of the text (and therefore the structure of the process being described).

This implicit implementation shows the user enough of the plan for the next action to be taken, but gives no overall visibility of the structure of the plan itself or the progress that is being made through it.

6.3 Goal-directed information retrieval

In common with the objective of browsing the text, the retrieval of answers to specific queries can best be served by a goal-oriented strategy such as semantic matching. A difference between this case and browsing is that the goal can probably be more easily specified, and is related primarily to the information content of the text, rather than to the overall structure.

In interface terms, the appropriate strategy can be supported in a number of ways. A simplistic (in user interface terms, thought not necessarily in terms of the implementation!) design is to provide a searching mechanism. This allows a user to phrase quite arbitrary "commands" that are closely related to goals. One disadvantage of search interfaces is that they often provide no external representation of what "actions" are available and what their effects will be. In other words, the user is not aware of what keywords have been indexed for searching, so interpreting the results of a search may be hard.

A alternative is to provide navigational help, by externalising affordance and action-effect resources, either as navigation links at appropriate points in the document. Of course, this requires the designer to have anticipated possible goals, so that the relevant resources can be implemented in the navigational structure. A simple use of this approach is the provision of indices and contents pages that give the user some higher-level visibility of how goals might be achieved.

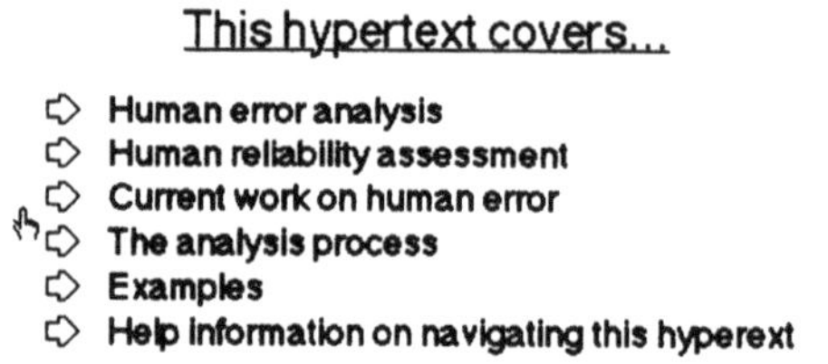

7. CONCLUSIONS

The paper has described a model for human-computer interaction based on the notions of *information resources* and the *interaction strategies* in which the resources may be deployed. The central message of the paper is that a single cognitive perspective isn't an adequate basis for designing interactive technology; the concept of strategy allows the model to generalise over a number of paradigms. Furthermore, the process of designing interactive systems can be seen as a progression from an understanding of the objectives of the system, through interaction strategies appropriate for the objectives, to decisions about how and where resources required by the strategies are to be implemented.

The kinds of domains used as examples in this paper could be classified as consisting of "user driven" interactions: the interactive artefact is a fairly passive component, it's behaviour being largely determined by user's inputs. In more dynamic domains such as aircraft flight decks or process control systems, however, the picture is much more complex. Here, the external world impinges on users' activity, generating events at unpredictable times and imposing temporal deadlines to satisfy higher level requirements (such as safety). Extending the concepts of resource and strategy into domains with such complex constraints is one of the main challenges for the future development of this work. One way of meeting the challenge is to consider not only the resources that might be employed in support of a strategy, but also the cognitive demands associated with using a resource, and the effect that this has on "metacognitive" issues like strategy switching.

A longer term aim of the work is to inform models of failure in interactive systems. Many existing approaches to understanding failure concentrate of errors at the subtask or action level. We aim to consider more of the contextual factors surrounding failure by looking at the ways that available resources can fail to support a strategy, and how this is affected by the demands of the work.

REFERENCES

Bornat, R. and Sufrin, B. (1996). Jape's Quiet Interface. In Merriam, N. A., editor, *International Workshop on User Interfaces for Theorem Provers*. Department of Computer Science, University of York. URL: *http://www.cs.york.ac.uk/~nam/uitp/proceedings.html*.

Carroll, J. and Mack, R. (1986). Learning to use a word processor: By doing, by thinking, and by knowing. In Thomas, J. and Schneider, M., editors, *Human Factors in Computer Systems*, chapter 2, pages 13–51. Ablex Publishing Corporation.

Fields, B., Wright, P., and Harrison, M. (1996). Designing human-system interaction using the resource model. In *APCHI'96: First Asia Pacific Conference on Human Computer Interaction*, pages 181–191. URL: *http://www.cs.york.ac.uk/~bob/papers.html*.

Green, T., Cañas, J., and Warren, C., editors (1996). *Proceedings of ECCE8: European Conference on Cognitive Ergonomics*. EACE.

Halverson, C. (1994). Distributed cognition as a theoretical framework for HCI: Don't throw the baby out with the bathwater – the importance of the cursor in air traffic control. Report 9403, Department of Cognitive Science, University of California, San Diego.

Hammond, N. and Allinson, L. (1989). Extending hypertext for learning: An investigation of access and guidance tools. In Sutcliffe, A. and Macaulay, L., editors, *Proceedings of the Fifth Conference of the BCS HCI Special Interest Group*, pages 294–304. Cambridge University Press.

Hardman, L. and Sharratt, B. (1990). User-centred hypertext design: the application of HCI design principles and guidelines. In McAleese, R. and Green, C., editors, *Hypertext: State of the art*, chapter 28, pages 252–259. Intellect Ltd.

Hutchins, E. (1995). *Cognition in the Wild*. MIT Press.

John, B. and Kieras, D. (1994). The GOMS family of analysis techniques: Tools for design and evaluation. Technical Report CMU-CS-94-181, School of Computer Science, Carnegie Mellon University.

Kirwan, B. and Ainsworth, L. (1992). *A Guide to Task Analysis*. Taylor and Francis, London.

Kitajima, M. and Polson, P. (1995). A comprehension-based model of correct performance and errors in skilled, display-based human-computer interaction. *International Journal of Human-Computer Studies*, 43(1):65–100.

O'Malley, C. and Draper, S. (1992). Representation and interaction: Are mental models all in the mind? In Rogers, Y., Rutherford, A., and Bibby, P., editors, *Models in the Mind: Theory, Perspective & Application*, chapter 6, pages 73–91. Academic Press.

Plowman, L. (1996). What's the story? narrative and the comprehension of educational interactive media. In (Green et al., 1996).

Suchman, L. (1987). *Plans and Situated Actions – the problem of human-machine communication*. Cambridge University Press.

Wright, P., Fields, B., and Harrison, M. (1996). Distributed information resources: A new approach to interaction modelling. In (Green et al., 1996), pages 5–10. URL: *http://www.cs.york.ac.uk/~bob/papers.html*.

Zhang, J. and Norman, D. (1994). Representations in distributed cognitive tasks. *Cognitive Science*, 18:87–122.

32

Teaching User Interface Design and Programming to Computer Science majors

Judy Kay
Bob Kummerfeld

Department of Computer Science
University of Sydney
{judy,bob}@cs.su.oz.au

ABSTRACT

This paper describes an innovative approach to teaching about human-computer interaction to a large class of students in their third year of a Computer Science major. Because of the tight time constraints on the course and the student's learning preferences and orientation, we have created a course which interweaves the learning of several programming tools for interface construction with the development of knowledge and skills in the design of user interfaces.

We present the structure of the course, especially its most unusual aspects. We also describe our rationale for the course design, our evaluation of student learning and the response to the course.

KEYWORDS HCI education, interface design, interface programming

1. Introduction

It is becoming increasingly important that students majoring in Computer Science should learn about creating good user interfaces. At the same time, typical Computer Science programmes are very full, with little time to add courses that teach students to build better interfaces. Indeed, as observed elsewhere (Greenberg 1996), traditional Computer Science degrees have rarely included courses in human-computer interaction.

We have designed an innovative one-semester human-computer interaction course. We needed to win over two sets of critics. First

Human–Computer Interaction: INTERACT'97 S. Howard, J. Hammond & G. Lindgaard (editors)
Published by Chapman & Hall

we had to convince our colleagues that this course should earn a place in a very tightly constrained computer science curriculum. With that battle won, we knew we would need to convince our students that they should take the course over other hard-core computer science options. We also wanted the course to mesh well with the student expectations and interests since that ensures better learning outcomes. Moreover, it had to be manageable with an enrolment of 80-120 students.

Essentially, our approach was to focus on three main elements:

- interface design - the core of most courses and texts in human-computer interaction;
- interface programming - several tools in current use for interface prototyping and production;
- reflection - about the relationship between these and the students' evolving understanding of interface design.

We knew that the students would value the skills acquired in the second, programming tool, part of the course. This would attract them to the course and would motivate them. At the same time, it could serve as a driving force for learning the interface design aspects. It would provide a context for learning activities that would make the interface design issues meaningful.

This is an unconventional approach. But it avoids several potential pitfalls of a course that deals exclusively with interface design. First, and most important, students may have elected to simply not do a typical course, staying with options closer to the usual technology-centred model of Computer Science. This would have meant large numbers of students continuing to graduate without learning anything about human-computer interaction. A second risk is that many students would find a pure human-computer interaction course so different from their previous studies that they would have difficulty seeing its relevance and importance for them.

This paper describes the course from two points of view: that of the student and our own design rationale. Then we outline how our course relates to more typical courses. We conclude with a summary of the student response to the course and our experience of teaching it.

2. The student's point of view

This section presents three central elements of the student's view of the course. First we describe the practical work since that is where the deep learning occurs. With this we describe the assessment since that is a major concern for students and we have been very careful to make it serve our goals. Finally, the sequencing of lecture material and practical work constitutes the last highly visible aspect of the course.

2.1 Practical work and assessment

All practical work was based upon a single problem: creation of an interactive interface to enable computer science researchers to search and update a database of bibliographic references. The major task of the semester required students to work in groups, usually of about five. Assessment was based on a group report and demonstration.

Students built prototypes using each of the following tools: World Wide Web's html with cgi interface, tk/Python (Ousterhout 1993, Rossum 1991) an X-toolkit (Patrick 1996) and Visual Basic. In addition students implemented a small search language using yacc and lex (Kernighan 1984).

Between each of these tools, students had lectures and practical work on various aspects of HCI and how it can inform better design of interactive systems. The primary text was (Newman 1995). Practical work was done in closed lab classes with approximately seven of these devoted to learning new technical tools for constructing interfaces, four to interface design aspects and the remaining two to practice and final demonstrations, activities the last being activities that encourage reflection and self-assessment of the work done. The four prototype implementations were done individually but with collaboration encouraged. These were assessed on a binary scale: satisfactory or not.

The final aspect of the work required students to write examination questions about the human-computer interaction lectures of the course. Each student was randomly assigned one week of lectures and required to write open-book exam questions, model answers and assessment schemes for these. Students were told that this would help them reflect on the lectures, deciding what was important and how one would assess knowing it. The best of these were made available to the class at the end of the semester. The students were told that the exam question also gave us a good idea of major problems or misconceptions. These aspects were reviewed in the last lecture.

The marks were awarded as follows:

Description	**Marks** %
Group Marks	
1. Demonstration	20
2. Report on system	10
Individual Marks	
3. Exam questions	10
4. Programming tools	10
5. Final exam	50

The report required a detailed explanation of the design of one screen in the system, an assessment of tools considered with reasons for selecting or rejecting each, evaluation of the interface created, its strengths and weaknesses and use of literature. The demonstration had to demonstrate the interface and explain its design and development process.

Note that the two main parts of the group assessment had a draft or trial run before the final one was submitted. This was to help students improve their work and also provide a low-risk opportunity to experiment with unusual ideas or one they may have been unsure about.

2.2 Course structure

The lecture and practical work schedule interwove the two elements of the course so that students could apply new interface design skills to the new prototypes they constructed. As one might expect, students were tempted to devote practical classes to developing their prototypes. This was avoided by making the interface design tasks serve the primary goal of the semester, the interface for the bibliographic database (and the report and demonstration for it). These tasks served a dual role in consolidating lecture material and as well as aiding in team-building and group communication and management.

The actual lecture topics and practical sessions are summarised below:

Lecture Topics	**Practical**
1. Overview of course, www/html	
2. forms/cgi	html, cgi
3. screen design	html, cgi
4. Python/tk	screen design
5. usability	Python/tk
6. usability	usability
7. X toolkit	usability
8. user-centred design	X toolkit
9. Visual Basic	design
10. formal notations	
11. yacc/lex	Visual Basic
12. interface problems, Java	
	draft reports
13. cognition, mental models	
theoretical foundations	practice demos
14. conceptual design, review	final demos

3. Design rationale - the teacher's view

There were many elements to our design. Here, we focus on two of the most important. In terms of learning effectiveness, the major aspect is the students' practical experiences. So we explain their rationale first. The other quite unusual aspect is our ordering of the teaching and learning elements of the course. Both these are inspired by a problem-based approach to learning where the demands of a problem are used to motivate the learning.

3.1 The role and management of the practical work

The course is dominated by the single major practical problem. Since the students had to make individual attempts at the prototypes they built with each of the tools, they had the opportunity to rebuild the same system four times before creating their final work in the interface as part of the group effort. This had several advantages:

- with each new prototype, they had a growing knowledge of interface design to draw upon;
- and they had a growing body of experiences both of building the earlier interfaces and seeing the efforts of their peers;
- there was no additional start up cost for getting into each new programming task as they were rebuilding interfaces for the same tasks and, at the same time, working towards the semester's main problem;
- the comparison between the tools were meaningful in two senses: they were doing the same tasks; and they were part of working towards a goal, the group's final project;
- reflection about what had been learnt was a natural part of the process.

Overall, we believe that the whole practical and learning sequence constitute an 'authentic' problem for real world interface design, involving just the stages practiced in the course: prototyping to explore interface tools and designs, learning about HCI that can improve the design and self-assessment at each stage to inform future work.

The role of groups in the major submissions is important. Since the students had built prototypes individually, they had to come to terms with the differences in their individual approaches when they came to create the group's interface design. Each group had to reach agreement on the tool they would use. The decision balanced ease of programming againats power for interface construction. We encouraged each practical class to try diverse tools and to look at each other's work. In the end, the bulk of implementations were split between use of www-html with various languages in the cgi-scripts and the X-toolkit.

The group was critical to effective learning about the range of usability and design approaches. Group work helped students reflect about their work and reasoning since they needed to discuss it with group members and justify it.

It also allowed work to be planned by the group, with a sharing of the effort required to do the actual construction, evaluative and research tasks and the whole group would assess and review outcomes.

Another critical aspect of our course management is that we took great care to ensure that students should not be overloaded. The course load was spread right through the semester and students were encouraged to collaborate at all stages of the programming work. We wanted students to have the time to stand back from their work and reflect on the learning experiences. To permit that, we had to make sure there was enough time for students to reflect as well as do the required tasks in the curriculum.

The overall effect of the practical work design was that the final products were extremely impressive. The demonstrations were very good, enhanced considerably by the practice sessions and the reports also demonstrated that students learnt from feedback on their draft submission. The class atmosphere was positive and cheerful as students worked co-operatively and purposefully towards the semester's goals.

3.2 The learning sequence

Two principles underly our ordering of the course elements:

- the programming and design elements were to

be tightly linked and interwoven so presentation alternated between them;

• aspects that students were likely to relate to were presented early in the course and these formed a basis for the others that were treated later.

Given these principles, it is easy to see that we would start with a programming tool. It represents the sort of learning our students are familiar with and value. Moreover, the choice of www/html/cgi programming enabled students to devote time learning about an area that is currently of great interest to them, employers and the public.

At the same time, it makes a very natural route for exploration of some truly ghastly screen designs, the first part of the human-computer interaction side of the course. But this is not the primary reason for teaching that very early. Screen design has several aspects that make it perfect for introducing a user interface design course. Firstly, there are many, well-defined facts one can learn. Applying these will reduce some of the most terrible screen design errors. This aspect can be taught in terms of very concrete guidelines with solid theoretical, empirical or physiological bases. For example, use of saturated blue text is demonstrably unreadable and we can explain why. Essentially, screen design makes a *concrete* element which has high payoff for a little learning. It makes for a rewarding start to the course.

While the practical classes consolidated the lectures on screen design, lectures introduced Python/tk. This was primarily to introduce an example of a scripting language and the language, Python, which was also useful for cgi-scripts.

The choice of usability as the second main interface design topic was driven by its immediate relevance and applicability. We linked this to the familiar software engineering concern with testing and made it clear that this was a new collection of strategies to build testing into the design process as well as the final evaluation. Students responded well. Their application of these aspects was visible in the final products (especially when compared with the prototypes). The reports of usability and the excellent exam questions submitted indicated a good level of understanding.

The next programming tool was GraphApp, an example of an X-toolkit designed to be easy to learn. For programmers familiar with C, it is a painless introduction to central concepts of this style of event driven interface programming.

At this point, we gave a brief overview of user-centred design and drew heavily on the student's background in software engineering as a basis both a foundation and as a basis for comparison. With the time available, our primary concern in this topic was that students have some experience and awareness of approaches they should draw upon in later work. We consider this satisfactory since we feel that the next significant level of learning in this area would require far more time than we had. Our introduction gave a useful foundation.

The next tool, Visual Basic, was chosen because it is so widespread that we felt our students would value meeting it. It was very easy to make simple prototypes and represents a style of interface that has an important place.

From this point we began the aspects of HCI that were less immediately useful for the project but which were useful for the report and demonstrations. We introduced various formal notations, as communication tools during the design process and on completion. Students seemed to like object-state transition diagrams and the User-Action Notation and other formal approaches: most of the exam questions written for these lectures focused on the most formal aspects. We linked this to our very brief survey of interaction styles. The lecture material simply summarised the interface styles that were familiar from the practical work and then introduced those interaction styles not available in the practical work.

The final tool may seem unusual in any interface course. It introduced students to yacc and lex, tools for building parsers for small languages. By careful construction of a practical task closely linked to the main project and by providing scaffolding, students could see the potential of these tools. There are many situations where the user may benefit from the power of a small command or programming language. This part of the course aimed to ensure that when our students met these cases, they would look to such tools to facilitate building that part of the interface well.

The last three weeks of lectures were mainly devoted to theoretical and psychological aspects that are foundations for all the pragmatics of the earlier HCI material. So, for example, it was at this stage that we introduced the human information processing model: students were readily able to see how this related to the GOMS analyses they met earlier. (We know this because our lecture style involves stopping at suitable points in the lectures and posing questions for small group discussion then sharing with the class. This case is typical of how we used this lecture style, asking students to stop and think about how new material related to what they already knew.) This section included some of the classical and entertaining examples of interface failures. These introduced mental models, various cognitively based theories, models of task performance, theories of exploration and conceptual design methods.

Rather than detail all topics discussed, we note that the lectures took a similar perspective to the textbook (Newman 1995) and covered all of its content except the chapter on statistical bases for design and analysis of experiments. We also supplemented lectures with some material from books (Baecker 1987, Borenstein 1991, Mayhew 1992, Galitz 1993, Preece 1994) and these also served as class references. As a brief interlude of change in this period, there was one lecture on Java.

4. Related courses

The most unusual aspect of our course is the integration of programming and design aspects of interface creation.

Another innovative aspect of the course is the ordering of the HCI material which differs from most texts, (Baecker 1987, Preece 1994, Thimbleby 1990, Dix 1993, Lewis 1996) including our prescribed text (Newman 1995) as well as the excellent ACM SIGCHI curriculum materials that include example curricula (SIGCHI).

It is interesting that a study of practicing user interface designers (Howard 1993) identified three central knowledge bases that practitioners should have: the technology of the user interface, facility with interface design and, particularly for the software engineer, skill in programming the user interface. The underpinning and history as well as theoretical aspects were judged as being of less importance. Our approach should enable students to build strongest foundations in areas that Howard's study suggest are critical.

5. Evaluation

There have been several indications that students have responded well to this course. Firstly, it attracted and held the bulk of the eligible candidates. Students responded energetically to all elements of the course: lecture and practical class attendance were good.

In terms of learning outcomes, the standard of the final systems was incomparably better than those as prototypes. They reflected the usability assessments students had done and the formal material from lectures. Some showed the effects of considerable research, exploring similar classes of systems and insightful analysis of user trials. The reports indicated that students were often aware of shortcomings of their designs as well as the trade-offs they had to make against conflicting goals. The demonstrations were also a good indication of student awareness of interface design issues. We received unsolicited positive comments from staff taking major software projects where they were struck by the dramatic rise in quality of interface design by students doing our course.

The student's examination questions, answers and grading schemes indicated a good understanding of major issues. A small number of students sat take-home final examinations and these indicate a good understanding of the main HCI aspects of the course. The final examination performance was consistent with our other source of evaluative information.

There are, as one would expect, several small areas where we would like to see improvements. For example, students should be encouraged to read more. Another serious concern to address in future is that students need more consolidation of the fact that their intuition is not enough. Some did appreciate that this was one of the central messages of the course. However, some casual student' comments indicated they only knew this at a superficial level because they made slips in conversation, belying the lack of deeper understanding.

Finally, student response to the course has been very positive. On the final course evaluation questionnaire, only two responses of the 71 received were clearly negative: these two students seemed to dislike the HCI part and did not see its relevance. Overall the responses were resoundingly positive, with many students taking the time to write quite detailed comments on what they appreciated about the course. We have also had several inquiries from students who would like to continue this work into Honours year projects.

6. Conclusions

For each of the elements of the HCI part of the course, one could easily justify far deeper study than our course permitted. Indeed, each aspect is the subject of whole texts that are designed for use in full semester courses. We cannot claim to have given our students the depth of understand that a half dozen HCI courses could give! However, we did aim for a useful foundation. For each area, we aimed to achieve the following:

• students met central ideas, terms, concerns and practical value of that area. This gave more than a mere literacy level of learning: it provided a foundation for further learning when problems demand it;

• students should be aware of the limits of their knowledge so that they will *know* that they need to go to the literature and learn more as problems demand serious application of elements of the course;

• students apply something of what they heard in each set of lecture topics to the main task of the semester and so built a deeper understanding strongly linked to their other knowledge;

• concrete and high leverage learning areas were treated early and more theoretical foundations were treated later when students could see them as the underpinnings of the concrete detailed knowledge they had by then applied to building better interfaces.

The common thread of the practical work served as an important way to unify and link the series of learning experiences. We are convinced that the time taken by the interface programming parts of the course provided advantages for learning the HCI aspects: the new HCI knowledge could immediately be linked to an authentic problem and the motivational and learning benefits help to offset the fact that the HCI aspects had to share time with the programming. Moreover, we believe there should not be a line between design and programming since a useless or difficult-to-use program may as well not be written at all. The pure technology has meaning and utility only when it can be combined with design knowledge. Our innovations in this course for teaching interface design and programming make it an excellent HCI basis for students who can only fit one HCI course into their computer science major.

References

Baecker 1987.
Ronald Baecker and William Buxton in *Readings in human-computer interaction : a multidisciplinary approach,* Morgan Kaufmann (1987).

Borenstein 1991.
N S Borenstein, *Programming as if people mattered: friendly programs, software engineering, and other noble delusions,* Princeton University Press, Princeton, New Jersey (1991).

Dix 1993.
Alan Dix, *Human-computer interaction,* Prentice Hall (1993).

Galitz 1993.
Wilbert Galitz in *User-interface screen design,* QED Pub. Group (1993).

Greenberg 1996.
S Greenberg, "Teaching Human Computer Interaction to Programmers," Research report 96/582/02, Department of Computer Science, University of Calgary (1996).

Howard 1993.
S Howard, *What do user interface designers say they need to know about HCI?,* OZCHI'93, Canberra Australia (1993).

Kernighan 1984.
B W Kernighan and R Pike in *The Unix programming environment,* Prentice-Hall (1984).

Lewis 1996.
Clayton Lewis and John Rieman, *Task-Centered User Interface Design,* ftp.cs.colorado.edu in: /pub/cs/distribs/clewis/HCI-Design-Book (1996).

Mayhew 1992.
Deborah J. Mayhew in *Principles and guidelines in software user interface design,* Prentice Hall (1992).

Newman 1995.
W M Newman and M G Lamming, *Interactive System Design,* Addison-Wedley (1995).

Ousterhout 1993.
John K Ousterhout, *TCL and the TK Toolkit,* Addison-Wesley (1993).

Patrick 1996.
Lachlan Patrick, *GraphApp,* http://www.cs.su.oz.au/~loki/graphapp/ (1996).

Preece 1994.
Jenny Preece, Yvonne Rogers, H Sharp, D Benyon, S Holland, and T Carey in *Human-computer interaction,* Addison-Wesley (1994).

Rossum 1991.
Guido van Rossum and Jelke de Boer, "Interactively Testing Remote Servers Using the Python Programming Language," *CWI Quarterly,* 4, 4 (1991).

SIGCHI .
ACM SIGCHI, *Curricula for Human-Computer Interaction,* (http://www.acm.org/sigchi/cdg/cdg3.html.

Thimbleby 1990.
Harold Thimbleby, *User interface design,* Addison-Wesley (1990).

33

Balloons, Boats and Ponies: Interface manipulation style and learning in a constraint-based planning task

Shirley J. Holst, Elizabeth F. Churchill and David J. Gilmore

Psychology Dept
University of Nottingham
Nottingham, NG7 2RD, UK

sjh@psychology.nottingham.ac.uk; churchill@pal.xerox.com;
dg@psychology.nottingham.ac.uk

ABSTRACT: The role of the interface in structuring student learning and in directing the learner's cognitive effort toward relevant material has become increasingly centralised in recent years. Specifically, interface designers have been called on to design interfaces which keep the learner focused on or "engaged" in the domain material, with the view that such engagement will have learning benefits. In this paper we operationalise the notion of cognitive engagement in terms of familiar cognitive psychological principles: planning and learning. Following laboratory studies, we have taken the view that cognitive planning can be induced by increasing the "cost" of selecting and executing actions by designing *less* direct interfaces. A study is reported which contrasts direct and indirect manipulation interfaces for a constraint-based planning task. Results from the study suggest that manipulation style can indeed affect users' information search and task solution strategies.

KEYWORDS: empirical, education, input devices, interaction design, theory, 'cognitive cost'

1. INTRODUCTION

Case studies of educational software indicate that children can successfully complete computer based tasks, whilst retaining little domain knowledge (e.g. maths; Moore, 1993). For cognitive psychologists, educators and educational software developers this is clearly a worry, as more educational software appears in schools. To overcome such problems, design guidelines encourage developers to ensure that the learner is active

Human–Computer Interaction: INTERACT'97 S. Howard, J. Hammond & G. Lindgaard (editors)
Published by Chapman & Hall

schools. To overcome such problems, design guidelines encourage developers to ensure that the learner is active (Jackson *et al*, 1996), engaged (Norman and Sporher, 1996), "cognitively immersed" in the material or motivated (Mallone, 1981). In this paper we report an attempt to draw on sound psychological theory and practice to operationalise the notion of cognitive engagement in terms of familiar cognitive psychological principles: planning and learning. Here, the role of the interface in structuring students' cognitive activities is centralised. Far from being a seen as a passive window onto the domain (as suggested for example by Laurillard, 1993), the interface and interaction style are seen as important for structuring learning activities; students' attention and cognitive processes can be directed to appropriate material for reflection through careful design of the interface and interaction style. In the following sections, we elaborate on this and present a comparative study.

1.2 Interfaces and learning

Studies indicate that increasing the 'cost' of actions by providing indirect, command-based interfaces and by increasing delays in system response encourages active problem solving and facilitates retention, recall and transfer of information. Svendsen (1991) and O'Hara and Payne (1994) empirically supported their prediction that certain forms of cost improve learning on computer-based problem-solving tasks. Command-based interfaces, delayed feedback and difficult error-recovery routines actually enhanced learning. Conversely, increasing ease-of-use through direct manipulation results in recognition or display-based performance (Svendsen, 1991; O'Hara and Payne, 1994; Gilmore, 1996). Such counter-intuitive results can help to explain why case studies like that cited above demonstrate little transfer of domain material away from the interface.

Applying this to the development of educational software, this analysis suggests that learning can be best facilitated by making the interface *less* easy-to-use for certain tasks by reducing the directness of the interface manipulation and thus forcing explicit cognitive processes like planning and problem solving (Churchill and Ainsworth, 1995; Gilmore, 1996). In this view, it is suggested that way in which the learner physically manipulates objects on-screen will affect the focus of their cognitive activity. By 'forcing' the learner to cognitively process curriculum appropriate information, concept formation and domain knowledge retention will be facilitated. There is some evidence from evaluation of intelligent tutoring systems that this assertion is well-founded; students using menus performed worse on post tests than students who were required to type responses into the tutor (Corbett, Anderson and Fincham, 1990).

Although these results are promising, there is still a need to understand fully the extent of this effect, to develop a clearer understanding of this effect and to consider the extent to which it "scales up" to more complex problem solving domains. In this vein, we studied a constraint based planning task to observe whether interface design and manipulation style affects students' information seeking behaviours, pre-action planning and post task knowledge.

2. HONEY BEARS TASK

2.1 Introduction

From the above discussion, we predicted that a less direct interface manipulation style will result in more "cognitive cost" in the form of pre-planning before action. To empirically test this hypothesis, two interfaces were developed for an on-line, constraint based planning task couched in the form of an adventure game: the Honey Bears task (Littleton et al, 1994).

The task and interfaces

In the Honey Bears task three bears (Airbear, Waterbear and Ponybear) plan a picnic, but on arrival at their destination (Almwood) discover they have forgotten their honey. The honey is at Flint on the other side of the river, but in the river there are Honey Monsters who will steal the honey if the bears attempt to move it by boat (see Figure 1). The goal of the task is for bears to use appropriate means of transport (boat, balloon or pony) to get the honey, whilst avoiding the Honey Monsters. Clearly the task requires planning of a route, whilst ensuring that the "correct" bear is in the appropriate place to use the most appropriate form of transport. (e.g. Ponybear can only use the pony and so on).

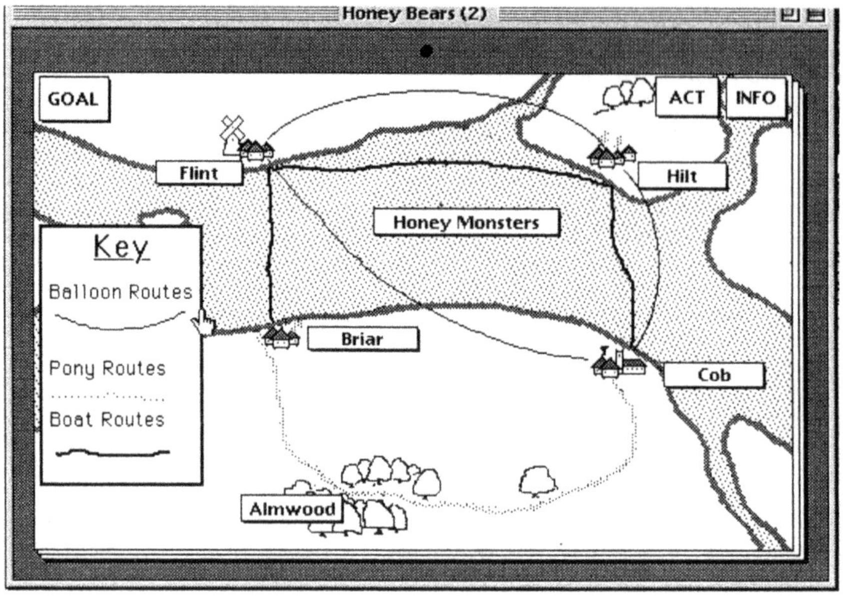

Figure 1: The Honey Bears map, taken from the "select elements" interface.

Two interfaces were developed for this task. The two interfaces were equivalent in terms of the task structure and goals, but one was designed to be more computationally costly in cognitive terms than the other, implementing O'Hara and Payne's notion of cognitive cost and action. Specifically, the "select elements", indirect manipulation interface offers a basic map with a key showing transport routes with no visual representation of where bears, transport and honey are located. Information must be sought and moves must be issued from a separate radio-button screen (Figure 2) away from the central map. This requires the learner to explicitly seek information about the location of items, and then to maintain a mental representation of their location throughout the task. This radio button screen not only required the user to move from the map, but also broke the possible task moves into means ends analysis format, forcing the user to think explicitly about the task requirements, task goals and task moves. By contrast, the second interface, the 'drag and place', direct manipulation interface, shows where both people and transport are currently located and allows moves to be made on a focused subsection of the map by dragging and placing items (shown in Figures 3 and 4). It therefore requires less information search, and can visually represent the effects of the user's previous action.

Hence, the 'select elements' interface was identified as being more costly to the user since actions are a more lengthy diversion, require explicit search for information and a non-visually based solution structure to be devised, whilst the second, 'drag and place' interface was identified as being less costly to the user as minimal information search is required and no mental transformation of the interface elements was needed. Notably, the 'drag and place' interface also keeps error costs low by directly presenting possible moves on a subsection of the map. Only a small number of constraints remain 'implicit' in the interface. (e.g. that the pony bear is needed to drive the pony). In contrast, 'select-elements' allows radio-button selection of impossible moves (e.g. travelling in one journey from

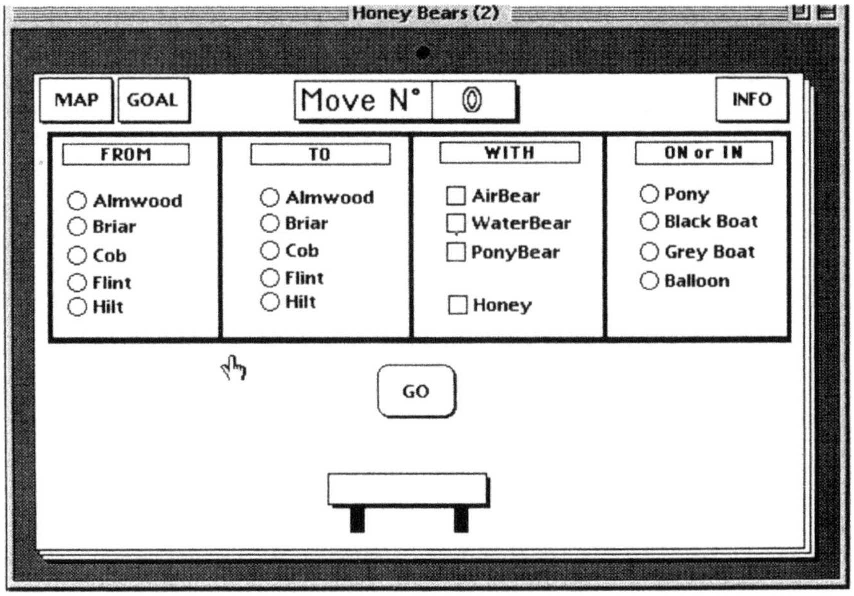

Figure 2: The "select elements" radio button interface for making moves

Flint to Almwood) and responds with an error-message only once the full set of radio-button selections is made.

An isomorphic second task was developed. Here, the bears were replaced by a king's loyal subjects, the honey monsters were replaced by pirates and the goal was to retrieve a crown. The transfer task was devised as a test of what was learnt on the Honey bears task and therefore all subjects needed to share a *common* interaction method; all subjects used a 'select elements' interface. For both tasks, there was one crucial piece of information which enabled the development of the correct task solution: that Honey Monsters eat honey and that pirates steal jewels, and that they should therefore be avoided by taking the balloon across the water.

2.2 Method

Design

A mixed design was employed. The independent variable was the type of interface experienced by subjects in their initial task, with two levels: 1) "high-cost", select-elements version of Honey bears used for the initial task and (2) "low cost", drag-and-place version of Honey bears used for the initial task. Both groups experienced the same transfer task, implemented with a 'select-elements', indirect manipulation interface. Dependent measures taken were number of information searches in total, number of information searches which were made before the first move (where information search was defined as moving to another screen to find out information about objects and locations), number of moves made before discovery of the main task constraint (that the Honey Monsters eat honey and must be avoided), percentage of move attempts which were successful (i.e. no error messages received on execution) and level reached by subjects during the trial (Levels 1-6). The percentage of successful moves made was a score constructed by taking *n*(moves made without error message on execution) divided by *n*(total number of moves attempted, including attempted executions which failed and did result in an error message). Information searches before the first move were used as an indication that subjects were seeking to discover in advance which routes are viable (i.e. planning), rather than moving

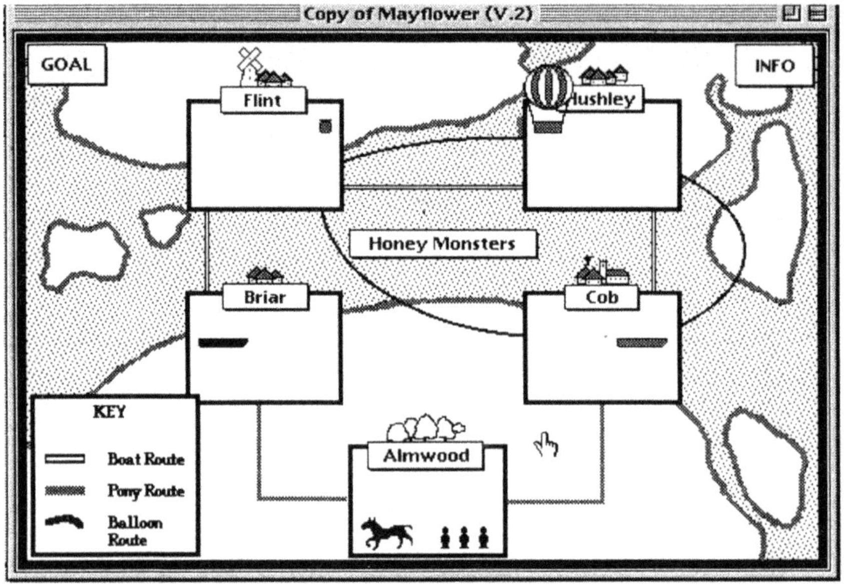

Figure 3: The Honey Bears interface, taken from the "drag and paste" interface

characters around the map by trial-and-error. Level was defined by how far they got towards delivering the honey; thus 6 was complete task success and 1 was moving the pony, the first move in an ideal task solution.

Materials

Written instructions were given to all participants, which detailed the task goals and possible actions. The tasks themselves were implemented in Hypercard on an Apple Macintosh LC II with single button mouse. Post task questionnaires asked participants to reflect on the interfaces in terms of cost.

Study participants

22 undergraduates from the University of Nottingham, aged between 18 and 23 took part in the study. Computer experience was mixed, but all had some experience of mouse-based computer interfaces. Participants were divided into two groups, with 11 participants per group.

Procedure

Study participants were randomly allocated to one of the conditions. Participants in Condition 1 trained on the "low-cost", drag-and-place version of the task before transferring to the Pirates task. Participants in Condition 2 trained on the "high-cost", select-elements version of Honey Bears before doing the Pirates task. The experimenter set up the starting screen; clicking on a START button began the session. Each participant was instructed to solve the problem as quickly as possible. Data was stored automatically to a separate Hypercard stack, as the subject completed each task. A questionnaire and debriefing followed the experimental session.

2.3 Results

Information searches

The 'select elements' group made a mean of 20.36 (sd = 20.63) information searches on the Honey Bears

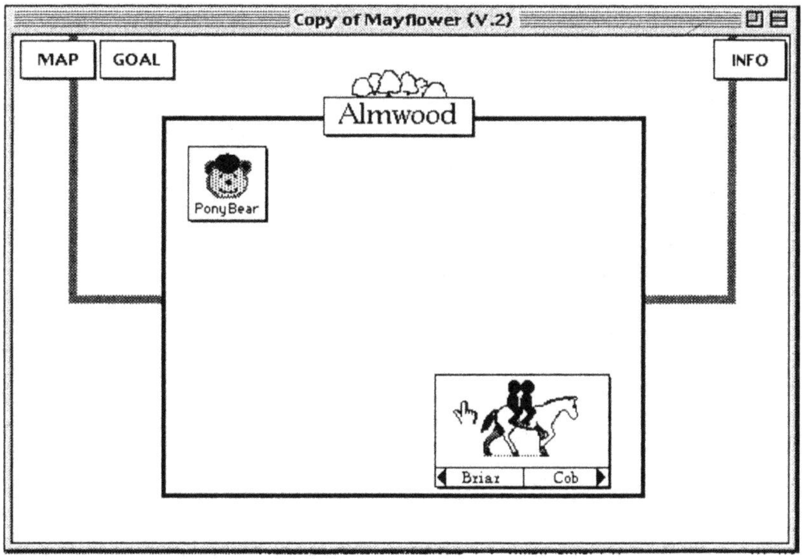

Figure 4: The Honey Bears interface: close up of the map from the 'drag-and-place' interface.

task compared to 11.73 (sd = 10.96) searches on the transfer (Pirates) task. The 'drag-and-place' group made 21.27 (sd = 12.6) searches at training and 27.55 (sd = 27.55) searches at transfer. An analysis of variance revealed no significant main effects but a significant interaction between group and trial ($F_{(1,20)} = 7.93$, $p<0.01$).

The two experimental groups were compared for the total number of information searches made before making the first move. If information gathering can be equated with planning activities, this should enable us to distinguish how users respond to the increased cost of making a move given the alternative representations. At training, subjects using the 'select-elements', indirect manipulation interface made an average of 12.27 (sd = 15.5) information searches before making the first move, whilst subjects in the 'drag-and-place', direct manipulation group made an average of 1.41 (sd = 4.5) moves before making the first move. At transfer, the 'select-elements' group made 8.46 (sd = 7.5) while the 'drag-and-place' group made 16.9 (sd = 7.3) information searches before the first move. An analysis of variance revealed a significant main effect of trial ($F_{(1,20)} = 6.62$ $p<.02$) and a significant interaction between group and trial ($F_{(1,20)} = 18.38$ $p<0.004$). These results indicate that the interface had a strong effect on the way in which subjects solved the task. The increased number of information searches before the first move made by the 'drag-and-place' group suggests that they were required to find information to solve the transfer (Pirates) task, information which the 'select elements' group had already discovered - that breaking down the goal into subgoals with constraints was an effective solution strategy.

Number of moves before and after discovering the constraint

The number of moves made before discovering the crucial information (that Honey Monsters eat honey) were assessed. These were compared to the number of moves made *after* discovering the constraint; means are presented in Table 1. At training, an unpaired t-test revealed a significant difference between the groups on moves taken before discovering the crucial information ($t = 2.83$, $p < .01$). This supports the assertion that the interface directed the subjects to pre-plan and search for information to a far greater extent in the 'select-elements' group than in the 'drag-and-place' group. Having found out that honey monsters eat honey and therefore a balloon must be taken across the water (requiring the presence of Airbear), the two groups were not distinguishable in their performance: there was no significant difference between the groups on number of moves made *after* the information has been discovered. There were no significant differences between the groups on the transfer (Pirates) task, either on moves before or moves after discovery that Pirates steal jewels. Of course, the relevance of this information had already been established through practice on the isomorphic Honey Bears task, so this is not surprising.

Group	Moves	Training	Transfer
Select elements	before	1.30 sd=1.83	0.40 sd=.96
	after	6.3 sd= 4.67	8.3 sd= 5.1
Drag and place	before	7.18 sd = 6.3	1.5 sd=2.14
	after	6.55 sd = 4.3	9.0 sd= 4.6

Table 1. Moves before and after discovery of the main constraint

Percentage of successful moves

The percentage of successful moves reflects how many actions were taken without receiving an error message. The means for the 'select-elements' group were 46.3% (sd = 35.96) at training and 62.5% (sd = 38.5) at transfer. The means for the 'drag-and-place' group for the 73.1% (sd = 28.2) at training and 86.8% (sd = 13.17) at transfer. There was a significant main effect of trial ($F_{(1,20)}$=9.63, p<0.01) and a significant main effect of group ($F_{((1,20)}$=4.46 p<0.05). The main effect of trial shows that both groups made moves more effectively at transfer. The main effect of group reflects the extra error-constraints experienced in the 'drag-and-place' interface. Some subjects reported using the radio-button screen to find out information: each time they triggered an error message, they gained new information about the problem. The high rate of error by the 'select-elements' group during training seems to reflect use of this strategy.

Level of problem solution achieved

For the training task, the mean level achieved by the 'select-elements', indirect manipulation interface group was 3.5 (sd = 2.2) and 3.2 (sd = 2.0) for the 'drag-and-place' interface group. On the transfer task, participants in the 'select-elements' interface group achieved a mean score of 4.6 (sd = 2.3), whilst the participants in the 'drag and place' interface group achieved a mean score of 5.4 (sd = 1.3). An analysis of variance revealed a main effect of trial (Honey bears versus Pirates) ($F_{(1, 20)}$ = 7.70, p <0.01). There was no main effect of group and no significant interaction between group and trial.

2.4 Discussion

It appears from these results that the interfaces did indeed result in different information search and task solution strategies for the two groups. The group presented with the 'drag and place' interface were much more inclined to use trial-and-error and took the opportunity to try things out in the interface rather than search for information or explicitly break the goal into subgoals with constraints to be satisfied. This was reflected in the greater number of moves taken before discovery of the main task constraint. Indeed, when presented with a 'select elements' interface at the transfer phase, subjects who had moved from the 'drag-and-place' interface expressed that the 'select-elements' interface was harder to use, but provided better task support by forcing thought about goals and moves. Further, the percentage of moves made without error support the notion that the 'drag and place' interface offers more information to users. In terms of learning effects, however, our measure of task success (level) did not provide enough support to suggest that the different manipulation styles had long lasting effects for this task. We believe this may have been due to the relative simplicity of the task, however.

3. CONCLUSIONS

This study has shown how laboratory based results in cognitive psychology can contribute to our understanding of how users interact with interfaces and can contribute to the development of broad brush guidelines for the development of learning interfaces. It also illustrates, however, that results from psychological studies cannot be taken off-the-shelf but must be put into clear context. Specifically, we believe that this study raises the need for a clearer definition of "cognitive cost" than that offered by O'Hara and Payne and by Svendsen. O'Hara and Payne's definitions of cost were so broad as to range from physical, to strategic, to mental costs. There are a number of different types of cost, with potentially very different effects on learner strategies. The effects of cost in the two Honey Bears interfaces ranged from provoking information search, to memory strategies, planning ahead to avoid wasted effort, and finally, mere diversion away from the domain in favour of the interface itself.

The issues of cost and of information presentation, and information available at the time of making a move will be developed in subsequent studies. The educational value of costliness in an interface seems to lie in its directive properties; such that the manipulation style encourages attention to be given to certain domain relationships rather than others. Cost will be beneficial to learning when it induces cognitive mechanisms which are integral in the learning process. Conversely, cost will be damaging to learning when it induces cognitive mechanisms which are superfluous to the learning process and the worst possible scenario is when superfluous cognitive processes are highly demanding on the learner's limited attentional resources.

ACKNOWLEDGEMENTS

This work was completed as part of a doctoral thesis, supported by EPSRC grant 94315041. The second author is supported by a EPSRC grant GR/J97786.

5. REFERENCES

Churchill, E. F., & Ainsworth, S. (1995). "Making Claims about Teaching Systems." in K Norby, P.H. Helmersen, D.J. Gilmore, S.A. Arnesen (Eds) *Human-Computer Interaction. Interact '95.* Chapman & Hall

Corbett, Anderson, J. R., & Fincham (1990). "Menu Selection versus Typing: Effects on Learning in an Intelligent Programming Tutor." in C. Frasson & G. Gauthier (Eds) *Intelligent Tutoring Systems: At the Crossroads of Artificial Intelligence & Education.*

Gilmore, D. (1996) The Relevance of HCI Guidelines for Educational Interfaces. *Machine Mediated learning, 5 (2)* 119-133.

Jackson, S., Stratford, S.J., Krajcik, J and Soloway, E. (1996) A Learner-centred Tool for Students Buidling Models. In *Communications of the ACM,: Special issue on Learner Centred Design 39, 4,* 24-27.

Laurillard, D. (1993) *Rethinking University teaching: A Framework for the effective use of educational technology.* London: Routledge.

Littleton, K., Light, P., Joiner, R., Messer, D and Barnes, P. (1994) Gender and software interaction in children's computer-based problem solving. Internal report: ESRC Centre for Research in Development, Instruction and Training, Department of Psychology, University of Nottingham, Nottingham, UK.

Malone, T. (1981). "Toward a theory of intrinsically motivating instruction." *Cognitive Science 4*: 333-369.

Moore, A. (1993) Siuli's Maths Lesson: Autonomy or Control. In J. Benyon and H. Mackay (eds) *Computers into Classroom. More Questions Than Answers.* The Falmer Press, Sussex, UK.

Norman, D. and Spohrer, J. (1996) Introduction. *Communications of the ACM: Special issue on Learner Centred Design, 39, 4,* 24-27.

O'Hara, K. and Payne, S (1994). "Cost of operations affects planfulness of action." Unpublished internal report, School of Psychology, Cardiff College, University of Wales, Wales, UK.

Svendsen, G. B. (1991). "The influence of interface style on problem solving." *International Journal of Man-Machine Studies 35:* 379-397.

34

Specifying Relations between Research and the Design of Human-Computer Interactions

John Long

Ergonomics & HCI Unit, University College London, UK
j.long@ucl.ac.uk

ABSTRACT. This paper argues the need for more effective: human-computer interactions; design of such interactions; and research to support such design. One contribution to more effective research would be the specification of relations between research and the design of human-computer interactions. The aim of this paper is to propose such a specification. Meeting this specification renders HCI knowledge coherent, complete and 'fit-for-design-purpose'. The absence of such relations renders Cognitive Science knowledge not coherent, complete nor 'fit-for-design-purpose' (as opposed to 'fit-for-understanding-purpose'). The paper concludes that specification of relations is required for more effective research support for the design of human-computer interactions.

KEY WORDS: research; design; human-computer interactions; effectiveness

1. INTRODUCTION

1.1. Human-Computer Interactions

Computing technology continues its inexorable advance. Computer applications pervade the home, the factory and the office. Computer developments continue to extend the limits of the technology - from novel hardware, such as speech recognisers, to novel software, such as spreadsheets. Novel complete technologies have been developed, such as integrated broadband communication and virtual reality (Long, 1991). Once the requirement was the computer and 'getting it to work at all', that is more effective computers. Now the main requirement might be said to be human-computer interaction, and 'getting the computer to work for us effectively', that is more effective human-computer interactions (Long and Dowell, 1996).

1.2. Design

Design of human-computer interactions has also continued to advance. Design includes both the specification of interactions and their subsequent evaluation, as well as the selection and training of users. Initially, the design of such interactions was a craft, which resided in the practices of programmers, designers, and user managers (Long and Dowell, 1989). Subsequently, attempts have been made to change these design processes by the behavioural sciences, such as Psychology and Sociology (also Cognitive Science - see Section 3), and the computing sciences, such as Software Engineering (Long, 1987). More recently, Human-Computer Interaction (HCI) research has also attempted to contribute to these design practices. Taken together, such design practices have achieved some notable successes. However, the success can also be viewed as limited. Notable failures have also been associated with such practices.

This view of current interaction design as being limited is reinforced, if the design practices are considered in terms of the 'capability maturity' model (Paulk, Curtis, Chrissis and Weber, 1993). The model has five levels of maturity. It would be difficult to classify current design practices as higher than Level 3,

Human–Computer Interaction: INTERACT'97 S. Howard, J. Hammond & G. Lindgaard (editors)
Published by Chapman & Hall

that is 'defined'. Without the specification of such practices (and their relationship to research), their process cannot rise to the maturer levels of 4 'managed' and 5 'optimised'. Indeed, many design practices, currently, would be unlikely to achieve even Level 2, that is 'repeatable', that is, from project to project. There is a need, then, for more effective design (Dowell and Long, 1989).

1.3. Research

Research has also continued to advance the acquisition and validation of new knowledge to support design. Technically, the behavioural sciences have acquired new knowledge concerning the phenomena of interactions. Technically, HCI research has acquired new knowledge concerning techniques, methods, and tools to support design. Institutionally, a number of initiatives have funded research to support design. Although much useful research was conducted under various initiatives, little is known about the effectiveness of such knowledge, to support design. What has been established is often negative. In addition, little of the research has been validated. As a result, little of the knowledge acquired has been incremented. Failure to increment constitutes a failure in progress. As a consequence, the potential for applying such knowledge has been limited (Long and Dowell, 1996). There is a need, then, for more effective research.

1.4. Specifying Relations

More effective research for design would result in more effective human-computer interactions. Such research would require the validation of new knowledge. Thus would knowledge be incremented, and so progress made. However, such incrementation would only be effective, if the new knowledge were 'fit-for-design-purpose', that is to support design practices. The criterion here is relevance. If research is not relevant to design, the application of such knowledge could only be by trial and error. A pre-requisite for more effective research is the specification of relations between research and design. Specification of these relations would constitute one contribution to more effective research. Only if such relations are specified, and subsequently implemented, will new research knowledge be incrementable with respect to its effectiveness. Only then will validation of knowledge result in more effective human-computer interactions. The specification of such relations is the aim of this paper.

2. SPECIFYING RELATIONS

2.1. Pre-requisites for Specifying Relations

Informally, research should support design. Relations, then, might be identified and enumerated. Such a scheme, however, is inadequate. First, 'research' is a more general expression than 'designing human-computer interactions'. Second, 'designing human-computer interactions' is too rudimentary an expression to provide support for research. An expression is required, which is more coherent, complete and 'fit-for-research-purpose'. These requirements indicate the following pre-requisites.

The first pre-requisite is a framework for disciplines. Such a framework should generalise design of human-computer interactions, so that it can be expressed at the same high level as that of research. Such a framework could then be used to model, and so to specify, relations between HCI research and design. The second pre-requisite is a framework for the HCI general design problem. The framework must be more coherent, complete and 'fit-for-research-purpose' than 'design of human-computer interactions'. However, it must also be expressed at a high enough level to support the modelling of alternative lower level descriptions of design. The model would specify the relations within the scope of the design to support research. The third pre-requisite is a framework for validation. The framework should be expressed at a high enough level to model both research (characterised as a discipline), and design of human-computer interactions (characterised as the HCI general design problem). Together, resulting models would, thus, embody, and so specify, the relations between research and design to support validation (see Figure 1). Meeting these pre-requisites would support more effective design.

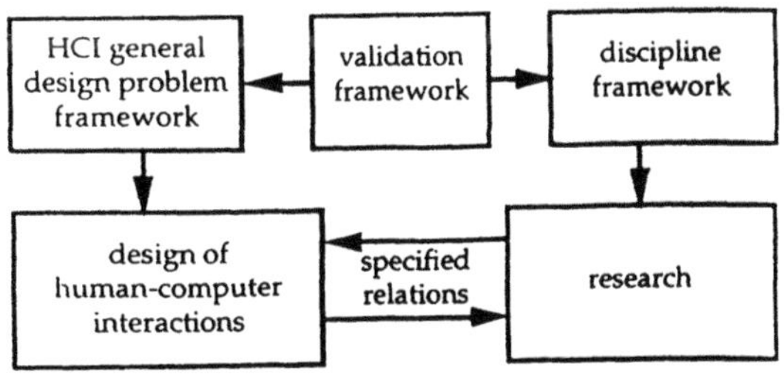

Figure 1. Frameworks to specify the relations between research and design of human-computer interactions to support the validation of knowledge.

The discipline framework proposed here to model relations between HCI research and design of human-computer interactions is taken from Long and Dowell (1989). A **discipline** (concepts are highlighted on first introduction) is assumed to possess three characteristics: **knowledge**; **practices**; and a **general problem**. **Research**, by its **research practices**, acquires knowledge. Knowledge supports practices solving the general discipline problem. Disciplines are, thus, distinguished by the general problem which they address. General discipline problems, however, also have a scope. Decomposition of a general problem, with respect to its scope, exposes general problems of **particular scope**. This decomposition allows the further division of disciplines into sub-disciplines. A discipline can thus be defined as: 'the acquisition by research practices, and use of knowledge to support practices, seeking solutions to a general problem having a particular scope' (see Figure 3).

2.1.2. General Design Problem of HCI

The HCI general design problem framework, proposed here to model alternative descriptions of design of human-computer interactions, is taken from Dowell and Long (1989). A **domain of application** of an HCI **worksystem** is where **work** originates, is performed, and has its consequences. **Goals** express a requirement for work. Goals are allocated to worksystems by organisations. A domain is distinct from, and delimits, a worksystem. A worksystem comprises at least two separate, but interacting, sub-systems - namely **human(s)** and **computer(s)**. Humans interact with computers to perform effective work. **Effectiveness** expresses how well the worksystem performs the work. The HCI general design problem, thus, can be expressed as: 'design humans interacting with computers to perform effective work'.

2.1.3. Validation Framework

The validation framework proposed here was used by Dowell and Long (1989) and Long and Dowell (1989). However, it is quite standard. Validation involves four processes: conceptualisation; operationalisation; test; and generalisation, and so four changes in the resulting products. **Conceptualisation** involves specified, and so explicit, representation. **Operationalisation** involves the mapping of concepts onto observables and eventually metrics. **Test** involves the evaluation of the assertions implicated in the concepts, which have been operationalised. Lastly, **generalisation** involves the abstraction and generification of the outcomes of the tests. The framework can be applied generally to knowledge, problems, etc. which are validated, if conceptualised; operationalised; tested; and generalised. Validation is required to ensure knowledge, problems, etc. are 'fit-for-purpose'. The pre-requisites for specifying the relations between research and the design of human-computer interactions have now been met. It remains to apply the frameworks to specify those relations.

2.2. Specified Relations

To specify the relations between research and the design of human-computer interactions, it is necessary to specify: the relations between HCI research and the HCI general design problem; and the relations within the particular scope of HCI to support HCI research, both with respect to the validation of knowledge, and so more effective design.

2.2.1. HCI Research and the HCI general design problem

The discipline framework and validation framework proposed earlier are now used to model the relations between HCI research and the HCI general design problem. Following Long and Dowell (1989) (see Section 2.1.1) the specification of the particular scope of HCI is: 'humans interacting with computers to perform effective work'. Given this particular scope of HCI, its general problem can now be specified as: 'the design of humans interacting with computers to perform effective work'. Given this HCI general problem, its practices can now be specified as: 'diagnosis (of work (in)effectiveness) and prescription (of humans interacting with computers)'. Such practices solve the general design problem of humans interacting with computers to perform effective work. HCI knowledge supports HCI practices to solve this general design problem. Research, as supported by its practices, can now be specified as: 'the acquisition and validation of HCI knowledge'. Given HCI research, the validation of its knowledge can be specified as: 'the conceptualisation; operationalisation; test; and generalisation of its HCI knowledge'. Hence, a coherent and complete model of the discipline of HCI can be specified as: 'research supporting the acquisition and validation by research practices, as: conceptualisation; operationalisation; test; and generalisation, of HCI knowledge to support HCI practices of diagnosis and prescription, to solve the general HCI design problem of humans interacting with computers to perform effective work' (see right-hand panel of Figure 2). This specification relates research to design of human-computer interactions.

2.2.2. *Particular scope of HCI to support HCI research*

The HCI general design problem framework and the validation framework are now used to model the relations within the particular scope of HCI, to support HCI research. It might, of course, be thought that such specification exists - 'the design of humans interacting with computers to perform effective work'. However, this expression is not adequate to support research. Concerning the validation of HCI knowledge, the expression is insufficiently conceptualised to support: operationalisation, test and generalisation. Concerning the application of HCI knowledge, that is HCI practices, the expression is insufficiently conceptualised to support design, as diagnosis and prescription. A more completely conceptualised definition is thus required.

Following Dowell and Long (1989) (see Section 2.1.2) to model the general design problem of HCI, it is necessary to specify: work; the worksystem, which performs the work; the goals of the worksystem; and the effectiveness with which the worksystem achieves its goals. The particular scope of the HCI general design problem is: 'humans interacting with computers to perform effective work'. Dowell and Long (1989) have proposed a conceptually more complete specification of HCI design as a general problem.

In the conception, a **domain of application** (of an HCI **worksystem**) is where **work** originates, is performed, and has its consequences. It comprises one or more **objects,** constituted of **attributes,** which have **values. Goals** express a requirement for change in the value of these attributes, and goals are allocated to worksystems by organisations. A domain is distinct from, and delimits, a worksystem. A worksystem comprises at least two separate, but interacting, sub-systems - of **human behaviours** interacting with **computer behaviours**. These behaviours are supported by mutually exclusive **human structures** and **computer structures**, and are executed to perform work effectively. Effectiveness is expressed by the concept of **performance**, that is, how well a worksystem achieves its goals - that is, **task quality**, and the **system costs** that are incurred in so doing. Costs are incurred by both the human and the computer and are **structural** and **behavioural**.

Given this conception of the particular scope of HCI, the validation of its general design problem (and solution) can now be specified as: 'the conceptualisation; operationalisation; test; and generalisation of the HCI general design problem (and solution)' (see left-hand panel of Figure 2).

The particular scope of the HCI discipline is the design of 'humans interacting with computers to perform effective work'. More completely, its particular scope would be the design of behaviours constituting a worksystem {S}, whose actual performance (P_A) conformed with some desired performance (P_D). The design of {S} would require the design of human behaviours {H} interacting with computer behaviours {C}. Hence, conception of the general HCI design problem would be:

design {H} and {C},
such that {H} interacting with {C} = $\{S\}_{P_A=P_D}$
where $P_D = fn\{Q_D, K_D\}$.
Q_D expresses the desired quality of work for the domain of application.
K_D expresses acceptable costs incurred by the worksystem (both human and computer).

Design here should be understood to include both the specification of interactive worksystem behaviours and the evaluation of actual and desired performance. Design also includes: the physical and organisational environment; and selection and training of humans, to the extent that these factors determine interactive worksystem behaviours, and so actual and desired performance.

This model of the HCI general design problem specifies the relations within the particular scope of HCI to support research. Thus, according to this general design problem model, research is only 'fit-for-design-purpose' if it meets these specifications, that is, acquires and validates knowledge which supports the solution of HCI general design problems, so expressed. The specification of relations within the particular scope of HCI, to support HCI research is now complete.

2.2.3. *HCI research and the HCI general design problem and particular scope of HCI to support HCI research*

Specified relations between HCI research and the HCI general design problem were modelled in Section 2.2.1. Specified relations within the particular scope of HCI to support research were modelled in Section 2.2.2. To specify the relations together, it suffices to integrate the two earlier sets of specified relations into a single model (see Figure 2].

Thus, according to these models of the HCI discipline and the HCI general design problem, research is only 'fit-for-design-purpose', if it meets these specifications, that is acquires and validates knowledge which supports the solution of the HCI general design problem, so expressed. The specification of relations is

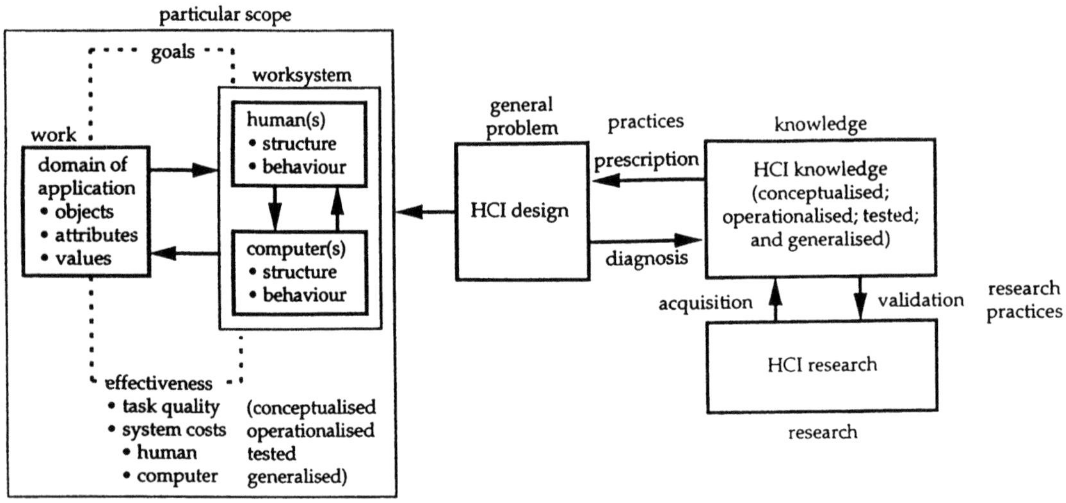

Figure 2. Model of the HCI discipline and model of the HCI general design problem specifying the relations between HCI research and the HCI general design problem, and within the particular scope of HCI, to support HCI research.

now considered to be complete. Taken together, these relations constitute one possible specification of the relations between research and design of human-computer interactions.

3. OTHER RESEARCH

3.1. Other research and HCI research

It has been proposed how relations can be specified between research and the design of human-computer interactions. The question can now be posed, as to what relations obtain between other research, HCI research and the design of human-computer interactions. In particular, the concern is with research not conducted to support the design of human-computer interactions. The example selected here is Cognitive Science. Note that Cognitive Science is not unique. Similar relations, proposed later, could similarly be suggested for: Sociology; Ethnomethodology; Ethnography etc. The same frameworks and models used earlier will also be used here.

3.2. Specified relations with Cognitive Science research

Cognitive Science generally seeks to understand knowledge-based behaviours. Such behaviours include: perceiving; categorising; thinking; reasoning; communicating; problem-solving, etc. Cognitive Science might be defined non-controversially as: 'understanding the general principles underlying natural and artificial forms of intelligence'.

3.2.1. Specified relations between Cognitive Science Research and the Cognitive Science general understanding problem.

To specify the relations between Cognitive Science research and understanding natural and artificial forms of intelligence, it is necessary to model the Cognitive Science discipline. Given the particular scope of Cognitive Science, as natural and artificial forms of intelligence, its general problem can be specified as: 'the understanding of natural and artificial forms of intelligence' (understanding being the general problem of science as a discipline). Given this general problem, the understanding practices can be specified as: 'explanation and prediction'. Cognitive Science knowledge supports such practices. Cognitive Science research practices acquire and validate such knowledge as: conceptualised; operationalised; tested; and generalised (see right-hand panel of Figure 3). (Compare with the HCI model in Figure 2.)

3.2.2. Particular scope of Cognitive Science to support Cognitive Science Research

For present purposes, the particular scope of Cognitive Science, as natural and artificial forms of intelligence, is assumed to include at least: natural, that is human, intelligence and behaviour; artificial, that is, artefact

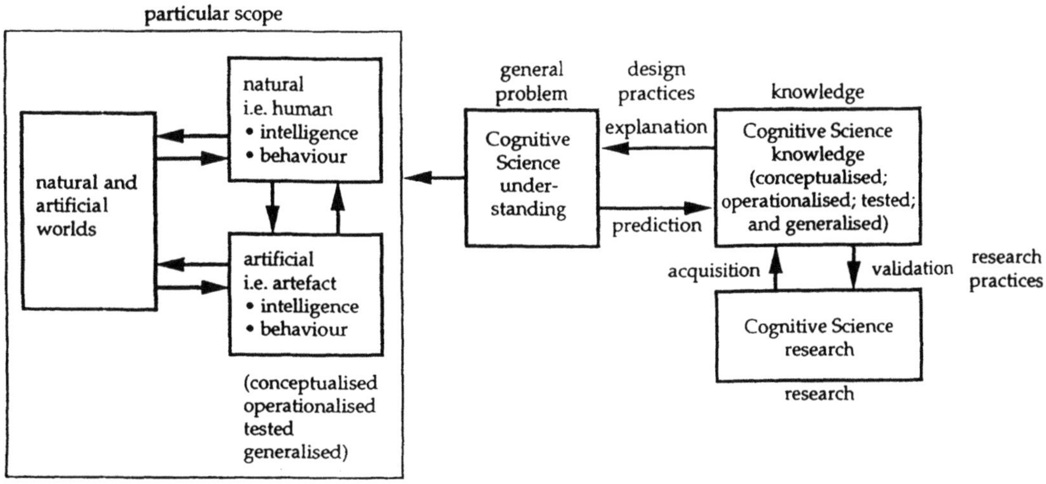

Figure 3. Model of the Cognitive Science discipline and model of the Cognitive Science general understanding problem specifying the relations between Cognitive Science research and the Cognitive Science general understanding problem, and within the particular scope of Cognitive Science, to support Cognitive Science research.

intelligence and behaviour; and natural and artificial worlds. Humans and artefacts are assumed to interact with one another, and with the world. Cognitive Science seeks to understand the: intelligence; behaviour; and interactions (see left-hand panel of Figure 3). (Compare with the HCI model in Figure 2.)

3.2.3. Cognitive Science discipline and the Cognitive Science general understanding problem

Specified relations between Cognitive Science research and the Cognitive Science general understanding problem are modelled in Section 3.2.1. Specified relations within the particular scope of Cognitive Science, to support Cognitive Science research are modelled in Section 3.2.2. To specify the relations between the Cognitive Science discipline and the Cognitive Science general understanding problem, it suffices to integrate the two earlier sets of specified relations into a single model (see Figure 3).

Thus, according to these models of the Cognitive Science discipline and the general understanding problem, research is only coherent, complete and 'fit-for-understanding-purpose', if it meets these requirements. That is, it acquires and validates knowledge, which supports the solution of the Cognitive Science general problem, so expressed. The claim is the same as made earlier for HCI. Knowledge produced by Cognitive Science research, and intended to support understanding, which embodies these relations, is more effective, than knowledge not embodying such relations.

3.3. Cognitive Science Research and Design

The question posed earlier can now be addressed. What relations obtain between other research, in this case Cognitive Science, and the design of human-computer interactions? An assessment of possible relations can be made by comparing the relations within Cognitive Science (shown in Figure 3), with the relations within HCI (shown in Figure 2). Inspection of these figures shows there to be no specified relations between Cognitive Science research and the design of human-computer interactions. For example, Cognitive Science understanding practices have no specified relations with the diagnosis of general design problems and the prescription of general design solutions. The Cognitive Science general understanding problem has no specified relations with the performance (of worksystems). Thus, there are no specified relations between Cognitive Science research and the design of human-computer interactions. Cognitive Science research is, therefore, not coherent, complete, nor 'fit-for-design-purpose'.

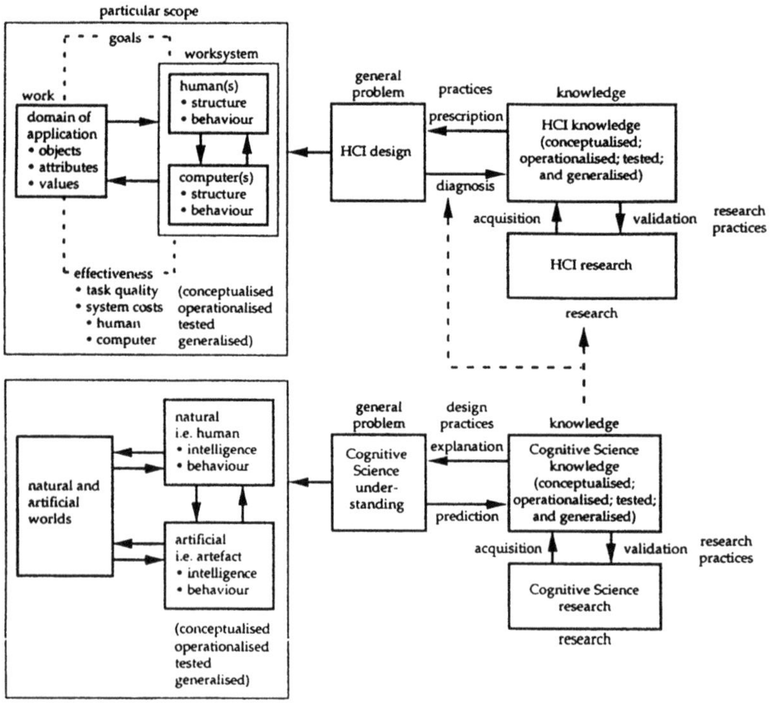

Figure 4. A model showing the unspecified relations (as dotted lines) between the HCI discipline and the HCI general design problem (Figure 2) and the Cognitive Science discipline and the Cognitive Science general understanding problem (Figure 3).

Note that a comparable conclusion must necessarily be drawn concerning the relations between HCI research and understanding natural and artificial forms of intelligence. Inspection of Figures 2 and 3 shows there to be no specified relations between HCI research and the understanding of natural and artificial forms of intelligence. For example, HCI design practices have no specified relations with the explanation of general understanding problems and the prediction of general understanding solutions. The HCI general design problem has no specified relations with (natural) intelligence, as expressed by humans.

It is, thus, concluded that research, not exhibiting the relations specified here with the design of human-computer interactions, such as that undertaken by Cognitive Science, is not coherent, complete or 'fit-for-design-purpose'.

3.4. Unspecified Relations between Cognitive Science Research and Design

It has been concluded that Cognitive Science research is not coherent, complete nor 'fit-for-design-purpose'. However, some researchers claim such a relationship. How might such a claim be understood with respect to the specified relations for Cognitive Science and HCI proposed here? This question can be addressed, if some relationship can be established between the HCI discipline and its general design problem (Figure 2) and the Cognitive Science discipline (Figure 3). The relevant models are shown in Figure 4. The models suggest two ways in which Cognitive Science might contribute to design. First, Cognitive Science knowledge might contribute to HCI research practices of the acquisition and validation of HCI knowledge, such practices having specified relations with the design of human-computer interactions. Second, Cognitive Science knowledge might contribute to HCI practices of diagnosis and prescription, and so of design, such practices having specified relations with design.

However, in both cases, the relations between Cognitive Science knowledge and HCI research, and HCI practices are unspecified. Hence, any relations could only be implicit. Such implicit relations could only be realised via the explicit relations specified between HCI research and the design of human-computer interactions. Further, the realisation of such implicit relations could only have the status of a 'craft'. That is, any 'knowledge' of transforming the Cognitive Science knowledge base to support either HCI research or HCI practices, is likely to reside only in the experience and skill of the individual researcher or design practitioner. Thus, there would be no validation of the transformation with respect to its support for the design of human-computer interactions. Cognitive Science knowledge, thus, is able to contribute to HCI design and research practices. However, such contributions can only be implicit, since unspecified. They cannot as such be known.

3.5. Other Research, HCI Research and Design

Readers might be interested to assess the relations between their own research (and that of others) and the design of human-computer interactions, in terms of the relations specified here. First, research can be assessed against the model of the HCI discipline and the model of the HCI general design problem (Figure 2). The research can be further assessed against the relations within the particular scope of HCI, to support HCI research (Figure 2). Second, research can be assessed against the model of the Cognitive Science discipline and the model of the Cognitive Science general understanding problem (Figure 3). The research can be further assessed against the relations within the particular scope of Cognitive Science, to support Cognitive Science research (Figure 3). Third, research can be assessed for unspecified relations between Cognitive Science research and the design of human-computer interactions (Figure 4). However, if research is neither HCI nor Cognitive Science (for example, Ethnomethodology, etc), then, the frameworks proposed for disciplines, the HCI general design problem and for validation, must be used to construct models of the kind appearing in Figures 2 and 3. Relations can then be specified. Assessment of the research can then be made against the models of specified relations.

4. SUMMARY & CONCLUSIONS

This paper began by summarising current and past technical and institutional developments, as they concern the design of human-computer interactions and research. The paper argues the requirement for more effective: human-computer interactions; design of such interactions; and research support for such design. Greater effectiveness of interactions, practices and research will derive from the validation of new HCI knowledge, and the specification of relations between HCI research and the design of human-computer interactions, such that research is 'fit-for-design-purpose'. This paper attempts to specify such relations. It is suggested how research with unspecified relations to the design of human-computer interactions, such as Cognitive Science, can only contribute implicitly to the design of human-computer interactions. Such implicit contributions can only be realised via the specified relations of HCI.

In conclusion, if a serious attempt is to be made to improve the effectiveness of: human-computer interactions; the design of such interactions; and the research support for such design, there is a need to ensure coherence, completeness and the 'fitness-for-design-purpose' of research to support the design of humans interacting with computers to perform work effectively, including validation for that purpose. All disciplines, which conduct research claiming to contribute to the design of human-computer interactions for effective work, need to specify the relations between their research and the design of human-computer interactions. Specifying relations between HCI research, and the HCI discipline, and within the design of human-computer interactions, expressed as the general HCI design problem, to support HCI research, as proposed in this paper, is one means of so doing.

Acknowledgments

I would like to acknowledge my debt to colleagues at the Ergonomics & HCI Unit, UCL, and especially to John Dowell by whom or with whom all the important ideas in this paper have been developed.

References

Dowell, J. and Long, J. (1989). Towards a Conception for an Engineering Discipline of Human Factors. *Ergonomics*, **32** (11), 1513-1535.

Long, J. (1987). Cognitive Ergonomics and Human Computer Interaction. In *Psychology at Work*, P. Warr (ed). Harmondsworth, UK: Penguin.

Long, J.B. (1991). Human-Computer Interaction and the Information Technology Revolution, or Getting Computers to Work for Us Effectively. In British Gas White Paper series.

Long, J. and Dowell, J. (1989). Conceptions for the Discipline of HCI: Craft, Applied Science and Engineering. In A.Sutcliffe and L.Macaulay (eds), *People and Computers IV, Proceedings of the Fifth Conference of the BCS HCI SIG*. Cambridge, UK: CUP. 9-32.

Long, J. and Dowell, J. (1996). Cognitive Engineering or 'getting users and computers interacting to perform work effectively'. *The Psychologist*, **9** (7), 313-317.

Paulk, M.C., Curtis, B., Chrissis, M.B. and Weber, C.V. (1993). Capability Maturity Model, Version 1.1. *IEEE Software*, 18-27.

35

Seeking the heart, brain and nerve in Oz: moving Internationalism beyond a cloak for commercial dominance or intellectual snobbery

Brian Shackel,

Founder Director, HUSAT Research Institute,
Loughborough University, U.K.

In a more famous journey to Oz, the travellers' quest was for a heart, a brain and 'the nerve'. This panel explores a parallel contemporary quest in the field of HCI from an international perspective.

In the quest for market dominance, there is a risk that computer companies will only do enough to internationalise software to be able to say that "we have an international product so you should buy it". In comparison with what COULD be done, current efforts to internationalise seem tokenistic at best and patronising at worst---i.e. HCI needs to move in a heartfelt way beyond effort which could be characterised as "we'll let you understand the language (else you won't buy the product), but we're not too interested in your customs and culture".

Such a development needs to re-examine the way that western society thinking (brain) tends to equate 'more' with 'better', proving slow to learn about the importance of intermediate and ultra-simple technology. Other parts of the world hold the concept of 'appropriate technology' where technology does not become an end in itself, and where more 'bells and whistles' are not good but bad technology. Rather, there is an argument that it is time for the western computing industry to realise that people do not NEED heaps of functionality as they only ever use a small proportion of it.

To adopt such a quest requires nerve---and demonstrable benefits. This panel will discuss some of the benefits to be achieved through internationalism, and will include an Australian business perspective.

Human–Computer Interaction: INTERACT'97 S. Howard, J. Hammond & G. Lindgaard (editors)
Published by Chapman & Hall

Effective Illustrations in Interactive Media: What Works?

Barbee Teasley

Human Factors
Ameritech
2000 W. Ameritech Center Drive
Hoffman Estates, IL 60196 USA
01-847-248-1400
FAX 01-847-248-6043
e-mail: teasley@acm.org

Keith Instone, Laura Marie Leventhal and Eric Brown

Computer Science Department
Bowling Green State University
Bowling Green, OH 43403 USA
01-419-372-2765
FAX 01-419-372-8061
e-mail: instone@acm.org

ABSTRACT Illustrations are often used in interactive media with the goal of enhancing information retrieval and learning. Yet prior work has shown that illustrations on a screen are not necessarily used effectively, and may not even be used at all. Two studies examined factors related to the successful use of illustrations. Study 1 contrasted three interaction styles. In one style, only text appeared when a term was selected. The second presented text as a caption, while the third revealed the text next to the relevant portion of the illustration. The last style produced superior learning of both illustration-related and unrelated material. The caption condition was no better than the control, no-illustration condition. Study 2 showed learning is just as effective if the user selects from a list and reads near the illustration, or selects from the illustration and reads a caption, suggesting that the most important factor is compelling users to direct their attention to the illustration.

KEY WORDS illustrations, interactive media, multimedia, learning

1. INTRODUCTION

Illustrations are ubiquitous in interactive media such as web sites, CD-ROMs and computer-based instruction. They can be used for many purposes, ranging from purely decorative, to supplemental, to crucial information (Waddill and McDaniel, 1992). While graphic design principles provide guidelines on the aesthetic aspects of illustrations and layout, there is little guidance available on how to make illustrations effective as a means of transmitting information which enhances or supplements information presented in text. In the absence of such rules, designers may use intuition—a practice which may or may not be effective (Teasley, Leventhal, Blumenthal, Instone and Stone, 1993). Furthermore, there is no clear understanding of the general cognitive principles which underlie learning from interactive, illustrated text.

Given the well-known phrase that "a picture is worth a thousand words," most would intuit that a computer-based presentation of information including illustrations would be easier to learn from and seek information in than text-only forms. In some situations, this is certainly true. For example, Ogozalek (1994) showed that elderly users performed better on information retrieval tasks using either of two computer-based forms of a document than a printed paper document. The computer-based version containing video, graphics, and audio, as well as text, produced better performance than the text-only computer version. The multimedia presentation was also the most highly preferred. The most commonly cited reason was that it overcame vision problems associated with aging. Similarly, Harrison (1995) found that online help incorporating either still or animated graphics improved performance on procedural tasks, compared to text-only help.

Human–Computer Interaction: INTERACT'97 S. Howard, J. Hammond & G. Lindgaard (editors)
Published by Chapman & Hall ©IFIP 1997

However, a surprising number of other studies have found that simply integrating illustrations and text on a computer screen does not, ipso facto, increase performance. For example, Wright, Hull and Black (1990) looked at subjects' willingness to study diagrams presented as an adjunct to text and at the amount of information gained from the diagrams. They found that when subjects had free access to diagrams (e.g., a button present on the screen labeled "Diagram"), they spent relatively little time studying the diagrams and made minimal use of the information in the diagrams. This was true despite variations in the diagrams and in the instructions. However, when compelled to look at diagrams because they came up unexpectedly, performance improved. This suggests that simply adding a button or notation to on-screen text to signal that additional information is available may not be a truly effective way to enhance learning.

Glenberg and Kruley (1992) investigated the impact that pictures presented with text on a computer had on the resolution of anaphors. An anaphor is a word or phrase that is interpreted in relation to previous elements in a discourse. An example of an anaphor is using a pronoun, such as: "The insect had spots. *It* was a ladybug." Earlier work had indicated that the greater the distance separating the antecedent (the initial reference) and the anaphor, the poorer the comprehension. In the study, subjects read texts that contained short descriptions of objects. Four or five parts of the objects were described in the text. In the text, antecedents described the name and location of the part. The anaphor repeated the spatial location of the part described in the antecedent, and also elaborated on its function. One-third of the texts had no pictures, one-third had an accompanying picture that was always present, and one-third had a picture that either disappeared or appeared late. They found that the presence of pictures did generally help, but did not differentially improve comprehension of texts requiring far anaphor resolution. "We are still somewhat puzzled. The pictures did not assist anaphor resolution, but there is no logical reason why they should not have done so" (Glenberg and Kruley, 1992, p. 471). These findings suggest that subjects did not use the information in the picture effectively to resolve the anaphors. The authors suggest that using illustrations to improve reading comprehension is a skill that must be learned. It could also be the case that illustrations which merely accompany the text in a passive way do not improve comprehension.

A study of hypermedia usability compared question-answering performance using a hypermedia encyclopedia to an equivalent paper version (Leventhal, Teasley, Instone, Rohlman and Farhat, 1993). While users were quite successful in most tasks with the hypermedia encyclopedia, they were not particularly effective in using illustrations as a source of information. In a later study, two hypermedia versions of the same encyclopedia were compared (Instone, Teasley and Leventhal, 1993). One version (the one used in the earlier study) included overlapping windows and several alternative ways to accomplish the same task. The other version used tiled windows and had simplified tools. While the content was identical in both cases, users were more successful at using illustrations in the new, simpler version (and were also much better at using other tools, performing better than paper book users in many instances). The results offered no definitive explanation of this unexpected result. It is possible that improving the interface as a whole improved users' ability to comprehend the text and illustrations, due to a reduced cognitive load. That is, fewer cognitive tasks may have been necessary to use the tools and attain access to information, allowing the user to spend more effort on remembering the content itself.

A study by Egan, Lesk, Ketchum, Lochbaum, Remde, Littman and Landauer (1991) found that chemists had great difficulty performing a task called "analogous transformation" while using a hypermedia/document browsing version of a collection of journal articles. The analogous transformations task requires that the user access a number of illustrations and draw inferences based on the illustrations. In the hypermedia, the user had to first find the appropriate article, and then perform an action to pop up the illustration. Subjects had problems both in coding the pictorial representation of the problem correctly (causing them not to find the appropriate article), and in failing to pop up the illustration, even when they did access the correct article. The authors note that "given that information linked to a text is displayed only at the option of the user, how should that information 'make itself known' to the user?...Having linked information call attention to itself at appropriate times is an unsolved and difficult problem" (Egan, et al., 1991, p. 310). These findings, similar to those of Instone, Brown, Leventhal and Teasley (1993), suggest that illustrations which are not well integrated with the text will be poorly utilized.

Finally, a series of studies looked at readers' willingness to use a glossary containing the definitions of words used in a text, and which also included pictures of the terms being defined (Black, Wright, Black and Norman, 1992). The studies showed that people were more inclined to use the glossary when the terms in the text were marked by a superscript black dot than when they were unmarked. They also found that moving the list of available glossary terms to the left side of the screen and requiring the user to access the items through that list reduced readers' willingness to access the items and their associated pictures. The authors suggest that there are cognitive costs associated with changing modality (e.g., switching from text to illustrations) and that this cost impacts on the processing of the main text.

These studies all show that it is not sufficient to simply add relevant illustrations to text and expect them to automatically aid comprehension. In particular, it appears that the amount of effort required to choose and access the illustration influences its use. Having the user perform an added action such as clicking on a button, or requiring the user to refer to information presented peripherally (e.g., from a list off to the side) deters the effective use of illustrations. Even passive display of an illustration (i.e., the Glenberg and Kruley result) does not insure its use. What did appear to encourage integration of the information from both modalities was the unexpected appearance of an illustration. This approach requires no action from the user, and uses a centralized (not peripheral) display of the information. Unfortunately, while this technique does enhance learning, it violates a central principle of user interface design by not allowing the user to control the interaction. We wished to explore alternative ways to involve the user with an illustration, without taking control away from the user.

The goal of the present studies was to explore factors which influence the effectiveness of integrating text and illustrations. We hypothesized that the way a user interacts with illustrations influences their effectiveness, and that an interaction style which essentially compels the user to interact with an illustration would be most effective. To that end, the first study contrasted text-only and traditional caption-style presentation of an illustration, to a style in which the text was visually next to the relevant portion of the illustration. As a control, all three conditions required the user to perform a point-and-click action to expose the text.

2. STUDY 1

The hypothesis of the first study was that compelling the user to interact with an illustration would result in enhanced learning through more integration of the textual and graphically presented information. The means chosen for compelling interaction was to present the illustration first, and to reveal textual information directly adjacent to the relevant portion of the illustration. The illustration contained "hot spots" (areas that could be clicked on with a mouse) that, when activated, revealed the relevant text. We labeled this an *integrated* interaction style. (See Figure 2.)

Two other interaction styles served as control conditions. One was a text-only condition. In this case, there were hot spots on the screen which were small circles next to text terms. When the user clicked on a hot spot, the text appeared directly to the right. The second control condition, the caption style, was exactly like the text-only condition, except that an illustration was present in the area above the hot spots and text (Figure 1). This style mimics a typical paper publication, with a captioned illustration. Note that all three conditions require the user to use the mouse and cursor to click on a hot spot and activate the text. Thus, the use of mouse and cursor is constant across all three conditions, as is the need to perform an action to reveal the pertinent text, providing control for these factors. By controlling for use of a mouse and cursor, and by always requiring the user to perform an action to see the text, we hoped to isolate just the effects of 1) presence or absence of an illustration, and 2) captioning versus integrated text and illustration.

We hypothesized that the subjects would learn the best when the text was integrated with the illustration. We also expected that having the text below the illustration would be no more effective than text alone, due to the relative isolation of the text from the graphic.

2.1 Materials

The materials consisted of a series of topic screens. Each topic was related to incidents from the Sherlock Holmes detective stories, by Sir Arthur Conan Doyle, and contained information about geographic entities or devices of interest to Sherlock Holmes. Sample topics are: the reproductive system of spaghnum sporophyte, areas near Ireland, obscure names for parts of a horse, and sections of Scotland. For each topic, there were four or five items. Each item consisted of one piece of spatial (directional) information and one fact related to a Sherlock Holmes story or about the object. For example, for the topic of Switzerland, one item was the town of Lausanne. The spatial information about Lausanne was "A town in west Switzerland." The fact was "Lady Frances Carfax was last heard from here."

The topics were presented in three interaction styles: *text-only*, *caption* and *integrated.* In the text-only interaction style, there was no illustration. Four or five item names were listed at the bottom of the screen. When users moved the cursor over the item name, text information about that item popped up to the right of the name. The text appeared in the same location on the screen for each item. (The text-only style was identical to what is shown in Figure 1, except there was no illustration. Note that in the figure, the user has selected "Davos Platz" and the text has appeared to the right).

The caption interaction style was similar to the text-only, except that an illustration (map or picture) appeared above the list of items, as shown in Figure 1. As in the text-only style, the text appeared to the right of the list of items. Each item name also appeared in the illustration in bold text.

In the integrated style, users pointed directly at the item on the illustration to reveal the text information. As shown in Figure 2, the information appeared near the location of the relevant item on the illustration.

In order to vary the materials, not every topic was geography-based. Several of the topics dealt with objects. For example, one topic showed the different parts of a gasogene, a device Holmes used for making soda water.

Each subject saw 12 topics, in a within-subjects design. The three interaction styles were randomly distributed across the topics, with the limitation that each user saw four topics in each interaction style. The order of the topics was also randomly generated.

Following the presentation of each topic, users saw a screen which directed them to work on a word search task (on paper) for 30 seconds. The word search task served as a distracter, so that the users could not answer the subsequent questions based on short term memory. At the end of 30 seconds, they answered a series of eight multiple choice questions presented on the computer. Four of the questions concerned the fact information from the topic and four concerned the spatial information. All eight questions were the same for each topic, regardless of interaction style used to present the topic. In addition to scores on the questions, the time spent studying each topic was recorded.

2.2 Subjects

The subjects were 27 students from an introductory computer science class. All had previous experience using a mouse for pointing. All rated themselves as "not very familiar" with the Holmes stories.

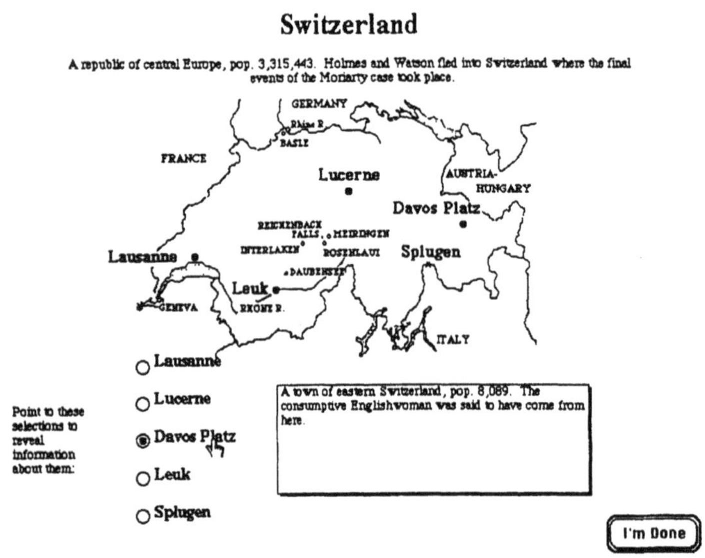

Figure 1: The caption interaction style

2.3 Procedure

The subjects were first given training for the task by viewing a sample topic and demonstrations of the three interaction styles. In these examples, instructions appeared on the screen along with the text and illustrations. The instructions explained where to point and what button to press when they were finished with each topic. Next, a sample topic was presented in one of the three interaction styles (randomly chosen), with no instructions present. This initial topic was the same for all users, and served as a practice trial. They then performed the primary task, which consisted of 12 trials. Each trial included the presentation of the topic (which the users were allowed to study as long as they wished), followed by 30 seconds of distracter task, followed by the eight multiple choice questions. Time for answering the questions was not limited.

2.4 Results

For each topic, there were a total of four spatial information questions and four factual information questions. A score of one was given for each correct answer and a zero for each incorrect answer. There were four topics presented in each of the three interaction styles. Thus, the maximum score for each type of question (spatial or fact) for each of the three interaction styles was 16. The mean number correct (out of 16) for each condition is shown in Table 1.

	Interaction Style			
	Text-only	Caption	Integrated	Overall
Spatial	8.6	9.9	11.3	9.9
Fact	10.2	11.0	12.3	11.1
Overall	9.4	10.4	11.8	

Table 1: Mean scores on the multiple choice questions in Study 1 as a function of type of question (spatial vs. fact) and interaction style. N = 27.

Using a repeated measures ANOVA, the main effects of question type and interaction type were significant ($F(1,34) = 16.1$, $p < .001$ and $F(2,34) = 9.7$, $p < .001$, respectively). The mean total correct was higher for the fact questions (mean = 11.1) than for the spatial questions (mean = 9.9). This suggests that the spatial information was more difficult to learn overall than the factual information, in spite of the fact that for two-thirds of the topics, the illustration was present and might have been expected to serve as an aid to learning the material. The factual information, on the other hand, would not be particularly enhanced by the illustration (e.g., the fact that "Lady Frances Carfax was last heard from here" is not actually illustrated or demonstrated by the illustration). Overall, the total number of correct answers for the integrated style was higher than for either of the other two styles (mean =11.8 versus 10.4 for caption and 9.4 for text-only). This suggests that the integrated style is the most effective way to present either factual or spatial information.

To explore whether the presence of any illustration was useful, two sets of pairwise t-tests were performed. One was done on the spatial data, and another on the fact data. Comparisons of the spatial question data indicated that there was no significant difference between the text-only and caption conditions, indicating that the presence of the illustration did *not* enhance learning of spatial information when the textual material was presented as a caption. In addition, scores on spatial questions for the integrated interaction style were significantly higher than the caption style (paired t, two-tailed = 2.0, DF = 26, $p < .05$). This shows that the critical factor which enhanced the learning of the spatial material was the integration of the text with the illustration, and not solely the presence of the illustration.

A second set of pairwise t-tests was done on the fact questions. The results parallel those found for the spatial questions. For the fact questions, the text-only and caption styles were again not significantly different from each other, suggesting that the simple presence of an illustration did not enhance learning. On the other hand, the comparison of the caption scores to the integrated style scores was significant ($t = 2.4$, DF = 26, $p < .05$), indicating that the integrated style, and not just the presence of the illustration, was responsible for the improved learning.

The time spent studying each topic card was also analyzed. The mean times were 70.5 seconds for text-only, 73.7 seconds for caption and 67.6 seconds for integrated. These differences were not significant.

2.5 Summary of Study 1

The results of Study 1 show that an integrated style is the most effective way to present text and illustrations when the user wishes to remember the information presented. Furthermore, the presence of an illustration is of no added benefit unless the text and illustration are integrated.

Surprisingly, enhanced learning occurred for both factual and spatial information. One might assume that the integrated style would be more of an aid to memory, because the text is presented in a spatially-related way, thus reinforcing the information in the illustration. There is no *a priori* reason why the integrated style would aid recall of the factual information, which was not represented by the illustration. The results, however, show that learning of both sorts of information was enhanced. Perhaps this stems from the fact that the integrated style helped the reader learn the organizational framework inherently present in the illustration, and provided "hooks" for the factual information. The time data, which was not different for the three styles, indicates that the advantages of the integrated style were realized with no additional time requirements.

3. STUDY 2

Study 1 demonstrated that integration is superior to either text alone or an illustration with a caption for learning both factual and spatial information. We then speculated about exactly what aspect of the integrated style contributes to this enhancement. Considering the actions of people when they use the integrated style suggests that they actually do two things:

• they point to the relevant part of the illustration to activate the related text, and

• they read the text which appears near the relevant portion of the illustration. (e.g., moving the hand in a "north" direction to click on a city located in the north on a map).This is similar to the way clapping a rhythm with your hands might reinforce hearing a rhythm with your ears. A second question is whether the placement of the text is critical. When the user reads the text, is it important that the text be next to the relevant portion of the illustration? Perhaps readers can be seeing, at least peripherally, the illustration at the same time they are reading, thus getting more information. Perhaps learning is facilitated because readers do not have to shift their eyes up and down between the illustration and the text. Or perhaps it requires a combination of these processes to achieve the enhanced learning. Study 2 attempted to answer these questions by comparing three somewhat different styles of interaction, all of which used an illustration, but involved different ways of revealing the text.

The content of the instrument was the same as in Study 1, including both factual and spatial questions. Three styles of interaction were used. One was the integrated style from Study 1. That is, the user pointed to an item name on the illustration to reveal the text, which appeared nearby. A second interaction style, called *illustration point*, had the user point to the item name on the illustration, while the text appeared as a caption. The purpose of this condition was to see if the action of moving the cursor onto the relevant part of the illustration was more important than having the text appear nearby. In the third style, called *illustration read*, the item names appeared in a list underneath the illustration. When the user moved the cursor over an item name, the related text appeared next to the relevant part of the illustration. The purpose of this condition was to see if having the text next to the illustration was more important than moving the cursor onto the relevant part of the illustration. The population of subjects for Study 2 was identical to that of Study 1. There were 20 participants.

3.1 Results

Thé mean number of questions correct for each of the conditions is presented in Table 2. (Recall that the maximum score for any condition is 16.) As in Study 1, performance was better on the fact questions than the spatial questions ($F(1,38) = 17.6$, $p < .001$). No other differences were significant. As Table 3 shows, the three integrated styles (point, integrated and read) clearly emerge as the better strategy for presenting text and illustrations. Comparing the characteristics of these three styles to the caption and text-only conditions, a common feature of the integrated styles is that users must at some time during the process move at least their eyes (and possibly the cursor) onto or near the relevant portion of the illustration. In the integrated style, the user moves the cursor onto the item name in the illustration, and reads the text near the illustration. In the illustration point style, the user moves the cursor onto the item name in the illustration, and in the illustration read style, the user reads the text near the illustration. In contrast, with the caption style, the user need never look at the illustration. (Of course, there was no illustration in the text-only style.) This suggests that the critical factor for enhanced learning is that the user must be somehow compelled to interact visually with the illustration at some point in the study period.

	Interaction Style			
	Integrated	**Illustration Read**	**Illustration Point**	**Overall**
Spatial	11.8	11.5	11.6	11.6
Fact	13.6	12.1	12.9	12.8
Overall	12.7	11.8	12.2	

Table 2: Mean scores on the multiple choice questions in Study 2 as a function of type of question (spatial vs. fact) and interaction style. N = 20

Interaction Style	N	Fact	Spatial	Mean
Illustration Point	20	12.8	11.6	12.2
Integrated	47	12.8	11.5	12.1
Illustration Read	20	12.1	11.5	11.8
Caption	27	10.9	9.8	10.4
Text-only	27	10.2	8.6	9.4

Table 3: Combined results from Study 1 and Study 2.

3.2 Discussion of Study 2

The results of Study 2 indicate that neither the movement of the cursor nor the placement of the text is more important to the enhanced learning from the integrated style. However, consider the results of both studies together, as shown in Table 3. (For the integrated style, the mean score combined across the two studies was used. The difference between these two means was not significant.)

4. CONCLUSIONS

One of the exciting aspects of interactive media is that they can provide a more efficient and effective way of presenting information and of promoting learning than through the use of more traditional media. However, prior studies have found that illustrated information presented on a computer display is not always used effectively. In fact, an illustration can be of no additional value at all, compared to plain text. In order to create effective presentations, designers need an understanding of the factors that make illustrations effective.

One factor which had been shown in a prior study to enhance learning from illustrations was compelling users to look by having the illustrations appear unexpectedly (Write, Hull and Black, 1990). However, this approach violates usability principles, and may not be suitable in many situations. In what we call the integrated style of interaction, the user must actively select the portion of the illustration of interest in order to reveal the textual information, which then appears adjacent to the illustration. This turns the user from a passive reader of text who has the option of looking at an illustration (the style typical of paper media), to an active user, who must look at and process the illustration to at least some extent in order to reveal the text. Our first study showed that this style of presentation enhanced learning by 20%. Interestingly, we also found that learning of factual information (which was *not* illustrated by the illustration) was improved just as much as spatial information (which was illustrated by the illustration). This finding is especially encouraging, because it means that the active style increases all learning, not just that directly related to the illustration.

The second study attempted to determine if either the act of moving the cursor onto the illustration or the fact that the text appeared closely adjacent to the illustration was the critical feature in enhancing learning in the integrated style. The study found no differences between these two conditions and the original style. These results, taken in conjunction with Study 1, suggest that the critical feature is simply that the user must interact with the illustration at some point in the study period. Thus, our findings support Wright, Hull and Black (1990), and extend their conclusions: learning is enhanced when the user either encounters an illustration unexpectedly, or is required to interact with the illustration.

The present studies support the following design guidelines concerning illustrations when the goal of the system is to inform the user:

• Have the user interact in some way with the illustration. Simply presenting a captioned illustration will not aid learning.

• Having the illustration appear unexpectedly will also enhance learning, but violates usability principles. Nonetheless, the technique could be effectively used in moderation.

• Reverse the usual order of saliency of text and illustrations. That is, make the illustration what users see first, and have them perform an action to bring up the associated text.

• Even if some of the information is not directly related to an illustration, associate it in a meaningful way with other text that is directly related to the illustration. Learning for the associated information will be enhanced, as well.

Additional work needs to be done to extend the basic finding to other uses of illustrations. For example, it seems likely that the integrated interaction style might be more effective than paper media for teaching definitions, contrasts and comparisons. Consider a person who wants to learn the names of and differences among various styles of architecture. The learner might explore diagrams or pictures of various examples. As they move the cursor over the illustrations, textual information appears which points out the characteristics of each style. An additional challenge would be extending this work to interactive animation or videos. For example, research done by Pane, Corbett and John (1996) showed that students did not learn declarative information any better from multimedia educational software than they did from static text and images. Clearly, there is much that needs to be understood before we can take full advantage of all that multimedia can offer toward enhanced learning and information seeking.

5. REFERENCES

Black, A., Wright, P., Black, D. and Norman, K. 1992, Consulting on-line dictionary information while reading. *Hypermedia*, 4 (3), 145-169

Egan, D. E., Lesk, M. E., Ketchum, R. D., Lochbaum, C. C., Remde, J. R., Littman, M. and Landauer, T. K. 1991, Hypermedia for the electronic library? CORE sample results. *Hypermedia '91 Proceedings*, 299-312.

Glenberg, A. M. and Kruley, P. 1992, Pictures and anaphora: Evidence for independent processes. *Memory & Cognition*, 20 (5), 461-471.

Harrison, S. M. (1995) A comparison of still, animated or nonillustrated on-line help with written or spoken instructions in a graphical user interface. *Human Factors in Computing Systems*, CHI 95, 82-89.

Instone, K., Brown, E., Leventhal, L. and Teasley, B. 1993, The challenge of effectively integrating illustrations into hypertext. *EWHCI '93 Proceedings*, Vol. 1, 78-86.

Instone, K., Teasley, B. and Leventhal, L. M. 1993, Empirically-based re-design of a hypertext encyclopedia, *INTERCHI '93 Proceedings*, 500-506.

Leventhal, L. M., Teasley, B. M., Instone, K., Rohlman, D. S. and Farhat, J. 1993, Sleuthing in HyperHolmes: Using hypertext vs. a book to answer questions. *Behaviour and Information Technology*, 12 (3), 149-164.

Ogozalek, V. Z. 1994, A comparison of the use of text and multimedia interfaces to provide information to the elderly. *Human Factors in Computing Systems*, CHI 94, 65-71.

Pane, J. F., Corbett, A. T. and John, B. E. Assessing dynamics in computer-based instruction. *Human Factors in Computing Systems*, CHI 96, 197-204.

Teasley, B., Leventhal, L., Blumenthal, B., Instone, K. and Stone, D. 1994, Cultural diversity in user interface design: Are intuitions enough? *SIGCHI Bulletin*, 26 (1), 36-40.

Waddill, P. J. and McDaniel, M. A. 1992, Pictorial enhancement of text memory: Limitations imposed by picture type and comprehension skill. *Memory & Cognition*, 20 (5), 472-482.Wright, P., Hull, A. and Black, D. 1990, Integrating diagrams and text. *The Technical Writing Teacher*, 17 (3), 244-254.

A Multimedia Interaction Space

Frank Vetere, Steve Howard and Ying Leung

Swinburne University of Technology
Swinburne Computer Human Interaction Laboratory
PO Box 218 Hawthorn Vic 3122 AUSTRALIA
{fvetere, showard, yleung}@swin.edu.au

ABSTRACT Multimedia is often described simply as a combination of media. The list of possible media usually includes text, graphics, images, sound, animation, video and others. What constitutes media however is not well understood, and so the list becomes somewhat arbitrary. There is a need for a more comprehensive model of multimedia. This paper suggests 'a Multimedia Interaction Space': a three dimensional space based on the notion of media as language with a particular grammar. It distinguishes between 'base media' associated with particular sensory channels and 'composite media'. Composite media are composed of more than one base medium. The Multimedia Interaction Space provides a framework to represent multimedia interactions from an HCI perspective.

KEYWORDS multimedia interaction space, multimedia, media, mode, metaphor, language, engagement

"Our languages are our media. Our media are our metaphors. Our metaphors create the content of our culture" (Postman 1985).

1. INTRODUCTION

Given the plethora of research and development in multimedia over the last two decades (e.g. Kjelldahl 1992, Blattner & Dannenberg 1992), one would expect a well formulated body of knowledge about multimedia interactions which establishes basic principles and provides a basis for future research. Instead much of multimedia research and discussion is based on descriptions which are characterised by using more than one medium through some computer system.

A description which typifies the general understanding of multimedia is "A multimedia computer system is one that transacts or interacts in more than one medium, ie. carriers of information such as text, audio, still graphics, animation, and video" (Baecker, Grudin, Buxton & Greenberg 1995 p.400). This description of multimedia is based on exemplification rather than a robust definition.

Baecker's description is not intended to provide the foundations of multimedia research. It is a general description which reflects current understanding of multimedia. Nonetheless it captures the flavour of many multimedia applications. A computer system that uses a combination of text, audio, still graphics, animation, and video is unquestionably considered multimedia. Such descriptions have become a de facto definition.

Human-Computer Interaction: INTERACT'97 S. Howard, J. Hammond & G. Lindgaard (editors)
Published by Chapman & Hall

Yet this type of description is not based on any rigorous understanding of multimedia. There is a need for a suitable structure upon which to base HCI research into multimedia.

The type of definition which views multimedia as simply an integration of text, sound and pictures is problematic. The problems arise from adopting a technology centric view rather than a user centric view to multimedia (Alty 1991, Marmolin 1992), and from conceptualising media as information carriers.

2. MEDIA AS TECHNOLOGY

When multimedia is seen as a combination of discrete media, undue emphasis is placed on the enabling technology rather than the interaction. Definitions based on audio and video representations lead to discussions about technological capabilities, such as compression techniques and transmission bandwidth. These are undoubtedly important, but from an HCI perspective they are at best only part of the picture.

The discrete media in arbitrary media lists are predominantly associated with output interactions. Animation, for example, is used only as an output medium. It has not been used as an input medium. This bias of multimedia representations towards output is in contrast to the HCI bias, whose research is largely about input. Many HCI models are concerned with input interactions (e.g. Payne & Green 1989, and Card, Moran & Newell 1983) and an analysis of interaction devices (Baecker & Buxton 1987, Helander 1991) shows a predominance of input over output devices.

Computer systems which focus on output rather than input tend to be more concerned with presentations rather than interactions (Mayes 1992). They then begin to resemble other systems that have little or no input mechanisms (e.g. television)

A technological view of multimedia does not capture the richness of the interaction. Multimedia is more than the sum of its media parts. New semantic and syntactical elements are created when media are combined (Alty 1991). When text and graphics are placed on a screen, a new representation is created. The text and graphics do not remain discrete entities. Together they form complex conceptual links that permit new forms of interactions. We recognise this new type of interaction in print by calling it 'newspaper' or 'magazine' or 'book'. In computer systems the new representation is called 'text and graphics' or 'multimedia' – a title which makes it indistinguishable from other media combinations. If multimedia is simply a combination of media then it cannot adequately represent the structures associated with media combinations.

So when multimedia is described as being a combination of media from some media list (e.g. text, audio, still graphics, animation, and video) it becomes more concerned with the capabilities of the hardware than with the interaction from the user's point of view, it becomes more concerned with the output rather than input media and it is unable to speak accurately about the interactions resulting from the media combinations.

3. MEDIA AS INFORMATION CARRIERS

A medium is often considered the carrier of information (Blattner & Dannenberg 1992, Baecker et al. 1995). This conceptualisation of media is potentially the source of confusion and ambiguity. A carrier of information could be the text, the CD-ROM, the CPU, the VDU, the computer network or the space between the eye and the screen. If they are all information carriers then they are all media. A system which uses a floppy disk and a VDU could then be considered multimedia. This ambiguity makes it difficult to compare research results and interpret progress in multimedia. Blattner & Dannenberg (1992) acknowledge this ambiguity by accepting that a medium may or may not be of a physical form. Steinmetz & Nahrstedt (1995) get around this problem by describing six categories of media; perception, representational, presentation, storage, transmission and information exchange. Both authors attempt to manage the difficulty, but neither address the problem through a basic reconceptualisation of media.

Conceptualising media as information carrier does not provide adequate granularity. Video and sound, for example, are both information carriers. Yet video is clearly a complex combination of many representations, including sound. Video is a 'higher order' medium. Simply considering video as another information carrier does not distinguish it from 'lower order' media. As a consequence video is often included in lists of possible media combinations (Blattner & Dannenberg 1992, Baecker et al. 1995). If all media were of equal status then adding sound to video would create a multimedia system. Again, this is misleading and ambiguous.

So media, as information carriers, leads to confusion about the nature of the information, confusion about the nature of the carrier and allows trivial media combination by not clearly discriminating between media types. A new concept of media is required.

4. MEDIA AS LANGUAGE

Alty (1996) suggests that the medium is the *language* through which the information is exchanged rather than the *carrier* of the information. He says that the valid language is defined by the restrictions of three communication mechanisms; the creation mechanism (e.g. a loudspeaker), the transmission mechanism (e.g. air) and the reception mechanism (e.g. the ear).

Conceptualising media as language is important. If media is considered language, then a grammar can be used to describe media. Discussions about the 'information' or 'information carrier' are no longer central to understanding multimedia. A simple device (e.g. a CD-ROM) cannot be considered a medium unless it is associated with a language and a corresponding grammar. 'Media as language' gives every medium a range of valid tokens (lexicon) that can be arranged in a particular ways (syntax) and that have particular meaning (semantics) depending on the context in which they are presented (pragmatics).

Alty (1991) also suggests that there be 'base' media (text, graphics, speech, sound, gesture and motion) and 'composite' media (e.g. video and animation). These two groups of media introduce a hierarchy that was lacking in Baecker's description. Combinations of base media are all valid (unlike combinations of media from an arbitrary media-list). Meaningless media combinations, like sound and video, are not possible because video is a composite media of which sound is already one its parts.

Composite media have a particular language with emergent features that are captured by the grammar. Animation, for example, is not simply a combination of graphics and sound, but a particular medium in its own right that is fully described by its grammar.

'Media as language' deals with many of the difficulties that arise from conceptualising media as information carriers, but there is still a need for a framework and notation in which multimedia can be suitably represented.

5. MEDIA AS METAPHOR

Hutchins, Hollan and Norman (1986) developed a 'space of interfaces' in order to better understand 'directness' in direct manipulation. The two dimensions of this space are distance and engagement. Distance is concerned with the gap between the system goals and the user's goals. Engagement is based on two interaction metaphors, conversation and model world. In the interface space, direct manipulation occurs when there is a small distance between user and system goals and there is a 'feeling' of engagement. This engagement occurs when the user has a sense of direct involvement with a world of objects (model world metaphor) rather than of communicating with an intermediary (conversation metaphor).

Engagement is related to the concept of interactivity. Laurel (1992) outlines four variables which help to characterise the level of interactivity; frequency (how often one interacts), range (the number of available choices for interaction), significance (whether those choices really affect matters) and the ability to act within a representation. This last variable is the degree to which one feels like they are actually participating in the ongoing action. This is comparable to engagement. Therefore, engagement is an important measure of interactivity.

Frohlich (1992) proposes that the two interaction metaphors (conversation and model world) be used as the basis for a 'design space of interfaces'. The conversation metaphor becomes Frohlich's language mode and the model world metaphor becomes the action mode. The 'mode' (or metaphor) is the first of four characteristics which define Frohlich's interface design space. The other three are 'channel', 'medium' and 'style'.

Frohlich defines two groups of channels; the human interface channels (voice & movement for output; hearing, sight & touch for input) and the computer interface channels (audio, visual & haptic). The term 'haptic' is used broadly to include both tactile information (specifying surface contact) and kinaesthetic information (specifying effector position).

He nominates six media; three associated with the language mode (speech, text, and gesture) and three with the action mode (sound, graphics, and motion). These are the base media that Alty (1991) used as a foundation for the composite media.

Frohlich's styles are a list of interaction techniques based on the work of Baecker & Buxton (1987)

Frohlich's use of terminology is unique. He gives a particular meaning to 'mode' which is not shared by many others. 'Mode' is often referred to as being a sensory channel (Mayes 1992), an interaction style (Blattner & Dannenberg 1992) or a computer state (Marcus 1995). Some researchers also differentiate between modality (channel and style) and mode (computer state) (Nigay & Coutaz 1993).

In Frohlich's interface design space, the interface mode or modality (as distinct from the system mode or modedness) refers to the two fundamental interaction metaphors.

The interface design space provides a detailed and comprehensive structure. It integrates media with interaction metaphors and then incorporates sensory channels and styles.

6. A MULTIMEDIA FRAMEWORK

Alty (1991) uses Frohlich's interface design space (later discussed in Frohlich 1992) to create a multimedia framework. This framework captures the concepts of interaction metaphors through the language and action modes and the concept of 'media as language' through the use of the creation and recognition mechanisms (these are equivalent to Frohlich's 'channel').

Alty (1991) recognises that this framework could be a basis for a model of multimedia interactions. There are nonetheless, some difficulties that need to be addressed before a comprehensive model is established.

Alty's multimedia framework loses the dimension of engagement. There is no longer a continuum from the conversation metaphor to the model world metaphor as is represented by the model of interface spaces in Hutchins et al. (1986). Instead the two metaphors are represented as discrete modalities.

Alty's multimedia framework does not permit adequate representation of video or animation. The concept of composite media is introduced, but there is no structure to represent it. Alty suggests that time could be added to the graphics medium to create animation, but the framework does not currently support this type of notation.

The use of language (as a conversation metaphor) to describe one of the interaction modes is a potential source of confusion given that media is also described as language (with grammatical constructs).

A suitable model of multimedia interaction would capture the detail of Alty's framework and also address the problems concerning lack of continuum for engagement, the representation of composite media and the possible confusion with the term 'language'.

7. A SPACE OF MULTIMEDIA INTERACTIONS

It is possible now to create a three dimensional space to model multimedia interactions (figure 1). This space incorporates interaction metaphors and is based on the concept of media as language.

The three sensory channels, visual, auditory and haptic, define the three axes. The haptic channel includes both tactile and kinaesthetic information (Frohlich 1992).

The six base media occupy space along the axes; text and pictures on the visual channel, speech and sound on the auditory channel, gesture and motion on the haptic channel. Any point within the space is specified by its grammar. So, the interaction associated with any point in the space has a particular semantic and pragmatic meaning for each of its lexical tokens and a particular syntactic structure.

The 'graphics' medium is renamed 'pictures' and includes moving as well as static pictures. A 'moving picture' is literally any graphic that moves, albeit with no accompanying sound. This could include silent film or silent animation. A moving picture has a different language structure from a static picture and so occupies a different region in the space. Video and animation can be represented in this three dimensional space by a region which includes sound, speech and pictures.

Further, the 'language' mode (Frohlich 1992) is renamed 'conversation'. This avoids possible confusion and is consistent with the earlier work of Hutchins et al. (1986) on interface spaces.

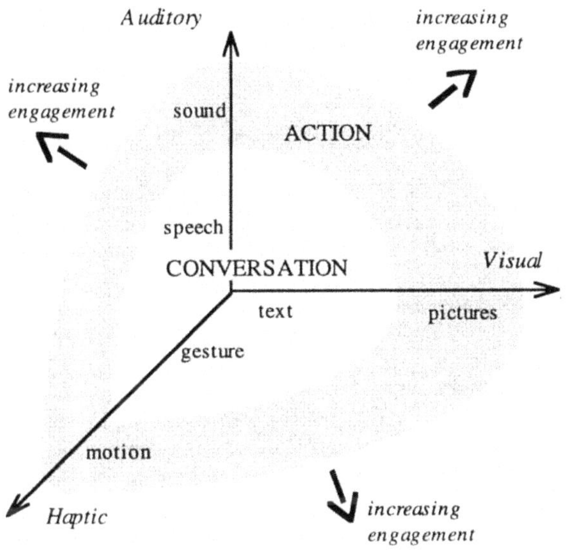

Figure 1: The Multimedia Interaction Space

The media closest to the origin (speech, text, gesture) are associated with the conversation metaphor (Hutchins et al. 1986). Those further away (pictures, sound, motion) are associated with the action or model world metaphor. The radial distance from the origin reflects the engagement of the interaction (as defined by Hutchins et al. 1986).

The Multimedia Interaction Space (MMIS) (figure 1) permits representations of multimedia interactions and helps to clarify the concept of media. According to the model, a multimedia interaction is characterised by the language constructs (semantic, syntactic, pragmatic, lexical) of the media, by the sensory channel (the three axes) and by the interaction metaphor (radial distance from the origin)

A representation of the complete human interaction with a multimedia system requires two diagrams, one for input and the other for output. These two diagrams would represent the nature of multimedia interaction (both input and output) and the level of engagement for any particular computer system. The complete interaction would be represented by spaces in both the input and output diagrams.

At any particular time, the interaction is represented by a point or region in the space. At some other time, the interaction will occupy another place. It is theoretically possible to show how the interaction changes over time. The conglomeration of these interactions produces a diagram which is a representation of the entire interaction over time. This diagram could be considered a 'map' of the interaction.

It is significant that engagement is included in the MMIS model. Engagement is an important feature of interactivity and interactivity is often associated with multimedia. This model of multimedia interaction captures three of the Laurel's (1992) four variables; frequency (amount of interaction), range (the number of available choices for interaction) and engagement.

It is also possible to use the model to represent new types of multimedia interactions that have yet to be fully exploited or developed. This is particularly relevant for media along the haptic channel.

The model is presently restricted to three of the five human sensory channels. It is conceivable that a five dimensional space could be created if there were a computer system that made use of the gustatory or olfactory senses.

8. APPLYING THE MODEL

If extended, the MMIS model could be used to represent input or output interactions of a computer application. The Encarta® encyclopaedia by Microsoft® is a typical example of a multimedia product which could be represented using the MMIS model (figure 2).

Two diagrams are required to represent the input and output interactions, but only the output diagram is presented here. Encarta's output uses media along two channels. It does not use haptic media, so the output media interaction can be represented along two dimensions, auditory and visual.

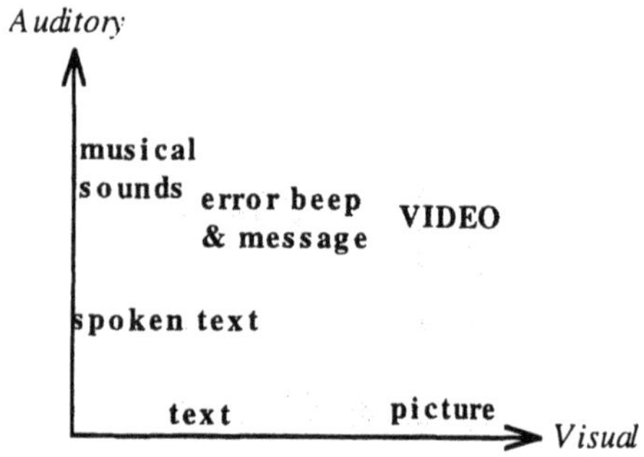

Figure 2: Using MMIS to represent the output media interaction of Microsoft® Encarta®

The MMIS model is used to represent the media associated with the output interaction. It is not a complete representation of the interaction. It is only intended to exemplify the model. Not all the media combinations have been included.

The diagram also makes many assumptions about the nature of the media and the level of engagement. A complete and thorough representation requires operationalisaton of the grammar for each media and for the characteristics of engagement. This would provide a basis on which to determine the size and position of the regions in the space. Presently, the model offers a framework on which operationalised characteristics may be build.

The Multimedia Interaction Space provides an elegant mechanism for representing the use of media in a computer application. As alluded to in figure 2, interactions with different multimedia systems would yield different MMIS maps. For example, short musical compositions would be differentiated from other sounds such as 'beeps' (which may contain textual error messages) and video (which contains moving pictures). In principal, the MMIS model supports descriptions of media types in a computer system and allows meaningful comparisons between systems.

9. CONCLUSION

The Multimedia Interaction Space makes progress towards a better understanding of multimedia interactions. The model provides some immediate benefits. These include:

- replacing general definitions of multimedia with a structured model which permits comprehensive representations of multimedia interactions
- reconceptualising media as language rather than as an information carrier
- allowing input as well as output media representations
- distinguishing between base media and composite media
- representing multimedia interactions from a user perspective by incorporating interaction metaphors
- combining the concepts of engagement and interactivity within a model of multimedia interaction.

The model also provides other advantages that could be exploited with further research. These include:

- being unconstrained by existing media representations and allows for the representation of undeveloped media (especially using the haptic channel)
- the possibility of representing changing interactions over time
- providing a potentially calculable conceptualisation of multimedia interactions

More work needs to be done in operationalising the concepts and in representing the possible relationships between the shaded areas. Nonetheless, the model makes a contribution towards creating a comprehensive structure upon which to base HCI research in multimedia. It does not explicitly represent interaction styles, as in Frohlich's (1992) design space, but it does attempt to integrate the key concepts of language and metaphor within a multimedia framework.

The integration of language and metaphor with multimedia echoes Postman's (1985) aphorism which prefaced this paper. He suggests that the use of language and metaphors through media has cultural implications. This is true for multimedia which is having a significant effect on society and culture. The Multimedia Interaction Space begins to acknowledge the role of language and metaphor in multimedia interactions.

10. REFERENCES

Alty, J. L. (1996) "Multimedia Interface Design" Tutorial notes at OzCHI 96

Alty, J. L. (1991) "Multimedia - What is it and how do we exploit it?" in Diaper, D. & Hammond, N.(Eds.) *People and Computers VI: Proceedings of the HCI '91 Conference* Cambridge University Press, Cambridge UK, pp 31-41

Baecker, R. M., Grudin, J., Buxton, W. A. S. & Greenberg, S. (1995) *Readings in Human-Computer Interaction: Towards the Year 2000 (second edition)* Morgan Kaufmann, San Francisco CA.

Baecker, R. & Buxton, W. A. S. (1987) *Readings in Human Computer Interaction* Morgan Kaufmann, Los Altos CA

Blattner, M. M. & Dannenberg, R. B. (1992) *Multimedia Interface Design* Addison Wesley, Reading MA

Card, S. K., Moran, T. P. & Newell, A. (1983) *The Psychology of Human-Computer Interaction* Lawrence Erlbaum, Hillsdale NJ

Frohlich, D. M. (1992) "The Design Space of Interfaces" in Kjelldahl, L. (Ed.) *Multimedia: Systems, Interaction and Applications*. Springer-Verlag, Berlin pp 53-69

Helander, M. (1991) *Handbook of Human-Computer Interaction*. Elsevier Science, Netherlands

Hutchins, E. L., Hollan, J. D. & Norman, D. A. (1986) "Direct Manipulation Interfaces" in Norman, D. A. & Draper, S. W. (Eds.) *User Centered System Design*. Lawrence Erlbaum, Hillside New Jersey pp 87-124

Kjelldahl, L. (1992) *Multimedia: Systems, Interaction and Applications*. Springer-Verlag, Berlin

Laurel, B. (1992) *Computers as Theatre*. Addison Wesley, Reading MA

Marcus, A. (1995) "A Comparison of Graphical User Interfaces" in Baecker, R. M., Grudin, J., Buxton, W. A. S. & Greenberg, S. *Readings in Human-Computer Interaction: Towards the Year 2000 (second edition)* Morgan Kaufmann, San Francisco CA, pp 457-468

Mayes, J. T. (1992) "The 'M-Word': Multimedia Interfaces and Their role in Interactive Learning Systems" in Edwards, A. D. N. & Holland, S. (Eds.) *Multimedia Interface Design in Education*. Springer-Verlag, Berlin pp 1-22

Marmolin, H. (1992) "Multimedia from the Perspective of Psychology" in Kjelldahl, L. (Ed.) *Multimedia: Systems, Interaction and Applications*. Springer-Verlag, Berlin pp 39-51

Nigay, L. & Coutaz, J. (1993) "A Design Space for Multimodal Systems: Concurrent Processing and Data Fusion" in *Proc. INTERCHI '93 Human Factors in Computing Systems* ACM Press pp 172-178

Payne, S. & Green, T. R. G. (1989) "Task-action grammar: the model and its developments" in Diaper, D. (Ed.) *Task Analysis for Human-Computer Interaction* Ellis Horwood, Chichester

Postman, N. (1985) *Amusing Ourselves to Death*, Heinemann, UK

Steinmetz, R. & Nahrstedt, K. (1995) *Multimedia: Computing, Communications and Applications* Prentice Hall, Upper Saddle River NJ

A Framework to Support Creativity in Multimedia Information Design

Kumiyo Nakakoji[1,4], Kouhei Suzuki[2], Nobuo Ohkura[3], Atsushi Aoki[1]

[1]Software Engineering Laboratory, Software Research Associates, Inc., 3-12, Yotsuya, Shinjyuku, Tokyo, JAPAN
[2]Information Technology Promotion Agency, MITI, Tokyo, JAPAN
[3]PFU Inc., Tokyo, JAPAN
[4]Cognitive Science Laboratory, Graduate School of Information Science, Nara Institute of Science and Technology, JAPAN

kumiyo@sra.co.jp, k-suzuki@ipastc.stc.ipa.go.jp, ohkura@pfu.co.jp, aoki@sra.co.jp

ABSTRACT Creating good multimedia information design requires a variety of domain knowledge, including knowledge about color, sound, movies and multimodal effects. Our eMMa (Environment for MultiMedia Authoring) project has focused on designing, building and assessing a computational system that supports casual users in designing multimedia information, such as creation of world-wide-web home pages. Exercising creativity in such design tasks is to find a "right" balance between innovativeness and usefulness of designed artifacts. This paper presents a framework of eMMa to support creativity in the both dimensions, with a brief scenario to illustrate how the eMMa system is used. We discuss case studies we have conducted in several academic and industrial sites, which demonstrates that users showed some creative aspects in their multimedia information design.

KEYWORDS multimedia information design, creativity, knowledge-based support

1. MULTIMEDIA INFORMATION DESIGN

Multimedia information design requires a wide range of design knowledge. Designers need to know how people perceive representations of text, color, sound, visual images and movies, as well as their psychological and cultural associations. In addition, there are some studies that specifically focus on the effectiveness of multimedia information design (Bearne, Jones, Sapsford-Francis1994, Tufte, 1983, Faraday, Sutcliff, 1997).

A well-designed multimedia information communicates its underlying intention to readers (or audience) as precisely, as concisely, and as rapidly as possible. On the other hand, poorly designed multimedia information, for example, arbitrary colored home pages on world-wide-web, is not only aesthetically unpleasant but also misleading. It may

Human–Computer Interaction: INTERACT'97 S. Howard, J. Hammond & G. Lindgaard (editors)
Published by Chapman & Hall

unfocus the point of the message, being unable to "correctly" communicate its intention to readers.

While many textbooks and courses are available for studying about each media, it is impossible to expect casual users to attend to such a wide range of information resources. By casual users, we mean those who are not professional multimedia title designers but those who use multiple media as a means to communicate their intention in their everyday practice. On-line manual for software products of a small company, personal recipe for home cooking, and a World-wide-web homepage for a local restaurant are example of such casual uses of multimedia information.

To support multimedia information designers in casual occasions (as opposed to support for professional multimedia title designers), we have developed a knowledge-based authoring support system, eMMa (Environment for MultiMedia Authoring) (Nakakoji et al. 1995, Nakakoji, Aoki, Reeves, 1996). Based on a human-computer collaborative problem solving model (Terveen 1995), eMMa supports users in selection of colors in their creation of visual images and search of a library of hundreds of reusable images. Experiences and "know-how's" are encoded as rules in eMMa's community knowledge-base, and used to map user's high-level requirements (e.g., to create a home page for young consumers) to detailed design decisions (e.g., which color to use as a background).

One goal in supporting users in multimedia information design, or in other design domains, is to build a computational support in such a way as to enhance users' creativity rather than imposing users of a single "right way to design." While the meaning of the term *creativity* may vary widely, we use the term to mean *to bring existing design concepts into unseen and even unthought, yet valuable ways of usage* (McLaughlin, Gero 1989). A multimedia information design is creative if synthesis of concepts and media usage is *innovative* and at the same time *useful*.

eMMa amplifies users' creativity by automatically volunteering information relevant to the users' current design situation (Fischer, Nakakoji, 1994). The system makes suggestions for users, which the users may have never thought of before, help them become aware of new aspects for their design tasks, leading to innovative artifacts. The system criticizes users' partial designs for improvement using its knowledge-base, leading to useful artifacts. In addition, the system's knowledge-base is shared and evolved by a community of users. Thus, their creative design can be supported in the social context (Csikszentmihalyi, Sawyer, 1995). By integrating the two dimensions of creativity with respect to social factors, the system supports people to produce creative multimedia information design.

We have conducted case studies by asking ten subjects to use eMMa to assess our approach. They are from both industry and academia, ranging from industrial design, architectural design, software engineering, web-page design, artificial intelligence, and cognitive science. We asked them to perform seven tasks to create visual images (e.g., design of background for a certain purpose) followed by interviews. We observed that based on the subjects' background, their approaches toward the tasks are quite different. In any cases, however, eMMa's knowledge-based support helped them produce artifacts in unpredicted (therefore psychologically innovative) and valuable ways.

In what follows, we first briefly describe how eMMa is used to create multimedia information design illustrated with a scenario. This scenario is drawn from a real task-flow conducted by one of the subjects in our case studies. Then, we outline a framework for computer-supported creativity. We describe theories behind our approach, and system requirements based on the framework. Next, we discuss our case studies to demonstrate how eMMa supports creativity based on the framework.

2. THE eMMa SYSTEM

eMMa (Environment for MultiMedia Authoring) (Nakakoji et al. 1995, Nakakoji, Aoki, Reeves, 1996) is a prototype system built on VisualWorks Smalltalk 2.5, which runs on PCs, Macintoshes, and Sun Workstations, to support casual users in producing good multimedia information designs. The system is designed for a single user, but its knowledge-base can be shared and evolved by multiple users, thereby supporting asynchronous collaboration.

2.1 Overview of eMMa

eMMa helps users in a collaborative manner (Terveen 1995). That is, users of the system make design decisions, and create and evolve design artifacts. The system monitors users' design tasks, and uses its knowledge-base to make suggestions for improvement or to identify potentially problematic situations in the users' current design. Contents of the knowledge-base can be modified by users as the system is used.

With the current implementation, the system helps users in three ways. First, the system helps users decide which colors to use in which combinations and in what proportions, based on the Munsell Color Theory (Sidelinger 1985). This functionality is called eMMaC – eMMa's Color-critiquing component (Nakakoji et al. 1995). Users specify a region anywhere on the screen, and asks eMMaC to criticize the balance of strength of each color used in the specified region with respect to each area. eMMa computes the balance by quantifying colors for each pixel of a specified image region using the Munsell Color system. Detailed descriptions of eMMaC are provided in (Nakakoji et al. 1995).

Second, the system helps users search for reusable visual images from a library of hundreds of GIF images. eMMa's ImageSearcher component (Aoki et al. 1995) allows users to formulate a query using image properties, such as color luminance, the center of gravity in terms of darkness of the image, colors used in specific areas of the image, free-hand border sketch and another image to retrieve similar images. ImageSearcher uses the information specified in the query to rank-order images of a set of GIF images by the degree of "match." Aoki et al. (1995) provides detailed descriptions of its matching algorithms.

Third, the eMMa-SPEC component (Nakakoji, Aoki, Reeves 1996) allows users to specify abstract requirements for their information design task, such as an intended type of audience, atmosphere to bring in, or a purpose. The system then, makes suggestions about color usage or other design decisions based on the specified requirements. Such inference is made through rules stored in its knowledge-base. Users can browse the rules and add or modify rules if desired.

In what follows, we present a scenario illustrating how to use eMMa in designing multimedia information. The scenario is based on an actual task-flow performed by one of the subjects we used in our case studies. Detailed discussions of eMMa's implementation can be found in somewhere else (Nakakoji et al. 1995, Nakakoji, Aoki, Reeves 1996, Aoki et al. 1995). Section 4 presents more detailed discussions about the case studies.

2.2 A Scenario of Using eMMa

A subject is given a task to design the background for a given image of a chair (see Figure 1). The goal is to design a poster for an industrial exhibition to demonstrate the chair.

Given the requirements, the subject first specified conditions for the task using eMMa-SPEC (Figure 2). By considering that the image is for an industrial exhibition, he thought that most of attendees for the exhibition would be *engineers* in their *forties*. He wanted to make the image *precise*, with a purpose of *marketing* in his mind.

Figure 1: A given task: to decide background for industrial exhibition

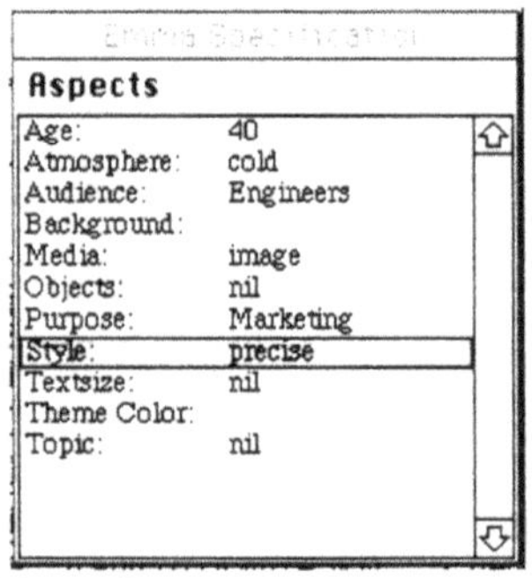

Figure 2: eMMa-SPEC

When the subject finished choosing aspects for his task using eMMa-SPEC, eMMa presented him a list of suggestions to use *purple*, *blue*, and *green* (see Figure 3). Those suggestions were associated with eMMaís rules (see the middle window in Figure 3). The system described why those suggestions were made; for example, suppose he wondered why *blue* is suggested. The bottom window in Figure 3 described that it is because he specified that intended audience would be engineers and blue brings in seriousness, which engineers would prefer.

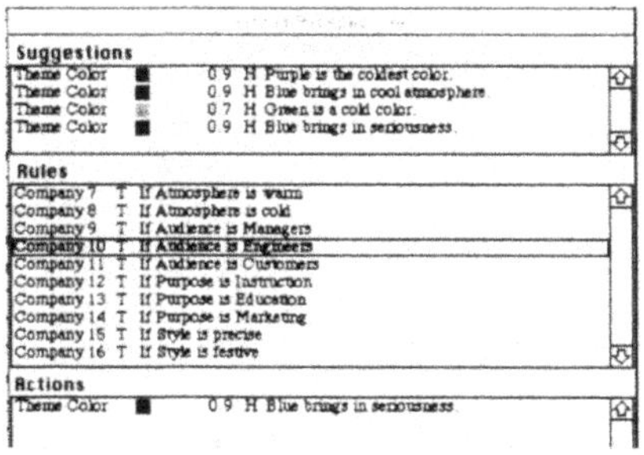

Figure 3: Suggestions made by eMMa

By looking at the suggestion, he decided to use something blue. Additionally, terms that appeared in the suggestions, such as seriousness and cold, reminded him of something "engineer-ish." He then remembered that there are images available in eMMa that he could use as background. So, he decided to search for pictures with straight lines. Using eMMaÍs ImageSearcher, he drew a sketch consisting of several orthogonal lines (see Figure 4). He also specified that he was interested in blue (not shown).

Figure 4: Free-hand sketch produced to retrieve "engineering-ish" photo images

Figure 5: Ordered photo images based on the subject's query (see Figure 4)

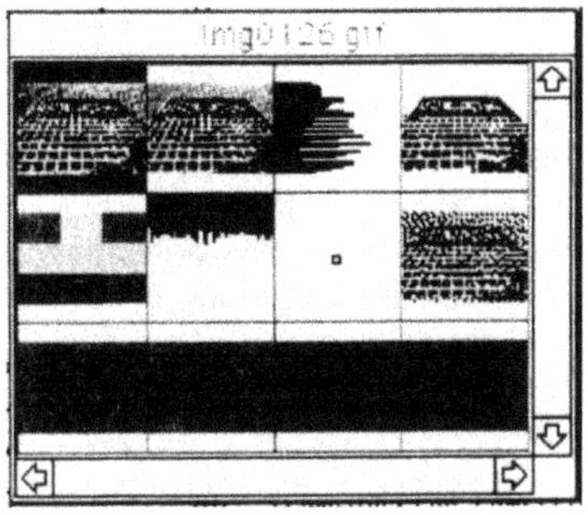

Figure 6: Automatically identified properties of an image

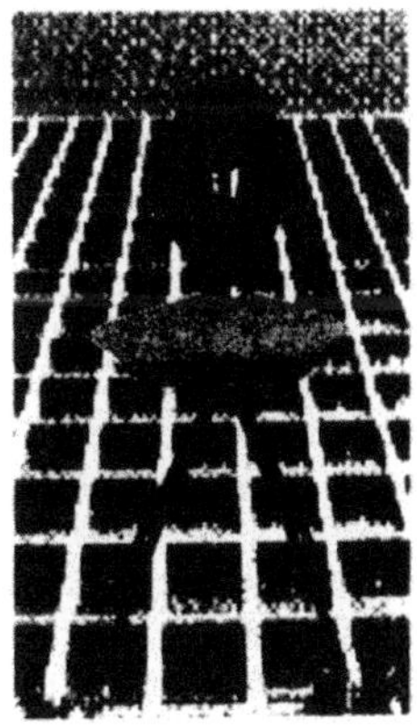

Figure 7: The subject's final design

Based on his queries, ImageSearcher ordered pictures according to the degree of match to the query (Figure 5). eMMa used automatically identified properties of each image to compute the degree of match (Figure 6 illustrates a set of identified properties from the building image). He found a nice picture of a building with blue sky, and decided to use it as background for the given task. Figure 7 illustrates his final design.

3. CREATIVITY

3.1 A Model for Creativity

While creativity is often associated with art, we are concerned with creativity that is required in everyday work practice. This type of creativity is in most cases not historical, but psychological (Boden, 1991). A resulting product is not necessarily novel or original to a community but is personally or psychologically novel to the individual who produced it.

While professional multimedia title authors may demonstrate historical creativity in their media usage, creativity in designing multimedia information in casual situations, such as a design of personal home pages in the World-Wide-Web, is in most cases, psychological. Owners of homepages, for example, demonstrate their own creativity using unfamiliar colors and fancy graphics in their background, and attaching sound to their homepages by looking at other people's home pages.

Creative artifacts needs to be both innovative and valuable. The product must be novel so that it is not a part of existing well-known solution. On the other hand, if the product is not useful, or of little value, it cannot be regarded as creative.

Our approach to use computer systems to support creativity is to integrate the two dimensions (see Figure 8). The system helps people become aware of new ideas by presenting information relevant to the people's current problem situation. Since the relevance is measured based on the system's domain knowledge, the system's volunteered information sometimes surprises users. It is left to the users to judge the usefulness of this volunteered information.

The system helps people improve their designed artifacts. The system has design knowledge and can identify problematic situations in the users' partial designs in the form of critiquing messages (Fischer, et al. 1993, Nakakoji, Sumner, Harstad 1994). Our previous work has identified that it is important to criticize the artifact at the "right" time, and to provide rationale behind the criticisms (Fischer et al. 1993).

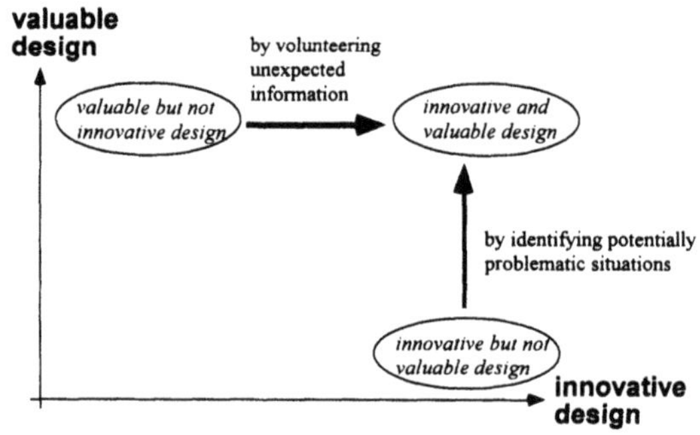

Figure 8: Two dimensions of creativity and their system support

Csikszentmihalyi and Sawyer (1995) argue that although the moment of creative insight usually occurs in isolation, *it is surrounded and contextualized within an ongoing experience that is fundamentally social.* They have developed a model that illustrates creative processes in social context. A creative process consists of four steps: preparation, incubation, insight, and evaluation. In the preparation phase, people identify problems, goals and constraints for achieving a task. In the incubation phase, people filter information from conscious awareness to the subconscious to be used for creative insight. In the insight stage, people actually produce something creative, finding new associations among existing objects. Finally, in the evaluation phase, people assess whether their insight is valuable.

Csikszentmihalyi and Sawyer stress the importance of embedding the creative process in social context, and the preparation, incubation, and evaluation processes use input from the community. That is, people use outside information to prepare, acquire potentially useful information from the community, and when they come up with creative insight by themselves, they use information from outside to evaluate their insight.

3.2 Creativity Supported by eMMa

As we discussed above, the preparation and incubation phases help people produce innovative ideas, and the evaluation phase assures that their products are useful.

Figure 9 illustrates how our eMMa system supports creativity based on this model.

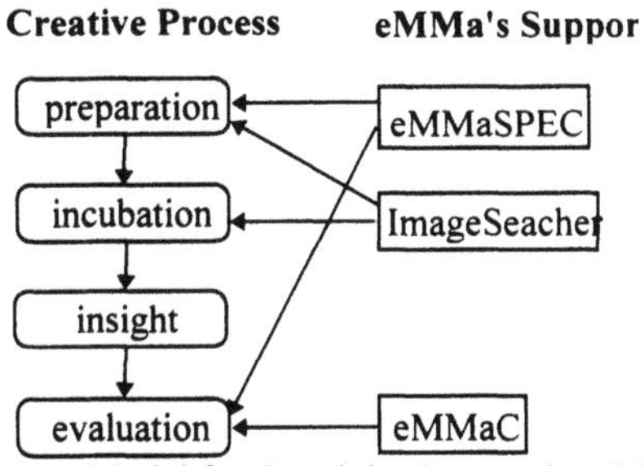

Figure 9: A Model for Creativity Support by eMMa

As illustrated in the scenario presented in Section 2.2, the system volunteers information for users relevant to the task at hand (Fischer, Nakakoji, 1994). In the scenario, the system made suggestions for the subject to use *blue* if he was designing for engineers as audience. This information was helpful for the subject to improve his design for the purpose as he had no idea how to map the audience-engineering requirement to a concrete design decision. Terms appearing in the suggestions, such as "seriousness" also helped the subject during the incubation phase as he gathered information relevant to his task. These rules are accumulated through the use of other users - users added rules as they used the eMMa system. Therefore, the subject indirectly communicated with a community of users through the eMMa's knowledge-base.

eMMa also helped the subject to produce an innovative artifact. The subject did not have a concrete idea for the background until he saw the picture of a building (see Figure 6). His query did not exactly state "please find a picture of a building." Instead, he drafted a sketch representing something "engineering-ish" using several orthogonal lines. He came up with a picture of a building, which he liked, and used it as background for his task.

4. Case Studies

As we designed and built the eMMa system to support casual users in multimedia information design, a concern has emerged that users of eMMa may just follow eMMaís suggestions and end up with the same final product. Our hypothesis was that as eMMa is built based around the model for creativity described above, products should be diverse with the help of eMMa as opposed to converging into a single outcome.

To test our hypothesis, we have conducted case studies of eMMa. We asked ten subjects to perform seven tasks using eMMa. The tasks are to design background and foreground colors and frames for given outlines and images of objects. The task presented in Section 2.1 was one of the task. Table 1 illustrates the distribution of subjects' background.

Table 1: Distribution of Subjects' Background

Architecture	1
Industrial Design	1
Artificial Intelligence	2
Web Homepage Design	1
Software Engineering	2
Cognitive Science	3

We prepared task descriptions on our web-site, and asked them to perform tasks at their local sites. Then, they are asked to describe what they have done through post-task interviews. Final and intermediate products are collected.

Rather than describing details of each study in detail, this paper focuses on the task presented above - to design background for a chair for industrial exhibition.

In short, no subjects produced exactly the same results. Variation of their outcomes is quite phenomenal. One used pictures as background, two subjects produced gradations of color using other drawing tools and used them as background, the others simply colored the background.

There were a variety of usage patterns of eMMa among different subjects. Two subjects simply used eMMa like a spelling checker - they designed background and asked eMMaC to criticize the color balance. Some used ImageSearcher extensively to find interesting usage patterns of background. One subject used a retrieved image as background. Three subjects used eMMa-SPEC to decide a main color based on the suggestions made by the system.

We have found three distinctive patterns of design processes using eMMa by subjects who have three different background: an artificial intelligence researcher, a web-homepage designer, and a software engineer. We briefly characterize each pattern and discuss how their creativity is supported by eMMa.

• Case 1: an artificial intelligence researcher

His case was basically the same as illustrated in the scenario 2.1. As discussed in Section 3, he effectively used eMMa to produce creative artifacts.

• Case 2: a web-homepage designer

She used eMMa-SPEC to characterize the task. She specified almost the same conditions as in Case-1. Once she was told by eMMa that blue should be used as a suggestion, however, she started exploring different variations of blue. She used eMMaC to find the right balance between the yellow of the chair and a variety of blues. She used another drawing tool to produce gradations of blues and used one of them as background for her final design. She browsed the image library, but did not do anything with it.

During the interview, she told us that it was helpful for her to be instructed to use blue by eMMa. Once being told, however, she wanted to explore for herself possible design spaces based on blue. It was relieving for her that she could use eMMaC to make sure her design decision "is good enough for the system's knowledge (originally transcribed in Japanese)."

• Case 3: a software engineer

A software engineer started trying to fill conditions using eMMa-SPEC. He mapped the industrial exhibition requirement to "audience: customer" and "style: festive" and "atmosphere: cheerful." The system, then, suggested to use warm colors to be cheerful, thereby to use yellow. He colored background to the chair yellow and asked eMMaC to adjust the balance between two yellows. The system suggested several variations of lighter yellows to use instead of his original yellow background. He agreed with the system, and finished his design with light yellow background.

It was interesting that this subject specified eMMa-SPEC in a totally different way from the previous two cases. The concept "for industrial exhibition" was mapped to something festive and cheerful, as opposed to something "engineering-ish" as illustrated in Case-1. Based on this different mapping, the system made completely different suggestions for color: yellow, a warm color, not blue. Subsequent design processes were different from those of Case-1 because of this different suggestion.

Through his interview, he also appreciated that the system suggested to use yellow, as he "had no idea what to do, and completely agreed with the system's suggestion." He also liked that eMMaC adjusted background and foreground yellows to assure him that his product is "okay." He was aware of the existence of ImageSearcher, but "never thought of using it because he found no need to find anything."

5. DISCUSSION

The above three cases we found in our case studies have demonstrated variations of usefulness of eMMa. While assigned tasks are quite simple (e.g., to design background), no final products were even similar to each other. This assured us that using eMMa will not impose users of a single outcome. In fact, subjects demonstrated quite a variation in their design decision making processes.

For example, the Case-3 subject mapped the requirements to concrete conditions very uniquely. The phrase "industrial exhibition" did not remind him of engineering, but more of festive events. Based on his understanding of the problem space, the system retrieved information relevant to his framed problem (i.e., suggested to use yellow). eMMa thus helped him increase usefulness of his design and did not prevent him from exploring new problem spaces.

Case-2 subject enjoyed exploring the solution space based on the system's suggestion - to use blue. As she finished her design, she wanted to create a rule to state that "if a purpose is for industrial exhibition, you should use not blue in general but this particular blue (that she used)," but did not dare to create one. The interview with her revealed that the rule occurred to her as she was performing her task. This type of "creative insights" should be able to stored in the system easily. While eMMa currently requires users to directly edit Smalltalk-style predicates to add and modify such rules, an end-user modifiable rule interface needs to be built.

As future considerations for the system, many subjects wanted to have smoother integration of the components of eMMa. Seven subjects first specified their requirements, looked at the suggestions made by the system, and used the suggestion as a query to search images in ImageSearcher. Retrieved images were then evaluated using eMMaC. If this sequence of actions is automated, however, there would be no room for users' subjective interpretations. For example, Case-1 subject mapped the concept "engineering" to several orthogonal lines. We need more studies to explore the role of creativity in these mapping processes.

ACKNOWLEDGMENTS

The work is supported by IPA (Information Promotion Agency), Ministry of International Trade and Industry, Japan. We would like to thank Brent N. Reeves, Kaoru Rin Hayashi, Kouichi Kishida, Akira Kumagai, members of the CCC Lab at NAIST, and members of the L3D Center at University of Colorado at Boulder, for their valuable contributions to the project. We would also like to thank people who participated in our case studies.

6. REFERENCES

Aoki, A., Nakakoji, K., Suzuki, H., Mizushima, K., (1995) Experience and Analysis of ImageSearcher in the Smalltalk Environment: an Image Retrieval System by Analyzing Properties of Images, Proceedings of the Object-Oriented Symposium'95, IPSJ, Tokyo, Japan, June, pp. 253-260, (in Japanese).

Bearne, M., Jones, S., Sapsford-Francis, J., (1994) Towards Usability Gudelines for Multimedia Systems, Proceedings of ACM Multimedia'94, ACM Press, San Francisco, CA, October, pp. 105-110.

Boden, M. (1991) The Creative Mind: Myths & Mechanisms, Basic Books.

Csikszentmihalyi, M., Sawyer, K., (1995) Creative Insight: The Social Dimension of a Solitary Moment, *The Nature of Insight* (R.J. Sternberg, J.E. Davidson Eds.), MIT Press, Cambridge, MA, Chap. 11, pp. 329-364.

Faraday, P. and Sutcliffe, A. (1997) Designing Effective Multimedia Presentations. Proceedings of CHI'97, ACM Press, Atlanta, GA, (forthcoming).

Fischer, G, Nakakoji, K, Ostwald, J, Stahl, G, Sumner, T (1993) Embedding Computer-Based Critics in the Contexts of Design, *Human Factors in Computing Systems, INTERCHI'93 Conference Proceedings* (Amsterdam, Netherlands), ACM, pp. 157-164.

Fischer, G. and Nakakoji, K., (1994) Amplifying Designers' Creativity with Domain-Oriented Design Environments, *Artificial Intelligence and Creativity* (T. Dartnall ed.), Kluwer Academic Publishers, the Netherlands, pp.343-364.

McLaughlin, S, Gero, J.S., (1989) Creative Processes - Can They Be Automated?, Modeling Creativity and Knowledge-Based Creative Design (Reprints of the International Round-Table Conference: Modeling Creativity and Knowledge-Based Creative Design), Heron Island, Queensland, December, pp. 69-94.

Nakakoji, K. Sumner, T, and Harstad, B (1994) Perspective-Based Critiquing: Helping Designers Cope with Conflicts Among Design Intentions, *Artificial Intelligence in Design'94*, J. Gero and F. Sudweeks (eds.), Kluwer Academic Publishers, Lausanne, Switzerland, August, pp. 449-466.

Nakakoji, K., Reeves, B.N., Aoki, A., Suzuki, H., Mizushima, K., (1995) eMMaC: Knowledge-Based Color Critiquing Support for Novice Multimedia Authors, *Proceedings of ACM Multimedia'95*, ACM Press, San Francisco, CA, pp. 467-476, November.

Nakakoji, K., Aoki, A., Reeves, B.N., Knowledge-Based Cognitive Support for Multimedia Information Design, *Information and Software Technology*, Elsevier Science, Vol. 38, No.3, pp.191-200, January.

Sidelinger, S J (1985), Color Manual, Prentice-Hall, Inc., (Englewood Cliffs, NJ).

Terveen, L.G., An Overview of Human-Computer Collaboration, *Knowledge-Based Systems Journal*, Vol. 8, No. 2-3, April-June 1995, pp. 67-81.

Tufte, E.R., (1983) *The Visual Display of Quantitative Information*, Graphics Press, Cheshire, CT.

User-centred design in the development of a navigational aid for blind travellers

Helen Petrie[1], Valerie Johnson[1], Thomas Strothotte[2], Rainer Michel[2], Andreas Raab[2] and Lars Reichert[3]

1 Sensory Disabilities Research Unit,
University of Hertfordshire,
Hatfield AL10 9AB, U.K.
email: {h.l.petrie|v.johnson}@herts.ac.uk

2 Department of Simulation and Graphics,
Otto-von-Guericke University of Magdeburg,
Universitätsplatz 2, D-39106 Magdeburg, Germany
email: {tstr|raab|rainer}isg.cs.uni-magdeburg.de

3 Department of Computer Science,
Free University of Berlin,
Takustrasse 9, D-14195 Berlin, Germany
email: reichert@inf.fu-berlin.de

ABSTRACT Modern technology can assist disabled people in two ways: either technology can be used to design devices specifically to meet the needs of disabled people, or technology that is already used by able-bodied people can be adapted to become usable by disabled people. This paper presents an example of the former. The MoBIC (Mobility of Blind People Interacting with Computers) project is developing a new navigational aid which gives blind travellers navigational information based on the new technologies of geographical information systems (GIS) and the global positioning system (GPS) of satellites. The aid includes two components: a pre-journey planning system and a system which will assist travellers on journeys. The process by which initial prototypes for the system were developed is outlined and the elicitation of user requirements is discussed. Some results of initial evaluations conducted in the United Kingdom and the first field trials conducted in Germany are also presented.

KEY WORDS: visually disabled users, navigational aid, user-centred design, evaluation

Human–Computer Interaction: INTERACT'97 S. Howard, J. Hammond & G. Lindgaard (editors)
Published by Chapman & Hall

1. INTRODUCTION

New technological innovations often fail to take account of the needs of elderly people and those with disabilities who find themselves at a disadvantage in many areas of life. For example, the facility to draw cash from an Automatic Teller Machine (ATM) is one many of us appreciate, but for those who use wheelchairs and cannot reach the card slot and those with impaired vision who cannot see the card slot or the instructions on the screen, the benefits of this facility are not so readily apparent. Increasingly, the benefits of new technology rely on the ability to interact visually i.e read a screen or use a mouse, and ATMs are just one example. Other examples include screen telephones and GUI-based computer applications.

Nonetheless, new technologies can be used to great advantage by people with disabilities and elderly people. Two ways in which technology can help these groups can be distinguished. Firstly, one can make mainstream technology accessible to a wider range of users, with differing needs and abilities. This will be referred to as "adaptive technology", as it adapts mainstream technology for use by a broader range of users (McMillan, 1992; Petrie, in press). The GUI problem mentioned above is an area in which this approach has been applied. Many people with visual or physical disabilities need to use computer systems and applications for employment or leisure. For example, people with visual disabilities have traditionally worked as telephone operators and more recently have found computer programming an employment area in which their disability is irrelevant to their productivity. But software in both these areas, and many others, is rapidly moving to GUI-based platforms and this is jeopardizing the employment opportunities for disabled people. Numerous efforts have been made to adapt GUI-based platforms for use by disabled people (Mynatt and Weber, 1994; Petrie, Morley and Weber, 1995).

The second way in which technology can help disabled and elderly people is to use technology to enable disabled and elderly people to perform tasks which they are currently unable to do or find extremely difficult. This domain of technological innovation will be referred to as "assistive technology", as disabled and elderly people are assisted in undertaking particular tasks by the technology. In this area, the ways these technologies are used may be completely different from the original intention, but assistive technology can use developments in many areas to greatly increase the quality of life of disabled and elderly people.

Two recent technological innovations are now available which allow the development of a new assistive technology for blind people. These technological innovations are computer-based geographical information systems (GIS) which give access to map information via a computer and the Global Positioning System (GPS) of satellites which provides information about the precise latitude and longitude of any position on the earth's surface, via a small receiver. These technologies are already being used in various navigational situations, for example to guide cars and planes.

The MoBIC (Mobility of Blind and elderly people Interacting with Computers) Project, funded by the European Union, is employing GPS and GIS technologies to guide blind travellers on a route which they can also plan on a home-based computer. This makes MoBIC an especially good example of assistive technology in that it is employing technologies already being used for other purposes to help disabled people to do something which was previously very difficult, if not impossible.

Whether one is designing for all the population, or only for a specific group with special requirements, it is important to include users in the design process to ensure that designers understand their requirements and capabilities. Much has been written about different methods for the involvement of users in designing interfaces to complex systems and the different methodologies which can be employed, such as user-centred design, participatory design and usability engineering (e.g. Nielsen, 1993; Norman and Draper, 1986; Schuler and Namioka, 1993; Whiteside, Bennett and Holtzblatt, 1988). These methodologies can also be applied to designing for disabled and elderly people, although a different set of problems and issues may arise.

This paper will outline initial designs for the two components of the MoBIC Travel Aid (MoTA). Some HCI techniques employed in the initial elicitation of user requirements which lead to the design of the MoTA aid and its progressive refinement will be discussed. Finally the evaluations and field trials of the first prototype implementations will be presented.

2. COMPONENTS OF THE MoBIC TRAVEL AID

The MoTA consists of two basic components: the MoBIC Pre-Journey System (MoPS) and the MoBIC Outdoor System (MoODS).

2.1 The MoBIC Pre-journey System

The MoBIC Pre-journey System (MoPS) allows blind people to explore a map and plan their journey before setting out. These activities can be carried out using a standard PC computer with appropriate output (synthetic speech or Braille) and the specialized MoBIC software.

The heart of the MoPS is a database used to organize the information which is relevant to users' exploration and planning tasks. It contains such data as:

• map information obtained from public sources. This includes street names and building numbers, locations of pedestrian crossings and public buildings (for example post offices, libraries, police stations); and

• personal information, such as addresses and preferences (for example, avoiding uncontrolled street crossings or flights of steps).

In addition, there are data which are specific to the needs of blind travellers:

• notes on the traversability of certain streets and areas (for example, a particular street may have parking meters, trees or a great deal of clutter outside shops) and

• information on specific surfaces underfoot (for example tactile tiles, cobbled pavements, grassed areas).

Users interact with MoPS to explore a map either using standard cursor keys or a touchtablet with a tactile overlay. To assist users in planning a particular route for a journey MoPS incorporates a route-calculation program which takes into consideration user preferences (e.g. use controlled crossings only; avoid steps; provide the shortest route to walk or by public transport). Figure 1 shows an example of the visual representation of digital map information. Such a presentation may be enlarged for those with partial vision and is also useful for sighted people assisting blind users.

2.2 The MoBIC Outdoor System

The MoBIC Outdoor System (MoODS) takes the journey plan developed with MoPS and assists travellers in reaching their destination by matching the information in its GIS against the traveller's position provided by a GPS receiver integrated into the MoODS system and a differential GPS signal which increases the accuracy of the GPS calculation. A Trip Management System advises the traveller by giving directions, warnings or other relevant information. The user interacts with the system by asking questions using a small, hand-held keypad and receiving answers verbally via an earphone which does not block other sounds from the environment. Special keys are reserved for questions such as "Where am I?" and "Where should I proceed from here?" It is important to note that the MoBIC system is primarily intended for the informational needs of travellers with respect to their overall journey. Most information about the immediate environment (e.g. an obstacle temporarily blocking the way) should still be provided by the long cane or guide dog.

3. INITIAL DESIGN OF THE MoTA

The first step in designing the MoTA was an extensive study of what blind people might find useful from such a system and how the information should be presented to users. A number of user requirements studies were conducted including in-depth interviews with both potential users of the system, mobility officers and others involved in the training and rehabilitation of blind people. Group discussions with potential users also took place. Finally, "Wizard of Oz" simulations of how the MoPS and MoODS components might function were made for potential users to try out to give them a concrete experience of what the system might be like and enable them to comment on different possibilities.

3.1 User Requirements

To understand the needs of blind and partially sighted people in relation to the MoBIC aid, a number of user requirements studies were undertaken within the MoBIC Project. Firstly, interviews were conducted with blind and partially sighted individuals concerning their current travel habits and problems which they encounter travelling in both familiar and unfamiliar environments, their ideas on what information the MoTA could provide and how that information should be presented. Secondly, interviews were conducted with teachers of mobility training and other individuals involved in this area, such as trainers of these teachers. Discussion groups were also held with blind, including elderly blind, people to elicit more general information about their views on the MoBIC aid. In addition further studies were conducted in which potential users were given mock-ups of aspects of the travel aid for assessment. A more detailed report of the elicitation of user requirements for the MoBIC Project can be found in Jansson (1995), and Petrie and Johnson (in press).

3.2 "Wizard of Oz" study of the MoODS system

Although the interviews and discussion groups yielded much useful information for the design of the MoTA, it was felt that many participants were having difficulty

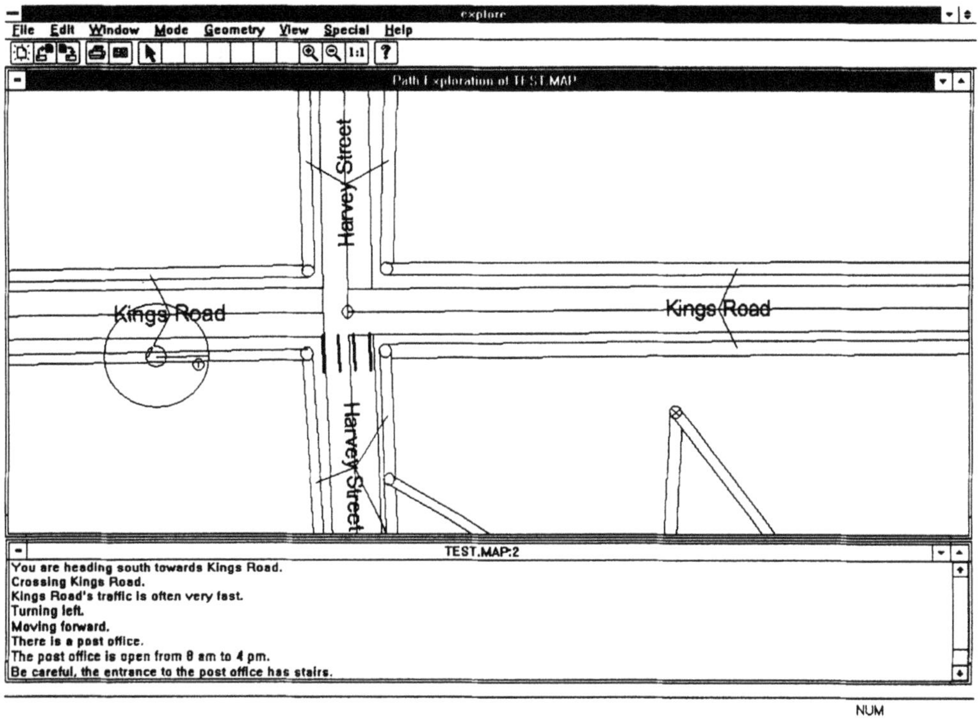

Figure 1: Example of the visual representation of digital map information

imagining what the systems might actually be like and how they could work. This is not surprising, as this is a completely new type of travel aid for blind people which no-one has had any experience with as yet. As an attempt to overcome this difficulty, a "Wizard of Oz" study of the MoODS system was conducted. Wizard of Oz studies are sometimes conducted in the design of complex computer systems (Landauer, 1987; Nielsen, 1993).

In the case of the MoODS system, when the study was conducted, work on the integration of the GPS and GIS components was still being undertaken, so a human being acted as the GPS receiver for the blind traveler. This was achieved in the following manner. Both authors walked a short route working out what instructions the MoODS system may give a traveler at different points on this route. These instructions were then recorded on a cassette tape with brief pauses in between each instruction. Then a number of blind people walked the route individually with their usual mobility aid, carrying a Walkman cassette player on which to listen to the instructions and accompanied by a sighted person (the second author). The pre-recorded instructions guided them from point to point along the route. At each point they paused and listened to the next instruction before proceeding. At the end of the route participants were asked a number of questions about their experience and asked to rate the system on a number of scales. It was stressed that what they were experiencing was only a simulation of part of the eventual MoODS system. This procedure allowed us to give potential users a more concrete idea of what using the MoODS system while travelling might be like and to see whether the nature of the speech messages given was appropriate (e.g. level of detail, format etc.)

Eighteen blind people took part in this study and all felt they had gained a much clearer idea of what MoBIC would be like and were able to give further suggestions for its design. They also gave positive feedback on the nature of the speech messages which was used to design the eventual format.

In order to find acceptable solutions to specific problems, both high and low fidelity prototypes of particular hardware components were presented to users. The interviews had identified a strong reluctance on the part of blind people to use earphones for receiving output from the MoODS and this extended to any device which might detract from the auditory cues on which those without sight depend so heavily. This problem was addressed as part of the Wizard of Oz study. Users evaluated three different earpiece and headset alternatives. The Sony Sports Headset MDR A17 (which has small earphones which can be placed in the ears or which sit in front of the ears, the latter configuration was used for this study), the Sony SR12 earpiece and the Sennheiser earpiece with earbow (both earpieces have a small earphone which sits in front of the ear). These were high fidelity prototypes in that they were fully functional and allowed users to experience genuine interaction. Participants rated alternatives on the following criteria:

Q1. How easy was it to hear the instructions?
(1 = Very difficult - 7 = Very easy)
Q2. How easy was it to use this device?
(1 = Very difficult - 7 = Very easy)
Q3. Did you feel at all conspicuous wearing it?
(1 = Very conspicuous - 7 = Not at all conspicuous)
Q4. Did you feel the device masked useful environmental sounds? (1 = Greatly - 7 = Not at all)
Q5. How happy would you be to use such a device?
(1 = Definitely would not use - 7 = Perfectly happy)
Q6. Overall rating of the device (1 = Very poor - 7 = Excellent)

The mean ratings given are shown in Figure 2. Of the three headset and earpiece alternatives considered, the earpiece produced by Sennheiser was the most positively received. The Sony SR12 earpiece was not felt to have sufficient volume. However, participants indicated that could the volume be improved the earpiece would be quite an acceptable device. The Sony Sports Headset MDR A17 delivered information at an acceptable volume, but some people felt that wearing a headset of any kind would make them more conspicuous. The headset was also felt to be more awkward to use than an earpiece which simply clips round the ear.

In the case of input to the MoODS an initial prototype of a wrist worn keypad was presented to users along with several cardboard mock-ups representing a number of variations. Whilst users were not able to fully interact with these low fidelity prototypes they were able to judge what it would be like to wear them and how easy or difficult it would be to identify and operate the keys. Users also provided ratings on the usability of the prototype keypad as well as various features of the keys, including spacing, identification (i.e knowing which key is which), configuration and responsiveness (all rated on a 1 to 7 scale, with 7 being the most positive rating). These ratings are shown in Figure 3 below. These evaluations lead to a number of recommendations (see Table 1) which greatly influenced the final design of the MoODS keypad.

4. INITIAL EVALUATIONS IN THE UNITED KINGDOM

Throughout the MoBIC project components of the system were evaluated as they became available. An example is the evaluation of the use of cursor keys to navigate through a digital map when using the MoPS. Potential users had indicated that they felt they would be able to learn about an area in this way and such a simple solution would obviously be very cost-effective for blind people, as it would only require the purchase of a software component to use with their existing PC.

The evaluation was conducted at the University of Hertfordshire on and close to the Hatfield campus. Four blind people participated in this initial evaluation, two male and two female. Two were congenitally blind and two adventitiously blind. The term congenitally blind refers here to those who were born with some kind of visual impairment though they may have had some residual vision for the first few years of life. Two of the participants were guide dog users and two long cane users. Ages ranged from 29 to 45 years. Two routes were devised and employed in the evaluation which involved two phases. Although the routes were matched in terms of length and complexity the order of presentation was counterbalanced to control for any extraneous variables.

In Phase 1 of the evaluation the four participants were asked to familiarise themselves with a simulated route on a computer at the university. In Phase 2 participants were taken out to the actual route and asked to walk from the start point to the finish. At this stage there was no MoODS component available and a researcher undertook to provide the information which would ultimately be provided by the MoODS in another Wizard of Oz simulation. In addition to the recording of time, errors and requests for help in both phases, rating scales and open ended questions were administered to

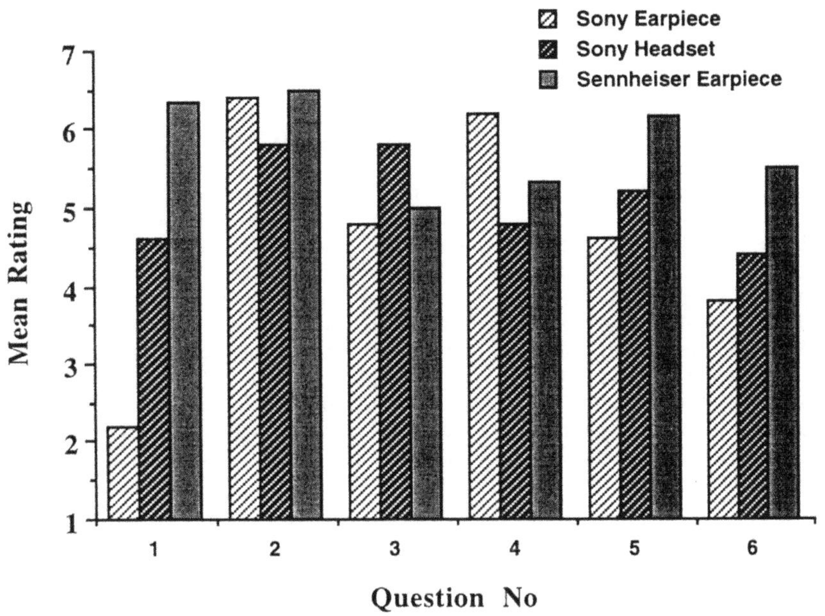

Figure 2: Mean usability ratings for headset/earpiece alternatives

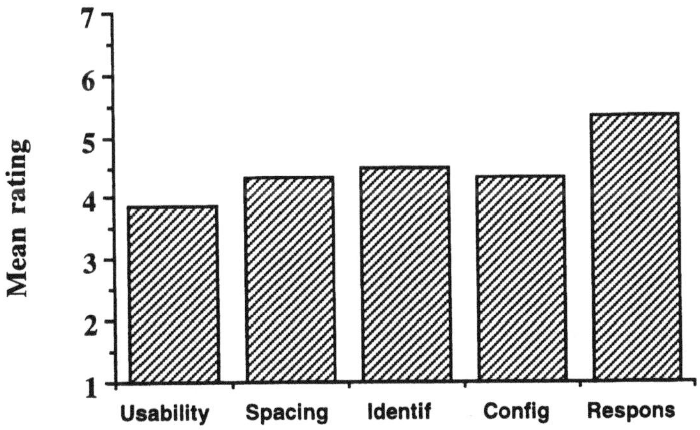

Figure 3: Mean ratings of features of the prototype keypad

Table 1: Recommendations for overall features of keypad

Feature	Recommendation
Shape	Circular, provided the measurements below are not exceeded
Diameter of keypad	No more than 6 centimetres (smaller if possible)
Thickness of keypad	The keypad should be as thin as possible
Connecting Cable	This should be as thin as possible, preferably so that it will fit inside the user's sleeve
Wrist fastener	Wrist strap must fasten firmly but also needs to be adjustable.

assess usability and learnability of and satisfaction with the MoPS component.

No participant studied the route for longer than 30 minutes before going out to walk it and only one participant requested help when using the MoPS. There were no requests for help while walking the route and only one of the participants made one error in walking a route. Figure 4 shows that mean ratings of usability, learnability and satisfaction were all close to the top of the 7 point scale as were ratings of the usefulness of various types of information provided by the MoPS. Although all participants completed the route walk without difficulty and were very positive in their assessment of the MoTA this evaluation was also successful in identifying a number of areas in which the MoPS software could be improved and these improvements were implemented in subsequent versions of the system.

5. FIELD TRIALS IN GERMANY

The field trials in Germany were conducted at the Free University of Berlin. Six participants attended a total number of 25 tutorial sessions using prototype versions of both the MoPS and MoODS components. Four of the participants were blind and two were partially sighted, five were male and one female and ages ranged from 25 to 61 years. Onset of visual disabilities varied with some having problems from birth and some only recently. The trials lasted for three months and during this time the software was regularly updated to incorporate suggestions made by participants.

The general feedback from all participants at the end of the trial indicated a high satisfaction with the latest version of the MoPS software and provided encouraging comments on the MoODS component. Figure 4 shows that, as in Hatfield, mean ratings for the usefulness of various types of information were well above the mid-point on the scale for all types of information and that the lowest mean rating given was for distance information in both cases. Although this is still above the mid-point, distance information was considered more useful by some people than others because some find distance difficult to judge.

Figure 4 shows the mean ratings for usability and learnability of and satisfaction with the MoPS component when using cursor keys for navigation as given by participants in both the Hatfield evaluations and the Berlin field trials. In both cases mean ratings for all questions are well above the mid-point on the scale and indicate a high level of satisfaction with this method of map exploration.

6. CONCLUSIONS

The MoBIC Travel Aid is a new type of aid designed to increase the independent mobility of blind and partially sighted people. The development of the aid was based on an extensive study of user requirements and the continued involvement of users is an important feature of the project. Evaluations have been conducted with prototypical components of the device throughout the project and realistic field trials have been undertaken. Results of these studies indicate a high level of satisfaction with the MoTA. It is anticipated that a commericial version of the MoPS component will be available for both Germany and the U.K. from our industrial partner, F.H. Papenmeier GmbH, in the course of 1997, followed by later commercialization of the MoODS component.

Acknowledgements

The work described in this paper was conducted for the MoBIC Project (TP 1148) supported by the Telematics Applications for the Integration of Disabled and Elderly People (TIDE) Programme of the Commission of the European Union (DG XIII). We would like to thank our project partners and the many people who participated in the MoBIC user studies for their time and assistance.

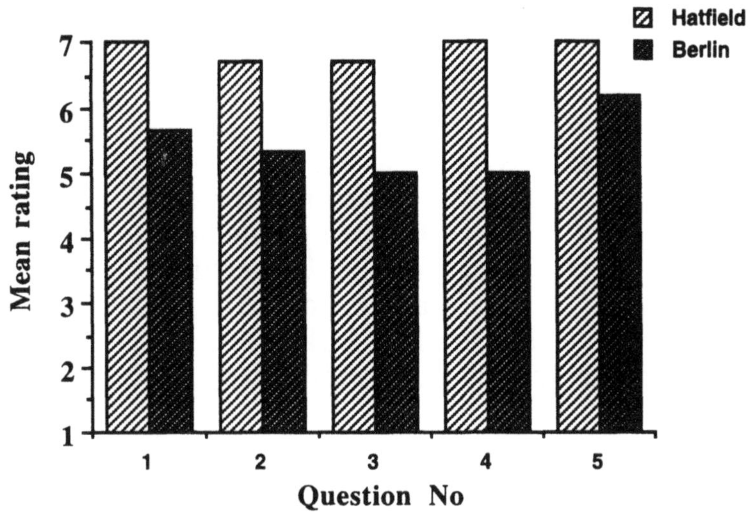

Q1 Overall how easy did you find it to operate this system?
Q2 How easy was it to learn to use this system?
Q3 How efficient did you think the system was for giving information?
Q4 How easy did you find it to build up a meaningful picture of the route exploring it in this way?
Q5 How satisfied are you with this method of obtaining map information

Figure 4: Ratings of cursor key method of map exploration in Hatfield and Berlin

References

Jansson, G. (1995). (Ed.), *Requirements for effective orientation and mobility by blind people*. London: Royal National Institute for the Blind.

Landauer, T.K. (1987). Psychology as the mother of invention. *Proceedings of CHI+GI '87: Conference on Human Factors in Computing Systems and Graphics Interface*. New York: ACM Press.

McMillan, W.W. (1992). Computing for users with special needs and models of computer-human interaction. *Proceedings of Conference on Human Factors in Computing Systems (CHI '92)*. New York: ACM Press.

Mynatt, E. D., & Weber, G. (1994). Nonvisual presentation of graphical user interfaces: contrasting two approaches. *Proceedings of Conference on Human Factors in Computing Systems (CHI '94)*. New York: ACM Press.

Nielsen, J. (1993). *Usability engineering*. Boston: Academic Press.

Norman, D. A., & Draper, S. W. (1986). *User-centered system design*. Hillsdale, NJ: LEA.

Petrie, H. (in press). User-centred design and evaluation of adaptive and assistive technology for disabled and elderly users. *Informationstechnik und Technische Informatik*.

Petrie, H. and Johnson, V. (in press). MoBIC: designing a travel aid for blind and elderly people. *British Journal of Visual Impairment*.

Petrie, H. Morley, S., and Weber, G. (1995). Tactile-based direct manipulation in GUIs for blind users. *Proceedings of Conference on Human Factors in Computing Systems (CHI '95)*. New York: ACM Press.

Schuler, D., & Namioka, A. (1993). *Participatory design: principles and practices*. Hillsdale, NJ: LEA.

Whiteside, J., Bennett, J., & Holtzblatt, K. (1988). Usability engineering: our experience and evolution. In M. Helander (Ed.), *Handbook of human computer interaction*. Amsterdam: North-Holland Press.

The Use of Music in a Graphical Interface for the Visually Impaired.

Dimitrios I. Rigas and James L. Alty
LUTCHI Research Centre
Dept. of Computer Studies
Loughborough University
Loughborough
Leicestershire LE11 3TU, UK
d.rigas@lboro.ac.uk and j.l.alty@lboro.ac.uk

ABSTRACT: The possibility of using music to communicate information of a spatial nature to visually impaired users is explored. The development of a tool - the AUDIOGRAPH - which enables visually impaired users to appreciate and manipulate objects contained in a graphical area is described. Early results show that the musical metaphors used did successfully communicate the general spatial layout and the types of objects contained in the space. Music was also successfully used to control the interface.

KEY WORDS: Interface Design, Visually Impaired Users, Music, Graphics, Auditory Interfaces.

1. Introduction

Graphical User Interfaces (or GUIs as they are often known) are now ubiquitous. They are offered as User-Friendly interfaces with a high utility. Whilst this is almost certainly true, resulting in better usability for a much wider user base, they also represent a serious step backwards for blind or visually impaired users. Traditionally, blind users have been successful in exploiting computer technology using devices such as Screen Readers to replace the visual sense. However, Screen Readers are not effective when applied to Graphical Interfaces, and this fact has begun to seriously limit visually impaired use.

The communication of graphical information to blind users is difficult to achieve using speech. The intensely serial nature of the speech medium, together with its language basis, requires continual translation and is very slow and error prone. We therefore decided to explore an alternative auditory medium which could suggest graphical shapes directly in some way. The most highly structured auditory medium being music, we expected that a study into the use of music for conveying graphical information could be fruitful.

2. Auditory Interfaces

The use of audio in human computer interfaces can be traced back to Bly (1982). Gaver (1986) later proposed the use of Auditory Icons and used them in the SonicFinder (1989) to assist visually impaired users with editing. Auditory Icons, however, are short bursts of familiar sounds rather than music. Edwards (1989) developed the Soundtrack system to assist blind users in editing, but again the use of music was very limited. Blattner et al, (1989) moved neared to exploiting music by proposing the use of Earcons - short musical melodies which share a common structure such as rhythm. Blattner also used the properties of musical structures to communicate the flow in a turbulent liquid, interestingly, utilising musical compositional techniques which were

Human–Computer Interaction: INTERACT'97 S. Howard, J. Hammond & G. Lindgaard (editors)
Published by Chapman & Hall

hundreds of years old. Brown and Hershberger (1992) used music and sound to support the visualisation of Sorting Algorithms, and Alty (1995) has developed purely musical mappings for the Bubble Sort and the Minimum Path Algorithm. Recently some progress has been made in assisting program debugging using music, for example, Bock (1995), and Vickers and Alty (1996). However there are very few recorded experiments to evaluate the use of music in human computer interaction.

3. Rationale behind the Investigations

The main objective behind the set of experiments reported in this paper, was to determine if blind users could, by the use of music alone, appreciate the spatial layout of objects in a graphical area and successfully perform a set of graphical operations on them using musical feedback. Because of the emphasis on music, and the fact that there was little previous work on the use or evaluation of musical representations, we decided to use music alone to communicate all information about the interface. We appreciate that in a real interface, such as a commercial tool, it would be sensible to use speech in addition to music (particularly for conveying exact information), but we felt that the inclusion of other auditory modes of interaction would risk confusion in the interpretation of the experimental results.

4. The AUDIOGRAPH system

We have therefore constructed an experimental prototype tool on which to carry out the investigations into the use of music in a graphical tool, (called the AUDIOGRAPH). AUDIOGRAPH has both a visual interface (for the experimenter) and a completely auditory interface for blind users. Because of the graphical nature of the domain it is easiest to describe it in terms of its visual interface first.

Input interaction with the system is exclusively via the keyboard. This mode was chosen after extensive discussions with blind users who pointed out the mouse has a number of disadvantages for blind and visually impaired users. The arrow keys are used for moving the cursor round the area, and other keys (usually any key) are used to confirm actions. All musical output is produced by MIDI output from Visual Basic, communicated to a stereo sound system using a Creative Labs Soundblaster 16-bit card. The actual sounds were created using a Roland MT32 Multi-timbre output device. All output information was communicated using music alone.

It is important to note that the AUDIOGRAPH tool was aimed at the average user (from a musical ability point of view). No special musical ability was expected for any of the experiments performed. A musical questionnaire was given to all participants to check their musical experience and knowledge.

5. Musical Mappings

A number of different types of information need to be communicated

1. the current position of the cursor or a graphical object
2. the nature of a graphical object (e.g. its type, size and shape)
3. the selection and application of graphical operations
4. the occupancy of the space around the cursor
5. file names for storage and retrieval

Furthermore it was postulated that user interaction would be best supported by a consistent use of music, that is, similar metaphors would be used over a range of domain items.

One of the most important aspects to communicate is that of spatial position. It was considered that a mapping from a number into pitch would provide a reasonably good mapping. This mapping had been used in the Bubble Sort of Alty (1995), where good correlations had been obtained between number and pitch. It is well known that users cannot achieve a completely accurate mapping to pitch, and problems have been reported in the use of intervals greater than an octave Deutch (1982). However, the objective in AUDIOGRAPH is not to communicate accurate positions but rather, a good sense of relative positions in the graphical space. Furthermore, the horizontal and vertical co-ordinates needed to be communicated separately and be easily identified. It was decided to use separation in time (i.e. the X co-ordinate would always be communicated before the Y co-ordinate, and the two would be communicated serially with a short pause inbetween). We felt that some additional redundancy would also be helpful and expected that timbre would assist in this respect (i.e. use of different instruments for X and Y). However the use of timbre is potentially problematic. If a user is told that the X co-ordinate is played on a trumpet, and the Y co-ordinate on a Piano, can the average musically untrained user successfully identify each instrument?

5.1 Identification of the Co-ordinate using Timbre

Users were first asked to name the instruments which they felt they could recognise.

Musical Instrument	% of Confidence	Musical Instrument	% of Confidence
Guitar	96	Xylophone	30
Piano	94	Trombone	39
Timpani	83	Pan Pipes	27
Violin	82	Tuba	20
Saxophone	76	Oboe	17
Flute	55	Piccolo	16
Harp	53	French Horn	13
Trumpet	42	Bassoon	10
Castanets	40	Celeste	3
Cello	37	Contrabass	3
Harmonica	37	Harpsichord	2
Organ	35	Mandolin	1
Clarinet	34	Cor Anglais	1

Table 1 Instrumental Timbres which Users thought they could identify

There are some instruments which almost all users thought they could identify (for example, Piano, Timpani and Guitar) whereas other instruments had very poor ratings (e.g. Mandolin, Harpsichord and Celeste - though this is probably because they did not associate the name with the sound). There was no significant difference between the sighted and blind users.

	Piano	Wind	Timp	Brass	Strings	Organ
Piano	65	0	0	2	3	4
Wind	4	59	0	5	13	15
Timp	0	0	15	0	0	0
Brass	8	7	0	18	11	4
Strings	2	9	0	5	14	2
Organ	1	4	0	3	5	15

Table 2 Users actual Timbre recognition performance

Then, all the instrumental timbres in the list were played to subjects, who then had to assign them to named instruments. A truncated form of the results is shown in Table 2 and are interesting because they do not always reflect the users' anticipations in Table 1.

The instruments in Table 2 have been grouped according to their conventional musical families (strings, woodwind, brass and drums), though we have departed from this classification by grouping Piano, Celeste, Xylophone and Guitar as one family (plucked or hit instruments) since the average user would not group Piano and Xylophone with Percussion. Similarly we have grouped Organ and Harmonica together. Certain instruments were readily recognised (Piano, Organ, Guitar, Flute, Drums etc..) and confusion within families was more common than between families. This suggests that instruments such as Piano and Organ can easily be distinguished by most non-musicians, but that designers should avoid the expectation that such users can distinguish timbre within musical families (e.g. a Cello and a Violin).

We therefore decided to use the Piano for the horizontal co-ordinate and the Organ for the vertical co-ordinate.

5.2 Communication of the Co-ordinates using Pitch

The next question to be solved was how to communicate the *length* of the co-ordinate. We had already decided to use pitch, but a number of options were open to us.

1. Use the Chromatic or Diatonic scale. The former provides more intervals, but the latter may be more familiar.
2. Using a particular note as origin, play all the notes between the origin and the value required. This has the advantage of communicating length both through pitch *and* time. We call this the *Note-Sequence* technique.
3. Play only the origin and the final value note. This has the advantage of brevity, but may run into problems because of octaves. We call this the *Note-Pair* technique.

A set of experiments was carried out with 12 blind users for all three conditions. In every case the range was 40 notes. No users in the sample were professional musicians. The experimental procedures were as follows:

1. the scale (Diatonic or Chromatic) was sounded over the 40 notes. Then the X co-ordinate was sounded, followed by a pause. Then the Y co-ordinate was sounded.. The user was asked to identify the co-ordinate being communicated. The order of presentation of the co-ordinates was randomised.

2. the experiments were carried out in order, Chromatic-Sequence, Diatonic-sequence, Chromatic pair, Diatonic Pair.

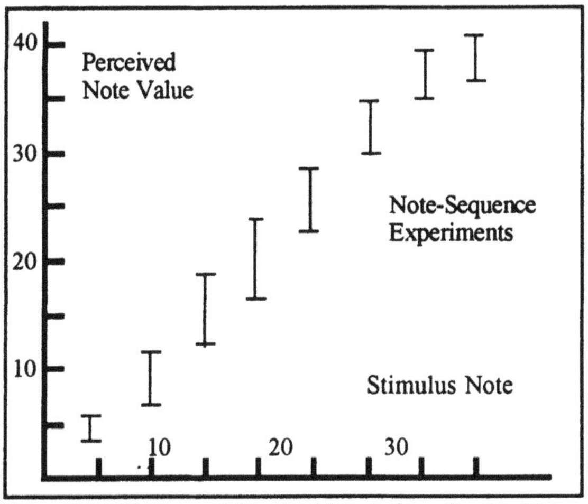

Figure 1(a) Means and Standard Deviations for the Note Sequence Results

The stimulus and response measures in Figures 1(a) and 1(b) are relative tone values based upon the E below middle C. Thus, middle C corresponds to the number 9 in the Chromatic scale. Overall, there was no significant difference between the Chromatic Scale and the Diatonic Scale.

Figures 1(a) and 1 (b) show the variation of the means and standard deviations of the perceived co-ordinate against the stimulus, for both X and Y co-ordinates and for the Note-Sequence and Note-Pair experiments for the Chromatic scale. Thus there was expected to be some learning effect for the Note-Pair experiment.

The variance is much greater in the Note-Pair-Pair results than in the Note-Sequence results, and this is in spite of some learning which must have taken

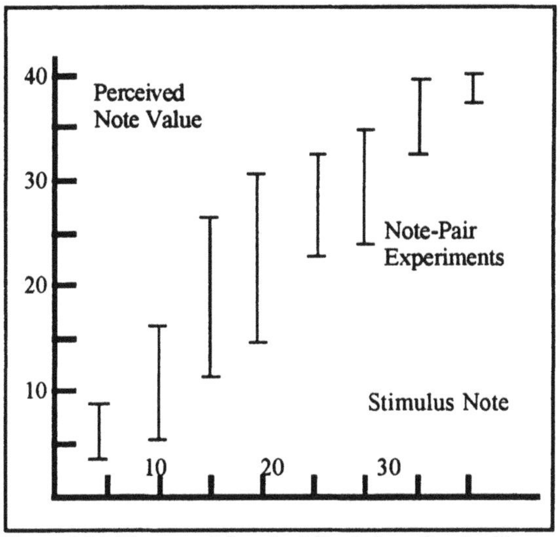

Figure 1(b) Means and Standard Deviations for the Note-Pairs results.

place because the Note-Pair experiment was second.

The difference between the two approaches can be seen in the global error table (which shows the error distribution independent of position) in Table 3.

Interface	Correct	±1	±2	±3
Note-Sequ.	22.27%	34.45%	17.45%	11.53%
Note-Pair	5.6%	12.66%	15.38%	10.89%

Table 3 The Global error distribution for the Note-Sequence and Note-Pair experiments.

Thus 75% of users could locate a position to within ±2 on the 40x40 grid using the Note-Sequence method, but this figure dropped to about 34% for the Note-Pair method, and this is in spite of increased exposure to the use of music. The figure of 74% for a ±2 error for the Note-Sequence method, (or 85% for ±3 error) is a good result, indicating that a user can obtain a general appreciation of the content of a graphical space using this technique, and the result is probably no worse than general visual memory for a similar task (people do not remember accurately the position of visual objects in a space).

Although Figure 1(a) shows that the location error in the Note-Sequence technique showed a steady worsening of performance as the co-ordinate value increased (there was an edge effect at the top end which arbitrarily reduced the errors there), performance was rarely worse than ±4 either way. As might be expected there was no difference in the performance with vertical and horizontal co-ordinates.

We conclude that blind users can use the Note-Sequence approach successfully to determine the co-ordinates of graphical objects to an accuracy acceptable for the general appreciation of space content. One reason why the approach works so well is that it uses three parallel mappings to communicate the co-ordinates - sequence length, counting of the notes, and pitch difference. Users can therefore trade-off between these three measures. It is also interesting to note that, with prolonged use, users became very adept at using the system.

5.3 Cursor Control

At first sight it might be thought that the Note-Sequence approach could not be used for cursor navigation because it would simply take too much time and this initially suggested that the less reliable Note-Pair technique would have to be used. However, it turns out that we can still use the Note-Sequence technique for cursor navigation without the time penalty. With a visual cursor, cursor movement is always shown incrementally, rather than absolutely. The cursor is never returned to the origin before each movement. Thus the musical feedback for an audio cursor only needs to communicate the incremental changes as the cursor navigates. As this happens, users effectively hear the relative Note-Sequence technique between the initial and final cursor positions. Furthermore, the total movement will normally be less than, say, ±15, so an accuracy, at least as good as, and often better than, the average obtained with co-ordinate location is achieved.

5.4 Identifying Graphical Objects

Graphical objects were also communicated using a spatial metaphor based on pitch. As far as possible the musical description was designed to have a one-to-one mapping with the graphical shape, and the mapping chosen was the same as the Note-Sequence mapping (used for both location and cursor navigation). This was expected to offer a number of advantages including the rapid generation of a mental model of the shape and consistency with the other three mappings simultaneously operating in the space-co-ordinate location, cursor navigation and control actions. The musical shapes communicated are shown in Figure 2.

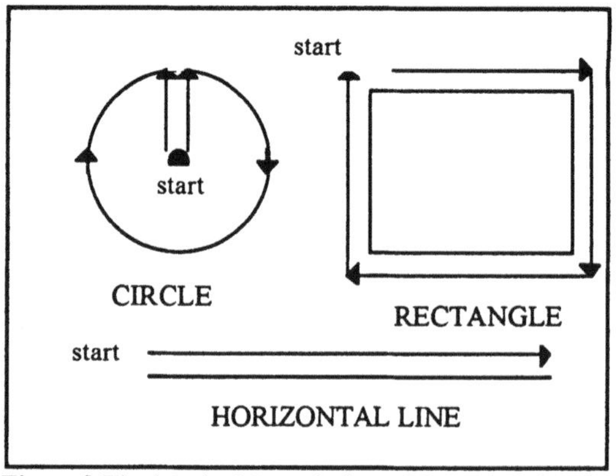

Figure 2 The Musical Description of Graphical Shapes

Without any prior training, 50% - 60% of subjects were able to recognise the shapes without training (particularly the circle and the horizontal line). Even with very limited training, the recognition rate increased to nearly 100% for the Circle, and the Vertical and Horizontal lines, and to over 80% for the Rectangle and Square. With more training subjects could easily reach 100% recognition rates for all shapes.

With graphical objects it is also important to be able to obtain an indication of the size as well as the shape itself. The experimental results here were more variable. The overall means of the sizes of the various objects were reasonably accurate (so there was no systematic error as the size increased). However, the standard deviation varied with both the size and shape. Apart from the Circle, the error worsened with size. This is probably because, in general, the lengths being communicated are larger for the other objects (the Circle radius was communicated, not the diameter). Recognition and Size determination performance are good enough to allow qualitative measurements in the Graphical space to be made.

5.5 Understanding the Musical Meanings of the Control Actions

The three main editing operations (Contract, Expand and Undo) were communicated by Earcons. In these cases a specific meaning had to be communicated in a short time. Rather than use rhythmically based Earcons (as in the case of Blattner), the Earcons were constructed using musical patters which were expected to have strong semantic perceptual properties for the listener. Taking earlier work (e.g. Alty 1996, where users have been shown to be capable of recognising and drawing short tunes), compound Earcons were designed which communicated a change of shape over time signifying the control action. Thus, Expand consisted of a short tune which expanded in length from one to four items. Contract was the inverse of this. Undo consisted of a short rising tune with an "error" in it which was corrected in the second playing.

The results for Expand and Contract were astonishingly good. Most users picked up the meaning without needing to be prompted (of course they did know that the Earcon had to represent one of the three control actions). Undo was not recognised on the first pass, but became instantly recognisable once the underlying idea had been communicated. This latter point emphasises the importance of context in musical interaction. Once users had been told that the first section of Undo was a rising scale with an error, and that the second tune corrected it, they immediately understood.

5.6 Other Facilities - Scanning

AUDIOGRAPH also provided users with techniques for scanning the area, generally, and in the neighbourhood of the cursor, though the available space in this paper precludes a full description of the techniques and the results obtained. The techniques available were Top-Down (scanning for the centre positions of objects by X and then by Y from the top of the diagram). Centre (scanning outwards from the cursor, locating objects centres as the spiral increased), and Ascending (scanning from the cursor to locate objects in ascending size). Users were able to successfully use the techniques to get a general impression of the contents of the graphical area.

6. An Example Use of the AUDIOGRAPH

To give an indication of how successful music was in conveying a diagram, blind users were presented with a number of diagrams and asked to "draw" out the content of the space. They used different scanning techniques to achieve this. An example diagram together with the user response is shown in Figures 3(a) and 3(b).

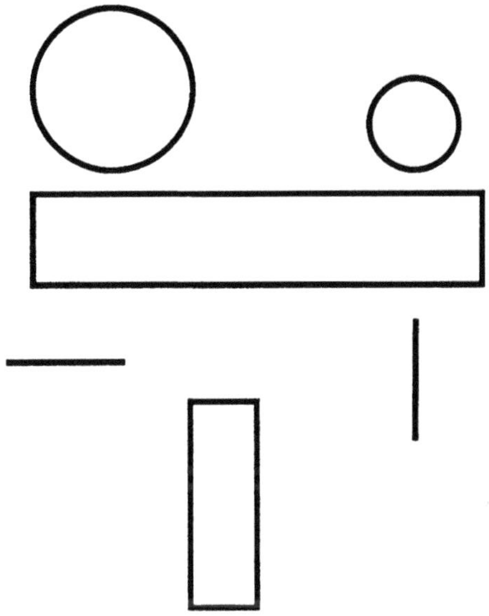

Figure 3 (a) The stimulus for a Blind User using AUDIOGRAPH who was required to interpret the diagram.

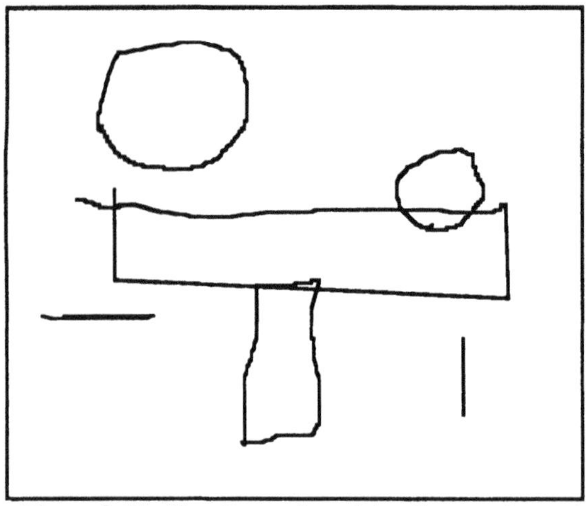

Figure 3 (b) User Perception of the diagram shown in 3(a) using the AUDIOGRAPH.

It should be appreciated that it is difficult for Blind users to accurately draw what they perceive. To assist them they were provided with paper which had a raised grid on it. However, the raised grid itself caused some deviations in the drawings. It can be seen that the user has perceived a successful overall view of the space.

Table 4 summarises the results from three drawn diagrams (from three different users) using the three different scanning methods. It details some comparative measures of how three diagrams were perceived, in terms of the number of shapes successfully reported, their relative sizes and an overall estimate of the spatial layout.

	Centre Scan	Top Down Scan	Ascend Scan	actual
No. Circles	2	2	2	2
No. Rects	1	2	2	2
No. Hor. lines	3	1	1	1
No. Ver. lines	3	1	1	1
Rel Size Circles	good	good	good	2;1
Rel Size Rects	good	good	fair	3:1
Spatial Overall	fair	good	good	

Table 4 Output from the same stimulus for three scanning methods

There were some discrepancies, for example, a subject in one example drew three lines (two Horizontal and one Vertical) which traced out three sides of the missing rectangle (line 2 of Table 4) so agreement was better than implied in Table 4. Agreement with the overall diagrams communicated (in terms of number of objects, relative size, and relative position) was quite good in most cases. It must be remembered that drawing on the raised paper was not easy and would contribute to errors. Some of the communicated diagrams were not so well perceived.

Although these results were satisfactory, it was felt that they might have been better given the results from the earlier location experiments. On reflection it was felt that the above experiment did not really represent the real-world situation, where most perceiving subjects would have some idea about the nature of the collection of objects being communicated.

In a second set of experiments in which a hint about the diagram ("Car", "Number", "Letter") was given, the importance of the perceptual context communicated was shown. When the subjects knew the diagram was a car, identification rose from 0% to 100%. Similar results (though not always quite so dramatic) were obtained for the other contexts, for example an "E" shape. These results will be reported in detail, separately.

7 Users Views of the Utility of the AUDIOGRAPH.

Overall ratings for AUDIOGRAPH from blind users were 60% (Good or Very Good), with 30%(Average). Only 10% of users thought it was Poor. Users really liked the Graphical Drawing Area representation (85% Good or Very Good), the Control Panel (85% Good or Very Good), and the Auditory Cursor (85% Good or Very Good). Less well thought of were, Sequential Pitch (35% Good or Very Good, with 60% considering it Average), Graphical Object Description (65% Good or Very Good and 25% Average) and Scanning (55% Good or Very Good and 30%Average), though all these were within acceptable levels. Most users pointed out the initial mappings were learned relatively easily and that any initial difficulties rapidly disappeared.

8. Conclusions

Overall, the results from the AUDIOGRAPH are encouraging, both technically, and from a user point of view. Users could obtain a general "graphical" view of the space and interact with the system. Users, in general were pleasantly surprised by the effect of music (as opposed to speech). With a relatively short training period they were able to use the system successfully to locate, move and modify graphical objects. All users responded very positively when asked if music could be used for a graphical drawing tool, particularly in addition to speech. Only 20% responded that they would not wish to use music. Finally, all answered "yes" to the question "should this research continue to investigate music as a communication metaphor ?" However a number of limitations have come to light:

1. Listening to a reasonably complex diagram can take some time.
2. the support for communicating relationships between objects is poor
3. Memorability for large non-meaningful graphical spaces is low

From our observations of the interaction between the blind users and the system we wish to make three points about the use of music in the human computer interface. Firstly, with musical stimuli, context is everything. A musical stimulus can be interpreted in many ways, so providing users (blind or sighted) with the appropriate context in which to interpret the music is very important. Secondly, the use of multiple messages within one musical stimulus is also crucial. In our examples, the use of pitch, length and counting considerably aided comprehension. Thirdly, it is very important to design all musical messages within a consistent framework. In our work, the communication of co-ordinates, cursor position, graphical shape and scanning all used a similar metaphor, and we believe that this greatly aided overall comprehension.

9. References

Alty, J.L., (1996), "Can we use Music in Human-Computer Interaction?", in People and Computers X (Proc. HCI'95), Kirby, M.A.R., Dix, A.J., and Finlay, J.E., (eds.), Cambridge Academic Press, pp 409 - 424.

Blattner, M.M, and Dannenberg, R.B., (1991), "Multimedia Interface Design", ACM Press, New York, Addison Wesley.

Blattner, M.M, Sumikawa, D.A., and Greenberg, R.M., (1989), "Earcons and Icons: Their Structure and Common Design Principles", in Human Computer Interaction, Vol. 4., pp 11 - 44.

Bly, S.A., (1982), "Communicating with Sound", Proc. CHI82, ACM Press, Addison-Wesley NY, pp 371 - 375.

Bock, D.S., (1995), "Auditory Software diagnosis Using a Sound Domain Specification Language", Ph.D. Thesis, Syracuse university, Syracuse.

Brown, M., and Hershberger, J., (1992), "Colour and Sound in Algorithm Animation", IEEE Computer Vol. 25, No. 12, , pp 52 - 63.

Deutch, D., (1982), The Psychology of Music, Academic Press.

Edwards. A.D.N, (1989), "Soundtrack: An Auditory Interface for Blind Users", Human Computer Interaction, Vol. 4, No. 1, pp 45 - 66.

Gaver, W., (1986), "Using Sound in Computer Interfaces", Human Computer Interaction, Vol. 2, No. 2, pp 167 - 177.

Gaver, W., (1989), "The SonicFinder: An Interface that Uses Auditory icons", Human Computer Interaction, Vol. 4, No.1, pp 87 - 94.

Vickers, P., and Alty, J.L., (1996), "CAITLIN: A Musical Program Auralisation Tool to Assist Novice Programmers with Debugging", in Proc. of ICAD'96, Santa Fe Institute, 1996.

41

Designing Auditory Cues for Mercator

Elizabeth D. Mynatt

Xerox PARC
mynatt@parc.xerox.com

ABSTRACT. The practice of designing human-computer interfaces requires synthesizing knowledge about the intended users, their tasks and interface design guidelines. This task is even more challenging for designers of auditory interfaces since few useful guidelines exist. To provide some general intuition about how people identify and conceptualize various auditory cues, we conducted two experiments. The purpose of this paper is to discuss how we used the results of these experiments to guide the selection of sounds for Mercator. As a screen reader for blind users, Mercator transforms graphical interfaces into auditory interfaces. The selection of the specific auditory cues used to convey objects and events in the Mercator interface is the result of this work. This design process was not solely the consumer of these experimental results, but also produced further insight into the selection and use of auditory cues.

KEYWORDS: Auditory Interfaces, Auditory Icons, Design Methodology, Audio, User Interfaces

1. INTRODUCTION

The practice of designing human-computer interfaces requires synthesizing knowledge about the intended users, their tasks and interface design guidelines. These guidelines, abstracted from the previous experiences of numerous designers, often provide ideas as well as constraints, but they rarely point to one, unquestionable answer. Additionally designers often face practical constraints such as a limited palette of colors or restricted screen space. Thus, the designer must work within this space of users, tasks, guidelines and practical constraints to carve an artifact balanced across these dimensions.

This task is even more challenging for designers of auditory interfaces. Few useful guidelines exist. Most interface guidelines simply advise not using audio at all. Acknowledging that audio is often useful in many human-computer tasks, designers still struggle with deciding what kinds of sounds to use, not to mention which specific sounds to use.

This paper reports on the process of deciding which sounds to use in an interface design. The design context is a system called Mercator. Mercator, described in more detail in the following section, transforms graphical interfaces into nonvisual interfaces for blind users. One class of sounds, called auditory icons, was particularly attractive for this design task since auditory icons operate much like graphical icons in that they leverage knowledge of the everyday world.

To provide some general intuition about how people identify and conceptualize various auditory cues, we conducted two experiments. In the first experiment, we analyzed descriptions of sounds. In the second experiment, we asked subjects to match sounds to concepts in graphical interfaces to understand how these aspects of graphical interfaces could be translated into sounds. In this paper, we briefly summarize these experiments and describe observations from the data analysis.

The purpose of this paper is to discuss how we used the results of these experiments to guide the selection of sounds for Mercator. Like other guidelines in human-computer interface design, the experimental results rarely pointed to one answer, in this case, a particular sound. More often they offered multiple hints, sometimes contradictory, during the selection process. This design process was not solely the consumer of these experimental results, but it also produced further insight into the selection and use of auditory icons.

Human–Computer Interaction: INTERACT'97 S. Howard, J. Hammond & G. Lindgaard (editors)
Published by Chapman & Hall

2. BACKGROUND

2.1. Auditory Icons

Gaver introduced the concept of auditory icons based on the premise that people describe sounds relative to the objects interacting to make the sounds. Computers and other man-made devices make a variety of beeps, buzzes and other artificial noises that otherwise we would never hear. Conversely, we typically hear things crumbling, things sloshing, things colliding - we hear the results of objects interacting together. When asked to describe a sound, we tend to describe it in terms of the objects that generated the sound such as a door slamming, stairs creaking or glass breaking. In other words, we describe sounds in terms of their sources, not in classical terms such as pitch and duration.

What this realization means to an interface designer is that we can use sounds to make users think of familiar objects in the same way as icons in GUIs. Gaver first demonstrated the use of auditory icons with his interface SonicFinder. In SonicFinder, Gaver added auditory cues to the graphical Finder environment on the Macintosh. Dragging a file icon with the mouse sounded like dragging something along the floor. Dropping an icon into the trashcan sounded like dropping a large object into a metal trashcan.

Auditory icons are not limited to simply reflecting categories of events and objects, but can be *parameterized* to reflect their relevant dimensions as well. For example, the auditory icon for a file can be manipulated to convey the size of the file. Although Gaver has successfully parameterized auditory icons in a number of interfaces, he notes the difficulty in parameterizing auditory icons due to the difficulty in controlling sampled sounds along the relevant dimensions and suggests synthesis as an alternative to sampled sounds.

Auditory icons appear to be a good match for this design task. Since they mimic the use of graphical icons, they seem well suited to conveying the components of graphical interfaces. Likewise, since their design potentially leverages existing knowledge, their use may help minimize the blind user's cognitive load.

2.2. Mercator Interfaces

Mercator is a system that automatically generates nonvisual interfaces for graphical applications. It was primarily designed to provide access to graphical interfaces for people who are blind. As a graphical application is executing, Mercator creates an off-screen model of the application interface. From that model, Mercator generates a nonvisual interface to the graphical application. As users interact with the nonvisual interfaces, Mercator translates their input to the input expected by the graphical application; translating keyboard input to mouse input for example. Thus while a graphical application is executing, Mercator users are able to interact with a parallel nonvisual interface.

Users navigate Mercator interfaces by traversing the structure of the application interface. This hierarchical structure is based on the objects used to construct the graphical interface. Moving up or down accesses different levels (parent/child) of the hierarchy while moving left or right accesses sibling objects. Users cannot move out of the bounds of the interface structure. Keyboard shortcuts allow users to jump to different portions of the structure and switch between windows on the screen. Separate controls are provided for manipulating the interface. This separation of navigation and control allows the user to navigate the interface without fear of accidently causing an event to occur.

Auditory icons convey the types of objects in the interface as well as provide feedback for interface events. For example, when the user navigates to a text-entry area they hear the sound of a typewriter. These auditory icons are parameterized to convey attributes of the objects. For example, a grayed-out toggle button sounds like a muffled pull-chain light switch.

Synthesized speech is used to read the text in the interface, such as the label on a button, as well as provide context-sensitive help. To access controls for scanning and editing large text areas, users switch Mercator into *text mode*. While in text mode, the keyboard controls are remapped to text controls.

3. USING AUDITORY ICONS

Evaluations of auditory interfaces reveal a number of factors that affect the usability of auditory icons:

- **Identifiability** - The user must be able to recognize the sound. The ecological frequency (how common the sound is) versus the relative uniqueness of the sound help determine its overall identifiability. If the user is unable to correctly identify the sound, then the usefulness of the sound is likely to be reduced. For example, in Cohen's ShareMon interface, the sound of a key turning in a lock represented a registered user logging into a computer system. Although the mapping between the sound and the interface concept is intuitive, the sound was not identifiable and therefore not utilized.

- **Conceptual Mapping** - How well does the sound map to the aspect of the user interface it is representing? Sound seems to lend itself to storytelling. Evaluators of auditory interfaces are often amazed at the stories users will build to explain the sounds that they hear. A favorite example is again taken from the ShareMon system where a knocking sound immediately followed by the sound of footsteps indicated that a user had logged onto a computer system and was accessing the shared file space. One test subject explained the sounds by describing a father expecting a baby who was knocking at a door (no one responds) and then pacing back and forth. The metaphorical power of auditory icons is immense, but controlling these mappings is a difficult design task.
- **Physical Parameters** - The physical parameters of the sound such as length, intensity, sound quality (for example, sampling rate) and frequency range may affect its usability. These physical parameters not only affect the user's reaction to the auditory cue, but they also affect the usability of the cue from the designer's perspective. The overall quality of the sound is largely determined by the sampling process. Users may negatively react to cheap (phone quality) or noisy sounds. The frequency composition of the cue may affect how it can be manipulated with standard filters.
- **User Preference** - How the user responds emotionally to the auditory icon is also important. Is the sound harsh or too cute? Almost all evaluations of auditory interfaces uncover sounds that users do not like.

The auditory icons used in an interface must also be evaluated as a cohesive set, again addressing the above issues. Concerning identifiability, the cues must be relatively distinct from each other so that they can be individually identified. The conceptual mappings in the interface must not be counterintuitive. The physical parameters of the auditory icons such as length, intensity and sound quality must also be carefully controlled as the user might attempt to attribute some meaning to any perceivable differences. These issues are important even if the sounds are not simultaneously presented. In addition to the above issues, concurrent presentation of auditory cues must also address basic psychoacoustic issues such as masking and streaming.

4. IDENTIFYING AUDITORY ICONS

To assess the identifiability of common auditory cues, we collected 64 sounds (short "everyday" samples from ten sound effects CDs with minimal editing). During the experiment, the sounds were played over two speakers to a classroom of 83 students. Under tight time constraints, subjects were asked to describe (free-form) the sounds as best they could.

The subjects' responses were analyzed by transforming their answer into a point in a 4x4 matrix. One axis on the matrix indicates how well the subject identified the object associated with the sound. The other axis indicates how well the subject identified the action associated with the sound. Per object and action, four scores were possible.

Y	Correct identification
P	(Partial) Either the subject identified a base material, an object with the same affordance or a similar action.
A	(Alternate) The subjects commonly selected a consistent (alternative), yet incorrect answer.
N	Incorrect or no answer

Table 1: Possible Identification Scores

4.1. Observations

Identifiability Scores are Low

The first result to note is that, in general, the identifiability scores were low with few sounds (13) showing an overall score over 80 (eighty) percent. This result is not surprising given the difficulty of the task and the short length of the sounds (under two seconds).

Distinction between Actions and Objects

The distinction between identifying a sound as an object or an action is clearly evidenced. Many sounds are consistently identified as objects (camera, typewriter, door, zipper) while other sounds are consistently identified as actions (closing, tearing, winding, locking). For example, for the sound of a camera taking a picture, specifically the shutter operating, subjects easily identified the object as a camera, but were unable to identify the correct action (taking picture, flashing, winding film). Another sound of winding a parking meter was easily identified as winding but the object (parking meter, typewriter, music box) was not identified. This separation supports the guideline for choosing some sounds to represent objects while using other sounds to represent actions. In general, the designer should decide if an action or an object (or both) need to be conveyed, and then choose the appropriate auditory cue.

Partial / Alternative Answers Merit Research

Many of the sounds resulted in high partial (P) or alternative (A) scores. In other words, the subjects heard some of the information in the sound. A partial answer for the object was recorded if the subject identified the base material of the object, or identified an object with the same affordance. For example, for the sound of closing a metal mailbox, recognizing the metallic material or answering "closing a file cabinet" resulted in a partial object score. For actions, identifying similar actions resulted in partial scores such as dropping or throwing, swinging or striking, or closing, latching or locking.

An alternative answer was scored if the pool of subjects tended to identify the object incorrectly but consistently. Cultural biases may partially explain alternative answers. For example, in our pool of undergraduate Georgia Tech students, whip cracks were identified as gun shots and popping a cork out of a champagne bottle was identified as making a popping noise with one's finger and cheek.

The large number of sounds with partial and alternative scores motivates future work in the learnability of auditory cues. One hypothesis is that sounds with high partial answers are easy to learn whereas sounds with high alternative answers are difficult to learn since it would require the subject to break the existing mapping between the sound and the alternative concept.

Sounds Naturally Conflict

Many sounds naturally conflict. For examples, machines that afford typing such as typewriters, keyboards, cash registers are naturally confused. Likewise printing and copying sounds are often mistaken for each other. These conflicts indicate when it may be difficult to present two similar concepts in an interface using auditory cues. For example, although the sounds of a copier and printer may be quite distinct, it may be difficult to correctly identify them when they are both used in the same interface.

5. MAPPING AUDIO ICONS TO GUIS

This experiment assessed how users expected auditory cues to be used to represent concepts common in graphical interfaces. Twenty-eight sounds were selected from the initial collection of sounds used in the first experiment. The sounds selected had high identifiability scores from the first experiment. Fifteen concepts (objects and actions) from graphical interfaces were chosen as the independent variable. During the experiment, each subject was presented with the graphical interface concept and five sounds. Their task was to choose which sound best matched the interface concept.

5.1. Observations

The observations reported here are based on debriefing the subjects and a quantitative analysis of the numerical data gathered during the experiment.

Four Types of Selection

During the debriefing, the subjects described why they had chosen a particular sound for an interface concept. The reasonings used to guide their selections seem to fall into four major categories. First, the subjects (as predicted) chose sounds that they felt represented the *semantics of the interface concept*. For example, the sound of typing on a typewriter (multiple keystrokes) was a common choice to represent an editable text field. Likewise, for closing a window, the sound for closing a car door was a common choice, followed by the sound of closing a zipper. This observation is not surprising, but it does indicate that sounds can be used to represent semantic information in the interface.

Second, several subjects indicated that they choose sounds that mapped well to the perceived *importance of the interface concept*. For example, the sound of a short tap on a typewriter was the most common sound for the check boxes that implement nonexclusive choices. Subjects reasoned that selecting a check box is easily undone, and therefore less important than pushing a button that was represented by a longer, more complex sound such as cracking a whip.

Third, subjects also indicated that they chose sounds that mapped to the perceived *length of the interface concept*. For example, selecting a radio button (common sounds: short and long pops) was described as taking less time than opening a folder (common sounds: opening door and slide whistle-pitch ascending).

Fourth, the subject choose sounds that mapped to the *physical appearance of the interface concept*. For example, a slide whistle (pitch descending) was the most common sound for a pull-down menu. Subjects explained that pop-up menus would have a different sound although the menu concept was shared by both objects. Several subjects explained that the sound of a camera shutter mapped well to the concept of a window appearing on the screen since the sound reminded them of square shapes being presented in quick succession.

Feedback is the Expected Use of Sound

Subjects' comments during the debriefing indicated that they expected the auditory cues to be used as feedback in the interface, usually as the result of a direct manipulation task. This use is in contrast to using sound to simply convey the identity of interface objects independent of a particular action. For example, in Mercator, navigating to an object causes a sound to be played that conveys the type of object. This distinction between conveying the identify of an object separate from feedback resulting in manipulating the object is important in auditory-only interfaces where the contents of the interface must be conveyed aurally.

6. UTILIZING RESULTS IN MERCATOR

The primary purpose of running the identification and mapping experiments was to gain insight into how people described auditory cues, and how they expected those cues to be used in computer interfaces. A secondary purpose was to select cues to be used in Mercator. The collection of sounds used in the experiments were samples taken from over ten sound effects CDs. When copying sounds from the CDs, we chose sounds that were good candidates for use in Mercator. For example, we looked for short, generic sounds for actions such as closing, opening, latching, winding and so on. We also looked for sounds involving objects such as typewriters, doors, file cabinets. We avoided two major types of sounds, animal sounds, and ambience sounds. For the most part, the experiments did not result in clear choices for which sounds to use in Mercator, but offered guidelines for the selection. This selection process is described in the following sections.In most cases, we attended to multiple guidelines when choosing sounds for Mercator. Table 2 illustrates the guidelines that we were able to use in the design.

6.1. Isolating Optimal Auditory Icons

Prior to performing the experiments, we hypothesized that a typewriter sound should represent text areas while a printer sound should represent read-only text areas such as message bars. But the question of which typewriter and printer sounds to use remained. The initial identifiability experiment helped isolate sounds that were readily identified as typewriters and printers. In the case of the typewriter sound, the mapping experiment confirmed that a typewriter sound would work. The mapping experiment did not distinguish that a printer sound was a good match for a message area. However, debriefing test subjects indicated that some subjects interpreted the message bar as only being used for conveying errors. These subjects choose alarm sounds instead. In general, the current printer sound is not ideal and we are still looking for a better one.

6.2. Action- & Object-oriented Sounds

One surprising result of the identifiability experiment was that some sounds were more often described as actions, while some sounds were more often described as objects. This bias in identification is useful in Mercator where some sounds need to represent objects independent of an action. When choosing sounds for objects, we looked for an indication of this bias. For example, we tried to identify push button sounds where the user did NOT think that they had just pressed a push button.

The opening door sound for containers is still problematic. Novice users typically believe that they have *entered* a container, not that they can look into a container. Previous sounds of rattling lids or shaking boxes with objects in them were not readily identified.

To represent selection, we needed a sound that had a strong action bias that did not remind the user of any specific object. The ripping paper sound has been successful. Most users do not identify the object as paper. Some do not recognize the action as ripping, but all users seem to believe that they have caused something to occur.

Obviously how users interpret sounds is also dependent on their input to the system. If users press the Enter key, they should anticipate that a selection is occurring. But selecting an object is generally followed by a series of sounds to represent actions and new objects appearing on the screen. Users have never identified the selection sound as a new object.

6.3. Controlling the Length and Complexity

Based on their selections and comments during the mapping experiment, subjects indicated that the length and complexity of an auditory cue should be consistent with the concept that it represents. Although not fully defined, complexity seems to be based on the range of pitch conveyed in a sound and the transitions between those pitches. Check boxes appear to be the simplest interface concept so they are conveyed with a short sound somewhere between a click and a keypress. As push buttons appear to be more complex since selecting a push button is harder to undo, this sound is longer and more complex.

The whistling sounds were popular choices since these sounds are particularly engaging. We use these sounds to represent pop-up windows since these sounds are relatively long and complex, matching the relatively lengthy and important occurrence of a pop-up window.

In a similar manner, a relatively long winding sound is used to indicate when an application is connecting to Mercator. Winding seems to imply waiting for an indeterminate period of time. In contrast, disconnecting an application is a short process and is accompanied by a succinct flushing sound.

6.4. Mapping Cues to Visual Events

Although some aspects of the visual interface are not directly conveyed to the Mercator user, representing visual events with sounds is sometimes useful. As previously discussed, whistling sounds indicate the appearance and disappearance of a pop-up window. As the pitch rises, it sounds like something is coming toward the user, to the forefront. This experience is like a pop-up window appearing on top of other windows. Although other sounds could indicate the presence of something new, the whistling sound helps solidify the concept of an appearing pop-up window. A pop-up window (the object) is conveyed with the sound of a spring for the same reason. We are still looking for a good "pulling down" sound to represent a pull-down menu.

Windows are often described as pieces of paper in the desktop metaphor. For this reason, switching between windows is accompanied with the sound of shuffling through paper. Again, the sound conveys a change in stacking order on the screen. Although the windows are not visible to the Mercator user, it is helpful to reinforce common concepts in graphical interfaces. In this way, Mercator users can more knowledgeably talk to their sighted colleagues about the behavior of a graphical application.

6.5. More Abstract Representations

Although our initial designs focused on concrete representations, some concepts in the interf^ce did not map well to concrete auditory icons. The most difficult concept to find a sound for was entering and exiting text mode. Concrete representations such as the sound of turning on a typewriter, or winding paper in the typewriter were more confusing than helpful. Since switching into text mode is caused by the user hitting a reserved key, the user only needed a simple feedback sound confirming the action. We chose the sound of a drawer being pulled out of a chest of drawers. The sound is simple, short and its low pitch helps it to be non-intrusive. The rolling and rocking sound indicates a change of state that does not sound alarming.

Radio buttons and toggle buttons were difficult to represent because in both cases, we wanted a simple, two-stage sound. The two parts of the toggle button sound needed to indicate that something could be latched, or unlatched. The two parts of the radio button sound needed to indicate that selecting one button might result in another button being deselected. We used a pull chain light switch sound for the toggle button. This concrete representation should remind the user of a control that can be turned on and off. For the radio button, we used a more abstract push button sound where the first part is shorter and lighter, indicated the deselection, than the second part. We also looked for a cue that sounded ***round*** since radio buttons are usually round as opposed to other push button controls[1]. Indications of roundness included no sharp attacks or decays and a simple, harmonic structure.

For the navigation error sound, we needed an action-oriented sound, but it needed to convey an attempted action. We wanted the sound to be non-alarming, no harsh buzzers or beeps, and to reinforce the concept of the hierarchical navigation scheme. We decided on a sound akin to a ball rebounding against a wall. It is a highly, action-oriented sound that hopefully conveys the walls of the explicit interface structure. When played successively (if the user hits too many keys in one direction), it creates a nice drumming effect. Although its low pitch is relatively non-intrusive, one frustrated test user working with Mercator described the sound as "banging his head against the wall!"

6.6. Designing Sets of Auditory Cues

The identification and mapping experiments focused on the design of individual auditory cues. These experiments were useful in that they highlighted general design guidelines. The net result, however, was that we used these guidelines to design a *set* of auditory icons for Mercator. Like many interface design tasks, it is difficult to design components of the interface separate from the context of the interface. One reason this statement is true for designing auditory icons is that the icons must be designed as a cohesive set. For example, the sound for flipping papers should not be louder than the sound for

1. In graphical interfaces radio buttons are generally round. In contrast, real world radio buttons are generally rectangular. In this design decision, the conventions of graphical interfaces overrode real world experience.

opening a door. The design guidelines for controlling the length and "complexity" of sounds are useful when comparing relative differences between sounds.

Another difficulty is choosing sounds for similar concepts in the user interface. For example, we needed sounds for push buttons, menu buttons, radio buttons, toggle buttons, and check boxes. These controls are all pushed (selected) to trigger an action in the interface. In Mercator, we used a combination of concrete and abstract sounds attempting to control the length and complexity of the individual cues. There is little chance that a successful set of icons would result from designing the auditory icons independently.

6.7. Practical Considerations

Mercator's interface design also placed two practical constraints on the selection of sounds.

- **Interruption** - When navigating an interface, the user may opt to move quickly through the interface without waiting to hear the full length of the auditory cues. Although the sounds are short, a user with any reasonable level of expertise tended to move faster than the sounds could be played. To accommodate faster navigation, sounds needed to be identifiable in the shortest time possible. The initial pitch and complexity of the sounds seemed to influence their identification.
- **Filtering** - Multiple levels of information are often conveyed in one auditory cue such as representing a grayed-out push button or a relatively small text area. A common technique to add an additional layer of information is to filter the sound with a high- or low-pass filter. These filters dampen a range of frequencies present in the sound resulting in a cue that sounds muffled or excited. These filters combined with modifying the overall intensity of the sound are both fairly powerful and cheap to implement. The use of these filters, however, constrained the initial selection of sounds for Mercator. For a filter to affect a sound, it must have an appropriate range of frequencies. In short, all of the sounds used in Mercator have a reasonably large bandwidth of frequencies so that filtering can be used.

7. A NEW PERSPECTIVE

When we began designing Mercator's auditory interfaces, our view of using auditory icons was limited to using concrete representations to represent concepts in the interface. The typewriter and printer auditory icons are examples of concrete representations where we want the user to identify the auditory icon. By thinking of a typewriter, the user is reminded that the object is an editable text area. As we designed cues for more abstract concepts such as switching text modes, we began paying more attention to the metaphorical qualities of everyday sounds. Realizing that auditory icons did not have to utilize concrete representations, we began experimenting with sounds where we did NOT want the user to be able to identify the source of the sound, but we still wanted the user to apply everyday listening skills when interpreting the sound. This strategy is not novel as foley artists rarely use concrete sounds when designing sound effects for films.

This realization made us question recent work where designers compared real world and musical sounds. The study concluded that musical sounds should be used because "users consistently preferred musical sounds to real world sounds." This result is not surprising since a professional designer created the musical sounds, but did not design the real world sounds. What the researchers did not acknowledge was that many of their "musical sounds" had significant real world qualities to them. For example, the musical sound for terminating a phone call ended abruptly and sounded like a metaphorical representation of placing the phone handset back into the cradle. Likewise, the musical sound for ringing was repetitive with a tempo akin to a real world phone ringing.

An interesting goal for future work is understanding what are the attributes or affordances of everyday sounds that help people leverage their everyday listening skills. In the previous examples, the amplitude envelope, pattern and tempo helped one to interpret the musical sounds in terms of everyday listening. The partial identification scores in the identification experiment may point to some of these underlying attributes.

8. REFERENCES

Albers, M. The Varese System, Hybrid Auditory Interface, and Satellite-Ground Control: Using Auditory Icons and Sonification in a Complex, Supervisory Control System. In *Proceedings of the Second International Conference of Auditory Display, ICAD '94*, Sante Fe, New Mexico, 1995, pp. 3-14.

Ballas, J. A. Delivery of Information Through Sound, In *Auditory Display: Sonification, Audification and Auditory Interfaces*, edited by G. Kramer, SFI Studies in the Sciences of Complexity Proc. Vol. XVIII, Addison-Wesley, 1994, pp. 79-94.

Butler, D. *The Musician's Guide to Perception and Cognition*. Schirmer Books. 1992.

Concept	Sound	Concrete or Abstract Representation	Action or Object	Control length and complexity	Map to Visual Events
Editable text area	Typewriter, multiple keystrokes	Concrete			
Read-only text area	Printer printing out a line	Concrete			
Push button	Keypress (ca-chunk)	Abstract		X	
Toggle button	Pull chain light switch	Concrete		X	
Radio button	Pa pop sound	Abstract		X	X
Check box	One pop sound	Abstract		X	
Window	Tapping on glass (two taps)	Concrete			
Container	Opening a door	Concrete	Object???		
Pop-up dialog	Spring compressed then extended	Concrete	Object	X	X
Application	Musical sound	Abstract			
Selection	Ripping papers	Abstract	Action		
Switching between applications	Paper shuffling	Concrete	Action		
Navigation error	Ball rebounding against wall	Abstract	Action		
Entering text mode	Rolling / rocking sound (drawer pulled out)	Abstract	Action		
Moving edit cursor in text area	Click (pitch based on position in text)	Abstract			X
Popup appearing / disappearing	Whistle up/down	Abstract	Action	X	X

TABLE 2: Choosing Sounds for Mercator

Cohen, J. Monitoring Background Activities, In *Auditory Display: Sonification, Audification and Auditory Interfaces*, edited by G. Kramer, SFI Studies in the Sciences of Complexity Proc. Vol. XVIII, Addison-Wesley, 1994, pp. 499-532.

Edwards, W.K. and Mynatt, E.D. An Architecture for Transforming Graphical Interfaces. In the *Proceedings of UIST'94: User Interface Software and Technology Symposium*, Marina Del Ray, CA., Nov. 2-4, 1994, 39-47.

Gaver, W. W. Everyday listening and auditory icons. Doctoral Dissertation, University of California, San Diego. 1988.

Gaver, W.W. Using and Creating Auditory Icons. In *Auditory Display: Sonification, Audification and Auditory Interfaces*, edited by G. Kramer, SFI Studies in the Sciences of Complexity Proc. Vol. XVIII, Addison-Wesley, 1994, pp. 417-446.

Mynatt, E. and Weber, G. Nonvisual Presentation of Graphical User Interfaces: Contrasting Two Approaches," in the *Proceedings of the ACM Conference on Human Factors in Computing Systems*, 1994.

Mynatt, E. Auditory Presentation of Graphical User Interfaces, In *Auditory Display: Sonification, Audification and Auditory Interfaces*, edited by G. Kramer, SFI Studies in the Sciences of Complexity Proc. Vol. XVIII, Addison-Wesley, 1994, pp. 533-556.

Mynatt, E. Evaluating Mercator. Submitted to CHI '97.

Sikora, C., Roberts, L. and Murray L. T. Musical vs. Real World Feedback Signals. In *CHI '95 Conference Companion, Human Factors in Computing Systems*. ACM. 1995, pp. 220-221.

Automating Tasks for Groups of Users : A System-Wide "Epiphyte" Approach

Zeiliger R. *, Kosbie D. **

* CNRS-GATE, 93 chemin des Mouilles
69130 Ecully
FRANCE
zeiliger@gate.cnrs.fr

** Microsoft Corporation, One Microsoft Way
Redmond, WA 98052
USA
dkosbie@microsoft.com

ABSTRACT End-users have to use macro-recorders when they want to automate tedious tasks. Their tasks often include actions from multiple applications. While some application-specific macro facilities or PBD systems have proved efficient to automate single-application tasks, system-wide - and hence application-independent - systems are few. Most system-wide recorders operate on low-level events whereas most repetitive activities are repetitive at a somewhat higher level of abstraction. We present a so-called "epiphyte" approach allowing automation of some of the repetitive tasks only, but working with unmodified applications. It uses external and partial application models to allow recording of hierarchical event histories which in turn facilitate the detection, generalization, anticipation and completion of repetitive sequences of actions. In this approach, experts are in charge of building external application models. We present some features which facilitate and quicken their work particularly in the context of a group of users.

KEYWORDS Programming By Demonstration, Macro commands, End User Programming, Interface agents, Hierarchical Event Histories.

1. INTRODUCTION

People often use generic applications developed by distant, unknown programmers to handle tasks similar to theirs (Cypher, 1993). In the process of mapping their activities into the capabilities of these generic applications, end-users are inevitably led to perform tedious repetitive actions. Automation of these tasks would be possible if only end-users were also programmers. But programming is difficult : Potter

Human–Computer Interaction: INTERACT'97 S. Howard, J. Hammond & G. Lindgaard (editors)
Published by Chapman & Hall

(Potter, 1993) identified the obstacles users have to overcome to achieve "just-in-time" programming defined as the "implementing of algorithms during task-time" : inaccessible data, the effort of entering the algorithm, limited computational generality, effort of invoking the algorithm, and risk. Various techniques have been developed to allow programming by end-user : preferences, script languages, macro-recorders and programming-by-demonstration (PBD). In most modern commercial systems, end-users have to use macro-recorders when they want to automate tedious tasks. Macro-recorders are either application-specific (such as EXCEL macro recorder) or system-wide (such as Quickeys or Automator). While the former can be efficient, the latter would be more useful because user's tasks often include actions from multiple applications. Unfortunately system-wide macro-recorders are still too "literal" (Cypher,1993) : "they replay a sequence of keystrokes and mouse-clicks, whereas most repetitive activities are repetitive at a somewhat higher level of abstraction". PBD goes a step further in creating generalized programs from the recorded actions. But again most successful PBD programs today are application-dependent (the best example is EAGER which is dedicated to Apple's Hypercard (Cypher, 1991)). Architectures have been proposed to facilitate system-wide PBD (Piernot, Yvon, 1993, 1995) (Kosbie, Myers, 1994, 1995) but none of the proposed architectural enhancements have yet been incorporated into popular systems such as Microsoft Windows.

In the next section we are presenting some of the issues related to building a system-wide Microsoft-windows based PBD system.

2. SYSTEM ARCHITECTURE OVERVIEW AND RELATED ISSUES.

The proposed system has to record system-wide user actions, detect repetitive action sequences and generalize to produce a program automating the task, under user's control. It matches the definition of software agents as suggested by P. Maes : "a set of programs which have a specific user-understandable competence, which are capable of learning about their environment and to which the user can delegate tasks that she is unwilling to perform" (Maes, 1996). Our agent has to go through the following steps :

1. Capturing in the system the low-level events (LLE) such as mouse-click and keyboard strokes. This module should not contain any application-specific code. The successive events constitute a history.

2. Generating higher-level events (HLE). This is a crucial step. A good example of a high-level event is "save-file"; different low-level events map to this higher-level event : the "control-S" keyboard stroke, the selection with the mouse of the "Save" item from the "File" menu or a mouse-click on the "save-file button" in the tool bar. In LLE history - based on mouse-clicks and key strokes - those events will be different, while the events will appear identical if we record an HLE history, thus resulting in an increase in power of the inference engine. Two sequences of actions which have the same meaning for the user can differ considerably in their expression. Crow and Smith showed that incorporating minimal knowledge about the underlying system (particularly a "small amount of low-level domain syntax") greatly improves the performance of a PBD system (Crow, Smith, 1993).

3. Including context. Events must also include application context if they are to be adequately reasoned over. The canonical example here is deleting all mail messages from a certain person. The only way to infer this behavior is to be able to reason over "who sent" the messages. This information should be part of the **context** of a "delete-mail" event. The problem, of course, is how much context should be included : in the case of an email event, we may include the entire header, but probably not the body, so any inferences requiring the body cannot be made.

Another problem when working with existing, unmodified applications is how a software agent can access this context : user interaction with applications such as text editors or graphical editors is achieved through the use of controls (buttons, menus, dialog-boxes) which have a well-defined system-wide semantic : clicking on a check box for example results in setting an option to "on" or "off" and the check box caption usually indicates the option name. On the contrary, interaction through the edit-window of a graphical editor has a specific semantic determined by the editor itself : a mouse-click in such a window may result for example in selecting or on the contrary de-selecting an object, depending on what was the previous state of this object. The information about the state of an editable object - which can be an important contextual information - is stored in the application itself and cannot be accessed by an external agent without modifying the application. This is an important drawback when working with unmodified applications.

4. Storing and accessing history. Two aspects of history have to be considered here (Cypher, Kosbie, Maulsby, 1993) : after a bit of user's interaction with the system, a good deal of event-history has accumulated. This is called the **static history**. From this static history, the system can infer templates of repetitive events, or patterns to search for. This process of inferring templates can be very expensive and thus may have to be done **off-line** (for example over night). Then the system has to deal with a part of history which is called the **dynamic history.** It encompasses the more recent user's activity which the system has to process in order to recognize that a patterned activity is beginning : that is, the system has to match the user's actions against part of one of the stored templates. This is obviously an on-line process and so must be very efficient.

5. Inferring templates of repeated activities in the static history. Various machine learning techniques can be used here but basically most PBD systems use symbolic techniques.

6. Matching dynamic history against the stored templates : specific algorithms have been developed to resolve this problem (Cypher, 1991)(Maulsby, 1993)(Frank, 1994). They rely on linear event histories.

7. Interacting with the user to control the completion of the task in a mixed-initiative fashion. There are many important issues here such as how the system informs the user that a possible match has been inferred? How the system completes the task (step-by-step or monolithically with an undo facility) ? How can the user help disambiguate when there are multiple reasonable generalizations? Can the user directly modify the stored procedure, effectively parameterizing it (thus the user demonstrates deleting every message from "Bill", but then can invoke this routine to delete all messages from anyone)? How can the user explicitly invoke a stored procedure ?

8. Completing the repetitive task, that is generating the events to be sent to the application in order to perform the task.

A simple prototype agent was first built and field tests were conducted in our lab over 3 month with 8 users. It was based on flat low-level event histories. Two main things were learned and informed the work which is partly reported here : i) very few repetitive sequences were found in the LLE histories we had recorded, while a human observer watching a user at work could quickly identify repetitive tasks, ii) repetitive tasks should not be confused with habits : when users perform repetitive tasks they are still conscious; they perform an intentional activity; they are still intentional users. If a software capable of automating their repetitive tasks was available, they want control over it.

We will now present the new prototype agent under development within the framework of the ACCEL project, focusing particularly on solutions we have developed to overcome the issues mentioned in points 2 and 3 above : the use of external application models to generate hierarchical event histories.

3. THE ACCEL PROJECT "EPIPHYTE" APPROACH

The research work within the framework of the ACCEL project is supported by French CNRS[1] and CNET[2]. It aims at building a Microsoft Windows-based agent capable of automating repetitive user tasks involving any unmodified applications. This system is qualified "epiphyte" : a term coming from the domain of biology and first coined by S. Giroux (Giroux, 1996) in the domain of information systems to refer to a system which is developed on the surface of an unmodified pre-existing system with the aim to

[1] Centre National de la Recherche Scientifique

[2] Centre National d' Etude des Telecommunications

empower it.

3.1. Capturing low-level events.

Low level events (LLE) - also called device-level-events- are captured through the standard Windows hook mechanism : mouse events, keyboard events and system messages are processed by the ACCEL agent **before** they reach the target application. On-line LLE processing at this stage encompasses **aggregation** and **enrichment** :

- aggregation : several "very low-level events" can be grouped and recorded as one basic user's operation : for example opening the open-file dialog box through the file-menu necessitates several mouse operations (main-menu-selection and then menu-item-selection) generating a set of events whose details are not important in our project : they are grouped and recorded as a "open-open-file-dialog-box-thru-menu" unique operation (a unique LLE). This aggregation is based on an external model of the target application described in the next chapter.
- enrichment : LLE are then enriched with contextual information including the current date and time, the target application name and the currently opened file if any. More contextual information can be added depending on the specifications attached to the current event in the target-application model : for example, if the LLE is a selection in a list-box, the text (name or value) of the selected item is incorporated to the context; if the LLE is a click on a check-box or a radio-button, the final value (ON or OFF) of the control is recorded. If the LLE concerns an untitled widget (a list-box for example) then the system searches for a title in the form of a text-label aligned either horizontally or vertically with the list-box in the same parent window. In the example shown in figure 1 a mouse-click in the combo-box will be recorded as the LLE : "Font.SetSize(10)" which is composed of : i) the basic low-level operation : SELECT 10, ii) enriched with the contextual information : SIZE (found in a text-label aligned with the combo-box and closer to it than any other label), iii) and enriched with the contextual information : FONT (found in the caption of the parent window).

This on-line enrichment mechanism could not apply automatically to every LLE : as we will see it is controlled through the specifications incorporated by a human expert in the target application model. Recording enriched LLEs facilitates the generation of structured HLEs which is the next operation performed by the agent.

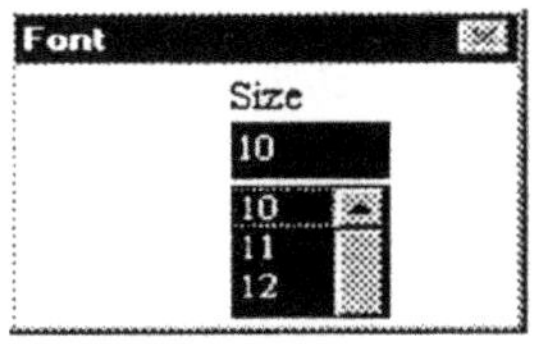

Figure 1 : set font size to 10 example

3.2. Generating high-level events.

Incoming LLEs are then aggregated again and structured to constitute mid-level events. This process is then repeated again to form even higher-level events. With this technique users' actions are recorded in the form of hierarchical event histories. This step is performed on the base of external models of the targeted applications which have to be built by expert users. This solution constitutes the key aspect of our approach.

Advantages of imposing a hierarchical structure on events' history have been exposed by D. Kosbie : hierarchical event histories are closer to user's task structure, they are more robust in the generalization process, they facilitate script matching (point 5 and 6 in previous chapter), they are more intuitive when read-controlled by end users, they are more efficient when played back. Detailed argumentation can be found in (Kosbie, Myers, 1993, 1994).

Unfortunately, the hierarchical structure of events cannot be fully inferred from the read-write patterns of the event handlers which do not provide enough information (Kosbie, Myers, 94). Due to heterogeneity in applications interface, the "enriched" LLE mechanism we have used cannot be fully automated and moreover it does not completely determine the event's hierarchical structure.

For hierarchical event histories to be feasible, there must be a way for applications to generate the event hierarchy. Different architectures have been proposed to allow application designers to incorporate the generation of hierarchical events in the new applications they build : the hieractors model (Kosbie, Myers, 1994), hierarchical command objects (Myers, Kosbie, 1996), AIDE events (Piernot, Yvon, 1994) or the AppleEvents model.

In the ACCEL project, since we want to work with **unmodified** off-the-shelf applications running under Microsoft Windows, we need an **"external" model** for every involved application : i.e. a complementary knowledge source which is not originally built-in the application but which can be built separately by an expert user to allow the hierarchical structuring of the stream of low-level events. This approach is named "epiphyte" because of the analogy - in the domain of biology - with plants which grow at the surface of other plants without being parasitic. Making a complete model of an application would be a great deal of difficult work; our system is designed to enable an expert user to make a more limited model which allows rich inferencing over a subset of user actions only.

In the context of our project, six hierarchical levels have been considered :

- low-level (or device-level) events (LLE) correspond to the basic operations with the mouse and the keyboard.
- mid-level (or widget-level) events (MLE) correspond to user's interaction with the various controls : list and combo boxes, edit controls, buttons, etc.
- high-level-events (HLE) aggregate several MLEs such as those generated by the use of a modal dialog-box; "Open-file(foo.doc)" is a typical HLE description.
- application-level-events (ALE) aggregate MLEs and HLEs resulting from user's interaction with the same application : EXCEL events and then WORD events for example.
- modeled/specific level (MSLE) is introduced here in response to point 3 mentioned above; a MSLE aggregates a set of events which are generated through the user's use of modeled controls, as opposed to a set of events resulting from user's interaction with application specific unmodeled features. This level doesn't correspond to a structure in user's task but it is mandatory in our approach to differentiate between segments of modeled and un-modeled events.
- session-level events (SLE) aggregate lower events which are generated as long as a user works without resting. SLE are segmented on the basis of time and rhythm statistics.

While hierarchical levels 1 to 4 reflect the inherent structure of "wimb" interfaces, level 5 is project-specific and it is assumed that level 6 corresponds more or less to low level tasks; further field tests will inform on the appropriateness of incorporating new intermediate levels in this hierarchy.

In figure 2, we present an example of a hierarchical history structured on the basis of this model. Two applications (WORDPAD and TOOLBOOK) are involved in a repetitive task : text files (texte1.txt, texte2.txt ...) are successively opened in WORDPAD, text is selected, copied into the clipboard and pasted into TOOLBOOK. Some unmodeled features of WORDPAD have been used before the beginning of the repetitive sub-task. In figure 2, the history structure is partly expanded to show only the full hierarchy of the first modeled WORDPAD event : HLE :OpenFile(texte1.txt) which was started by MLE :OpenDialog(Open), which was itself triggered by LLE :"msg CmdId 7935...". File name (texte1.txt) was extracted from the enriched LLE part of MLE :SetFileName (not detailed in figure 2) and transmitted to its parent HLE.

3.3. Including context : every event descriptor in an application-model includes a section describing the contextual information which is required and a method to access it. When identifying the event, the ACCEL agent obtains the contextual information and incorporates it into the history.

3.4. Storing and accessing history : each time it captures a new LLE, the ACCEL agent selects the model (.HAM file) of the target-application (the application to which the event is destined) and it performs the 6-level hierarchical structuring. It is an on-line process whose result is the recording of a hierarchical event static history (.HEH file).

3.5. Inferring templates. In the ACCEL project, this is a heavy off-line process which is achieved by a specialized agent : a "light" agent is installed on every end-user's computer; it permanently captures the LLE, includes the context, generates the hierarchical history and transmits the history data (through TCP/IP protocol) to a distant specialized agent which records it. The specialized agent searches for templates of repetitive activities. If some templates are detected, then the specialized agent informs the local agent which can then start to match the dynamic history against those templates. The specialized agent is supervised by an expert user.

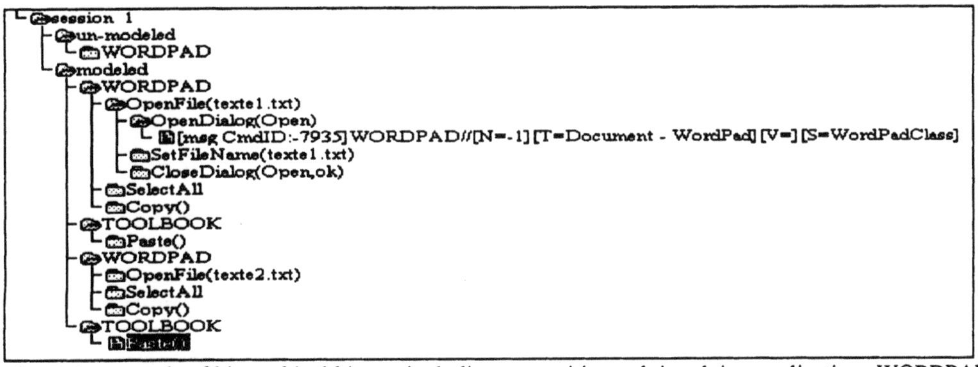

Figure 2 : example of hierarchical history including a repetitive task involving applications WORDPAD and TOOLBOOK (partly expanded).

Advantages of a hierarchical history when searching for templates can be easily seen in the example shown in figure 2 : at ALE level, the pattern is obvious : WORDPAD, TOOLBOOK and so on; it is still obvious at HLE level (thanks to the processing of the file name as a contextual information) and at MLE level (thanks to hiding equivalent LLEs).

3.6. Inferring matches against templates : existing algorithms (mentioned above) have been generalized to apply to hierarchical histories (instead of "flat" histories). These will be described in a forthcoming paper. The remaining steps (interacting with the user and performing the task) are still under development and cannot be presented here.

We will now focus on some aspects of the modeling task which is to be achieved by expert users. We present some features which facilitate and quicken their work particularly in the context of a group of users.

4. EXTERNAL APPLICATION MODELS

4.1. Application models overview

There is one model for each application. Model files are collections of event descriptors. Event description is inspired from the "hieractor model" (Kosbie, 1994) which was developed to express arbitrary high-level application behavior. This model was intended for application designers building new applications, however it is used in our approach to make an a-posteriori modeling of application behavior. The basic idea behind hieractors is that most application behaviors are naturally defined in terms of the events which **start**, **run**, **end** and **abort** them. Here is an example of an HLE event descriptor (from WORDPAD model) :

HLE : SetFont (<name>,<style>,<size>,<color>)
start-when : MLE : OpenDialog(font)
end-when : MLE : CloseDialog(font,ok)
abort-when : MLE : CloseDialog(font,cancel)
run-when : MLE : SetFont(<name>)
or MLE : SetStyle (<style>)
or MLE : SetSize(<size>)
or MLE : SetColor(<color>)
or MLE : Null()

Every event is described in terms of the events of level below which start, end, run and abort it. An HLE is described by MLEs and an MLE is described by LLEs. For example, we have the following description :

MLE : SetFont(<name>)
start/end-when :
LLE : [click]WORDPAD/<mfn> - WordPad / Font/ [T=&Font :][V=<name>]

The MLE named Nul() corresponds to user's actions (and thus LLEs) which are of no consequence on the behavior described by their parent HLE (for example : using a scrollbar in a list-box). Parameters are transmitted from an MLE to their parent HLE : MLE :SetSize(10) will have for parent : HLE :SetFont(-,-,10,-).

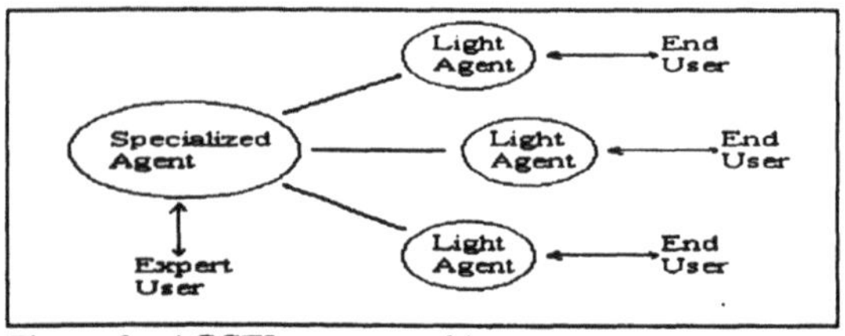

Figure 3 : ACCEL agents architecture.

The MLE OpenDialog(font) can be started by different LLEs depending whether a menu, shortcut or button is used : corresponding events are part of its "start-when LLE :" section.

In the LLE section of the MLE described above, <mfn> is an abstraction of the name of the file currently opened in WORDPAD : it is part of the context.

4.2. Building application models

Using external applications models is a key factor in our approach but the building of such models might also appear as a very time-consuming task. Rather than attempting to improve a fully automated agent based on sophisticated machine-learning techniques, we prefered to appeal to a human expert.

So the current situation involves a group of end-users aided by software agents under control of an expert-user. The expected benefit is an increase of the robustness of the agent's detection module; dependence on a human expert is a cost which can be i) minimized in developing dedicated tools aimed at facilitating and quickening the modeling task, ii) shared among a group of users having similar and time critical tasks. The entire system evolves toward a kind of groupware environment which facilitates the automation of end-users' tasks.

As we have said above, every end-user has a light-agent running permanently. Light agents (LAs) communicate with a specialized agent which runs on the expert-user computer (figure 3). The specialized agent (SA) provides also features to facilitate the modeling task :

- SA collects all LLEs sent by LAs; statistical analysis of all LLE histories gives the list of the most intensely used applications across the group of end-users. Using a simple pattern-matching technique (editing distance) it gives also the list of those functions in the applications which seem to be involved in repetitive activities. In short, statistics indicate those parts of applications which the expert-user will have to model first. The expert user does not work for individuals : when a part of an application get modeled, it benefits to every end-user.
- Enriched LLEs bring default contextual information and the system maintains a list of LLE templates which facilitate extracting of contextual parameters The enrichment mechanism - which was not robust enough in a fully automated approach - becomes very helpful when supervised by a human expert.
- Application models are fully editable while the agent and the application itself are running, so that the application model can be built in a nearly demonstrational mode.
- the specialized agent (SA) provides a debug-mode allowing the expert user to instantly "click-check " in a given application and control that the resulting events have been correctly modeled.

5. RESULTS, FUTURE WORK AND CONCLUSION

Eight ACCEL agents are currently installed in ARDEMI (http ://www.ardemi.fr/), a software company developing multimedia courseware. Text, sound, graphic editors and authoring tools are to be used in conjunction to achieve multimedia authoring. Users often complain that their tasks involve tedious repetitive operations they cannot automate. Users' actions were permanently recorded there since December 1995, however no result was achieved primarily because the agents reasoned over low-level events. This was our principal motivation for appealing to hierarchical event histories. Generating such histories necessitates that the agents incorporate at least a minimal knowledge of the underlying system and applications.

We have recently undertaken the external (and partial) modeling of applications WORDPAD and TOOLBOOK in order to validate the mechanism which generates hierarchical event histories. First results show a clear increase in power of the inference engine, but the application modeling task is still too cumbersome; we are pursuing ways to simplify this task. More applications need to be modeled before a real field test can be made.

Research efforts are being pursued in two complementary directions, both of which are related to "Programming-by-Demonstration" : the development of the light-agents interface allowing end-users to control the automation of their tasks, and the development of a "modeling-by-demonstration" interface, i.e. an interface allowing expert-users to build application models in a more "demonstrational" fashion.

6. ACKNOWLEDGMENTS

Support for the work described in this paper was provided by CNRS and CNET (ACCEL project N°941B107). The idea of "Hierarchical event histories" was introduced by the second author who is completing a PhD thesis at Carnegie Mellon University.

7. REFERENCES

Crow, D., Smith, B. (1993), The Role of Built-In Knowledge in Adaptive Interface Systems, *proceedings of International Workshop on Intelligent User Interfaces*, ACM press, NewYork.

Cypher, A. (1991), EAGER : Programming Repetitive Tasks by Example, *in proceedings of CHI'91*, ACM press, NewYork.

Cypher, A. (1993), Watch What I do, Programming by Demonstration (ed. A. Cypher), MIT press, Cambridge, Ma., USA

Frank, M., Foley, J. (1994), A Pure Reasoning Engine for Programming by Demonstration, in *proceedings of UIST'94*, ACM press, New York.

Frank, M. R. (1996), Standardizing the Representation of User Tasks, in *Acquisition, Learning & Demonstration : Automating Tasks for Users*, AAAI Symposium, Technical Report SS-96-02, AAAI press, Menlo Park, Ca., USA

Giroux, S., Paquette, G., Pachet, F., Girard, J. (1996), EpiTalk, a Platform for Epiphyte Advisor Systems Dedicated to both Individual and Collaborative Learning, in *proceedings of ITS'96*, Springer-Verlag Lecture Notes in Computer Science, to appear, 1996 (http ://www.laforia.ibp.fr/~fdp/EpiTalk.html).

Kosbie, D., Myers, B. (1993) A System-Wide Macro Facility Based on Aggregate Events : A proposal, in *Watch What I Do* (ed. A. Cypher), MIT press, Cambridge, Ma., USA

Kosbie, D., Myers, B. (1994) Extending Programming By Demonstration With Hierarchical Event Histories, in *proceedings of EWHCI'94* (eds. Blumenthal, Gornostaev, Unger) ICSTI, Moscow.

Maulsby, D. (1994), PhD Thesis, University of Calgary, Canada.

Myers, B., Kosbie, D. (1996), Reusable Hierarchical Command Objects, *in proceedings of CHI'96*, ACM press, NewYork.

Piernot, P., Yvon, M. (1993) The AIDE Project : An Application Independant Demonstrational Environment, in *Watch What I Do* (ed. A. Cypher), MIT press, Cambridge, Ma.

Potter, R. (1993) Just-In-Time Programming, in *Watch What I Do* (ed. Cypher), MIT press, Cambridge, Ma.

Yvon, M., Piernot, P., Cot, N. (1996), Programming by Demonstration : Detect Repetitive Tasks in Telecom Services, in *proceedings of OZCHI'96* (eds. Hasan, Nicastri), Ergonomics Society of Australia, Canberra, Australia.

Maes, P., Wexelbat, A. (1996), Interface agents, CHI'96 tutorial notes, ACM press.

43

Object-based Linear Undo model

Chunbo Zhou

Dept. of Computer Science
Yamanashi University
4-3-11 Takeda, Kofu
Yamanashi 400, Japan
shou@cluster.esi.yamanashi.ac.jp

Atsumi Imamiya

Dept. of Computer Science
Yamanashi University
4-3-11 Takeda, Kofu
Yamanashi 400, Japan
imamiya@yamato.esi.yamanashi.ac.jp

ABSTRACT The simplicity of traditional linear undo model makes it easy to understand, easy to use and widely adopted in a lot of software products on the market. But the traditional linear undo model cannot support object-based recovery operations. In order to solve this problem, we propose the object-based linear undo model in this paper. In our model, the traditional linear recovery history is reorganized into main history and subhistories. The main history represents the sequence of interactive cycles. The subhistories record the operations on corresponding objects. Traditional linear undo mechanism is improved and applied to both main history and subhistories so that the main history can support traditional linear undo/redo operations and the subhistories can support object-based undo/redo operations. The object-based linear undo model has been implemented on the platform of TRIBASE, a UIMS system developed by SEIKO Instruments Incorporation.

KEY WORDS usability engineering, interaction design, recovery model, undo, redo

Human–Computer Interaction: INTERACT'97 S. Howard, J. Hammond & G. Lindgaard (editors)
Published by Chapman & Hall

1. INTRODUCTION

Recovery facility is very important for enhancing the usability and learnability of human-computer interaction systems. So far a lot of undo models have been proposed. All the undo models can be classified into primitive undo models or meta undo models(Yang, 1988). In a primitive undo model, all the user-issued commands including both task-oriented commands and recovery commands are regarded as primitive commands. The recovery history is the list of such primitive commands which have been issued. There is only one recovery command, undo, that reverse the effect of last user-issued command. So primitive undo model is a single level undo model and seldom studied nowadays. In a meta undo model, only task-oriented commands are recorded in the recovery history. Recovery commands such as undo, redo and skip are meta commands which work on the history of task-oriented commands. The meta commands are never recorded in the history.

Furthermore, meta undo models can be classified into linear undo models or nonlinear undo models (Berlage, 1994 Yang, 1988). In a linear undo model, undo and redo commands can only work on the history by the order that task-oriented commands are recorded. A nonlinear undo model allows the user to undo or redo an arbitrary command in the history. Typical nonlinear undo models include script model (Archer, 1984), US&R model (Vitter, 1984), Triadic model (Yang, 1988), script-defined selective undo model (Prakash, 1994), direct selective undo model (Berlage, 1994), etc.

Event-object recovery model of Wang and Green is also a kind of nonlinear undo model (Wang, 1991). It divides the global recovery history into subhistories which corresponds to the objects of an object-oriented system. Our undo model discussed in this paper is derived from this model.

Although so many undo models have been proposed, it is the linear undo model that has been widely adopted in software products on the market. Let us regard the linear undo model adopted in those software products as traditional linear undo model so as to differentiate from our linear undo model. In the rest of this paper, we shall analyze the traditional linear undo model, point out its problems, and propose the solution.

2. TRADITINOAL LINEAR UNDO

2.1. Principle

In a traditional linear undo model, all the executed commands are recorded in a history list that may become arbitrary long (Figure 1). The last command in the list can be undone. When it is undone, it is removed from the history list and put into a redo list. The undo operation can be repeated until the history list empty (all of the commands are in the redo list). The last command put into redo list can be redone and again be appended to the history list. New commands are appended to the history list without affecting the redo list. It is important to note that undo and redo in this model are meta commands, they do not appear in the history (Berlage, 1994).

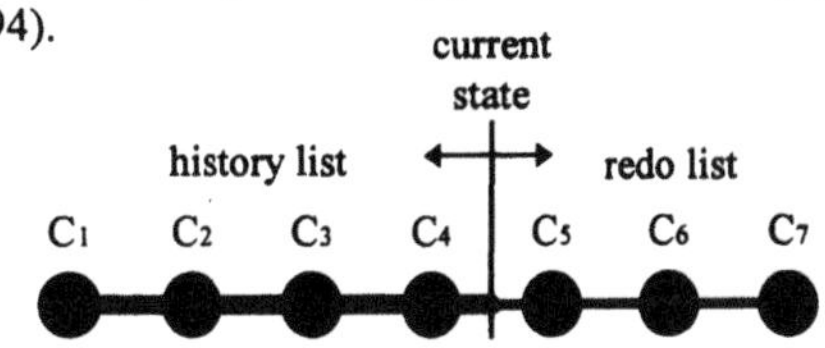

Figure 1. Traditional linear undo model

Sometimes linear undo model cannot work well. Suppose the user has drawn a circle on the screen and has later moved the circle to a new position. Now if the user undoes the move command and submits a new command to delete the circle, then the move command cannot be redone since the circle no longer exists.

The only case where linear undo model may not work well is when a new command is submitted while the redo list is not empty (Berlage, 1994). In some software products such as GINA and Microsoft Word, the redo list will be cleared when any new command is submitted. We adopt this method in our model as well. Another method to deal with this problem is to create new branches in recovery history (Figure 2).

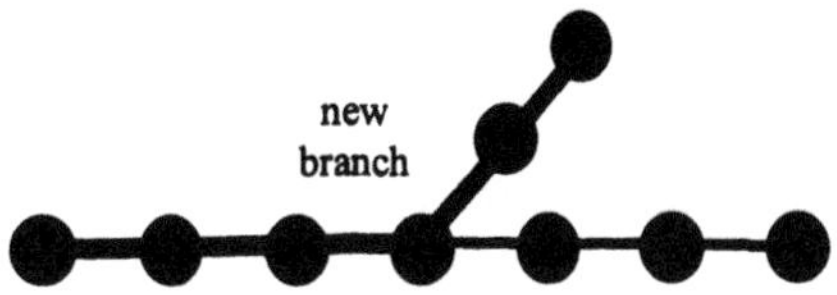

Figure 2. Creating a branch in the history

2.2. Advantages

Advantages of traditional linear undo model:

1. Its principle is simple and easy to be implemented.
2. Executing undo/redo by the order that the task-oriented commands have been submitted is in keeping with the imagination of users so that it is easy to be understood and accepted.
3. The user needn't know the details of commands. So its panel can be simplified as items of a menu. In contrast, for many nonlinear undo models, the commands stored in a recovery history must be displayed on screen so that the user can select a command from the history to undo or redo (Berlage, 1994 Myers, 1996). The nonlinear undo model may be hard to use for some end users who don't know much about commands.

2.3. Disadvantages

Disadvantages of traditional linear undo model:

1. The user can only execute undo/redo by the order that the task-oriented commands are recorded in the history list. However, the user may prefer to make his own choices during his recovery operations. Generally, the choices include,
   - to select an arbitrary command in the history list to undo/redo. For this purpose, many nonlinear undo models have been proposed. We don't discuss this problem in this paper.
   - to select an arbitrary object and change its states by undo/redo. Traditional linear undo model cannot support such operations. We mainly discuss this problem in this paper.
2. When a new command is appended to the history list while redo list is not empty, the linear undo model may not work well (Berlage, 1994). Two methods are available for this problem, to clear the redo list or create new branches in the history.
   - On clearing the redo list, some recovery information are lost so that further redo is impossible.
   - On creating new branches, the data structure of recovery history might become complex and unpredictable. The user has to make choice on a branch node. It would not be easy to use for some end users, so we don't adopt this method.

3. OBJECT-BASED LINEAR UNDO

As mentioned above, the user may prefer to select an arbitrary object and change its states by undo/redo. But the traditional linear undo model cannot support such operations. It is reasonable to reorganize the commands stored in a traditional linear history into subhistories based on the objects so as to support the user's purpose. To divide the traditional linear history into subhistories is not so simple as it is supposed. We must analyze the relationship among the commands in advance.

3.1. Relationship among commands

In order to analyze the relationship among the commands, we must know how the commands are submitted, executed and recorded.

The human-computer interaction can be described as a sequence of interactive cycles (Yang, 1988). Every interactive cycle has two phases, a planning phase and an execution phase. During a planning phase, the user evaluates the current state of an object, selects a command and inputs it. The submission of the selected command terminates the planning phase. The execution phase is the period during which the system executes the submitted command. The feedback from system terminates the execution phase.

Commands executed in the same interactive cycle are defined as synchronous commands. Commands executed in different interactive cycles but influencing each other are defined as asynchronous commands.

Generally, it can be supposed that only the command submitted by the user is executed in an interactive cycle. Therefore, it is reasonable to create a recovery history correspondingly to the sequence of interactive cycles by recording user-issued commands only. However, it should be noted that not only user-issued commands but also system-issued commands might affect the states of objects. Let us use the following example to explain why system-issued commands should be taken into account in creating an object-based recovery history.

Suppose there is a circular dependency (Vander Zanden, 1994) between rectangle A and B as follows.

A.right = B.left - 5
A.bottom = B.bottom
B.left = A.right + 5
B.bottom = A.bottom

In interactive cycle 1, the user may select A and move it to a new position. Then the constraint solver of the system evaluates the new values of B and moves B to a new position.

C_{a1} : Move(A, p_{a1}) *from user*
C_{b1} : Move(B, p_{b1}) *from system*

In interactive cycle 2, the user may select B and move it to a new position. Then the constraint solver of the system evaluates the new values of A and moves A to a new position.

C_{b2} : Move(B, p_{b2}) *from user*
C_{a2} : Move(A, p_{a2}) *from system*

In a traditional linear undo model, the history list of this example is $C_{a1}C_{b2}$. The constraint solver is also used to support undo and redo operations. When the user undoes C_{b2}, the state of A will be set back to its state before C_{a2} is executed automatically by the constraint solver of the system.

Now let us simply divide the traditional linear history $C_{a1}C_{b2}$ into subhistories based on objects A and B.

A: C_{a1}
B: C_{b2}

Suppose the user selects A to undo. In the subhistory of A, only C_{a1} is recorded so that only C_{a1} is to be undone. However, undo C_{a1} is meaningless because that the position of A has been changed by another command C_{a2} when C_{b2} was executed. The current position of A is not the result of C_{a1} but the result of C_{a2}. So C_{a2} should be also recorded in the subhistory of A in order to enable the user to select A to undo/redo. For the same reason, C_{b1} should be recorded in the subhistory of B.

A: $C_{a1}C_{a2}$
B: $C_{b1}C_{b2}$

Suppose the user selects A to undo. In the subhistory of A, C_{a2} can be undone. It is important to note that C_{a2} and C_{b2} are synchronous commands so that they should be undone or redone together in order to keep the dependency between A and B. So we need a method to record the synchronous relativity between C_{a2} and C_{b2}. Since synchronous commands are executed in the same interactive cycle, we can define a kind of record which can represent an interactive cycle. Now we are ready to build a new recovery model for object-based recovery operations.

3.2. Framework of our model

The framework of our model consists of three components (Figure 3). The Recovery Unit (RU) is the representation of an interactive cycle. All the objects manipulated in the same interactive cycle are recorded in the same recovery unit record. The Object Record (OR) describes the identity of an object created in an application. Each OR record corresponds to each object. The Recovery Information (RI) records the data necessary to execute recovery operation. A RI record corresponds to a RU record by the recovery unit identity code RUID.

The components are organized into three layers. The top layer is the list of RU records which represents the sequences of interactive cycles. The list of RU records is defined as main history which is similar to the recovery history of traditional linear undo model. The middle layer is the list of OR records. In the third layer there are different lists of RI records. One list of RI records belongs to one OR record uniquely and is defined as a subhistory. The linear undo mechanism is applied to both main history and subhistories. It is the subhistories that can support the user to select an arbitrary object to undo or redo.

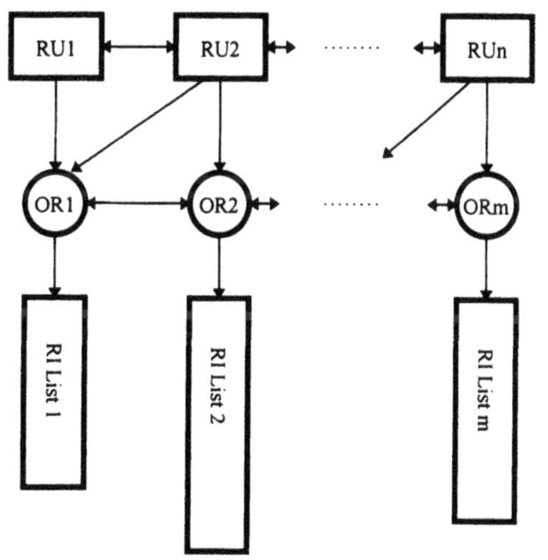

Figure 3. Framework of our model

3.3. Recovery operation

Our model allows the user to carry out undo/redo in both main history and subhistories. Undo/redo in main history is defined as global undo/redo. Undo/redo in subhistories is defined as local undo/redo. Let us use an example to explain how the framework of our model works. Suppose the user has operated as follows,

Step 1:	CreateRect (A)
Step 2:	CreateCircle (B)
Step 3:	Move (A, pa_1)
Step 4:	Move (B, pb_1)
Step 5:	Select (A, B)
Step 6:	Color ((A, B), red)
Step 7:	Color ((A, B), green)
Step 8:	Release (A, B)
Step 9:	Color (A, pink)
Step 10:	Color (B, yellow)

Where pa_1 and pb_1 are the positions on the screen. The commands working on A and B are divided into subhistories of A and B. The records of subhistories are illustrated in figure 4. The main history is shown in figure 5. We can see that object A and B are manipulated together from Step5 to Step8. The synchronous relativity between A and B from step5 to step8 is recorded in main history from RU5 to RU8. We define the area from RU5 to RU8 in the recovery history of our model as a synchronous zone (Figure 6).

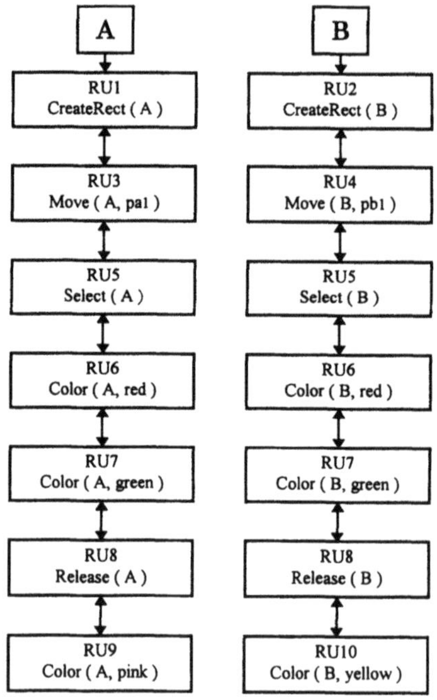

Figure 4. Records of subhistories

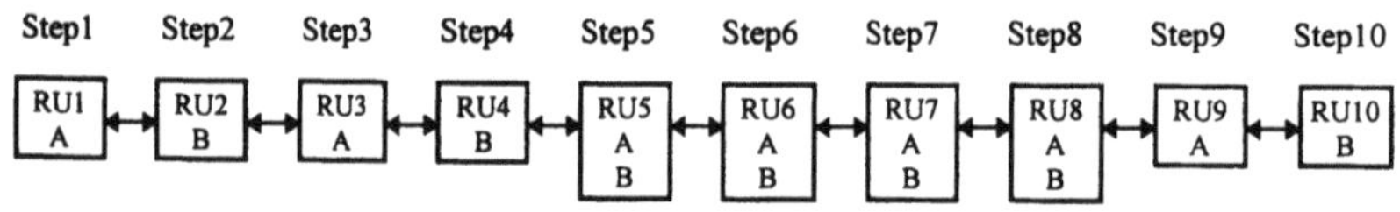

Figure 5. Records of main history

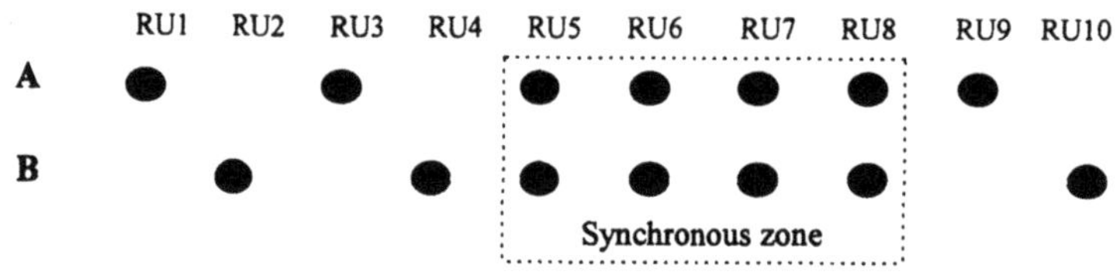

Figure 6. Synchronous zone in recovery history

Global linear undo/redo

The traditional linear undo mechanism (Figure 1) is applied to the main history of the object-based linear undo model. So the objet-based linear undo model can work as traditional linear undo model when the user do recovery operation in the main history only.

Suppose the user undoes the RU record identified as RU6 in the main history (Figure 5). The framework reads the set of objects recorded in this RU record. In this example, it reads object A at first and locates the subhistory of A to find the RI record identified as RU6 (Figure 4). If the command recorded in this RI record, Color (A, red), has not been undone, the framework undoes it, else does nothing. Then the framework reads the next object B and undoes it in the same way. This undo procedure continues until all the objects recorded in this RU record are undone. Naturally, redo function is implemented in the same way.

Global linear undo/redo method can preserve the dependencies among objects since it always undoes or redoes synchronous commands together.

Local linear undo/redo

Dependencies among objects should be considered when the traditional linear undo mechanism is applied to the subhistories of our model. For an independent object, its subhistory is independent. So the recovery operations can be executed in its subhistory independently without influencing each other with any other subhistory. For a dependent object, its subhistory relates to other subhistories. The undo/redo method of traditional linear undo should be modified to deal with this condition. The rules of local linear undo/redo is give as follows.

- when current undo/redo operation is out of any synchronous zone, the framework executes it in current subhistory independently.
- when current undo/redo operation goes into a synchronous zone, the framework displays a dialog box to remind the user that undo/redo operation is entering a synchronous zone and ask the user if he/she wants to undo/redo related objects together. On the answer 'Yes', it undoes or redoes other objects automatically. On the answer 'No', it undoes or redoes the selected object independently (Figure 8).

For instance, Objects A and B are independent from step1 to step4, dependent from step5 to step8, and independent again in step9 and step10 (Figure 5). It is obvious that A and B are independent out of the synchronous zone (Figure 6). So the states of A and B can be undone or redone independently out of the synchronous zone. A and B are dependent in the synchronous zone. Generally it is supposed that the dependencies among objects should be preserved. So the local linear undo/redo on A or B should be switch to global linear undo/redo on Both A and B in the synchronous zone.

Suppose both A and B are green and the user selects A to undo. At first, the framework locates the subhistory of A to find the current RI record which identified as RU7 and searches in the main history to find the RU record identified as RU7. Then the framework uses the global linear undo method introduced above to undo the commands Color(A, green) and Color(B, green) in the subhistories of A and B.

However, we have to note that the user may change his idea sometimes. For instance, when the user selects object A to undo/redo, the user may regard A as an independent object and undo/redo the states of A only. In other words, the user may want to break the dependency between A and B sometimes. Although it conflicts with the common assumption that the dependencies among objects should be preserved during recovery operations, we must support the user's purpose. Our solution to this problem is, when current operation of local linear undo/redo enters a synchronous zone, the framework asks the user if he/she wants to undo/redo the synchronous commands together. On the answer 'Yes', the framework will undo/redo synchronous commands automatically, else it will regards the current object as an independent object and undo/redo its states only. If the user changes his idea again and wants to keep the dependencies among objects, he can use the global linear undo/redo method or click on 'Yes' in the dialog box to make the framework switch local linear undo/redo to global linear undo/redo (Figure 8). Therefore the object-based linear undo model is flexible for the user to recombine the states of objects in a system.

Redo list

It is very often that the user does several steps of recovery operation and then submits a new command. For the traditional linear undo model, when a new command is submitted and appended to history list while redo list is not empty, one of the two methods would be taken: to clear the redo list or create a new branche in the history. We adopt the former method in our model.

When the new command is submitted out of any synchronous zone, only the redo list in current subhistory is cleared.

Suppose the user selects object A to undo (Figure 4). After several steps of undo operation, the current state of A is the state after the command 'Move (A, P_{a1})'. In the subhistory of A, the history list includes the RI records of RU1 and RU3, the redo list includes the RI records from RU5 to RU9. Now the user submits a new command 'Delete (A)'. This command is executed and its RI record is inserted at the position after the RI record of RU3, and then the redo list in this subhistory is cleared. In the main history (Figure 5), all the records of A from RU5 to RU9 are also cleared while the new RU record is inserted after RU3.

When the new command is submitted in a synchronous zone, the method on redo list depends on what kind of recovery operation that the user has chosen for this synchronous zone.

- If the user has chosen to undo/redo the current object only, then the new command can affect on the current object only because the synchronous dependency has been broken. If the redo list in the subhistory of current object is not empty, the framework will clear it and then clear its corresponding records in the main history.
- If the user has chosen to undo/redo synchronous commands together in this synchronous zone, the new command can affect on all the objects in this synchronous zone. The framework will assign the new command into the subhistories correspond to the objects. If any redo list in these subhistories is not empty, the framework will clear it and then clear its corresponding records in main history.

4. IMPLEMENTATION

The implementation of our model is based on TRIBASE, a UIMS system which is developed by SEIKO Instrument Incorporation (SEIKO, 1995). TRIBASE can support cooperation among multiple applications. It has been applied to commercial software products such as VLSI CAD systems.

The implemented system consists of three parts (Figure 7). The kernel part is TRIBASE which manages interfaces of applications through the user interface database (UIDB) and supports communication among applications. The sample application (SP) is a simple graphical editor which has its own UIDB records and a Command Reference Table that contains the definition of primitive commands and corresponding reverse commands. The recovery handler (RH) has its own UIDB records as well. The framework of our model is built in RH.

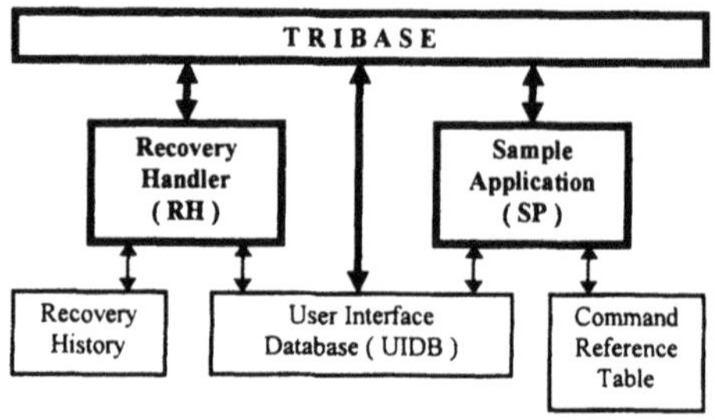

Figure 7. Architecture of the implemented system

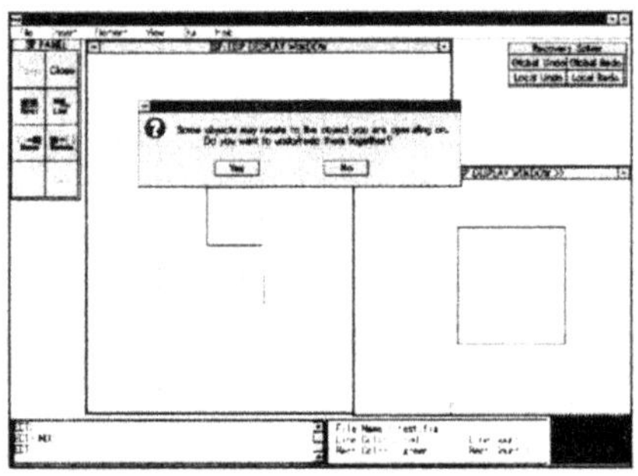

Figure 8. An example display of the sample application with the recovery handler panel and the synchronous undo/redo confirmation dialog box.

When SP begins to run, its application ID and Command Reference Table are sent to RH. When the user works on SP, the primitive commands are packed into recovery messages and sent to RH. All the recovery messages are written in a standard format. When a recovery message is transmitted from SP to RH, Do procedure of RH is invoked to create corresponding records of recovery history. When the user works on RH with undo or redo commands, the reverse commands or original commands are packed into recovery messages and sent to SP to be executed without creating any recovery message. Figure 8 is a sample display.

5. RELATED WORK

Our model is derived from the event-object recovery model of Wang and Green (Wang, 1991). In their model, the global history is divided into subhistories and encapsulated in corresponding objects. The framework is composed of a set of Recovery Objects (RO) which are nested in the user interface objets and organized in a predefined hierarchical structure. Each RO has its own list of Recovery Information (RI) and accepts recovery commands. The undo/redo method for each RI list is similar to US&R model. We use the concept of recovery unit of this model to represent interactive cycles and deal with synchronous commands. However, instead of encapsulating recovery histories into corresponding objects, we organize main history and subhistories into a global control framework. In this way, we can separate recovery utility from concrete applications. The separation makes it possible for us to design a common recovery handler which can serve multiple applications.

6. CONCLUSION AND FUTURE WORK

The object-based linear undo model proposed in this paper is derived form both traditional linear undo model and event-object recovery model. The framework of this model consists of a main history which represents the sequence of interactive cycles and subhistories which record the operations on corresponding objects. The main history can support traditional linear undo/redo operations and the subhistories can support object-based recovery operations. The framework of our model is flexible for the user to recombine the states of objects. Furthermore, the framework of our model can be separated from concrete applications. The separation makes it possible to design a common recovery handler which can serve multiple applications. It should be mentioned that the framework of our model can support not only linear undo mechanism but also nonlinear undo mechanism. We plan to propose object-based nonlinear undo model and improve object-based linear and nonlinear undo models to support collaborative systems.

7. REFERENCES

Archer, Jr., J. E., Conway, R. and Schneider, F. B. (1984), *User Recovery and Reversal in Interactive Systems*, ACM Trans. on Programming and Systems, Vol.6, No.1, January 1984, 1-19.

Berlage, T. (1994), *A Selective Undo Mechanism for Graphical User Interface Based on Command Objects*, ACM Trans. on Computer-Human Interaction, Vol.1, No.3, September 1994, 269-294.

Myers, B. A. and Kosbie, D. S. (1996), *Reusable Hierarchical Command Objects*, CHI 96, April 13-18, 1996, 261-267.

Prakash, A. and Knister, M. J. (1994), *A Framework for Undoing Actions in Collaborative Systems*, ACM Trans. on Computer-Human Interaction, Vol.1, No.4, December 1994, 295-330.

SEIKO Instruments Incorporation (1995), *TRIBASE Manuals*.

Vander Zanden, B., Myers, B. A., Giuse, D. A. and Szekely, P. (1994), *Integrating Pointer Variables into One-way Constraint Models*, ACM Trans. on Computer-Human Interaction, Vol.1, No.2, June 1994, 161-213.

Vitter, J. S. (1984), *US&R: A new Framework for Redoing*, IEEE Software, Vol.1, No.4, October 1984, 39-52.

Wang, H. and Green, M. (1991), *An Event-object Recovery Model for Object-oriented User Interfaces*, UIST 91, November 11-13, 1991, 107-115.

Yang, Y. (1988), *Undo Support Models*, Int. J. Man-Machine Studies **28**, 457-481.

44

The Role of Culture in Interface Acceptance

Vanessa Evers[1] and Donald Day[2]

[1] Faculty of Mathematics, Computer Science, Physics and Astronomy,
The University of Amsterdam,
1000 GG Amsterdam, the Netherlands
Vanessa@infosys7.infosys.unsw.edu.au

[2] School of Information Systems, The University of New South Wales,
Sydney NSW 2052 Australia
Donald_Day.chi@xerox.com

ABSTRACT In order for global software to be marketed successfully, the design of interfaces should accommodate users' cultural differences. This study examines users' culturally specific design preferences, and evaluates the attitudinal and behavioural consequences of satisfying or not satisfying such preferences. Participants consist of 206 international students, plus a control group of 38 Australian students. Results indicate that design preferences do affect interface acceptance, but that the path of influence leading from preference to attitude and behaviour varies from culture to culture. In particular, unexpected differences are noted between Chinese and Indonesian subjects. Conclusions emphasise the need for confirmatory research, both in terms of interface acceptance and in the design of information systems.

KEY WORDS globalisation, culture, interfaces, attitudes, user behaviour

1. INTRODUCTION

This paper discusses cultural factors in user acceptance of human-computer interfaces. It is grounded in beliefs that culture is a discernible variable in interface acceptance, and that interfaces designed for globally marketed software should accommodate users' cultural differences.

Most studies in this area approach acceptance issues from an ease of use and usefulness point of view (Davis, 1993; Hubona, 1996; Igbaria, 1994; Thovtrup, 1991). Some international interface design literature discusses the "internationalisation - localisation strategy" from an implementation point of view (Taylor, 1992; Luong et al, 1995; Uren et al., 1995). Other work, however, uses a more conceptual approach (Russo, 1993; Teasley et al, 1994; del Galdo, 1990; del Galdo et al, 1996). Russo and Boor (1993) deal with

> A range of cross-cultural elements that need to be considered by the interface designer: Text, Number, Date and Time Formats, Images, Symbols, Colours, Flow and Functionality.

Russo and Boor also discuss social norms and intuitive behaviour that influence the use of such elements. Fer-

Human–Computer Interaction: INTERACT'97 S. Howard, J. Hammond & G. Lindgaard (editors)
Published by Chapman & Hall

nandes (1995) gives developers specific interface design advice, based on his experience developing international software at Claris Corporation, and modelled on various countries' *non*-IT consumer products, advertising, traffic signs and architecture.

Studies comparing cultures in terms of information technology find significant differences in attitudes toward computers (Igbaria and Zviran, 1996; Choong & Salvendy, 1997; Omar, 1992). The cultural environment people live in is assumed to have a strong effect on how they conceptualise reality (Allwood, 1990).

To a certain extent, the interface is a marketing tool, just as vital to sales as is packaging for soft drinks. de Kerckhove (1991) describes design as a technology's public relations, sharpening its image in the marketplace. It is the "visible, audible or textual outer shape of cultural artefacts".

In the pilot study reported here, we address only globally marketed software packages. We ignore Usenet, Internet and other cyberspace facilities. We examine the extent to which culture influences user preferences in interface design. We also review whether these influences are consistent with established theories of cultural orientation (Hall, 1959; Hofstede, 1991; Trompenaars, 1993).

2. RESEARCH MODEL

This research uses the modified technology acceptance model (Figure 1), first proposed in Day (1996a). That model is based on Davis (1993), whose approach has been changed to incorporate cultural aspects.

2.1 Culturally specific design preferences

This first construct represents what users want the system to look like and what functionality should be included. For example, Sukaviriya et al (1990) tells us that in some Asian scripts there is no upper or lowercase letter writing. Under these circumstances, a function to change case would be completely useless. It would be irrelevant to user expectations.

2.2 Beliefs about system usefulness

This construct represents "the degree to which an individual believes that using a particular system would enhance his or her job performance" (Davis, 1993).

2.3 Perception about system ease of use

This construct represents "the degree to which an individual believes that using a particular system would be free of mental or physical effort" (Davis, 1989).

Ease of use may be defined experientially as well as culturally. For example, for people in the Arabic world a right-to-left flow of information seems natural. However, many Arabic users are so familiar with American software that they might find a different, culturally adapted design hard to adjust to -- even if it were more intuitive.

2.4 Attitude of satisfaction in using

This construct represents the degree to which a user's perceived personal needs and the need to perform specific tasks satisfactorily are met by a system (Goodhue and Straub, 1991).

3. RESEARCH PROPOSITIONS

Five propositions were developed directly from the research model (Figure 1).

1. Users' culturally specific design preferences influence their beliefs about system usefulness while using globally marketed software.
2. Users' culturally specific design preferences influence their perceptions about system ease of use while using globally marketed software.
3. Users' beliefs about system usefulness influence their attitudes of satisfaction while using globally marketed software.
4. Users' perceptions about ease of use influences their attitudes of satisfaction while using globally marketed software.
5. Users' attitudes of satisfaction in using globally marketed software influence their anticipated system use behaviour with such products.

4. METHOD

4.1 Sample

The international subjects were 206 students from the Foundation Studies Program of The University of New South Wales (UNSW), Sydney, Australia. Subjects

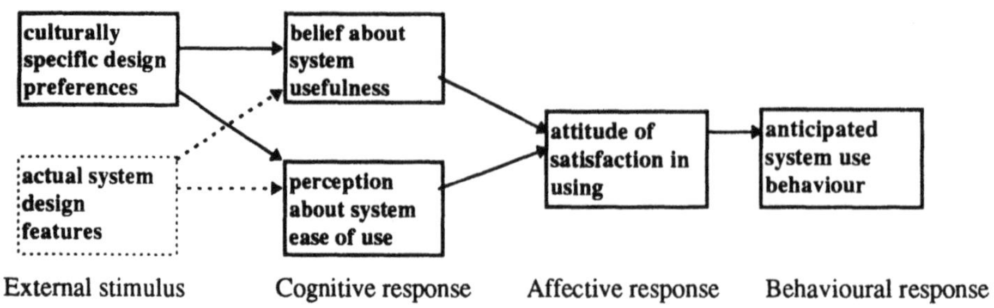

Figure 1. Modified Technology Acceptance Model (after Davis, 1993)

were chosen because of participation in an orientation program, which we felt would encourage their co-operation.

The sample consisted of three main groups: Indonesians (44 males, 31 females), Chinese and Hong Kongese (27 males, 39 females), and "Others" (33 males, 27 females). This latter group was largely from other Asian countries like Taiwan, Singapore and Japan. Thus, subjects were excluded from data analysis because their numbers would not support statistical significance. The majority of subjects were between 18 and 21 years old, had some computer experience, and had a fair knowledge of English. Chinese and Indonesian subjects were assigned to their groups on the basis of language, cultural identification, amount of exposure to other cultures, and length of time family had lived in a specific area.

An Australian control group consisted of 38 undergraduate students from UNSW, selected for dominant culture homogeneity and relative lack of multicultural influence. Twenty-seven of these students were male, 11 female. Most were between 18 and 21 years old, and had some computer experience. This control group was included to ensure that observed effects would in fact be due to cultural differences, rather than to extraneous non-cultural factors. (If an effect were similar in both the main sample and in the control group, cultural differences could not be presumed to be the cause.)

4.2 Materials and procedure

Data were collected by means of an eight-page questionnaire. The questionnaire was reviewed in advance by both the UNSW Institute of Languages and the UNSW Institute of English Language, to ensure that questions were culturally neutral (Day & Evers, 1997). This instrument consisted of 39 anchored Likert-scale items, 22 open-ended questions, 15 forced-choice selections, and one battery of three scenario-based options.

The survey was administered during a pre-session orientation sponsored by the UNSW Foundation Studies Program. Subjects were allowed 40 minutes to complete the questionnaire. Control group data were collected in two tutorials at the UNSW School of Information Systems.

4.3 Measures

Key research model constructs were operationalised as follows.

Culturally specific design preferences. Eighteen interface design features were presented to subjects. Response options were anchored on a 6-point Likert scale.

Belief about system usefulness. This construct was measured by asking to what extent computers would be better in performing certain actions. This was operationalised as preferences.

Perception about system ease of use. The perceived ease of use of a culturally adapted interface, and users' input device.

Attitude of satisfaction in using. Subjects were asked how satisfied they would be in using culturally sensitive software.

Anticipated system use behaviour. Subjects were asked whether it would take more or less time to learn a system designed for their culture, compared to one with a universal interface.

In addition, potential confounds such as age, gender, experience, economical situation, opportunity in education, direction used while reading scripts, contact with technology, and contact with other cultures were assessed to evaluate potential extraneous influences in the findings.

Since the study was designed to assess the cultural bases of interface acceptance, several culturally specific variables were examined to judge their impact on key constructs in the research model. Included were variables addressing

- *uncertainty avoidance* (whether uncertainty is perceived as threatening; Hofstede, 1991),
- *need for significant others*,
- *parallel versus sequential actions* (to do 'more things at once' or 'one thing at a time'),
- *diffusion versus specificity* (whether business and personal relationships are separated clearly; Trompenaars, 1993),
- *particularism versus universalism* (whether behaviour is rule-based versus relationship-based; Trompenaars, 1993),
- *collectivism versus individualism* (whether people like to work and make decisions in groups versus alone; Hofstede, 1991; Trompenaars, 1993),
- *high context versus low context* (whether meaning resides in context, or that information instead should be stated explicitly), and
- *transference* (the extent to which a person blames others or one's self).

A description of these variables can be found in (Hoft, 1990).

4.4 Statistical analysis

Following data entry using SPSS-PC, univariate statistics were generated for all questions. Response items were combined using reliability analysis techniques, to create scales for design preferences (α = .8), to assess system usefulness (α = .77), and for creation of a culture of origin profile (α = .62). Reliability levels for all three scales are high enough to be deemed sufficient (DeVellis, 1991). Data were corrected for a 12.3 percent item response bias, then re-categorised into 5-point response scales.

Next, Pearson correlations were run for interconstruct effects as predicted by the research model, and cross-tabulations were generated to add texture to the interpretation of significant correlations.

5. RESULTS

5.1 Descriptive statistics

In this section, statistics from the largely Asian main sample are followed (in parentheses) by corresponding results from the Australian control group.

In terms of user expectations, 72.9% *(28.9%)* liked lots of different colours, 68.3% *(31.6%)* liked soft colours, 54.2% *(63.2%)* liked pull down menu's, 54.3% *(31.4%)* liked fixed menu's, 43.1% *(8.3%)* liked text based interfaces, and 63.8% *(78.4%)* liked GUI interfaces.

In regard to input and output devices, we found that 88.5% *(72.2%)* liked using a mouse, 66.2% *(21.1%)* liked joysticks, and 73.1% *(47.1%)* liked touch screens. In all, 86.5% *(64.9%)* strongly liked sounds.

In examining user satisfaction, we found that 67.9% *(86.8%)* would be satisfied using technology adapted to their culture. Only 34% *(65.8%)* thought it would take less time to learn a culturally adapted interface. And 52.7% *(34.2%)* preferred to instruct a machine with detailed commands rather than providing only general direction.

In examining cultural variables, we found that 68.7% *(39.5%)* scored high on uncertainty avoidance. About 75.6% *(57.9%)* were found to be diffuse, and 40.8% *(18.4%)* tended towards universalism. About 40.8% percent *(36.8%)* were collectivist, and 59.7% *(100%)* had a high context orientation.

In analysing these univariate results, we drafted the following interface preferences profile for Asian users of globally marketed software. Its validity will need to be verified in future research involving subjects responding from within their home cultures.

Asians prefer soft colours, fixed (versus pull-down) menus, and explicit, text-based (not symbolic) interfaces. They like the mouse as an input device best, with the touch screen second. Sound is somewhat important, as well.

Asians place relatively low value on the cultural adaptiveness of software, possibly because they believe

Table 1.
INTERFACE DESIGN PREFERENCES, CHINESE VS. INDONESIANS

Chinese (n = 66)			Indonesian (n = 75)		
Mean	SD	Interface Design Features	Mean	SD	F1, p<.05
3.09	1.2	Strong bright colours	3.55	1.2	NS
2.56	1.0	Soft colours	2.09	0.8	5.2
2.00	.9	A lot of different colours	2.37	1.1	5.3
4.45	1.0	Black and white displays	3.95	1.3	15.9
3.06	1.0	Text based interfaces	2.70	0.9	NS
2.34	.9	GUI	2.36	1.1	NS
2.32	.8	Windows	2.37	0.8	NS
2.41	1.0	Pop-up menus	2.15	0.8	5.7
2.60	0.8	Pull-down menus	2.59	1.0	NS
2.69	0.8	Fixed menus	2.33	0.9	NS
1.74	0.8	Mouse	1.64	0.8	NS
2.35	1.2	Joystick	2.22	1.1	NS
2.13	1.1	Touch screen	1.88	0.8	6.9
2.22	1.0	Data glove	1.81	0.8	4.5
1.76	0.8	Sounds	1.52	0.7	3.6
1.62	0.8	Multimedia	1.41	0.5	12.8

Notes (1) NS = non-significant; (2) In terms of means, the smaller the number the more strongly the feature is preferred.

it would take longer to learn culturally adaptive interfaces. They also prefer to instruct computers using detailed commands.

In terms of intercultural anthropology, Asians tend to mix private and business matters, see uncertainty as threatening, consider relationships and trust important, and prefer to work in teams.

That Asians prefer to instruct computers using detailed commands, find uncertainty as threatening, and prefer text-based rather than symbolic interfaces is not what one would expect from the orthodox intercultural literature.

One of the key findings of this study was that there are not only interface-relevant cultural differences between Asians and Australians (as expected), but that significant differences also exist within Asian groups -- specifically, between Indonesians and Chinese.

Table 1 shows the mean interface design feature preferences expressed by these two Asian subsamples. These data suggest that Indonesians like soft colours, black and white displays and pop-up menus more than do Chinese. Also, Indonesians seem to like new technology and alternative input and output (e.g., sounds, touch screens, data gloves and multimedia) more than do Chinese. On the other hand, the use of many different colours seems more appropriate for Chinese.

5.2 Associative statistics

Figure 2 summarises significant correlation results. Although correlations were not very substantial, we found enough significant relationships to support the research model.

Culturally specific design preferences relate significantly to system usefulness in all three groups (Proposition 1). The relation seems to be the strongest for the Chinese.

Design preferences influence ease of use (Proposition 2) for the total sample and for the Indonesian subgroup. There are significant relations between system usefulness and attitude of satisfaction (Proposition 3), between ease of use and attitude of satisfaction (Proposition 4), and between attitude of satisfaction and anticipated system use behaviour (Proposition 5).

It is interesting to note that the acceptance process seems to flow differently for the two subgroups. For the

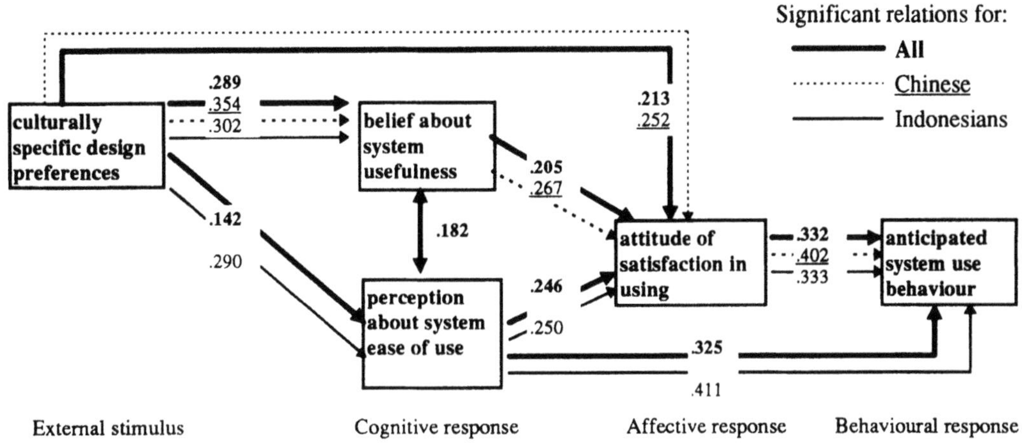

Figure 2. Significant Correlation Results

Note Every significant interconstruct relationship is represented by an arrow. Correlations are in **bold** for the entire sample, underlined for the Chinese, and in regular type for the Indonesians.

Chinese, acceptance is routed through preferences, usefulness and attitude of satisfaction. However, for the Indonesians it seems to move along the ease of use side of the model. Also, ease of use seems to influence behaviour more strongly than does attitude of satisfaction.

This implies that for the Indonesians, user preferences do influence both their beliefs about system usefulness and their perceptions about ease of use. However, it seems that the Indonesian user is only satisfied by the usability of the system. System use behaviour also is affected by perceived ease of use.

In contrast, results suggest that Chinese attitudes of satisfaction are attributable to user preferences and beliefs about usefulness. System use behaviour is attributable to attitudes of satisfaction, as expected.

We found that cultural variables relate significantly to interface design preferences for the main sample, as well as for the Chinese and Indonesian subgroups.

System ease of use and system usefulness affect each other only in the main sample, with a very weak correlation. Because of this, we can assume there is no interconstruct relationship between ease of use and usefulness.

The most interesting observation in the Australian control group is that neither ease of use nor usefulness seem to drive attitude of satisfaction (propositions 3 and 4). Attitude of satisfaction is influenced by culturally specific preferences in design and by cultural variables.

6. DISCUSSION

6.1 Conclusions

This research sought to extend previous research by examining the Davis (1993) model in a cultural context. Findings demonstrate the existence of cultural differences in terms of interface acceptance in globally marketed software. Not only do groups have different preferences in design features, but there also are differences in the acceptance process.

It seems that Chinese find usefulness a more discernible variable, while ease of use (which also directly influences system use behaviour) is more important for Indonesians. This suggests that Chinese will try to work with a useful interface, even when it is hard to use. Indonesians, however, will tend to give up more easy when an interface is hard to understand. This finding could be related to anthropological literature that describes Indonesians as higher in uncertainty avoidance than the Chinese (Hofstede, 1991). It could explain as well the importance of a usable interface for Indonesians.

Also interesting is the fact that Indonesians' beliefs about ease of use directly influence their anticipated system use behaviour. This implies that when they find a system easy to use, they expect to be happy in using the system. It seems that being genuinely satisfied with the system is less important than the knowledge that it will be easy to use.

It is hard to explain why preferences in interface design directly influence Chinese attitudes of satisfaction. This effect implies that when preferences for design features are met, users will be satisfied with the interface. There seems to be no need to find out whether the interface is easy to use. Maybe Chinese find that their demands for ease of use are met when the interface looks the way they want it to. Usefulness influences their attitudes of satisfaction as well. Therefore, we can assume that a system's external design features are not enough to satisfy the Chinese. Certain functionality levels must be met, as well.

Within the Australian control group, attitudes of satisfaction also were influenced directly by design preferences. This suggests that in this sense Australians are similar to Chinese. However, the Australians' lack of a need to fulfil ease of use and usefulness demands in order to feel satisfied is worth noting. It seems that Australians find an interface satisfactory when it meets their preferences in interface design *even if the system is either hard to use or not useful to them.* It could be that Australians separate interface satisfaction from system satisfaction; perhaps they can be dissatisfied with a system, while at the same time being satisfied with the interface they are using. This would suggest they put more emphasis on the way an interface looks than on the functionality it provides.

The finding that different groups form different paths through the research model (Table 2) supports the supposition that human-computer interface acceptance is indeed influenced by culture.

These subjects are not believed to be atypical in any substantial way versus their reference populations. Therefore, these findings are at least generisable to Asians of the age group from which these subjects were drawn.

Table 2.
CULTURALLY BASED ACCEPTANCE PATHS

Chinese
preferences ⇒ usefulness ⇒ satisfaction ⇒ behaviour
Indonesians
preferences ⇒ ease of use ⇒ satisfaction ⇒ behaviour
Australians
preferences ⇒ satisfaction ⇒ behaviour

6.2 Future research

The current study is the pilot for a larger, multi-year effort. The authors are aware of its several methodological shortcomings (Day, 1996b). In particular, the lack of strong correlations and the use of international students rather than workplace subjects are of concern.

Future research will include alternate data collection modes such as interviews, direct observation of user behaviour, and focus groups. Also, questionnaires will be administered to overseas subjects in their home cultures, to minimise potential cultural contamination problems.

REFERENCES

Allwood, C. & Wang, Z-M. (1990). Conceptions of computers among students in China and Sweden. *Computers in Human Behaviour* 6, 185-199.

Choong, Y-Y & Salvendy, G. (1997). Design of icons for use by Chinese in mainland China. In "Shared Values and Shared Interfaces", a special issue of *Interacting with Computers* (forthcoming).

Davis, F. (1989). Perceived usefulness, perceived ease of use, and user acceptance of information technology. *MIS Quarterly* 13, 319-340.

Davis, F. (1993). User acceptance of information technology: system characteristics, user perception and behavioural impacts. *International Journal of Man Machine Studies* 38, 475-487.

Day, D. (1996a). Cultural bases of interface acceptance: foundations. In *People and Computers XI*, 35-47. Proceedings of HCI'96 (August 20-23, 1996, Imperial College). London: Springer-Verlag.

Day, D. (1996b). Cultural bases of interface acceptance:

methods. In *Proceedings, 2nd AIS Americas Conference*, 716-718. (August 15-18). Phoenix: Assn. for Information Systems.

Day, D. & Evers, V. (1997). Instrument development for multicultural usability studies. Submitted to People and Computers XII (HCI' 97). Bristol, UK, 13-15 August

DeVellis, R. (1991). *Scale Development: Theory and Applications*. Newbury Park, Calif.: Sage.

Fernandes, T. (1995). *Global Interface Design*. London: Academic Press.

Del Galdo, E. (1990). Internationalisation and translation: some guidelines for the design of human - computer interfaces. In J. Nielsen (Ed.), *Designing User Interfaces for International Use*, 1-10. New York: Elsevier.

del Galdo, E. & Nielsen, J. (1996). *International User Interfaces*. New York: Wiley.

Goodhue, D. & Straub, D. (1991). Security concerns of system users. *Information & Management* 20(1), 13-27.

Hall, E. (1959). *The Silent Language*. New York: Doubleday.

Hofstede, G. (1991). *Cultures and Organisations: Software of the Mind*, 125. New York: McGraw-Hill.

Hoft, N. (1990). Developing a cultural model. In J. Nielsen & E. del Galdo (Eds.), *Designing User Interfaces for International Use*, 41-73. New York: Elsevier.

Hubona, G. & Blanton, J. (1996). Evaluating system design features. *International Journal of Human Computer Studies* 44, 93-118.

Igbaria, M., Schiffman, S. & Wieckowski, T. (1994). The respective roles of perceived usefulness and perceived fun in the acceptance of microcomputer technology. *Behaviour and Information technology* 13, 349-361.

Igbaria, M. & Zviran, M. (1996). Comparison of end-user computing characteristics in the US, Israel and Taiwan. *Information and Management* 30, 1-13.

de Kerckhove, D. (1991). *Brainframes: Technology, Mind and Business*. Utrecht, the Netherlands: Bosch & Keuning BSO/ORIGIN.

Luong, T., Lok, J., Taylor, D. & Driscoll, K. (1995). *Internationalisation: Developing Software for Global Markets*. New York: John Wiley & Sons.

Omar, M. (1992). Attitudes of college students towards computers: a comparative study in the Middle East. *Computers in Human Behaviour* 8, 249-257.

Russo, P. & Boor, S. (1993). How fluent is your interface? designing for international users. *Human Factors in Computing Systems*, 24-29. Proceedings of INTERCHI '93, Amsterdam. New York: ACM.

Sukaviriya, P. & and Moran, L. (1990). User interfaces for Asia. In J. Nielsen (Ed.). *Designing Interfaces for International Use*, 189-218. New York, Elsevier.

Taylor, D. (1992). *Global Software: Developing Applications for the International Market*. New York: Springer-Verlag.

Teasley, B., Leventhal, L., Blumenthal, B., Instone, K. & Stone, D. (1994). Cultural diversity in user interface design: are intuitions enough? *SIGCHI Bulletin* 26(1), 36-40.

Thovtrup, H. & Nielsen, J. (1991). Assessing the usability of a user interface standard. *CHI'91 Human factors in Computing Systems*, 335-341. Proceedings of CHI'91. New York: ACM.

Trompenaars, F. (1993). *Riding the Waves of Culture: Understanding Cultural Diversity in Business*, 6-10. London: Nicholas Brealey.

Uren, E., Howard, R. & Perinotti, T. (1995). *Software Internationalisation and Localisation: An Introduction*. New York: Van Nostrand Reinhold.

45

Free Usability Data

Randolph G. Bias

BMC Software, Inc.
10415 Morado Circle
Austin, Texas 78727
USA
rbias@bmc.com

ABSTRACT Convergent software industry thrusts of user-centered design, cost-justifying usability, and discount usability engineering drive usability engineers toward gathering the least expensive user data possible. What could be better than free data? This short paper encourages usability engineers to capture user data that already exist in their organizations, and points them to likely sources of these data.

KEYWORDS usability, discount usability, user data, user-centered design

1. FOUR ASSERTIONS

- Human beings are remarkably similar.
- Computer programmers are human.
- Human beings are remarkably different.
- Product development resources are finite.

These conspire to make usability key in software development. Human beings are seductively similar – most have two functioning eyes and arms, fingers roughly the same size, memory ranging only from fair to "I wish it was better." Too, programmers are human, and understandably tend to think if they can use a computer program, other humans likely can too.

These superficial similarities mask vital differences in cognitive capabilities and experiences. Thus we differ wildly in what we find "usable." This, and the programmers' tendency to depend on their own intuitions, has led to a long, inglorious history of unusable user interfaces (UIs). The solution is a strong focus on "user-centered design" (Norman, 1990), whereby user data inform product designs.

Plus, product development resources being finite, "discount usability methods" (Nielsen, 1993) for collecting these user data have emerged as a key approach to user-centered design.

2. DISCOUNT USABILITY

Discount usability engineering methods, such as usability walkthroughs, can be employed by usability professionals (and sometimes the software developers themselves) at low cost, and yet yield ample, high quality usability data to help steer product re-designs.

3. WHY IS USABILITY A PROBLEM?

There are various reasons why software UIs are not wondrously usable. An organizational inhibitor to good UI design is "the limitation of contact between

Human–Computer Interaction: INTERACT'97 S. Howard, J. Hammond & G. Lindgaard (editors)
Published by Chapman & Hall

designers/developers and users" (Mayhew & Bias, 1994, p. 296). Whether for reasons of corporate propriety, or expense, or a fear of allowing customers to meet with "bit heads," software developers have tended not to communicate directly with users.

4. A SOLUTION: "DEVELOOPS"

One rich yet nearly free solution is to establish feedback loops between product development and other organizational groups (thus, "develoops"), to capture user data that are in-house already, the least expensive data imaginable. At BMC Software, these feedback loops met with unanimous support, but they required a tailored, one-group-at-a-time approach.

4.1. Customer Support

Customer support is a rich source of quantitative and qualitative user data. Often in a company there's a structured feedback loop between customer support and R&D; indeed, customer support may be the primary source of new product features. At BMC there are regular meetings between support and R&D.

4.2. Sales and Pre-sales Support

Any sales force is busy enough without forming new communications links. But sales has much direct customer contact, especially with first-time users, so are likely to have unique wisdom about a product. At BMC, the corporate intranet site is used for the R&D-sales loop. The pre-sales folks maintain, and share with R&D, a LotusNotes database for each product.

4.3. Training

It is easy to imagine a course instructor thinking, "I hate this part of the class, it's so hard for me to explain." **THAT** part of the product needs to be communicated back to R&D. At BMC, the intranet site is used for this feedback loop.

4.4. Services

Consultants who serve customers in various roles – set-up, trouble-shooting, tailored configurations – represent another source of user data. The intranet site, again, is the feedback vehicle used at BMC.

4.5. Caution Zones

First, a loop is a loop, implying information flow in both directions. R&D must track reported usability problems, and alert the initiator when a fix is implemented. Further, other groups benefit from early notice about optimal current product work flows.

Second, you may hear that someone had fed back information to R&D, but was not convinced that it did any good. Problem tracking is an imperative.

Third, drive feedback loops from all directions. Individual product developers should be convinced about the value of user data to the success of their designs. Other groups need to recognize the value of their efforts to the usability (and therefore customer satisfaction and therefore sales) of the company's products. Further, each group (and manager) may need help appreciating how ancillary benefits address their central charter, benefits such as fewer calls to customer support and additional marketing help.

Fourth, what's GOOD about these products? Encourage all of the people in your organization to communicate particularly usable and well-liked areas of your products. This affords R&D positive reinforcement for their good work. Further, it identifies areas that require **no** further usability attention, and should be left alone (and, indeed, used as models for further extensions).

6. REFERENCES

Mayhew, D. J., & Bias, R. G. (1994) Organizational inhibitors and facilitators. In Bias, R. G., & Mayhew, D. J. (Eds.), Cost-justifying usability. Boston: Academic Press.

Nielsen, J. (1993). Usability engineering. Boston: AP Professional.

Norman, D. A. (1990). The design of everyday things. New York: Doubleday Currency.

Automated Theory-based Procurement Evaluation

Andrew Howes, Stephen J. Payne, David Moffat

School of Psychology
Cardiff University of Wales, PO Box 901,
Cardiff CF1 3YG. WALES, U.K.
HowesA@cardiff.ac.uk

ABSTRACT In this paper we report progress on software for evaluating computer interfaces for the purposes of procurement. The software takes a description of the interface to be evaluated and outputs metrics describing the consistency of the interface. The output metrics are determined by automatically constructing a Task-Action Grammar from a manual description. We illustrate the evaluation tool with examples of evaluations of abbreviation structures and syntactic/semantic alignment.

KEYWORDS Metrics, Usability evaluation, Automatic tools, Task-Action Grammar, Consumer product

1. INTRODUCTION

Purchasers of new applications are often presented with a host of competitors, from which a choice must be made partly on the basis of which is easiest to learn and use. The most learnable and usable package will reduce training costs and, with a confident user community, be more effective during its life span. However, limited information is provided by manufacturers about the usability of their own software.

This information gap is partially bridged by trade magazines that review the usability and learnability of new software products (Bawa, 1994). Such magazines serve software purchasers who have become suspicious of the manufacturers' guarantee that their own software is easy to learn and use. We refer to this use of evaluation as procurement evaluation and contrast it to design evaluation, which has been much more widely studied in HCI. Ideally, procurement evaluation might be performed by purchasers, and therefore requires techniques that assume less expertise from the evaluator than does design evaluation. Procurement evaluation need only deliver summative information: It need not inform redesign, and therefore must report only on the quality of a system, not on the determinants of quality. Furthermore, despite its modest ambitions, successful procurement evaluation could have a long-term impact on the quality of design, because well-informed purchasers create an increased pressure on designers and manufacturers.

Consider an example of the procurement evaluation context: PC Magazine, which is published by Ziff Davis Ltd., and which advertises itself as a "lab-based magazine", prints reports on software usability compiled by their own in-house usability laboratory. In the March 1995 issue of this magazine there is a usability report on a number of available Personal Information Manager packages (PIMs) which provide diary-like functions. Each package is tested empirically by a number of evaluators and is scored on a number of indices of usability (page 178). Two of these indices are: productivity, or "the proportion of correctly-completed tasks measured against the time taken to finish them"; intuitiveness, which is "the effectiveness of the on-line help and the manuals, and how many references were made to them, measured against the number of calls to the supervisor."

We have been investigating how to automate the generation of indices similar to productivity and intuitiveness with a computer-based tool. Others have started to explore this idea (Barnard & May, 1993; Byrne, Wood, Sukaviriya, Foley & Kieras, 1994; Farenc, Liberati, Barthet, 1996). An automatic evaluation tool can be thought of as a function E that takes as input a description of the system, S, and outputs metrics indicating the usability and learnability of the system. In this paper we focus on measuring

Human–Computer Interaction: INTERACT'97 S. Howard, J. Hammond & G. Lindgaard (editors)
Published by Chapman & Hall

consistency (Payne & Green, 1986). Consistency is a measure of the degree to which the methods used to achieve goals share the same structure, and is one factor that influences the learnability of the device. Despite the amount of research that has been done on consistency new computer interfaces are still being produced with inconsistencies. For example, the Psion Organiser 3c used the keys "Psion-D" to change an entry in "Agenda" mode but in "Time" mode "Psion-D" means "delete". In this paper we specify E such that it gives a number C indicating how consistent the interface is, thus:

$$C = E(S)$$

where an improvement in the design of the interface would increase the value of C. (A more sophisticated version of the function would output further metrics.). In this paper we refer to three descriptions of the interface: The *input description* (S); the *intermediate description* (some psychologically motivated description of the knowledge required to use the device); and the *evaluation description* (C).

As Long (1989) and Barnard (1990) point out, work on interface evaluation in Human-Computer Interaction has tended to focus on specifying constraints on the intermediate description (e.g. Card, Moran, Newell, 1983; Payne & Green, 1986), rather than on determining how to deliver the psychological knowledge embedded within this description to the analyst.

The evaluation function must be both useful and usable for evaluators involved in the procurement process. To be usable, the input description needs to be readily available and the resulting evaluation description has to use simple and intuitive representational forms.

In this paper we report an evaluation tool that takes as input a description derived from a manual. Many manuals provide precise and formalised statements of how commands are achieved (e.g. the Unix command manual), or an on-line list of command specifications (e.g. Microsoft-Word provides a text-file listing of 337 commands, each with its menu location and keyboard accelerator).

To address usefulness we have based the evaluation function on Task-Action Grammars (Payne & Green, 1986, 1989). TAG is a formal notation for representing the knowledge necessary to use computer interfaces (Payne & Green, 1986, 1989 -see also D-TAG, Howes & Payne, 1990). The model uses semantic features within a rewrite grammar to expose how similarities and differences between interface tasks and methods can affect perceived consistency. TAG's sensitivity to the users' tasks means that it is not subject to the criticisms of Grudin (1989). By embedding psychological constraints within an intermediate description, TAG can achieve considerable savings in the expertise required for the inference of evaluation descriptions. However, the production of the rewrite grammar is itself a highly specialised and rather demanding skill. It is the process of producing a grammar that we describe how to automate in this paper.

The sections below illustrate two evaluation tools that we have built. The first introduces the general idea of automating evaluation and focuses on the evaluation of abbreviation consistency and performance time and the second looks at the evaluation of aspects of consistency that are dependent on the task semantics.

2. AUTOMATED EVALUATION

As an example of automated evaluation, consider the Unix C-shell. In this device the command to "remove a directory" is communicated by the user typing the character sequence "rmdir" and then typing the name of the directory. This method of communicating commands is not only used in command-oriented operating systems such as Unix and Ms-Dos, but also in text processing systems such as LaTeX, and to define "accelerators" in highly display-based (Graphic User Interface) environments like the Apple Macintosh and Windows. It is not, as is sometimes claimed, a mode of communication that has been entirely replaced by display-based devices. Moreover, the problem of designing consistent command syntax is not bound to keyboard-based inputs. It is also a potential problem for the design of voice activated systems and gestural interfaces, and is a very real problem for the design of consumer products such as Video Recorders. (There are many millions of Video Recorders, only a few are operated with a mouse.)

Here we talk through an evaluation scenario in which an evaluator compares the Unix commands for manipulating files and directories with the file manipulation commands for another (in this case

Interface: Unix (or NewUnix)		
Command Syntax	**Abbreviation**	**Words**
rmdir directory-name	rmdir	"remove directory"
mkdir directory-name	mkdir	"make directory"
cd directory-name	cd	"change directory"
ls directory-name (or lsdir)	ls (or lsdir)	"list directory"
more file-name	more	"more file"
rm file-name	rm	"remove file"

Table 1. The description of the (New)Unix interface(s) provided to the Evaluation Tool.

hypothetical) interface called NewUnix. The evaluation tool (written in Prolog) produces outputs that describe the consistency of the interface and the average performance time. The evaluation steps are:

(1) Provide a description of the relevant aspects of the interface. For our demonstration the description of the interface is provided in the form of the manual's description of the action sequence required for the command and the words that the command is an abbreviation of (see Table 1 for a description of some aspects of Unix).

(2) Run the evaluation function over the device description to learn that the average optimal performance time is 667 milliseconds and that the index of consistency is 1.2 (see Table 2 for an idea of how this information might be presented).

(3) Having evaluated the Unix interface, we can now move on to evaluating the NewUnix interface. This involves the same procedure. The description of NewUnix differs from Unix only in that the abbreviation for communicating the words "list directory" is "lsdir" rather than "ls" (see Table 1 again). This small change will illustrate the sensitivity of the consistency and performance time measures.

(4) The evaluation function can now be run over the NewUnix description. It says that the average optimal performance time is 767 milliseconds and that the index of consistency is 1.5 (Table 2).

(5) We have now generated two evaluations for two different interfaces: Unix and NewUnix. It can be seen from the output of the evaluation function that NewUnix (with a consistency coefficient of 1.5) is more learnable than Unix (with a consistency coefficient of 1.2) but that Unix (with an average performance time of 667 milliseconds) offers marginally more efficient performance times than NewUnix (with an average performance time of 767 milliseconds). This kind of trade-off is a common feature of interface designs.

These simple metrics raise many questions. For example, should the index of consistency be weighted for the frequency of use of the commands? We discuss these issues later.

Our prototype demonstrates the coarse properties of an automated evaluation tool, but no more. The important features to note are: (a) that a person using this tool need only specify the actions required for a command as they appear in the manual (grammatic analysis is not required), (b) that the tool in the form of a computer program performs an evaluation, and (c) that the output of the function can be quickly interpreted by someone who is not trained in psychology. Comparing consistency indices of 1.2 and 1.5 immediately reveals that the NewUnix interface is superior to Unix in this respect. We believe that indices of this form are

Interface Evaluator Report	Unix	NewUnix
Consistency coefficient	1.2	1.5
Average performance time	667ms	767ms

Table 2: Output of the evaluation tool for the two interfaces.

suitable for use in procurement evaluation and perhaps for publication in reviews such as those found in PC magazine.

3. SEMANTIC/SYNTACTIC ALIGNMENT

One of the most important features of the Task-Action Grammar (TAG) notation (Payne and Green, 1986, 1989) is that it can be used to evaluat semantic/syntactic alignment: The degree to which the different syntactic structures used in an interface correspond to the major semantic categories of the tasks.

The evaluation tool described in this section utilises this feature by constructing a database of TAG rules that capture how task-descriptions are mapped into the required action-sequences. A rule takes a set of semantic features of the task-description, and returns a sequence of syntactic tokens, i.e. a fully specified action-sequence. The consistency index is calculated on the basis of the number of rules required to represent all of the tasks.

One of the hardest problems that a human analyst faces when constructing a TAG is selecting semantic features to describe the tasks. The evaluation tool solves this problem by taking the English language sentence that is given as the manual definition of the command and using each word in the sentence as an individual semantic feature. We assume that the manual contains meaningful definitions and that the same words are used for the same concepts throughout the manual (the use of synonyms will cause the evaluation tool problems). In the current version, some simplification of sentences may be necessary before they are passed to the evaluation tool.

Rules are found from the set of manual-derived exemplars by examining their semantic and syntactic properties, and grouping the exemplars into classes that can be described by a single rule. The largest classes are preferred. In order to explain how this is achieved we introduce the concepts of a semantic characterisation and a syntactic class of commands. A set of semantic features is said to characterise a set of commands if those commands all share those features, and if no other commands share them. A general syntactic form can represent a set of commands if the syntactic form of each of those commands can be seen as a special case of that general form. For example, in Table 1, the commands that take a "directory-name" parameter are exactly the ones that are defined by the word / feature "directory". Mappings from a feature-set to a syntactic form are constructed only when a semantic characterisation and a syntactic class capture exactly the same set of commands, i.e. they are aligned.

The TAG constraints are not sufficient to specify a single grammar for a language: There are typically many grammars that satisfy its constraints. Here we assume that the most compact grammar for a set of tasks is the most useful for determining metrics.

In order to apply this assumption the evaluation tool needs heuristics to guide it to the most efficient grammar first. The prototype follows a locally-guided strategy which leads to an approximation of the most efficient grammar. The algorithm is:

1. Find the set CS1, that contains the largest number of examplars and that is semantically characterisable by some feature-set, call it FS1;
2. Check that there exists a syntactic form for every exemplar in CS1, call this syntactic form, SF1;
3. If (2) holds then:
    4. There exists a mapping rule FS1 $\rightarrow$ SF1;
    5. Remove the features that are common to all exemplars that are in CS1 and apply this algorithm to the remainder (recurse to step 1).
    6. Apply this algorithm to the commands that were not in CS1 (recurse to step 1).

7. else, if (2) does not hold then:
    8. Backtrack to step 1 and repeat the algorithm with the next-largest command-set, CS2.

In initial tests this algorithm has lead to a good approximation of the most efficient grammar.

The algorithm constructs rules that satisfy the TAG-constraints because of the checks in steps 1 and 2 that the set CS1 (or CS2 etc.) is simultaneously characterisable by the task semantics and by the command syntax. It also finds the most general rules because it tries the feature sets that characterise the largest number of exemplars first.

The algorithm terminates when there are no more commands in step 1 to be covered. The grammar is the collection of rules of the form FSi → SFi that were found each time the algorithm went through step 4.

To illustrate this algorithm we describe how it constructs a grammar for exemplars from an artificial interface called the "Toy Post Office" (Payne & Green, 1989). Payne and Green reported an experiment using three languages numbered 1, 2 and 3, in order of decreasing consistency. It turned out that Language 1 was easiest for subjects to learn, and is also describable (in a hand-written TAG grammar) in the fewest rules. While Language 3 was the hardest, and required several rules more at the highest level to describe it.

The "Toy Post Office" does not have a manual from which to select task descriptions. Instead we have used the English Language descriptions of tasks used by Payne and Green in their published paper. For example, Payne and Green (1989), page 219, state that to achieve the task, "high priority request for information about a missing brown boxer dog" then the user should type "DOG BOXER HIGH BROWN."

Each of the three grammars took the evaluation tool about 10 seconds to generate on a 486-PC running SWI-Prolog on the Linux OS. As expected, the grammars were similar to those written by Payne and Green. They only differ where the evaluation tool is unable to handle null-rewrites (where a sub-phrase may sometimes be allowed to be empty).

In describing how the tool constructed the grammars we look only at the second half of the languages (commands s17 to s32) and we only compare languages 1 and 2. We will not explain what the tasks achieve, we are only interested here in the relationship between their semantics and their syntax.

In Table 3 the task-description given to the evaluation tool for command s28 was: "Change person X's password to Y, with low priority." The program takes all of these words to be semantic features. Notice that the task features are not identical to their action tokens. The program determines correspondences by looking for configural alignments in the whole set of exemplars. For example, the feature "person" goes with the token name, because they both occur in the same command set. Also notice that apparently superfluous features, which occur in every command, like "priority," are ignored because they do not serve to distinguish between commands. These features, therefore, only appear in a rule if the entire set of commands is syntactically unifiable, in which case one can say that they do indeed turn out to characterise a degenerate command-set: namely, the whole language.

The right-hand part of Table 3 shows the grammar deduced by the consistency evaluator. The top of the grammar is 'sentence', which expands via one rule into a sequence of subtasks, such as 'sub1(PsF1)'. The subtasks themselves expand into tokens. Alternative expansions of the subtasks are possible. These are numbered. The variable 'PsF1' occurs twice in the 'sentence' rule, which means that the expansion chosen for 'sub1' should agree with the expansion for 'sub3'. Thus, the grammar does not allow commands in which 'job(X)' occurs in the first position and 'password(Y)' in the third, because that would require the 'PsF1' variable to be simultaneously bound to the constants '4' and '3' in the same expansion. A particular variable can only be bound to one constant in a particular instantiation.

The variable 'PsF2' occurs uniquely in the top-level rule (for 'sentence'), so that there are no binding restrictions on it. Therefore any priority can occur embedded between any possible first and third tokens.

The variables (e.g. 'PsF1') are what we call pseudo-features. They are synthesised by the program as it builds the grammar, simply to support the binding restrictions we want in order to enforce co-occurrences of the right terms with each other. How this synthesis is accomplished is not so important here, but we do view these pseudo-features as a minor inconvenience. Our aim is that the evaluation tool should use the task-description derived features, that constrained the grammar construction, in the output.

Having constructed a grammar the evaluation tool calculates a complexity metric for the grammar. The

Sentences of Language 1
s17. bluff, very_high, bluff_game_type(X)
s18. bluff, very_low, bluff_game_type(X)
s19. bluff, high, bluff_game_type(X)
s20. bluff, low, bluff_game_type(X)
s21. quote, very_high, quote_game_type(X)
s22. quote, very_low, quote_game_type(X)
s23. quote, high, quote_game_type(X)
s24. quote, low, quote_game_type(X)
s25. name(X), very_high, password(Y)
s26. name(X), very_low, password(Y)
s27. name(X), high, password(Y)
s28. name(X), low, password(Y)
s29. job(X), very_high, town_office(Y)
s30. job(X), very_low, town_office(Y)
s31. job(X), high, town_office(Y)
s32. job(X), low, town_office(Y)

Grammar	
sentence	→ sub1(PsF1) sub2(PsF2) sub3(PsF1)
sub1(1)	→ bluff
sub1(2)	→ quote
sub1(3)	→ name(X)
sub1(4)	→ job(X)
sub2(1)	→ very_high
sub2(2)	→ very_low
sub2(3)	→ high
sub2(4)	→ low
sub3(1)	→ bluff_game_type(X)
sub3(2)	→ quote_game_type(X)
sub3(3)	→ password(Y)
sub3(4)	→ town_office(Y)

Table 3. Language 1 and its deduced grammar.

current metric is very simple: Count the alternatives in the top-level rule. In the case of the grammar in Table 3, there is just 1 alternative.

Language 2 is made more complex than Language 1 by the different position of the priority tokens in some of the command (see Table 4). The evaluation tool fails to find a syntactic form that covers all of the sentences. Instead, it breaks them into two groups on the basis of distinguishing task features, and finds a rule that fits each group. As a consequence, the grammar in Table 4 has two alternatives in its top-level rule instead of Language 1's single possible expansion for 'sentence'. According to our simple metric, therefore, Language 1 is the better than Language 2. The predictions made by the evaluation tool thereby match Payne and Green's prediction, which is supported by their data.

The figures arrived at by the evaluation tool summarise the consistency scores of the three whole languages as follows. We take consistency to be inversely proportional to the size of the languages optimally small rule-set, as suggested by Payne & Green:

Language 1: $C = 1/2 = 0.50$
Language 2: $C = 1/3 = 0.33$
Language 3: $C = 1/7 = 0.14$

These indices or metrics could be used in a procurement evaluation context to determine which interface is best on this dimension. We emphasise that they have been produced automatically using a program that works from manual-like descriptions and that they are sensitive to configural aspects of the semantics of the tasks being analysed.

4. DISCUSSION

We have described in general terms what automated theory-based procurement evaluation might mean and in addition we have described Prolog implementations of consistency evaluators that take manual-like descriptions as input. We have demonstrated that an automatic evaluation tool can derive representations, closely related to Task-Action Grammars, that previously had to be written by hand, and in addition

Sentences of Language 2

s17. very_high, bluff, bluff_game_type(X)
s18. very_low, bluff, bluff_game_type(X)
s19. high, bluff, bluff_game_type(X)
s20. low, bluff, bluff_game_type(X)
s21. very_high, quote, quote_game_type(X)
s22. very_low, quote, quote_game_type(X)
s23. high, quote, quote_game_type(X)
s24. low, quote, quote_game_type(X)
s25. name(X), very_high, password(Y)
s26. name(X), very_low, password(Y)
s27. name(X), high, password(Y)
s28. name(X), low, password(Y)
s29. job(X), very_high, town_office(Y)
s30. job(X), very_low, town_office(Y)
s31. job(X), high, town_office(Y)
s32. job(X), low, town_office(Y)

Grammar

sentence $\rightarrow$ sub1(PsF1) sub2(PsF2) sub3(PsF2)
sentence $\rightarrow$ sub4(PsF1) sub1(PsF2) sub6(PsF1)

sub1(1)	$\rightarrow$ very_high
sub1(2)	$\rightarrow$ very_low
sub1(3)	$\rightarrow$ high
sub1(4)	$\rightarrow$ low
sub2(1)	$\rightarrow$ bluff
sub2(2)	$\rightarrow$ quote
sub3(1)	$\rightarrow$ bluff_game_type(X)
sub3(2)	$\rightarrow$ quote_game_type(X)
sub4(1)	$\rightarrow$ name(X)
sub4(2)	$\rightarrow$ job(X)
sub6(1)	$\rightarrow$ password(Y)
sub6(2)	$\rightarrow$ town_office(Y)

Table 4. Language 2 and its deduced grammar

we have shown that the evaluator predicts the learnability of previously reported experimental results.

A potential problem with the evaluation tool arises from the fact that it is essentially a hill-climber, and as a consequence it can be trapped by local maxima. Whilst the algorithm has produced good results on small toy problems we are currently investigating whether it scales up to full application-size sets of commands (> 200).

In addition, there are a number of issues with the evaluation description (the metrics given as output) that interest us. The productivity and intuitiveness indices used by PC magazine have given us an initial guide as to what is required. However, there are many issues unanswered. For example, (a) Should task-action mappings that are used more frequently have a larger effect on the overall index? It might be that it is more important that infrequently used commands are consistent so that they can be readily inferred. (b) Should the indices be affected by the size of the interface? For example, should a device that has 300 commands and only two syntactic forms be rated as more consistent than a device that has 10 commands and two syntactic forms? (c) Is it useful for the tool to provide different metrics at different levels of analysis? The prototype described above gives only the top-level of summary analysis. At the next level, consistency might be unpacked to reveal particularly problematic commands (hot spots; Howes & Young, 1991, 1996), and performance time might be unpacked to give worst-case and best-case tasks. (d) Will it be useful to determine some of the indices relative to larger scale benchmark tasks (e.g. write a letter) rather than the simple-tasks (e.g. open a file) considered in the prototype tool?

5. REFERENCES

Barnard, P.J. (1990) Bridging between basic theories and the artifacts of human-computer interaction. In J.Carroll (Ed) *Designing Interaction - Psychology at the Human-Computer Interface*. Cambridge: Cambridge University Press.

Barnard, P.J. & May, J. (1993) Cognitive modelling for user requirements. In P.F. Byerley, P.J. Barnard & J.May (Eds) *Computers, Communication and Usability: Design Issues, Research and Methods for Integrated Services*. Elsevier Science Publishers B.V.

Bawa, J. (1994) Comparative usability measurement: the role of usability lab in PC Magazine UK and PC/Computing. *Behaviour and Information Technology, 13*, 1 & 2, 17-19.

Byrne, M.D., Wood, S.D., Sukaviriya, P., Foley, J.D., & Kieras, D.E. (1994) Automatic interface evaluation. In *Proceedings of Human Factors and Computing Systems: CHI'94*. Boston, April, 1994.

Card, S.K., Moran, T.P., & Newell, A. (1983) *The psychology of human-computer interaction*. Hillsdale, NJ: Erlbaum.

Farenc, C., Liberati, V., & Barthet, M. (1996) *Proceedings of CADUI'96 2nd International Workshop on Computer-Aided Design for User Interfaces* - Namur, Belgique, June 1996.

Grudin, J. (1989) The case against user interface consistency. *Communications of the ACM, 32*, 1164-1173.

Howes, A. & Payne, S.J. (1990) Display-based competence: Towards user models for menu-driven interfaces *International Journal of Man Machine Studies, 33*, No. 6, 637-655.

Howes, A. & Young, R.M. (1991) Predicting the learnability of task-action mappings. In S.P. Robertson, G.M. Olson, J.S. Olson (Eds.) *Reaching Through Technology - CHI'91 Conference Proceedings: Human Factors in Computing Systems*, New Orleans, Louisiana. Addison-Wesley. 113-118.

Howes, A. & Young, R.M. (1996) Learning consistent, interactive and meaningful device methods: a computational model. *Cognitive Science, 20*, 301-356.

Long, J. (1989) Cognitive ergonomics and human-computer interaction. In J.Long and A.Whitefield (Eds.) *Cognitive Ergonomics and Human-Computer Interaction*. Cambridge University Press.

Payne, S.J. & Green, T.R.G. (1986) Task-action grammars: A model of the mental representation of task languages. *Human-Computer Interaction, 2*, 93-133.

Payne, S.J. & Green, T.R.G. (1989) The structure of command languages: an experiment on task-action grammar. *International Journal of Man-machine Studies, 30*, 213-234.

47

Adaptive Navigation Support in Educational Hypermedia on the World Wide Web

Peter Brusilovsky

Human-Computer Interaction Institute, School of Computer Science
Carnegie Mellon University Pittsburgh, PA 15213, USA
plb@cs.cmu.edu

John Eklund

Faculty of Education
University of Technology, Sydney NSW Australia
j.eklund@UTS.edu.au

Elmar Schwarz

Department of Psychology
Carnegie Mellon University Pittsburgh, PA 15213, USA
eschwarz@andrew.cmu.edu

ABSTRACT Adaptive navigation support is a new direction of research within the area of adaptive and user-model based interfaces. The goal of adaptive navigation support (ANS) techniques is to help users find an appropriate path in the learning and information space by adapting link presentation to the goals, knowledge, and other characteristics of an individual user. This paper briefly reviews several methods of adaptive navigation support and discusses their applicability in WWW context. We suggest some reasonably simple but effective ANS methods for Web-based systems: history-based, knowledge-based and prerequisite-based adaptive annotation. We describe of two developing Web-based educational systems, InterBook and KBNS-WEST to demonstrate the manner in which these key methods could be incorporated into a Web-based educational system and to provide a working example of ANS methodology.

KEYWORDS adaptive hypermedia, educational hypermedia, navigation, user model, WWW

Human–Computer Interaction: INTERACT'97 S. Howard, J. Hammond & G. Lindgaard (editors)
Published by Chapman & Hall

1. INTRODUCTION

The World Wide Web (WWW) is both a freely navigable and largely unstructured collection of documents, and a distributed medium for implementing specific educational applications. Its exponential growth in recent years has underscored the need for navigation support mechanisms which are specially tailored to accommodate the current knowledge and information seeking tasks of the individual user. The WWW is increasingly being used as a delivery means for what could loosely be termed courseware, that is, content-based, sequenced instructional materials designed to achieve a specific learning objective. Navigation support in this closed corpus context (Ibrahim and Franklin, 1995) attempts to address the problems of a user's unproductive wandering, refocussing them on their learning objectives, suggesting logical next steps to inform them about the knowledge structure of the hyperspace, or re-sequencing materials according to their demonstrated knowledge of content. In these cases, the knowledge implicit in the hypermedia is well defined and carefully structured, similar to that found in a textbook.

Adaptive hypermedia systems are capable of altering the content or appearance of the hypermedia on the basis of a dynamic understanding of the individual user. More specifically, Adaptive Navigation Support (ANS) is a generic name for a group of techniques used in adaptive hypermedia systems (Brusilovsky, 1996) which use this model to provide directional assistance to the user. For example, suggesting where the user should proceed, or annotating what is learned and ready to be learned.

This methodological paper is specifically concerned with adaptive navigation support on the Web, and describes some reasonably simple yet effective ANS methods for Web-based systems. Firstly, we briefly review several ANS methods and discuss their applicability in the context of the WWW (see also Eklund and Zeiliger, 1996). We then suggest two specific methods of adaptive navigation support based on adaptive annotation technology. These methods have shown to be especially efficient in educational hypermedia (Brusilovsky and Pesin, 1995; Zeiliger, Reggers, and Peeters, 1996). Using two Web-based adaptive educational systems which use ANS, InterBook (Brusilovsky, Schwarz, and Weber, 1996) and WEST-KBNS (Eklund and Sawers, 1996), we demonstrate how adaptive annotation technologies may be implemented.

2. TECHNIQUES OF ADAPTIVE NAVIGATION SUPPORT

Adaptive navigation support techniques can be classified in several groups according to the way they adapt presentation of links (Brusilovsky, 1996) *direct guidance*, *sorting*, *hiding*, and *annotation*.

Direct guidance can be applied in any system which can decide what is the next "best" node for the user to visit according user's goal and other parameters represented in the user model. WWW example of direct guidance is ELM-ART (Schwarz, Brusilovsky, and Weber, 1996), which generates an additional dynamic link (called "next") connected to the next most relevant node to visit. Direct guidance is quite a relevant technology for WWW context. A problem of direct guidance is that it is "too directive": it provides almost no support for the users who would like make their own choice rather than simply follow the system's suggestion.

The idea of *adaptive ordering* technology is to sort all the links of a particular page according to the user model using some easily recognisable means of conveying this to the user, such as having the more relevant links closer to the top (Hohl, Böcker, and Gunzenhäuser, 1996). Adaptive ordering has a limited applicability: it can be used with non-contextual links, but it can hardly be used for indexes and content pages (which usually have a stable order of links), and can never be used with contextual links and maps.

The idea of navigation support by ***hiding*** is to restrict the navigation space by hiding links to irrelevant pages. A page can be considered as irrelevant for several reasons: for example, if it is not related to the user's current goal (Brusilovsky and Pesin, 1994; Vassileva, 1996) or if it presents materials which the user is not yet prepared to understand (Brusilovsky and Pesin, 1994; Pérez, Gutiérrez, and Lopistéguy, 1995). Hiding has a wide applicability, it protects users from the complexity of the unrestricted hyperspace and reduces their cognitive load. Hiding has, however, another problem: as noted by some psychologists, hiding can provoke the formation of incorrect mental models of the hyperspace.

Adaptive annotation technology augments the links with a comment which inform the user more about the current state of the nodes behind the annotated links (Brusilovsky, Pesin, and Zyryanov, 1993; de La Passardiere and Dufresne, 1992; Hohl, Böcker, and Gunzenhäuser, 1996; Schwarz, Brusilovsky, and Weber, 1996). Link annotations can be provided in textual form or in the form of visual cues, for example, using different icons, or colours, font sizes, or font types. The typical kind of annotation considered in traditional hypermedia is static (user independent) annotation. Adaptive navigation support can be provided by dynamic user model-driven annotation. Adaptive annotation in its simplest history-based form (outlining the links to previously visited nodes) has been applied in some hypermedia systems including several World-Wide Web browsers. Even this form adaptive annotation which can distinguish only two states of links (links to visited/not visited nodes) appears to be quite useful.

Annotation appears to be a good means of implementing adaptive navigation support. Annotation can be naturally used with all possible forms of links, and this technique supports stable order of links and avoids problems with incorrect mental maps. Annotation is generally a more powerful technology than hiding: hiding can distinguish only two states for the related nodes - relevant and non relevant - while annotation, as mentioned above, can distinguish up to six states (for example, Hyperadapter (Hohl, Böcker, and Gunzenhäuser, 1996) uses annotations to show several levels of relevancy).

An example of annotation-based adaptive navigation support technique can be provided by systems ISIS-Tutor (Brusilovsky and Pesin, 1994) and ITEM/PG (Brusilovsky, Pesin, and Zyryanov, 1993) The backbone of the hyperspace in these systems is formed by a conceptual network which represents the pedagogical structure of the subject being taught. Each concept of the conceptual network and each learning units (such as presentation units, problems, and examples) is represented by a node of the hyperspace. Each learning unit is connected to all concept nodes which are required to work with this unit. The weighted overlay student model represents separately the level of the student's knowledge of each of the concepts. Using this student model and the conceptual network, the systems can distinguish four educational states for each node represented by a hypermedia page: not-ready-to-be-learned (i.e., has unlearned prerequisites), ready-to-be-learned, in-work (concept node is visited and learning started), and learned (student has solved the required number of problems for the concept). The idea of ANS in ISIS-Tutor and ITEM/PG is that concepts with different educational states have different meanings for the student and making educational states visible will help the student in hyperspace navigation. To make educational states visible, links to the concepts with different educational states are annotated with different colours and some special characters.

The methods of annotation-based ANS applied in ISIS-Tutor and ITEM/PG are relatively simple, but they have shown to be very efficient. The adaptive and non-adaptive versions of ISIS-Tutor have been compared in a recent experiment (Brusilovsky and Pesin, 1995). The results of the experiment showed that the overall number of navigation steps and the number of repetitions of previously studied concepts are about twice as less for a version with ANS (and this difference is significant). This implies that ANS methods methods applied in ISIS-Tutor and ITEM/PG can improve user performance in hypermedia by significantly reducing navigation difficulty. With these kinds of ANS, the user can achieve the same result using a smaller number of navigation steps and visits to hypermedia nodes.

3. KNOWLEDGE-BASED AND PREREQUISITE-BASED ANNOTATION FOR WWW

As we mentioned in the previous section, adaptive annotation is familiar to WWW users because any WWW browser allows them to distinguish visited and unvisited nodes, showing them in different colours. This simple "history" - based annotation has shown to be very useful. We claim that more advanced ways of adaptive annotation could be also very helpful for WWW users. In this section we would like to generalise the experience of ISIS-Tutor and ITEM/PG systems and suggest some more annotation-based ANS methods to be used on WWW. These methods take into account the user's knowledge of the subject represented in the hypermedia system. All these methods are based on the three main decisions about representing the knowledge about the domain, the course, and the student described below.

The knowledge about the domain is represented in the form of a concept-based domain model. The simplest form of domain model is just a set of domain concepts. These concepts can be named differently in different systems - topics, attributes, knowledge elements, objects, learning outcomes, but in all the cases they are just elementary pieces of knowledge for the given domain. Depending on the domain and the application area, the concepts can represent larger or smaller pieces of domain knowledge. A more advanced form of the domain model is a network with nodes corresponding to domain concepts (and with links reflecting several kinds of relationships between concepts. This network represents the structure of the domain covered by a hypermedia system.

The domain model provides a structure for the representation of the user's knowledge of the subject. For each domain model concept, an individual user knowledge model stores some value which is an estimation of the user knowledge level of this concept. This can be a binary value (known – not known), a qualitative value (good-average-poor), or a quantitative value, such as the probability that the user knows the concept. This type of model, which is called an *overlay model,* is most often used in adaptive hypermedia systems. An overlay model of user knowledge can be represented as a set of pairs "concept - value", one pair for each domain concept. The overlay model is powerful and flexible, it can measure independently the user's knowledge of different topics.

The knowledge about the course is represented by indexing hypermedia nodes containing various units of learning material (presentations, tests, examples, problems) with domain model concepts which are related to the content of the unit. This is a relatively popular direction for the development of education-oriented hypermedia systems. There are two major types of indexing: content-based indexing and prerequisite-based indexing. With content-based indexing, a concept is included in a page index if some part of this page presents the piece of knowledge designated by the concept (Brusilovsky and Pesin, 1994; Schwarz, Brusilovsky, and Weber, 1996; Zeiliger, 1993). With prerequisite-based indexing, a concept is included in a page index if a student has to know this concept to understand the content of the page (Schwarz, Brusilovsky, and Weber, 1996).

We identify two further methods for intelligent ANS on WWW: knowledge-based annotation and prerequiste-based annotation. The idea of the "knowledge-based" method is to distinguish different levels of the user's knowledge of the node. We suggest the use of three graduations: not-known, in-work (partially known) and well-learned, and annotate differently the links to the nodes of these three classes as in (Brusilovsky, Pesin, and Zyryanov, 1993; de La Passardiere and Dufresne, 1992). Here by "not-known" we mean that the user has never heard about some of the concepts from the node's outcome. "In-work" means that the user has acquired some information about all the concepts presented in this node (it does not necessarily imply that the user has just visited this node!). "Well-known" means that the user confirmed his or her knowledge of all the concepts presented in this node by answering tests or solving problems. This method requires a user model which could distinguish three levels of user knowledge of the concept: the user has never heard about a concept, the users has read some information about a concept, and finally that the user has correctly answered a test or solved a problem which requires this concept.

The idea of the second "prerequisite-based" method is to distinguish nodes which are ready and not-ready to be learned as in (Brusilovsky and Pesin, 1994). The node is considered as not-ready-to-be-learned in two cases: first if any of the concepts in the prerequisite section of node index is not-known and second is any concept from the outcome section of node index has a not-known prerequisite concept. This method could be implemented with the simplest form of overlay model which only distinguishes known from not-known.

4. IMPLEMENTING ANNOTATION-BASED ANS ON WWW

In this section we will demonstrate how these two knowledge-based ANS methods could be implemented in WWW context. We describe briefly two educational Web-based systems, InterBook and WEST-KBNS.

4.1. Adaptive Navigation Support in InterBook

InterBook[1] (Brusilovsky, Schwarz, and Weber, 1996) is a system for authoring and delivering adaptive electronic textbooks on WWW. All InterBook-served electronic textbooks have generated table of content, a glossary, and a search interface. In InterBook, the structure of the glossary resembles the pedagogic structure of the domain knowledge. Each node of the domain network is represented by a glossary entry. Likewise each glossary entry corresponds to one of the domain concepts.

[1] http://www.contrib.andrew.cmu.edu/~plb/InterBook.html

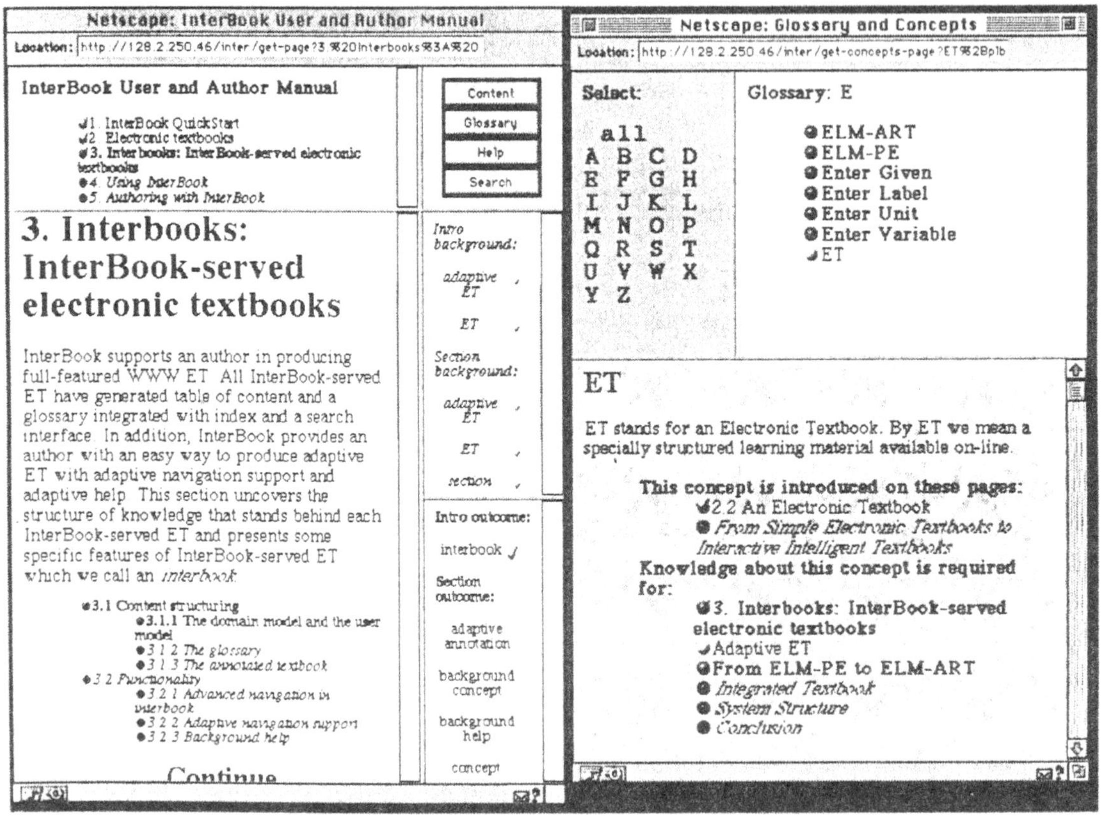

Figure 1. Adaptive navigation support in InterBook. Green bullet (bold fond) means recommended, red bullet (italic) means "not ready to be learned", while bullet (normal font) means "nothing new".

All sections of an electronic textbook are indexed with domain model concepts. For each section, a list of concepts related with this section is provided (we call this list spectrum of the section). The spectrum of the section can represent also the role of a concept in the section (each concept can be either an outcome concept or a background concept).

The knowledge about the domain and about the textbook content is used by InterBook to serve a well-structured hyperspace. In particular, InterBook generates links between the glossary and the textbook. Links are provided from each textbook section to corresponding glossary entries for each involved background or outcome concept. Similarly from each glossary entry describing a concept InterBook provides links to all textbook units that can be used to learn this concept. It means that an InterBook glossary integrates features of an index and a glossary. These links are not stored in an external format but generated on the fly by a special module that takes into account the student's current state of knowledge represented by the user model.

InterBook uses special icons (coloured bullets) and different fonts to provide adaptive navigation support (Figure 1). Wherever a link appears on InterBook pages: in the table of content, in the gossary or on a regular page, its font and colour of its bullet will tell the user about the status of the node behind the link. InterBook integrates all three methods of annotation: history-based, knowledge-based and prerequisite-based.

Currently four colours and three fonts are used. Green bullet and bold font means 'ready and recommended', ie., the node is ready-to-be-learned but still not learned and contains some new material. A red bullet and an italic font warns about a not-ready-to-be-learned node, while white means 'clear, nothing new', ie., all concepts presented on a node are known to the user. Violet is used to mark nodes which have not been annotated by an author. A check mark is added for already visited nodes. Currently, InterBook does not support tests and can not provide "well-learned" annotation.

4.2. Adaptive Navigation Support in WEST-KBNS

WEST-KBNS[2] (WEST-Knowledge Based Navigation Support) (Eklund and Sawers, 1996) is a system under development in which the user is offered annotated links on an overview map generated from a Web-delivered course. WEST-KBNS uses an existing online course authoring and delivery tool WEST[3] as its central component, and involves the application of elements of formal concept analysis for the domain model.

Students enter the course via a web page which uses a script to hide the Netscape location, toolbar and the directory buttons, and establishes a frameset with a large frame at the top of the screen in which the WEST pages appear, and a smaller bottom frame in which a clickable overview map is generated for each student showing the annotated hypermedia nodes. The courseware is sectioned into chapters, each containing a number of pages of instructional material with text, hypertext, and graphics. Each chapter has a set of automarked multiple choice tests. Presently, the overview map shows the links as visited, unvisited, current and suggested. With further development it will show the links in one of four states: unvisited, visited, current, and learned. This means it will be both history-based and knowledge-based according to the methods we have suggested earlier in this paper.

The overview map is generated dynamically with Javascript, and loaded by a script placed in each of the WEST course pages in the top frame extracting the context in which the course page is being delivered. In other words the map is individual for the particular user, extracting not just the connection ID (particular to the user) but also the URL of the page in the top frame. KBNS-WEST does not generate the link set automatically (although this is being considered for development), so as pages are added to the WEST course in the top frame, some manual rewriting of the Javascript is required.

This system uses a relatively simple component of concept analysis (Willie, 1982), an unsupervised learning algorithm, that produces a containment lattice called a concept lattice. The basic structure of formal concept analysis is the *context*. A context is comprised of a set of *objects* (denoted by G), a set of *attributes* (denoted by M), and a relation that describes which objects possess which attributes. The attributes are the finest-grained elements of knowledge. An attribute may be a simple declarative term, or represent some structural knowledge which relates terms. A cross-table marks if an attribute exists on a page, or in a test. For instance if attribute 1 is related to a page 1, an x is placed in the lattice cell, if attribute 2 is not related to page 1 an x is not placed in the corresponding cell. The same attributes are located in each multi-choice test item using another cross-table. Implicitly a cross-table links the test items to the pages in the courseware through an attribute set. Attributes in this system play the same role as concepts in InterBook. The hypermedia nodes or pages represented in the overview map represent the objects. From the context a set of concepts is derived. This means that the concepts are not hypermedia components within themselves, such as nodes or terms, but are implicitly defined by the context. Each concept is a pair (A,B) where A is a set of objects and B is a set of attributes, and each of these is translated into an individual test question. Thus a concept is defined by a set of objects and a set of attributes, and is represented by one or more test questions. The test questions are the hypermedia components which best represent the concepts. The rationale for this structure is that concepts are not necessarily explicity identifiable hypermedia components, but may be distributed over many pages of instruction or may be in the "subtext" of the learning material; however, when we test student's learning, we wish to test their acquisition of concepts. The system records which node, or object, has been visited, and this permanently changes the colour of the node for that student. Students answer the auto-marked multi-choice tests and the data is then interpreted to create the student's overview map, along with the data about where the

2http://www.education.uts.edu.au/west/KBNS/

3http://www.west.ie

student has been. Together this will show which of the pages are current, learned or visited. A page is marked as learned (and thus annotated on the overview map with a different colour) when a certain percentage of the attributes that belong to that page are recorded in the student model as known.

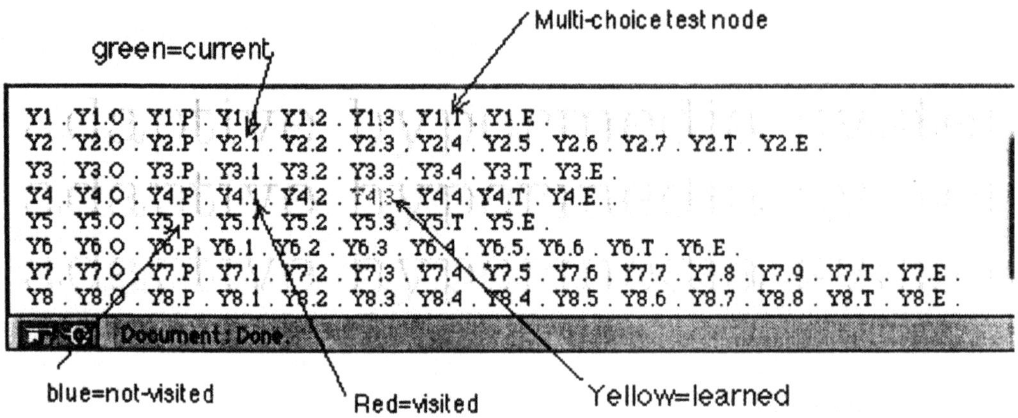

Figure 2. Colour-annotated clickable overview map of the pages in the WEST course

The structure of the courseware itself somewhat negates the need to suggest the next best link for the user to follow, as the well-structured and goal-oriented content of the hypermedia makes it clear to the user which node to revisit before proceeding. In other words, it is which suggests prerequisites to the user, who may assume that Chapter 3 is a prerequisite to Chapter 4, for instance. It should be noted that it would be relatively simple using this annotation to also direct the user to remedial or extension material depending on the outcomes of the tests.

The history-based mechanism in KBNS-WEST extends beyond that provided by the browser, and is accomplished by recording which nodes the student has visited and writing this to a file. This is the history component of the student model and may be considered to be similar to the "partially learned" annotation, if we assume that by visiting a node the student will acquire at least a partial knowledge of its content. However, this does not take into account students browsing ahead, similar to quickly flipping the pages of a book before beginning a close reading.

5. CONCLUSION

In this paper we have specifically discussed adaptive navigation support (ANS) on the Web, describing some reasonably simple yet effective ANS methods. After placing adaptive navigation support in the context of adaptive hypermedia systems implemented on WWW, we have discussed several methods of ANS and suggest a specific method of adaptive navigation support based on adaptive annotation technology. Using two Web-based adaptive educational systems which use ANS, InterBook and WEST-KBNS, we have shown how adaptive annotation technologies may be implemented.

InterBook provides an authoring and delivery mechanism into which the content of a book may be structured through the identification of key domain concepts to create an adaptive electronic textbook (Schwarz, Brusilovsky, and Weber, 1996). Based on the user's path through the structured hyperspace using a domain model and a user model, InterBook annotates links as visited, learned, ready-to-be learned and not ready-to-be learned, integrating the history-based, knowledge-based and prerequisite-based methods of ANS.

WEST-KBNS is a system under development in which the user is offered annotated links on an overview map generated from a WEST course, and involves the application of concept analysis to provide the knowledge representation such that the overview map annotates nodes as visited and unvisited, learned and unlearned offering the student a visual representation of the student model. The ANS in this system is both history and knowledge-based. By describing these adaptive systems we have illustrated some simple but efficient ANS methods for Web-based systems, and highlighted the diverse ways in which they may be implemented. The history-based, knowledge-based and prerequisite-based methods of adaptive navigation support provide opportunities to provide individualised instruction in closed corpus WWW-based courseware.

6. REFERENCES

Brusilovsky, P. (1996) Methods and techniques of adaptive hypermedia. *User Modeling and User-Adapted Interaction* **6** (2-3), 87-129.

Brusilovsky, P. and Pesin, L. (1994) ISIS-Tutor: An adaptive hypertext learning environment. *Proceedings of JCKBSE'94, Japanese-CIS Symposium on knowledge-based software engineering.* Edited by H. Ueno and V. Stefanuk. Pereslavl-Zalesski, Russia, May 10-13, 1994, pp. 83-87.

Brusilovsky, P. and Pesin, L. (1995) Visual annotation of links in adaptive hypermedia. *Proceedings of CHI'95 (Conference Companion).* Edited by I. Katz, R. Mack and L. Marks. Denver, May 7-11, 1995, pp. 222-223.

Brusilovsky, P., Pesin, L., and Zyryanov, M. (1993) Towards an adaptive hypermedia component for an intelligent learning environment. In *Human-Computer Interaction*, Lecture Notes in Computer Science, Vol. 753, L. J. Bass, J. Gornostaev and C. Unger (eds), Springer-Verlag, Berlin. pp. 348-358.

Brusilovsky, P., Schwarz, E., and Weber, G. (1996) A tool for developing adaptive electronic textbooks on WWW. *Proceedings of WebNet'96, World Conference of the Web Society.* San Francisco, CA, October 15-19, 1996, pp. 64-69, http://www.contrib.andrew.cmu.edu/~plb/WebNet 96.html.

de La Passardiere, B. and Dufresne, A. (1992) Adaptive navigational tools for educational hypermedia. In *Computer Assisted Learning*, I. Tomek (ed) Springer-Verlag, Berlin. pp. 555-567.

Eklund, J. and Sawers, J. (1996) Customising Web-based course delivery in WEST® with navigation support. *Proceedings of WebNet'96, World Conference of the Web Society.* San Francisco, CA, October 15-19, 1996, pp. 534-535.

Eklund, J. and Zeiliger, R. (1996) Navigating the Web: Possibilities and practicalities for adaptive navigational support. *Proceedings of Ausweb96: The Second Australian World-Wide Web Conference.* , pp. 73-80.

Hohl, H., Böcker, H.-D., and Gunzenhäuser, R. (1996) Hypadapter: An adaptive hypertext system for exploratory learning and programming. *User Modeling and User-Adapted Interaction* **6** (2-3), 131-156.

Ibrahim, B. and Franklin, S. D. (1995) Advanced educational uses of the World-Wide Web. *Computer Networks and ISDN Systems* **27** (6), 871-877.

Pérez, T., Gutiérrez, J., and Lopistéguy, P. (1995) An adaptive hypermedia system. *Proceedings of AI-ED'95, 7th World Conference on Artificial Intelligence in Education.* Edited by J. Greer. Washington, DC, 16-19 August 1995, pp. 351-358.

Schwarz, E., Brusilovsky, P., and Weber, G. (1996) World-wide intelligent textbooks. *Proceedings of ED-TELECOM'96 - World Conference on Educational Telecommunications.* Boston, MA, June 1-22, 1996, pp. 302-307, http://www.contrib.andrew.cmu.edu/~plb/ED-MEDIA-96.html.

Vassileva, J. (1996) A task-centered approach for user modeling in a hypermedia office documentation system. *User Modeling and User-Adapted Interaction* **6** (2-3), 185-224.

Willie, R. (1982) Restructuring Lattice Theory: An approach based on heiracrchies of concepts. In Rival, I. (ed.) *Ordered Sets*, Reidel, Dordrecht-Boston, p. 445-470.

Zeiliger, R. (1993) Adaptive testing: contribution of the SHIVA model. In *Item banking: Interactive testing and self-assessment*, NATO ASI Serie F, Vol. 112, D. Leclercq and J. Bruno (eds), Springer-Verlag, Berlin. pp. 54-65.

Zeiliger, R., Reggers, T., and Peeters, R. (1996) Concept-map based navigation in educational hypermedia : a case study. *Proceedings of ED-MEDIA'96 - World conference on educational multimedia and hypermedia.* Boston, MA, June 17-22, 1996.

Improving Browsing Performance: A study of four input devices for scrolling and pointing tasks

Shumin Zhai **Barton A. Smith** **Ted Selker**

IBM Almaden Research Center
650 Harry Road, NWE-B2 , San Jose, California 95120, USA
{zhai, smith, selker}@almaden.ibm.com

ABSTRACT Navigating through online documents has become an increasingly common HCI task. This paper investigates alternative methods to improve user performance for browsing World Wide Web and other documents. In a task that involved both scrolling and pointing, we compared three input methods against the status-quo. The results showed that a mouse with a finger wheel did not improve user's performance; two other methods, namely a mouse with an isometric rate-control joystick operated by the same hand and a two handed system that put a mouse on the dominant hand and a joystick on the other, both significantly improved users' performance. A human factors analysis on each of the three input methods is also presented.

KEYWORDS Input Devices, Interaction Techniques, Web Browsing, Scrolling, Mouse, Isometric vs. Isotonic Devices, joystick, Wheel Mouse, IntelliMouse™, TrackpointIII™, Two-handed Input, Bimanual Interaction.

1. INTRODUCTION

Today's mainstream interaction style (WIMP - window, icon, menu and pointer), although with a long history (Smith, Irby, Kimball, Verplank & Harslem, 1982), is still gaining a wider range of applications and a larger user population. The rapidly developing World Wide Web (WWW) makes the use of such style of interaction even more frequent and intense. As a result, the limitations of existing WIMP features also become more severe and obvious. There have been numerous interface inventions and studies since the basic WIMP style was developed (e.g Buxton 1986), but they have been largely restricted to the research literature and isolated demonstrations. The unavailability of commercial hardware and software and an incomplete understanding of human factors both have contributed to the lack of major improvements in the mainstream interfaces.

One basic feature of the existing mainstream WIMP interfaces is that the user communicates with the computer system via a single stream of spatial input, physically driven by a 2 degree of freedom input device, typically a mouse, and graphically displayed as a cursor. The universal cursor travels around the entire interface, switching its functions from pointing, to selection, to drawing, to scrolling, to opening and to jumping, according to what virtual devices (widgets), such as the main document/window, a menu, a scrolling bar, an icon or a hyperlink, has been acquired and engaged. Such a single stream operation, needless to say, has offered the users many advantages such as the ease of understanding and learning the interaction mechanism. The disadvantage, however, is the limited communication bandwidth (Buxton 1986) and the costs in time and cognitive effort of acquiring widgets and control points (Buxton and Myers 1986, Leganchuk, Zhai and Buxton 1996). A particular case at point is document browsing, one of the most frequent tasks in interacting with computers. A document, such as a text file, a spreadsheet, a folder, and most importantly, a

Human–Computer Interaction: INTERACT'97 S. Howard, J. Hammond & G. Lindgaard (editors)
Published by Chapman & Hall

WWW page, is often larger than the viewing window that competes for space with multiple other windows on the same limited computer screen. When working on such a document, the user's point of interest often moves to outside of the viewing window, forcing the user to move (scroll) the document. With the traditional scroll bar method, there are at least the following three limitations:

1. It takes a certain amount of time, T_1, to acquire the scrolling bar. According to the well studied Fitts' law (Fitts 1953), T_1 is logarithmically proportional to the ratio of A and W. A is the distance the cursor has to travel and W is the size of the widget acquired. At the extreme case (travel across the entire screen to acquire the arrow widget at the end of a scroll bar), the Fitts index of difficulty can be up to 8 bits, which may take more than 2 seconds to complete.

2. There are three methods of using a scrolling bar, each has some limitations. First, the user can acquire the moving handle and drag it. The advantage with this method is that the user can scroll the document at a controlled speed that is suitable for the particular task. The disadvantage is that the dragging function, requiring maintaining pressure on a button while moving the input device, is more difficult and takes more time than pointing over the same Fitts' index of difficulty (MacKenzie, Sellen and Buxton 1991). The second method is to use the cursor to press the arrow buttons at the ends of the scrolling bar, causing the document to scroll at a speed that is not adjustable by the user. This is binary control: either move at a fixed speed or stop. The speed could be too slow when the user wants to move very far, or too fast when the user wants to visually track the document. The third method is to click on the rest of the space on the scroll bar, causing the document "jump" at a speed faster than the second method. The location of the window jumped to is often unpredictable by the user, causing visual discontinuity or "loosing track".

3. Perhaps most importantly, when the user has to go to the scroll bar to move a document, even by just one line, it takes the perceptual, cognitive and motor resources away from the target that the user focused attention on, breaking the work flow.

The above analysis shows that the standard, single input stream WIMP interface is inadequate for browsing, one of today's most common interaction tasks. This study looks into three alternative methods for browsing. We will conduct a human factors analysis on each of the three techniques and we will then present a formal experiment that compared these methods against the standard single stream method.

2. THREE ALTERNATIVE METHODS FOR BROWSING

2.1. Mouse with Isometric joystick

As shown in Figure 1, the first alternative device we studied is JSMouse, a two button mouse with a miniature joystick mounted between the two buttons. The Mouse retains all usual functions as in a standard mouse. The miniature isometric joystick, an IBM TrackPoint III™, is a rate controlled input device (Rutledge and Selker 1990, Barret et al 1995). Each of the two devices can function as an independent normal 2 degree-of-freedom input device. In the current study we assign the mouse for pointing and the miniature control stick for scrolling. We hypothesized that the isometric control stick is particularly suitable for scrolling tasks based on the following reasoning.

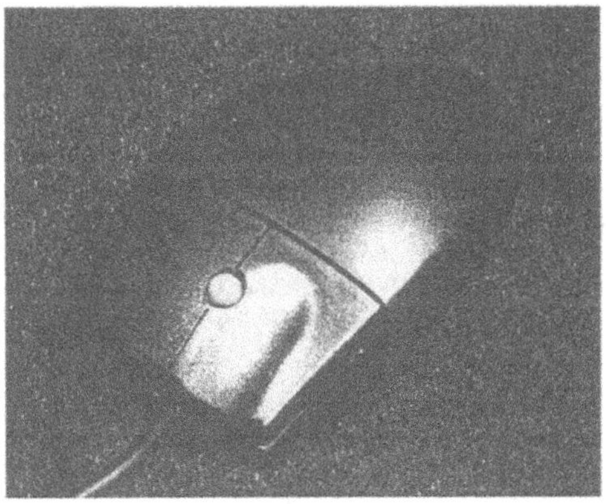

Figure 1 The JoystickMouse (JSMouse) is a mouse with an miniature joystick mounted between the two buttons. The users may use index or middle finger to manipulate the joystick.

First, let us briefly review the two basic types of transfer functions in input: position and rate control (see Poulton 1974 for detailed review). Position control, also referred as zero order control, maps the user input variable to the cursor displacement according to a constant, or a variable gain. Rate control, also called first order control, maps the user input variable to cursor *velocity*. As shown in recent six degree of freedom input control studies (Zhai and Milgram 1993, Zhai, Milgram and Drascic 1993, Zhai 1995), position control is better conducted with isotonic, free moving devices, such as the mouse; and rate control is better conducted with isometric or elastic devices. The key factor to this compatibility issue is the self-centering effect in isometric or elastic devices. With self centering, rate control can be easily done. Without it, rate control requires conscious effort. Either position control or rate control can give user certain ability to control all aspects of movement, including displacement, movement speed or higher order derivatives, but each mode corresponds to only one aspect directly: displacement or speed.

Scrolling, or navigating through a document, requires the user not only to control the final displacement of the document to make the target appear in the viewing window (a rather easy requirement by Fitts' index of difficulty because of the large effective "width" - the difference between the viewing window size and the target area), but also to control the speed of the movement so that the user can comfortably scan the document to look for the target. An isometric rate control device apparently meets these requirements. On the other hand, if we use an isotonic position control device, such as the mouse, the user may not be able to control the speed of movement continuously. In particular, due to physical constraint (of either the human arm or the mouse pad), position control allows the user to move only within a certain distance at one stroke. The user has to release (by lifting the mouse) and re-engage the position control device repeatedly in order to scroll over a longer distance.

When using the JSMouse, the user can either use the index finger or the middle finger to operate the control stick. When using the index finger, the user has to switch the same finger between the left button and the control stick. Due to the close proximity, the user can rely on kinesthetic memory to locate the stick without looking at it.

2.2. Mouse with a track wheel

The idea of adding an additional sensor onto a mouse is not new. As described in (Venolia 1993), a thumb wheel can be mounted onto a standard mouse for additional degree of freedom in 3D interface. More recently, the Microsoft IntelliMouse™ provides a finger wheel on the top of a mouse. The later, which was called WheelMouse, is the second device we included in the current study.

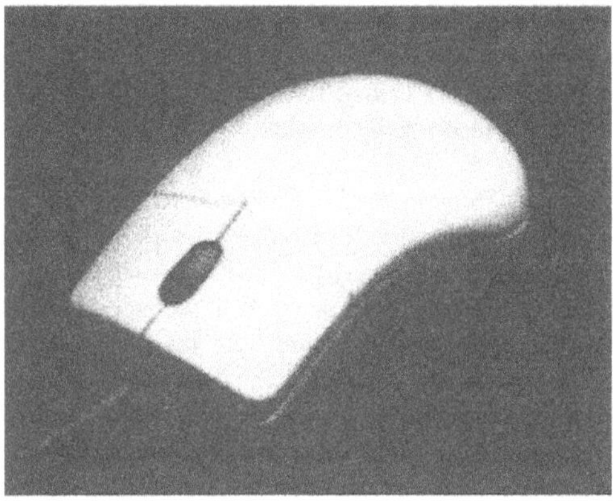

Figure 2 The WheelMouse used in the study was a Microsoft IntelliMouse™. It works in three modes: Wheel rolling, press (the wheel) and move (mouse) to do rate control, and click and move.

The track wheel in the IntelliMouse is largely free moving (isotonic) but with a detent mechanism. Each detent step corresponds to one line of scrolling. The wheel works in position control mode. Position control requires repeated release-reengage for long movement. In the case of the track wheel, the user can quickly repeat the stroking of the wheel. The IntelliMouse provide two additional modes of scrolling; both turn the mouse itself into a rate control device. As analyzed earlier, an isotonic device lacks the self centering effect that is desirable in rate control. In one mode of the IntelliMouse, the user presses down the wheel, which is also a button, to engage in rate control scrolling. The more the mouse is moved from where the wheel is pressed down, the faster the document scrolls. When the user releases the wheel, scrolling stops. In the second mode, the user presses and releases the wheel (click) to start the rate control scrolling. Any following click, either on the wheel or on other buttons stops the scrolling. In both cases, a visual anchor is left on the screen to indicate where the rate control scrolling starts. This may help the lack of centering effect in the mouse for rate control, but such a centering feedback comes from the visual channel, not the haptic feel.

As with the JSMouse, the user can use either the index finger, or the middle finger to roll the track wheel for scrolling. Pointing is done by normal mouse movement.

2.3. Two handed joystick and mouse

The third method we studied was a two-handed input method. A keyboard with a TrackPoint III™ (between the G, H, B keys, as in IBM Thinkpad computers) and a standard mouse were used in this method (Figure 3). The user operates the control stick with non-dominant hand to do scrolling and manipulates the mouse with the dominant hand to do pointing.

The idea of using the non-dominant hand for a scrolling task has been advocated by researchers such as Buxton (1986) for over a decade. Scrolling was also one of the first scenarios in which two handed input was experimentally demonstrated to be superior to the standard one handed input. Equipping subjects' non-dominant hand with two strips of touch-sensitive tablet and their dominant hand with a puck on a graphics tablet, Buxton and Myers (1986) studied users performance in a text document navigation (jump or scroll) and selection (pointing) task. In that experiment the subjects used their non-dominant hand to jump (one strip that was absolute position sensitive) or scroll (another strip that was relative movement sensitive) the document and used the dominant hand to select targets. With such a two-handed set-up, 15% (for expert users) to 25% (for novice) performance improvement was measured.

The present two-handed system studied here differs from that of Buxton and Myers, and from any other published two-handed techniques to our knowledge such as (Kabbash, Sellen and Buxton, 1994; Leganchuk, Zhai and Buxton, 1996), in terms of the physical devices used in two-handed interaction. One of the two devices in the system is an isometric rate control joystick. There are four potential advantages to including an isometric joystick in a two-handed system.

First, there will always be some individual preference for a certain type of device. Some users may prefer one type over another. Having one joystick and one mouse in the system gives the user a choice when they need only one device. Second, device performance is task dependent. A unique advantage of in-keyboard isometric joysticks is that the user's fingers do not have to leave the keyboard, making mixed typing and pointing task much faster (Rutledge and Selker, 1990). Including an isometric joystick in the dual device system gives the user the choice when needed for a particular task.

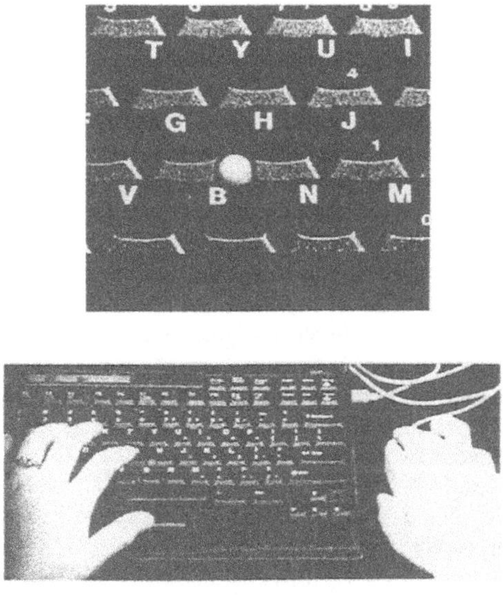

Figure 3 In-keyborad Isometric Joystick (top), operated by the non-dominant (left for this user) hand for scrolling while the dominant hand moves a mouse for pointing (bottom). Note that the system can be easily set for left-dominant user.

Third, an isometric joystick requires less space, or "footprint", than any other device (mouse, tablet or trackball). This is not only important for portable computing, but also important for a two-handed desktop environment where a keyboard with a mouse has already crowded the workspace. Fourth, as pointed out earlier, a rate control technique that is compatible with isometric devices can be particularly suitable for scrolling tasks, no repetitive release-reengage problem exists as in position control techniques.

However, the joystick-mouse two handed system also poses an unanswered theoretical question: with those two handed systems that have been demonstrated to be advantageous, both hands were engaged in isotonic position modes (consistent or similar motor action across two hands). In the current system, the two hands are engaged in *different* motor control mechanisms: one in isotonic position control one in isometric rate control. Is such a combination still superior to the standard one handed input system?

What is also conceptually interesting is the contrast between the two-handed system (Figure 3) and the Joystick Mouse (Figure 1) both included in the current study. Identical transducers were used in the two input methods. The difference was entirely the location of the joystick. In the case of JSMouse, the joystick was on the mouse and was manipulated by the same hand that operates the mouse. In the current case, the joystick was in the keyboard and was manipulated by a different hand. In other words, we are distributing two streams of input in two ways: one puts both streams into one hand and the other separates them to two hands. It is interesting to find out how user performance differs between the two methods.

We should briefly mention a human bimanual action theory: Kinematic Chain model (Guiard 1987). The KC model strongly suggests that the two human hands work in a cooperative but asymmetric manner. The non-dominant hand, like a base link in a chain, tends to take precedence (act first), work on a larger but coarse scale, and set the frame of reference. The dominant hand, like a terminal link in a chain, tends to act later, work in a smaller but finer scale and operate within the frame-of-reference. The current two-handed system coincides with these characteristics very well: the non-dominant side acts first (scroll first), sets the frame of reference, and moves at a larger distance (rate control). The dominant hand acts later and operates within that frame on a smaller scale. This is also what we do in natural life: hold and move a document with our non-dominant hand and write within the page with our dominant hand.

3. THE EXPERIMENT

3.1. Experiment Design

We choose to model our experimental task after one of the most frequent interaction tasks today's computer users do: Web browsing. A web page, stored as a local file to avoid transmitting delay, was presented to the subject. The document contains texts from an IBM computing terminology dictionary (Figure 4). A hyper link is embedded at an unpredictable location in each page. The user's task was to scroll the document until he/she found the target hyperlink (Figure 4, bottom). Clicking on the target word "Next" would bring the subject to the beginning of the next web page. Each test of the experiment consisted of 10 pages of browsing (scroll and point). The size of the web pages was set as such that the scroll handle was 1.3 cm (so it was not too difficult to acquire for the standard mouse condition, see Figure 4, bottom). The web browser viewing area was 24 cm wide and 15 cm long on a CRT display. Subjects were allowed to adjust the positions of mouse, keyboard, and display on the desk to suit their own preferences.

Four interaction methods were tested in the experiment: Standard Mouse (Mouse), Mouse with a track wheel (WheelMouse), Mouse with Joystick (JSMouse), and Mouse with in-keyboard joystick (2hand). Note that pointing mechanism is the same with all four methods: mouse movement by the dominant hand. A total of 12 volunteer subjects participated in the experiment. An order balanced within subject design was used. Each subject performed the tests with all four methods in a pre-assigned order of the four methods. With each method, the subjects were first given one practice run, during which they were asked to explored all modes (in the cases of Mouse and WheelMouse) and strategies (aggressive or careful). They could take as much time as they liked to finish these 10 pages of browsing. The subjects were then asked to performed two consecutive tests (10 pages each test) as quickly as possible. The same 10 web pages were for all tests.

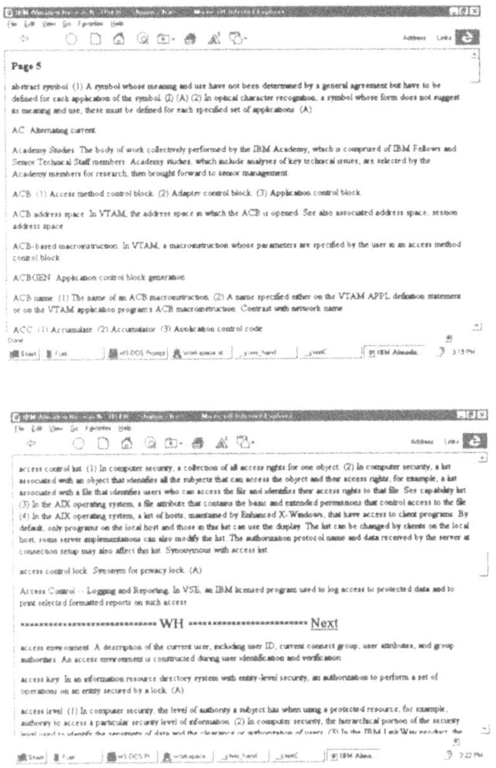

Figure 4 Web page browsing was used as the experimental task. The subjects had to scroll and point at a hyperlink to proceed in the task. Shown here are the beginning (top picture) and the middle (bottom picture) of page 5.

Of the 12 subjects, all had extensive experience with using a mouse; five had much experience with using the in-keyborad isometric joystick; all but one had no experience with the three alternative methods; one subject had a little experience with the three alternatives.

Trade marks on the devices were covered in order not to bias subjects' opinion on each of the methods. After completing all four methods, subjects were asked to rate each of the four methods on a -3 (terrible) to +3 (great) scale based on their experience.

3.2. Results

Figure 5 shows the mean completion time and 95% confidence bars in each of the two consecutive tests. A repeated measure variance analysis showed that subjects completion time was significantly affected by input method ($F_{3,11} = 20.3$, $p < .0001$). Although Test 2 was significantly faster than Test 1 ($F_{1,11} = 12.4$, $p < .01$), such an improvement did not alter the relative performance pattern of the input methods (Method X Test insignificant: $F_{3,11} = 1.1$, $p = .37$).

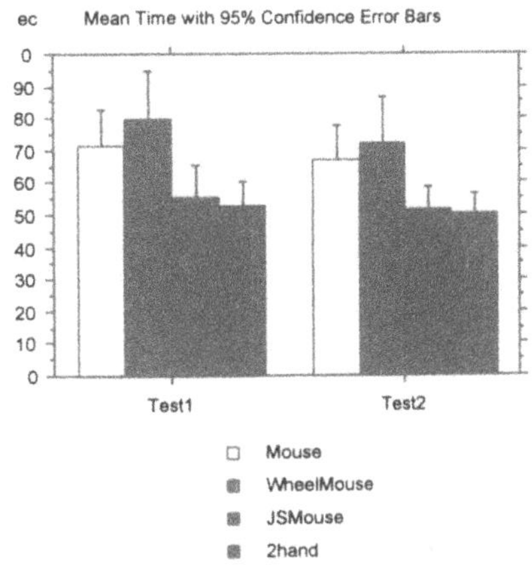

Figure 5 Completion time of web browsing task

Taking the Mouse condition as the reference, the JSMouse and 2Hand conditions were 22.4 and 25.5 percent faster, and the WheelMouse condition was 8.7 percent slower than the standard mouse condition. Statistically, the difference between Mouse and Wheel-Mouse conditions ($p = .086$) and the difference between JSMouse and 2Hand ($p = .57$) were not significant. All other pair wise comparisons were significant ($p < 0.0001$, t-Test).

Subjects subjective rating based on their experience were similar to the performance measurements (Figure 6) except for the difference between Mouse and Wheel-Mouse. Subjects gave the WheelMouse a significantly lower rating than the standard mouse ($p < .05$, t-Test). sThe JSMouse and 2Hand conditions were rated significantly higher than the other two methods (p value from .01 to .0001), but the difference between the two was not significant ($p = .86$).

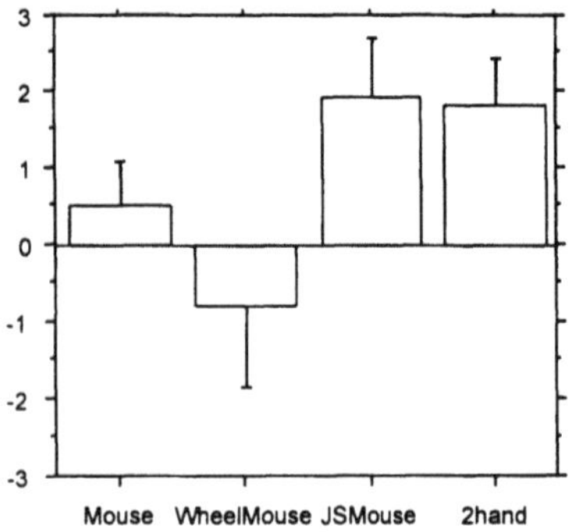

Figure 6 Mean subjective ratings, with 95% confidence error bars, on the four input methods: 3 = great, 2 = very good, 1 = good, 0 = OK, -1 = poor, -2 = very poor, -3 = terrible.

4. DISCUSSION

WheelMouse. Surprisingly, although it offered dual-stream input, the WheelMouse did not outperform the standard mouse, despite the fact that with a single stream mouse one has to switch between target selection and acquiring the scroll bar. Three subjects commented that it was tedious and tiring to repeatedly roll the wheel to scroll a long distance, although this was an intuitive mode. Although encouraged to explore all three modes in the practice phase, only 6 subjects used the two additional rate control modes in addition to wheel rolling in the real tests. It was felt that the rate control mapping functions in the IntelliMouse could be improved. However, we believe the lack of self-centering in the isotonic device (mouse) places it at a fundamental disadvantage to do effective rate control (Zhai and Milgram 1993, Zhai et al. 1993, Zhai 1995). Alternatively, if the mouse functioned in position control mode when the button was pressed, user's performance might have been much higher. The low performance of the WheelMouse in this task shows that a dual-stream solution is not guaranteed to outperform the status-quo single stream input.

JSMouse. Supporting our analyses in the introduction, this dual-stream input device outperformed the standard single stream input significantly. Subjective ratings also verified its advantages. Comparatively, although both the JSMouse and the WheelMouse used one hand to handle two streams of input (even with the same fingers), the JSMouse significantly outperformed the WheelMouse, by a mean magnitude of 29 percent.

2Hand. Interestingly, no significant performance or rating difference was found between the two handed system and the JSMouse, even though the two streams of input were assigned very differently. Nonetheless, the results showed that an asymmetric two handed design, one hand with isometric rate control and the other hand with an isotonic position control worked well, outperforming the status-quo by 25 percent for the browsing task. Concerns were raised if such a two handed system would work at all and if the user would confuse the functions of the two hands. Clearly this is not the case. For more demanding tasks, such as a graphical mail sorting task in which the user needs to drag a mail icon into a folder window, scroll the window while keeping the dragged object and then drop it into an intended folder, we have observed more advantage with the two handed system than the one handed dual-stream solution that might be overloaded. Furthermore, it is extremely difficult, if not impossible, to use the one handed solutions in tasks that requires parallel actions, such as scaling, translating, and rotating a 2D geometry by controlling two vertices (Leganchuk, Zhai, Buxton, 1996).

5. CONCLUSIONS

Three dual-stream input systems , two single handed and one two handed, were analyzed and compared in a web browsing task that require scrolling and pointing. Results showed that a mouse with a joystick all controlled by one hand, or a mouse in one hand and joystick on the other, significantly outperformed the current standard single stream mouse input. However, the mouse with a track wheel device did not performed any better than the standard mouse. In order to take advantage of additional input streams, the types of input devices must be appropriately matched to the tasks being performed. In addition to much evidence in the literature, this study indicates that it is time to add multi-stream input into mainstream commercial systems, although each step of new design has to be guided by thorough human factors research to avoid very possible mistakes.

Acknowledgment
We sincerely thank our colleagues who made significant contributions to the project that this study is based on, in particular Bobby Lee, Ron Barber and Bob Olyha for software development, Kim May for hardware development and Satoru Yamada for commenting on the experimental design.

6. REFERENCES

Barrett, R.C., Selker, E.J., Rutledge, J.D. and Olyha, R.S. (1995) The Negative Inertia: A dynamic pointing function, in *CHI'95 conference companion: Human Factors in Computing Systems*, 316-317.

Buxton, W. (1986) There is more to interaction than meets the eye: some issues in manual input, in Norman, D.A and Draper, S.W. (Eds) *User Centered System Design*, Lawrence Erlbaum Associates, 319-337.

Buxton, W. and Myers, B. (1986) A study of two-handed input, in *Proc. of CHI86*, 321-326.

Fitts, P. (1954) The information capacity of the human motor system in controlling the amplitude of movement. *Journal of Experimental Psychology*, 46, 199-210.

Guiard, Y. (1987) Asymmetric division of labor in human skilled bimanual action: The kinematic chain as a model. *Journal of Motor Behavior*, 19(4) 486-517.

Kabbash, P., Buxton, W., Sellen, A. Two-handed input in a compound task, in *Proc. of CHI94: ACM Conference on Human Factors in Computing Systems*, 417-423.

Leganchuk, A., Zhai, S. and Buxton, W. (1996) Manual and Cognitive factors in two-handed input: an experimental study. submitted for publication.

MacKenzie, I. S., Sellen, A., and Buxton, W. A comparison of input devices in elemental pointing and dragging tasks (1991), in *Proc. of CHI'91: ACM Conference on Human Factors in Computing Systems* New Orleans, Lousiana, 161-166.

Poulton, E.C. (1974) *Tracking skill and manual control*. New York, Academic Press.

Rutledge. J. and Selker, Force-to-motion function for pointing, in *Proceedings of INTERACT90: The IFIP Conference on Human Computer Interaction*, 701-705.

Smith, D.C., Irby, C., Kimball, R., Verplank, W. & Harslem, E. (1982) Designing the Star user interface. *Byte*, 7(4), 242-282.

Venolia, D. (1993). Facile 3D direct manipulation. In *Proc. of INTERCHI'93: ACM Conference on Human Factors in Computing Systems, Amsterdam. The Netherlands*, 31-36.

Zhai, S. (1995) *Human Performance in Six Degree-of-Freedom Input Control*, Ph.D. Thesis, University of Toronto. http://vered.rose.toronto.edu/people/shumin_dir/publications.html

Zhai, S. Milgram, P (1993) Human Performance in evaluation of manipulation schemes in virtual environments, in *Proc. of VRAIS'93: IEEE Virtual Reality Annual International Symposium*, Seattle, USA, 155-161.

Zhai, S. Milgram, P, Drascic, D. (1993) An Evaluation of four 6 degree-of-freedom input techniques, in *Adjunct Proc. of INTERCHI'93: The IFIP Conference on Human Computer Interaction*, Amsterdam, The Netherlands , 155-161.

49

From Command to Control: interface design for customer handling systems

Nicola Millard*, Linda Hole# & Simon Crowle#

*BT Laboratories, Martlesham Heath, Ipswich, England[1]
#Bournemouth University, Wallisdown, Bournemouth, England

nicola.millard@bt-sys.bt.co.uk
lhole@bournemouth.ac.uk
scrowle@bournemouth.ac.uk

ABSTRACT This paper describes interface design activity which focused on the tasks performed by call centre advisers. The advisers' work is supported by a large database, which offers them a command line interface. Contextual observation revealed that more effort was needed to interrogate the database than to communicate with the customers. A subset of advisers' tasks was used to provide scenarios for the design of a 2D/3D graphical user interface, which was prototyped in Macromind Director™ and evaluated by a user group. Initial feedback indicated that the design metaphor and dialogue style have the potential to radically improve the advisers' interaction with the system.

KEY WORDS case study database GUI design

1. INTRODUCTION

Systems which support the telephone interaction between a customer adviser and their customers in a call centre environment present numerous challenges to the user interface designer. These user interfaces need to:

- present a large amount of complex information;
- present the right information at the right place at the right time in the right format;
- provide the customer adviser with a navigation mechanism that does not distract them from their conversation with the customer;
- provide a coherent, efficient and effective method for getting information to the customer at their first point of contact.

Typically, customer service centres provide their customer service advisers with a command line interface to these systems. These tend to fulfil the first criteria but are difficult to use, require a high commitment for training and place a significant cognitive load onto the customer adviser, thus distracting them from their principle task: talking to the customer. A forms driven interface is also common in customer service centres and solves some of these problems. This research was initiated to investigate whether a prototype graphical user environment could be introduced into an operational service centre and fulfil these criteria. The prototype was intended to provoke discussion among systems designers as to the viability of introducing such interfaces into

[1] Thanks are due to Mike Ward of BT Laboratories and the staff of the BT Customer Service Centre, Bournemouth, for their support and encouragement throughout the project.

Human–Computer Interaction: INTERACT'97 S. Howard, J. Hammond & G. Lindgaard (editors)
Published by Chapman & Hall

operational environments. The research team was given access to a customer service centre in the South of England taking incoming calls on a wide range of topics relating to their telephony services.

The study was carried out in three phases:

1. observation of the advisers working with the command line interface;
2. design of the graphical user interface;
3. evaluation of the new interface.

2. PHASE ONE: PROBLEM IDENTIFICATION

Phase one of the study provided an overview of the use of the customer service database to:

- show how the system represented the requirements of the advisers' tasks;
- demonstrate the methods the advisers used to perform those tasks;
- relate the methods used to performance of the task itself.

The research team needed to obtain a users' (adviser's) view of the command language access to the database so that a true picture of call handling activity could be developed. The study began with passive observation of the customer advisers' interaction with the database within their work context. A total of 365 calls were observed with 11 advisers as they performed the tasks of receiving and responding to customer enquiries. During the call, the advisers performed actions such as: browsing the database; writing a note; looking for information off-line. The data consisted of sequences of the command language codes used to browse the database during each call, plus any other actions the advisers performed during the call.

Three call scenarios were identified during analysis: bill enquiries; features sales; moving house. Actions were collated and analysed for 180 calls which fell within the three scenarios. It was found that within each scenario, 83% of adviser activity was focused on a central 16 typical actions. A task flow analysis was obtained from the bank of taped verbal protocols of customer calls. Approximately 10% of the calls in each category were transcribed from the tapes to produce an activity flow, illustrating how the conversation between customer and adviser mapped onto the adviser's work with both the system and off-line facilities.

The findings from the task analysis were as follows:

1. Only a comparatively small subset of database screens were used during call handling, and, within the subset, activity was primarily focused on a few key screens.
2. Movement between the screens did not follow the prescribed menu-driven route: the experienced advisers had learnt the three-letter commands to access the area of the database they required.
3. Interaction with the database in this fashion sometimes caused problems with the saving of entries in certain fields. Hence a lot of note-taking activity was required for the advisers to maintain the information they had collected from the customer or their records.
4. Information presented on a screen was sometimes needed in conjunction with other screens. This added to the users' cognitive load as they were required to flick backwards and forwards between screens to follow their thoughts about the customer enquiry.
5. The advisers rarely used the system menus or help facilities; when they forgot how to access areas of the database, they relied on one another for help.
6. Customers' personal data were repeatedly noted, whereas the system might have been expected to carry that data throughout the interaction.
7. Accessing the database via this interface meant that a disproportionate number of actions were required to complete each task.

Passive observation was chosen as a method which would not disrupt the advisers' natural work pattern. However, it did mean that none of the advisers' views could be elicited during data collection. A questionnaire was administered to 30 advisers to ascertain their overall impression of the database; approximately 43% were returned for analysis. The findings indicated that:

1. Advisers suggested that the system was 'easier' rather than more 'difficult' to use. A possible explanation of this could be the experience of the users, none of whom could be classified as a novice or intermediate user. Since it is the nature of the job that advisers should be competent in their knowledge and use of the system, it is not unreasonable for persons of this level to consider the job 'easy'.
2. Although the advisers found the database adequate for their jobs, they felt that the system was sometimes a hindrance to them doing the job to the best of their abilities.

3. The single largest area of concern was the speed of interaction required to meet the call handling time, which was targeted at 240 seconds per telephone call.
4. Many advisers enjoyed their jobs and took a pride in successfully and efficiently dealing with the customer enquiries and problems. They basically viewed themselves as the database access provider for the customer, mastering the interface on the customer's behalf.

The database provided all the information that the advisers could ever need, although it wasn't necessarily on one screen. Its command line interface relied heavily upon fast and accurate typing. Interaction with the system was powerful, flexible, and user controlled: experienced advisers could access the information held within the database with speed and efficiency; they could gain instant access to all areas of the database within their level of authorisation. However, this interface made a heavy demand on the adviser's long term memory to recall the three letter screen commands, making the system difficult to learn and to remember. The reliance upon typed input made the use of the system error prone as the advisers attempted to work at a speed which enabled them to meet their call handling targets. The advisers did not always work in the manner required by the system, and hence they had to undertake lots of note-taking as parameters were lost from screen to screen. During a call, the advisers browsed the database to gain an understanding of the customer's circumstances as they were speaking, holding information from the various locations in their working memory.

3. PHASE TWO: INTERFACE DESIGN

Phase two generated the prototype interface, POW (Personal Office Workspace), which was a result of:

- addressing some important HCI issues that are problematic in command-language interfaces;
- reviewing actions the advisers took to perform the three scenarios;
- synthesising modern interface metaphors and interaction styles with the advisers' activities.

3.1 Scenario based design

A scenario-based approach looks at the user, their environment and the context of the work. In the particular case of these customer advisers, the customer exists as part of the scenario and the interaction between the adviser and the customer (not just the adviser and the system) must also be considered (Carroll, 1995). The design of the interface focused on the advisers, their work and how the system could most effectively support their activities. The functionality was defined in terms of adviser activities, the information requirements for those activities and how the activities supported the advisers' work. Developing a system using scenarios allowed both the designers and advisers to communicate using a common point of reference (the office environment).

Prototyping from scenarios begins with a relatively simple model of the system. Users test the prototype with real-world work scenarios suggested by both the designer and user. Using this method, the designer and user can quickly pick up errors in design, identify areas that need development and capture usability problems.

3.2 System analysis

POW's 3D, graphical user interface reduces cognitive load and provides user-controlled methods of interaction. For example, users need only recognise information sources (Phonebook, Streetfinder, etc) rather than having to recall them (3-letter command codes), and the objects offer affordances (Norman, 1988) which inform the users about their potential behaviour. The system also provides some automation (with automatic retrieval of telephone numbers) and alleviates the need to note system status.

Information is presented in a more manageable and meaningful way; POW objects are taken from real-world scenarios that both customer and adviser are familiar with and that encapsulate information in a recognisable format (eg presenting billing information as the customer sees it). This graphical *ad hoc* manipulation interface (Kappel & Min Tjoa, 1992) enables the adviser to manipulate the environment to carry out a task. By using direct manipulation interface metaphors to access/process information, POW allows its users to concentrate on what they are doing rather than how they are doing it (Weller & Hartson, 1992).

3.3 Interface design

In designing the interface, the team took a craft approach, relying on the three scenarios to guide the design decisions. Lansdale, Scrivener and Woodcock (1996) comment that in HCI, disciplines such as task analysis or cognitive psychology are insufficiently developed to prescribe exactly how design should proceed in any given situation. Wallace and Anderson (1993) suggest there is a need to synthesise the sources of interface design quality: talent from the craft approach; principles from the cognitive engineering approach.

The prototype interface addressed the problems of:

- maintaining the power and flexibility of access offered by the database, to provide an interface which would still offer the advisers control and flexibility in their work;
- removing the need to flick backwards and forwards from one screen to another: the information scattered across numerous screens needed to be provided on one screen without overloading the screen;
- ensuring that data entries were saved when moving from one information source in the database to another;
- avoiding hand-written notes which duplicated information held on the system.

In order to maintain the powerful interaction with the database which was provided via the command line interface, a graphical, direct manipulation interface was chosen: this would be flexible, easy to learn and remember, and less error prone because far less keyboard entry would be required (Mayhew, 1992). Just as the command line dialogue enabled the advisers to travel anywhere in the database, so the graphical interface would provide direct access to all of the stored data via objects on the screen. It offered easily reversible actions, instant, visual feedback, and exploited the use of visuo-spatial cues, to utilise recognition rather than recall memory.

The provision of a GUI shifted some of the advisers' cognitive load to their perceptual system. Rather than keeping the task requirements within their working memory, the advisers would be able to obtain visual cues from the objects on the screen to remind them which procedures they had/had not completed. The declarative actions using semantic memory in the command line dialogue were replaced with procedural actions using episodic memory in the direct manipulation dialogue (Anderson, 1980). Wright and Lickorish (1994) observed that in any complex task that makes many demands on memory processes, people will select procedures that result in fewest additional demands on their working memory.

The proposed new interface built upon the desktop metaphor which users may already know and expect to find (Sawyer & Mariani, 1995): it transformed the desktop into a cubicle. This provided the customer advisers with a visual image of their own, virtual, 3D workspace, enclosed by "walls" which could be enhanced by the adviser's own personal pictures, notes, etc. The cubicle, at desktop level, housed a variety of objects the adviser needed to perform the call handling tasks.

"Books" of information provided pages of data on the same screen without the advisers having to change screens or refresh screens. The advisers' knowledge or intuition about the contents of these "books" would reduce the need to hold the numerous command codes in their memories. Data was shown to be stored 'within' the objects and was consistent with the adviser's conception of information storage and retrieval with these objects in everyday life.

"Peel-off notes" took the role of information holders; in everyday life we jot things on them and move them around, so why not transfer this process to the screen? Data was manipulated by the use of these "peel-off notes", which could be: written on and dragged to a file to instigate a search for the customer record; peeled off record A and dragged to record B to effect an update of the customer records; written on and stuck onto a customer's page to annotate the customer record.

4. PHASE THREE: INTERFACE EVALUATION

The POW prototype, based on the three call handling scenarios, was engineered with a small amount of data to enable some data manipulation to take place. During phase three of the study, POW was shown to a new group of twenty customer advisers to assess their initial reactions to the interface. Individual interviews were conducted to obtain detailed views from users who were of varied experience.

Prior to seeing POW for the first time, the advisers were encouraged to focus their thoughts on the customer service database interface currently used by means of a brief questionnaire. The questionnaire presented strengths and weaknesses of the command language dialogue style (Mayhew, 1992) to elicit the advisers' judgements of how their system measured up against these criteria. This was an attempt to highlight the power of the command language interface, so that the advisers might take a more critical view of the direct manipulation interface, rather than being swayed by its novelty.

The interviews were video-recorded to collect all the advisers' interaction on screen, plus their comments. The interviews were used to establish the adviser's: previous computer experience; interpretations of the system metaphor; expectations of the interactive objects displayed on screen; reactions and comments regarding system design. All participants were informed before the session began that their interview was strictly confidential and that it was not a test of intelligence or aptitude. The video camera was pointed at the computer monitor, not at the participant.

4.1 Results

The questionnaire data confirmed some of the phase one findings from the first group of advisers. There was overall disagreement that the command line interface to the customer service database:

- was fast and efficient;
- was flexible;
- offered screens which were consistent in appearance;
- allowed the users to customise the screens;
- allowed the users to enter multiple commands;
- trapped errors;
- allowed the users to undo any erroneous actions.

There was a 50/50 divide of opinion that the customer service database:

- was easy to learn;
- enabled them to enter and exit the screens as they wished;
- offered screens which were well designed.

There was overall agreement that the customer service database:

- was clear and easy to understand;
- used the keyboard as a satisfactory input device;
- allowed access to customer information;
- allowed the user to check input before it was actioned;
- provided a useful HELP facility.

From the open-ended questions it was apparent that:

- the best aspect of their current system was the sense of power the advisers experienced by having the ability to access information directly, and by being familiar with the system;
- the worst aspects were both design and performance related: the customer service database was considered to be slow, cumbersome, unreliable, complex, inflexible, unclear and suffered from a lack of prompts;
- some advisers felt the system relied too heavily on jargon, and the information provided on-screen was difficult to understand or use;
- the most common mistakes that they encountered were due to typing errors, incorrect input and general systems errors.

The advisers suggested that the design of the customer service database could be improved by: less typing; reordering of the information with an emphasis on keeping the relevant information together and having direct access to that information; an error correction facility; fewer screens; having a list of customer options; having the ability to page back and forward without having to save information; increasing the speed between screens to allow quicker access to frequently used screens.

The interview data was organised into a set of keywords or phrases describing:

a) initial adviser reaction to aspects of the system;
b) in-depth comments on aspects of the system;
c) features advisers would like to see added to/changed in the system;
d) how the advisers would handle the three call scenarios with the system.

It was interesting to note the wide variety of abilities amongst the advisers. Those who had gained previous experience with direct manipulation system metaphors were more capable of grasping the concepts behind the interface and expressing their expectations of the system. Those with no previous computer experience and/or who had used the customer service database for many years appeared to try to interpret the new system in terms of the current system's functions. However, almost without exception the reception to the new system was positive and very encouraging.

65% of the advisers recognised the whole environment to be a representation of an office or a room. Others broke the scenario down into smaller components such as a filing cabinet, or a shelf of books. Some of the more literal minded described it as an 'integrated database' or '3D outlines' (of books).

35% of the advisers guessed that the "peel-off-note" was something to do with accessing the customerfs details; 25% of advisers thought it to be a page from one of the books, a diary or a piece of paper; 30% could not identify it; 10% could not actively use the system (could not use the mouse), they only gave comments.

The prototype caused one or two interaction difficulties (eg closing the books and putting away the flipchart), and some advisers said that it 'would take a bit of getting used to'. Despite these problems, the overwhelming response to the interface was encouraging.

How the advisers would handle the three call scenarios with the system was categorised in terms of the use of an object (or objects) on screen. Some advisers were able to elaborate on how they would use the information from each object within the context of a) the scenario and b) the system as a whole, whilst others could only identify which objects they would use to achieve their goal. All advisers had little or no difficulty in proposing a solution to the call handling scenarios using the system, which suggests that they had become engaged in the POW environment (Weller & Hartson, 1992).

5. DISCUSSION

Testing the POW prototype and receiving user feedback was an essential part of the development strategy. By analysing the video recordings of the interviews it was possible to determine how the POW objects matched up to the advisers' expectations; for example which "book" the adviser expected to contain what information. An interaction study shows how users most commonly attempt to use the system (such as methods of opening and closing books). Also, discussions with the advisers during and after using the system revealed areas that need development (moving house using the Streetfinder) and individual differences in working practice. Interestingly, exposure to the new interface promoted active thinking on the part of the advisers, who frequently suggested new features that would help with their work. For example, one adviser suggested including spatial information on customers' addresses.

POW incorporates the best of the customer service database system whilst making considerable HCI progress, but still has many steps to make before it can become a reality. However, even in the first prototype stage, POW has received a positive response from the advisers.

Call centres have been established within a wide variety of organisations, each of which aim to provide a fast, friendly and efficient customer response. The customer advisers handling the incoming calls are under pressure to present a warm and co-operative human interface whilst possibly wrestling with a sterile and unyielding systems interface. If they are provided with an interface which closely resembles the real world, the advisers will feel supported by a system which more naturally maps on to the focus of their work: co-operating with their customers to solve problems.

Whilst the design of these empowering environments (Weller and Hartson, 1992) should become the focus of serious endeavour in order to release the advisers from the stress of less usable interfaces, it would be useful to also examine the possibility of enabling the advisers to *enjoy* their customer handling work: Norman (1986) gives this as his second goal for cognitive engineering. If the advisers find themselves perceiving their use of the computer system as *fun* (Igbaria, Schiffman & Wieckowski, 1994), then their call handling behaviour will change to produce a better level of interaction with their customers.

Only 22% of the companies (of 100+ employees) surveyed by the Henley Centre (The Henley Centre, 1994) appeared to have the appropriate level of investment in technology, telecoms services, customer research and human resources to enable them to perform an effective customer handling function. 60% of the major organisations contacted could not access their customer data either quickly or easily. 9% of companies were classed by the Henley Centre as 'advanced call handlers'. These companies are beginning to recognise that effective user interface design is the way to fulfil their complex information management needs as they interact with the customer.

A large percentage of these 'advanced call handlers' are currently using systems which have command line interfaces. Use of forms based and Windows based interfaces are more common in companies who have not had large legacy systems to integrate into their customer service processes. Use of more innovative GUI environments are rare. However, development using tools which support graphical environments are becoming more common. These are beginning to change the standard forms based look and feel of the screen environment.

6. CONCLUSION

The role that user interface design plays in managing the critical interaction between a customer adviser and their customer is significant. The initial evaluation of the POW metaphor indicated that the location of commonly accessed items of customer data can be successfully represented in a graphical environment. Recognition of the elements within the POW environment made it easy to navigate and use without placing a significant amount of additional cognitive load on the customer adviser whilst interacting with the customer. Although the POW prototype was never intended to become an operational system, elements, such as the "peel off notes", have already been incorporated into operational customer handling interfaces.

The ability of the POW prototype to handle the high complexity, high volume amounts of customer data which occur in an operational environment has yet to be proven. When dealing with low level information which is less frequently accessed, a command line system is often more powerful and the POW metaphor may not be appropriate. Other issues which require further investigation are the effect of user experience on navigation and the practicality of a mouse driven user interface over keyboard driven or touchscreen in an operational environment.

Customer handling, however, is not just about innovative technologies. Peters (1989) stated that "service equals systems plus smiles". Technology can take the emphasis on process away from the human adviser so that they can concentrate on customer care. However, deskilling the adviser can take away some of the challenge and motivation of what can be a boring and repetitive task. Giving the adviser a good working environment, a supportive team and responsibilities for running the customer service centre and taking calls can all be motivating factors that promote delivery of a world class customer interface. Using the principles established in the design of the POW interface, the user's personal screen world can be used to complement and reflect the overall design of their working environment.

REFERENCES

Anderson, J R (1980) *Cognitive Psychology and its Implications* San Francisco: W H Freeman & Co

Carroll, J M (1995) *Scenario-Based Design: Envisioning Work & Technology in System Development* Wiley

Igbaria, M, Schiffman, S & Wieckowski, T (1994) The respective roles of perceived usefulness and perceived fun in the acceptance of microcomputer technology *Behaviour & Information Technology, vol 13, no 6, pp349-361*

Kappel, G & Min Tjoa, A (1992) State of art and open issues on graphical user interfaces for object-oriented database systems *Information & Software Technology, vol 34, no 11, pp 721-730*

Lansdale, M W, Scrivener, S A R & Woodcock, A (1996) Developing practice with theory in HCI: applying models of spatial cognition for the design of pictorial databases *Int. J. Human-Computer Studies, 44, pp777-799*

Mayhew, D (1992) *Principles & Guidelines in Software User Interface Design* London: Prentice-Hall

Norman, D (1986) 'Cognitive engineering' in Norman, D & Draper, S (eds) *User Centred System Design* Lawrence Erlbaum Associates

Norman, D (1988) *The Psychology of Everyday Things* New York: Basic Books

Peters, T (1989) *The Customer Revolution* BBC Video

Sawyer, P & Mariani, J (1995) Database systems: challenges and opportunities for graphical HCI *Interacting with Computers, vol 7, no 3, pp273-303*

The Henley Centre (1994) *Teleculture 2000*, July

Wallace, M D & Anderson, T J (1993) Approaches to interface design *Interacting with Computers, vol 5, no 3, pp259-278*

Weller, HG & Hartson, HR (1992) Metaphors for the Wright, P & Lickorish A (1994) Menus and memory load: navigation strategies in interactive search tasks *Int. J. Human-Computer Studies, 40, pp965-1008*

Nature of Human-Computer Interaction in an Empowering Environment: Interaction Style Influences the Manner of Human Accomplishment *Computers In Human Behaviour, vol 8, pp313-33*

50

Command/Shortcut Keys in WIMP User Interfaces: A Lost Cause?

Kee Yong LIM

School of Mechanical & Production Engineering
Nanyang Technological University
Nanyang Avenue
SINGAPORE 639798
mkylim@ntuvax.ntu.ac.sg

ABSTRACT In recent years, command/shortcut keys have proliferated exponentially in WIMP menus. However, it remains unclear whether the substantial resources spent on programming the functions of such keys, have resulted in real and/or significant benefits for user interaction. This paper reports a study to determine user interaction patterns for WIMP user interfaces and users' performance in exploiting command/shortcut keys. Subjects were served a questionnaire, a paper-based test and an on-line task to assess their preference for a particular style of interaction and their performance in respect of command/shortcut keys. The results of the study provide a new perspective for software development managers who are confronted with limited human/project resources. The work will support better decisions and resource planning in connection with value engineering, and with the effectiveness and productivity of user interface programmers.

KEYWORDS Command/Shortcut Keys, WIMP User Interfaces, Usability, Menu Design, Productivity and Effectiveness in Software Development.

1. BACKGROUND

For the past decade, graphical user interfaces have emerged as the predominant design for software applications. Today, WIMP (Windows, Icons, Menus and Pointer) user interfaces have effectively supplanted command-line user interfaces. This development is a direct endorsement of how the application of a simple human factors principle (recognition being superior to recall) could contribute significantly to the design of user friendly computer systems.

Paradoxically, there appears to be a shift in recent years, towards 'recall directed' interaction. Specifically, it may be observed that command/shortcut keys have been included rather pervasively in WIMP menus. It appears that the inclusion was made initially on the belief that the keys offer users a means of exploiting the best design features of both command line and WIMP user interfaces. This belief has gone unquestioned to the extent that command/shortcut keys have proliferated

Human–Computer Interaction: INTERACT'97 S. Howard, J. Hammond & G. Lindgaard (editors)
Published by Chapman & Hall

exponentially. Is the belief valid? Are the benefits of command/shortcut keys actually realised? Are there negative implications of increasing the number of command/shortcut keys? To address these questions, a study was conducted to determine users' interaction styles, preferences and performance with respect to their exploitation of command/shortcut keys.

2. THE STUDY

The study aims to determine:

- how well users remember different command/shortcut keys
- the extent (frequency and range) of use of particular command/shortcut keys
- the nature and frequency of errors for particular command/shortcut keys
- differences in interaction styles and performance between experts and novices in relation to command/shortcut keys
- users' preferences (if any) for particular devices to input command/shortcut keys.

The objective of the study is two-fold:

- to determine the actual effectiveness of command/shortcut keys
- to ascertain whether the (significant) resources invested by software companies to provide command/shortcut key functions have been worthwhile.

The study was conducted on two commonly used software applications. Subjects (university students) used in the test were generally computer literate ranging in age from 21 to 28 years old. 75 subjects were served a number of tests. First, a questionnaire was served to elicit their use of command/shortcut keys.

Second, the subjects were subjected to a paper-based multiple-choice answer test to determine their ability to recognise and recall the function of a set of command/shortcut keys. This test was structured into two sections as follows:

- Section 1: subjects were asked to match command names given in full (e.g. 'Save') to abbreviated representations of command/shortcut keys (e.g. 'Ctrl S').
- Section 2: subjects were asked to match abbreviated representations of command/shortcut keys (e.g. 'Ctrl S') against the correct command names which are typically indicated in full as menu items (e.g. 'Save').

The objective of the test is to ascertain the extent to which the abbreviated forms of command/shortcut keys is recognised by subjects. It is anticipated that subject performance would correlate with the appropriateness of the representations found in common software applications. In this context, 'appropriateness' was assessed according to established rules of abbreviations and semantics found in design handbooks (e.g. Helander, 1988). The complexity of the representation (e.g. length and syntax of the character string used to abbreviate the command/shortcut key) was also considered. Command/shortcut keys were thus classified into simple and complicated classes. In addition, representations associated with frequently used and/or generic command/shortcut keys were also noted. The latter classification refers to command/shortcut keys that are commonly found within one application and across different applications respectively. A third classification was also defined to uncover any optimisation by users (intentional or otherwise), of the physical effort required to use command/shortcut keys. It is conceivable that users may avoid using some command/shortcut keys not because they were unable to remember the keys, but because additional or awkward effort is required for their activation. In particular, some command/shortcut keys may require more than two-fingers and/or more than one hand to activate. It would be informative to ascertain the extent to which the economy of effort would affect users' interaction patterns. A final classification of command/shortcut keys addressed the consistency of the representations of generic commands found in different release versions of the same application, across different applications, and across platforms. Worse, with a fast growing set of command/shortcut keys, some applications have even used the same key to represent different access functions found in different screen displays. As in the case of the economy of effort, it is conceivable that users might avoid using command/shortcut keys if a significant set of generic commands have different representations across these applications. The resulting cognitive load and frustration due to the negative transfer of learning effects, may deter a user from learning let alone use command/shortcut keys. It would be 'natural' for users to avoid a situation that engenders a sense of helplessness. It should be noted that applications which provide functions to enable users to define their preferred representations of command/shortcut keys (according to those they have already learnt), would alleviate but not solve the problem. Although enforcing consistency of representations is a solution, it is made very difficult by the large (and still growing) set of command/shortcut keys that are found in existing applications.

The motivation for such a comprehensive classification of command/shortcut keys was two-fold:

- to support richer interpretation of the data to be collected. For instance, by serving the test to subjects with different levels of experience (of the software application), the extent to which user performance may improve with learning may be determined for each class of command/shortcut keys.
- to ensure a balanced set of test questions. Thus, the test questions used will address the complete spectrum of command/shortcut keys; i.e. covering simple keys such as Ctrl S, Ctrl C, Alt E to more complicated Ctrl-Shift, Alt-Shift combinations (see Windows Interface Guidelines, 1995). Command/shortcut keys associated with common/generic functions were similarly selected to make up half the set used in the test.

To avoid potential interaction effects due to the clustering of a particular class of command/shortcut keys, test questions were also randomised. A 'don't know' response was also included as one of the multiple-choice selections to minimise reckless guessing by subjects.

To complement the questionnaire and paper-based tests, a final objective assessment was also conducted. A subset of the 75 subjects were selected at random to participate in an on-line test involving a wordprocessing task. The task entailed typing and editing of a text passage and involved a set of command functions that may be activated by mouse-based menu selections, and/or keyboard inputs. No time limit was enforced for task completion in this test.

Subject inputs were recorded and analysed to ascertain their interaction patterns and the extent of their exploitation of command/shortcut keys. The subjects were also observed to determine the extent of their (actual) preferences for a particular style of interaction, i.e. mouse-based interaction with menu items or keyboard-based interaction with command/shortcut keys.

For both paper-based and on-line tests, the nature of errors committed by subjects with respect to the recognition and use of command/shortcut keys, were also analysed.

3. RESULTS

The study yielded rather rich information. A detailed discussion of the results will be reported at a later date. The present paper will only provide a summary of some of the results.

Generally, the study indicated the following:

(1) command/shortcut keys were remembered rather poorly. The performance of subjects was unsatisfactory even for common functions such as 'Find'. In this instance, only 11% of the subjects knew the appropriate command/shortcut key. With more complicated command/shortcut keys (e.g. those involving a modifier key, see Windows Interface Guidelines, 1995), correct identification of the key functions dropped drastically to about 4%.

(2) limited use (frequency & range) of command/shortcut

keys. The results indicated that subjects tend to use only command/shortcut keys that are simple and common/generic across software applications. The results seem to suggest that combination type command/shortcut keys were used so infrequently that subjects were unable to achieve a satisfactory level of competence. In particular, the subjects knew the function of only about 10% of the keys. Later observations of their performance of a wordprocessing task revealed a limited use of access keys (e.g. keying 'O' for Open). It was observed that subjects (mostly right-handed) were unwilling to release the mouse to key in access keys and combination type command/shortcut keys. They were also uncomfortable with using the left-hand to key in commands. It appeared that input using the mouse was more 'intuitive' and economic in effort (see also (5) below). Subjects also found it more disruptive to have to shift their visual focus from the screen to the keyboard, when they wanted to locate the keys to activate the more complicated command/shortcut keys. It would be interesting for future research to examine whether touch typists would also be similarly affected. Another observation made was that subjects were more inclined (consciously or otherwise) to move from the keyboard to the mouse when they needed to activate menu items. This inclination was observed even for subjects who knew the command/shortcut keys required to activate the desired command functions. However, the converse did not apply. Instead, when the subject's hand was already resting on the mouse, they were less inclined to release the mouse to use the keyboard, even if they know the command/shortcut key. For instance, observations during the on-line test revealed that some subjects would even use the mouse to 'Save' a file rather than key in 'Ctrl S'. This inclination of subjects was observed to be more pronounced when more complicated command/shortcut keys were involved. One explanation for this observation may be that moving the mouse would incur little or no additional mental resources (see also (4) below). Conversely, for more complex tasks, it is possible that competition for the same mental resources may arise if users need to recall complicated command/shortcut keys. Thus, users would tend to choose the easier style of interaction rather than suffer a higher mental load or lower task performance.

(3) more errors for meaningless or semantically weak command/shortcut keys. Subjects encountered more problems with combination type command/shortcut keys and function keys which were complex and semantically obscure, e.g. Ctrl-Shift P, Alt E P and F5. Such command/shortcut keys may be compared with semantically 'acceptable' keys such as 'Ctrl S' for 'Save'. Observations of subject performance of the on-line task revealed slower recognition of access keys with inappropriate abbreviations (e.g. keying 'T' for 'Help Topics', see Windows Interface Guidelines, 1995). It is indeed surprising to find that such poor designs of command/shortcut keys persist despite extensive recommendations for command 'naming' (see Barnard et al., 1982; Hirsh-Pasek et al., 1982; Ehrenreich, 1985; etc.).

(4) no significant difference between expert and novice performance in the use of command/shortcut keys. Before reporting the results, it is pertinent to acknowledge that there is no absolute or universally accepted definition of an expert or novice user. For the present study, an expert was defined generally as a user who:

- is generally knowledgeable about computers
- is generally knowledgeable about software applications
- has spent more than 6 hours per week on the software application under test
- has used the software application under test for more than a year

In this context, it was observed that the recognition and recall of command/shortcut keys by expert and novice users were equally poor. Subjects identified correctly only 10% of common command/shortcut keys; did not know the functions of 80% of the keys and gave wrong answers for the rest. The results suggested that the extent of use of command/shortcut keys did not increase with higher competency in using the software. These results contradicted observations by d'Ydewalle et al. (1995) that expert subjects used command/shortcut keys more frequently than menu selections via a mouse. A likely explanation of the difference is that subjects in the present study accumulated their expertise largely from using WIMP user interfaces only. As a result, they may be predisposed towards mouse-based interaction. In the case of d'Ydewalle et al., a significant number of the subjects 'graduated' from command-based user interfaces to WIMP user interfaces. Some of their subjects were also programmers. Thus, it may be postulated that users' past interaction experience can determine their interaction pattern/behaviour with WIMP user interfaces. For users who were exposed to WIMP user interfaces only, it appears that a form of 'transfer of learning' effect may manifest itself as a habituation or predisposition towards a particular style of interaction, i.e. mouse-based or keyboard-based interaction. The results of the study suggest that such users may go through a sequence of menu selections using the mouse, without even noticing the representations of command/shortcut keys displayed next to the menu items selected. Thus, these users may not learn the representations at all, or would only learn them after much longer exposure to the software application.

(5) overwhelming preference for mouse-based command input. The survey of subject responses indicated a negative attitude towards command/shortcut keys. Subjects reported that they used such keys rarely as they could not remember them. They also felt that inadequate guidance was given on the use of the keys. Later observations of their performance of a wordprocessing task revealed an overwhelming preference for mouse-based command input via menu selections. The ratio of mouse to keyboard input was determined to be about 88:12. This result compares well with the 90:10 ratio reported by d'Ydewalle et al. (1995). Thus, it may be concluded that mouse-based command input is by far the most dominant style of interaction for WIMP user interfaces.

4. DESIGN RECOMMENDATIONS

The results of the study indicated that for common software applications, the effectiveness of command/shortcut keys is very limited. This observation is aggravated further by the strong predisposition of users towards mouse-based interaction. This predisposition was particularly pronounced for users who have used only WIMP user interfaces since starting on computers. With the pervasive implementation of WIMP user interfaces, new and recent generations of users would fall into this category. Consequently, the use of command/shortcut keys by users would not only be limited presently, but may be expected to diminish in the near future. It may thus be concluded that the current emphasis on providing a comprehensive set of command/shortcut keys, is misguided and should be curtailed. In view of the reported worldwide shortage of IT staff, continued deployment of human resources to programme an extensive set of command/shortcut keys, is not only unproductive but highly irrational. Such a software development practice should be reviewed.

Existing user interface design guidelines for command/shortcut keys should also be revised. It is recommended that the set of command/shortcut keys provided should be small, and be confined preferably to simple and commonly used keys that are generic across software applications (see also Rosenberg and Moran, 1984). Design effort should thus be directed at defining an optimal set to balance efficiency trade-offs between mouse-based menu selection and keyboard-based input of commands (see Paap, 1988). Such a set of command/shortcut keys could be specified based on an understanding of their classifications and associated implications as described in this study. By abandoning the emphasis on providing an all-inclusive set of command/shortcut keys, it would also be easier to define more appropriate and consistent representations of command/shortcut keys. The problems reported earlier in this paper may thus be avoided.

5. REFERENCES

Barnard, P. J., Hammond, N. V., MacLean, A. and Morton, J., 1982, Learning and Remembering Interactive Commands in a Text Editing Task, Behaviour & Information Technology, 1(4), 347-358, Taylor & Francis.

d'Ydewalle, G., Leemans, J. and Rensbergen, J. V., 1995, Graphical vs Character-Based Wordprocessors: An Analysis of User Performance, Behaviour & Information Technology, 14(4), 208-214, Taylor & Francis.

Ehrenreich, L., 1985, Computer Abbreviations: Evidence and Synthesis, Human Factors, 27(2), 143-155.

Helander, M, 1988, Handbook of Human-Computer Interaction, Elsevier Science (North Holland).

Hirsh-Pasek, K., Nudelman, S. and Schneider, M. L., 1982, An Experimental Evaluation of Abbreviation Schemes in Limited Lexicons, Behaviour & Information Technology, 1(4), 359-369, Taylor & Francis.

Microsoft Windows, 1995, The Windows Interface Guidelines, A Guide for Designing Software, Microsoft Corp.

Paap, K. R., 1988, Design of Menus, In: Helander, M. (ed.), Handbook of Human Computer Interaction, 205-235, Elsevier Science.

Rosenberg, J. and Moran, T., 1984, Generic Commands, In: Shackel, B. (ed.), Human Computer Interaction - INTERACT'84, 245-249, Elsevier Science.

Developing the optimum help system using the LUCID method

Andy Smith, Lynne Dunckley, Diana Burkhardt and Alan Murkett[1] Ken Eason[2] and Johnathan Church[3]

[1] Department of Computing, University of Luton, Park Square, Luton, Bedfordshire, LU1 3JU, UK.
Tel: +44 (0) 1582 34111 Fax: +44 (0) 1582 489212
email: andy.smith@luton.ac.uk
[2] HUSAT Research Institute, Loughborough University of Technology, Leicestershire LE11 3TU, UK.
[3] Plasmon Data Ltd, Melbourne, Cambridgeshire, SG8 6EN, UK.

ABSTRACT In this paper the authors describe the application of the Logical User Centred Interface Design (LUCID) method to the development of a Windows based help system. LUCID is a participative method which, through the integration of Taguchi techniques from the domain of total quality management, attempts not only to develop usable human-computer interfaces, but to identify the optimum, or most usable, interface. An outline of the method together with detailed results from the first commercial implementation are presented. The method is shown to provide powerful support to the optimisation of a commercial on-line help system.

KEY WORDS: usability, evaluation, prototypes, design methods, Taguchi

1 INTRODUCTION

In a review of user interface development processes and methodologies, Hartson and Boehm-Davis (1993) recognise that although *'in one sense considerable progress has been made'* they identify a number of key specific research areas where there remains the need for *'real breakthroughs'*. In terms of methodologies for interface design Hartson and Boehm-Davis (1993, p109) state that:

- *'research in the area of formative evaluation needs to focus on interactive evaluation techniques that, in fact, lead to convergence on a good or at least an improved design'*

and

- *'there is especially a need for techniques that can assign credit and blame, pinpointing why user performance is not up to expected levels in terms of specific interface flaws and shortcomings'*

Bevan (1995) has suggested that *'quality of use'* should be the major design objective for an interactive software product using the criteria *'does the product enable the intended users to achieve the intended tasks, rather than does it merely satisfy its*

Human–Computer Interaction: INTERACT'97 S. Howard, J. Hammond & G. Lindgaard (editors)
Published by Chapman & Hall

specification'. Juran (1979) defines quality as being *'fit for purpose or use'.* It has seemed appropriate therefore to investigate the ways in which TQM techniques may contribute to meeting Hartson and Boehm-Davis's aims.

In order to address these issues Smith and Dunckley (1996) are currently developing a new interface design methodology called the Logical User Centred Interface Design (LUCID) method which integrates the application of Taguchi techniques from the arena of total quality management into the development approach. This paper describes a commercial application of the LUCID method to a Windows based help system, following two earlier pilot studies.

2 INTRODUCING LUCID

The discipline of human-computer interaction is maturing rapidly and a wide number of interface design methods, for example Supportive Evaluation (Robinson and Fitter, 1992) and Method for Usability Engineering (Lim and Long, 1994), have been developed within the last decade. It might at first, therefore, seem unnecessary to propose yet another method.

The rationale behind the LUCID method outlined here is to develop a more systematic and rigorous procedure for developing and optimising the user interface. LUCID is founded on the following underlying principles:

- *adoption of a user-centred development approach*, whereby users and developers can work together on the identification of factors which effect usability and which specify performance,
- *effective use of iterative and parallel prototyping*, so as to facilitate user participation, maximise the effectiveness of the interface evaluation process whilst minimising the time required for development,
- *integration of Taguchi techniques,* thereby providing the rigour necessary for the identification of the optimum interface,
- *systematic and logical integration of techniques,* so that the method can be applied by commercial interface designers.

The Taguchi approach to interface design is an evolutionary technique but, through a crucial parallel phase, places an emphasis on the design, rather than the iterative testing of the interface. Application of Taguchi techniques within the LUCID method will provide the following information:

- *What is the optimum interface design?*
- *What factors and associated levels give the optimum design?*
- *What is the expected quality characteristic (usability metric) for the optimum interface?*

The basic stages in the proposed method are outlined in Figure 1 and an outline diagrammatic comparison between the LUCID approach and alternative prototyping approaches is provided in Figure 2. Although a number of phases within LUCID are still in development, and full implementation data is not yet available, Figure 2 suggests that although the parallel prototyping phase is later in the process, the iterative prototyping stage is much shorter and the overall development time could be reduced whilst enhancing quality. The proposers of the methodology look forward to further validating such claims.

3 TAGUCHI DESIGN METHODS

3.1 Taguchi in general

Taguchi methods were developed by Genichi Taguchi in Japan and their use has spread to both the USA and Europe where, through the use of experimental design, aspects of quality can be pushed back from inspection to design. Taguchi aims to shift resources to the creative design process rather than relying on inspection methods to ensure quality. The majority of the applications of Taguchi methods are within production control where in order to investigate quality a quality characteristic (e.g. *strength* in a production environment) is identified and losses occur not only when a product is out of a permissible range for the quality characteristic, but when it deviates from its target value.

	Phase	Activities
1	Functional Analysis and Design	• requirements capture • task analysis etc.
2	Exploratory Investigation	• through brainstorming sessions users and developers identify key factors, associated level and performance criteria • *exploratory* prototypes tested
3	Taguchi Design	• selection of appropriate orthogonal array • investigate interaction between factors • design of experiments
4	Taguchi Testing	• user *assessment* testing • analysis of results: *first-shot* and *detailed* analysis • selection of optimum design
5	Refinement	• confirmatory *validation* testing • further iterative refinement

Figure 1 Stages in the LUCID Method

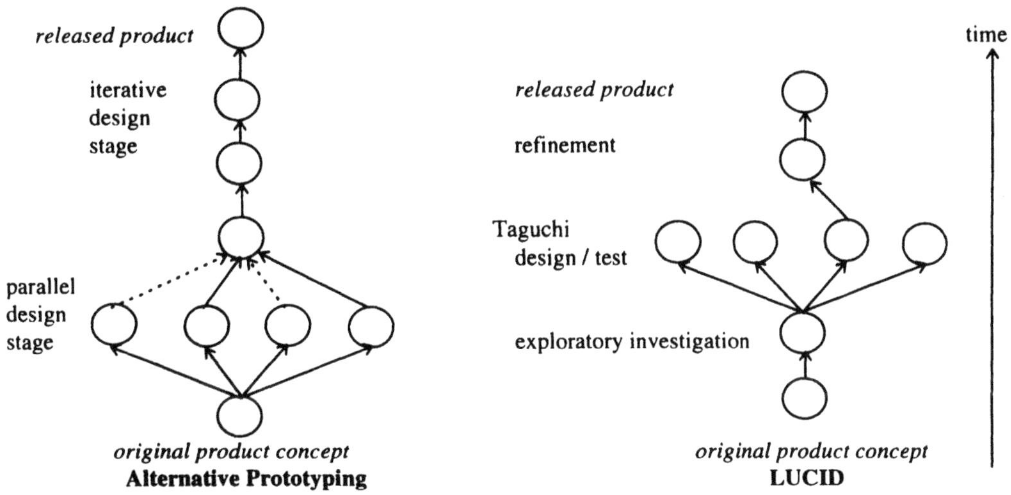

Figure 2 LUCID vs. Alternative Prototyping

Emphasis is given to the process of optimising production processes and product factors in such a way as to minimise variation in the product and performance. Underlying the Taguchi method is the concept that quality is affected by two types of factor: internal or *control* factors (such as materials) which can be controlled easily and external *noise* factors from the environment (such as maintenance of equipment) which cannot be controlled easily.

The search for the optimum production process often involves conducting a number of experiments where each of the control factors are systematically changed. The technique for systematic investigation of conditions is based on the factorial design method first introduced by Fisher in the 1920's and extensively applied in agrarian and social sciences. However the Taguchi method drastically reduces the number of experiments which have to be carried out by providing a framework for design, and also a simplified analysis of results which makes the factorial design accessible to non-statisticians. In many situations full factorial analysis will involve many experiments. By using fractional factorial experiments, identified through the use of orthogonal arrays, the number of experiments can be drastically reduced. In the case of fifteen two level factors only sixteen experiments would be necessary. Through statistical analysis techniques the optimum situation (any one of the 32,768 options) could be determined. Full details of the Taguchi process can be found elsewhere (Taguchi, 1986) but we summarise the standard Taguchi procedure below.

Design and Conduct of Experiments

The basic concept is for the design team to agree on the quality characteristic, or combination of characteristics, for measuring the performance of the product or process under study. The team then identifies the input factors and associated levels which are considered to influence the quality characteristic of the output. When applying Taguchi methods within LUCID an example factor might be *menu nesting level* which could have two levels of *broad and shallow* and *narrow and deep*.

When the factors and levels are agreed an orthogonal array is selected, the factors are assigned to columns, and experiments to rows, thereby determining the conditions for individual experiments. Experiments are then conducted to determine values of the quality characteristic associated with the factor levels determined from the orthogonal array. Figure 3 illustrates the first two orthogonal arrays, the L_4 array which would deal with up to three factors and the L_8 array which can cope with up to 7 factors. The orthogonal arrays are systematically named as $L_A(B^C)$ where A is the maximum number of experiments, or in our case interfaces (rows), B is the number of levels and C is the number of factors (columns). The two arrays shown relate to bivariate factors (just two levels), however it should be emphasised that other arrays allow for multivariate (many levels) factors.

The orthogonal arrays are independent: every column covers one factor and has the same number of occurrences of each level as every other column. This ensures that any differences in the results are only due to the change of levels.

Factor / Expt.	$L_4(2^3)$		
	A	B	C
1	1	1	1
2	1	2	1
3	2	1	2
4	2	2	1

Fac. / Expt.	$L_8(2^7)$						
	A	B	C	D	E	F	G
1	1	1	1	1	1	1	1
2	1	1	1	2	2	2	2
3	1	2	2	1	1	2	2
4	1	2	2	2	2	1	1
5	2	1	2	1	2	1	2
6	2	1	2	2	1	2	1
7	2	2	1	1	2	2	1
8	2	2	1	2	1	1	2

Figure 3 Orthogonal Arrays

Orthogonal arrays are balanced because there are always an equal number of occurrences of each level in every column. In some situations factors in the design may influence each other and may not be independent. The Taguchi method will allow the design study to investigate both the input factors and the suspected interactions between the factors. The number of columns dictates the number of single factors or interactions which can be investigated. An $L_8(2^7)$ can deal with seven factors or four factors and three interactions.

Analysis of Results

The main effects are evaluated and their influence determined quantitatively thereby determining the optimum conditions. ANOVA is performed on the results to identify the relative strengths of the factors. Multiple runs can be carried out and the results analysed and the signal to noise ratios (S/N) calculated. The S/N ratio represents a concept developed by Taguchi as an estimate of the relative strengths of the effects of the system factors versus the noise in the environment. After completing the analysis a further test of the optimum conditions must be made to confirm the performance.

3.2 LUCID and Taguchi

In terms of incorporating Taguchi techniques within interface design it is necessary for us to discuss the role of both the factors and quality characteristics. Within interface design there are an extremely large number of design factors. Indeed at the start of the design process there is an infinite space of design options. However, at particular stages within a prototyping process the design space, although still large, will become restricted. At this stage it will be possible to determine a range of factors, with their respective levels. The quality characteristic for the Taguchi approach to interface design will be either selected or calculated from a range of usability metrics. Normally it is expected that one single overarching, system specific, characteristic will be determined.

4 IMPLEMENTING LUCID

4.1 MANAGER help system

The particular application of the LUCID method which we report here relates to the optimisation of the on-line help system supporting a piece of software called *Manager*. Manager is available from Plasmon Data Ltd and allows a computer to have transparent access to one or more optical disk jukeboxes. The application area was concerned with the installation and configuration of jukeboxes for distributed systems with computing technicians as typical end users.

4.2 Overview of the Study

In this particular implementation we are focusing on the optimisation of an existing system. It was not necessary therefore to undertake Phase 1 of LUCID, Functional Analysis and Design. Furthermore it was possible to take the previously implemented version of the Manager Help File System as the exploratory prototype when initiating the analysis within Phase 2, Exploratory Investigation. Knowledge of usability issues such as common user errors and difficulties framed the construction of task scenarios used later in development. Following discussions within the design team it was possible to identify six separate factors, each with two levels, together with the likelihood of one interaction between two of the factors. Two points should be made concerning the selection of factors and levels. Firstly it should again be emphasised that the method could have coped with multivariate factors. Secondly whilst some of the factors may appear to have an obvious required level, based on well known guidelines, the total systems approach ensures that trade-offs between guidelines can be systematically managed. The factors and levels themselves are shown in Figure 4. In preparation for Phase 4, Taguchi Testing, the design team was able to identify three distinct usability metrics:

- total time to complete a task
- number of button presses required to complete a task
- user satisfaction level.

Phase 3, Taguchi Design, involves the detailed experimental design. With seven factors in total it was necessary to employ the L_8 orthogonal array (Figure 3) which indicated that eight interfaces would need to be produced and tested. The specification of the eight interfaces is shown in Figure 5. Whilst, at first, it may seem rather resource intensive to have to build eight distinct interfaces, in reality the modifications necessary required only minimal effort using current software development tools.

During Phase 4, Taguchi Testing, the usability tests were undertaken One particular aim of this implementation of the LUCID approach was to investigate the effect of restricted access to users for testing purposes. It was decided to involve just five computer services technicians as typical end users in the usability tests. In order to take account of the learning effect the users were tested on each interface in a random order which did not bias any one interface. Eight separate task scenarios were developed requiring the users to find out technical information from the help files. Whilst the scenarios included different queries they required very similar actions. Prior to formal testing each user was able to use a ninth interface and scenario for system familiarisation.

For each of the 40 tests the performance metrics identified above (total time and number of button presses) were determined. After each test the users completed a simple satisfaction questionnaire. One feature of LUCID is the identification of a single overarching systems specific quality characteristic. In this case it was possible to develop a composite metric based upon equal weighting and scaling of the three individual metrics (Figure 6).

Factor		Level 1	Level 2
A	method of help access	graphical	textual
B	menu nesting level	wide and shallow	narrow and deep
C	interaction A with B		
D	window size	large	normal
E	line spacing	single	1.5
F	font style	Arial	Bookman
G	colour of hotword	same as help text (i.e. black)	green

Figure 4 Factors and levels identified

	Levels of each factor (A - G)						
Interface	A	B	C	D	E	F	G
1	graphical	wide / shallow		large	single	Arial	same
2	graphical	wide / shallow		normal	1.5	Bookman	green
3	graphical	narrow / deep		large	single	Bookman	green
4	graphical	narrow / deep		normal	1.5	Arial	same
5	textual	wide / shallow		large	1.5	Arial	green
6	textual	wide / shallow		normal	single	Bookman	same
7	textual	narrow/ deep		large	1.5	Bookman	same
8	textual	narrow / deep		normal	single	Arial	green

Figure 5 Factors and levels by interface

4.3 Analysis of Results

One feature of the Taguchi / LUCID approach is the fact that a non-statistician can easily identify a *first-shot* optimum interface. By calculating the average metrics for all factors at each level the optimum interface can be suggested. In Figure 7 we present the average data for each level of every factor relating to the individual and composite metrics.

The results show a high degree of commonality. The data shown in bold is the lower of the two values (all metrics conform to a *lower the better* criterion) and indicates the required level for each of the factors. Overall the first-shot analysis predicted that the optimum interface is described by $A_2B_1C_2D_1E_1F_1G_1$ with Factors A (textual method of help access) and B (wide / shallow nesting level) being the most significant as indicated by the percentage difference between the levels.

Int	Time (sec.)	Button Presses	Satis. Rating	Comp. Metric
1	153.2	19.0	12.4	0.867
2	216.6	28.4	14.0	1.165
3	181.6	25.2	15.4	1.083
4	194.9	27.25	15.7	1.146
5	123.2	14.0	10.6	0.693
6	153.6	21.4	13.6	0.931
7	174.0	20.0	15.8	1.002
8	190.8	26.0	15.4	1.113

Figure 6 Summary of metrics by interface

Time				Button Presses		
Fac	L1	L2		Fac	L1	L2
A	187	**160**		A	25.0	**20.4**
B	**162**	185		B	**20.7**	24.6
C	184	**163**		C	23.4	**22.0**
D	**158**	189		D	**19.6**	25.8
E	**170**	177		E	**22.9**	22.4
F	**166**	181		F	**21.6**	23.8
G	**169**	178		G	**21.9**	23.4
Satisfaction Rating				Composite Metric		
Fac	L1	L2		Fac	L1	L2
A	14.3	**13.9**		A	1.07	**0.935**
B	**12.7**	15.6		B	**0.914**	1.09
C	14.4	**13.8**		C	1.04	**0.963**
D	**13.6**	14.7		D	**0.911**	1.09
E	14.2	**14.0**		E	**0.999**	1.00
F	**13.5**	14.7		F	**0.955**	1.05
G	14.4	**13.9**		G	**0.986**	1.01

Figure 7 Average data by factor and level

Within the detailed analysis stage the results were subjected to a detailed statistical analysis using Taguchi's adaptation of ANOVA for saturated designs in which the least significant factors are pooled and assigned to the error sum of squares in order to enable the calculation of the *F ratios*. Multiple trials were analysed using Taguchi's concept of the signal to noise ratio. This is a useful concept for estimating the strength of the noise involved in the experimental design in contrast to the effects of the main factors. The S/N ratio is the reciprocal of the variances of the measurement error. It is a maximum for the combination of factor levels that has the minimum error variance i.e. the optimum design. For the Composite Metric the S/N ratios of the factors are given in Figure 8.

The larger the difference the greater the significance for the factor. There would appear to be a close relation between these results and those indicated in the first-shot analysis. In this application the sources of noise were considered to be due to the users' abilities, learning styles and any differences in the task scenarios.

Factor	Level 1	Level 2	Diff.
A	-7.716	-6.644	*1.072*
B	-6.278	-8.082	*1.804*
C	-7.681	-6.679	1.002
D	-6.362	-7.999	*1.637*
E	-7.255	-7.106	0.149
F	-6.680	-7.681	1.001
G	-7.051	-7.310	0.259

Figure 8 S/N Ratios, Composite Metric

Figure 9 summarises the detailed statistical results giving the *F critical* values at 90% as a guide. However Taguchi recommends, based on his own experience, that factors which give rise to F values greater than 2 should all be taken into account. In the different cases, shown below, the three or four least significant factors in terms of percentage contribution were pooled together to form the error sum of squares so that the F variance ratio could be calculated. The table shows that, although there is some variation in the results using the different metrics, in general the three significant factors in this application are *method of help access, menu nesting level*, and *window size*. This indicates that further refinement of the interface should concentrate on these factors. In addition *font style* was a significant factor in terms of user satisfaction, although it does not appear to have an impact on user performance *whilst method of help access* was not rated as highly by the users. The possible interaction between *method of help access* and *menu nesting level* was investigated in this experimental design. It was found to be statistically significant for the *total time* metric but not in the other cases. This indicates that future refinement of the interface should bear this in mind.

Overall the detailed analysis provided confirmation of the first-shot analysis indicating that the LUCID approach can be applied at two levels:

- by all interface designers at the first-shot level without recourse to the statistical techniques
- with statistical back-up to confirm and provide additional information using the Taguchi variation of ANOVA.

Time			Button Presses		
Fcrit(1,3)=5.53			Fcrit(1,4)=4.54		
Fac	F	%	Fac	F	%
A	4.12	13.9	A	9.48	25.3
B	7.29	24.7	B	6.83	18.2
C	6.57	22.5	C	-	2.24
D	8.56	29.0	D	17.18	45.8
E	-	0.01	E	-	0.27
F	-	7.53	F	-	5.59
G	-	2.63	G	-	2.57
Satisfaction Rating			Composite Metric		
Fcrit(1,3)=5.53			Fcrit(1,4)=4.54		
Fac	L1	L2	Fac	L1	L2
A	-	2.26	A	4.77	18.4
B	37.5	70.6	B	8.34	32.1
C	-	2.75	C	-	5.75
D	5.54	10.4	D	8.84	34.1
E	-	0.26	E	-	0.01
F	6.07	11.4	F	-	8.85
G	-	2.26	G	-	0.80

Figure 9 Average data by factor and level

5 CONCLUSIONS

LUCID is in the relatively early stages of development. Current work is focusing on Phases 3 and 4 as these are clearly crucial to the total approach. Taken together the pilot study (Smith and Dunckley, 1996) and this more extensive study suggest that the LUCID / Taguchi approach to interface design is both feasible and worthwhile. It enables the interface designer to test a limited number of interface designs at an early stage in the development process and determine with a high degree of certainty the major factors within the optimum interface specification. Iterative prototyping, based upon the optimum interface, can later be used to refine other more minor factors which may not have been included. Future emphasis will need to be placed on Phase 2, Exploratory Investigation, where building upon current techniques for user-centred design, support will be provided for the identification of key factors and performance criteria.

Whether or not LUCID should be considered to be one of 'breakthroughs' that Hartson and Boehm-Davis (1989) seek, it certainly provides significant support for two of the issues which they highlight, as outlined in the introduction. The Taguchi parallel design and testing strategy ensures, subject to early prototype constraints and the identified quality characteristic, the identification of the optimum interface design. In addition the Taguchi variant of ANOVA provides a technique whereby the features most significantly effecting usability (credit and blame) can be determined.

REFERENCES

Bevan N, (1995), 'Measuring Usability as Quality of Use', *Software Quality Journal* **4** (2), 115-130.

Hartson, H. R. & Boehm-Davis, D. (1993), 'User Interface Development Processes and Methodologies', *Behaviour and IT* **12** (2), 98-114.

Juran, J. M. (1979), Quality Control Handbook, McGraw-Hill.

Lim, K. Y. & Long, J. (1994), *The MUSE Method for Usability Engineering*, Cambridge University Press.

Robinson, D. & Fitter, M. (1992), 'Supportive Evaluation Methodology', *Behaviour and IT*, **11** (3), 151-159.

Smith, A. & Dunckley, L. (1996), 'Towards the Total Quality Interface - applying Taguchi TQM Techniques within the LUCID method', in Sasse, M. A., Cunningham, R. J. & Winder, R. L. (eds.), *People and Computers XI*, Proceedings of HCI-96, Springer.

Taguchi, G. (1986), *Introduction to Quality Engineering*, Asian Productivity Organisation.

Beyond Belief: Representing Knowledge Requirements For The Operation Of Safety-Critical Interfaces

Chris Johnson

Glasgow Accident Analysis Group,
Department of Computer Science, University of Glasgow, Glasgow,
Scotland, G12 8QQ.

http://www.dcs.gla.ac.uk/~johnson
E-mail: johnson@dcs.gla.ac.uk

ABSTRACT: Human intervention has played an important role in many major accidents. The staff of the London Underground continued to allow trains to deposit passengers in Kings' Cross after the fire had started. The crew of the Herald of Free Enterprise left their bow doors open. One reason why human 'error' is such a significant factor in major disasters is that companies frequently fail to consider the detailed requirements that must be satisfied by operator training. Accident reports often criticise the lack of structure and content in the courses that are provided for safety-critical applications. The following pages address this problem. A mathematical notation is used to represent knowledge requirements for off-shore oil production. This provides an explicit representation of the factual and procedural information that must be included in training courses. This approach also helps to document the standards by which an operator's performance will be assessed. The application of a formal notation is appropriate because a range of organisations, including the UK Ministry of Defence and NASA, are advocating these languages for large-scale development projects. Logic-based formalisms, therefore, provide a common language for systems engineering and human-factors development. This helps to ensure that training issues are not relegated to an after-thought in the design and implementation of safety-critical systems.

KEYWORDS: Safety-critical interfaces; formal methods, training; human factors; logic.

1. INTRODUCTION

Recent accidents in the transportation, power generation and chemical industries have illustrated the importance of ensuring that operators understand the rules and procedures which govern the operation of their applications. For example, the Piper Alpha enquiry found that:

> "The lack of an exact format or content for the induction training; the brevity of time devoted to it; the almost cursory assessment of whether an individual required to attend the training...all point to the failure to ensure that all were properly informed on matters critical to their safety in an emergency. " (Cullen, 1990)

Such findings are surprising because national and international legislation emphasises the importance of adequate training. For example, the Australian Petroleum (Submerged Lands) Act states that:

> "...an employer contravenes (the act) if the employer fails to take all reasonable steps to provide to employees in appropriate language, the information, instruction, training and supervision necessary to enable them to perform their work in a way that is safe and without risk to their health".

If companies are to obey this legislation then they must provide the regulatory authorities with evidence which shows that they deliver appropriate training and supervision. Unfortunately, many companies document their training in terms of high-level objectives, such as "the operator shall be aware of the general operating procedures for this system" (Fennel, 1988). This makes it difficult for companies to defend their practices when failures do occur. Accident reports into Bhopal (Morehouse and Subamaniam, 1986), Kegworth (AAIB, 1990) and Three Mile Island (USNRC, 1980) all criticise the training practices of the companies involved.

Human–Computer Interaction: INTERACT'97 S. Howard, J. Hammond & G. Lindgaard (editors)
Published by Chapman & Hall

This paper argues that formal notations can be used to represent training objectives for safety-critical interfaces. This is appropriate because commercial and regulatory bodies have recommended the use of these notations in the development of safety-critical systems (MOD, 1991). Formal methods have also been used to support the design of human-computer interfaces (Harrison and Thimbleby, 1989). For instance, Dix (1991) has exploited a mathematical notation to investigate timing problems in multi-user systems. Elsewhere, we have shown that probabilistic logics can be used to analyse the stochastic processes that characterise interaction with safety-critical systems (Johnson, 1993, 1995 1995b). An important benefit of these techniques is that they provide a bridge between current practice in both human computer interaction, through task analysis (P. Johnson, 1992), and software engineering (Fidge, Kearney and Staples, 1993). Unfortunately, formal notations have not been used to represent training requirements. This makes it difficult for trainers to reason about the rules and regulations that are intended to guide an operator's interaction with a safety-critical system.

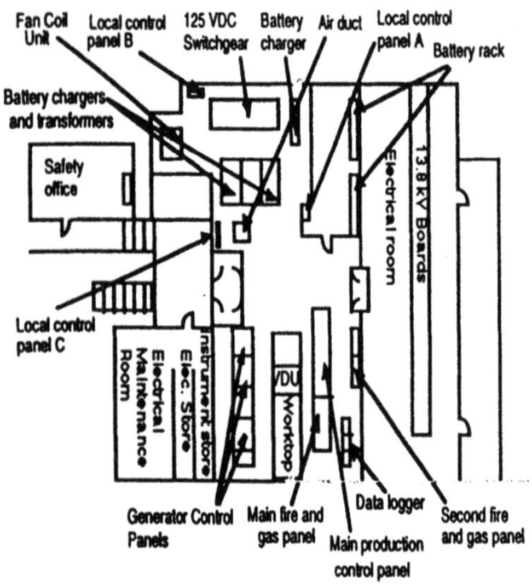

Figure 1: Plan of the Piper Alpha Control Room

Competency requirements for an off-shore oil production facility are used to illustrate the remainder of this paper. These systems have posed a significant challenge for both systems designers and human factors specialists (Wardell, 1989). Oil production facilities are complex applications. This is illustrated by the plan of the Piper Alpha control room, shown in Figure 1.

Operators must monitor the extraction of oil from geological structures under the sea-bed. They must also control the extraction and purification of any gas that is recovered with the oil. They must monitor repair activities and maintenance schedules. They must also watch for problems that threaten the safety of the rig. For instance, gas leaks pose a considerable risk of fire. If gas is detected then control room personnel must investigate the cause and identify potential solutions. These tasks involve almost continuous interaction with computerised sensing and control systems.

It is important to emphasise that this paper focuses upon the operating rules and procedures that form a critical component of any operator's training with safety-critical computer systems. Brevity prevents a detailed discussion of the physical training that also play an important role during induction courses and competency tests. This topic is addressed in a companion paper (Johnson, 1996).

2. Representing Training Requirements

Companies that operate oil production facilities are faced with a difficult problem. On the one hand, regulatory authorities, such as the Health and Safety Executive, are urging them to document their training procedures. On the other hand, there are few techniques that can be used to develop such documentation. Natural language reports are unwieldy and quickly become intractable if they are used to represent many different training requirements for many different operators (Johnson, McCarthy and Wright, 1995). An additional problem is that training reports frequently describe the procedures that are used to instruct operators. They do not describe the objectives for that training. This makes it difficult to identify the criteria that are used to gauge the success or failure of that training. User models provide a solution to these problems. In particular, they provide structures that can be used to represent the cognitive objectives for an operator's training (Green and Benyon, 1995). For example, Duke, Barnard, Duce and May (1995) use the following clause to describe what should happen when an operator is trained to delete warnings from a safety-critical application. This approach exploits Barnard's Interacting Cognitive Subsyetems model. A representation of the message is formed at the propositional level. This representation is then used to form the goal of deleting the message at an implicational level. Finally, the articulatory subsystem translates the goal into a process that activates the musculature to move the hand and complete the necessary action. The training would have failed if the operator could not recognise the message, could not form the correct goal, or failed to produce the correct articulatory response:

> *per(delete_message)* ⇒ *mesg@prop* ∧
> : *prop-obj::obj-lim::lim-hand:* ∝ *config* (1)
>
> This states that if the user can delete a message then they form a representation of the message at the proposition level, *mesg@prop*, and they form a goal to remove the object, *prop-obj*, this is translated through processes that activate their musculature, *obj-lim::lim-hand*, to complete the necessary action.

Practical problems prevent trainers from using this approach to represent training requirements. The level of detail in (1) would place heavy burdens upon any company that had to document training requirements for many different operators. The developers of this approach are aware of these issues and are currently developing tools to support the application of their user models (May, 1995).

3. Epistemics for Training Requirements

In anticipation of current research in user modelling, it is important that trainers have some alternative means of representing training requirements. Epistemology, or the study of knowledge, has a history stretching back to the Ancient Greeks (Fagin, Halpern, Moses and Vardi, 1995). This work has led to a number of epistemic logics that can be used to reason about the consistency and completeness of knowledge in areas such as Artificial Intelligence, Philosophy and Distributed Systems (Barwise and Perry, 1983).

Before showing how epistemics support the analysis of training requirements, it is first important to demonstrate the ways in which logic supports systems engineering. For example, the Piper Alpha accident was probably caused by a condensate injection pump being operated without a pressure safety valve. A systems requirement is, therefore, that a pump is started if it is protected by a safety valve and there is no permit to perform maintenance on the pump. This latter requirement is important because operators must not start a pump that is being repaired by their colleagues:

> *safe_start(injection_pump)* ⇐
> *working(ps_valve, injection_pump)* ∧
> *not work_permit(injection_pump).* (2)
>
> It is safe to start an injection pump if a pressurised safety valve is fitted and there is not a permit to perform maintenance work on that component.

This systems engineering constraint provides a focus for the development of training requirements. For example, the following clause uses the epistemic *Kn* operator (read as 'knows') to state that the user should only attempt to start a pump if they know that the safety valve is working and that there is no permit to work on that pump. This illustrates the close relationship between interface development and operator training. The human-machine interface must enable its users to start up the injection pumping equipment, *input(user, start_injection_pump)*. Training must be provided so that operators understand the conditions which must be satisfied if they are to issue this input. The following clauses exploit a first order variant of epistemic logic, the interested reader is directed to (Fagin, Halpern, Moses and Vardi, 1995) for more information on the formal under-pinnings of this notation. In contrast, the remainder of this paper focuses on the application of the logic:

> *input(user, start_injection_pump)* ⇔
> *Kn(user, working(ps_valve, injection_pump))* ∧
> *Kn(user, not work_permit(injection_pump))* (3)
>
> A user provides input to start an injection pump if and only if they know that the safety valve for that pump is in working order and they know that there is no permit to work for that component.

Such clauses provide a precise and concise means of representing the competency requirements that must be satisfied by the users of complex systems. They represent the minimum standards that operators must satisfy in order to be certified for particular applications. For example, the previous requirement might be used in an examination by posing questions such as:

> What checks should be made before you issue input to start up the condensate injection pumps?

An important benefit of clauses, such as (3), is that they strip away the clutter of implementation details that frequently obscure critical properties of safety-critical systems. Trainers and operators can identify high-level training objectives without being forced to consider low level device handling. For instance, permits to work can be revoked if maintenance has to be suspended for a short time. Under these circumstances, operators may start the equipment if they know that a suspension permit has been issued. Such high-level objectives can easily be lost amongst the many different output events and input sequences that must be considered during the later stages of training:

input(user, start_injection_pump) ⇔
Kn(user, working(ps_valve, injection_pump)) ∧
(Kn(user, not work_permit(injection_pump)) ∨
Kn(user, suspension(injection_pump))) (4)

The user provides input to start an injection pump if and only if they know that the safety valve for that pump is in working order and they know that there is no permit to work for that component or they know that there is a suspension permit on the pump.

Section 6 will describe how presentation details and input requirements can gradually be introduced into clauses, such as (4), to represent competency requirements during the later stages of training. For now it is sufficient to realise that previous clauses refer to 'generic' *users*. They do not demonstrate that epistemic logic can be used to identify training requirements for particular operators performing particular tasks.

4. Training For Particular Tasks

Many oil production operators will never need to start up the injection pumping equipment. Toolpushers, divers and rig electricians are not expected to perform such tasks during their routine duties. Fortunately, the allocation of training requirements can be represented by changing the *user* marker in previous clauses to describe particular roles in the operation of the system. For example, the lead production operator, *lpo*, is responsible for starting up the condensate pumping equipment:

input(lpo, start_injection_pump) ⇔
Kn(lpo, working(ps_valve, injection_pump)) ∧
Kn(lpo, not work_permit(injection_pump)) (5)

The lead production operator provides input to start an injection pump if and only if they know that the safety valve for that pump is in working order and they know that there is no permit to work for that component.

Additional clauses can be introduced to represent the training requirements that relate to other users. For example, it might be specified that the dive superintendent, *dsi*, should issue orders to start diving operations if they know that the diesel fire pumps have been switched from manual to automatic. This is a critical training requirement because fire-fighting pumps are fed with sea-water. If the pumps are activated while divers are working on the rig then they may be sucked towards the pump inlets. As before, it is important that trainers have some means of explicitly representing such requirements. Competent dive superintendents must check that the pumps are on manual if they allow divers to enter the water:

input(dsi, start_diving) ⇔
Kn(dsi, manual(diesel_fire_pumps)). (6)

The diving superintendent issues input to start diving operations if and only if they know that the diesel fire pumping systems have been turned from manual to automatic.

The previous clause will only be successful if operators can access the information that they have been trained to consider. For example, it would be little use training the dive superintendent to check on the state of the *diesel_fire_pumps* if they could not find out about the state of these components using the displays presented by the on-board information systems.

5. Training and Systems Engineering

It is important to emphasise that epistemic clauses, such as (5) and (6), do not guarantee the safety of an application. For instance, it is entirely possible for the diving superintendent to believe that the diesel pumps are on manual when they are, in fact on automatic. Similarly, the lead production operator might believe that the safety valve is operational when it is broken:

potential_accident ⇐
Kn(lpo, working(ps_valve, injection_pump)) ∧
not working(ps_valve, injection_pump) (7)

There is the potential for an accident if the lead production operator knows that the safety valve is working and it is, in fact, the case that the valve is not working.

This clause represents a situation in which the lead production operator holds an erroneous belief about the state of their application. Systems engineers, trainers and interface designers must co-ordinate their activities to ensure the operator only believes that the pressure safety valve is operating if and only if that component is working:

Kn(lpo, working(ps_valve, injection_pump)) ⇔
working(ps_valve, injection_pump) (8)

The lead production operator knows that the safety valve for that pump is in working order if and only if that component is, in fact, working.

Clause (8) represents a design objective that must be satisfied by the underlying systems engineering. Sensors must be deployed to accurately gauge the state of the valve. If these systems reported that the safety valve was working when it was broken then the operator might start the condensate pump. In such circumstances, the user's training might actually threaten the safety of the system. The operator simply follows the criteria laid down in clause (3). If, however, the systems engineers believed that the monitoring equipment might provide erroneous values then (3) might be altered so that operators were trained to perform additional checks.

6. Training and Interface Design

Norman (1990) argues that operator training must be supported by the development of 'appropriate' displays. The converse is also true. An interface is of little benefit if operators cannot be trained to exploit the information that it presents. The following clause demonstrates that epistemic logic can be used to represent the link between display objects and the information that operators have been trained to obtain before starting the injection pumps:

Kn(lpo, working(ps_valve, injection_pump)) ⇔
present(lpo, ps_valve_ok_icon) (9)

The lead production operator knows that the safety valve is in working order if and only if there is an icon to confirm this fact.

Clause (9) provides an extremely abstract description of an interactive system. This is an advantage because it does not force trainers to consider the low level details of particular presentation devices. Unfortunately, the logic provides little idea of the images that might be used to represent the valve icon. Logic can, however, be used to represent the structure and content of complex displays. For example, the following clauses describe the way in which the *condensate_display* might include the image of the *ps_valve_ok_icon*. This in turn includes the image of a feed adjuster. Finally, the feed adjuster is composed of the graphical primitives that are presented to the user:

part(condensate_display, ps_valve_ok_icon) (10)
part(ps_valve_ok_icon, feed_adjuster) (11)
line(feed_adjuster, 0.1, 0.2, 0.6, 0.2) (12)

The first clause states that the ps_valve_ok_icon is part of the condensate display. The second clause states that a feed flow adjuster is, in turn, part of the ps_valve_ok_icon. Finally, the third clause states that the image of the feed flow icon contains a line from Cartesian co-ordinates (0.1,0.2) to (0.6, 0.2).

Figure 2 presents the structure of the image that is described by the previous clauses. The resulting graphical structures can be directly executed using the Prelog prototyping system. A detailed discussion of this approach is presented in (Johnson, 1995a).

The significance of the formulae (9,10,11,12) is that they explicitly represent the information which interface designers intend to communicate through particular images. The *ps_valve_ok_icon* tells the user that the injection valve is working, *Kn(lpo, working(ps_valve, injection_pump)*. These clauses provide a focus for evaluation. Lead production operators can be asked to describe the information that is represented by the valve icon. If the users fail to recognise that the valve is working then the image must be redesigned or operators must be trained to recognise the meaning of the existing image.

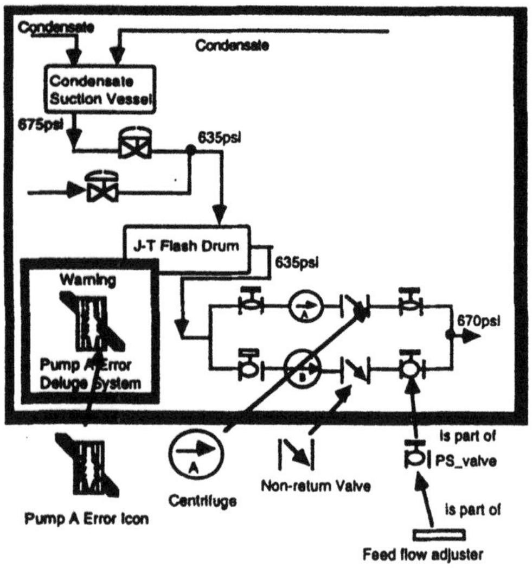

Figure 2: Image for the Condensate Display

7. Representing Training Violations

Previous sections have used epistemic logic to represent knowledge requirements for a safety-critical interface. The application of a formal notation does not, however, guarantee that operators will remember their training. For example, the lead production operator might attempt to start the pump with insufficient information about current maintenance activities. Under such circumstances, they would not know whether a permit to work had been issued, *not Kn(lpo, work_permit(injection_pump))* :

training_failure ⇐
input(lpo, start_injection_pump) ∧
Kn(lpo, working(ps_valve, injection_pump)) ∧
not Kn(lpo, work_permit(injection_pump)) (13)

A training failure occurs if the lead production operator provides input to start an injection pump and they know that the safety valve for that pump is in working order but they do not know that there is no permit to work for that component.

It is important to emphasise the difference between clause (3) and clause (13). In the former case the lead production operator definitely knows that there is no permit to work, *Kn(lpo,not work_permit(injection_pump))*. In clause (13), the operator does not know whether there is a permit, *not Kn(lpo, work_permit(injection_pump))*. These different situations can, in turn, be compared to one in which the user deliberately starts the pump even though they know that there is maintenance being performed on that component:

deliberate_training_violation ⇐
input(lpo, start_injection_pump) ∧
Kn(lpo, working(ps_valve, injection_pump)) ∧
Kn(lpo, work_permit(injection_pump)) (14)

A lead production operator deliberately violates their training if they start an injection pump and they know that the safety valve for that pump is in working order and they know that there is no permit to work for that component.

Clauses (13) and (14) are violations of the training requirements represented in (3). Regulatory authorities would expect a formal review if the lead production operator attempted to start an injection pump that was currently being worked on. If the enquiry could demonstrate that the operator was simply negligent, as represented in (13), then the sanctions would be less severe than the deliberate neglect described in (14).

8. Conclusion And Further Work

This paper has demonstrated that epistemic logic can be used to represent training requirements in terms of the knowledge that operators must possess in order to safely perform particular tasks. This approach provides a more precise and concise means of representing competency criteria than the high level objectives that are frequently criticised in accident reports. An important benefit of our approach is that it can be directly integrated with current techniques for software engineering. This is vital if operator requirements are to be explicitly considered during the detailed development of safety-critical systems.

Our approach is limited in the sense that it focuses on knowledge requirements for safety-critical interfaces. We have not attempted to represent the physical skills that form an important component of many training programmes. Elsewhere we have described how logic can be used to reason about the physical layout of complex working environments (Johnson, 1996).

Future work will build closer links with task analysis and user modelling. For instance, epistemic logics can be used to express the propositional and implicational information that. is represented in the ICS model. Alternatively, the logic notation can be used to formalise the structured notations in Green and Benyon's (1995) ERMIA user modelling techniques.

Finally, we are concerned to improve the usability of the approach described in this paper (Gray and Johnson, 1995). Mathematical requirements provide non-formalists with a poor impression of what it would be like to interact with a safety-critical system. We are addressing this problem by extending the Prelog prototyping. This enables designers to directly execute the logic clauses that are presented in this paper. At any point during interaction, designers can ask the user to justify their reasons for a particular action. These can then be compared to the epistemic, Kn, clauses to determine whether the operator has taken into account all of the information requirements that were identified during their training.

Acknowledgements

Thanks go to the members of the Glasgow Accident Analysis Group and the Glasgow Interactive Systems Group (GIST) and to the Formal Methods and Theory Group in Glasgow University. This work is supported by the UK Engineering and Physical Sciences Research Council, grants GR/JO7686, GR/K69148 and GR/K55040.

References

Air Accidents Investigations Branch, Department of Transport. *Report On The Accident To Boeing 737-400 G-OBME Near Kegworth, Leicestershire on 8th January 1989,* number 4/90, Her Majesty's Stationery Office. London, United Kingdom, 1990.

J. Barwise and J. Perry. *Situations And Attitudes.* Bradford Books, Cambridge, United States of America 1983.

Cullen, *Proceedings Of The Public Enquiry Into The Piper Alpha Disaster.* The Department of Energy, Her Majesty's Stationery Office, London, United Kingdom, 1990.

Dix, A. *Formal Methods For Interactive Systems,* Academic Press, London, United Kingdom, 1991.

D. Duke, P. Barnard, D. Duce and J. May. *Systematic development of the human interface.* In APSEC'95-Second Asia-Pacific Software Engineering Conference 1995.

R. Fagin, J. Halpern, Y. Moses, and M. Vardi. *Reasoning About Knowledge.* MIT Press, Boston, United States of America 1995.

D. Fennel, *Investigation Into The Kings' Cross Undergr*ð*und Fire.* Department of Transport, Her Majesty's Stationery Office, London, United Kingdom, 1988.

C. Fidge, P. Kearney and J. Staples, *Formal Verified Real-Time Software: An Integrated Development Strategy,* Technical Report, Software Verification Research Centre, Department of Computer Science, University of Queensland, Australia, June 1993.

P.D. Gray and C.W. Johnson, *A Critical Analysis Of Interface Specification Notations.* In P. Palanque and R. Bastide, editors, The Specification And Verification Of Interactive Systems, 113-133, Springer Verlag, Berlin, 1995.

T.R.G. Green and D. Benyon, *Displays As Data Structures: Entity-Relationship Models of Information Artefacts.* In K. Nordby, P. Helmersen, D. Gilmore and S. Arnesen (eds.), Interact'95, 55-60, Chapman Hall, London, 1995.

M.D. Harrison and H.W. Thimbleby, (eds.), Formal Methods In Human Computer Interaction, Cambridge University Press, Cambridge, United Kingdom, 1989.

C.W. Johnson, *A Probabilistic Logic For The Development of Safety-Critical Interactive Systems.* International Journal of Man-Machine Systems, 39(2):333-351, 1993.

C.W. Johnson, *The Formal Analysis Of Human-Computer Interaction During Accident Investigations.* In G. Cockton, S.W. Draper and G.R.S. Weir, editors, People And Computers IX, 285-300. Cambridge University Press, Cambridge, 1994.

C.W. Johnson, *The Application of Petri Nets to Represent and Reason about Human Factors Problems During Accident Analyses* In P. Palanque and R. Bastide, editors, The Specification And Verification Of Interactive Systems, 93-112, Springer Verlag, Berlin, 1995.

C.W. Johnson, *Using Z to Support the Design of Interactive, Safety-Critical Systems* Software Engineering Journal, (10)2:49-60, 1995a.

C.W. Johnson, *Decision Theory and Safety-Critical Interfaces.* In K. Nordby, P. Helmersen, D. Gilmore and S. Arnesen (eds.), Interact'95, 121-127, Chapman Hall, London, 1995b.

C.W. Johnson, Impact of Working Environment upon Human-Machine Dialogues: A Formal Logic for the Integrated Specification of Physical and Cognitive Ergonomic Constraints on User Interface Design. Ergonomics (39)3:512-530, 1996.

C.W. Johnson, J.C. McCarthy and P.C. Wright, *Using A Formal Language To Support Natural Language In Accident Reports.* Ergonomics, (38)6:1265-1283, 1995.

P. Johnson, *Human Computer Interaction: Psychology, Task Analysis and Software Engineering,* McGraw-Hill, London, United Kingdom, 1992.

J. May, Dual-task configuration in ICS: An ART* enterprise application. Technical report, MRC Applied Psychology Unit, Cambridge, United Kingdom. Reference EC Amodeus-2 technical report UM/WP34. 1995.

Ministry Of Defence, Requirements for the Procurement of Safety Critical Software, MOD DEF-STAN 00-55, London, United Kingdom, 1991.

W. Morehouse and M.A. Subamaniam, The Bhopal Tragedy. Technical Report. Council for International and Public Affairs, New York, United States of America, 1986.

D. Norman, *The 'Problem' With Automation : Inappropriate Feedback And Interaction Not Over-automation.* In D.E. Broadbent and J. Reason and A. Baddeley (eds.), Human Factors In Hazardous Situations, 137-145, Clarendon Press, Oxford, United Kingdom, 1990.

J. Reason, *Human Error,* Cambridge University Press, Cambridge, United Kingdom, 1990.

United States Nuclear Regulatory Commission, Three Mile Island: A Report To The Commissioners and the Public. Technical report NUREG/CR-1250-V (The Rogovin Report), Washington D.C., United States of America, 1980.

R.W. Wardell, *An Ergonomic Perspective On Safety In The Oilfield.* In D.L. Pettigrew, editor, Proceedings of the 33rd Annual Meeting Of The Human Factors Society, pages 999-1003. United States of America, 1989.

Formal Specification as a Tool for Objective Assessment of Safety-Critical Interactive Systems

Philippe Palanque[1,2], Rémi Bastide[2], Fabio Paternò[3]

[1] CENA,
7 avenue Edouard Belin,
31055 Toulouse Cedex,
France
palanque@cict.fr

[2] LIS,
University of Toulouse 1,
1 pl. Anatole France,
31042 Toulouse Cedex,
France
bastide@cict.fr

[3] CNUCE - CNR,
36, via Santa Maria,
56128 PISA,
Italy
f.paterno@cnuce.cnr.it

ABSTRACT The design of safety critical systems calls for advanced software engineering models, methods and tools in order to guarantee safety requirements that can put human life at stake. When the safety critical system encompasses a substantial interactive component, the same level of confidence is required towards the human-computer interface. Conventional empirical or semi-formal techniques, although very fruitful, do not provide sufficient insight on the reliability of the human system cooperation, and offer no easy way, for example, to quantitatively compare two design options. The aim of this paper is to present a method with related tools and techniques for engineering the design and development of usable user interfaces for safety-critical applications. The specific application area which we will consider is air traffic control but most of the results will be valid for any application areas with similar requirements.

KEYWORDS Formal specification, Interaction Techniques, Task Models, Petri nets, Air Traffic Control

1. INTRODUCTION

The usability and safety requirements in the design and specification of Interactive Systems are usually investigated in separate and limited ways. There is a lack of structured methods and related tools which can drive the work of designers and developers, especially for applications domains which require sophisticated interaction techniques such as Air Traffic Control. We believe that the formal modelling of task and system can be a valid answer to these problems.

Air Traffic Control (ATC) is an important application area, and one in which many problems are still to be solved: for example a number of air traffic control incidents routinely occur because of the undesired effects of interactions between human actors, or because of the lack of efficiency of current systems, which ends up by wasting time both for air traffic controllers and for pilots. The main reason for this seems to be the misunderstanding resulting from the fact that interaction between controllers and pilots is done exclusively through phone communications. Airlines have estimated that an improvement in air-traffic control could lead to savings up to 20% of fuel costs.

This class of application represents a challenge for people involved in specification, design and development of user interfaces. One promising technique to address this problem is the use of formal methods because they are based on the use of notations

Human–Computer Interaction: INTERACT'97 S. Howard, J. Hammond & G. Lindgaard (editors)
Published by Chapman & Hall

with precise semantics and make it possible to reason about properties of the application specifications and to predict the performance of the future interactive system. Although formal methods have already been used for safety critical applications such as ATC (Hall 96), they are yet to be applied to the design of the user interfaces in safety critical applications, apart from some limited work (Johnson 95, Paternò 95) which can be considered as a useful starting point even though several key problems have not been addressed.

This paper addresses the problem of specification and verification of safety critical application and presents how formal methods can be applied on a full scale case study. The first section of the paper presents the case study that comes from the air traffic control domain. Section 3 is devoted to tasks modelling and presents how tasks models can vary in complexity according to technological facilities. System modelling is presented in section 4. This section shows that the same formalism can be applied for describing both high level and low level interaction techniques such as specific pop-up menus. Section 5 presents how the requirements introduced in section 2 are met in the specification.

2. THE CASE STUDY

This paper is based on a real case study on air traffic control. Nowadays, the airspace is divided in sectors, each of them being controlled by two air traffic controllers managing different tasks and working in a cooperative way[1]. The air traffic controller has at his disposal a workstation for handling the traffic over a given sector, by communicating with the pilots in the planes currently flying in the sector.

2.1 The current system

The whole system is thus divided in two main parts: the controller workstation and the pilot board.

[1] For the sake of simplicity we will consider in the remainder of this paper that all the work is done by a single controller, and merge the actual tasks of the two controllers into a single one.

The controller workstation:

- the information about the plane are displayed on a radar screen. This radar screen is slightly more complex than classical ones, as several information about the plane are displayed aside each plane, several past positions are displayed as well as the speed vector.
- the controller has a kind of note pad organised in a set of paper ribbons called strips. Each strip is initially emitted by a computerised system that fills up the initial information according to the flight plan of the plane. When controllers ask pilots to modify flight parameters of the flight (such as speed, heading, ...) they write down the information on the strip.
- a VHF radio equipment for communicating with the pilots. It is important to notice that there is no way to select a given plane as all aircraft are connected to the same frequency and thus receive all the information for and from all the planes in the sector.

The pilot board:

- the pilot has a set of physical devices for piloting the plane. These devices are used according to the information sent by the controller. For example it is possible to change speed, heading, ... (all the flight parameters)
- the pilot has a special device for handling the frequency of communication. Changes of frequency are to be done each time the plane enters a new sector.

Nowadays, the only way for pilots and controllers to communicate is using the VHF radio device and all the information is exchanged by voice.

This kind of communication induces a set of problems and part of them are at the origin for air traffic control agency to provide new communication media between pilots and controllers.

- The bandwidth limit. For each sectors, all the communications are done using a given frequency and all the planes in the sector are sharing this frequency. This induces a lot of exchanges and at some time the traffic is so dense that controllers and pilots have to hurry in order not to use to much bandwidth.

- Misunderstanding : The use of voice for the only channel introduces a lot of possibilities for the pilot to misunderstand what the controller said. For example NASA (Grayson 81) has analysed 5402 incidents reports in 1981 and has shown that 1991 incidents due to too low level auditory quality have been reported. 792 incidents reports were due to a misunderstanding of words during the communication.
- The identification of the plane. As all the planes are listening to the same frequency the identification of which pilot the controller is talking to is crucial. Consequently, all the messages start and end with the identification of the controller and the identification of the plane. This adding of information increases the potential problems described in the previous paragraphs.

2.2 Data link applications

An alternative system called Data-Link is currently studied in most country. This system tries to solve the bandwidth problem by providing another communication channel between pilots and controllers. This system implies a modification of both the controller workstation and the pilot board. In this paper we will mainly focus on the air traffic control workstation.

The problem in modifying these systems is that the level of reliability of the air traffic control applications as to be guaranteed at the same level as before. This level is very high as no air plane accident has ever occurred due to an error made by air traffic control.

Several systems offering data link facilities are currently studied at CENA. An example of a data-link application (called Druides) under development at the CENA is shown on Figure 1.

This Figure presents a hard copy of the screen of Druide. Only part of the application is shown here. The screen can be split in 3 different regions:

• the light grey part which correspond to the sector handled by the controller. In this sector, white line represent plane routes. On these routes planes are represented by a succession of white dots the first one being the actual position of the plane and the smaller ones the previous positions. Along with these dots information concerning the flight are displayed: the callsign of the flight, its speed, its heading and the next beacon it is supposed to fly over.

• the dark grey part which represent all the outside of the controlled sector,

• the open menu used by the controller for entering information. This menu is a pop-up menu that appears when the user clicks on the label of a flight. When it pops-up, the menu is split in two parts:

  • On the left side the direct command menu (no parameter is needed) which offers three commands, SEND and ABORT (for sending or cancelling the current data-link command) and VOICE for asking the pilots to call the controller using the radio.

  • On the right side of the menu the user can select one of five commands which need parameters: FREQ (for asking the pilot to switch form one radio frequency to another one), CFL (for changing the Current Flight Level of the plane), SPEED (for changing the speed), HEAD (for changing the heading of the plane) and BEACON (for changing the route of the plane i.e. the next beacon it has to fly over). Each time the controller selects one of these commands, another pop-up menu appears (see Figure 1) that allows for entering the parameter of the command. By pressing CNC (cancel) this pop-up menu is closed, by selecting a value, the parameter is set, and by clicking on the arrows, the values presented are scrolled.

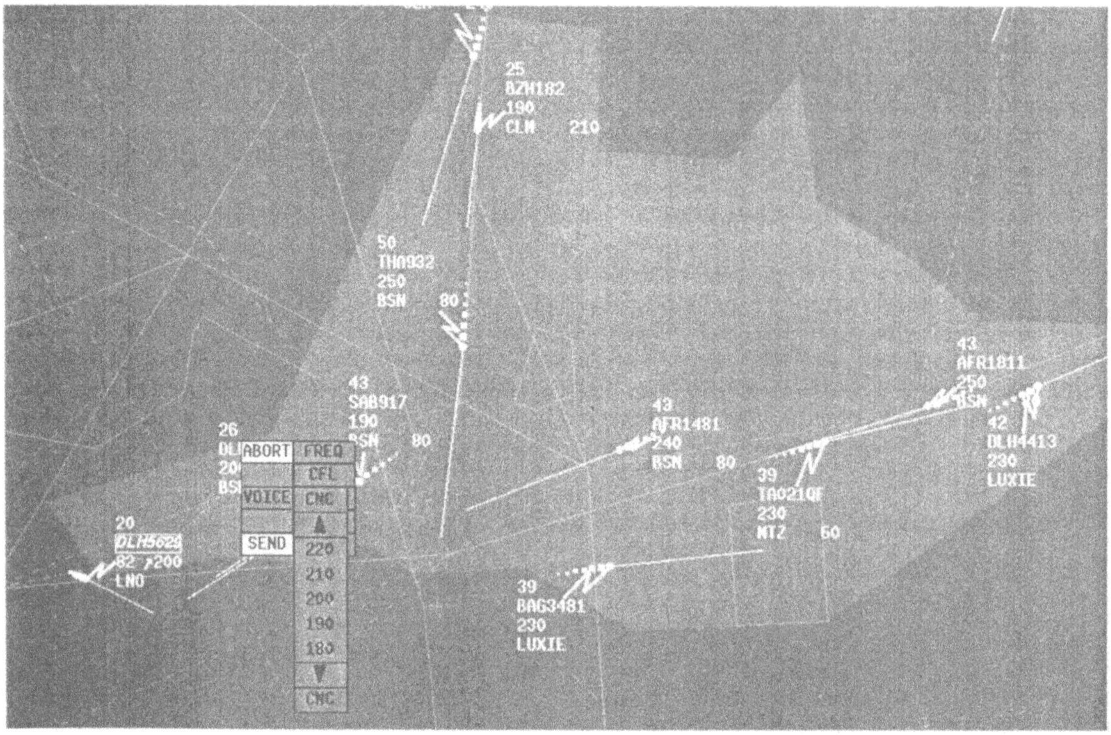

Figure 1 : The ATC System Allowing Data Link Commands

2.3 The requirements

A set of requirements that have to be fulfilled by the data link applications are expressed below in ACTL (Emerson 88) for those that imply temporal constraints, or using set theory for the other ones.

Requirements can be classified in two categories : high-level requirements related to the very semantics of air-traffic control, and lower level ones, related to interaction techniques.

- A control order is only received by one plane
- Any request sent by a controller will be received at some time by a pilot.
- A control order is sent to only one plane (only one plane can be selected at a time)
- For each control order, only one information is sent
- All control orders finish by either Abort or Send
- It is not possible to build several orders at a time

Requirement 1 : Each request sent by a controller to a plane *p* is received by that plane

Let Planes be the set of planes in a sector, let DLRequest be the set of possible data-link requests sent by a controller, let Vrequest be the set of all the possible voice requests (requests sent using radio) :

∀ p ∈ Planes, ∀ req ∈ DLRequest,

AG[send(req,p)]AF<receive(req,p)>true

For all the possible futures (A operator) and for all the states (G operator), if the controller send a request *req* to a plane *p* then for all the possible futures (A operator) in the sequence of states (F operator) there will be a state in which the plane *p* will receive the request *req*. The angled brackets means that it is mandatory that it exists such a state.

Requirement 2 : A data-link request sent by a controller to a plane *p* is received by only that plane

∀ p,p' ∈ Planes, ∀ req ∈ DLRequest,

AG[send(req,p)]AG[not(receive(req,p'))]true

Requirement 3 : A voice request sent to a plane p is received by all the planes in the sector

∀ p ∈ Planes, ∀ req ∈ VRequest,

send (p, req) ⇒ ∀ p' ∈ Planes, receive (p', req)

Requirement 4 : It is not possible to build several orders at a time

∀ p ∈ Planes, ∀ req, req' ∈ DLRequest,

AF[start_send(req,p)]A[True{not(start_send(req',p)} U(end_send(req,p)}true]

which means that if a request order has been started then it will not be possible to start another one until (U operator) the first one has been terminated.

3. TASK MODELLING

This section is devoted to describe the tasks that have to be managed by the controller. We will mainly focus on the ones that are addressed by data link applications but of course they can potentially be done in parallel with all the others tasks of the controller (cooperation with the other controller, resolution of conflicts, take over, ...).

The fundamental tasks are first analysed in an abstract and hierarchical way, and are later detailed with an operational formalism that allows to express more precisely concerns such as data-flows and synchronisations.

3.1 Tasks in the application domain

We use ConcurTaskTree to specify the tasks: it is a diagrammatic notation which shows the task hierarchy and indicates the temporal relationships among tasks at the same level. T1 ||| T2 indicates that the tasks can be performed in concurrent way, T1 >> T2 means that when T1 is terminated then T2 is activated, TX* indicates that task TX is repeatable (when it terminates it can be executed again until another task will disable it), T1 [> T2 indicates that when the first action of the T2 task occurs then T1 is disabled.

The following task model describes how planes are managed by the air traffic control. When a plane enters a given sector, its pilot has to contact the controller for that sector. The controller then manages the flying over his/her sector, and terminates by « shooting » the plane, i.e. transferring it to the next sector.

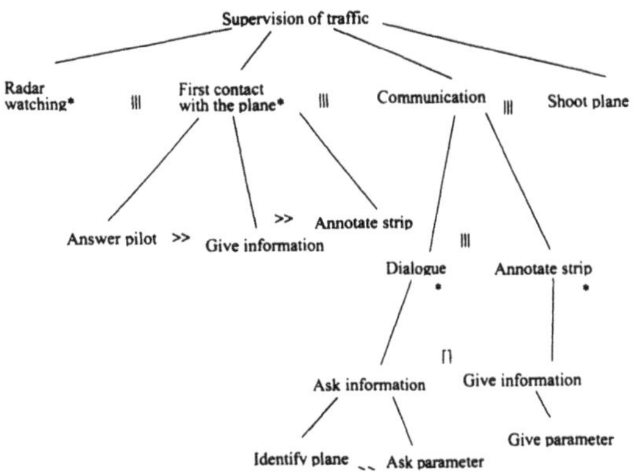

Figure 2 Hierarchical description of tasks

3.2 Tasks in the current system

We have chosen high-level Petri nets as the formalism for detailed task modelling. This formalism features a graphical notation which makes the models more readable, but more importantly it also has a high degree of formality, which makes possible the proof of properties on the task models.

3.2.1 The Petri net formalism

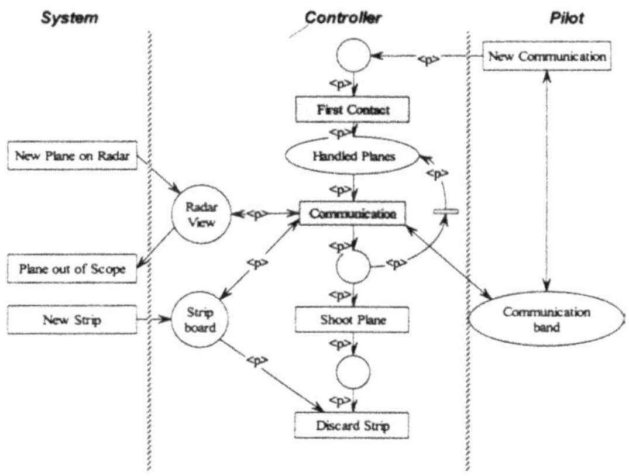

Figure 3 Top-level Petri net task model

When modelling with Petri nets (Murata 89), a system is described in terms of state variables (called *places*, depicted as ellipses) and by state-changing operators (called *transitions*, depicted as rectangles), connected by annotated *arcs*. The state of the system is given by the *marking* of the net, which is a distribution of *tokens* in the net's places. In coloured Petri nets, the tokens assume values from predefined types, or *colours*.

State changes result from the *firing* of transitions, yielding a new distribution of tokens. Transition firing involves two steps: (1) tokens are removed from *input* places and their values *bound* to variables specified on the input arcs, and (2) new tokens are deposited in the *output* places with values determined by *emission rules* attached to output arcs. A transition is *enabled* to fire when (1) all of its input places contain tokens, and (2) the value of those tokens satisfy the (optional) Boolean constraints attached to the input arcs.

Figure 3 shows the Petri net description of the user's task in the current system, before the introduction of data-link features. This task model is presented in an « organisational » style, where the different operations to be performed are classified according to the actor who holds the responsibility for this action. We distinguish between operations to be performed by the system itself (detecting new planes or printing out new paper strips on the controller's desk), by the pilot (initiating a new communication with the controller) and by the controller.

The task model of Figure 3 is hierarchical, the shaded transitions being actually macro-transitions that can be further refined by more detailed nets.

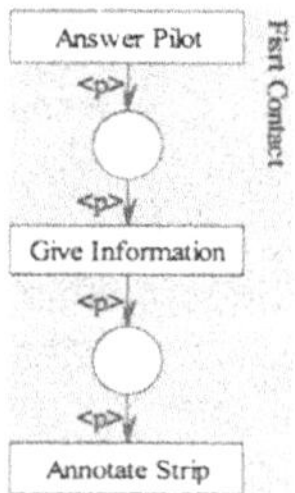

Figure 4 : Macro-transition « first contact »

Figure 4 shows such a macro-transition, which details the operation « first contact » as a mere sequence of simpler subtasks.

The main focus of this model is the controller's task. The operations performed by the other actors are only present to describe the data and the control flow between the different entities involved in the system.

The task model shows that the handling of a plane by a controller is initiated by the pilot of a plane, who makes a phone call to the controller. A precise sequence of actions has then to be undertaken to confirm this contact (Figure 4, Macro-transition « First Contact »).

The controller is then involved in several communication with all the planes that he/she handles, and this task involves watching the radar view and manipulating the strips on the strip board (Figure 5, Macro-transition « Communication »).

It is important to note that, in this version of the system, the communication band is shared by all the pilots : any message emitted is listened to by all the other pilots flying over a given sector. The inconveniences brought by this shared resource have been highlighted in the first section of this paper. However, this can also be considered as a valuable feature of the system : it happens that pilots point out misunderstandings in a conversation between the controller and another plane.

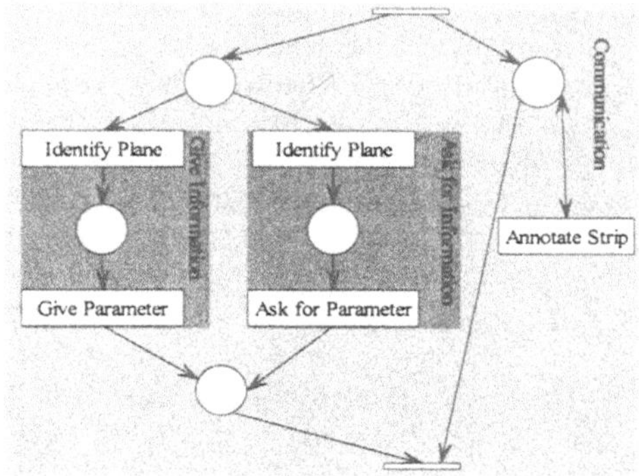

Figure 5 : Macro-transition « Communication »

The subtask « Communication », illustrated in Figure 5, is the most complex in this model : there is a choice between two lower-level tasks (« Give Information » and « Ask for Information ») while the subtask « Annotate Script » can be performed concurrently.

3.3 Tasks including data link features

The introduction of data-link features in the systems allows to migrate to the system's responsibility several operations that were previously of the controller's responsibility, thus diminishing the controller's workload.

A particularly difficult operation for the controller in the initial system is the matching of plane identifiers (provided through voice communication with pilots) with planes that are displayed on the radar screen and with the related paper strip on the strip board. This operation actually gives rise to numerous identification errors in the conversations between controllers and pilots.

This problem can be noticed in the task model in Figure 3, as the macro-transition « Communication » requires the same variable <p> (standing for Plane) coming from three different places (Radar view, Strip board and Handled planes). In the Petri net model that we use, this is akin to the semi-unification mechanism of languages like prolog, and the presence of such a configuration in a task model indicates a significant workload for the user. We have already presented a method for accurately calculating the workload of the users using performance evaluation techniques available in the Petri net theory (Palanque 96).

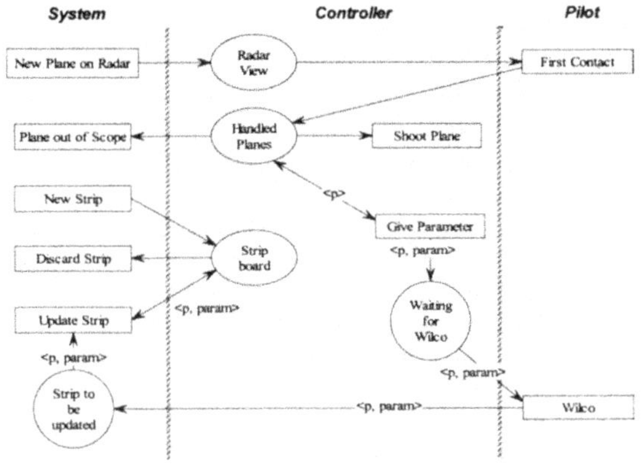

Figure 6 Task model with data-link features

The new task model in Figure 6 clearly shows that the introduction of data-link features allows for a significant reduction of the task model's complexity. Actually, macro-transitions are not needed in this diagram, and the whole task model fits in a single schema.

4. SYSTEM MODELLING

4.1 Interaction Technique Modelling

This section is devoted to the modelling of the interaction techniques for entering data-link commands. In Figure 7 we can see the coarse grain of dialogue for this interaction.

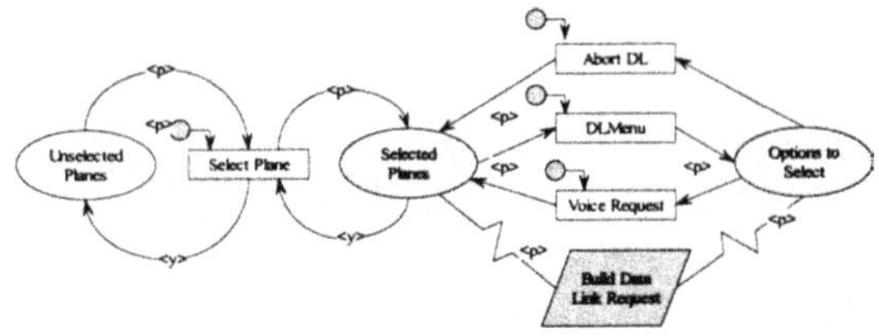

Figure 7 : Coarse grain of interaction

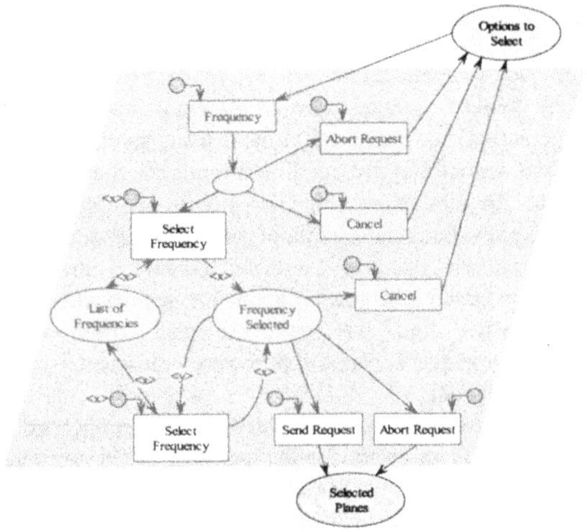

Figure 8: Subnet for « Build Data-Link Request »

Figure 8 presents how a specific data link command can be built by the controller. This model corresponds to the refinement of the greyed out transition in Figure 7. This kind of interaction is the same for the five different data link commands. For this reason only the one corresponding to the "Change frequency" command is presented.

4.2 Verification of the requirements

A necessary step in the life cycle is to prove that the requirements presented in section 4.1. In this section we show how to check on the models that the system fulfils. This kind of verification techniques are based on the computation of marking graph and the verification of the temporal formula on this marking graph. Proving Temporal Logic formulas over Petri net based specifications has already been studied (Jancar 90), and most of the results can be reused for our purposes. For space reasons, the detailed proofs are not shown here, but we have dedicated a paper to the topic of verification of specifications (Palanque 95).

5. CONCLUSION

We have shown in this paper that formal models and techniques can provide fruitful insights at various stages of the development life cycle of safety critical interactive applications. All the models (requirements, task models, coarse grain of dialogue and low-level interaction) have been expressed using mathematically based formalisms. It is of first importance that, at every stage, the models provided are precise enough in order to express behaviour without ambiguity. Besides, this will provide designers with mathematical tools that make it possible to reason about the specification. The formalisms that we have selected offer cross-verification mechanisms that ensure consistency of the various models.

A reproach often addressed to the supporters of formal methods in HCI is the lack of real life examples supporting the feasibility of their use. Even though only a small excerpt of the case study is presented here we hope that this example demonstrates the scalability of our approach to life-size applications.

ACKNOWLEDGEMENTS

The authors would like to thanks Stéphane Chatty and Muriel Preux as well the DRUIDES team at CENA, namely: Sylvie Courteix, Stéphane Marché, Arthur Mustieles, Luc Novalès, and Sophie Tahmassebi that provided us with all the information about the data-link application. The authors would like to acknowledge the Italian CNR and the French CNRS (by the way of the GDR-PRC-CHM) which partially supported this work under the cooperation project n° 3226.

Last but not least we would like to thanks anonymous reviewer for helping us in improving the final version of the paper.

REFERENCES

(Emerson 88) Emerson E.A., Srinivasan J. Branching Time Temporal Logic, in LNCS 354 p.122-172, Springer-Verlag 1988.

(Hall 96) A.Hall, "Using Formal Methods to Develop an ATC Information System", IEEE Software, pp.66-76, March 1996.

(Jancar 90) Jancar P. Decidability of a temporal logic problem for Petri nets. Journal of Theoretical Computer Science, vol. 74, pp. 71-93, 1990.

(Johnson 95) C.Johnson, "The Application of Petri Nets to Represent and Reason About Human Factors Problems During Accident Analyses, Proceedings DSV-IS'95, pp. 93-112, Springer Verlag.

(Mackenzie 94) D.MacKenzie, "Computer-related accidental death: an empirical exploration", Science and Public Policy, 21, , August, pp.233-248.

(Murata 89) T.Murata, "Petri net Properties, analysis and applications". Proceedings of the IEEE (77), 4, 1989, pp.541, 580.

(Palanque 1996), Palanque P & Bastide R. Performance evaluation as a tool for evaluating the formal design of user interface. Proceedings of the IEEE CESA'96 conference, IEEE Press 1996, pp. 235-245.

(Palanque 95), Palanque P & Bastide R. Verification of an interactive software by analysis of its formal specification. Proceeding of Interact'95 conference Chapman et Hall. pp. 191-196.

(Palanque 96) Palanque P., Paterno' F., Bastide R., Mezzanotte M. Towards an Integrated Proposal for Interactive Systems design based on TLIM and MICO. Proceedings of DSV-IS'96, Springer Verlag 1996.

(Paterno 95) F.Paterno', M.Mezzanotte, "Formal Analysis of User and System Interactions in the CERD Case Study", Proceedings of EHCI'95, Chapman & Hall Publisher, 1995.

Reasoning about Human Error and System Failure for Accident Analysis

Chris Johnson

Glasgow Accident Analysis Group,
Department of Computer Science, University of Glasgow, Glasgow,
Scotland, G12 8QQ.

http://www.dcs.gla.ac.uk/~johnson
E-mail: johnson@dcs.gla.ac.uk

ABSTRACT: Accident reports are produced by regulatory and commercial authorities, such as the UK Air Accident Investigation Branch and the US National Transportation Safety Board, in response to most major accidents. These documents describe the human and system failures that lead to major accidents. Recommendations are then made so that the operators and regulators of safety-critical systems can avoid future accidents. Unfortunately, it is often difficult for readers to trace the way in which particular conclusions are drawn from the many hundreds of pages of evidence in these reports. Natural language arguments often contain implicit assumptions and ambiguous remarks that prevent readers from understanding the reasons why a particular conclusion was drawn from a particular account. Operator error is frequently blamed for accidents that might equally have been blaimed upon poor systems engineering or interface design. This paper, therefore, argues that mathematical proof techniques can be used to support the findings of accident investigations. These techniques enable analysts to formally demonstrate that a particular conclusion is justified given the evidence in a report. The later sections of this paper then introduce Conclusion, Analysis and Evidence diagrams. These can be used to communicate the results of a formal analysis. The intention is not to replace the natural argumentation structures that are currently used in accident reports. Rather, our aim is to increase confidence that particular conclusions are well supported by the evidence that is presented within a report.

KEYWORDS: accident analysis; formal methods; human factors; design rationale, CAE diagrams.

1. INTRODUCTION

Accident reports are intended to ensure that major failures do not recur. They are produced by a wide range of national (Cullen, 1990, Fennel, 1988) and international bodies (Morehouse and Subamaniam, 1988). Typically, these documents begin by providing a brief synopsis of the events leading to an accident. The synopsis is then followed by a number of expert analyses. These identify and prioritise the failures leading to the accident. Finally, conclusions are drafted from the experts' findings. These form the basis of any actions that companies or regulatory authorities might take to prevent future failures.

Unfortunately, it is not always easy for readers to understand the justifications that support particular conclusions (Johnson, 1994). Accident reports are often many hundreds of pages in length. The evidence that supports a particular line of analysis may be lost amongst the paragraphs of contextual detail. A further problem is that natural language can be ambiguous. For example, accident reports often refer to situations of 'high workload' and 'operator error' without explaining the precise meaning of these terms (Reason, 1990). Many accident reports are also inconsistent in the sense that the same term is used to refer to several different objects or people (Johnson, McCarthy and Wright, 1995). These problems create considerable confusion for the reader and may even lead them to doubt the accuracy of the final report.

Formal proof techniques can be used to avoid the ambiguity and inconsistency of natural language (Austin and Parkin, 1993). A number of authors have also used these techniques to support the design of dynamic, interactive systems. For example, Dix (1991) has used

Human-Computer Interaction: INTERACT'97 S. Howard, J. Hammond & G. Lindgaard (editors)
Published by Chapman & Hall

an algebraic notation to reason about high level properties of multi-user systems. Paterno, Sciacchitano and Lowgren (1995) have used the LOTOS notation to examine interaction with complex multimedia applications. Palanque and Bastide (1995) have applied Petri Nets to examine safety and liveness properties of distributed systems. None of this work has been applied to reason about accident reports. In particular, there has been no attempt to use mathematical techniques to prove that conclusions are well-founded with respect to the analysis that is presented in an accident report.

2. THE CASE STUDY

The events leading to the Kegworth disaster are used to illustrate the argument that is presented in this paper. The Air Accident Investigation Branch's (1990) report concluded that the accident was caused by a complex interaction between system and human failures. The main events leading to the accident can be summarised as follows. A British Midlands Boeing 737-400 took off from Gatwick on course for Belfast. Thirteen minutes later the turbofan in the number one (left) engine fractured. This caused a series of compressor stalls in that engine. The pilots were unsure about what had happened. There were excessive vibrations throughout the airframe. Loud noises and a smell of fire could also be detected in the cockpit. There were transitory fluctuations on the primary instrument displays and a maximum reading on the airborne vibration meter (AVM) for the left engine.

The crew's initial reaction was to diagnose a fire. The commander dis-engaged the auto throttle and asked the First Officer to throttle the right engine back. This was a mistake because it was the left hand engine that was faulty. Surprisingly, when the First Officer did this all indications of trouble in the left engine went away except for a maximum reading on the AVM for the left engine. The pilots did not notice this warning. The aircraft was then diverted to East Midlands Airport. The aircraft appeared to be flying normally and there was no reason to suspect that the wrong engine had been shut down.

Approximately fifteen minutes later, as the aircraft was being manouvered for its final approach to runway twenty-seven at East Midlands Airport, there was a sudden fall in power in the left engine. Attempts to re-start the right engine failed. The commander then tried to stretch the glide of the aircraft. He failed and the aircraft crashed on the embankment of the M1 motorway two hundred yards short of the start of the runway. A total of forty-six passengers died and a further seventy-four suffered serious injury.

3. MODELLING THE ACCIDENT

In order to reason about the findings of an accident report, it is first necessary to model the events leading to the failure. The first stage in this process is to identify the critical operators, tasks, communications, systems and process components that helped to shape the course of the accident.

3.1 Critical Components

A limitation with natural language approaches to accident reporting is that it can be difficult to identify critical information from a mass of background detail. For example, the Air Accident Investigation Branch's report into the Kegworth crash includes the following account:

> "During the 11 seconds that elapsed between the disengagement of the autopilot and the throttling back of the No. 2 engine, the aircraft rolled slowly to the left through 16 degrees but the commander made no corrective movement of the aileron or rudder." [Page 3]

Additional information, such as the degree of roll, is included to help the reader form a picture of the accident even though this information is not used in the subsequent analysis. Unfortunately, such details may actually obscure the underlying causes of operator 'error' and system 'failure'. Our previous work on accident analysis has, however, identified a number of categories that can be used to identify critical components in an accident (Johnson, 1995, 1995a, 1996):

- **operators.** It is necessary to represent the people involved in an accident so that readers can follow the way in which operator intervention affects the course of system failures;
- **tasks.** It is necessary to identify the tasks that operators were, or should have been, performing during accidents;
- **communications.** It is vital to represent communication between the operators that are involved in an accident. Misunderstandings have a profound impact upon the safety of many applications;
- **information and control systems.** This type of information is included because the quality of information that is available to system operators is

often determined by the channel that is used to support their observations;

• **physical components.** Components failure often forms the starting point for many accidents involving interactive systems.

"During the 11 seconds that elapsed between the disengagement of the autopilot and the throttling back of the No. 2 engine, the aircraft rolled slowly to the left through 16 degrees but the commander made no corrective movement of the aileron or rudder." [Page 3]

The paragraph from the Air Accident Investigation Branch (AAIB) report, cited above, can be used to identify an operator, the Commander. It is also possible to identify information and control systems such as the autopilot. We can identify physical components including the aileron and rudder. The following table shows part of the results that were obtained by extending this analysis throughout the AAIB report.

Operators	**Tasks**	**Messages**
commander	*program_FMS*	'It's the le...it's the right one'
first_officer	*navigation*	'Shut it down'
london_ATC	*radio_ATC*	'Okay throttle it back'

Systems	**Components**
eis	*engine_1*
	engine_2

Table 1: Critical Entity Table for Kegworth

In formal terms, the elements of this table define the types that model the Kegworth accident.

3.2 Axiom for the Accident System

The identification of such critical entities is of little benefit if analysts cannot represent and reason about their role in an accident. For example, the following quotation describes the crew's activities prior to shutting down the working engine:

"Immediately after throttling back the number 2 engine, the first officer advised London Air Traffic Control that they had an emergency situation which looked like a fire. The commander then ordered the first officer 'SHUT IT DOWN'." [page 4]

The following clause captures the observation that the first officer issued input to throttle-back the number two engine. This formula is constructed using the critical entities which were identified in table 1:

input(first_officer, throttle_back(engine_2)). (1)

This states that the first officer issues input to throttle back the number two engine.

The problem with such representations is that they strip out the temporal information that frequently has a critical impact upon the course of an accident. This can be introduced using a simple temporal logic. The following clause states that there exists a time at which the first officer throttled back the number two engine. Unfortunately, we cannot be more precise than this because the previous citation does not state the exact moment at which this occured:

$\exists t$ *:input(first_officer, throttle_back(engine_2), t).* (2)

This states that the first officer issues input to throttle back the number two engine at some time *t*.

In fact, the AAIB report does provide a precise timing for the first officer's action. This is presented in Figure 2 of Appendix 4 on page 170, well away from the previous quotation from page 4. This scattering of temporal information throughout a report can make it extremely difficult for readers to construct an accurate time-line of the events leading to major failures. The following clause illustrates how logic can be used to avoid this limitation:

input(first_officer,
throttle_back(engine_2), 20_05_24). (3)

This states that the first officer issues input to throttle back the number two engine at 20:05:24.

Given this starting point it is now possible to reconstruct the sequence of events that were described in the previous quotation. We know that the command to 'SHUT IT DOWN' occured after the input described in clause (3):

$\exists t$ *: message(commander,*
first_officer, SHUT_IT_DOWN, t) $\wedge$
after(20_05_24, t) (4)

This states that the commander told the first officer to SHUT IT DOWN at some time after 20:05:24..

It is important to note that the previous clause does not capture all of the temporal constraints in the accident report. For example, the previous paragraph stated that the commander's order was issued 'immediately after'. the engine was throttled back. Additional clauses could be introduced to specify that the order must have been issued within five, ten, fifteen seconds of the first officers input. This would only be justified, however, if analysts conducted further investigations into the cockpit interaction immediately before the accident.

4. REASONING ABOUT OPERATOR ERROR

Clauses, such as (3) and (4), provide a number of additional benefits for accident analysis. In particular, they provide a precise and concise means of reasoning about the system failures that lead to operator 'error'. For example, the AAIB report found that:

> "Throughout the period of compressor surging, the No. 2 engine showed no parameter variations but because the first officer was unable to recall what he saw on the instruments, it has not been possible to determine why he made the mistake of believing that the fault lay with the No. 2 engine. When asked which engine was at fault he half-formed the word 'left' before saying 'right'. His hesitation may have arisen from genuine difficulty in interpreting the readings on the engine instruments or it may have been that he observed the instruments only during the 6 second period of relative stability between the second and third stages." (page 97)

This quotation reveals how accident reports may not provide a single, definitive analysis of the events leading to a major failure. Either the First Officer observed the engine information systems and experienced 'genuine difficulty in interpreting the readings' or 'he observed the instruments only during the 6 second period of relative stability'. The following clauses represent the two hypothesised causes for the operator error. As before, the timings for the period of quiescence could not be obtained from the pages surrounding the quotation. These were obtained from a trace of the critical engine parameters in Appendix 4 to the main report:

∃t, ∀t' :
input(first_officer, throttle_back(engine_2), t) ⇐
not(observe(first_officer, pei(engine_1), t') ∨
observe(first_officer, pei(engine_2), t')) ∧
before(t', t). (5)

This states that the first officer throttles back the number 2 engine at some time, *t*, if they fail to observe the primary engine information systems for the number 1 or number 2 at any time before they issue the input.

∃t, ∀t' :
input(first_officer, throttle_back(engine_2), t) ⇐
observe(first_officer, pei(engine_1), t') ∨
observe(first_officer, pei(engine_2), t')) ∧
before(20_05_10, t') ∧ before(t', 20_05_16) ∧
before(t', t) (6)

This states that the first officer throttles back the number 2 engine at some time, *t*, if they observe the primary engine information systems for the number 1 or number 2 engine between 20:05:10 and 20:05:16 and the input is issued after the observation.

It is possible to use formal reasoning as a means of demonstrating that these hypotheses are supported by the description of the accident that is presented elsewhere in the report. *If such a proof cannot be constructed then either there is a mistake in the formalisation or there is an omission in the accident report itself.* For example, Finding 7 states that:

> "The flight crew did not assimilate the readings on the engine instruments before they decided to throttle back the No. 2 engine. after throttling back the No. 2 engine, they did not assimilate the maximum vibration indication apparent on the No. 1 engine before they shut down the number 2 engine 2 minutes 7 seconds after the onset of vibration, and 5nm south of EMA (East Midlands Airport). The aircraft checklist gave separate drills for high vibration and for smoke, but gave no drill for a combination of both." (Finding 7, page 142)

The following clause formalises this using the timing for throttling back the engine that was given in (3):

∀t: not(observe(first_officer, pei(engine_1), t) ∧
observe(first_officer, pei(engine_2), t)) ∧
before(t, 20_05_24) (7)

∀t: not(observe(commander, pei(engine_1), t) ∧
observe(commander, pei(engine_2), t)) ∧
before(t, 20_05_24) (8)

Clause 7 states that the first officer did not observe the primary engine information systems before 20:05:24. Clause 8 states that the commander failed to regard these instruments before 20:05:24. We assume her e that values of *t* range from the initiating event for the accident.

In order to formally prove that the finding of page 97 is supported by the evidence given on page 142, we must apply the following inference rule to (5) and (7). This states that if at all times we can conclude Q given some fact P and at some time we know that P is true then we must know that at some time Q is also true:

$$\forall t: P(t) \Rightarrow Q(t),\ \exists t': P(t') \vdash \quad \exists t': Q(t') \qquad (9)$$

Informally, this argument can be expressed as follows. From analysis on page 97, clause (5), we know that the first officer throttles back the number two engine if he fails to observe the primary engine instrument systems. From the evidence of page 142, clause (7), we know that the first officer failed to observe the primary engine instrument systems before 20:05:24. We can, therefore, infer that the first officer did indeed throttle back the number two engine:

∀t':input(first_officer,
throttle_back(engine_2),20_05_24) ⇐
not(observe(first_officer, pei(engine_1), t') ∨
observe(first_officer, pei(engine_2), t')) ∧
before(t', 20_05_24).

[Instantiating 20_05_24 for t in (5) given (3)] (10)

input(first_officer, throttle_back, engine_2, 20_05_24)

[Applying (9) to (10), given (7)] (11)

This formal analysis helps to identify an important conflict between the human factors chapter in the report and the AAIB's overall findings. The human factors account admits the possibility that the First Officer did observe the engine information systems but that he did so during the seconds of quiescence, see clause (6) and the quotation from page 97. In contrast the overall findings of the report, used in the previous proof, do not consider this possibility, see clause (7) and the quotation from page 142. The First Officer's error was explained in terms of their failure to monitor the systems rather than the failure of the systems to provide information about the engine problem throughout the failure. The report does not provide any explanation of why operator 'error' was a more likely cause of the accident than the failure of the systems to indicate a potential problem during the period of quiescence.

5. FINDING EVIDENCE FOR ANALYSIS

It is important to emphasise that there might have been a number of different reasons why the operators failed to assimilate the readings on their computerised instrumentation systems. The previous analysis stated that the crew failed to observe their displays, *not(observe(first_officer...* The human factors account also suggests that there may have been presentation problems which might have prevented an accurate diagnosis even if the crew had observed the displays:

> "Unlike the transient fluctuations that would have appeared on the primary engine instruments, the reading on the No. 1 engine vibration indicator rose to maximum and remained there for about three minutes On the EIS (Electronic Engine Information Systems) however not only is the pointer of the vibration indicator much less conspicuous than a mechanical pointer but, when at maximum deflection, it can be rendered even less conspicuous by the close proximity of the No. 1 engine oil quantity display, which is the same colour as the pointer and is the dominant symbology in that region of the display." (page 100)

This illustrates further problems with natural language argumentation structures in accident reports. The quotation documents human factors concerns about the presentation of the EIS. This issue was ignored in the overall findings of the AAIB report which focussed upon operator error. In other words, the overall findings focussed upon the crew's failure to correctly monitor their instruments rather than on the problems with the presentation of the systems themselves. Such inconsistencies between the different sections of a report might be blaimed upon the problems of coordinating diverse teams of experts from many different backgrounds. Logic can, however, provide a common means of reasoning about human error, interface design and systems engineering. For example, the following clause relates the first officers command to throttle-back the functioning engine to the sampling and presentation of the oil quantity indicator on the number 1 engine:

$\exists t, \forall t'$: *input(first_officer, throttle_back(engine_2), t)* $\Leftarrow$
close(avm(engine_1), oil_quantity(engine_1), t') $\wedge$
same_colour(avm(engine_1),oil_quantity(engine_1), t') $\wedge$
before(t, t') (12)

This states that the first officer issues input to throttle back engine 2 at some time, if at all previous times the AVM display is close to the oil quantity indicator and both displays are the same colour.

It is important to emphasise, however, that the formalisation process does not ensure that the relationship is 'correct'. The link between the oil quantity indicator and the First Officer's failure must be proven by conventional accident analysis techniques. In other words, given that we know about the detailed presentation and layout of the EIS, is it safe to conclude that at some time the commander will fail to monitor the AVM? The AAIB have addressed this issue by conducting a survey:

> "The overall results, however, showed that a large majority of pilots considered that the EIS displayed engine parameters clearly and showed the rate of change of parameters clearly. Fewer that 10% of pilots reported any difficulty in converting to the EIS from the earlier hybrid instruments and only a few reported minor difficulty in alternating between the EIS and hybrid displays. 64% of pilots stated that they preferred instruments with electromechanical pointers to the EIS" (page 69).

The results of this survey are inconclusive; they do not directly support the argument presented in (12). Further evidence might be gathered through the experimental analysis of pilot performance with the AVMs. This illustrates the way in which formal analysis provides a means of explicitly linking the products of an accident investigation with the findings that are documented in a report. Surveys, such as that cited above, and other forensic investigations help to establish the validity of clauses, such as (12). Failure to confirm a hypothesis indicates the need to conduct further investigations to establish alternative clauses all to treat any consequent inferences with a degree of scepticism in the final report.

6. PRESENTING FORMAL ARGUMENTATION

Mathematical analysis provides non-formalists with an extremely poor idea of the argumentation processes that support particular conclusions. This section, therefore, argues that elements of design rationale might be recruited to communicate the formal analysis of accident reports.

6.1 Design Rationale

Semi-formal, design rationale notations avoid the communications problems of mathematical specifications. For instance, the graphical Issue Based Information System (gIBIS) uses a complex web of issues, positions and arguments to record the rhetorical events in a design meeting (Conklin and Begeman, 1989). Rank Xerox's Questions, Options and Criteria (QOC) notation identifies key concerns that must be addressed during the development of interactive systems (Buckingham Shum, 1995). For example, Figure 1 shows that automatic cancellation might be used to answer the question of how to cancel a particular warnings. This approach is justified by the criteria that it reduces the burdens on system operators. This option is not supported by the criteria that it helps the operator to observe the warning. The diagram shown in Figure 1 is relatively simple in that it only shows a single option for the design question. In practice, these diagrams tend to show a number of alternative clauses each of which represents a different design option for the problem being considered. The interested reader is directed to Johnson (1996a) for more detail on the application of this approach.

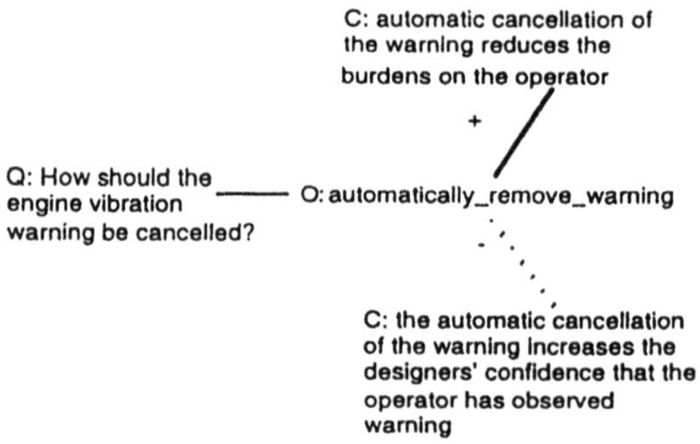

Figure 1: QOC for the Cancellation of a Warning .

Design rationale notations are appropriate for our purposes because they provide an explicit structure for many different forms of argumentation. In design rationale, they represent the reasons for and against particular development decisions. In accident analysis, they might represent the evidence for and against particular causes of an accident.

6.2 Conclusion, Analysis and Evidence(CAE) Diagrams

The Questions, Options and Criteria notation can be translated into a form that directly supports the formal analysis of accident reports. Instead of using questions to represent critical design issues, diagrams can represent the conclusions that are presented in a report. The options of a QOC diagram correspond to alternative interpretations of the events leading to a conclusion. Criteria can be compared to the evidence that supports or weakens the interpretation of an accident. Figure 2 presents a Conclusion, Analysis and Evidence (CAE) diagram for the Kegworth Accident

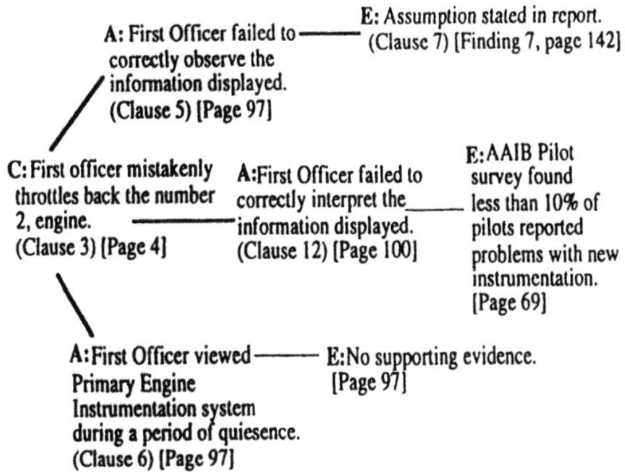

Figure 2: Conclusion, Analysis, Evidence (CAE) Diagram for the Kegworth Accident

The first officer mistakenly throttled back the number 2 engine. This conclusion is taken from page 4 of the report and is formalised by clause 3. It relies upon an analysis which suggests that the first officer failed to correctly interpret the information on their instruments. This is supported by the analysis in Page 97 of the report and is formalised in clause (5). The analysis rests upon an assumption that is presented as evidence in page 142, [Finding 7], of the report. The conclusion is also supported by an analysis which suggests that the operator failed to correctly interpret the information because of the display layout. This analysis is formalised in clause 12 and is taken from page 100 of the AAIB report. The analysis is not supported by survey evidence which suggests that less than 7% of pilots reported any problems with the displays. Finally, the conclusion is supported by an analysis that the first officer viewed the instrumentation during a period of quiescence. This is taken from page 97 and is formalised in clause 6. No supporting evidence was offered for this assertion.

7. CONCLUSION AND FURTHER WORK

This paper has argued that formal methods support the use of natural language in accident reports. They provide a precise and concise means of representing critical events during the course of major disasters. These representations effectively form a model or a time-line for the accident. Formal proof techniques can then be applied to determine whether the model actually supports the findings that are contained in an accident report. In the case of the Kegworth report, we have shown how the overall finding neglect the evidence of problems in the cockpit layout by focussing almost exclusively upon the evidence for operator error.

Further work intends to develop this approach in a number of ways. The task of maintaining CAE diagrams, such as Figure 2, clearly requires some form of tool support. One direction for further work is to exploit hierarchical, graphical representations of formal proofs, such as tableaux . Hypertext display strategies might also be used to filter out the associated prose, or conversely, the mathematics at different stages during the analysis (Johnson, 1996a).

The techniques that are described in this paper can also be applied to represent and reason about the bias that is often embodied in accident reports. This is achieved by examining the factual information and the inferences that are presented in each account. Formal analysis can then be used to identify the impact of factual omissions. For example, very different interpretations might have been produced if the Kegworth report had removed information about the possible period of quiescence. Such an omission not only affects the timeline of events leading to failure, it also restricts the valid inferences that can be made about an accident. For instance, readers would have been forced to accept operator error as the primary cause of the accident. Formal analysis can identify these differences because it would no longer be possible to prove theorem (6). We have already demonstrated that this approach can be used to identify 'biases' in the reporting of nuclear power accidents (Telford and Johnson, 1996). It remains to be seen whether these techniques can be applied to accident reports from other domains.

Acknowledgements

Thanks go to the members of the Glasgow Accident Analysis Group and the Glasgow Interactive Systems Group (GIST) and to the Formal Methods and Theory Group in Glasgow University. This work is supported by the UK Engineering and Physical Sciences Research Council, grants GR/JO7686, GR/K69148 and GR/K55040.

References

Air Accidents Investigations Branch, Department of Transport. *Report On The Accident To Boeing 737-400 G-OBME Near Kegworth, Leicestershire on 8th January 1989,* number 4/90, Her Majesty's Stationery Office. London, United Kingdom, 1990.

S. Austin and G.I. Parkin, *Formal Methods: A Survey*, The National Physical Laboratory, Sponsored by the United Kingdom Department of Trade and Industry, Teddington, United Kingdom, 1993.

S. Buckingham Shum, *Analysing The Usability Of A Design Rationale Notation.* In T.P. Moran and J.M. Carroll (eds.) Design Rationale Concepts, Techniques And Use, Lawrence Erlbaum, Hillsdale, New Jersey, United States of America, 1995.

J. Conklin and M.L. Begeman, *gIBIS: A Tool For All Reasons,* Journal Of The American Society For Information Science, 200-213, May, 1989.

Cullen, *Proceedings Of The Public Enquiry Into The Piper Alpha Disaster.* The Department of Energy, Her Majesty's Stationery Office, London, United Kingdom, 1990.

Dix, A. *Formal Methods For Interactive Systems*, Academic Press, London, United Kingdom, 1991.

D. Fennel, *Investigation Into The Kings' Cross Underground Fire.* Department of Transport, Her Majesty's Stationery Office, London, United Kingdom, 1988.

C.W. Johnson, *The Formal Analysis Of Human-Computer Interaction During Accident Investigations.* In G. Cockton, S.W. Draper and G.R.S. Weir, editors, People And Computers IX, 285-300. Cambridge University Press, Cambridge, 1994.

C.W. Johnson, *The Application of Petri Nets to Represent and Reason about Human Factors Problems During Accident Analyses* In P. Palanque and R. Bastide, editors, The Specification And Verification Of Interactive Systems, 93-112, Springer Verlag, Berlin, 1995.

C.W. Johnson, *Decision Theory and Safety-Critical Interfaces.* In K. Nordby, P. Helmersen, D. Gilmore and S. Arnesen (eds.), Interact'95, 121-127, Chapman Hall, London, 1995a.

C.W. Johnson, Impact of Working Environment upon Human-Machine Dialogues: A Formal Logic for the Integrated Specification of Physical and Cognitive Ergonomic Constraints on User Interface Design. Ergonomics (39)3:512-530, 1996.

C.W. Johnson, Literate Specification. Software Engineering Journal, (11)4:225-237, 1996a.

C.W. Johnson, J.C. McCarthy and P.C. Wright, *Using A Formal Language To Support Natural Language In Accident Reports.* Ergonomics, (38)6:1265-1283, 1995.

W. Morehouse and M.A. Subamaniam, The Bhopal Tragedy. Technical Report. Council for International and Public Affairs, New York, United States of America, 1986.

P. Palanque and R. Bastide, *Formal Specification and Verification of CSCW Using The Interactive Cooperative Object Formalism,* In M.A.R. Kirby, A.J. Dix and J.E. Finlay (eds.), People and Computers X, 213-232. Cambridge University Press, Cambridge, 1995.

F. Paterno, M.S. Sciacchitano and J. Lowgren, A User Interface evaluation, Mapping Physical User Actions to Task-Driven Formal Specifications. In P. Palanque and R. Bastide (eds.), Design, Specification and Verification of Interactive Systems '95, 35-53, Springer Verlag, Berlin, 1995.

J. Reason, *Human Error*, Cambridge University Press, Cambridge, United Kingdom, 1990.

A.J. Telford and C.W. Johnson, *Extending the Application of Formal Methods to Analyse Human Error and System Failure During Accident Investigations.* To appear in the Software Engineering Journal, Novermber 1996.

55

Mental Representations Constructed by Experts and Novices in Object-Oriented Program Comprehension

Jean-Marie Burkhardt*, Françoise Détienne*, and Susan Wiedenbeck**

* Ergonomic Psychology Group, INRIA
Domaine de Voluceau, Rocquencourt, BP 105,
78153, Le Chesnay, cedex, France
Jean-Marie.Burkhardt@inria.fr, Francoise.Detienne@inria.fr

** Computer Science and Engineering Department,
University of Nebraska
Lincoln, NE 68588-0115, USA
susan@cse.unl.edu

ABSTRACT Previous studies on program comprehension were carried out largely in the context of procedural languages. Our purpose is to develop and evaluate a cognitive model of object-oriented (OO) program understanding. Our model is based on the van Dijk and Kintsch's model of text understanding (1983). One key aspect of this theoretical approach is the distinction between two kinds of representation the reader might construct from a text: the textbase and the situation model. On the basis of results of an experiment we have conducted, we evaluate the cognitive validity of this distinction in OO program understanding. We examine how the construction of these two representations is differentially affected by the programmer's expertise and how they evolve differentially over time.

KEY WORDS mental representation, situation model, program model, object-oriented programming, program comprehension, text comprehension, expertise

1. OBJECTIVES

The object-oriented (OO) paradigm is growing fast in popularity, but not enough scientific evidence has been amassed about it. The research that exists is mostly focused on program design and reuse (see for example: Détienne, 1995; Pennington, Lee and Rehder, 1995). Furthermore, there is, as far as we know, no empirical work on the comprehension processes of OO programmers. Our objective is to investigate the mental representations constructed by programmers in the course of tasks involving the comprehension of software, e.g., reuse of parts of past designs and documentation of code. Previous studies on the comprehension of software texts were carried out in the context of procedural or functional languages. Based on the van Dijk and Kintsch's model of text understanding (1983), Pennington (1987a, 1987b) developed and tested a model of procedural program comprehension. One key aspect of the van Dijk and Kintsch's model is the distinction between two kinds of representation the reader might construct from a text: (1) the textbase which refers to what is said in the text and how it is said and (2) the situation model which represents the situation which is referred to by the text. The purpose of this work is to develop and evaluate a cognitive model of OO program understanding. More specifically, we will evaluate the cognitive validity of the distinction between the textbase (or program model) and the situation model in OO program understanding.

Section 2 presents our theoretical framework for studying OO program understanding and our research questions. In section 3, we present the methodology used in our empirical study. In section 4 we present and discuss the results of this study.

Human–Computer Interaction: INTERACT'97 S. Howard, J. Hammond & G. Lindgaard (editors)
Published by Chapman & Hall

2. THEORETICAL FRAMEWORK

2.1. The mental model approach to text comprehension

Current models of text comprehension (Johnson-Laird, 1983; Schmalhofer and Glavanov, 1986; van Dijk and Kintsch, 1983) assume, in addition to the surface form (or verbatim) representation, two distinct, but interacting, levels of cognitive representation: (1) the textbase or propositional representation and, (2) the situation model or mental model. Level 1 is the linguistic representation of the text. It is isomorphic with the text structure and reflects what is contained in the text at a propositional level, i.e., it represents the microstructure and the macrostructure of the text. Level 2 is seen as an a-linguistic representation of the text that is isomorphic or homomorphic with the situation described by the text. Theory assumes that the propositional representation is built by mean of automatic processes from the verbatim representation. The building of the situation model, by contrast, is optional (Mills, Diehl, Birkmire, and Mou; 1995). It is produced by inferences and it makes extensive use of the subject's existing domain knowledge.

2.2. The mental model approach applied to procedural program comprehension

Pennington (1987a, 1987b) adapted van Dijk and Kintsch's text comprehension model to procedural program comprehension and tested it empirically. Pennington distinguished between two different mental representations which may be built while comprehending a program: 1) the **domain model** which is equivalent to van Dijk and Kintsch's situation model and reflects entities of the problem domain and their relationships, and 2) the **program model** which is equivalent to van Dijk and Kintsch's propositional textbase and reflects the text-based representation of the program.

Pennington argued that control flow and elementary operations information belong to the program model, while function and data flow information belong to the domain model. Her experimental paradigm was to give subjects a program to read for a limited time and then ask them questions reflecting different information categories, presumed to make up the situation and program models. The correctness of the responses to the questions then served as an indicator of the nature of the representation. Her experiments (Pennington, 1987a; 1987b) generally supported the dual model. She showed that control flow and elementary operations representations, which make up the program model, emerge first during program comprehension, perhaps because the programmer initially segments the elementary operations of one line or less into larger text structure units representing control flow. Function and data flow knowledge, which makes up the domain (or situation) model, emerge later with continued processing of the program.

2.3. Taking into account the OO nature of programs and the size of programs

There are several limitations to this approach related to the procedural nature of the languages used by Pennington and to the small size of the program she used. Pennington conducted her experiments with procedural languages and she did not examine at all representations about objects or even data structures. However, objects are central entities in OO programs and the construction of the representation of objects should be taken into account in a model of OO program understanding. We assume that the representation of objects is part of the situation model inasmuch as it reflects the objects of the problem situation.

Furthermore Pennington's model accounts for understanding of short programs but does not scale up easily to larger programs. Two aspects are not accounted for: the representation of delocalised plans and the representation of text macrostructure. Pennington assumes that the reader uses plan knowledge to construct the situation model. A plan is a set of actions that, when placed in a correct order, achieves some desired goal. Programmers have knowledge about patterns of program instructions which typically go together to accomplish certain functions or goals (Soloway, Ehrlich and Bonar, 1982). Pennington assumes that plan representations of a program are primarily based on data flow relations. In long programs, particularly in OO programs, it happens that many plans are delocalised. According to Rist (1996), plans and objects are orthogonal in OO systems. A plan can use many objects and an object can be used in many plans. In an OO system, the actions in a plan are encapsulated in a set of routines, and the routines are divided among a set of classes and connected by control flow. In our model we take the view that the construction of these complex delocalised plan representations is primarily based on client-server relationships, in which one object processes and supplies data needed by another object.

The macrostructure of long programs is not accounted for at all in Pennington's model, at the level of the program model. She accounts for the representation of elementary units, such as elementary operations and control flow between these operations, but she does not account for the representation of larger text units such as routines. Our model considers these text units as reflected by the macrostructure of the program model.

2.4. Proposed model of comprehension of object-oriented programs

As in Pennington's model, our **situation model** contains information about goals and data flow. In order to take into account the OO nature of programs and the size of programs, we have added information about objects as well as client-server relationship between objects. Information about objects and goals represents the static aspects of the problem solution, whereas information about data-flow and client-server relationships represents more dynamic aspects of the solution to the problem.

To summarize, the static aspects of the situation model refer to:

(1) the problem objects which directly model objects of the problem domain;

(2) the relationship between those objects, i.e., the inheritance/composition relationships between objects;

(3) the computing or reifed objects (e.g., a string class which is not a problem domain object). They are also represented at this level inasmuch as they are necessary to complete the representation of the relationships between problem objects, i.e., they bundles together program-level elements needed by the domain objects;

(4) the main goals of the problem. They correspond to functions of the program viewed at a high level of granularity. They do not correspond to single program units. The complex plan which realizes one goal is usually a delocalized plan in an OO programs.

The dynamic aspects of the situation model represent the communication between objects at a high level of granularity and the communication between variables at a fine level of granularity. These relationships trace the delocalized plans and the local plans involved in the problem solution. They are:

(1) Communications between objects correspond to client-server relationships in which one object processes and supplies data needed by another object. These connections between objects are the links connecting units of complex delocalized plans. In an OO system, the actions in a complex plan which performs a main goal are encapsulated in a set of routines, and the routines are divided among a set of classes and connected by control flow. Client-server relationships represent those connections.

(2) Communications between variables correspond to data flow relationships connecting units of local plans in a routine.

The **program model** contains two levels:

(1) at a microlevel, elementary operations constitute basic text units and control flow information constitutes the links between text units. Control flow, at this fine level of granularity, represents the control structure (either sequence, loop or test) linking individual operations;

(2) at a macrolevel, larger text units are represented. These are functions corresponding to units in the program structure, i.e., routines attached to objects.

As in text understanding theory, we assume that the construction of the situation model makes extensive use of the subject's existing domain knowledge. This representation is produced by inferences and is also a source of new inferences. Two kinds of knowledge, generic and episodic, and two knowledge domains, the problem domain and the programming domain, may be involved in this construction. Inferences may be drawn on the basis of schematic knowledge from the programming domain, such as plan knowledge. Knowledge about the problem situation, either generic knowledge or episodic knowledge, may also be activated and used as a source for inferences. On the contrary, the construction of the program model is based mostly on text structure knowledge and on local inferences for connecting propositions.

An important idea is that, whereas the construction of the textbase is systematic/automatic, the construction of the situation model is optional. Also, the building of the situation model requires time. It depends on the subject's knowledge and also on the task.

2.5. Research questions

We wish to evaluate the cognitive validity of the distinction between the program model and the situation model in OO program understanding. In particular, we wish to examine how the construction of these two kinds of representation is differentially affected by the programmer's expertise and how they evolve differentially over time.

Our first question is how expertise in programming affects the construction of the two representations. Here we must make clear that we do not manipulate expertise in the problem domain (all subjects have knowledge in this domain), but rather we manipulate the expertise in the programming domain. We compare expert programmers in OO programming with advance computer science students learning OO programming.

According to our model, the expertise of subjects should affect the construction of the situation model but not the construction of the program model, provided that our novices are advanced students.

However, it is worth noting that a different hypothesis would be made by advocates of OOP. They have made strong claims about the naturalness, ease of use, and power of this design approach (Rosson and Alpert, 1990). It has been argued that there is a direct correspondence between the OO paradigm and the way people naturally think about problems (Borgida, Greenspan and Mylopoulos, 1986). If this is true, decomposition of a problem into objects may be easier in the OO paradigm because it is driven more by knowledge about world structure and less by knowledge about design schemas (or programming plans) representing classes of solutions in the programming domain. On this basis it could be argued that constructing the situation model, in particular the static part of it, would be easy in OO program comprehension, whatever the programmer's level of expertise. Thus, it would be expected that expertise in programming would not affect the construction of the situation model.

Our second research question concerns how the program model and situation model evolve over time. We examine the representations constructed after a first phase of comprehension then after a second phase of comprehension. The question is whether there is an order of construction of representations in OO program comprehension.

Another research question is the effect of the task (or purpose for reading) on the construction of the representations in OO program comprehension. We chose two tasks, a reuse task and a documentation task, because these are two realistic purposes for reading in program comprehension and because the problem solving component involved is more important in the former than in the latter. This question will not be addressed directly in this paper as the data are still being analyzed.

In order to analyze these research questions we conducted an experiment on OO program understanding by experts and novices. Our experimental paradigm is similar to the one used by Pennington. Subjects answered questions after having studied a program for a certain period of time. The question categories were revised in accordance with our model.

3. DESIGN AND METHODOLOGY

3.1. Experimental design

A three-factor mixed design was used, as shown in Figure 1. The between subjects factors were expertise (OO expert vs. OO novice) and task orientation (documentation vs. reuse). The within subjects factor was phase (preliminary comprehension phase vs. task performance phase) and information category. Half the subjects were given a documentation task and half a reuse task.

The comparison between question set 1 after the preliminary comprehension phase and question set 2 after the task performance phase addressed the research question about the order of acquisition of knowledge in comprehension. Data came from both correctness of responses to questions and reaction times. The comparison between experts and novices provided data relevant to the research question about comprehension differences between expert and novice OO programmers.

3.2 Subjects

The subjects were 30 object-oriented experts and 21 object-oriented novices. The experts were professional programmers with experience in object-oriented design with C++. The novices were advance computer science students who were experienced in C but had only a basic knowledge of object-oriented programming and C++.

	OO experts		OO novices	
	Documentation task	Reuse task	Documentation task	Reuse task
Preliminary comprehension phase	Study pgm with documentation orientation, then question set 1	Study pgm with reuse orientation, then question set 1	Study pgm with documentation orientation, then question set 1	Study pgm with reuse orientation, then question set 1
Task performance phase	Documentation of pgm, then question set 2	Reuse to solve target problem, then question set 2	Documentation of pgm, then question set 2	Reuse to solve target problem, then question set 2

Figure 1 Experimental design

Thirty of the subjects were speakers of English and 21 were speakers of French.

3.3 Materials

The materials consisted of a database program of approximately 550 lines which managed personnel, student, and course information for a small university. The program was composed of 10 classes. It was written in object-oriented C++ and presented in 23 files. The domain of the problem allowed us to write a program which took good advantage of the OO paradigm, including ease of conceptualization in terms of objects, classes, and inheritance. As in Pennington's study (1987a), little documentation was included in the text of the program. During the task performance phase, reuse oriented subjects were given a variation of the library problem (Wing, 1988) to design and implement. This problem was partially isomorphic to the database program and allowed for reuse by template copying and modification or by inheritance. Documentation oriented subjects were asked to comment the code for the use of another programmer who would later maintain it.

Elementary operations
Does the program contain the code fragment: if ((number == search) ll (name == search)) return TRUE; else return FALSE;?
Control flow
In "initialize" are the professors initialized before the courses ?
Elementary functions
Does "Collection::maintain" print out a list and ask the user to input a selection.?

Table 1 Example of questions from categories composing the program model

Problem objects
Does the program define a "Schedule" class?
Computing objects
Does the program define a "Collection" class?
Object relationships
Does the "Researcher" class inherit from the "Employee" class?
Goals
Does the program allow you to create a new schedule for an upcoming semester?
Client-server
Does the "Schedule" class call a member function of the "Course" class?
Data flow
In "Schedule::maintain" does the value of "selection" affect the value of "offerings"?

Table 2 Example of questions from categories composing the situation model

Two matched sets of yes/no questions were developed, one to be used at the end of each phase. The questions fit conceptually into two classes targeting knowledge making up the program model and the situation model. Three information categories reflected information composing the program model (see **Table 1**).

Six information categories reflected information composing the situation model (see **Table 2**). The first four represent the static part of the situation model and the last two represent the dynamic part.

Two matched questionnaires were used. Each questionnaire contained 54 questions (3 yes questions * 3 no questions * 9 question categories). Two versions, a French and an English version, of each questionnaire were created. The order of presentation of the questionnaires was counterbalanced. The questions were randomized for presentation to subjects.

3.4 Procedure

Experts and novices were assigned randomly to the documentation or reuse groups. They were given an orientation to study the program for later reuse or documentation, as appropriate. Subjects were then given the database program and asked to study it for 35 minutes. Verbal protocols were collected. After this preliminary comprehension phase oriented by documentation or reuse goals, subjects answered the first question set on-line. Correctness and reaction times to the questions were recorded. In the performance phase, subjects were asked to carry out the documentation or reuse task for 90 minutes. Again verbal protocols were collected. Finally, subjects answered the second set of comprehension questions.

Subjects were provided with a paper version as well as an electronic version of the program files. They were allowed to run the program but could modify it only in the second phase of the experiment.

4. RESULTS

In this section we first present the global results with respect to the factors under study: expertise, phase, and information category. Then we present more detailed results concerning the model of comprehension of OO programs presented earlier. Most of the analyses involve the correctness of responses to the questions, but reference is made to reaction times when appropriate. Whatever the comparison we made, we calculated the scores considering 6 as the maximum correctness value. We do not report results from the protocol analysis.

Assignment of subjects to novice or expert levels was initially done on the basis of a self-report questionnaire. To verify the group assignments a posteriori, a qualitative data analysis was done on subjects responses patterns by using a dynamic cluster method. The results strongly supported our original grouping. A preliminary analysis showed few effects of language and those restricted largely to the reaction time data, so language is not treated further here.

Initially a three-way mixed model Analysis of Variance was performed on the number of correct responses to questions. The between subjects factor was expertise (novice or expert). The within subjects factors were phase (1=preliminary or 2=task performance) and question category (nine categories as described in section 3.3). The results showed that there was a significant overall effect of expertise ($m_{expert} = 4.23$, $sd = 1.32$; $m_{novice} = 3.89$, $sd = 1.29$; $F(1, 44) = 11.08$, $p < .0018$). There was a significant effect of phase ($m_{phase1} = 3.93$, $sd = 1.34$; $m_{phase2} = 4.25$, $sd = 1.28$; $F(1, 44) = 23.87$, $p < .0001$). Category was significant, as well ($F(8, 352) = 36.68$, $p < .0001$). The two-way interaction of expertise and category was significant ($F(8, 352) = 3.16$, $p < .0018$). The two-way interaction of expertise and phase was not significant, nor was the two-way interaction of phase and category, nor the three-way interaction. See Figure 2 for the means of the interactions.

Our model of OO program comprehension contrasts the situation model with the program model. We carried out further analyses to test this model. The model-based analysis compared the six information categories making up the situation model (problem objects, computing objects, object relationships, goals, client-server relationships, and data flow) with the three information categories making up the progam model (elementary operations, control flow, and elementary functions). We found an overall difference between the situation and progam models ($m_{situation} = 4.36$, $sd = .61$; $m_{program} = 3.55$, $sd = .65$; $F(1, 43) = 110.94$, $p < .0001$). Scores for the situation model improved significantly between phase 1 and phase 2 ($m_{situation\text{-}p1} = 4.17$, $sd = .65$; $m_{situation\text{-}p2} = 4.55$, $sd = .51$; $F = 10.83$, $p < .002$), while scores for the program model did not. Experts had significantly higher scores on the situation model than did novices ($m_{situation\text{-}expert} = 4.56$, $sd = .54$; $m_{situation\text{-}novice} = 4.10$, $sd = .61$; $F(1, 44) = 19.17$, $p < .0001$). However, there was no expert/novice difference on the program model.

As described above, the situation model may be considered to have two aspects: static information vs. dynamic information. To investigate the representation further we compared these two with each other and with the program model. The static situation knowledge contained problem objects, computing objects, object relationships, and goals. The dynamic situation knowledge contained client-server relationships and data flow. There was a significant overall difference between the static and dynamic information ($m_{static} = 4.74$, $sd = .68$; $m_{dynamic} = 3.62$, $sd = .96$; $F(1, 45) = 106.20$, $p < .0001$). Also, the reaction times (corrected

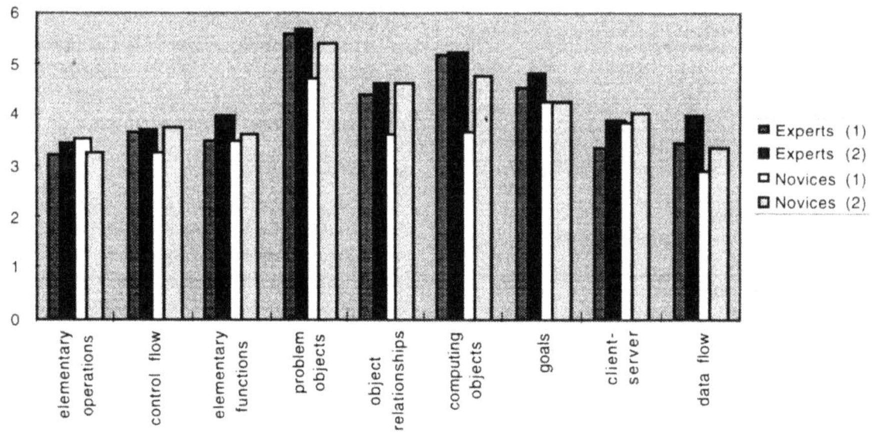

Figure 2 Mean correctness score by question category for novices and experts in phase 1 and in phase 2 (max. = 6)

for question length) for the program objects and goals categories of the static part were faster than any other categories. There was a significant difference between phase 1 and phase 2 for static information ($m_{static-p1}$ = 4.57, sd = .71; $m_{static-p2}$ = 4.90, sd = .59; F(1, 45) = 7.15, p < .0104) and also for dynamic information ($m_{dynamic-p1}$ = 3.38, sd = 1.09; $m_{dynamic-p2}$ = 3.85, sd = .75; F(1, 45) = 9.36, p < .0037). For the static information experts scored significantly higher than novices ($m_{static-expert}$ = 5.00, sd = .49; $m_{static-novice}$ = 4.36, sd = .73; F(1, 46) = 34.23, p < .0001). However, for the dynamic information there was no difference between experts and novices. There was a significant overall difference between the static part of the situation model and the program model (means given previously; F(1,45) = 237.92, p < .0001). Finally, for the comparison of the dynamic part of the situation model and the program model, there was no significant difference.

5. DISCUSSION

Our results tend to show that the distinction between the situation model and the program model has cognitive validity for OO programmers. First, our findings show that there is an overall difference between these two representations. The situation model appears to be stronger (based on the correctness of responses) than the program model. Second, our findings show that these two representations are affected differentially by the expertise and phase factors. Expertise has an effect on the construction of the situation model, whereas it has no effect on the construction of the program model. Furthermore, phase affects the construction of the situation model but not the program model, i.e., there is an enrichment of the situation model over time whereas the program model remains "stationary".

Our results also indicate an overall difference between the static and dynamic parts of the situation model. Based on the correctness scores, the static part of the model appears to be better developed than the dynamic part in the mental representation of OO programmers. The expertise factor affects the construction of only the static part, whereas the phase factor affects the construction of both the static and dynamic parts. In particular, experts develop a better static situation model than do novices. Both static and dynamic parts improve over time. Interestingly, the dynamic part of the situation model is not better developed than the program model. This implies that the marked difference between the situation model and the program model is accounted for by the effect of the static part.

According to our results, the situation model is more fully developed than the program model, even in an early phase of comprehension. This contrasts with the results of Pennington (1987a, 1987b) for procedural programmers. She showed that the program model developed more fully in the early stages of comprehension, whereas the situation model emerged later, after performance of a meaningful programming task. Perhaps this difference between our results and Pennington's can be explained by the programming paradigm. It appears that the OO paradigm, with its emphasis on objects and relationships of objects, may facilitate the construction of a situation model earlier in program comprehension. This is consistent with the naturalness claims of advocates of the OO paradigm. On the other hand, the situation model constructed by experts is stronger than that constructed by novices. This suggests that the construction of the situation model is not based solely on problem domain knowledge but also on knowledge acquired through experience in the programming domain. These latter findings are consistent with results on object-oriented design (Détienne, to appear) which show a greater benefit of this paradigm for expert designers than for novice designers.

With respect to the program model, our results show that it is not enriched over time as is the situation model. Rather it remains essentially constant. Perhaps this ceiling effect is related to the size of the program. In a larger program, it may be difficult to keep in working memory a representation of program level information. This resource limitation hypothesis requires further verification. Another possible explanation of lack of growth of the program model is the comprehension strategy of the programmer. A programmer may concentrate on certain parts of a program at the expense of others, as observed in the "as-needed" comprehension strategy (Koenemann and Robertson, 1991; Littman, Pinto, Letovsky and Soloway, 1986). The use of an as-needed strategy appears to be task related. In further analyses, we will use our quantitative and qualitative data together to understand the relation between the construction of the mental representation and comprehension strategies.

In our results, both the static and the dynamic parts of the situation model evolved, becoming more elaborated over time. However, the static part always remained more developed than the dynamic part, even for experts. The program objects and goals were also the more accessible, as shown by reaction times. The dynamic part reflects the mental representation about plans, either local or delocalized. It appears that the OO paradigm facilitates the construction of the situation model most strongly in its static part. It may be hypothesized that the dynamic part is important for linking the static aspects of the situation model to the program model. Our results suggest that the OO paradigm does not strongly support this linking of the dual mental representations, at least not early in program comprehension.

6. LIMITATIONS AND FUTURE DIRECTIONS

There are several limitations of this study related to the methodology. Subjects worked with a single program which implemented a database. To generalize the results it is necessary to repeat the study with other programs in other problem domains. Furthermore, while the program was larger than often used in this kind of study, it was still a small program by industrial standards. Thus, we do not know whether the mental representation of a much larger program would conform precisely to what we found here. In our study subjects worked with the program for approximately 2 hours, and most did not have time to finish the reuse or documentation task they were given. We might have observed further evolution of the mental representation if they had worked with the program over a longer time.

One future direction will be to analyze the influence of our task factor on program comprehension. As shown in recent studies on text comprehension (Mills et al. 1995), the purpose for reading exerts an important influence on the construction of the mental representation. We expect that similar effects will be found in the domain of programming. In addition to analyzing the effects of a reuse or documentation task, we are interested in extending this study to other comprehension-related tasks, such as program modification.

Another direction of this research will be to analyze the comprehension strategies used by subjects performing different tasks and subjects at different levels of expertise. We plan to use qualitative data from our think-aloud protocols to link specific comprehension strategies to outcomes in the development of the mental representation.

REFERENCES

Borgida, A., Greenspan, S., and Mylopoulos, J. (1986). Knowledge representation as the basis for requirements specifications. In C. Rich and C. R. Waters (Eds): *Readings in Artificial Intelligence and Software Engineering*. Los Altos, CA: Kaufmann. 561-570.

Détienne, F. (1995) Design strategies and knowledge in object-oriented programming: effects of experience. *Human-Computer Interaction*, 10 (2 & 3), 129-170.

Détienne, F. (to appear) Assessing the cognitive consequences of the object-oriented approach: a survey of empirical research on object-oriented design by individuals and teams. Interacting with Computers.

Johnson-Laird, P. N. (1983). *Mental models: Towards Cognitive Science of Language, Inference, and Consciousness*. Cambridge: Cambridge University Press.

Koenemann, J. and Robertson, S.P. (1991). Expert problem solving strategies for program comprehension. In S. P. Robertson, G. M. Olson, and J. S. Olson (Eds): *CHI'91 Conference Proceedings*, NY: ACM. 125-130.

Littman, D. C., Pinto, J., Letovsky, S., and Soloway, E. (1986). Mental Models and Software Maintenance. In E. Soloway and S. Iyengar (Eds): *Empirical Studies of Programmers*, Norwood, NJ: Ablex. 80-98.

Mills, B. C., Diehl, V. A., Birkmire, D. P. & Mou, L-C. (1995) Reading procedural texts: effects of purpose for reading and predictions of reading comprehension models. *Discourse Processes*, 20, 79-107.

Pennington, N. (1987a). Comprehension strategies in programming. In G.M. Olson, S. Sheppard, and E. Soloway (Eds): *Empirical Studies of Programmers: Second Workshop*. Norwood, NJ: Ablex. 100-113.

Pennington, N. (1987b). Stimulus Structures and Mental Representations in Expert Comprehension of Computer Programs. *Cognitive Psychology*, 19, 295-341.

Pennington, N., Lee, A. Y., & Rehder, B. (1995). Cognitive activities and levels of abstraction in procedural and object-oriented design. *Human-Computer Interaction*, 10 (2 & 3), 171-226.

Rist, R. (1996) System structure and design. In W. D. Gray, & D. A. Boehm-Davis (Eds): *Empirical Studies of Programmers, Sixth*. Norwood, NJ: Ablex. 163-194.

Rosson, M. B., and Alpert, S. R. (1990). The cognitive consequences of object-oriented design. *Human-Computer Interaction*, 5(4), 345-379.

Schmalhofer, F., and Glavanov, D. (1986). Three Components of Understanding a Programmer's Manual : Verbatim, Propositional, and Situational Representations. *Journal of Memory and Language*, 25, 295-313.

Soloway, E., Ehrlich, K., & Bonar, J. (1982) Tapping into tacit programming knowledge. *IEEE Transactions on Software Engineering*, SE-10, 595-609.

van Dijk, T.A. and Kintsch, W. (1983) *Strategies of Discourse Comprehension*. New York: Academic.

Wing, J.M. (1988) A study of 12 specifications of the library problem. *IEEE Software*, 5, 66-72.

An empirical investigation of memory for routes through menu structures

Juliet Richardson, Andrew Howes and Stephen J. Payne

School of Psychology, University of Wales, College of Cardiff.
PO Box 901, Cardiff, CF1 3YG, U.K.
RichardsonJ@Cardiff.ac.uk

ABSTRACT Menu structures are a pervasive mechanism for interacting with computers. However, whilst a number of investigators have studied the effects of different types of menu structure on initial search performance, there is little empirical work on how routes experienced through exploration, are committed to memory. This paper reports a preliminary empirical investigation of human memory for this kind of skill. Specific predictions are derived from a functional model, called AYN (Howes, 1994). The predictions of the model and the actual performance of the subjects are compared and the implications of the findings for the model are discussed.

KEYWORDS Cognitive Models, Computer Menus, Interactive Search, Displays, Recognition Memory.

1. INTRODUCTION

We report a preliminary experiment designed to investigate memory for routes through menu structures. We are particularly interested in how subjects remember routes that have been experienced during exploration. An understanding of memory for this kind of experience could be useful in designing a wide range of interactive systems including world wide web pages and browsers.

Several researchers have studied human exploratory search of menus, and a number of important observations have been made. Most of these relate to the strategies used in the search process rather than to memory for this process, but nonetheless they help uncover the nature of what needs to be remembered.

The most immediate and important observation is that menu search is semantically guided. Empirical investigations of subjects learning to use various versions of the CA Cricket Graph and MS EXCEL graphing packages have been carried out (Franzke, 1994; Franzke, 1995). Subjects were set tasks such as "change the line and symbol style of the plotted graph," some of which involved the use of menu structures. Response times were measured for menu labels that (a) were also words in the task description; (b) were synonyms with words in the task description; (c) were semantically related to the task and (d) had no link at all to the task. Response times during an initial exploratory trial were found to be fastest for the overlapping words and slowest for the words that had no links at all. These differences were reduced with practice.

Of course, in real applications it is rarely the case that the everyday semantics of labels are sufficient to guide the novice user through the correct route. In such circumstances, users have to combine semantic guided search with less knowledge-dependent and more general purpose search strategies. In situations where the semantics are not sufficient, subjects using Cricket Graph have been observed to manage search by using an "iterative deepening" procedure: subjects search both the external world defined by the menu structure and an internal world of possible interpretations of menu labels (Rieman, 1994). A model, IDXL, of "iteratively deepening" exploratory search has been developed (Rieman, Young and Howes, 1996). A central mechanism is that for any selection the model must make a choice as to whether to search the internal world

Human–Computer Interaction: INTERACT'97 S. Howard, J. Hammond & G. Lindgaard (editors)
Published by Chapman & Hall

of knowledge, or the external world of the device. If it decides to search the internal world then it elaborates its semantic interpretation of the visible menu labels. If it decides to search the external world then it chooses the item that is judged most likely to lead to the goal. This item may be on a menu other than the current menu.

Rieman *et al.*'s model is of novice behaviour, which is obviously different from the behaviour of experts who will have extensive knowledge of menu functions to guide their search and who should therefore rely less on strategies such as semantic guidance and "iterative deepening". Kitajima and Polson (1995) report a model of skilled use of the Cricket Graph package. The model uses representations of the user's goals and of the task environment. These representations are linked by an action cycle consisting of two stages: an evaluation stage and an execution stage. During the evaluation stage the model generates a representation of the objects present in the display. This representation only contains limited information on object appearance. The model then elaborates this representation by a memory sampling process using the goals and the display objects as cues for retrieval from long term memory. During this process information is retrieved about the functions of objects and their links with the goals and with the actions to be performed. For example, the initial representation of a menu item might be elaborated to include knowledge that the menu item can be pulled down as well as information about what items will be present on that pull-down menu. This elaboration process is probabilistic and even with all of the relevant information present in long term memory the model may fail to elaborate the display representation fully leading to errors as a result of incomplete information. During the second phase of the cycle, the execution stage, three candidate objects from the display are selected and the possible actions that can be carried out on them are considered. Eventually one action-object pair is selected and that action is executed on the selected object thus changing the task environment and restarting the action cycle.

The two models described above are candidate models of how experts and novices search during exploration but they leave open the question of how memories are encoded during the search process. How do people perform a menu search task for the second, third or fourth time? How does performance improve?

Howes (1994) reports a functional model, called AYN, of the exploratory acquisition of menu knowledge. AYN acquires two types of knowledge as it interacts with a menu structure: *recognition* knowledge and *control* knowledge.

In AYN, recognition knowledge consists of episodic chunks that are encoded into memory for every combination of goal, menu and action that the model experiences regardless of whether the action leads to the goal. AYN also acquires recognition knowledge that the goal has been achieved. Recognition knowledge, of course, does not directly support recall, merely identification of the menus that have been previously visited, which selections made and which goals visited.

AYN uses recognition knowledge to help guide search in the menu structure both during initial exploration and during subsequent trials. A set of rules determines how the model applies this knowledge: (1) if the goal has not yet been achieved then avoid recognised selections; (2) if the goal has been achieved and there is a recognised selection then it should be applied; (3) if there are no recognised selections and the goal has been achieved then AYN should apply a backup operator. These rules help limit the size of the search space but they are not sufficient to determine a single correct route to the goal (for further detail see Howes, 1994).

Control knowledge determines which menu selections lead to the goal and which lead to dead-ends. It is acquired through exploration of the menu structure. However, exploration often makes control knowledge hard to acquire because the goal is temporally remote from the initial choices that must be made. For example, in Microsoft Word for the Apple Macintosh, if a user is trying to change a document from single to double columns their initial choice might be between "Format" and "View". If the selection is "Format", then the user will not know until after three further selections whether or not this choice was correct. In AYN working memory is bounded to store only the previous action. Thus, when the goal is achieved AYN only learns positive control knowledge for the selection immediately preceding the goal. On the next trial, when AYN reaches the selection known to be right (i.e. the one before the goal), it learns positive control knowledge for the immediately preceding selection that led to it. In this way positive knowledge is passed back up the structure in a *final-first* way until positive knowledge has been learnt for all the selections leading to the goal. AYN acquires negative control knowledge in a similar way for selections that lead to dead-ends.

The acquisition of recognition and control knowledge leads to two emergent behaviours: (1) over a number of trials the number of actions required to achieve the goal is reduced; (2) the model's reliance on recognition knowledge models the fact that users remain dependent on the display.

Whilst computer implementations of AYN successfully search and learn about menu structures, AYN itself remains largely untested. It is therefore clear that a more detailed empirical investigation is needed. The experiment reported in this paper was designed to test the following assumptions of the AYN model: reliance on recognition knowledge; the order of learning of correct actions at different levels within the menu tree (positive control knowledge); the learning of negative control knowledge.

In addition to testing AYN's assumptions, the experiment was also designed to examine the effect of extra information that might aid search (in this case, cues to level within the menu structure). Many researchers have studied the coarse-grained properties of various design heuristics (e.g. Mehlenbacher, Duffy and Palmer, 1989; Pierce, Parkinson and Sisson, 1992; Snowberry, Parkinson and Sisson, 1983) and also support tools (e.g. Howes and Payne, 1990; Van Hoe, Poupeye, Vandierendonck and De Soete, 1990; Webb and Kramer, 1990) for menu-based systems but these studies are not guided by a deep understanding of what the underlying cognitive mechanisms are. Instead, studies are designed to look for a measurable effect on a property such as overall task performance time. Unfortunately, this too frequently leads to non-significant results.

Level cues have been investigated previously, along with other search aids such as a trace of all previously selected options, a representation of the menu structure and a display of the entire previous menu (Van Hoe *et al.*, 1990). None of these aids was found to affect the time taken to achieve the goal. However, this could be due to the fact that unlike many real-life menus, the experimental menus were too easy: the semantic relationship of the labels to the goal frequently determined the correct selection In situations where labels do not offer such clear guidance, search aids might have a greater effect on performance.

1.1. Methodological issues

Before we describe the experiment it is first necessary to discuss the problem of conducting experiments with menus with semantically unhelpful labels. The obvious problem in using semantically unhelpful labels rather than meaningful labels is that it changes the user's task. Thus, findings obtained with menu trees with semantically unhelpful labels might not apply to meaningful menus in actual devices. However, we argue that many menu labels in "real-world" devices are initially unhelpful to users despite the care taken in design. For example, a novice user of Microsoft Word for the Apple Macintosh might consider both the "Edit" and "Format" menus to be equally close in semantic terms to the goal of changing the text style. The task of choosing good menu labels may not be that much easier than the task of choosing good command-line words (cf. Furnas, Landauer, Gomez and Dumais, 1987).

One advantage of using menu structures with labels that give no semantic guidance to the user is that all subjects have the same prior semantic knowledge relevant to the task, namely none that can guide their choices. This avoids the problem of being unable to determine exactly what is influencing each decision in menus with meaningful labels where each subject will make selections on the basis of their prior semantic knowledge.

In the experiment presented here subjects were given menu structures in which the choices at each selection were pairs of words which were semantically unrelated to the goal but which were close semantic associates of each other (for example, "Pistol" and "Revolver" were the two choices at one node). The use of semantic pairs of words should ensure that the nodes are recognisable on subsequent visits, for example, the node with the options "Pistol" and "Revolver" might be recognised as a "gun" node.

2. METHOD

2.1. Subjects

32 undergraduate students from the Psychology Department at Cardiff University participated in this study for course credits.

2.2. Materials and design

Each subject was given four menu trees, each randomly generated from a set of 31 noun pairs. Each tree consisted of five levels with binary choices between a top and a bottom option at each node, as illustrated in Figure 1. A backup option was also provided at each node. The two options at a node were semantic noun pairs placed in alphabetical order (for example, "Carbon" and "Charcoal"). These noun pairs were carefully selected so that there was no overlap in meaning between any two pairs (both within and between trees).

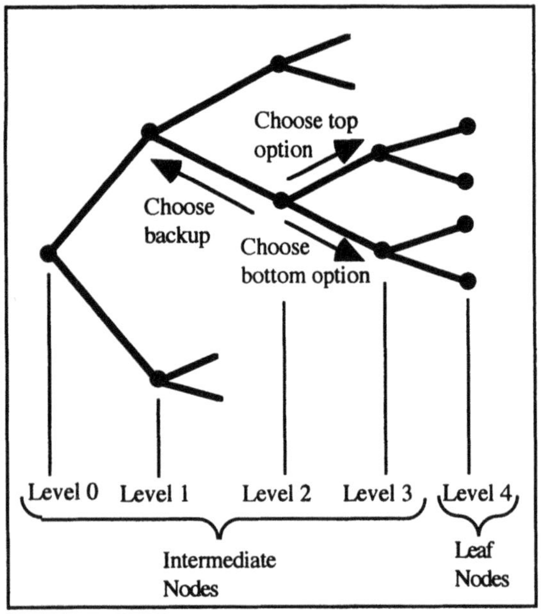

Figure 1. Partial illustration of the design of the trees used in the experiment.

One within-subjects factor was manipulated in this experiment. In addition the effect of practice on a number of variables was measured. The within-subjects factor concerned the presence or absence of a level cue. In two of the trees subjects were given a level cue which indicated the level of the current node within the tree (shown by a number between one - for the top level - and four - for the lowest level). In the other two trees there was no cue to level. For half the subjects the level cue was present in the first and the third trees, for the other half the level cue was present in the second and the fourth trees.

Two other factors were manipulated in order to balance the design. The first of these was the order of presentation of the trees. Each subject was presented with the four different trees in one of four different presentation orders. These orders were based on a Balanced Latin Square to ensure that each tree was presented equally often before and after each of the others. The second factor that was manipulated was the order of presentation of the goals. All subjects had to search for the same four goals (one per tree) which were defined by their position in the menu (e.g. one goal was reached by first selecting the top option, then the top option, then the bottom option, then the bottom option and then the top option). At each level in the tree two of the goals required the top choice to be made and two required the bottom choice to be made. As for the trees, there were four presentation orders for the goals based on a Balanced Latin Square. Thus there were sixteen conditions in total formed by combining the four possible presentation orders for the goals and the trees.

2.3. Procedure

The experiment was presented on an Apple Macintosh computer using a program written in MacProlog32. Each subject was first shown the experimental instructions which contained information on the structure of the trees. Each subject was then given a practice task similar to the tasks used in the main part of the experiment. This practice task required the subject to search for a goal in a tree which had four levels (rather than the five levels used in the main part of the experiment). Level cues were present on the practice trial for all subjects. This should ensure that if any subject was unsure about the meaning of the level cues then s/he would ask about them during the practice trial and not during the experimental trials. After completing the practice task each subject was given the opportunity to review the instructions or to retry the practice task prior to starting the experimental trials.

The main part of the experiment consisted of ten trials. On each trial the subject was asked to search for the first goal in the first tree followed by the second goal in the second tree, and so on, as determined by the condition. The tasks were interleaved to prevent rehearsal from trial to trial. The choices made by the subject and the time taken to make each of those choices were automatically recorded by the program.

As outlined above, at each node in the tree, subjects were presented with a top and a bottom option together with a backup option. When one of the two options was selected the next choice point appeared. Selecting backup allowed subjects to backup to the previous node. It should be noted that the backup option was not present either in the top-level root node (where backup is not possible) or in the goal node (where backup would allow the subject to review the choices leading to the goal).

The duration of the experiment was between 45 minutes and one hour.

3. RESULTS

3.1. Total number of actions per task

The total number of actions taken by each subject on each task on each trial was calculated. These data were subjected to an Anova to check for main effects of trial and level cue and for interactions between these variables. There was a significant main effect of trial, $F(9, 270)=87.429$, $p<0.01$: the number of actions made decreased significantly over trials 1 to 4, after which there were no significant changes. There was also a significant main effect of level cue, $F(1, 30)=11.055$, $p<0.01$: when a level cue was present subjects took significantly fewer actions (18.5 actions per task, on average) than when a level cue was absent (23.9 actions per task, on average). There was a significant interaction between trial and level cue, $F(9, 270)=4.205$, $p<0.01$. The facilitatory effect of the level cue was only significant on trial 1, thereafter there was no difference between the number of actions made when the level cue was present and absent.

3.2. Percentage of correct actions taken on the success path

For each node on the success path leading to the goal the percentage of correct actions made by subjects on their first visit to that node on each trial was calculated. The first visit to each node on each trial was used because the action taken on this visit should reflect the effects of long term memory rather than the effects of local, short-term search strategies. These data were subjected to an Anova to check for main effects of trial, level and level cue and for interactions between these variables.

There was a significant main effect of trial, $F(2, 60)=168.04$, $p<0.01$: the percentage of correct actions made increased with trials. In addition, there was a significant main effect of level, $F(3, 90)=4.15$, $p<0.01$: a higher percentage of correct actions were made at level 0 (the top level in the tree) than at levels 1 or 3 (level 0: 84.8% correct, level 1: 77.7% correct, level 2: 80.0% correct, level 3: 78.8% correct). There was no significant effect of level cue on success path actions.

There was a significant interaction between level and level cue, $F(3, 90)=5.170$, $p<0.01$. At level 3, a significantly higher percentage of correct actions were made when there was no level cue than when a level cue was present. At all other levels the presence or absence of a level cue made no significant difference to the percentage of correct actions, as shown in Figure 2.

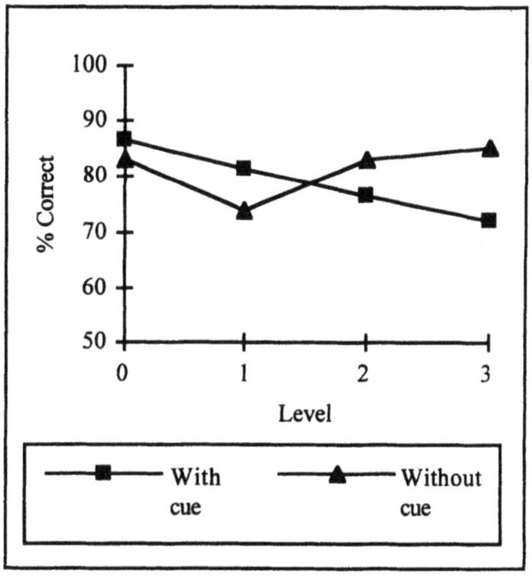

Figure 2. Graph showing mean percent correct at each level with and without a level cue present.

There was also a significant three-way interaction between trial group, level and level cue, $F(6, 180)=4.531$, $p<0.01$. The interaction between level and level cue was significant only on trials 2-4. On trials 5-10 there was no significant interaction between these two variables.

3.3. Exhaustive search sequences

The mean lengths of sequences of exhaustive and non-exhaustive search were calculated for each subject on each task on each trial. Exhaustive search was defined as consisting of only the following types of action: select either option at a node where neither option has been tried; select the untried option at a node where only one has been tried; select backup at a node where both options have been tried; select backup at a leaf node or a dead-end (where tried and untried actions were defined only in terms of the current search sequence - as soon as an exhaustive search sequence was broken, all actions were redefined as untried). In addition, in order to qualify as exhaustive search the following actions had to be included in the sequence: a back up from two tried actions, a visit to a leaf node.

These data were subjected to an Anova to test for main effects of trial, level cue and "exhaustiveness" and for interactions between these variables. There was a main effect of trial, F(9, 270)=54.245, $p<0.01$: the length of both exhaustive and non-exhaustive search sequences decreased significantly over the first four trials but did not decrease further over trials 4 to 10. There was a main effect of level cue, F(1, 30)=7.445, $p=0.01$. Both exhaustive and non-exhaustive search sequences were shorter with a level cue (6.26 actions, on average) than without a level cue (7.53 actions, on average). There was also a main effect of exhaustiveness, F(1, 30)=40.356, $p<0.01$. Exhaustive search sequences were significantly shorter (4.31 actions, on average) than non-exhaustive search sequences (9.48 actions, on average).

On trial 1 alone, non-exhaustive search sequences were longer when there was not a level cue present than when a level cue was present. There was no effect of level cue on the length of exhaustive search sequences on trial 1 or any other trials: F(9, 270)=3.874, $p<0.01$, for the interaction between trial, level cue and exhaustiveness.

3.4. Backups

The percentage of actions that were backups at each node off the success path was calculated. These nodes were then grouped according to the number of previous forward moves made from them: no previous forward moves, between one and five previous forward moves, between six and ten previous forward moves or more than eleven previous forward moves. A forward move is one where the subject moves down the menu rather than backing up. The means are shown in Figure 3. Statistical analyses could not be carried out on these data due to the high number of missing data points.

On all trials it appears that more backups were made from nodes where there had been no previous forward visits than from nodes where there had been one or more previous forward visits.

On trial 3 only, more backups were made from nodes where there had been more than eleven forward visits than from nodes where there had been between one and ten previous forward visits. In addition, on trials 4 and 5, more backups were made from nodes where there had been more than eleven forward visits than from nodes where there had only been between six and ten forward visits but not from nodes where there had been between one and five backups.

Over trials, the proportion of actions that were backups increased more rapidly for nodes where there had been no previous forward visits than for nodes where there had been one or more previous forward visits.

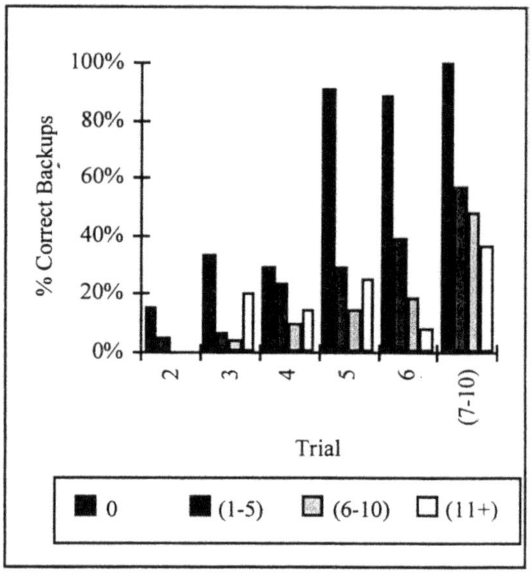

Figure 3. Graph showing the mean percentage of backup actions at each node according to the number of previous forward moves from that node.

4. CONCLUSIONS AND DISCUSSION

The main findings of the experiment were:

• When a level cue was present subjects took fewer actions to complete tasks on trial 1. However, when a level cue was present subjects learnt the last action in a sequence more slowly than when there was no level cue.

• On trial 1, non-exhaustive search sequences were longer when the level cue was absent than when it was present. There was no effect of level cue on the length of exhaustive search sequences.

• On all trials subjects were better at backing up from nodes where they had not previously made a forward move than from nodes where they had.

• Over trials, subjects got better at backing up from nodes where they had not previously made a forward move.

• On trials 3, 4 and 5 subjects were better at backing up from nodes where they had made eleven or more previous forward moves than from nodes where they had made between six and ten previous forward moves.

As stated in the introduction, AYN uses recognition knowledge to help determine which option to choose at each selection point. A number of the results summarised above support this assumption of the model. In particular, subjects were better at backing up from nodes that they had not made a forward move from before than they were at backing up from nodes where they had made one or more previous forward moves. This indicates that visited and unvisited nodes are distinguished in subjects behaviour.

In addition, with practice subjects backed up from an increasing percentage of nodes from which they had not previously made a forward move. This improvement of recognition of nodes that have not been previously selected may occur for a similar reason to the reason for behaviour observed in IDXL (Rieman *et al.* 1996). The IDXL model selects the menu item that best matches the current task. In some cases this "best match" might be a previously ignored item at a higher node in the menu. Thus the IDXL model will choose to backup when an item at a higher node in the menu is a better match to the task than any of the choices at the currect node. In the case of the interactive search task, subjects might be making a similar relative judgement between the familiarity of the current node and the expected familiarity of a correct node and using this judgement as the basis for the decision whether to go forward from the node or whether to backup. Over trials the expected familiarity of the correct nodes will increase, consequently the difference in familiarity between correct and unvisited nodes will also increase and the relative judgement will become easier leading to an improvement in backing up from unvisited nodes. At present AYN does not account for relative familiarity judgements.

As well as using recognition knowledge AYN acquires control knowledge that determines both which actions lead to failure and which to success. The results do give some support to the hypothesis that subjects acquire negative knowledge. In particular, on trials 3, 4 and 5 subjects were more likely to backup from nodes where they had previously made more than eleven forward moves than from nodes where they had only made between six and ten forward moves. Whilst this is supportive, it also indicates that the learning appears not to be one-shot and instead requires a number of experiences. This is consistent with more gradual learning mechanisms (e.g. an instance theory of memory, Logan, 1988) than are embodied in AYN. However, it should be noted that on all trials subjects are much more likely to backup from nodes where there have been no forward moves whatsoever. This indicates that, if there is any learning of negative knowledge, then it contributes much less to performance than subjects' ability to recognise untried nodes does.

Whilst subjects clearly acquire knowledge of the correct route with practice, the data does not support the hypothesis that this route is acquired in a final-first order. Instead, all subjects seemed to learn the first action in the sequence before the others. AYN does not account for this result, and if anything would predict that the last action should be acquired first. Initial analyses not described above indicate that the result was not due to subjects visiting the first node more frequently than other nodes. However, the result may be due to a rehearsal strategy during initial search giving rise to a primacy effect. In addition, we note that learning the first choice first could be a rational strategy: (1) if a subject learns the correct selection to make at the first node in the menu tree then the space within which the goal must lie is halved; (2) the first node in the structure is a special case in that one of the two possible selections at this point *must* be on the route leading to the goal. This is true of no other node in the menu structure.

Finally, the presence or absence of a level cue had two main effects on performance.

(1) When a level cue was present subjects took fewer actions on the first trial to complete each task. This seems to be due to the fact that when there was a level cue, subjects' sequences of non-exhaustive search were shorter: the level cue seemed to reduce the lengths of the periods of time for which subjects searched unsystematically.

(2) Unexpectedly, when there was no level cue, subjects learned the last action of the route better than when there was a level cue. One possible explanation for this finding is that subjects might have been using the level cue to guide their exhaustive search rather than looking at the actual labels of the selections made. As a consequence, when there is no level cue subjects learn the labels of the selections leading to the goal. However, when a level cue is present the change in search strategy means that learning is disrupted.

Thus, overall the effect of providing level cues is not completely beneficial. Whilst the level cue helps initial exploration of the menu structure it appears to stop subjects from paying attention to the actual labels of the operators that they select.

In summary, through the initial, preliminary experiment reported here, we have moved towards developing an empirical understanding of how subjects remember routes through menus with labels that do not initially relate to the goal. Through practice subjects seem to acquire recognition knowledge and control knowledge that associates particular selections with the goal. In particular, we have tested some of the assumptions of the AYN model and found some supporting evidence and some challenges to its underlying mechanisms. We have also looked at the more applied issue of providing a level cue search aid and found that the effects are not all beneficial. We believe that these results are relevant to real-world interactive menu systems where the semantics of the menu labels do not determine a unique best selection.

Obviously, in order to develop a more detailed and complete account of interactive search, further work is required. In particular, we plan to follow two lines of future research: (1) Current work that we are undertaking investigates how subjects remember routes through menus which have some semantic structure. For example, it appears that "plausibility" probably interacts with the familiarity of menu items to determine subjects' choices. (2) In addition, we plan to investigate in more detail particular results obtained in this experiment, such as the order in which the correct choices are learnt, the effect of a level cue and the factors that lead subjects to make correct backups.

ACKNOWLEDGEMENTS

This work was supported by the ESRC Cognitive Engineering Initiative.

REFERENCES

Franzke, M. (1994) *Exploration, acquisition and retention of skill with display-based systems.* Ph.D. Thesis, Department of Psychology, University of Colorado, Boulder.

Franzke, M. (1995) Turning research into practice: characteristics of display-based interaction. *Proceedings of the Conference on Human Factors in Computing Systems* (New York, NY.), Association for Computing Machinery, 421-428.

Furnas, G.W., Landauer, T.K., Gomez, L.W., and Dumais, S.T. (1987) The vocabulary problem in human-system communication. *Communications of the ACM, 30*, 11. 964-971.

Howes, A. (1994) A model of the Acquisition of Menu Knowledge by Exploration. In B. Adelson, S. Dumais and J. Olson (Eds.) *Proceedings of Human Factors in Computing Systems CHI'94* (Boston, MA.), ACM Press, 445-451.

Howes, A. and Payne, S.J. (1990) Supporting exploratory learning. In D. Diaper, D. Gilmore, G. Cockton & B. Shackel (Eds.), *Human-Computer Interaction - INTERACT'90.* Amsterdam: Elsevier Science Publishers, B.V. 881-885.

Kitajima, M. and Polson, P.G. (1995) A comprehension-based model of correct performance and errors in skilled, display-based, human-computer interaction. *International Journal of Human-Computer Studies, 43*, 65-69.

Logan, G.D. (1988) Toward an instance theory of automatization. *Psychological Review, 95*(4), 492-527.

Mehlenbacher, B., Duffy, T. M., and Palmer, J. (1989) Finding information on a menu: linking menu organisation to user's goals. *Human-Computer Interaction, 4*(3), 231-251.

Pierce, B.J., Parkinson, S.R., and Sisson, N. (1992) Effects of semantic similarity, omission probability and number of alternatives in computer menu search. *International Journal of Man-Machine Studies, 37*, 653-677.

Rieman, J. (1994) *Learning strategies and exploratory behaviour of interactive computer users.* Ph.D. Thesis, Department of Computer Science, University of Colorado, Boulder.

Rieman, J., Young, R.M. and Howes, A. (1996) A dual-space model of iteratively deepening exploratory learning. *International Journal of Human-Computer Studies, 44*, 743-775.

Snowberry, K., Parkinson, S.K., and Sisson, N. (1983) Computer display menus. *Ergonomics, 26*(7), 699-712.

Van Hoe, R., Poupeye, K., Vandierendonck, A. and De Soete, G. (1990) Some Effect of Menu Characteristics and User Personality on Performance with Menu-Driven Interfaces. *Behaviour and Information technology, 9* (1), 17-29.

Webb, J.M., and Kramer, A.F. (1990) Maps or analogies? A comparison of instructional aids for menu navigation. *Human Factors, 32*(3), 251-266.

Adaptation of a task analysis methodology to the design of a decision support system

Sandrine Balbo and Craig Lindley

CSIRO, Mathematical and Information Sciences
Locked Bag 17, North-Ryde NSW 2113
AUSTRALIA
Emails: [Sandrine.Balbo|Craig.Lindley]@cmis.csiro.au

ABSTRACT The aim of this article is to describe the use of an analytical method for task analysis (MAD) within an industrial development project, APLCRATES. The method has previously been used within research contexts, and has been limited to task analysis and user interface design. Within the APLCRATES project, we not only used the method for defining the user tasks and interfaces, but we also used it for knowledge acquisition and as a powerful communication tool between the different development teams addressing decision support system development, database definition, on-line help, user manual definition, and for communication with the clients. We explain briefly the aim of the APLCRATES project and what MAD is, and then describe in detail how MAD was used and modified to meet the needs of the project.

KEYWORDS

Usability engineering, task analysis, decision support systems, user requirement specification, user participation.

1. INTRODUCTION

CSIRO Mathematical and Information Sciences (CMIS), in collaboration with Integrated Systems Solutions Corporation (ISSC), has developed the Expert Module of a spares assessment expert system (called APLCRATES) for the Manager Codification, Cataloguing and Allowances (MCCA) department of the Royal Australian Navy (RAN).

Activities of the CMIS team included knowledge acquisition, the design and development of the core decision support functions, and the design of the graphical user interfaces (GUI) of the decision support system.

ISSC provided the overall management of the project, as well as the database development (eg. definition, creation, population, report generation functions, import and export functions), choosing and organising the hardware, developing the on-line help information, development of an integrated electronic book, and the development of a tutorial to learn how to use the system and its key concepts.

A key feature of this project was the application by the CMIS team of the MAD methodology (Méthode Analytique de Description, or in English: Analytical Description Method). MAD had previously been used as a user task modelling methodology in research

Human–Computer Interaction: INTERACT'97 S. Howard, J. Hammond & G. Lindgaard (editors)
Published by Chapman & Hall

environments. In this development project, MAD was used for modelling user tasks as a framework for interface and general Expert Module application development, as a high-level knowledge model within which detailed knowledge models were developed, and as a communication mechanism between the diverse groups collaborating on project development.

The objective of this paper is not to present a comparative study of task analysis methods, but to show how the MAD task analysis method has been transferred from a pure research environment and successfully applied in an industrial development project and for a type of application, namely a decision support system, for which it was not originally designed.

The paper presents the RAN problem, the MAD methodology, and describes the use of MAD for system requirement specification leading to the development of the APLCRATES User Requirement Specifications (URS).

2. MCCA REQUIREMENTS

The primary task of the Navy MCCA department is the creation of Assembly Part Lists (APLs). Each APL decomposes an assembly (from a simple chair to more sophisticated pieces of equipment embedded on a ship) into the parts it is composed of. Each part within an APL is associated with assessment codes that provide the necessary information for computing the quantity of the part that needs to be stored on board a ship prior to its mission. Decision-making involves a tradeoff between having sufficient spares carried on board ships for them to remain operational, and reducing the total inventory costs involved in the acquisition and storage of parts.

To manage the creation of APLs, five different categories of staff are involved: the system administrator, MCCA managers, MCCA technical staff, MCCA non-technical staff, and trainees. Briefly, the system manager is in charge of managing the database, the managers make sure that the decisions taken are correct, the technical staff associate assessment codes with parts and build the APLs, while non-technical staff conduct data entry and research in the database.

The old MCCA system used for the process of APL creation provides only a character-based user interface. It has many limitations, constituting requirements that a new system must address. The main limitations of the old system are:

- it provides very inefficient access to the database: the end-user has to know the identifier of an APL to access it,
- no download facilities exist from or to the database, ie. to copy an APL from another database, the end-user works from a listing and must retype the complete APL in order to enter it into the new database,
- to exit the system, the end-user has to go back to the main menu,
- learning how to use the system takes a long time, mainly due to its complex methods for navigation, and the use of function keys and shortcut keys,
- very little explanation or help is provided,
- repetitive information must be entered to satisfy the system.

In addition to redressing these deficiencies, the new system must:

- reduce the training time; since it takes approximately 6 months of on-the-job training before a new staff member becomes effective. This problem is compounded by short posting cycles in military forces, resulting in a high staff turnover rate for particular jobs and roles.
- encourage higher quality and more standardised assessment. Trained operators are proficient, but do not constitute "experts" in assessment; the new system is required to take a standardised approach to assessment representing the best of current expertise, and make this accessible to all operators.

These functional requirements for reduced training time and standardised decision making result in the following technical software requirements:

- to automate decisions whenever possible,
- to provide computer supported copy/paste functions between the APLCRATES database and other databases when possible,
- a strong help facility, relevant to the context and available from any stage of the assessment process,

- strong guidance in the decision-making process: asking questions rather than directing the choices,
- improved search facilities.

These requirements meant that is was necessary for the APLCRATES development team to have a good understanding of APL creation and definition tasks, and the requirements pertaining to those tasks from the viewpoint of managers and all other RAN staff involved in the process of APL creation and maintenance. The application experts themselves did not have a single consistent understanding of how assessment should be carried out. A major aspect of the analysis phase of the APLCRATES project was the development of a common and agreed model of assessment expertise. This was done by CMIS human-computer interaction specialists and knowledge engineers working together with expert RAN and Defence Department staff to define a common model.

The APLCRATES project schedule allowed two calendar months to develop the first prototype and complete the User Requirement Specification (URS) for the system. It is during this analysis phase that MAD was most heavily used, providing a systematic foundation for subsequent system design and implementation, including detailed knowledge engineering activities.

3. DIFFERENT VIEWS AND SINGLE TOOL

During the analysis phase at CMIS, we performed two different tasks:

- a complete task analysis to define what the GUI should provide, and how it should be organised. The resulting models provided the basis for screen design, specification of detailed functions associated with each screen, and a high level modularisation of task knowledge as a framework within which detailed knowledge acquisition could occur.
- detailed knowledge acquisition to design the decision support system, resulting in rules, decision trees, and decision tables that could be embedded throughout the extensive interfaces of the system to provide specific decision support for subtasks.

The common basis for these two tasks was a series of interviews with the users; the interviews were performed by the knowledge engineers (who were primarily in charge of knowledge acquisition) and the human-computer interaction specialists (who were primarily in charge of the design of the GUI). Even if the overlap between the two tasks is extensive, very different formalisms were used to transcribe on to paper the understanding obtained from these interviews. The knowledge engineers used flow charts, decision tables, and rules, while the human-computer interaction specialists used MAD.

We will discuss very briefly the technique initially used by the knowledge engineers; in practice the whole team very quickly shifted to the use of MAD. To find a complete discussion from the knowledge acquisition point of view, refer to [Lee 97].

For knowledge acquisition, flow charts were used to get the overall organisation of APL creation and definition tasks. The limits of effectiveness of flow charts were quickly reached, particularly the fact that they can only represent strict sequential activities, while the work performed at the MCCA department is not simply sequential, but also involves a lot of interleaving tasks. Building an APL can take several months, and is certainly not done in one uninterrupted sequence.

For the task analysis, MAD was used. MAD provides a methodology to perform task analysis, following a hierarchical decomposition of the tasks; MAD is described in detail in the next paragraph. The human-computer interaction specialists used MAD because the method is well documented, has been proved to work in many different research contexts, and because it is easy to use (as demonstrated in the next sections below). Unfortunately, there was no time to perform a comparative study among different task analysis methodologies before the start of the project.

A few weeks after the beginning of the project, as the knowledge engineers reached the limitations of flow charts, we decided to adopt the MAD formalism as a common formalism within the CMIS team. As explained in section 5.2, the MAD formalism not only was used as the basis for both knowledge acquisition and GUI design, but also by the ISSC team, and as a communication tool with the clients. A brief description of the MAD methodology is provided in the next section. Use of the MAD formalism in the context of the project is explained in section 5.

4. THE MAD METHODOLOGY

MAD provides a methodology to gather information on the operational tasks performed by users, based upon extensive interviews and leading to the formalisation of task descriptions. The interviews with the end-users are semi-directed by the MAD specialists. In the first part of the interview, the end-user will not be interrupted and will be asked to describe how s/he is working. This allows the analysts to gather the user's representation of their work. The second part of the interview is more closely directed: the "Why and How" technique is used to split the end user's goals from the methods they follow to achieve these goals [Sebillotte 95]. This second part of the interview process enables the completion of high level task representation using the MAD formalism. "The MAD formalism offers an extension of the key-concept of hierarchy (in the sense of structural parsing) of abstraction levels, using logic-and-time graphs of objects, from the most general (root) to the most specific (task leaves, ie. elementary tasks). In addition, an object-based structure has been chosen to offer both declarative and procedural statements; each object is an independent entity, which corresponds to the requirement of representing conceptual entities significant to the user" [Scapin 90]. The concept of a task is represented using this object-based structure. Each object is characterised by the following [Sebillotte 95]:

- the name: a short and clear description of the task under consideration.
- the goal: states the objective achieved by executing the task.
- the initial state: a list of objects representing the part of the world in which the task will be carried out, and that might be modified by the execution of the task.
- the preconditions: a set of predicates expressing constraints upon the objects of the initial state.
- the body of the task: expresses how the task is executed. It can be either an elementary or a composite task:
  - * an elementary task is generally represented by a verb that expresses the action that it refers to,
  - * a composite task can be decomposed further into a set of sub-level tasks (that will be either elementary or more composite tasks) linked together by one of the following constructs:
    - SEQ (sequential): subtasks are executed one after the other,
    - PAR (parallel): no constraint on the execution order of the subtasks,
    - SIM (simultaneous): true parallelism in the execution of the subtasks,
    - ALT (alternative): only one of the subtasks needs to be executed.
- the postconditions: are a set of predicates expressing constraints upon the objects of the final state.
- the final state: a list of objects representing the part of the world in which the task was carried out, and that was modified or created by the execution of the task.
- The task attribute: a characteristic of the task and may be any of the following:
  - * @ (iterative): the task may be repeated, several times,
  - * OPT (optional): the task does not necessarily have to be carried out,
  - * PRIOR (priority): the task can interrupt other tasks,
  - * INT (interruptible): the task is or is not interruptible.

5. ADAPTATION AND USE OF MAD

A few modifications to the MAD formalism were necessary while characterising each task during the interviews with the MCCA managers and staff (ie. when building the tree and associating with each task a name, goal, pre- and post-conditions, etc.). We explain below what these modifications are and why they were necessary, before presenting what we used

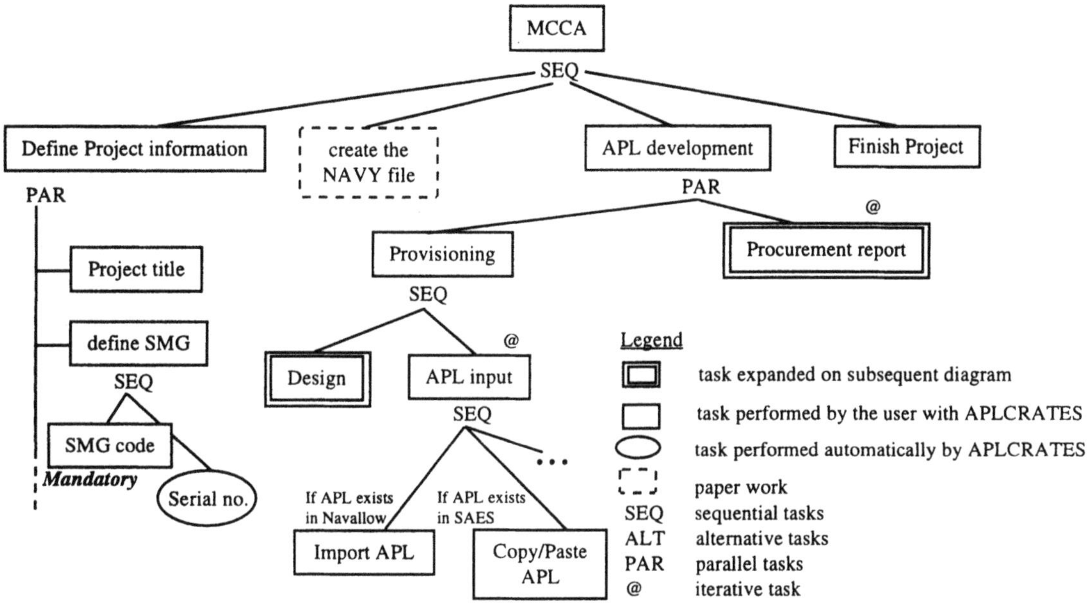

Figure 1: Example of use of the MAD formalism

the MAD formalism for, within the analysis phase of the project. Figure 1 and table 1 illustrate our discussion. Figure 1 presents an example of how the MAD formalism was used within the project. Table 1 summarises MAD usage and the different actors involved in APLCRATES development. Four actors are distinguished: the CMIS development team, the ISSC development team, the MCCA managers and the MCCA staff (technical, non-technical, system administrator and trainee).

5.1. MAD modifications

The three main modifications were:

- the dropping of pre- and post-conditions,
- the addition of a comment slot to group information specific to knowledge acquisition,
- the addition of the source of information.

The first and most significant modification concerns dropping the initial state, precondition, postcondition and final state. Dropping the precondition follows the addition, in the tree, of some conditions (for example in figure 1: 'if APL exists in Navallow' prior to the 'Import APL' task) to be realised prior to the execution of a task. It seemed more natural and easy to formulate conditions that way, instead of using objects to be defined in the initial state, and then used in a postcondition. We did not need the definition of these objects for our initial goal to acquire a general understanding of the tasks performed by the MCCA staff. The same applies to the postconditions and final state.

For the knowledge engineers, the initial MAD formalisation was very useful for organising the information as it was gathered. Since the MAD formalism did not provide a structure, or a slot, in which to place this information, we created one by adding a comment slot to each task (similar to the name or goal slots). The comment slot allows us to associate information with the appropriate task in a structured way. Information used in the comment slots included algorithms to be applied, databases accessed, default values, field length and so on.

The third important modification done to the MAD formalism was the addition of another slot for specification of the source of information. The source of information clarifies whether the task is performed on paper or on the computer, when it is carried out with the help of the computer, and whether the end-user or the computer is performing the task. This source of information was represented in the tree by a plain rectangle box for tasks performed by the end-user within the system (for example, in figure 1, entering the 'Project title' in the system), a round box for automatic tasks (for example, in figure 1, the computation by the system of the serial number, depending on the SMG code entered by the end-user), and a dashed-line rectangle box for manual tasks (for example, in figure 1, the opening of a folder including various papers concerning the project being created).

A few minor modifications were done as well, concerning the use of constructors and attributes.

For tree constructors, we only used SEQ, PAR and ALT. We did not need the SIM constructor since there is no true parallelism in the procedures followed for constructing and managing APLs (to control database consistency, the same data cannot be modified by two people at the same time).

The only task attribute we used was the iterative (symbolised by @). We did not use the optional attribute, but added the mandatory one to some elementary tasks, essentially when it concerned entry of mandatory database fields (for example, in figure 1, the field 'SMG code'). The non mandatory elementary tasks are not optional either, they have to be performed at one stage for the high-level task to be completed, but do not need to be performed to start the other tasks. In the example, to start the 'APL development' task, only the mandatory fields of the 'Define Project information' must be completed. The notation could be extended to deal with cases like this by incorporating separate symbols to distinguish mandatory but non-sequential subtasks.

5.2. Use of MAD

We used MAD in many different ways; for task analysis, knowledge acquisition, the design of both the decision support system and the help/tutorial related items, and as a communication tool among all actors involved in the APLCARTES project.

First of all, MAD provided us with a reliable way of organising our understanding of the MCCA task. While performing the first rounds of interviews, we also used MAD as a tool for presenting the results of the analysis to the MCCA managers and staff to demonstrate we understood their tasks: both the hierarchical decomposition of tasks and the components of acquired knowledge. In this way MAD not only helped us to make sure that our understanding of the task was correct, but also helped to fix the vocabulary used subsequently within the APLCRATES system.

Having constructed the MAD trees for the MCCA tasks, the design of the GUI for the decision support system was made easy. There is no doubt within the development team that the understanding we had of the organisation was reflected through the user interfaces with the help of the MAD descriptions. The MAD trees indicated groups of items that had to be kept together within the GUI, as well as ones that could be split through different sets of screens; for example, from figure 1, all information under the'Define Project information' task block is presented in one screen. These trees also provided the basis for the organisation of menus and buttons, and, more importantly, they provided the general map for navigation through the different screens. The generic

Actors involved	MAD usages
CMIS, MCCA managers & staff	structuring our understanding of the task
CMIS, ISSC, MCCA managers	fixing vocabulary
CMIS, MCCA managers	structuring knowledge acquisition
CMIS, MCCA managers & staff	design of the GUI
ISSC, MCCA managers	defining topics to be covered within the help system and the tutorial
CMIS, ISSC, MCCA managers	writing the URS

Table 1: Summary of the MAD usages

nature of this process for going from the task description to the GUI design would be worth investigating.

In fact, working on the MAD formalism of the MCCA task provided a very good understanding of the work environment. In addition, this representation provided a constant communication loop between the development teams and the MCCA managers and staff for validation purpose.

The use of MAD was so well accepted by all actors of the APLCRATES project that the models expressed by the MAD formalism were used to compose the heart of the User Requirement Specifications for the project.

6. CONCLUSION

The APLCRATES system answers the users' needs and follows the work organisation that was successfully understood by the development team through the MAD description. This successful understanding critically relied upon strong collaboration with the end-users. The first prototype has been intensively tested by the human-computer interaction specialists (for usability) and by the MCCA managers (for the correctness and completeness of business rules), and the major changes that came out of these tests were limited to the organisation of the decision making process. Today, the implementation of the first version of the product is in use by MCCA staff and the only complaint received so far concerns some slow access to the database in the RAN busy networking environment. We are planning shortly to conduct some more usability tests on the RAN site.

The fact that MAD was successfully used for high-level knowledge formalisation opens the possibility of applying task models to new domains such as knowledge-based systems. Some of the modifications that were brought to MAD in the context of this project must be seen and understood in this light.

It may be noted that using the MAD description helped us gain an understanding of MCCA tasks and their decomposition, but the context of the work itself was only understood later on in the process. In fact, the MAD methodology assumes that the work context is already well understood. To understand the context of the work, some other tools like the contextual design methodology developed by [Holtzblatt 96] could be used, and this would complement MAD to provide a comprehensive analysis methodology.

ACKNOWLEDGEMENT

Thanks to the various reviewers of this paper for their helpful comments and to all members of the APLCRATES project (development team, MCCA managers and end-users) for a dynamic working environment.

REFERENCES

[Holtzblatt 96] Karen Holtzblatt & Hugh Beyer, "Contextual design: principles and practice", in Field methods for Software and systems design, John Wiley & Sons, 1996.

[Scapin 90] Dominique Scapin & Christine Pierret-Golbreich, "Toward a method for task description: MAD", in Work with display units 89, L. Berlinquet & D. Berthelette (Eds), Published in Elsevier Science Publishers B.V. (North-Holland) 1990.

[Sebillotte 95] Suzanne Sebillotte, "Methodology guide to task analysis with the goal of extracting relevant characteristics for interfaces", Technical report for Esprit project P6593, INRIA, Rocquencourt (France), April 1995.

[Lee 97] Maria Lee, Sandrine Balbo, Craig Lindley & Mikhail Prokopenko, "Combining Rule-Based Knowledge Acquisition with Task-Oriented User Analysis for Dispersed, Embedded Expert Systems", PACES'97 conference proceedings.

58

ConcurTaskTrees: A Diagrammatic Notation for Specifying Task Models

F. Paterno', C.Mancini, S.Meniconi

CNUCE-C.N.R.
Via S.Maria 36
56126 Pisa
Italy
{fabio, cristian, silvia}@cnuce.cnr.it

ABSTRACT In this paper we discuss a notation to describe task models, which can specify a wide range of temporal relationships among tasks. It is a compact and graphical notation, immediate both to use and understand. Its logical structure and the related automatic tool make it suitable for designing even large sized applications.

KEYWORDS Task models, formal notations, model-based user interface design, tools for design.

1. INTRODUCTION

The use of task models in user interface design and development has recently been recognised as an important contribution to obtain more user-oriented interactive applications. A new generation of model-based (Foley et al., 1991) tools such as Trident (Bodart et al., 1992), TLIM (Paterno' et al., 1996), Mastermind (Szekely et al., 1995), Adept (Johnson et al., 1994), ICO (Palanque et al., 1995), and AIDE (Sears, 1995), all use, in different ways, task-models to support user interface design.

It is becoming increasingly common for the various specialists involved in this process (developers, designers, psychologists, application domain experts) to discuss the tasks that the system should support. To this end it is very important to have notations to develop task specifications so that:

- they are easy to understand and use, thus improving communication among people discussing the design;
- they are able to structure large sized specifications which are developed in industrial applications;
- their semantics is precisely defined to avoid ambiguities in the communication.

When choosing the notation we found that some important features have to be supported:

- hierarchical logical structures which were introduced by GOMS (Card et al., 1983) have proved to be a useful way to represent task models because they allow designers to reason about the design at different abstraction levels and they support the refinement design process better;
- modern user interfaces are characterized by highly interactive behaviours in multimedia environments, it is thus important to be able to express a wide variety of temporal relationships;
- a task model for an industrial application may be complex, it is thus important to be able to express relevant relationships precisely and to have information on more detailed aspects in an interactive way.

When we started our work on task models we considered UAN (Hartson and Gray, 1995) as a good starting point. UAN supports hierarchical specifications and has operators to express temporal relationships among tasks. However we found it had two main limitations: it has a textual specification which makes it difficult to read and interpret (for example to find cross-references among tasks): and it gives limited support for deriving a software architecture, as its main purpose is to specify only the

Human–Computer Interaction: INTERACT'97 S. Howard, J. Hammond & G. Lindgaard (editors)
Published by Chapman & Hall

externally perceivable behaviour of the user interface by associating tables indicating above all user actions and system responses.

Thus our first contribution was (Paterno' and Mezzanotte, 1995) to provide a graphical representation of the hierarchical structure and to use LOTOS (ISO, 1988) operators to express the temporal relationships among tasks at the same abstraction level since they have a more formally defined semantics. Furthermore LOTOS is an international standard notation already used in various industrial and research centers to specify applications which have, as an important feature, temporal ordering among possible actions.

We found this approach useful but, especially when we started to apply it to industrial applications, we found some points which required further improvements:

- ambiguity in the priority among operators used at the same level of the task tree;
- the need to specify which component of the Interactive System considered will perform the task;
- additional information about the tasks that could be used in the user interface development;
- the necessity to define better the relationships between a father task and its subtasks;
- new operators for a compact specification of common situations.

In this paper we describe how we overcame these problems. We first introduce the main concepts which drive how we build task models. Next we show pieces of ConcurTaskTrees specifications for expressing examples of interactive applications. Then we show how the tool supporting these specifications works, and finally some concluding remarks are given.

2. TASK MODEL

A task defines how the user can reach a goal in a specific application domain. The goal is a desired modification of the state of a system or a query to it.

A task in our approach is described by the following attributes:
Name : used to identify the task
Type: there are four possible types: abstract, user, application, interaction
Subtask of: name of father task
Objects: vector of objects, each element defines: name of object, type of object (internal, perceivable), list of input object actions, list of output object actions
Iterative: a Boolean indicating whether the task is iterative
First action: The set of possible initial actions is indicated
Last action: The set of possible final actions is indicated.

At each level the task specification is built in two steps: first the objects are identified and then the actions which allow the communication among them are defined.

2.1 Objects

Objects are entities which are manipulated to perform tasks by the associated actions.
The objects are user-perceivable and internal objects, which are both manipulated to perform the tasks by using the associated actions.
Perceivable objects are items which users can interact with using their senses, for example menus, icons, windows, voice, sounds, and so on. They can belong to application or interaction tasks.
Internal objects are entities which belong to the application and which need to be mapped onto perceivable objects to be presented to the user. Examples of internal objects are: the state of a request for a data base, the data base itself.

Each object can belong to one or more tasks. In the task decomposition process when we consider a new task level in the task-tree, objects, which were defined in the previous task level, may receive two types of manipulation:

- decomposition (one object at a task-level is decomposed into two or more objects at the next task level);
- refinement (the set of actions associated with one object is increased when we consider the next task level).

2.2 Actions

Actions are associated with objects. Actions can be cognitive, logical, or physical. For tasks which are not iterative we have to indicate what the last action is. We need to specify the possible initial actions because they are used when we are evaluating expressions which indicate a possible choice ([] operator, which means that at the beginning, both tasks are available and once one of them is started the other is no longer available) between tasks or disabling among tasks ([> operator, which means that once the first action of a task occurs then the other task is deactivated).

2.3 Specification of the component performing the task

We can identify four types of tasks depending on the allocation of their performance:

- *user tasks* are performed entirely by the user, they require cognitive or physical activities without interacting with the system. Possible examples are when the user reads a list of flights satisfying some constraints and selects one of them for his/her journey or, in a video conference application, the possibility to analyze the content of some information received and evaluate whether or not it is sufficiently clear; if not, the user asks for clarification. Thus user tasks are associated with some processing performed by the user on information received from the environment.
- *application tasks* are completely executed by the system. They receive information from the system and they can supply information to the user. They are activated by the application. For example, compiling a program and sending messages when some errors are detected, or receiving network messages and displaying them.
- *interaction tasks* are performed by user interactions with the system. These interactions are activated by the user. Examples are editing a diagram or formulating a query to a data base.
- *abstract tasks* are tasks which require complex actions, and their performance does not completely fall into one of the three previous cases.

In the task specification the types of tasks are presented differently either by different icons or different geometric shapes as in Figure 1:

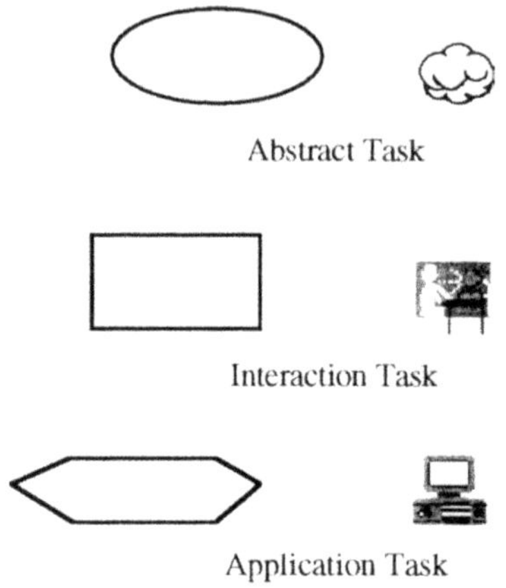

Figure 1: The two possible presentations of Task types.

We make a further distinction. Tasks can be:

- *processing tasks,* given an input they perform some processing and then provide a related result;
- *control task,* their main purpose is to generate an event control: they inform other tasks that a given condition has been reached.

3. CONCURTASKTREES

The task model is built in three phases:

- a hierarchical logical decomposition of the tasks represented by a tree-like structure;
- an identification of the temporal relationships among tasks at the same level;
- an identification of the objects associated with each task and of the actions which allow them to communicate with each other. The identification process is performed layer- by- layer.

The temporal relationships among tasks are expressed by using an extension that we have defined of the operators of the LOTOS notation which is a concurrent notation. ConcurTaskTrees thus allows designers to describe concurrent tasks, unlike the GOMS proposal which uses hierarchical task decomposition but is only able to analyse sequential tasks (though some more recent proposals have tried to overcome this limitation).

Unlike UAN, two tasks can synchronise (|[]| operator) in the approach proposed. This happens when they have to exchange information: the output information of one task is the input information for the other task. Tree-like structures with concurrent operators to indicate temporal relationships among tasks at the same level allow designers to specify more complex behaviours than those associated with finite state automaton.

The operators that we use to describe the temporal relationships are:
T1 ||| T2, *interleaving*: the actions of the two tasks can be performed in any order;
T1 |[]| T2, *synchronization*: the two tasks have to synchronize on some actions in order to exchange information;
T1 >> T2, *enabling*: when the first task is terminated then the second task is activated;
T1 []>> T2, *enabling with information passing*, in this case we want to highlight that when T1 task terminates it provides some value for task T2 besides activating it;
T1 [> T2, deactivation, when one action from the second task occurs the first task is deactivated;
T1*, *iteration*, the task is iterative;
T1(n) *finite iteration*, how many times the task will be performed is specified;
[T1], *optional task*, its performance is not mandatory;
T, *recursion*, the possibility to include in the task specification the task itself.

3.1 Solution to the ambiguity problem

If we simply build task models using these operators the first problem is the possible ambiguity of some expressions. For example in Figure 2, we can interpret the specification in two ways: either (T1 [] T2) ||| T3 or T1 [] (T2 ||| T3).

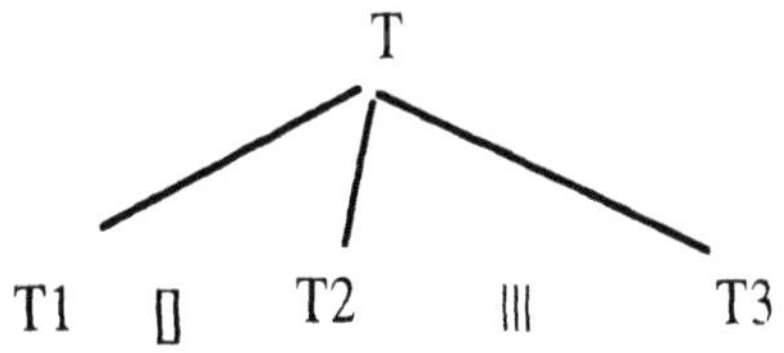

Figure 2: An example of possible ambiguity.

To solve the ambiguity there are two possibilities: we can use the priority order among operators defined in the standard LOTOS (choice > parallel composition > disabling > enabling), or we can introduce a task which disambiguates the expression, as in Figure 3. Parallel composition can be either completely interleaving among tasks, or interleaving with synchronization on some actions.

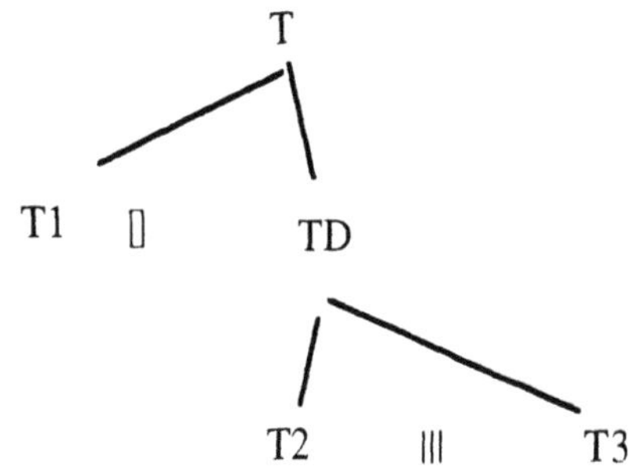

Figure 3: A solution to solve the ambiguity.

3.2 Relationships between father task and its subtasks

If we use these operators in a hierarchical context we can achieve a lot of flexibility in terms of being able to specify different behaviours. For example in the next diagram there are two possibilities: the same tasks are involved, T1 and T2 are performed in interleaving in both cases but if the iteration is at the father level then we mean *order independence performance*: tasks can be executed in any order but before executing them again both tasks have to be terminated. In the second case, with iteration introduced at the subtask level, we have a *continuous interleaving among tasks* which means that once one task is terminated it can be executed again without waiting for the termination of the other task.
An example of order independence is when specifying a request for a flights database then users have to specify both departure and arrival towns but the order is not meaningful. Once the request is transmitted then a new one can be composed in the same way. In the same application we have continuous interleaving between the task specifying a request and the one clearing it: they can both be executed many times without any limitation on their order.

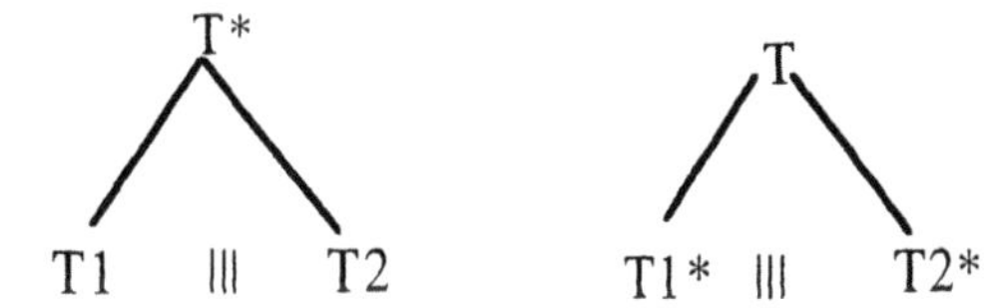

Order independence performance Continuous interleaving

Another example which gives a clear indication of the possibilities of this type of representation is shown in Figure 4. In both cases we have a selection and then a choice of two possibilities which provide different ways to modify the element selected. However, there is one important difference. In one case the choice of task to perform is made by the application which detects how many elements have been selected, and depending on the result, allows the user either to choose between editing and deleting (if there is only one selected element) or just deleting (if there is more than one selection element). In the other case the choice of task (changing an object size or an object colour) is made directly by the user. We express these different behaviours by specifying the type of task which is the father of the tasks that can be chosen: if the father task is an application task, this means that the choice is made by the application (though the performance of the selected task can still be made by the user or his/her interactions) otherwise, if the father task is an interaction task, the choice is made by a user interaction.

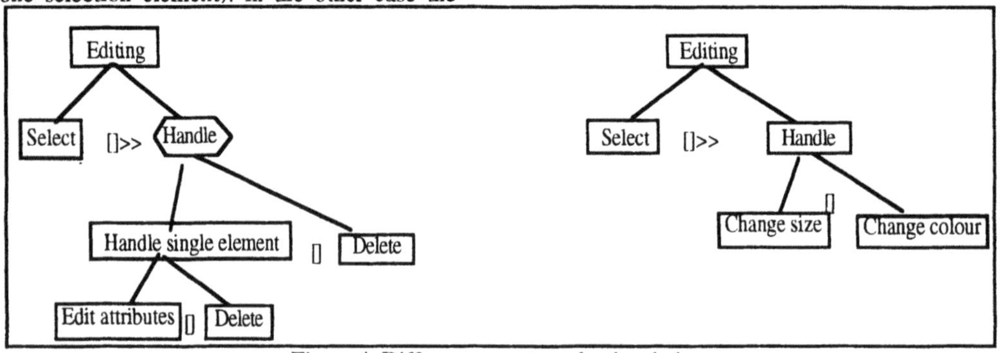

Figure 4: Different ways to make the choice.

3.3 Recursion

We assume that we want to describe the example described in Figure 5. Whenever an edit button is selected then a new order is activated. At some time the set of orders can be deactivated by the close button and the activated orders remain active.

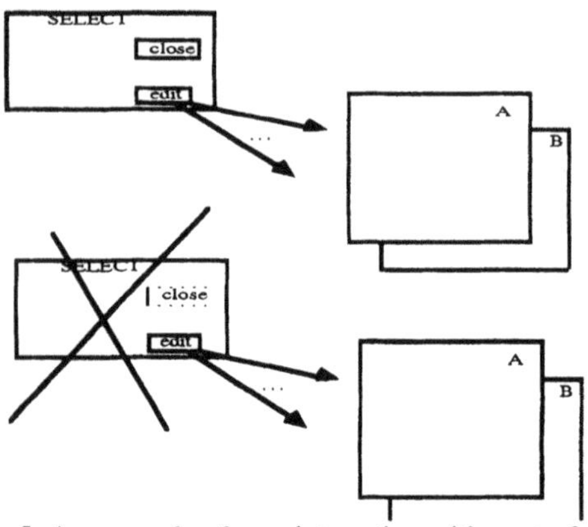

Figure 5: An example of user interaction with a set of orders.

In ConcurTaskTrees this behaviour can be described in the following way where we have a recursive definition of the Application task.

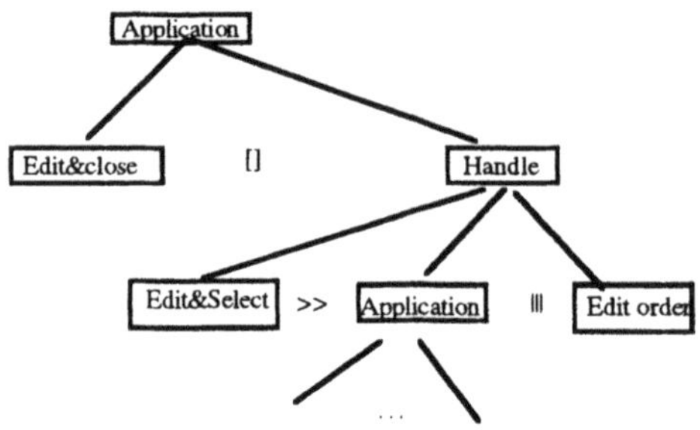

Figure 6: An example of recursive task specification.

The difference between iterative and recursive specifications in ConcurTaskTrees is that in the first case, when we use the * operator, the performance of the related task is repeated in the same modalities until another task deactivates it. The second case, when in the definition of a task we find the task itself again, allows us to describe the cases when, depending on some condition (in our example the selection which activates a new order form), we want to perform a task again without knowing in advance how many times we will perform it and, for each new performance, we will give the possibility to perform a new, additional task (in our example editing a new form). In the task tree it is sufficient to specify the possible recursion at only one level to indicate that it may happen more than once.

In our example the user can stop the recursion by selecting the Edit&close task. Once this task has been selected then we stop the possible recursion (because it is in the other option of the choice) but we do not stop the Edit order tasks created, which can be terminated separately. We had to introduce the handle task to manage correctly the priorities among operators.

3.4 Examples of specifications in ConcurTaskTrees

One common situation is the need for the user to cancel a modification which has just been specified. This can be described by the tasks represented in Figure 7. We have a generic application during which the user can edit various possible modifications. Once a modification has been specified the user can either perform it or cancel it. In both cases, as editing is an iterative task, then the user will be able to specify a new modification until the close task is performed.

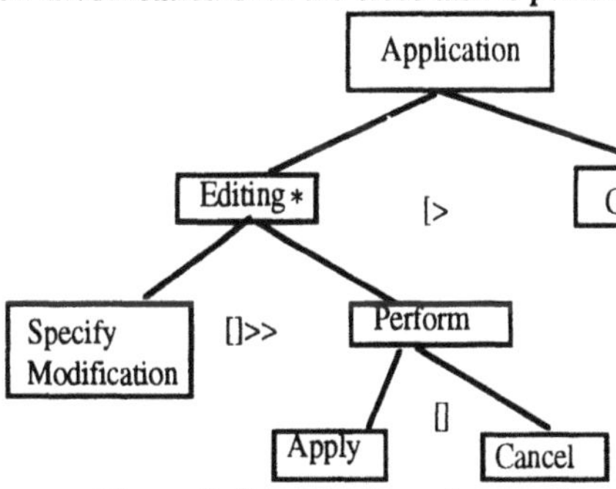

Figure 7: Specification of cancelling.

Another interesting situation is *exception handling*: a request is transmitted to the functional core which sends a message to the user indicating that something exceptional has happened. If we consider the structure of the previous example we have to add an Exception task, as a subtask of the Perform task. This Exception task has a first phase, performed by the application, which generates a warning message and a second part, an interactive subtask, which allows the user to manage the exception in some way.

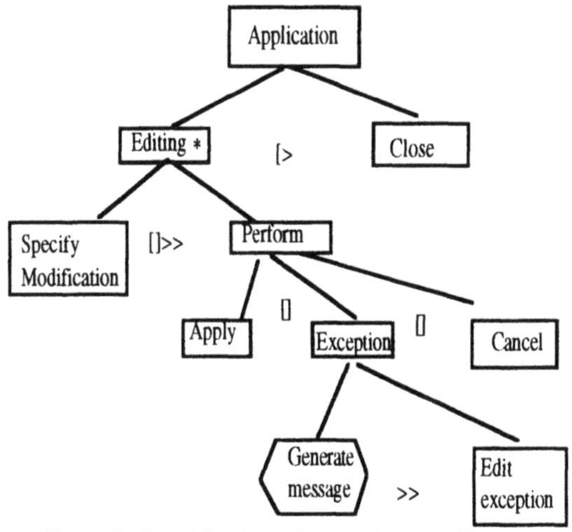

Figure 8: Specification of exception handling.

4. THE TOOL SUPPORTING TASK MODELS DESIGN

We have developed an automatic environment (Paterno' et al., 1997) which supports designers in developing task and architectural models (Coutaz, 1993), and in identifying their relationships. It is implemented in Java. At the beginning there are three choices:

- editing a task model;
- transforming a task model into an architectural model in semi-automatically;
- analysing the relationships between a task and an architectural model.

Whatever choice the designer has made it is always possible to select again the other possibilities. The task editor is a direct manipulation task which allows the designer to build the task tree and to use the LOTOS operators to indicate their temporal relationships. When a task is selected then by selecting one of the icons associated with the possible four task types, new subtasks are automatically created and located in the editing area.

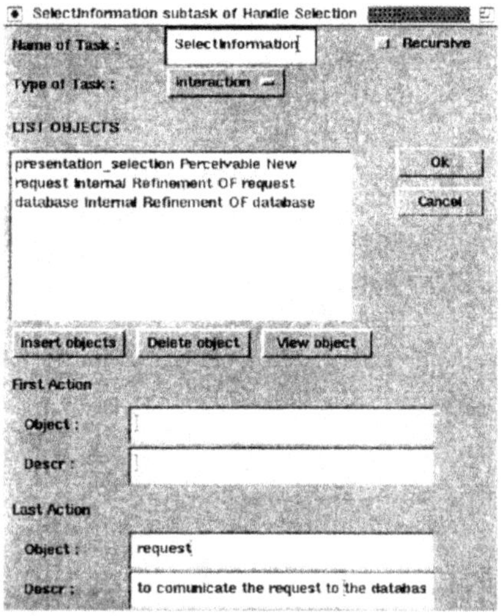

Figure 9: An example of the specification of objects.

It is also possible to select a task and to provide additional information about it (Figure 9): the objects that it manipulates and what the possible first and last actions are. For each of these objects, it is possible to activate dialogue boxes which allow the designer to specify the actions which they require (see Figure 10).

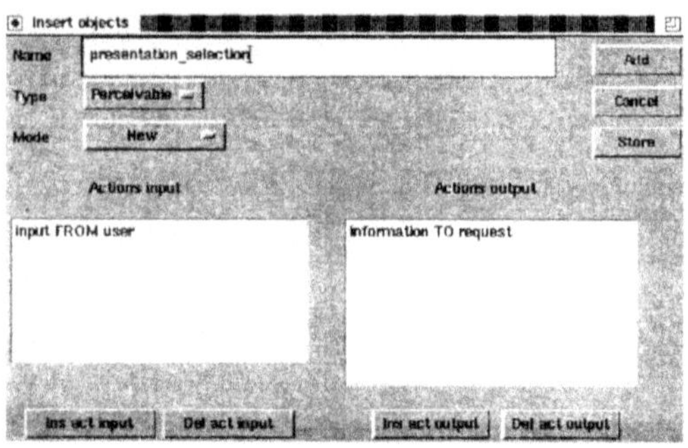

Figure 10: An example of specification of actions.

Actions are classified depending on whether they are input or output actions. Actions are used to allow objects defined at the same level of the task tree to communicate. At any task level it is possible to check the semantic consistency which means, for example, given an input action of an object, at the same task level, there must be an object with the corresponding output action. A task specification can be saved in order to be reused and edited again later on.

Figure 11 shows a simple example of a task model for interacting with an electronic museum. At the beginning we identify a session (Handle selection task) which can be disabled by a specific task (CloseSession task). The session first allows the user to select a type of work of art (sculptures, paintings, and so on). Once a type has been selected, the application presents information related to the selected type of work. Further selection criteria can be recursively specified and cancelled until the user has made a specific request to indicate all the information satisfying the desired requirements. Finally, the user can select one of them and the application will present it.

5. CONCLUSIONS

We have presented a notation supported by a related tool to build task models. It uses graphical constructs and operators derived from a formal specification. The resulting notation gives a compact specification of a wide variety of dynamic task behaviours. The tool which supports ConcurTaskTrees is available to the public at http://verdolo.cnuce.cnr.it/task.tgz. We have applied our approach to various applications (videoconference, museum systems, business applications) which confirmed its ability to address many possible situations.

To facilitate its use in industrial applications we are designing a set of templates which allow models for common patterns in user interactions to be reused.

We have developed a method (Paterno' et al., 1997) able to derive architectural models and implementations which are consistent with the temporal and semantical requirements indicated in task models obtained following the approach described in this paper.

ACKNOWLEDGEMENTS

We wish to thank Ilse Breedvelt and Camjel Severins for useful discussions on the topics of the paper, and Progetto Finalizzato Beni Culturali for partially supporting the work presented.

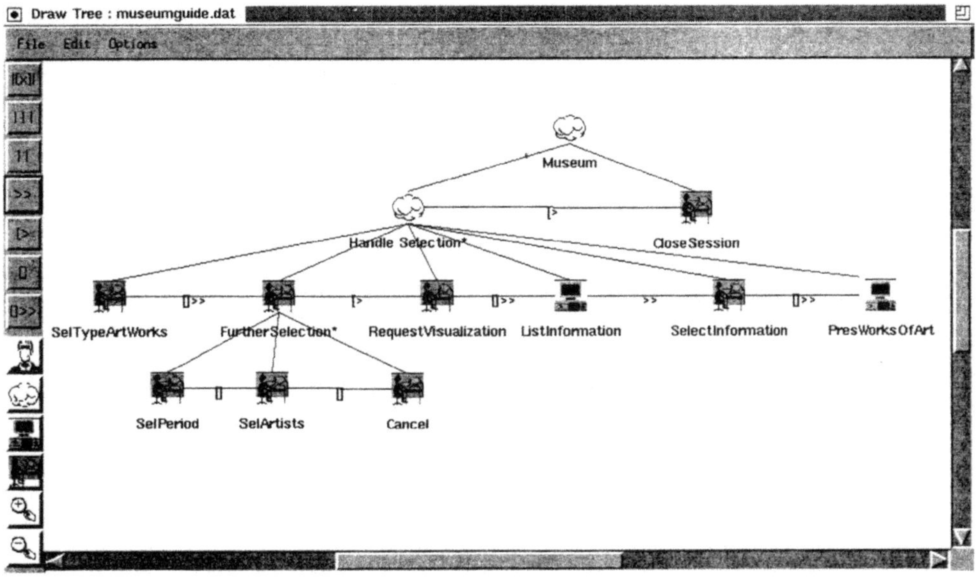

Figure 11: An example of task model obtained with the support of the automatic tool.

6. REFERENCES

F.Bodart, A.Hennerbert, J.Leheureux, J.Vanderdonckt, (1995) "A Model-based approach to Presentation: A Continuum from Task Analysis to Prototype", in Interactive Systems: Design, Specification, and Verification, pp.77-94, Springer Verlag.

S.Card, T.Moran, A.Newell, (1983) "The Psychology of Human-Computer Interaction", Lawrence Erlbaum Ass. Publ., Hillsdale, N.J., 1983

J.Coutaz, (1993) "Software Architecture. Modelling for User Interfaces", in the Enciclopedya of Software Engineering, pp.38-50, 1993, Wiley.

J.Foley, W.Kim, S.Kovacevic, K.Murray, (1991) "UIDE - An Intelligent User Interface design Environment" In Sullivan and Tylor (eds.), Intelligent User Interfaces, ACM Press, 1991, pp.339-384.

R.Hartson, P.Gray, (1992) "Temporal Aspects of Tasks in the User Action Notation" Human Computer Interaction, Vol.7, pp.1-45, 1992.

ISO (1988) Information Processing Systems - Open Systems Interconnection - LOTOS - A Formal Description Technique Based on temporal Ordering of Observational Behaviour. ISO/IS 8807, ISO Central Secretariat.

P.Palanque, R.Bastide, V.Senges, (1995) "Task model - system model: towards an unifying formalism", Proceedings HCI95 International, Japan, September 1995.

F.Paterno', M.Mezzanotte, (1995) "Formal verification of undesired behaviours in the CERD case study", Proceedings EHCI'95, pp.213-226, Chapman & Hall, 1995.

F.Paterno', C.Mancini, S.Meniconi, (1997) "Understanding Task and Software Architecture Relationships", CNUCE Internal Report, February '97

P.Szekely, P.Sukaviriya, P.Castells, J.Muthukumarasamy, E.Salcher, (1995) "Declarative Interface Models for User Interface Construction Tools: the Mastermind Project", Proceedings EHCI'95, pp.120-150.

Sears, A.. (1995) "AIDE: A step toward metric-based user interface development tools". Proceedings of UIST'95. ACM Press, pp.101-110.

S.Wilson, P.Johnson, C.Kelly, J.Cunningham, P.Markopoulos, (1993) "Beyond Hacking: a Model-based Approach to User Interface Design, Proceedings HCI'93.

Positioning Usability in an Organisation: Can usability really help organisations achieve their business objectives?

Janice Anne Rohn, Manager
Usability Labs and Services
Sun Microsystems
2550 Garcia Avenue
Mountain View, CA 94043-1100
USA
rohn@sandybeaches.eng.sun.com

Sarah Bloomer, Director
The Hiser Group
P.O. Box 312
Prahran, Victoria 3181
AUSTRALIA
sarahb@mel.hiser.com.au

TOPIC

This panel addresses the question of whether usability can help organisations to achieve their business goals through the integration of usability methods during the design and development of software.

Usability is beginning to be sold to managers at a strategic level with the promise that it can impact and support business goals and initiatives: cost-justification figures seem to indicate that usability really can impact the bottom line, whether in improving customer service and satisfaction or creating a greater market share for a particular product. But can usability actually fulfil this promise? And what is preventing usability from being as readily accepted as other strategic initiatives such as change management, business process re-engineering or training initiatives?

Our aim is to take a critical look at usability and the benefits that it claims by bringing together professionals who include usability in their strategies. We will compare usability to other techniques which aim to make organisations more competitive, reduce costs or enhance productivity, in order to gain an understanding of how usability complements or conflicts with these techniques and thereby deliver business benefits.

PANEL MEMBERS

Panel members consist of practitioners from areas related to usability, specifically, business process re-engineering, change management, training, and software development, as well as a discussant familiar with introducing usability into organisations. In the spirit of Interact's international focus, we have attempted to bring together panelists from a range of organisations, professions as well as continents to draw together a broad spectrum of experiences.

The positions focus on the value of usability and experiences of whether the benefits (such as reduced training costs, enhanced productivity, greater user acceptance, and reduced development time) can actually be realised. They will provide hard evidence of the success of their own techniques, such as statistics, testimonials and case studies. The following questions will be considered:

1. How is usability positioned in your organisation, and does it vary from organisation to organisation?
2. Can usability deliver significant business benefits that support an organisation in becoming more competitive?
3. How does usability complement or conflict with other methods and techniques designed to enhance the competitive advantage?
4. How can the usability practitioner achieve buy-in for usability across an organisation, from end-users to developers to upper management?

Usability Manager - Janice Rohn, Sun Microsystems, USA

The usability manager is often tasked with the job of convincing upper management, project leaders and often end-users (in the case of in-house software development) of the benefits and reasoning for allocating resources to usability. This can be

Human–Computer Interaction: INTERACT'97 S. Howard, J. Hammond & G. Lindgaard (editors)
Published by Chapman & Hall ©IFIP 1997

particularly challenging in technology companies given the emphasis on technology-driven products and increasingly shortened development cycles. With an increasing emphasis on internet products, there is a tension between just getting a product out versus taking some initial time to define users, requirements, and usable design. Usability can only succeed by demonstrating the importance of performing these activities and by keeping pace with accelerated development schedules.

Janice Rohn is Manager of Usability Labs and Services at Sun Microsystems. Janice joined Sun in 1992, when she founded the usability group and designed and built usability labs for Suns sites in California and Colorado. Janice has been working on human-computer interaction and strategy issues across Sun, and has led several efforts to improve the integration and usage of HCI methods. Janice is President of the Usability Professionals Association. Prior to joining Sun, Janice worked at Apple on the usability and design of products such as System 7, QuickTime, the PowerBooks, and the Quadras. Prior to Apple, Janice was a research assistant at Stanford University in expert systems and medical informatics. Janice has a number of publications including a chapter in Cost Justifying Usability.

Business Process Re-Engineering - Mark Andrew, ALARA, Australia

Business process re-engineering is becoming increasingly popular in the current climate of downsizing and restructuring. Changes to business processes are often facilitated through technology since new processes require new systems. This puts usability practitioners in a good position to have an impact on new business processes.

Usability is commonly defined as an outcome during these assignments, rather than as a consulting effort. It is sometimes recognised by clients as a performance indicator for employees (i.e. are the people and the work "demonstrating usability"?) but rarely recognised as a progressive journey. Consequently, a consulting culture of "trojan horse usability" has developed (i.e. ensure usability by subterfuge first, then reveal the process). Along the way, both the client's, and consultant's "culture" changes as a result of such partnering efforts. Mark will be in a position to talk about such experiences.

Mark Andrew works with industrial clients in transport, mining and manufacturing. He aims to help them understand their operational risks, in order to improve business process efficiency. Assignments usually involve task analysis and work methods design, and result in redesigned equipment, procedures and communication. Before returning to ALARA to head up their Victorian office in 1995, Mark consulted in business process re-engineering and strategic management.

Change Management - Dianne Saker, Andersens Consulting, Australia & USA

Usability as a *discipline*, and if implemented well, can impact the business bottom line, not just for IT development methodologies, but for entire user communities and the organisation as a whole. Usability demands a paradigm shift in behaviour, work processes and people change. A usability practitioner must effectively understand broad change management principles and the weighting of usability in managing small or large scale change. To convince upper management to commit resources, money and time to usability requires an understanding of such change and the pressures of large scale implementation.

Dianne Saker is a Change Management Manager for Andersen Consulting and leads the Australian Usability team for her practice. Dianne has pioneered usability and HCI methods as a discipline to a number of key Australian organisations in the Financial Services and Government industries. Dianne is a global usability expert and has consulted to organisations around the world on building business need for usability and establishing usability disciplines into large technology, process and people change projects.

Client Management - Malcolm Keys, Optus Communications, Australia

Improving job performance while reducing training costs is the goal of performance support initiatives. Usability and user interface design complement this goal by providing practical methods for improving computer systems. However, for usability to deliver benefits, it must be integrated into the development life cycle and culture. When it is not integrated into the mainstream practices of the organisation, usability appears to provide only bad news at the wrong time, and is therefore often ignored.

At Optus, usability has been introduced through the training and performance improvement initiative and is therefore inherently cross-disciplinary. Our most successful activity has been to measure the usability of each of our systems as they are delivered and publicise the results within the organisation. This is leading to culture which places a high importance on usability of its products and makes use of the available usability infrastructure.

Malcolm Keys is a Usability Manager with the Optus Communications Systems Training where he leads the usability initiative. Since joining Optus, Malcolm has established a set of usability techniques tools designed to be used by systems development teams. Prior to joining Optus, Malcolm worked as a senior usability consultant at The Hiser Group and was an independent consultant in multimedia.

Discussant - Randolph Bias, BMC Software, USA

Randolph Bias is Manager of Usability Engineering for BMC Software, Inc. He has a Ph.D. in human experimental psychology from the University of Texas at Austin, and 15 years' experience in software usability engineering at Bell Labs and IBM. Randolph is a "Certified Human Factors Professional" and is co-editor of _Cost-Justifying Usability_ (R. G. Bias & D. J. Mayhew, Eds., Academic Press: Boston, 1994).

Format For Running The Panel

A panel format was selected for this topic in order to explore various viewpoints regarding the impact of usability at the corporate level, providing an opportunity to explore these viewpoints, and resulting in a stimulating debate about whether usability can have an impact on business objectives. The panel format facilitates the exchange of practical knowledge between panelists and audience members.

This is a comparative panel. Although it doesn't directly compare approaches and techniques within an area, it does look at the approaches between areas, and how each area potentially influences each other, positively or negatively. The common ground in this panel is the passing of knowledge between several groups of practitioners who may impact each other on a strategic project.

This panel will aim to be highly interactive. The audience will be asked to submit their questions on cards which are handed out when they arrive. The concept of organisational usability will be briefly presented (5 minutes) by one of the panel organisers. To open the debate, each panelist will give a short presentation (5 minutes) of their view of how usability supports or conflicts with their business orientation or area of expertise. The discussant will then summarise the four positions (5 minutes).

The second half hour will focus on a set of pre-defined questions prepared to focus the discussion on strategic questions. An overhead projector will be used to capture key issues raised by each panelist. Input from the audience will be encouraged. The last half hour will address questions from the audience as submitted by the cards. Throughout the session, we will capture things that work and things that don't work from the panelists and the audience, thereby building up a total picture of the debate as it unfolds.

Defining a Family of Feedback Signals for Multimedia Communication Devices

Cynthia A. Sikora and Linda A. Roberts

Lucent Technologies: Bell Labs Innovations
200 Laurel Avenue, 4E-508
Middletown, New Jersey 07748
USA
Tel: (908) 957-6135
Email: csikora@lucent.com and lin@lucent.com

ABSTRACT A family of auditory feedback signals was created for multimedia business devices. This family was derived from a wide variety of options, including real world, musical and communications sounds. In Experiment I, typical business users mapped 48 sounds to functions and rated the pleasantness and appropriateness of the sounds. Experiment II tested the best sounds for each function (based on the findings of Experiment I) within the context of a graphical user interface business communications simulation. Users rated the pleasantness and appropriateness of each sound and selected the best sound option for each function. Experiment III evaluated the resultant family of auditory signals for discriminability using similarity ratings. Results showed that, real world sounds mapped most reliably to the functions; users consistently preferred musical sounds to the real world sounds. Of the eleven feedback signals selected for specific functions, four were communications based and seven were musical. None of the real world auditory signals were acceptable. The resulting family of sounds was generally discriminable with the exception of one pair. The apparent dimensions used to make judgments about the sound pairings were duration, average pitch and harmonic complexity.

KEYWORDS Auditory Feedback, Auditory Icons, Earcons, Sound, User Interface Design

Human–Computer Interaction: INTERACT'97 S. Howard, J. Hammond & G. Lindgaard (editors)
Published by Chapman & Hall

1. INTRODUCTION

In today's market, the use of sound as feedback has become more possible with advances in technology and the widespread availability of computer equipment. However, auditory feedback is still lacking in many communications products supporting multimedia and graphical user interfaces. The emphasis in most products has been on visual feedback provided to the user, which is not always sufficient for communications tasks. However, as multimedia applications become viable, there has been an increasing interest in developing auditory signals that can ease the complexity of the user's interaction with the applications. The introduction of these new multimedia devices and services also provides an opportunity to include signature "look" and "listen" elements.

During the past decade, two classes of sounds have been proposed as auditory feedback signals (Brewster, Wright and Edwards, 1993). The first, auditory icons, use environmental sounds that have a strong semantic link with the object represented by the sound. An example of this may be the sound of a door closing when a file is closed. The use of these "real world" sounds has been advocated due to the discernible functional mappings inherent in these sounds (Blattner, Sumikawa and Greenberg, 1989; Gaver, 1986; Mynatt, 1994). The second class of sounds, earcons (Brewster et. al., 1993), refer to abstract synthesized sounds. Implicit in this latter category are the sounds that are more musical in origin, with well-defined pitches, rhythms, harmonies and timbres. Jones and Turner (1989) showed that, whereas subjects preferred earcons, they were better able to associate auditory icons to functions.

One issue regarding the implementation of real world sounds concerns users' reactions to listening to them repeatedly over time in an actual business application. One of our concerns is that users may perceive the real world sounds as annoying and trite. More abstract, musical sounds may be less intrusive, providing appropriate feedback without being distracting to the user or others.

Abstract sounds (i.e., earcons) that may provide a successful alternative to real world sounds include communications and musical sounds. We refer to communications sounds as relatively simple signals derived from traditional electronic tones used in telecommunications products. We refer to musical sounds as more complex abstract musical signals that are unconstrained by currently used telecommunications audible feedback tones.

Table 1: Auditory signals were sought for eleven functions which are labeled and described.

FUNCTION	DESCRIPTION
Confirmation	Sound associated with performing a task correctly.
Distinctive Ring	Ringing that can be associated with a particular type of call.
Drop from Conference	Auditory feedback to indicate that an individual has left a conference call in progress.
End Call	Auditory feedback that a call has been terminated.
Error	Auditory indication that an error condition or incorrect action has occurred.
Hold Reminder	Alerting signal that a call is placed, or remains, on hold.
Join Conference	Sound indicating that a new individual has joined a conference call.
Logo	Auditory signal associated with the start up of a product.
Personalized Ring	A selectable ring used to distinguish one user's phone from others.
Send Call	Auditory indicator provided for buffered dialing to confirm that the digit string has been sent.
Status Indicator	Auditory signal indicating wait time during system activity.

A professional sound designer/musician designed both communications and musical feedback signals for eleven different communications functions (shown in Table 1). The musician was asked to create one communication and one musical sound for each function, but he created many more alternatives than requested (due to his enthusiasm for the project). Real world signals for the functions were selected from sound libraries.

In Experiment 1, we investigated which feedback signals (i.e., real world, communications, and musical) mapped best to the eleven functions. In addition, we asked subjects to evaluate the sound's pleasantness and its appropriateness for use in a business setting. Based on the results of this experiment, we derived three candidate sounds for each function. In Experiment 2, we tested the pleasantness and appropriateness of the candidate set of sounds within the context of a simulated business communications application. Results of the second study enabled us to then select the single best feedback sound for each of the eleven functions. The primary goal of Experiment 3 was to ensure sufficient distinctiveness within the resultant family of 11 sounds. In addition, we sought to determine which dimensions of sound users evaluated when listening to the signals in order to guide future research in this area.

2. EXPERIMENT I: SOUND EXPLORATION

The experiment was designed to find any natural mapping of the sounds to the functions. The sounds were also evaluated for their overall pleasantness, and their appropriateness for a business environment. Thirty-eight computer literate office workers participated as paid subjects. The subjects were tested in four groups of approximately 10 per group.

The 48 sounds that were evaluated consisted of 22 musical sounds, 14 communications oriented sounds and 12 real world sounds. The 12 real world sounds were selected from an initial set of 30 real world sounds. The ideas for the 30 real world sounds were generated using brainstorming techniques with a small group of college students who volunteered to participate during their internship at our company (Lucent Technologies, formerly AT&T). The real world sound ideas were then investigated for availability from sound libraries. Due to difficulty in recognizing some of the sounds, the real world sounds were limited to those that provided an adequate auditory representation of the referent. Examples of real world sounds and the intended functions include footsteps (wait status indicator), paper crumpling (error), door opening (join conference), door closing (drop from conference), knocking on door (hold reminder), phone hanging up (end call) and applause (confirmation).

Each group of subjects was provided with a study packet. After filling out a brief demographic questionnaire, subjects were given verbal instructions about the task. Subjects were also encouraged to read the written version of the instructions provided in the study packet. The subjects were told that they would hear sounds and be asked to select the function that best matched the sound as a feedback signal and to rate the sound for pleasantness, appropriateness and confidence of the function chosen. The instructions emphasized that the sounds were intended for a state-of-the-art business application. The subjects were also requested to assume that all telephone activity was presented in a multimedia application on a personal computer.

The subjects were provided with a sheet with definitions of the 11 communications functions that require auditory feedback. Subjects were instructed to read through the list of functions and their definitions and to ask questions about anything that was unclear. The function description list was available to the subjects throughout the study. Definitions for the constructs being rated were also provided:

- Functional Mapping refers to the function that is best represented by a given sound.
- Pleasantness refers to the pleasing quality of the sound.
- Appropriateness refers to how well the sound is suited for a business application.
- Confidence refers to their degree of confidence that the sound provides a good match with a function.

The subjects were instructed that they would hear each sound twice and that they should listen very closely. Subjects were advised that any given sound could be modified to accommodate the needs of a specific function (e.g., repeated for ringing or lower volume for hold reminder). They were also invited to write in any comments they might have.

The subjects were given two practice trials, and any questions they had were addressed. Each group of subjects was then presented the 48 sounds, in a different random order. Each sound was played twice. After each sound was presented, the subjects indicated which of the 11 functions the sound best mapped to, and then rated the sound for its overall pleasantness, appropriateness in a business setting, and the confidence they had in selecting that function for that sound. For each of the three latter tasks, a 9-point scale was used where 9 denoted "very pleasant", "very appropriate" and "very confident". After an intermediate task, the groups were presented with the sounds again in a different randomized order and made the same mapping and rating judgments.

The data were analyzed to determine which sounds mapped most often to the functions. Overall, the real world sounds mapped most predictably to the functions. The communications sounds mapped to the functions with reasonable consistency. The musical sounds mapped least consistently to the functions.

The results for the pleasantness ratings are shown in Figure 1. There was a reliable main effect of time [F(1,36)=7.36, p=.01], demonstrating that listeners gave higher ratings upon the second hearing of them. There was also a reliable effect of sound class [F(2,72)=252.55, p<.01]. In this case, the musical and communications sounds received significantly higher pleasantness ratings relative to the real world sounds. There were no significant interactions.

Ratings of the appropriateness for a business environment are shown in Figure 2. As occurred for the pleasantness ratings, there were main effects of time [F(1,36)=5.26, p=.027] and of sound class [F(2,72)=168.62, p<.01] and no interactions. Communications and musical sounds were judged to be reliably more appropriate for a business setting than were the real world sounds.

Based on these results, we derived three auditory signals for each function for further evaluation in Experiment II. Eleven real world sounds, 7 communications sounds and 15 musical sounds were selected. The eleven real world sounds each mapped very well to their respective functions, but achieved very low ratings for pleasantness

Figure 1: Pleasantness ratings for the classes of audibles are shown. Ratings are based on a nine point scale where 9 is very pleasant and 1 is very unpleasant.

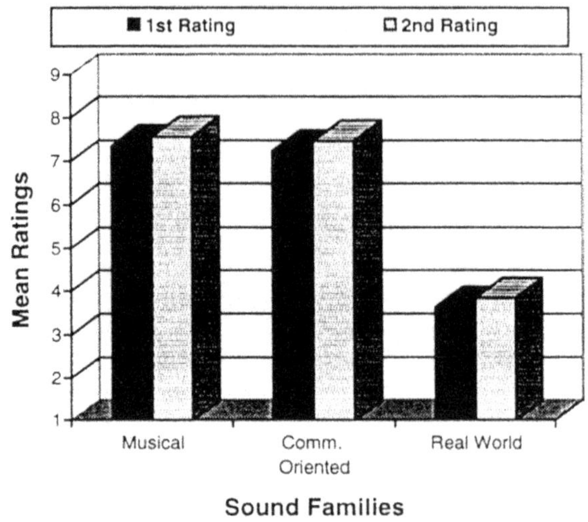

Figure 2: Appropriateness ratings for the classes of audibles are shown. Ratings are based on a nine point scale where 9 is very appropriate and 1 is very inappropriate for a business environment.

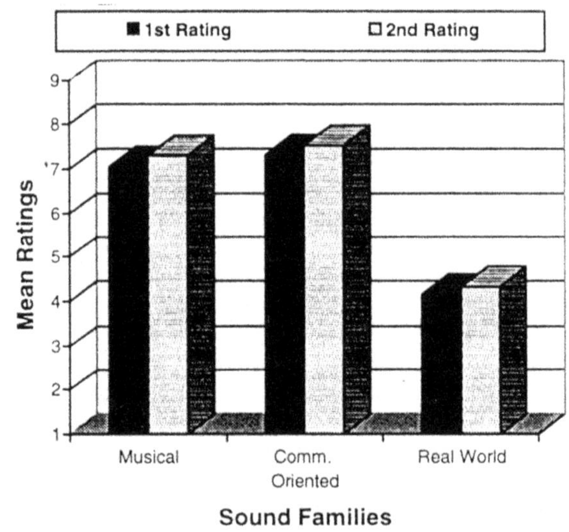

and appropriateness. The remaining two candidates for each function were those musical or communications sounds that had the best mapping. When no clear mappings to functions were evident (e.g., two or more sounds mapped relatively well to a given function), sounds were selected that had the highest pleasantness and appropriateness ratings.

3. EXPERIMENT II: EVALUATING SOUNDS IN A BUSINESS CONTEXT

The subset of sounds selected from Experiment I was based primarily on functional mapping. Experiment II was designed to test the sounds further within the context of a simulated business communications PC application. Twenty-two computer literate office workers who were not tested in the previous study participated as paid subjects. The subjects were tested in groups of two to four.

Each group of subjects was given a study packet which included written instructions, questionnaires and rating sheets. The business application simulation was used to present the sounds in a business scenario within a graphical telecommunications application. Subjects were told that they would be rating auditory feedback sounds for pleasantness and appropriateness within a business application. They were also instructed that, within a trial, they would select the one sound that they felt was best for that function. As in Experiment I, it was emphasized that the sounds should be envisioned for a multimedia telephone in a state-of-the-art office environment. Subjects were told that they would only hear each sound once within the scenario before being asked to make the ratings. The constructs being rated (i.e., pleasantness and appropriateness) were defined prior to the task.

Projected from an LCD projector attached to the PC, subjects were shown a simulation that provided a context and scenario for each of the functions. Subjects began with a practice scenario with three different sounds for a function not included in the study. After making individual ratings and then selecting the best sound for the function, any questions were answered before continuing. Before each scenario, the function being depicted was defined. The scenario was shown three times with three different sounds, presented in different orders for each group. After hearing each sound, the subjects rated its pleasantness and appropriateness on a 9 point scale. The subjects then heard all three sounds in the scenario again before selecting the sound that they would most prefer for that function.

Figure 3 shows the mean ratings for pleasantness and appropriateness of the sounds included in Experiment II. There was a significant difference among the sound families for both the pleasantness [$F(2,702)=46.23$, $p<.01$] and appropriateness [$F(2,702)=28.89$, $p<.01$] ratings of the sounds included in Experiment II. Overall musical sounds received the highest ratings for both pleasantness and appropriateness. In both cases real world sounds received the lowest ratings.

Figure 3: The mean pleasantness and appropriateness ratings of the auditory signals included in Experiment II are shown based on a nine point scale where 9 reflects a positive response.

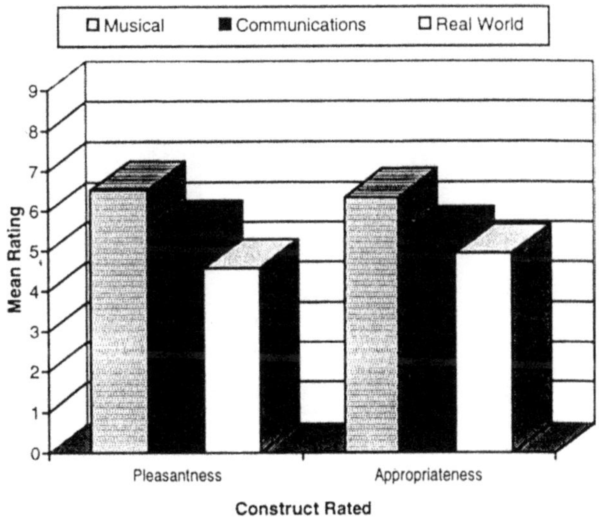

As occurred in Experiment I, the real world sounds were consistently rated poorly on pleasantness and appropriateness. In addition, subjects seldom chose a real world sound as the best choice for any of the functions.

The musical sounds had consistently high pleasantness and appropriateness ratings and were most frequently selected as the best choice. Communications sounds varied in subjective ratings and occasionally proved to be the best selection for a given function. None of the real world sounds were viable choices due to low ratings.

Figure 4 shows the mean pleasantness and appropriateness ratings for the sounds derived based on best choice judgments. Although all sounds selected were rated positively for pleasantness and appropriateness there was still a significant difference between the musical and communications sound families. There was a main effect of sound class for both pleasantness [$F(1,236) = 30.13$, $p<.01$] and appropriateness [$F(1,236) = 11.35$, $p<.01$]. Musical sounds were rated more highly on both constructs than communications oriented sounds.

Figure 4: The mean ratings of pleasantness and appropriateness for the auditory signals chosen as best for the functions are shown, based on a nine point scale.

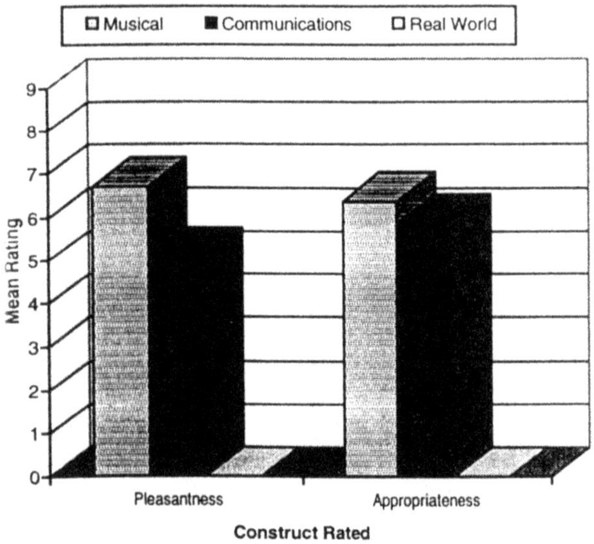

Eleven sounds, one for each function, were subsequently selected for use as auditory feedback. The selections were based primarily on the frequency of the sounds being selected as "best" for that function. Rating data for pleasantness and appropriateness was used to verify that the selected sounds were considered pleasant and appropriate within the business application task. Seven of the sounds were musical sounds and four were communications sounds. None of the real world sounds was selected.

4. EXPERIMENT III: EVALUATING THE DISCRIMINABILITY OF THE RESULTANT FAMILY OF SOUNDS

The final sound selections for the eleven functions requiring auditory feedback were chosen based on the preference data from subjects in Experiment II. Although each sound selected mapped adequately to the function and was rated highly for overall pleasantness and appropriateness in a business environment, the question of discriminability within the family still existed. Experiment III was designed to evaluate the discriminability of the eleven sounds within the sound family identified.

Subjects rated the similarity of the eleven sounds and described the dimensions they used to make their judgments. Thirty-eight computer literate office workers, who were not involved in either of the previous studies, participated in the study and were compensated for their time. The subjects understood that the sounds being evaluated were intended to provide auditory feedback in a business application, but the eleven functions were not described to them.

Subjects filled out a brief demographic questionnaire and were then given verbal and written instructions describing the task. The subjects were tested individually using a computer simulation. The task required judging the degree of similarity of each pairing of the 11 sounds using a five point scale, where 5 denoted "very similar" and 1 denoted "very dissimilar". Subjects were given a brief introduction to the task and then completed the task at their own pace.

To listen to a pair of sounds, the subject clicked on each of two buttons to play the sounds. The subject was able to play each sound as many times as necessary prior to making a rating. Subjects indicated perceived similarity by clicking one of the buttons on the five point scale.

After each rating, the subject clicked on the "next" button to indicate their readiness for the next pair of sounds. There were 55 sound pairings of the 11 sounds. Subjects completed a questionnaire which inquired about the strategies used for making the similarity ratings.

The data from the sound similarity ratings revealed that the discriminability within the sound family was quite good with the exception of one pair of sounds. The sound for the Error and End Call functions were judged to be very similar.

Based on subjective reporting in conjunction with a multidimensional scaling analysis of the data, three dimensions appear to be used by the subjects to make their similarity judgments. The dimensions are best described as duration, average pitch and harmonic complexity of the sounds. The complexity of the sound was described by subjects using various terms, but in each case it seemed to reflect the degree to which the sound was simple or complex. The two sounds that were judged to be too similar to be easily discriminated were both short, low pitched simple sounds.

4. DISCUSSION

An investigation of functional mapping revealed that, for real world sounds, subjects generally selected the function for which the sound had been intended. The communications sounds, whose abstract musical tones were based on learned pairings, had less consistent functional mappings. The musical sounds, which had no previous learned association, were more randomly mapped to the functions.

To further investigate which sounds should be selected for use, the subjective ratings of the sounds were analyzed within the context of a business application. The more musically oriented sounds were most preferred. Clearly, our results support earlier findings (Jones and Furner, 1989) that the type of auditory feedback most preferred by subjects is not the same as those sounds that provided the best functional mapping. Rather, the users' reactions indicate that real world signals are less appropriate for actual applications relative to abstract musical feedback. These results emphasize the need to solicit judgments in addition to functional mappings when choosing appropriate audible feedback signals. Indeed, our results demonstrate that subjective ratings of pleasantness and appropriateness are more reliable selection criteria.

Once individual sounds were identified for each function and the preferences for the sounds were verified, the discriminability of the sounds as a family was investigated. Overall, the sounds were easily discriminable. An exception was that the auditory feedback for Error was rated as being very similar to End Call. The sound for the Error function was replaced as a result of this data.

Discriminability data provided a glimpse at the strategy used to make similarity judgments about auditory feedback signals. Although described in various terms, pitch, duration and harmonic complexity seem to be critical, observable aspects of sounds. In fact, the two sounds that were rated as very similar were similar on all three dimensions. These results do not, however, preclude the importance of other aspects of sound since our results may simply be a reflection of our particular sound stimulus set.

In summary, results of these experiments indicate that real world sounds are less appropriate for business communications applications than are more abstract musically based sounds. Considering the richness and complexity of the graphically based products users have available today, it is a natural progression for the accompanying auditory feedback to rise to a similar level of sophistication and appeal.

These conclusions must, however, be treated with some caution since there were several flaws in our methodology. First, there were more musical sounds in the stimulus sets in Experiment I than communications and real world sounds and subjects may have assumed an experimenter bias when making their judgments. Second, the real world sounds may have been disadvantaged since they were selected from sound libraries and were not privy to the same creativity and technical manipulation as were the communications and musical sounds. However, we have recently carried out research that addresses these limitations in the present studies and preliminary results demonstrate patterns that mirror the current results. Another concern is that, since the more musical signals are not as intuitively mapped to the functions relative to real world sounds, there may be issues relative to end user training particularly for visually impaired users. The long term use of these sounds may also be questioned. For example, it may be that abstract sounds become concrete enough to be perceived as annoying at some point. The study was also limited to testing subjects in the United States. These sounds are being tested in other countries to ensure they are appropriate and pleasant to people in other parts of the world. At this point, these sounds have been tested in Singapore, Turkey and India. Those results are currently being compared to equivalent testing done in the United States.

5. ACKNOWLEDGMENTS

The authors would like to thank Mark Barasch of Mark Barasch Music Productions LTD for his creative musical contributions, La Tondra Murray and Andrea D'Amico for running subjects and Dan Teibel for his technical input and support.

6. REFERENCES

Blattner, M., Sumikawa, D. & Greenberg, R. (1989). Earcons and icons: Their structure and common design principles. *Human-Computer Interaction*, **4**, 11-44.

Brewster, S., Wright, P. & Edwards, A. (1993). An Evaluation of Earcons for Use in Auditory Human-Computer Interfaces, in Proc. *INTERCHI'93 Human Factors in Computing Systems* (Amsterdam, April 24-29, 1993), ACM Press, pp. 222-227.

Gaver, W. (1986). Auditory icons: Using sound in computer interfaces. *Human-Computer Interaction*, **2**, 167-177.

Jones, S. & Furner, S. (1989). The constructions of audio icons and information cues for human-computer dialogues. Contemporary Ergonomics, *Proceedings of the Ergonomics Society's 1989 Annual Conference*, T. Megaw (Ed.)

Mynatt, E. (1994). Designing with Auditory Icons: How Well do We Identify Auditory Cues?, *in Proc. CHI'94 Human Factors in Computing Systems* (Boston, April 24-28, 1994), ACM Press, pp. 269-270.

ConcertTalk: A Weekend With a Portable Audio Space

Henry B. (Hank) Strub
Interval Research Corporation
1801-C Page Mill Rd.
Palo Alto, CA 94304 U.S.A.
+1-415-842-6088 *strub@interval.com*

ABSTRACT This paper describes a study of the ConcertTalk system, a portable audio space that was used for two days. Two-way radios were provided to attendees at Lollapalooza rock concerts, and their use was recorded and analyzed. The study's participants quickly began using the system, used it throughout the day, and found many creative ways for the radios to improve the Lollapalooza concert experience. ConcertTalk's results suggest the utility of studying CHI technologies outside of work places, both to validate and expand the foundational theory of our growing domain of knowledge in practice.

KEYWORDS Portable user interfaces, Speech & voice, Social issues, Audio space, Observational study.

1. INTRODUCTION

The ConcertTalk system involved giving two-way radios to Lollapalooza concert attendees. The motivation for this study was to explore a different setting for a media space, which was specifically implemented as a portable audio space. Lollapalooza brings together national and local alternative rock in outdoor venues that hold 20,000 - 30,000 people [13]. The data for this study are recordings of ConcertTalk traffic and interviews of ConcertTalk users after the concerts. Its two sets of users liked the system and used it extensively. This study is also notable for being of an audio-only media space (an audio space).

The ConcertTalk study created an audio space with unique properties as a media space. ConcertTalk was a portable and wireless system, designed for a recreational setting without structured tasks to be performed. ConcertTalk was used intensely, although each user group had only one day with the system.

This paper begins by looking at two widely-held beliefs about media spaces that this study challenges. It then describes the study, and unique characteristics of running a study at Lollapalooza concerts. Results are presented descriptively. Special attention is devoted to creative uses of the system. The discussion suggests that foundational theory on media spaces can be expanded through broadening the domains of media space use.

2. MEDIA SPACES: FOR WORKPLACES, WITH HIGH-QUALITY AUDIO

Media spaces tend to support visual and audio communication, and often let users directly present, annotate and edit documents on computers. The users of media spaces are either not in the same place, not available at the same time, or both. The workplace or the school have been the assumed domains for the media space since its inception [3]: this is one belief about media spaces that is challenged in this study.

Most of the previous studies on media spaces have either been directly related to work of some sort or have simulated work situations ([3, 11] both include reviews). Rather than look at a media space as a work tool that functioned as a "medium for social activity" ([3], p. 39), the current study found a social activity and inserted an audio space to see what behaviors would emerge. Technology envisionments (two instances were from AT&T and Microsoft) portray videoconferencing for social situations, and low-end videoconferencing is being marketed to consumers—but these domains have not been the subject of media space studies.

As an audio space's use depends on its communication being comprehensible, one issue to investigate was whether ConcertTalk's use would be negatively influenced by its low-quality audio. Having high quality audio is considered important for media spaces, even more important than having high-quality video [2, 3, 14]: this is the second belief about media spaces that is challenged in this study.

In the system studied by Tang and Isaacs [14], most of the audio problems were caused by delays, echo, and incomprehensible audio. Although their users were generally unwilling to wear headsets that would have reduced audio problems, the users would run the system with telephone-quality audio (which reduced audio bandwidth and decreased the overall quality but minimized delays and echo). Bly, Harrison, and Irwin [3] mention further audio problems caused by room noises like fans, and the inability to hold side conversations through a media space.

Human–Computer Interaction: INTERACT'97 S. Howard, J. Hammond & G. Lindgaard (editors)
Published by Chapman & Hall ©IFIP 1997

Although most experimental media spaces have been used and studied in workplaces, they have not been used only to discuss work-related tasks. Hindus, *et al.* [6] had much less task-oriented interaction on the system they studied than expected, though this may have been a function of their users' work style. Hindus *et al.'s* system use also depended on having a critical mass of users, often influenced by the presence or absence of key participants.

These media space issues were relevant to ConcertTalk, as were issues of privacy and accessibility to other users as well as to non-users. In fact, non-users' reactions to ConcertTalk influenced its use and judgment. Also, ConcertTalk's low-quality audio actually had advantages for its use at rock concerts.

3. THE STUDY

The ConcertTalk study took place at Lollapalooza rock concerts, one weekend in August 1994 in Mountain View, California. Roughly ten concert attendees per day received portable two-way radios. The initial goal for the project was to see how these attendees used the radios. Its methodology was motivated by Flanagan's Critical Incident Technique [7], looking for repeating patterns and exceptions in the data.

All radio communications were recorded, except during a technical problem that lasted for less than an hour on the second day. Most of the participants were interviewed two days after the show they attended. The study's participants were reminded that their radio use was monitored and that radio transmissions recorded. Participants also knew that anyone with a scanner could listen to their communications.

3.1. The Setting

Lollapalooza concerts were an interesting setting for a portable audio space. There was much to see and do over the course of a concert day; shows lasted ten hours with two stages of music (sometimes both stages had bands playing concurrently). Concert venues hosted vendors representing local organizations; selling food, drink, and clothing; or offering opportunities to participate in arcade-like activities. One other activity was the Electric Carnival—a tent with art-oriented multimedia that was free to attendees [10].

Lollapalooza attendees were an interesting user community for trying ConcertTalk. A majority of them were in their late teens, which is a social time of life [5]. Teens get stereotyped as spending a lot of time talking to friends both in person and on the phone. The author expected that they might find creative uses for ConcertTalk. Also, there were questions about how ConcertTalk users and the people around them would react to the presence of radios.

3.2. The Subjects

Different groups of subjects used the radios each day of the study. The two groups of participants will be referred to by the day on which the people used the system: Day 1 and Day 2 participants. The goal in recruiting subjects was to find groups of teenagers in their "last year" of high school. Groups of friends were recruited through the author's coworkers. Parental release forms were obtained for participants younger than 18 years old.

The ten Day 1 participants all knew each other before the concert. All of Day 1's participants were given lawn tickets in return for their participation, and therefore none of them had access to reserved seating sections of the amphitheater. As result, Day 1 participants were expected to spend much of the day with each other. Most of the Day 1 participants had recently graduated from high school. They ranged from 17 to 20 years old; six were female and four were male.

The relationships among Day 2 participants were more complex. The main group consisted of four people who had reserved seats, along with five who were given lawn tickets. Two other teens, who were strangers to the rest of the group, were provided with lawn tickets. In the larger group, six participants were male and three were female; in the other pair one was female and one was male. Their ages ranged from 16 to 21. Only ten radios were available for participants to use. The three young women in the main group (who spent the day together) volunteered to share two radios between them. The couple showed up late and kept the radios only part of the day.

3.3. Audio Equipment

Fourteen Motorola GP-300 radios were rented for this study. Figure 1 shows a ConcertTalk participant wearing a radio. The radios were of noticeably lower audio quality than telephones[1]. The radios, which can handle up to eight different channels, were configured with just two channels to ease analysis and to minimize the chance that users would split up on different channels and not find each other. Remote speaker/microphone units, which plugged into the radios, were given to participants. When using remotes, people with a radio could attach the radio to their waist or store it in a pack while keeping the speaker/microphone at hand or clipped at shoulder level. Two radios were used for recording the two channels, and the final two radios were used by researchers to monitor ConcertTalk traffic in case the study's participants needed assistance.

4. OVERALL USAGE RESULTS

The radios were well used throughout the time that participants had them. On Day 1, participants arrived at 3 p.m. Except for one twenty-minute period of silence the

[1]These radios have a rated audio bandwidth of 300-3000 Hz. This 2700 Hz bandwidth is substantially narrower than the 3300 Hz bandwidth of telephone service in America.

radios were almost constant used until they were collected at 9 p.m.. On Day 2, participants used the radios from 1 p.m. until 9 p.m., but there were a few silent periods that lasted longer than ten minutes. All cases of extended silence coincided with musical sets by popular performers—the ConcertTalk participants apparently ignored the radios only to listen to music.

New conversations commonly began less than a minute after others ended, and it was rare to have silent periods of longer than two or three minutes. Most conversations, on both days, were on one channel. There was only one period where two or three participants switched to the alternate radio channel, stating it was because they could not carry on a conversation due to too much conversation on the primary channel.

On both days, participants needed little encouragement to use the radios. The only instruction necessary was on the need to engage the radios' transmit button for perhaps half a second before the radio would start transmitting.

Although not large or heavy, the radios (along with the remote microphone/speaker assemblies) looked like technology worn by police and security guards. One question was how concert attendees, both participants and the people they met, would react to the radios. There was concern that these radios might be considered "nerdy," and that participants might resist wearing and using the radios or hide the radios.

Figure 1. A ConcertTalk participant with a radio.

The ConcertTalk study's participants did not mind carrying radios with them. In fact, they commented on how other people thought of them as undercover security and treated them with more respect than they were used to at a rock concert. Users said it was easy to traverse through crowds, and that no one complained when someone with a radio accidentally stepped on a blanket that demarcated a group's sitting space.

5. COMMON USES FOR THE RADIOS

Most of the conversation on ConcertTalk was about people, mainly the participants themselves but sometimes other friends. Discussion of facts (even information exchange about the concert) was rare. As a result, most of the categories in this analysis relate to human interactions as opposed to informational categories.

5.1. Identifying Individuals

After learning to use the radios, initial discussions on both days were devoted to finding people and identifying when specific individuals were listening. When beginning a set of interactions, participants usually began by asking if a specific individual was listening (or "on"). Much less common were requests directed to a location, for example, a call to "anyone at home base." Participants did not respond to the few requests for everyone listening to identify themselves. It is unclear whether no one was listening at those times or whether participants did not care to identify themselves.

5.2. Discussing Locality

A radio conversation was usually started for some purpose (often a social one). Once a requested individual was identified as listening to ConcertTalk, participants usually determined each other's whereabouts. Knowing location often had practical value in deciding whether or where to meet. For example, some participants often used the system to find who (of the few participants of drinking age) was near a beer vendor.

A common basis for discussing locality was to coordinate getting together. On both days, participants set up blankets on the lawn so all could sit together. That was the most common place to gather, though participants also met by the "Ice Cold Beer" sign at the top of the lawn. One day's participants met in front of a landmark they called "the outhouse" (this structure was centrally located on the lawn), while the other day's participants met by a prominent yellow balloon.

Both days' participants had to establish common frames of reference to find each other. For instance, participants had to agree whether "to the left of the stage" referred to left from the perspective of looking out from the stage or from the field looking at the stage. These discussions arose both for finding people on the field and for meeting at exits from the amphitheater.

5.3. Arranging Activities

Another popular use of the radios was arranging to do something together. Participants commonly did not use the radios to explain *why* they wanted to meet up with someone else (which in itself is interesting). When a meeting's purpose was mentioned, it was often eating. On both days, there were arrangements about possibly illicit activities. On one day, participants used code words while on the other day they openly discussed these activities.

6. CREATIVE USES OF THE RADIOS

Although other authors have reported on media spaces used for social interactions (especially [6]), ConcertTalk's focus was social interactions. Its social use was especially interesting for the variety of creative and fun ways the radios were used.

6.1. Pretending to Work for Security

All the participants in this study said they enjoyed other concert attendees perceiving them as working for security, often talking or reacting to them as undercover security or even police officers. Concert attendees spontaneously asked ConcertTalk participants whether they worked for security, or what they were doing with radios. In a few cases, participants were confronted by attendees for trying to "sneak around" the concert as undercover security. Many participants described situations where people reacted to them upon seeing the radios, before anything was said. The recordings contain cases where participants started using radio codes that sounded official, like when a participant started using codes after announcing he was going to the restroom, "521 mission found, ready to complete mission, over."

Both days' participants took advantage of the common perception of their working for security. Many described the ease of moving through crowds when radios were visible or audible. Both days' recordings have examples of participants speaking as security might, asking for "backup" or describing the location of "a bad situation" (in one case, participants approached an inebriated person who was obviously unwell). A Day 1 participant brought a flashlight to the concert, and said she used it at night with her radio to startle people as she walked through a crowd. Some Day 2 participants described how announcing "security coming through" would get people to move out of their way.

6.2. Guest Radio Users

On both days of Concert Talk, people not formally participating in the study tried the radios. On Day 1, where the participants all knew each other, guests tended to be friends of a participant. Some Day 1 guests were only acquaintances of the participant whose radio they used; these guests tried to contact their friend who was on another radio. On Day 2 the participants were not as familiar with each other, and most of the guest users seemed to have just met the person whose radio they used.

Day 2's guest users were varied. For example, a young woman described a "hot looking guy" their group had met. In this case, the radios served the social function of enabling flirting. This whole transaction is otherwise incongruous since the people listening (all were male) knew the young women and probably did not care about their meeting a cute guy. Another fellow, nicknamed by participants as "the Motorola guy," used the radios to give a short monologue on his appreciation of Motorola and Motorola radios.

Two other guests during Day 2 were also noteworthy. At one time, the young women said they had met a "cute woman" (named Candy) they "wanted to introduce to the radios." During the post-concert interview, they said they had tried to set her up with a male participant. The male participants did not express interest in meeting her. The other interesting guest on Day 2 was Mark, introduced as a participant's brother. The young women wanted to meet him since he sounded "cool and together." However, Mark was an imaginary person, made up by the male participants. During the post-concert interview, Day 2's female participants stated their disappointment upon learning that Mark was not a real person.

6.3. Development of a Group Lexicon

Both sets of participants fell into a unique radio lexicon that seemed consistent with how radios are portrayed in the media. For example, both days' participants commonly ended transmissions with "over" to signify that they were done and waiting for a reply. "Do you copy?" was a standard way for Day 2 users to ask whether someone was listening, while Day 1 users varied between saying "copy" and "come in." When transmissions were unintelligible, it was common for Day 2s to request repeat of transmissions by saying "come again."

On both days, there was an interesting evolution of language to describe where participants had set up a meeting place on the lawn. Each day began with detailed descriptions of the meeting place's location and how to find it. As the days progressed, the directions became ever shorter. This evolution of contracted descriptions, from phrases to a few words has been identified as a general phenomenon in human communication[4].

6.4. Miscellaneous Uses

Some of the participants' creativity was exhibited in poking fun at, and having fun with, other participants. For example, Day 2's transmissions began with the first participants annoying the person who organized their group while he waited outside the concert venue to distribute tickets as others arrived. Another early activity on Day 2 was spontaneous calls of "Red Leader, Red Leader." Two of Day 2's participants started the day by referring to each other as "Woodchuck" and "Gray Squirrel." It is not known whether these nicknames had been used prior to the concert.

There are also instances of spontaneous dialogues related to commercial entertainment, especially among Day 2's participants who often acted out dialogue from the movie *Top Gun* and the television show *Star Trek*. An odd phenomenon during Day 2 were infrequent requests to "maintain radio silence." Apparently, only one user uttered this statement, commonly between conversations but at least once during a dialogue.

On both days, there was radio discussion about specific participants heading off to restroom facilities. In particular, Day 2 participants repeatedly announced their entrance and when "mission completed, leaving structure," twice transmitting the flushing of toilets.

Two other unique radio events took place during Day 2. In one, participants pretended they were security asking for backup to help with a "riot" that started when a "new kid on the block" was spotted. This was followed by description of a fellow needing a "nose cast" due to "hitting his nostril with a pedal while riding a unicycle." Later in the day, it sounded as if security used ConcertTalk's channel 2 to request assistance to get a duck off the field. This was an odd event since it sounded serious and was not followed by joking. Even during the post-concert interview, one participant admitted to thinking the duck incident had been real.

7. CONCERTTALK RADIOS AS ARTIFACTS

So far, this paper has described how radios were used by the participants in social activities and in enjoying the concert. This section looks at how these radios' size, form, features, and characteristics worked for the ConcertTalk participants.

7.1. Radios as Fashion

The Lollapalooza audience is known for being fashion conscious [13]. The Motorola radios used in this study were rugged commercial devices, not at all designed for the fashion or style of Lollapalooza. Even so, neither day's participants commented about the radios looking unfashionable. Comments from non-participants about the radios were always oriented towards their purpose and why they were being carried, rather than to their appearance. The radios' practical styling did not seem to negatively influence the participants' attitudes toward their use of the radios.

7.2. Use of the radios' multiple channels

This section reviews observations regarding how ConcertTalk participants took advantage of the two channels they were configured with. On Day 1, participants were told that they could request assistance on channel 1. They interpreted this as a request not to use channel 1 except for emergencies, and Day 1's radio use was restricted to channel 2. Day 2's participants were told that researchers would monitor both channels, though each radio was set to channel 2 before it was distributed. There was little radio traffic on channel 1 during Day 2 other than rare instances when a participant spoke to a researcher, though on one occasion some participants wanted to carry on a dialogue when others were already talking. On that occasion, another participant interrupted them on channel 1. Perhaps that person was monitoring channel 1, or switched channels when the others switched to channel 1.

7.3. Radios as instruments of safety

Women on both days described that the radios made them feel safer at the concert. If a problem arose, they knew they could call to nearby friends for help. During both post-concert interviews, women talked about walking off by themselves, which would have made them uncomfortable had the radios not linked them to friends. On Day 2 one woman walked away from her friends in a "test loss" to get experience using the radios to find each other.

7.4. Radios as Portable Artifacts

The radios used in this study were too large to be carried in a pocket comfortably. Besides the radios and their antennas, ConcertTalk participants were also supplied with a remote speaker/microphone connected to the radios by means of a coiled cord.

Still, no users complained about the weight or size of the radios; in fact some users said the radios were easier to pay attention to since they had bulk. About 25% of the users reported carrying the radios in backpacks. Three or four users carried the radio in their hands and used it without the remote speaker/microphone assembly.

Many participants did comment that the remote speaker/microphone units were less comprehensible than the radios. This influenced some to not use the remote units, even though they had to hold the radios in their hands during use, and they still needed to carry the remotes all day.

Although this study demonstrates that radios can be enjoyable and easy to use, there is other evidence for this point. There are many types of radios (in the U.S. they include Citizen Band, GMRS, and other low-power FM handhelds), which are popular among many communities of users[9]. Also, Julian Orr has studied the adoption and use of radios among copier technicians [12]. The radios Orr studied were well liked and judged as contributing to more efficient repair work.

8. DIFFERENCES BETWEEN DAY 1 AND DAY 2

When a study only has two different user groups, it is hard to know the basis for performance differences between them. This section discusses group differences and their implications. Day 1's participants all knew each other to some degree, and were of similar ages. Day 2's participants were more heterogeneous in age and each one in the main group knew only three or four of the other participants. Additionally, Day 2 included two other users who were strangers to all the other participants.

Day 1's conversations reflect its participants' familiarity with one another. There was a fairly constant stream of conversations, which were usually for practical purposes. Day 2 users' conversations contained more instances of fun and creativity. Perhaps this was due to their not knowing each other well. The radios may have been a medium for showing off and impressing others. A few Day 2 participants said ConcertTalk helped them get to know the other participants.

An interesting Day 2 phenomenon was the tendency for only a few people to talk at any time. The active participants divided themselves into three or four groups. In the post-concert interview, they said that all could hear incoming transmissions but only one member of any group would tend to respond.

The couple on Day 2 who were strangers to the rest of the group never became integrated into conversations; in fact, they returned their radios early. In the post-concert interview, one said it was hard to break into conversations due to not even knowing people's names.

An interesting sequence of dialogues during Day 1 was due to a unique event: the headline rock group Smashing Pumpkins played a surprise set on the second stage. A series of conversations preceded this event. It was first mentioned at 6:15 p.m. as "a surprise gig" by the group Porno for Pyros, which would start at 6:30 on the second stage. This led to excited conversation about meeting at the second stage. The first participants announced their arrival there at 6:30, but saw the equipment from another group being broken down. Discussion continued about Porno for Pyros, and some of participants met while others gave up and requested that radios be used to announce when the group showed up. About 7:00, a rock group's equipment was being set up. Word went out that the surprise group was the Smashing Pumpkins, but some of the radio traffic argued over which group was actually playing.

8.1. Consciousness about being recorded

There were early comments during Day 2 about the recordings being monitored. Later in the day, a Day 2 participant spoke to the researchers (on channel 2, which was Day 2's main channel for conversations) about not being able to see the concerts. Additionally, a Day 2 participant apologized to the person listening to the recordings for missing a great concert. Although Day 1's participants did not talk about being recorded or monitored, their early use of code words for illicit activities may have reflected planning regarding ConcertTalk's use being recorded.

9. CONCERTTALK'S AUDIO QUALITY WAS ACCEPTABLE

The radio's poor audio quality did not appear to impair ConcertTalk's use. Retransmission requests occurred only when transmissions were made with loud background noise, or when statements were not transmitted due to participants starting to speak immediately after engaging the radio transmit button. In the post-concert interviews, no one complained about the radios' audio quality. Participants said they had no problems with comprehensibility. On both days, participants seemed to have no difficulty identifying each other.

9.1. Being Loud Enough at the Right Time

Ideally, a portable communication system should always be at the right volume for whatever its users are doing. This was not the case with ConcertTalk. Some participants turned off their radios when they listened to music, making them unavailable to other participants. Others turned the radio volume up when they were in a noisy situation, but then were embarrassed by the radios being loud (and calling attention to themselves) just after they left the noisy area. Yet, while sitting on a blanket in the concert area, a few participants found it easier to use the radios to communicate with someone sitting four people away rather than talking directly to those people.

9.2. Mediocre Audio can have Benefits

The radios' low audio bandwidth might be considered a feature for the Lollapalooza setting. In the midst of the noisy ambient background of a festival rock concert, radio transmissions had a distinct sound. As long as radios were loud enough to be audible over the ambient noise (that was not always the case, especially when participants were close to an active stage), transmissions were distinctive. Had radios provided better quality, participants may have had trouble distinguishing transmissions from the live acoustic environment. Although this phenomenon should not be taken as a recommendation for poor audio, there should be consideration of making media space communications distinctive from those in their users' local spaces.

10. CONCERTTALK AND MEDIA SPACES

This paper began by raising questions on whether siting an audio space outside of a workplace might inform the theoretical foundation of media spaces. This final section discusses ConcertTalk as a media space.

Using ConcertTalk, someone speaking had no feedback from listeners except after ending a transmission, and after a listener responded with a transmission. This feature was in direct opposition to the property of seamlessness that is often considered a virtue for media spaces [8]. There were loud background noises around the concert site and they would have been distracting had they been constantly transmitted over ConcertTalk. The tradeoffs involved in such issues should be considered in the design of personal systems for communication.

This "push to talk" feature also helps ConcertTalk results argue for modifications to the general rule that audio quality is important in media spaces [2, 3, 14]. Participants did not complain about the system's audio quality, though they occasionally asked that transmissions be repeated. However, the narrow bandwidth and low fidelity of the radios' speakers helped participants differentiate between sounds in the world and the system's sounds. There are disadvantages to half-duplex systems like ConcertTalk (for example, it required turn taking, and did not allow interruptions of long statements). ConcertTalk was immune from the common media space problems of echo and delay.

What factors will contribute to successful use of a group-oriented audio space like ConcertTalk? The number of users can make or break a system. It is hard to have more than one conversation running on a single audio channel for more than a brief period since additional transmissions often result in the channel's becoming inaudible. A group needs to be large enough so there are responses to requests or questions, but not so large that users cannot break in to say something. Multiple radio channels can be available when a primary channel is over-used, but this advantage is a risk for the system: once people divide up across other channels it can be difficult to find specific people. Also, a successful system like ConcertTalk needs social users who talk but not all the time. Ten participants worked well for ConcertTalk, but it is worth investigating how the size of an audio space's user community influences its use. Hindus, *et al.* [6] suggest that an audio space needs a critical mass of users to be successful. The system they described needed the presence of key users to run well, though ConcertTalk had no key users.

Another issue relevant to media spaces is the possible conflict between group availability and person-specific accessibility [1]. People sometimes want to be available to a specific sub-group and still be accessible to individuals who are not part of that group. ConcertTalk's constraints and simplicity helped turn those issues inside out. Group exclusivity was established by the radios being set to reserved frequencies, and by their only going to known individuals (except for the two strangers on Day 2, who did not successfully integrate with the other users). Individual accessibility was easy to control through turning a radio's volume down, shutting it off, or simply by ignoring it. It was also easy to expand accessibility by letting guests listen and speak into a radio.

Indeed, any technological system exists within social practices that help the technology be more or less effective. Features that are advantageous in some situations will prove problematic in others. ConcertTalk was considered a success by its participants, but this may reflect properties that are tied to Lollapalooza which might not transfer to other situations.

10.1. ConcertTalk's Intentionality and Privacy

ConcertTalk can be said to have offered no privacy to participants, since all radio traffic was recorded and anyone with a scanner may have listened in on conversations. However, a significant privacy-related difference between the ConcertTalk radios and many media spaces is that nothing was transmitted over ConcertTalk without someone pushing a button to transmit. Although this step can be viewed as an impediment to communication, intentionality was behind every utterance that was broadcast. The intentionality of ConcertTalk utterances is in sharp contrast to media spaces that have open audio channels, which often result in users forgetting that fellow users can hear comments addressed to someone nearby (or to something, like a phone)[6]. Additionally, although participants were good at recognizing each others' voices, there was some anonymity on the system[2]. Finally, participants could see anyone standing nearby who might overhear ConcertTalk transmissions.

11. METHODOLOGICAL ISSUES

It would have been interesting to have microphones and recorders, separate from the radios, with each participant. There are records on how people coordinated activities and get-togethers, but there is no data on what happened once people met up. Also, people experience varied personal audio environments, yet there is no data on how non-radio noises interacted with radio transmission and reception. Additionally, it would have been interesting to observe participants as they decided to use radios, either were or were not successful over the airwaves, and how participants reacted to radio transmissions.

12. CONCLUSIONS

This study began as an exploration of an audio space, used away from work places or schools. It was expected that such a different environment would result in new questions and issues about audio spaces in particular, and media spaces in general. This study also shows the general value of studying concepts from unique perspectives.

The ConcertTalk system can be considered successful. Its participants used the system heavily and creatively. ConcertTalk contributed positively to how participants experienced Lollapalooza concerts. Much of its activity was purposeful, and can be viewed as being like work even though discussion topics were social.

[2]This was especially in evidence by "Mark," the imaginary brother and visitor to the system, who fooled Day 2's females.

Allan MacLean has suggested that one framework to use when analyzing a CSCW system is to see how it changes activities that people perform (personal communication). ConcertTalk was a success from this perspective in that it appears to have helped participants perform activities they would probably have already engaged in. For example, the primary ConcertTalk activity was making arrangements for getting together. Many of the other activities can be viewed as cases of flirting or showing off. The popular "playing security guard" game might appear to violate this assertion, but it is consistent from the perspective that playing security helped participants move through concert crowds, and thereby became a means for helping the participants show off.

ConcertTalk's results should not be overgeneralized. A Lollapalooza concert is a unique type of event. The day is too long for attendees to stay in one place, yet it provided a set of activities that a group could enjoy together. Common interests in similar types of information[3] encouraged communication and may have in fact made the system's "party-line" nature especially useful. However, participants were not engaged in attention-demanding tasks so there were no activities to be interfered with due to radio interruptions. Even in non-work environments, it is likely that different activities will be more and less amenable to their users' being interrupted by small talk from an audio space.

The ConcertTalk study was a theoretically-based system that situated an audio space in the outside world. It was used and appreciated by its participants; in fact both sets of participants asked about the cost of renting the equipment. ConcertTalk demonstrates that some of the theory growing around media spaces is a function of their being studied only in work places, and broadens the range of issues to consider regarding audio quality in media spaces.

13. ACKNOWLEDGMENTS

Andrew Singer provided the spark for this project. Anthony Wagner and Lisa Hagström helped set up and run the study. Debby Hindus helped improve this manuscript. David Gessel, Bud Lassiter, Jason Lewis, and Wayne Burdick helped with technical details. Laura Dimario, Andrew Singer, Elin Pedersen, and Sue Faulkner provided contacts to participants. Noel Hirst; and staff from Shoreline Amphitheater and Lollapalooza all helped this study take place.

14. BIBLIOGRAPHY

1. Bellotti, V., S. B. Shum, A. MacLean and N. Hammond. Multidisciplinary modelling in HCI design ...In theory and in practice. Proceedings of CHI '95: Conference on Human Factors in Computing Systems, 1995: 146-153.

2. Bielski, L. *Bellcore's videoconferencing research: Bigger displays are less visible and more powerful.* Advanced Imaging. 8: 32-34, 1994.

3. Bly, S. A., S. R. Harrison and S. Irwin. Media Spaces: Bringing people together in a video, audio, and computing environment. *Communications of the ACM*, 1993, 36(1): 28-46.

4. Clark, H. H. and D. Wilkes-Gibbs. Referring as a collaborative process. *Cognition*, 1986, 22: 1-39.

5. Cole, M. and S. R. Cole. *The development of children.* Scientific American Books, New York, 1993.

6. Hindus, D., M. S. Ackerman, S. Mainwaring and B. Starr. Thunderwire: A field Study of an Audio-Only Media Space. *Proceedings of Computer Supported Cooperative Work '96*, 1996: 238-247.

7. Flanagan, J. C. The critical incident technique. *Psychological Bulletin*, 1954, 51(4): 327-358.

8. Ishii, H., M. Kobayashi and J. Grudin. Integration of interpersonal space and shared workspace: Clearboard design and experiments. *ACM Transactions on Information Systems*, 1993, 11(4): 349-375.

9. Kneitel, T. *Two-way radio: Uncensored.* Popular Communications. 13: 8-9, 1995.

10. Markoff, J. *An impresario's high-tech big top.* New York Times. C1-C2, 1994.

11. Olson, J. S., G. M. Olson and D. K. Meader. What mix of video and audio is useful for small groups doing remote real-time design work? *Proceedings of CHI '95: Human Factors in Computing Systems*, 1995: 362-368.

12. Orr, J. E. Ethnography and organizational learning: In pursuit of learning at work. Xerox PARC, Systems & Practices Lab, SPL-93-040, P93-00090, 1993.

13. Pond, S. *The trick is to be loved but not embraced.* New York Times. 1994.

14. Tang, J. C. and E. A. Isaacs. Why do users like video? Studies of multimedia-supported collaboration. CSCW, 1993, 1: 163-196.

[3]For example, who to meet or eat with, or whether a group was still on stage.

Making menus musical

Stephen A. Brewster and Murray G. Crease

Department of Computing Science
University of Glasgow, Glasgow, G12 8QQ, UK.
Tel: +44 (0)141 330 4966 / Fax: +44 (0)141 330 4913
stephen@dcs.gla.ac.uk or murray@gtnet.com
www.dcs.gla.ac.uk/~stephen/

ABSTRACT Future human-computer interfaces will use more than just graphical output to display information. In this paper we suggest that sound and graphics together can be used to improve interaction. We describe an experiment to improve the usability of standard graphical menus by the addition of sound. One common difficulty is slipping off a menu item by mistake when trying to select it. We designed and experimentally evaluated sonically-enhanced menus to try and overcome this problem. The results from the experiment showed a significant reduction in the subjective effort required to use the new menus along with significantly reduced error recovery times. A significantly larger number of errors were also corrected with sound.

KEY WORDS Menus, audio, multi-modal widgets, earcons, sonification.

1. INTRODUCTION

Human-computer interfaces currently rely almost entirely on graphical feedback to present information to the user. However, research is now showing that sound combined with graphics can significantly improve usability by taking advantage our natural ability to share tasks across sensory modalities, for example Alty (1995), Beaudouin-Lafon & Conversy (1996) and Brewster *et al.* (1995). Such multimodal interfaces allow a greater and more natural communication between the computer and the user. They also allow the user to employ appropriate sensory modalities to solve a problem, rather than just using one modality (usually vision) to solve all problems. We believe that for these reasons sound should become a standard, integrated component in human-computer interfaces of the future. One question that remains is how should sound be used to improve usability?

This paper describes an experiment to investigate the integration of sound into standard graphical menus to overcome usability problems. Menus are a standard feature of most graphical interfaces because they are a convenient way of grouping commands to improve usability. Norman (1991) has a detailed discussion of all aspects of menus and their use. The design of menus has become almost standard across systems. However, they are not without problems. One of these is the mis-selection of menu items due to inadequate feedback. Norman has very little discussion of the feedback required to indicate a selection. He does say (p 157) "...the system should provide feedback to the users confirming selection and informing them of its progress". He does not suggest how this should be done. It is normally assumed that the visual highlighting of the menu item is sufficient. We believe that this is not the case.

1.1 The problem with menus

Pull-down menus are operated by pressing the mouse button down in the menu bar (or on hot-spot to bring up a pop-up menu). On some systems (e.g. the Macintosh) the mouse button must be held down so that the menu

Human–Computer Interaction: INTERACT'97 S. Howard, J. Hammond & G. Lindgaard (editors)
Published by Chapman & Hall

remains visible, on other systems (e.g. Windows95) the menu may stay pulled down until the user presses the mouse button again. This paper concentrates on the former. Moving the cursor along the menu bar highlights the menu title the cursor is in and displays the items in that menu. When the cursor is moved into the menu the items are highlighted as the mouse moves over them (unless the item is a divider or greyed-out). If the cursor is moved out of the menu the menu remains displayed but the highlight is removed. This provides a back-out facility in case the user decides that no menu item is to be chosen. If the cursor is over a valid item when the button is released that item is selected and the menu is removed. On some systems (e.g. the Macintosh) the user can set the item selected to flash between zero and three times to indicate that it has been selected. If the button is released when the cursor is not over a valid menu item, the menu is simply removed. For more details on menu interactions see Crease (1996).

A study of menu interactions showed three possible outcomes of a selection: A correct selection, an incorrect selection and no selection.

An incorrect selection could occur for one of two reasons: 1) The wrong menu item was mistakenly selected - a mis-selection. In this case the user simply chose the wrong item; 2) The cursor slipped onto the wrong menu item accidentally as the button was being released - an *item slip*. Our study of menus showed that, sometimes, just as the mouse button was released users could slip into an adjacent menu item. This happened partly because the action of releasing the mouse button could move the mouse a little and also because users often started to move the mouse to the location of the next action before the mouse button was released.

Similarly, no selection could happen for one of three reasons: 1) The user decided not to select anything and moved the cursor out of the menu before releasing the button; 2) The cursor slipped off the edge of the menu as the button was being released - a *menu slip*; 3) The user selected a disabled item or a divider.

Menu and item slips reduce the usability of menus and can sometimes cause more serious problems. For example, if the user slipped off when trying to save and did not notice, the data would not be saved with perhaps serious consequences. We decided to investigate these problems further to see if menus could be improved.

1.2 Action Slips and Closure

Why do item and menu slips occur? As mentioned, they can occur because the release of the mouse button can move the mouse itself. However, the errors are also both examples of *action slips* (Reason, 1990). These errors occur with expert users who perform many simple operations (such as button clicks and menu selections) automatically and do not explicitly monitor the feedback from each interaction. Lee (1992) describes such errors thus (p 73): "...as a skill develops, performance shifts from 'closed loop' control to 'open-loop' control, or from monitored mode to an automatic, unmonitored mode of processing." As users become familiar with a simple task they no longer monitor the feedback from it so closely. In this case the automatic task is the menu selection (which most users are very familiar with). The user will be concentrating more on the main task he/she is trying to perform than on the menu selection.

One problem that exacerbates the difficulties of actions slips is *closure* (Dix *et al.*, 1993). Closure occurs when a user perceives a task as being completed. In some cases the task may appear to be completed when it is not. The user may experience closure and carry on to do something else and cause an error. Brewster *et al.* (1995) and Dix & Brewster (1994) investigated such a situation that could occur with graphical buttons. In this case, users could slip off a button by mistake and not press it. This happened because as the graphical button highlighted (when the mouse button was pressed), users experienced closure and carried on to their next task. In fact the graphical button was not actually pressed until the mouse button was released. After analysis, Brewster *et al.* suggested three criteria necessary to make action slips and closure a problem. In terms of menus these would be:

i) The user reaches closure after the cursor is moved into the desired menu item and the text is highlighted.

ii) The visual focus of the next action is at some distance from the target menu item.

iii) The cursor is required at the new focus.

In this case, when the desired menu item has been highlighted the user experiences closure. The task is, in reality, not completed until the mouse button is released over the desired menu item. However, because of closure the user may begin to move on to his/her next task before the menu selection has been completed. If this task requires the cursor and visual focus to be away from the menu, all the conditions for an action slip have been met.

An example of this error consider selecting 'Save' from the file menu in a word processor. The user will be more concerned with the document being saved than the mechanics of the menu, making action slips likely. He/she would be typing in the document and decide to save. The mouse (and visual attention) would be moved up to the menu to select save, the menu item would be highlighted, the user would see the highlight, reach closure and then begin to move back to the document to continue typing. If this return movement is done too soon, the mouse may slip on to another item or out of the menu before the interaction is complete. In many systems no feedback is given to indicate a save has been performed, so the user would have no indication of his/her error.

1.3 Overcoming the Problems

In order to solve the problems of action slips and accidental mouse movements users must perceive the feedback from the menu. Therefore the right feedback must be given to ensure users know what is going on (Reason, 1990). The Macintosh-style multiple flash goes some way to dealing with this problem, but is not a complete solution because any feedback from the menu requires the user's visual attention to be on the menu and if the second criterion above is met, this will not be the case. In this paper we suggest using auditory feedback to solve the problems. Why use sound, why not just use extra graphical feedback? It is difficult to solve these problems with extra graphics. Graphics displayed on the menu will not be seen by users because their attention will have moved back to the main task they engaged in. The visual system has a narrow area of focus which means that users cannot look at the menu as well as their main task (Brewster, 1994). Information could be displayed at the mouse location but we do not know if users are looking there either. In this case, non-speech sound has certain advantages. It can be heard from all around, it is good at getting our attention whilst we are looking at something else and it does not disrupt our visual attention. It is also language independent. If we give menu information in sound then we do not need to know where users are looking. If users must look at the menu then it forces them to stop what they are doing for their main task and causes the interface to intrude upon the task they are trying to perform, sound does not have such drawbacks.

1.4 Previous Work in the Area

As mentioned above, Brewster *et al.* (1995) investigated the use of sound to improve interaction with graphical buttons. Buttons have a subset of the problems of menus because users can slip off a button in a similar way to a menu. To solve the problems sounds were added for when the mouse button was pressed down in a graphical button and when a correct selection was made. The results of adding sound to buttons significantly improved their usability. Error recovery was significantly faster and required fewer mouse clicks than standard buttons. Participants also significantly preferred them to standard graphical buttons. The knowledge gained from that experiment suggested that we might be able to overcome some of the problems of menus in the same way.

Other work on sonifying widgets, for example scrollbars Beaudouin-Lafon & Conversy (1996) and Brewster *et al.* (1994), have proved successful in improving usability. We therefore believed that sound would allow use to improve the usability of menus.

Much work has been done on the optimal layout and design for menu structures (see Norman for a full review) but little has been done to investigate the selection of items from menus. A notable exception is the research by Walker *et al.* (1991) who proposed some design improvements for graphical menus to increase their usability by decreasing the time taken to move the cursor to the desired item. Their two main approaches were: The use of impermeable borders around menus and to increase the size of items further away from the start point in the menu to make them easier to hit. It was found that the use of impermeable borders (ones that the mouse could not move through) reduced the time taken to make a selection. The user could move the mouse to the top, bottom or right edge of the menu and not be able to move through. Therefore, the user could aim to overshoot the menu item at the edge where there was an impermeable border knowing that it was not possible to do so. This eliminated the time taken to make the secondary movement required to correct the initial overshoot. The user could leave the menu without making a selection by moving the mouse out the left edge of the menu. One problem was that it did make the menus less flexible because users had to leave them from the left side only.

Walker *et al.'s* other solution was to increase the point size of items as their distance from the top of the menu increased, i.e. increasing the size of the target area. This allowed the user to make a movement towards the target more quickly. It did however also make the distance to the target greater. If the menu became too long, two movements would have to be made to reach the target, thus eliminating any benefits gained.

There has been some previous work on adding sound to menus, although to solve different problems. Karshmer *et al.* (1994) added sounds to a menu system to aid navigation for blind users. He was not trying to overcome the slip off problems but to aid users in navigating around menus structures. The navigation was implemented by either changing the tones and timbres of the items in the menus, or by using synthetic speech to tell users their position in the hierarchy. Navigation was not the focus of our work here, our aim was to overcome slip off problems in graphical menus for sighted users.

2. EXPERIMENT

As there had been no other work to try and overcome menu selection errors with sound we decided to design an experiment to discover if auditory feedback could improve usability. For the experiment we needed to be able to differentiate three types of errors: An item slip, a menu slip and a slip onto a divider or disabled item. We could easily differentiate the latter two (because we knew where the participants were supposed to be clicking) but the former was more difficult. How could we tell if users slipped off a menu item or were really choosing the one on which they released the mouse?

We conducted an initial investigation into menu interactions to investigate ways in which we might be able to find out if an item slip had occurred. We noticed that when users selected an item correctly they stayed on the item longer than when an item slip occurred. We therefore decided to use timing information to help us identify correct selections and item slips. In a pre-test we added a timer to a simple menu system so that we could investigate how long it took users to select items (Crease, 1996). From this we discovered that for a correct selection users held the mouse over the item for an average of 265 msec before releasing. When an item slip was made the cursor was over the item for just 17 msec. For correct selections users moved the mouse to the item and did some cognitive processing to ensure it was the correct menu item before releasing the mouse button. For an item slip there was no cognitive processing, just the mouse button release time. This gave us a method for identifying correct selections and item slips.

2.1 Experimental Hypotheses

The extra feedback heard by participants should make the task easier because they will be able to tell they have made errors and recover from them more readily. This should result in an overall reduction in subjective workload and in particular a reduction in the effort required for the task. There should be no increase in annoyance due to the sounds as they will be providing information that the participants need.

The time taken to recover from item and menu slips should be reduced because users will know that they have made errors more quickly. The number of errors corrected by the participants (i.e. corrected before the error dialogue comes up to say that an error has been made) should also be increased as the demanding auditory feedback will be noticed.

2.2 Main Task

Figure 1 shows the interface to the task the participants had to perform. It was based on a car parts ordering system. Participants had to send car parts to destinations using a menu system. In the figure the Parts and Destinations menus are shown. At the bottom of the screen the boxes with 'fan belt' and 'Auchterarder' in them show the participants the part and destination they must choose. Once a part and destination pair had been chosen, the participants had to select 'Accept' on the File menu. This terminated the interaction. If one or both of the chosen items was incorrect an error dialogue was displayed and corrections had to be made before participants could continue. If an item or menu slip occurred on any of the Parts, Destinations or File menus then the participant would not be able to carry on to the next pair until they had noticed and corrected the error.

The task was designed to be simple so that the participants could easily learn it and reach a level of automaticity in the task where slip-off errors would occur.

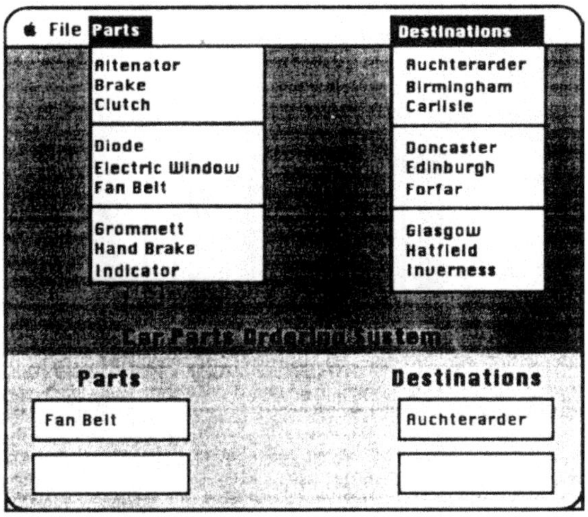

Figure 1: The screen of the menu testing program. The parts and destinations menus are shown.

2.3 Sounds

The sounds used were based around structured audio messages called *Earcons* (Blattner *et al.*, 1989, Brewster *et al.*, 1993). Earcons are abstract, musical tones that can be used in structured combinations to create sound messages to represent parts of an interface. The sounds were created using the earcon guidelines proposed by Brewster *et al.* (1995).

Three earcons were needed to deal with the problems described above:

1. An earcon was played when a menu was displayed. We used a family of organ sounds to indicate that the menus were related (part of the same application). The File menu had a percussive organ, the Parts menu a drawbar organ and the Destinations menu a rock organ. A low intensity, continuous note at pitch C_3 (523 Hz) was played for each of the menus. The sound continued as long as the cursor was in the menu. If the user moved the cursor out of the menu the sound stopped. The method proved effective in the design of sonically-enhanced buttons (Brewster *et al.*, 1995) so was used again here.

2. To deal with item slips a combination of two earcons was used. A highlight sound was created that was similar to the standard graphical highlight. This was again a continuous, low intensity tone which used the timbre of the menu that the cursor was in. The sound alternated in pitch from B_2 (987 Hz) for odd numbered items and E_3 (329 Hz) for even numbered items. So the first item in the menu would be played at E_3, the second at B_2 and the third at E_3. This sound started when the mouse had been over an item for half a second. Only two sounds were needed to indicate the movement from one menu item to another. These pitches were chosen to make the two earcons sound distinct. This sound was stopped if the user moved the mouse out of the menu or moved over a divider or disabled item.

3. The final earcon indicated a selection. This could be either a correct selection or an item slip. For a correct selection (in a menu item for longer than 17 msec) the earcon was based around the timbre of the menu the cursor was in and the pitch of the sound was based on the highlight sound for the menu item. Using these as a base, two 40 msec duration tones were played at a higher intensity. To indicate an incorrect selection the timbre of the current menu was again used. However, this time a fixed rhythm of three notes of 40 msec each at pitch C_2, B_2 then F_2 was played (these sounded discordant and therefore attention-grabbing). This was not dependent on the highlight sound for the current menu item. This sound was always the same, indicating the item slip error in each of the different menus. If the user released the mouse over a divider then no sound was played.

To avoid any potential annoyance due to the earcons we made sure they were all played at low volume. The menu earcon (1) indicated a menu slip by a lack of sound and the highlight earcon (2) didn't start playing until the participant had been over an item for half a second. In a normal, fast interaction this sound was not played, the user only heard the menu sound (1) and the selection sound (3).

2.4 Participants

Twelve participants were used. They were undergraduate and postgraduate students from the Department of Computing Science at the University of Glasgow. All were experts with more than three years experience of graphical interfaces and menus.

2.5 Experimental Design and Procedure

The experiment was a two-condition, repeated-measures within-subjects design. The order of presentation was counterbalanced to avoid any learning effects across conditions. One group of six participants performed the auditory menu condition first and the other used standard visual menus first. Ten minutes of training was given before each condition. During each condition the participants had to enter 150 parts to destinations pairs as quickly as possible. Instructions were read from a prepared script.

To get a full measurement of usability we used a range of quantitative and qualitative measures. These were error rates, error recovery times and workload (Hart & Staveland, 1988).

Hart & Staveland (1988) break workload into six different factors: Mental demand, physical demand, time pressure, effort expended, performance level achieved and frustration experienced. We used the NASA-Task Load Index (TLX) for estimating workload. To this we added a seventh factor: Annoyance. One of the main concerns of potential users of auditory interfaces is annoyance due to sound pollution. This is often given as a reason for not using sound at the human-computer interface. In the experiment described here the annoyance due to auditory feedback was measured to find out if it was indeed a problem. We also asked our participants to indicate overall preference, i.e. which of the two interfaces they felt made the task easiest. Participants had to fill in workload charts after both conditions of the experiment.

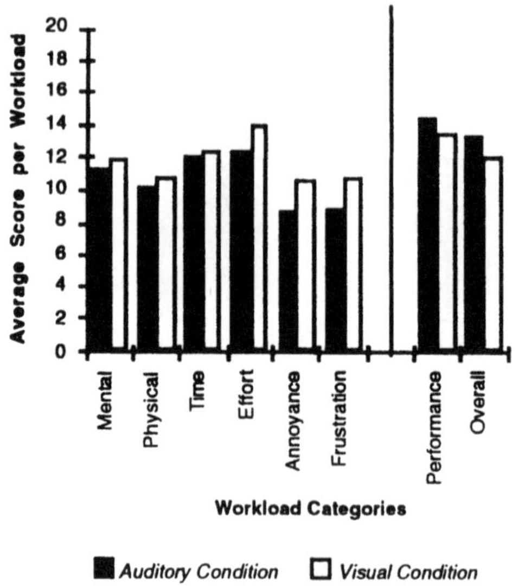

Figure 2: Average workload scores for the two conditions. In the first six categories higher scores mean higher workload. The final two categories, performance and overall preference, are separated because higher scores mean less workload.

3. RESULTS

3.1 Workload Results

Figure 2 shows the average workload score for each category. They were scored in the range 0-20. The average workload (based on the six standard workload factors: Mental, physical, time, effort, frustration and performance) was 10.02 for the auditory condition and 11.04 for the visual. This difference was significant (T_{11}=4.42, p=0.007) indicating that the participants found the task easier with the sonically-enhanced menus. This confirmed the hypothesis.

Paired T-tests were carried out on the auditory versus visual conditions for each of the workload categories. Average effort was reduced significantly from 13.9 in the visual condition to 12.5 in the auditory condition (T_{11}=2.43, p=0.03) confirming the hypothesis.

There was no significant difference in terms of annoyance (T_{11}=1.43, p=0.18). Six of the participants rated the visual condition more annoying, five the auditory condition more annoying and one rated them the same. This indicated that the participants did not find the auditory feedback to be annoying confirming the hypothesis.

3.2 Time and Error Results

The overall number of errors corrected (i.e. before the error dialogue appeared) increased significantly from 55% to 92% in the auditory condition (T_{11}=3.982, p=0.002), confirming the hypothesis. The percentage of item slips corrected increased significantly to 70% in the auditory condition from 17% in the visual (T_{11}=4.21, p=0.001), again confirming the hypothesis. The percentage of menu slips corrected increased to 83% in the auditory condition from 63% in the visual. This was not a significant improvement (T_{11}=1.11, p=0.289). Two participants made no menu slips at all in the auditory condition.

The average time taken to recover (detection and correction of the error) from all errors decreased significantly in the auditory condition (2.38 secs) compared to the visual (4.18 secs) (T_{11}=4.04, p=0.0009). Figure 3 shows the average time each participant took to recover from an error in each condition (both item and menu slip errors are included).

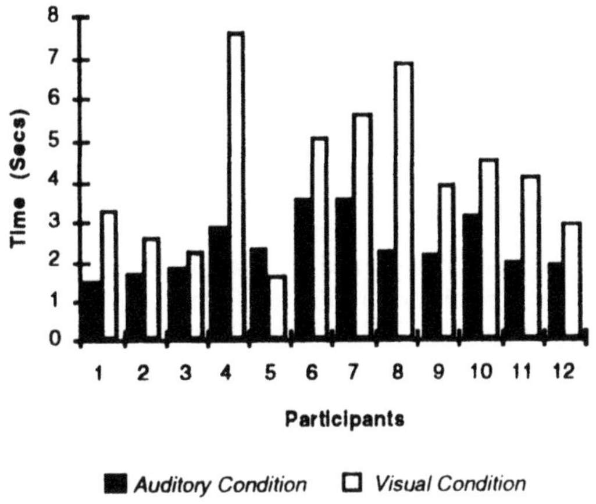

Figure 3: Average error recovery times for all errors.

The average time taken to recover from an item slip decreased significantly from 4.1 secs in the visual condition to 2.53 secs in the auditory (T_{11}=2.55, p=0.03). The recovery time from a menu slip decreased from an average of 3.07 secs in the visual condition to 1.57 secs in the auditory. A wide variance in the times in the visual condition meant that an F-Test was conducted. This showed a significant reduction in the variance in the auditory condition (F_{11}=18.11, p=1.76x10^{-5}). The range of times decreased from a minimum of 1.87 secs and a maximum of 11.25 secs in the visual condition to between 1.73 secs and 2.08 secs.

3.3 Discussion

The workload analysis showed that the overall workload, and in particular effort expended, was reduced significantly when using the sonically-enhanced menus. It was reduced because the sonic enhancements meant that participants needed to expend less effort to notice and recover from menu and item slips. This was not at the expense of making the menus more annoying to use. This, along with previous results from sonifying graphical widgets indicates that sound can provide a significant qualitative improvement in a user's experience with a system.

The results also showed that the integration of sound allowed faster recovery from errors. Both menu and item slip error recovery rates showed a significant improvement in the auditory condition. Participants could tell they had made an error and correct it significantly faster than in the visual condition. The menu slip off results showed that the earcons reduced the variance in the time taken to recover from an error. The data indicated that the better performers stayed at a similar standard, whilst the poorer performers improved greatly.

The reason the sonic feedback improved error recovery rates was that the participants' visual focus moved to the next menu before the previous selection was completed. In the visual condition the avoidable menu-selection feedback was missed, whereas in the auditory condition the demanding feedback ensured the user was alerted.

Although the item slip recovery rate was significantly improved, the item slip sound was occasionally played incorrectly. This happened if a participant interacted with the system very slowly and their items slips took longer than 17 msec. These false positives occurred as some users moved the mouse around much more slowly than others. To solve this problem a future the system could include a control panel, similar to the one that allows a user to set their preferred double-click speed, which would allow a user to set their preferred menu selection speed.

4. FUTURE WORK

This work is part of an overall project to develop a sonically-enhanced interface toolkit (Brewster, 1995). The toolkit will consist of all of the standard widgets but they will be enhanced with sound to improve their usability.

One interesting area of future work would be to investigate the use of automatic error correction. Our pre-test showed that we could identify item slips by the time they took. This means that we could add an auto correction feature to the menus so that if a selection took place that the system identified as an item slip then it could be rejected and the adjacent item where the mouse had been for a longer amount of time could be selected. This would avoid errors of this type occurring. We will investigate the use of sound together with automatic error correction in a future experiment.

5. CONCLUSIONS

This work has demonstrated the power of multimodal interactions. By combining the advantages of the visual and auditory senses, problems of interacting with menus can be overcome. The results have shown that integrating earcons into graphical menus can reduce the subjective workload required to use them. It can also increase the number of errors corrected and reduce the time taken to recover from errors. These advantages were gained without making the menus more annoying to use.

Using sound in this way means that users can concentrate on their main task without the interface intruding. The combination of graphics and sound provided a significant qualitative and quantitative improvement in the participants' experience with the menus. Future interface designers can use sound in this way and know that they will be improving the usability of their systems.

6. REFERENCES

All of the references by Brewster along with sounds samples are available from http://www.dcs.gla.ac.uk/~stephen/

Alty, J.L. (1995). Can we use music in human-computer interaction? In Kirby, Dix & Finlay (Eds.), *Proceedings of People and Computers X, HCI'95*, (pp. 409-423), Huddersfield, UK: Cambridge University Press.

Beaudouin-Lafon, M. & Conversy, S. (1996). Auditory illusions for audio feedback. In Tauber (Ed.), *CHI'96 Conference Companion*, (pp. 299-300), Vancouver, Canada: ACM Press, Addison-Wesley.

Blattner, M., Sumikawa, D. & Greenberg, R. (1989). Earcons and icons: Their structure and common design principles. *Human Computer Interaction*, **4**, 11-44.

Brewster, S.A. (1994) *Providing a structured method for integrating non-speech audio into human-computer interfaces*. PhD Thesis, University of York..

Brewster, S.A. (1995). The development of a sonically-enhanced widget set. In Blumenthal, Gornostaev & Unger (Eds.), *Proceedings of EWHCI'95*, (pp. 126-129), Moscow, Russia: International Centre for Scientific and Technical Information.

Brewster, S.A., Wright, P.C., Dix, A.J. & Edwards, A.D.N. (1995). The sonic enhancement of graphical buttons. In Nordby, Helmersen, Gilmore & Arnesen (Eds.), *Proceedings of Interact'95*, (pp. 43-48), Lillehammer, Norway: Chapman & Hall.

Brewster, S.A., Wright, P.C. & Edwards, A.D.N. (1993). An evaluation of earcons for use in auditory human-computer interfaces. In Ashlund, Mullet, Henderson, Hollnagel & White (Eds.), *Proceedings of INTERCHI'93*, (pp. 222-227), Amsterdam: ACM Press, Addison-Wesley.

Brewster, S.A., Wright, P.C. & Edwards, A.D.N. (1994). The design and evaluation of an auditory-enhanced scrollbar. In Adelson, Dumais & Olson (Ed.), *Proceedings of CHI'94*, (pp. 173-179), Boston, Ma.: ACM Press, Addison-Wesley.

Brewster, S.A., Wright, P.C. & Edwards, A.D.N. (1995). Experimentally derived guidelines for the creation of earcons. In Kirby, Dix & Finlay (Eds.), *Adjunct Proceedings of HCI'95*, (pp. 155-159), Huddersfield, UK

Crease, M. (1996) *Making Menus Musical*. Undergraduate Thesis, University of Glasgow.

Dix, A., Finlay, J., Abowd, G. & Beale, R. (1993). *Human-Computer Interaction*. London: Prentice-Hall.

Dix, A.J. & Brewster, S.A. (1994). Causing trouble with buttons. In *Ancillary Proceedings of HCI'94*, Sterling, UK: Cambridge University Press.

Hart, S. & Staveland, L. (1988). Development of NASA-TLX (Task Load Index): Results of empirical and theoretical research., In Hancock & Meshkati, Eds., *Human mental workload*. Amsterdam: North Holland B.V.

Karshmer, A., Brawner, P. & Reiswig, G. (1994). An experimental sound-based hierarchical menu navigation system for visually handicapped use of graphical user interfaces. In Proceedings of *ACM ASSETS'94*, (pp. 123-128), Marina Del Rey, CA, USA: ACM Press.

Lee, W.O. (1992). The effects of skill development and feedback on action slips. In Monk, Diaper & Harrison (Eds.), *Proceedings of HCI'92*, (pp. 73-86), York, UK: Cambridge University Press.

Norman, K. (1991). *The psychology of menu selection*. Norwood, NJ, USA: Ablex Publishing.

Reason, J. (1990). *Human Error*. Cambridge, UK: Cambridge University Press.

Walker, N., Smelcer, J. & Nilsen, E. (1991). Optimizing speed and accuracy of menu selection: A comparison of walking and pull-down menus. *International Journal of Human-Computer Studies*, **35**, 871-890.

63

Collaboration Awareness and its Use to Consolidate a Disperse Group

Tracy Narine, Andrea Leganchuk, Marilyn Mantei, William Buxton

University of Toronto
Dept. of Computer Science
10 Kings College Road
Toronto, Ontario
CANADA M5S 1A4
{tracyn,andrea,mantei,willy}@dgp.utoronto.ca

ABSTRACT Communication often drops dramatically between group members who move a significant distance from their work group despite the provision of mediated communication support. Although the poor quality of the communication exchange via mediated communication is certainly responsible for a significant portion of this drop, lowered suggestion, availability and comfortableness of the communication contact may also cause a drop. With the intent of re-creating these background contact characteristics found in a co-located group, low resolution video pictures of widely dispersed co-workers were exchanged and displayed on each others' workstations via a system called Postcards. The study found that all users (close and far) tended to use the system extensively for coordinating telephone calls and visits. Users also reported knowing more about what is happening at work and knowing more about their co-workers time pressures. They saw no change in the amount of telephone traffic, E-mail or informal meetings that took place. Thus, Postcards provided useful cues for contact coordination but did not affect the frequency of communication. Overall, the results suggest that the continued awareness of both the presence of one's co-workers and a knowledge of their contactability state are a useful part of maintaining distant contacts.

KEYWORDS Postcards, Portholes, Awareness, Video Desktop Conferencing, Media Spaces, Coordination, Collaboration

1. INTRODUCTION

When co-workers are not co-located, project deadlines slip, miscommunication is more common and optional projects never get carried out (Kraut & Egido, 1988). In the modern world, the extensive amount of electronic communication possibilities suggest that distant work collaborations should not be a problem. This is especially true with the widespread use of the cellular phone, electronic mail and video conferencing. Researchers argue that this is because existing media are too limited. Media spaces were developed with the belief that a properly managed video exchange would encourage collaboration (Tang, Isaacs & Rua, 1994). It has been difficult, however, to find much difference in the work performed when telephone is compared to

Human–Computer Interaction: INTERACT'97 S. Howard, J. Hammond & G. Lindgaard (editors)
Published by Chapman & Hall

video in experimental settings (Short, Williams & Christie, 1976; Williams, 1977).

Hollan and Stornetta (1992) argue that communication systems differentiate co-located workers from distant workers because they fail to add the richness of face-to-face communication. They further suggest that communication media can add value to communication only if they move away from attempting to be a poor second to face-to-face encounters. We agree with this approach and argue that one mechanism that could enhance both mediated and face-to-face communication is *collaboration awareness*.

We define collaboration awareness as one case of background awareness (Buxton, 1994; 1995) in which a co-worker is peripherally made aware of the potential for collaboration with a colleague. We use a variation of the Portholes system developed at Rank Xerox EuroPARC (Dourish & Bly, 1992) called *Postcards*. Postcards, like Portholes, takes frequent low resolution video snapshots and broadcasts them via computer network for display on workstations. It is these updated pictures of co-workers which we believe make co-workers collaboratively aware.

2. THE CASE FOR COLLABORATION AWARENESS

In attempting to demonstrate what value collaboration awareness might have for co-workers, we need to explore why communication drops off so dramatically when colleagues are not co-located. Co-located workgroups engage in multiple forms of communication creating a social network (Scott, 1991). Consider a co-located workgroup that uses telephone, voice mail and E-mail extensively. If one or more group members moves to a new location that is non-proximal the communication links between these individuals and the rest of the network soon drop below a typical threshold. This is strange especially in light of Haythornthwaite *et al's* study (1995) which describes a co-located workgroup whose members had weakly overlapping work schedules but yet maintained strong contact through E-mail communications. These individuals were co-located in space but certainly not in time. One argument given for the drop in communication is a failure of the communication media to provide sufficient richness to the contact making contact with co-located colleagues preferable. We do not discount the studies that show that mediated communication is not as rich as face-to-face, but we suggest that the drop in communication may also be due to weak support for the intent to communicate.

We see this intent thwarted by three different mechanisms at play. They are the lack of:

- intent stimulus
- intent opportunity
- intent comfort

Intent stimulus is any event which triggers an intent to communicate. In the design rationale for the Cruiser system, this was a colleague walking down the hall and seeing someone available in their office for conversation (Root, 1988). This form of stimulus is self-reinforcing when workers are co-located, but dwindles when workers are distant because of the need to maintain the exchange of faxes, E-mail or phone calls to continue the stimulus. Once one of the parties involved travels or is extremely busy, the chain is broken and the contact dwindles. Even in the workgroup with widely diverse work times, scheduled meetings where attendance from all workshifts was required, tended to restart the communication exchange.

Intent opportunity is the probability of making a communication contact once the intent to communicate is formulated. In a group with electronic mail support, this opportunity is always there, but its use also depends on the information to be communicated. As an asynchronous medium, it lacks the spontaneity and immediacy of synchronous forms. A common example of thwarted intent opportunity is the frustration of playing telephone tag. In co-located environments, intent opportunity will be much higher because so many more opportunities for communication will exist. Even in the diverse time workgroup, individuals modified their schedules to increase opportunities for contact when needed.

Intent comfort is the sense of the social acceptability of making the communication contact. When people are co-located, they cannot help but have contacts in the hallway or lunchroom, all of which make the contact more natural and less intrusive. When people are not co-located, these easily enacted contacts go away and there is more of a social barrier for making the contact. In addition, there is less shared information to use as conversation starters.

We argue that despite its lack of richness and depth, mediated communication might be used more extensively at a distance if a form of background awareness enhanced the three communication intents. We study Postcards usage to examine this possibility. We have not looked at a widely separate group for our study but at one that is slightly separated. Face-to-face communication in the organization studied requires walking either up or down or opening locked doors. Thus, we are eliminating any mediated characteristics of communication and looking at how Postcards affects the intent to communicate when the face-to-face communication has a large startup cost.

We expect the presence of the video snapshots to cause co-workers to think about others and thus, generate a communication exchange. If this is so, we should find an increase in telephone calls and visits with the installation of the system. We also expect the video snapshots to indicate the availability of the other person. Thus, once the intent to communicate is established, we should see the snapshots being used to ascertain if the communication can take place. We should also see the use of the sensing agent that is built into Postcards, which lets a person know when the person with whom communication is desired returns to their office.

Finally, people can use Postcards to observe their co-workers and learn more about them. If a group is already co-located, this would not seem to be necessary. Thus, if the group is using Postcards in this fashion, it suggests that it is a useful tool for increasing the comfort intent by providing an understanding of one's fellow workers and their work characteristics. There is a possible fourth form of collaboration awareness that we will call intent aggregation which we do not cover in this paper. Monge *et al* (1985) were able to predict optimal meeting times after studying four days of co-workers' organizational proximity. We view this intent as a correlation to intent opportunity.

3. THE INSTALLATION

In Postcards, we extend the concept of Porthole's awareness by characterizing three forms of awareness mechanisms that might be at play. Postcards has been built with additional tools to support these mechanisms. Having a good image of one's co-workers availability at all times provides intent stimulus. Providing a mechanism that maintains the intent to communicate despite a co-worker's temporary absence also supports intent stimulus. Providing contact tools for instantly initiating a contact and images to indicate the availability of the contact support intent opportunity. Intent opportunity is also supported by listing contact information through other media, e.g., E-mail address and fax and telephone numbers. Providing regularly updated images of co-workers supports intent comfort. The features Postcards provides are described in the following paragraphs.

3.1. The Postcards Application

The main window of the Postcards user interface is shown in Figure 1. Each image is a grayscale picture 104 pixels wide and 80 pixels high. We have intentionally kept the pictures small and unobtrusive to avoid invasions of privacy. Smaller pictures also save bandwidth and screen real-estate. We display the title and the time the snapshot was taken.

A user can select which pictures of others to view from any of many Postcards sites. A list indicates which pictures are available and which ones the user is currently receiving. Support for operations such as video or voice contact are provided if Postcards resides in a media space. User Information is provided, like phone number and E-mail address. Users can also turn their own picture taking on or off.

The *Sense* option is used to notify the user when activity is next "sensed" in the selected person's office. This option acts like a secretarial agent who lets the user know that a given person has returned to their office. When activity is noted, a dialog box appears on the user's screen. It will timeout and disappear after 20 seconds in case the user is not around. Sensing continues to function until canceled by the user.

Sensing uses a simple image differencer which compares the amount of pixels that have changed between the previous image and the most recently captured image. If the change is above a set threshold, a sensing alert is sent.

3.2. The Site and Participants of the Study

The site chosen for this study was a high-tech company.

Eight individuals participated in the study. We have divided the study group into *team* and *peripheral* members. The *team* members form a close knit group of six individuals. The *peripheral* members are two individuals in the company who do not carry out the same work as the team but either performed support work for them or served as a liaison between them and the rest of the company.

The team is made up of a senior manager, a project manager and four workers. This team is dispersed within the company having offices on three separate floors. Figure 2 gives an approximate measure of this dispersal. Distances between offices are shown in number of footsteps, doors, locked doors and stairs. As Figure 2 illustrates, there is a mix of open and closed offices within the study group. Only the three managers have offices with doors. To travel between floors, security doors and doors into stairwells must be opened. Only two participants (1 team member, 1 peripheral) are within a line of sight of each other. Given the distributed nature of the group, the cost to initiate any face-to-face communication is high, not unlike that of distant group members.

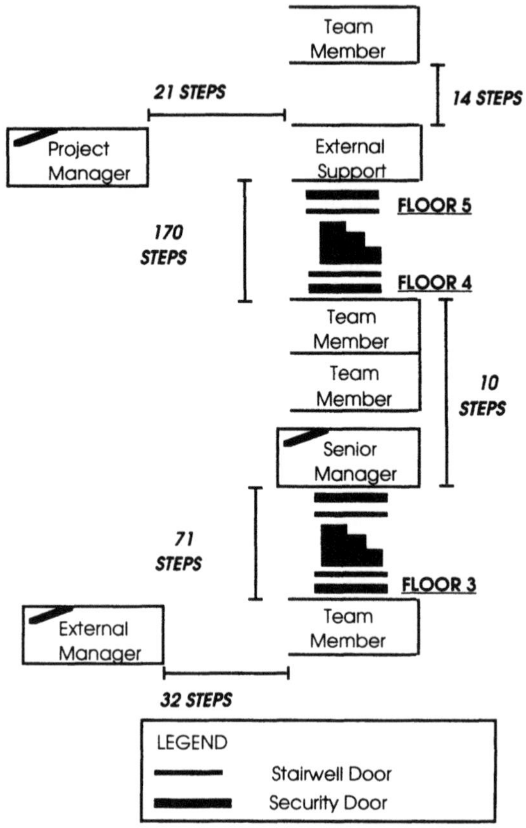

Figure 2: Footsteps between users in study group

Figure 1: Postcards main screen

3.3. Group Organization

The team's senior manager is extremely busy and travels frequently. A queue of people often form at his door when he is in town. When the senior manager is not available, the team's project manager guides the team's work. Three team members report directly to the project manager. The other team member works independently and reports to the senior manager. The team has one regularly scheduled meeting per week. Peripheral members of the study group do not meet regularly with the other members but do have informal spontaneous meetings with one or more of the team's members.

4. MEASURING POSTCARDS USE

Postcards usage data was collected for a total of three weeks. We logged user actions, distributed a questionnaire, conducted informal interviews with subjects and gathered E-mail comments.

The Postcards client logged the total time it was running, all user actions and the duration of any user requests. We logged the number of pictures that the users displayed, an indication of the formation of subgroups of communication. We also measured how many times the participants made use of the Sense and User Information options to provide support of our belief that Postcards provided the initial stimulus for a communication and provided appropriate support for enacting that stimulus.

The questionnaire we distributed to the eight participants in the study focused on their perceptions and memory of what they did when they initiated a communication with a co-worker. It also asked what strategies they used to find a co-worker and what sparked a communication to take place. Answers to these questions would examine the validity of our collaboration awareness claims. On a more practical note, we also wanted to know how users felt about the operation and features of the system and what items they thought would be useful to add to Postcards.

Informal interviews with each of the study's participants provided us with usage anecdotes plus a suggestion list for problems to fix. E-mail comments also gave us insights into problems users encountered with the system

5. RESULTS

The responses to our questionnaire were uniformly similar and provided evidence that all three forms of collaboration awareness were being used to facilitate communication. Participants in the study used Postcards heavily to support finding the window of opportunity for their intent to communicate. They used it less as a reminder to communicate (intent stimulus) but reported that Postcards contributed to increasing their familiarity with co-workers (intent comfort). Anecdotes of more personal expressions via Postcards suggest that users feel quite comfortable with each other, but we have no evidence that Postcards in any way fostered this familiarity.

We asked a series of questions on how group members used Postcards when they wished to contact another group member. Table 1 illustrates that users used Postcards for verifying the availability of a co-worker whenever they telephoned or visited a colleague especially if the person resides on another floor. Six of the eight users always checked Postcards before traveling to another floor and exactly half of the users always check Postcards before phoning others. The two users who never check Postcards when visiting someone on the same floor are close enough to hear and see the people they wish to visit.

Question	Always	Sometimes	Never
Before I do the following, I check Postcards:			
telephone	4	4	0
visit on another floor	6	2	0
make a same floor visit	2	4	2
I wait for a new picture before:			
visiting that individual	1	3	4
telephoning someone	0	2	6
The pictures remind me that I need to talk with the person			
about a work issue	0	3	2
about a non-work isssue	0	0	5

Table 1: Use for making contact with co-workers

Users usually did not wait for a picture to be updated before they telephoned or visited suggesting that they assumed that contact opportunity has remained the same since the last image capture. Our questionnaire also asked if the images prompted a communication to take place. Their responses indicated that this happened occasionally for work related issues but not for social exchanges. Although this suggests that Postcards is not used for intent stimulus, it is unlikely that users can accurately report this phenomena as Nesbitt and Wilson (1977) demonstrate in their classic paper. These answers indicate that users do not perceive that Postcards gives them any intent stimulus.

Intent opportunity was also supported by a question which asked what types of strategies people used when they wanted to make contact with a co-worker. Table 2 lists the responses to this question. The results indicate that all participants used Postcards daily for checking the contactability of others. Since Postcards was not an available strategy until its installation, this 100 percent adoption by all group members indicates the usefulness of this intent opportunity support that Postcards provides. Users did not report using the sensing function for setting up a future contact possibility. This is corroborated by the logged data and individual interviews. We believed that use of the sensing function would be related to Postcards provision of intent stimulus, but the lack of immediacy of a contact is already supported by the voice and E-mail media which are used more than sensing.

Strategies for making Contact:	
use Postcards sensing tool	0.75
periodically check Postcards pictures	3.00
continue to walk by their office	1.13
leave voicemail with a request	2.13
leaving an E-mail with a request	1.88
leaving a note with a request	0.88
Meaning:0=never, 1=few times/month, 2 = few times/week and 3 = daily use.	

Table 2: Strategies employed for finding a co-worker

We asked users to give their perception on changes that Postcards made to their work habits. On average, the results show increased intent opportunity. In particular, users reported less travel between floors because of Postcards and less frustration in finding their co-workers. They saw no increase in their informal meetings, telephone conversations, or E-mail exchanges. Users also indicated that they have a better sense about what is happening with their co-workers and what their co-workers' work pressures are. This was also reported anecdotally when one co-worker indicated that he saw that another colleague was very busy with meetings in his office. These results are shown in Table 3.

Changes in work habits:	
informal meetings	1.88
telephone conversations	2.00
travelling from floor to floor	2.75
writing notes to co-workers	2.13
writing E-mail to co-workers	2.00
frustration with finding co-workers	2.63
knowing what is going on at work	1.50
sense of other's work pressures	1.63
going to lunch with co-workers	2.00
Meaning: 1=more, 2=same, 3=less	

Table 3: Perceived changes in work habits

We also asked how Postcards was used and the results are shown in Table 4. Users readily used the system to find lunch and dinner companions and also to check for an intent opportunity. They also simply used the system to view their co-workers. We interpret this viewing as a form of intent comfort, that is, a building of familiarity with one's co-workers.

How Postcards is used daily:	
seeing who is avail. for lunch	0.88
seeing if a colleage is avail. for a phone call	1.63
seeing what a colleage is doing	0.63
glancing at co-workers	1.50
seeing if a colleage is avail. for a visit	1.75
Meaning: 0 = never use this way, 1 = once per day, 2 = 2-5 times per day, 3 = > 5 times per day	

Table 4: How Postcards is used daily

We also asked users if Postcards had increased their awareness of working in a group. Users responded to a five point Likert scale with 1=strongly agree, 2=agree, 3=neutral, 4=disagree and 5=strongly disagree. The average of the responses was 1.75.

Most of our results are based on user's perceptions of how they use Postcards. The reliability of their responses is corroborated by log data on their use of the sensing and information functions which are quite low, as reported. The other results, however, are suspect until correlated with a behavior measure. The anecdotes about usage and the active user maintenance of the system suggest that Postcards' collaboration awareness is useful to the group. The user's responses to our queries of how it is useful fits our model of providing useful information for the three proposed types of pre-communication planning.

5.1. Postcards Usability

The questionnaire also asked users to evaluate various features of Postcards. About half of the study group found the sound played before picture capture to be disruptive and annoying. Most of the members who did not like the sound recorded their own. One of the participants situated in an open-office environment complained that the sound annoyed surrounding workers. This problem ceased when the user recorded a quieter sound. Some users were uncomfortable with the picture being taken immediately after the warning sound. Consequently, a 2 second delay was added.

An important attribute of the system is the interval between subsequent snapshots. Within the study group, 4 out of 7 members were content with a 3 to 5 minute interval. The other 3 members wanted updates to be every 1 to 2 minutes. No-one requested a longer interval between snapshots.

5.2. New Features

There were several features that the users mentioned that they would like to see in a later release of the software. This included the ability to send out a standard set of messages to other users such as busy, not busy, lunch, in a meeting or on vacation. They were also interested in being able to send electronic Post-its to other users or to attach Post-its to their Postcard display. This would support a simple reminder system.

Another feature that was discussed several times throughout the duration of the experiment is the ability to immediately update any Postcards picture. We felt that supporting this functionality would infringe on the rights of users of the system. Especially in the case when any individual attempts to continuously update another's picture. In the current implementation, there is no method for a user to control accessibility of their picture. This type of functionality would be necessary before supporting instant updates of any individual's picture.

6. ANECDOTAL USAGE

The questionnaire asked users to list any anecdotes about how they or a colleague used the systems in ways that were unique or different than what was expected. We elicited this information because it often suggests design changes and because it provide some insight into how the system is being incorporated into the workplace and worklife.

Three anecdotes are of interest for these purposes. In one case, a team member put a stuffed animal in front of the Postcards camera whenever they was away from their office or desirous of privacy. The use of the animal for both purposes conveyed a confusing message to co-workers. However, its very ambiguity provided a privacy protection that Postcards had taken away. Colleagues could not know if the person was actually absent from their office or intensely working on a project. The stuffed animal message did not thwart any of the intents to contact because it clearly said that contact was not possible but was removed at other times when contact was possible.

Two users were also observed to be making faces (presumably at each other) but humorously shared with the entire work group. This suggests a high degree of comfortableness with other members of the work group since the "faces" remain displayed for four minutes.

If members of the study group forgot to tell visitors about Postcards, visitors were often "spooked" by the sound announcing the picture capture. The sound is supposed to sound like a camera shutter clicking but if heard out of context, it is difficult to guess what it was. This suggests another problem with the design of Postcards. Visitors have not agreed to have their images broadcast to others, yet by visiting a Postcards office, they are suddenly visible to the entire work group. The work group is also visible to them creating the effect of visiting a virtual open office (Li & Mantei, 1992). Fortunately, the choice to limit the quality of the images also limits the invasiveness of visitor image capture.

7. CONCLUSIONS

Overall, we have found that Postcards was being used by the co-located group, but not completely in the ways we anticipated. Its primary usage was that of managing the intent opportunity - seeing if an individual was available for contact. Its secondary usage was that of co-worker observation which can be weakly interpreted as supporting intent comfort. We saw little evidence of intent stimulus. However, the group, although dispersed in the company, was not separated sufficiently so that other forms of intent stimulus were not already available. Indeed, it can be argued that because the group already had a communication network in place with tight links between all participants, that intent stimulus was not necessary and therefore not measurable. A different form of study would need to enacted, one in which communication links had fallen below a given threshold and were rejuvenated by the use of Postcards.

As a collaboration awareness tool, the Postcards usage demonstrates its simple effectivity in a co-located environment for coordinating communication. As such, it meets Hollan's criteria that a CSCW tool, to be used by both distant and local groups, must provide the same added value to both groups. Postcards appears to do this.

8. ACKNOWLEDGMENTS

Many thanks to those who participated in this study, Canada's National Science and Engineering Research Council, Alias|Wavefront Inc. and British Telecomm which helped fund this research. Also, we thank Xerox for providing us with the Portholes code. and the developers that have been associated with this project

9. REFERENCES

Buxton, W. (1995) Integrating the Periphery and Context: A New Taxonomy of Telematics, in *Proc. GI'95 Graphics Interface Conference*, ACM Press, 239-246.

Buxton, W. (1994) Metaphors that Keep us on the Periphery, *Human Computer Interaction*, **9**, 1, 50-52.

Dourish, P. and Bly, S. (1992) Portholes: Supporting Awareness in a Distributed Work Group, in *Proc. CHI'92 Conf. on Human Factors in Computing Systems*, ACM Press, 541-547.

Haythornthwaite, C., Wellman, B., and Mantei, M. (1995) Putting Computerized Communications in Perspective: Media Use and Work Relationships in a Research Group. *Group Decision and Negotiation*, **4**, 3.

Hollan, J. and Stornetta, S. (1992) Beyond Being There, in *Proc. CHI'92 Conf. on Human Factors in Computing Systems*, ACM Press, 119-125.

Kraut, R. and Egido, C. (1988) Patterns of Contact and Communication in Scientific Research Collaboration, in *Proc. CSCW'88 Conf. on Computer-Supported Collaborative Work*, ACM Press, 1-11.

Li, J. and Mantei, M. (1992) Working Together Virtually, in *Proc. GI'92 Graphics Interface Conf.*, 115-122.

Monge, P. R., Rothman, L. W., Eisenberg, E.M., Miller, K. L. and Kirste, K. K. (1985) The Dynamics of Organizational Proximity. *Management Science*, **31**, 1129-1141.

Nisbett, R.E. and Wilson, T. D. (1977) Telling More than We can Know: Verbal Reports on Mental Processes. *Psychological Review*, **84**, 231-259.

Root, R. (1988) Design of a Multi-Media Vehicle for Social Browsing, in *Proc. CSCW'88 Conf. on Computer-Supported Cooperative Work*, ACM Press, 25-38.

Scott, J. (1991) *Social Network Analysis*. London, Sage.

Short, J., Williams, E., and Christie, B. (1976) *The Social Psychology of Telecommunications*. London: John Wiley and Sons.

Tang, J. C., Isaacs, E. A. and Rua, M. (1994) Supporting Distributed Groups with a Montage of Lightweight Interactions, in *Proc. CSCW'94 Conference on Computer-Supported Cooperative Work*, ACM Press, 23-34.

Willliams, E. (1977) Experimental Comparisons of Face-to-Face and Mediated Communication: A Review. *Psychological Bulletin*, **84**, 963-976.

Representing Activity in Collaborative Systems

W. Keith Edwards

Xerox Palo Alto Research Center
3333 Coyote Hill Road
Palo Alto, CA 94304
+1-415-812-4405
kedwards@parc.xerox.com

ABSTRACT. Awareness is an important concept in coordination and collaboration at large. Based on prior research in awareness for collaboration, this work presents a data model for representing information about user activity. Fine-grained activity information can be an important tool for facilitating awareness in workgroups. Further, unlike some forms of information used for awareness, activity data is easily stored and parsed. This representational model is implemented atop the Intermezzo collaboration framework and provides a systematic approach to capturing information about users spread across a network.

KEYWORDS: computer-supported cooperative work, awareness, coordination, Intermezzo.

1. INTRODUCTION AND PRIOR ART

Collaborative software, by definition, involves the interaction of multiple people working together to accomplish some task. In most current collaborative settings, these users are likely to be distributed in space or, in the case of asynchronous systems, even distributed in time. To interact more effectively, users need to be aware of others: their presence, actions, and so forth. The goal of awareness is to promote *coordination* among users: making their interactions more efficient and fluid.

In the "real world," users maintain an awareness of others through a number of sources: peripheral sounds, quick glances, information passed along from others. In an attempt to provide some of the benefits of real-world awareness in the computer domain, a number of computer-augmented approaches have proven useful for promoting awareness information among participants and potential participants in a collaborative endeavor.

Computer-mediated awareness can be roughly categorized into two forms: awareness in *application-dependent* and *application-independent* contexts.

In the application-dependent domain, programs must convey a sense of the actions of users within the application: what objects are they manipulating, and what actions are they taking, in the space of objects and actions provided by the application. Examples of systems that provide this form of awareness include ShrEdit (McGuffin, 1992), and PREP (Neuwirth, 1990). For example, in the ShrEdit shared editor, users are presented with a "Gestalt" view, which shows the (virtual) location of participants in the editing session, and highlights their foci in the document.

In the application-independent domain, awareness systems try to convey a sense of the user's place within the world, instead of the user's place within an application. The goals of this form of awareness closely resemble those of "real world" awareness: provide information about location and activity to support coordination, and be useful in a pan-application context. Most current examples of application-independent awareness are *mediaspace*-like (Bly, 1993) systems in which the computer is used as a facilitating device for propagating video from cameras mounted in the physical work space. We can see and hear the context of users in the physical world, and these real-world cues are translated into the computer-mediated world.

Human–Computer Interaction: INTERACT'97 S. Howard, J. Hammond & G. Lindgaard (editors)
Published by Chapman & Hall

Both the sheer volume and the richness of prior work illustrate the perceived value of augmented awareness by the research community. Perhaps more importantly, the reported experiences of users when participating in such systems is indicative of their value—users *like* working with these awareness systems (Fish, 1990).

This paper presents a model of human awareness based on *activity monitoring* which is useful in either application-dependent or -independent settings. Activity-based awareness can provide a wealth of useful information for coordination. Further, it can deliver information that is complimentary to other approaches. This model has been implemented using the Intermezzo collaboration support environment (Edwards, 1995). We present a systematic format for representing activity, examine the utility of this approach to awareness, and compare it to other awareness schemes.

2. AWARENESS THROUGH ACTIVITY

Gutwin and Greenberg report in (Gutwin, 1996) a set of facets of awareness that should be considered when developing computer-augmented awareness systems:

- *Presence.* Who is participating in the activity?
- *Location.* Where are they working?
- *Activity Level.* How active are they in the workspace?
- *Actions.* What are they doing?
- *Intentions.* What will they do next?
- *Changes.* What changes are they making and where?
- *Objects.* What objects are they using?
- *Extends.* What can they see? How far can they reach?
- *Abilities.* What can they do?
- *Sphere of Influence.* Where can they make changes?
- *Expectations.* What do they need me to do next?

The activity-based awareness approach used by Intermezzo can facilitate a number of these components of awareness. In particular, this approach provides information about presence, location, activity level, actions, changes, and objects.

This work presents a model in which applications cooperate to capture activity information. That information is then represented in a form that makes it readily available to other applications—and to users via applications—that need awareness of others.

3. AWARENESS IN INTERMEZZO

This research takes the approach of promoting awareness by modeling user activities. Activities are represented as a tuple called an *activity record*:

$$A_n = \{S_n, V_n, O_n\}$$

S is the ***Subject***, or the user involved in the activity. *V* is the ***Verb***, or the current task the user is engaged in. *O* is the ***Object***, or the "thing" being operated on. The activity record tuple captures the notion of one user engaged in a single particular task, on an object or set of objects.

This approach has a number of important benefits:

- Information can be collected by a relatively minor set of extensions to applications or toolkits.
- Activity-based awareness satisfies many of the facets of awareness.
- Activity information is easily parsed and stored, and access can be controlled at a fine granularity.

This model has been implemented and explored using the Intermezzo collaboration support environment.

3.1. Implementation

Intermezzo presents to application writers a simple replicated object store. Intermezzo objects, called *resources*,. can be shared, searched, and protected via access control lists. A server process coordinates access to shared resources from client applications. The abstract activity model presented in this paper has been implemented directly atop the Intermezzo object foundation: subject, verb, and objects are represented as types of Intermezzo resources. Each of these types has its own set of *slots* (member data) that maintain information relevant to instances of that type.

As we shall see, the generation of subjects and verbs is quite simple. Reliable and semantically-meaningful generation of objects, on the other hand, requires much support from the runtime environment.

By convention, all Intermezzo-aware applications publish activity records when they run. Thus, applications are responsible for keeping the "picture" of the user up-to-date. Users are known in terms of their activities, and the objects of those activities. In essence, users are modeled in terms of their behaviors.

Consider an example: the user "keith" edits a file using an Intermezzo-aware editor. The editor retrieves the information needed to construct resources representing the user, the application, and the edited file. These resources are combined into an activity record and is published to the Intermezzo runtime service. Once published, the activity record and its components are available to any application that has the proper authorization to examine them.

The global "context" in which collaborative applications are operating comprise a number of resources, which represent a space that may be searched using sophisticated search operations (see). Figure 1 shows an application running on a client machine publishing an activity record on the Intermezzo server.

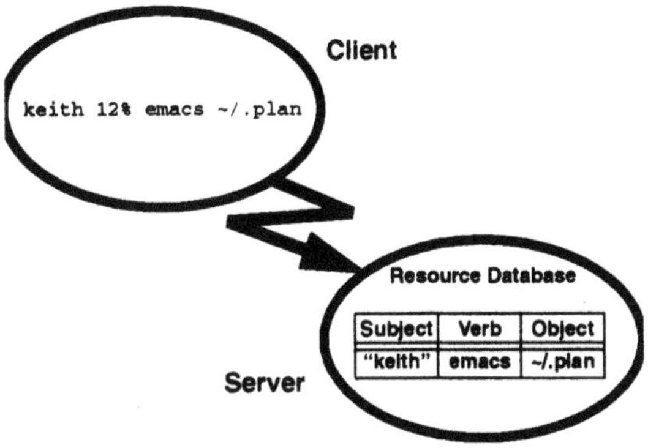

Figure 1: An Application Publishes an Activity Record

3.2. Activity Components in Detail

In large part, the degree to which the Intermezzo model satisfies the facets of awareness mentioned in Section 2 depends on two factors:

- The information associated with each resource.
- The conventions followed by applications and users for publishing activity records.

By pushing a large amount of information about user activity into the environment, we can satisfy a wider range of awareness needs. A richer array of information means that more applications can benefit from the data collected by the awareness system. This section details the information that Intermezzo stores in the global environment as represented by the resources used by the awareness system.

Activity Resources

The Activity resource captures the notion of a single user engaged in a single task on some particular artifact. Activity resources serve as containers for the individual components of an activity: Subjects, Verbs, and Objects. The individual attributes of an Activity resource are links to instances of these resource types, which are described in more detail below.

Subject Resources

Subject resources represent single users of the system. The slots in a subject resource constitute a "single-source" repository of information about a user, and can be used by a variety of applications. Applications are free to access and, given authorization, update slots in subjects.

The slots present in the resource are extensible—applications that need to associate new data with users can add slots as needed. By convention a number of slots are always present—their availability is guaranteed when Intermezzo generates subject resources.

Subject slots include general identifying information such as name, email address, and so on. Subjects also include "back links" to the activities that contain it. From the activity resource, current tasks and objects may be derived. Thus it is possible to generate a complete list of current applications and open files from a given user.

Note that subject resources represents fairly static data. With the exception of the activities slot which, by convention, is updated whenever new activities are created, the data maintained by subjects represent rarely-changed attributes of a given user. For this reason, subject resources are persistent by default (they are long-lived, and survive the termination of any given session or user program). Without persistence it is impossible to refer to a user who is not engaged in any activities.

Other resources in the activity record—verbs and objects—are not persistent by default, since they represent transient states. Human beings, in contrast, are by-and-large long-lived entities, at least in the time span represented by computer applications.

Verb Resources

Verbs represent single tasks. A user engaged in multiple tasks will have multiple activity records, each containing a unique verb representing the task. Multiple verbs will be instantiated if the user is running multiple instances of the same task.

Verbs capture information associated with a single active process in the system. Like subjects, the slots associated with verbs can be extended by applications. A set of common slots are agreed upon by convention and implemented by Intermezzo. Common slots include the application name, start time, idle time, location (hostname), and a back link to the activity resource containing the verb.

Some of this information is static and can be determined at application start-up time (application name, start time, location). Other information, namely idle time, requires application intervention to maintain.

Object Resources

Objects represent the focus of a task: the "thing" on which the task is operating. Objects can represent an essentially infinite set of entities on which applications can operate. Common types of objects include files, calendars, database selections, and so forth.

Because of the need for flexibility in representation, objects are more complex than either subjects or verbs For any given task, Intermezzo must be able to generate an object instance that uniquely identifies the thing on which the task is operating, no matter what the type of that thing may be.

We require objects to have the property that there is a one-to-one mapping between an instance of an object resource and the physical entity to which it refers. That is, given an object, one can determine the physical thing it is modeling; and given any physical artifact, it is possible to generate a unique object for it.

The Intermezzo toolkit provides support for objects in the form of a framework for generation, comparison, and retrieval of objects. Individual applications must implement code to generate unique objects for the particular data types on which they operate. Since the object of a given application is domain-dependent, Intermezzo cannot know *generally* how to interpret a given artifact, or even how to generate a one-to-one-mapping to an object instance.

Intermezzo does provide support for generating objects for the most common artifact type: files. The system can uniquely generate objects for any file anywhere in the network. Note, however, that because of application requirements, even the interpretation of files varies from application to application. Developers are free to interpose their own interpretations into the object generation sub system. The section "Granularity and Hierarchy" has more information on defining objects.

Many of the slots in objects are domain-dependent, based on the type of the object. Hence conventions about the definition of these slots are left to the applications that use them. The generic framework established by Intermezzo does enforce a set of slots that are present in all objects and are used for generation and comparison.

The "namespace" of an object defines a particular type of object. For example, files, calendars, and database selections are all represented by different namespaces. Within a given namespace, the name slot uniquely identifies the object as distinct from "siblings" that share its namespace (that is, they are different instances of things with the same type).

The common slots in the generic object framework are represented in Table 1 below.

Attribute	Description
Namespace	The type of the object, represented as a string.
Name	A domain-dependent identifier for the object, valid within its given namespace.
Printable Name	A human-readable string which can be used to identify the object.
Activities	Back-links to the activities containing this object resource.

Table 1: Object Resource Attributes

Comparison of object resources requires comparison of both the namespace and the name. The namespace ensures that no "apples and oranges" comparisons are performed (files and calendars for example); names ensure distinction within a particular type of object ("file1" and "file2" for example).

4. GRANULARITY AND HIERARCHY

One consideration when generating a resource that represents the focus of a task is that applications differ in what aspect of that focus is relevant. For example, consider a user editing a file with a drawing tool. Applications may consider any of a number of characteristics of the object (the file) salient. A project manager tool may need to track when changes are made to any files within a certain directory. Tools specifically built for collaboration may have an even finer-grained focus: a collaborative drawing tool may consider the particular figure within the file currently being manipulated a salient feature of awareness.

Because of the fact that different applications may consider any number of attributes of an artifact salient, simply representing objects as single entities is insufficient. We need a scheme that represents the artifact at a number of granularities: from the machine the artifact resides on, to any containers the artifact may be embedded in (directories in the case of files), to individual components of the artifact that represent the user's current focus (such as figures in a drawing). Objects are represented as hierarchies, with each layer in the hierarchy providing a *view* of the object at a given granularity. As we descend the hierarchy, features hidden in the "large-scale" view become apparent.

In many cases, layers in the hierarchy will be domain-independent. For example, many applications manipulate files. An infrastructure that can generate objects representing the host the file resides on, and the directory of the file, as well as the file itself, will be generally useful to a number of applications.

Other layers will be domain-dependent. Practically anything below the granularity of "file" will only be understood by applications that have the domain knowledge to interpret the object. For example, the notion of figures in a drawing only has meaning to drawing applications; other tools do not have the domain knowledge or infrastructure to interpret such constructs.

The Intermezzo model represents objects as a list of resources that model the particular artifact at a range of granularities. The toolkit supports several domain-independent layers, namely files, directories, and hosts. Applications are responsible for supporting new layers of the artifact hierarchy that represent domain-dependent views of the artifact—the toolkit *cannot* provide this support, since it is domain-dependent.

Table 2 shows an example of an object list representing the hierarchy used to model a particular artifact, in this case a figure in a drawing. The first

Artifact	Description	Domain
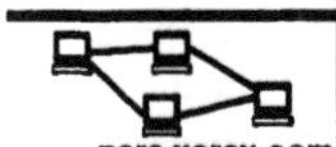	Network domain of host.	Environment
	Host fileserver	Environment
	Directory path.	Environment
	Document.	Environment
	Figure within file.	Application

Table 2: Example of Object Hierarchy

column denotes the artifact, viewed at a particular granularity. The second column provides a description of the artifact viewed at this granularity. The third column represents whether the view is domain-dependent or domain-independent. The example shown here uses a number of layers to represent the artifact: the network domain containing the host the artifact resides on, the host itself, the components of the path leading to the file containing the figure, the document containing the figure, and the figure itself.

Note that there are any number of possible additional layers in this hierarchy. Coarser-grained interpretations are possible, as are domain-specific intermediary layers representing constructs such workgroups and projects.

The hierarchical representation of artifacts provides information needed by applications to interpret user activity. Applications can decide at what granularity a given artifact is relevant to them, and interpret the artifact accordingly.

5. EVALUATION

5.1. Comparison with the "Real World"

Comparing the activity-based approach to awareness with the non-machine augmented, "everyday" awareness of others that we commonly experience is instructive, because the comparison offers a common point of reference, and can help identify deficiencies in the activity-based approach.

The most problematic limitation with the activity-based approach is that information is not "free for the taking." In the real world, users simply look around to gather a rich array of information about user activities, locations, and so forth. Humans are adept at determining interruptibility, and other socially-influenced aspects of awareness. As Rouncefield, *et al.*, (Rouncefield, 1994) state, the "ecology of the office provides, to those who know it, the 'at-a-glance' availability of what people are doing, what state they are at, how quickly they are getting the work done, and so on."

In comparison, the activity-based approach requires extensive application cooperation to function effectively. In fact, awareness is one of those situations in which nearly total "buy-in" is required for maximum utility. Similar effects are seen in group calendar tools, where virtually everyone in a work group must use the system without fail for it to function at all (Grudin, 1988). With the Intermezzo approach, applications must cooperate with the runtime system to facilitate awareness.

This requirement for application cooperation is not present in some other computer-based awareness systems, notably mediaspaces, where there is only one stand-alone application that must be run to enable awareness. Users do not have to change their behavior to take part in the system, since mediaspaces essentially "transplant" the remote physical space, along with its associated cues, to the user.

A second important limitation is that some user states are not well-captured by activity. For example, user moods cannot be modeled by this approach. Physical location must be inferred from where applications are being run. Systems that are more like mediaspaces may be able to capture some of these complex user states, although even they still have limitations, due to artifacts in the quality of video and audio for example.

A final limitation is that the computer must still decide how to present and use awareness information once it has been collected. In the real world, collection and presentation of awareness information are synonymous, at least when performed first-hand: a user sees a coworker and is instantly aware of a wealth of information. The Intermezzo model only specifies a structure for the representation of awareness data. It does not specify how this information will be presented, or even when or if it will be presented. Again, applications must make intelligent decisions about the presentation of awareness for the information to be usable at all.

5.2. Comparison with Other Computer-Based Approaches

Comparison with other computer-mediated awareness systems is also useful. While the activity-based approach has certain limitations and benefits with respect to "real world" awareness, we shall see that it has a different set of strengths and weaknesses relative to other computer-based schemes.

Two common approaches to computer-supported awareness have been investigated. The first and most common is awareness through computer-mediated audio and video. The second is the use of active badges. Each approach has its own strengths and weaknesses relative to the activity-based scheme, and yet these approaches can be integrated together to complement one another.

Video monitoring systems, generally characterized as mediaspaces, support awareness of the locations and actions of others through a near-constant video presence (Cavecat (Mantei,1991), and so on). Some go beyond the simple connected-office approach to provide a locality-based metaphor for interaction (Cruiser (Root, 1988), Jupiter (Curtis, 1993)). In these systems, awareness is regulated and filtered by co-presence in a virtual space.

Video-based systems, rather obviously, provide high-quality indications of events and situations in the physical world: physical location, physical tasks, facial expressions, and so forth. Such systems, however, provide few if any cues about computer-based tasks and activities. Information about the virtual world can only be inferred from physical side effects.

Another difference is that the awareness information received from a video monitoring system is readily available to humans, but difficult to mechanically parse and store. Activity-based approaches have an opposite set of trade-offs. They provide information that is easily machine-representable, but applications must bear the burden of parsing and presenting the data to users.

The second common computer-based approach to awareness is the use of active badges (Want, 1992). Active badges are devices worn by users which update a global location database as the position of the wearer changes. Rooms in the work area must be equipped with sensor devices to receive the data transmitted by the badges.

Information about physical location and co-presence is the only *direct* information provided by active badges. Other types of awareness information must be inferred from location. For example, the location of a coworker in a boss's office may be an indication of interruptibility.

An advantage of active badge systems over video monitoring is that the information is available in a convenient machine-parsable format.

5.3. Summary of Comparisons

A summary of the three computer-based awareness approaches, video monitoring, active badges, and activity-based, as well as "real world" awareness, is presented in Table 3 below. The last row in the table

	Activity Based	**Active Badges**	**Video Monitor**	**"Real World"**
Location	◍	●	●	●
Tasks	●	○	◍	●
Interrupts	◍	○	◍	●
Co-pres	◍	●	●	●
Parsable?	●	●	○	○

● = Supported

○ = Not Supported

◍ = Partially Supported

Table 3: Comparison of Awareness Approaches

indicates how amenable the approach is to automated machine-parsing. Some approaches generate data that is more easily represented and stored by computer; the aspect of parsability will be discussed more fully in the next section.

Together, the strengths and weaknesses of the activity-based approach along with those of other approaches suggest that an augmentation may be effective—by combining multiple approaches better "coverage" and more robust solutions may be obtained. The activity approach supports integration through the use of "controller" applications that directly modify the resource database whenever some condition occurs. In essence, controllers act as proxies on behalf of non-Intermezzo-aware applications. For example, an "active badge controller" can update the location slots of subject resources with physical position information.

6. NOTES ON AWARENESS

As we have seen, the activity-based approach to awareness is capable of bringing a wealth of information into the application domain so that it can be presented to users. There are other interesting repercussions implicit in the activity-based approach that may not be immediately obvious however. This section investigates these.

6.1. Input to Applications, Not Just Users

In most awareness systems to-date, awareness data has *typically* been used directly by users. For example, in most mediaspaces, activity is not captured in a machine-readable form. Rather, it is displayed as video and left for humans to interpret. The salient components of awareness are not directly represented in any computer-based form; they must be extracted by users from the video.

A number of "activity monitor" applications have been built that are similar in principle to the awareness approach used by Intermezzo (Manandhar, 1991, and Newman, 1991), but still these systems generate data for direct human consumption only. Typically the activity data is sent to a client application which presents it in a window on the user's desktop.

In contrast, one of the goals of the activity-based approach used by Intermezzo is to make it possible for applications to behave intelligently in the presence of information about user activity. That is, just as users are aware of the presence and activity of other humans, so can applications be made aware of their users.

As an example, consider a computer-based teleconferencing application that could be made aware when one of its users is on the phone. The application could mute the audio from the conference, and notify other participants that the user is engaged in another task that demands auditory attention.

As another example, consider a collaborative editing system in which a user invites another to join the session. The editing tool could be written to analyze the potential collaborator's location and tasks in an effort to determine if the recipient should be disturbed, or if the request for collaboration should be delayed.

Further, the collaborative toolkit itself can use awareness information to enhance its functionality. Intermezzo uses awareness data as an input to regulate its policy (Edwards, 1996), access control, and session management mechanisms (Edwards, 1994).

6.2. Policy and Access Control is Essential

One obvious concern about bringing awareness into the environment is that the availability of such information is potentially a huge privacy violation. Capturing and potentially storing detailed information about the whereabouts and activities of users requires provisions for strong security guarantees about access to this information.

Acknowledgment of the security risks inherent in awareness systems has been noted many times, particularly in the case of mediaspace systems (Smith, 1995). In almost all mediaspace studies, there are a number of potential users who refuse to use the system even though (a) there is strong physical security (users can simply cover the camera), and (b) storage and machine processing of mediaspace data is not feasible with current technology.

Certainly the security concerns present in mediaspace systems are present in an activity-based awareness system. If anything, the concerns are greater since a machine-parsable representation of the information is readily available. Thus, security and access control schemes are of paramount importance in a coordination support system that makes awareness data available to users and applications. Intermezzo uses a novel approach in which the awareness system itself is used to regulate access control to awareness data objects. This scheme is discussed in detail in (Edwards, 1995).

6.3. Persistence Adds Value

A third point to make about activity-based modeling is that persistence can significantly increase the power of the system. The activity-based approach is particularly useful for capturing the real-time aspects of awareness: the instantaneous condition of the collaborative world and the users in it. The ability to support some persistent data (subjects, for example) is quite useful, and persistence has other uses that have not been fully explored by this research. Two obvious uses are the collection of user statistics, and a form of organizational memory "on the cheap" (by remembering who within an organization has written to a document, for example).

7. SUMMARY

This paper has presented a general model for machine-generated representations of information useful for awareness. This model uses logging information about user activities, and has a number of interesting properties relative to other awareness schemes.

One of the strengths of the activity-based approach is that it makes awareness information available in a format that is easily machine-parsable and -storable, unlike some other media, such as video. This trait makes activity-based awareness useful as input to applications, in addition to as input to users, which has been the traditional use of machine-augmented awareness.

We have presented an implementation model that can be used to capture, store, and disseminate awareness information. This model captures activity as a set of tuples representing users, their actions, and the objects of those actions. The object framework, in particular, is extremely flexible and can represent a wide array of data types useful to either application-dependent or -independent awareness.

Finally, we have compared the activity-based approach to a number of other schemes, including the awareness information we are presented with in the physical world. The information available in the activity-based model can be leveraged by other approaches to awareness to "fill in the gaps" in the information presented to users and applications.

REFERENCES

Bly, S.A., Harrison, S.R., and Irwin, S. (1993). "Media Spaces: Bringing People Together in a Video, Audio, and Computing Environment." *Communications of the ACM*, 36: 1.

Curtis, P., Dixon, M. Frederick, R., and Nichols, D. (1995). "The Jupiter Audio/Video Architecture: Secure Multimedia in Network Places." *Proc., Third International Multimedia Conference*, ACM.

Edwards, W.K. (1994). "Session Management in Collaborative Applications." *Proc., Conference on Computer-Supported Cooperative Work (CWCW'94)* , ACM.

Edwards, W.K. (1995). *Coordination Infrastructure in Collaborative Systems*. Ph.D. Dissertation, Georgia Institute of Technology.

Edwards W.K. (1996). "Policies and Roles in Collaborative Applications." *Proc. Conference on Computer-Supported Cooperative Work (CSCW'96)*, ACM..

Fish R.S., Kraut, R.E., Chalfonte, B.L. (1990). "The VideoWindow System in Informal Communications." *Proc. Conference on Computer-Supported Cooperative Work (CSCW'90)*, ACM.

Grudin, J. (1988). "Why CSCW Applications Fail: Problems in the Design and Evaluation of Organizational Interfaces." *Proc., Conference on Computer-Supported Cooperative Work (CSCW'88)*, ACM.

Gutwin, C., and Greenberg, S. (1996). "Workspace Awareness for Groupware," *Proc., Conference on Computer-Human Interaction (CHI'96)*, ACM.

Manandhar, S. (1991). "Activity Server: You Can Run But You Can't Hide." *Proc., USENIX Conference*, USENIX Association.

Mantei, M.M, Baecker, R.M., Sellen, A.J., Buxton, W.A.S., Milligan, T., Wellman, B. (1991) "Experiences in the Use of a Media Space." *Proc., Conf. on Computer-Human Interaction (CHI'91)*, ACM.

McGuffin L, Olson, G. (1992). "ShrEdit: A Shared Electronic Workspace," CSMIL Technical Report, Cog. Sci. and Machine Intelligence Lab., U. of Michigan.

Newman, W., Eldridge, M., Lamming, M. (1991). "Pepsys: Generating Autobiographies by Automatic Tracking," *Proc. European Conference on Computer-Supported Cooperative Work (ECSCW)*.

Neuwirth, C. M., Kaufer, D. S., Chandhok, R., and Morris, J. (1990). "Issues in the Design of Computer Support for Co-authoring and Commenting." *Proc., Conference on Computer-Supported Cooperative Work (CSCW'90)*, ACM.

Root, R.W. (1988). "Design of a Multi-Media Vehicle for Social Browsing," *Proc., Conference on Computer-Supported Cooperative Work (CSCW'88)*, ACM.

Rouncefield, M, Hughes, J.A., Rodden, T., and Viller, S. (1994). "Working with Constant Interruption: CSCW and the Small Office." *Proc. Conference on Computer Supported Cooperative Work (CSCW'94)*, ACM.

Smith, I., and Hudson, S. (1995). "Applying Cryptographic Techniques to Problems in Media Space Security." In *Proc., Conference on Organizational Computing Systems (COOCS'95)*, ACM.

Want, R., Hopper, A., Falcao, V., and Gibbons, J. (1992). "The Active Badge Location System." *ACM Transactions on Information Systems*, 10:1, Jan. 1992.

What Happened to our Document in the Shared Workspace? The Need for Groupware Conventions

Gloria Mark and Wolfgang Prinz

GMD-FIT, German National Research Center for Information Technology
Schloß Birlinghoven
53754 Sankt Augustin, Germany
E-mail: {Gloria.Mark, Wolfgang.Prinz}@gmd.de

ABSTRACT Conventions for conducting work with groupware are essential. They include rules for how the groupware functionality should be used for communication about work, for how data should be processed, and for decision-making. Based on user experiences with POLITeam, a large groupware system implemented in a German ministry, we report how conventions are difficult to establish and to follow. We illustrate how conventions are necessary in practice, through a cooperative task using a shared workspace. Two solutions are presented to aid users in following conventions.

KEYWORDS Groupware, CSCW, conventions, awareness, shared workspace

1 INTRODUCTION

A shared workspace in a groupware system has no idea about managerial work. For that matter, it has no idea about secretarial work. Nor does it have any idea about how people should work on shared documents: how the files should be edited, where the documents should be stored, or which data files should be retained. Moreover, a groupware system cannot predict the actions that users take, nor the effects that they will have on others using the system. A groupware system is like a Tabula Rasa; the system provides the functionality, and the users define their procedures with it. However, the users must coordinate their procedures so that the work can be conducted smoothly.

Although user studies in CSCW have addressed the problem of how groups coordinate their work (e.g. Hughes et al., 1992; Posner and Baecker, 1992) only a few studies have addressed how groupware features can aid coordination. Some examples include Quilt, which offers users a choice of styles to coordinate editing (Leland, et al., 1988). In the Colab project, the need for a shared reference was realized as an important design consideration (Tatar et al., 1991). PREP is a collaborative editor which employs role assignment and explicit annotation to aid coordination (Neuwirth et al., 1990). However, groupware functionality is becoming increasingly complex, and as users in PoliTeam, a large groupware project, pointed out, coordination problems exist not only with their work, but also in coordinating the use of the functionality itself. In this paper we will discuss how the user requirements have led us to develop a technical solution for how group conventions can be supported, and which allows personal conventions for some work.

1.1 The POLITeam project

The goal of the POLITeam groupware system is to build a "telecooperation bridge" between Bonn and the new German capital of Berlin. Federal agencies will relocate over time, resulting in a large division of labor

Human–Computer Interaction: INTERACT'97 S. Howard, J. Hammond & G. Lindgaard (editors)
Published by Chapman & Hall ©IFIP 1997

in departments spread between the old and new capitals. The main function of the POLITeam system is to supplement paper work processes with electronic work processes in a government ministry. To accomplish this, POLITeam offers a shared workspace and electronic circulation folders (Prinz and Kolvenbach, 1996). An already existing groupware system (LinkWorks) was chosen and adapted to specific user and situation requirements. For further information, see Klöckner et al. (1995).

Our strategy was to implement prototypes in three representative areas of the government, which enables us to understand how users are adapting, and to correct mistakes early (Orlikowski, 1992). Further, an evolutionary cycling approach was used in the design, allowing modifications to be made over time and which designers and users reported as beneficial (Mambrey et. al, 1996). The project began in May 1994, and the system has been installed since January, 1995. A new version of the system was installed in February, 1996.

The focus of obtaining our user requirements was done with users at the Federal Ministry of Family Affairs, Senior Citizens, Women, and Youth, located in Bonn. In the department where the system is installed, we find varied employee roles: 1 unit leader, 6 ministry employees (responsible for specific content areas of the ministry), and 3 typists in their own service unit. The employees collaborate using the shared workspace and email. Their activities include services such as responding to citizens' requests, doing tasks for the Minister, and collaborative speechwriting. In addition, the manager is responsible for activities such as information dissemination and decision-making.

2 CONVENTION REQUIREMENTS

2.1 Method

The requirements for user conventions emerged over the course of several workshops. In the most recent workshop, held in June, 1996, the new system version was discussed. The unit leader spoke as representative of the users and stated that the number one user requirement at this time was the need to establish conventions among the users. An in-depth discussion ensued, where all of the users named conventions necessary for their system use, and reasons for them. The POLITeam design team, along with the users, then discussed the points one by one trying to find solutions to enable the users to set conventions. We did not conduct a formal analysis of this conversation, since we felt that the users presented a straightforward request, and had spent a long time themselves considering how conventions could be set. We attribute this straightforward request to the regular relations established between the users and design team via direct designer-user interaction, and user advocates, which resulted in a long list of other user requirements which were introduced (Mambrey et al., 1996). The earlier discussions of conventions in previous workshops could also have set precedents for the topic.

2.2 What are conventions?

We define conventions as rules established in the group, common to all members, for carrying out the following transactions via a groupware system, in particular POLITeam: *communication transactions*, e.g. who to inform about document changes; *data processing transactions*, e.g. should a document be created and distributed as a share or as a copy; and *decision-making transactions*, e.g. who is responsible for a document, or for maintaining the order of a workspace?

2.3 Conventions in a shared workspace

In this section we illustrate how the use of shared workspaces raised the need for the agreement on and support of conventions. With POLITeam, shared folders and email support communication and cooperation. The shared workspace supports a document production task between two units in the ministry: the writing office and a ministry unit (referred to as Unit 57, not its real name). The task of the writing office is to type a draft provided by members of Unit 57.

The shared workspace has two purposes: First, it provides shared access to documents for the writing office and the Unit 57 members for the following: to exchange a text initially produced by the writing office, and to have access to a text for the production of a clear copy that has been produced or that will be modified later by a Unit 57 member. Second, it provides access to all documents that have been produced within the unit to the unit leader.

In the case when the electronic version of the document is modified and then forwarded on paper for further processing, the writing office must incorporate the annotated paper changes into the electronic version. Therefore, the writing office requires retaining access to the latest electronic version of the document.

The solution in practice is as follows. Documents are exchanged by all using shared workspaces. For each member of Unit 57 a workspace exists which is shared between this member and members of the writing office. All these workspaces are contained in another folder, called the unit-folder. This allows the writing office to organize documents according to the units and members of a unit. Whenever a document is produced by the writing office, this document is placed in the appropriate unit/person workspace and the person is informed about the new document by an event notification. This convention for how the shared workspaces are organized is logical for the writing office members' work process. It is determined by the name of the user (Unit 57 member) for whom it was typed and the date of production. We refer to this as the *order* view. The sorting criteria for the documents in a workspace is the date when the document was typed.

This solution seemed appropriate for the users initially. But after some time of practical experience, the following problem occurred. The Unit 57 members wanted to organize their documents according to their work processes, i.e. they wanted to collect documents produced by the writing office in a task or process-specific folder, rather than according to unit members. Their sorting criteria for documents in a workspace depends not on the date of production, but rather on the content of a document, e.g. a speech on a transit problem, or on an economic issue. We refer to this as the *work-process* view. With the current configuration only one view, the order view, is supported.

Thus, we found that users prefer to structure their information using their own pattern. We also found that the different views of the users corresponded to different level structures: the typists prefer to use a relatively flat information structure, and for some of the unit leaders, they prefer a deep multi-level structure. The problem for the group arises when the different users collaborate in a shared workspace which requires one common information structure for the groups' documents. Some users often could not find documents among the vast array of information in the shared workspace because the system supported the order view, which was not their view.

A second example of a convention is one that was set via a workshop: work must occur in the shared folder, i.e. a document must not be removed. However, in practice, the Unit 57 member would drag the document out of the folder shared with the writing office into their task-specific folder. After that operation, the writing office no longer had access to the electronic document, which was crucial for changes. Thus, the Unit 57 member violated the conventions that were established for the use of the shared folder. Even documents which are produced only by the Unit 57 members must be stored in the folders shared with the writing office, to provide an electronic version for the clear copy production.

2.4 The user requirements

The above scenario illustrated how establishing common views of the information, and how agreements about working on shared documents are necessary conventions in a shared workspace. Additionally other conventions that users named in the workshop were:

- *Naming conventions for documents.* Different users prefer to store and access documents using different naming conventions. The typists preferred naming a document by the creator (or owner) whereas the ministry employees preferred naming documents according to content and semantics.
- *Storing old and current documents.* The users' one file storage cabinet has become too huge to manage and since more information can be stored electronically, "old" and "new" documents need to be defined.
- Conventions regarding *shared tasks.* These include what changes to accept in a document; who should make the changes; a model for access rights for different classes of documents; different "closets" (based on an office metaphor, used in POLITeam): working on a document as a share, vs. a copy; editing text; ownership of documents; and conventions for producing new documents.
- Conventions for determining *borders between public and private work,* in a shared workspace. These also include access rights and document storage.
- *Substitution rules* for when a workspace member is absent. In the paper world, one can simply lock drawers with personal items, but with groupware, it is not so straightforward, e.g. reading another person's email.

Conceptual vs. physical owner of a document. One person may be the coordinator of the document, yet another person may have created the document.

Although we present a long list of user requirements, in this paper we focus on presenting general solutions and concepts for the provision of conventions and views in a shared workspace environment.

3 CONVENTIONS IN THE COURSE OF GROUP DEVELOPMENT

3.1 The stages of group development

To help us design solutions for supporting groupware conventions, we can draw upon behavioral studies to see how groups establish common routines. Although group members bring their own prior experience into a group, a new group starts out without its own culture. Only as members begin to interact does the group develop common goals, means, working procedures, and rules of interaction (Schein, 1985). This process has been modeled extensively as a series of stages that a group evolves through until such common ground is reached (e.g. Bales, 1950; Bion, 1961; Bennis and Shepard, 1956). Members gather information about the group and use a reciprocal process of accommodation of a group toward the individual, while the individuals attempt to get the group to conform to their style (Moreland and Levine, 1989). This accommodation process continues as the group gradually establishes common procedures and goals.

3.2 The User Group's Evolution with POLITeam

We have observed that since the introduction of the POLITeam system, our user work group has also evolved in its use of the system. We can also characterize the development of our user work group, with respect to its system use, in terms of rough stages. What we have identified over time are changes in attitudes and use of the system. It is important to note that the time span of stages can only be roughly determined, since we could only interview users and hold workshops at specific time points. We believe that although there was probably concurrence with some events, most likely the stages are sequential, i.e. users could not have asked for group conventions without first learning system basics (Table 1).

With respect to the user group in Table 1, we found two interesting phenomena concerning conventions. First, it took about six months of regular use with the system for the users to discover that they needed conventions for using the system (Stage II in Table 1). Initially, these first conventions that users recognized concerned individual information structuring. It is our view that the users first needed to gain familiarity with the system before it became clear to them that conventions were needed and this required time. When the users became more experienced with the possibilities of the system, they developed ideas for a

Stage	Time Span	Characteristics of stage: major problems/events
I. Learning basic functionality; mostly single-user idea of system	1st 6 months after system introduced	Problems with windows, hardware, basic computer skills: • struggling with text processing • transferring individual work practices to system • adapting group functionality to meet the group's needs
II. Discovering alternatives for structuring information	between 6 - 9 months	Developed own style for structuring information: • structuring information according to own work process • collecting information (finding semantic connections)
III. Developing awareness of group use of system	1 ½ years after system introduction	Began to develop awareness of cooperative work with the system • discussed conventions for group use in workshop • discussed consequences of other members' actions
IV. Mature group working with the system	?	We would expect the following: • new, unanticipated use of tools • conventions would be learned • implicit conventions would be developed

Table 1. Stages of user group development with POLITeam

better task and process-oriented support. This resulted in a task-oriented organization and structuring scheme for some users, which conflicts with an initial text-processing oriented configuration of the system.

It also took time and experience for the users to realize that they needed conventions in order to interact as a *group* with the system (Stage III). User advocates of POLITeam made regular site visits to the users' worksites and their support included not only training in system use but also with conventions, such as how the system could support their work practices (Mambrey et. al, 1996). However, it was only with regular use of the system with their unique tasks that made it clear to the users (and to us) that it is not always possible to predict in advance what conventions a group needs in order to use a system like POLITeam. This suggests to us that the process of establishing conventions is on-going and whatever feedback the system can provide about others' activities could benefit this process.

4 ESTABLISHING CONVENTIONS

4.1 The difficulty of setting conventions

In this section, we discuss why conventions might be difficult to establish with a groupware system, based on our observations during site visits, reports from the user advocates, and conversations with the users during workshops.

1. *Restricted feedback and communication makes it difficult to establish conventions.* In a face to face group, communication, visual information, and feedback sources are rich, which facilitates the negotiation and agreement of work routines. In contrast, working in distributed locations with groupware restricts social and visual information. In a distributed group, the restricted communication makes it not only more difficult to explicitly set conventions, but also more difficult for people to understand them.

2. *The groupware environment lacks cues for conventions.* Cues such as type of dress, posture, and tone of speaking in a face-to-face meeting immediately provide information on whether the group is formal or informal, what type of language is appropriate, and whether the group might be following strict rules of procedure or not. A groupware environment lacks such cues, making it difficult for people to know what is appropriate behavior to use with the system.

3. *Individuals may be reluctant to give up their individual conventions.* Initially POLITeam users spent a great deal of effort in developing their own styles for sorting information (see Table 1). It may be difficult to give up a style that is meaningful and possibly logical for one's own task. Even in the paper world, people are often reluctant to give up personal conventions.

4. *Some conventions with groupware are totally new for the group.* With some conventions, users had no analogy from the paper world to apply, such as not knowing when they should distribute documents as 'shares' (a Linkworks feature) or as copies, since the share facility has no counterpart in the paper world. Another example is that a transcriber of a document becomes the owner in a groupware system, and must learn to change the access rights for the actual owner.

5. *Unfamiliarity with the system.* As outlined in Table 1, users may be unfamiliar with the system, making it difficult for them to understand what conventions might be necessary. System support may also focus too much on teaching functionality, and not enough on coordinating use of the functionality.

4.2 Means for Supporting Conventions

Derived from these observations, we consider now methods for how conventions can be established.

In POLITeam, workshops were conducted to set conventions using user advocates as mediators (Mambrey, 1996). These workshops covered conventions for maintaining public information documents, for document naming conventions, and general concerns. Whereas communication is generally restricted during groupware use, a workshop offers the advantage of face-to-face communication. Users can freely discuss conventions that are needed, along with their goals and purposes. Whereas a groupware environment lacks cues for appropriate behavior, especially for new users, a workshop can help users orient themselves to the groupware context. Setting conventions via workshops can help to overcome the first two difficulties mentioned in section 4.1.

5 TECHNOLOGICAL SUPPORT

Technological support can be applied to target the remaining difficulties identified in 4.1. It can facilitate convention use in three ways. First, support can be given in the form of awareness. Second, for many routines, default conventions can be implemented into the system. And third, support can enable users to retain individual conventions.

5.1 Awareness and convention use

A groupware system, such as a shared workspace, is a social environment. Here, people's actions are not independent. For example, one may make changes to a shared document, which are visible to all others. Not only do people's actions interact with one another, but one's actions can have adverse consequences for others. If a document is removed from a shared workspace, then others may not find it. If someone rearranges files within a folder, creating subdirectories, then others will not readily find them. If someone renames a document, then another user will have serious difficulties.

Many groupware systems, such as a multi-user database, act like single user systems; one can see their own actions, but may be unaware of the actions and their effects from other users. However, a shared workspace is an example of a groupware system where each one's actions and their effects are experienced by those who are cooperating.

In a synchronous shared workspace environment, the effects of users' actions can be immediately seen. For example, Dourish and Bellotti (1992) describe the shared feedback which is available in ShrEdit, a multi-user text editor, where users can see the views of others, or "find" other users in the shared document. Additionally, one has access to activity information; users can see whether others are tracking them or others. This provides information on other users' actions, but not their effects. However, the authors noted that the users would ask each other about effects, such as who had written certain parts, or they would caution each other about consequences of actions.

The immediacy with which actions can be seen in a synchronous environment lends itself to easier learning of the relationship between action and effect, since actions and effects are contiguous in time (e.g. Moeller, 1954). However, asynchronous shared workspaces inhibits learning the relationships of actions-effects, since the time separation makes it more difficult for people to make this connection. One experiences many actions and many effects and along with a time difference, pairing them together can be difficult.

It is for this reason that we argue for awareness information in three time periods. One may see the effects of others, e.g. a missing document in the shared folder, but not know the actions that caused it, e.g. whether a convention was violated. Therefore, *past* history of actions is important in a shared workspace in order to reconstruct what actions have been done. *Present* actions and effects are necessary in order to be aware of the state of the documents. Awareness of *future* effects are necessary since one may see the current actions of others yet needs to learn their consequences. We argue that all three types of awareness information are necessary in order to overcome the cooperation difficulties raised by restricted feedback to aid users in establishing and maintaining conventions for groupware use.

5.2 Providing cues for conventions

The system should also provide cues about appropriate behavior in a shared workspace. Four levels of support are possible: signaling conventions by *visualization*; *notification and provision of feedback* about action, to support active learning of conventions; *automatic ensurement* of conventions, and *enforcement* of conventions, to avoid inappropriate user behavior.

The *visualization* of conventions through different workspace appearances is an implicit way of signaling conventions in a shared workspace. This can be achieved using appropriate interface metaphors such as rooms. Thus, the appearance of that workspace signals its type, and the conventions that apply to that type of workspace.

The metaphors applied by our groupware platform, LinkWorks, all stem from single user objects, e.g. cabinets, folders, and drawers. These are appropriate for the organization of a single user environment, but not for the organization of a shared environment. The semantic of these metaphors is applied to govern and control how containers are nested. They have no implication for their use as shared workspaces, nor do they change their behavior when they are shared. Often users were not aware whether the workspace they are using is shared or not.

Notification and the provision of feedback can support users in learning what behavior is appropriate. Notification can be used as reinforcement when a convention is correctly followed, and it can also promote active learning when the convention is broken. This technique increases the awareness of the users of the consequences of their actions, e.g. that moving an object out of a shared workspace makes that object inaccessible for other members of the shared workspace.

The *automatic ensurement* of conventions in our case means that an alias of a document is automatically created when it is dragged out of the folder. However, this automatic ensurement of the convention has the drawback that the user will not become aware of his/her actions, since the user does not actively perform the action. Thus, active learning does not occur.

The *enforcement* of conventions can hinder inappropriate behavior of users in a shared workspace. However, the enforcement of conventions can be too rigid of a solution since it may hinder cooperation. Enforcement would imply that users are not allowed to remove a document out of the shared folder, but that could prevent users from storing and representing documents in different folders when that is necessary for a specific task.

This discussion illustrates that an easy and straightforward solution for the support of group conventions in shared workspaces does not exist. The choice of the support level depends on the particular convention, its importance for the functioning of the group, and the groupware experience. For example, an essential convention in an inexperienced group can be supported by a combination of notifications and the provision of feedback to support the active learning and collection of experiences together with enforcements to warn users from unintended but harmful actions. In a more experienced group, the automatic ensurement of conventions becomes relevant combined with sporadic notification to refresh the users' awareness about the conventions. This multi-level support for conventions requires a very flexible approach that can adapt to the level of experience of a group (see Syri, 1997).

5.3 Supporting individual conventions

When individual conventions may be difficult for users to give up, a technical solution is to enable users to retain them. Not only does this offer the large advantage that users may keep conventions that might logically relate to their task, but also when users must assume other roles, such as substitutes, they can manage other users' files in a shared workspace using their own familiar routines.

In our case, different views of the shared documents were required by members of the writing office and Unit 57 members. The writing office prefers the order view, which requires a two level structure of the documents. The Unit 57 members prefer the work-process view, which requires that documents are further organized into folders where each folder represents a distinct process. But the writing office has no knowledge about the structure, so they cannot directly browse. The provision of a search facility is also not acceptable since a document is remembered by its location, not by its name.

The provision of different views is possible by the creation of additional aliases. By placing the alias of a document in a task specific folder, the unit members can organize documents in their individual views. However, subsequent changes to the document are still accessible for the writing office. Thus, the alias provides a translation between the different views.

We must now consider some problems that are raised when users have different views on shared information. Although a document is shared within a group, everybody has a different view to the document without a common reference, or group view. For example, a member of the Unit and a typist may refer to the same document differently, because they see the document from different views: different folders or workspaces. We must provide functions that map the individual views to a common group view. For a common reference, we must consider the identity and locality of shared objects in the individual views.

Object identity: users must be able to confirm whether two objects they are referring to are identical. This can be achieved either by a unique object share that is accessible by the users, or by a function that tells the users whether the object they both have currently selected are the same.

Object locality: to become aware of the structuring preferences of other users, it should be possible to get information about the locality of a shared object on another users' desk. This will allow a better understanding of other users who they collaborate with. However, a user might not want to publish certain information, e.g. if a user placed a shared document in the waste basket of his/her electronic desktop. Thus, it must be possible to assign appropriate access rights.

Thus, users can retain their own information structure while collaborating in the shared workspace. A common group view is available which is independent of the number, and configuration, of individual user views. Individual views are cognitively easier, especially when: 1) group membership is dynamic, i.e. new members can always adapt a file structure to their own needs, 2) the information becomes vast, and 3) one is a substitute for another member: they can simply access their own information structure to manage another user's workspace.

6. CONCLUSIONS AND OUTLOOK

In this paper we have presented our experience with the development of a user work group with POLITeam. We discovered that the users need conventions for using the groupware as they gained experience with the system functionality and their electronic work process. We presented their user requirements for conventions and then illustrated a typical work scenario with POLITeam, where following the conventions was critical. A technical solution was proposed for supporting group conventions, and for retaining some individual conventions using the groupware.

One might ask whether supporting individual conventions would lead users to think that the groupware system should be viewed as a single user, rather than group system, as Orlikowski discovered was prevalent thinking with one user group (Orlikowski, 1992). However, we argue that this would not be the case. First of all, other group conventions are required with the system, such as those for shared editing. Secondly, the emphasis on establishing conventions, both group and individual, using workshops, helps to reinforce a perspective that it is a group system where actions from each user produce consequences for others. And third, along with individual information structures, a reference view is available that represents a common view for the group, which users can refer to.

ACKNOWLEDGMENTS

We give special thanks to Alex Bordetsky, Ludwin Fuchs, Peter Hoschka, Markus Sohlenkamp, Anja Syri, and Volker Wulf for their valuable comments.

REFERENCES

Bales, G. (1950). *Interaction Process Analysis.* Chicago: University of Chicago Press.

Bennis, W. G. and Shepard, H. A. (1956). A theory of group development. *Human Relations* 9 (4), 415-437.

Bion, W. R. (1959). *Experiences in Groups.* London: Tavistock.

Dourish and Bellotti, V. (1992). Awareness and coordination in shared workspaces. In *Proceedings of CSCW '92*, Oct. 31-Nov. 4, Toronto, 107-114.

Hughes, J. A., Randall, D., and Shapiro, D. (1992). Faltering from ethnography to design. *Proceedings of CSCW'92*, Toronto, ACM Press, 115-122.

Klöckner, K., Mambrey, P., Sohlenkamp, M., Prinz, W., Fuchs, L., Kolvenbach, S., Pankoke-Babatz, U., Syri, A. (1995). PoliTeam: Bridging the Gap between Bonn and Berlin for and with the Users. *Proc. ECSCW'95*, Stockholm, Kluwer Academic, 17-31.

Leland, M. D. P., Fish, R. S, Kraut, R. E. (1988). Collaborative document production using Quilt. *Proceedings of CSCW'88*, Portland, OR, ACM Press.

Mambrey, P. Mark, G. and Pankoke-Babatz (1996). Integrating User Advocacy into Participatory Design: the Designers' Perspective. *Proc. of PDC '96*, 251-259.

Moeller, G. (1954). The CS-UCS interval in GSR conditioning. *Journal of Exper. Psych.*, 48:162-66.

Moreland, R. L. and Levine, J. M. (1989). Newcomers and oldtimers in small groups. In P. Paulus (ed.) *Psychology of Group Influence.* Hillsdale, N.J.: Lawrence Erlbaum.

Neuwirth, C. M., Kaufer, D. S., Chandhok, R., and Morris, J. H. (1990). Issues in the Design of Computer Support for Co-authoring and Commenting, *Proceedings of CSCW'90*, Los Angeles, CA., Oct. 1990.

Orlikowski, W.J. (1992). Learning from Notes: Organizational Issues in Groupware Implementation, *Proc. of CSCW '92*, Toronto, ACM Press, 362-369.

Posner, I. R. and Baecker (1992). How people write together. *Proc. of the Twenty-fifth Hawaii Inter'l Conference on System Sciences*, 127-138.

Prinz, W. and Kolvenbach, S., (1996). Support for workflows in a ministerial environment, *Proceedings of CSCW'96* Boston, ACM Press, 199-208.

Schein, E. H. (1985). *Organizational Culture and Leadership.* San Francisco: Jossey-Bass.

Syri, Anja (1997). Tailoring Cooperation Support through Mediators. To appear in *Proceedings of ECSCW'97*, Lancaster, Kluwer Academic.

Tatar, D. G., Foster, G., and Bobrow, D. G. (1991). Design for conversation: lessons from Cognoter. *Int. J. Man-Machine Studies*, 34, 185-209.

Enhancing the usability of usability design tools: The case of information requirements specification

Juliet Richardson and Thomas C. Ormerod

Department of Psychology, Lancaster University, Lancaster, LA1 4YF, U.K.
RichardsonJ@Cardiff.ac.uk, T.Ormerod@Lancaster.ac.uk

ABSTRACT In this paper we report the development of a tool for information requirements specification (IRS), designed to support the application of a particular IRS methodology, the Sub-Goal Template scheme (Shepherd, 1993; Shepherd and Ormerod, 1992), and the use of a notation embodied within that methodology. First, an empirical study was conducted to determine typical errors made by users of the IRS notation which was subsequently re-designed to avoid these errors through the provision of templates. Second, the tasks involved in using the IRS methodology were articulated in order to develop a process model for a computer-based support tool. Finally, an evaluation of the usability of the tool showed that it achieved the main aims of supporting both the notation and the methodology. We argue that, in developing methods that address usability issues, the usability of design aids to support the methodologies should also be subject to scrutiny.

KEY WORDS Usability, Methodologies, Notations, Requirements Specification, Design Support Tools

1. INTRODUCTION

A large number of tools and methodologies have been developed to support complex activities such as design. However, the notations and representations embodied in such supporting technologies are rarely subjected to close scrutiny. In this paper, we report a number of studies that examine the usability of a notation for information requirements specification (IRS). The IRS methodology is based upon the Sub-Goal Template scheme of Shepherd (1993; see also Shepherd and Ormerod, 1992), which employs a variant of Hierarchical Task Analysis (HTA: Annett, Duncan, Stammers and Gray, 1971), to identify stereotypical user tasks and their associated information needs at a level of detail that is useful but not overly constraining for subsequent interface design. The studies resulted in the development of a computer-based IRS tool which delivers information requirements in a form that can be used as a tendering document for interface design.

Design in domains such as architecture, engineering and software development is generally conceptualised as a complex problem-solving activity (Simon, 1969), entailing processes such as problem definition and decomposition, and solution development and simulation. The extremely ill-defined nature of design tasks, and the time lag between the specification of requirements and feedback upon the viability of solutions, have been proposed to differentiate design from other kinds of problem-solving activity (Goel and Pirolli, 1989). In order to support designers, many tools and methodologies have been developed (e.g. Ashworth and Goodland, 1990; Jackson, 1980). Typically such supporting technologies are developed by domain specialists, and tend to reflect a focus upon desirable characteristics of a design product rather than an understanding of the design process (Guindon, 1992; Lansdale and Ormerod, 1994). Whilst psychologists have increasingly been involved in the development of design methodologies, to date there has been little psychological research into the utility of the notations underlying such methodologies.

Human–Computer Interaction: INTERACT'97 S. Howard, J. Hammond & G. Lindgaard (editors)
Published by Chapman & Hall

Our research into design support technologies has focused upon the development of an IRS methodology for process control displays, that is, identifying the information that an operator needs to undertake each task entailed in the control of plant and equipment. Identifying information requirements is an inherently psychological task and one that is critical for effective display design, yet it is rarely given the prominence it deserves. This is in part because designers tend to focus upon specifying functional requirements for displays, and also because it entails expertise in human factors.

In the domain of interface design there are four essential characteristics of a requirements specification:

(1) The requirements specification should be complete in order that the final system designed will support the whole range of operator tasks.

(2) Both the functional requirements of the system and the information requirements of the human operator(s) should be specified. However, information requirements are often neglected and many methodologies focus only on functional requirements (Harker, Olphert and Eason, 1990). Interface design can end up being an afterthought which is considered only after the rest of the system has been designed.

(3) The requirements specification should be independent of details arising from any existing or potential implementations (Parnas and Clements, 1986). This will allow the designers to freely choose the best solutions for the design.

(4) The process of requirements specification needs some degree of guidance and formalism. This can be achieved through following formal design methodologies. Such methodologies provide a structure within which the design process can occur, helping break the design task down into manageable units.

There are numerous methodologies which aim to support the process of requirements specification (see Appendix A of Olle, Hagelstein, Macdonald, Rolland, Sol, Van Assche and Verrijn-Stuart, 1988 for an overview of 34 methodologies). However in this paper we shall focus on specific issues by considering only one methodology, the Sub-Goal Template (SGT) scheme as developed by Shepherd and Ormerod (1992; Shepherd, 1993) to support information requirements specification for process control interfaces.

2. THE SGT SCHEME

The SGT scheme sets out to meet the needs outlined above by taking an HTA as the basis for a requirements specification. HTA, developed by Annett *et al.* (1971), is a well established technique for task analysis. An HTA involves identifying the immediate subgoals of a task. Each of these subgoals can then be taken in turn and themselves redescribed in terms of subgoals. This redescription process is repeated until the level of the analysis is of a fine enough grain to be useful for design. However, care must be taken that the task analysis is not a description of the existing technology: the analysis should cease at a point where the tasks describe simple implementation-independent operations such as "Open valve C" rather than specific tasks such as "Press button B" which are tied in to the existing interface. Not only does an HTA consist of a detailed redescription of tasks but it also contains plans that describe relationships between the tasks and constraints acting on them. Plans allow sequence information to be captured which can then be used to determine the organisation of information requirements.

The SGT scheme provides a notation for taking the output from an HTA and using it as the basis for an IRS. There are two parts to this process.

(1) Firstly, the information requirements of the lowest level tasks in the HTA are specified through the use of templates known as SGT elements. Each task is redescribed using the SGT notation as an instance of a more generalised stereotypical task, such as "Adjust equipment" or "Read" or "Monitor rate of change". For example, the task of altering the opening of a valve might be classified as "Adjust equipment" as might the task of altering the temperature of a liquid or of varying a pipe flowrate. Each of these tasks has associated stereotypical information needs. For example, in order to carry out the task "Adjust equipment" the operator would need to know the possible operating states of the equipment together with feedback confirming its actual state. In this way the information requirements for each operational task can be specified.

(2) In addition to the information requirements the SGT scheme also provides a notation for specifying the organisation of that information. This is achieved by taking the plans from the HTA, which detail sequences and interdependencies between tasks, and re-writing them using the sequencing elements of the SGT scheme. There are four of these elements as shown in Table 1. The designer can use the information captured by these sequencing elements to ensure that the organisation of information on the interface is optimal. For example, information required for tasks that are performed at the same time should be displayed in one location.

Sequencing elements.	
Code	*Label*
S1	*fixed procedure: then do*
S2	*choice: if Z then do X if not Z then do Y*
S3	*parallel: then do together X and Y*
S4	*optional sequence: do in any order X and Y*

Table 1. The sequencing elements (from Shepherd and Ormerod, 1992). Note: X and Y refer to tasks and Z refers to an operation condition.

Thus the SGT scheme provides a notation which can be used to redescribe an HTA to produce an information requirements specification. It not only specifies the full set of information required by the operator but also gives some detail of how to organise that information. The SGT scheme meets three of the four pre-requisites for a successful requirements specification given above: firstly, the specification should be complete as long as it is based on a complete HTA; the specification should be independent from implementation as it is based on an HTA that focuses on tasks and goals rather than on the specific mechanisms used to achieve those goals; the specification of information requirements is at the heart of the SGT scheme and is therefore not sidelined. However, by itself the SGT notation does not really give any guidance to users or introduce any formalism into the process of design. This can only be achieved by a methodology.

A methodology for using the SGT scheme is shown in Figure 1. There are two ways in which the SGT scheme can be used to produce an information requirements specification: an existing HTA can be translated into SGT elements, or an HTA can be constructed from scratch using SGT elements. Either process will produce a formal analysis of the operators' tasks together with the information needs of these tasks.

The first stage in producing an SGT-based IRS is to select a goal. This will either be the initial goal in a plan or the next goal in the plan currently being explored. Once a goal has been selected the analyst must first decide whether that goal should be assigned to the system or to the operator. If the goal can be automated then it is assigned to the system; if not then it is assigned to the operator and the analyst must then attempt to redescribe the goal as a single SGT element. If this is possible then the appropriate SGT is recorded, the information requirements are added and the next goal, if any, is identified.

If redescription as a single SGT element is not possible then the current goal must be decomposed into a set of subgoals governed by a plan. The plan should be hypothesised in terms of sequencing elements and evaluated against the goal constraints. Once an

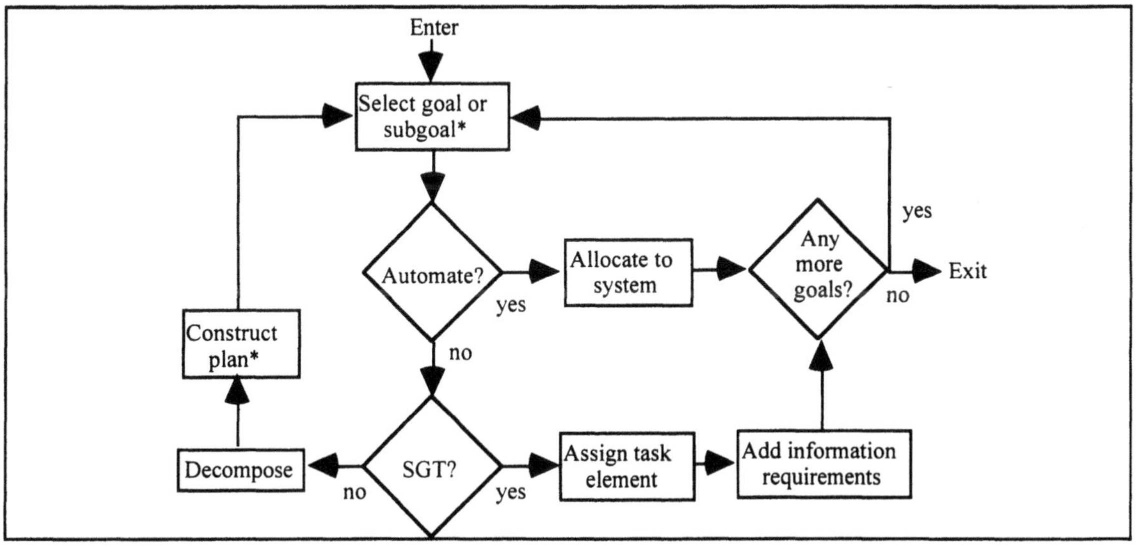

Figure 1. An illustration of the process of HTA translation and generation using the SGT scheme. Asterisks (*) indicate the points at which an existing HTA can be used to provide information.

acceptable plan in terms of sequencing elements has been identified then it is recorded and the next goal, if any, should be selected. If the goal cannot be decomposed then attempts should be made to redescribe it or to loosen the goal constraints if possible.

Thus the stage labelled "Decompose" in Figure 1 covers a large number of different tasks involved in capturing the information required to produce an HTA. In particular, during this stage the analyst should collect information to determine the constraints acting on operational goals, the subgoals into which these goals can be decomposed and the possible sequences in which these subgoals can be carried out. If the analyst finds it impossible to decompose a goal then it might be necessary to consult the end-users to see if there is any way in which the constraints can be relaxed. For example, more funding may be made available.

If an HTA is available then the process is essentially the same except that the HTA can be used to provide input at certain stages. In particular, an HTA can be used to identify subgoals and their governing plan which can then be translated into sequencing elements. Therefore although the tasks of redescribing an existing HTA into SGT elements and constructing an HTA appear to be quite different, they are in fact essentially similar. The only difference is that if there is an existing HTA then it can be used to identify higher unexplored goals as well as subgoals and plans governing them.

3. AN EMPIRICAL STUDY OF THE SGT NOTATION

A preliminary evaluation of the SGT notation was carried out using 14 novice subjects. These subjects were given a pen and paper-based plan redescription task: they were presented with paragraphs containing descriptions of sequences of actions carried out on a fictional process control plant and were asked to express these sequences as plans using the sequencing elements of the SGT scheme. This task required subjects to work out the constituent tasks, their order and inter-dependencies and then write this using the SGT sequencing elements. Subjects were given sequences of varying levels of complexity: some were simple sequences of actions, others were more structurally complex sequences of interdependent actions.

The main result from this evaluation was that subjects' use of the SGT sequencing elements was by no means perfect. Given six plans to redescribe, on average subjects got only 3.3 correct on the first attempt, if they were allowed to attempt to correct their errors this figure rose to 4.5 correct. Over these six redescription tasks, subjects made, on average 4.6 errors, of which 2.25 were syntactic and 2.35 were semantic. Syntactic errors are defined as those in which an element is written down incorrectly or is used in an incorrect situation. Semantic errors are those in which the sequence is syntactically correct but is still wrong. The main types of syntactic errors made by subjects were to add extra items into the elements or to miss out parts especially when building complex embedded sequences of elements.

4. A TOOL TO SUPPORT THE USE OF THE SGT SCHEME

There are several reasons for constructing a tool to support the use of the SGT scheme. For example, Tse and Pong (1991) argue that a structured framework, such as that provided by a computer tool, to support requirements specification would allow the completeness and the consistency of the specification to be checked. In addition, Farooq and Dominick (1988) argue that design support tools can encourage different designers to use the same techniques, they can reduce time and cost and they can increase consistency between different interfaces.

Whilst these are all legitimate reasons for producing computer tools to support requirements specification we will focus here on two issues that are more specific to the SGT scheme: the problem of how to support use of the notation and the problem of how to support the methodology.

4.1. Supporting the notation

The notation of the SGT scheme requires subjects to use the sequencing elements to describe the interdependencies and ordering of tasks. The evaluation of the SGT notation reported above found that subjects tended to make several errors. In particular, they often missed out parts of the notation or added in extra items. Obviously, it is important that a computer tool should support the use of the SGT notation in such a way as to prevent these errors.

One possible solution is suggested by research carried out into the problem of supporting computer programming notations. Writing plans using the sequencing elements involves describing sequences of actions using a formal language. A similar task is involved in writing computer programs where the programmer has to translate sequences of activities into formal code. Sime, Arblaster and Green (1977a; 1977b) have investigated ways of reducing errors when subjects are asked to write programs using different forms of conditional statement. Sime *et al.* (1977a) investigated how subjects could be helped to make fewer syntactic errors when programming in a "mini-language" containing conditional statements. They found that subjects who were given a dictionary that automatically provided templates for whole conditional constructions solved more problems correctly at the first attempt than subjects who were taught a procedure for constructing programs. Sime *et al.* (1977b) obtained a similar result for subjects writing programs in another mini-language.

Sime *et al.* (1977a; 1977b) have demonstrated that an automated syntax can help computer programmers. It seems likely that this result can be generalised to the SGT scheme as there are parallels between the type of task used by Sime *et al.* and the task of using the sequencing elements. Both tasks involve using a formal, restricted language to describe relationships between different items. Thus an automatic syntax was incorporated into the SGT tool. When users of the tool select a sequencing element to put into a plan, they have to indicate the location of that element within the plan. An appropriate template is then inserted with spaces for filling in the subgoals. For example, if the user selects an S3 element to link two subgoals then the following template is written:

Then do together
• _________
And
• _________

The user must fill in two subgoals in the spaces given. In this way the user cannot either add extra items into the elements or miss out parts. In addition, the tool automatically checks that the points at which subgoals or elements are inserted are legitimate. For example, a subgoal can only be put into a plan to a location inside an element. Thus, the tool should support the notation and prevent user errors.

4.2. Supporting the methodology

The SGT tool must not only prevent errors in the use of the notation but it should also support the use of that notation within the methodology outlined above (Green, 1989). The SGT methodology can be split into two parts: checking to see if there are further unanalysed goals so that one can be selected and recording the information associated with the selected goal. In order to carry out the first of these processes, users of the tool will need a representation of the HTA which allows them to see which goals remain to be analysed in order to select one of them. In order to carry out the second process, users will need to be guided through the process of recording the appropriate information. The SGT tool was therefore designed with two main parts: (1) A Tree Diagram Window which contains a representation of the HTA which can be used to access information on individual goals and plans; (2) A Goal Information Window which guides the user through the process of inputting information related to a single goal.

The main component of the Tree Diagram Window is a representation of the HTA which is automatically updated as the HTA is built up. The representation consists of a hierarchical tree with each goal at each level represented by a node consisting of a box containing the goal's number and short label.

The Goal Information Window for an individual goal is opened when the user clicks on that goal in the Tree Diagram Window. This window guides the user through the process of recording the information associated with the current goal as defined by the methodology shown in Figure 1. Figure 2 gives a detailed illustration of exactly how this is achieved. For each goal the user is guided to record a short label, a longer description, an SGT element, if any, and the associated information requirements or, if no SGT element is assigned, the constraints, subgoals and plan. The parts of Figure 2 that are labelled with numbers map directly onto Figure 1 as follows:

(1) This is a dialogue window in which the user is asked if the goal can be automated. If they decide that it can be then this is recorded and no more information need be recorded for that goal. This supports the part of the process labelled "Automate?" in Figure 1.

(2) This indicates a window in which the user must chose the SGT element, if any, that describes the current goal. In this window the user is presented with a menu of the SGT elements. Further information on selected elements can be obtained as required. This supports the part of the process labelled "SGT?" in Figure 1.

(3) If an SGT element is chosen then it is assigned automatically to the goal. This supports the part of the process labelled "Assign task element" in Figure 1.

(4) Once an SGT element has been chosen then the user has to fill in answers to questions that elicit the information needs associated with the selected element. These information requirements are then filled into an appropriate template. Once the requirements have been recorded the information set for the goal is complete. This supports the part of the process labelled "Add information requirements" in Figure 1.

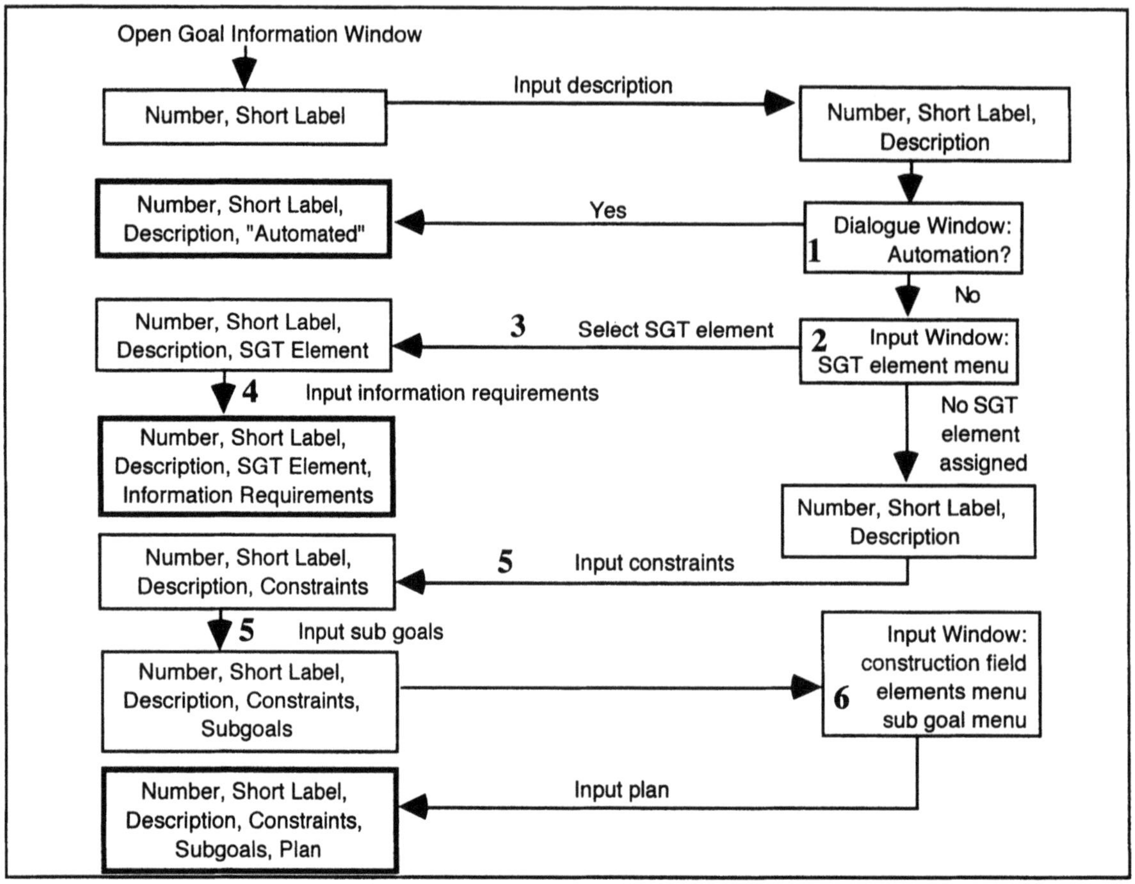

Figure 2. Illustration of the process of inputting individual goal information into the Goal Information Window.

(5) If no SGT element can be assigned to the goal then the user must specify the constraints acting on the goal. Once these have been specified the subgoals of the current goal must be identified. This supports the part of the process labelled "Decompose" in Figure 1. The numbering of subgoals is automated, so that the user is freed from having to work these out, and is able to concentrate on other parts of the analysis.

(6) Once the subgoals have been identified the user can open the Plan Construction Window. This contains a field into which the plan can be written, a menu of sequencing elements, information about the sequencing elements and a menu of the subgoals. The user constructs the plan by selecting a point in the construction field then selecting an element or a subgoal from one of the menus. The selected element or subgoal is then written to the chosen point as long as it is a legitimate location. This supports the part of the process labelled "Construct plan" in Figure 1.

The SGT tool thus not only guides the user through the process of inputting goal information but also provides the information that is needed for the various tasks involved in that process. In particular, information on the SGT and sequencing elements is provided at the points where the user has to select between these elements. The tool also guides the user through the process of collecting information by indicating at each point what type of information is required.

5. EVALUATION OF THE SGT TOOL

There were two parts to this evaluation: the first part was designed to check whether the tool supported the use of the SGT notation whereas as the second part was carried out to check the extent to which the tool supported the SGT methodology.

5.1. Evaluating support for the notation

This evaluation was essentially a replication of the notation evaluation reported above. 16 novice subjects were used and they were given the same set of six plan redescription tasks. The only difference was that subjects were asked to carry out the task using the SGT tool rather than pen and paper.

Generally the results indicated that the SGT tool was successfully preventing errors in the use of the SGT notation. T-tests were carried out to test the significance of these effects. Out of the six tasks, subjects got, on average 4.5 correct on the first attempt. This is significantly more than the number of correct solutions achieved on the first attempt with pen and paper (3.33 correct, $p<0.05$). In addition, over the six tasks, on average subjects made only 1.83 errors, again this is significantly less than the number of errors made when using pen and paper (4.58 errors, $p<0.05$). Of these 1.83 errors, 0.33 were syntactic and 1.5 were semantic. The number of syntactic errors is significantly lower than the number made with pen and paper ($p<0.05$) whilst there is no difference for the number of semantic errors. This shows that whilst the tool can help subjects to write down their interpretation of a sequence of actions with more accuracy it cannot increase the actual accuracy of the interpretation itself.

Thus, overall the features, such as templates, that were built into the SGT tool do seem to have had the desired effect of improving the level of accuracy with which the SGT notation is used to record sequences of activities.

5.2. Evaluating support for the methodology

This second evaluation was carried out to check whether the tool supports the SGT methodology as defined above. This evaluation was essentially a case study of an expert process control interface designer using the SGT tool. The designer was closely observed whilst he used the SGT tool to try and develop a user requirements specification for a computer tool to simulate and analyse a gas network.

In general the designer felt that the tool guided him through the use of the SGT scheme in a useful way. In particular, the tool made the subject think in detail about the sequences in which subgoals should be carried out and the conditions governing these sequences. This information is obviously central to good interface design. In addition, the user felt that it was easy to switch between different parts of the specification because of the good support provided by the tool: if he left a task half completed and then returned to it later he found it easy to pick it up again.

However, the subject did encounter a couple of difficulties in using the tool. Firstly, he felt that the way in which plans had to be constructed was too inflexible. The tool restricts plan construction to a strictly sequential process: the elements and subgoals have to be added into the plan in order. This aspect of the tool should therefore be altered to provide better support for the important task of specifying plans: users should be allowed to add elements and subgoals into the plan in any order.

The second problem that the subject encountered was that he felt that there was a lack of guidance on how to collect the information required by the SGT scheme. He thought that it would be useful if the tool could provide guidance on the type of information required, possible sources for that information and possible collection methods. As outlined above, the collection of information is an important aspect of the SGT methodology and the tool should be altered to provide better support for it.

Thus, in general the tool provided good support for the SGT methodology with just a couple of problems which were the inflexibility of plan construction and a lack of guidance on data collection. Both of these are important aspects of the SGT methodology (see Figure 1) and should be better supported by the tool. Carrying out a detailed evaluation in this way has highlighted these potential problems at an early stage.

6. SUMMARY AND CONCLUSIONS

The main conclusion to be drawn from this work is that care must be taken in designing usability-oriented tools. In particular, there should be two main inputs to the process of designing tools: (1) A high level analysis of the tasks involved in using the methodology should be carried out so that the tool can be designed to support them. In this way a tool can be produced that will guide users through the process of applying the methodology. (2) A lower level more detailed analysis of the use of the particular notation embodied within the methodology should also be carried out. The results from this can then be used to ensure that the tool prevents errors in using the notation as far as possible.

In addition to carefully designing the tool to support both the methodology and the notation, evaluations should be carried out at an early stage to check the extent to which the tool succeeds in these aims. In the case reported in this paper, it was found that the tool supported the use of the notation well, preventing errors found when subjects used pen and paper. The tool was also found to provide mainly good support for the methodology, although there were two important aspects of the methodology that were not well supported.

It is perhaps ironic that good design and careful evaluation of the usability of usability tools are often neglected. However, as this work demonstrates, both are of vital importance to the production of tools that will support designers and prevent simple errors. If the aim is to encourage the design of simple and effective system interfaces, then the tools that are used in interface development must be equally simple and effective.

ACKNOWLEDGEMENTS

The work reported in this paper was carried out as part of the first author's Ph.D. research and was funded by a studentship from British Gas plc. The second author's design research is currently supported by the ESRC Cognitive Engineering Initiative Grant No. L127251027.

REFERENCES

Annett, J., Duncan, K.D., Stammers, R.B. and Gray, M.J. (1971). *Task Analysis*. London: HMSO.

Ashworth, C. and Goodland, M. (1990). *SSADM: a practical approach*. London: McGraw-Hill Book Company.

Farooq, M.U. and Dominick, W.D. (1988). A survey of formal tools and models for developing user interfaces. *International Journal of Man-Machine Studies*, *29*, 479-496.

Goel, V. and Pirolli, P. (1989). Motivating the notion of generic design within information-processing theory: the design problem space. *AI Magazine*, *Spring*, 18-36.

Green, T.R.G. (1989). Cognitive dimensions of notations. In A. Sutcliffe and L. Macaulay (Eds.), *People and Computers V*, (pp. 443-460). Cambridge: Cambridge University Press.

Guindon, R. (1992). Requirements and design of design vision, an object-oriented graphical interface to an intelligent software design assistant. In Proceedings of CHI'92, 499-506.

Harker, S.D.P., Olphert, C.W. and Eason, K.D. (1990). The development of tools to assist in organisational requirements definition for information technology systems. In D. Diaper (Ed.), *Human-Computer Interaction - INTERACT '90*. North-Holland: Elsevier Science Publishers B.V.

Jackson, M. (1980). *The design and use of conventional programming languages*. London: Academic Press.

Lansdale, M.W. and Ormerod, T.C. (1994). *Understanding interfaces: a handbook of human-computer interaction*. London: Academic Press.

Olle, T.W., Hagelstein, J., Macdonald, I.G., Rolland, C., Sol, H.G., Van Assche, F.J.M. and Verrijn-Stuart, A.A. (1988). *Information systems methodologies: a framework for understanding*. Wokingham: Addison-Wesley Publishing Company.

Parnas, D.L. and Clements, P.C. (1986). A rational design process: how and why to fake it. *IEEE Transactions on Software Engineering*, *12(2)*, 251-257.

Shepherd, A. (1993). An approach to information requirements specification for process control tasks. *Ergonomics*, *36(11)*, 1425-1439.

Shepherd, A. and Ormerod, T.C. (1992). *Development of a formal method of user requirements specification for process plant displays*. Report: Loughborough University of Technology, Loughborough.

Sime, M.E., Arblaster, A.T. and Green, T.R.G. (1977a). Reducing programming errors in nested conditionals by prescribing a writing procedure. *International Journal of Man-Machine Studies*, *9*, 119-126.

Sime, M.E., Arblaster, A.T. and Green, T.R.G. (1977b). Structuring the programmer's task. *Journal of Occupational Psychology*, *50*, 205-216.

Simon, H.A. (1969). *The sciences of the artificial*. Cambridge, MA: MIT Press.

Tse, T.H. and Pong, L. (1991). An examination of requirements specification languages. *The Computer Journal*, *34(2)*, 143-152.

Experiences using situated and non-situated techniques for studying work in context

Andrew M. Dearden & Peter C. Wright

HCI Group, Department of Computer Science,
University of York, York, YO1 5DD, UK
telephone: (44)-1904-433376
email:{andyd,pcw}@minster.york.ac.uk

ABSTRACT In this paper, we draw a distinction between situated techniques and non-situated techniques for studying work context. We define a situated technique as one in which the data collection takes place in the normal working environment of the person being studied. We describe our experience of a case study in which we applied a combination of situated and non-situated techniques to analyse work practice in context. To co-ordinate these different types of technique, and to provide adequate validation, we adopted an iterative model building approach.

Our case study demonstrates the feasibility and the value of combining these different techniques, and emphasises the value of model building and validation.

KEYWORDS Contextual inquiry, soft systems analysis, situated techniques, requirements gathering.

1. THE NEED FOR CONTEXTUAL TECHNIQUES IN HCI

There has been a growing awareness in the HCI and CSCW communities of the need to understand the contexts in which the technology we design is to be used. Holtzblatt and colleagues have developed a methodology, called contextual inquiry (Holtzblatt & Jones, 1993; Beyer & Holtzblatt, 1995; Holtzblatt & Beyer, 1996), which provides a number of techniques for studying work context. The need to study the context of work is also evident in the popularity of broadly ethnographic approaches to requirements gathering (Suchman 1995).

Outside of the HCI and CSCW community, the problem of understanding context has been recognised by some systems analysts. Soft Systems Analysis (Checkland, 1981; Checkland & Scholes, 1990; Patching, 1993) is a methodology for studying human activity systems with a view to specifying requirements for management intervention, often in the form of changes to information technology (IT) provision. This work has provided a number of interesting techniques for studying context which have not yet penetrated the HCI community.

Soft Systems Analysis can be characterised in terms of a number of steps. Initially, analysis begins with an unstructured problem situation. By using interview techniques and a recording method known as rich pictures (see below) the analyst seeks to express the problem situation. An important goal at this stage of analysis is to understand the problem situation in its real world context. Following the expression of the problem situation, the next stages of analysis involve defining relevant systems and developing models of these systems. These 'ideal' models are then compared with the problem situation, and the comparison is used to identify desirable and feasible changes.

Comparing the soft systems approach with methods of studying context in HCI such as contextual inquiry and ethnography, reveals important differences. Firstly, in ethnography and contextual inquiry, data gathering takes place in the normal working environment of the subject. We may characterise these techniques as *situated* data collection techniques. In contrast, soft systems analysis typically collects data using interviews

Human–Computer Interaction: INTERACT'97 S. Howard, J. Hammond & G. Lindgaard (editors)
Published by Chapman & Hall

in a *non-situated* manner. Secondly, soft-systems analysis places a strong emphasis on the use of models as tools to aid understanding of the work context.

In this paper, we report on a study which sought to combine situated and non-situated data gathering techniques in analysing the 'quality of fit' between the work done by a group of office workers and the IT provided to support that work.

2. THE STUDY

The organisation referred to in this study (which has to remain anonymous for confidentiality reasons) processes financial claims made by customers. Staff in the organisation receive claim forms from customers and have to assess whether the customer is eligible for payments, often over an extended period of time. Customers who are currently eligible may cease to be eligible and cases must therefore be updated and reviewed. Performance measures such as speed of claim processing and accuracy of payments calculation are also important aspects of the work of the assessors.

Our study had a very specific brief, to investigate and report on three related issues.

1) *To describe the work of the assessors.*

2) *To analyse the 'quality of fit' between the IT and the work of assessors.*

3) *To survey new technologies that might be of use to the organisation in the short, medium and long term.*

The study was subject to time constraints. The total workload was 22 person days, with 12 half days being allocated to on-site data gathering activities. This constraint was significant when compared to the time-scales that relate to the processing of a customer's claim. For example: the targets for processing of a claim are of the order of a few days; some of the assessor's work may involve issuing requests for information with a turnaround measured in weeks; and the total period of a customer's claim may be a number of months or years.

These time constraints had a significant effect on our selection of appropriate techniques. We decided that there was a prima-facie case for using some situated data gathering techniques (Beyer & Holtzblatt, 1993; Suchman, 1993). However, we were concerned that, using these techniques alone, we might not obtain a sufficiently broad sample of the work within the time available (Hughes et al., 1995). Consequently, we chose to supplement these techniques with non-situated data collection techniques drawn from soft systems analysis. To co-ordinate the use of these two different data gathering methods, to support synthesis of the data, and to support validation, we introduced an iterative model building activity. In practice, we found that the model building activity delivered an additional benefit in highlighting issues that required further investigation.

3. THE TECHNIQUES SELECTED

In considering the techniques that we used, we group them under three headings: techniques to support situated data collection; non-situated techniques to investigate aspects of context outside of the immediately observable situation; and techniques to support validation.

3.1. Situated data gathering

Contextual interviews

Our primary situated data gathering technique was the use of contextual interviews, as described by Beyer & Holtzblatt (1995) and Holtzblatt & Jones (1993). In a contextual interview the investigator observes the interviewee carrying out his or her normal work. The investigator uses the interviewee's activities and artefacts in the work environment as cues for inquiry. For instance, if the interviewee is observed using some tool, the place of the tool in the work can be discussed, and the interviewee can be asked about other tools that are available in the environment. Similarly, when the interviewee is conducting some activity, the ordering and the structure of the activity can be discussed.

This technique seemed particularly appropriate for gathering information about how the IT was used within the work, and how well the structure of the software matched to the assessors' preferred structure for the work.

Train me and cramming

The work of assessors is highly technical and considerable subject matter expertise and domain-specific language pervades the work. This presents a problem for a contextual interview, since much valuable interview time could be lost negotiating terminology. To overcome this problem we invested a significant amount of our available time on a 'train me' session with one of the organisation's training staff using standard training materials; and on cramming, i.e.

studying documentation to learn the structure of the computer system. Whilst this work was not *situated* in terms of our definitions, we include it here because it we used it to support situated data collection.

Although we cannot claim this as a new 'technique' we believe that this activity should not be overlooked by any practitioner seeking to use situated data collection techniques to study human-computer interaction.

Action Recorder

One possible exercise within a contextual interview is to record a 'day in the life' of the worker being studied. We supplemented this high level, low granularity description of the assessors' work with a more fine grained analysis of activities over a shorter time window using 'Action Recorder' (Watts et al., 1996).

Action Recorder allows an observer to monitor the changing activities of a person and a set of tools by making a single key press whenever either the person's activity changes, or the state of a tool changes.

We used Action Recorder to produce logs of assessors' activities, and changes to the computer system state, over forty minute periods. Conventionally, this would be done by video recording the activity and then analysing the video back in the laboratory. In our study, time constraints did not allow for this, instead, we entered the data points in real time.

3.2. Going beyond the immediate situation

Some of the events that we needed to consider in analysing the context of work, were beyond the scope of the immediately observable situation. For instance, a customer's claim may run over many months, and the history of a claim may be relevant to our understanding of an assessor's work. Similarly, some of the work may involve outside bodies or agents that are not persistently represented in the situation of work. We used non-situated techniques to explore these issues.

Semi-structured interviews and rich pictures

Semi-structured interviews are a standard data gathering technique, and are used within the Soft Systems Analysis methodology (Patching 1993) to elicit information about the context of a 'problem situation'. We used such interviews to investigate: the contact that assessors had with external bodies and individuals; the assessors' attitudes to their work and the tools available; the sources of information used in the work; particular problems that they had identified etc. The interviews were recorded on audio tape. Also, during the interview, we worked with the interviewees to produce 'rich pictures'.

Rich pictures are freehand sketches drawn during an interview session to represent aspects of the information being discussed. Elements of rich pictures may include: actors and artefacts in a situation; the roles of actors, relationships between actors, and between actors and artefacts; communications between actors; issues relating to those actors or artefacts. In fact, any information that the person drawing the picture thinks may help in understanding the situation. The rich picture should be regarded primarily as an *aide memoir* for the interviewer, rather than as a complete recording of a set of specific observations. Figure 1 shows an example of a rich picture representing the context of a public house, taken from Patching (1993).

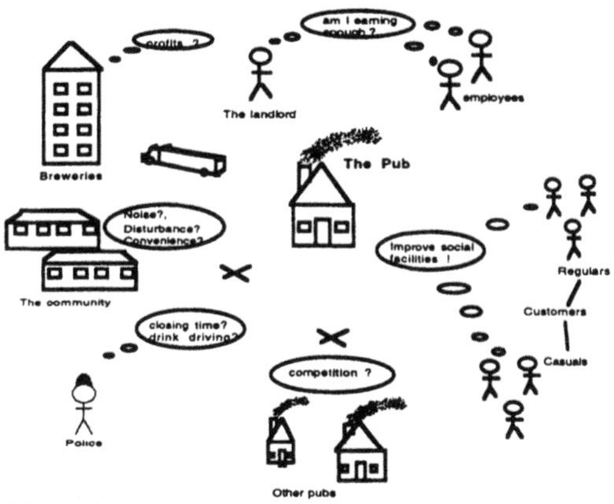

Figure 1: An example of a rich picture of a pub (based on Patching 1993). Crosses indicate possible conflicts.

Scenario analysis

The organisation's concern for accuracy, led us to consider techniques for gathering data about the possible causes of errors in claims processing. Errors present a major challenge for situated observation techniques, since errors are unlikely to occur during observation sessions and, when errors do occur, they may not be recognised by the observer due his or her limited domain knowledge.

In conjunction with quality controllers, we constructed a number of error scenarios, to find out more about the nature of errors in the assessors' work. We then used these error scenarios in a focus group discussion with assessment team leaders, to identify possible problem areas in the work or in the IT support that might have been related to these particular errors.

3.3. Validating our understanding of the work

The process of producing a report that may lead to changes in a work-system, places an obligation on the writer to ensure that the information in the report is valid and respects the viewpoints of the people within the work-system. We used three techniques to support validation.

Model building

We used model building to co-ordinate our data gathering using these heterogeneous methods, and to support validation of our understanding of the data. The models were in the form of informal diagrams that expressed particular aspects of our understanding. An example of one of the models is shown in figure 2.

The process of model building forces the analyst to explicate his or her understanding of the situation. This helps to clarify that understanding, and to identify hidden assumptions, contradictions or gaps in the analysts' knowledge. Having an explicit representation of this understanding may generate new insights and provoke new questions.

Challenging assumptions

The second validation technique was the technique of 'challenging assumptions'.

Using our understanding of the work, and our models, we produced a series of statements that were either consequences of the models, or contradicted our models. Many of the statements were designed to be provocative or extreme, in order to involve assessors in debating points of contention, and to provide stronger tests of our hypotheses.

The statements were presented to two focus groups. The first focus group consisted of five assessors. The second group involved two assessment team leaders, a trainer and a quality controller.

Wish lists

The final validation technique was a wish list exercise. All of the off-line interviews had terminated with questions about the best and worst aspects of the work and the tools provided, and 'wishes' for possible changes. Because the assessors' knowledge of available technology was constrained by their experience, we supplemented their wishes with additional possibilities based on our own knowledge. To avoid bias, we did not indicate to participants which wishes were generated by their peers and which by us.

Each of these wishes was written on a small (A6) piece of card. Within the focus groups, we asked the participants to write down new wishes on more cards. The final collection was then displayed, grouped and discussed.

4. EVALUATING THE TECHNIQUES

In this section, we report on the data that we found using each of the techniques, and consider what general lessons can be learned about the technique, from this case study.

4.1. Situated data gathering

Contextual Interviews

One of the most important things we discovered about the work during the study was that change and history are very significant when assessing a customer's claim and planning payments. The following observations (among many) from a contextual inquiry session made this apparent:

> When customers made telephone enquiries, assessors were observed to visit one particular screen more often than others. The screen is a free text notes page. The notes page is 12 lines long and, when full, is dumped to a paper copy, before new information is inserted. It is standard practice, in one of the offices visited, to use two lines of the page to record the customer's previous address(es). Given the space available, this indicates the importance that the assessors (and their managers) attach to this historical information.
>
> An assessor dealing with a complex claim left her desk and went into a separate office to use a stand-alone PC. On the PC she used a spreadsheet, then returned to her desk and used the output from the PC to update the customer's file on the main computer system. Further questioning revealed that the work on the PC was a comparison of the customer's entitlements and payments from the organisation over the last 18 months, to identify possible arrears or overpayments.

These kind of incidents are very easy to detect using a contextual interview. Both incidents were quite unexpected to us as observers, and consequently it is unlikely that we would have been able to lead the assessor to talk about these in a more structured off-line interview. Meanwhile, the assessors might have seen use of the free text notes, for example, as so obvious that it was not worthy of mention in the interview, or at too low a level of detail for a rich picture.

A second important aspect of the work, that was easily identified using situated observation, was the frequency with which work was interrupted by telephone calls, or requests from other staff for information about a customer's claim. Such interruption occurred often and at times when the assessor was in the middle of a complex investigation. The interruptions were invariably concerned with matters unrelated to the assessor's current claim.

'Train me' and cramming

A major benefit of this exercise was the improvement to our ability to follow the work of the assessors without being overwhelmed by the complexity of their navigation around the computer system. Assessors typically visit between 5 and 10 out of more than 50 available different dialogue screens in the course of a 5 minute telephone call. By cramming, we learned the most important screen numbers, which were displayed in a common location across all the dialogue screens. This enabled us to observe the order in which the work was conducted, without interrupting after every navigation.

A secondary, more intangible benefit may have been in giving us as observers more credibility when working with the assessors.

Finally, having some understanding of the ideal view of the work embodied in procedural guides and in the design of the computer system, gave us a reference point to compare against the flow of work as it is actually practised.

Action Recorder

Although we were unable to collect sufficient data using action recorder to generate significant statistical results, analysis of the records provided us with useful supporting evidence about the distribution of assessors' activities.

In particular, we were able to demonstrate our contention that most of the work was concerned with investigating a few complex cases, rather than processing large number of simple cases. During one recording session (of 45 minutes), the assessor was primarily working on a single case, switching back after each of 4 telephone interruptions, and 2 interruptions by colleagues which took up over 35% of the recording session.

4.2. Going beyond the immediate situation

Semi-structured interviews and rich pictures

Some major issues were identified through the off-line interviews, that might have been difficult to uncover using contextual observations alone. Some typical examples are given below.

> A number of assessors felt that the speed with which new products were introduced and old products revised, made it difficult for changes to `bed down'. As with any organisation, new systems inevitably encounter `teething troubles'. The assessors that we interviewed felt that dealing with such problems was a significant source of pressure for them.
>
> In one interview the assessor compared the current situation with the previous paper-based arrangements. In the clerical system, where multiple customers claims were related in a particular way, their files were kept together as a single unit. In the computer system this link is recorded using the free text notes, and the assessor has to retrieve the other customers' details manually.

As the above examples illustrate, the kind of issues made apparent by the off-line techniques, were concerned with the organisational and historical context of the work, i.e. aspects of the work that were largely beyond the day-to-day work of claims processing. Such issues need to be considered in HCI design.

The importance of the telephone also arose in the off-line interviews. Whilst our situated observation had established the fact that telephone interruptions occurred frequently, it was the off-line interview that allowed us to explore the organisational context that explains why the work is the way it is.

> During one interview an assessor described how the management were promoting a 'single point of contact' for customers. The single point of contact meant that a customer should be able to talk to one person who could explain precisely what point the customer's claim had reached. This philosophy led to the situation where a customer would be put through from the switchboard to the assessor who was dealing with their claim. This in turn led to the high level of telephone interuptions

that we had observed. Previously, the role of assessing claims was separated from the role of dealing with customer enquiries.

Taking the assessors out of the situation, and allowing them to step back and reflect on their work, allowed them to voice general concerns that they might normally ignore in their day-to-day work.

Scenario analysis

For all of our selected error scenarios, we found that the focus group participants quickly reached a consensus on those components of the work that were the most likely sources of the error. We asked the participants to map each scenario description to one of the components of our process model (figure 3). The results suggested that the information gathering part of the process, which was not well supported by the IT, was a very common source of error.

The exercise had the additional benefit of providing some validation of our process model.

4.3. Validating our understanding

Model building

We constructed two major models.

The first model, figure 2, illustrates the context in which the assessors work. In the model, three separate environments are identified: the assessors office environment, the external environment and the systems environment. The systems environment contains representations (denoted by *s) of aspects of the other two environments. For example, the fact that knowledge about the administrative world is encapsulated in the computer system's behaviour is represented by 'administrative world*' in the systems environment. Similarly, the system's knowledge about the customer is denoted as 'customer's world*'. The model also highlights the fact that the assessor has only a limited 'window' on the external and systems environments. Information flows between the three environments.

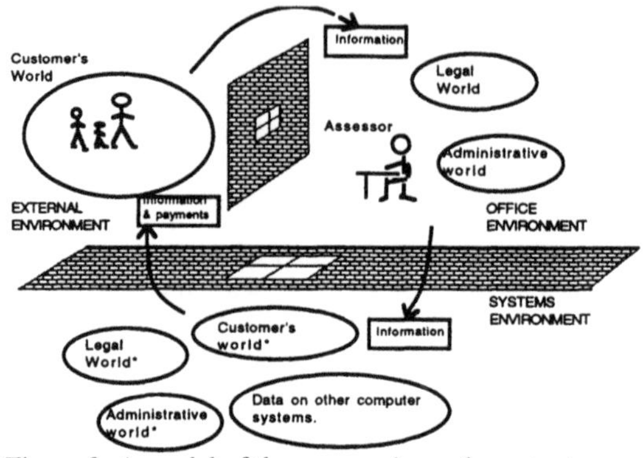

Figure 2: A model of the assessor's work context.

The model building activity helped us to articulate a number of key aspects of the work context. In particular: that all the worlds are subject to change at different rates; that time lags between changes in the customer's, administrative and legal worlds and the corresponding worlds in the systems environment are unavoidable; and the dynamic nature of the assessors work in controlling the system to maintain a balance between the payments made by the system, and the customer's entitlements.

The second model was more closely related to classical human information processing models. Figure 3 shows the processing of an individual claim as a network of actions and decisions. The model divides the work of processing a single claim into a number of phases. Following some alerting signal, such as a letter, phone call, or a printed message from the computer system the first major phase is an information gathering and recording phase. This is followed by a decision whether to proceed with changes to the customer's file (shown as the box 'Ready?'). The next phase is a process of updating the customer's file, reviewing the changes, adjudicating (accepting the changes), planning payments and then setting case controls to alert the assessor when a need for further action may be expected.

The model building took place in between two phases of data collection, the latter being shaped markedly by the model building activity. The activity of the observer reporting back to a colleague who had not done any observation at this stage, proved to be extremely valuable. It offered a chance to reflect on the data collected, explicate assumptions that the observer had made, and highlight possible areas of uncertainty where further data collection was required.

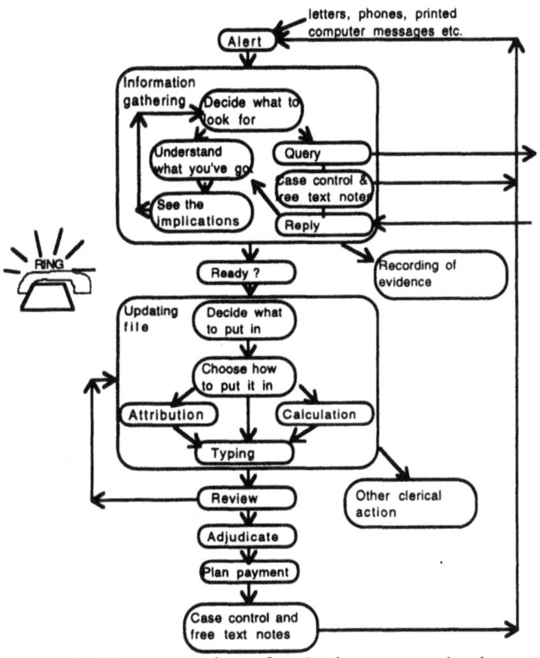

Figure 3: The processing of a single customer's change of circumstance.

For example, in developing the process model shown in figure 3, we were suspicious of the strict sequential division between the 'information gathering' and 'updating file' activities. On purely intuitive grounds we would have expected these to be concurrent and iterative. By further investigation, we were able to confirm that there was a hard divide between information gathering and file updates, this being a consequence of the need to maintain strict consistency between the customers recorded circumstances and the current value of payments. During the information gathering activity, partial information is recorded using the notes page, and only when a full set of changes and evidence had been collected, is the main body of the customer's file updated. This point served to clarify the role of the notes page as a tool in managing the investigation of the customer's claim.

Examples of issues arising during the construction of the context model were: the relationship between the various computer systems that held information about the customer; and how much of the communication between the computer system and the customer could be observed by the assessor. In fact, the computer system automatically generates letters composed of multiple standard paragraphs then sends them to the customer, without the assessor being able to inspect the content of the letter either before or after they are sent. This occasionally leads to the customer telephoning to ask for an explanation about a letter, the content of which is unknown to the assessor.

Challenging Assumptions

In the challenging assumptions exercise we presented the focus groups with provocative statements derived from, or contradicting the models, and designed to promote discussion. This exercise allowed us to engage the assessors in debating detailed points of our model and our understanding, where merely presenting the model might have provided us with less useful feedback.

Examples of statements that we used to promote discussion were: (1) the free text notes page is the most important screen; (2) automated interfaces to other computer systems are more trouble than they are worth; (3) Making the system more intelligent (e.g. reducing the number of clerical components) would not save me much time in a typical day; (4) 10% of the customers take up 90% of my time.

The participants greeted a number of our assumptions with scepticism and we were able to use this to encourage them to elaborate on the topics referred to by the assumptions. In some cases, this led us to new information about exceptions to our generalisations; in others it led us to temper the strength of our conclusions; in still others it led us to qualify our assertions. For example, in response to assumption (2), participants said that in fact, interfaces to other systems are invaluable in their day-to-day work, and were ultimately worth the extra effort that was required from them during their introduction. Their main concerns about the introduction of new software were that the software should be robust and that they should recieve adequate training.

Wish Lists

The wish list exercise was our final validation technique. The discussion based around the wish lists were extremely fruitful in allowing us to gauge people's opinions about the possible software changes. Among the possibilities discussed were: improvements to the facilities for recording free text notes, electronic cut and paste, electronic mail and on-line decision support systems. Improvements to the free text facilities were solutions based on existing technologies suggested by the participants themselves. Discussion here helped us to validate our belief in the importance of this resource. Issues such as electronic cut and paste took some participants beyond their current experience, but were recognised as possibly useful tools. Decision support systems were greeted with scepticism.

The discussion and emerging consensus allowed us to validate which requests were of genuine benefit to a large number of the assessors, and which were specific to one particular part of the work, or even peculiar to an individual.

5. DISCUSSION & CONCLUSIONS

The constraints on our study led us to combine situated and non-situated techniques for studying the context of work, co-ordinating these different approaches through iterative model building and validation. As we expected, the different data collection techniques proved effective for studying different aspects of the work context.

The situated techniques of contextual interviews supported by cramming, and use of Action Recorder provided important information about the work as practised and the day-to-day interaction with the computer system.

The non-situated techniques helped us to open out the organisational context and study issues that were physically or temporally located beyond the range of the immediately observable situation. The issues covered by these techniques included accuracy and errors, the history of work practices and artefacts, and significant events or processes that occur outside the assessors workplace.

Conceptual model building not only supported synthesis of these different data sources, suggested new insights and new questions to investigate during data collection, but also allowed us to engage assessors in the validation of our understanding before that understanding was embedded in the final report. Without such articulation and validation we do not feel we could have given sufficient voice to our participants.

From our experiences, we conclude that these elements: situated study, non-situated study, model building and validation can be successfully combined to produce an integrated approach to the study of work context, and that some of the techniques developed within soft systems analysis deserve the attention of HCI practitioners.

One question that remains is what types of conceptual models are most effective for studies of work context? The style of our conceptual models, and our method of using them, differs substantially from the style and methods used in soft system analysis (Checkland, 1981), or in Contextual Design (Holtzblatt & Beyer, 1996). We cannot say whether or not these alternative modelling approaches could offer similar benefits.

REFERENCES

H. Beyer & K. Holtzblatt, 1995. Apprenticing with the Customer. *Communications of the ACM* 38(5), pp 45 - 52.

P. Checkland, 1981. *Systems Thinking, Systems Practice. John* Wiley & Sons, Chichester.

P. Checkland and J. Scholes, 1990. *Soft Systems Methodology in Action*. John Wiley & Sons, Chichester.

K. Holtzblatt & S. Jones, 1993. Contextual Inquiry: A Participatory Technique for System Design. In Schuler & Namioka (editors), *Participatory Design: Principles and Practices.* Lawrence Erlbaum Associates, Hillsdale, NJ., pp 177 - 210.

K. Holtzblatt & H. Beyer, 1996. *Contextual Design: Using Customer Work Models to Drive Systems Design.* Tutorial notes from CHI 96. In Context Enterprises, Harvard, MA.

J. Hughes, J. O'Brien, T. Rodden, M. Rouncefield & I. Sommerville, 1995. Presenting Ethnography in the Requirements Process. In *RE95, Proceedings of the Second IEEE International Symposium on Requirements Engineering,* pp 27 - 35. IEEE Press.

D. Patching, 1993. *Practical Soft Systems Analysis.* Pitman, London.

L. Suchman (editor), 1995 Representations of Work. *Communications of the ACM* 38(9), pp 33-68.

L. Watts, A. Monk & O. Daly-Jones, 1996. Interpersonal awareness and synchronization: assessing the value of communications technologies. *Int. J. Human-Computer Studies,* 44: 849-873

User requirements capture for a multimedia CSCW system

Janni Nielsen* Gitte Lindgaard* Lone Dirckinck-Holmfeld**
Morten Vendelø*, Oluf Danielsen*, Marianne Georgsen****

* Institute of Informatics, Copenhagen Business School
** Institute of Communication, Aalborg University
*** Institute of Computer Science, Learning, Roskilde University
Denmark
janni.nielsen@cbs.dk

ABSTRACT: The early stages of a Europen Union funded multimedia CSCW project scheduled to run for several years are described. The project, called Manicoral, concerns the definition, design, development and implementation of a CSCW as well as a study of cultural, collaborative and communications aspects of a scientific community to whom the interaction media are new. The CSCW system encompasses both data visualisation and communications tools. These are being developed iteratively together with user requirements which are expected to change as the project matures and the user groups become accustomed to using the tools. The Scandinavian perspective and Human Factors analyses are broughttogether in a wholistic conceptual framework in the project to cover both technical requirements and collaboration, communication and cultural issues. Methods applied so far and early results are reported.

KEY WORDS: Multimedia, CSCW system, user requirements, Scandinavian perspective, human factors

1. INTRODUCTION

Early investigations into user needs and cultural aspects characterising a European scientific research community, the future users of this multimedia CSCW system, are reported in this paper. The project is a longitudinal study of emerging commuinication patterns, learning, collaboration and cultural characteristics of a technologically sophisticated set of user groups. In addition, it aims to define, design, develop and implement the supporting CSCW system which has two major components: communication tools and data visualisation tools. The project partners and their roles and objectives are described first. This is followed by a discussion of two major traditions brought together to provide a wholistic account of user-related needs, changes and developments of tools and behaviour during the project. These perspectives are the Scandinavian and Human Factors. Investigative methods applied so far are discussed with a focus on field studies already conducted and video analysis of two kinds of sessions in which users are defining their initial requirements. Preliminary data are reported, and research to be undertaken in the near future is discussed.

Human–Computer Interaction: INTERACT'97 S. Howard, J. Hammond & G. Lindgaard (editors)
Published by Chapman & Hall

2. MANICORAL

2.1 The project

Manicoral (Multimedia And Network In COoperative Research And Learning) is an international, interdisciplinary, user-driven research and development project involving partners from Denmark, Great Britain, The Netherlands, Austria, Italy and Greece. Disciplines represented in the project include natural science, humanities, behavioural and social science as well as technology. Manicoral is funded by the European Union's 4th Frame Program, Telematics for Research. It commenced in January 1996 and is expected to run for four years. The objective is to define, develop, implement and evaluate a multimedia Computer Supported Co-operative Work System (CSCW) among a geographically distributed European research group. It is anticipated that use of CSCW tools will provode better access to scientific methods, results and raw data, and that this will enhance collaboration in the user groups. This should enable these to develop sophisticated products such as global gravity maps.

2.2 The partners: User groups

The user group, AFRICAR (Altimetry For Research In Climate And Resources) is a network of European geoscientists who investigate the use and exploitation of radar altimetry data. The AFRICAR groups have collaborated for many years through conventional technology and infrequent face-to-face meetings. Their research seeks to utilise methods for measuring the distance from satellites to the ocean surface, or to the surface of ice caps. Change in the height of the ice caps may indicate climatic change. On the ocean, the location of currents and eddies may be observed, and changes in these contribute both to a basic understanding of climatic changes and to use in weather forecasting. The location of currents is also of importance for navigation and shipping, since time and fuel may be saved by following or avoiding currents. Observations made by groups such as AFRICAR are also used for gravitational field calculations. This is important for mapping resources, for example, oil, volcanic activity or deeper processes in the earth, such as earthquakes.

Vast quantities of raw data obtained from a number of sources are stored in large databases located in different geographical locations. The accuracy of the data varies, as does their format, scale and granularity. It is difficult and cumbersome to locate, recognise, diagnose and remove noisy or erroneous data from a database. In order to compare data from different sources, these must be calibrated. This is very difficult, even for data pertaining to a particular geographical area or a certain time frame. This is partly because no common standards are imposed on the data format, database interaction methods, search and retrieval mechanisms, or on ways to extract or mark subsets of data. In an effort to inspect data effectively and efficiently, raw data are transformed into visual maps, wave forms, line graphs, and so forth. A variety of non-standard data manipulation tools are being used in these processes, many of which users themselves have developed.

2.3 The Human Communication, Collaboration, and Cognition group (HCCC)

Researchers in the Danish HCCC group represent the humanisties as well as the behavioural and social sciences. Their task is to develop a conceptual and methodological framework for studying, analysing and specifying user requirements for a CSCW system for scientific cooperation. This framework will also be used for evaluating the constitutive influence of collaborative technologies on the AFRICAR research community.

2.4 The technical group

The task of the technical experts at the Rutherford Appleton Laboratories (RAL) in the UK is to provide a system for Distributed Cooperative Visualisation (DCV). The DCV system will be based on the user requirements specification generated by the HCCC group, and will also be building on existing visualisation systems already used by AFRICAR. Another European project, the Telematics MERCI project, will supply CSCW tools. These will be revised and enhanced iteratively throughout the duration of the Manicoral project to fine-tune the technology so as best to match users' emerging, and probably changing, requirements.

3. OBJECTIVES OF THE HCCC GROUP

Manicoral is unique in that it commenced before the CSCW tools were introduced into the AFRICAR groups. This enables a longitudinal study of how an international research community evolves, of how technology may enable new ways of collaboration and change the roles of community members, and also to study the evolution of novel ways to generate, combine and interpret scientific data.

The HCCC objectives are to:

- develop a conceptual framework and methods for developing user-driven requirements and functional specifications
- study how communication and collaboration evolve in a distributed research community over time
- study the constitutive influence of CSCW technologies on a community

3.1 Perspectives

In order to satisfy the HCCC objectives, two major theoretical traditions are brought together. These virtually represent two ends of a philosophical and methodological continuum that spans investigative approaches ranging from the empirico-mathematical to the culture-understanding (see Mc Garland & Polgar, 1994 for elaboration). The culture-understanding end is represented by what has been labeled the "Scendinavian" perspective, and the empirico-mathematical end is represented by a more traditional Human Factors perspective. Relevant characteristics of these are described below.

3.1 A Scandinavian perspective

In Scandinavia there is a long tradition for Participatory Design (PD), or user centred design, where Union representatives and participants were involved in the systems developmental process (Greenbaum & Kyng, 1991; Ehn, 1988; Bødker Grønbæk, & Kyng, 1993). However, this framework alone was insufficient to satisfy the myriad of factors to be studied in the development and implementation of a CSCW tool for a technologically sophisticated user group such as AFRICAR.

To take account of these factors, a new approach, Dialogue Design, is being developed. Dialogue Design differs from the traditional Danish version of PD in that all the participants are researchers and highly experienced in using advanced technologies. Dialogue Design draws on Dialogue Research tClausen, Lorenzen & Rasmussen., 1992), a Danish research tradition focusing on mutual dialogues between researchers and project participants as the tool for development and assessment (Cronberg, Duelund, Jensen et al., 1991). The concept of dialogue is borrowed from Habermas' ideal of a dialogue free from power games (Habermas, 1987), a true dialogue with no hidden agendae, and where participants meet with open mind and with the understanding that the 'best arguments will win'. A reasonably open-ended dialogue-oriented approach is taken to accommodate and even highlight cultural and disciplinary differences between the Manicoral partners. Thus the methods applied in investigating the relevant aspects of the research community are adaptable and applied in accordance with a collaborative understanding and mutual learning processes.

In the initial step, we have applied different methods to capture the inter-dependent user requirements and their visions. Requirements cannot be captured adequately without also capturing users' vision of their future work to be supported by a new system. Visions Capture aims to outline a possible future. The notion of a 'possible' future is stressed to denote the uncertainty associated with predicting any future. Any technological tool is implemented in an existing organisational culture, into a community where clearly defined, as well as unspoken, practices are the order of the day; it will be used by people who bring their organisational and idiosyncratic understandings to the interaction. These factors influence the development- and implementation process as well as later usage patterns. Design of tools is also design of work tasks, the implementation of which may require users to obtain new qualifications. Implementation of tools thus changes organisations as well. Because the technological systems are such forceful change-agents, user driven design requires rich visions and imagination, which are fundamental cognitive tools in the design process (Nielsen, 1993).

3.3 The Human Factors perspective

From a human factors angle, it is important to derive user requirements specifications that can be readily translated into user interface design. Usually, one would perform a thorough User Needs Analysis (Lindgaard, 1994) which includes some kind of task analysis. However, there are no routine tasks in the present project. Therefore, alternative methods must be explored for capturing user requirements and writing functional specifications. From the human factors perspective, it is important to understand what users want to communicate with each other, how they want their data to look, how they want to be able to identify, mark, manipulate and transpose data, and what data views they want to show, compare, and discuss.

The CSCW tools provided are novel to AFRICAR interactions which adds further elements of uncertainty the the requirements specification process: users cannot state precisely what they want; no one can predict exactly what data manipulation tools will be able to provide, and new interaction and communication patterns are likely to emerge as users gain experience using the tools. For these reasons, requirements specifications will proceed through at least two major phases. In the first phase, the aim is to understand how users expect to interact using the future CSCW. Preliminary data from this phase are presented later. In the second phase, the specifications will be adjusted iteratively according to how users are found actually to interact via these tools, and as the tools themselves evolve. It is commonly found that users' requests, outlined before the technology is available, vary substantially from the ways their interactions evolve once technological support tools are provided (Lindgaard, 1995). The iterative, concurrent refinement of requirement specifications and tools is a novel approach to systems development.

In order to study the evolution of new communication patterns and forms of collaboration, data are currently being collected on existing communication patterns within AFRICAR to determine what is being communicated by whom, how often, using which technologies, and so forth. Sampling communication among members at regular intervals over the next four years should capture any changes to existing communication patterns.

In an effort to trace the constitutive influence of a CSCW tool in this community, different meeting types undertaken by AFRICAR without the CSCW tools are currently being analysed from video recordings, but results are not yet available. In the first instance, this analysis will highlight differences and similarities between such meeting types identified to date. As with communication patterns, regular sampling of meetings should allude to any changes in meeting culture, structures or participant roles occurring over time.

4. METHODS

The range of methods applied so far include field studies of daily practice in some of the local research communities as well as recordings of AFRICAR meetings and discussions. In addition, two types of workshops have been held to capture user requirements: a so-called vision workshop and a mind mapping worhshop These were videotaped, and the preliminary analysis is presented later. During the field studies, a range of methods were used for data capture, including observations, video recordings, in depths interviews, photographing, and dialogue discussions.

4.1 Field studies

The field study methodology was partly inspired by ethnographic traditions, partly by a critical hermeneutic framework, and partly by a learning approach building on planned dialogues. In order to understand the needs and visions of the AFRICAR groups as a coherent scientific community and to investigate the constitutive role of technology field studies aiamed to elucidate daily practice in local communities. Three of the six AFRICAR communities took part. These were selected to represent the geographical spread of the community as well as varying levels of technology usage, and also to contrast the research foci within AFRICAR. The field studies aimed to gain insight into similarities and differences between the various research communities.

An observations-and-interview guide was developed from the theoretical perspectives of learning, cognition and scientific knowledge cultures which have been combined in a preliminary conceptual framework (Danielsen,

Nielsen & Dirckinck-Holmfeld, 1996). This is not discussed further here.

The categories in the guide included descriptions of artefacts, photographs as a still life documentation of the research institutions, listing of the technological equipment (what, where and when it is used), and a description of the local group members (educational background, research focus, employment status). Also the scientific visualisations the groups worked with/produced, (graphs, topographical maps, computer-generated visualisations and animation) and observations of learning situations (interactions between members, seminars) were noted .

The local AFRICAR communities have different characteristics. In some communities the development of visualisations of scientific data using different software tools is an indispensable part of the geophysical research; in others such tools are rarely used. The number of researchers in a local AFRICAR group varies from two 12. Some communities have recruited new members from their own students, others have recruited candidates from related disciplines. Each local research community is thus unique in some respect which has now been documented.

Observations and note-taking were used during all field studies. In one community in which all computers were located in a computer room with several PCs and work stations, activities and collaboration were sampled in this room at regular intervals. Another community had a very small room with a coffee machine. The adjacent hallway had become an informal, but central meeting place.

Video recordings were made of sessions in which AFRICAR researchers were demonstrating how they work. Video-taping was also used to document group-interviews.

In depth, semi-structured interviews were carried out key AFRICAR members. A number of topics had been formulated in preparation, based in the theoretical model and the categories from the field guide. Parts of the interview used a more conflicting technique, called the double perspective change (Nielsen, 1987) which encourages the interviewee to change perspective during the interview.

Still Life photographs were taken systematically throughout the institute, including hallways and offices. They capture the work environment and serve as memory aids of places, layouts, people and incidents.

Dialogue Discussions were used when one of the HCCC representative stayed with the family of the local AFRICAR manager and spent several hours travelling to and from work every day. This gave ample time for informal talks. A topic would be defined as important and would then be explored freely, but persistently during the drive. Immediately after arrival, field notes would be taken to summarise the dialogue.

4.2 AFRICAR meetings

Face to face meetings are an important part of the AFRICAR collaboration. As it is believed that the nature, frequency, content and duration of meetings is likely to change with the introduction of the CSCW tools, examples of these meetings have been recorded before these tools were available to enable comparisons later in the project. Preliminary analyses of these data suggest there are three distinct types of meetings. Characteristics of these are currently being studied from video recordings, note taking and collection of all documentation tabled. The outcome of this analysis is unavailable at the time of writing.

4.3 Capturing user requirements

Three techniques have been applied to capture initial user requirements: (1) a mind mapping workshop, (2) a face-to-face discussion following hands-on experience with the current CSCW tools, and (3) a vision workshop . The first two of these were captured on videotape and highlights of the human factors analysis of these are presented later. Outcomes of the vision workshop were too general to use as a basis for drafting user requirements specifications. They are thus not presented here, but a summary may be found in Vendelø (1996).

A mind mapping workshop conducted in two sessions on consecutive days was being held at the outset of the Manicoral project to explore the possibilities for a joint project, and to identify a possible focus for the work within and between scientific groups. Mind mapping enables one to sketch and acquire an overall view of a given problem field. Participants work in small groups. In the first of two phases, the groups are asked to draw, sketch or write key concepts as they come to mind. All inputs are equal, but rationales may be requested. In the second phase, participants are asked to organise and add infrastructure to the concepts noted in phase 1, resulting in a map showing goals and relationships between the concepts discussed.

Just prior to the vision workshop, a hands-on session of the current CSCW tools was conducted. This was followed by a group discussion focusing on the perceived merits and shortcomings of these existing tools. Some of the AFRICAR members had prepared a number of subject-specific themes to be discussed during the session and which were typical for their scientific work. Their task was to collaborate on the themes while trying out the CSCW tools. With this experience fresh in mind, the videotaped discussion proved to be an excellent source for obtaining relevant user requirements. Selected data from the analysis are presented later.

5. RESULTS

5.1 Field studies

The analysis of field study data revealed a number of dimensions along which the three communities varied. These are outlined below:

Institution: Members of the AFRICAR groups work in traditional European universities or in government research laboratories.

Politics: Ranges from geodesy and geophysics being barely tolerated to these being high priority fields

Local meetings: Colloquia and regular seminars are held in some communities; irregular discussions only in others

Teaching obligations: Ranges from none up to presenting eight lectures per week in areas such as surveying; teaching is at undergraduate and/or graduate levels

Local communities: The size of the local groups varies from two to eight senior, and a small number of junior scientists working together. In some cases, the entire group is located on a single floor; in others they are placed in different buildings.

Academic background: Geodesy, geophysics, mathematics, physics, and engineering

History of collaboration: Ranges from 24 years to recent arrivals

Publication record: Ranges from editorial board membership and frequent international publications to none

Scientific focus: Ranges from empirical estimates of satellite positioning to purely theoretical work and applied geodesy

Organisation of technology: Computers are either in common computer rooms or in people's offices. the amount of equipment varies from a PC to large work stations, plotters and other advanced machines.

Role of visualisations: Some work requires no visualisations although they may have illustrative value, whereas visualisations are central to other kinds of work

Visions for AFRICAR: AFRICAR is seen by some as a data sharing group and by others as a forum for scientific discussion and collaboration as well as specification of joint projects.

5.2 Human factors videotape analysis

Three videotapes were analysed, in the first instance by transwcribing all utterances spoken and the time at which they occurred. Two of the tapes were recordings from the mind mapping workshop (November 1994), and the third recorded the post-CSCW interaction meeting (March, 1996). The duration of meetings varied with the first mind mapping workshop (MM1) taking 90 minutes, the second one (MM2) taking 110 minutes, and the CSCW discussion (CSCW) taking 60 minutes respectively. Space does not allow reporting of these results in detail. Attention will therefore be brought only to the most important highlights. First, the number of unique ideas concerning a relevant aspect of the technology, possible common AFRICAR projects, and future interactions were ascertained for each meeting. These totalled 63 at MM1, 54 at MM2, and 44 at the CSCW meeting. It is not surprising that the group runs out of new suggestions over time; on that score alone, one would expect the most recent meeting to be least productive. The data appear, superficially, to support that contention.

Yet, it is interesting to note that, despite some similarities between meetings, the focus clearly shifted from one meeting to the next. At all meetings, between seven and ten topics were discussed, and roughly a quarter of the time was devoted to discussing possible data manipulation tools for the future (MM1 27.17%, MM2 25.76%, CSCW 27.17% of the meeting time). However, at MM1, the first 28.24% of the time was spent just getting the discussion going and ideas emerging. People clearly felt embarrassed and awkward about using this method for generating and discussing ideas. However, once they became involved, the discussion flowed freely. At MM2, roughly one third (30.18%) of the meeting time was devoted to discussing possible projects AFRICAR might undertake in the course of the Manicoral project. This subject had not been broached in MM1 at all. In the CSCW meeting, close to one half of the time (44.05%) was spent talking about possible ways to conduct meetings using the tools. This compares with 5.40% and 6.49% of time devoted to that topic at MM1 and MM2 respectively. At the CSCW meeting, one might have expected members to concentrate on the scientific themes in the ensuing discussion. Instead, it is striking that was the human-human interaction and the barriers to same caused by the technology that occupied members the most directly following this experience rather than discussing the technological merits of the tool.

In terms of deriving actual user requirements for the CSCW tools, a high proportion of the ideas tabled at the three meetings were bearing directly on specifying what users would like to be able to do interactively. At MM1 such technological ideas comprised 55.56% of the 63 ideas; at MM2 this figure was 64.81% of the 54 ideas, and at the CSCW, it was 65.09% of the total of 44 ideas. At the time of writing the data ae still being calibrated to determine exactly how many of these technical ideas and suggestions are unique. It is expected that there will be a certain amount of overlap between the three data sets. However, it is clear already now that, in MM1 and MM2, that is before they had been exposed to the CSCW tool, users were expressing their ideas in much broader terms (eg. "it would be nice to be able to see the relationship between different data and data formats layered in one visualisation") than was the case in the CSCW session ("We want two overhead projectors"). Ideas in this latter case were to a large extent constrained by the technology in its current form. Depending on the amount of overlap of ideas yet to be determined, this could support the notion that users of future technology should generate their initial ideas away from, and thus unconstrained by, the technology. The final data analysis should shed light on this argument.

6. CONCLUSION AND FUTURE WORK

The preliminary data provided here show that Manicoral provides an excellent opportunity for deriving user requirements before users have been exposed to the technology, and also to develop new investigative tools to accomplish this. In addition to the usual human factors analyses designed to specify the tool per se, the project also offers an opportunity to trace ongoing, probably changing, communication and interaction patterns, learning and cooperation in an emerging scientific community. In the near future, scenarios will be drafted and explored for feasibility with the users. These scenarios will be based on users' expressed wishes taken ad verbatim from the video tapes. The scenarios will probably need to specify short-term, medium and long-term realisations which will then serve to guide the further development of the tool together with other observations. The scenarios will, in the short term, be central to a participatory design workshop to be conducted soon.

REFERENCES

Clausen, C., Lorentzen, B. & Rasmussen, L. B (eds.) (1992). *Deltagelse i teknologisk udvikling*, Fremad, Copenhagen.

Cronberg, T, Duelund, Jensen, & Qvortrup, L. (eds.) (1991). *Danish Experiments - Social Constructions of Technolog,*. Copenhagen: New Social Science Monographs

Danielsen, O. Nielsen, J. & Dirckinck-Holmfeld, L. (1996). *Conceptual Framework - introductory reflections upon fundamental theoretical concepts in Manicoral*, Manicoral, Working Paper-Deliverable 3.1

Greenbaum, J. & Kyng, M. (1991). Introduction: Situated Design, in J. Greenbaum and M. Kyng (eds.), *Cooperative Design of Computer Systems*, Lawrence Erlbaum Ass. London, pp 1-25.

Habermas, J. (1987). *The Theory of Communicative Actions*, Policy Press, Cambridge, vol I & II,.

Lindgaard, G. (1995). WOW - 568 smart features on your PABX: What reallydetermines the uptake of technology? *Proceedings HFT '93 International Symposium Human Factors in Telecommunications*, Darmstadt, Germany, May 11-14.

Lindgaard, G. (1994). *Usability testing and system evaluation: A guide for designing useful computer systems*, Chapman & Hall, London.

McGarland, M. & Polgar, S. (1994). Paradigm collapse in psychology: The necessity for a "two methods" approach, *Australian Psychologist*, 29 (1), 21-28.

Nielsen, J. (1987). Datamater og erkendelsesprocesser - en teoretisk analyse af erkendelsesparadigmer, set i relation til nogle 8.klasses elevers arbejde med datamater, Danmarks Lærerhøjskole, PPP publikation nr. 42.

Vendelø, M. (1996). Work task 03.2 in MANICORAL: [ID] Index and overview of initial requirements capture, working document, Copenhagen Business School, Copenhagen.

Constrained vs spontaneous speech and gestures for interacting with computers: A comparative empirical study

Sandrine Robbe*, Noëlle Carbonell*, Pierre Dauchy**

*CRIN-CNRS & INRIA-Lorraine, BP 239, F54506 Vandœuvre lès Nancy cedex
**IMASSA-CERMA, BP 73, F91223 Brétigny sur Orge cedex
robbe@loria.fr, carbo@loria.fr pierre@cerma.fr

ABSTRACT In the framework of a prospective ergonomic approach, we simulated two multimodal user interfaces in order to study the usability of constrained vs spontaneous speech. The first experiment, which served as a reference, gave subjects the opportunity to use speech and gestures freely. Contrastingly, in the second experiment, subjects had to comply with multimodal constraints. We conducted a comparative study between these two experiments which aims to provide designers with useful knowledge concerning the requirements, preferences and expectations of potential users of future multimodal interfaces. The paper presents both experiments together with the conclusions of our analyses of the collected data.

KEYWORDS Design rationale, Interaction design, Speech and voice, Usability evaluation, Multimodal user interfaces

1. INTRODUCTION

Fuller transparency of Human-Computer Interaction (HCI) ranks among users' major expectations; in particular, it is much sought after by occasional users and the general public, inasmuch as the cognitive cost of learning an artificial language is higher for them than for users who intend to become experts or frequent users (Shneiderman, 1987).

Thanks to recent advances in both automatic continuous speech recognition and natural language (NL) interpretation, it is now possible to process large subsets of spoken NL accurately, and to substitute them for existing artificial query or command languages (Seneff et al., 1996), with a view to offering users "natural" (hence transparent) HCI. Nevertheless, researchers in computational linguistics have not yet reached a thorough understanding of spatial reference phrases and anaphora mechanisms. Thus, the implementation of oral NL as a substitute for direct manipulation (Shneiderman, 1983) cannot yet be considered, since the control of iconic interfaces requires the ability to indicate locations on the screen, and to select a specific icon from a set of similar graphical objects. An attractive solution for achieving robust quasi-"natural" HCI soon is to design HCI languages that include, as well as oral statements from a given subset S of NL, multimodal[1] commands associating oral statements from S with pointing gestures. Research on the implementation of multimodal HCI is developing rapidly ((Bellalem and Romary, 1995) (Nigay and Coutaz, 1993)). In addition, field studies (Falzon, 1991) indicate that operators spontaneously develop specific operative sublanguages for professional exchanges; these languages consist of subsets of natural language with a restricted syntax and a limited non-ambiguous vocabulary.

We are currently investigating, within a prospective ergonomic research framework, utility and usability issues pertaining to the implementation of this short-term ap-

[1] Subsequently, "multimodality" and "multimodal" will refer to the association of speech and gestures only.

Human–Computer Interaction: INTERACT'97 S. Howard, J. Hammond & G. Lindgaard (editors)
Published by Chapman & Hall

proach. The main goal of the comparative empirical study reported here is to assess the influence of realistic expression constraints on the behaviours of potential users of future multimodal interfaces. More precisely, we address the following issues, with a view to providing designers with useful knowledge concerning the requirements, preferences and expectations of multimodal interface users:

- Is it possible to define realistic constraints on users' spontaneous forms of multimodal expression, which they will comply with easily, as well as learn rapidly and reliably (mostly through the interaction)?
- What is the influence of such constraints (especially system recognition failures) on users' activities, their use of multimodality, and the efficiency of the interaction?
- Which design methods will guarantee the generation of "good" expression constraints, that is: constraints which are easy to apply, do not interfere with users' activities, and maintain the efficiency and the appeal of the interaction?

To answer these questions, we considered two experimental situations: in the first, which served as a reference, subjects could use speech and gestures freely, whilst in the second they had to comply with multimodal constraints.

We first describe the experimental setup. Then we analyse and interpret the resulting empirical data. Finally, we summarize our main results from which we infer useful conclusions for the design of multimodal HCI.

Whilst constrained oral HCI has motivated numerous experimental or empirical studies (Hauptmann and McAvinney, 1993), few empirical studies have been devoted to multimodal constrained HCI (Catinis and Caelen, 1995); and, to our knowledge, no comparative study has been published thus far. The issues we mentioned earlier have not yet been addressed.

2. EXPERIMENTAL SETUP

2.1 Overview

Two groups, of eight subjects each, interacted, during three weekly sessions, with two different multimodal interfaces whose functionalities were simulated thanks to the Wizard of Oz technique. The average length of a session was about half an hour (per subject). Both groups carried out identical tasks; but subjects in the reference group (SP) could use speech and/or 2D gestures spontaneously, while subjects in the experimental group (CS) had to comply with expression constraints.

Although human face-to-face communication involves 3D gestures more often than 2D gestures, we restricted the nonverbal expression of subjects to 2D gestures – i.e. gestures on the surface of the screen – in order to offer them a realistic HCI environment, that is, a user interface that could be implemented in the near future. In addition, as application objects were represented by 2D icons, gestures in a 3D space were not needed.

The application domain and the tasks that subjects had to perform were chosen so that all the necessary actions for achieving the scenarios could be expressed easily using just speech, or just gestures, or a combination of both modalities.

2.2 Expression constraints

In order to obtain a tractable multimodal artificial language that would impose minimal constraints on the spontaneous expression of CS subjects, we selected an appropriate subset of the overall set of utterances and gestures used by SP subjects. The gestural component of this language included two categories of elementary gestures: pointing gestures (PG) and simulation gestures (SG), that is, gestures (akin to mouse drags) that mimed requested translations or rotations of graphical objects. Ambiguous gestures and constructs, and no others, were eliminated from the simple gestural "vocabulary" and "syntax" used by SP subjects.

We adopted the following selection criteria for defining the oral component of the language:

- Utterances should be reliably interpretable using current continuous speech recognisers; therefore, the size of the vocabulary was restricted to a hundred lexical items or so, and the syntax was simplified so that it could be described by a CF grammar (the static branching factor of this grammar is 5.5 and its dynamic branching factor is 2.6);
- The language expressiveness (i.e. its semantics) should be equivalent to the union of the semantic interpretations of all the utterances issued by SP subjects over the three sessions – we wanted to sepa-

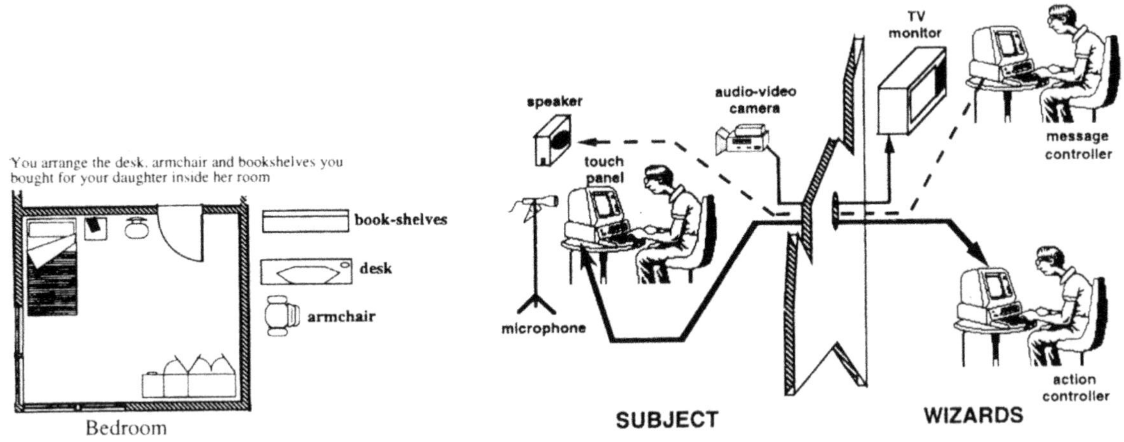

(A) (B)

Figure 1: (A) First scenario: text and initial display. (B) Experimental setup.

rate the possible effects of lexical and syntactic constraints on the expression and activity of CS subjects from the influence of semantic restrictions, so that the effects of lexical and syntaxic constraints could be assessed accurately through a comparison of CS and SP subjects' behaviours;

- Synonyms and ambiguities (at the lexical and syntactic levels) should be eliminated, as they are excluded from operative sublanguages consisting of subsets of NL defined spontaneously by operators.

CS subjects were given a written description of this multimodal artificial language (MAL), and the experimenter helped them to perform the examples included in this short manual before the execution of the first scenario; this initial training stage lasted less than 10 minutes on average. SP subjects had no initial training, but they could, before launching the first scenario, explore the capabilities of the interface in the presence of the experimenter who just answered their questions.

2.3 Subjects

All subjects had previously used software intended for the general public, and most of them were familiar with direct manipulation; some had basic programming knowledge, but none was an expert in computer science. Their backgrounds and professions were similar.

2.4 Application domain and tasks

Subjects were asked to perform design tasks relating to furniture arrangement. They had to modify the layout of various furnished rooms according to instructions specified in scenarios of increasing complexity. Initial layouts were displayed on the screen in the form of 2D plans. Figure 1(A) reproduces the first scenario and the corresponding initial layout.

2.5 Implementation of the WOZ technique

Two human operators were in charge of the simulation of the functionalities of both multimodal interfaces.

One of them interpreted the subject's commands and activated the relevant software functions; results were displayed simultaneously on the subject's and the wizards' screens. The other operator, who was taking care of dialogue management, selected and activated pre-recorded oral messages in response to incoming utterances and gestures from the subjects. The experimental setup is described in Figure 1(B).

In addition, the CS setup included a commercial continuous speech monospeaker recognizer, since the wizards could not decide accurately, in real time, whether or not an oral command belonged to the oral component of the MAL language. Wizards interpreted oral utterances from the subjects using the results of the recognition system (which were displayed on the subject's and the wizards' screens).

2.6 Recordings and transcripts

Subjects were videotaped throughout both experiments. Written descriptions of the video recordings consist of orthographic transcripts of utterances, and standardized descriptions of subjects' gestures and system actions.
Results of the speech recognizer were included in the transcripts of the CS group.
Transcripts of both first sessions (one scenario) were analysed and compared. Results of the comparisons are summarized in the next section.

3. RESULTS AND INTERPRETATIONS

Results, interpretations, discussions and conclusions are grouped according to the issues presented in the introduction.

3.1 Application of expression constraints

Subjects in the CS group complied very easily with gestural constraints: we picked out only three "incorrect" gestures in the transcripts. This result is not surprising since subjects were allowed to use only a few gestures based on simple forms.
On the other hand, all subjects resorted to words outside the vocabulary, at least once. Most of these lexical items are semantically related to words in the vocabulary (e.g. by synonymy or antonymy). All subjects corrected some of their lexical errors spontaneously, generally after the first rejection of the corresponding utterances by the system; half of the subjects corrected all of them. Such lexical errors are not frequent, although their frequency varies greatly from one subject to another: the percentages (per subject) of utterances including such errors range from 1% to 30%, but rates for five subjects are lower than 10%.
Syntactic errors are fewer than lexical ones (23 vs 32 in the whole corpus of transcripts), and only five subjects are concerned. But these errors were detected and corrected less easily (30% vs 56%).
On the whole, subjects in the CS group, although they had gone through a very short initial training, managed to confine the oral components of their requests within the boundaries of a restricted subset of NL without apparent difficulty (few errors). As the MAL language can compare with standard command languages, with respect to the vocabulary size and structural complexity, the reasons for this success may be ascribed to specific properties of this artificial language, and thus to the method used for its design, that is:

- MAL is a subset of NL;
- its power of expression has been defined from the analysis of the oral commands and statements uttered spontaneously by SP subjects; it is then equivalent to the power of expression of the spontaneous oral statements formulated by users interacting with the same application, performing similar tasks, and aiming to achieve identical goals;
- synonymy and polysemy (i.e. lexical ambiguity) have been excluded, as well as structural synonymy and ambiguity, in order to emulate the efficiency of operative languages.

Nevertheless, this method has some drawbacks that may preclude its application in industrial environments. The observation of users interacting freely with the application (cf. the SP study) is costly, and the definition of an appropriate but tractable subset of NL may prove tricky[2]. Moreover, the bulk of this investment is application-dependent and then not reusable in other application domains.
An inter-group comparison suggests that subjects from the CS group benefited from the linguistic constraints with which they had to comply. Hesitations and grammatical incorrections are significantly (Wilcoxon test[3]: Σ_{CS}=43 W(8;8)=]49;87[; $p<0.05$) less frequent in their oral statements than in those from SP subjects: 13% vs 53%, and 1.9% vs 23.5% respectively[4]. These results are detailed in Table 1.
In addition, CS subjects formulate their oral requests more precisely than SP subjects: half of the subjects in

[2]For instance, words divide the user's activity into elementary tasks that do not necessarily coincide with the application functions.

[3]We used a Wilcoxon test when there was a significant difference between variances and a t-test in other cases.

[4]Percentages represent numbers of relevant tokens normalized by the total number of oral and multimodal commands per group.

	Hesitations								Incorrections							
	S1	S2	S3	S4	S5	S6	S7	S8	S1	S2	S3	S4	S5	S6	S7	S8
SP subjects	3.1	12.5	1.6	3.1	7.8	4.7	12.5	7.8	7.8	12.5	-	-	-	-	1.6	1.6
CS subjects	2.3	1.5	1.1	0.8	1.9	1.5	3.8	3	0.4	-	-	-	-	0.4	0.8	0.4

Table 1: Percentages of hesitations and grammatical incorrections over the total number of oral and multimodal utterances per subject (S1, ...,S8)

the SP group vs two in the CS group expressed one (or more) imprecise or ambiguous oral request. But it would be rash to draw conclusions from a few instances per group only. Further empirical or experimental studies are needed to evaluate what appears as a mere observed tendency.

This positive influence of the linguistic constraints imposed on CS subjects may be due to the fact that the protocol of the CS study met a request formulated by most SP subjects in the post experiment questionnaires. They stated that they would have greatly appreciated an initial presentation of the interface, including actual instances of commands and interaction sequences. As a justification for this request, they complained that they had been disconcerted, at first, by the new interface they had to test. The attitudes of SP subjects suggest that beginners require illustrated presentations of the capabilities and functioning of new interfaces and HCI paradigms, even in the case when the new interface or mode of interaction may be viewed as an implementation of the concept of "transparency".

We analyse, in the next section, the possible effects of the expression constraints that we selected on the activity of users, on their use of multimodality and the efficiency of the interaction.

3.2 Side-effects of expression constraints

3.2.1 On the use of modalities

There are marked differences between the two groups as regards their use of speech and gestures (cf. table 2). But these differences are not statistically significant by reason of intra-group pronounced inter-individual variations ($\Sigma_{CS} = 67$ W(8;8)=]49;87[; $p<0.05$). The comparison is focused solely on the initial formulations of commands, due to the low number of repetitions and reformulations expressed by SP subjects, whose requests are interpreted by human wizards. Contrastingly, CS subjects are induced to make multiple repetitions and reformulations since their oral statements are interpreted by a commercial speech recognizer with limited accuracy.

According to table 2, the multimodal commands issued by CS subjects involve pointing gestures (PG) exclusively (MP multimodality), while SP subjects, in the same context, slightly favour the use of simulation[5] gestures (SG) over PG gestures. This contrast, which is not statistically significant (Σ_{CS}=74,5 W(8;8)=]49;87[; $p<0.05$), might derive from differences in the experimental setups. CS subjects were shown instances of both types of multimodal commands; they had then the opportunity to discover the redundancy of multimodal commands involving SG gestures (MS multimodality) and, by comparison, to appreciate the conciseness and accuracy of semantically equivalent MP statements. On the other hand, SP subjects could only rely on their previous experience of direct manipulation to elaborate multimodal commands. This result constitutes an additional argument in favour of the necessity of a minimum initial training, and illustrates the limitations of users' discovery and exploration capabilities.

The fact that CS subjects resort to speech more frequently than SP subjects (cf. table 2) may be viewed as a consequence of their reluctance to use MS formulations, since there is no significant ($t(7,7)=0.0002$; $p<0.05$) difference between the two groups as regards the use of gestural (PG or SG) commands.

The use of speech and gestures for expressing reformulations is influenced by factors other than individual preferences, previous experience or the information content of requests. Table 3 describes the modalities selected by CS subjects for reiterating oral requests that the speech recognizer had failed to recognize accurately; repetitions and reformulations of gestural commands are ignored because of their very low frequency (23 occurrences, mak-

[5] That is, they simulate translations and rotations of pieces of furniture with gestures akin to mouse drags.

	SP subjects										CS subjects									
	S1	S2	S3	S4	S5	S6	S7	S8	Tot	%	S1	S2	S3	S4	S5	S6	S7	S8	Tot	%
O	1	2	1	4	3	10	6	2	29	33	37	33	5	1	7	10	15	5	113	49.5
SG	5	7	8	-	-	-	-	2	22	25	3	4	-	1	-	-	35	16	59	26
PG	1	-	1	-	-	1	-	9	12	14	23	1	-	2	1	1	1	1	30	13
MS	15	4	-	-	-	-	-	-	19	21	-	-	-	-	-	-	-	1	1	0.5
MP	1	2	-	-	3	-	-	-	6	7	1	-	2	-	1	-	21	1	26	11

O: Oral commands
SG: Simulation Gestures
PG: Pointing Gestures
M...: Multimodality involving simulation gestures (MS) or pointing gestures (MP)
Tot: Total number of requests per type of modality and per subject
%: Percentage of O (or SG,...) requests over the total number of requests per group (i.e. SP: 88, CS: 229)

Table 2: Use of modalities (initial formulations of requests)

	reformulations								final reformulations							
	S1	S2	S3	S4	S5	S6	S7	S8	S1	S2	S3	S4	S5	S6	S7	S8
O	9	66	12	1	5	7	8	7	3	13	2	1	-	2	3	1
SG	4	12	1	-	1	1	4	-	4	12	1	-	1	1	4	-
PG	2	2	1	-	2	3	-	-	2	2	1	-	2	3	-	-
MS	-	-	-	-	-	-	-	-	-	-	-	-	-	-	-	-
MP	-	-	2	-	2	-	-	-	-	-	2	-	1	-	-	-
Tot	47	100	21	2	13	18	47	15	47	100	21	2	13	18	47	15

Tot: Total number of oral and multimodal requests (initial formulations + reformulations)

Table 3: Use of modalities (reformulations of unrecognized oral requests)

ing up 10% of all repetitions and reformulations). Results in Table 3 show that six CS subjects resort occasionally to gestural or multimodal expressions after the recognition failure of an oral command, and that the tendency to switch over to SG, PG or MP formulations increases as the number of consecutive recognition failures increases: from 21% of the intermediate (unsuccessful) reformulations to 59% of the final (successful) reformulations. Multimodality appears thus as a useful feature for user interfaces that implement unreliable communication media.

Finally, subjects from both groups favour monomodal commands (72% and 88% of initial formulations, for the SP and the CS groups respectively; cf. table 2) over the simultaneous use of speech and gestures. This observation contradicts a widespread assumption within the relevant scientific community, namely: the naturalness of multimodal commands such as " Put this (+ pointing at an object) here (+ pointing at a location on the screen) ". Further empirical or experimental research is needed in order to address this issue which is crucial for the design of future multimodal HCI.

3.2.2 *On the activity and interaction*

Expression constraints may have influenced the activities of the CS subjects to some extent. The comparison between the two groups yields results that are difficult to interpret for the following two main reasons.

Firstly, subjects had to perform design tasks; it is then impossible to evaluate the efficiency of their activities, and to draw conclusions from quantitative cues such as: the global time spent on performing the scenario, the average execution time of the various types of elementary actions, the adequacy of intermediate and final results to

	S1	S2	S3	S4	S5	S6	S7	S8
SP subjects	5.7	5.7	3.4	3.4	1.1	2.3	1.1	2.3
CS subjects	0.5	0.5	0.5	-	-	-	0.9	1.7

Table 4: Simple vs complex commands - Percentage of complex requests over the total number of requests (initial formulations)

the requirements expressed in the scenario, etc. Within the framework of design tasks, such cues are either irrelevant or ambiguous. The results presented here should be considered as tentative. In order to assess their reliability and the soundness of our interpretations, it is necessary to compare them with results obtained in the context of other activities.

Secondly, creative tasks promote the expression of idiosyncrasies; this may explain why we observed large inter-individual differences, and obtained no statistically significant result even though we detected group tendencies, that is, behaviour patterns from which one or two subjects only (in the considered group) departed.

CS subjects performed a greater number of actions than SP subjects, but this result is not significant (Σ_{CS}=79; W(8;8)=]49;87[; $p<0.05$). On the contrary, their actions were significantly (Σ_{CS}=38; W(8;8)=]49;87[; $p<0.05$) less complex than those performed by SP subjects[6].

The second inter-group difference suggests two plausible interpretations. The first one is based on the following observation that has been reported in several psychological studies of oral human communication (Harris et al., 1980). That is, interlocutors adapt their behaviours to the capabilities and competences of their dialogue partners, the extent of which they infer from a priori knowledge and/or guess from the first dialogue exchanges. The CS subjects decomposed their activities into smaller and simpler units because they inferred from the poor speech understanding capacity of the simulated system that its functional capabilities were also limited. Thus they made no distinction between linguistic and functional limitations in their evaluation of the system competences. Such confusions have been observed in the context of Wizard of Oz empirical studies of complex oral HCI (cf. (Amalberti et al., 1993) for information dialogues).

On the other hand, it might be assumed, within the framework of a cognitive load model, that CS subjects requested the execution of simpler actions as a compensation for the additional cognitive cost of their adaptation to expression constraints; one might conclude then, that expression constraints have a negative side-effect on users' activities inasmuch as they reduce the efficiency of "natural" multimodal HCI.

We also analysed other aspects of the activity of CS and SP subjects: the scope of their action plans, their reactions to irrecoverable communication failures and impossible actions, the strategies they adopted for arranging pieces of furniture in the room, among others. But intergroup comparisons did not reach statistical significance, by reason of the intra-group variability and/or the insufficient amount of relevant tokens.

To summarize, inter-individual differences, together with insufficient empirical data, make it impossible to reach a clear conclusion as regards to the influence of linguistic constraints on the activities of subjects and their use of modalities.

4. GENERAL CONCLUSION

We designed, within the framework of a prospective ergonomic approach, two multimodal user interfaces in order to study the usability of constrained vs spontaneous speech and gestures. The functionalities of both interfaces were simulated according to the Wizard of Oz experimental paradigm. Each interface was used during three weekly sessions by eight subjects who carried out simple design tasks.

Comparative analyses yielded empirical results that suggest useful conclusions for the design of the next generation of multimodal user interfaces for the general public, namely:

- Even drastic linguistic constraints will be well ac-

[6] Subjects could move pieces of furniture and orientate them (simple actions), or combine both types of actions in complex commands such as the permutation of two pieces of furniture, for example: "Put the television set in the North-West corner of the room, facing the settee."

cepted and easily complied with by users, provided that the resulting language is a subset of NL which does not impose semantic restrictions on the expression of users. We propose an efficient but costly method for designing such tractable artificial languages in the context of interactive applications involving a restricted pragmatic domain.

- A short initial training period or tutorial is useful for beginners, even with "transparent" interfaces.

- Constraints that satisfy the requirement mentioned in the first alinea may have positive side-effects on users; in particular, they may entail a reduction of hesitations and incorrect statements.

As for the side-effects of expression constraints on users' activities, it is impossible to draw clear conclusions from the empirical data we analysed and compared.

Our results have been obtained from the transcripts and videotapes of the first session (one scenario only). During this session, several SP and CS subjects (one SP, and at least two CS) explored and tested the capabilities of the simulated multimodal interface systematically, while the others just performed the scenario. This may explain why the comparisons between the two groups yielded few significant results. The empirical data collected during the two following sessions should be easier to interpret, since subjects are likely to have given up previous exploration strategies and activities.

Moreover, as behaviours and strategies tend to stabilize under the influence of practice, evolutions during sessions 2 and 3 should be slower than during the first session. Therefore, the effects of expression constraints on subjects' behaviours should be more noticeable during these sessions. A careful analysis, subject-by-subject, of the data collected during sessions 2 and 3 might even contribute to a better understanding of the behaviours of subjects during the first session.

Acknowledgements

We express our thanks to R. Amalberti and C. Valot, researchers at CERMA, for their significant contributions to the definition and implementation of the experimental setup. This comparative study was partially supported by the French Ministry of Defence (D.G.A./D.R.E.T. contract N° 95-125).

References

Amalberti, R., Carbonell, N., and Falzon, P. (1993). User representations of computer systems in human-computer speech interaction. *International Journal of Man-Machine Studies*, 38:547–566.

Bellalem, N. and Romary, L. (1995). Reference interpretation in a multimodal environment combining speech and gesture. In *First International Workshop on Intelligence and Multimodality in Multimedia interfaces*, Edinburgh.

Catinis, L. and Caelen, J. (1995). Analyse du comportement multimodal de l'usager humain dans une tâche de dessin. In *IHM'95*, pages 123–129, Toulouse: Cépaduès.

Falzon, P. (1991). Studying functional dialogues and operative languages. In Queinnec, Y. and Daniellou, F., editors, *Designing for everyone. XI Congress of the IEA.*, Paris. Londres: Taylor and Francis.

Harris, G., Begg, I., and Upfold, D. (1980). On the role of the speaker's expectations in interpersonal communication. *Journal of Verbal Learning and Verbal Behavior*, 19:597–607.

Hauptmann, H. and McAvinney, P. (1993). Gestures with speech for graphic manipulation. *International Journal of Man-Machine Studies*, 38:231–249.

Nigay, L. and Coutaz, J. (1993). A design space for multimodal interfaces: concurrent processing and data fusion. In *InterCHI'93*, pages 172–178, New York: ACM.

Seneff, S., Goddeau, D., Pao, C., and Polifroni, J. (1996). Multimodal discourse modelling in a multi-user multi-domain environment. In *Fourth International Conference on Spoken Language Processing*, pages 1922–195, Philadelphia.

Shneiderman, B. (1983). Direct manipulation: a step beyond programming languages. *IEEE computer*, 16(8):57–69.

Shneiderman, B. (1987). Designing the user interface: Strategies for effective human-computer interaction. New York: Addison-Wesley Publishing Company.

Speech timing prediction in multimodal human-computer interaction

Marie-Luce Bourguet & Akio Ando

Nippon Hoso Kyokai (Japan Broadcasting Corporation)
Science and Technical Research Laboratories
1-10-11 Kinuta Setagaya-ku Tokyo 157 Japan
bourguet@acod1.strl.nhk.or.jp, ando@strl.nhk.or.jp

ABSTRACT This paper proposes a quantitative model of natural modality integration for speech and pointing gestures. An experiment is described that study temporal synchronization between speech and pointing gestures during multimodal interaction. The end of a pointing gesture (MT) is shown to be synchronized with either the key word of an expression or the deictic marker of a deictic expression. It is also shown that MT tends to be slightly behind the beginning of its associated word; this tendency becoming more marked for lengthy expressions (more than 6 syllables). All correlation scores were found to be above 0.9.

Automatic understanding of natural multimodal interaction may advance only through good models of spontaneous communication. Specifically, the model proposed here can be efficiently used in the speech recognition system or in the interface management system to predict speech timing according to gesture timing.

KEY WORDS Multimodal Interaction, Speech Recognition, Pointing Gestures, Synchrony, Predictive Model

1. INTRODUCTION

Natural communication between people and computerized systems inevitably involves voice interaction. This is because speech is the most natural and widely used human mode of communication. But speech is seldom used alone. In fact, natural communication also involves a variety of bodily movements that actively participate in the communicative process. For example, verbal communication is often accompanied by hand gestures, eyes and head movements, face expressions that fulfill divers communicative functions. These nonverbal acts usefully accompany the spoken words by adding nuance of meaning (facial expressions), maintaining good quality of communication (glance, smile), or clarifying an expression (hand signs).

Researchers in experimental psychology, have described different aspects of natural speech and gesture integration. It has been shown for example that human perception of speech is achieved via a variety of bottom-up and top-down sources of information. When people watch a speaker, they are influenced both by what they see and what they hear (see the McGurk effect [McGurk, 1976]). Research is currently being done on multimodal systems that integrate auditory and visual information at low-level signal processing (automatic lip-reading), for better overall speech recognition.

But natural communication is much more than just speech and lip-reading. [Rime, Schiaratura, Hupet & Ghysselinckx, 1984] have shown that verbal encoding was not dissociable from body movement. In an experiment, they immobilized the head, arms, hands, legs and feet of subjects during a conversation, and observed the effect of immobilization on the content of speech. Not only a significant decrease for vividness of imagery in the dialogues was found, but a significant

Human–Computer Interaction: INTERACT'97 S. Howard, J. Hammond & G. Lindgaard (editors)
Published by Chapman & Hall

increase in the activity of the body zones that remained free to move (the eyebrows, eyes, mouth and fingers) was also noted. These data suggest that the gestural motor activity of a speaking person is inextricably linked to his or her verbal encoding activities.

One of the most visible manifestations of speech-related non verbal behavior is hand gesturing. Various classifications have been proposed for hand movements that occur with speech [Freedman 1972, Cosnier 1982, McNeill 1985] although all of them rely on a system proposed earlier by [Efron, 1941/1972]. The [Rime & Schiaratura, 1991] "revised Efron system of gestures" distinguishes four types of hand gestures within the broader category of "depictive gestures" (gestures that refer to the object of the speech):

1. **iconic gestures** used by a speaker to display information about the shape of objects, spatial relations and actions.
2. **pantomimic gestures** involving the manipulation of some invisible object or tool in contact with the speaker's hand.
3. **symbolic gestures** that can be translated directly to some verbal meaning (e.g. the "OK" posture made with the fingers).
4. **deictic gestures** such as pointing to direct the listener's attention to objects or events in the surrounding environment.

With regard to temporal synchronization between speech and gestures, several studies suggest that gestures usually precede speech. [Dittman & Llewellyn, 1969] observed that hand movements were particularly concentrated around the first word of utterances. [Kendon, 1972] concludes from a speech sample analysis that when a bodily movement is precisely related to a word in a sentence, the movement in question begins before the corresponding word. Finally, [Butterworth & Beattie, 1978] conclude from similar analyses, that the initiation of iconic gestures usually precedes the word with which they are associated.

All models that have been proposed so far, to describe the temporal relationships between speech and gestures, are essentially of a qualitative nature. They can not be easily used in the human-computer interface. In contrast, the goal of our research is to begin specifying quantitative models of temporal synchronization between speech and gestures, to guide the design of robust multimodal systems.

In the following sections, we briefly review the difficulties inherent to speech and gesture integration in the human-computer interface. Then an experiment that was designed to study how people integrate their use of spoken and gesture input is described. It is followed by a discussion on the application of a predictive model of speech and gesture integration in the interface management system and in the speech recognition system.

2. SPEECH AND GESTURE INTEGRATION IN THE HUMAN-COMPUTER INTERFACE

The technology of automatic speech recognition has advanced to the point where rudimentary conversational interaction can be reliably accomplished for well-delimited tasks. Also, systems that can isolate and track a user's body, recognize gestures performed by his/her hands and face are currently under experimentation. These technologies, speech recognition along with computer vision, although still imperfect, have developed enough that it is critical to address now the question of their integration in the human-computer interface.

This is not an easy task however. Speech recognizers are still prone to recognition errors, which is particularly true in noisy environments and for degraded auditory inputs. We are forced to note that even after decades of effort, speech recognition by machine remains far inferior to human performance. Position trackers also show inaccuracies. Moreover, with these new devices (speech recognizers, eye trackers, body trackers, etc.), the user is set free to behave and communicate with the machine in a natural and spontaneous way; but on the other hand, it becomes increasingly difficult for the interface management system to determine when input has occurred and the precise value of that input.

Even the integration of speech and rather easily recognizable pointing gestures is not a straightforward operation. As shown in the previous section, the use of speech and gestures by human beings, is fully integrated and coordinated. But unfortunately, the devices used to interact with computers have not been designed to cooperate. The flexibility of interaction they offer is not addressed appropriately by current software tools.

Nevertheless, the integration of speech and pointing gestures in the human-computer interface has already been implemented in several experimental systems. Most of these systems use pointing to help prevent ambiguity in a recognized speech utterance. Pointing, associated with speech, can provide additional information about the user's intentions through phenomena of redundancy, disambiguation or complementarity. This additional information is successfully exploited at the semantic or pragmatic levels of analysis.

Our approach to the problem is somewhat different but complementary. We believe that, to the extent that human behavior can be quantified, communicative behavior models are necessary to perform a good integration of audio and visual information in the interface management system. The following section describes a small scale experiment designed to begin specifying how people integrate their use of pointing gestures and spoken input during multimodal human-computer interaction. Our assumption is that speech occurrence time can be predicted according to pointing gesture timing.

3. METHOD

3.1. Subjects, tasks and procedure

Twelve subjects, presenting various degrees of familiarity with computers, participated as unpaid volunteers in the experiment. All subjects were right-handed and native speakers of Japanese.

The experiment was divided in three tasks involving increasing semantic efforts as well as increasing levels of freedom in the use of gestures and speech.

For the first task (the "single word task"), subjects were shown on the computer screen sets of square figures of various sizes and colors. They were instructed to point at each figure while uttering the figure's color. Pointing gestures had to be performed with the right hand, starting from a fixed location on the desk, and ending with one finger touching the computer screen. After each gesture, the hand had to be brought back onto the desk. Subjects could move on the next figure at their own pace, but the pointing gesture (movement between the desk and the computer screen) had to be executed as quickly as possible. Possible colors were: "ao" (blue), "midori" (green), "murasaki" (purple) and "nezumi iro" (gray).

For the second task (the "question/answer task"), subjects were shown on the computer screen sets of pictures representing various musical instruments, or sports, or animals, or Japanese dishes, etc. Subjects were then asked questions related to the pictures such as "Which dish is made of rice and fish?", "Which sport is practiced on the snow?", etc. Each question had to be answered using unconstrained speech and simultaneous pointing gesture. Gestures had to be executed as for the previous task except that no speed constraint was imposed.

For the third task (the "drawing task"), subjects were asked to manipulate computer objects in order to build consistent drawings. A model to be reproduced as well as the constituent parts of the model were simultaneously provided on the computer screen (see an example on Figure 1). Objects' manipulation could be done by ordering commands to the computer ("Put the red triangle here", "Remove that", etc.) using speech and pointing gestures. No constraint was imposed on the use of speech and gestures. An operator, acting on a duplicated display, was actually monitoring the drawing editor. Subjects were aware of the operator's job and were asked to speak and act as naturally as possible.

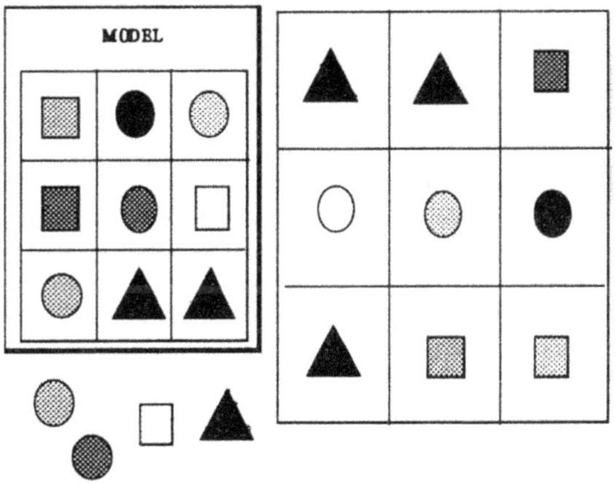

Figure 1: Example of a "drawing task". Subjects are asked to manipulate the graphical objects, using spoken commands and pointing gestures, to produce a drawing similar to the model shown on the left side of the figure.

3.2. Data collection

The three tasks, performed by the twelve subjects, were videotaped. The relative timing of speech and pointing gestures was then carefully measured in terms of video frames (30 frames per second).

For the first and second task, a "multimodal record" is made of one utterance and its associated pointing gesture. A new time reference is calculated for each multimodal record and corresponds to the initiation of the gesture (when the hand quit the desk). The end of a gesture, which also corresponds to the movement duration (or movement time: MT), is calculated when the finger reach the computer screen (Figure 2).

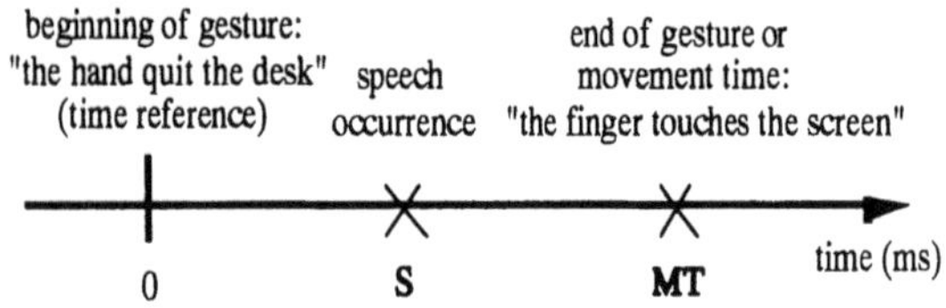

Figure 2: Calculation of movement time.

Speech occurrence time (S) is calculated according to the type of utterance. For a single word (first task), S corresponds to the beginning of the first syllable of the word. For deictic expressions, S corresponds to the beginning of the first syllable of the deictic marker ("kore", "kono" (this), "sore", "sono" (that), "koko" (here), etc.). For the other types of utterance, S corresponds to the beginning of the first syllable of the most significant word (keyword). This way of calculating speech occurrence will be discussed later.

For the third task, timing is measured in a similar way, except for compound commands which are made of two gestures (e.g. "kore ha, koko ni oite kudasai" (put this here)). In that case, the time reference is calculated at the beginning of the first gesture and used as such for the whole command thus for two consecutive multimodal records (Figure 3).

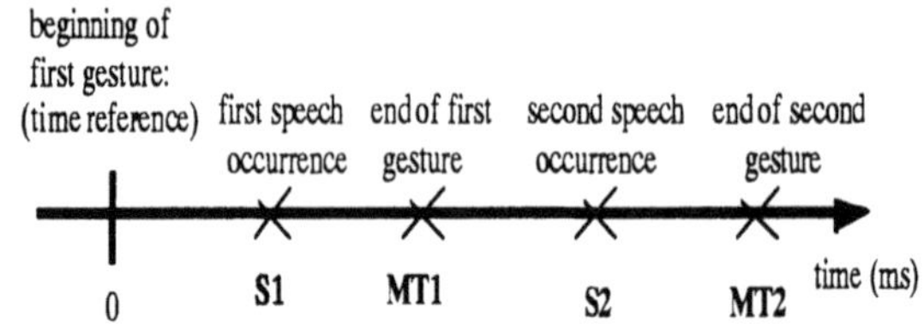

Figure 3: Speech occurrence time and movement time calculation for complex commands.

4. RESULTS

4.1. Using the Fitts' law ("single word task")

The Fitts' law [Fitts, 1954; MacKenzie, 1992 for a review of the Fitts' law) is used in HCI to measure and predict movement time for tasks such as text or object selection with a pointing device. The Fitts' law states that a movement tasks' difficulty (ID, the "index of difficulty") can be quantified using information theory by the metric "bits". Specifically,

$$ID = \log_2 (2A / W) \quad (1)$$

where A is the distance or amplitude to move and W the width or tolerance of the region within which the move terminates. From Equation 1, the time to complete a movement task is predicted using a simple linear equation, where movement time (MT) is a linear function of ID,

$$MT = a + b\, ID \quad (2)$$

In a Fitts' law experiment, multiple trials are conducted for each task condition (A, W), then measurements are generally aggregated across subjects resulting in one data point for each task condition.

During the first task of our experiment we collected a total of 1440 trials. Each square figure was characterized by an index of difficulty ranging from 2.5 to 7 (for a total of 10 different IDs), as well as a color (among the 4 possible colors). 40 different task conditions were thus defined, and for each task condition 36 trials were collected (1440 / (10 * 4) = 36). Data is represented in Figure 4. After applying tests of correlation and linear regression, we found that movement time (ms) could be predicted as:

$$MT = 345 + 36\, ID \quad (3)$$

with a very high correlation score of r = 0.99.

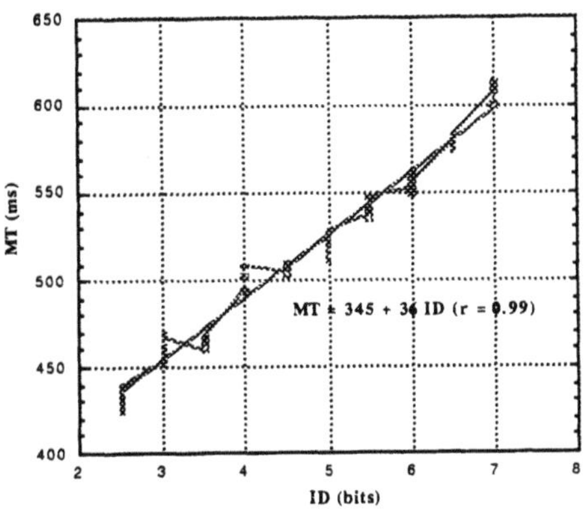

Figure 4: Plot and regression line for MT = f(ID) (first task). Each data point is the mean of 36 trials. There is a strong correlation between MT and ID (Fitts' law).

The next step of our research was to relate speech occurrence time to movement time. First, the effect of the length of speech (total number of syllables) on movement time was examined. Correlation and linear regression tests were applied again separately for each color variable. Let's recall here that the four possible colors were "ao" (2 syllables), "midori" (3 syllables), "murasaki" (4 syllables) and "nezumi iro" (5 syllables). The four equations of regression line that were found are as follows:

ao:	MT = 334 + 38 ID (r = 0.994)	(4)
midori:	MT = 345 + 35 ID (r = 0.994)	(5)
murasaki:	MT = 343 + 37 ID (r = 0.991)	(6)
nezumi iro:	MT = 357 + 34 ID (r = 0.99)	(7)

Equations 3, 4, 5, 6 and 7 are very similar (time differences are smaller than measurement precision: 1 video frame = 33.33 ms), which let us suppose that the length of speech had no sensitive effect on movement time during the first task.

Second, the effect of movement tasks' difficulty (ID) on time delay between MT and S (D = MT - S) was studied (Figure 5). A low correlation score was found between D and ID (r = 0.202). For ID ranging from 2.5 to 7, D is always positive. In other words, S always precedes MT.

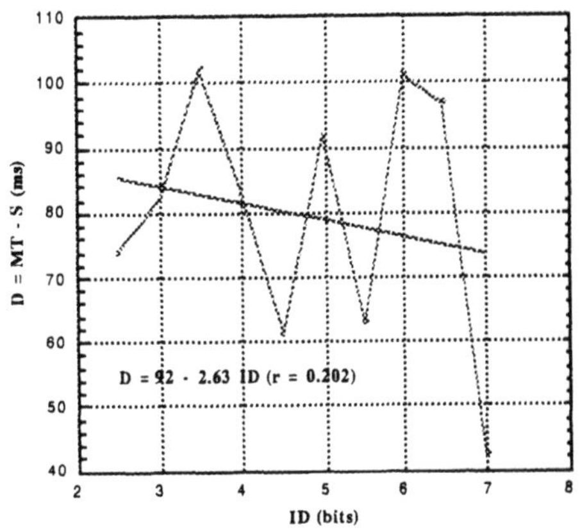

Figure 5: Plot and regression line for D = f(ID) (first task). Each data point is the mean of 144 trials.

Next, the effect of the length of speech (n) on D was examined (Figure 6). Again, linear regression test was applied and a very strong correlation score was found between n and D:

$$D = 37 + 12\,n \quad (r = 0.962) \tag{8}$$

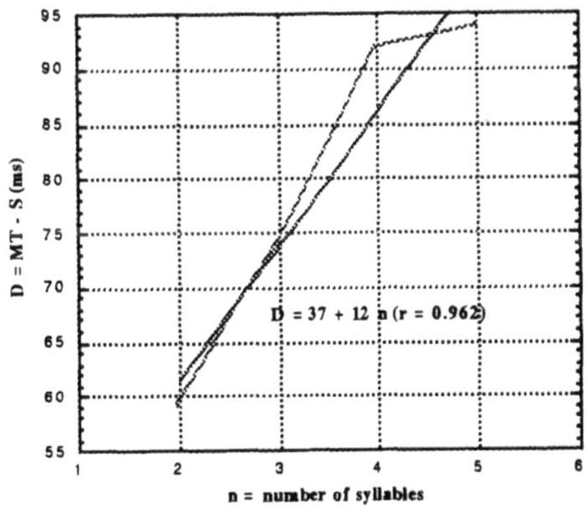

Figure 6: Plot and regression line for D = f(n) (first task). Each data point is the mean of 360 trials.

From Equation 8, it can be seen that D increases with n, thus that the advance of S on MT increases with n. This means that the end of gesture (MT) doesn't always coincide with the beginning of the first syllable but tends to coincide with a syllable of more central position in the word. The calculation of D for n varying from 2 to 5, gives the following values (ms): 61 (n = 2), 73 (n = 3), 85 (n = 4) and 97 (n = 5). On average, the length of a syllable is about 100 ms, thus MT coincide with the first syllable for $1 < n < 6$. For n varying from 6 to 14, MT coincides with the second syllable, etc.

Finally, tests of correlation and linear regression were applied again as shown in Figure 7 to study the relationship between S and MT. The following equation of regression line was found:

$$S = -128 + 1.15\ MT\ (r = 0.979) \quad (9)$$

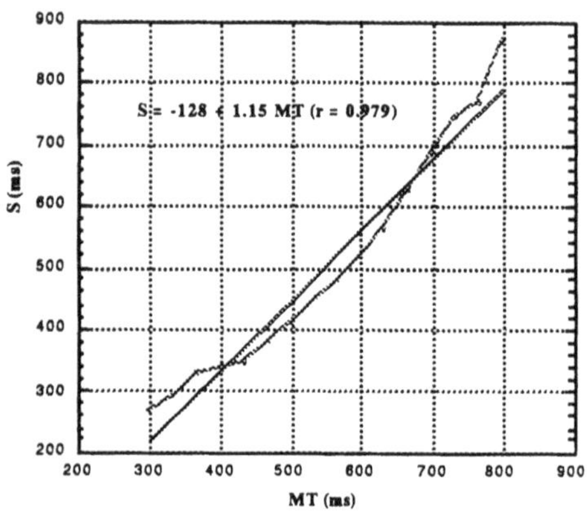

Figure 7: Plot and regression line for S = f(MT) (first task). Each data point is the mean of several trials (from 1 trial to 269 trials) for a total of 1440 trials.

A very high correlation score was found between S and MT. Equation 9 confirms the observation that S tends to precede MT. However, the tendency is inverted for MT ≥ 853.33 ms (out of data range). For MT that ranges from 300 to 800 ms, S varies from 217 to 792 ms and D from 8 to 83 ms. MT always coincide with the first syllable of the word.

4.2. Speech timing prediction (second and third tasks)

During the second and third tasks, no constraint on the use of speech and gestures was imposed. MT was observed to be synchronized with either the deictic marker of a deictic expression, or the key word of other expressions (see previous section "data collection").

For the data collected during the second task (the "question/answer task") the following equation was calculated:

$$S = -184 + 0.97\ MT\ (r = 0.929) \quad (10)$$

Each data point was the mean of several trials (from 1 to 38 trials) for a total of 420 trials.

For the data collected during the third task (the "drawing task"), the following equation was calculated:

$$S = -80 + 0.94\ MT\ (r = 0.967) \quad (11)$$

Each data point was the mean of several trials (from 1 to 35 trials) for a total of 734 trials.

Equations 10 and 11 are very similar. As expected, natural integration of speech and pointing gestures is task independent. Unlike what is suggested by Equation 9 (first task), D tends to increase with movement time. Within the range of the collected data ($300 < MT < 5000$), MT is found to take place between the first and the fourth syllable of either the key word or the deictic marker (or the first syllable of the following word). This can be explained in two ways. Longer gestures actually correspond to:

(1) hesitation, movement time is then delayed;

(2) the second part of a complex command ("drawing task"). If speech is short, the gesture is slightly behind (e.g. "kore ha, koko desu" (this is here) + two pointing gestures).

5. DISCUSSION

The results of our experiment are in accordance with previous findings on temporal synchronization between speech and gestures (see the Introduction of this paper). In particular, [Kendon, 1972] says that bodily movements, when precisely related to a word in a sentence, begin before the word in question. We found that hand pointing gestures always start before their associated spoken word (the key word or the deictic marker of an expression), and that they terminate in synchronization with (or slightly behind) the beginning of the word.

Such a quantitative model of natural speech and gesture integration can be used in both the speech recognition system and the interface management system.

In automatic speech recognition (ASR), errors are typically divided into three categories: substitution (misrecognition of a word), insertion (abusive recognition of noise or unintentional utterance) and false rejection (non-recognition of a word). The correct association of speech and gesture, according to a predictive model, could prevent an erroneous rejection decision. Similarly, in case of bad association of speech and gesture, insertion error could be avoided. With regard to substitution errors, one of the main difficulty in ASR, is word boundary detection, especially in noisy environment. A quantitative model of natural modality integration that provides information on speech timing (beginning time of a word in an utterance) could help solving the problem.

In the interface management system, it is often difficult to determine which input is related to which input and if two inputs are actually related. Alternate usage of concurrent multimodality and compound multimodality makes things even more difficult [Bourguet, 1992] (Figure 8).

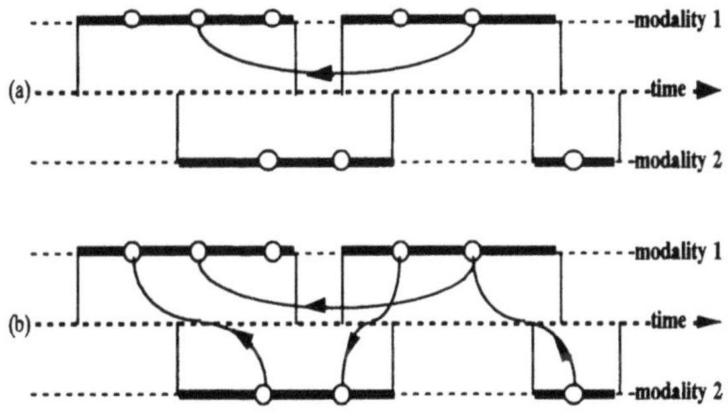

Figure 8. Concurrent multimodality (a) allows a system user to simultaneously input two independent commands by means of two different modalities. Information merging (symbolized by an arrow), if needed, is unimodal (e.g. anaphora resolution in natural language). Compound multimodality (b) allows a single command to be given by means of two or more modalities. Information merging is made across modalities.

The choice of good criteria to guide information fusion is of great importance. In most current multimodal systems, information merging is done at a high level of abstraction (semantic or pragmatic level), which minimizes the risks of erroneous fusion. Such fusion mechanisms are certainly robust but generally application-dependent. Conversely, information fusion based on temporal criteria is currently less reliable but allows the design of more generic multimodal interface tools. This lack of reliability is due to the lack of good quantitative models of natural modality integration.

6. CONCLUSION

Our assumption, prior to the experiment, was that speech timing could be predicted according to pointing gesture timing. The results of the experiment suggest that it is true. The predictive equations that were calculated on the different sets of data (Equations 9, 10 and 11) actually show that speech occurrence time and movement time are closely related. All correlation scores were found to be above 0.9 (correlations above 0.9 are considered very high for any experiment involving measurements on human subjects). The end of a pointing gesture (MT) has been shown to be synchronized with either the key word of an expression or the deictic marker of a deictic expression. It has also been shown that MT tended to be slightly behind the beginning of its associated word; this tendency becoming more marked for lengthy expressions (more than 6 syllables).

The model that was proposed here is based on a small set of data and needs to be refined. With more data, it would be possible to closely examine the relative timing of speech and gestures in many different circumstances and for different types of utterances. This is part of our future work.

We chose to study speech timing according to gesture timing because in the case of speech and hand pointing gestures (that can be easily recognized using a touch panel), most of the inaccuracy lies in the speech recognition process. However, for more complex gestures, or for pointing gestures performed at distance, a similar model could be calculated to predict gesture timing according to speech timing.

ACKNOWLEDGEMENTS

Many thanks to Mr. Takehiro Izumi, Executive Research Engineer (and former Director General) at NHK Science and Technical Research Laboratories; and to Mr. Taiji Nishizawa, Director General of NHK Science and Technical Research Laboratories for inviting me in their laboratory. Special thanks to Dr. Eiichi Miyasaka, Director of the Auditory Science & Acoustics Research Division at NHK Science and Technical Research Laboratories for supporting this research.

REFERENCES

Bourguet, M.L. (1992). Conception et realisation d'une interface de dialogue personne-machine multimodale. PhD dissertation, Institut National Polytechnique de Grenoble, France.

Butterworth, B. & Beattie, G. (1978). Gesture and silence as indicators of planning in speech. In R.N. Campbell & P.T. Smith (Eds.), Recent advances in the psychology of language, 347-360. New York: Plenum.

Cosnier, J. (1982). Communications et langages gestuels. In J.Cosnier, J. Coulon, J. Berrendonner & C. Orecchioni (Eds.), Les voies du langage: communications verbales, gestuelles et animales, 255-303. Paris: Dunod.

Dittman, A.T. & Llewellyn, L.C. (1969). Body movement and speech rhythm in social conversation. Journal of Personality and Social Psychology, 11 (2), 98-106.

Efron, D. (1941/1972). Gesture, race and culture. The Hague: Mouton.

Fitts, P.M. (1954). The information capacity of the human motor system in controlling the amplitude of movement. Journal of Experimental Psychology, 47, 381-391.

Freedman, N. (1972). The analysis of movement behavior during the clinical interview. In A.R. Siegman & B. Pope (Eds.), Studies in dyadic communication, 153-175. Elmsford, NY: Pergamon.

Kendon, A. (1972). Some relationships between body motion and speech. In A.R. Siegman & B. Pope (Eds.), Studies in dyadic communication, 177-210. Elmsford, NY: Pergamon.

MacKenzie, I.S. (1992). Movement time prediction in Human-Computer Interfaces. Proc. Graphics Interface' 92, Morgan Kaufmann, 140-150.

McGurk, H. & MacDonald, J. (1976). Hearing lips and seeing voices. Nature, 264, 746-748.

McNeill, D. (1985). So you think gestures are nonverbal? Psychological Review, 92 (3), 350-371.

Rime, B., Shiaratura, L., Hupet, M. & Ghysselinckx, A. (1984). Effects of relative immobilization on the speaker's nonverbal behavior and on the dialogue imagery level. Motivation and Emotion, 8, 311-325.

Rime, B. & Schiaratura, L. (1991). Gesture and speech. In R.S. Feldman & B. Rime (Eds.), Fundamentals of Nonverbal Behavior, 239-281. The Cambridge University Press.

Talking to the Conversation Machine: An Empirical Study

Catherine G. Wolf*, Max Kassler, Wlodek Zadrozny, Lukasz Opyrchal

IBM Thomas J. Watson Research Center
30 Saw Mill River Road, Hawthorne, NY 10532 USA
*cwolf@watson.ibm.com

ABSTRACT This paper describes an empirical study of a prototype conversational speech system, the Conversation Machine. The system allowed users to carry out a number of common banking transactions using a conversational-style interface over the telephone. The study reports detailed findings on how users interacted with the Conversation Machine, categories of error, measures of accuracy and goal success, subjective reaction to the Conversation Machine, and correlations between objective measures and important measures of user satisfaction. Among the findings of interest are that users preferred the speech system over a telephone keypad system and that goal success was more highly correlated with measures of user satisfaction than was recognition accuracy. Implications for the design of conversational user interfaces based on an analysis of errors are also discussed.

KEY WORDS speech recognition, speech interface, natural language

1. INTRODUCTION

Jenny is about to board the plane for a two-week vacation. A thought suddenly flashes through her mind: She forgot to pay her Mastercard bill! She dashes for the nearest phone, dials the number for her automated speech banking system and says, "Please pay my Mastercard bill." Her request is recognized and the system voice responds, "Your Mastercard balance is $2005.56. You do not have enough money in your checking account to pay this bill. Would you like me to transfer money from your savings account and pay the bill?" Jenny responds, "Yes," and the system gives a message confirming payment of the bill. Jenny boards the plane, relieved that all is in order.

When typical consumers think of using speech to interact with a computer, they usually imagine a conversational interaction in which the computer recognizes not only their words, but understands their intentions as well. The possibility of carrying on an unconstrained conversation with a computer in which the computer understands its partner in a completely human-like way is not likely to be realized in the foreseeable future. However, interactions such as the one illustrated by the scenario above are likely to become a reality in the next few years. As suggested by Danis and Karat (1995), researchers can accelerate the development of usable speech interfaces and the underlying speech technology by picking applications whose requirements are a good match to the strengths and limitations of the technology.

This paper describes an empirical study of a prototype conversational speech system, the Conversation Machine. The domain of application was home banking. The system allows users to carry out a number of common banking transactions using a conversational-style interface over the telephone. The study had several purposes:

Human–Computer Interaction: INTERACT'97 S. Howard, J. Hammond & G. Lindgaard (editors)

•To understand how people interact with the system in order to improve the usability of the system. For example, we wanted to know what strategies people used when the system made an error.

•To collect data about the way people spoke to the system in order to more adequately cover the variety of utterances people use.

•To assess the system's accuracy in recognizing users' utterances.

•To assess users' success in accomplishing their goals with the system, and their reactions to the system.

This work benefits from the earlier research of Yankelovich, Levow and Marx (1995), Marx and Schmandt (1996), Halstead-Nussloch (1989), and Clark and Brennan (1991) on the design of conversational interfaces, and the work of Hansen, Novick and Sutton (1996) on the design of effective speech prompts. The study presented here contributes to the field by reporting detailed empirical findings on how users interacted with the Conversation Machine, categories of error, measures of accuracy and goal success, subjective reaction to the Conversation Machine, and correlations between objective measures and important measures of user satisfaction. The paper also discusses the implications of these findings for the design of conversational speech interfaces.

A conversational speech interface offers a number of potential advantages over keypad input for telephone-based services such as the current banking application:

•A conversational interface allows users to make requests in their own words. In a keypad interface, the burden is on the users to figure out which of the system options best matches their goals.

•A conversational interface may have a flat, nonhierarchical command structure which allows users to accomplish their goals directly (e.g., "What is my checking balance?"). Keypad interfaces require the users to learn and navigate several levels of a hierarchical menu structure to accomplish their goals.

•A conversational speech interface allows users to make compound requests (e.g. "Pay my phone and electric bills."). Keypad interfaces typically require users to accomplish their goals as a series of discrete tasks.

While a conversational speech interface promises considerable benefits for an application such as banking over the telephone, there are also a number of challenges in the design of such systems. Due to the imprecise nature of speech recognition, there may be a mismatch between the user's utterance and what is recognized by the system. Since speech recognizers often fail in non-human ways, the user may be surprised by the result (Rhyne and Wolf, 1993). Furthermore, the user may have little idea how to recover from a recognition error. In addition, the appearance of some human-like language ability may make it difficult for users to distinguish what the system can and cannot do. Such issues as these cannot be solved by improvements to the speech and natural language technology alone, but must also be addressed by the design of the user interface.

2. THE SYSTEM

2.1 User Interface Design and Application Functionality

The system allowed users to do the following operations: get checking and savings account balances, transfer money between checking and savings accounts, get the balance for four bills, pay these bills, summarize the bills, summarize all bills and accounts, get help, and cancel a transaction.

The system was capable of some compound actions, such as paying several bills at once, and understood some forms of deictic reference, such as pronouns.

The command structure was flat, and the top-level prompt, "What else can I do for you?" simply signaled that the system was ready to accept another request. Some dialogs required additional information from the user for completion. In these sub-dialogs, the users were asked for the additional information and only responses appropriate to the dialog were accepted. For operations which changed the balance of an account, the user was asked to confirm the transaction before it was executed.

For greater accuracy, dollar amounts were entered using the keypad. Even if users spoke the amount in a request, they were prompted to enter it using the keypad.

When a recognition failure occurred at a top-level dialog, the user was asked to rephrase the request. When an acceptable response was not given within a sub-dialog, several levels of prompting were used, giving progressively more explicit instructions.

The prompts consisted of pre-recorded human speech by a female speaker. The prompts used a polite, first-person style.

2.2 System Components

The Conversation Machine consists of three major modules: Natural Language/Dialog Machine, Computer Telephony System, and Continuous Speech Recognition. The modules communicate through TCP/IP. The system is modular.

The Conversation Machine ran on an RS/6000 model 370 under AIX.

Natural Language -- The natural language grammar is represented as a collection of constructions (Goldberg, 1995), i.e. data structures where syntactic, semantic and pragmatic information are combined in one record. This representation has important computational advantages of being general, compact and object oriented (Zadrozny, 1996).

Dialog Machine --The Dialog Machine works in the conversation-for-action paradigm, i.e. it tries to find out which action to perform and what the parameters of the action are. In other words, it is a finite collection of states and transitions plus a small number (<20) of global, contextual variables that help determine the next state and the utterance interpretation. If the whole utterance cannot be interpreted within a given context, the largest subpart that makes sense is tried. Because of the possible ambiguities, there is a small set of rules (5 clauses) expressing the preferences in interpretation (cf. Zadrozny, 1995).

Speech Recognition -- The system as tested used the BBN Hark Continuous Speech Recognition System. The IBM Continuous Speech Recognition System, has more recently been integrated into the Conversation Machine. Both recognizers support large vocabulary, and both work best if at any point of a conversation the active vocabulary does not exceed a few hundred words.

Computer Telephony System – The IBM DT/6000, version 1.6 system was used.

3. THE STUDY

3.2 Tasks and Procedure

Since one of the goals of the study was to collect information on how people spoke to the system, we did not want to "put words in their mouths" by presenting the tasks they were to do in words they might use to accomplish these tasks. Accordingly, we created scenarios that either described a situation the study participants were to resolve or required the participants to fill in missing information in a table, without using phrases they might employ to accomplish the goal. An example of the first kind of scenario is: "You are at the airport leaving for a two-week vacation. You have an uneasy feeling that you forgot the electricity bill. Check to see if it needs attention, and if so, take care of it."

Eight scenarios were used, with the intention that these would give participants an opportunity to use all of the functions of the system. The scenarios were given to the participants in a paper booklet. The first two scenarios were designed to be relatively simple, in order to allow participants to become familiar with the experimental procedure.

Participants were given verbal and written instructions about the procedure, including an example task. They were told they would be interacting with a computerized voice recognition system and to "make requests as if you were speaking to a human."

Participants spoke to the system using a telephone handset over a dial-up connection.

It took approximately 45 minutes to one hour to complete the session.

3.2 Participants

Twenty-two people participated in the study. Sixteen were recruited from a temporary employment agency and were paid for their services; six were internal employees who volunteered for the study. All participants were native speakers of American English and none had worked in the area of speech recognition or natural language understanding. There were eleven males and eleven females. Participants were asked to give their ages in terms of five age categories. The youngest participants were in the 18-20 year-old category and the oldest were in the 51-65 category.

3.3 Data Collection

An audio recording which contained both the human participant's utterances and the system's responses was made for each session. In addition, a log file was generated for each session which contained what the system recognized for each utterance as well as the system's response. The transcript of the audio recording and the computer-generated log were merged for data analysis.

In addition, participants filled out a questionnaire about their reactions to the system at the end of the session.

4. RESULTS

4.1 Variety of Speaking Styles

The 22 participants exhibited a considerable variety of speaking styles. A few adopted a telegraphic, command-like style (e.g., "pay telephone bill"), others used a more conversational style (e.g., "I would like to pay my telephone bill"), while others rambled on (see examples in section 4.5). Many made deictic reference (e.g. "pay the bills we just spoke about"), and quite a number used polite forms (e.g. "Please pay...." "Could you tell me...").

The average utterance length was 5.95 words, but ranged from an average of 4.28 for the top-performing quartile of participants (based on the goal success measure described in section 4.3) to 7.98 words for the lowest- performing quartile. This relationship between utterance length and recognition success may be mediated by the greater disfluency rate for longer utterances (Oviatt, 1995) and the tendency for longer utterances to be syntactically more complex.

4.2 Accuracy

One measure of accuracy assessed how well the system understood the participant on an utterance-by-utterance basis. This measure is based on analysis of three aspects of a user-system interaction: the user's spoken utterance, the words recognized by the system (recognized result), and the system's response. Each spoken utterance was classified into one of three categories: 1. Exact match -- the recognized result exactly matched the speaker's utterance. 2. Exact to user -- the recognized result and speaker's utterance were not an exact match, but the system's response was the same as it would have been for an exact match. Because many different recognized results may be mapped to the same system response, it is possible for the appropriate response to be given to the user, even if the system does not recognize the user's utterance exactly. For example, consider the following interaction:

User: The balance of my checking account.
System recognition: about my checking balance.
System response: Your checking balance is $70.00.

3. Error -- the system did not give the user the appropriate response.

Thirty-eight percent of the utterances fell into the exact match category, 20% were in the exact to user category, and 42% were errors. Thus, the average effective utterance accuracy rate (exact + exact to user) experienced by the participants was 58%. This number had a wide range, from 16% to 82% across the 22 participants.

The percentage of utterances in each category as a function of scenario is shown in Figure 1. This graph shows a tendency for the percentage of exact matches to increase and the percentage of errors to decrease as users gain more experience with the system. The outlier point at scenario 5 is due to a large number of competence errors (see section 4.4) in which participants asked the system a question it was not designed to answer.

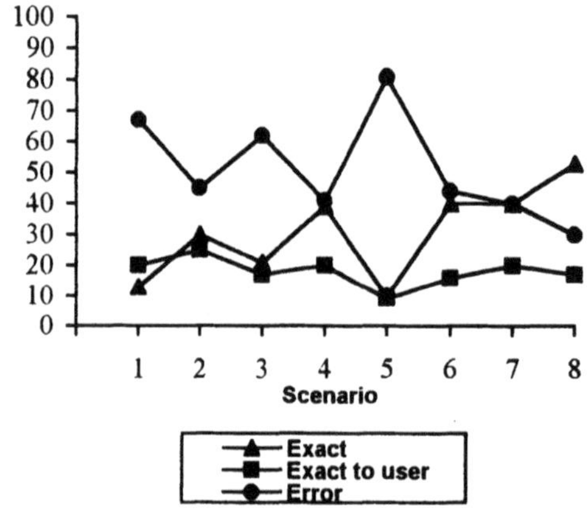

Figure 1. Percentage in each Accuracy category as a function of scenario

Perceived accuracy is likely to be a contributor to overall satisfaction, so it is interesting to compare perceived and actual accuracy. Figure 2 shows participants' estimate of the percentage of time the system correctly understood their request and the estimate of the percentage of time it misunderstood their request (collected in independent questions), as well as effective percentage correct (exact + exact to user) and error percentage. This graph reveals that study participants tended to overestimate the accuracy of the system and, correspondingly, underestimate the error rate. Participants' perceived and actual error rates were significantly correlated (r=.43, p <.05), but perceived and actual percentage correct were not significantly correlated.

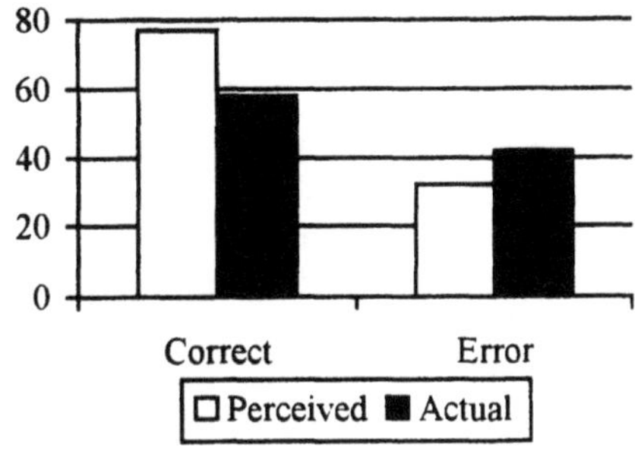

Figure 2. Perceived and Actual Accuracy

4.3 Goal Success

Another measure of the effectiveness of the system is whether or not participants were able to accomplish their goals using the it. Almost all of the scenarios required users to perform a number of sub-goals, such as getting the checking balance, paying the phone bill. We scored whether or not a participant was able to accomplish each sub-goal attempted, regardless of the number of consecutive attempts it took. Participants were able to accomplish 92% of the sub-goals attempted. This number ranged from 75% to 100% for the 22 participants. Thus, although accuracy as measured on an utterance-by utterance basis was 58%, the goal success rate was considerably higher. As might be expected, the goal success measure and effective accuracy were highly correlated (r=.81, p<.05).

4.4 Error Categories

Errors were classified into a number of categories as shown in Figure 3. The largest proportion of errors (26%) were misrecognition errors, in which the system recognized the user's utterance as a different, legitimate request. This includes cases in which the system responded with the required information or action but gave unrequested information as well, cases in which the system was "on the right track" but gave only a partial response, as well as outright errors. About 20% of the errors were recognition failures, in which the system was unable to produce a match for the user's utterance. For both these categories, the problem resulted from an error of speech recognition and the utterance would have been handled correctly by the natural language component.

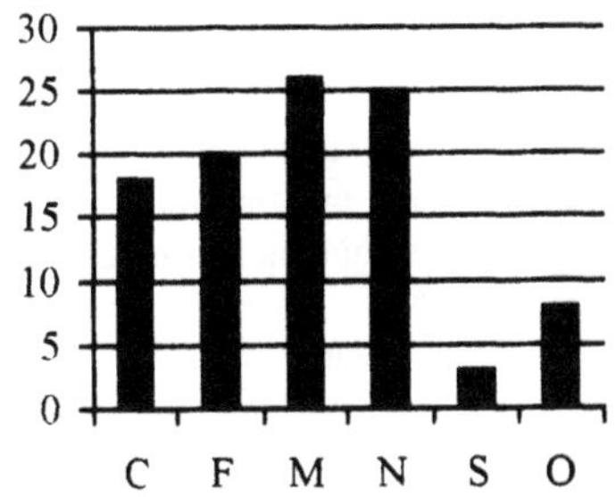

Figure 3. Percentage of Errors due to Competence (C) . Recognition Failure (F), Misrecognition (M), Noise (N), Sub-dialog (S) and Other (O)

About 25% of the errors were due to noise, in which the system picked up background noise or breathing noises when nothing was spoken, or speech intended for the experimenter. These errors are due to the combined effects of the sensitivity of the telephone microphone to background sounds, the speech recognizer's ability to distinguish signal from noise, and the fact that the system as tested could not be put on hold or mute.

About 18% of the errors were competence errors, in which the user made a request which was outside the system's competence. For example, one user made the request, "If I write a check for $200, will it bounce?" Some of the requests in this category were for information or actions which the system could handle if phrased in a different way, such as this example. Other requests were beyond the system's capabilities, such as providing a history of bill payments.

Sub-dialog errors were errors in which the participant was in a sub-dialog but made a top level dialog request. In many of these cases, the participant had gotten into the sub-dialog as a result of an earlier recognition error and essentially repeated the earlier request.

4.5 How People Respond to Errors

As described in section 4.4. the major sources of error were speech recognition errors. noise. competence errors. and sub-dialog errors. The problem for users is that they often have little idea why the error occurred and what they can do to recover from it. This is related to the what-can-I-say problem (Yankelovich, 1996). As a starting point in designing user interfaces that help people recover from errors. we did a qualitative analysis of the strategies participants used in dealing with errors. We have not yet done a rigorous validation of the classification or a tally of the error strategies. but present this information because of its value in stimulating thinking about how to facilitate error recovery.

Repetition — Often people were at a loss to rephrase their request in a different way and simply repeated the request. This never worked in the case of competence errors. but occasionally worked for recognition errors.

Semantic/syntactic substitution — Participants rephrased a request by making semantic or syntactic substitutions (or both). The first example illustrates a semantic change with a minor syntactic change: the second illustrates a larger syntactic change. Our impression is that rephrasings that involved larger changes tended to be more successful.

Original: Uhm. what is my current insurance bill?

Follow-up: What is the balance on my insurance?

Original: I would like to know my checking balance.

Follow-up: How much is in my checking account?

Elaboration – Participants elaborated on a failed request, adding redundant or new information. In the few cases where a very brief original request was expanded, this strategy worked. Although elaboration often works with human conversation partners, in most cases, the elaboration strategy produced a long request which failed. The following example comes from the participant with the highest utterance error rate.

Original: Uhm. how much would my electric company bill bé this month?

Follow-up (1): My electric bill for the month. uh. just wondering how much would come out to this month?

Follow-up (2): My electricity bill. I want to know. uhm. what the amount will be at the end of the month, how much will I owe?

Simplification – Participants simplified a request. resulting in a briefer request. This sometimes also involved breaking a compound request into parts. This strategy often worked. For example.

Original: I would like to take care of my bills. and I would like to know the checking account balance.

Follow-up: What is my checking account balance?

Ignore sub-dialog prompt – When participants found themselves in a sub-dialog due to a recognition error. they sometimes ignored the prompt because it did not offer them acceptable alternatives. Because the system was designed to handle responses to the prompt only. this strategy failed. For example.

Original: I want a transfer...

System: Which bills should I pay?

Follow-up (1): I want a transfer. of a hundred dollars...

System: Which bill? Phone. insurance. Mastercard. or electricity?

Follow-up (2): No. no bills {pause}. I just want to transfer money from my savings account into the checking...

Goal shift – On occasion. participants changed their goal when faced with an error. There are at least three situations when this happened: 1. The system responded with information or began a transaction that was relevant to the scenario (although not the correct response to the user's request). and the participant changed his/her goal to match the response. 2. The participant had attempted a request that was beyond the application's competence (such as providing bill payment history). and the changed his/her goal to one within the system's abilities. 3. The user gave up on the goal and tried something else.

Help request – Although study participants listened to an introductory message at the beginning of the session that told them they could ask for help. and one of the error prompts reminded them of this. there were an average of only 1.7 help requests per participant. Nine participants never used the help command.

4.6 Subjective Ratings of System and Correlations with Objective Measures

At the end of the session. we gave participants a questionnaire which asked them to rate the system on a number of dimensions using a 6-point rating scale (1 to 6). The means suggest a favorable reaction to the system (see Table 1 for selected means).

Dimension	Mean
Felt in control (not at all-very much)	4.50
Ease of use (rather difficult-very easy)	4.41
Keypad-Speech preference	4.23

Table 1. Mean ratings (1 - 6) on selected questions

The Keypad-Speech question asked participants which system they would be more likely to use if both a keypad and speech system like the current one were available. Forty-five percent of the participants responded in the highest category in favor of speech, indicating that a large group of people had a strong preference for the conversational interface.

The control and ease of use dimensions were significantly correlated with the objective goal success measure ($r=.53$, $r=.46$, respectively, $p<.05$). The utterance accuracy measure was moderately, but not significantly, correlated with these measures. This result suggests that the ability to accomplish one's goal may be a more important factor in user satisfaction than utterance level accuracy.

4.7 Personality Ratings

It has been observed that people have social reactions to computer systems, particularly those that use speech in the user interface (Nass, Steuer and Tauber, 1994). In the questionnaire, we asked participants to rate the system on 12 personality attributes using a 6-point semantic differential scale. Table 2, which shows a subset of these attributes, indicates that people rated the personality of the system quite positively. Of particular note is that the system was perceived as efficient, competent, and reliable.

Attribute	Mean
Friendly-Unfriendly	2.05
Active-Passive	3.00
Intelligent-Unintelligent	2.41
Helpful-Unhelpful	2.64
Cooperative-Uncooperative	2.36
Efficient-Inefficient	2.27
Reliable-Unreliable	2.00
Competent-Incompetent	1.82

Table 2. Mean Personality Ratings (1-6)

5.0 DISCUSSION AND CONCLUSION

This study suggests that state-of-the-art conversational interfaces, such as the Conversation Machine, may be preferred over keypad interfaces by typical consumers. The system tested in this study was preferred to a keypad interface by a majority of the participants. It was rated as easy to use, gave the users a sense of control, and was perceived as competent, efficient and reliable. It should be noted that the characteristics of the domain (e.g. number and complexity of potential requests) are critical to the applicability of a conversational interface.

Our results indicate that recognition accuracy may not be the best predictor of user satisfaction. The important subjective measures of ease of use and sense of control were significantly correlated with goal success, but not with utterance accuracy. Goal success was also correlated with both the perceived percentage correct and the perceived percentage error, whereas actual accuracy was correlated with only the perceived error rate, and not the perceived percentage correct. This supports the claim that the user's ability to accomplish his/her goals may be a more important measure of the acceptability of this system (and others like it) than objective accuracy.

The study analyzed categories of errors and participants' error recovery strategies as a starting point in improving both goal success and accuracy. Misrecognitions and recognition failures due to the speech recognition component were responsible for the largest proportion of the errors. These errors may be addressed by improvements to the underlying speech technology and also by changes to the user interface which help users avoid and recover from errors. Another significant category of errors was noise. As mentioned above, these errors are due to the sensitivity of the telephone microphone, the speech recognizer's ability to distinguish signal from noise, and the fact that the system tested had no way to mute or pause the recognizer. We have now added a pause function to the Conversation Machine, which gives the user some control over when the system is listening for speech. A third category of errors consisted of competence errors. In some cases, these errors represent the need to add additional functionality to the banking application or additional constructions to the natural language/dialog component. However, there is a tradeoff between increasing the coverage of these components and decreasing the speed and accuracy of the system. Furthermore, it is unlikely that a system could be designed to handle some of the utterances produced by our users (see section 4.5). The approach required in these cases is to design the user interface to help people avoid and recover from errors.

Our analysis of participants' strategies in dealing with errors suggests that their intuitions based on human-human conversation did not always work, although some strategies were more likely to be successful than others. The appropriate error recovery strategy may depend on the source of the error. However, the user is not likely to understand the cause of the error and the system may have limited ability to diagnose the cause (or even detect that an error occurred). Consequently, approaches to error recovery must be based on a combination of giving the user generally useful advice, giving the user information sufficient to determine the state of the system, and whatever limited information the system can provide in diagnosing an error. We are currently trying out several approaches to dealing with errors.

Recognition failures are perhaps easier to deal with than other errors since the system has detected that it is in an error state. One approach we are experimenting with is to provide increasingly directive prompts. For example, since simplification tends to be a successful user strategy, one prompt suggests the use of "short, simple requests." If the user is still not successful, examples of acceptable requests are given. The goal is to give users some insight into the style of speech which is acceptable as well as what they can request, without giving the impression that they are constrained to use just the speech given in the examples. Another approach, which can be combined with the above, is to prompt the user to ask for help on a particular topic. See Yankelovich (1996) for a discussion of current wisdom on how to deal with the what-can-I say problem.

Misrecognitions are more difficult to handle, since the system has not detected the error. We are exploring the possibility of using the dialog history as a way to detect repeated misrecognitions.

Errors that occur in a sub-dialog can be addressed in several ways. First, it may be necessary to give the user explicit feedback for state in each prompt, even if that feedback has just been given in the preceding prompt. Second, as our system and many others do, the acceptable responses to the sub-dialog can be presented in a prompt. Finally, there should always be a way for the user to get out of the sub-dialog (e.g. say "cancel"), and the user should be reminded of how to do this.

6.0 REFERENCES

Clark, H. H. and Brennan, S. E. (1991). Grounding in communication. In J. Levine, L. B. Resnick, and S. D. Behrand (Eds.), *Shared Cognition: Thinking as Social Practice*. APA Books, Washington.

Danis, C. and Karat, J. (1995). Technology-driven design of speech recognition systems. In G. Olson and S. Schuon (Eds.) *DIS '95: Symposium on Designing Interactive Systems*. ACM, New York, 17-24.

Goldberg, A. E. (1995). *Constructions: A construction grammar approach to argument structure*. The University of Chicago Press, Chicago.

Halstead-Nussloch, R. (1989). The design of phone-based interfaces for consumers. *CHI '89 Conference Proceedings*, 347-352.

Hansen, B., Novick, D. G., and Sutton, S. (1996). Systematic design of spoken prompts. *CHI '96 Conference Proceedings*,. 157-164.

Marx, M. and Schmandt, C. (1996). MailCall: Message presentation and navigation in a nonvisual environment. *CHI '96 Conference Proceedings*, 165-172.

Nass, C., Steuer, J. and Tauber, E. R. (1994). Computers are social actors, *CHI '94 Conference Proceedings*, 72-78.

Oviatt, S. Predicting spoken disfluencies during human-computer interaction. (1995). *Computer Speech and Language*, 9, 19-35.

Rhyne, J. R. and Wolf, C. G. (1993). Recognition based user interfaces. In R. Hartson and D. Hix (Eds.), *Advances in Human-Computer Interaction*, 4, Ablex, 191-250.

Yankelovich, N. (1996). How do users know what to say? *interactions*, 3.6, 32-43.

Yankelovich, N., Levow, G. A., and Marx, M. (1995). Designing SpeechActs: Issues in speech user interfaces. *CHI '95 Conference Proceedings*, 369-376.

Zadrozny, W. (1995). From utterances to situations: Parsing with constructions in small domains. *Language, Logic and Computation: The 1994 Moraga Proceedings*.

Zadrozny, W. (1996) Natural language processing: Structure and complexity. *Proceedings of the Eight International Conference on Software Engineering and Knowledge Engineering*, 595-602.

Storing and Retrieving Documents in a Shared Workspace: Experiences from the Political Administration

Volker Wulf

Institute for Computer Science III
University of Bonn
Römerstr. 164, D-53117 Bonn, Germany
Email: volker@informatik.uni-bonn.de

ABSTRACT In the following we will describe experiences made when introducing a shared workspace in a German federal ministry to support the cooperative typing of documents. It will be shown how the shared workspace improved the typing process, how storing and retrieval conventions evolved during a two-year period, and which technical improvements of the system functionality have been required by the users to ease document retrieval. Finally, it will be discussed which organizational and technical factors support the establishment of common storing and retrieving conventions in shared workspaces.

KEYWORDS Groupware, Shared Workspaces, Classification Scheme, Document Retrieval, Field Study

1. INTRODUCTION

As the production of documents is increasingly based on the application of personal computers, storage and retrieval of electronic documents are an important research topic. Nevertheless, studies on storing and retrieval habits of office employees have focused up to now mainly on the handling of paper documents. There exist only few empirical studies dealing with the file organization in the electronic office (cf. Barreau and Nardi 1995; Rao et al. 1994). These studies look at the organization of electronic documents from a single user perspective. Since the production of documents gets more of a cooperative activity with networked computers, additional research on the organization of electronic documents in shared workspaces is required.

From a methodological point of view, most of the studies on the organization of electronic and physical files have taken a static perspective in the sense that the data were gathered at just one point in time (e.g. Malone 1983; Suchman and Wynn 1984, Barreau 1995; Nardi, Anderson and Erickson 1994). Since the organization of documents - especially in collaborative environments - might evolve considerable during time, a more long term research approach could lead to interesting results. The period following the introduction of a new computer system seems to be an especially interesting time span. Here we assume to observe how conventions for the organization of electronic documents are established based on prior experiences and how they evolve later on.

In the following, we will report on the evolution of storing and retrieving habits in a shared workspace. The shared workspace was introduced to ease the cooperative production of typed documents in a German federal ministry. Based on the experiences made during a two years span, we will draw some conclusions on how to support the establishment of storing and retrieving conventions in shared workspaces.

Human–Computer Interaction: INTERACT'97 S. Howard, J. Hammond & G. Lindgaard (editors)
Published by Chapman & Hall

2. STORING AND RETRIEVING IN INDIVIDUAL WORKSPACES

As the focus of this study has been influenced by the results of already existing research work, I will give a brief survey on its results. Interviewing ten office workers on the physical organization of their desks, Malone (1983) distinguishes files and piles as mayor units of desk organization. While in files the individual documents are titled and ordered, in piles there is not any structure of the containing documents. Piles themselves are not named, either. The organization of the documents seems to be related to their contend.

As the result of an empirical study on 15 experienced Macintosh users of different professional background, Nardi, Anderson and Ericson (1994) distinguish three types of information represented on electronic documents: "ephemeral", "working", and "archived". While ephemeral information is needed only for a short period of time (e.g.: "to do"-lists, memos, ...), working information is created by the users when carrying out their actual tasks. It has a typical shelf time of weeks or months. By contrary, archived information is only indirectly relevant to users' actual work. It represents completed work and has a shelf time of months or years. The authors found out that different types of information are stored in different ways by the users. While ephemeral information is kept rather in "electronic piles" either unstructured on the desktop or loosely filed at the top directory level, working and archived information is more systematically filed.

Barreau (1995) has interviewed seven managers of a large information management company to find out how they store and retrieve electronic documents. In comparing the classification schemes applied by the interviewees in her study with those of an earlier study carried out by Kwasnik (1989) on the organization of paper documents, she found that "...(m)any of the same types of documents were identified, and many of the same dimensions were used in making classification decisions" (p. 336). Nevertheless, comparing the classification schemes of different individuals she found "completely different rules for classifying documents based upon the level of granularity required to support the workload" (p. 337). Malone (1983) had already pointed to the fact that different office workers showed great variations in how precisely they organized their offices. Performing interviews about the work practice of 16 office workers of a large office equipment manufacturer, Suchman and Wynn (1984) have come to a similar result. They state that the most efficient and satisfactory pattern of desktop organization are discovered rather than prescribed (cf. Suchman and Wynn 1984, p. 150). Moreover, Barreau (1995) stated that classification "(r)ules that are applied for a period of time to reflect the priorities of the moment may soon be abandoned or forgotten..." (p. 337).

Concerning the methods to search for an electronic document, Barreau and Nardi (1995) distinguish between "location based" and "logical" finding. In location based finding a user makes a guess for the folder or directory where he thinks a document might be located, goes to that location, and browses the documents located there. This process is iterated if needed. In logical finding the user specifies an inquiry by filling in attribute values or keywords related to the document he is searching for. As a result he gets listed all the documents which correspond to the inquiry. While location based finding is similar to the searching process for paper documents, logical finding can be just applied for electronic documents. Both of the studies, which look at the users' habits to search for electronic documents indicate an overwhelming preference for location based search. The authors attribute this fact to the higher level of control the users exercise over the location based search process and problems in remembering the right attribute values (e.g. the document's name) of the desired document (cf. Barreau and Nardi 1995, pp. 40).

Looking at search processes for paper documents on colleagues' desks, Suchman and Wynn (1984) point to problems resulting from the fact that the way papers are organized on one person's desk is not easily apparent to other workers. Therefore, Barreau and Nardi (1995) assume that for search outside of the individual desk, tools for logical finding might be more appropriate than for searching on the individual desk.

Moreover, empirical studies have indicated that the allocation of documents on the desk has a critical reminding function. Malone (1983) has already hinted to this fact when looking from an individual perspective at the physical organization of papers on desks. Suchman and Wynn (1984, pp. 147) add that the localisation of documents on an employee's desk often indicates the state of processing to his colleagues. The reminding function of the allocation of documents has also been observed in the studies on the organization of electronic documents (cf. Barreau and Nardi 1995).

3. THE RESEARCH SETTING

This research took place in the context of the POLITeam project. Within the POLITeam project a groupware application is developed in an evolutionary and participative way. The first system version is generated by configuring the commercial product LinkWorks by Digital (POLITeam I). Based on the experiences gained by introducing the first system version in three different fields of application, we develop advanced versions of the system. The functionality mainly consists of an electronic circulation folder, shared workspaces, and an event notification service. Looking at the means to organize files, the system is based on the desktop metaphor and offers an electronic folder hierarchy. These folders can be either used only on one's personal desktop or they can be shared with other users (cf. Klöckner et al. 1995, Mambrey, Mark and Pankoke-Babatz 1996).

In the following we will report about experiences made in one of the three different fields of application of the POLITeam project. The field of application is a section of a federal ministry. The section consists of about five employees and one section manager. The work of the section is supported by typists and a worker in the registrar. The typists belong to the central typing pool whose offices are located in another part of the building. The registrar is allocated on another floor of the same building. Before introducing the POLITeam system, the typing pool was equipped with net-worked PCs, using a common server to store the text documents. The employees of the operating section and in the registrar were not equipped with computers for their daily work.

This report is based on results of initial interviews with the users concerning their work practice before the introduction of POLITeam, on interviews carried out after the introduction of POLITeam, on experiences gained by providing regular system support after the introduction of POLITeam, and on an evaluation of several workshops held in this field of application. Within the first workshop, we presented the prototypical configuration to the users (workshop A), half a year after the introduction of POLITeam I we held a workshop to discuss problems the users were facing when applying POLITeam I (workshop B), about another half a year later we presented the POLITeam II version to the users (workshop C) and the most recent workshop was held half a year after the introduction of POLITeam II to represent some features of the new system version and to discuss problems of use (workshop D). In all of the workshops employees of the section of the ministry, the section manager, employees of the typing pool, the head of the ministry's computer department and members of the project-team working as system support and as designers participated.

4. STORING AND RETRIEVING DOCUMENTS BEFORE THE INTRODUCTION OF POLITEAM

One of the main tasks of the ministry's section observed, consists of the development of concepts for a certain field of politics. Some of these concepts are developed just within the section. Others are worked out in cooperation with other sections of the ministry. These concepts (e.g. manuscripts for speeches of the minister, answers to inquiries from the parliament, or answers to letters sent by citizens) are documented on paper and provided by means of circulation folders for the upper level of the ministry's hierarchy. All the paper documents, for internal as well as for external use, are typed.

Before the introduction of POLITeam all type work for the ministry was carried out by the central typing pool. Therefore, members of the section sent hand-written texts or tapes with voice recording to the typing pool. After typing, the texts were sent back to the sender who checked the document. If he found a mistake, he had to send it back to the typist who did the correction. This version of the document was finally given to the section manager who was responsible to process it and who might have asked for further modifications. As the transportation of the material between the employees of the section and the typists was normally done by internal messengers and as the typists had to schedule their different tasks, it normally took three to four days for the typing of the first version of a document. Thus if a task was very urgent, the section members used to bring their manuscripts to the typists personally and asked for a preferential treatment. But even this procedure took time, especially if the typed version contained mistakes. These problems were the reason why the introduction of POLITeam led to a change in the typing process. This process innovation influenced the storing conventions for typed documents strongly.

Before the introduction of POLITeam typed documents were stored twice in the ministry, electronically and physically. These stores served different purposes and thus were built up in a very different way. The - still existing - physical store of the whole ministry is handled by the employees of the registrar. Within the registrar individual paper documents are filed in folders. A folder contains all paper documents related to a specific task of the ministry. All the tasks of the ministry can be classified according to a ministry-wide classification scheme. The employees in the registrar create folders for all the tasks performed in the ministry as soon as they receive paper documents related to them. For instance, if tasks are initiated by an incoming mail these letters are normally routed via the registrar before they reach the individual sections. Thus the registrar classifies it, looks whether there exists already a corresponding folder (ongoing task), or creates a new folder (new task). A new folder receives an index according to the task classification scheme of the ministry. The registrar uses this index to store and retrieve the folders because their physical placement in the registrar is related to the index.

If the ministry is working on certain tasks the corresponding folders are taken out of the registrar to the sections which are responsible for them. For instance, in case of a task created by an incoming letter, the registrar will send the newly created folder to the organizational unit responsible for its performance. Members of a specific operative section responsible for the task will hold the folder as long as they work on it. Though members of a section are not allowed to store folders in their offices for a longer period of time, the arrangement of different piles of folders in certain areas of their offices is used by them to remind themselves of the corresponding tasks. To remind section members of tasks which have to be performed in the future, the employees of the registrar provide a corresponding service. They keep a list of these tasks and send the corresponding folders at the predefined dates to the sections. The physical reception of a folder reminds the members of the operation sections of the tasks. Thus, folders containing all the paper documents related to a especial task are the basic units for storing and retrieving physical documents in the ministry.

By contrary the storage of electronic documents was based on individual documents. Before the introduction of the POLITeam system, the typing pool was the only organizational unit which stored documents electronically. The typing pool had created directories for each section of the ministry, containing subfolder for each member of the sections. Within these subfolders all the documents which any typist had written for a certain client were stored. On the third level of the folder-hierarchy, the typists distinguished among five different types of documents to be stored in the same subfolder. Thus, if a client would ask for corrections on a certain type of document, any typist knew in which subfolder to search. To ease finding within the subfolders, all typists used a common convention for the naming of documents. Using the DOS operation system, they were restricted to the use of eight symbols to name documents. The first five symbols of the documents' name were used to indicate the date of a document's first creation, expressing day, month and year in reverse order. Thus, it was possible to search within the subfolders using a temporal structure. This naming and storing conventions were convenient for the search needs of the typing pool because they eased location based finding of individual documents. Nevertheless they were incompatible with the conventions for storing paper documents. This fact became obvious when other parts of the ministry started to work electronically, as well.

5. STORING AND RETRIEVING DOCUMENTS AFTER THE INTRODUCTION OF POLITEAM

After the introduction of the POLITeam system the mode to produce typed documents has changed. It was decided to create a shared workspace consisting of a folder which could be accessed by the operative section and the typing pool. Within this folder all documents were stored which the typing pool produced for the members of the section. The folder contained subfolders to store documents produced for each member of the section.

The introduction of folders shared between the section and the typing pool allowed new modes for the division of labour. Being equipped with a word processing tool and having the chance to gain access to typed documents, the members of the section could decide flexibly what to type themselves and when to ask the typing pool. Each of them developed in the following an individual strategy. Moreover, the section manager who checked all the documents leaving the section typed his corrections himself by accessing the shared folder. Though there was a change in the way typed documents were produced within the section, the handling of typed documents outside of the section did not change. As the other sections, the hierarchy of the ministry, and the registrar were not yet equipped with computers, all documents got printed out and left the section in traditional circulation folders.

When POLITeam I was introduced, the shared workspace consisted of a two level hierarchy of folders. In the folder shared between section and typing pool there were subfolders containing the documents for each member of the section. To maintain their location based search strategy, the typists changed the naming convention by starting the name of each document with a letter indicating the document type and continuing with numbers, indicating the date of a document's creation. The access to the shared folder was implemented in a way that the head of the section and the typists could read and write all documents in the whole folder while the other members of the section could just access documents in their subfolders.

During workshop B on problems of use, half a year after the introduction of POLITeam I, the members of the operative section expressed their dissatisfaction concerning these patterns of naming and storing. When searching for documents they do not think of document types, but of their tasks. Working on a task means to create various documents of different types. Thus, the mode of storing and naming did not reflect their needs for the support of a location based finding strategy. Discussing this topic, a conflict of interest between the section and the typing pool became manifest. As both organizational units classified the documents in a different way a single location based organization of the documents would not satisfy both sides. In this situation the members of the POLITeam project proposed different solutions. First, one member of the POLITeam project suggested to keep the naming and storing system like it was, but to tell the members of the section to display the documents in the temporal order of their creation. She assumed that such a display would come close to a task-oriented structure of storage, because documents concerning the same task would be created around the same time. This proposal was perceived positively within the workshop but it was not possible to implement because POLITeam I just allowed to display documents according to the time of their last modification. The members of the section felt that such a display would not be sufficiently task-oriented. Thus, this compromise which had allowed to generate two different patterns to organize documents within a folder could not be implemented due to a lack of flexibility of the interface display function.

The solution agreed on finally in the workshop, was to allow the members of the section to introduce a third level in the folder-hierarchy, where documents could be allocated according to the section member's task they belong to. The naming of the documents was kept like it was. Thus, the classification scheme of the operative section became the base for the storage of the documents. Nevertheless, it turned out that the compromise found in the workshop was not put widely into practice.

Another problem became obvious after the introduction of the POLITeam I version. As the cooperation between the section and the typing pool was based on shared folders, the typed documents were neither sent electronically nor physically from the typists to the section members. Before the introduction of POLITeam, the reception of a typed document informed the members of the section that the typing process was finished and reminded them of the corresponding task. After the introduction of POLITeam the typists stored newly typed documents in the shared subfolder. Thus, the members of the section were not notified explicitly, they had to look themselves in their folder to check whether a document has been typed. Therefore, the members of the section asked in the workshop B for technical functions which make typed documents visible to them. They wanted to see by means of the colour of an icon, whether the typists have finished working on the corresponding document. Moreover, they wanted to recognize newly created files by a different colour of icon. As POLITeam I did not offer these options, we discussed different intermediate solutions. First of all, it was suggested that the typists should send a mail whenever they finished working on a document. The typists found it too labour-intensive and the members of the section feared the flood of incoming mails. As an intermediate solution, they agreed to use the rudiment features of the already existing event service.

About 12 months after the introduction of the POLITeam I version, we equipped the users with a new system version (POLITeam II). In this version we had realized those user requirements which where rather simple to implement within the base system. Concerning the storage and retrieval of documents the following features were most relevant. Location based finding got supported by the introduction of a viewer which allows to scan into individual documents without opening the corresponding application. Moreover, a function was implemented which allowed to select between different display-modes of documents within a folder. For instance, the users could organize documents according to their names, their date of creation, or their index which has become an additional attribute of the electronic documents. Thus, within a folder the individual users could select among different modes to allocate documents.

Furthermore, the POLITeam II version offered a tool for logical finding of documents. Though the LinkWorks product version contained already such a search tool, it had been deactivated when configuring the POLITeam I version. This was due to the fact that the original search tool allowed to find any document within the system independent of the location where it was stored. Thus, users could have retrieved, accessed and modified documents which were allocated on the private desktop of other users. As we assumed that such a search tool would have endangered the acceptance of the whole system, we decided to deactivate this feature. For the POLITeam II version we had modified the search tool in such a way that users could only find documents which were accessible on their own desktop (cf. Kahler 1996). In the following we will report on the further development of the file organization in the shared folder and the experiences made with the new features of the POLITeam II version.

Looking at the file organization in the shared workspace about one year after the agreement in workshop B, the majority of the members of the section still worked with a two level folder-hierarchy. Nevertheless, in interviews several of them complained that the amount of documents within their subfolders which made it very troublesome to find any document.

For instance, one member of the section pointed out that she had not used subfolders in her subdirectory because their creation and the classification of documents led to additional work. She appreciated very much the additional features to display documents according to different criteria. This was the only way for her to find documents in her vast subfolder. Nevertheless, after a year of document production her subfolder is meanwhile that crowded with documents that she has real problems in finding them. This is especially the case for older documents which she reuses occasionally. Thus, on the one hand she regreted that she did not build up a third level in the folder hierarchy to ease document-retrieval. On the other hand she avoided the additional workload. Moreover she stated that the classification and archiving of documents is not her job. She told us that she is not familiar with the classification scheme of the ministry and expects support from the registrar concerning the electronic storage of documents.

By contrary, one of her colleagues has developed an own classification scheme by creating task-related subfolders to store documents. When asking the typing pool to get a document typed, she indicates the corresponding subfolder on the manuscript. She finds this organization of documents to be very helpful to support her daily work.

Thus, the members of the section have developed rather individual strategies for the organization of the documents in the folder shared with the typists. Therefore, the storage scheme within this folder became a topic of discussion in workshop D. The manager of the section brought up a controversy. Though he had advocated the compromise negotiated within the workshop B, he was meanwhile of the opinion that there should not be any third level within the folder hierarchy of the shared workspace. He stated that the newly introduced display function should offer sufficient support to search for documents. A further level of the folder hierarchy made it very difficult for him to retrieve documents within the other section member's subfolders. He especially insisted on the fact that the index attribute should be filled in every electronic document. A display of the documents according to this index should be a sufficient support for location based retrieval.

In the following the members of his section who had created a third level in the folder hierarchy explained how helpful such an organization was for their work. A member of the project-team supported them by explaining how a third level of the folder hierarchy together with the newly introduced display function can support location based finding. As the section manager insisted on a standardised file organization, the member of the project-team suggested to allow only subfolders on the third level of the hierarchy, which are created according to the organization-wide classification scheme. After discussing details like which version of the classification scheme should be valid and on which level of granularity the scheme should be applied, the new convention was agreed upon by all the users.

Though the search tool has been introduced in the POLITeam II version the facts presented up to now indicate that most of the documents are still retrieved by location based finding. For instance, one of the section members stated in an interview that she uses the search tool less than once a week. She needs it mainly if she cannot remember the folder a document is stored in or if a document has been mistakenly moved into a wrong folder.

In workshop D the question arose whether it should be possible to apply logical finding to those documents which can not be accessed by location-based finding. The typists were in favour of such an implementation because they had made the experiences that the members of the section did not keep all the relevant documents stored in the shared folder. Thus they would prefer to be able to search on the section member's private desks. Moreover, they are sometimes asked by members of the section to search for a specific document in another section member's shared subfolder because the typists can access the whole shared workspace. Thus, they had to provide manual services to the section which an extended search tool could provide electronically.

By contrary, the members of the section were less enthusiastic about an extended function for logical finding. On the one hand they argued that finding documents on the desktop of a colleague with whom they do not co-operate at all does not make much sense.

On the other hand they fear that their privacy would get violated if, for instance, somebody of the hierarchy of the ministry could check all documents an employee has created during a certain period of time. Moreover, documents been stored on their private desk are often in an unfinished state and they would not like to allow access to them before they get ready. After discussing this topic for a while a member of the project-team suggested a redesign of the search tool which would allow to differentiate the behaviour of the search tool according to the location a document is stored. Thus, documents stored in certain locations should not be found at all, in other locations the search tool would just display the location of the documents while in other cases the documents could be accessible directly. Such a design of the search tool was thought to be a viable way to extend the search tools scope beyond a user's own desktop.

6. CONCLUSION

In the case study reported we saw how storing and retrieval habits on working and archived information evolved after the introduction of groupware. Introducing a groupware system which is based on the desktop metaphor, we observed strong preferences of the users for location based finding in comparison to logical finding. This finding might be due to the fact that the system did not contain a search tool before the POLITeam II version. Nevertheless this finding concerning shared workspaces is consistent with results on single user's workspaces. Thus, it seems to be important to focus research and tool development on location based finding.

Concerning logical finding in groupware, the users require that these tools should be sensitive to the location a document is stored. To avoid information overload and to protect the privacy of certain locations, search-tools should not display all the documents fitting to the specification of an inquiry. Moreover, it seems to be reasonable that search tools provide different mechanisms to control access to documents which are allocated outside of the searchers own workspace. This leads to a different design of search tools for collaborative environments in comparison to those for single user systems (cf. Kahler 1996, Wulf 1997).

Looking at the establishment of a classification scheme for the location based storage of electronic documents, we have experienced a long lasting negotiation process. Within this process, we are facing two different problems. On the one hand two contradicting collective classification schemes had to be reconciled. Looking at the development of collective storage convention one sees that first of all the system of the typing pool was applied. Contrary to the operative section, in the beginning of the project, the typing pool had already experiences with the electronic storage of documents, and thus, could present a viable solution for the problem. At that time the members of the operating section were not yet aware of the implications resulting from this decision. After producing an increasing amount of electronic documents and getting used to computer based work, the members of the section got sensitive to this problem. Being in the stronger position within the organization, they were able to modify the established conventions according to their perceived requirements. Nevertheless even at this point the section manager had still problems to anticipate his particular interests which were different from the other members of the section. Nevertheless, in the following he was able to re-negotiate and modify the existing conventions for storing documents.

On the other hand we were facing the problem on how to reconcile different individual preferences. The research on the document organization on individual desks has revealed already a big variety of different storing schemes. These individual differences threatened the implementation of the storing conventions agreed upon in the workshops. Indeed the compromise for organising the shared workspace was just put into practice by those members of the section who felt that an additional level within the folder hierarchy would be helpful for them. Thus, beyond the problem of finding appropriate conventions for location based storing there is the other problem on how to motivate individuals to put these agreements into practice.

To avoid such problems, Malone (1983) has suggested to simply allow multiple classification schemes. Indeed LinkWorks provided functionality to create multiple folder hierarchies. It allowed to generate different aliases for one document. By organising the aliases in the individually created folder-hierarchy each user could realize his own view on the shared workspace (cf. Mark and Prinz 1997). In this way a shared view realising the negotiated convention and an arbitrary amount of individual views could have been created. Nevertheless the user did not make use of this feature. They pointed out that the maintenance of their individual folder hierarchy was too troublesome and labour-intensive because they had to create and store aliases for every newly created document. By contrary, multiple classification schemes which were provided by different display options for documents within one folder were highly appreciated by the users because the different schemes could be easily generated. Thus, the experiences reported on indicate that as long as the individual organization of documents has to be performed manually, one should try to establish a common classification scheme for location based storing in a shared workspace.

Looking at this negotiation process, it turns out that experiences concerning the storage of electronic documents and the power-position of the different collective and individual stakeholders influence its outcome considerably. Moreover, the facilitation of members of the project-team played an important role in the negotiation process. As the members of the project team had a rather profound knowledge about the work practice of the different users and a clear idea of the options the system's functionality offered, they were able to suggest possible approaches to solutions. Though facilitators disposing of technical and organizational knowledge might ease negotiations, the establishment of a classification scheme to store documents in a shared workspace has to be seen as an evolutionary process. This is due to the fact that individual users and groups of users do not perceive their requirements immediately and that new technical search and display functions might effect the users' requirements for a classification scheme. Moreover, if the participants in electroniccly supported work processes change, changes of collective classification schemes might be required. In our case a widening of the field of application within the ministry which will introduce electronic document handling within the registrar and within further levels of the ministry's hierarchy is likely to affect the storing scheme.

Let´s look at the reminding function of a document's allocation. The case study reveals that besides the organization of documents on a desktop the reception of paper documents can serve as a reminder to carry out tasks with them. Working in a shared workspace means to loose the reminding function of the document reception. Therefore, the users asked for a compensation by an additional functionality, the event service.

As a sophisticated event service was not foreseen in the design of the LinkWorks system, we could not implement it in the POLITeam II version. A more tailorable design of the base system would have eased to satisfy the users' requirements at this point (cf. Henderson and Kyng 1991). Looking at the benefits the users got from the quick implementation of the new display function, it becomes obvious that evolutionary negotiation processes on storage and retrieval conventions benefit strongly from a tailorable design.

7. REFERENCES

Barreau, D. K.: Context as a Factor in Personal Information Management Systems, in: Journal of the American Society of Information Science, Vol. 45, No. 5, 1995, pp. 327 - 339

Barreau, D. K.; Nardi, B. A.: Finding and Reminding - File Organization from the Desktop, in: SIGCHI Bulletin, Vol. 27, No. 2, 1995, pp. 39 - 43

Henderson, A.; Kyng, M.: There's No Place Like Home: Continuing Design in Use; in: J. Greenbaum; M. Kyng (eds): Design at Work - Cooperative Design of Computer Artifacts, Hillsdale, 1991, pp. 219 - 240

Kahler, H.: Developing Groupware with Evolution and Participation: A Case Study, in: Proceedings of the Forth Biennial Conference on Participatory Design (PDC´96), Boston, MA, Nov. 13 - 15, 1996, pp. 173 - 182

Klöckner, K.; Mambrey, P.; Sohlenkamp, M.; Prinz, W.; Fuchs, L. Kolvenbach, S.; Pankoke-Babatz, U.; Syri, A.: POLITeam – Bridging the Gap between Bonn and Berlin for and with the Users, in: H. Marmolin; Y. Sundblad; K. Schmidt (eds): Proceedings of the ECSCW´95 Conference, Dordrecht, 1995, pp. 17 - 32

Kwasnik, B. H.: The Influence of Context on Classification Behavior, Doctoral thesis, Rutgers University, 1989

Malone, T. W.: How do People organize their Desks?, in: ACM Transactions on Office Information Systems, Vol. 1, No. 1, 1983, pp. 99 - 112

Mambrey, P.; Mark, G.; Pankoke-Babatz, U.: Integrating User Advocacy into Participative Design in: Proceedings of the Forth Biennial Conference on Participatory Design (PDC´96), Boston, MA, Nov. 13 - 15 1996, pp. 251 - 260

Mark, G; Prinz, W.: The Establishment and Support of Conventions for Groupware, in this volume

Nardi, B.; Anderson, K.; Erickson, T.: Filing and Finding Computer Files. Technical Report # 118, Cupertine: Apple Computer, Inc. 1994

Rao, R.; Card, S.; Johnson, W.; Klotz, L.; Trigg, R.: Protofoil: Storing and Finding the Information Worker´s Paper Documents in an Electronic File Cabinet, in: Proceedings of the CHI´94, Boston, MA, April 24 - 28, ACM-Press, New York 1994, pp. 180 - 185

Suchman, L.; Wynn, E.: Procedures and Problems in the Office, in: Office Technology and People, Vol. 2, 1984, pp. 133 - 154

Wulf, V.: On Conflicts and Negotiation in Multi-User Applications; in: Kent, A.; Williams, J. G. (eds): Encyclopedia of Microcomputers, Dekker, New York et al., 1997 (in press)

Models and Metaphors in Groupware: Towards a Group-Centered Design

Gloria Mark and Peter Mambrey

GMD FIT
German National Reserch Center for Information Technology
Institute for Applied Information Technology
Research Group CSCW
Schloß Birlinghoven
53754 Sankt Augustin, Germany
E-mail: {Gloria.Mark,Peter.Mambrey}@gmd.de

ABSTRACT This paper reports on user experiences with the introduction of a groupware system in a government ministry. Our findings suggest that users understood the system as supporting collaboration, yet they had difficulties in understanding and using the groupware due to: 1) the lack of corresponding representation in the user's actual working life, 2) the reluctance to change personal work habits in order to develop shared group conventions, 3) the organization's influence through strict codes and procedures, and 4) the different models of cooperative work that users and designers developed. We recommend that designers and practitioners focus training and analysis on developing a shared representation of the group toward its work and the groupware system.

KEYWORDS groupware, metaphor, mental model, organizational influences, user studies

1. INTRODUCTION

Learning to work with a groupware system is a complex feat. In recent years, some attention has been directed toward the user's cognitions as an important approach in which to understand how the user comprehends and works with a new system (e.g. Davidson, 1996; Orlikowski, 1992, Rogers and Ellis, 1994). A user's acceptance and behavior toward a technology has been proposed by Orlikowski and Gash (1994) to be related to the clarity of the user's understanding of the technology.

Training people in a groupware system is difficult since there are few experiences reported with actual groupware use. Those that have generally report difficulties that users have in adapting to technology (Bowers, 1994; Bullen and Bennett, 1990; Grudin, 1988; Orlikowski, 1992; Rogers, 1994). The lack of user experiences makes it difficult to develop a conceptual teaching model which can be used as a basis to introduce groupware.

The purpose of this paper is to report on user experiences during the introduction of a large groupware system, POLITeam. Our focus of the user investigation was to discover ideas and attitudes that the users had developed of the system and of their collaborative process. When the project started, we realized that users would be faced with difficult problems: they would not only have to learn new functionality (and for most users, learn basic computer skills as well), but they would also have to learn new work patterns which were not based on anything similar in the users' actual working life.

Human–Computer Interaction: INTERACT'97 S. Howard, J. Hammond & G. Lindgaard (editors)
Published by Chapman & Hall

2. THE ORGANIZATIONAL SETTING

2.1 System use

In 1991, the German government voted to move the capital from Bonn to Berlin. Not all federal agencies and ministeries will relocate at once; thus, departments will be distributed between the two cities during the move. The goal of the POLITeam groupware system is to connect government employees through telecooperation between Bonn and Berlin. An existing groupware system (LinkWorks) was chosen and adapted to specific user and situation requirements. (For further information, see Sohlenkamp et al., forthcoming).

Prototypes were implemented in three areas of the government: the Federal Ministry of Family Affairs, Senior Citizens, Women, and Youth (FM), the State Representative body of Mecklenburg-Western Pomerania (SR), and the Ministry of Justice (MJ) in Schwerin. The project began in May 1994, and the system has been installed since January, 1995. The design approach integrated three different aspects: evolutionary cycling, direct designer-user contact, and user advocacy (Mambrey et al., 1996).

Although all locations have the full system installed, use is concentrated in particular applications, depending on the work practices of each ministry. In the FM, there are currently 10 users: 7 are employees responsible for specific content areas of the ministry, and 3 are typists in the central typing pool. The employees collaborate using the shared workspace, (e.g. writing speeches for the minister) and they exchange documents with each other and with the typing pool, who type intermediate and final versions.

In the SR, there are currently 8 unit leaders who use the system. Collaboration is primarily with the "Reference" application which allows people to work on a shared electronic document remotely and asynchronously. The users use this system to record votes for their respective ministers. The German House of Representatives meets every two weeks, and discusses approximately 80 issues. The unit leaders use the groupware for information dissemination and the Reference application to record their votes on 80 shared documents, one per issue.

The third location, the MJ, has approximately 20 users, mostly lawyers. Because of the distance from Bonn, site visits and interviews were conducted, but less observation was possible at this site than at the others.

2.2. Method of observation

We present our observations from a collection of experiences: workshops, site visits, discussions between designers and users, and user interviews. One of the authors was involved in the project since its inception and participated as an observer in design workshops, work requirements analyses, training workshops, a number of structured background interviews, regular user interviews, and simply "being present and chatting with the users". Transcripts were taken for most of these activities. This field work was done continually since May 1994. This author also actively discussed work scenarios with the users. In addition, a study was conducted to identify how the government's formal code of procedures (GGO) actually was implemented in the organization and to what extent it was followed by the employees. Both authors conducted additional interviews with users, after the system was in use about 6 months, and were observers in workshops and design discussions. The goal in observing the work requirements analysis was to try to understand what the users' work practices were, and how the users understood their working relationships.

3. MODELS AND METAPHORS OF GROUPWARE

Although with more user experiences we can better define a normative mental model of groupware, we began by following Johnson-Laird's (1983) notion: mental models are internal representations that are developed through experience. Mental models:

> *...play a central and unifying role in representing objects, states of affairs, sequences of events, the way the world is, and the social and psychological actions of daily life (p. 397).*

A mental model for a groupware user is not only a representation of how the system works, but it also contains a representation of the group work with the system. Although we discuss models *of* groups, it is important to emphasize that mental models are individual constructs. A person's mental model of a system is one's own representation of how and why the system works: it can generate descriptions of the purpose and form of the system, it can explain its functions, and can be used to make predictions about future states. Models develop naturally. They need not be technically accurate, but they must be functional and fit for a purpose (Fischer, 1991).

People have different perspectives, and this often becomes evident when people use groupware. Designers' perspectives have been observed to be different than those of users (Davidson, 1996; Orlikowski and Gash, 1994). The groupware use may be affected not only by users' understanding or misunderstandings of the system, but also by different mental models that group members have about the group and its goals. Generally, when people work in groups, they develop a set of common norms, assumptions, goals, and procedures, and members strive to attain a common understanding of these as the group becomes a reference for them (Newcomb, 1959). Since people are individuals, it is not possible that their cognitive representations can be identical, yet if they are interacting in a group sharing the same experiences, common perceptions develop (Fiske and Taylor, 1984). Especially when working together in an organization, people develop similar representations: experiences, activities, or attitudes which they recognize as common, referred to as "shared understanding" by Schein (1990). These can be centered on task goals, knowledge about the work and organization, or their informal and formal social communication, etc. However, when different representations among group members exist, they can become manifest as problems when a new technology is implemented (Orlikowski and Gash, 1994).

Metaphors can be vehicles to develop mental models, to explore them, and to communicate them. Metaphors enable us to create new perceptions, to conceptualize, and to think imaginatively about artifacts and mentifacts as well. As exploratory tools, metaphors can be used to help people restructure their models and generate new ideas, and can be valuable in system design (Mambrey and Tepper, 1996).

As researchers, we are trying to understand the models of the users. The problem with mental models is that they are individual, and often difficult to externalize. Unlike a scientific conceptual model of a system, which can be operationalized and described with formal notation, mental models are not standardized. Metaphors can provide valuable clues to the researcher as to what a user's model might be. For example, the researcher can observe what metaphors the person applies to learn new experiences, and how literally it is applied. A person may also explain an operation with the wrong metaphor, indicating that the user has a false model of the process. For example, one might believe that they "own" a document, enabling them to change access rights, when in effect, one is actually using it through WYSIWIS.

4. THE USERS' MODELS

In this section, we present selected scenarios which illustrate the range of models that the users developed.

4.1 Models of cooperation

Whereas before the implementation of the system, users used the expression "cooperative work" in an abstract and general way, after the users began working with the system, they began using the term "cooperative work" in a more personal, however sometimes idiosyncratic way. Thus, we found that users developed different notions of cooperation.

During an instructional workshop, the users referred to "searching" for a file as a cooperative activity, since this action may be performed if your colleague asks you for a document. This was an idea which did not occur to us. One unit leader's view of cooperation was very feature specific; using the Reference function to record votes, or looking to see whether others are logged on made him feel that he was working cooperatively, or "electronically connected". Otherwise, he did not have a sense of working cooperatively with others. To another unit leader, his model of the collaborative nature of the system was a function of his work role. As a coordinator, the system is a tool that he uses to distribute work; it saves time for him. As a coworker, it is a "shared" system, where he uses it in the same capacity as his colleagues, and as an information provider, it is a communication device, to disseminate information.

However, the users also expressed wanting to put a limit on cooperation. This occurred during a workshop where the users were taught a new version of the Search tool. The Search tool is designed so that a found object automatically is produced as a Reference. As a Reference, anyone searching and finding this object (searching is limited to access rights) could make changes to it and it appears on the original. When this feature was demonstrated to the users, they protested strongly. They claimed that this idea went against their idea of cooperative work. They did not want to allow the complete freedom for all to make changes to a found object. They felt that the original should remain intact, in the owner's "desktop space". They preferred that the found object should be a copy instead, where making changes does not affect the original. The automatically produced Reference was a design feature in Linkworks, and the designers felt that the design philosophy was to promote sharing and strengthen groupwork. We interpret the users' reaction as an expression of "bounded" cooperation, contrary to what the designers expected.

Different ideas about cooperation also developed between the unit employees and the typists in the FM. To the unit employees, who do conceptual work such as writing speeches, their interaction with the central typing pool is not cooperation. To them, typing is a "mechanistic" process like reformatting, and they feel there is no "add-on" value from the typist. However, the typists feel that they are a necessary part of groupwork and cooperation. The typists believe that they are "manipulating" the documents, which makes their jobs a part of the group work. Here the metaphors that the employees use to convey group work conflicts with the typists' notion. The "add-on" metaphor of the civil servants assumes intellectual modification is a requirement for group work. As will be discussed shortly, this differing notion of cooperation translated into differences in conventions of system use.

4.2 Models of the organization

We found that many aspects of the organization were applied as metaphors by the users in their use of the groupware. These include the idea of responsibility, which is associated with one's position in the vertical line, and with the idea of private and public work that is officially prescribed in the government's codes. This formal set of codes, the GGO, are strict regulations about how work is to be organized and conducted.

Organizational responsibility

In a study of the organizational hierarchy, Mambrey and Robinson (1994) found that the employees hold specific models of the hierarchical direction: cooperation is associated with the horizontal strata, is self-organized, and revolves around the task, whereas coordination and "controlling of work" is associated with vertical lines. Responsibility is a key difference. In horizontal cooperation, the responsibility is shared by the group. In vertical cooperation, the responsiblity is shifted to the upper ranks, which relieves the employee of the responsibility. Using the metaphor "chiefs" in connection with work indicates always a vertical structure of "those above us" who are responsible.

We see this notion of responsibility affecting the employees' use of the shared workspace in the FM. People maintain their personal workflows that they are responsible for on the shared workspace, but no one maintains the group work that no one is personally designated responsible for. This collection, consisting of old mail, memos, old speech versions, etc. has simply built up on the shared workspace like a junk drawer. However, sometimes users need material from it and they complain that they cannot find it. What we see happening here is a 'social dilemma' (Dawes, 1980). In a social dilemma, each group member must decide to cooperate or not to cooperate for all members to receive benefits. One can be a 'good citizen', as in the case of contributing to public television, or one can be a 'free rider', and hope that others will contribute to keep public television alive. If all are free riders, as in the case with the shared workspace, then the work does not get done, and no one receives the benefits of having an organized workspace.

However, in contrast, all the users are careful to maintain a common address book which they all receive benefits from, consistent with Grudin's (1988) observation. The address book tool has a closer representation to what is familiar in the paper world than does a shared workspace; the benefits of having a common address list may be easier to understand and appreciate than the benefits of an organized workspace.

One brief note of observation: when a person is personally responsible for shared work that is transferred through the workspace, then the documents are maintained (e.g. the exchange process of a speech between the typist and the employee who is responsible for it). The pattern we observe is that if it is a group member's responsibility to make sure that the task is completed, then they take care that the work is done. Otherwise, they look for personal benefits.

Organizational property

Acording to the GGO, only official documents exist. The only work allowed is official work, done on behalf of, and by rules that substitute for the Minister in person. The public nature of work is emphasized in the detailed work flow process, e.g. the specific path that an incoming letter takes, and how it will be archived and therefore remain public for several years (Mambrey and Robinson, 1994).

In work practice, the hierarchical, strictly formal bureaucracy is intertwined with officially "invisible", informal work. A ministry is a vivid social construction, which needs the self-organized informal interaction of persons and formal structure to work (Mambrey and Robinson, 1994). Despite this idea of public work within the organization, the employees have their own private work which refers to privacy during the process of doing a task, such as writing a speech. The early versions are considered private work.

We found that this notion of private and public work was reflected in the users' use of their physical desks. Everything which is within a drawer is strictly private; everything which is upon the desk top is public, at least to the colleagues of the unit. You do not need to control access to your desktop since everyone who is allowed to walk around in the office area can look at your desk top. By social protocol nobody searches in your drawer, which in addition often is locked by a key.

The situation is quite different if we change from the physical world to the electronic world. Because of the "official" nature of public work, the users wanted to be very clear about maintaining a distinction between public and private work. In the requirements analysis, users requested that they have a personal desk drawer in the system to store their private documents (although this requirement was against the formal GGO). For example, one unit leader has special links to the ministry of the coalition in Schwerin which is headed by a social democrat. He of course does not want that all of his work is transparent, and is not interested that all his work is seen by his department head, who is in the CDU, the other party in the coalition. The users are very careful as to which documents they put in the shared folder, knowing that all would have access to it, e.g. "I put only files into this folder, that I think are really public". The users consider the working process as private, and want the system to allow them to maintain their privacy during this process.

4.3 Models of personal work

We also found that people were reluctant to give up their personal style of working, which is necessary in order to establish some shared group conventions.

Different work styles: storage and "piles"

One of the authors made sketches of, and talked with users about their desktops, in order to identify common patterns. Desktops exist which are nearly blank; other desktops are overloaded with all kinds of artifacts of the office work. Nevertheless all the different groups share a common storage principle: they think and organize in piles (of documents). The piles are generally not arbitrary; there is a structure according to the owner's personal scheme: usually piles affiliated with tasks. For example, for one unit head, the following rules existed: urgent and important piles lay close to the center, urgency overrules importance, and future work is situated at the periphery of the desk. Each pile itself is structured by importance (top being most important) rather than chronological ordering.

In using the shared workspace, users had to learn a new way of structuring their electronic desktops. The task of the users was to transfer a 3-D structuring system that they were used to in the paper world, into building a 2-D structure with nested documents. The users know their own desktops; it is intuitive to them where documents are stored, and search is easy. However, not only did users report difficulty in adapting to an electronic desktop structure, but also with changing their personal organization of work to adapt to a shared group organization.

Personal information structuring

The users in the FM strongly rejected the idea of having a shared common organization of information. The unit employees prefer nesting their documents in a hierarchical structure on the shared desktop; the typists want all information to be stored on one level without hierarchical structuring. It is our speculation that both may be applying analogy from the paper world to the electronic desktop. The employees of the unit, as described above, structure their information on their physical desktops in pile arrangements. The typists, by analogy, may be using the same physical structuring that they use in the paper world: an "in-box" and "out-box" on their desks. One employee reflected her resistance to change by commenting that people are "creatures of habit". What we observe is that users are pulling their files out of the joint registrar (i.e. the "nonjunk drawer") on the shared desk tops and storing them in their personal archives. In fact, the users also report that they do not even want to see files or folders of colleagues on the shared desk top because this is viewed as unneccessary infomation overload.

4.4. Models of electronic work

We found a very different type of problem with the users in the SR. The Reference application, primarily used to record the votes of ministers, was difficult to learn and understand. Moreover, a useful metaphor for the Reference could not be developed. In the following, we discuss some of these conceptual difficulties.

What you see is not what you own

The users did not understand the distinction between being the owner and possessor of a document. The users believed that if the document appeared on their screen (The WYSIWIS feature of the Reference), then they were owners, with full ownership rights. Here are common errors which illustrate the incorrect model that the users had of the application. The owner produces the document with public access rights. It is then forwarded to another unit leader who opens it, and changes the access rights to private. He later wants to work on it but can't open the document because the access profile belongs to the owner, and not to him. Another common error is that a user may try to erase the Reference, thinking all others would also lose their documents. If the user is not the owner, he only succeeds in erasing his own Reference.

What you don't see is what you have

Applying analogous reasoning of paper documents to electronic documents can lead to misunderstandings. Our service staff had to help both FM and SR users who could not find documents although they were sure that they existed electronically. It turned out that documents "existed" for the users only when they could see them on the electronic desk top, e.g. as an icon or as an abbreviation. Although elaborate search mechanisms exist (e.g. a Search tool) they relied on the well known structure of the paper world for analogy, i.e. you identify papers by their appearance and only if you physically are in possession of them can you manipulate them. The users had difficulty understanding that they could manipulate a file without visually seeing the document. For example, the access right of a folder can be changed from public to private, which affects all files which are included in the folder. When a document becomes private, then it does not appear visually on the desktop any more to people who do not have the access rights.

5. DISCUSSION

We found that users carried many metaphors from the paper world into the electronic world. These metaphors came from the organization, from their physical desktops, and from their experiences with paper documents. Unfortunately, too many of these "paper world" metaphors were applied too literally. Despite the intensive training, it proved to be very difficult to communicate the idea of the Reference to the users. We surmise that the reason was that the Reference application had no familiar representation in their "paper world". The role of prior experience cannot be underestimated in the development of models of new processes, since prior experience can help guide the user on what might be appropriate strategies in learning a system (Carroll and Thomas, 1982).

Designers and users had different perspectives of group work: different expectations about learning and understanding a remote asynchronous shared application, and in developing shared group conventions. This suggests to us that designers must develop an appropriate representation of the group, its work practice, and realistic expectations about what the group can accomplish.

Different perspectives also existed between the employees and typists of the FM: different notions of cooperation, different file structuring conventions, and lack of maintainance of the shared workspace. A groupware system brings people together to form new types of work relationships. Designers and trainers must consider these work relationships, and suggest common discussions if necessary when issues arise.

Two very basic yet different kinds of problems emerged in the different ministries. In the SR, the main problem for the users seems to be the lack of understanding of the system, leading to frustrating errors (one user described the Reference as his "main nemesis"). In contrast, in the FM, although the users also made errors with the system, the main problem seems to be due to the nature of the work group collaboration. We attribute the inflexibility in adapting to a shared group convention, and the lack of maintenance of the public space, more to the work group than to the nature of the system. The work groups are different in the two ministries. In the SR, cooperation using the system is horizontal, among unit leaders at the same level of the hierarchy. In the FM, cooperation is between employees and typists who have many differences: different jobs, education levels, career path orientations, salaries, etc. which could certainly play a role in the development of the problems that we observed.

It is our general belief that users viewed the system as collaborative, rather than single-user, in contrast to Orlikowsi's (1992) finding with Lotus Notes. Unlike our users, the Notes users did not receive intensive training in the collaborative aspects of the system, and system metaphors were not used.

The strict codes and procedures of the organization influences the people's work habits, and this in turn, influences their use of the system. Whereas Orlikowski (1992) reports that the competitive and individualistic nature of the organization was against supporting cooperation, our finding was similar, except that people's models of cooperation is associated with particular horizontal lines of the organization's hierarchy. The vertical line, which connotes career paths, and superiors, competes with the notion of working together cooperatively. The model of responsibility which the organization fosters also surfaces with the use of the shared workspace. The users do not maintain documents unless a specific individual is responsible for them. Unlike Grudin's (1988) dilemma, only one or a few need to make the effort to organize material and all would benefit from an organized shared workspace where documents would be easy to find.

We feel that the users were able to accept problems, such as the constant system errors they made, because they saw real benefits in using the system, such as in saving time. One unit leader in the SR claimed that he received the electronic work about one day earlier than he would ordinarily receive the paper work. As a coordinator, this is a big relief for him. The employees in the FM reported a faster turn-around time for working and reworking versions of documents, using the shared workspace.

6. DEVELOPING SHARED MODELS

In this paper, the lesson that we have learned is that is essential to consider the group's shared representation of the new technology. We propose that designers use a *group-centered* design approach, where system design and training emphasizes an appropriate shared representation of the group members. We present some suggestions in this direction.

- Initial experiences play an important role in forming an appropriate mental model. It is more difficult to change attitudes later, than earlier.
- Models must be continually developed over time, since groups need time to develop common factors: assumptions, understanding of roles, procedures, etc.
- Designer-user communication must consider group issues. This could also be done using user advocates, an approach which we found to be effective, since the user advocates developed close working relationships with the users (Mambrey et al., 1996).
- Trainers must support the design process through the constant training and reinforcement in the idea of collaborative work with the system. From our experience, we found training in collective groups to be valuable.
- In performing work analyses, distributed cognition can be a useful means to identify the shared and individual knowledge of groups, and how it is communicated, adapted, and used (Rogers and Ellis, 1994).
- Metaphors can help develop common experiences, as with the case of the POLITeam metaphor (i.e. "teams between cities"), the project name which we use to build a social identity for users and designers. Metaphors can be valuable teaching aids, but only when they are the right ones. From our experience, different perspectives can result in the selection of the wrong metaphor. Not all metaphors are appropriate, and metaphors in the paper world cannot transfer literally to the electronic world. We lose information when information is transferred from the paper to the electronic world and for this reason, a literal mapping from source to target can create confusion. Metaphors are highly contextual, are tied to experience, are nonliteral expressions, and must be understood so.

This study has raised challenging questions for us. What is the implication for groupware if users have different notions of cooperation? How can groups develop ideas about group work that are less under the influence of the organization and more relevant for the group? How can personal conventions and work styles be integrated to create standards for a shared group work style when it is required in groupware? What are appropriate metaphors to represent work processes which have no representation in the workers' actual life? We intend with further observation to gain more insight into what these early findings might mean.

Acknowledgements

The authors would like to thank the following people for their valuable comments and insights: Wolfgang Dzida, David England, Margarete Boos, Richard Bentley, Alfred Kobsa, and Klaas Sikkel.

References

1. Bowers, J. (1994). The Work to Make a Network Work: Studying CSCW in Action, in *Proceedings of CSCW '94* Chapel Hill, October 1994, ACM Press, 287-298.
2. Bullen, C. and Bennett, J. (1990) Groupware in Practice: An Interpretation of Work Experience. *Proceedings of. CSCW '90*, Los Angeles, October, 1990, ACM Press, 291-302.
3. Carroll, J.M. and Thomas, J.C. (1982). Metaphors and the Cognitive Representation of Computing Systems. *IEEE Transactions On Systems, Man, And Cybernetics*, Vol. SMC-12, No. 2.
4. Davidson, E.J. (1996). *Framing Information Systems Requirements: An Investigation of Social Cognitive Processes in Information Systems Delivery.* Dissertation, Massachusetts Institute of Technology.
5. Dawes, R.M. (1980). Social dilemmas. *Annual Review of Psychology*, 31, 169-193.
6. Fischer, G. (1991). The importance of models in making complex systems comprehensible. In Tauber, M.J. and Ackermann (Eds.), *Mental Models and Human Computer Interaction 2*, North-Holland.
7. Fiske, S.T. and Taylor, S.E. (1984). *Social Cognition.* New York: Random House.
8. Grudin, J. (1988). Why CSCW applications fail: problems in the design and evaluation of organizational interfaces. *Proceedings of CSCW '88*, ACM Press, 85-93.
9. Johnson-Laird, P. (1983). *Mental Models.* Cambridge: Harvard University Press.
10. Mambrey, P., Mark, G., and Pankoke-Babatz (1996). Integrating User Advocacy into Participatory Design: the Designers' Perspective. In J. Blomberg, F. Kensing, E. Dykstra-Erickson (Eds.) *Proceedings of the Participatory Design Conference'96*, Cambridge, M.A., 251-261.
11. Mambrey, P. and Robinson, M. (1994). Preparing a speech for the minister: notes towards understanding the role of artifacts in a flow of work. *Unpublished manuscript.*
12. Mambrey, P. and Tepper, A. (1996). Metaphors and System Design. In P. Hoschka (ed.): *Assisting Computer. A New Generation of Support Systems.* Lawrence Erlbaum Assoc. Hillsdale N.J.
13. Newcomb, T.M. (1959). Individual systems of orientation. In S. Koch (Ed.), *Psychology, A Study of Science*, Vol. 3, New York: McGraw-Hill.
14. Orlikowski, W.J. (1992). Learning from Notes: Organizational Issues in Groupware Implementation, *Proceedings of CSCW '92*, Toronto, ACM Press, 362-369.
15. Orlikowski, W.J. and Gash, D.C. (1994). Technological frames: making sense of information technology in organizations. *ACM Transactions on Information Systems*, (12) 2, 174-207.
16. Rogers, Y. (1994). Exploring obstacles: integrating CSCW in evolving organisations. *Proceedings of CSCW '94*, Chapel Hill, Oct. 1994, ACM Press, 67-77.
17. Rogers, Y. and Ellis, J. (1994). Distributed cognition: an alternative framework for analysing and explaining collaborative working. *Journal of Information Technology* (9), 119-128.
18. Schein, E. (1990). *Organizational Culture and Leadership.* San Francisco: Jossey-Bass.
19. Sohlenkamp, M., Mambrey, P., Prinz, W., Fuchs, L., Syri, A., Pankoke-Babatz, U., Klöckner, K., and Kolvenbach, S. (Forthcoming). Supporting the distributed German government with POLITeam. *International Journal of Multimedia Tools and Applications.*

Handling Conflicts in Groupware: Concepts and Experiences made in the POLITeam-Project

Volker Wulf

Institute for Computer Science III
University of Bonn
Römerstr. 164
D-53117 Bonn, Germany
Email: volker@informatik.uni-bonn.de

ABSTRACT The activation of certain functions in groupware affects different users who might have conflicting interests. We will develop technical mechanisms to support users in regulating these conflicts. Contrary to current implementations of groupware, these mechanisms strengthen the position of the users which are affected by the activation of a function. Therefore, they provide visibility of activation, a channel for communication, or the right to intervene. After presenting the general concept, it will be shown how these mechanisms are used within the POLITeam project to support users in handling conflicts when activating certain functions.

KEYWORDS Groupware, Conflict Regulation, Evaluation, Field Study, Implementation Architecture

1. INTRODUCTION

In the CSCW literature it is widely assumed that cooperative work implies the existence of conflicting interests among individuals (cf. Schmidt 1991; Easterbrook et al. 1993). Conflicts may be related to a wide spectrum of different occasions and topics. In this paper a specific type of conflict will be examined. These conflicts occur when one user activates a function which produces a state transition of the groupware system. As groupware provides channels to transmit or to share data, a state transition resulting from the activation of a function might affect the interests of other users. For instance, a shared window system provides to the users a function which allows to choose among different floor control policies (cf. Greenberg 1991, pp. 21). The activation of this function to change the actual policy by one user will affect the interests of the other users of the section.

To examine conflicts resulting from the activation of groupware functions, we will distinguish among different conflict-constellations by using the concept of roles. A role describes a specific position held by users within a technically mediated interaction. In the following section we will just look at a single conflict-constellation per function: the one between the activator who uses a function actively and the role of the user affected who might suffer from disturbances caused by this action.

Conflicts resulting from the activation of a function have not yet been investigated systematically within the CSCW literature. There are only few case studies reporting empirically on this type of conflicts (cf. Cool et al. 1992; Dourish 1993; Kahler 1994). Nevertheless, looking at the design of certain applications, one can find occasionally functions equipped with a technical mechanism to regulate such conflicts among the users

Human–Computer Interaction: INTERACT'97 S. Howard, J. Hammond & G. Lindgaard (editors)
Published by Chapman & Hall

(cf. chap. 2). But these mechanisms appear to be rather the result of accidental than of well grounded design decisions being aware of different alternatives.

Therefore, at first we will develop a classification scheme for technical mechanisms to support users in regulating conflicts in groupware. Furthermore, we will show how these mechanisms can be used to satisfy user requirements within a participative software development project.

2. TECHNICAL MECHANISMS TO REGULATE CONFLICTS

Looking at the state of the art in the CSCW literature there are two modes for handling conflicts caused by the activation of a function. They are either masked out from the ordinary users or they are solved in favour of the activator. In the first case conflicting activations of a function are solved either by a rigidly implemented automatism (e.g. concurrency control in traditional information systems) or they are solved automatically according to a specification provided by a privileged user (e.g. access control in traditional information systems) (cf. Wulf 1997). In the second case conflicting activations of a function are executed by the system in the way the activator intended it. Affected users do not get technical support to perceive the conflict or to influence the activation of a function. Whatever functional alternative the activator selects, it will be automatically executed. Thus, the system performs directly the state transition intended by the activator.

To overcome the masking out of these conflicts, their regulation has to become a design issue of the interface of ordinary users. To strengthen the role of the users affected when handling these conflicts, the deterministic relationship between the activator's choice and its execution has to be broken up.

To motivate our design approach to support users in handling this type of conflicts, we look at proposals developed in conflict theory. The underlying assumption of the mainstream in conflict theory is that the interests of the different parties involved in a conflict can be satisfied by a solution which all parties experience as mutually beneficial. Thus, it is assumed that endemic conflicts should become overt. Overt conflicts should be solved among the parties involved in a conflict by negotiations. If the parties involved cannot find a consentaneous solution a third party should be asked for mediation (cf. Dahrendorf 1961; Glasl 1992).

Assuming that users of groupware do not always work at the same time or at the same place, technical mechanisms should be offered to support them in solving conflicts caused by the activation of a function. They could make conflicts visible to users affected and offer a channel for communication among them. To offer a base for communication the user affected should have the right to intervene against the activation of a function. In case of disagreement among users these mechanisms could contain a strategy for mediation.

Though technical support seems to be crucial to regulate conflicts in groupware, social practice in handling conflict should not be replaced (cf. Dourish 1993). Therefore, we will present technical mechanisms to handle conflicts which can be embedded in social practice in different ways. Thus, they allow even for modes of conflict regulation which are not in accordance with the mainstream of conflict theory.[1] The technical mechanisms for conflict management can be classified whether they allow the user affected to intervene against an activation, whether they make a conflict visible and whether they offer a channel for communication. Figure 1 gives a classification scheme for these mechanisms.

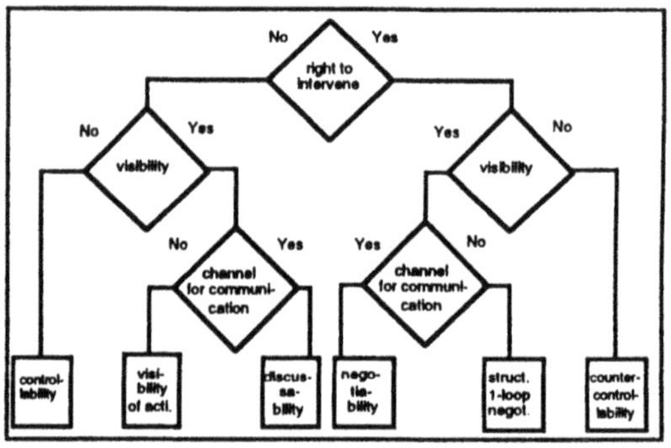

Figure 1: Classification scheme for technical mechanisms to moderate conflicts between activator and affected users

In case of controllability, there is not any technical mechanisms to support users in regulating a conflict. It is either intended to allow the activator to decide on usage of the function autonomously or conflict regulation fully depends on social practice.

In case of visibility of activation the user affected automatically get a notification about the activation of a

[1]This is of special importance as recent research in the field of CSCW has questioned the validity of the assumptions in mainstream conflict theory (cf. Egger and Wagner 1992).

function which causes conflicts. This information can be either sent to him or be kept available for his access. During the design or configuration of this mechanism the exact content of the data set has to be determined. In case it is not sent to the user affected, the duration of its accessibility has to be decided, too. Thus, this mechanism makes endemic conflict overt which is a precondition for its solution.

Visibility of activation is realized for instance in the RAVE video communication systems. Whenever a channel is built up to another person's office, a special sound is automatically produced to inform the user affected (cf. Gaver 1991, p. 305). Moreover, visibility of activation can be reached by a pop-up message on the workstations screen (cf. Dourish 1993, p. 129). If the user affected is in his office at the moment the channel is built up he can adapt his behaviour accordingly. Though he cannot intervene against the channel by technical means, he may be able to move out of the focus of the camera or redirect the focus of the camera. Thus, the right to intervene might be achieved through social practice. Nevertheless, in certain situations it might be annoying for the users affected to adapt their own behaviour to someone´s activation of a function.

Another example for visibility of activation as means for conflict regulation is given by Condon (1993, pp. 180). Conflicts which are coming up when two users attempt to change the same object at the same time on a shared whiteboard are handled by displaying each person's action on the other's screen. As the application provides an additional video channel for the users working on the whiteboard, they can use this channel of communication to negotiate a solution of the conflict. As there exists a means for communication within the application in this case visibility of activation may initiate a negotiation process. If there is not a consentaneous solution different versions of the same object can be stored.

Beyond making a conflict overt, technical support for its communicative solution could be provided. If the activation of a function has become visible by technical means, a technical channel of mutual communication could be built up in that moment. Such a channel can be realized in different ways. The messages transmitted via this channel of communication among the users involved could be structured, semi-structured or unstructured (cf. Malone et al. 1988). Structured communication would just allow to express the intended alternative for use or tailoring of a function. Thus, in this case just highly structured acts of communication would be offered to the users. Additional to these highly structured acts a semi-structured channel would allow to the users involved to express further explanations on the desired alternatives. In this sense the co-ordinator (cf. Winograd 1988) offers a semi-structured channel of communication. Contrary to these types of communication channels, an unstructured version would allow to the users involved to provide their point of view without following strict formal patterns. According to the application and its environment such an unstructured channel could be based on textual, audio or video communication. It could be synchronous or asynchronous. For instance in case of a conflict a telephone or a video communication line could be built up among the users involved. Thus, a channel of communication makes a conflict always visible to users affected by technical means.

As long as technical mechanisms are restricted to give visibility to the users affected and to build up a channel for mutual communication, we will talk about discussability. Discussability could be implemented in the following way. The functional alternative is executed immediately and the users affected are technically supported to establish a communication channel with the activator. By this means they may convince the activator to modify the state-transition performed. As the way a conflict is solved strongly depends on how well the users affected can express his argument, a semi-structured or unstructured version of the communication channel should be applied. Right now discussability has not yet been implemented for conflict regulation.

If the users affected have additionally the chance to intervene against the activator's decision by technical means we will talk about negotiability (cf. Herrmann 1995; Wulf 1995). In this case the activation of a function will only take place if activator and users affected have found an agreement. In case of structured and semi-structured negotiability the speech acts are clearly defined by the structured part of each message. Therefore, it is technically simple to detect the outcome of a negotiation and to realize the right to intervene of the user affected. In case of unstructured negotiability there is not any data available for the technical mechanism to detect the outcome of a conversation between activators and the users affected. To realize their right to intervene against the activators decision, in this case the negotiation mechanism should be designed in a way that the users affected will have to input the result of the conversation.

In case activator and user affected cannot find a consentaneous solution within a certain period of time, strategies for mediation have to be implemented. Assuming that during the application of groupware a third party for mediation will not always be available, the negotiation mechanism has to be configured in advance in a way that it will activate a default option according to the state of the conversation (cf. Wulf 1995).

Negotiability have not yet been widely implemented. Hammer et al. (1993, p. 143) propose to handle conflicts concerning the activation of the forwarding function in in-house telephone systems by unstructured negotiability. Whenever the activator wants to establish a call forwarding, a telephone line will be built up automatically to the user affected. Via this line they can negotiate, finally the user affected has to confirm the activation. In this case the negotiation process is entirely supported by technical means. The users involved are forced to communicate with each other to find a solution of a potential conflict. The default option in case of disagreement is selected by the user affected – the forwarding function will not get active.

A special case of negotiability is the structured single loop version. In this case communication among users is not technically supported. The user affected just gets a notification on the activator's decision. He can intervene against this decision by technical means expressing a disagreement. Again strategies for mediation have to be realized to handle cases where a consentaneous solution cannot be found within in a certain period of time.

Structured single loop negotiability as a means for conflict management has been proposed for instance in video communication systems. Dourish (1993, pp. 128) presents it as a solution to privacy problems. A channel is only built up when the user affected has agreed on it by pushing a button. Similar solutions were described by Cool et al. (1992) and Belotti and Sellen (1993). This mechanism is already well known in ordinary telephone systems. A telephone line is just established when the recipient (user affected) has agreed on it by picking up the receiver.

The final type of technical mechanisms for conflict regulation is called counter-controllability. In this case the activation of a function is neither made visible to the users affected by technical means nor are the users affected supported to negotiate with the activator via a technical channel of communication. Nevertheless users affected get technical support to intervene against the activation of a certain function. They are equipped with another function whose state transitions will be checked whenever the activator tries to activate function F. If the state transitions resulting from the activation of the counter-controlling function allow for the intended activation, it will be executed immediately, else the function which was supposed to be activated will take a default state in case of disagreement among the users. Thus, contrary to all the other mechanisms proposed so far the users affected decide about their position held in a conflict before the conflictious function is activated.

Counter-controllability as a means to handle conflicts can be found in several CSCW applications, as well. Dourish (1993) has implemented a program within the RAVE video communication which allows users to cut off incoming video calls automatically. The cut off mechanisms can be specified for certain groups of users and periods of time. Malone et al. (1988) and Terveen and Murray (1996) have proposed a similar mechanism for e-mail systems to filter incoming mails. In these cases counter-controllability rather contributes to an automatic solution of a conflict than encouraging negotiation. As it hinders to establish a channel of communication, a negotiation had to be performed by the help of another communication channel. This strict option of conflict solution was intended by the designer of these mechanisms to protect the users affected right for privacy and communicative self-determination.

3. REQUIREMENTS FROM THE POLITEAM PROJECT

In the following we want to show how these concepts were applied within a groupware development project. Within the POLITeam Project we develop a groupware application in an evolutionary and participative way. Its functionality mainly consists of an electronic circulation folder, shared workspaces, and an event notification service. Based on the experiences gained by introducing a commercial product (LinkWorks by DEC) in three different fields of application, we develop advanced versions of the system (Klöckner et al. 1995, Sohlenkamp et al. 1997). An important means for user involvement are different types of workshops in which users, support staff, and designers participate. In the design-centered workshops users and support staff report on their experiences and articulate requirements, to which the designers respond by presenting their concepts for the next version of the system. Conflicts among users caused by the activation of a function have been discussed within several of these workshops.

Conflicts concerning the activation of the delete-function were discussed within a section of a federal ministry. This workgroup had decided to build up a folder to share mailing lists for different groups of recipients. Usually, one of the members of the unit started to build up such a list and made it available for his colleagues by storing it in the shared folder. The colleagues used and updated the list for their purposes. By this work practice, the folder became more and more crowded. Thus, the users felt a need to delete mailing lists which were not used any more. Nevertheless, whoever would do so, would violate the interests of those users who were still using the list.

After the users had brought up that topic within the workshop, a designer proposed verbally certain of the mechanisms developed in section 2 to be integrated in the next version of the system. It was generally agreed among the users that mechanisms which provided a technical channel for communication (negotiability and discussability) were not needed. As the offices of the users of this section are located around the same hallway, technical channels of communication would replace face-to-face contact which was regarded as undesirable. Counter-controllability would force each individual user to specify in advance whether a certain mailing list should get protected from being deleted. There were concerns whether these a priori specifications would represent the users' intention in the moment a certain list should get deleted.

A structured single loop version of negotiability which gave any group member the right to veto the execution of the delete function was discussed controversially among the uses involved. One user assumed that such a mechanism would lead to a further bureaucratisation of his work, if anybody had to agree before. He therefore preferred just receiving before hand a notification (visibility of activation). One other user feared the additional workload resulting from permanent decision making. Other users liked the idea that the application of this mechanism would allow all the users affected to participate in the decision making ("It is helpful to get an okay. In this case you know what is the matter"). As a result of this discussion, the designers proposed a variant of structured single-loop negotiability. The mechanism for conflict regulation should give the users affected a longer period of time (e.g. one week) to react to the activator's decision. If individual users do not react by then, their agreement would be taken as default option in case of time delay. The voting rule should give any member of the group a veto-right to intervene against the execution of the delete function. Such a configuration was generally accepted by the members of the group. As technical mechanisms for conflict-regulation were not available in that system version, the members of the group agreed upon sending a mail before activating the delete function on one of the mailing lists. Thus, a social convention was used to replace technical mechanisms.

Within another workshop we presented a new function to the members of the same group. The new function allows to the creator of an object to stop object-sharing with other users. This function had been required to handle documents which had to be shared just for a short period of time within a group. During the workshop the users mentioned other types of documents on which they would not like the creator to determine the level of object-sharing. For instance, the head of the unit argued that most of the documents were created by one of his colleagues while he would just modify or read them before sending them out. His interests were affected by this function because he could not reaccess these documents after its activation by the creator. Concerning certain type of documents he demanded to equip this function with structured single-loop negotiability. For other documents visibility of activation seemed sufficient to him to protect his interests.

Presenting a newly designed search tool in a workshop, we found conflicts between the activator and the users affected, too. The participants of this workshop belonged to a different field of application - an organizational unit of a state ministry. The search tool presented allows the activator to specify certain criteria to search for document in the whole groupware system. The result of the search is displayed in a window. Out of this window, the activator can manually select relevant documents. These documents will be displayed on his desktop even if they were not accessible for the activator before. Thus, this function allows the activator to access other peoples documents.

Obviously such a design affects the interests of the users affected. For instance one user imagined that his boss would sit at night on his computer searching for documents containing certain keywords. Therefore, all of the users asked for counter-controllability to be able to create private domains where other users' access via the search-tool would be impossible. This mechanism was already realized in the prototype presented. Moreover, they asked for visibility of activation in case of non-private documents got shared as a consequence of the activation of the search-tool.

Stating that for certain types of documents (e.g. circulation folders) search activities should not result in document-sharing, they criticised the a lack of technical flexibility of the search-tool. Concerning this type of documents they rather preferred to provide for the activator only a copy or just some information on the document's state (e.g. name of the current owner). Only in case the user affected had explicitly agreed on document sharing, this functional alternative should be activated. Thus, they proposed a structured single loop version of negotiability where the intermediate state and the default option provided the activator with restricted possibilities while documents sharing was just executed after an agreement of the user affected. The user asked to be able to choose the intermediate state and the default options in a way that they should still provide enough information to allow the activator to continue his tasks without waiting for the users affected reaction.

4. APPROACH FOR IMPLEMENTATION

The experiences from the POLITeam project show that there are different functions of the application which cause conflicts among users. For sake of conformity with user expectations, mechanisms which support users to regulate conflicts concerning the activation of these functions should be designed in a similar way. Furthermore, an implementation architecture for groupware should offer technical flexibility. Thus, it should ease to tailor the ordinary functionality as well as the linkages between conflict constellations and technical mechanisms for conflict regulation. To support technical flexibility as well as conformity with users' expectations, we implemented mechanisms for conflict regulation centrally in a component apart from the functions they refer to (conflict manager). Thus, instead of implementing these mechanisms for every function separately, all the function of an application, which contains a potential for conflict, are just equipped with configuration data which indicate the mechanism to apply. These data have to be created and stored for each conflict constellation in the configuration store.

The structure of the configuration data has to be determined for each function and allows to specify the mechanism applied depending on the actual context of a function's usage. In case of the delete function in POLITeam the context of usage consists just out of the name of the document to be deleted. In this architecture the linkage between a conflict constellation of a function and a technical mechanism for conflict regulation is tailored by just modifying the configuration data. Technical mechanisms themselves could be tailored centrally for the whole application.

Based on these considerations, we have implemented the technical mechanisms for conflict regulation in the way displayed in figure 2. LinkWorks offered an application programming interface which we used to extend the code of the three functions in a way that after the activation and before the execution of the conflictious state transition the technical mechanisms for conflict regulation are executed (extension of the function).

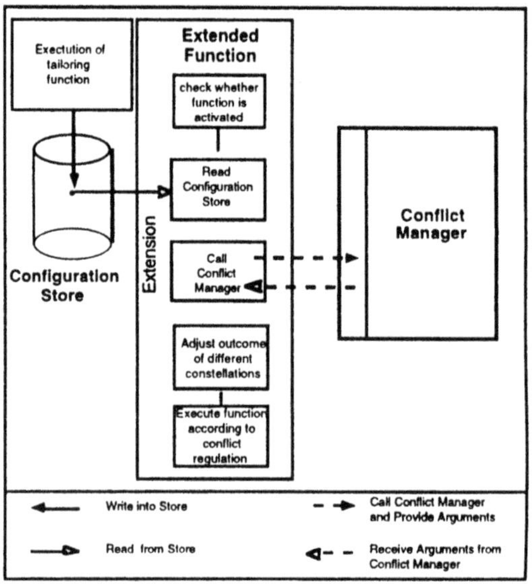

Figure 2: Overview of an architecture to implement technical mechanisms for conflict regulation

Thus, whenever a user activates one of the three functions the relevant configuration data for each of the function's conflict constellations is read from the configuration store. The conflict manager is called and the functional alternative resulting from the conflict regulation is sent back to the process initiated by the extended function. If a function contains more than one conflict constellation, the solutions worked out within the different constellations have to be adjusted according to predefined rules. Finally, the resulting functional alternative determined within this process of technically supported conflict regulation will be executed.

In section 2, we assumed that the role of the user affected was just held by one individual. This assumption is not always given. For instance, when activating the delete function in POLITeam depending on the document more than one user may be affected in the same way. In this case, we just have to handle a single conflict constellation, where a group of users is in the role of the user affected. Such groups have to be taken into consideration when designing technical mechanisms to regulate conflicts (cf. Wulf 1995). To satisfy the user requirements concerning the "delete"-function, a group-oriented version of the mechanism: single loop structured negotiability was implemented in the conflict manager which transformed the individual users´ reaction into a group's decision. In case of the search tool a group-oriented version of the mechanism visibility of activation grants notifications to a whole group of users affected.

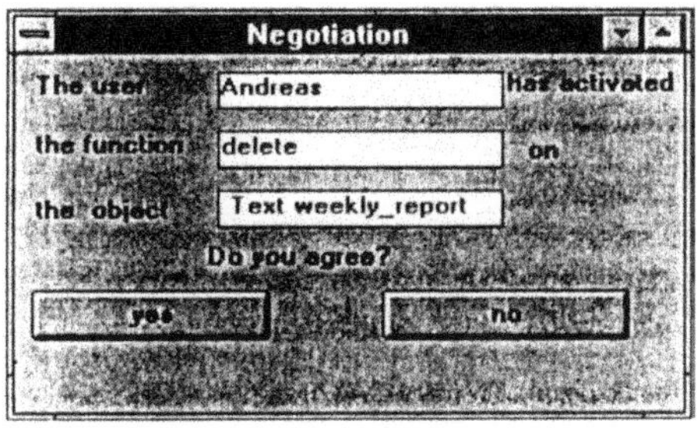

Figure 3: Negotiation window received by the users affected of the "delete"- function

Taking the example of the "delete" - function, we will describe how the mechanisms for conflict regulation are seen from a user's point of view. If a user tries to delete an address-list, he is notified by a system created message indicating that the document can only be deleted in case none of the other users disagrees within a weeks span. Then the conflict manager sends a negotiation window to the users affected (cf. figure 3). They receive it in a especial mail folder for conflict handling. If they open this folder, they see all the messages generated by the conflict manager. They can access and react to them individually. If all of the users affected have reacted the activator receives a message which tells him depending on the result either that the deletion is not possible or to click a button to finally delete the document.

5. CONCLUSION

We have proposed a classification scheme for technical mechanisms which support users in regulating conflicts concerning the activation of certain groupware functions. Discussions with users in workshops showed that the technical mechanisms presented in this paper are a useful means in regulating conflicts between users. Therefore, we have implemented a first prototype.

As a next step, the design of these mechanisms has to be evaluated by the users. The prototypical implementation of additional mechanisms effects the performance of the application. Therefore, further research towards efficient implementations is needed. Furthermore, we have to support the configuration activities by an appropriate user interface. Assuming that there are even more potentially conflictious functions within an application and for each of their conflict constellations a configuration matrix has to be filled, there is an obvious need for innovative approaches which allow to reuse configurations for conflict regulation.

Looking at the implementation architecture for technical mechanisms of conflict regulation, it resembles that one of access control. Indeed, approaches to implement access rights in groupware distinguish more than just reading and writing permissions. They allow to specify access rights concerning a wide variety of functions (cf. Shen and Dewan 1992). To realize access control, one has to extend the code of each function in a similar manner as we have proposed. Access control lists used in these approaches can be seen as configuration data for conflict regulation. Nevertheless, compared to the approach proposed in this paper, access control in groupware has just regarded counter-controllability as a technical mechanism for conflict regulation. Thus, our results would plea to extend these approaches to offer users more than just a single technical mechanism for conflict regulation.

6. ACKNOWLEDGEMENTS

I would like to thank Andreas Pfeifer and Markus Rohde for valuable discussions on the topics addressed in this paper. Dirk Fischer has implemented the prototype. This research has been supported by the German Ministry of Education and Research within its "Polikom" research program under the grant No. 01 QA 405/0.

7. REFERENCES

Belotti, V.; Sellen, A.: Design for Privacy in Ubiquitous Computing Environment, in: de Michelis, G.; Simone, C.; Schmidt, K. (eds): Proceedings of the Fourth Conference on Computer Supported Cooperative Work - ECSCW '93, Kluwer, Dordrecht, 1995, pp. 77 - 92

Cool, C.; Fish, R.S.; Kraut, R.E.; Lowery, C.M.: Interactive Design of Video Communication Systems, in: CSCW '92. Sharing Perspectives. Proceedings of the Conference on Computer-Supported Cooperative Work, (ACM Press, New York) 1992, pp. 25 -32

Dahrendorf, R.: Elemente einer Theorie sozialen Konflikts, in: Dahrendorf, R. (ed.): Gesellschaft und Freiheit, München 1961, pp. 197 - 236

Dourish, P.: Culture and Control in a Media Space, in: de Michelis, G.; Simone. C.; Schmidt, K. (eds): Proceedings of the Third Conference on Computer Supported Cooperative Work - ECSCW '93, Dordrecht, NL, Kluwer 1993, pp. 125 - 138

Condon, C.: The Computer Won't let me: Cooperation, Conflict and the Ownership of Information, in: Easterbrook, S. (ed.) CSCW: Cooperation or Conflict, Springer, London u. a. 1993, pp. 171 - 185

Easterbrook, S. M.; Beck E. E.; Goodet, J. S.; Plowman, L.; Shaples, M.; Wood, C. C.: A Survey of Empirical Studies of Conflict, in: Easterbrook, S. (ed.) CSCW: Cooperation or Conflict, Springer, London et al. 1993, pp. 1 - 68

Egger, E.; Wagner, I.: Time Management: A Case for CSCW, in: CSCW '92. Sharing Perspectives. Proceedings of the Conference on Computer-Supported Cooperative Work, ACM-Press, New York 1992, pp. 249 - 256

Gaver, W.: Sound Support for Collaboration; in: L. Bannon, M. Robinson; K. Schmidt, (eds.): Proceedings of the Second European Conference on Computer Supported Cooperative Work, Amsterdam, 1991, pp. 276 - 292.

Glasl, F.: Konfliktmanagement, 3rd ed., Bern 1992

Greenberg, S.: Personizable Groupware: Accomodating individual roles and group differences, in: L. Bannon; M. Robinson; K. Schmidt (eds.): Proceedings of the Second European Conference on Computer Supported Cooperative Work, Amsterdam, 1991, pp. 17 - 31.

Hammer, V.; Pordesch, U.; Roßnagel, A.: Rechtliche Gestaltungsanforderungen an betriebliche ISDN-Telefonsysteme, Berlin Heidelberg, Springer, 1993

Herrmann, T.: Workflow Management Systems: Ensuring Organizational Flexibility by Possibilities of Adaptation and Negotiation, in: Proceedings of COOCS, August 13 - 16, 1995, Milpitas, CA, ACM-Press, New York 1995, pp. 83 - 96.

Kahler, H.: Von der Empirie zur Gestaltungsanforderung - Beispiele für den Einfluß explorativer Empirie auf die Entwicklung von Gestaltungsanforderungen für Groupware, in: Hartmann, A.; Herrmann, Th.; Rohde, M.; Wulf, V. (eds): Menschengerechte Groupware - Software-ergonomische Gestaltung und partizipative Umsetzung, Stuttgart, Teubner 1994, pp. 109-124

Klöckner, K.; Mambrey, P.; Sohlenkamp, M.; Prinz, W.; Fuchs, L. Kolvenbach, S.; Pankoke-Babatz, U.; Syri, A.: POLITeam – Bridging the Gap between Bonn and Berlin for and with the Users, in: H. Marmolin; Y. Sundblad; K. Schmidt (eds.): Proceedings of the Second European Conference on Computer Supported Cooperative Work, kluver, Dordrecht, 1995, pp. 17 - 32

Malone, T. W.; Grant K. R.; Lai, K.-Y.; Rao, R.; Rosenblitt, D.: Semistructured Messages are Surprisingly Useful for Computer-Supported Coordination, in: I. Greif (ed.): CSCW: A Book of Readings, Morgan-Kaufmann Publisher, San Mateo, California, 1988, pp. 311 - 334

Schmidt, K. : Riding a Tiger or Computer Supported Cooperative Work, in: L. Bannon, M. Robinson; K. Schmidt, (eds.): Proceedings of the Second European Conference on Computer Supported Cooperative Work, Amsterdam, 1991, pp. 1 - 16

Shen, HH. and Dewan, P.: Access Control for Collaborative Environments, in: Computer-Supported Cooperated Work ´92. Sharing Perspectives. Proceedings of the Conference on Computer-Supported Cooperative Work, ACM Press, New York, pp. 51 - 58

Sohlenkamp, M.; Fuchs, L.; Klöckner, K.; Kolvenbach, S.; Mambrey, P.; Pankoke-Babatz, U.; .; Prinz, W.; Syri, A.: Supporting the Distributed German Government with POLITeam, in: International Journal on Multimedia Tools and Applications – Special Issue on Multimedia Projects in Governments, 1997 (to appear)

Terveen, L.; Murray, L.: Helping Users Program Their Personal Agents. In: Proceedings of CHI '96, April 13.-18, ACM-Press, New York 1996, pp. 355-361

Winograd, T.: A Language/Action Perspective on the Design of Cooperative Work, in: I. Greif (ed.): CSCW: A Book of Readings, Morgan-Kaufmann Publisher, San Mateo, California, 1988, pp. 311 - 334.

Wulf, V.: Negotiability: A Metafunction to Tailor Access to Data in Groupware; in: Behaviour & Information Technology, Vol. 14, No. 3, 1995, pp. 143 - 151

Wulf, V.: On Conflicts and Negotiation in Multi–User Applications; in: Kent, A.; Williams, J. G. (eds): Encyclopedia of Microcomputers, Dekker, New York et al., 1997 (invited paper)

Wearable Computers: Field-Test Results and System Design Guidelines

Chris Esposito

Virtual and Augmented Reality Group
Boeing ISS Research and Technology
PO Box 3707, MS 7L-48
Seattle, WA 98124 USA
chrise@atc.boeing.com

ABSTRACT Since the summer of 1994, a group of partners, led by Boeing and including Carnegie Mellon University, Virtual Vision, and Honeywell have developed or provided significant design input on several generations of wearable computer systems, head-mounted displays (HMDs), and field-tested several application prototypes using these systems. Some of these applications include KC-135 skin inspections at McClellan Air Force Base in Sacramento, California, autopilot troubleshooting for the Boeing 777, and fuel system problem diagnosis and repair for the Boeing 757. This paper will address three questions: Why would someone wear a computer? What is a wearable computer? How does application and user interface design for these systems differ from that for more conventional office desktop applications?

Keywords Wearable Computers, Head Mounted Displays, Input Devices, Speech Interfaces

1 INTRODUCTION

Since the summer of 1994, a group of partners, led by Boeing and including Carnegie Mellon University, Virtual Vision, and Honeywell have developed or provided significant design input on several generations of wearable computer systems, head-mounted displays (HMDs), and field-tested several application prototypes using these systems. Some of these applications include KC-135 skin inspections at McClellan Air Force Base in Sacramento, California, autopilot troubleshooting for the Boeing 777, and fuel system problem diagnosis and repair for the Boeing 757. A separate branch of this project has been investigating the use of 'Augmented Reality' in several manufacturing applications, although this work will not be reported on here - see (Caudell, 1992) or (Janin, 1994) for more information on this area.

This paper will address three questions: Why would someone wear a computer and its peripheral devices? What is a wearable computer? How does application and user interface design for these systems differ from that for more conventional office

Human–Computer Interaction: INTERACT'97 S. Howard, J. Hammond & G. Lindgaard (editors)
Published by Chapman & Hall

desktop applications? Since this is a relatively new and unfamiliar topic, we shall begin by describing some of the representative tasks and environments that can benefit from these new systems. This will be followed by a brief description of current hardware and probable future systems. The final section will describe the Boeing 757 application in more depth, including some design guidelines and lessons learned from the field tests.

2 WHY A WEARABLE COMPUTER?

One of the most basic characteristics is that these systems are used for work that cannot be done in a conventional office environment. This includes tasks like aircraft maintenance and vehicle inspections but excludes tasks like using a laptop on an airplane for text editing.

Another characteristic is that the user needs real-time read/write access to more information while doing the work than can be conveniently manually carried to and organized at the worksite. Examples of this may be as simple as a inspection checklist scenario, or a more complex one such as a troubleshooting and repair scenario that requires access to stored diagnostic procedures and schematics, along with keeping a record of what maintenance was actually done. This second scenario raises the issue of just how much data may need to be available at the worksite. For example, the total amount of operational, diagnostic, and repair data for most modern aircraft easily runs to tens of thousands of pages, but only a dozen of these pages may be needed to identify and repair the problem. Identifying and providing timely access to the right subset of the database raises issues that are broader than the scope of this paper, but to the extent that a wearable is seen as a potential delivery vehicle for this data, there is considerable overlap in these issues.

A third characteristic has to do with the manual nature of the application tasks. If the users' hands are already busy, then a system that provides access to this information in a substantially hands-free fashion can provide significant operational advantages over a system that requires frequent physical context switches between doing the work and using a paper manual or a laptop.

The physical environments these systems are used in provide their own unique set of challenges. These include extremes of temperature and humidity, and lighting conditions that can range from complete darkness to full sunlight. In some cases, dirt, grease, oil, sand, hydraulic fluid and various fuels may be common in the environment, all items seen as serious contaminants in the office world. The users may be required to wear gloves, hard hats, safety shields and uniforms, and wearable systems must integrate into this setup as comfortably and non-intrusively as possible or there is likely to be significant resistance from users. In some specialized and exotic applications currently being developed, the wearable systems are woven directly into the clothing worn by a soldier and are designed to run without any intervention from him; in this case they are designed to constantly monitor life signs (heart rate, blood pressure, etc.) and report any deviations due to hazards such as gunshot or knife wounds. As we shall see in later sections, all of these task and environmental characteristics significantly affect the design of the wearable hardware and the applications that run on them.

3 WHAT IS A WEARABLE COMPUTER?

In this section we will describe the hardware and software components used to develop our field-tested systems and how they are likely to evolve in the near future; a more detailed description of the application will be in the next section.

3.1 Current Hardware

Our current prototype systems are from the Flexible PC Company, and consist of:

- 100 MHz 486 CPU with power management
- 32 MB memory
- standard set of I/O connectors
- standard 15-pin VGA connector
- 4 Type III PCMCIA slots

These slots are currently filled with 2 340 MB PCMCIA hard drive cards and 1 PCMCIA speech recognition / sound card from Speech Systems, Inc.

The remaining slot may be filled by a wireless networking card or other device as needed by the task. The standard serial ports mean that we can attach a variety of input devices, such as touchpads, dials, or devices as required.

Our current HMD prototypes are from Virtual Vision, Inc. and feature:

- 8-bit grayscale VGA monocular display
- adjustments for display position and orientation
- adjustments for focus and brightness
- eye safety shield
- optics that focus the image at arms length
- integrated earphone
- integrated noise-cancelling microphone

The dial input device that was used in the final field evaluations was constructed by Carnegie-Mellon from one of their cannibalized Vu-Man 3 wearable computers.

The 777 and 757 applications were built by the author using Visual Basic 3.0 and the PE500 Speech Application Development Environment from Speech Systems, Inc., to run under Microsoft Windows for Workgroups 3.11. The Flexi-PC has a flexible system backplane which allows it to wrap around the user's waist, and physically resembles a money belt. The dial was put into a modified camera case, and was also worn on the waist strap of the Flexi-PC.

3.1 Future Development

Many of the developments in wearables are mirrored by (and often driven by) changes in the enormously larger laptop market but as time goes on and wearables grow into their own category of significant size, we can expect some divergence to take place. The probable future directions for most wearable systems can be divided up into the following four categories:

- CPU, System Bus, and Graphics
- Storage
- Power
- Packaging, Expandability, and Connectivity

3.1.1 CPU, System Bus, and Graphics

Now that most Pentium power management has evolved so that laptops have these CPUs, we can expect to see wearables with 133-150 MHz Pentium CPUs in early 1997, with continued evolution towards Pentium Pro and PowerPC CPUs in the later part of 1997 and into 1998.. The current combination of slow and narrow ISA and PCMCIA buses is expected to give way to some combination of CardBus (a laptop version of the desktop PCI bus), Accelerated Graphics Port, Zoomed Video, and Universal Serial Bus by late 1997 or early 1998. This will obviously and dramatically improve system performance in almost all areas. In addition to the dedicated buses for graphics and video just named, we can expect the integration of low-cost 3D graphics hardware (approximately equal to an SGI Reality Engine 1) onto the motherboard by sometime in 1998. This is a specific instance of a more general trend towards greater integration of functions that used to require separate add-in cards (wireless networking, cellular phone, speech recognition) onto the motherboard.

3.1.2 Storage

Current storage solutions such as PCMCIA disks are a focus for a disproportionately large number of problems associated with current wearables. Some of these, such as a difficulty in continuing to function after being dropped 6 feet onto a concrete floor, are intrinsic to the design of the devices themselves. Disks are also one of the two largest consumers of battery power (the display is the other), although the disk hardware is not entirely to blame here. Several modern popular operating systems, such as Windows 95, Windows NT and most flavors of UNIX, are constantly accessing the disk for virtual memory support regardless of the amount of physical memory in the system. Whether or not current capacities are adequate is obviously application-dependent, although for our applications the more storage the better. One solution may be to rely more on dynamically downloading and caching data when it is needed over a wireless link instead of preloading it to begin with. Another expected solution is the development of large (500MB - 1GB) flash memory modules that can serve as solid state disks. These devices would be much faster, have much lower power consumption, and be far more shock resistant than current drives. Intel has promised such devices by 1998.

3.1.4 Packaging, Expandability, and Connectivity

There is already something of a split in the nascent wearables market between fixed-function units that are not easily (or at all) reconfigurable or expandable and more general purpose wearables with available expansion slots that are accessible by end-users. We expect that the smallest of the fixed function units will soon fit in a shirt pocket, and that some sort of convergence with the current handheld systems and PDAs will then happen. The current tangle of cables and physical connectors that link the central system with the various peripherals will give way to a scheme that takes local advantage of the wireless communications that are also expected to be built in. The notion of a `personal area network', or a human-sized wireless network that connects all of the body-worn devices is in the early stages of development.

4 FIELD TEST RESULTS AND DESIGN GUIDELINES

In this section we will discuss some of the lessons learned during the development of the 757 application, describe the field tests and discuss some of the early results. The lessons and results have to do with input devices, head-mounted display issues, and the software portion of the system user interface, so the discussion is divided into these three sections following the description of how the test evaluations were organized.

4.1 Field Test Setup

The 757 field tests were done at Renton Field, in Renton, Washington, using flight test mechanics with between 8 and 15 years of experience. Their job is to make sure that the plane is ready to fly before its first flight test. Because these planes have not yet flown, the problems the mechanics encounter can be in any system or location on the plane, so their troubleshooting experience is substantially broader and deeper than most aviation mechanics. Each subject first filled out a demographic questionnaire that gathered data about work history and previous computer usage. They were then given a brief (2-5 minute) demo and hands-on training on how to use the user interface for the fuel system troubleshooting application.

Each subject was timed and videotaped while using the system - this meant moving around the aircraft out on the tarmac while performing the tests or measurements required by the scenario. Each was asked to provide a stream-of-consciousness think-aloud verbal report of goals, problems, and impressions as they did this. After the scenario was complete, they filled out a post-test survey about the usage of the system and we conducted a videotaped debriefing. The problem scenario itself involved telling the mechanic what diagnostic messages had been reported, and asking them to follow the standard procedures and use the standard manual pages and fault isolation logic trees for the reported problem. The data loaded into the prototype application included all of the manual pages and fault isolation logic trees that a sample of mechanics had asked to see during a documentation of the baseline process for solving this particular problem. This set of pages exceeded what any single mechanic asked for, and at no time during any of the trials did a mechanic ask to see information not available on the wearable at the time of the test.

4.2 Input Device Issues

A general observation about developing applications for use on a wearable is that although some of the user interface issues are the same as for conventional desktop systems, going from a mouse and keyboard in an office to body-worn devices, displays, and voice input in a wide variety of environments challenges a great many assumptions and conventions that have developed over the last 15 years or so.

Recognizing that a conventional 2-button mouse was probably going to be a thoroughly unsuitable input device, we bought, built, or borrowed a wide variety of input devices to try out with the applications we were developing. The list of devices is show below.

- Trackballs
- Touchpads
- Rotary dials with buttons
- Ring mice
- Force-sensitive joysticks
- 3D mice
- Speech Recognition

Speech recognition is included for completeness in this list, although it has it's own set of associated issues that will be dealt with separately in a later section.

After several months of experimentation, it became clear that many of the observations, problems, and principles were clustering around four larger and interacting groups of ideas

1. The mapping between physical device and interaction task
2. The physical environment the system was to be used in
3. Device orientation
4. Device location and size

4.2.1 Device/Task Mapping

The ubiquity of the mouse is something of a mixed blessing. It is well suited for some types of 2D tasks and has undoubtedly contributed to the popularization of what we now regard as conventional graphical user interfaces. On the other hand, it's ubiquity has also led to the development of interface techniques that are varying mixtures of cumbersome and clever solely for the purpose of allowing a mouse to be used for tasks that it is relatively unsuited for - interactive control of many-degree-of-freedom human figures in animation packages, for example (Esposito, 1995).

The absence of a ubiquitous or default input device for wearables squarely raises the question of what device ought to be used for a given task or application. The basic considerations of device/task mapping that arise in conventional user interface (UI) design, as described in (Jacobs, 1992), also arise here. However, for many desktop applications the analysis need not go too much further than this because it can be reasonably assumed that the user is indoors, sitting down facing the monitor and has a mouse and keyboard available. The next three sections discuss additional factors that need to be considered when designing systems for use on a wearable out in the field.

4.2.2 Physical Environment

Many of the devices in the list just above were not designed to work or tested in the environmental conditions described earlier in this paper. Some fail immediately and some fail soon after becoming dirty or clogged, while a few stand up reasonably well to what we have subjected them to so far. Many touchpads, for example, are capacitive rather than resistive and depend on the electrical characteristics of a bare finger to complete a circuit in order to function properly. Simply putting on a pair of gloves renders these devices useless; the presence of grease or oil usually has the same effect. Pressure-sensitive touch pads depend only on a pair of membranes coming into contact at a point underneath the finger, and so will continue to work where capacitive ones will not. Unfortunately, this capacitive/resistive distinction is rarely noted in product packaging or documentation. In much same way that the chamber on a mechanical mouse can get dirty and need cleaning, a trackball used by oily dirty gloves can require almost constant cleaning. A force-sensitive pointing device like a Trackpoint that can be easily used with bare hands becomes a lot more difficult to precisely control if the user is wearing a pair of thick gloves that muffle the force cues being sensed by the finger.

A device that has worked well for us was a dial device built by the Wearable Computers Group at Carnegie-Mellon University (CMU). It consists of a large central dial that clicks as it rotates to provide tactile and audible feedback, with 2 small buttons (which act as duplicate right mouse buttons) and 1 large (left) button around the perimeter of the dial. It is well sealed against the set of contaminants already described and can be easily used with or without gloves.

4.2.3 Device Orientation

This is one of those areas in which, perversely enough, the more experience a user has with desktop devices, the more this experience can work against them. The standard 2D pointing devices provide a mapping between the physical motion of a mouse or finger and the virtual motion of a cursor on the screen. The fixed horizontal orientation of these devices and constant use of these devices in this orientation mean that this particular mapping is so ingrained that interaction techniques like Pie Menus can be very successful relying only on the muscle memory that this constant use provides.

The relative absence of desks in most outdoor environments and the desire for more hands-free operation mean that physical input devices will more likely be worn somewhere on the body rather than constantly held, and worn at different orientations than they had on the desktop. This change in orientation changes the physical - virtual motion mapping that the user may have learned. For example, wearing a resistive touchpad vertically on a belt so that the left and right buttons are still on the left and right makes moving the cursor up and down somewhat awkward because in order to move the cursor up, the finger must physically move down, and vice versa. Rotating the device 180 degrees so those up and down motions are correct now reverses left and right. In some cases the device driver can adjust for these reversals in software, in some cases it can not. In all cases it is an issue that needs to be explicitly dealt with. Rotating the central dial part of the dial device we have been using is orientation independent, but locating the buttons is not.

4.2.4 Device Location and Size

The notion of wearing devices on one's body brings up the obvious question of where one is to wear them. Application requirements may rule out some locations as unsuitable - in a car/truck inspection task, lying on your back underneath the vehicle is common, so the front of the body is a preferable location. During part of our 757 fuel system scenario the mechanic is on his stomach behind a seat in the flight deck checking a circuit breaker near the floor, so we mounted the dial device on the side of one hip or another, based on user preference. Using these devices in tight spaces suggests that devices that are small or at least conform to the body will cause fewer problems than larger devices or ones that protrude more. One of the frequent problems we had with the dial was that subjects kept bumping it against equipment in the wheel wells as they were climbing up or climbing down; this caused spurious input to the system that they then had to detect and undo. Unlike a desktop mouse that is always in the users peripheral field of view, the body-worn device may not be visible at all for part or all of the time it is being used. Not only is the potential for eye-hand coordination reduced or lost, but now such things as device orientation (if that matters) and button locations may need to be discoverable by touch alone. CMU achieved this with the dial by giving it an asymmetric rounded trapezoid shape, and giving the buttons different sizes, shapes, and numbers of raised plastic dots on each.

4.3 Head-Mounted Display Issues

As described earlier, our HMD had a right-eye monocular grayscale VGA display, with the virtual image focused at about arm's length from the eye. The optics were sufficiently opaque that the outside world could not be seen through them. Two ball joints back near the ears and two near the temple allowed the front visor and eyepiece either to be flipped up out of the way or raised slightly and angled downward for a glance-up style of viewing.

The strongest reaction we received was to the notion of wearing an HMD at all. Some subjects in both evaluations were either positive or neutral about wearing one, while others were adamantly opposed to wearing one. Upon closer examination, the distinguishing factor in most cases was the extent to which the subjects' work was primarily outside the aircraft (generally opposed) or inside the aircraft (neutral or positive). For safety reasons, those subjects that worked on the outside of the plane place an extremely high priority on a completely unobstructed field of view so that they can see anything that might be coming towards them, especially from above.

There were also a number of age-related vision issues to deal with. As already mentioned, the optics focused the image at about arms' length away from the user. In a `baseline' condition (office light, eyepiece fully down in front of the eye), all subjects had no difficulty reading the 14-point text used in the HMD, or in switching back and forth between looking at a monitor at arms length and the HMD image. However, in full sunlight we had to cover the frontmost surface of the display unit (the side away from the eye) to prevent ambient light from washing out the display. In addition, there are several places in the scenario when the point of interest was nearer or farther away than arms length, and switching back and forth to read the text of the diagnostic procedure or work on the part required frequent refocusing. The effort required for this repeated refocusing was too noticeable to several subjects over 40. An unexpected interacting factor was the presence of bifocals on many of the older subjects. The near-focus part of their lens was in the lower portion, and the far-focus in the upper portion. Those that used the glance-up style of wearing were then looking at some or the entire arms-length image through a far-focus lens, which contributed to some of the difficulty in reading the text clearly. We are currently in the very early stages of considering a new display design in which the display elements sit beneath the eyes, angled upward as way of dealing with this problem.

4.4 Software Issues

4.4.1 Screen Real Estate

One of the most challenging (but temporary) problems in designing these applications was coping with grayscale VGA screen real estate during a time when 19" or 21" monitors running at least 24 bit color at 1280 x 1024 has become common. Having only one fourth of the screen real estate meant that pixels were doled out with an eyedropper, metaphorically speaking. Since the dial device did not support general 2D positioning and speech input generally makes a poor and imprecise pointer; the user could not manually move or resize the application windows. There was quite a bit of experimentation juggling the variables of window size, window location, font size, and font style to make sure that enough information was visible and that the visible information was readable. We decided against trying to display wiring diagrams and schematics since these images were several feet on a side and plotted at 300 dpi; given the limited resolution currently available this would have been a bit like looking at a map through a soda straw. Since we had no graphics, it turned out that for these applications the lack of color was not a problem. We finally settled on 14-point type and used a mix of regular and boldface type, using the boldface to indicate selectable hyperlinks in displayed manual pages. Since managing screen real estate was primarily the responsibility of the application, it maintained a record of which windows were open and what their sizes were. As a window opened or closed, the surrounding open windows automatically resized to make best use of the available screen space. Higher resolution (1280 x 1024) displays and color VGA displays are expected in 1997 which will reduce some of these design difficulties.

4.4.2 Speech Input

The speech recognition system that we used, after considerable evaluation of alternatives, was from Speech Systems Inc., and supported speaker-independent continuous speech that is mapped into the best fit from a context-free grammar that we built. There was considerable concern early in the development that speech would not function acceptably well (as reliably as a physical input device) in the noisy environment of an airstrip. There was a deliberate design decision to provide a bit of redundancy by making speech and the dial parallel and equivalent input channels so that if either failed the application could still be used with the other. This had the side benefit of allowing us to look at user preferences for speech or the dial for giving commands to the system. Some early results from the evaluation data suggest that while both devices worked well, users preferred speech over the dial because they viewed it as a more direct way of giving a command; in the rare case that speech did not work they fell back to using the dial.

Early recognition rates were not acceptable, so we set about tuning the vocabulary. We had 10 subjects say every word in the vocabulary and looked for words that were repeatedly misrecognized. Ironically, most of the word and phrase recognition errors came from the presence of `yes' and `OK' in the vocabulary; two words that are common in

Windows dialog boxes. After removing these words and substituting `confirm', recognition rates rose so that on average we had 1 misrecognition per subject.

The last issues to deal with have to do with providing feedback to the user. More specifically, how does the user know what he can say, and how does he know what the system thinks he has said? The second of these was easy - a fixed area of the screen labeled `I heard' always contained the text of the last utterance. Solving the first was a bit more involved and driven by two goals. The first was the notion of parallel and functionally equivalent input channels. The second goal was to minimize the required training time and make this system as `walk-up-and-use' as possible. Since the subjects were able to successfully use this system with at most 5 minutes of instruction, we believe we have largely succeeded. After examining quite a few variations, the solution we settled on was to have all of the voice commands visible in one portion of the screen and 1 standard Windows button corresponding to each voice command visible in another portion of the screen. The sets of buttons and voice commands were shown side by side, each in 2 columns of 4, to suggest the parallel and equivalent nature of these channels. Rotating the dial caused the Windows input focus to change from one button to the next, skipping over any buttons that were grayed out because those commands were not available at this point in the application. The post-test usability scores for both of these features were both quite positive - 9 out of 10 for the last utterance, and 8.5 out of 10 for command availability. The application as a whole received an 8 out of 10.

5 FUTURE WORK

Based on the debriefings with the mechanics, two requirements consistently came through. The first was that of all the graphics data that is available to a mechanic, the single most important piece is the wiring diagram. It is not often needed, but when it is, it is essential and there is no real substitute. Higher resolution HMDs and sourceless head orientation trackers will allow us to experiment next year with some ideas for using head orientation as a `head cursor' to control panning and zooming around graphic images. We also plan on extending our work to look at collaborative work, by enabling groups of mechanics, either all on the plane or some back at the central hangar, to share voice, video, and application data (like wiring diagrams) as they collectively try to do troubleshooting and repair tasks.

REFERENCES

Caudell, T., Mizell, D. (1992) Applications of Augmented Reality. Proceedings of HICSS 92.

Esposito, C. (1995) Of Mice and Monkeys: A Specialized Input Device for Virtual Body Animation. Proceedings of the ACM 1995 Symposium on Interactive 3D Graphics.

Jacob, R. and Sibert, L. (1992) The Perceptual Structure of Multidimensional Input Device Selection. CHI 92 Conference Proceedings.

Janin, A. (1994) A Videometric head tracker for augmented reality applications, Proceedings SPIE East.

76

Human Interface and Applications on IdeaBoard

Masaki Nakagawa, Tsuyoshi Oguni and Takashi Yoshino

Dept. of Computer Science
Tokyo Univ. of Agri. & Tech.
Naka-cho 2-24-16, Koganei, Tokyo, 184, Japan
nakagawa@cc.tuat.ac.jp

ABSTRACT This paper describes a new style of human interface and several applications on an interactive dynamic whiteboard. If current GUIs are just expanded to the whiteboard size, the teacher would have to frequently move from side to side and stretch their hands from edge to edge, as well as the teacher's body would cover the board. In order to avoid these problems, operability from an arbitrary standing position of the teacher with a reasonable amount of hand movement, thus no hiding of the board by the body, and easy operations by electronic markers have been sought. Moreover, various applications have been prototyped. A programming education system is one of these, where the teacher writes a program on the board and can have it recognized, compiled and executed in front of the students. Another is an arithmetic education system where children write arithmetic equations on the board and the system answers them.

KEYWORDS pen interface, handwriting recognition, electronic whiteboard, direct pointing, GUI

1. INTRODUCTION

This research has been motivated from our experience in programming education.

So far, we have been teaching programming on a white/black board and telling students to try the programs that we have explained after the class. Next week, their answer is often that the programs have not worked. The reason is quite simple. Programs that we write on a white/black board are not always syntactically perfect and moreover students often misread them or miscopy them in their notebooks.

Then, the students ask us to lecture in a computer room. Now, they can try programming immediately. But, the problem is that they focus their attention on their PCs and do not pay attention to our explanations. It is very difficult to present intrinsic materials in a computer room.

On the other hand, the advantage with the white/black board is that we can focus the attention of students on our writing and present new materials while confirming their understanding by watching their faces. But, we cannot show the execution of programs in front of them.

Although practice on a PC is essential for each student to learn programming for themselves, to computerize the white/black board and provide it with the capability of showing program execution brings about new potential for programming education.

We decided to develop a system to combine the merit of the white/black board and that of computer processing as a part of pen interface research. The system may open the way for new applications other than programming education.

Human–Computer Interaction: INTERACT'97 S. Howard, J. Hammond & G. Lindgaard (editors)
Published by Chapman & Hall

The Liveboard by XEROX is well-known as such a system (Elrod et al. 1992, Pedersen et al. 1993, Weiser 1991, 1993). The effect of capturing audience's attention and the benefit of recording and replaying handwriting has been reported. These observations apply to our system as well, but our system differs from the Liveboard in the following respects.

Firstly, the Liveboard and especially its applications developed at XEROX PARC avoid handwriting recognition except that for gestures (Pedersen 1993). On the other hand, we employ handwriting recognition, which is essential to compile and execute handwritten programs, to exploit the power of computing.

Secondly, the Liveboard uses gesture commands while we are not positive about employing them because of the reasons described below. We try to enhance the desktop GUI to make it suitable for the large interactive display and electronic markers.

The reason that the Liveboard employs them is that a simple expansion of the desktop GUI to the board size requires the user to push top left button as well as bottom right buttons, thus making the user's body cover the board. But, we try a different possibility.

Thirdly, the Liveboard seems to be oriented for meetings and presentations, but our system is mainly designed for educational use. To develop educational applications is an important part of our research.

Fourthly, the resolution of 640 x 480 and the brightness of the 67-inch color display of the Liveboard is not satisfactory. Even the updated resolution of 1024 x 768 of the Liveboard 3 is not good enough to be used as a whiteboard.

Enlarging a computer display and the sharing of it by participants makes collaboration easier by itself. To be used as an electronic whiteboard, however, brightness and resolution seem to be very important. Without a sufficient level of quality in these respects, the merit of the whiteboard will be reduced.

We considered employing the Liveboard, but decided to use a temporary hardware to develop software while preparing a new hardware described later. We call our system "*IdeaBoard*" (interactive, dynamic, electronic assistant board).

The basic concept of the *IdeaBoard* is not the enlargement of the computer display, but the coupling of the merits of a whiteboard with those of computer processing. This requires the very high resolution of a large display (more than 1600 x 1280 resolution of the 70-inch size) with electronic markers as well as a new interface design and applications which inherit the conventional and familiar interfaces from a whiteboard while exploiting the dynamic processing of contents by computing.

In this paper, we present user interfaces and applications on *IdeaBoard*.

2. TEMPORARY HARDWARE

The temporary hardware is composed of a 70-inch tablet, an LCD projector and a Windows machine. Its appearance is shown in Figure 1. The display of the Windows machine is projected on the tablet from the LCD projector.

The tablet has a size of 1,331.1 x 998.4 mm and approximately 4,000 x 3,000 resolution with 3 cordless markers and an oval-shaped eraser which are all battery free. A marker sends its position and touched/untouched information which corresponds to the mouse's left button on the PC, but it is not equipped with a switch corresponding to the mouse's right button. The oval-shaped eraser has two point-indicators so that the system can sense the position and orientation of the eraser. Each pen or eraser sends its own identification code so that its role can be changed by software. One of the hardware limitations is that multiple pens and the eraser cannot be used at the same time.

The LCD projector has a resolution of 640×480, a brightness of 250 lumen and 16 M colors, which restricts the specification of the temporary *IdeaBoard*.

Figure 1. The temporary *IdeaBoard* in use.

3. DESIGNING THE *IdeaBoard* UI

3.1. UI for a Large Surface with Markers

If we just expand the usual GUI for the desktop machine to the whiteboard size, problems occur in its usability. A teacher has to move from side to side, stretch hands from button to button, which not only makes the teacher practice gymnastics but often hides the board from the students. Often, operations too minute are also required which are difficult for the hand of a standing person. Moreover, double tapping with a marker is not as easy as with a mouse. Concurrent use of markers and a keyboard is far more difficult than that of a mouse and a keyboard because their manipulation scales are so different.

In order to design the interfaces, the size of the board, its vertical position, operability by markers, body actions by a teacher as well as the consistency with the desktop GUI must be taken into consideration.

3.2. Gestures Considered Harmful

Gestures have been an attraction of pen interfaces. The Liveboard has also employed gestures. We are reluctant, however, to employ gestures because of the following reasons:

(1) Design of gestures is very difficult. Often, gestures are difficult to remember and easy to forget.
(2) Gestures have simple shapes and simple shapes are hard for machines to recognize.
(3) There is little context to augment gesture recognition.
(4) Mode change for inputting gestures is troublesome and easy to forget.
(5) Misrecognition of a gesture or forgotten mode change yields an abrupt and unexpected result which must be canceled. It not only interrupts lectures or presentations very badly but also shocks the teacher or presenter.
(6) Because of the above problems, users fear that gestures might be misinterpreted and may hesitate to use gestures.

We think that pattern recognition can be more usefully employed for contents rather than for commands.

3.3. Extension of the Desktop GUI

We are now very familiar with the desktop GUI. It has apparent advantages against the old style of user interfaces as well as being refined to be accepted from a majority of users.

Even if a simple expansion of the desktop GUI to the whiteboard size is not usable, to employ or extend its styles or elements in a form that they are consistent with the desktop while enhancing the usability of the *IdeaBoard* can still be effective.

3.4. Guidelines

In the process of reviewing the desktop GUI, we have set the following guidelines:

(1) Operability from any standing position
To operate *IdeaBoard* without crossing the surface, gestures or pop-up menus can be considered. In order to invoke the pop-up menus, a gesture or an extra action is required. We tried to solve the problem by a different method with the temporary hardware.

(2) Operability by body size movement
Too large a movement, required for a user to operate the *IdeaBoard,* is hard and ends up hiding the board, but too minute a movement is also difficult for the standing user. Body size movement with direct pointing and manipulation is not only natural to the user but also appealing to the audience and it navigates their focus of attention.

(3) Easy operability by a marker
To keep pushing a marker horizontally at one point on the vertical board is hard for a person. His/her hand becomes tired in trying to remain steady. Compared with this, dragging (drawing) a marker is easier and more direct for the audience so that its employment is considered.

(4) Natural extension of the desktop GUI
We try not to create new styles or elements of GUI as far as those of the desktop GUI can be effectively employed. When we need to extend or modify them, we try to be as consistent as possible with the desktop so that the users do not feel a big difference.

(5) Smooth movement of displayed objects
Very smooth and continuous movement of displayed objects such as shown in Pad (Perlin 1993) seems more important for the shared large display. We try to execute the actions on the board as smoothly as possible so that the audience can keep their focus of attention

without being annoyed by the sudden change of contents.

4. ELEMENTS OF THE *IdeaBoard* UI

4.1. Scroll

Being different from the common scrolling by tapping or dragging a button or a bar at a fixed position, the *IdeaBoard* enables a user to scroll in any direction from any standing position.

We place the scroll bar around the board as shown in Figure 2. If you touch a marker to any point in the scroll bar and drag it in any direction, then the window is scrolled in that direction. You can scroll from any standing position and you do not have to move to the scroll button and keep pushing it. If you move the marker (x, y) after touching the scroll bar, then the window is scrolled by (kx, ky) where k is determined by the velocity of the marker movement.

Figure 2. Scrolling from any point in the window frame.

4.2. Window Movement

We propose the following method for window movement. If you touch a marker to the title bar and drag it to (x, y), the window is moved to (kx, ky). The coefficient k is adjusted so that the window can be moved around in the display if you stretch your hand with the marker from any standing position.

By drawing a line between (x, y) and (kx, ky), you can easily observe what and how you are moving. Its appearance has already been shown in Figure 1.

4.3. Tool Bar

We propose a tool bar as shown in Figure 3. Function buttons in the tool bar extend or shrink as the window is widened or narrowed. One might have to stretch one's hand, but even the most distant function button is extended as the window is widened so that one is unlikely to hide the window.

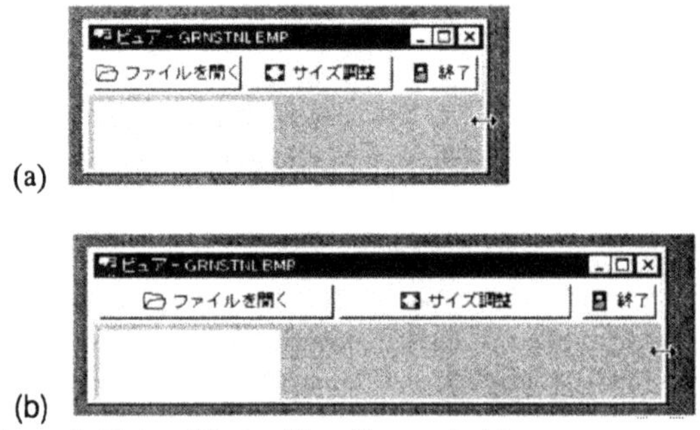

Figure 3. Extensible tool bar (from a to b).

4.4. Counter

Common counters are as shown in Figure 4 (a). If you push or keep pushing the up/down button, the counter is increased/decreased.

We propose a counter as shown in Figure 4 (b). The up button and down button are merged to provide a bigger button. If you touch a marker to any point in the button and drags up or down, the counter is increased or decreased in proportion to the amount of the marker's movement. This dispenses with the need to keep touching the marker or touch it many times at the same point.

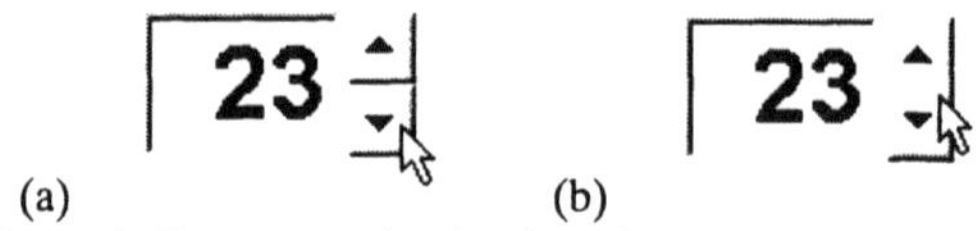

Figure 4. Counter setting by dragging.

4.5. Tab

Tab is used to turn a page. We propose the following type of tab as shown in Figure 5. When a tab is shown on the right side in the page, tapping at the left side causes the tab to be displayed there. When it is shown on the left, tapping at the right brings the tab to the right.

A user need not move to the other side to tap the tab.

Moreover, touching a tab item with the marker and dragging it up or down causes a jump to upper or lower tab items according to the amount of the marker's movement. This dispenses with careful tapping to the right destination since the destination can be reached by just dragging the marker up or down while confirming the visual feedback.

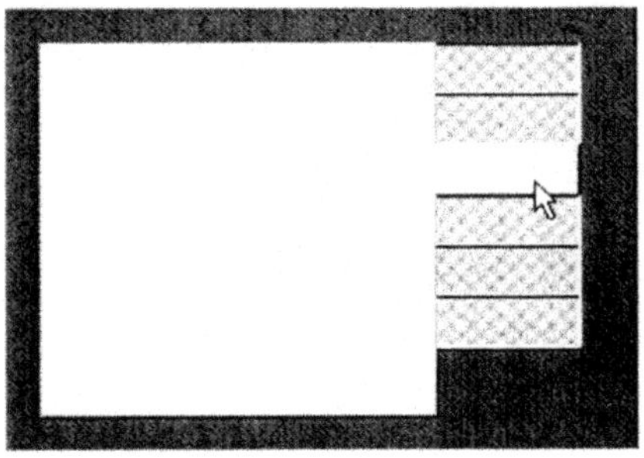

Figure 5. A proposed tab.

4.6. Turning Pages

We propose page turning by dragging the marker to the direction that one wants to go rather than pushing page turning buttons. Figure 6 shows an example. When pages are just for viewing, touching the marker at any position and dragging to right/left causes the page to be turned to the right/left. One need not tap the marker in specified positions. Whether you are touching the marker on the right page or the left page is not important. Page turning direction is just determined by the direction of dragging. Thus, a teacher can turn the page to either right or left direction whether standing at right or left of the board. When the pen is dragged by x, the page is turned by kx. The coefficient k is adjusted so that amount of hand movement is appropriate.

5. APPLICATIONS ON THE *IdeaBoard*

Applications on the *IdeaBoard* employ handwriting recognition when necessary, but they do not blindly try to recognize handwriting whatever and whenever it is. The following applications have been prototyped.

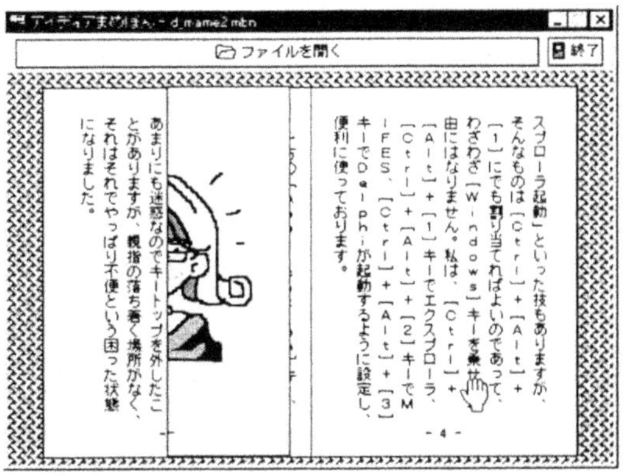

Figure 6. Page turning by dragging.

5.1. Programming Education

A teacher writes a program, explains it, then makes the system recognize and execute it. Here, program recognition is not for program input but for programming education and demonstration.

Figures 7, 8, and 9 show a handwritten program, the result of its recognition using the context of a C program, and the result of its execution, respectively.

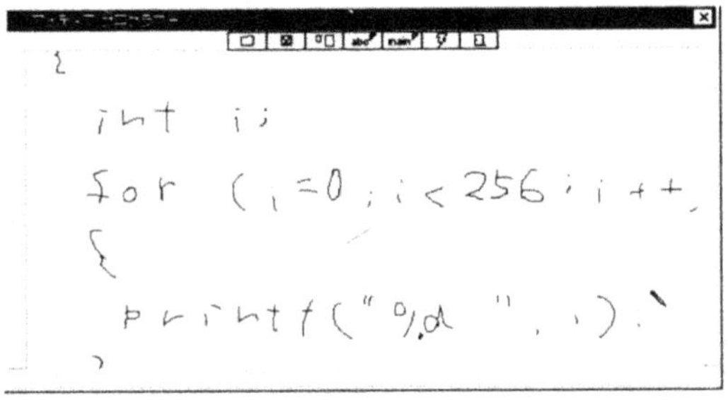

Figure 7. A handwritten program.

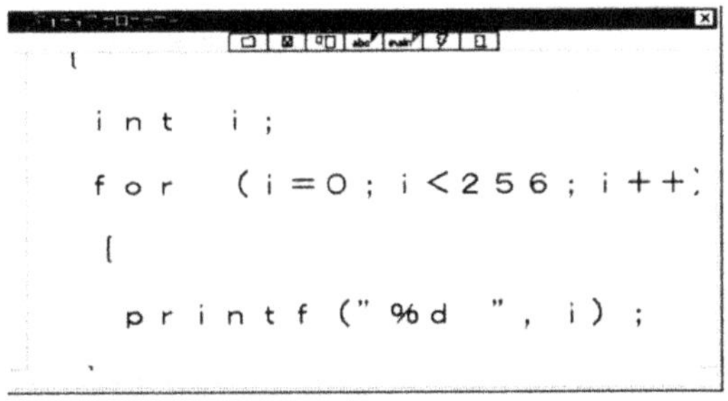

Figure 8. Result of program recognition.

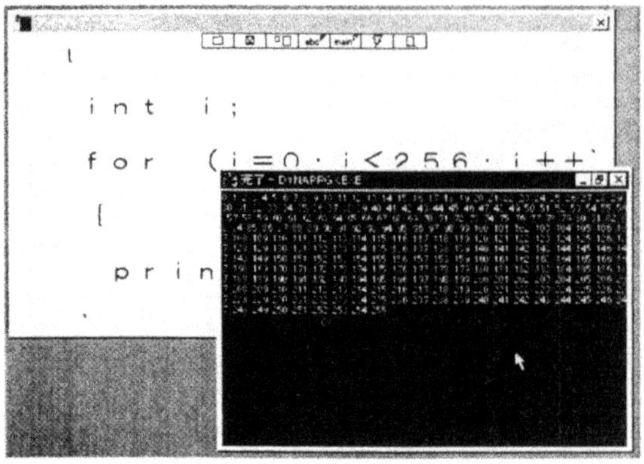

Figure 9. Result of program execution.

Here, we follow the lazy recognition scheme which delays the display of recognition until needed. Lazy recognition also provides an easier structure to employ context processing (Nakagawa et al. 1993a, 1993b).

When a teacher is writing a program and explaining it, machine recognition is not only unnecessary for the teacher and students, but it is even worse than when no recognition is employed. Recognition immediately after a pattern is written causes interruption because of the correction of incorrect recognition and the verification of recognition even if a pattern is correctly recognized.

When the teacher wants to show the execution of a handwritten program, however, program recognition is highly convenient and effective. Although the teacher might have to correct some misrecognitions, it is worth the trouble since the machine can show the execution of the program that the teacher has just written in front of the students.

Editing functions for space insertion and deletion of characters and lines can be triggered by tapping a marker between lines and dragging right or left (blank insertion or character deletion) or dragging down or up (blank line insertion or line deletion). They are executed smoothly.

Smoothness has been sought to realize move and copy functions as well. If you tap a marker between lines and wait for a certain period, then the color of the upper line is reversed. If you drag the marker up/down without detaching it, the color of more upper/lower lines are reversed. This shows that lines of text have been selected. Then, when you tap the marker at some place outside the reversed area, the selected lines are copied. On the other hand, if you tap the reversed area again, the selected lines are drawn into the marker smoothly. Then, when you tap the maker at some place, the saved lines are released there.

5.2. Arithmetic Education

Children write arithmetic equations on the board and the system answers whether they are correct or not. They can share calculations with others, teachers and the system. The same editing functions as the programming education system are provided. Figure 10 shows the *IdeaBoard* with this application running.

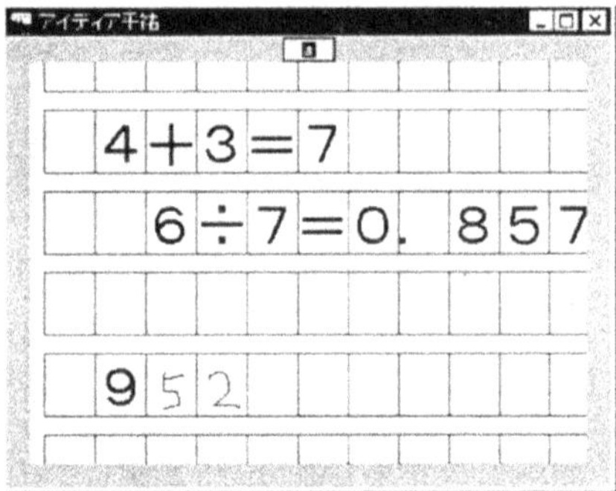

Figure 10. Arithmetic education on *IdeaBoard*.

5.3. WWW Browser

The *IdeaBoard* is expected to be useful for visiting electronic museums and libraries where a teacher can focus the attention of students on the shared picture on the *IdeaBoard*.

This application also employs the enlargement of hand movement. A distant object can be pointed to by a pointer which can be stretched from any point in the window frame as shown in Figure 11. You only have to touch the marker anywhere in the frame and drag it to the direction of the destination. Your hand movement is enlarged so that the pointer head can point to the destination without requiring you to move to the destination with your body hiding the board. With this pointer, pointing to an anchor then detaching the marker causes a jump to its linked page. URL addresses or key words for search can be input through the front end of a handwriting recognizer.

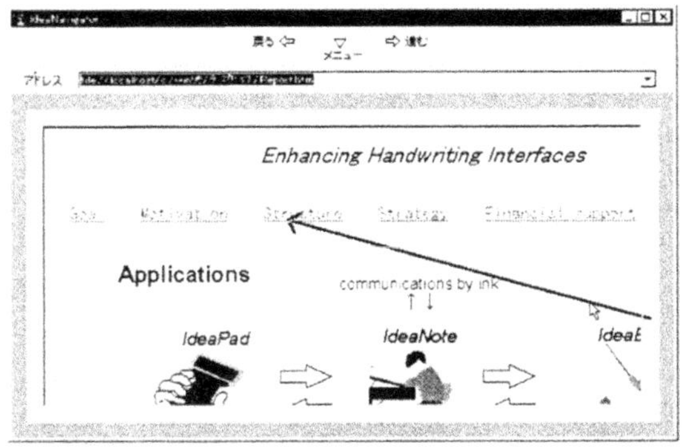

Figure 11. WWW Browser on *IdeaBoard*.

5.4. Other Applications

In addition to the above, handwriting training where a student writes Kanji and the system evaluates the correctness of handwriting using the recognition engine, and brainstorming support where idea cards are arranged on the board and they are recognized and summarized into a document are the major applications proposed to be run on the *IdeaBoard*. For these applications, handwriting recognition is useful if it has more than a certain level of quality and it can be upgraded by context processing. We have developed a highly robust and customizable character recognition engine (Nakagawa et al. 1996a, 1996b).

The difference in the stance towards pattern recognition thus described makes the *IdeaBoard* system different from the Liveboard system.

6. FUTURE WORK

6.1. Enhancement of UI and Applications

Following the current design principle, some more UI elements would be required to run some other applications. Moreover, each of the current applications must be elaborated through the iterative design method. Effectiveness of the *IdeaBoard* must be evaluated through the expansion of its scope as well as the enhancement of each application.

A better way to invoke multiple applications must be considered. When switching from one application to another, relocation and resizing of windows are needed as on a desktop environment. The problem is that they are more troublesome on the large board than on the desktop environment. Seamless combination of multiple applications must be studied.

We decided not to employ gestures since their misrecognition disrupts lectures and presentations in unexpected ways. There is another serious problem with the gestures, which is the mode change required to input them. It is troublesome if a teacher must touch some button every time to change the mode of the pen. Moreover, the teacher might forget to change the mode with the result that an ink pattern might be misinterpreted as a gesture or vice versa, which all must be canceled.

Nevertheless, a limited number of gestures are still appealing to the pen UI design. With an appropriate design, a robust recognition method, good interface design that avoids mode selection, gestures might be able to provide expected benefits.

6.2. Development of a New Hardware

The hardware that we are currently using is unsatisfactory. Front projection is dazzling to the teacher's eyes and its display is hidden by the teacher's body. A resolution of 640 x 480 is too coarse since 1 pixel is about 2mm x 2mm in size when enlarged to the 70-inch size. When we write a character of size of 20 mm x 20mm, it has only a resolution of 10 x 10 dots. If it is a English font, it may be legible. For handwritten Kanji characters, however, the resolution is too poor for them to be displayed as they are written. Therefore, we cannot write Japanese text or mathematical formulas as we can on a whiteboard. It is also very difficult to carry out brainstorming while displaying tens or hundreds of electronic idea cards which have been written on PDAs. Brightness of the display is also a problem. If a class room has to be dark like a theater, the demerits overwhelm than the merits. The display must be usable in a well-lighted environment so that students can see the teacher's face and actions as well as the screen. Then, both the real explanation by the teacher and the virtual contents of the display are merged on the students' retinas. With the limited hardware, the possibility of software will be restricted and the evaluation of the system is destined to be poor.

We started to make a new hardware based on a rear-projection 70-inch High Vision TV which has a 680 cd/m^2 brightness, a 180:1 contrast rate and a 1600 x

1280 resolution. With better hardware, various possibilities for software can be studied and issues will be clarified without putting the blame on hardware.

6.3. Total System for Pen Interface

Pen is a scalable interface unlike mouse or keyboard, i.e., it can be used commonly between PDAs, desktop display integrated tablets and large interactive boards. The total system is one in which you write down your idea memos on a PDA wherever you might be, then download them to a desktop environment and have them recognized when necessary, or you prepare materials for a lecture on the desktop and carry out the actual lecture on the *IdeaBoard.* The live lectures can be recorded and reviewed on a desktop or PDA. The lazy recognition scheme is employed throughout the total system.

Although the total architecture, composed of small, medium-size, and large pen input devices, is again similar to the ubiquitous computing at PARC (Weiser 1991, 1993), our aim is to provide the power of computing to our behaviors of handwriting which are made on media including various sizes of papers, notebooks and a white/black board. In contrast to this, the PARC's research is oriented more for collaboration where the small device (ParcTab) is mainly used to locate where the user is rather than for writing down memos.

7. CONCLUSION

This paper has described the *IdeaBoard* interface and application prototypes which are expected to succeed the merit of the white/black board as well as to provide users with computing powers to manipulate and interpret handwriting for education.

Enhancement of the *IdeaBoard* environment based on the evaluation of the prototypes as well as the development of the better hardware are being carried out.

8. ACKNOWLEDGMENT

This work is being supported by the Advanced Software Enrichment Project of IPA under MITI, Japan. We would also like to thank Hitachi, Hitachi Software and Fujitsu for their collaboration.

9. REFERENCES

Elrod, S., Bruce, R., Gold, R., Goldberg, D., Halasz, F., Janssen, W., Lee, D., McCall, K., Pedersen, E., Pier, K., Tang, J. and Welch, B. (1992) Liveboard: A Large Interactive Display Supporting Group Meetings, Presentations and Remote Collaboration. *Proc. CHI'92*, 599-607.

Nakagawa, M., Machii, K., Kato, N. and Souya, T. (1993a) Lazy Recognition as a Principle of Pen Interfaces, *INTERCHI'93 Adjunct Proc.* 89-90.

Nakagawa, M., Kato, N., Machii, K. and Souya, T (1993b) Principles of pen interface design for creative work, *Proc. ICDAR'93*, 718-721.

Nakagawa, M. and Tu, L.V. (1996a) Structural Learning of Character Patterns for On-line Recognition of Handwritten Japanese Characters, in *Advances in Structural and Syntactic Pattern Recognition* (eds. P. Perner, P. Wang and A. Rosenfeld), Springer-Verlag, 180-188.

Nakagawa, M., Akiyama, K., Tu, L.V., Homma, A. and Higashiyama, T. (1996b) Robust and Highly Customizable Recognition of On-line Handwritten Japanese Characters, *Proc. 13th ICPR*, Ⅲ, 269-273.

Pedersen, E.R., McCall, K., Moran, T.P., Halasz, F.G. (1993) Tivoli: An Electronic Whiteboard for Informal Workgroup Meetings, *Proc. INTERCHI'93*, 391-398.

Perlin, K. and Fox, D. Pad: An Alternative Approach to the Computer Interface, *Proc. 1993 ACM SIGGRAPH Conference*, 57-64.

Weiser, M. (1991) The Computer for the 21st Century, *Scientific American*, 94-104.

Weiser, M. (1993) Some Computer Science Issues in Ubiquitous Computing, *C. ACM*, **36**, 7, 74-84.

Towards gaze-mediated interaction: Collecting solutions of the "Midas touch problem"

Boris Velichkovsky, Andreas Sprenger and Pieter Unema

Applied Cognitive Research
Dresden University of Technology
D-01062 Dresden, Germany
Fax +49 (351) 4637741
E-mail velich@psy1.psych.tu-dresden.de

ABSTRACT: For a development of truly user-centered interfaces we need to take into account not only generic characteristics of human beings but also actual dynamics of attention and intentions of persons involved in an interaction. Modern eyetracking methods are indispensable tools in such a development, as they allow the use of eye movement data for control of output devices, for gaze-contingent image processing and for desambiguation of verbal as well as nonverbal information. The main obstacle on the way to these applications is the so-called "Midas touch problem": how to differentiate "attentive" saccades with intended goal of communication from the lower level eye movements that are just random or provoked by external stimulation? We report results of our investigations of the problem and present a solution based on a functional classification of fixations correlated with their duration. Several additional solutions are also considered together with the data on the trainability of the human oculomotor system.

KEYWORDS: Attention, eyetracking, fixations, levels of processing, user-centered approach

INTRODUCTION

Technological changes often grow up silently in interdisciplinary neighborhoods. New methods from cognitive neurosciences may well soon initiate such changes in human-computer interaction. For the first time, neuroimaging and eyetracking methods provide evidence about the actual course of human information processing and brain structures involved (Velichkovsky & Hansen, 1996). This is exactly the type information we would need to adapt our interfaces to momentary fluctuation in abilities, performance and intentions of users. In particular, the new eyetracking methods have reached the threshold of ergonomic acceptance for the alternative forms of interaction (Hansen, Andersen & Roed, 1995, Jacob, 1995) and are considered in professional publications as one of the most promising technologies for the development of cognitive ergonomics in the short and middle term perspective (Joch, 1996). In our contribution we consider some empirical questions which have to be answered on the way to a broad practical use of these methods.

EYETRACKING AND HUMAN-COMPUTER INTERACTION

The new generation of eyetracking systems do afford different applications with a relatively low load for their users. They are increasingly fast, precise and non-intrusive,. As a rule, the systems are video-based, which means that the gaze direction is computed on the basis

Human–Computer Interaction: INTERACT'97 S. Howard, J. Hammond & G. Lindgaard (editors)
Published by Chapman & Hall

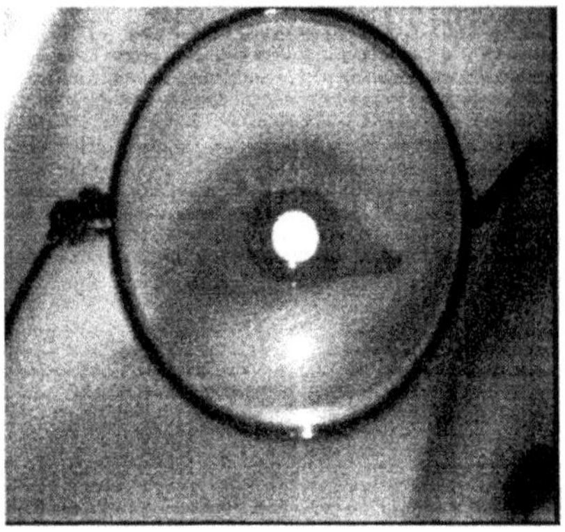

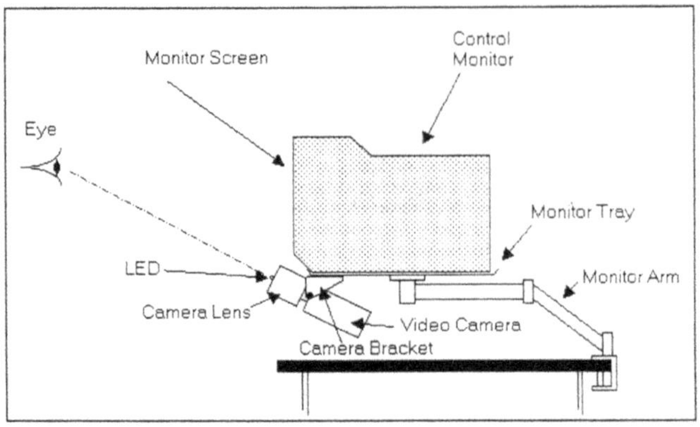

Figure 1: Human eye in infrared light of an eyetracking camera. Right: A non-intrusive eyetracker at the work place.

of picture of the pupil and the corneal reflex from infrared light sources. In the non-intrusive versions the only demand on the user is a more or less constant sitting position whereby the head movements are usually permitted (see Figure 1). The precision of the systems is a 0.5 degree of arc and is independent from blinks that are indentified as such by software. Temporal resolution (50 or 60 Hz) however is too low for recognition of short fixations (Starker & Bolt, 1990, Velichkovsky, Hillers & Sprenger, in preparation). Head-mounted systems can be much faster, up to 600 Hz, and are even more precise in terms of spatial resolution, especially with the interfaces based on the self-organized neural networks (Ritter, 1993) that lead to a further improvement of resolution up to 30%. (Baluja & Pomerleau, 1994, Pomplun, Velichkovsky & Ritter 1994). The precision of about 0.5 degree of arc seems to be sufficient for most of the applications. During the session users only notice the light head-mounted device. Their head movements and slight body movements are permitted. Modern eyetracking systems are built according to the TCP/IP standard, so a transmission of data via Internet is possible (Velichkovsky & Hansen, 1996).

Depending on the system one can measure different parameters, such as blinks, pupil's diameter and, last but not least, the gaze direction and the fixation time. These parameters are interesting primarily as indices of the focus of visual attention of the users. Indeed, the gaze direction is considered to be the most reliable, though unfortunately not ideal (Helmholtz, 1896, Hoffman, 1996), index of the focus of attention. Combining of all these parameters one can find indices for the type of processing and the human emotional state (Velichkovsky, 1995). The most obvious application of the methods is the "gaze-mouse", as e.g. in situations where it is no longer possible to rely on the fine manual coordinations or on the speech control of the interface, but the gaze direction can be *interpreted* in an intentional way (Stampe & Reingold, 1994, Starker & Bolt, 1990). A more sophisticated approach to gaze-based interaction is less connected with the idea of using gaze as a substitute for the computer mouse. Instead, the data are to be *interpreted* at a higher level for a reconstruction of user's perception (Pomplun, Ritter & Velichkovsky, 1996, Raeithel & Velichkovsky, 1995) or to be used in a new type of "noncommand interface" (e.g., Nielsen, 1993, Velichkovsky & Hansen, 1996). In other words, eye movements are used as a continues measure of attention being paid to individual objects on the display. Even more complex *interpretation* of the data may be needed for development in the direction of "interest and emotion sensitive" media (Engell-Nielsen et al., 1997 in press).

We are now coming to the main issue. As already mentioned the gaze direction is not an ideal indicator of attention: e.g., we cannot jump to point B while attending point A, but we can well attend B while fixating A. During an average working day our eyes make more than 100.000 saccadic movements. Which of them is attentive or intiated with a communicative intention and which is not? How should computers decide? No wonder that some of the previous attempts to use eyetracking data for an interacting with a computer have not been particularly successful (Starker & Bolt, 1990). Jacob (1995) pointedly termed this difficulty the "Midas touch problem". Obviously, one should try to filter out the tremendous amount of data, but according to what criteria and for what tasks?

A MODEL OF VISUAL INFORMATION PROCESSING

To answer these questions we need a model of eye movement control in relation to information processing tasks. In the last time this was the discovery of *express saccades* that raised an interest to eye movement data (e.g. Fischer & Weber, 1993). The movements have an extraordinary short latency of less than 100 ms, the shortest latency of any movements in humans. Fuctionally they seem to belong to the organism's orienting response: they are in a sense reflexes imposed on us by our environment and they resist any conscious control. This means that their potential importance for the interaction with computer is "zero".

A classification of the higher order tasks for eye movements still is a somewhat speculative matter (see however Challis, Velichkovsky & Craik, 1996, Deacon. 1996, Velichkovsky, 1994). First of all, a very basic function of eye movements (which is performed in a synergy with other motor systems of the organism) is *search.* If a potentially important object or feature has been discovered it should be perceptually described. Such an *identification* is hardly possible without eye movements, thought these mevements can be of another type than during the search. After identification the information can be semantically categorized. Some of the information may receive also additional *self-referential* (or perhaps *other-referential*) interpretation. Only at this point the information may be considered to be ready for a possible *communication.* That also at this last stage eye movements are important has been claimed more than 100 years ago (Hering, 1977), but remained almost unexplored. In a series of experiments we recently investigated parameters of eye movements in all these tasks.

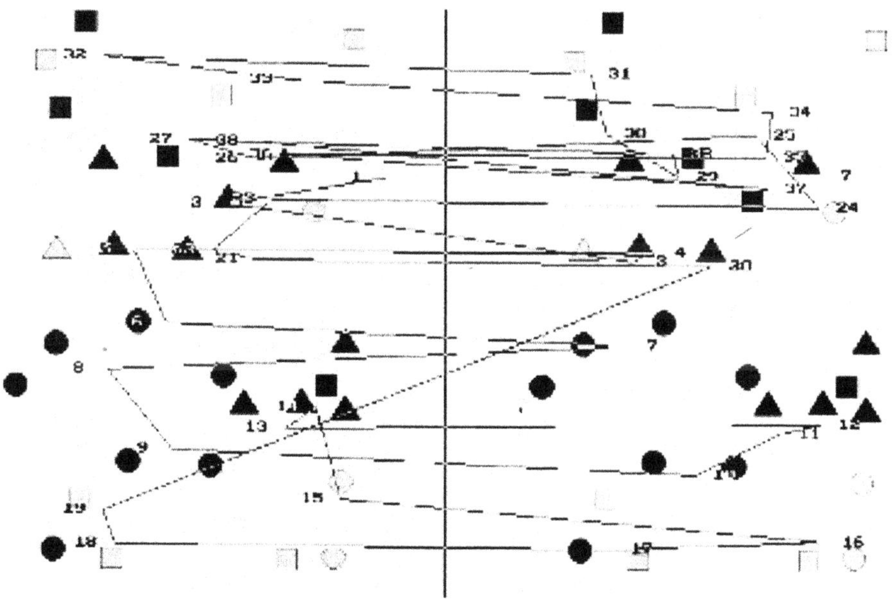

Figure 2: Typical pattern of saccadic eye movements in a search task

Eye movements in search tasks

A typical pattern of search saccades is shown in Figure 2 (Velichkovsky, Challis & Pomplun, 1995; Pomplun et al., 1997 submitted). The task was in detection of one single difference between left and right parts in the display of objects which varied in color and form. One can easily see the high amplitude saccades scanning the picture in the way that an immediate repetition of the visit to the same region is being blocked. There is a neurophysiological mechanism behind this variant of the "travelling salesmen problem" known as the IOR (Inhibition of return). It inhibits after a fixation (probably only in the search modus) all the saccades directed to this particular region of the space (Hoffmann, 1996).

The fixation time found in these experiments usually lies between 120 and 250 ms. The time may be longer in the vicinity of the critical elements of the display shortly before an answer. This probably demonstrates an interference from the higher levels because repeated fixations of the same region are possible in the final phase. From the point of view of possible applications, this all means that the diapason of fixation times immediately above the region of express saccades, until at least 250 ms, has to be regularly closed for a command initiation in gaze-mediated interfaces.

Levels of processing and fixation time

If a potential source of information is found it can be processed so-to-say to different "depths": either one remains "on the surface" of encoding of physical features or one tries to reconstruct semantic and personally relevant relations of the data as well. The actual level of processing is a function of the situation, the task and the user's skills and abilities. The investigation of the levels is a traditional chapter of cognitive studies, whereby one usually differentiates at least three levels, that of perceptual, semantic and self-referential processing (Challis, Velichkovsky & Craik, 1996, Velichkovsky 1994, Velichkovsky, Challis & Pomplun, 1995). There is recent evidence from investigation in our lab that eye movements correlate with the level of the encoding tasks. Figure 3 shows an example of material from some of these studies (Velichkovsky, Hillers & Sprenger, in preparation) that allows a control of levels of processing and the difficulty of perception.

A systematic effect observed in such levels of processing experiments is that in the case of perceptual encoding (i.e. encoding oriented to physical features of objects) there are relatively many fixations with duration between 120 and 250 ms. With a deeper encoding – semantic or self-referential – the number of fixations within the segment of 250-450 ms grows significantly. What do these data tell us? Obviously even after time of fixation of 250 ms there has to be some further internal information processing aimed at a reconstruction of semantics and personal relevance of the situation. Before this higher-order information is extracted it is simply too early to use the gaze position for communication. In what segment of fixation time are there traces of our communicative intentions?

Are there specific "communicative fixations"?

To take the gaze direction into account for communicative purpose is a natural human ability. Early in the development of the face-to-face interaction we learn to coordinate our attentional ressources with

Figure 3: Stimulus material from the levels of processing experiments (three grades of sensory reduction is shown)

those of other people, so that the state of "joint attention" becomes possible: we attend the same object at the same time as our partner and the problem of the high referential ambiguity of natural language disappears (Velichkovsky, Pomplun & Rieser, 1996). The lacking support for the "joint attention" states may be one of the reason for the ergonomic problems of electronic communication, especially in transmission of spatial and practical knowledge. In Figure 4 one can see the layout of one of our recent experiments aimed at investigation of these issues (Velichkovsky, 1995,).

The task consisted in a cooperative solution of a puzzle game. One of the two subjects was an expert, who solved the task many times before, the other – a novice, who saw the puzzle for the first time but should find a solution in practice. We registred verbal communication of the partner and their eye movements in the following three modes of communication:

- "Voice": expert and novice could communicate only by voice.
- "Voice and mouse": in addition to verbal remarks it was possible for the expert to show relevant parts of puzzle with the mouse.
- "Voice and gaze": in addition to verbal communication actual position of fixations (either of expert or of novice) were shown on the monitor of the partner.

For the present context the data on the eye movements of partners are of special interest. An explicit intention to support verbal instructions by the gaze leads to a significant rise of the proportion of

Figure 4: Experiments on the transfer of gaze direction data in cooperative problem solving

extremely long fixations – around 500 ms and more. There is also a negative correlation of the number of such fixations in experts and the puzzle solution time in novices. In other words, the long fixation can be indeed used as a source of information in a situation of an indirect communication with other people mediated by computer.

CONCLUSIONS AND TASKS FOR THE FUTURE

With respect to the questions formulated at the beginning of the paper these experiments give us a rather straightforward answer. Different segments of fixation time may have a different functional interpretation. In the order of tasks from the initial detection and search to a more "in-depth" processing leading to understanding of the information and its communication to partner in cooperative problem solving, there is a systematic increase in the duration of fixations. Particularly, in the case of communicative intentions one finds extremely long fixation of 500 ms and more. A simple visualization of the results is presented in Figure 5. Additional neurophysiological studies recently demonstrated that these changes in levels of processing also involve different brain mechanisms (Challis, Velichkovsky & Craik, 1996, Velichkovsky et al. 1996). This corresponds to the known data about hierarchical organisation of the control mechanisms of eye movements (Fischer & Weber, 1993).

The practical solution to the "Midas touch problem" is therefore to set up the temporal filter for the "gaze-mouse" applications on the values of 450-500 ms. The threshold seems to be of importance also for other reasons. In the course of verbal description of a scene (as well as in reading), eyes are often a little bit ahead of speech, so that there is a temporal gap between voice and eyes – Eye-voice span. The span is variable, but as a rule it is about 400-500 ms or less (Velichkovsky, Pomplun & Rieser, 1996). In other words, only when the gaze position will be explicated with a latency of about 500 ms, the intended focus of speech and the actual focus of visual attention will converge on the same object. Such a redundancy supports the verbal instructions and creates a context for the "joint attention" states.

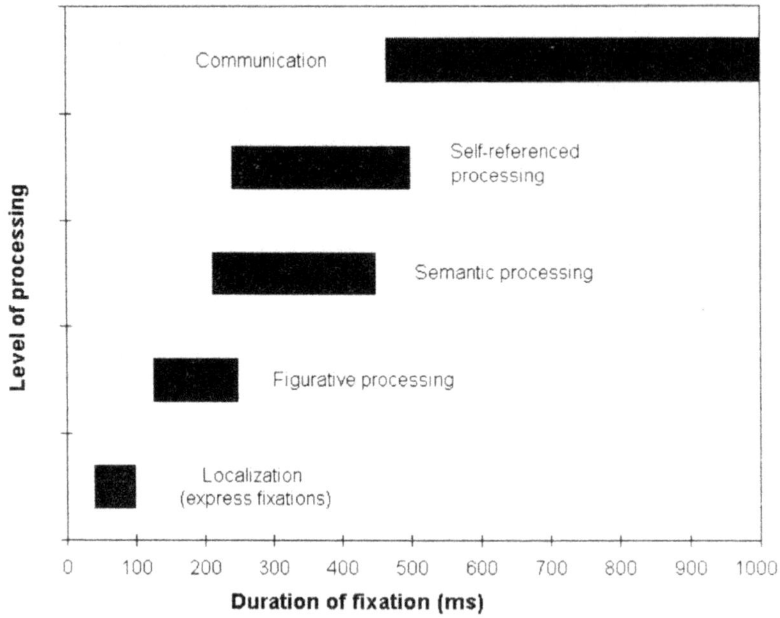

Figure 5: Fixation time as an indicator of the level of processing

There are further technological options of updating the "gaze-mouse" to a completely reliable communication tool. The "gaze-mouse" does not need a visual feedback in contrast to the usual, manually controlled computer mouse. However such a feedback (e.g. in the form of "eyecons" – a dynamic visualization of eye closing and initiating commands, if fixated during the time of more than 500 ms) seems to be helpful from the point of view of users (Hansen, Andersen & Roed, 1995, Velichkovsky & Hansen, 1996). A later development can be an eclectic combination of gaze direction, fixation time, pupil diameter and possibly blinking frequency as a measure of interest or different interpretation of the display recognized by an individually tuned neural network (Nielsen, 1993, Ritter, 1993, Velichkovsky & Hansen, 1996).

With this possibility we would bridge the gap between the traditional "gaze-mouse" story and the second, more advanced group of applications based on a continuous monitoring in distribution of attention. In this case it is the set of fixations over the time which defines the course of interaction with computer. A particularly interesting technique is the method of "attentional landscapes" illustrated by the Figure 6. Here two more traditional ways of representing the eye movement data (as fixation points (**a**) and as clusters of fixations (**b**)) are confronted with the "attentional landscape" - a more graded representation of the resolution of details based on the idea of an idealized fovea (as in (**c**)). The "attentional landscape" can be used as an image filter function (see Figure 6(**d**)) to reconstruct the subjective view of the initial picture, so-to-say "as seen by the user's cortical homunculus".

We were able to show in recent time that the use of attentional landscapes as a filter function for the gaze-contingent processing of visual displays does allow to adequately visualize the actual subjective perception, e.g., of ambiguous pictures (Pomplun, Ritter & Velichkovsky, 1996, Velichkovsky, Pomplun & Rieser, 1996). With the data summarized in the present paper we can in the future improve the interface design by visualizing of a "first look" of an interface or by reconstructing - in the form of images - the history of user's attempts to go beyond the information given, as in efforts to understand semantics of one or another

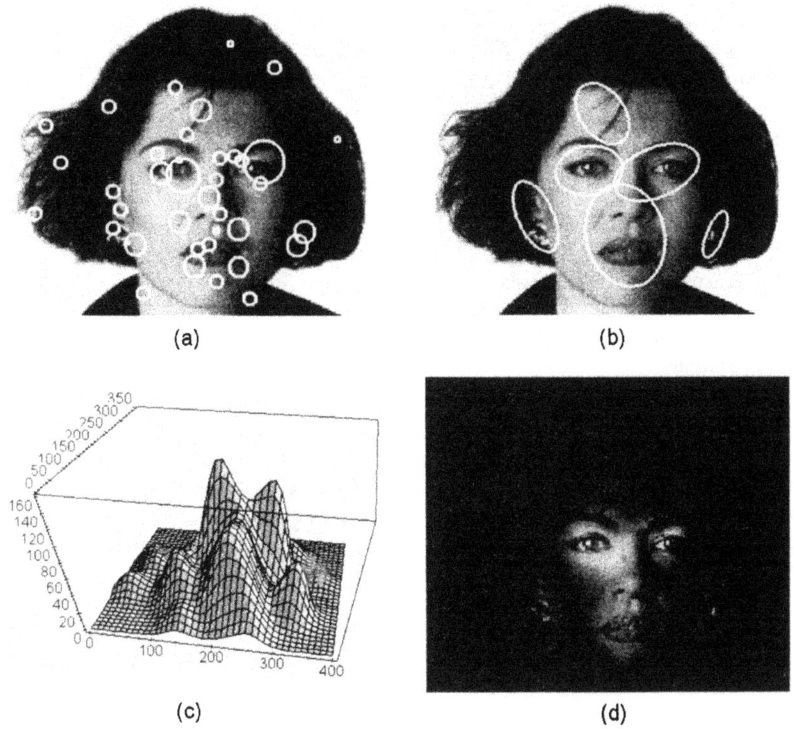

Figure 6: Different ways of representing eye movement data: (a) as points or circles, (b) as clusters, (c) as "attentional landscapes", (d) as subjective view of the picture (after Velichkovsky, Pomplun & Rieser, 1996))

element of the display. The knowledge about functional significance of different classes of eye movements is an indispensable step on the way to this goal, because the selection of eye movement parameters for gaze-mediated interaction has to be task-dependent. What we cannot say at present is how eyetracking may change the parameters of human eye movements. According to some reports (Cleveland & Cleveland, 1996) a systematic use of "gaze-mouse" devices permanently improves user's performance, so that even thresholds as low as 250 ms can be finally managed. Perhaps our eyes can in a sense repeat the evolution of the hand – to an instrument of new, specifically human skills shaped by the development of technology.

ACKNOWLEDGMENTS

We appreciate support of our colleagues and co-workers in Dresden, Bielefeld and Toronto. Thanks are also due to Nancy and Dixon Cleveland (LC Technologies, Inc., Fairfax, VA) for their data on trainability of human oculomotor system.

REFERENCES

Baluja S. and Pomerleau D.(1994). Non-intrusive gaze-tracking using artificial neural networks. In: *Neural information processing systems, Vol. 6*, New York: Morgan Kaufman Publishers.

Challis, B.H., Velichkovsky, B.M. and Craik, F.I.M. (1996). Levels-of-processing effects on a variety of memory tasks: New findings and theoretical implications. *Consciousness & Cognition, 5*, 63-89.

Cleveland, D. and Cleveland, N. (1996 September) Personal communication.

Deacon, T. W. (1996). Prefrontal cortex and symbolic learning. In B.M.Velichkovsky and D.M.Rumbaugh (Eds.), *Communicating meaning*. Mahwah, NJ: Lawrence Erlbaum Associates.

Engell-Nielsen, T., Glenstrup, A.J. and Hansen, J.P (1997 in press). Eye-gaze interaction: A new media – not just a fast mouse. *International Journal of Human-Computer Interaction Studies*,

Fischer, B. and Weber, H. (1993). Express saccades and visual attention. *Behavioral and Brain Sciences, 16*, 553-610.

Hansen, J.P., Andersen, A.W. and Roed, P. (1995). Eye-gaze control of multimedia systems. In Y.Anzai, K.Ogawa and H.Mori (Eds), *Symbiosis of human and artifact*. Amsterdam: Elsevier Science Publisher.

Helmholtz, H.v. (1896). *Handbuch der physiologischen Optik, 3d edition*. Hamburg und Leipzig: L.Voss.

Hering, E. (1977). *The theory of binocular vision*. New York: Plenum Press [first German edition, 1868].

Hoffmann, J.E. (1996).Visual attention and eye movements. In H.Pashler (Ed.), *Attention*. London: University College London Press.

Jacob, R.J.K. (1995). Eye tracking in advanced interface design. In W.Barfield and T.Furness (Eds.), *Advanced interface design and virtual environments*. New York: Oxford University Press.

Joch, A. (1996). What pupils teach computers. *Byte, 21*, 99-102.

Nielsen, J. (1993). Noncommand user interfaces. *Communications of the ACM, 36(4)*, 83-99.

Pomplun, M., Ritter, H. and Velichkovsky, B.M. (1996). Disambiguating complex visual information: Towards communication of personal views of a scene. *Perception, 25(8)*, 931-948.

Pomplun, M., Velichkovsky, B.M. and Ritter, H. (1994). An artificial neural network for high precision eye movement tracking. In B.Nebel & L.Drescher-Fischer (Eds.), *Lectures notes in artificial intelligence*. Springer Verlag, Berlin.

Pomplun, M. et al. (1997 submitted). Comparative visual search. *Journal of Experimental Psychology: Human Perception & Performance*.

Raeithel, A. and Velichkovsky, B.M. (1995). Joint attention and co-construction of tasks. B.Nardi (Ed.), *Context and consciousness: Activity theory and human-computer interaction*. Cambridge MA: MIT Press.

Ritter, H. (1993). Parametrized self-organizing maps. In S.Gielen and B.Kappen (Eds.), *ICANN93-Proceedings*, Berlin: Springer.

Stampe, D.M. and Reingold, E. (1994). Eye movement as a response modality in psychological research. In *Proceedings of' the 7th European conference on eye movements*, Durham, University of Durham,.

Starker, I. and Bolt, R. A. (1990). A gaze-responsive self-disclosing display. In *CHI 90 Proceedings*. New York: ACM Press.

Velichkovsky, B.M. (1994). The levels endeavour in psychology and cognitive science. In P.Bertelson, P.Eelen and G.d'Ydewalle (Eds.), *International perspectives on psychological sciences: Leading themes*. Howe UK: Lawrence Erlbaum Associates.

Velichkovsky, B.M. (1995). Communicating attention: Gaze position transfer in cooperative problem solving. *Pragmatics and Cognition, 3*, 199-222. 23.

Velichkovsky, B.M., Challis, B.H. & Pomplun, M. (1995). Working memory and work with memory. *Zeitschrift für experimentelle Psychologie, 42*, 672-701.

Velichkovsky, B.M. and Hansen, J.P. (1996). New technological windows into mind. In: *CHI 96 Proceedings: Human factors in computing systems*. New York: ACM Press.

Velichkovsky, B.M., Hillers, R. and Sprenger, A. (1996 in preparation). Encoding, eye movements and memory performance in the processing of non-verbal information.

Velichkovsky, B.M., Pomplun, M. and Rieser, H. (1996). Attention and communication. In W.H.Zangemeister et al. (Eds.), *Visual attention and cognition*. Amsterdam: Elsevier Science Publisher.

Velichkovsky, B.M. et al. (1996). Evoked coherences of EEG: Communication of brain regions and levels of processing. *Zeitschrift für Elektroenzephalographie, Elektromyographie und verwandte Gebiete, 27*, 111-118.

Tree Structure Operation for Video Editing Utilizing Image Recognition Technology

Hirotada Ueda
Research & Development laboratory,
Hitachi Denshi, Ltd.
32 Miyuki-cho, Kodaira,
Tokyo 187, Japan
hiro-u@po.iijnet.or.jp

Takafumi Miyatake
Central Research Laboratory,
Hitachi, Ltd.
1-280 Higashi-koigakubo, Kokubunji,
Tokyo 185, Japan
miyatake@crl.hitachi.co.jp

ABSTRACT This paper proposes an approach to integrate image recognition technology into nonlinear video editing system and discusses the results of a prototype development. The prototype consists of five support functions for video editing; automatic scene separation during disk recording, tree structure story editing, quick review with micon, film metaphor interface and integrated information management. The automatic scene separation is the exact solution for the complaint of the current system users. The tree structure story editing and the integrated information management provide methods to author video structure in several different detail levels and relieves the constrain of limited size of the window. The quick review with micon is a convenient shot comparison method. The film metaphor interface offers a intuitive and speedy operation for video strings.

Keywords video editing, video structure, film metaphor, scene separation, image recognition

1. INTRODUCTION

Multimedia technology is a rapidly growing one. One of the typical applications is a nonlinear video system. In the nonlinear video system hard disk recording technology offers a quick and random access capability to handle video contents. This fact removes loss time of tape winding a lot. Computer technology also offers good GUIs (Graphical User Interface).

Another feature of a nonlinear video system is the capability of combine different type of information in a integrated manner [1]. Keywords and annotations and so on are easily attached and managed in a efficient way. These are grate advantage when comparing with previous tape oriented editing systems. However, in current nonlinear video systems, computers seem to be used only as controllers for the hard disk devices or as generators for GUIs. We do not yet use full computing power of data processing effectively in this field. Consequently video handling is still time consuming work and needs trained operators.

Recently an approach combining image recognition technology with multimedia technology is getting popular [2]. There are two application types in this approach: editing [3] [4] and archives [5] [6] [7] [8]. In these applications temporal-spacial video contents structure is automatically analyzed and the results are used to help users handle video contents. Functions utilized image recognition technology offer descriptions of scene separations, motion of the camera and filmed objects, tracks and

Human–Computer Interaction: INTERACT'97 S. Howard, J. Hammond & G. Lindgaard (editors)
Published by Chapman & Hall

contour lines of objects, existence of objects, periods of existence and automatic linking of identical objects.

There are many good research results. However there are few real products. Are those not so attractive nor usable for users? One of the reason is the fact that integration of those functions has not been sufficient. In this paper we propose new design concepts to integrate those and utilize full computing power for the nonlinear video editing. We also show the results of our prototype system.

2. DESIGN CONCEPTS

Through the discussion with the users of current nonlinear editing system, we found that they have a common complaint. That is a manual scene cutting process as a preparation for the nonlinear icon based editing. Even after the long waiting time for digital copy recording, they cannot start editing yet. They first have to carefully watch the contents and choose the point to cut scenes.

Another users request for more effective video editing is a method that can show the total video structure in several levels of detail seamlessly.

Because of the similarity with film based editing, where they can really directly move a shot very quickly, users who are familiar to the computer like the icon based editing very much. However motion picture oriented users complain that such a operation is a directly imported one from the computer world.

Users also require a good method to manage informations that are generated in the video editing process from shooting, editing to the end of archiving stage. Huge amount of informations are generated. Typical examples are dates, still pictures, written/voice memos, contract conditions, copy rights information and so on. They are valuable but cannot be stored with the video in current systems.

To relief these users inconveniences, we developed following five new functions:

- Automatic scene separation during disk recording
- Tree structure story editing
- Quick simultaneous shots review
- Film metaphor interface
- Integrated multimedia information management

We had developed the automatic scene separation technology in 1990[2]. At that moment the power of workstation is not sufficient and we could just do non-real-time scene separation and hard disk recording separately. However now we have more CPU power even with a smallest (cheapest) workstation. We also found that some workstation has multiple video data paths that can be used to achieve real-time scene separation during compression recording. This is a main issue to answer the above users complaint. This feature removes time consuming manual separation process and user can immediately start editing after the hard disk recording.

Our solution for a effective video editing is the tree structure story editing. We employ the combination of the tree structure and links between objects. Figure 1 shows this structure. Here the scenario is an entire story composed of a number of scenes. Each scene consists of one

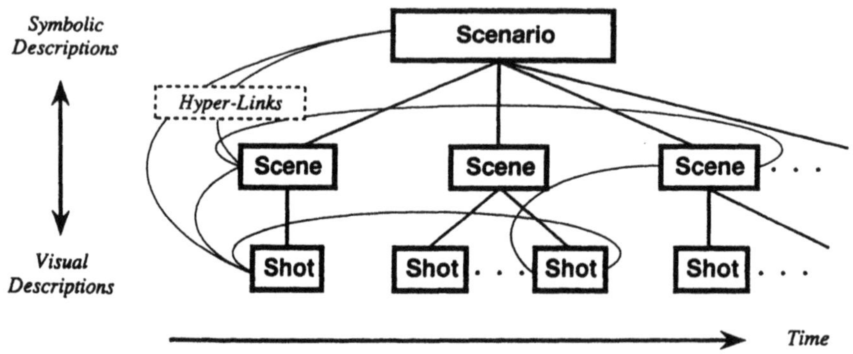

Figure 1. Tree Structure of Video

or more shots. Scenes may have sub-scenes. In this tree structure, the upper parts have symbolic descriptions and the lower parts have more visual descriptions. The lowest parts (i.e., shots) of this structure contain raw video data. According to this scheme we designed a new GUI that enables the user to easily understand the video structure and to edit story through this visual structure. Using this tree structure the user can handle video contents in any size of blocks like chapters, sections, paragraphs and words in a book.

One important idea of this design is a capability to partly hide this structure. For instance, when some scene is already edited enough, the user hides the lower part of this scene and can concentrate upon the rest of the story. This technique offers a efficient use of the limited computer screen size.

We also add a convenient method to check the contents of each shot. We borrow the idea of micon (moving icon) from Davenport group [9]. Using this technique the user can view the miniature size play back of multiple shots simultaneously. This method gives the user, for example, a capability of quick comparison of shots to select the best one.

We introduced the film metaphor interface in the special effect operation. Most TV station people said, this operation, utilizing simple thumbnail and time line editing window, was one of the inconvenient part of current systems.

To achieve the integrated multimedia information management we found that the tree structure for editing story is good to store these informations on it. Any information could be attached to the objects on the arbitrary level of the tree depending on its nature.

3. PROTOTYPE

3.1 Hardware

Hardware specification of our prototype system is the followings:

- Low cost off the shelf workstation
  (SGI INDY with Indy Video)
- Motion JPEG compression board
  (SGI Cosmo Compress).

To achieve the simultaneous operation of automatic scene separation and compression recording, we assign two video capturing paths; VINO (originaly equipped) and Indy Video (optional one). Using the VINO video path we get a miniaturized image of each frame and compare a pair of these images frame by frame to detect scene change points. When a scene change point is detected, the system records the time code of this frame. At the same time all miniaturized images are stored into the hard disk. These images are used for the micon play back. The video data given through the Indy Video path is feed into the Cosmo Compress and compressed video is recorded into the hard disk.

3.2 Software

The size of the software of our prototype system is about 90K steps. The language is C. Operating system IRIX and control software for SGI hardware are the normal one came with the hardware. Therefore this software is easily transported to the SGI family systems.

3.3 Functions

Our prototype application program is a nonlinear video editing system that has five new functions. Figure 2 shows a typical screen image of the system.

Automatic scene separation

There is no special operation for the Automatic scene separation. When the user set up the video source and start the hard disk recording in the same manner as current systems, our system automatically start the Automatic scene separation. This process runs simultaneously with the digital compression and hard disk recording process. During the recording a monitor window opens in the center of the screen.

Tree structure story editing

The lower window in Figure 2 is a pool of shots. After the digital recording process, automatically separated shots are visually listed in this window. Each micon is displayed as a box with a depth which indicates the time length of the shot as shown in Figure 2. This representation compactly visualizes the temporal structure of the video. Then the user chooses appropriate shots and drugs them into upper window.

The upper window is an editing area. Here we introduced the tree structure story editing. The user connects several shots into a block as shown in Figure 2. This operation makes a pert of the tree. When shots are

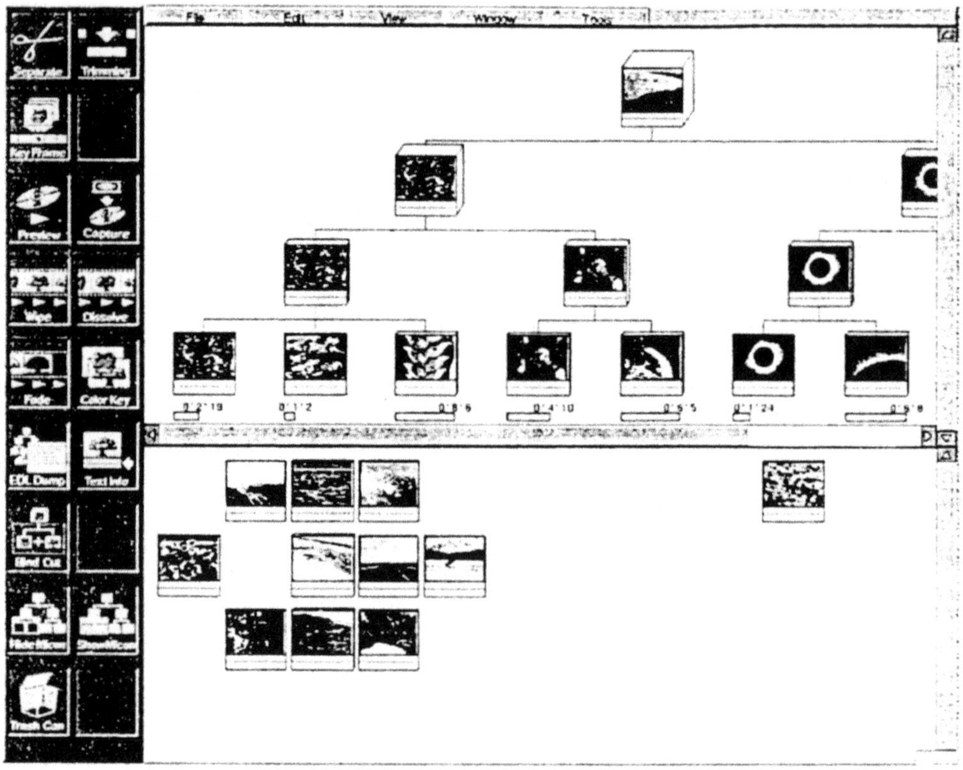

Figure 2. A screen of the prototype system

connected a new higher layer micon is generated. The user repeat such steps and create whole tree structure. This structure corresponds to the one shown in Figure 1. Time axis is left to right and logical abstraction level is bottom to top.

Raw video data (shot) is located at the lowest level of the tree. The user can attach annotations to any level of icons using the dialogue windows. The abstraction level of these annotation might differ according to the height of the tree structure. All micons has a thumbnail image of the first frame of the shot or the group of the shots by default setting. The user can change this with any frames within the duration of the shot or the group of the shots.

While editing, the user moves shots one by one along the time axis as a usual editing system. The user also can move a block of shots with a single action by picking the upper level icon of the tree. Using this function the user, for

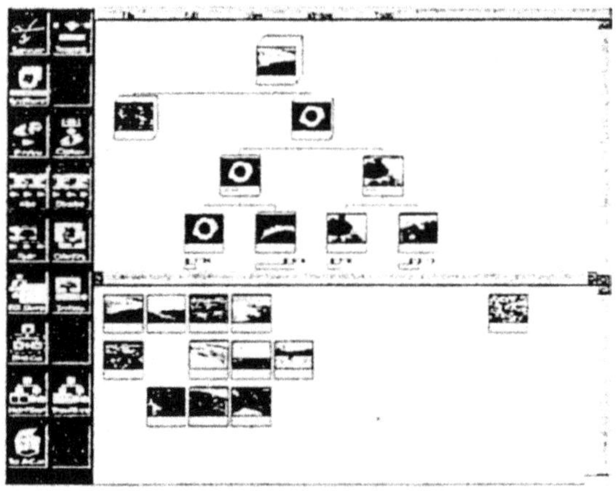

Figure 3. A screen of the hidden tree

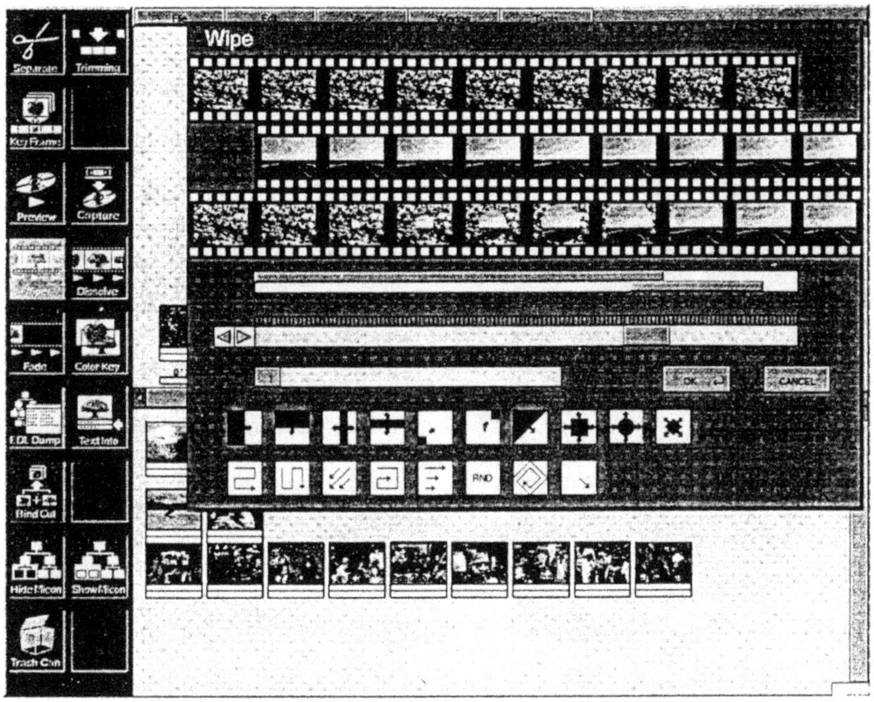

Figure 4. A screen of the special effect operation

instance, can easily change the order a scene consists of flower shots and a scene of mountain shots. In both cases, when a icon moved to any place at the same level of the tree the order of the block is changed.

When the user think that some block is well constructed and want to concentrate in the rest of the story, the user select the top icon of that block and hide the lower part of the block. This situation is shown in Figure 3. The block at the left side in Figure 2 is hidden and a right side block (those are out of the window and not visible in Figure 2) comes into the window in Figure 3. Thus the user overcomes the problem of the limited area of the window.

Quick simultaneous shots review

Shots are presented as micons so that the user can play back arbitrary numbers of them simultaneously in any time without the operation to open monitor windows. Therefore the user can check the content within a structure at a glance.

The size of a miniaturized video frame is only 80x60 pixels (15K byte) instead of 640x480 of a full frame. This size is fairly less than a compressed frame (around 100K byte). Father more miniaturized video frames does not require decompression that cause some overhead to fill the buffer memory etc. In fact the play back of micon is immediate but play back of compressed video has 0.5 to 1 seconds idle time after the users button operation in our prototype. Micon play back is very light process for the computer and we can play even ten or more micons simultaneously. This is a big benefit for the user when the user compare multiple similar shots.

Film metaphor interface

The miniaturized video frames also offer a good function for the user interface of special effect operations. Figure 4 shows an example. This is a situation when the user does a wipe effect. A wipe operation window is opened in the center of the screen. Here the upper film metaphor shows

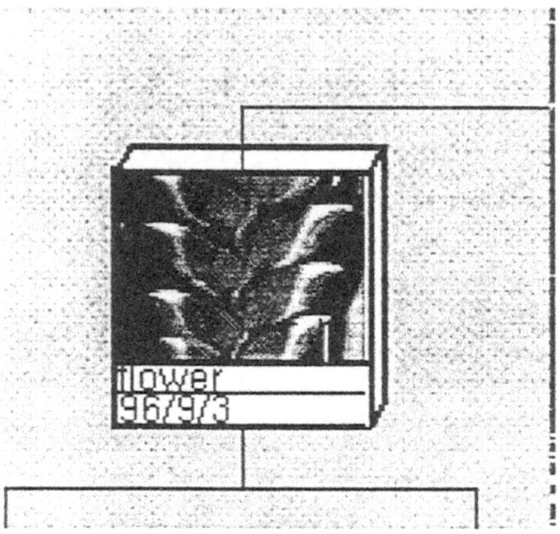

Figure 5. A close up of the micon with annotation

an A-roll video shot, the middle shows a B-roll shot and the lower film metaphor shows a result of a wipe effect. The set of scroll bars under the film metaphors controls the overlap amount of A and B-roll. The simple scroll bar below them controls the viewing position. Using the lowest slider the time resolution can be changed by the correspondence between one film flame and the number of the video flames.

As the size of miniaturized frames is fairly small, regeneration of result film metaphor according the change of the effect pattern is immediate. When we generate it using compressed video it requires about three times of a real time before showing the special effect result. The operation of the overlap amount is also as smooth and intuitive as real film handling.

Integrated multimedia information management

We provide a dialog box for each nodes of the tree structure. Thorough the dialog box the user can attach any information to the appropriate nodes. Any kind of multimedia information can be linked to any nodes using this dialog box. Therefore the user can manage all information related to the video in a layered structure very easily. Some portion of the information selected by the user (e.g. date, the title of the section of the story etc.) can be shown in the lower part of the micon as shown in Figure 5.

4. DISCUSSION

Through the evaluation of earlier version of our prototype that has not the simultaneous scene separation nor the tree structure story editing [3], we found that visual listing of video structure is efficient support for video editors. Conventional video editing system requires numerous repetitions of fast-forward and rewind operations until an overview of the structure, as shown in the components window of Figure 3, is firmly fixed in the user's mind; this is very time consuming. Image recognition technology removes this time-consuming step in video editing.

To answer the further users request we realized a simultaneous scene separation during the hard disk recording. Professional users are very much sensitive to the accuracy of separation point (a frame rate accuracy is required). If processing time is not quick enough, the system cannot catch the accurate timing of the scene change. So we have to perform frame by frame image comparison in every 33 msec. We had to try many fine tuning of our program to achieve this functionality. Finally we found that this program uses almost full computing power and data transfer capability of the newest workstation (that is the lowest cost one though). The recognition accuracy is also important issue. The total error rate of our scene separation is less than 1%.

Miniaturized video frames are valuable to improve the system performance. Their data size are fairly small and do not use complicated compression. Consequently they do not require heavy process. However they efficiently offer intuitive visual interface such as the special effect operation interface and the film metaphor interface.

We have just finished our prototype and we did not have field evaluations yet. However when we show the demo, almost all users of current nonlinear editing system say that the simultaneous scene separation is really valuable. They also say the tree structure story editing with the hidden lower structure and the integrated multimedia information management attached to this tree structure may fit in drama and documentary video editing well.

As described earlier we developed our prototype on the standard hardware and system software. So it is easily transported to the any SGI family systems. One exception is the simultaneous automatic scene separation. If the system does not have dual video paths, this is not possible. Further if the control software for the video paths given by the hardware vender is not API compatible, some part of our program needs modification. In fact we now has two versions, one for INDY and the other for Indogo2. But the Indigo2 version does not have the simultaneous automatic scene separation capability because we could not find the way to open two video paths in parallel.

Through the experience of this development we strongly request more powerful standard multimedia data paths in the workstation (also PC) as well as the power of the CPU. When we get more powerful data paths and CPU we can produce more intelligent functions that work simultaneously to analyze video contents in various point of view. Then we can create more usable nonlinear video systems.

5. CONCLUSION

We proposed a new approach to design a nonlinear video editing system. It consists of five funtions; Automatic scene separation during disk recording, Tree structure story editing, Quick simultaneous shots review, Film metaphor interface and Integrated multimedia information management. According these concepts we have developed a prototype. The automatic scene separation is the exact solution for the complaint of the current system users. This was the most difficult one and we use almost full computing power and data transfer capability of the newest workstation. The tree structure story editing provides a convenient method to edit video structure in several different detail levels. It also offers a way to change the order of a group of shots quickly. The hidden lower structure technique also relieves the constrain of limited size of the window. The quick review with micon gives the user a convenient shot comparison method. Miniaturized video frames also achieves a speedy and intuitive interface for the special effect operation. The integrated multimedia information management method utilizing the tree structure is powerful tool to maintain informations generated through out the video creating procces.

5. REFERENCES

[1] Davenport, G., Aguierre-Smith, T. and Pincever, N. "Cinematic primitives for multimedia," IEEE Computer Graphics and Applications, 11(4), pp. 67-75, (1991).

[2] Ueda, H., Miyatake, T. and Yoshizawa, S. "IMPACT: An Interactive Natural-Motion-Picture Dedicated Multimedia Authoring System," ACM CHI'91; pp. 343-350 (1991).

[3] Ueda, H., Miyatake, T., Sumino, S. and Nagasaka, A. "Automatic Structure Visualization for Video Editing," ACM INTERCHI'93, pp. 137-141 (1993).

[4] Mackay, E. W. and Davenport, G. "Virtual Video Editing in Interactive Multimedia Applications," Communications of the ACM, 32(7), pp. 802-810 (July 1989).

[5] Nagasaka, A., and Tanaka, Y. "Automatic Video Indexing and Full-Video Search for Object Appearances," IFIP WG 2.6 2nd Working Conference on Visual Database Systems, pp. 119-133 (1991).

[6] Zhang, H. J., Low, C. Y., Smoliar, S. W. and Wu, J. H. "Video Parsing, Retrieval and Browsing: An Integrated and Content-Based Solution," ACM Multimedia'95, pp. 15-24 (1995).

[7] Taniguchi, Y., Akutsu, A., Tonomura, Y., and Hamada, H. "An Intuitive and Effisient Access Interface to Real-Time Incoming Video Based on Automatic Indexing," ACM Multimedia'95, pp. 25-33 (1995).

[8] Smith, M. A., Christel, M. G. "Automating the Creation of a Digital Video Library," ACM Multimedia'95, pp. 357-358 (1995).

[9] Brendmo, H. P. and Davenport, G. "Creating and viewing the elastic Chrals - a hypermedia jarnal," Hypertext, State of the art. McAlesse, R. and Greene, C. (eds.), Intellect Ltd. (1990).

Improving Access to a Digital Video Library

Michael G. Christel	David B. Winkler	C. Roy Taylor
HCI Institute and Software Engineering Inst. Carnegie Mellon University Pittsburgh, PA 15213 USA mac@sei.cmu.edu	Department of Computer Science Carnegie Mellon Univ. Pittsburgh, PA 15213 dwinkler@cs.cmu.edu	Department of Computer Science Carnegie Mellon Univ. Pittsburgh, PA 15213 crt@cs.cmu.edu

ABSTRACT Quick access to short, relevant video segments enables efficient use of a digital video library. This study evaluated an interface designed for such access, an interface that allows the user to browse a set of segments generated by a search query. Subjects' performance and attitudes were measured while they performed a fact-finding task to determine the relative effectiveness of three presentations: a text list, naively chosen visual imagery, and query-based visual imagery. Results show little difference in performance and subjective satisfaction between text lists and naively chosen imagery, but significant improvements when the images that represent video segments are based on the query that returned the segments (query-based poster frames). This result applies to the organization and representation of information in digital video libraries.

KEYWORDS multimedia, display design, evaluation, digital video library, video abstraction

1. INTRODUCTION

The near future will see a massive conversion of information into digital formats, a recasting of "The Information Age" as "The Digital Information Age" in which users can access almost any tidbit of data via the network — from anywhere, at any time. The resulting information will overwhelm users unless they are armed with powerful browsing and filtering support.

Digital information will include full-motion video as well as the text and single-image media found on today's Web. As digital video libraries emerge, users will need tools that handle effectively the dynamic nature of video; they will not likely invest hundreds of hours to find a single, relevant segment within a 1000-hour library. Thus future digital video libraries must support *content*-based indexing and retrieval of brief video segments (Brown, 1995; Taniguchi, 1995; Wactlar, 1996).

Carnegie Mellon University's Informedia Project plans to field a 1000-hour digital video library by 1998. An initial, 45-hour library that supports content-based searching was segmented into 1600 "video clips," typically 1 to 2 minutes in length, and field-tested during the spring of 1996. Image processing, speech recognition, and natural language processing techniques were collectively applied to the video data for content extraction and temporal segmentation (Hauptmann, 1997; Smith, 1996).

1.1. Video abstraction

The Informedia digital video library provides users with alternate representations, *video abstractions,* of library materials. Users can cheaply (in terms of access, transfer, and viewing times) review a video abstraction

Human–Computer Interaction: INTERACT'97 S. Howard, J. Hammond & G. Lindgaard (editors)
Published by Chapman & Hall

before deciding to incur the cost of accessing richer information layers or a complete video clip. Video abstractions used in the Informedia library include:

- Poster frame: a single "thumbnail" image representing a video clip and computed by selecting one frame from the clip and reducing it to a quarter of its original resolution, so that several representative images can be displayed simultaneously (as shown in Figures 1 and 2).
- Filmstrip: a set of images extracted from a video clip and displayed in chronological order, as shown in Figure 3. Such filmstrips have been used since the advent of digital video (Mills, 1992) and remain popular today (Taniguchi, 1995; Zhang, 1995).
- Skim: a compact representation that summarizes the original clip by concatenating its significant subsets of video and audio data.

This paper examines the impact of video abstractions, specifically poster frames, on digital video library use for a well-defined information retrieval task.

1.2. Construction of poster frames

Each library clip can be decomposed into *camera shots*, which are sets of "contiguous frames representing a continuous action in time or space" (Zhang, 1995). Informedia researchers have developed an algorithm that identifies, for each camera shot, a *shot frame*, the individual frame that best represents the whole shot (Smith, 1996). By default the algorithm chooses the shot's middle frame. If camera motion is detected and that motion stops within the shot, then the frame where the camera motion ends is selected. Other image processing techniques, such as those that detect and avoid low-intensity images, further refine the selection process. Thus a library clip consists of a sequence of shots and can be represented compactly by a sequence of shot frames.

Psychological research suggests that poster frames, when accompanied by text titles, allow a user to identify a video clip more quickly and accurately than do access mechanisms that present information as text only. According to theories of brain function localization and parallel cognitive processing (Guastello, 1989; Benbasat, 1993), information presented in text and pictorial form together will be processed faster than a purely textual display. Recognition may also be faster for pictures than for text (Egido, 1988; Benbasat, 1993).

However, empirical studies have not confirmed definitive advantages for iconic and pictorial representations. Specifically, studies of browsing and database navigation have found little or no performance differences between pictures and text (Egido, 1988; Benbasat, 1993). These authors conjecture that the novelty and visual appeal of pictures may slow users and offset any inherent, low-level processing advantages hypothesized for pictorial representations.

This lack of significant results may also derive from the sparse attention paid to *which* pictures an interface uses. Our study compared poster frames to text lists for a fact-finding task. We also examined implications of *how* the visual images are selected, that is, which shot frames serve as poster frames.

2. EXPERIMENT

2.1. Subjects

Thirty participants were recruited from Carnegie Mellon University students and Pennsylvania Governor's School for the Sciences high school scholarship students during the summer of 1996. Each student received $5 for participating in this study.

Subjects were asked in an online questionnaire to rate certain experiences of the prior two weeks and six months. All subjects reported comparable experience with digital information services and little prior experience with digital video. Subjects were then randomly assigned to one of six treatment order permutations, as shown in Table 1.

2.2. Materials

Subjects participated in the study individually. Each used a computer with a 17-inch color monitor, headphones, and hardware support for smooth, full-motion video playback.

	Question Set 1	Set 2	Set 3
5 subjects	Treatment 1 (T1)	T2	T3
5 subjects	Treatment 2 (T2)	T1	T3
5 subjects	Treatment 3 (T3)	T1	T2
5 subjects	T1	T3	T2
5 subjects	T2	T3	T1
5 subjects	T3	T2	T1

Table 1. Experimental design (four questions per question set)

The library for this study contained 45 hours of video from three Public Television series: "The Infinite Voyage," "Planet Earth," and "Space Age." These videos were manually segmented into 1600 clips (average length 1.7 minutes), that served as the elemental units for indexing the library. Each clip was identified with a unique seven-character text string.

Descriptive titles for each clip were added manually and speech recognition aligned each clip's text transcript with its video information (Hauptmann, 1997). This data was checked and corrected for accuracy, and the library was successfully field-tested at a local K-12 school in the spring of 1996.

To simplify the subjects' tasks, our experiment severely restricted access to the library. While recognizing the pedagogical importance of student-initiated questions (Wallace, 1996), this study focused on the effects of different displays of query results rather than on strategies for formulating questions and search-queries.

Following a careful analysis of the library material, we composed three question sets: "The Reign of the Dinosaurs", "Early Humans", and "Life Cycles of All Things." Pilot testing trimmed each set to four questions that:

- Were nontrivial and potentially interesting to our subjects
- Were answered completely by at least one video clip in the library
- Could be naturally rephrased into queries that return at least 12 clips from the library (the best 12 clips were presented in the study)

Each subject answered the same 12 questions (3 sets of 4) by examining the results of preformulated queries. The result set always contained 12 clips, as shown in Figure 1. An answer key was generated independently by other Informedia Project members. A clip in the result set was given a score of 100 if it completely answered the question, 50 if it partially answered the question, and 0 if judged not relevant.

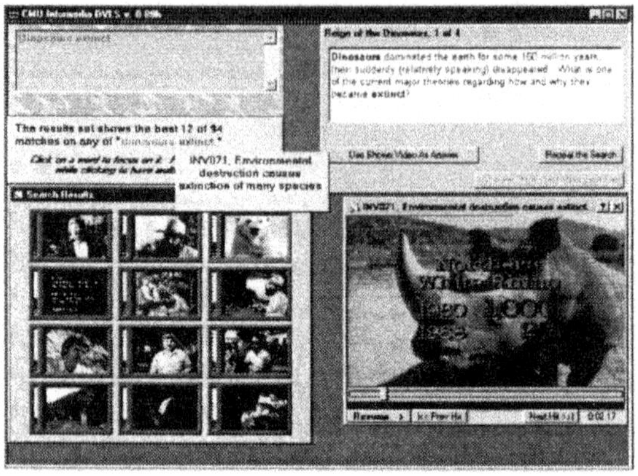

Figure 1. Screen shot (12-item result set at lower left)

2.3. Design

The experiment varied how video clips matching a given query were displayed in a result set: conventional text, naively chosen poster frames, and query-based poster frames. For the query illustrated in Figure 1, Figure 2 shows these three treatments. The result set was always the same size and always located at the lower left of the screen. In each treatment, moving the mouse over a result item displayed the full title text for that result item in a separate window. For example, Figure 1 shows the title window for the "polar bear" result, beginning with "INVO71."

For the text treatment, T1, each clip in the result set was represented by one line of text containing a unique ID and as many characters of its title as fit into the displayed result set area. Similar result set displays have been used by others (Brown, 1995; Hearst, 1995). A numeric query relevance score was also shown with each result line, with each result set containing 12 lines of text.

For poster frame treatments T2 and T3, the result set consisted of a 4 X 3 array of poster frames, one for each result. Within the border around each poster frame, a thermometer graphically indicated the query relevance score.

[1.00]	INV0641	The Great Dinosaur Hunt in Paris, Gould consid
[0.47]	INV0638	Nanotyrannus resembles Troodon, and many livi
[0.30]	INV071	Environmental destruction causes extinction of
[0.30]	INV061	The study of dinosaurs has been dynamic over
[0.24]	INV069	Paleontologists recreate and display the creatu
[0.21]	INV0637	The nanotyrannus was similar to the Tyrannosa
[0.20]	INV0629	Today scavengers at flood sites are birds, maki
[0.20]	INV066	In the 18th century, extinction was a controver
[0.17]	INV0636	One can find new species and ideas on the she
[0.17]	PLE0436	A new theory links the extinction of dinosaurs t
[0.16]	PLE0444	The existence of Nemesis may illuminate human
[0.14]	INV0642	Dinosaurs roamed the earth for far longer than

Treatment T1: Text list

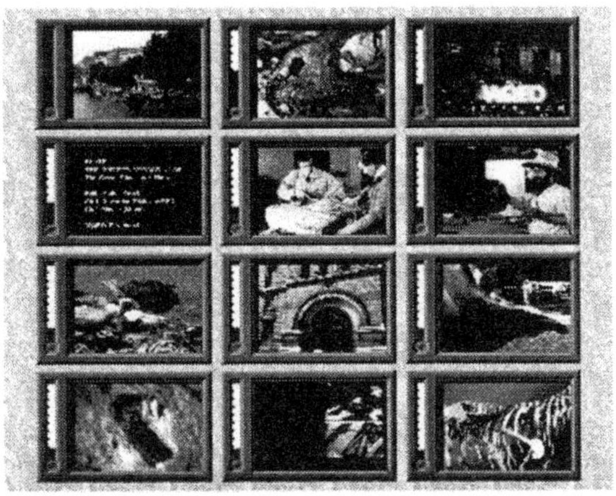

Treatment T2: Opening shot poster frames

Treatment T3: Query-based poster frames

Figure 2. Results set shown in different treatments

For both treatments T2 and T3, the poster frames were computed automatically rather than manually selected. Treatment T2 used the shot frame for the first shot in the clip to represent that clip. Treatment T3 used a query-based poster frame for a clip based on the clip's set of shot frames, the time-aligned transcript, and the query text:

1. Every clip in the digital video library has a sequence of shots, each represented by a shot frame (Smith, 1996), and a transcript that is tightly aligned with the clip's video times (Hauptmann, 1997).
2. For a given query in the experiment, there are 12 clips in the result set. For each clip, words in its transcript that match the query are identified. These words each have an associated video time and a strength of match (score).
3. Each scoring time is then mapped to a single shot, and contributes to the query-matching score for that shot.
4. The shot frame for the highest scoring shot is selected as the representative image, i.e., poster frame, in the result set presentation.

This algorithm is outlined graphically in Figure 3.

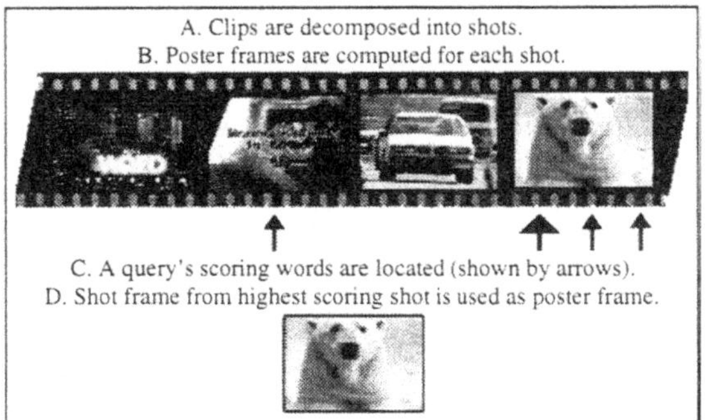

Figure 3. Treatment 3 (T3) poster frame algorithm

To counteract any inter-subject variability, a within-subjects design was chosen for the experiment. Each subject experienced each treatment. All sequences of the three treatments were used to address carry-over effects, with five subjects randomly assigned to each of the six permutations of treatment order.

The dependent variables in this experiment were the grades received for each question set, the time spent to answer each question set, and the subjective satisfaction with the interface used for that question set. The question sets were presented in the same order to every subject. With 30 subjects, any given question set for a given treatment was seen by 10 subjects (see Table 1).

2.4. Procedure

Each subject received the same online multimedia tutorial which discussed the use of the digital library system to accomplish fact-finding tasks. Subjects answered online questionnaires concerning their backgrounds. They subsequently received instructions on the screen informing them that they would be presented with three sets of four questions each, which should be answered as quickly yet accurately as possible.

Text on the screen introduced the topic of "The Reign of the Dinosaurs." Then the first question in this set was displayed, along with the text for a related query and 12 results for that particular query (see Figure 1). The result set presentation was one of T1, T2, or T3.

The subject browsed this result set and selected video clips to open and play until satisfied that a particular result clip was the answer to the given question. After confirming the choice, the subject was presented with the next question in the set. After all four questions in a set were answered, the subject filled in an online questionnaire concerning that set.

This procedure was then repeated two more times, for the "Early Humans" question set and "Life Cycles of All Things" question set. Each question set used a different treatment (T1, T2, or T3) for their results presentations.

The Questionnaire for User Interface Satisfaction (QUIS) is a usability testing tool designed to gauge a user's subjective satisfaction with the computer interface. A subset of QUIS 5.5b-S was used for evaluation in this study, specifically all six questions concerning overall user reactions, three questions on the screen presentation (4.1, 4.2, 4.3), and three questions on learning to use the system (6.1, 6.2, 6.4) (QUIS, 1994). These questions were selected based on their applicability to our video library interface and the goals of this study. They formed the contents of the questionnaire filled in by each subject after each question set.

3. RESULTS AND DISCUSSION

No significant differences in the dependent variables were expected for treatment ordering (i.e., the random assignment to one of the six treatment permutations), nor were any found. Significant differences at the 0.05 level or better were found in a number of cases concerning the treatment variable, i.e., the manner in which the result sets were presented.

3.1. Question set scores

The mean question set scores for the three treatments are given in Table 2. Score differences among the treatment groups, $F(2, 48) = 3.103$, were significant at the $p < 0.1$ level but not for $p < 0.05$. We did not expect to find any significant difference for question set scores because we were using very bright high school students and college students already familiar with electronic searching and online data. These subjects were given a fairly simple task of picking a video clip from a set of 12 that contains the answer to the current query, and doing this just 4 times per question set. The trend reflected in Table 2 merits further study, however. Poster frames appear to improve scores when compared to text presentation. Differences in result set presentation may have significant effects for more difficult or more extensive fact-finding tasks.

T1 (text list)	**T2 (first shot poster frame)**	**T3 (query-based poster frame)**
315.00	346.67	353.33

Table 2. Mean question set score per treatment (perfect score = 400)

3.2. Performance time

The mean time to complete a question set for each treatment is shown in Table 3. The treatment had significant effects on the performance time, $F(2, 48) = 14.737$, $p < 0.001$. The query-based poster frame presentation resulted in a 36% reduction in time necessary to complete the fact-finding task.

T1	**T2**	**T3**
921.9	952.0	590.7

Table 3. Mean time (seconds) to complete question set

The difference between T2 and T3 times is especially interesting, implying that simply replacing the text list with *any* poster frame graphical menu is not good enough. In fact, the first shot poster frame treatment had a slightly longer mean question set completion time than did the text list treatment. Only when the poster frame selection is query-based is there a significant drop in the time needed to complete the fact-finding task.

Recall that the experimental design eliminated the necessity for subjects to formulate and execute their own queries. The tasks necessary to answer the presented question were reduced to:

- Browsing the 12 video clips for candidate answers
- Playing candidate answers for appropriateness
- Selecting a video clip as the answer

Table 4 presents the mean number of video clips opened by a subject before deciding on his or her answers to a question set. Since each question set contained 4 questions, and a video clip could only be selected as an answer after it was opened, the absolute minimum number of video opens for a question set is 4. The treatment had significant effects on the number of video opens performed in completing a question set, $F(2, 48) = 4.374$, $p < 0.05$. However, this data does not explain the time difference shown in Table 3: treatments T2 and T3 both should have had much quicker task performance times based on Table 4 but Table 3 shows only T3 exhibiting such differences.

T1	T2	T3
11.63	9.07	9.83

Table 4. Mean number of video opens for question set

In support of the browsing task for finding candidate answers, subjects could move the mouse over a result set item and have a separate text box display the ID and full title string, as shown in Figure 4 for "INV071." Table 5 presents the mean number of text box titles opened by a subject in this way, referred to hence as result item browsing. The treatment had significant effects on result item browsing performed in completing a question set, $F(2, 48) = 8.13$, $p < 0.001$. Furthermore, the large difference between T3 and the other treatments helps explain the difference in time shown in Table 3.

T1	T2	T3
74.7	74.2	55.5

Table 5. Mean number of browsed text titles for a question set

Using the opening shot's poster frame to represent a video clip (T2) does not adequately distinguish a particular clip from others in the result set given the context of a specific query. Under T2, subjects browsed the result set as frequently as with the text lines (T1) to see the full text titles displayed for clips. When the poster frame selection is based on the query (T3), then it better identifies and distinguishes the clip, allowing users to more quickly browse the result set for candidate answers. The result is significantly less time spent browsing text titles (Table 5), good selections for candidate answers (Table 4), and an overall drop in time necessary to complete the task (Table 3).

3.3. Subject satisfaction

The answers to questions on screen presentation and learning to use the system produced no significant differences between the three treatment groups. The same multimedia tutorial was given to all the subjects before they began using the system. This tutorial did not bias the subjects toward a better understanding of either the text or poster frame treatments. It did serve the subjects well: the mean score for the learning questions across all subjects was 7.00 (from a 9 point scale with "9" representing the most favorable rating) and the mean score for screen presentation was 7.28.

T1	T2	T3
6.13	6.30	6.87

Table 6. Mean rating "terrible-wonderful" 9 pt. scale

When subjects were asked for their "overall reactions to the system as shown by this particular question set," the treatment had a significant effect on the "terrible - wonderful" 9 point scale, $F(2, 48) = 3.515$, $p < 0.05$. Experiences in the poster frame treatments were reported as more wonderful, and the query-based poster frame treatment receiving the most favorable rating of the three treatments. The mean scores for this question are reported in Table 6. The other 5 questions used to evaluate overall subjective satisfaction revealed no significant differences.

4. FUTURE WORK

The results reported in the preceding section can be extended in a number of ways, including the following:

- Apply query-based techniques to other video abstractions
- Apply query-based techniques to clip boundaries
- Augment poster frames with other information visualization techniques
- Extend query-based techniques based on greater knowledge of what the user is trying to do
- Test query-based poster frame benefits for libraries containing other styles of video besides documentaries

The improvements in performance time and satisfaction brought about by the use of query-based poster frames may also be realized with other query-based video abstractions. Instead of only using a single poster frame, all scoring shots' shot frames for a particular query could be used as an abstraction for a video clip result. These frames could be displayed simultaneously in a filmstrip view, or could be presented temporally in sequence using the same screen layout as the poster frame display shown in Figure 1. Likewise, the algorithm used to define "significant" audio and video to be included in a "skim" could be strongly weighted to use the scoring data from a query. Skim videos could be dynamically adjustable with parameters both for collapsed playback rate (e.g., 0 to 50% of original playback time) and the amount of influence of a query in composing the skim. Empirical studies will have to be conducted to determine the benefits of query-based modifications to a video abstraction when that abstraction has a temporal component.

Perhaps the query-based modifications should be extended to the clip boundaries as well for material in a digital video library. A physical segmentation of the video library into clips imposes a fixed segmentation on the video data. These clips are separated from their original context and may not meet the future needs of the library user (Davis, 1994). A more flexible alternative is to logically segment the library into clips but keep the video data intact in its original context, as is done with the Informedia library (Wactlar, 1996). Tests can be run to determine the effects of dynamically modifying clip boundaries based on the query or other user action which retrieves that clip.

A number of other browsing mechanisms could be added to the query results display for the video library. To enable better filtering and browsing, the features deemed important by the user should be emphasized and made visible. For example, if the distribution behavior of query terms within a video clip is important to a user, TileBars could be used in presenting the query results (Hearst, 1995). Further work must be done to explore the effects of using browsing mechanisms like TileBars in combination with video abstractions when accessing digital video libraries.

To determine which browsing mechanisms are appropriate to a user's needs, the user's identity and primary tasks must be better understood. Query-based poster frames produced improvements when the task centered about the query results and browsing the 12 video clips for candidate answers. For tasks not as dependent on queries, other browsing mechanisms may become critical or the query-based poster frame selection may need to be refined. For example, digital libraries for the sciences in support of inquiry-based learning should allow students to investigate driving questions by "asking and refining questions, making plans, designing experiments, debating ideas, collecting and analyzing information and data, drawing conclusions and communicating their ideas and findings to others" (Wallace, 1996). The use of query-based poster frames would likely benefit the analysis task when viewing a collection from a query. If given a larger context, however, such as inquiry-based learning, then video abstractions could be further refined for added benefit within that domain.

The library used in the experiment reported here contained all documentaries. The results should be verified across other classes of video, such as news footage which is often the focus of other research groups (Brown, 1995; Zhang, 1995; Hauptmann, 1997).

5. CONCLUSIONS

Full content retrieval in a video library can be a difficult and time-consuming process, as evidenced by anyone trying to find a clip of interest in a videotape or, worse, from a stack of videotapes. In order to improve access to relevant information, a digital library can be logically partitioned into clips and can provide alternate abstractions of video content. These abstractions can effectively represent a clip and be viewed in less time than the full clip. The experiment reported here shows that a single, representative image for a clip — when based on query criteria — improves performance time and subjective satisfaction.

The future promises to deliver increasingly more powerful computer processing and greater bandwidth. Digital video will no longer be relegated to the multimedia research labs or a few precious hours on a home machine, but will become as commonplace as text and graphics. The difficulties in quickly accessing a video clip of interest will remain, however, underscoring the importance of improving video abstractions.

6. ACKNOWLEDGMENTS

This material is based on work supported by the National Science Foundation, DARPA, and NASA under NSF Cooperative Agreement No. IRI-9411299. We thank Howard Wactlar for his project leadership, Michael Smith for his work with video abstractions, and Bryan Maher, Ricky Houghton, Craig Marcus, King Sun Wai, Don Marinelli, Michael Wagner, and the rest of the Informedia Project team for their efforts in preparing the library for experimentation.

7. REFERENCES

Benbasat, I. And Todd, P. (1993) An experimental investigation of interface design alternatives: icon vs. text and direct manipulation vs. menus. *Int. Journal of Man-Machine Studies*, **38**, 369-402.

Brown, M.G., Foote, J.T., Jones, G.J.F., Jones, K.S., and Young, S.J. (1995) Automatic Content-Based Retrieval of Broadcast News. In *Proceedings of the ACM Multimedia Conference*, 35-43.

Davis, M. (1994) Knowledge Representation for Video. In *Proceedings of AAAI '94*, 120-127.

Egido, C. and Patterson, J. (1988) Pictures and Category Labels as Navigational Aids for Catalog Browsing. In *Proceedings of the ACM CHI'88 Conference on Human Factors in Computing Systems*, 127-132.

Guastello, S.J., Traut, M., and Korienek, G. (1989) Verbal versus pictorial representations of objects in a human-computer interface. *Int. Journal of Man-Machine Studies*, **31**, 99-120.

Hauptmann, A.G., and Witbrock, M.J. (1997) Informedia: News-on-Demand - Multimedia Information Acquisition and Retrieval. To appear in *Intelligent Multimedia Information Retrieval* (ed. M. Maybury), MIT Press, Menlo Park, CA.

Hearst, M.A. (1995) TileBars: Visualization of Term Distribution Information in Full Text Information Access. In *Proceedings of the ACM CHI'95 Conf. on Human Factors in Computing Systems*, 59-66.

Mills, M., Cohen, J., and Wong, Y.Y. (1992) A Magnifier Tool for Video Data. In *Proceedings of the ACM CHI'92 Conference on Human Factors in Computing Systems*, 93-98.

QUIS 5.5b. (1994) University of Maryland at College Park. Available through http://www.lap.umd.edu/QUISFolder/quisHome.html.

Smith, M. and Kanade, T. (1996) Video Skimming for Quick Browsing Based on Audio and Image Characterization. Carnegie Mellon University, School of CS Technical Report CMU-CS-95-186R, Pittsburgh, PA.

Taniguchi, Y., Akutsu, A., Tonomura, Y., and Hamada, H. (1995) An Intuitive and Efficient Access Interface to Real-Time Incoming Video Based on Automatic Indexing. In *Proceedings of the ACM Multimedia Conference*, 25-33.

Wactlar, H.D., Kanade, T., Smith, M.A., and Stevens, S.M. (1996) Intelligent Access to Digital Video: Informedia Project. *Computer*, **29**(5), 46-52.

Wallace, R., Krajcik, J., and Soloway, E. (1996) Digital Libraries in the Science Classroom: An Opportunity for Inquiry. *D-Lib Magazine*. URL http://www.dlib.org/dlib/september96/09contents.html.

Zhang, H.J., Smoliar, S.W., Wu, J.H., Low, C.Y., and Kankanhalli, A. (1995) A Video Database System for Digital Libraries. In *Digital Libraries: Current Issues (Digital Libraries Workshop DL '94, Newark, NJ, May 1994, Selected Papers)* (eds. N.R. Adam, B.K. Bhargava, and Y. Yesha), Springer, Berlin.

Eigen-Space Coding as a Means to Support Privacy in Computer Mediated Communication

Joëlle Coutaz*, James L. Crowley, François Bérard***

CLIPS-IMAG, BP 53, 38041 Grenoble Cedex 9
(**) INPG, 46 av. Félix Viallet, 38330 Grenoble Cedex
FRANCE
{Joelle.Coutaz, jlc, Francois.Berard}@imag.fr

ABSTRACT The current solutions to disclosing privacy in computer-mediated communication are two-fold: either the connection is permitted and an audio-video link is opened providing a full-blown perceptual view on the distant location, or the connection is denied and the distant visitor has no perceptual access to the remote site. We claim that the disclosure of private data is more complex than these simplistic binary solutions. In this article, we present the concept of published observability as a system property to characterize the disclosure of private data. We propose a technical solution as an instantiation of this property using an eigen-space coding for private video data. This technique has been implemented within CoMedi, a mediaspace under development.

KEY WORDS privacy, computer mediated communication, mediaspace, eigen-space coding, computer vision

1. INTRODUCTION

Computer Mediated Communication (or CMC) covers multiple forms of person-to-person communication supported by a computer network infrastructure. CMC may occur asynchronously as with E-mail or synchronously as in desk-top video conferencing and mediaspaces. In typical mediaspace settings such as Cavecat (Mantei, 1991), Cruiser (Fish, 1992) and Montage (Tang, 1994), users can teleglance at a remote office, open a Vphone connection or maintain a permanent link with a distant shared location. Although these systems are intended to support informal encounterings and provide a global sense of a shared community, they may also be used abusively and highjack our own privacy.

Access control to privacy may rely on social protocols as in the very first mediaspace developed at PARC (Stults, 1986); it may rely on technical solutions as in Cruiser, or it may include a combination of both imperative and indicative controls as in Montage. The current solutions to disclosing privacy are two-fold: either the connection is permitted and an audio-video link is opened providing a full-blown perceptual view on the distant location, or the connection is denied and, with the exception of Cruiser, the distant visitor has no perceptual access to the remote site. We consider that the disclosure of private data is more complex than these simplistic binary solutions.

In this article, we present the concept of *published observability* as a system property that characterizes the disclosure of private data to distant users. We propose a technical solution as an instantiation of this property using an eigen-space coding for private video data. This technique has been implemented within CoMedi, a mediaspace under development.

Human–Computer Interaction: INTERACT'97 S. Howard, J. Hammond & G. Lindgaard (editors)
Published by Chapman & Hall

2. COMEDI, A MEDIASPACE PROTOTYPE

CoMedi (Communication and Media-space) is being tested on four Silicon Graphics Indy workstations communicating over the Ethernet. Each workstation is equipped with a motorized pan-tilt-zoom color camera, and microphones placed on the four corners of the computer monitor. It provides users with typical facilities such as glancing at someone, Vphoning and exploring a remote location using a virtual window (Gaver, 1995): the distant camera is remotely controlled by the user's head movement.

In its current state, the originality of CoMedi lies in the integration of multiple active and cooperative computer vision processes: three visual processes (eye blink detection, skin-driven color histogram (Schiele, 1995), and cross-correlation (Crowley, 1995)) are used in cooperation to detect and track mediaspace occupants with robust and real time performance (Coutaz, 1996). The availability of complementary visual processes permits the system to interpret the user's movements by activating the set of processes that are appropriate to the situation. In particular, users can accomplish their tasks without distractions of remaining in a narrow field of view. They can move around and adjust their own views on remote sites without being tied up to the workstation.

The cooperation of multiple visual processes is primarily intended for improving the robustness and the flexibility of the tracking system. It also serves as the foundation for increasing the transmission bandwidth. Low bandwidth is an important source of discontinuities within the human communication process (Sellen, 1995). It can be improved by using high speed ATM based-technology, complemented with compression techniques. In CoMedi, we obtain very high video compression ratio by stabilising the image of the user using our visual cooperating processes. Stabilisation provides the position, scale and illumination normalisation which makes possible efficient compression using an eigen-space. In CoMedi, eigen-space coding was initially intended for increasing transmission bandwidth. Early experiments led us to exploit this technique for an additional purpose: that of a magic filter for published private video data.

3. THE CONCEPT OF PUBLISHED OBSERVABILITY

A number of properties have been developed in the literature to structure and reason about the design, the implementation and the evaluation of interactive systems (IFIP WG2.7, 1996; Dix, 1991). One of these properties is "Observability": the property that the presentation of the system contains sufficient information to allow the user to determine the functional state of the system (Salber, 1994; Salber 1995). In principle, the information to be made observable is motivated by the task model.

In groupware, observability may be in conflict with the protection of the private space. The private space is the set of variables that model personal data, for example, the fact that I am currently in my office reading my E-mail. The quality of being "personal" for a particular state variable is decided at the analysis stage of the design process. Clearly, the observability of personal state variables is relevant to group awareness (Dourish, 1992) but may conflict with privacy. Our concept of published observability allows designers to reason about this antagonism (Salber, 1995).

A personal state variable relevant to a group activity is made observable only if its owner has authorized its publication. The authorization for publication may be static (i.e., decided at the design stage) or dynamic (i.e., may be changed at run time). For ethical reasons, the owner of a state variable should be the user whose state is conveyed by the variable but the owner may lend the state variable to others.

The binary duality "authorization-interdiction" of publishing a state variable does not convey the subtlety of human social relations. We introduce the concept of publication filter to support this requirement. A filter is both a mapping and a transformation function. As shown in Figure 1, a publishable variable P is linked to at least one representative variable R. In turn, R is rendered by at least one presentation object that makes R perceivable to remote observers. Dependencies between P and R and between the representatives and the presentation objects are maintained by the publication filters. The type of filter depends on P, on the role of the owner, on social relationships, etc. The identity function is one such basic filter. The eigen-space coding described in Section 4, provides an innovative filter for private video data.

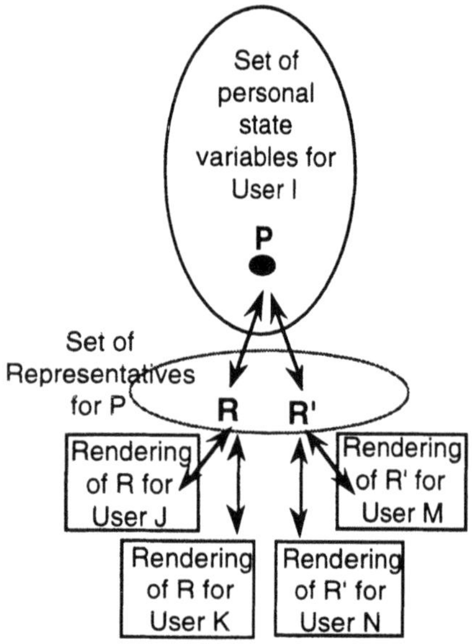

Figure 1. Published and filtered observability. Arrows denote publication filters. In this illustration, personal state variable P is published as two representatives R and R' for two different groups of users. In turn, R and R' are rendered depending on the final observer in each group.

For example, "current activity" can be defined as a personal state variable P that memorizes the current activity (e.g., reading E-mail) of a user engaged in a mediaspace. The user may decide to publish this variable as is for his collegues (therefore, the filter is the identity function) but, for unknown users, he may decide to hide himself behind a smoke screen. For example, one possible representative R for P would be the level of availability. R would then be rendered by an interaction object (e.g., an icon) using the door metaphor as in Cavecat, or the venitian blinds metaphor as in Cruiser, or even the shadow filter as proposed in (Hudson, 1996).

In this section, we have introduced the concepts of published observability and publication filter. We have illustrated these notions with known solutions as developed for current mediaspaces. In the next section, we describe a new way of handling video images using our concept of published and filtered observability.

4. EIGEN-SPACE CODING AS A PUBLICATION FILTER

Eigen-space coding employs principal components analysis to determine an optimal basis space for coding a signal for transmission(Loève, 1963; Watanabe, 1965). This mathematical tool has been used recently in computer vision for recognition: identifying faces (Turk, 1991), interpreting hand gesture (Martin, 1995), and indexing documents. As discussed above, we have used eigen-space coding as a compression technique for video-phone images as well as for the basis of a publication filter. The computational details of the technique is available in the Annexe as well as in (Brégeon, 1996). In this section, we only outline the principles.

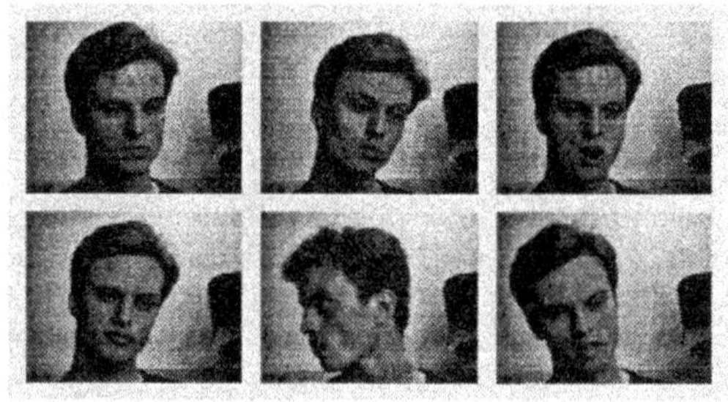

Figure 2. Sample images $I_0, I_1, \ldots I_5$ used to build an eigen-space for Laurent.

Video images that are sent over the network through a publication filter are coded as their coordinates in an N-dimensional orthogonal space: an eigen-space. This space is defined as the principal components computed from a set of representative video images. Figure 2 shows a sample of 6 initial images $I_0, I_1, \ldots I_5$ used to build the eigen-space $J_0, J_1, \ldots, J_4$ shown in Figure 4. Figure 3 shows the mean image of the sample images. The received image is rebuilt in real time on distant sites using the mean image and a linear combination of the basis images.

Figure 3. The mean image $\Gamma = \frac{1}{n}\sum_{k=0}^{n-1} I_k$

Figure 4. The resulting eigen-space $J_0, J_1, \ldots, J_4$ for sample images of Figure 2.

Figure 5 shows a live source image of Laurent and its reconstruction as perceived by a distant observer. It illustrates how the publication filter works. We observe that the reconstruction process has filtered out Laurent's arm: his representative published set, $I_0, I_1, \ldots I_5$, does not include any image with an arm raised. As a result, any person appearing in the background, Laurent picking his nose, or even Laurent being naked would not be published to distant observers. Laurent could even use a John Wayne eigen-space to reconstruct his live images on the fly. (We have played this trick using another student's eigen-space to reconstruct Laurent's live faces.)

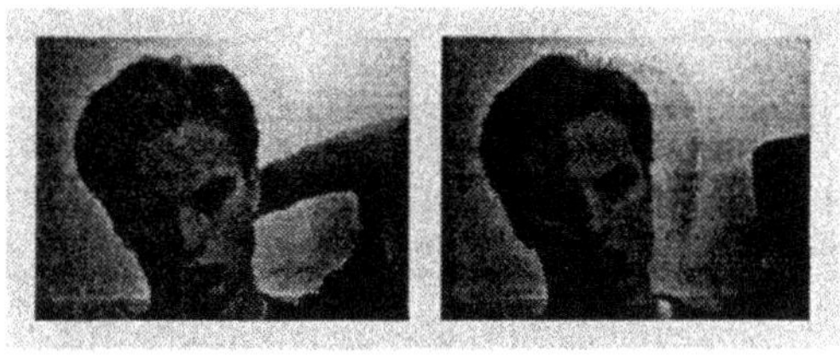

5a) W = Source live image 5b) $\tilde{W}$ = Received rebuilt image

Figure 5. A source live image W of Laurent (5a) and its reconstruction $\tilde{W}$ as perceived by a distant observer (5b) $\tilde{W} = \Gamma + \sum_{i=0}^{i=p-1} c(i) \cdot J$ where $c(i)$ denote the coordinates of W in the eigen-space $J_0, J_1, \ldots, J_4$ of figure 2.

The reconstruction is perfect when the live image is identical to one of the sample images. When not identical but reasonably similar, the reconstructed image is slightly distorted (see Figure 6). Real life requires more precision. To support this new requirement, we have developed an incremental eigen-space coding capable of adjusting dynamically to local changes: when the energy of the current live image exceeds a threshold, the local as well as the distant eigen-spaces for that user are updated accordingly (Brégeon, 1996).

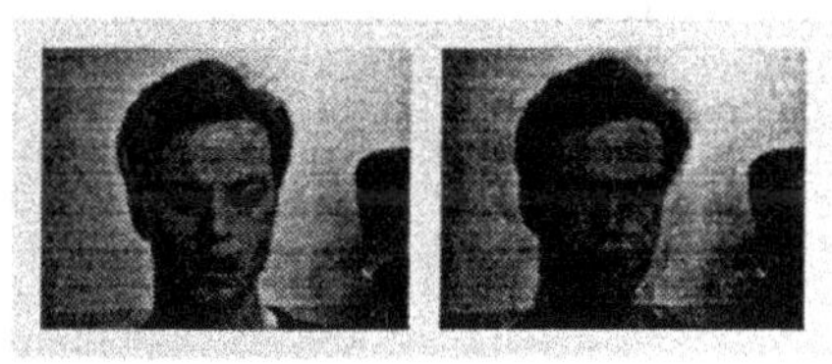

Figure 6. Live source image (left) and its real time reconstruction (right) when the source image is within a reasonable distance in the eigen-space.

5. CONCLUSION

The concept of published observability and its companion, the notion of publication filter, provide a new dimension for reasoning about privacy in multi-user systems. We have exploited a new way of using eigen-space coding for publishing private video data in an innovative and flexible manner. So far, we have demonstrated the technical feasibility of our ideas through a real time implementation of the eigen-space filter on workstations linked over Internet. Clearly, ATM-based technology would significantly improve the incremental version of the eigen-space filter.

We have not yet performed usability studies. We need to evaluate the impact of image distorsion in relation to communication tasks as well as the social implication of hiding or transforming "real pixels". In the current implementation of CoMedi, we do support reflexivity (the user sees his reconstructed image) in order for the sender to check the image received on remote sites.

We also claim that one filter does not fit all. Filters should be composed over areas of the live scene to provide a flexible and fine grain level of privacy for video data. For example, I would like the system to replace the area of the blackboard in my office that discloses my latest scientific results with a nice poster image. I would also like to provide the remote observer with a sense of coming and going activities at my office door using a shadow filter (Hudson, 1996). In addition, I would like to use the eigen-space filter for my face so that no one sees when I am sucking my pen while typing at the terminal. To this end, we have developed a robust face tracker (Coutaz, 1996, Crowley, 1997) that controls a pan-tilt-zoom camera and provides the eigen-space filter with a normalized source image.

Composing video filters with sound information is another interesting avenue for novelty and questions: How eigen-space coding can be extended to speech and sound to provide remote users with sufficient awareness of local sound events without having access to the real wording? More generally, how should filter composition be made amenable to non specialist users?

6. ACKNOWLEDGEMENT

This work is supported by France Telecom-CNET. We are grateful to Denis Brégeon and Laurent Le Corre for the implementation of the eigen-space coding algorithms.

7. ANNEX

Eigen-Space Coding

Notations

Upper cases denote vectors and matrices. Lower cases correspond to scalar values.

A source image whose definition is w x h pixels is represented by a vector composed of w*h components. Each component represents one pixel of the source image.

The number of images in the initial sample set is n.

The number of dimensions retained for the Eigen-Space is p.

Initial set of sampled images: $I_k \quad \forall$ k = 0, 1, ... n-1

A mean image is computed from the initial sampled set: $\Gamma = \frac{1}{n}\sum_{k=0}^{n-1} I_k$

The sampled images are recentered on the mean image: $\Gamma_k = I_k - \Gamma \qquad \forall$ k = 0, 1, ... n-1.

Matrix of recentered images: A = $[\Gamma_0 \;\; \Gamma_1 \;\; \dots \;\; \Gamma_{n-1}]$

Covariance Matrix: A A^t (A^t denotes the transpose of A)

Working matrix: A^t A = Q

Eigen vectors of the working matrix: $V_k \; \forall$ k = 0, 1, ... n-1 (ranked according to decreasing eigen-value)

Eigen vectors of the sampled set: $Z_k = \sum_{i=0}^{i=n-1} V_k(i) \cdot \Gamma_i \;\; \forall$ k = 0, 1, ... p-1

Eigen-space is composed of the normalized eigen vectors : $J_k = \frac{Z_k}{\|Z_k\|}$ $\forall$ k = 0, 1, ... p-1

Algorithm

The construction of the eigen-space follows the following steps:

1. Sample n initial images representing publishable scenes (see Figure 2): $I_0, I_1, \ldots I_{n-1}$
2. Compute the mean image Γ of the sampled set (see Figure 3) as well as the set of initial images recentered on the mean image, e.g., for every i compute Γ_i and build the matrix A = $[\Gamma_0 \ \Gamma_1 \ \ldots \ \Gamma_{n-1}]$

   Reduce A to a set of orthogonal images using principal component analysis (see figure 4). The orthogonal images are defined as the eigen vectors of A A^t. However A A^t has a size which is the square of the number of pixels in each image. In most cases it is unreasonable to compute such a matrix. To avoid this problem we consider the matrix of inner products between the images, Q = A^tA . We note that the Eigen-vectors of Q are $QR = \lambda R$. We note the following identity:

   $$(A^tA)R = \lambda R$$
   $$A(A^tA)R = A\lambda R$$
   $$(AA^t)AR = \lambda AR$$

   Thus λ AR give the eigen-vectors of AA^t.
3. Order V_i according to their decreasing eigen-value

so as to select the p vectors among n that are the most discriminants. Chose p so that the sum of the eigen-values attains a threshold.

The eigen-space of publishable scenes is used locally to code source images in real time as a vector of p numbers. This vector is transfered to the remote site where the image is reconstructed using the eigen-space sent once at connexion time.

Source live image : W

Projection vector : C = {c(i)} with c(i) = $\langle W-\Gamma, J_i \rangle$, i = 0, ...p-1

C is a column vector built from the projection of W recentered with the mean image.

Rebuilt images are computed as:

$$\hat{W} = \Gamma + \sum_{i=0}^{i=p-1} c(i)\cdot J$$

8. REFERENCES

Brégeon, D. and Le Corre L. (1996) *Technique de Codage par Eigen Vecteurs*, Rapport de projet de fin d'étude ENSIMAG, 1996.

Coutaz, J. , Crowley, J. L. and Bérard, F. (1996) Coordination of Perceptual Processes for Computer Mediated Communication, *in proceedings of the second International Conference on Automatic Face and Gesture Recognition*, IEEE Computer Society Press, pp. 106-111.

Crowley, J. L. and Martin, J. (1995) Experimental Comparison of Correlation Techniques", in *proc. IAS-4, International Conference on Intelligent Autonomous Systems*, Karlsruhe.

Crowley, J. L. and F. Bérard (1997) Multi-Modal Tracking of Faces for Video Communications, *IEEE Conference on Computer Vision and Pattern Recognition CVPR '97*, Puerto Rico.

Dix, A. (1991) *Formal Methods for Interactive Systems*, Academic Press.

Dourish, P. and Bly, S.A. (1992) Portholes : Supporting Awareness in a Distributed Work Group, in *proceedings of the CHI'92 Conference on Human Factors in Computing Systems*, pp. 541-547.

Fish, R.S., Kraut, R.E., Root, R.W., and Rice R.E. (1992) Evaluating Video as a Technology for Informal Communications, in *proceedings of the CHI'92 Conference on Human Factors in Computing Systems*, pp. 37-47.

Gaver, W., Smets, G. and K. Overbeeke (1995) A Virtual Window on a Media Space, *Proc. CHI'95*, ACM publ., pp. 257-264.

Hudson, S. & Smith, I. (1996) Techniques for Addressing Fundamental Privacy and Disruption

Tradeoffs in Awareness Support Systems. In *Proc. CSCW'96*, ACM Press, pp. 248-257.

IFIP WG 2.7 (1996) *Design Principles for Interactive Software* (C. Gram & G. Cockton Eds.), Chapman&Hall.

Loève, M. (1963) *Probability Theory*, 3rd Edition, Princeton, Van Nostrand.

Mantei, M., Backer, R.M., Sellen, A., Buxton, W., Milligan, T. and Wellman B. (1991) Experiences in the use of a Media Space, in *proceedings of the CHI'91 Conference on Human Factors in Computing Systems*, pp. 203-208.

Martin, J. (1995) *Suivi et Interprétation de Geste : Application de la Vision par Ordinateur à l'Interaction Homme-Machine*, Rapport DEA Informatique, IMAG - INPG.

Salber, D. (1994) *The System Modelling Glossary*, Amodeus Project Document: System Modelling/WP 26.

Salber, D. (1995) *De l'interaction Homme-Machine individuelle aux systèmes multi-utilisateurs: l'exemple de la communication homme-homme médiatisée*, Thèse de doctorat de l'Université Joseph Fourier, Grenoble.

Schiele, B. and Waibel, A. (1995) Gaze Tracking Based on Face Color, in *proc. International Workshop on Face and Gesture Recognition*, Zurich.

Sellen, A. (1995) Remote Conversations: The Effects of Mediating Talk with Technology, in *Human Computer Interaction*, Lawrence Erlbaum Publ., Vol. 10(4), pp. 401-444.

Stults, R. (1986) *MediaSpace*, rapport technique Xerox PARC.

Tang, J.C. and Rua, M. (1994) Montage: Providing Teleproximity for Distributed Groups, in *Proc. of the Conference on Computer Human Interaction (CHI'94)*, pp. 37-43.

Turk, M. and Pentland, A. (1991) Eigenspaces for Recognition. *Journal of Cognitive Neuroscience*, **3(1)**, pp. 71-86.

Watanabe, S. (1965) Karhunen-Loève Expansion and Factor Analysis: Theoretical Remarks and Applications, *Transaction of the Fourth Prague Conference on Information Theory, Statistical Decision Functions and Random Processes*, 1965.

81

The populated web: Browsing, searching and inhabiting the WWW using collaborative virtual environments

Steve Benford, Dave Snowdon, Chris Brown, Gail Reynard and Rob Ingram

Department of Computer Science
The University of Nottingham
Nottingham, NG7 2RD,UK
email: {sdb, dns, ccb, gtr, rji}@cs.nott.ac.uk

ABSTRACT. This paper presents new approaches for accessing the World Wide Web using multi-user three dimensional spaces, or collaborative virtual environments (CVEs.) The major sections of the paper deal with the aspects of browsing and navigating, searching, populating and displaying information within, and about the WWW. The methods described are illustrated with examples of working applications developed by the authors which together present an image of a possible future for Web access and collaboration based around the Web and its contents.

KEYWORDS. virtual reality, world wide web, visualisation, collaboration, virtual environments.

1. INTRODUCTION

The goal of this paper is to present new services for accessing, exploring and collaborating via the World Wide Web. Between them, these services demonstrate new approaches to browsing and searching and, perhaps more importantly, seek to transform the Web into an environment where users are naturally aware of one another's presence and are easily able to communicate with one another. Our approach utilises Collaborative Virtual Environment (CVE) technology (i.e. multi-user, distributed virtual reality) in order to provide navigable 3-D graphical, textual, audio and video representations of the structure of the Web and also of its users. Put another way, we aim to transform the Web from being a series of discrete locations which can be visited one at a time into being a landscape of many related locations which is visibly populated by its users.

This work has been motivated by a number of problems with the Web in its current form.

Browsing and navigating - the problems of navigating hypermedia systems are well known (see below). A key aspect of these problems is that current Web browsers constrain the user to see only one page at a time instead of allowing them to get a sense of where they are currently located within a more general context.

Searching - searching is an intellectually demanding task which may involve iteratively comparing the results of many queries in order to home in on useful information. However, current Web search engines only allow users to enter a single query at a time and provide little opportunity for interactively comparing the results of many different queries.

Populating - although many users may be simultaneously accessing the same Web information, the current generation of Web browsers hides their presence from one another. Furthermore, although there have been

Human–Computer Interaction: INTERACT'97 S. Howard, J. Hammond & G. Lindgaard (editors)
Published by Chapman & Hall

attempts to add real-time communication facilities to the Web (e.g. audio telephones), these have so far been limited in their capabilities and have not been well integrated with general Web browsing. In contrast, automatic awareness of the presence of other people and an ability to communicate with them is taken for granted in physical information environments (e.g. we are automatically aware of other people reading a notice board, browsing a newspaper stand or using a library without even having to think about it).

Displaying- the typical picture of Web access is of a single user browsing information via some kind of personal computer or workstation. Part of our work has involved considering alternative ways of displaying Web information within people's working environments (e.g. the use of larger scale projected displays) in order to enable new kinds of Web access and usage.

The remainder of this paper explores each of these issues in turn, presenting a series of Web-based applications and services which have emerged from our recent research. Between them, these applications offer a vision of future Web access which is radically different from that provided by the current generation of Web browsers.

2. BROWSING AND NAVIGATING - FROM PAGE TO LANDSCAPE

We begin our exploration with the issues of browsing and navigating. Jacob Nielsen addressed the problems of navigating large hypermedia structures, citing cases where users were unable to return to given locations [Nielsen90]. A number of solutions have been proposed to these kinds of navigation problems, including guides, tours and various backtracking mechanisms. Indeed, variants of these have been integrated in the current generation of World Wide Web browsers. These techniques, however, introduce their own problems; for example, the passive movement mode in guided tours may inhibit learning of the system and reduces the hypertext to a linear form. As a result, Nielsen has proposed the use of overview diagrams (effectively maps) and fish-eye techniques to show both local detail and global context. Some more recent browsers have made use of this idea to show a user's current location with respect the broader structure of the web (e.g. the Harmony browser for Hyper-G). With reference to our own work, this idea of accessing specific Web pages while still having a view of the surrounding context (i.e. other nearby pages) has motivated the development of the WWW3D browser.

Like all of the applications described in this paper, WWW3D is realised as a a Collaborative Virtual Environment - a multi-user distributed virtual reality system. This means that many users who are connected by a computer network can experience a shared virtual world constructed from interactive 3-D graphics, audio, video and text. Each user can freely navigate their own viewpoint within this world, can directly interact with the objects they find there, can see other graphically embodied users and can talk to them via audio and text channels. Users may access the world using a conventional workstation, a projected display or possibly a head mounted display (though in practice, few people have access to the latter and the quality of display provided is so low that they would be almost useless for accessing any textual information). The applications described in this paper have been built using the DIVE CVE platform from the Swedish Institute of Computer Science (SICS) [Fahlén93], a widely used CVE toolkit within the research community. More information on CVEs can be found in [Benford94].

For the time being, we will focus on the browsing functionality of WWW3D. We shall address multi-user issues in section 4 below. WWW3D provides a single 3-D graphical display which integrates 3-D representations of individual web pages (HTML), the structure of the part of the web that the user has explored and history information showing the links the user has followed in the recent past.

WWW3D uses the information contained in HTML tags to produce a representation of an HTML document in 3-D space. Each web document is represented as a sphere which is labelled on the outside with the document's title. The contents of the document are placed around the inside surface of the sphere and become visible when the user flies into the sphere. Textual information is represented by icons that can be unfolded to reveal an entire text. Images are displayed by texture mapping them onto polygons on the inside surface of the sphere. Finally, links to other documents are represented as icons, labelled with their destination. To reduce the visual complexity of the virtual environment WWW3D makes extensive use of Level of Detail (LOD) operations. When viewed from outside a document is represented as an opaque sphere and the actual document content is not displayed. When a user enters a document to view it, the sphere is drawn in wireframe so that the rest of the virtual environment is still visible outside. Figure 1 shows the contents of an example web document as displayed by WWW3D.

When the user selects a link icon, WWW3D creates a new sphere representing the target document, locates it near the original document and draws an arrow between them. As more links are followed, so more spheres and arrows are added to the structure resulting in the gradual construction of a 3-D graph of the area of Web space that the user has explored. An incremental version of the Force Directed Placement (FDP) [Fruchterman 91] algorithm is used to dynamically regenerate the layout of this graph. This algorithm is based on a physical simulation of spring forces such that the spheres are treated as masses, the links as springs and the action of the springs on the masses is simulated until the whole structure settles into a stable state. As a result, the 3-D graph that is generated has the useful effect of pulling tightly interlinked Web pages into local clusters, thereby making the structure of the Web more legible.

Several other visual cues are provided to aid navigation. For example, the brightness of both the spheres and the link arrows is dependant on the time since the user last visited them, thereby providing the user with a visual representation of their browsing history. As WWW3D parses a newly retrieved document, it checks for links to documents that the user has already explored and also draws arrows to represent them. This means that at any given moment the complete set of links between document is displayed without the user having to follow every link. This is intended to aid the user by indicating links between documents of which the user might have been unaware. Figure 2 shows the display produced by WWW3D after a user has browsed a number of documents.

A user may start a WWW3D browsing session either by specifying one or more initial URLs from which to begin browsing or simply continuing where they left off, using the saved state from the last session.

In summary, WWW3D represents an innovative approach to browsing and navigating the Web in that it shows the detail of individual pages situated within the broader context of a 3-D map of the structure that a user has browsed so far and allows the user to easily move between these two levels of detail (e.g. by flying into a sphere to read a single page or pulling back their viewpoint to obtain an overview of structure).

Figure 1: A WWW3D representation of the contents of a web document.

Figure 2: A collection of web documents showing the links between them.

3. SEARCHING - GRAPHICAL REPRESENTATION AND MANIPULATION OF QUERIES AND RESULTS

Next we focus on the problem of searching. The typical operation of a current Web search engine is that the user enters one or more keywords and in return is presented with a list of matching pages, rank ordered according to how well they matched. The problem with this approach is that it is difficult for the user to compare the results returned by different queries in order to home in on pages that match successive or multiple combinations of keywords. We have therefore developed the VR-VIBE application in order to allow users to dynamically compare the results of multiple search queries [Benford95]. VR-VIBE is based on an earlier 2-D system by Olsen et al. called VIBE [Olsen93] and works as follows:

1. The user enters a number of queries, each consisting of several keywords.
2. Each query is assigned a position in 3-D space, either directly by the user (i.e. by picking it up and dragging it) or automatically by the system if the user wishes.
3. The application matches each page in its local catalogue against each query, resulting in a score that represents the *relative attraction* of that page to that query. From this, the *overall relevance* of a specific page to all of the queries can be calculated (the sum of all scores for this page), as can the *overall significance* of each query (the sum of all scores across for this query).
4. A 3-D representation of the search space is then constructed in the following way. An icon representing each matched page is located at its relative centre of attraction to all of the currently active queries. Thus, a page which is attracted to only one query will be located next to that query, whereas a page which is attracted to several queries will be located somewhere between them, with its exact position depending on the relative strengths of the attractions. In other words, it is as if the queries exert a gravitational pull on the pages. The overall relevance of each page is mapped onto the size and shade of its icon.; thus, the bigger and brighter it is, the greater its overall relevance to all of the queries. Similarly, the overall significance of each query is mapped onto its brightness; thus, the brighter it is the greater its "pull" on the pages in the space. The resulting 3-D visualisation gives the user a sense of which pages are generally interesting (big and bright ones) and also which pages are most relevant to which specific keywords (spatial position).

However, perhaps the most important aspect of VR-VIBE is the way in which users may dynamically manipulate the visualisation. Current functionality includes:

- Flying through the 3-D scene in order to home in on specific areas or zoom out for an overview.
- Selecting the icons of pages in order to retrieve them from the Web and display them.
- Selecting queries in order to activate or de-activate them.
- Dynamically adding new queries to the visualisation.
- Repositioning queries either by dragging them or asking the system to "tidy" them into a sensible configuration.
- Running an additional temporary search and highlighting pages which match it.
- Using a relevance filter widget to remove all pages whose overall relevance falls below a set threshold.

We anticipate that it is this ability to dynamically manipulate the visualisation, adding and removing queries, moving them about and so forth, that is the real power of this approach over the current generation of "one query at a time" interfaces to Web search engines.

Figure 3 shows VR-VIBE being used to browse a catalogue of 1500 documents on the subject of CSCW. We can see the documents arranged into the shape of a pyramid, and simple embodiments of other users.

4. POPULATING - EMBODIMENT AND COMMUNICATION

So far we have considered how to visualise the underlying structure of the Web and also how to visualise the results of searching the Web. In this section we turn our attention to the issue of populating the Web - making its users directly visible to one another and enabling them to communicate. We separate this discussion into two parts: embodiment and communication for 3-D users (i.e. the users of future multi-user VR based Web browsers) and tracking and representation of 2-D users (i.e. the users of the current generation of 2-D Web browsers).

4.1. Embodiment and communication for 3-D users

Both of the above visualisations are inherently multi-user. This means that several people may share the same virtual world at the same time, freely navigating their own viewpoints. Each person sees the visualisation from their own autonomous perspective in 3-D space in much the same way as we perceive shared physical space. Each person may also be represented by an embodiment, a graphical object which is attached to their viewpoint and which shows that they are present, where they are located

FIGURE 3: Multiple users browsing a document space using VR-VIBE

and where they are looking in the virtual world. Embodiments (sometimes called avatars or clones), may range from simple graphical objects which essentially act as 3-D tele-pointers through to complex animated graphical forms which track the physical movements of their owners (through VR tracking devices), support gestures and even facial expressions (e.g. through the use of texture mapped video as discussed below). Embodiments may also support some other more subtle aspects of communication in virtual worlds including:

- **Degree of presence** - our experience with VR tele-conferencing has shown that the presence of an embodiment in a virtual world does not necessarily mean the active presence of its owner "inside" of it (particularly where simple, relatively static, embodiments are involved) [Greenhalgh95]. Users are often distracted by events in their physical space and sometimes even leave their terminal equipment unattended. This can cause some social embarrassment for other 3-D users (e.g. talking to an uninhabited body). As a result, our embodiments can show various degrees of presence (e.g. people may put them into a "sleeping" position if they have to absent themselves from the virtual world).
- **Points of presence** - an extension of the above idea involves adding some simple agent functionality to an embodiment so that it may carry out rudimentary communication functions on behalf of its owner while they are absent. For example, we have extended some of our embodiments to record messages, to give out messages and to try to alert their owner when directly "prodded".
- **Capabilities** - As we shall see below, we anticipate that the Web will continue to be a heterogeneous environment in that people will access it using a wide range of equipment, network services and so forth. For example, some people may be audio capable and some only text; some may have 3-D browsers and some 2-D. A key aspect of embodiments is that they should naturally convey the underlying communication capabilities of their owners. Thus, if one of our bodies has ears then it is audio capable; a letter "T" on its head indicates text capability and a clear distinction is made between representations of 2-D and 3-D users.

In addition to embodiment, our applications support direct real-time communication between users through a combination of audio, text, graphics and video. Thus, on encountering another's embodiment one may directly address them using whatever combination of media is appropriate as is indicated by their embodiment. In the case of video, one or more real-time video streams can be texture mapped onto polygonal surfaces in the virtual world. For example, a video image of a face may be attached to the front of an embodiment, so that the video window moves and turns in the virtual world as the user does, or a video view into a remote physical scene may be realised as a "video window" pasted on a wall in the virtual world (see the Internet Foyer application below). Figure 4 shows an example of a three person virtual meeting from the point of view of one of the participants. The users are embodied with simple graphical objects but greater detail and identity is provided by the real time video faces.

Our integration of real-time media into virtual environments utilises an underlying mechanism called the spatial model of interaction which is intended to support scaleability in terms of number of simultaneous participants whilst maintaining flexibility of communication [Greenhalgh95]. The model allows users to scope their interaction in terms of maintaining only a limited network connectivity to others as they move about the virtual world and also to flexibly control the quality of service provided across these different connections. To quickly summarise, connectivity is enabled through a concept called *aura* - a personal subspace which scopes ones presence. Quality of service is controlled through a concept called *awareness*, a measure of how much each object is aware of each other connected object. In turn, awareness is controlled by two further concepts called *focus* and *nimbus*. A focus represents the spatial allocation of a users attention and a nimbus the spatial projection of their information. Thus, A's awareness of B is some function of A's focus on B and B's nimbus on A. Finally, various *adapter* objects change a users aura, focus and nimbus allowing them to reconfigure their communication capabilities (e.g. standing at the virtual podium expands one's aura and nimbus allowing one to address a greater number of people than usual). The net effect of aura, awareness, focus and nimbus is that users move around a virtual space and use various objects in order to manage connectivity and quality of service. More specifically, audio, textual, graphical and video are sensitive to relative positions and orientations (e.g. transmitted audio may become quieter or the frame rate of video images may be reduced as one moves or turns away from them).

In summary, we have discussed a number of issues concerned with representing the presence of other VR-based users of Web visualisations and of enabling and managing communication between them over different media. Next, we consider the issues involved in tracking and representing the presence of the users of the current generation of Web browsers.

4.2. Tracking and representation for 2-D users

Our browsers also support users in being aware of the presence of so called 2-D users (i.e. the users of current graphical multi-media browsers such as Netscape and Mosaic). This involves three key issues: tracking, representation and mutuality.

- **Tracking** - we have developed a module that tracks the presence of users as they access our Web server and move from page to page and notifies the various visualisation tools that were described above. This module works with both live data and also from Web logs.
- **Representation** - we represent the presence of these tracked users through embodiments. 2-D users' embodiments are placed close to and facing the page that they are currently browsing. Animated movements then show their progress as they move from page to page across the visualisation. Thus, one can directly see their progress as they wander about.
- **Mutuality** - tracking and representation raise the further issue of privacy. Our approach is based on a general principle of mutuality, whereby anyone who enters a server that supports tracking is warned of this in advance and is given the opportunity to decline being tracked (our Web pages carry a standard form allowing people to sign in and identify themselves). On electing to be tracked, a 2-D user gets to see a textual list of other visitors (3-D and 2-D) appended to each Web page. If they decline, then they do not see this list. Thus, either users are mutually aware or mutually invisible.

5. DISPLAYING - BOUNDARIES BETWEEN PHYSICAL AND VIRTUAL

Our final issue in this exploration of future Web interfaces concerns the nature of physical displays. The current picture of Web access is of users sitting down at individual machines and browsing through the Web as a focused activity. Although we would not expect this kind of access to disappear, there are other interesting possibilities that might be considered. In particular, in considering the Web as a navigable space in its own right, we have become interested in its relation to people's existing physical spaces. This has led us to experiment with new forms of Web access based on the use of shared projected displays which enable more peripheral and casual awareness of the Web and its use. We shall illustrate this idea through an example application - the Internet Foyer - which integrates many of the techniques described in previous section [Benford96].

5.1. Goal of the Internet Foyer

We begin with the goal of the Internet Foyer. Foyers are important areas of physical buildings for a variety of reasons. First, they present the public face of a building and the organisation(s) which it houses. The significance of this function alone should not be underestimated; large sums of money are spent on making foyers interesting and impressive places. Second, foyers provide a context for locating useful information for visitors such as maps, directories and displays. Third, they may be home to various people whose job it is to help these visitors (e.g. receptionists). Fourth, they enhance security by providing a single point of entry into the organisation within which incoming and outgoing people are made publicly visible and hence accountable. Fifth, they provide public meeting places, either for arranged rendezvous or for chance encounters.

Turning to the Web, it is clear that, in parallel to the physical manifestation of buildings, many organisations are increasingly acquiring an electronic manifestation through the World Wide Web. In such cases, the public "home" pages of an organisation on the WWW could be considered to be a kind of foyer: a public entry point into the organisation's We space. There is certainly evidence that organisations are investing considerable effort into turning their WWW pages into interesting and impressive places. However, when compared to physical foyers, WWW pages leave much to be desired. For example, the people who pass through them are not generally visible to one another and there are no opportunities for rendezvous and social encounters.

There are therefore two main goals to the Internet Foyer. First, by using a combination of the techniques described above, to construct a virtual foyer based on a populated visualisation of an organisation's WWW space which might come closer to the functionality of a real foyer. Second, to merge this virtual foyer with a real physical foyer so as to provide an integrated shared space which spans both the physical and virtual worlds. Thus, visitors entering an organisation's WWW space would be able to interact with those entering its physical space and vice versa.

5.2. Functionality of the Internet Foyer

The overall concept of the Internet Foyer is summarised below. Visitors in a traditional physical foyer see a graphical representation of a virtual foyer projected onto the wall. This virtual foyer is a 3-D graphical visualisation of an organisation's home pages whose electronic visitors are mutually embodied (i.e. visible to one another) and are able to communicate with one another through open audio channels. A video window in the virtual foyer affords its occupants a corresponding view back into the real foyer and an open audio channel allows communication between the two spaces. There are therefore three ways to experience the Internet Foyer:

As a visitor to the physical foyer one users enter a normal physical space. Projected onto a wall of that space is the graphical representation of the virtual foyer. This representation is based on the approach described in section 2. Both 3-D and 2-D visitors to this visualisation and represented using the techniques described in section 4 and an open audio link allows communication with the virtual reality users in the virtual foyer.

As the user of a VR-based Web browser, one sees the same basic visualisation as those in the physical foyer. However, one is able to freely navigate around this visualisation, homing in on specific details or backing off in order to obtain a perspective view. A real-time video window which is texture mapped onto a wall of the virtual foyer allows CVE users to look out into the physical foyer and to see its occupants looking back at them.

As the user of a traditional (2-D) WWW browser one sees the Internet foyer as a series of WWW pages. On entering the foyer one is asked to register. Beyond this, additional pages provide information about current and recent visitors, displayed as simple textual lists and may display captured images from both the real and virtual foyers.

Figures 4(a)and 4(b)present images of the Internet Foyer as it appears to different users. Figure 4(a)shows an overview of the Internet Foyer as it appears to a VR-based user, with a 3D graph style visualisation of a set of WWW pages, as described earlier, and a real time video window onto the physical world. Figure 4(b) shows how the Internet Foyer appears to visitors in the physical foyer.

In summary, the Internet Foyer represents an interesting Web application from several points of view. First it combines all of the ideas of visualisation, embodiment, tracking and communication as described above. Second, the use of combined projection and video texturing techniques has enabled us to create a new kind of display where the Web is seen more as an extension to a normal physical space (i.e. where access is shared and casual), rather than as a specific application which is launched on an individual computer.

6. Conclusion

Many people talk about the Web as if it were a space. Indeed, the populist term "Cyberspace" has become synonymous with the Web. In this paper, our aim has been to consider how the utilisation of Collaborative Virtual Environment technology might actually help transform the Web into being a truer space than it is today - specifically, into being a space that is both navigable and populated. Our paper has presented a series of applications which, between them, offer a vision of future Web browsers and services. The paper has also explored a number of key issues which underlay this vision, including:

- Allowing users to perceive the inherent structure of a region of the Web through the use of 3-D visualisation techniques, thus aiding navigation.

- Supporting more dynamic and interactive forms of searching.
- Embodying both 3-D and 2-D Web users so that they are mutually aware.
- Supporting integrated and scaleable real-time communication (including audio and video) between users through the concepts of aura, focus and nimbus which provide new ways of managing network connectivity and quality of service based on spatial proximity.
- Supporting the tracking of users as they progress across the Web, coupled with the notion of mutuality so as to maintain personal privacy.
- Considering the use of projected displays to enable new forms of Web access.

We hope that kinds of techniques may soon become an integral part of Web browsers. The necessary infrastructure is certainly maturing rapidly in the form of low-cost, high performance 3-D graphical platforms and the recent emergence of 3-D standards for the Web (i.e. VRML). Given this emerging infrastructure, we believe that it may soon be possible to develop a new generation of more usable, dynamic and populated Web services and tools.

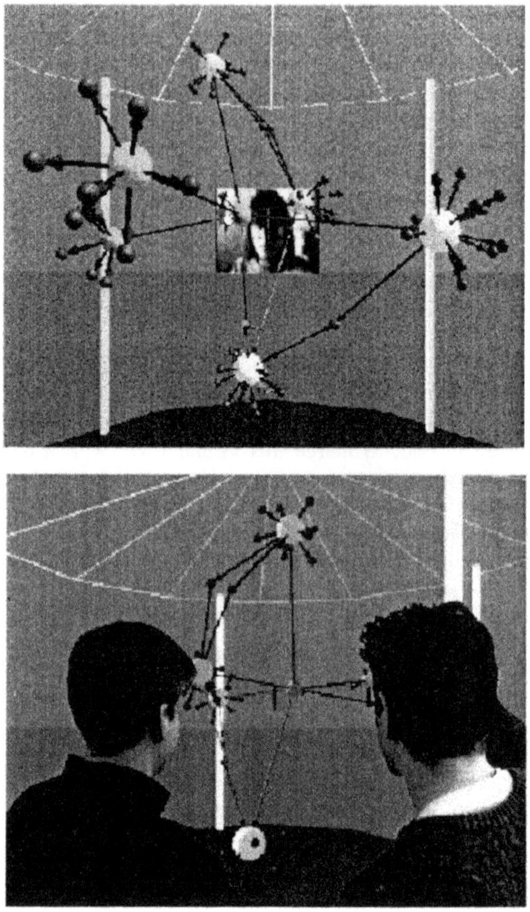

FIGURE 4: The Internet Foyer as viewed (a) from within the virtual world and (b) from the physical world using a projection display.

REFERENCES

[Benford94] Benford, S. D., Bowers, J. M., Fahlén, L. E., Mariani, J. and Rodden, T. R., Supporting Co-operative Work in Virtual Environments, The Computer Journal, 37 (8), Oxford University Press, 1994.

[Benford95] Benford, S., Snowdon, D., Greenhalgh, C., Ingram, R., and Knox, I., VR-VIBE: A Virtual Environment for Co-operative Information Retrieval, *Computer Graphics Forum*, 14, 3, 1995, NCC Blackwell.

[Benford96] Benford, S. D., Brown, C. C., Reynard, G. T. and Greenhalgh, C. M, Shared Spaces: Transportation, Artificiality and Spatiality, Proc. ACM Conference on Computer Supported Cooperative Work (CSCW'96), Boston, ACM Press (in press).

[Fahlén93] Fahlén, L. E., Brown C. G., Stahl, O., Carlsson, C., A Space Based Model for User Interaction in Shared Synthetic Environments, in Proc.InterCHI'93, Amsterdam, 1993, ACM Press.

[Fruchterman91] Fruchterman, T. M. J. and Reingold, E. M., Graph Drawing by Force Directed Placement, *Software Practice and Experience*, Vol. 21 (11), 1129-1164.

[Greenhalgh95] Greenhalgh, C. M., and Benford, S. D., MASSIVE: A Virtual Reality System for Tele-conferencing, ACM Transactions on Computer Human Interfaces (TOCHI), 2 (3), pp. 239-261, ISSN 1073-0516, ACM Press, September 1995.

[Neilsen90] Nielsen, J., The Art of Navigating Hypertext, *Communications of the ACM*, 33, 3, pp. 297-310, ACM Press.

[Olsen93] Olsen, K. A., Korfhage, R. R., Sochats, K. M., Spring, M. B. and Williams, J. G., Visualisation of a Document Collection: The VIBE System, *Information Processing and Management* 29 (1), pp. 69-81.

GroupScape: Integrating Synchronous Groupware and the World Wide Web

T.C. Nicholas Graham

Department of Computer Science
York University
4700 Keele St., North York
CANADA
graham@cs.yorku.ca

ABSTRACT Synchronous groupware applications support people collaborating in real time over a distance. The world wide web supports asynchronous collaboration by allowing people to share distributed information repositories. This paper presents a new technique for creating applications that tightly integrate synchronous groupware with the world wide web. The key points of the technique are: two new HTML tags allow synchronous views to be embedded within WWW pages *without programming*; lightweight connection of WWW documents and applications is achieved through the use of *constraints*, and the use of the model-view-controller architecture allows easy integration of applications and WWW pages that were developed separately. This technique has been demonstrated in the context of the new multiuser *GroupScape* HTML browser, developed using the *Clock* groupware development toolkit.

KEYWORDS CSCW, Groupware Development, HTML, WWW

1. INTRODUCTION

Synchronous groupware applications support people collaborating in real time over a distance. Example applications include multiuser text editors, teleconferencing applications and collaborative software engineering tools. The defining property of *synchronous* groupware is that it helps people to work together at the same time, allowing participants to immediately see the effects of other participants' actions. Synchronous groupware is meant to create *group awareness*, allowing people to work with the kind of direct communication they would have if they were all in the same room.

The world wide web (WWW) supports a different kind of collaboration, allowing distributed groups to share information, but not supporting the direct person-to-person communication of synchronous groupware. For example, the WWW has been effectively used to support the collaborative development of documentation in a software reengineering project (Finnigan et al., 1997) and in the collaborative development of an information repository on the Boreal forest (Freemantle et al., 1996). The web therefore supports *asynchronous* group work.

With the growth of the WWW as a dominant technology for information dissemination and collaboration, it is natural to want to integrate synchronous and asynchronous collaboration in a WWW-based tool. Such integration should support people in collaboratively finding and analyzing information on the WWW (Greenberg and Roseman, 1996) and should support the integration of web browsing and applications. Current approaches typically provide restricted integration between web pages and synchronous applications (Rees and Woo, 1994) or require complicated programming in CGI, Java or Olé (Rex, 1996).

This paper presents a new technique for tightly integrating synchronous groupware applications with the

Human–Computer Interaction: INTERACT'97 S. Howard, J. Hammond & G. Lindgaard (editors)
Published by Chapman & Hall

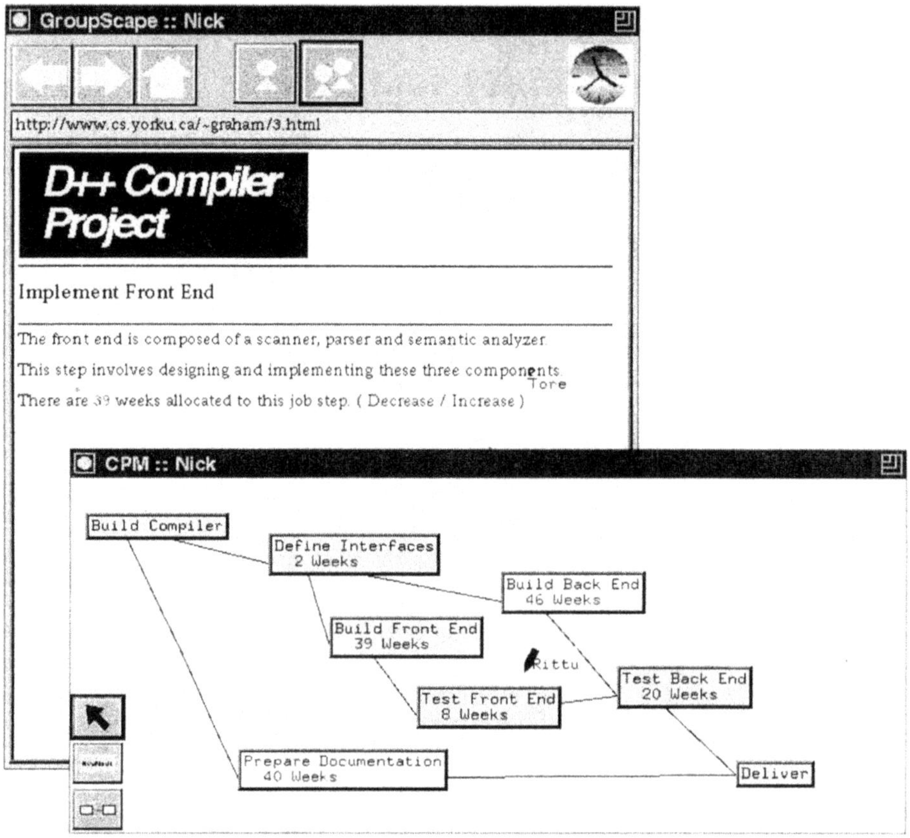

Figure 1: A collaborative project scheduling tool integrating the GroupScape web browser and a synchronous critical path planning application.

world wide web. The technique provides tight coupling of WWW pages and synchronous applications without programming. The technique has three features:

- An object-oriented design pattern, based on the model-view-controller architecture (Krasner and Pope, 1988), is used to permit easy integration of synchronous groupware and a multiuser web browser;
- To bring synchronous functionality into web documents, two new HTML tags are introduced. These tags support synchronous functionality without programming;
- The connection of synchronous applications and web documents is achieved through declarative constraints, allowing a web browser to be connected to synchronous applications without programming.

To demonstrate this technique, we have developed the *GroupScape* browser, a multiuser HTML browser supporting our extended HTML language. GroupScape itself was written using the Clock groupware development tool (Graham et al., 1997).

The paper is structured as follows. The next section introduces an example application to motivate the problems in integrating a synchronous application with the WWW. The following sections introduce the design pattern used to structure applications, the extended HTML language, and the use of constraints to connect the GroupScape browser to standalone applications.

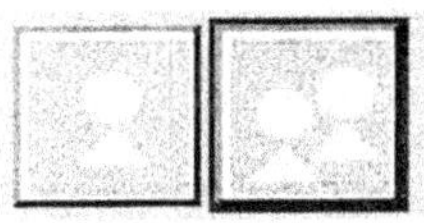

Figure 2: Users can select between private and group browsing modes

2. A GROUPWARE PROJECT SCHEDULER

Figure 1 shows an example application integrating synchronous groupware and the world wide web. The application allows a group of people to schedule resources in a fictional compiler development project. The application window shows the steps involved in carrying out the project and the number of weeks allocated to each step. The critical path through the network is shown in grey. The participants in the planning session can add new nodes to the network, connect nodes and move nodes. This is an example of a synchronous groupware application since all participants see the same network, and changes perfomed by one participant are immediately reflected on the displays of the other participants. When this application is augmented by a voice channel (e.g., using a telephone), managers in the compiler development project can use it to negotiate the allocation of project resources. To help increase group awareness, telepointers are used to show the positions of the other participants' pointers.

The GroupScape browser window is used to view information describing the project phases. By default, all participants see the same page, and all navigation commands apply to the displays of all users. If a participant selects the private viewing mode, however, his/her browser decouples from the shared page, allowing browsing independent of the other participants (figure 2). The telepointers from the application window also apply to the GroupScape window, allowing participants to see who else is viewing the same WWW page as they are.

The application window and the GroupScape browser are connected in several ways to allow them both to be used in the planning and negotiation process:

- Whenever a participant clicks on a node in the network, the page describing that node is displayed in the browser on all participants' displays;
- In the browser, the text describing a given project step contains the number of weeks allocated to the project. When the allocation is changed, the value displayed in the browser changes in real time;
- In the browser, buttons allow allocations to be increased or decreased. When these buttons are clicked, the allocation on the WWW page is changed, the allocation on the node in the application window is changed, and the critical path is updated as necessary. These effects are carried out in real time on the displays of all participants.

2.1 Requirements of Integration

This application contains a set of features that serve to motivate the ways in which synchronous group interaction may be integrated with web browsing. These forms of integration are:

Group web browsing: Facilities should be available to allow a group to browse the web together. Participants should be able to synchronize the pages they are viewing, to drop out of the group and rejoin it, and to easily see who else is on the same page.

Application based browsing: It should be possible for the groupware application to control which page is being viewed. In our example, clicking on a node in the critical path network directs GroupScape to load that page.

Embedded synchronous views: It should be possible to embed application-dependent views in web pages. These views should be updated in real time, without requiring the page to be reloaded. In our example, the number of weeks allocated to each job step is embedded as a synchronously updated view.

Embedded application events: It should be possible for web pages to control the application. In our example, web pages have embedded hot areas allowing participants to modify the time allocated to job steps.

This paper presents a technique for performing all these styles of integration without programming. Section 3 presents an object-oriented design pattern for integrating the GroupScape browser with synchronous groupware applications. This pattern is expressed in the *Clock* groupware development language (Graham et al., 1997), but should be adaptable to other object-oriented user interface development languages. Section 4 then shows how extending HTML with two new constraint tags makes it easy to introduce application functionality into web pages without programming.

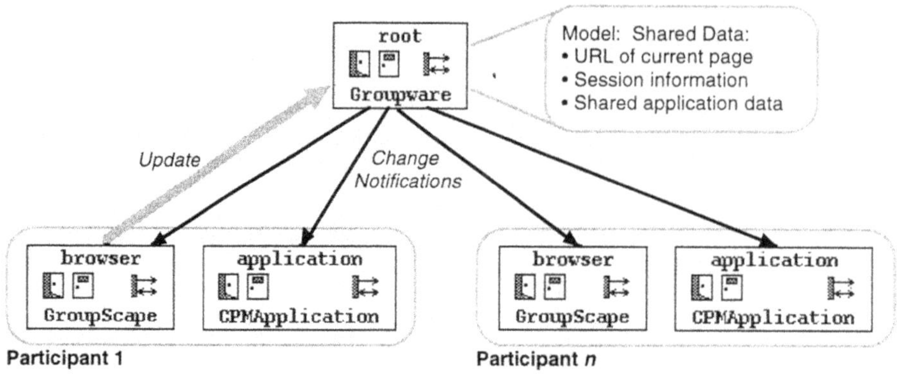

Figure 3: An MVC-based run-time architecture integrating GroupScape and synchronous applications. Each participant node contains view and controller components implementing that participant's user interface.

3. INTEGRATION ARCHITECTURE

In order to integrate web browsing and synchronous applications, we adopt a layered *model-view-controller* (MVC) architecture (Krasner and Pope, 1988) for the run-time organization of the multiuser browsing and application session. This architecture reduces the direct links between components in the session, simplifying the programming of inter-component communication. To allow the use of this model without programming, an object-oriented *design pattern* is provided that captures the details of the MVC communication protocol. To link a synchronous groupware application to the GroupScape browser, the programmer simply instantiates the pattern with the application. As will be seen in section 4, the GroupScape browser recognizes two new *constraint tags* that allow the browser to interact with the application without programming.

This design pattern was developed in the Clock groupware development toolkit, but should be easily adaptable to other object-oriented languages.

3.1. Run-Time Architecture

MVC has proven to be a natural way of organizing groupware applications, and can be implemented efficiently in a distributed context (Graham et al.,1996b, Kindberg et al., 1996). MVC allows the GroupScape browser to be connected to applications without any direct communication between the application and the browser. This means that GroupScape can be integrated with applications without reprogramming either the application or GroupScape itself.

To demonstrate how this architecture works, figure 3 shows the run-time organization of the integrated scheduling application of figure 1. A *model* component implements all data shared by the application and the browsers of the participants in the groupware session. The model contains information about who is in the session, the URL of the page currently being viewed, and shared application information such as the structure of the critical path network and the number of weeks allocated to each job step. For each participant, an instance of the application and of the GroupScape browser is connected to the model.

All communication between components in the run-time architecture is performed through the model. When a participant performs an action, an update is sent to the model to indicate the change that has taken place. The model then notifies the application and browser components of all participants that they must update their displays. For example, if a participant decreases the number of weeks allocated to a job step (by clicking on the "decrease" button in the browser), an update is sent to the model to set a new time for that job step, and all participants are notified of the change.

The advantage of this architecture is that the browser and application do not need to communicate directly. This means that the browser does not need to know what kind of application it has been connected to, or how to communicate with that application. Section 4 shows how this allows us to use constraint tags to embed application knowledge in the browser without programming.

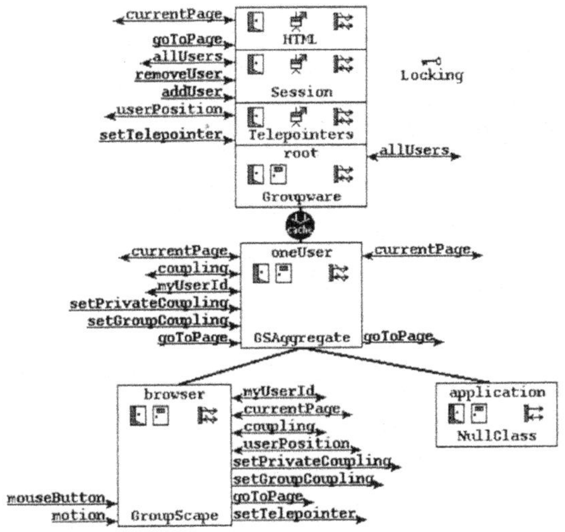

Figure 4: An object-oriented design pattern for coupling GroupScape to synchronous applications.

3.2. A Pattern for Integration

Object-oriented design patterns encode standard ways of organizing programs (Beck and Johnson, 1994). Patterns help programmers apply an existing program organization in new contexts by showing what program components are required, and how they are parameterized to the new context.

Figure 4 shows a pattern for integrating the GroupScape browser with synchronous groupware applications. This pattern was developed using the visual *ClockWorks* programming environment (Graham et al.,1996a), and was used to implement the application of figure 1. In ClockWorks, patterns are available from a library, and can be instantiated and manipulated visually.

In the pattern, the *Groupware* component is used to implement the shared data of the model. The abstract data types implementing this data are attached to the component: the *HTML* ADT represents the URL of the current page, with methods *goToPage* to set the current page and *currentPage* to return the current URL; the *Session* ADT represents information on the current participants in the session, and the *Telepointers* ADT represents the positions of each participant's mouse pointer.

For each participant, an instance of the *GSAggregate* class is created, in turn creating an instance of the browser and the application. *GSAggregate* is responsible for maintaining the coupling status of the browser, supporting group and private navigation.

The *GroupScape* component implements the multiuser browser. The browser always displays the page at URL *currentPage*, so that whenever the current page is modified in the *HTML* ADT, the browser automatically updates the page displayed.

The application itself is given class *NullClass* in the pattern. The application is a *parameter* to the pattern that must be filled in when the pattern is instantiated. To integrate an application with the browser, the programmer instantiates the pattern, fills in the correct application class, and makes any shared application data visible in the model. Normally, this can be done with no programming whatsover, simply by positioning objects in the visual environment.

This pattern encapsulates the difficult programming problems of the run-time architecture of figure 3, so that programmers do not have to solve them every time the browser is integrated with a groupware application. In order to instantiate the pattern, the programmer must fill in the class of the *application* component, and add any new shared ADT's to the model. In ClockWorks, this can be done purely visually, with no programming whatsoever.

4. CONSTRAINT TAGS

In the application of figure 1, the GroupScape browser is used to display pages that are integrated with the project planning application. These pages contained views that needed to be updated in real time (the time allocated to each project) and hot areas that invoked functionality in the application (the *increase* and *decrease* buttons.) Using the GroupScape pattern, this linkage is achieved by embedding special constraint tags in the HTML document being viewed, requiring no modification of the browser code itself. The constraint tags are: the CLOCKVIEW tag which allows a synchronous view to be embedded in an HTML document, and the CLOCKUPDT tag, which allows hot areas to be defined that will cause updates to the application state.

Figure 6 shows the complete HTML code for the document displayed in figure 1. This document contains a description for step "3" in the project, the step of implementing the front-end of the compiler. Other than the new CLOCKVIEW and CLOCKUPDT tags, this document is composed of standard HTML, and will therefore display correctly in any browser (but without the groupware functionality.)

```
<HTML>
<HEAD>
<TITLE>Build Front End</TITLE>
</HEAD>
<BODY BGCOLOR="#FFFFFF">
<img src="d++.gif">
<HR>
<H1>Implement Front End</H1>
<P>
<HR>
The front end is composed of a scanner,
parser and semantic analyzer.
<P>
This step involves designing and
implementing these three components.
<P>
There are
<CLOCKVIEW VIEW=(
  TextColour red (NumText (jobTime "3")))
>???</CLOCKVIEW>
weeks allocated to this job step. (
  <CLOCKUPDT UPDT=(
    setJobTime "3" (jobTime "3"-1))
      >Decrease</CLOCKUPDT>/
  <CLOCKUPDT UPDT=(
    setJobTime "3" (jobTime "3"+1))
      >Increase</CLOCKUPDT>)
</BODY>
</HTML>
```

Figure 6: The HTML code displayed in figure 1.

The CLOCKVIEW tag is used in this document to embed a synchronously updated view in the HTML page. The general form of the tag is:

```
<CLOCKVIEW VIEW=view>alt</CLOCKVIEW>
```

which states that the given *view* is to be embedded in the document at this point. The *alt* text provides an alternate view (expressed in HTML) that will be displayed by browsers that are not aware of GroupScape tags. In the example of figure 6, the document contains the tag:

```
<CLOCKVIEW
  VIEW=(
    TextColour red (
      NumText (jobTime "3")))
>???</CLOCKVIEW>
```

which states that the current job time of step "3" is to be displayed as red numeric text. If the browser does not support GroupScape tags, the text "???" will be displayed.

The view embedded in the tag is a *constraint* that is implicitly attached to the model. The request 'jobTime "3"' is used to obtain the time currently allocated to job step "3". As was seen in figure 4, this request is implemented in the *JobTimes* ADT in the model. Therefore, whenever the time allocated to this step is modified by any participant, the MVC functionality of the GroupScape pattern will ensure that the embedded view is automatically updated. The CLOCKVIEW tag therefore allows synchronously updated views to be embedded in HTML documents, and ensures that they will be connected to the shared application data in the model, and automatically updated in response to any changes. It is important to note that these changes do not require the page to be reloaded, only the view to be updated locally by GroupScape.

The view constraints themselves are expressed in Clock's view language, allowing arbitrarily complex views involving text, graphics, sound and video.

The CLOCKUPDT tag allows updates to the model to be embedded within HTML documents. The general form of this tag is:

```
<CLOCKUPDT UPDT=updt>text</CLOCKUPDT>
```

The effect of the tag is to display the text *text*; whenever a participant clicks on the text, the message *updt* is sent to the model. In browsers that do not handle GroupScape tags, the text is displayed but is not sensitive to input. For example, the tag:

```
<CLOCKUPDT
  UPDT=(
    setJobTime "3" (jobTime "3"-1))
>Decrease</CLOCKUPDT>
```

implements the *Decrease* button of figure 1. Whenever a participant clicks on *Decrease*, the time allocated to job step "3" is decreased by 1 week: the *setJobTime* method is invoked to set the time of step "3" to 1 week less than the current time allocated to the step (as obtained through the method invocation *jobTime "3"*). The MVC functionality of the GroupScape pattern allows simple modifications in the model to implicitly update the application state, so the application windows and browsers of each participant are automatically informed of the change in the time for the job step, and can update their views accordingly.

Embedding constraint tags into HTML documents provides a flexible means of integrating the GroupScape browser with synchronous groupware applications. The CLOCKVIEW tag allows documents to contain synchronous views that are updated in real time without reloading the page; the CLOCKUPDT tag allows documents to contain hot areas that cause real time modification to applications. Since these tags embed communication with the application, no reprogramming of the browser itself is necessary.

5. ANALYSIS

The technique described in this paper simplifies the process of integrating group web browsing with synchronous groupware applications. By making it easier to connect a groupware web browser with applications, we hope it will be easier to experiment with different styles of collaboration based both on the information repositories of the web and on the immediate communication of synchronous groupware applications.

Through the example of figure 1, we have shown that there are four important ways that synchronous groupware should be integrated with the world-wide-web: through multiuser web browsing, through embedding synchronous views in web documents, through navigation controls in the application, and through application controls in the browser.

The techniques described in this paper support all four of these integration forms: the GroupScape browser is itself a synchronous groupware application, supporting browsing both privately and in a group. Through two new constraint tags (CLOCKVIEW and CLOCKUPDT), GroupScape allows synchronous views and application events to be embedded with HTML documents. Through an object-oriented design pattern, programmers can easily couple synchronous applications to GroupScape without programming.

The main advantage of this approach is the ease with which integrated WWW/groupware applications can be created. Once the design pattern has been developed once and placed in a library, programmers can rapidly develop new integrated applications. Once the application itself has been created, programmers can customize the integrated behaviour by experimenting with the definitions of the tags, without having to modify the application itself. The tags are designed so that people using a standard browser will still see a reasonable result, but will not receive the synchronous functionality. This allows pages designed for GroupScape to be used for standard browsing as well.

The primary disadvantage of our approach is that the design pattern and the new constraint tags require the custom-built GroupScape browser. To be successful in practice, an integration technique should be based on the features of the standard web browsers that are installed on millions of machines. We view our work as providing direction for how standard browsers could be extended to better support synchronous interaction.

5.1 Related Research

There has been substantial earlier research on the integration of synchronous groupware with the WWW. Many of these systems have been a strong influence on our own work.

Systems integrating synchronous groupware and the WWW can be roughly divided into two categories: those that provide multiuser web browsing and those that allow on-the-side synchronous groupware applications to be invoked through web pages. A major goal of the GroupScape project is to combine these two styles, facilitating tight integration of group web browsing and on-the-side applications.

5.1.1 Group Web Browsing

A number of tools aim to allow groups to browse the web together. The *GroupWeb* browser (Greenberg and Roseman, 1996) allows multiple participants to view the same web page simultaneously, slaving views so that as one participant changes pages, the views of the other participants are also updated in real time. To promote group awareness, telepointers, a multiuser scroll bar and a group annotation facility are provided.

The *Sociable Web* browser (Donath and Robertson, 1994) aims to make web browsing a more communal activity by providing dynamic information about who else is viewing the same page, and by providing chat communication tools that can be invoked directly from the current page. People browsing the web can therefore not only find out information about a given topic, but can also find out who else is looking for similar information at the same time.

Group web browsers provide excellent facilities for collaborating on finding and analyzing information. Group browsers (including GroupScape) have the disadvantage, however, of requiring a custom-built browser that supports its synchronous use.

5.1.2 Applications on the Side

Another approach to integrating synchronous groupware and the WWW is to use a standard browser, but to permit web pages to invoke synchronous applications that run on the side. Typically these approaches require participants to run a separate client application for the synchronous application, and provide only limited interaction between web browsing and the synchronous application.

One of the earliest applications in this style was *Yarn Web* (Rees and Woo, 1994), an electronic meeting system. Yarn Web combines a chat program for synchronous communication with web pages for session management and activity logging. Despite being based on a standard browser, Yarn Web allows a simple form of view slaving by having Yarn clients send page change notifications to the browser.

The *Como* system (Rex, 1996) allows synchronous groupware applications to be launched *within* web pages. Como applications are written as Java applets, and include chat, voting and shared drawing programs.

The *Mushroom* system (Kindberg et al.,1996) also takes this approach, providing the abstraction of the *MROOM*, a virtual room in which shared work can be carried out by one or more participants. MROOMS can be accessed by clicking on links in standard HTML documents,but are themselves synchronous applications. MROOMS are in effect places for synchronous interaction that can be found by traversing the web.

6. CONCLUSIONS

This paper has demonstrated a technique for integrating synchronous groupware applications with the WWW. The technique allows applications to be coupled with the new multiuser GroupScape browser. The connection is performed using a design pattern based on the model-view-controller architecture. To provide a wide range of integration styles, the GroupScape browser supports two new constraint tags, permitting application views to be embedded in HTML pages, and permitting pages to contain application controls.

7. ACKNOWLEDGEMENTS

GroupScape was developed by the author using the Clock groupware development toolkit. Clock and ClockWorks were developed by the author, Tore Urnes, Catherine Morton, Roy Nejabi and Gekun Song. This work was partially supported by NSERC and the ITRC.

8. REFERENCES

Beck, K. and Johnson, R. (1994) Patterns Generate Architectures, in *Proceedings of the European Conference on Object-Oriented Programming (ECOOP'94),* 139-149.

Donath, J.S. and Robertson, N. (1994) The Sociable Web, in *Proceedings of the Second International WWW Conference.*

Freemantle, J.R., Shepherd, P.R., Dunlop, J.D., Gray, L. and Miller, J.R. (1996) An Integrated Approach to Collection and Dissemination of Airborne Remote Sensing Imagery, in *Proceedings of the Second Annual Airborne Remote Sensing Conference and Exhibition.*

Finnigan, P.J., Holt, R., Kalas, I., Kerr, S., Kontogiannis, K., McDaniel, J., Müller, H.A., Mylopoulos, J., Perelgut, S., Stanley, M., Tourlakis, I., Tzerpos, V., Uhl, J., Wong, K. (1997) The Software Bookshelf. *IBM System Journal* (to appear).

Graham, T.C.N., Morton, C.A., Urnes, T. (1996a) ClockWorks: Visual Programming of Component-Based Software Architectures. *Journal of Visual Languages and Computing* 7, 175-196.

Graham, T.C.N., Urnes, T. and Nejabi, R. (1996b) Efficient Distributed Implementation of Semi-Replicated Synchronous Groupware, in *Proceedings of the ACM Symposium on User Interface Software and Technology (UIST'96),* ACM Press, 1-10.

Graham, T.C.N., Rasouli, R. and Urnes, T. (1997) *The Clock Language Reference.* http://www.cs.yorku.ca/~graham/reference.html.

Greenberg, S. and Roseman, M. (1996) GroupWeb: A WWW Browser as Real Time Groupware. In *Human Factors in Computing Systems, CHI Companion Proceedings,* ACM Press, 271-272.

Kindberg, T., Coulouris, G., Dollimore, J. and Heikkinen, J. (1996) Sharing objects over the Internet: the Mushroom approach. In *Proceedings of Global Internet '96*, IEEE Press, 67-71.

Krasner, G.E. and Pope, S.T. (1988) A Cookbook for Using the Model-View-Controller Interface Paradigm. *Journal of Object-Oriented Programming.*(1):3,26-49.

Rees, M.J. and Woo, T.K. (1994) A World-Wide-Web User Interface for an Electronic Meeting Tool. In *Proceedings of OZCHI,* 187-192.

Rex, M. (1996) Welcome to COMO Professional 1.0. http://www4.informatik.uni-erlangen.de/Projects/como/www/products/comopro1.0/www/doc/index.html

Where to locate user profiles of personalized applications? - A user profile management agent -

Tomonari Kamba and Laurent Freléchoux

C&C Research Laboratories, NEC Corporation
4-1-1, Miyazaki, Miyamae-ku, Kawasaki,
Kanagawa, 216
Japan
{kamba | laurent}@mmp.CL.nec.co.jp

ABSTRACT This paper describes a user profile management agent on the World Wide Web. To help web users to get relevant information efficiently, various sites are providing personalized services and the number of such sites is rapidly increasing. However, deciding where to locate user profiles of personalized applications is a difficult problem. To date, there have been two solutions to this problem: storing user profiles on the server side or storing them on the client side, which is a terminal that runs a web browser. Both these methods have advantages and disadvantages. When the user profiles are stored on the server side, it is impossible for the users to use the same profiles to access other personalized servers. When they are stored on the client side, it is difficult for the server to compare different users' profiles and to provide a so-called collaborative filtering service. Our method solves these problems by storing the user profiles on an agent. The agent keeps the user profiles of a group of users and mediates the communications between the users and personalized servers. When a server requests a user profile, the agent gives it to the server. When a user profile needs to be updated, it is done so on the agent. This agent not only discharges the personalized servers from the user profile management tasks but also gives users the possibility of getting new functions such as collaborative filtering using their own user profiles. We have implemented the user profile management agent as an extended proxy server of the web and have demonstrated that the proxy server is useful for sharing user profiles both between different personalized servers and between different users.

KEYWORDS user profile, personalization, agent, World Wide Web, proxy server

1. INTRODUCTION

We often hear the word "personalization" these days, especially within the context of the World Wide Web (WWW). The word is similar to "customization" but there seems to be a slight difference between the two. For example, the appearance attributes of the X-Window system are called customizable because the user can change them by editing an attribute file. Automatic customization is important for the so-called adaptive user interface. For example, if a system can automatically find an operation sequence that a user does often and if it can create a short-cut for the operation sequence spontaneously, the user interface of the system will be called "automatically customizable". In these cases, most people will agree that we should call the mechanism behind them "customization" rather than "personalization".

Human–Computer Interaction: INTERACT'97 S. Howard, J. Hammond & G. Lindgaard (editors)
Published by Chapman & Hall

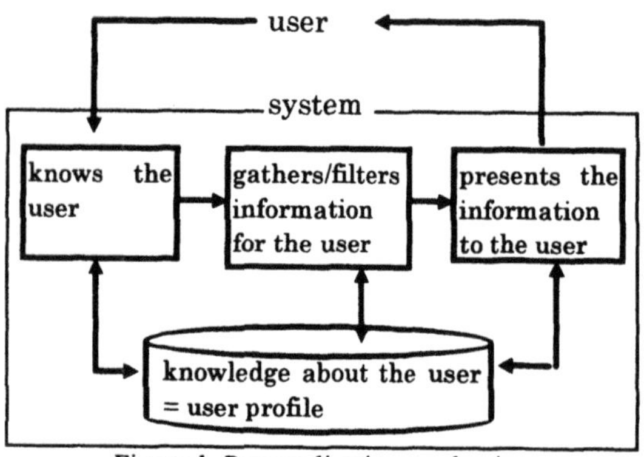

Figure 1. Personalization mechanism

On the other hand, there are some cases that are usually called "personalization", not "customization". One of the typical examples is a personalized news system. It is a system that picks up articles for each user from a large amount of sources so that the user can read relevant articles in a short time.

When we compare these examples, it seems that "customization" is related to the syntactic aspect of the system, and "personalization" is related to more semantic aspects. When the appearance or operations is adapted to each user, it will usually be called customization; however, when the information content is adapted to each user, it will be called personalization. We think the reason why personalized services are so popular now is that people really need them. Contents accessible on the Web are very widespread and heterogeneous, and thus people need a way to filter them. Search engines such as AltaVista (http://altavista.digital.com/) are useful when looking for documents about a specific topic. However, when they want to get relevant (but not so pinpoint) information constantly, as when people read newspapers everyday, a personalization mechanism is useful to filter the information on the WWW.

Then, from the technical point of view, what is needed for personalization? First, a personalization engine has to know the user (see Figure 1). The knowledge about users is usually called the user profile. Then, the engine has to filter or gather information considering the user profile. Lastly, it has to present the gathered or filtered

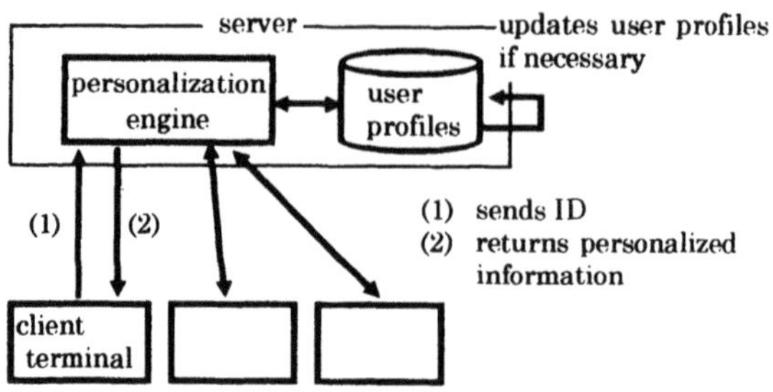

Figure 2. Centralized user profiles on the server

information to the user. As can be seen in Figure 1, one of the key factors of personalization is the user profile.

It is of course important to discuss what information should be included in the user profile with what format, but the answer to this question depends on the applications. Sometimes we need the users' names for personalization, and sometimes we may need to know which color they like. On the other hand, where to locate user profiles is a more common problem.

To provide a personalized service, we can build a system that stores user profiles on the server side. It is also possible to store the user profiles on the client side, which is, a terminal that runs a web browser. As we will discuss in the next section, the difference of these two architectures directly affects the system functions, and both have advantages and disadvantages.

In this paper, we will propose another architecture based on this discussion, which is to build a user profile management agent. This agent is placed between servers and clients and manages the user profiles. We have implemented such an agent as an extended proxy server of the WWW and will show how it works.

2. RELATED WORK AND PROBLEM STATEMENT

2.1. Having user profiles on the server

One way to build a personalized service is to manage all the user profiles on the server (see Figure 2). When the user accesses the server, the server identifies the user in some way, retrieves the user's profile from the database, gathers or filters information considering the user profile, and presents the personalized information to the user. The identification of the user is usually done

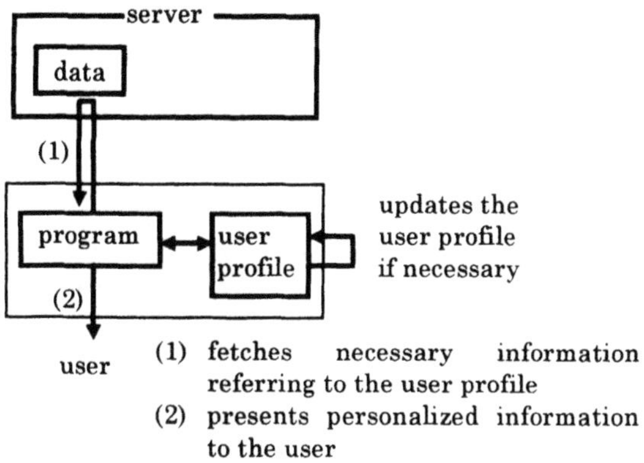

Figure 3. User profiles stored and managed on the client side

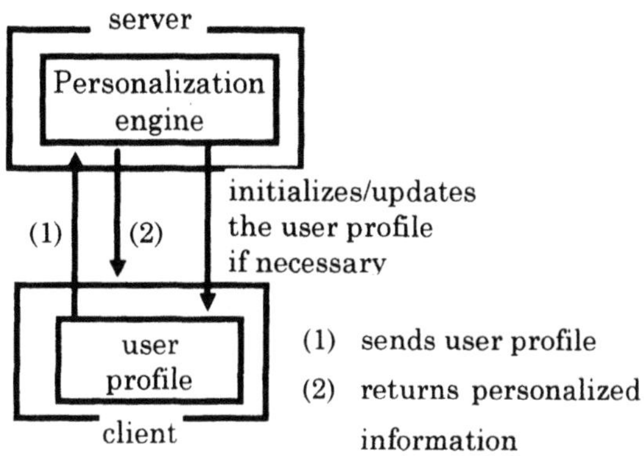

Figure 4. User profiles stored on the client side and managed by the server

by asking the user to type in an ID and password. We can find a lot of applications built with this architecture on the WWW.

The Krakatoa Chronicle developed by Kamba et al. is one example (Kamba, 1995). In this system, the user profiles of all the users are stored on the WWW server. The user can access it with a WWW browser. When a user gives an ID and password to the system, the system scores newspaper articles using the user profile and sends the article contents and article scores to the client. The appearance of the newspaper is created on the client side using the article scores.

2.2. Having user profiles on the client

We will explain the following two methods of storing user profiles on the client side.

- The user profile is stored and managed on the client side.
- The user profile is stored on the client side but is managed by the server.

An architecture for the first method is shown in Figure 3. The server works just as a document database. Considering the user profile stored on the client side, the client program fetches the necessary pieces of information from the server and presents them to the user. This architecture seems to have been adopted by PointCast Network (http://www.pointcast.com/). On the client side, the users can select news categories, areas where they want to know the weather, companies on which they want to get related news, and so on. The files that store such information can be called a user profile. The client program automatically accesses the server and gets articles related to the genres specified in the user profile.

An architecture for the second method is shown in Figure 4. In this architecture, the personalization engine is on the server, and the server manages the user profile but uses a client terminal to store a user profile. When the user accesses the server, the client sends the user profile to the server, then the server personalizes information using the received profile and sends the personalized information to the client. The server also sends a modified user profile to the client if necessary. Personalization with this method can be implemented on the WWW using the Cookie mechanism (http://home.netscape.com/newsref/std/cookie_spec.html). Cookie defines an interface between the server and the client (WWW browser) that manages a special file on the client, called the cookie data. In the cookie data file, the address of a personalized web server is associated with a set of attributes and values that should be sent to the server. Whenever the browser accesses a personalized web site listed in the cookie data file, the browser sends the corresponding attributes and values to the server. When the server sends a message that includes the "Set-Cookie:" string to the browser, the browser modifies the cookie data file based on it.

2.3. Problem statement

Before discussing the problems of current architectures, we will point out one of the popular trends of personalized services. To provide a personalized service to a user, his or her user profile is of course needed. However, it is not enough. Other users' profiles are also very useful for personalization. This is called collaborative filtering or social filtering. Let us look at an example. If a person X likes a book A, the system can analyze the content of the book and deduce what kind of information person X likes. Then, the system can find documents similar to book A and show them to person X. This technique is called content-based filtering and is often used to provide personalized services. Collaborative filtering is quite different from this. When a person X likes a book A, the system looks for other users who also enjoyed book A, and finds what other books are popular among the users who like book A. Based on this information, the system can propose a book that will be relevant to person X without analyzing the content of book A at all. This collaborative filtering has been demonstrated successfully in various systems (Hill, 1995; Shardanand, 1995) and is also an important and powerful technique for personalization. It is important to notice that personalization by this method is quite difficult unless the user profiles are centralized.

The advantages and disadvantages of each personalization architecture will now be discussed.

- **Storing and managing user profiles on the server:** The advantage here is that both content-based and collaborative filtering can be easily performed on the server. One of the disadvantages is that the server needs to have a large amount of disk space to store all the user profiles. Another disadvantage is that the user profile cannot be shared between different web services. For example, if keywords that a user is interested in were stored on the client side, the user would be able to access various personalized services, such as personalized newspapers and magazines, by using the same profile. In addition, there are some privacy concerns associated with this method. In other words, not only the personalized service but also user profiles are controlled by the server with this architecture. This is not desirable from the users' point of view.
- **Storing and managing user profiles on the clients:** With this method, the user can control the user profile and can also use it for another objective if necessary. However, it is quite difficult to get a collaborative filtering service. Since all the user profiles are on the client side, no one can gather all the users' profiles to compare or group them.
- **Storing user profiles on the clients and managing them on the server:** For practical purposes it is almost impossible to do collaborative filtering with this method too. Since the server controls personalization, it would be possible in theory to gather all the users' profiles and do collaborative filtering. However, in comparing and grouping user profiles the server will need to store the same profiles as those on the clients and guarantee the synchronization between the profiles on the server and the clients. This is quite redundant and needs much work on the server.

In short, there is no way of performing both content-based and collaborative filtering services easily, while ensuring the users have reasonable control over their own profiles.

3. A USER PROFILE MANAGEMENT AGENT

3.1. Concept

To solve the problem described in the previous section, we propose a user profile management agent. It stores user profiles of a group of people and mediates the communications between personalized servers and the users within the group (see Figure 5).

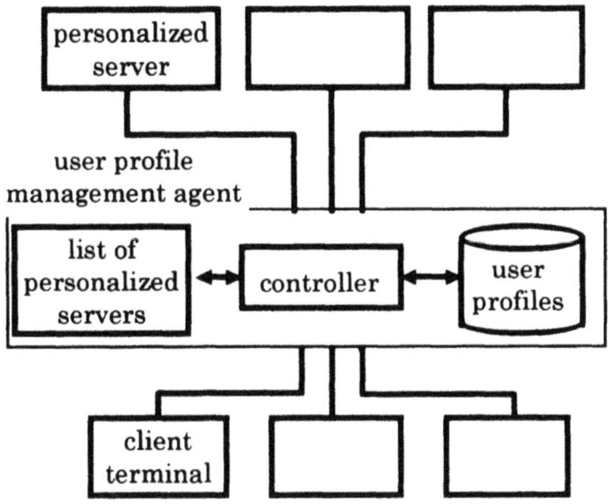

Figure 5. A user profile management agent

The following list shows the functions provided by the agent.

- When the server requires a user profile from the agent, the agent returns the requested profile if it is allowed by the user beforehand.
- When the server asks the agent to forward personalized information to a specific user, the agent does so.
- When the server asks the agent to update a user profile, the agent does so if it is allowed by the user beforehand.
- When a user requires a user profile from the agent, the agent returns the requested profile if it is allowed by the owner of the profile beforehand.
- When a user asks the agent to send his or her profile to a specific server, the agent does so.
- When a user asks the agent to update his or her profile, the agent does so.

In other words, the agent exists in the middle of the users and personalized servers, and both of them can read/edit the stored user profiles if allowed to by the owners beforehand. Therefore, the servers can share the user profiles and the users can share the profiles within a group of people.

3.2. Implementation as an extended proxy server

To show how a user profile management agent works, we have implemented one as an extended proxy server of the WWW. It mediates the communications under the Hypertext Transfer Protocol (HTTP) and manages Cookie-based personalized services. All the user profiles are stored on the extended proxy. The server can set a user profile on the extended proxy in the same way as when it sets the profile on a client terminal using Cookie. When a user tries to access a personalized service that needs the user's profile, the extended proxy server automatically sends the user profile to the server by adding it on a message from the user to the server. Since this extended proxy is transparent for the communication between the users and non-personalized services, it can be used as a gateway between an Intranet within a company and the Internet open to the world. By using this extended proxy server, people within a company can share user profiles. They can even add a collaborative filtering function to the personalized services provided by an outside service provider. This proxy server can also be used by information providers. If a provider provides multiple personalized services, it will be desirable to share customers' profiles among different services. By using our extended proxy server, the user profiles can be centralized on the user profile management agent. Implementation details are described below.

Our extended proxy server is implemented on a UNIX platform using the proxy server developed at CERN as a base (http://www.w3.org/pub/WWW/Daemon). We call it a user profile extended proxy. It works as a regular proxy for any web address (URL) that does not provide a personalized service using Cookie. Whenever the proxy receives an HTTP request for a personalized server, it requires the user to type in an ID and password, then it looks in its database to see if the "URL-user ID" pair is registered. If it is already registered, the content of the user profile is retrieved, added to the HTTP request in the Cookie-format header, and sent to the web server that provides the personalized service (Figure 6). When the server needs to update a user profile, it will include the updated profile again as a header within the regular HTTP response. As this response goes through the proxy, the content of the user profile is extracted and

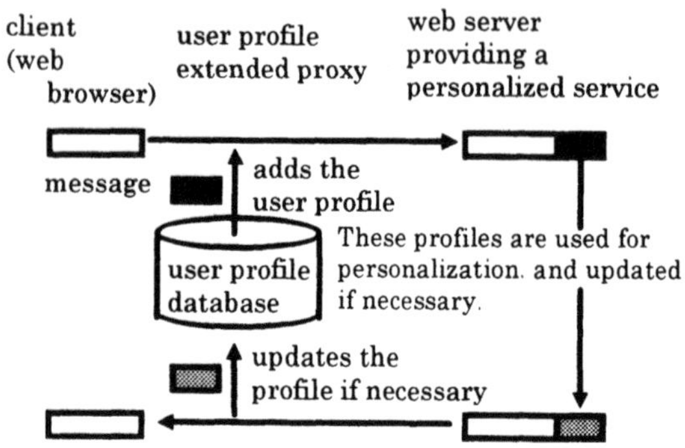

Figure 6. Communications through the extended proxy

stored in the database on a proxy. After extracting the content of the user profile, the proxy forwards the HTTP response to the client. This process assures complete transparency both for the client and the server: they send and receive the same messages as when they do so without an extended proxy.

When a user accesses a personalized service for the first time, the HTTP request will not contain any user profile. The server then informs the proxy, by including a Cookie-format header in the HTTP response, that the server in fact provides a personalized service and needs to store a new user profile. The proxy then adds an entry to the database and stores the user profile. This user profile extended proxy has the following advantages.

- **Ease of server maintenance:** discharges the web service providers from the user profiles management tasks and simplifies the programming of the web services since they are not required to interface with a large database of user profiles. The management tasks are distributed onto multiple proxies.
- **Ease of authentication:** centralizes and simplifies the authentication of the user. Once the user logs in to the proxy, all the log-ins to personalized servers are managed by the proxy. This also allows the user to use different terminals to access personalized web services with the same user profile as long as the access to the Internet is done through the same proxy.
- **User profiles sharing among servers:** enables the user profiles to be shared among different web services. Once a user profile is created for a personalized service, another service can also use it if the owner of the profile allows it.
- **User profiles sharing among users:** enables users to implement collaborative filtering services on the proxy since the profiles of a group of people are centralized on it.

3.3. Application examples

We have implemented two applications that share the same user profiles using our user profile extended proxy. One is a personalized newspaper service and the other is a personalized technical report. These two services are implemented on different web sites and provide different contents, but both use the user profiles of the same format within the mechanism of Cookie. In these applications, a user profile is a set of keywords and their weights. Since a Cookie data file consists of "attributes" and "values", our applications just interpret attributes as keywords and values as weights. When a user is interested in documents that include a specific keyword, the word's weight is high in the user's profile. Each of these systems gathers newspaper articles or technical reports from external sites, extracts keywords from them, and stores them on the server. When a user accesses the server, the server compares the user's profile with the keywords of each document, and scores all the documents. The more keywords in the user profile are included in a document, the higher the score the document gets. When a document gets a high score, it is shown at a former position within a list of document titles (Figure 7).

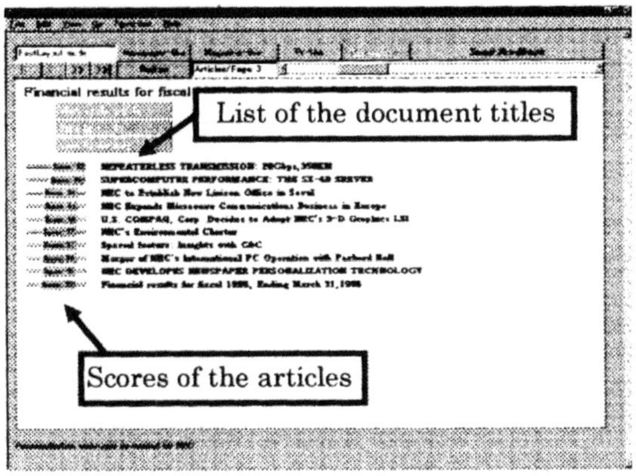

Figure 7. An example screen of our personalized technical reports

If there is no extended proxy, the Cookie file is stored on the client terminal, and the two similar personalized services cannot share the user profile written in this file. When the user profile extended proxy is used, however, the two services can share the user profile. This is useful for both services. Even when a regular user of one of the services accesses the other service for the first time, he or she can get the personalized information because the user profile is already on the extended proxy. For example, if the user has already registered the word "Internet" as a keyword for the newspaper, the user will get technical documents related to the Internet on the other server without setting his or her profile for the personalized technical reports service.

In addition, the user profiles can be shared among multiple users on the proxy. As an example, we have implemented a primitive collaborative filtering service. When this collaborative filtering does not work, the scores of the articles for a user are computed using only the user's profile as described above. When a program to support collaborative filtering exists on the proxy, the program automatically creates a group profile which is the average of all the users' profiles. When the proxy sends a user profile to the server, the program automatically mixes the group profile with the user's profile before it is sent to the server. Generally, a group of people who use the same proxy server often have similar interests, and they exchange ideas to get new information. This collaborative filtering function automatically supports such activities.

It should be noticed that this collaborative filtering function can be added by the users, not by the personalized service provider. By using the extended proxy, even when the server provides only a content-based filtering service, the group of users can start a collaborative filtering service by themselves as long as the user profile format is open to the users and Cookie is used for transporting the user profiles.

4. DISCUSSION AND FUTURE WORK

4.1. Security and privacy

Personalization and privacy are closely related issues. When we want to get personalized services on the Web, there is some possibility that our personal data will be stolen by a malicious third party. However, storing the user profiles at the proxy can be considered secure in the sense that they are stored within a usually trusted organization. In many companies, proxies are used to implement a firewall, and therefore access to the user profiles is impossible from the outside. In any case, storing personal data on the proxy will be better than letting outside providers keep the data.

In addition, in our system, access to the user profile is protected by a password so as to prevent any abuse from the inside. As long as the user is not requesting a URL associated with a user profile, no authentication is required. The first time the user requests a URL associated with a user profile, the proxy requires the user to authenticate him or herself with his or her user ID and password. This happens only once per browser's session, as it does when accessing a restricted web server.

4.2. Storage

As the proxy will centralize the storage of the user profiles, the amount of data to be stored can be significant. If it is considered that the users will use more and more personalized services, the size of each user's profile will tend to increase, but rarely decrease. This problem will certainly be accentuated by users surfing on the Web, accessing personalized services that require storage of a user profile, and never accessing these services again. To avoid storage problems, the proxy must be able to recycle the disk space for unused user profiles.

One solution that enables recycling is to ask web applications to specify an expiration date for each user profile that they want to be stored. This mechanism is provided by the Cookie. The disadvantage of this solution is that it relies on the "good will" of web applications for setting reasonable values for the expiration.

Another solution, and complementary to the first one, is to stamp each user profile with the current date/time when it is accessed. This stamping is done by our extended proxy and consequently does not rely on the web applications. Whenever a storage shortage occurs, the system starts deleting the oldest user profiles, considering that they are not relevant anymore. In addition to this stamping method, a counter is associated with each user profile, and this counter is increased each time when the profile is accessed. This prevents the omission of a profile that is accessed regularly, for example every month, even if the stamp is the oldest.

4.3. Future work

To date, we have implemented only a primitive collaborative filtering service on our extended proxy, but we are planning to design various filtering services. For example, we are planning to do grouping of our extended proxy users automatically. Even in our laboratory, whose members share fairly consistent interests, there are some groups that have different research themes. Each group member will have similar but different interests. To get group scores, we should consider which group a user belongs to.

In order to make our extended proxy widely useful, it is required that more personalized service providers make the format of their Cookie files open to public. Then, similar personalized services can share the user profiles, and the users need not register their profiles for each service. The opening of the format of the Cookie file will be necessary also when we consider the privacy issue.

5. CONCLUSION

We have pointed out the problems of current user profile management architectures and have proposed a user profile management agent that mediates the communication between personalized servers and users. This agent stores user profiles in itself and manages them. We have implemented the agent as an extended proxy server of the WWW. By using this extended proxy server, different personalized services can share the same user profiles, and at the same time, a collaborative filtering service can be implemented on the proxy server.

Personalization is an important technology to help people to get relevant information efficiently, but it should be implemented deliberately since it relates to the privacy issue. We believe our user profile management agent helps web service providers to manage personalization services more easily than now and helps users to get useful services such as collaborative filtering under their own control.

ACKNOWLEDGMENT

We would like to thank Shiro Sakata and Yoshiyuki Koseki for their constant support during our research. We would also like to thank Hidekazu Sakagami for his help in building our personalized applications.

REFERENCES

Hill, W., Stead, L., Rosenstein, M., and Furnas, G. (1995) Recommending and Evaluating Choices in a Virtual Community of Use, *CHI'95 Conference Proceedings*, pp.194-201.

Kamba, T., Bharat, K., and Albers, M.C. (1995) The Krakatoa Chronicle - An Interactive Personalized Newspaper on the Web, *Proceedings of the Fourth International Conference on the World Wide Web*, pp.159-170.

Shardanand, U. and Maes, P. (1995) Social Information Filtering: Algorithms for Automating "Word of Mouth", *CHI'95 Conference Proceedings*, pp.210-217.

HCI at CSIRO: Practical Research

Nadine Ozkan, Duncan Stevenson and Sandrine Balbo

CSIRO, Mathematical and Information Sciences
Locked Bag 17, North-Ryde NSW 2113, Australia
[nadine.ozkan|duncan.stevenson|sandrine.balbo]@cmis.csiro.au

Abstract The CSIRO division of Mathematical and Information Sciences (CMIS) and its predecessors the Division of Information Technology and the Division of Computing Research, have a long history of research in data visualisation and data interaction. More recently, the division has also started a research focus in HCI: a group was formed in 1995 to support research in both HCI and visualisation. This paper looks at the nature of the earlier work, at the integration of HCI skills into the development of data visualisation applications and at the emergence of HCI research within the division.

Key words usability engineering, data visualisation, user and task modelling, virtual reality

1. INTRODUCTION AND CONTEXT

The Commonwealth Scientific and Industrial Research Organisation (CSIRO) is Australia's national research organisation. Its role is to conduct research and to help the Australian industry through both the application of research results and knowledge transfer.

The HCI-Visualisation research group was formed within CSIRO's Division of Mathematical and Information Sciences (CMIS) in 1995. Today, the group consists of 6 researchers and 3 PhD students. Much of the research carried out within the Division is in the form of strategic research centred around problems posed by industrial partners. The work in HCI is multi-disciplinary in nature, involving close collaboration with scientists from many fields (image processing, multi-media, artificial intelligence, knowledge engineering, software engineering). The results of this work are strategic research in the form of case studies and prototypes, illustrating novel approaches to the problems industry has posed. Other more tactical work is shorter-term, responding to requests from industry to solve specific problems, and involves drawing on a skills base which is not otherwise available in the IT community in Australia.

2. VISUALISATION

A common thread in the work on data visualisation, dating from the late 70's, is the handling of large complex data sets with numerically demanding applications. This often involved anticipating by several years the hardware and software needed to do the job. For example, in the early 90's, massively parallel hardware was used to simulate interaction for an animation of particular scenarios. The system was

Human–Computer Interaction: INTERACT'97 S. Howard, J. Hammond & G. Lindgaard (editors)
Published by Chapman & Hall

1000 times slower than a production interactive system would have required, but was still able to provide the required test-bed for studying algorithms and techniques. Today the HCI-Visualisation group explores the use of small-scale immersive Virtual Reality systems and haptic force-feedback devices to study 3D geology for the mining industry. Each system costs upwards of $200 000 and the algorithms are in their infancy, yet our industrial partners expect that by the time we have a reasonable mastery of the situation, such systems will be affordable at the site.

The early work was often done in a near-absence of user requirements simply because the users and their applications did not exist. With the growth of HCI as a mature discipline and with a more computer-literate industrial base, we are now finding that we can take a more integrated approach combining techniques from data visualisation, user requirements and HCI.

3. HCI

Current activities in HCI are task analysis and task modelling, user-centred design and evaluation (especially for multimedia and web-based user interfaces [Yap & al. 1996]), user modelling for adaptive interfaces (specifically student for intelligent training systems [Yacef and Alem, 1996]) and data sonification [Barrass, 1996]. Due to lack of space, this paper only describes a subset of these.

3.1 Task and knowledge representation

Task analysis and task modelling techniques are one of the group's main area of expertise. Consequently, we are exploring their use in domains which lie outside their traditional scope of application, for example expert knowledge elicitation and representation. The division has been involved recently in the design and development of a decision support system for the Royal Australian Navy. The various partners in the project adopted the MAD formalism for task representation as the common formalism both for interface design and for knowledge representation [Balbo and Lindley, 1996].

3.2 Usability evaluation

In this area, the group has two main foci: automatic user interface evaluation and the new evaluation problems posed by recent technologies such as multimedia interfaces or web-based interfaces.

In the first stream of research, a robust automatic analyser for the evaluation of user interfaces is currently being developed. The approach is based on a comparison between the end user's actions and a data-flow oriented task model. The discrepancies between the two are analysed using behaviour rules based on ergonomic criteria [Balbo, 1996].

For the second stream of research, the group has developed and is constantly updating methods and templates for the usability evaluation of recent technologies. The problems posed by these new technologies include multimedia software typology and the adaptation of usability methods to software used in contexts different from the work environment such as home, kiosk, classroom, etc. We have also been closely associated with the setting up of a usability lab specialised in multimedia evaluation [Ozkan and Balbo, 1996].

4. FUTURE DIRECTIONS

In addition to the various streams of research briefly described here, we plan to initiate activities in automatic text generation and human-computer dialogue in the near future.

REFERENCES

S. Balbo and C. Lindley. 1996."Adaptation of a Task Analysis Methodology to the Design of a Decision Support System", Interact'97 proceedings.

S. Balbo. 1996. "An automatic analysis mechanism for ergonomic evaluation", CSIRO T.R. 96/44.

S. Barrass. 1996. "Sculpting a Sound Space with Information Properties", Organised Sound, 1, 2, Cambridge University Press.

N. Ozkan and S. Balbo. 1996. "Requirements Analysis for a Multimedia Usability Lab". CSIRO T.R. 96/61.

K. Yacef and L. Alem. 1996. "Student and expert modelling for operational simulation-based training" in Proceedings of Intelligent Tutoring Systems (ITS'96), Montreal, June, pp 614-622.

K. Yap, B. Simpson-Young and U. Srinivasan. 1996. "Enhancing Video Navigation with Existing Alternate Representations". in International Workshop on Image Databases and Multi-Media Search. Amsterdam, August, pp. 91-98.

Interdisciplinary research in practice at CMD, Uppsala University

Bengt L. Sandblad

CMD, Center for Human-Computer Studies
Uppsala University
Lägerhyddvägen 18, S-752 37 Uppsala, Sweden
Phone: +46 18 18 33 21, E-mail: Bengt.Sandblad@cmd.uu.se
http://www.cmd.uu.se

ABSTRACT CMD, Uppsala University Center for Human-Computer Studies, is an interdisciplinary research unit where researchers from different departments of the university closely co-operate in research concerning computer applications in working life. Scientific disciplines such as psychology, computer science, systems analysis, physics, ergonomics, medicine and dentistry are represented. Main characteristics of the research are integration of different HCI-related competencies into a homogenous interdisciplinary team and the strong involvement in 'real working life' development projects. Through this, new integrated theories, methods and techniques have been developed.

KEY WORDS Interface design, participatory design, cognitive load, development tools, work environment problems, HCI in organisations.

1. THE INTERDISCIPLINARY EXPERIENCE

Research concerning the introduction of information technology in working life must by necessity be interdisciplinary. However, the advantages of *inter*disciplinary research can only be achieved if it is paired with strong *intra*disciplinary competencies. If the researchers co-operating in the interdisciplinary research do not continuously develop their traditional knowledge, the interdisciplinary advantage will soon be lost. It also takes time and efforts to develop functioning interdisciplinary research co-operation. Success requires long time engagement, mutual respect, scientific methodology and, at least in the beginning, focus on concrete applications. Interdisciplinary knowledge is more then 'the sum of the parts'. At CMD, we have in this way been able to develop new approaches to studies of human-computer interaction in working life applications. Examples are methods for analysis of skilled professionals' every day use of information and methods and tools for design and construction of efficient user interfaces to be used in dynamic work situations.

2. WORKING LIFE APPLICATIONS

At CMD, the research focus is on working life applications of information technology. When developing computer systems for skilled professionals in different work environments, the role of the user interface is especially central. Badly designed interfaces will result in low user acceptance, high costs, inefficient work, negative stress and sometimes even health problems (Nygren, 1992). Interface requirement specifications for specific professional use will often differ significantly from more general design rules. Domain specific style guides, specifying interaction requirements for advanced use in specific work environments can significantly improve the design process. If the work organisation, the functionality of the computer support system or the user interface to the system is not properly designed, the possibilities for the professionals to perform efficiently will often be drastically reduced. We call such hindrances *cognitive work environment problems*. Research and field studies at CMD indicate that such problems are becoming increasingly important in today's working life.

Human–Computer Interaction: INTERACT'97 S. Howard, J. Hammond & G. Lindgaard (editors)
Published by Chapman & Hall

3. COGNITIVE WORK ENVIRONMENT PROBLEMS

A main research goal is to identify new knowledge concerning cognitive work environment problems and to specify system development methods and techniques that can minimise such problems. Research activities include experimental studies of cognitive work load and relations to design of user interfaces. Prototypes have been developed and tested in working life applications. (Nygren, 1996)

4. RESEARCH AREAS

In order to integrate traditional academic research with the introduction of improved methods and techniques in practical interface design and system development, our 'in house' laboratory research is combined with participation in 'real life' development projects. In such projects our research results can be tested in evaluated.

New interface methods and techniques

• Formulation of a method for *analysis of information utilisation* in professional work situations. The result of such an analysis is a set of requirement specifications for the interaction between user and system.

• Development of methods for specification of *domain specific style guides* for defined classes of work situations. In a domain specific style guide we incorporate high level design knowledge into interface element classes and related design rules (Borälv, 1994).

• The development of graphical user interfaces is today too resource consuming and leads to severe constraints when it comes to the use of experimental techniques. We are developing a prototype for object oriented, model based, user interfaces. Here the design and functionality of the system is described in a declarative language, stored in a database and interpreted at run-time.

• Several research activities concern aspects of visualisation techniques, such as e.g. the use and interpretation of colours in user interfaces and dynamic visualisation in virtual reality (VR) environments.

Operator-Process Interaction

Research is here directed towards analysis of human capabilities and technological conditions for control of complex, dynamic systems. Operator support systems must allow development of efficient mental models of the process and support complex decision making. Application projects concern present problems in train traffic control and in control of high speed crafts at sea. Next generation operator systems will be based on 'control by awareness' rather then 'control by exception'.

Organisational development and IT design

There is a need for a new paradigm of system development, focusing on development of organisation and work activities as such. Methods for analysis, requirement specifications, system design and construction, must consider all relevant aspects simultaneously, and not focus only on technical information support systems. We are currently, in co-operation with the Swedish National Tax Board, studying organisational development in a case handling domain, integrating development of organisation, information systems and professional competencies (Gulliksen, 1996).

Usability evaluation methods

In co-operation with occupational health care units we have developed a practical method for 'semi-expert' usability evaluation of existing computer systems in a work environment. The method is based on a combined observation and interview technique, and focuses on functionality and cognitive aspects of human-computer interaction.

5. EDUCATIONAL PROGRAMS

CMD is active in undergraduate programs at the university, where interdisciplinary courses are given e.g. in the computer science programs. Graduate students at CMD participate in the programs of their 'home' departments of the university, e.g. in the systems analysis and psychology programs.

6. REFERENCES

Nygren E., Johnson M., Lind M. and Sandblad B. *The art of the obvious.* Proceedings of CHI'92, Monterey, California, May 1992.

Borälv E., Göransson B., Olsson E. and Sandblad B. *Usability and efficiency. The HELIOS approach to development of user interfaces.* Comp. Methods and Programs in Biomed.45, Suppl.(1994), S1-152.

Nygren, E. *From paper to computer screen. Human information processing and user interface design.* Ph.D. thesis. Faculty of Science and Technology, Uppsala, Sweden (1996). ISBN 91-554-3699-4.

Gulliksen, J. *Designing for usability - Domain specific human-computer interfaces in working life.* Ph.D. thesis. Faculty of Science and Technology, Uppsala, Sweden (1996). ISBN 91-554-3700-1.

PART THREE

Posters

Use of Internet facilities in education

Jaroslav Sklenar

University of Malta
Department of Computer Information Systems
Msida MSD 06
Malta
jskl@cis.um.edu.mt

ABSTRACT Hypertext documents offer completely new opportunities in all aspects of communication both among humans and between humans and computers. The poster shows typical screens of a web document that is used as a means of communication between a lecturer and a quite big population of students involved in various courses at the University of Malta. The spectrum of students goes from the Junior College (sixth form) through various undergraduate courses to candidates preparing for their B.Sc. theses.

KEYWORDS Education, World Wide Web, INTERNET

1. INTRODUCTION

We all know how the mass use of all Internet based facilities has changed our lives in recent years. There are many aspects of this phenomenon that has both positive and negative consequences (recently my son has downloaded a complete "Terrorist Handbook" with detailed guides how to prepare explosives and similar stuff). Whatever are the consequences, the Internet is here, it will be here, and young people will use it definitely more and more. So the only thing we should do is to make the best possible use of it.

2. TEACHER - STUDENT

The most typical way of using web documents in education is probably distribution of notes, extracts of lectures, various charts, worksheets, demonstration programs and sometimes complete textbooks. The advantages are obvious. A lecturer can transfer a lot of data to practically unlimited number of recipients in a very short time. What is maybe even more important is the possibility of keeping materials permanently up to date. All changes are done only once in the original document in the home directory of the owner of the page, all recipients get automatically a latest updated version at each connection. This is broadcasting.

Web documents can also complement e-mail in point to point communication. Very often there are problems with attachments to e-mail messages. In the UNIX environment the attachment has to be often converted manually. If the message is not saved properly, it must be retransmitted. All these can cause troubles, especially if there is a very heterogeneous group of potential recipients (from hackers that are totally in to beginners, who have never used computers before). An alternative way is a simple special purpose document (maybe with a not standard extension to its name) that contains a reference (URL) to the file to be transferred together with a guide how to use it. The name of the document is then given (for example e-mailed) to the recipient or a group of recipients. The file is permanently available, the transfer is very easy even for

Human–Computer Interaction: INTERACT'97 S. Howard, J. Hammond & G. Lindgaard (editors)
Published by Chapman & Hall

complete beginners, and again its updating (maintenance) is very easy. When not used any more, both the file and the document should be deleted.

3. STUDENT - TEACHER

This flow of information is very useful for all teachers. We all need a sort of feedback from students. Especially at lower grades (in my case at the sixth form college) there is a permanent danger, that students might give up in certain more demanding topics. All teachers know how difficult it is to obtain this type of information. When asked in the class, many students are because of various reasons not willing to talk frankly about their problems. Of course personal contact lessons help a lot, but time is a very limiting factor. Here simple e-mail can help very much. First of all, the tutor must get student's confidence, that all the information supplied will be used by the educator only and will not be revealed to other students under any circumstances. Then it is possible, to get very useful ideas and hints from students. When writing e-mail messages at home, students can concentrate, and so they tend to be more open. This is another reason why all Web documents should have an option to e-mail to the author.

Forms that can be created by the facilities of the HTML language offer another way how to obtain information from students, but their preparation is not an easy task to do and they actually just replace traditional questionnaires.

4. STUDENT - STUDENT

All teachers know what a powerful tool is proper motivation. The possibility of being adequately rewarded makes many people (not only students) work very hard. A very efficient way of rewarding students is a sort of public appreciation of their abilities. For this purpose a Web document can be very useful. For example in my Web page there is something I call "Student's corner". It is used for presentation of nice solutions to various problems, so far mostly as a place to show Turbo Pascal programs that are either interesting, not traditional, have educational value, or have simply a nice graphics. (We use Turbo Pascal both at the sixth form and in most under graduate courses).

Of course all presented programs are available to all students (to be downloaded in compressed form). It is very important to make it very clear since the very beginning, that a place like that can under no circumstances be used for any commercial purpose. There is this danger, because many students - especially the best ones - who contribute with their programs are actively involved in various software companies already during their studies. So an attempt to use a teacher's page for advertising is logical.

5. TEACHER - TEACHER

The name of this chapter is not the best one, but it was very tempting to use the fourth combination. In fact there are many other ways how Internet facilities can be used in research, organization of conferences (like this one), and generally in all activities that are based on transfer of information. Actually it is more difficult, but definitely shorter to list activities, that can not benefit from Internet facilities like e-mail, Web documents, News groups, File transfer, etc.

Among many others, Internet has helped very much in communication between authors of software products and their users. It used to be a very demanding task to keep all registered users informed about the latest development and especially to distribute patches, adds on, and new versions of the product. Internet offers an elegant solution to this problem. In fact practically all commonly used products have their home pages, that contain everything the company wants the users to know. Even for commercial products you can often find various adds on and updates (like for example Internet Assistant for Microsoft Word).

The poster shows typical screens from the home page of the program PetriSim, that is an editor and simulator of Petri Networks with the possibility to create user simulation models in Turbo Pascal. There are several demo examples, that are all full scale editors and simulators of Petri networks. For more see my home page: **http://www.cis.um.edu.mt/~jskl**

Usability Evaluation Techniques for Large-Scale Web Sites

Karyn Burger and Ellen Jackson

Interactive Multimedia Group, Logica Pty. Ltd.
30 Collins St., Melbourne, Victoria
AUSTRALIA
burgerk@logica.com
jacksone@logica.com

KEYWORDS World Wide Web, usability evaluation, user testing

1. INTRODUCTION

The combination of hardware and software limitations within World Wide Web site development has created a set of unique constraints on the choice of available interface elements and the user's interaction with them. Information about these users and the tasks they perform is also different from graphical user interface development, due to the diverse and constantly changing population on the Web and the more continuous, fluid nature of tasks such as browsing or entertainment most common to the Internet environment (Graphic, Visualisation and Usability Centre (GVU), 1996). It is also difficult to gain a detailed understanding of the user's environment in which they may access the site, which may include work, home, school/university and increasingly, Internet cafes.

Due to these factors, and the recent explosion of web sites over the Internet, usability for the web is playing "catch-up" to develop better ways of designing and testing for the user. Some design guidelines are beginning to emerge to point to ways that web pages can be more efficiently designed (for example, Sun web guidelines, Apple, Benjamin (1996)). This re-evaluation of design guidelines and the speed with which web sites are generally developed have called for an evolution of the evaluation techniques that were traditionally built upon character-based and GUI task-based applications.

2. HEURISTIC EVALUATION.

Heuristic evaluation is a technique whereby one or more usability professionals use and study the interface in detail to identify areas that, from their experience, will lead to usability problems (Nielsen & Molich, 1990). This technique is particularly useful for evaluation of World Wide Web applications, due to its time and cost efficiency in what is often an extremely rapid development environment. Ideally, heuristic evaluation is undertaken according to usability principles, or rules. These usability principles, as developed by Nielsen and Molich (1990), include; use simple and natural dialogue, speak the user's language, minimise memory load, maintain consistency, provide feedback, clearly marked exits, shortcuts and error messages, and prevent errors.

Our experience, however, suggests that although these basic principles also apply to Web site evaluation, they need to be adapted and expanded to most effectively evaluate Web interfaces through heuristic evaluation. For example, clearly marked exits and shortcuts are difficult to design for due to the non-linear, hypertext environment of the web. We have found navigation considerations such as minimise scrolling, inclusion of site maps and provision of alternative navigation methods for different users to be more useful in web evaluation. Other useful constructs have included:

- Is the text broken into small sections?
- Are graphs and tables used where appropriate?

Human–Computer Interaction: INTERACT'97 S. Howard, J. Hammond & G. Lindgaard (editors)
Published by Chapman & Hall

- Is data tailored to the user where possible?
- Is time sensitive-data up-to-date?
- Are the size and amount of graphics appropriate?
- Is the download time of graphics appropriate to the goal of the site?
- Is the user given a choice of how they view data?
- Is animation used appropriately?

3. INFORMAL USER EVALUATION.

Informal User Evaluation (Rubin 1994) is an exploratory test in which the effectiveness of preliminary or early design concepts can be assessed. Informal user evaluation is a fast means of evaluating a Web site, thus it also fits well within short turnaround requirements. Scenarios are used to guide the user's exploration of the site, although users can also be encouraged to investigate or browse the site as they might normally do in order to evaluate the browsing or information gathering task. Quantitative measures are rarely gathered at this stage, and qualitative findings can be quickly integrated as input to the next iteration. Because the emphasis of these sessions is on the evaluation of the appropriateness of the interface to the user's cognitive model, users are encouraged to "think aloud" and to suggest alternatives for areas causing confusion. A particular technique that we have found useful here is the paired-user walkthrough technique. This involves two users working through the interface together. The dialogue that results can provide a rich and direct commentary of the users' interaction with the system (Wildman, 1996). This commentary can be particularly revealing for Web site evaluation as it can provides user feedback on issues such as how useful, interesting and engaging the product is for the user.

4. USER TESTING.

Traditional formal user (or usability) testing involves the collection of empirical data through the observation of representative users using a product to perform representative tasks (Rubin, 1994). While the essential techniques used for usability testing are similar for evaluation of web applications, there are several differences that should be taken into account when undertaking usability testing for web sites.

- **Recruitment.** As it is very difficult to conduct a detailed user analysis on who will be using the site, user testing subjects should represent a wide range of characteristics and capabilities, including high, medium and low levels of web literacy.
- **Test Scenarios**. Information gathering, searching and interactive tasks can be well represented within task scenarios, although it can be very difficult to represent browsing or entertainment. It may be more realistic to test these constructs within informal testing.
- **Test Environment**. Because user's platforms may vary greatly, the site should be specifically tested for usability on the minimum platform environment specified, and then tested for adequate functionality on as many other combinations of devices as possible. Test scenarios should also represent the wider context of use, for example home or work tasks.
- **Analysis**. It is often difficult to empirically assess such constructs as interest and entertainment and the degree to which these are satisfied for the user by the web site. Alternatives include debriefing interviews or questionnaires, as well as the "Write to Us" area of the site once it has been released

5. REFERENCES

Apple Computer. (1996) *Apple Web Design Guide.* http://www.cybertech.apple.com/HI/web_design/intro.html.

Benjamin, B. (1996) *Elements Of Web Design* http://www.cnet.com/Content/Features/Howto/Design/

Graphic, Visualization & Usability Center (1996) *GVU's 5th WWW User Survey.* Graphic, Visualization & Usability Center, http://www.cc.gat

Nielsen, J. & Molich, R. (1990) Heuristic Evaluation of User Interfaces, in *Proceedings of CHI '90* (Seattle, WA, April 1-5), 249-256.

Rubin, J. (1994) *Handbook of Usability Testing: How to plan, design and conduct effective tests.* John Wiley & Sons, Inc. New York.

Sun (1996) *Guide to Web Style.* http://www.sun.com/styleguide/

Wildman, D. (1996) "Getting the most from paired-user testing". *Interactions, Volume 2 Number 3.*

Pop-Up Windows and Information Retrieval

Stéphane Caro

INRIA Rhône-Alpes
655, av. de l'Europe
38330 Montbonnot Saint-Martin
FRANCE
Stephane.Caro@inrialpes.fr

ABSTRACT Paralinguistics organizers such as parenthesis, footnotes, and pop-up fields on screen, should play an important role signalling the writer's "minimization" intention when secondary points are concerned. This experiment investigated the role of pop-up fields compared to brackets in an information retrieval task. The results showed that, in this kind of task, putting secondary pieces of information into pop-up fields significantly speeded the search process compared to a condition in which the same information was displayed in brackets.

KEYWORDS Information Retrieval, Pop-up windows, Electronic Document Ergonomics

1. INTRODUCTION

A frequent task in a screen reading process is to find a piece of information in a set; either we are seeking information in a text (or a set of texts) in the hope of finding it, or we are seeking it knowing that it is in the content. In reading "from beginning to end", we admit that the reader does a categorization between main textual unit (TU) and secondary TU in order to modulate the depth of his processing. In a consultation for seeking information, the problem is to read the minimum of non-pertinent information before finding the pertinent. Categorization of TUs not only between main and secondary but also between various types of TUs could be crucial. We postulated that the use of pop-up windows could be a powerful means in order to facilitate the information retrieval task. If some TUs are hidden but correctly categorized, (with underlined words in the text for example) then the reader could either cheerfully ignore them, or explicitly seek the information in its locations; and in addition, such pop-up windowing of information decreases the amount of permanently displayed text and thus the text processing load.

2. THE EXPERIMENT

2.1. Overview

The objective of the experiment was to compare the effect of puting secondary TUs in pop-up windows with more classical para-linguistic organizers, like brackets, for a textual information retrieval task. Using the measurement of retrieval times for specific information (on main information TUs and secondary information TUs), we expected that the use of pop-up windows would decrease these information retrieval times.

2.2. Material

A small text database was constructed. The chosen texts present five cars. Each car description was five screen pages long. Two versions of this base were made: a «bracket» version in which the secondary TUs were at the same level as the main TUs but were between brackets (see Figure 1). In the «pop-up window» version, the same TUs were put in «pop-up windows». Underlined words (see Figure 1) enable the reader to: see the information in the pop-up with a mouse click, anticipate the type of information stored in the pop-up window.

Human–Computer Interaction: INTERACT'97 S. Howard, J. Hammond & G. Lindgaard (editors)
Published by Chapman & Hall

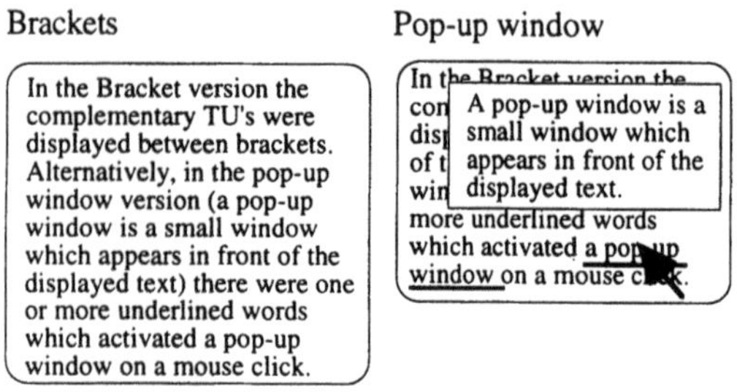

Figure 1: Brackets and pop-up window of the same text

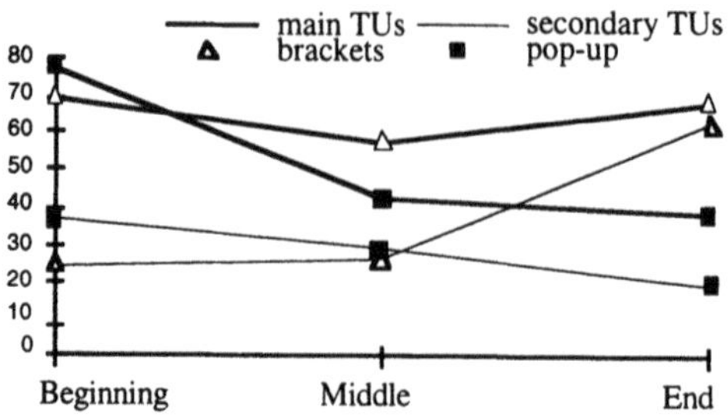

Figure 2: Response times (in sec.) at the 3 points

2.3. Subjects

Twelve volunteers participated in the experiment. They were all native French speaking adults (average age 26 years) with an education level of at least bachelor +3 years.

2.4. Retrieval Task

Twelve questions had to be answered, six on each type of TU. The time taken to answer each question was measured.

2.5. Experiment Plan

Six subjects had pop-up windows and six had brackets. Three questions about main TUs and three questions about secondary TUs were destined to measure the evolution of response time at three points in the experiment (at the beginning, in the middle, at the end).

2.6. Results

An ANOVA with repeated measures was calculated on the question response time logarithm for each information type (main/secondary). Figure 2 shows the observed data and the interactions. For the search on the main information, the analysis shows that neither the *presentation* effect (brackets vs. pop-up) nor the *moment* effect was significant (at the beginning, in the middle, at the end). But their interaction was significant [$F(2,20) = 5.66$; $p<.02$]. Then, for the main information, if the presentation in a pop-up tends to give longer search times than the brackets presentation at the beginning, it is the contrary at the end of the session. For the search times on the secondary information TUs, the effect of the factors is not significant nor is their interaction.

We considered the times needed for the main and secondary information TUs as two different measures and calculated a multivaried ANOVA. Globally, pop-up presentation gives significantly faster search times than brackets presentation [F- Wilks' Lambda = 4.6; $p <.05$]. It is possible to make the same search decision in both types of information in the text: for the secondary information TUs [$F(1,10) = 5.1$; $p<.05$] and for the main information TUs [$F(1,10) = 7.2$; $p<.03$].

2.7. Discussion

For a retrieval task in a small textual base, the secondary information TUs distinction with pop-up has a facilitation effect in relation to a condition where the information is equally distinguished but simply with brackets. Indeed, even when the subjects were not familiar at the beginning with pop-ups, this experiment enabled us to observe an evolution of the relative efficiency of the two presentation forms. At the beginning, the pop-up windows tend to increase search times compared with brackets, but at the end of the experiment the tendency reverses. However, this evolution is only significant for searches for the main information TUs. This phenomenon seems to be due to a progressive improvement of the subject search times for the pop-up windows, but equally and curiously to a performance deterioration at the end of the session for the bracket subjects. It could be that the end session search test presented an *a priori* unsuspected difficulty compared to the searches at the beginning and the middle of the session. At the same time, the pop-up window group continue to improve their performances. However that may be, the final test showed that the pop-up window subjects are faster than brackets subjects and this is true for the searches on the main and the secondary TUs.

A Concept Model for Maintaining Awareness of Document Configuration

Shi Tao

UNSECO Supported International Centre for Engineering Education (USICEE)
Monash University, VIC 3168, Australia
tao@eng.monash.edu.au

KEY WORDS: CSCW

CSCW is essentially a cooperative process and involves bringing expertise together in order to develop a document. The document components are worked on by collaborators independently and are assembled and reassembled based on the requirements of the working system. In order to ensure consistency within the document in a changing environment it is necessary to maintain awareness of document configuration among individual collaborators. In this poster, a multi-dimensional model is presented as a first step to explicitly represent the complex relationships among the components in the collaborative document preparation, with the objective of maintaining awareness of document configuration in asynchronous distributed cooperation. This proposal is primarily based on Prof. Igor Hawryszkiewycz' paper(Hawryszkiewycz, 1996). The prototype will be developed with *Java*.

The first dimension of the model shown below is project workflow. In general, the task sequence is neither linear nor parallel, but exhibits network behaviour with change being dynamic. Each task in the process is linked by a set of vectors which can be seen as the function of time. This means that the same task can be repeated at different times. This dimension is project oriented with the aim of producing the relevant document.

The second dimension consists of three layers. *The first layer* is the collaborative document preparation. It is a set of document preparation activities which are affiliated to each project task. The activities consist of task-cycles, and each cycle has several steps. It is document management oriented. *The second layer* represents the document's various states distinguished by different colours. The document evolves through the task-cycle as it progresses from one state to the next. The task-cycle steps can be mapped into document management at each state transition. The document states can, therefore, be links between tasks and document components, which can be used to model dynamics. *The third layer* is about **versioning policies**. The versioning policy can be seen as an integrative mechanism at conceptual level to combine activities with artefacts. Each of the version numbers correspond to certain activities during document preparation. The number changes should automatically be displayed to individuals. The versioning policy consists of two parts - coordination and private. The coordination policy is defined in terms of configuration, task-cycle and cycle-step. Each time

Human-Computer Interaction: INTERACT'97 S. Howard, J. Hammond & G. Lindgaard (editors)
Published by Chapman & Hall

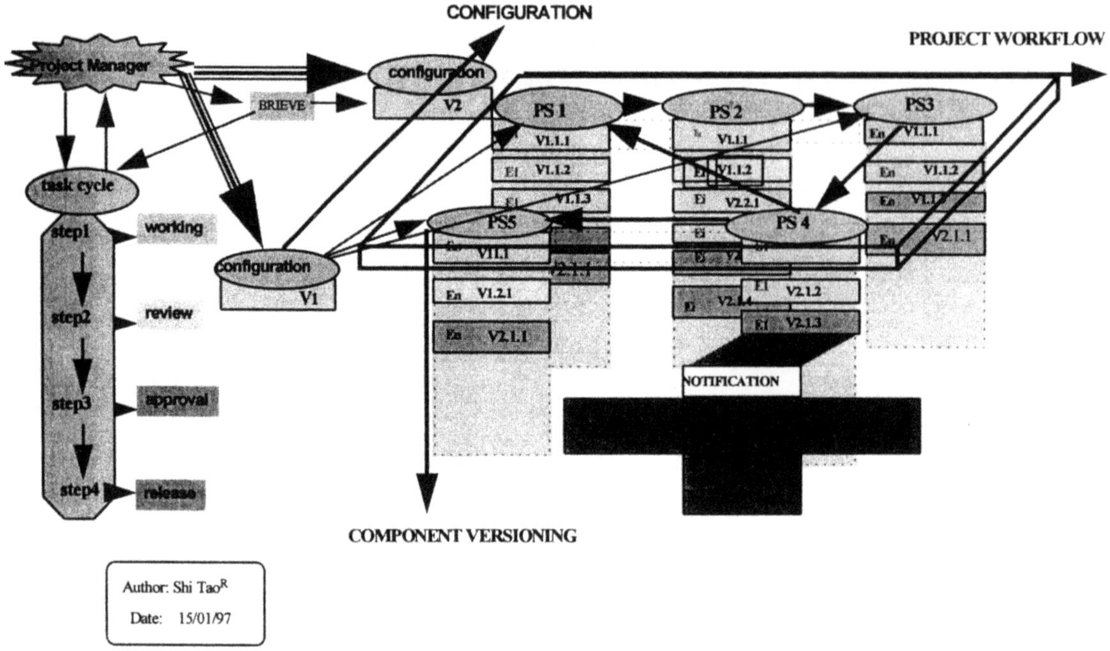

Figure 1: A multi-dimensional concept model.

a new configuration is constituted, the first number of the version in this part is changed and a new brief may be issued. Once the document goes through a task-cycle, the second number of the version is incremented. Except for step one, any task-cycle step can change the third number of the version. The private policy is a set of individual versioning conventions. The changes made by individual writers are hidden from all other collaborators.

The third dimension of the model is configuration. The **configuration** is meaningful compositions of document versions in a given state consistent with its ontology. The ontology is a set of specifications of physical elements at the semantic level. It is like a set of IP addresses acting as an invisible assembly line embedded in the document elements. For each configuration, the relevant components are combined and their first version numbers are changed. As the components are grouped and invoked, individuals are notified. This can be done by blinking the component in the model and informing the individual collaborator of the occurrence. Notification with a detailed description of the changes can be accessed by clicking the component nodes.

References

1. Hawryszkiewycz, I.T., *An architecture for supporting asynchronous processes*. (Unpublished) (1996).

Assessment of modal beliefs about using an electronic supermarket

Peter Roberts, Ron Henderson & Debra Rickwood
Centre for Applied Psychology
University of Canberra
ACT 2616
Australia

petrob@ozemail.com.au

ABSTRACT
36 users of a prototype electronic supermarket answered open ended questions regarding beliefs, social pressures and perceived control relating to the service. Results indicated mainly positive salient beliefs about the service, perceived behavioral control dominated by concerns about the system and the importance of social pressures on usage. Analysis revealed that convenience, time saving and money saving were the primary positive beliefs with lack of sensory cues the primary negative belief. The implications of the study for the use of predictive theoretical models are discussed.

KEY WORDS
Electronic supermarket, Theory of Planned Behavior, Technology Acceptance Model.

1. Introduction

The aim of the study was to identify modal salient beliefs, primary sources of social pressure and modal perceived behavioral controls arising from the use of the electronic supermarket service. Results are to be used in the application of the Theory of Planned Behavior as a predictor of the use of the service and to ascertain whether the Technology Acceptance Model has validity outside workplace and educational environments.

2 METHOD

2.1 Sample

A total of 36 users of a prototype electronic supermarket participated. Users were mainly working adults, with access to a computer and modem, predominantly female (24), and identified themselves as the main shopper in the household.

2.2 Measures

Using the procedures outlined by Ajzen and Fishbein, subjects were asked to respond to list advantages and disadvantages of the service, significant persons who approved or disapproved of their usage, as well as inhibiting and facilitating factors which could affect their use of the service. Subjects were also asked to list any other matters relating to the service they considered important. No indication was given to subjects as to the number of factors required under each category.

Human–Computer Interaction: INTERACT'97 S. Howard, J. Hammond & G. Lindgaard (editors)
Published by Chapman & Hall

In developing a predictive model, it would be normal practice to elicit salient beliefs from a sample before they commenced the behavior. Because of the highly innovative nature of the activity, it would have been very difficult for subjects to conceptualise the activity to a level where sufficient salient beliefs could be generated for analysis and therefore experienced subjects were used.

2.3 Procedure

19 users answered the seven open ended questions as part of a larger self-report questionnaire and 15 answered by telephone interview.

3 Results

In total 212 salient beliefs, 70 sources of social pressure and 90 behavioral control factors were listed. These factors were grouped into 22 categories. Using a cut off of 80% for categorised factors on each construct, the following have been identified as the modal beliefs.

Salient beliefs	
convenience	28.7%
negative system attributes	17.0%
lack of sensory cues	10.4%
saving time	7.1%
saving money	6.6%
positive system attributes	6.1%
enjoyment	4.7%
Subjective norms	
friends	24.3%
work colleagues	18.6%
family	17.1%
spouse	5.7%
"anti-computer" people	5.7%
traditional grocery retailers	2.9%
Perceived behavioural control factors	
specific assisting system factors	23.3%
specific system difficulties	16.7%
costs	15.6%
availability of equipment	14.4%
difficulties with technology	11.1%

4 Discussion

The study of the attitude-behavior relation arising from the introduction of innovative information technology has been examined largely in the workplace and educational environments. Much of this research has been conducted using the Technology Acceptance Model (TAM), a derivative of the Theory of Reasoned Action (TRA). Studies comparing the TAM with the TRA support the finding that the primary antecedent beliefs about predicting the use of innovative information technology are the perceived usefulness of the system to the user and the system's ease of use. Also this research indicates that perceived social pressures to use or not to use the system (subjective norms) are not an important factor in decisions on use in workplace and educational environments.

The electronic supermarket is an application of information technology outside those environments and is a quite radical departure from the socially significant activity from physically visiting shops. This study supports the necessity to revisit the fundamentals of the TRA in that it indicates that the salient beliefs go beyond those presumed by the TAM. Convenience was nominated as the most important factor which equates to usefulness and system attributes (both positive and negative), equating to ease-of-use, were together the next ranked factor. Additional factors (sensory cues, saving money and enjoyment) are outside the scope of the TAM, but rated as important by the users. The importance of subjective norms was highlighted by the high response rate to those factors, indicating a social perspective of electronic shopping.

The subsequent addition of perceived behavioral control factors to the TRA to form the Theory of Planned Behavior is a recognition that the attitude-behavior relation exists is not confined to purely volitional decisions. Further research will be needed to determine whether subjects view electronic shopping as a purely volitional activity or is significantly affected by the control factors nominated.

Acceptance of computers in human roles

Kylie O'Hare & Ron Henderson
Centre for Applied Psychology
University of Canberra
ACT 2616
Australia

ron@science.canberra.edu.au

ABSTRACT
The aim of the study was to examine attitudes towards computers full filling what would be labelled traditional human roles. A total of 114 individuals completed a questionnaire examining their attitudes and the hypothesised predictors of attitudes. It was found that there was marked differences in attitudes toward computers full filling traditional human roles and that key psychological variables were statistically, but weakly, related towards these attitudes.

KEY WORDS
Anthropocentricism and computers, Computer acceptance, social issues.

1. Introduction

Researchers have began to examine peoples attitudes towards computers full filling human roles. The argument is now being advanced that although computer based technology may be capable of performing certain functions, do people want them to perform these functions, or are there roles that people do not want computers to perform.(see Nass, Lombard, Henrikson & Steuer, 1995).

The current research aimed to examine peoples attitudes towards computers full filling what would traditionally been considered human roles in an Australian adult sample. The study also aimed to examine potential psychologically based predictors of these attitudes.

2 METHOD

2.1 Subjects

A total of 114 subjects voluntarily completed the self-report questionnaire. Subjects were from a range of occupations and background. Thirty-seven were male and 77 were female, with a mean age of 33. Seventy-nine percent of subjects used a computer on a daily basis.

2.2 Measures

The questionnaire assessed biographical data and a number of psychological attributes of the subjects. Section one assessed the participants cognitive attitudes towards general computer usage and three sub-scales from the Sixteen Personality Factor Questionnaire - Warmth, Abstractedness, and Apprehension which had previously been shown to be associated to acceptance of computers in non-traditional roles.

The final section of the questionnaire consisted of the acceptance of computers in human roles devised

Human–Computer Interaction: INTERACT'97 S. Howard, J. Hammond & G. Lindgaard (editors)
Published by Chapman & Hall

by Nass et al., (1995). In this scale asked the question "Assume that computers could do everything that humans can do. How comfortable would you be with computers as..." The 24 items that followed named a different role, such as baby sitter, bank teller etc. The scale was scored on a five point (very uncomfortable / very comfortable) scale. A factor analysis on the current data set revealed that a four factor solution provided the best fit to the data (acceptance of computers in: routine roles, interpretive roles, authoritarian roles, personal roles).

2.3 Procedure

The non-probability technique of convenience sampling was used (Jackson, 1995), with questionnaires distributed to people of varying ages and occupations.

3 Results

A one-way Analysis of Variance (ANOVA) was conducted on the four factor mean scores to determine whether the sample differed with respect to their attitudes towards the factors. The ANOVA revealed a significant effect, $F(2,452)= 63.36$, $p<.001$. A post hoc comparison with a Bonferroni adjustment revealed that there were significant differences between acceptance of computers in interpretive roles and authoritarian and personal roles, with people being more accepting of computers in interpretive roles than in authoritarian or personal. There were also significant differences between acceptance of computers in routine roles and acceptance of computers in interpretive, authoritarian or personal roles. People were more accepting of computers in routine roles (see Table 1).

Table 1: Means and Standard Deviations of dimensions of Acceptance of Computers in human roles.

Dimensions	Mean	SD
Acceptance of computers in		
routine roles	3.14	.90
interpretive roles	2.16	.88
authoritarian roles	1.72	.86
personal roles	1.82	.83

Stepwise regression analyses was conducted to identify predictors of attitudes towards acceptance computers in human roles. In the first analyses, cognitive attitudes was statistically selected to be entered on step 1, and accounted for 4.5% of the variance of acceptance of computers in interpretive roles, $R^2=.045$, $F(1,113)=5.36$, $p<.05$. Abstractedness also made a significant independent contribution, explaining a further 3.8% of the variance and was entered on step 2, $R^2=.083$, $F(1,113)=5.03$, $p<.01$.

The second regression was conducted on acceptance of computers in authoritarian roles. Age was statistically selected to be entered on step 1, and accounted for 4.3% of the variance, $R^2=.043$, $F(1,113)=5.12$, $p<.05$.

The regression run on factor three, acceptance of computers in personal roles, indicated that none of the independent variables were significantly responsible for the variance of acceptance of computers in these roles. The regression run on the acceptance of computers in routine roles indicated that 6.4% of the variance was caused by people's cognitive attitudes towards computers, $R^2=.064$, $F(1,113)=7.72, p<.01$.

4 Discussion

People appear to only accept computers acting in what could be considered routine roles. Acceptance of computer in authoritarian (e.g Judges) and personal (e.g baby sitters) was especially low. As would be expected cognitive attitudes were predictive of acceptance of computers in both interpretive and routine roles. It should be noted, however, that in all cases the amount of variance explained in the regression equation was low (under 10%), indicating that other factors must account for a large portion of variance in human roles.

5. References

Nass, C. I., Lombard, M., Henriksen, L. & Steuer, J. (1995). Anthropocentrism and computers. *Behaviour & information Technology, 7,* 103-135.

Robust Computer Vision for Computer Mediated Communication

François Bérard, Joëlle Coutaz

CLIPS-IMAG
BP 53
38041 Grenoble Cedex 9, FRANCE
{francois.berard, joelle.coutaz}@imag.fr

James L. Crowley

GRAVIR-IMAG
INPG, 46 av. Félix Viallet
38031 Grenoble, FRANCE
jim.crowley@imag.fr

ABSTRACT In Computer Mediated Communication, static video cameras provide a restricted field of view of remote sites. The concept of virtual window has been introduced to alleviate this problem. Although this technique is interactionally attractive, early implementations have proved unsatisfactory because of lack of robustness. In this paper, we demonstrate that robustness and accuracy can be increased by combining multiple computer vision techniques such as eye blink detection, skin color histogram and cross correlation, that adapt to a variety of operating conditions.

KEYWORDS Computer Mediated Communication, Virtual window, Computer vision, face tracking.

1. INTRODUCTION

In Computer Mediated Communication such as video conferencing, static video cameras provide a restricted field of view of remote sites. As a result, peripheral awareness of distant people, objects, and events is lost. In addition, static cameras imply extra articulatory tasks that interfere with real world activity. In particular, users must keep their head (or an object of interest) within the field of the camera in order to be perceived by distant parties. The concept of virtual window tends to alleviate this problem by slaving a remote controlled camera to movements of the user's head (Gaver, 1995): when the head moves to the left, the camera rotates to the right, and vice versa. The same control is used for vertical head translations. The resulting behavior is similar to that which people get when looking through a real window.

The implementations of the Virtual Window concept by Gaver (1995) and Cooperstock (1995) use a simplistic vision technique based on background subtraction. Although this technique is computationally inexpensive, it exhibits three weaknesses that impede usability: first, an initialization step is required to register the background image. For so doing, the user has to move out of the field of view of the camera. In addition, the technique tracks any movement. As a result, it is not reliable for varying backgrounds. Third, the technique is sensitive to camera noise, provoking jittering of the head position estimation and consequently an inaccurate remote camera control. Gaver admits that his system was not accepted by users due primarily to the lack of robustness of the tracking system.

In this paper we demonstrate that robustness and accuracy can be increased by combining multiple computer vision techniques such as eye blink detection, skin color histogram and cross correlation, that adapt to a variety of operating conditions.

2. THREE TECHNIQUES FOR LOCATING HEADS

A human must periodically blink to keep his eyes moist. The fact that both eyes blink together provides a redundancy which permits blinking to be

Human–Computer Interaction: INTERACT'97 S. Howard, J. Hammond & G. Lindgaard (editors)
Published by Chapman & Hall

discriminated from other motions in the scene. Blink detection is based on the difference of successive images. If the eyes happened to be closed in one of the two images, two small roundish regions appear over the eyes where the difference is significant. Eye blink detection can handle a wide range of lightning conditions. As a result, it doesn't need calibration. In addition, it is computationally inexpensive: the face can be searched in the whole image in a wide range of scales. Unfortunately, eye blink occurs very irregularly and not very often (about once every 30 seconds): we use it to boostrap the two other detection techniques.

The head position estimation provided by eye-blink detection is used to calibrate the color histogram from a region of the image (close to the eyes) that contains skin colored pixels. However, color detection shares the same limitation as background subtraction: since the pixels are not processed as a coherent set but as individuals, the technique is sensitive to camera noise resulting in jittering. To achieve accuracy, we use correlation tracking.

Cross-correlation operates by comparing a reference template (e.g., piece of the nose) to an image neighborhood at each position within a search region. Cross correlation is very accurate (i.e., 1 pixel): it provides the stability and accuracy needed for mapping fine grained movements of the user's head. It suffers however from two drawbacks: it is unable to track non-rigid motions such as a head rotation; and it is very expensive when it comes to comparing the target to the image in every position of the search region. We keep a high processing rate by reducing both the target size (we typically use 8x8 targets) and the search region. The counterpart is that the tracking often loses the head, either because the user has rotated his head, or moved abruptly. This problem is solved using the cooperation of the two other complementary detection techniques.

3. COOPERATION

In order to support cooperation, the output provided by each tracker is normalized and formalized: each tracker returns its estimation of the head position, a precision and a confidence factor. The fusion of the results is performed using a Kalman filter (Crowley, 1997). Figure 1 illustrates the cooperation of the three face trackers implemented as a Tcl supervisor. When tracking confidence is low, the supervisor runs blink detection to look for a face (eye blink is fast and does not need initialisation). When blink is detected, a color histogram is initialised, a correlation template is stored for each eye. As long as the tracking CF remains high, correlation is used to track the eyes (correlation is fast and precise). When a tracking CF with a low value (< 0.5) is obtained, correlation tracking has failed, the color histogram is used to recover the face (histogram always returns a result). If the tracking CF is high again (>0.5), the correlation template is re-initialised at an eye position estimated from the face position and the correlation is run again. If, on the other hand, the tracking CF drops below a threshold (i.e., CF<0.5), the supervisor draws upon the eye blink detector.

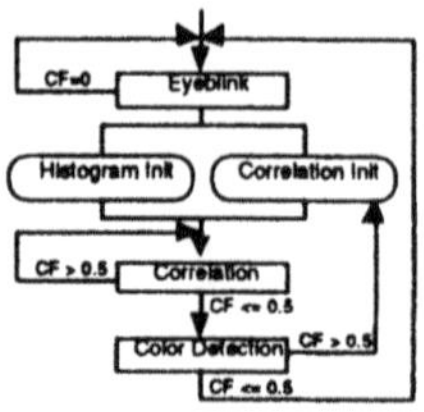

Figure 1: Cooperation of the three techniques.

4. CONCLUSION AND ACKNOWLEDGEMENTS

We have developed an autonomous, fast, accurate and robust face tracking system using the cooperation of multiple computer vision techniques. This work opens the way to the effective use of cameras as new input devices for interaction.

This work is supported by CNET France Telecom. We are grateful to F. Kirouche and F. Planchon for their participation in the implementation of the tracking system, and to N. Oliver for her insights on the color model.

5. REFERENCES

Cooperstock, J.R. Tanikoshi, K. and Buxton W. (1995) Turning Your Video Monitor into a Virtual Window. Proc. of *IEEE PACRIM, Visualisation and Signal Processing.*

Crowley, J. L. and F. Bérard (1997) Multi-Modal Tracking of Faces for Video Communications, *IEEE Conf. on Computer Vision and Pattern Recognition CVPR '97.*

Gaver, W. Smets, G. Overbeeke K. (1995) A Virtual Window on a Mediaspace. in Proc. *CHI'95*, ACM, Publ., pp. 257-264.

Colour Coding of Information Layers in Computer Displays

Darren Van Laar*, Terry Williams*, Ian Umbers† & Steve Smeaton†

*Department of Psychology
University of Portsmouth
Portsmouth P01 2ER
UNITED KINGDOM
vanlaard@psyc.port.ac.uk

†Computing Systems and MMI Group
Nuclear Electric PLC
Barnett Way, Barnwood
Gloucester GL4 7RS
UNITED KINGDOM

ABSTRACT A method is reported which enables designers to analyse computer displayed information into a task hierarchy, and then allocate sets of colour codes to reflect this information structure. These sets of colours are derived from principles of cartography and colour science, and give rise to the impression of layers of information, where elements of the display most relevant to the task appears more conspicuous and nearer to the user than less task relevant information. The application of this method to typical control room displays is described.

KEYWORDS interface design, cartography, colour coding, colour displays, design

1. INTRODUCTION

The nature of good interface design lies in the effective communication of information that is directly relevant to the completion of a user's task. Previous work in cartography has advocated the use of conceptual layers as a means to organise task relevant data elements on a map or display (Wood, 1968).

Although such an approach has proved its worth in cartography, much cartographic design pays little attention to principles of colour science and often leads to inadequate map design (Taylor, 1984). More recently, this approach has been applied to computer based air-traffic control displays with good initial results (Reynolds, 1994). Besides maps or schematic representations it may be possible to use colour science based cartographic principles to design alphanumeric, tabular or graphical displays of the type typically found in industrial or emergency control rooms.

This paper offers a method of producing hierarchical visual effects on control room computer displays. A set of palettes for producing the perceptual effect of layers of information has been identified, and a method of application developed.

2. AIMS AND OBJECTIVES

Nuclear power station control room displays in the UK are predominately monochrome, green on black or yellow on black. A methodology for colour coding using 24-bit colour displays was required by the Nuclear Industry with the following objectives:

- To provide the designer with a set of colours with which to code display formats according to current psychological principles and standards governing the perception of colour from emissive displays.
- Such colour sets should offer a way of visually emphasizing task relevant information.
- The entire set of colours should be dividable into smaller sets that will correspond to a series of information layers allocated by the designer according to task relevance.

Human–Computer Interaction: INTERACT'97 S. Howard, J. Hammond & G. Lindgaard (editors)
Published by Chapman & Hall

- The set should avoid the pitfalls associated with the application of colour to displays. Such factors include colour contrast effects, visual after effects, ambiguities, and unwanted chromostereopsis.
- The colour sets should be applicable across the range of different power station displays so as to maintain consistency.
- No significant alterations were to be made to the content and structure of existing displays.

4. DERIVATION OF COLOUR SETS

The effect of information layers on displays is intended to be similar to that within road maps, where more important information (e.g. main roads, motorways), appear more conspicuous and immediate than less important information (e.g. land use, contours), whilst maintaining the visibility and discriminability of all information.

Six 'palettes' of colours, one achromatic set, four layering sets, and an alarm set were developed according to principles of colour science rather than employing graphic designers. Each layering palette consisted of six colours, a grey and five colours which differed in hue, but which had the same level of lightness and saturation. As long as they are far apart in colour space, the actual hues of the five colours are unimportant, but have been selected to be a red, a brown, a green, a blue and a purple in the current version of the methodology.

Palettes differ in lightness and saturation between layers, but contain colours which have the same five hues. This enables conceptually similar elements to be grouped between layers. In this way, for example, related information of different levels of importance about the same power station area such as boiler area and boiler vessel, could be coded by different levels of green.

Using task analytical techniques, elements of the display are first categorized into one of six information layers, Layer One containing the least important elements of the display, and Layer Six containing display elements most relevant to the task. Colours are then allocated to each of the layers.

Layer One is the background layer, on which all other layers will be seen to rest. Besides the background colour, screen and display boundary lines, labels describing the display also appear on this layer. To further de-emphasise this information, all elements on this layer are from the achromatic palette. Layer Two contains low level task grouping areas, whereby regions of the display are grouped by background colour or 'wash'. Where mimic displays are required such as schematic boilers or turbines, these items also appear on Layer Two. Layer Three contains titles to areas of the display. These need to appear as more important than the background, but less important than other text. Level Four contains static reference text, such as the units in which temperature or pressure are measured, and similar labels. Level Five appears to lie upon all the previous levels and contains frequently updated information such as changing pressure values or graphics. A final, 'alarm' layer, Layer Six, shows infrequent but highly relevant information which needs to appear as immediately conspicuous and important. The colour coding of this layer is based on different principles to the other layers, and contains highly saturated colours chosen according to industry standards and conventions (e.g. bright red, yellow, orange).

The methodology described above has been applied successfully to a large number of control room displays, and has substantially improved the appearance and conspicuity of task relevant information. Prediction of the exact colours required produce the layering effect has been implemented in a spreadsheet. Experiments quantifying these improvements are currently being planned.

5. REFERENCES

Reynolds, L. (1994) Colour for air traffic control displays. *Displays*, 15, 215-225.

Taylor, S. (1984) Colour design in aviation cartography. *Displays,* 10, 187-194.

Wood, M. (1968). Visual Perception and map design. *Cartographic Journal*, 5, 54-64.

Searching for the biggest and the brightest; Selection of documents in VR-VIBE

Elizabeth F. Churchill[1], Dave Snowdon[2], Steve Benford[2] and Parmjit Dhanda[2]

[1] Dept. of Psychology,
University of Nottingham,
Nottingham NG7 2RD, UK
Elizabeth.Churchill@nottingham.ac.uk

[2] Dept. of Computer Science,
University of Nottingham,
Nottingham NG7 2RD, UK
{d.snowdon, s.benford}@cs.nott.ac.uk

1. INTRODUCTION

This poster presents a preliminary usability evaluation of VR-VIBE (Benford et al., 1995). VR-VIBE is a 3-D information visualisation system which offers a relevance-based, visual representation of documents within a bibliographic database. Perceptual metaphors are exploited to direct the user's attention to salient items, whilst also providing meaningful information about the query-related salience of other items and about an item's 'relative relevance' to more than one topic.

2. VR-VIBE

VR-VIBE defines a technique for displaying document icons within a 3-D spatial framework of queries, called Points of Interest or POIs (Benford et al, 1995). The spatial position of an icon indicates the relative attraction of a document to the different queries or POIs, where attraction is estimated in terms of thematic similarity. Thus, an icon equally spaced between two POIs is equally relevant to both, while an icon close to a particular POI is relevant to that POI only. Absolute relevance is depicted by the size and brightness of the document's representation; the more relevant the document the bigger the icon and the brighter the colour. Relative icon size and brightness thus differentiates documents which are slightly relevant to all POIs from documents which are highly relevant to all POIs. Figure 1 illustrates a VR-VIBE display with 5 POIs (represented by green octahedrons) and 1582 documents (represent by blue cuboids). A 3D scrollbar allows users to filter out less relevant documents from the display by changing the relevance threshold. Users can navigate within the 3-D space, select individual documents, control the display according to the dynamic relevance threshold, "drag" POIs to new locations and specify new searches by creating new POIs or specifying keywords.

Human–Computer Interaction: INTERACT'97 S. Howard, J. Hammond & G. Lindgaard (editors)
Published by Chapman & Hall

Figure 1: The world of documents in VR-VIBE.

3. THE STUDY

Although VR-VIBE has been designed to support multi-user, collaborative search and browsing, for the purposes of this preliminary usability study, we focused on individual users' search success and search strategies. Specifically, we considered: whether users are able to locate the most relevant document to a given query by exploiting the inter- and intra-icon cues, the methods used to specify searches and users' subjective assessments of the system.

15 graduate students from the University of Nottingham took part in the study. All participants were computer literate, although none had ever used 3-D information visualisation tools before.

Seven study tasks were designed to test interface knowledge and ability to conduct semantically driven spatial analysis of the document space with only limited training. For each task, a target document was specified and users' selections compared to the target. The tasks ranged from highly specified to less specified. In later tasks, participants were given more freedom to select their own keywords for a search.

Participants read two short introductory paragraphs on VR-VIBE and completed a number of practice tasks. The maximum time for practice was 40 minutes, after which participants completed the study tasks. Participants were video-taped throughout the sessions. Finally, a post-task questionnaire was presented and an interview conducted to establish participants' subjective judgements of and conceptual knowledge about the system. Item selections were evaluated in terms of time to make a selection and accuracy of that selection, determined by considering the overall relevance rating assigned to the selected document by VR-VIBE. Subjective measures were attained through presentation of a questionnaire.

4. CONCLUSIONS

This preliminary evaluation of VR-VIBE suggests that novice users with little training are able to select documents relevant to several POIs using spatial position and item features (size and brightness) as cues. Overall, less time for selection and better accuracy was achieved on the tasks with more POIs, but less document icons displayed. Analysis of the video tapes suggested that participants who scored the highest accuracy scores frequently used POI drags, exploiting the dynamic nature of the representation to disambiguate the spatial location of documents and thus their relative and absolute relevance. Tasks which required the specification of keywords resulted in the lowest accuracy measures. This suggests that whilst browsing an existing set of documents is facilitated by the visual display, specifying the keywords for the search presents more difficulties. This problem is not unique to search using VR-VIBE; selecting appropriate keywords often presents difficulties when using text-based systems (Borgman, 1986).

Although the results are promising, our study does not address the effect of practice on search strategy and success. Studies are currently being conducted to address this issue and to compare VR-VIBE with textually based search tools.

REFERENCES

Benford, S. Snowdon, D. Greenhalgh, C., Ingram, R., Know, I. and Brown, C. (1995) VR-VIBE A Virtual Environment for Co-Operative Information Retrieval, Proceedings of EuroGraphics '95, Maastricht, Holland.

Borgman, C.L. (1986) Why are online catalogs hard to use? Lessons learned from information retrieval studies. Journal of the American Society for Information Science, 37(6), 387-400.

BUILD-IT: a computer vision-based interaction technique of a planning tool for construction and design

M. Rauterberg[1], M. Bichsel[2], U. Leonhardt[2] & M. Meier[2]

Swiss Federal Institute of Technology (ETH)
[1]IHA & [2]IKB, Clausiusstrasse, CH-8092 Zurich, SWITZERLAND
http://www.ifap.bepr.ethz.ch/~rauterberg

ABSTRACT It is time to go beyond the established approaches in human-computer interaction. With the Augmented Reality (AR) design strategy humans are able to behave as much as possible in a natural way: behavior of humans in the real world with other humans and/or real world objects. Following the fundamental constraints of natural way of interacting we derive a set of recommendations for the next generation of user interfaces: the *Natural User Interface* (NUI). The concept of NUI is presented in form of a runnable demonstrator: a computer vision-based interaction technique for a planning tool for construction and design tasks.

KEYWORDS augmented reality, natural user interface, computer vision-based interaction

1. INTRODUCTION

The embodiment of computers in the work place has had a tremendous impact on the field of human-computer interaction. Mouse and graphic displays are everywhere, the desktop workstations define the frontier between the computer world and the real world. We spend a lot of time and energy to transfer information between those two worlds. This could be reduced by better integrating the virtual world of the computer with the real world of the user. Following the argumentation of Fitzmaurice, Ishii and Buxton [3] a graspable user interface has the following advantages:
"• It encourages two handed interactions; • shifts to more specialised, context sensitive input devices; • allows for more parallel input specification by the user, ... • leverages off of our well developed skills ... for physical object manipulations; • externalises traditionally internal computer representations; • facilitates interactions by making interface elements more 'direct' and more 'manipulable' by using physical artifacts; ... • affords multi-person, collaborative use" ([3] p.443).

Summarising we can conclude the following design recommendations: To empower the human to computer interaction, the user must be able to behave in a *natural way* bringing into action all of his or her body parts (e.g., hands, arms, face, head, voice, etc.). To interpret all of these natural expressions we need very powerful and intelligent pattern recognition techniques.

2. THE DEMONSTRATOR "BUILD-IT"

Inspired by the ideas of Tognazzini [5], the SUN StarFire video, and Wellner's digital desk [6] we designed a system that is based primarily on the concept of Natural User Interfaces (NUIs, see [4]). We choose the task context of planning activities for plant design. A patented system, called "BUILD-IT", has been realized and an application, supporting engineers in designing assembly lines and building plants, was implemented. The realized design room (see Figure 1) enables the users to sit around a table and to act in the interaction space with a mixture of virtual and real world objects on the table. The vertical area for (in the background of Figure 1) is used for a 3D perspective view into the designed plant.

The BUILD-IT hardware has five components:

1) A table with a white surface is used as a horizontal projection and interaction area (the top view). An ASK 960 high resolution LCD projector projects the top view of the computer graphics scene vertically down to the table.
2) A white projection screen provides a vertical projection area (the side view). An ASK 860 high resolution LCD projector projects the 3D perspective view into a computer graphics scene horizontally onto the projection screen.
3) A CCD camera with a resolution of 752 (H) by 582 (V) pixels looks vertically down to the table.

Human–Computer Interaction: INTERACT'97 S. Howard, J. Hammond & G. Lindgaard (editors)
Published by Chapman & Hall

4) A small brick with a special surface is the physical interaction 'device' (the universal interaction handler).
5) A low-cost Silicon Graphics Indy (IP22 133 MHz processor, R4600 processor, and the standard Audio-Video Board) provides the computing power for digitising the video signal coming from the camera, analysing the users' interactions on the table, and rendering the interaction result in the two views.

Figure 1: The design table of BUILD-IT

The BUILD-IT software consists of two independent processes communicating with each other through socket connection.
1) The real time analysis process of the video reads images from the camera, extracts contours of moving objects, analyses these contours [2], and determines the position and orientation of the universal interaction handler (the brick).
2) An application is built on top of the multi-media framework MET++ [1]. This application interprets the user action based on the position and orientation of the interaction handler, modifies a virtual scene according to the user action, and renders the top view of the new scene (for the vertical projector) and the side view into the scene (for the horizontal projector).

The application is designed for supporting providers of assembly lines and plants in the early design processes. It can read and render arbitrary CAD models of machines in VRML format. The input of a 3D model of the virtual objects is realized by connecting BUILD-IT with the CAD-System CATIA. So it was possible to import the original CAD-models into BUILD-IT.

BUILD-IT currently supports the following user (inter-)actions:
- Selection of a virtual object (e.g., a specific machine) in a 'virtual machine store' by placing the interaction handler onto the projected image of the machine in the menu area on the table.
- Positioning a machine in the virtual plant by moving the interaction handler to the corresponding position in the projected plant layout on the table. Positioning includes machine orientation that is coupled to the orientation of the interaction handler.
- Fixing the machine by covering the surface of the interaction handler with the hand and removing it.
- Re-selection of a machine by placing the interaction handler onto the specific machine.
- Deleting the machine by moving it back into menu area (the virtual machine store).
- Moving a virtual camera through the plant, rendering the perspective view of this camera, and displaying it on the vertical projection screen (the side view).

To change the side view the virtual camera can be moved on a level with the eyes of a virtual person of 1.7 m body height. The virtual camera is selected and moved exactly the same way as all other virtual objects. The current view position and viewing direction corresponds to the current position and orientation of the virtual camera icon in the plant layout.

The system has been empirically tested with several managers and engineers out of companies that produce assembly lines and plants. These tests showed that the system is intuitive to use, easy to learn, and that people could enjoy using it. Most persons were able to assemble virtual plants after only 30 seconds of introduction to the system.

3. REFERENCES

[1] Ackermann P: Developing Object-Oriented Multimedia Software Based on the MET++ Application Framework. Heidelberg: dpunkt, 1996.

[2] Bichsel M: Segmenting Simply Connected Moving Objects in a Static Scene. Transactions on Pattern Recognition and Machine Intelligence (PAMI), Vol. 16, No. 11, Nov. 1994, pp. 1138-1142.

[3] Fitzmaurice G, Ishii H, Buxton W: Bricks: Laying the Foundations for Graspable User Interfaces. In Proc. of the CHI '95, 1995, pp. 442-449.

[4] Rauterberg M, Steiger P: Pattern recognition as a key technology for the next generation of user interfaces. In Proc. of IEEE--SMC'96 (Vol. 4, 1996, pp. 2805-2810). Piscataway.

[5] Tognazzini B: Tog on Software Design. Addison-Wesley, Reading MA, 1996.

[6] Wellner P: Interacting with Paper on the Digital Desk. Communications of the ACM, 36(7), 1993, pp. 87-96.

Modelling Interaction for Virtual Reality Systems

Kulwinder Kaur and Alistair Sutcliffe

Centre for HCI Design, City University, Northampton Square
London EC1V 0HB
UNITED KINGDOM
K.Kaur@city.ac.uk
A.G.Sutcliffe@city.ac.uk

ABSTRACT There is practically no design advice on how to construct usable virtual reality systems, even though severe usability problems have been reported. This paper describes an interaction model for virtual environments developed from Norman's (1988) theory of action, as a first step in creating design guidance. The model consists of cycles of action for goal oriented, exploratory and reactive behaviour. User actions are linked to design properties required for successful interaction. The design properties represent desirable affordances of the virtual environment and can be presented as HCI design guidelines and in checklist questionnaires for evaluation.

KEYWORDS virtual reality, interaction models, interaction design

1. Introduction

Virtual Environments (VEs) are a novel interface type offering new possibilities for human-computer interaction. Notable features of VEs include their structure as 3D graphical models which the user navigates through and interacts with, typically using natural interaction styles, such as viewpoint control modelled on human head movements. However, guidance on how to design usable VEs are hard to find, even though significant usability problems have been reported. For example, in an evaluation of a submarine VE (Kaur et al. 1996) usability problems included getting and maintaining a suitable viewing angle, losing whereabouts after getting too close to objects (nose against the wall) and recognising interactive hot-spots in the environment.

2. Modelling interaction

As a first step in creating interface design guidance for VEs, we have developed models of interaction by elaborating Norman's (1988) generalised model of action to describe interactive behaviour in VEs.

Tasks in VEs are often loosely structured with exploration and opportunistic actions (Hayes-Roth and Hayes-Roth 1979). For example, in many simulation and tutorial applications, the user's task is to explore the environment so behaviour is primarily opportunistic following of cues. VEs are often active, with objects operating independently of the user's actions through system initiative (Bryson, 1995). Therefore, 3 inter-connected cycles have been used to model interaction:

Task/action cycle - describes purposeful, top-down behaviour in planning and carrying out specific actions as part of the user's task or goal.

Explore/navigate cycle - describes opportunistic and less goal directed behaviour when the user explores or searches for features of interest.

System initiative cycle - describes reactive behaviour to system events, and to the system taking interaction control from the user (e.g. taking the user on a pre-set tour of the environment).

Figure 1 shows a section of the explore/navigate cycle. The user scans the environment with either an intention to explore or an intention to search for an object to carry out actions from the task/action cycle. The user then continually navigates and scans until target objects are found or features in the environment arouse interest, possibly prompting exploratory actions.

Human–Computer Interaction: INTERACT'97 S. Howard, J. Hammond & G. Lindgaard (editors)
Published by Chapman & Hall

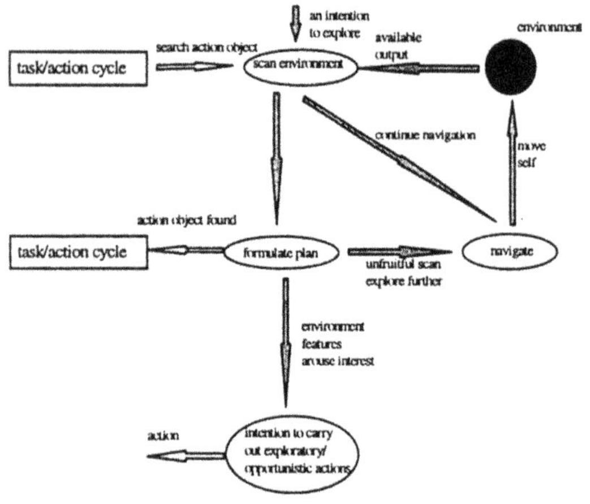

Figure 1: Section of explore/navigate cycle

The interaction models provide a clear breakdown of interactive behaviour and have been used to systematically reason about what properties are required in a design to support the user during each identified stage in interaction. Required design properties have been linked to usability problems by identifying difficulties likely to occur if the properties are missing or inadequate. For example, for the scan stage in the explore/navigate cycle, the properties 'distinguishable objects' and 'identifiable objects' are required. If these properties are not satisfied, a predicted problem is that the user will have difficulty determining what objects are in their immediate vicinity when scanning the VE.

We are evaluating the predictive power of the interaction models with experimental studies, using think aloud protocols and analysis of video footage. Observed patterns of mental and physical activity can then be checked against predictions in the interaction models. We are evaluating the importance of the design properties, by implementing them in an existing VE and then testing for differences in numbers of usability problems and task performance for users of the altered version over an original version. Results from the studies will be used to refine the interaction models and set of design properties.

3. Discussion

Our future work involves adapting the design properties into guidelines for design and checklist questions in evaluation methods. For example, for the scan stage in the explore/navigate cycle, a walkthrough evaluation method would include the check:

When scanning the VE, can the users distinguish and recognise many/few/none of the objects? Does the object appearance match the users' expectations?

In conclusion, an interaction modelling approach has been proposed as one promising way of addressing problems of interaction design for VEs. The models lead to design properties which are required for supporting important stages in interaction. The properties are being used to form the basis of design advice and criteria for the evaluation of VEs, from a usability perspective.

ACKNOWLEDGMENTS

Kulwinder Kaur is funded by the EPSRC.

References

Bryson S. (1995). Approaches to the successful design and implementation of VR applications, in *Virtual Reality Applications,* Ed Earnshaw R.A., Vince J.A. and Jones H. London, Academic Press.

Hayes-Roth B. and Hayes-Roth F. (1979). A cognitive model of planning. *Cognitive Science* **3**, 275-310.

Kaur K., Maiden N. and Sutcliffe A. (1996). Design practice and usability problems with virtual environments, in: *Virtual Reality World '96 conference, Stuttgart.* Proceedings. IDG Conferences.

Norman D.A. (1988). *The psychology of everyday things*. New York, Basic Books Inc.

Modelling the mock-up: towards the automatic specification of the behaviour of early prototypes

Chris Phillips and Chris Scogings

Department of Computer Science
Massey University
New Zealand
{C.Phillips, C.Scogings}@massey.ac.nz

ABSTRACT A shortcoming of current early prototyping tools is that although they permit the designer to construct a mock-up of the look and feel of the interface, they provide no model of the interaction. Such tools could be extended to produce such a model as a byproduct of the construction of the prototype. This research explores such an extension to HyperCard, and reviews its utility. The interaction model is specified in Lean Cuisine+, a semi-formal graphical notation for describing the behaviour of direct manipulation graphical user interfaces.

KEY WORDS early prototyping, interaction model, HyperCard, Lean Cuisine+

1. INTRODUCTION

Prototyping supports the view that good interfaces can only be constructed through iterative refinement. It involves constructing a smaller scale version or mock-up of a proposed system. A variety of prototyping tools and techniques are available to support iterative interface development, from pencil and paper mockups to full scale interface development environments (Hix & Schulman, 1991; Myers, 1993; Szekely, 1994).

The focus of this research is on support for *early prototyping*. A shortcoming of current early prototyping tools is that although they permit the designer to construct a mock-up of the look and feel of the interface, they provide no model of the interaction. The mock-up exists and can be exercised, but no specification or description of the interaction exists outside the code produced. The focus is rather on 'screens', i.e. on the *interface* rather than the interaction.

Early prototyping tools could be extended to produce a model of the interaction as a byproduct of the construction of the prototype. This research explores such an extension to HyperCard, and briefly reviews its utility. The interaction model is specified in Lean Cuisine+ (Phillips, 1995), a semi-formal graphical notation for describing the behaviour of direct manipulation graphical user interfaces.

2. EXTENDING HYPERCARD

HyperCard (Claris, 1992) is based on two primary abstractions: cards and stacks (of cards). Each card corresponds to one screen, and may contain buttons and text fields in addition to artwork. Backgrounds may be defined to contain features common to several cards. Each HyperCard object (button, field, stack etc) has an associated HyperTalk script which describes what it must do in response to messages (e.g. mouse clicks). Using HyperCard, the designer may define the appearance of screens, and also simulate the behaviour of menus, buttons etc in linking screens. Thus both the look and feel of the interface can be created.

A HyperCard stack has been developed to prototype an interface for a real estate application in which potential house buyers can select likely properties from

Human–Computer Interaction: INTERACT'97 S. Howard, J. Hammond & G. Lindgaard (editors)
Published by Chapman & Hall

a data base of the properties currently for sale in a given town. The 'Property' Stack consists of the following cards, each of which represents one screen in the prototype:

- *A Town Map Card:* Which shows a map of the town with the location of properties marked. Properties can be selected by direct manipulation.
- *A Search Card:* Which provides fields for the entering of selection criteria, and buttons for initiating the selection of properties.
- *Property Cards:* Each of which displays details of one property, and provides buttons for continuing the search.

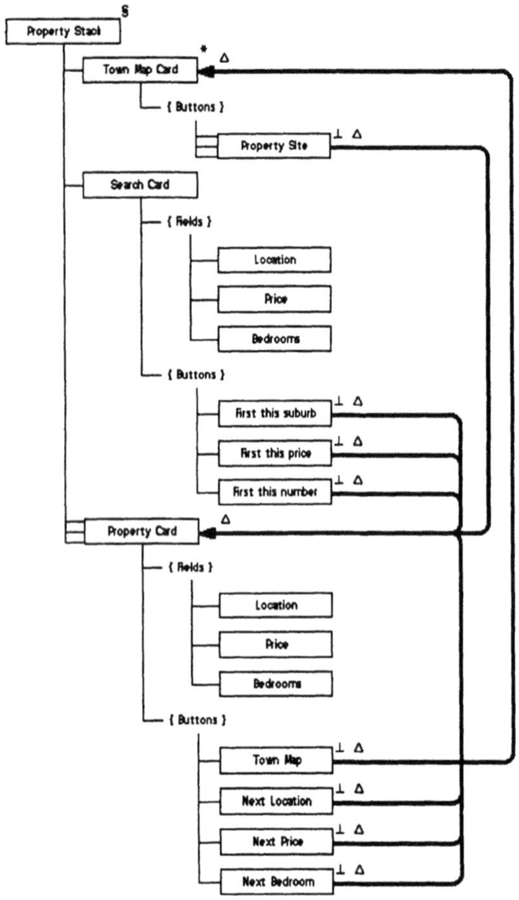

Figure 1: Property Stack: Lean Cuisine + diagram

The Lean Cuisine+ specification of this stack is shown in Figure 1. It has been produced semi-automatically from the associated HyperTalk scripts. The stack is represented by a dialogue tree, which shows inter-relationships and some of the constraints which impact the behaviour of the selectable primitives. Further constraints are captured in the form of selection triggers, represented by directed arcs.

3. REVIEW

A semi-formal model of the interaction associated with a HyperCard stack has been produced in the form of a graphical specification using Lean Cuisine+. The model provides information on the interaction which could otherwise only be uncovered by exercising the stack and committing the behaviour to memory. This information provides useful documentation, and can be analysed for structural shortcomings and inconsistency within the dialogue. For example, excessive navigation between screens in performing tasks can be uncovered.

HyperCard exhibits generic features of prototyping tools for GUIs - the representation of objects (including screens) and the links between them. The graphical modelling being explored in this research should thus be applicable to a wider range of interface development tools.

REFERENCES

Hix, D. & Schulman, R.S. (1991): Human-Computer Interface Development Tools: A Methodology for their Evaluation, *Comms. ACM*, 34, 3, 74-87.

HyperCard (1992): Claris Corporation.

Myers, B.A. (1993): State of the Art in User Interface Tools, In Hartson, H.R. and Hix, D. (Eds*), Advances in Human-Computer Interaction*, Ablex, Norwood, NJ, 11-28.

Phillips, C.H.E. (1995): Lean Cuisine+: An executable graphical notation for describing direct manipulation interfaces, *Interacting with Computers*, 7, 1, 1995, 49-71.

Szekely, P. (1994): User Interface Prototyping: Tools and Techniques, *Proc. ICSE'94 Workshop on SE-HCI*, Sorrento, Italy, Springer, 76-92.

Task analysis for collaborative work

Andrew Monk and Leon Watts
Department of Psychology, University of York, York, YO1 5DD, U.K.
Email: [am1 | law4]@york.ac.uk

ABSTRACT Collaborative work requires all participants to synchronise their separate activities through their awareness of each other. This paper proposes a diagrammatic scheme for reasoning about this synchronisation for the purpose of configuring communication technologies. The Comms Usage Diagram (CUD) was developed in the course of three field studies of medical teleconsultation.

KEYWORDS Task analysis, CSCW, telemedicine, collaborative work, communication technology.

1. INTRODUCTION

The diagrammatic representation described here was developed in the course of three studies of medical teleconsultation. The sites visited used videophone technology to connect the occupants of a treatment room in a primary care centre with a consultant in a hospital. A typical consultation would involve talking about a patient's problem and viewing some visual information such as an X-ray. A striking feature of these consultations was the role played by peripheral parties. When the GP was talking to the consultant the patient could generally overhear and interject. Patients are often accompanied by a relative, there may also be a nurse or technician present. Again, these peripheral participants are aware of what is going on and may take some part in the activity being undertaken. Of course, the communication technologies used restrict the information available to the remote parties. For example, the consultant will only be able to see whoever is sitting directly in front of the videophone. It is thus incumbent on the GP to make sure that the consultant is aware of the presence of everyone in the treatment room at the start of the consultation. The consultant is then able to use language that is appropriate to the situation.

This sensitivity to the identity and awareness of one's audience is typical of collaborative work (Clark & Schaefer, 1989). When deciding on how to best configure communication facilities to support collaboration one needs to reason about the requirements of different activities and phases of the work in this regard. This then is the purpose of the representation described here, to reason about collaborative work and the potential impact of communications technologies when configuring those technologies for some particular task.

A common abbreviation in engineering for communications technologies is "comms" hence the graphical representation proposed will be referred to as a Comms Usage Diagram or CUD. Graphical representations are commonly used in task analysis (Kirwan & Ainsworth, 1992) to summarise and reason about work and the CUD is in this tradition. An analyst will use any information available to come to some understanding of the work. Because of the diversity of these sources of information, e.g., interviews and direct observation, some common representation is required to integrate and reason about the understanding acquired.

2. A SAMPLE CUD

Figure 1. is part of the CUD created to reason about the work at one field study site. There are two locations a Minor Treatment Centre staffed by nurse practitioners in London and an accident and emergency department in Belfast. The first two columns indicate the activities going on at each of these locations and the people who are present.

Primary and peripheral participants:- Primary participants are named with the activity. For example, there is an activity where the nurse practitioner and consultant "discuss case". Here the primary participants

Human–Computer Interaction: INTERACT'97 S. Howard, J. Hammond & G. Lindgaard (editors)
Published by Chapman & Hall

are the nurse practitioner and the consultant but the patient and a relative of the patient are also present in the treatment room. They are considered as peripheral participants and represented by "(P, R)".

Sequence:- The CUD can be read from top to bottom giving the approximate order of events. Task phases are relatively invariant. These are signified by horizontal rules across the full width of the CUD (see Figure 1.) The sequence of activities within a task phase is more varied and does not have to be made explicit. Order is implied through the content of the activities and where joint activities have a strong sense of initiation or causation, through the use of single headed arrows. In the first task phase in Figure 1. the ordering of the events, placing a call and fetching the consultant is implied by the single headed arrows. The activities of "greeting" and "discussing" use double headed arrows. The ordering of these events is implied by their content.

Mediation and its effects:- Comms resources are listed in the first place at the same horizontal level as the activity to which they refer. Activities given further down the CUD are taken to inherit these. Any changes to the configuration are then noted next to the activity at which the change was made. The rightmost column records the relevant "effects": whether a point is positive or negative and the participant affected. They vary considerably in scope. The alternative course of action, had the videophone not been available, would have been to refer the patient on. Figure 1. notes an advantage for the nurse practitioner of a reduction in paper work relative to this alternative. This is an advantage of broad scope brought about by the new way of working that is made possible by the technology. At the other extreme there are points made that apply only to the operation of the mobile camera.

3. DISCUSSION

The notes made in the rightmost column of the CUD are the major reason for performing the analysis. They will normally originate in a comment from an informant. What the CUD adds is the possibility to locate the advantage or disadvantage more precisely within the work and to find other places in the work that could be affected similarly.

The CUD is an effective tool for reasoning about the technological support of collaborative work through communication technologies. By using this representation we were able to summarise and reason about the data given by our informants. It was possible to characterise how communication occurred between all participants in a way that could be made accessible to those informants so that they could comment on our conclusions. The account was compact, two sides of A4 for two sites and one for the other. By using this representation we were able to make strong recommendations about the use of video and audio technology for teleconsultation (Watts & Monk, 1997).

REFERENCES

Clark, H. H., & Schaefer, E. R. (1989). Contributing to discourse. *Cognitive Science*, 13, 259 - 294.

Kirwan, B. & Ainsworth, L. K. (1992). *The task analysis guide*. London: Taylor and Francis.

Watts, L. A. & Monk, A. F. (1997). Telemedical consultation: task characteristics. In *CHI'97*, New York: ACM.

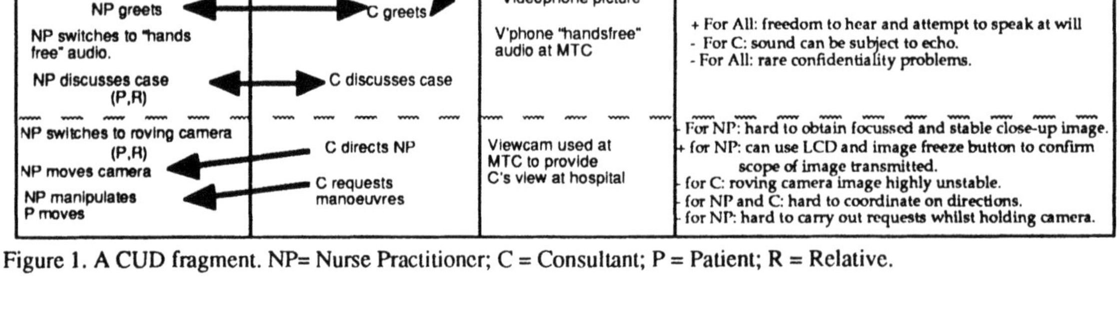

Figure 1. A CUD fragment. NP= Nurse Practitioner; C = Consultant; P = Patient; R = Relative.

The effect of goal setting on ability-performance relations during practice on a computerised pursuit tracking task.

Jennifer Waycott & Janice Langan-Fox

Department of Psychology
The University of Melbourne
Parkville 3052
Australia

ABSTRACT The study examined a theory proposed by Ackerman (1988) which predicts a dynamic pattern of ability-performance relations during the learning of consistent and moderately complex perceptual motor tasks. The theory is particularly relevant for explaining the development of automatisation at computerised tasks. In the present investigation, one group of participants were given a specific and difficult performance goal while another group was simply told to "do your best". All participants were then given 32 trials on a computerised pursuit tracking task, with performance scores on this task then correlated with ability scores. It was expected that the goal-setting manipulation would disrupt the normal pattern of ability-performance correlations. Although some group differences were found, overall the results failed to support Ackerman's theory. Thus, Ackerman's model may be theoretically underdeveloped and further investigation, including consideration of the effect of goal setting, is required to fully understand the relationship between abilities and performance on computerised tasks.

KEY WORDS: Skill acquisition, individual differences, cognitive models, ability, performance.

1. INTRODUCTION

This study examined how the assignment of a performance goal moderates the relationship between abilities and performance during the learning of a computerised pursuit tracking task. Specifically, the investigation was designed to test Ackerman's (1988) theory of ability-performance relations during skill acquisition. Ackerman's theory predicts a dynamic pattern of ability-performance relations during practice on consistent and moderately complex perceptual motor tasks. Therefore, the theory can be applied to skills involved in operating computerised tasks, which generally have consistent information-processing requirements, and are increasingly being utilised by employees in various occupational settings.

1.1 Ackerman's (1988) theory

Ackerman (1988) proposed that three broad classes of ability - general ability, perceptual speed ability, and psychomotor ability - determine performance as practice progresses through the three phases of skill acquisition, described by information-processing theories of learning (e.g., Anderson, 1976, 1987; Fitts & Posner, 1967; Schneider & Shiffrin, 1977). The three skill acquisition phases mapped to the abilities proposed by Ackerman, are outlined in the table below.

Human–Computer Interaction: INTERACT'97 S. Howard, J. Hammond & G. Lindgaard (editors)
Published by Chapman & Hall

SKILL ACQUISITION PHASE	ABILITY CLASSES
PHASE 1: Performance is slow, error-prone and requires conscious control.	**General ability:** *Represents a broad construct that underlies non-specific information-processing efficacy.* *eg: reasoning processes.*
PHASE 2: Attentional demands are reduced as task-specific productions are learned and refined.	**Perceptual speed ability:** *Refers to individual differences in the speed with which simple cognitive tasks can be completed.* *eg: searching through random letters to identify instances of a target letter.*
PHASE 3: Performance has become automatic, or procedural, and no longer requires conscious control.	**Psychomotor ability:** *Individual differences in the speed of response to tasks that require little or no cognitive processing.* *eg: reaction time*

Table 1. Ackerman's (1988) theory of ability-performance relations during skill acquisition.

The basic rationale behind Ackerman's (1988) theory is that as performance progresses from controlled processing (Phase 1) to automatic processing (Phase 3), the resources required by a task change. Correspondingly, the abilities determining performance also change. Initial individual differences in performance will be determined by general cognitive ability. Then, as the resource-dependency of performance is reduced (i.e., Phase 2), perceptual speed ability will primarily determine performance variability. Finally, when automaticity is reached (i.e., Phase 3), performance is said to correspond to predominantly noncognitive psychomotor abilities. Figure 1 (right) depicts the predicted pattern of ability-performance correlations across the three phases of learning.

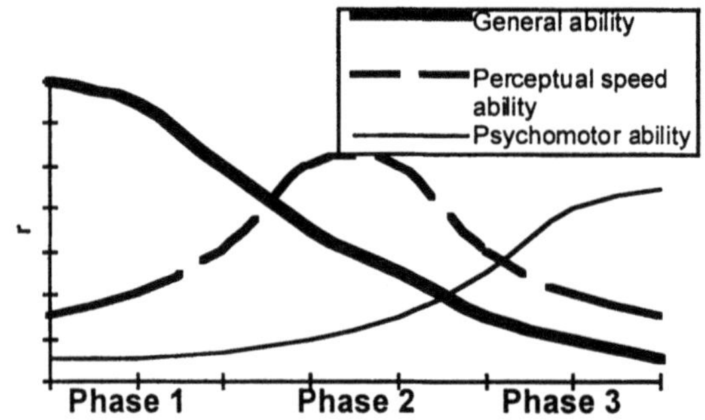

Figure 1. Ability-performance correlations proposed by Ackerman

1.2 The study

The current investigation aimed to examine how the setting of a specific and difficult performance goal might moderate the pattern of ability-performance correlations proposed by Ackerman (1988). Participants (60 first year psychology students at the University of Melbourne) were given 32 trials on a highly consistent computerised pursuit tracking task. The task involved following a target box moving horizontally across the screen with a cursor controlled by the computer mouse. The mouse controls were reversed, such that moving the mouse in one direction resulted in the cursor moving in the opposite direction across the screen. At the end of each 45-second trial a performance score (the percentage of time spent on target) was given. One group of participants (n = 31) were told that they must try to reach a score of 70% by the end of the session. The remaining participants (n = 29) were simply told to "do your best". Scores on each practice trial were correlated with three composite ability scores, obtained from the administration of nine ability tests which were previously used by Ackerman (1988) and were factor analysed to ensure each test loaded on the appropriate ability class.

2. HYPOTHESES

It was expected that, because motivational forces are said to interfere with the attentional resources available for on-task attention (Kanfer & Ackerman, 1989, 1996), the goal-setting manipulation would slow, or even preclude the progression of skill acquisition through the three learning phases. Therefore, it was predicted that the ability-performance correlations for individuals given a performance goal would depart from the pattern predicted by Ackerman, such that:

1. General ability-performance correlations would decrease later in task practice;
2. Perceptual speed ability-performance correlations would increase later in task practice;
3. Psychomotor ability-performance correlations would remain low throughout the practice session.

3. RESULTS & DISCUSSION

Curve estimates of the ability-performance correlations plotted against trial number, were obtained using linear regression for general and psychomotor abilities, and cubic regression for perceptual speed ability.

In contrast to predictions, there were no significant between-group differences for the pattern of general and perceptual speed ability-performance correlations. Thus, there was no support for the hypothesis that there would be a disruption in the normal process of ability-performance correlations for subjects in the goal condition. The prediction that there would be little evidence of the influence of psychomotor ability on performance was partially supported. For subjects who were given a performance goal, the psychomotor ability-performance correlations were actually negative, in comparison to the positive correlations for the no-goal group. This would suggest that, as expected, the goal manipulation precluded the development of Phase 3 (psychomotor) performance. Nevertheless, the psychomotor ability-performance correlations decreased, rather than increased across practice, suggesting that Ackerman's (1988) proposal that psychomotor ability is associated with performance during Phase 3 of skill acquisition may be inaccurate. Alternatively, it is possible that participants in both groups did not proceed past Phase 1 of skill acquisition, given that general ability-performance correlations remained high across task practice. This means that further practice trials would be necessary to examine the effect of goal setting on ability-performance correlations as automatisation at a computerised task develops.

On all three ability measures (i.e., general, perceptual speed, and psychomotor abilities), the correlations with performance exhibited quite substantial instability from trial to trial for subjects in both the goal and no-goal conditions. Thus, the correlations did not generally follow the pattern that Ackerman's (1988) theory predicted. It is possible that the computer game-like qualities of the pursuit tracking task may have tapped different abilities than those identified by Ackerman, and that the dynamic spatial qualities of the pursuit tracking task differed substantially from the reaction time tasks used in Ackerman's (1988) study. Nevertheless, the results do suggest that Ackerman's theory may have several flaws; for example, the ability classes he identified and mapped onto the phases of skill acquisition appear to be inaccurate.

4. CONCLUSION

It is apparent that motivational variables may moderate the relationship between abilities and performance, and the effect of goal setting on ability-performance relations during practice on computerised tasks, needs further examination. It may also be beneficial for future research to consider the interactive effects of goal setting and dispositional constructs. Such research could have important implications for industrial training, particularly with respect to consistent and repetitive computerised tasks which are becoming increasingly common in contemporary workplaces.

REFERENCES

Ackerman, P. L. (1988). Determinants of individual differences during skill acquisition: Cognitive abilities and information pocessing. *Journal of Experimental Psychology: General, 117*, 288-318.

Anderson, J. R. (1976). *Language, Memory and Thought*. NJ: Lawrence Erlbaum.

Anderson, J. R. (1987). Skill acquisition: compilation of weak-method problem solutions. *Psychological Review, 94*, 192-210.

Fitts, P. M. & Posner, M. I. (1967). *Human Performance*. Belmont: Brooks/Cole Publishing Company.

Kanfer, R. & Ackerman, P. L. (1989). Motivation and cognitive abilities: An integrative/aptitude-treatment interaction approach to skill acquisition [monograph]. *Journal of Applied Psychology, 74*, 657-690.

Kanfer, R. & Ackerman, P. L. (1996). A self-regulatory skills perspective to reducing cognitive interference. In I. G. Sarason, G. R. Pierce, & B. R. Sarason (Eds.) *Cognitive Interference: Theories, Methods, and Findings* (pp 153-171). Mahwah, NJ: Lawrence Erlbaum Associates.

Schneider, W. & Shiffrin, R. M. (1977). Controlled and automatic human information processing: I. Detection, search, and attention. *Psychological Review, 84*, 127-190.

Internationalising Media Production: Early Users of Remote Creative Collaboration Tools

Ellen Baker, John Geirland*, Annmarie Chandler, Tom Fisher, Rachel Moss

University of Technology, Sydney
PO Box 123 Broadway 2007 (Australia)
* Center for Executive Learning, Loyola Marymount University (USA)
E.Baker{A.Chandler, T.Fisher}@uts.edu.au Geirland@aol.com

ABSTRACT: During 1996 there was a sharp increase in the use of remote collaboration technologies within the advertising and film industries. There was even some international collaboration, driven by the need to use scarce expertise located elsewhere. This paper reports on a series of case studies carried out in Australia, the U.S. and the U.K. to assess the reactions of these forefront users and to try to determine 1) which CSCW tools will be most useful for international production applications and 2) what conditions will facilitate creative collaboration internationally.

KEYWORDS CSCW, Multimedia, Art and Media, New or Emerging Technologies, Management Issues.

1. INTRODUCTION AND METHOD

Global working encounters many difficulties (O'Hara-Devereaux & Johansen, 1994) and international collaboration on creative products presents additional challenges, because their failure rate is high and media production is costly. Anxiety levels are high and staff tend to be chosen on the basis of long-term relationships nurtured during previous projects. Media production is generally divided into three segments (pre-production, production, post-production) and remote collaboration may be needed within any of these stages. Creative staff generally carry out assigned work independently and then submit it periodically for approval.

Semi-structured interviews were conducted in seven organisations in L.A., London and Sydney that recently used remote international collaboration for motion-video production. Further information was obtained from two wide-area-network consortia, Sohonet in London and Hollynet in L.A. Most of the companies were in post-production, one was a major U.S. studio. Two of the companies have offices in both L.A. and London.

2. COLLABORATION TECHNOLOGIES

These early users confirm that close collaboration is possible in media production work internationally, even with the support tools available in 1996. Tools currently used fall into three categories.

1) *Electronic Delivery* is used instead of couriers, to get quicker decisions or approvals, or to transfer computer image files for additional processing, such as effects work. Some systems (e.g. the Videofax) have been specifically designed for media industry applications.

2) *Interactive access or control* extends the reach of the creative person beyond their own workstation. Some companies have high speed internal networks connecting all their equipment and these networks are now being extended internationally. Nominated files are accessed, modified and then returned to the host computer by the collaborators, which corresponds to the CSCW category 'different time, same place'.

3) *Synchronous collaboration systems* support person-to-person, real-time collaboration on visual material, the CSCW category 'same time, different place'. The most

Human–Computer Interaction: INTERACT'97 S. Howard, J. Hammond & G. Lindgaard (editors)
Published by Chapman & Hall

commonly used form is a combination of the telephone with some technology for simultaneously viewing a frame or film clip. Generally this uses only prior electronic delivery but a number of systems, specifically designed for media production work, with shared workspaces, are now available (e.g. Sprint Drums). The software supports scrolling and annotating of motion video in a shared workspace and has a small video-conferencing window for a view of users' faces.

One of our case study companies felt that the information participants would receive about each other on a workstation would be too limited, so instead they began with a room-based videoconferencing system and then integrated other functionality on an `as needed' basis. They use this system regularly between L.A. and London.

3. FACILITATING INTERNATIONAL COLLABORATION

Our case studies point to a number of propositions.

1) *Asynchronous vs synchronous* - Real-time collaboration will be needed but most communication will be asynchronous, due to time zone differences and the advantage of a quick response over scheduling a meeting. Collaborators will capitalise on time-zone differences, to maximise the effective working time at each location or to allow work to go on around the clock.

2) *Coordination needs* - Extensive coordination will be an important need, as is illustrated by one case study. Animation work for a film was being done in L.A. and London simultaneously and integration of these activities required continual use of auxillary support facilities, such as electronic mail.

3) *Increased creative control* - User acceptance of International collaboration will often depend on whether it results in increased creative control for the film/TV director or advertising/studio executive. Interviewees reported greater involvement in the details of productions by these people, even if they were in another country at the time.

4) *Security* - Current security concerns about the use of computer networks for media collaboration will decrease, along with current concerns about credit card information over the Internet.

5) *Trust, stress reduction, improved work practices* - Remote collaboration will require trust between media co-workers. Although there are strong bonds from similarity of norms within the worldwide media production community, prior in-person collaboration will still probably be necessary. Use of CSCW tools will result in creative production staff having shorter waiting times for feedback and everyone feeling more confdent that the desired product will emerge at the end. Work practices will also be normalised and become more efficient, with less shif work and fewer very long workdays.

6) *Videoconferencing* - Media production provides a good example of what Whittaker (1995) called `video as data', and also may provide support for what he called the `social cueing hypothesis', that visual information provides cues about emotion. Our interviewees (both those who use videoconferencing and those who don't) emphasised the importance of seeing the people you are collaborating with. Although people generally overestimate the usefulness of seeing the people they are communicating with, in this relationship-dominated industry seeing faces may be more valuable, and specially designed support systems may facilitate collaboration.

Overall, the successes reported by the early users studied indicate that, although there are challenges ahead, this is the future direction of media production.

We thank the companies that participated for their permission to publish these results, and the Australian Research Council (Grant A79530730), the Australian Film TV & Radio School and the Faculty of Business, UTS.

4. REFERENCES

O'Hara-Devereaux, M. & Johansen, R. (1994) *Global Work*. Jossey-Bass, San Francisco.

Whittaker, S. (1995) Rethinking Video as Technology for Interpersonal Communications. *International Journal of Human-Computer Studies*, 42, 501-529.

101

A Group Decision Support System by Externalizing, Sharing and Reflecting Individual Viewpoints

Naotaka Kato, Masanobu Chujo and Susumu Kunifuji

Japan Advanced Institute of Science and Technology, HOKURIKU
1-1 Asahidai, Tatsunokuchi, Ishikawa, 923-12, Japan
nkato@jaist.ac.jp, kuni@jaist.ac.jp

ABSTRACT This paper proposes a new type of group decision support system which focuses on facilitating processes of reaching a consensus. The system is characterized by the following points: (1) It is an interactive system which shows each decision maker in a group useful information for decision-making with GUI. (2) It extracts conflicts which should be adjusted among decision makers in the group by sharing their viewpoints. (3) It supports negotiation processes for resolving conflicts by using a tradeoff analysis based on sensitivity analysis. (4) It shows each decision maker the degree of agreements and the degree of compromises during the negotiation process. In this abstract, we describe the outline of our system and then show an implementation example. The experimental results shows some usefulness of the system for supporting negotiation processes by iterative interaction between each decision maker and the system.

KEYWORDS GDSS, Groupware, tradeoff analysis, Analytic Hierarchy Process

1. INTRODUCTION

Group decision support systems (GDSSs) (Gray, 1994) have a variety of methods for supporting consensus making processes. Generally, in these processes, each member has his individual viewpoint because he has his own standard of values. To reach a consensus effectively, each individual should externalize his viewpoint and then the members should reflect upon the viewpoints, and analyze them to reach a consensus. Our approach to decision-making based on reaching a consensus focuses on both disagreements and compromises that come from members' individual viewpoints, that is, which viewpoints lead to disagreements and which lead to compromises can be quantitatively represented.

In this abstract, we propose a novel interactive GDSS which brings to reality the above approach and includes two kinds of tradeoff analyses for resolving conflicts among the decision makers.

2. PROPOSED GROUP DECISION SUPPORT METHOD

Figure 1 shows a process of group decision-making based on alternative selection. It is composed of three steps. The first two steps are typical ones. The first step is for constructing an evaluation structure. All decision makers must have a common recognition of the decision-making problem. In this step, we use a well-known thinking support method for a group called the KJ method (Kawakita, 1975). It is used to analyze an unstructured decision-making problem and to construct a hierarchical evaluation structure for the problem.

Human–Computer Interaction: INTERACT'97 S. Howard, J. Hammond & G. Lindgaard (editors)
Published by Chapman & Hall

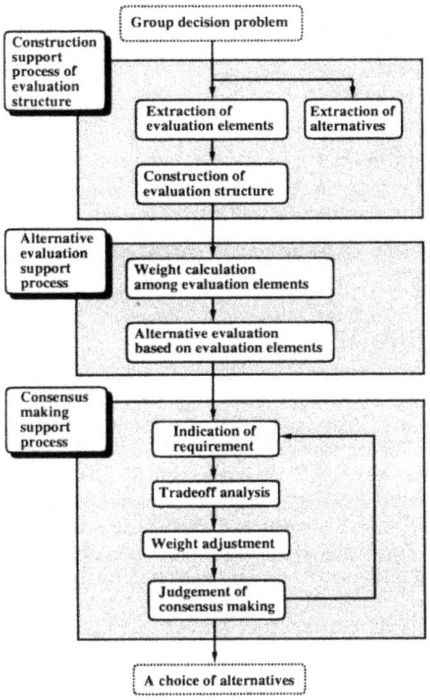

Figure 1 The proposed group decision support model

Second step is for evaluating alternatives based on the evaluation structure. AHP (Analytic Hierarchy Process) (Saaty, 1980) is used to evaluate alternatives quantitatively. It constructs an evaluation structure from individual's subjective judgements and then calculates the weights for each evaluation's attributes in the structure. A consistency ratio for member's judgements is also computed.

The last step is new proposed one for reaching a consensus among the members. Each individual viewpoint is represented as an evaluation structure with weights assigned to each attribute. Because members share their viewpoints, the viewpoint of one member may affect that of another. By analyzing the differences between viewpoints, we can find some conflicting parts of the viewpoints. Such conflicts are adjusted through negotiation processes based on tradeoff analysis. In the tradeoff analysis, we adapt the sensitivity analysis method (Masuda, 1987).

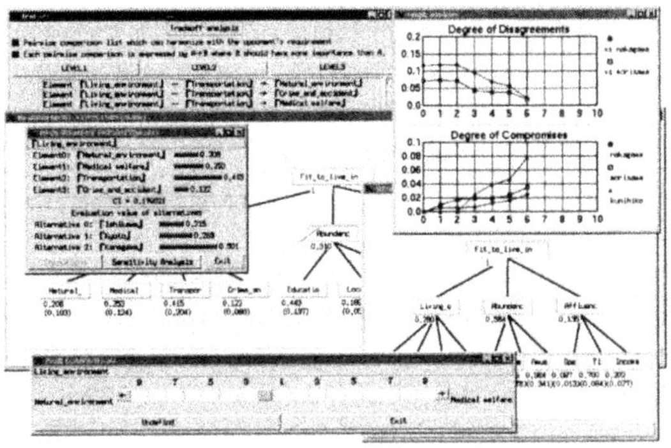

Figure 2 An example of windows for tradeoff analysis

3. IMPLEMENTATION

We have implemented a prototype system on a SUN work station with X window. The system has WYSIWIS (What You See Is What I See) function including GUI. Figure 2 shows a snapshot of operation windows in a process of the tradeoff analysis.

4. CONCLUSION

We observed the following usefulness of the system through some experimental evaluation: (1) The effect of individual variation in negotiation ability can be reduced in the negotiation processes. (2) Negotiation activity through this system becomes more persuasive or reasonable than conventional negotiation activity. (3) Decision makers become more amenable to compromising. (4) The system can also be used to enhance the effectiveness of the Delphi Technique.

REFERENCES

Gray, P (1994) Decision Support and Executive Information Systems, Prentice-Hall.

Kawakita, J. (1975) The KJ Method, Kawakita Research Institute.

Masuda, T. (1987) Sensitivity Coefficients of Consistency Index and Priorities Used in the Analytic Hierarchy Process, IEICE, A Vol.J70-A, No.11, 1562-1567 (in Japanese).

Saaty, T.L. (1980) The Analytic Hierarchy Process, McGraw-Hill.

Using 'Accident Fault Trees' in Conjunction With Traditional Accident Reports

Lorna Love and Chris Johnson

Glasgow Accident Analysis Group,
Department of Computing Science, University of Glasgow, Glasgow,
Scotland, G12 8QQ.

Email: {love, johnson}@dcs.gla.ac.uk

ABSTRACT Accident reports help to ensure that operator 'error' and system 'failure' do not threaten other applications. Unfortunately, a number of usability problems limit the effectiveness of these documents. Each section is, typically, drafted by a different expert; forensic scientists follow metallurgists, human factors experts follow meteorologists. In consequence, it can be difficult for readers to form a coherent account of an accident. This paper argues that fault trees can be used to present a clear and concise overview of major failures. Unfortunately, fault trees have a number of limitations. For instance, they do not represent time. This is significant because temporal properties have a profound impact upon the course of human-machine interaction. Similarly, they do not represent the criticality or severity of a failure. We have, therefore, extended the fault tree notation to represent human-machine interaction during major failures. The resulting Accident Fault Tree diagrams can be used in conjunction with an official accident report to better visualise the course of an accident. The Clapham Junction railway disaster (Department of Transport, 1989) is used to illustrate our argument.

KEYWORDS accident analysis, fault trees, operator 'error', system 'failure'.

1. FAULT TREES

Fault trees are, typically, used pre hoc to analyse potential errors in a design. They have not been widely used to support post hoc accident analysis. They do, however, offer considerable benefits for this purpose. The leaves of the tree can be used to represent the initial causes of the accident (Leplat, 1987). These basic events can be used to represent the phenotypical failures that lead to an accident (Hollnagel, 1993). Intermediate events can represent the operator 'mistakes' that frequently exacerbate system failures. An undeveloped event is a fault event that is not developed further, either because it is of insufficient consequence or because information is unavailable.

There are a range of important differences that distinguish the use of Accident Fault Trees from their more conventional application. Some arise from the semantics of the gates that are used to construct the diagrams. Conventionally, the output from an AND gate is true if and only if all of its inputs are true. Accidents cannot be analysed in this way. Most accident reports do not distinguish between necessary and sufficient conditions. In Accident Fault Trees, therefore, an AND gate represents the fact that an accident report cites a number of initiating events as contributing to the output event. No inferences can be made about the outcome of an AND gate if any of the initiating events do not hold.

The output of an OR gate is true if and only if at least one of it's inputs is true. An OR gate can be used in an Accident Fault Tree to represent a lack of evidence. Evidence can be removed accidentally or deliberately from an accident scene. Alternatively, evidence may be missing because the person holding the information died in the accident. The output of an XOR (exclusive OR) gate is true if and only if exactly one of the inputs are true. They are useful in Accident Fault Trees when we know an intermediate event was caused by either of two events, but not both.

2. ACCIDENT FAULT TREES

2.1 Introducing Paragraph References

The results of an initial usability test with accident analysts indicated that the standard fault tree notation did not support cross-referencing between the tree and the original document. Events in Accident Fault Trees are annotated to include a paragraph number. This number refers to the paragraph number of the accident report that the information in the node is taken from.

2.2 Representing Post-Accident Sequences

Fault trees typically stop at the 'undesired event'. In accident reports, events after the accident are important too. These, typically, include the operator actions that are taken to mitigate the effects of system failure. For example, the Ambulance service played an important part in the Clapham railway accident. Although their actions did not cause the accident, they reduced the *consequences* of the accident. It is, therefore, important that Accident Fault Trees include post-accident events. Accident Fault Trees explicitly frame the accident. Branches spread out both above and below the accident.

Human–Computer Interaction: INTERACT'97 S. Howard, J. Hammond & G. Lindgaard (editors)
Published by Chapman & Hall

The accident is at the centre of the tree. The roots below the centre represent the factors influencing the accident. The leaves above the centre specify the actions taken and the subsequent events following the accident.

2.3 Introducing Time

Temporal properties can have a profound impact upon the course of human-computer interaction. Delays in system responses can lead to frustration and error. Conversely, rapid feedback from monitoring applications can stretch an operator's ability to filter information during critical tasks (Johnson, 1996). Accident Fault Trees, therefore, include real-time. It is important to note, however, that is not always possible or desirable to associate an exact time with all of the events leading to an accident. Given limited evidence in the aftermath of an accident it is unlikely that operators will be able to recall the exact second in which they did or did not respond to a system failure.

2.4 Introducing Criticality

Many existing fault trees fail to represent the criticality of an event. This is surprising because different faults will carry different consequences for the continued operation of an interactive system. For example, keystroke errors may only have a marginal impact whilst more deep-seated mode confusion can have catastrophic consequences. Figure 1 illustrates a graphical extension to the fault tree notation that can be used to represent criticality.

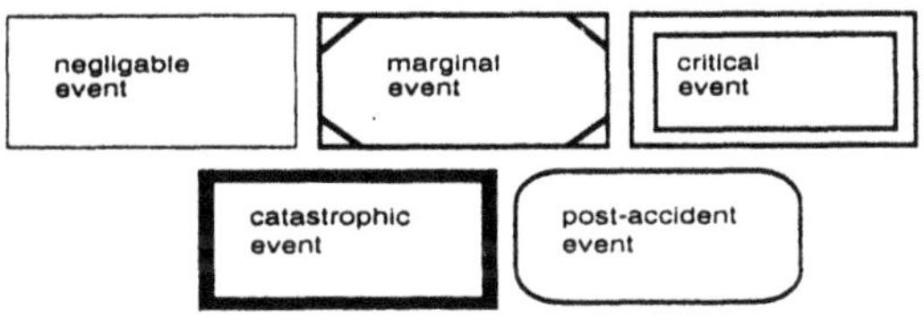

Figure 1: Weighted fault tree nodes

A negligible failure leads to a loss of function that has no effect on system. A marginal failure degrades the system but will not cause the system to be unavailable. A critical failure completely degrades system performance. A catastrophic fault produces severe consequences that can involve injuries or fatalities. It should be noted that we are currently evaluating a range of alternative presentation formats for these symbols.

It is important to emphasise that the criticality categorisation is a subjective assessment. What is important is not whether the reader agrees with our particular assessment, but that the diagram makes the categorisation explicit. Too often these assessments are left as implicit judgements within the natural language of an accident report.

3. THE CLAPHAM ACCIDENT FAULT TREE

Figure 2 illustrates an application of the extensions presented in the previous section. The Clapham Accident Fault Tree includes paragraph references and post-accident events. It also links the event nodes to the times at which they took place. Finally, the Accident Fault Tree makes explicit the level of criticality of each event.

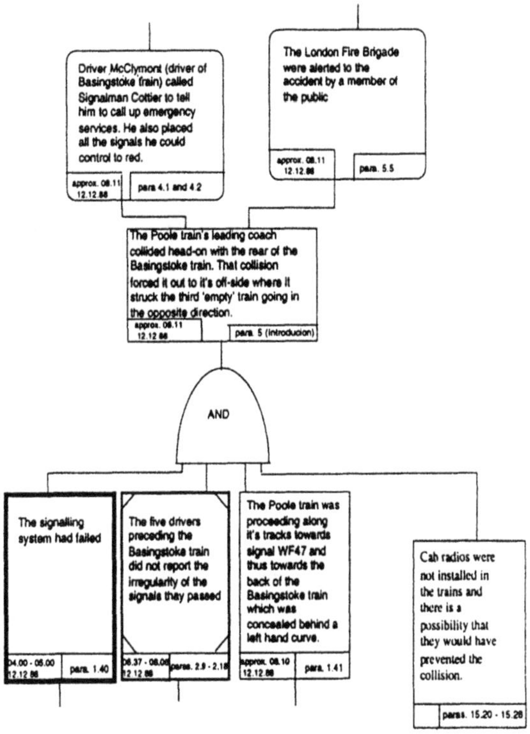

Figure 2: Extract from a Clapham Accident Fault Tree

REFERENCES

Department of Transport. *Investigation into the Clapham Junction Railway Accident.* Her Majesty's Stationery Office. London, United Kingdom, 1989.

E. Hollnagel, *The Phenotype Of Erroneous Actions*, International Journal Of Man-Machine Studies, 39:1-32, 1993.

C. Johnson, *Documenting The Design Of Safety-Critical User Interfaces*, Interacting With Computers, (8)3:221-239, 1996.

J. Leplat. *Accidents and Incidents Production: Methods of Analysis.* In J. Rasmussen, K. Duncan and J. Leplat (eds.), New Technology and Human Error. John Wiley and Sons Ltd, 1987.

J. Reason, *Human Error*, Cambridge University Press, Cambridge, United Kingdom, 1990.

Functional Evolution of Software: FOCUs Model of Design Rationale

Irene Au
Netscape Communications Corporation
Mountain View, CA 94043
i-au@netscape.com

Penelope Sanderson
SCHIL, School of Information Technology
Hawthorn, VIC 3122
Swinburne University of Technology
psanderson@swin.edu.au

ABSTRACT. In this poster we present the FOCUs model for representing design rationale. The FOCUs model assimilates the benefits of the MacLean, Young, Bellotti, and Moran's (1996) QOC model and the interdisciplinary constraints and pressures represented in Rasmussen, Pejtersen, and Goodstein's (1994) domain maps. A set of FOCUs maps for a particular design problem can be generated and organized into a lattice to represent design rationale from the most general to most specific detail. We have applied the FOCUs model to the development of a smart scheduling feature in two different but related software applications. We argue that the FOCUs model is particularly useful for tracking the evolution of functional prototypes and concept demonstrators.

KEYWORDS. Design rationale, software engineering, design space analysis, QOC model, interdisciplinary design

DESIGN RATIONALE

Software design and development is a dynamic process that involves forging a path from an initial need to a fully functional and usable product. HCI researchers have been seeking ways of better understanding, facilitating, and documenting this process (Moran & Carroll, 1996). In this poster we present a new model—FOCUs (Au, 1996)—developed to capture the design rationale invoked when we added a smart scheduling feature to the Advising Workbench (AWB) software for academic advising at University of Illinois (Sanderson, Iozzo, Buberel, & Au, 1995).

The smart scheduling feature takes a student's proposed list of courses and, from the multiple sections offered within each course, finds many possible weekly schedules to choose from. Because the design process for the smart scheduler was complicated by multiple constraints, we performed a post-hoc analysis of design rationale using MacLean, Young, Bellotti, and Moran's (1996) Questions-Options-Criteria (QOC) framework and Rasmussen, Pejtersen, and Goodstein's (1994) domain maps. The QOC notation successfully represented some of the design rationale for the smart scheduler but it had no compelling way of representing the effects of criteria imposed on the design by different constituencies involved in the product. In contrast, Rasmussen et al.'s (1994) domain maps showed how design is molded by the competing needs of different constituencies, but assumptions made about the problem, the tradeoffs considered between options, and the compromises made, were not reflected. Moreover, transitions between the domain map cells only represented temporal sequence, which did not express implications or design interactions that occur in parallel.

FOCUS MODEL

To cover the above inadequacies we developed the FOCUs model of design rationale (see Figure 1). FOCUs (Features, Organizational support, Computer science, and Users) is a descriptive model of software evolution and is a symbiosis between the QOC notation and Rasmussen's domain maps (Au, 1996).

Like the latter, FOCUs maps use a grid to lay out the design process (Fifure 1) Rows represent the features wanted (F), the organizational support available to provide access to resources during development (O), computational issues (C), and usability issues (Us). Columns represent the Goals (G) of the different interests represented, Requirements or Rationale (Rq), Constraints (Cn) imposed by some interest, and Resolution (Re).

Human–Computer Interaction: INTERACT'97 S. Howard, J. Hammond & G. Lindgaard (editors)
Published by Chapman & Hall

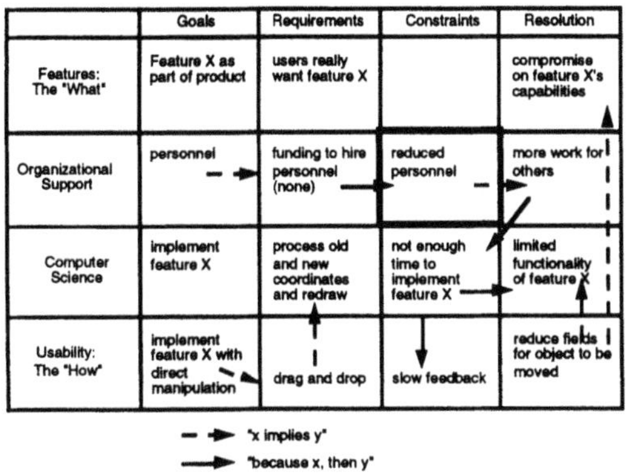

Figure 1: A sample FOCUs map from a simple design problem (not smart scheduling).

Because design resolutions may be linked or nested within each other, such relations must be shown. FOCUs maps can be organized into a lattice (see Figure 2) so that specific solutions to more general problems are visualized appropriately.

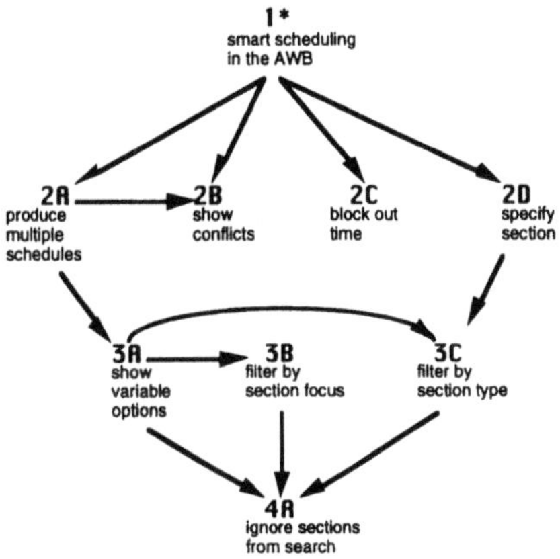

Figure 2: Lattice of nine FOCUs maps detailing design rationale for the smart scheduling feature of the AWB.

Overall, we found that the FOCUs maps throw into sharp relief the sources of compromise that shaped the current form of the smart scheduler. They illustrated the pervasive effect of particular constraints and helped us prioritize efforts to remove these constraints, some of which involved significant organizational negotiation.

EVALUATION OF FOCUS MODEL

For the smart scheduling prototyping problem, the FOCUs approach inherits the advantages but avoids some disadvantages of the QOC and Rasmussen approaches. (1) The lattice of FOCUs maps allows different levels of detail to be expressed. (2) FOCUs maps make it easy to see the constraints imposed on the design by the different domains and constituencies involved. (3) FOCUs maps are both descriptive and explanatory, revealing how the software evolved and why. (4) FOCUs maps are sensitive to differences in implementation, tradeoffs, and compromises. (5) The arrows linking cells entries allow developers to visualize the complexity of the design problem and to predict potential problems if requirements or constraints change. (6) A set of FOCUs maps highlights the pervasiveness of constraints during development—particularly when building functional prototypes—and helps prioritize efforts to remove such constraints.

CONCLUSION

We believe the evolutionary and multiply-constrained aspect of software design is captured well by the FOCUs model. The FOCUs approach is generalizable to a wide range of design and prototyping situations, but full assessments have yet to be performed. However, given its effectiveness with the smart scheduling problem, we are cautiously optimistic.

REFERENCES

1. Au, I. (1996). *The Advising Workbench: A case study in the functional evolution of software.* Unpublished master's thesis, Department of M. & I. E., University of Illinois at Urbana-Champaign, Urbana, IL.
2. MacLean, A., Young, R., Bellotti, V., & Moran, T. (1996). Questions, Options, and Criteria: Elements of Design Space Analysis. In T. P. Moran and J. M. Carroll (Eds.), *Design Rationale: Concepts, techniques, and use* (pp. 53-105). Hillsdale, NJ: Lawrence Erlbaum Associates.
3. Moran, T.P., & Carroll, J.M. (1996). Overview of design rationale. In T.P. Moran and J.M. Carroll (Eds.), *Design rationale: Concepts, techniques, and use* (pp. 1-19). Hillsdale, NJ: Lawrence Erlbaum Associates, Inc.
4. Rasmussen, J., Pejtersen, A. & Goodstein, L.P. (1994). *Cognitive engineering: Concepts and applications.* New York: Wiley.
5. Sanderson, P., Iozzo, N., Buberel, J., & Au, I. (1995). The Advising Workbench: Participation-Based Development of a Software Environment to Support Student Advising. *Proceedings of the 39th Annual Meeting of the Human Factors and Ergonomics Society* (pp. 1180-1184). Santa Monica, CA: Human Factors and Ergonomics Society.

GraphApp: A High-Level Toolkit for Building Prototype User Interfaces

Lachlan J. Patrick

Basser Department of Computer Science
University of Sydney
AUSTRALIA
loki@cs.su.oz.au

ABSTRACT GraphApp is a cross-platform high-level toolkit for the construction of graphical interfaces to applications. It has been designed specifically to be easy and quick to learn, and was used in a course teaching user interface design. This paper gives a brief outline of the motivations for the creation of this toolkit and the approaches taken to achieve the design goals. A brief summary of student usage of the toolkit is presented.

KEYWORDS prototyping, building user interfaces, teaching user interface design, cross-platform user interface toolkit

1. INTRODUCTION

There have been few graphics toolkits which have been designed specifically with learning in mind. The SUIT toolkit (Pausch, 1992) is one; Tk (Ousterhout, 91) is another which is sometimes used for teaching, despite not being made especially for beginners.

A graphics toolkit designed for learners should satisfy a number of conditions. It must be easy to learn and be sufficiently powerful to use in real-world programs. Good documentation is also important for learners.

GraphApp (Patrick, 1996) was used in a course teaching user interface design to computer science students, which introduces a number of stricter requirements for the design to satisfy.

The toolkit should be representative of event-driven graphics toolkits in general, so that students can transfer the lessons they learn to other systems. If it works on multiple operating systems, this is advantageous since students can take source code home and experiment.

Additionally, making programs easy to understand and fast to learn are important factors in a course with only a brief time allotted for teaching interface construction tools.

GraphApp met all of these design goals and was used with much success in the above-mentioned course, which also introduced students to HTML, Tk and Visual Basic.

This paper describes some of the design decisions made during GraphApp's development, and briefly describes its use in teaching.

2. THE DESIGN OF GRAPHAPP

GraphApp is a real-world, cross-platform, easy to learn graphics toolkit with a vocabulary and design optimised for user interface construction.

2.1. Cross-platform

GraphApp works on multiple platforms to facilitate the transfer of source code between the workplace and the home computer, or between different workplace

Human–Computer Interaction: INTERACT'97 S. Howard, J. Hammond & G. Lindgaard (editors)
Published by Chapman & Hall

computers. It implements many of the most common widgets available in modern graphical operating systems, is small and efficient and the source code is readily available.

The C language (Kernighan, 1988) was chosen as the target language for the toolkit, since this is a common, standard language for which compilers exist on most operating systems. Porting GraphApp was thus not impeded by language choice.

The students who were taught GraphApp as part of a third year computer science course already had a familiarity with the C language, and prior surveys had shown that many owned PC compatible computers at home. The practical part of the course made use of X-Windows terminals linked to a central file server.

GraphApp was useful in this course because it allows source code portability between X-Windows and Microsoft Windows (Petzold, 1992) platforms. The library is layered above each operating system so as to give access to widgets using the native appearance of each platform.

2.2. Easy to Learn

GraphApp is easy to learn for a number of reasons: the use of sensible defaults; initialisation and event handling on demand; short parameter lists; and sensible identifiers are all factors.

The use of sensible defaults is an example of how 'training wheels' (Carroll, 1984) can improve learning. The student need not know how to use colours, fonts or windows to begin programming, but these concepts can be learned as experience increases.

There is no need to explicitly initialise the library or write event handling routines, because this is all performed automatically as needed.

Function parameter lists have been kept short through the strategic use of a small number of global variables, the passing of structures in some cases, and appropriate function naming.

The use of verbs as function names reduces some parameter lists, simplifying learning and providing a better match between student expectations and GraphApp code than would be the case with some other systems. For instance there are polymorphic functions named 'show' and 'hide', which affect the visibility of graphical objects, rather than a single 'showhide' function which takes an extra parameter.

3. IN THE CLASSROOM

GraphApp was employed as part of a course teaching user interface design, and the response to the toolkit was positive. It was used both in a small exercise and a major task by many students.

Students were introduced to HTML, Tk, Visual Basic and GraphApp, and were given two one-hour lectures and four hours of practical work to learn each tool. The aim was for all students to be able to complete a small exercise by the end of that time, so each tool had to be easy to learn.

For a major assessment task, students chose one of the tools and extended the exercise task into a full program. GraphApp was used by almost 40% of students for this project, with HTML being more highly favoured at almost 50%.

The fact that GraphApp was often used is an encouraging sign. A survey of the perceived relevance of these tools was also conducted, and the 70% of the class who responded ranked the above tools in the same order as their use in the major assessment task.

4. CONCLUSION

GraphApp is a cross-platform graphics toolkit with a vocabulary and design optimised for learning, which has been used successfully in a course teaching user interface design.

5. REFERENCES

Carroll, J.M.; Carrithers, C.; "Training Wheels in a User Interface", *Comm. of the ACM*, Vol. 27, No. 8, (August 1984) pp 800-806

Kernighan, B.; Richie, D.; *The C Programming Language*, 2nd ed., Prentice Hall, (1988)

Ousterhout, J. K.; "An X11 Toolkit Based on the Tcl Language," USENIX, (Winter 1991)

Pausch, R.; Conway, M.; DeLine, R.; "Lessons Learned from SUIT, the Simple User Interface Toolkit", *ACM Trans. on Information Systems*, Vol. 10, No. 4, (October 1992), pp 320-344

Patrick, L.; http://www.cs.su.oz.au/~loki/graphapp

Petzold, C.; *Programming Windows 3.1*, 3rd ed., Microsoft Press, (1992)

PART FOUR

Videos

105

Image Browsing: a Space-Time Trade-off

Kevin Lam and Robert Spence

Department of Electrical & Electronic Engineering
Imperial College, London, England SW7 2BT
+44 171 594 6259
r.spence@ic.ac.uk

ABSTRACT

Browsing is defined as *the assessment of content*, and is different from searching. Whereas the browsing of text can be tedious and difficult, the browsing of images can often proceed more easily and at a much faster rate. For example, while images may well occupy more space than the associated descriptive text, their adequate appearance need only be brief. For this reason, the space that would be required to fully and continuously display a number of images can be traded for a much smaller space if those images are capable of being riffled, each image being displayed only momentarily. The space-time trade-off is illustrated by the example of a video-store whose contents can be browsed.

KEYWORDS

Browsing, Visualization

1. BROWSING

Browsing - a term often informally used to describe a variety of activities - is here defined solely as *the assessment of content*. A new book, for example, may be picked up, and its pages flicked through in a matter of seconds, to gain some awareness of structure, make-up, features and style - in general, an awareness of *content*. Browsing is also well illustrated by a diner viewing the menu in a new restaurant, or the person having a first glance at *The Times* newspaper.

Browsing is *not* the same as searching, the latter activity being characterised by a specific goal. While searching often follows browsing or, in some cases, is essentially concurrent with browsing, it is nevertheless important that interaction design should specifically address the needs of browsing as a distinct activity.

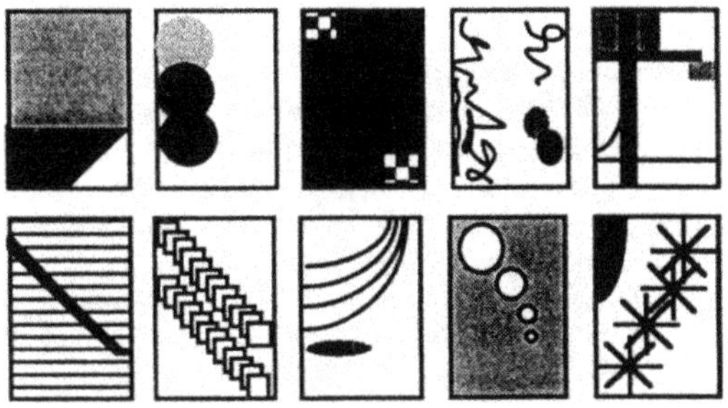

Figure 1 Images in full view

Figure 2 Images partially overlapped to conserve space

2. A SPACE-TIME TRADE-OFF

It can be tedious and time-consuming, for example, to browse a textual list of paintings in a collection. By comparison, even a brief glance at the paintings themselves may well be sufficient to gain some insight into the nature of that collection. However, if images are displayed in full (Figure 1), an immediate disadvantage with a display screen of finite size is a severe limit on the number of images that can simultaneously be displayed, at adequate resolution, for perception, retention and later recognition. Overlapping (Figure 2) of the images goes some way towards ameliorating this space limitation, but at the expense of only a partial presentation of each image.

Human–Computer Interaction: INTERACT'97 S. Howard, J. Hammond & G. Lindgaard (editors)
Published by Chapman & Hall

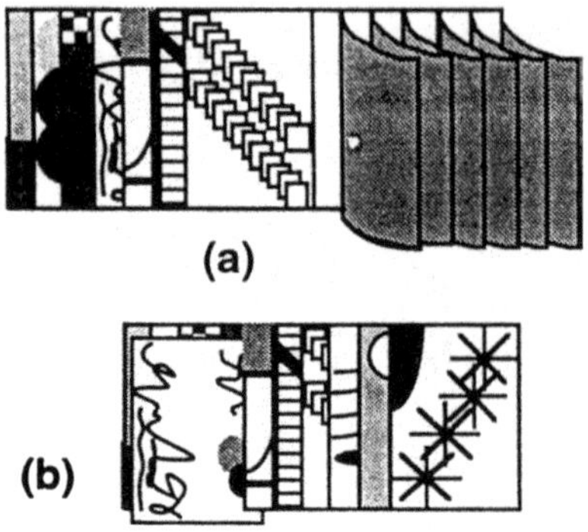

Figure 3 Each image is fully though momentarily displayed

A remarkably simple solution to the space limitation is to exploit the human being's ability [4] to perceive, retain and later recognise the features of an image following its relatively brief display. Thus, if the images are now displayed in full *only momentarily*, either by a riffling action (Figure 3a) or by a brief though complete display of each image in turn (Figure 3b), the 'browsing capacity' of the display can be significantly increased. With each of these approaches, space has been traded against elapsed time.

3. A VIDEO STORE

The 'space-time trade-off' approach to image browsing has been illustrated in the context of a video store in which a customer might first browse to see what videos are available, later gradually moving towards a search activity to select a video for viewing. Though our primary concern here is with browsing, the interface design fully recognises the need, additionally, to support effective search.

The appearance of the video store is shown in Figure 4. There are three rows ('shelves') of video posters. All except those in the centre region are overlapped to a considerable degree, though complete overlap is avoided because of the need to show context and approximate extent and to provide spatial reference. The bifocal concept [3] supports the concurrent display of 'focus and context', and is combined with the '3D' Perspective Wall [2] presentation technique thus, during and after browsing, some posters representing individual videos can be examined in more detail in the central region.

Browsing to assess the structure and content of the store is achieved by simple movement of the cursor over the overlapped collections of posters at each side. As the cursor moves over a poster, it immediately protrudes allowing full view. Typically, the entire row might be browsed in three or four seconds.

Other features are conventional. For example, as in the bifocal display [3], the entire 'shelving' can be moved to and fro to bring particular categories of video ('musical', 'education') into the central region, and to allow a poster-based menu to be used for additional browsing or search. The example is, of course, neither the only nor the first example of the appropriateness, for browsing, of the momentary display of an image. The Video Streamer [1], for example, is a superb and earlier example. The purpose of the video is to demonstrate an essentially dynamic technique by video.

4. CONCLUSION

Given that browsing is the assessment of content, the browsing of images can be achieved efficiently in limited space by the activity of riffling, with each image only displayed for a fraction of a second.

REFERENCES

1 Elliot, E. and Davenport, G. Video Streamer, ACM, CHI'94 Companion Proceedings, pp.65-66 (1994)

2. Mackinlay, J .D., Robertson, G.G. and Card, S.K., The Perspective Wall: detail and context smoothly integrated, ACM, Proc. CHI'91, pp.173-179 (1991)

3. Spence, R. and Apperley, M.D. Data-base navigation: an office environment for the professional, *Behaviour and Information Technology*, 1, 1, 43-54 (1982).

4. Standing, L. (1973) *Learning 10,000 pictures*, Quarterly Journal of Experimental Psychology, 25, 207-222 (1973)

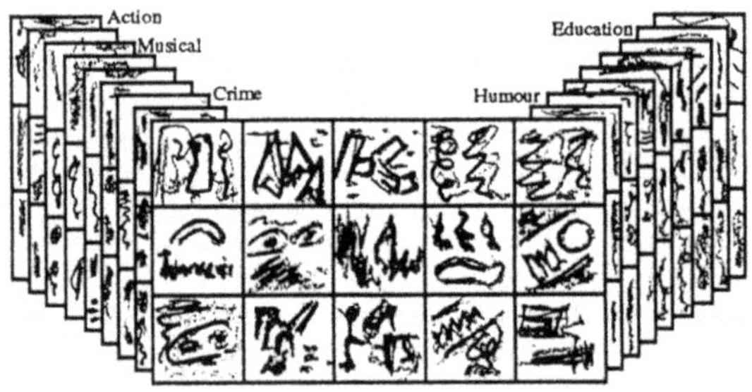

Figure 4 Sketch of the implemented video store

106

Demonstration of the IdeaBoard Interface and Applications

Tsuyoshi Oguni, Takashi Yoshino and Masaki Nakagawa

Dept. of Computer Science
Tokyo Univ. of Agri. & Tech.
Naka-cho 2-24-16, Koganei, Tokyo, 184, Japan
oguni@hands.ei.tuat.ac.jp

ABSTRACT This video demonstrates a new style of human interface and several applications on an interactive dynamic whiteboard (Nakagawa et al 1997). Its design issues have been how to realize easy and natural operation to the large board from an arbitrary standing position of its user with a reasonable amount of hand movement, avoidance of unreliable gesture commands as well as smooth and natural extension of the current desktop GUI.

KEYWORDS pen interface, handwriting recognition, electronic whiteboard, direct pointing, GUI

1. INTRODUCTION

A white/black board is one of the devices which are not fully computerized although it may open the new way of presentation and lecture. We decided to develop a system to combine the merit of the white/black board and that of computer processing as a part of our pen interface research.

The Liveboard by XEROX is well-known as such a system (Elrod et al. 1992, Pedersen et al. 1993, Weiser 1991, 1993). Our system mainly differs from the Liveboard in the following respects.

Firstly, the Liveboard and especially its applications developed at XEROX PARC avoid handwriting recognition except that for gestures (Pedersen 1993). On the other hand, we employ handwriting recognition to provide the power of computing to our behaviors of handwriting. However, we are not positive about employing gestures because of the reasons describe below.

One of the reasons that the Liveboard has employed gestures would be that a simple expansion of the desktop GUI to the board size requires the user to push top left button as well as bottom right buttons, with the result that the user's body often covers the board. We try to find a different solution.

Secondly, the resolution and brightness of the Liveboard seems unsatisfactory. Enlarging a computer display and sharing it by participants make collaboration easier by itself. To be used as an electronic whiteboard, however, brightness and resolution are very important.

We decided to use a temporary hardware to develop interface and applications while making a new hardware. We call our system "*IdeaBoard*" (Interactive, Dynamic, Electronic Assistant Board).

The basic concept of the *IdeaBoard* is not the enlargement of the computer display, but the coupling of the merits of a whiteboard with those of computer processing. This requires the very high resolution of a large display (more than 1600 x 1200 resolution of the 70-inch size) and sufficient brightness so that the students can watch the teacher's face as well as the contents on the board in a well-lighted room. Moreover, new human interface design as well as

Human–Computer Interaction: INTERACT'97 S. Howard, J. Hammond & G. Lindgaard (editors)
Published by Chapman & Hall

applications must be developed which inherit the conventional and familiar interfaces from a white/black board while exploiting the dynamic processing of contents by computing.

2. GESTURES CONSIDERED HARMFUL

Gestures have been an attraction of pen interfaces. The Liveboard has also employed gestures, but we are reluctant to employ gestures because of the following reasons:

1. Pattern recognition problem
   Gestures have simple shapes and simple shapes are hard for machines to recognize. Moreover, there is little context to augment gesture recognition.
2. Human interface problem
   Design of gestures is very difficult. Often, gestures are difficult to remember and easy to forget. Moreover, mode change for inputting gestures is troublesome and easy to forget. Misrecognition of gestures or forgotten mode change yields an abrupt and unexpected result and that must be canceled. They not only interrupt lectures or presentations very badly but also shock the teacher or presenter.

Because of these problems, users fear that gestures might be misinterpreted and may hesitate to use gestures.

Therefore, we avoid the human interface being dependent on gestures. Nevertheless, we do not avoid pattern recognition. Pattern recognition can be more useful for contents rather than for commands.

3. *IdeaBoard* USER INTERFACE

If we just expand the desktop GUI to the whiteboard size, a teacher has to move from side to side, stretch hands from button to button, which not only makes the teacher practice gymnastics but often hides the board from the students. To operate the *IdeaBoard* without crossing the surface, the elements of the desktop GUI should be examined and modified so that it can be operated from an arbitrary standing position.

Considering the body movement to operate the *IdeaBoard,* if it is too large, it is hard for the user as well as it hides the board, but if it is too minute, it is again difficult for the standing user. We think that body size movement with direct pointing and manipulation is not only appealing to the audience but also navigates their focus of attention.

To keep pushing a marker horizontally at one point on the vertical board is hard for a person. Our hands become tired in trying to remain steady. Double tapping is also not so easy as with a mouse. Compared with these, dragging (drawing) a marker is easier and more direct for the audience,

Smooth and continuous movement of displayed objects (Perlin et al. 1993) seems more important for the shared large display so that the audience can keep their focus of attention without being annoyed by the sudden change of contents.

Consequently, the styles and elements of the desktop GUI must be modified so that they can exploit the *IdeaBoard* features. However, the modification should be very natural so that users do not feel a big difference.

4. CONTENTS IN THE VIDEO

The styles and elements of the the *IdeaBoard* UI are shown in the video. Several applications which are effectively interacted by the UI are also demonstrated.

This work is being supported by the Advanced Software Enrichment Project of IPA under MITI, Japan.

5. REFERENCES

Elrod, S., Bruce, R., Gold, R., Goldberg, D., Halasz, F., Janssen, W., Lee, D., McCall, K., Pedersen, E., Pier, K., Tang, J. and Welch, B. (1992) Liveboard: A Large Interactive Display Supporting Group Meetings, Presentations and Remote Collaboration. *Proc. CHI'92*, 599-607.

Nakagawa, M., Oguni, T., Yoshino, T. (1997) Human interface and applications on IdeaBoard, to appear in Proc. *INTERACT 97*.

Pedersen, E.R., McCall, K., Moran, T.P., Halasz, F.G. (1993) Tivoli: An Electronic Whiteboard for Informal Workgroup Meetings, *Proc. INTERCHI'93*, 391-398.

Perlin, K. and Fox, D. Pad: An Alternative Approach to the Computer Interface, *Proc. 1993 ACM SIGGRAPH Conference*, 57-64.

Weiser, M. (1991) The Computer for the 21st Century, *Scientific American*, 94-104.

Weiser, M. (1993) Some Computer Science Issues in Ubiquitous Computing, *C. ACM*, **36**, 7, 74-84.

MANICORAL (Multimedia and network in cooperative research and learning).

Werner Fürst*, Roger Haagmans, Marc Naeije**, Janni Nielsen*****

*Technical University of Graz, **Delft University of Technology,
***Copenhagen Business School
***janni.nielsen@cbs.dk

KEY WORDS: Distributed geoscientific research community, communication, cognition, multimedia.

The fast development of new IT-tools and communication technologies provides new opportunities for computer mediated collaboration in geographically distributed groups. One of the fields suitable for application of these technologies is collaboration among scientists. This opportunity is especially important to many of the smaller European countries where it may be difficult to maintain competent scientific research within highly specialized fields. The new tele-communication technologies provide scientists in smaller countries with opportunities to maintain close collaboration with colleagues in foreign countries in spite of dispersion in time and geographical location, and combined with multimedia to enhance visual representations of scientific data they open up radically new dimensions in research.

The MANICORAL video introduces the MANICORAL project that aims at exploring, developing, implementing and evaluating a Computer Supported Cooperative Work System among a geographically distributed European research Group. This integrated system optimally combines various media and high speed networking. Consequently, it will enhance international collaboration, access to scientific methods, results and data. Hence, the MANICORAL life board may become a standard tool in everyone's local scientific environment, as it will support and improve everydays scientific work regardless of location.

Especially, the video shows how Distributed Cooperative Visualization (DCV) tools can facilitate collaboration within a distributed group of scientists. The distributed group has both teaching and research obligations and the DCV tools may facilitate both. However, of these two obligations support for research is the most obvious, as here the video clearly demonstrates how the DCV tools enables the scientists to share data, interpretations and ideas over the network, and thereby, enables them to become more productive.

MANICORAL belongs to the telematics program of the European Union and unites human factors expertise, technology providers and geoscientists.

Human–Computer Interaction: INTERACT'97 S. Howard, J. Hammond & G. Lindgaard (editors)
Published by Chapman & Hall

PART FIVE

Doctoral Consortium

Towards a method for user interface specification

Paul Chesson

Department of Computer Science
The University of Melbourne
Parkville, Australia, 3052
email: chesson@cs.mu.OZ.AU

ABSTRACT A major aspect of user interface specification is concerned with describing the structure of dialogue between an interactive system and its users. The goal of this work is to establish an effective and usable language and process by which the behaviour of a user interface can be completely and accurately defined. This method should enable the production and maintenance of well-structured, understandable, and concise specifications for a wide variety of systems. It should also support specification at multiple levels of abstraction and allow refinement between these levels.

KEYWORDS User Interface, Dialogue Specification, Requirements

1. Introduction

1.1 Motivations

A major aspect of user interface specification is concerned with describing the structure of dialogue between an interactive system and its users. Specifications produced from this process aim to facilitate the communication of requirements and design decisions between the participants in software development. In addition, the user interface specification enables developers to verify that any required constraints are maintained and to analyse various aspects related to the usability of an interface.

There is a need for a universal notation which is adaptable for use for multiple views of the interface behaviour, thereby increasing the scope of its use within software development (Bass, 1994). When applying notations to particular specification problems, rarely is any procedural guidance given. Such guidance would reduce the time needed to learn the language, and avoid the language being used inappropriately (Monk et al., 1993).

1.2 Proposed objectives

The goal of this work is to establish an effective and usable language and process by which user interfaces can be completely and accurately defined.

Development of a language suitable for user interface specification should aim to meet the following objectives:

- Communication and Expression
  - allow easy understanding of the notation and straightforward translation into an informal description,
  - enable the expression of requirements which cover a wide range of levels from the physical actions of a user to the goals which they aim to achieve, and
  - provide the ability to express temporal relations, including sequencing, repetition, order independence, interruptibility, mutual interleavibility and concurrency.
- Construction
  - facilitate the re-use of parts of a specification in the same system or other systems, where the same or similar functionality is required, and

Human–Computer Interaction: INTERACT'97 S. Howard, J. Hammond & G. Lindgaard (editors)
Published by Chapman & Hall

- allow parts of the specification to be smoothly coupled with or de-coupled from other parts of the system or other systems.

- Reasoning and Analysis
  - enable the resolution of questions related to the user's ability to reach a state or effect from various points within the dialogue space, and
  - provide potential to perform various types of usability analysis on a specified interface, including issues such as efficiency, complexity, cognitive consistency, and likelihood and consequences of user errors.

The development of a well-defined method for deriving the specification from a set of informal requirements should address how the following will be achieved:

- production and maintenance of a well-structured, understandable, and concise specification for a wide variety of problems,
- minimisation of the impact of decision-making and the amount of work needed from software developers in the specification process,
- support for task level abstractions,
- the use and mixing of multiple levels of abstraction, whilst maintaining an integrated and coherent specification, and
- refinement between between different levels of abstraction.

2. Method for language development

Development of a user interface specification language commenced with the investigation of various existing languages, and their application to a case study of a graphical drawing application. A set of characteristics and capabilities of user interface specification languages was derived for use in assessing and comparing the potential of languages. Various ways of classifying user interface specification languages were also investigated, in order to identify major paradigms for reasoning about and presenting specifications.

The language which was developed aimed to adequately address as many of the characteristics and capabilities as possible, as well as being able to support multiple paradigms to a significant degree. The central objectives were to allow a strong mapping between the components of the language and the natural language requirements with which they corresponded, and a low coupling between components in order to promote ease of modification of an existing specification.

In order to produce formal specifications, the language used to produce a specification must have formally defined semantics. The language under development was given formal semantics by developing a well-defined set of steps which are able to translate any given specification written in the language into a language or notation which has an established set of syntax and semantics.

The initial focus of development was on the lower levels of interaction. The next step was to move towards the specification of user tasks, paying particular attention to the way in which the state of a task is maintained from the history of operations performed. A graphical file manager was used as a test case for this step.

3. Results

This section describes the work performed towards the outlined objectives.

3.1 Case study

Investigation of various user interface specification languages yielded a list of useful characteristics and capabilities found in such languages (Chesson and Johnston, 1996b), the most important of which became objectives in the development of the new language (see section 1.2).

A case study of how well various languages were able to demonstrate such capabilities proceeded using the requirements for a core piece of functionality from the `xfig` drawing package. The languages which have been examined are Jacob's language for direct manipulation interfaces (Jacob, 1986), Interactive Cooperative Objects (Palanque et al., 1993), the CNUCE interactor model (Paternó and Faconti, 1992), and Dialogue Specification Notation (Curry and Monk, 1995).

Some of the observations which were particularly relevant to the development of the new user interface specification language include:

- there are dilemmas in choosing between different mechanisms within a language, which can achieve the same result,

- there are difficulties in specifying the behaviour of an interface without concern for the details of how this behaviour could be expressed,
- a poor design of framework or model will force developers to have to "work around" the model, rather than with it,
- specifying strong modalities in an interface, whereby the majority of user operations are ignored or have their normal behaviour suspended, can be difficult, and
- handling the creation and deletion of dynamic objects is a significant issue.

3.2 Classification of languages

It was found useful to consider languages in terms of how their individual components (states, variables, objects, user events, system actions, etc.) are integrated into a specification. Such paradigms may also closely relate to the way in which the participants in software development read or construct specifications. The following paradigms have been proposed:

State-based paradigm which expresses systems in terms of the status of the interface.

Event-based paradigm which expresses systems in terms of the reactive behaviour of the interface and the changes which may occur.

Grammatical-based paradigm which expresses systems in terms of a top-down hierarchy of operations.

Logic/Constraint-based paradigm which expresses systems in terms of what can be performed and the constraints to be maintained.

Further classification may be achieved by examining the components themselves and the abstractions they represent. For example, objects may represent active agents, visual objects, or conceptual objects in the application domain.

3.3 Development of FLUID

A language for specifying user interfaces, FLUID (Formal Language for User Interface Dialogue) (Chesson and Johnston, 1996a), has been developed. The language draws upon logic-based, event-based, and state-based paradigms. The rationale was to provide a wide range of views from which the specification can be read, including those which emphasise logical constraints, hierarchical control and data flow, and the visual status of an interface.

The central unit of abstraction in a FLUID specification is the requirement. Requirements may be elicited from a customer, or included as a result of user interface design decisions. Requirements are expressed declaratively by the use of natural language, allowing the specification to be presented, constructed, and maintained in an intuitive manner.

Individual requirements are related by a hierarchical structure which defines how each requirement constrains and is constrained by others. The dynamic behaviour of the interface is modelled by the propagation of events through this hierarchy.

The behaviour of each requirement is expressed procedurally. This expression is achieved through a combination of mechanisms, namely, the processing of events through the hierarchy, the states of the interface, and the triggering of actions. The mechanisms are provided though a combination of tables and simple coloured Petri nets.

The formal semantics for FLUID have been defined by a process which translates an arbitrary specification written in FLUID into coloured Petri nets. The various graphical components of FLUID are expressed using a set theoretic model whose constraints are also expressed using set theory. This model can then be translated into another set theoretic model which corresponds to a coloured Petri net with inhibitor arcs and priorities. This translation can be performed automatically using a well defined set of steps described in set theory.

The final Petri net generated by the translation process not only enables a precise definition of the behaviour of specifications for interactive systems described in FLUID, but also provides a basis for assisting software developers of such systems. Direct execution of the Petri net will enable validation of the system, and formal techniques may also be applied to verify properties of the interface being developed (Palanque and Bastide, 1995).

3.4 A framework for requirements

A three-layer specification model was proposed to provide a framework for the classification and organisation of requirements and their associated FLUID components:

The symbolic layer deals exclusively with concepts within the user interface environment itself, and excludes any reference to the domain of the application being specified.

The semantic layer deals with simple operations presented by the used, and presented within the context of the application domain.

The pragmatic layer deals with task which are able to be performed by the user, having a practical purpose in performing a piece of work within the context of the application domain.

This model is adopted by FLUID through the use of three constraint hierarchies, connected to each other via the events transferred between them. A set of guidelines describes how events and actions from a specification are used within a particular layer of the model.

High level user tasks and operations can be refined into a "chain" of constraint sub-dialogues which control access to the piece of functionality performed by the task.

4. Further work

Development of a method for user interface specification with FLUID will continue by examining natural language requirements from one or more case studies and classifying them according to their abstraction level, purpose, and effects. The purpose of a requirement may be to provide the user with access to the functionality of the application or to constrain such access. The effects of a requirement may relate to its interaction with the environment of the user, or the application.

Each requirement will then be specified through one or more alternative sub-dialogues, each of which satisfies the requirement. Frequently used strategies and steps used to specify particular classes of requirements (as determined in the previous stage), will determine hypotheses for rules which can be applied to other interfaces. Affirmation of this work will be carried out by testing the proposed method on new problems. A set of sub-dialogues will be established for common forms of interaction in user interfaces.

A similar process will be used to refine and extend requirements down through multiple levels of abstraction, using the three-layer model as a starting point.

References

Bass, L. (1994). Working group on formal methods in HCI and software engineering. In Taylor, R. and Coutaz, J., editors, *ICSE'94 Workshop on SE-HCI: Joint Research Issues*, pages 14–16, Sorrento, Italy.

Chesson, P. and Johnston, L. (1996a). FLUID: Specifying data flow and control for user interfaces. In Yong, L., Herman, L., Leung, Y., and Moyes, J., editors, *Proceedings of the First Asia-Pacific Conference on Computer Human Interaction*, pages 171–180, Singapore.

Chesson, P. and Johnston, L. (1996b). Objectives for user interface specification languages. In *Proceedings of the First Australian Requirements Engineering Workshop*, 10 pages, Melbourne. Department of Information Systems, Monash University.

Curry, M. and Monk, A. (1995). Dialogue modelling of graphical user interfaces with a production system. *Behaviour and Information Technology*, 14(1):41–55.

Jacob, R. (1986). A specification language for direct-manipulation user interfaces. *ACM Transactions on Graphics*, 5(4):283–317.

Monk, A., Curry, M., and Wright, P. (1993). Why industry doesn't use the wonderful notations we researchers have given them to reason about their designs. In Gilmore, D., editor, *User-centred requirements for software engineering*, pages 253–261, Berlin. Springer-Verlag.

Palanque, P. and Bastide, R. (1995). Verification of an interactive software by analysis of its formal specification. In *Proceedings of the IFIP Human-Computer Interaction Conference (Interact'95)*, pages 191–197, Lillehammer, Norway.

Palanque, P. et al. (1993). Design of user-driven interfaces using petri nets and objects. In Bodard, F., Rolland, C., and Cauvet, C., editors, *Conference on Advanced Information System Engineering CAISE'93*, pages 569–585, Paris, France. Springer Verlag, LNCS n.685.

Paternó, F. and Faconti, G. (1992). On the use of LOTOS to describe graphical interaction. In Monk, A., Diaper, D., and Harrison, M., editors, *HCI'92, People and Computers VII*, pages 155–173, London. Cambridge University Press.

Layout Complexity: Does It Measure Usability?

Tim Comber,
John R. Maltby
Southern Cross University
PO Box 157
Lismore, NSW 2480
Australia.
tcomber@scu.edu.au
jmaltby@scu.edu.au

ABSTRACT This research investigates the validity of the layout complexity metric to GUI screen design. This metric offers a simple method to gauge the complexity of the visual design of a computer screen by classifying screen objects into classes based on common dimensions and positions. However, though it has been used by other interface researchers, it is not clear that it is a valid metric for GUIs. Initial work suggests that users prefer more complex layouts rather than the simple ones suggested by guidelines. The pilot study showed that screens midway between complex and simple were the most usable. The next experiment is at the data collection stage. It uses four screens differing in complexity and a Latin-squares design to avoid experimental bias and nuisance variables. Twenty-four human participants are randomly assigned to blocks. The final experiment will attempt to gain a wider range of users with a more complex task.

KEY WORDS Layout complexity, GUI, interface, usability.

1. RESEARCH THESIS

Despite the importance of screen displays to computer users (Shneiderman 1992), there are few empirical studies relating to modern, bit-mapped screens, (Galitz 1993) even though clearly most new computer systems use some form of GUI. This research examines the use of one *static measure* of layout quality; layout complexity and compares it to other measures eg white space, balance, and symmetry, to assess the usability of screen designs.

Static measures are defined as those metrics that do not require any knowledge of the task. They are independent of the functioning of the application. They can be contrasted to *dynamic measures* such as Layout Appropriateness (Sears 1993) which require the designer to able to identify the functions of screen objects. The chief attraction of static measures is that they can be incorporated into the design environment, eg see DON (Kim and Foley 1993), which automates part of the generation of a particular GUI and then lets an evaluation module compute the metrics (balance, symmetry, and the associated index). However, before layout complexity can be used in such a way it needs to be shown that it does measure usability. Earlier research has shown that it does affect users' attitudes

Human–Computer Interaction: INTERACT'97 S. Howard, J. Hammond & G. Lindgaard (editors)
Published by Chapman & Hall

to alphanumeric screens (Tullis 1988) but GUI's are more complex and visually oriented.
The layout complexity metric (LC) provides a measure of the horizontal and vertical alignment of objects and their positional alignment (Bonsiepe 1968). The layout complexity formula states that the complexity of a system C is given by

$$C = -N \sum_{i=1}^{i=n} p_i \log_2 p_i \qquad (1)$$

where:

$$N = \sum_{i=1}^{n} n_i$$

and

$$p_i = \frac{n_i}{n}$$

where:

N = total number of objects (widths or heights, distance from top or side of page)
n = number of classes (number of unique widths, heights or distances)
n_i = number of objects in the *i*th class
p_i = proportion of the *i*th class.

2. HYPOTHESIS:

Layout Complexity: There is a trade-off between usability (U) and complexity C with a relationship of the form U = fC where U is a maximum for some intermediate value of C (Figure 1 and Figure 2).

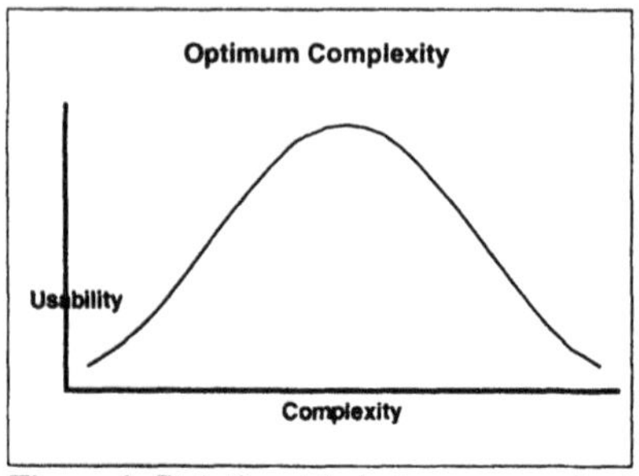

Figure 1: Relationship between complexity and usability

As the complexity figure becomes smaller, it becomes more difficult to distinguish different interface objects and the interface takes on an artificial regularity. On the other hand, the interface becomes more predictable. At the other extreme as the interface approaches maximum complexity, it looks artificially irregular. What is more important, it becomes impossible for the designer to group objects with similar functions on the basis of size or position. However, the increase in complexity does mean that the user has more information and therefore more choice of operations

3. METHODOLOGY

My hypothesis implies a causal relationship between layout complexity and usability of computer interfaces. Therefore an experimental design is the most appropriate methodology. The advantages of the experimental method are well known (Simon 1969), (Robson 1973). A Latin-square design will be used for the main experiment in order to detect learning effects and control for individual differences.
In the first instance a survey was used to determine whether complexity theory could be applied to GUI design and if indeed it measured some aspect of design "quality" (Comber and Maltby 1994). This was followed by a pilot experiment (Comber and Maltby 1995) with layout complexity as the independent variable and usability as the dependent variable. An important characteristic of usability testing is that it should be carried out "by real users carrying out real tasks in a real technical, physical and organisational environment" (Bevan and McLeod 1994) p136. Therefore it was important to build an application that had real utility, one that could be perceived by the particpants as being a real application rather than a contrived experimental one.

4. FINDINGS TO DATE

Initial work (Comber and Maltby 1994) focused on the use of the layout complexity metric (see (Bonsiepe 1968)(Tullis 1983; Tullis 1988; Tullis 1988)) applied to the opening screens of thirteen Windows 3.1 applications. It was found that the most complex screen was 66 times greater than that of the least complex screen. Screen dumps were made of these applications and presented to thirty people to determine whether Bonsiepe's technique would provide a predictive measure for users' ranking of different designs (Comber and Maltby 1994).

The subjects were asked to sort the screen prints from best design to worst design, with no ties. No attempt was made to define what was meant by "goodness" of design, this interpretation being left up to the individual. The expectation based upon the work of Tullis and Bonsiepe was that good layout design strives to be simple. This was not borne out by the results. A number of applications, including Microsoft Word and Excel, received rankings opposite to that expected. This suggests that users prefer more complex layouts. Having shown that layout complexity is both measurable for GUI's and that at least one aspect of usability, attitude, is affected by the metric, the next stage was to determine the metric's utility by building an application and measuring the effect of layout complexity on usability.

A pilot experiment (Comber and Maltby 1995) was designed to test three components of usability; effectiveness, learnability, and attitude. The pilot consisted of a simple application, running under Microsoft Windows, that calculated layout complexity for each design iteration. The screen with the lowest complexity score consisted of objects arranged in a neat grid with almost uniform sizes. The next two screens consisted of almost normal layouts and the final screen had every object with a different size and position. Seven experienced computer users volunteered to take part in the pilot study. It was found that the least and most complex screens were the least usable as expected (Table 1).

Usability	Screen 1	Screen 2	Screen 3	Screen 4
Complex	156	170	186	228
Error-free	36%	79%	86%	71%
Time	354	290	276	293
Rating	4	7	16	0

Table 1. Summary of results.

Table 1 summarises the results. The screens with a mid-range complexity, screens 2 and 3, rate better overall than the screens at either end of the complexity scale. However these results do need to be treated cautiously because of the small number of subjects and the limited number of screens.

The results from this pilot showed differences in usability between screens differing in complexity. However, the application required further development to improve its data collection capabilities and to make it more automated.

5. PLANS FOR FURTHER WORK

The next stage involves a controlled experiment with a Latin-square design. With four different layouts, this will require 24 people. The application has been written to allow the experiment to proceed without the presence of the experimenter making it more cost-effective to administer. The application now collects details of layout appropriateness (Sears 1993) and white space as well as layout complexity. At the time of writing there remains the coding for the symmetry and balance metrics (Kim and Foley 1993).

A separate application saves the dimensions and positions of each control (widget) in the interface to a file to enable the reconstruction of the screen layouts by the software. This application also calculates the static metrics.

A simple Microsoft Windows application, *Launcher*, originally designed as an example application for a Visual Basic tutorial, forms the basis for the experiment. The application was originally designed to allow some simple file management routines for Windows 3.1; viewing files, adding file names to a list and renaming them with any string, deleting files etc. Subjects were asked to complete a simple task with each screen.

The software records data for each screen:

- time between each click,
- distance between clicks,
- errors made,
- requests for help (pressing F1).

The program presents an ethics disclaimer and allows the person to exit the experiment at any time in accordance with university ethics policy. Each person has the same task to perform and can practice the task before attempting the experiment. The program asks for the age group, sex, occupation, years spent computing, computer experience, familiarity with Microsoft Windows and the amount of time spent using a computer per week. Each of the four screens is then presented in random order and the user is expected to complete the task on each screen. After each screen there is the opportunity to judge their opinion of the screen. At the conclusion the participants can review their choices and make comments.

Four different screen layouts were designed, each with a different complexity score The screen with the lowest score consists of objects arranged in a neat grid with almost uniform sizes. The next two screens consist of almost normal layouts and the final screen has every object with a different size and position. Table 2 shows the complexity ratings for each of the four screens used in the experiment. The theoretical minimum was not achievable in VB, when using different objects, as some objects could not be resized to match other objects ie objects in VB have a fixed size relationship to other objects.

Complexity Scores for 16 Objects						
	Theory min.	Scr. 1	Scr. 2	Scr. 3	Scr. 4	Theory max.
C	64	133	156	178	212	248
%	0%	42%	49%	57%	78%	100%

Table 2: Complexity scores for 16 objects

The experiment is now in the data collection stage. The final experiment will attempt to gain a wider range of users with a more complex task.

6. REFERENCES

Bevan, N. and M. McLeod (1994). "Usability measurement in context." Behaviour & Information Technology **13**(1 & 2): 132-145.

Bonsiepe, G. A. (1968). "A method of quantifying order in typographic design." Journal of Typographic Research **2**: 203-220.

Comber, T. and J. R. Maltby (1994). A Formal Method for Evaluating GUI Screens. ACIS'94 - Doctoral Consortium, Melbourne, Australia, Dept. of Information Services, Monash.

Comber, T. and J. R. Maltby (1994). Screen complexity and user design preference in windows applications. OZCHI'94, Melbourne, Australia, CHISIG.

Comber, T. and J. R. Maltby (1995). Evaluating usability of screen designs with layout complexity. OZCHI'95, Wollongong, CHISIG.

Galitz, W. O. (1993). User-Interface Screen Design. Inc., P. O. Box 812070, Wellesley, MA 02181, Q. E. D. Information Sciences.

Kim, W. C. and J. D. Foley (1993). Providing high-level control and expert assistance in the user interface presentation design. Proceedings of the INTERCHI '93. S. Ashlund. Amsterdam, Netherlands, ACM: 430-437.

Robson, C. (1973). Experiment, Design and Statistics. Harmondsworth, Middlesex, Penguin.

Sears, A. (1993). "Layout appropriateness: A metric for evaluating user interface widget layout." IEEE Transactions on Software Engineering **19**(7): 707-718.

Shneiderman, B. (1992). Designing the User Interface: Strategies for Effective Human-Computer Interaction. Reading, MA, Addison-Wesley.

Simon, J. L. (1969). Basic Research Methods in Social Science. New York, Random House.

Tullis, T. S. (1983). "The formatting of alphanumeric displays: a review and analysis." Human Factors **25**(6): 557-582.

Tullis, T. S. (1988). Screen design. Handbook of Human-Computer Interaction. M. Helander, Elsevier Science Publishers B.V. (North-Holland).

Tullis, T. S. (1988). "A system for evaluating screen formats: Research and application." Advances in Human-Computer Interaction: 214-286.

110

From Experience Feedback Towards an Evolutive Memory for Participatory Design

Markus D. Durstewitz

Man-Machine Systems Laboratory, IMAT-MMS, University of Kassel
Ph.D. Research Project carried out with Eurisco, Toulouse
Eurisco, 4 ave Edouard Belin, F-31400 Toulouse
FRANCE
Markus.Durstewitz@onecert.fr

ABSTRACT Previous experience plays a key-role in design problem-solving. Therefore we formalized experience feedback and access in order to improve the design process and the quality of products so designed. Groups of designers use shared design documents in their work. Therefore we introduced the concept of experience folders as a document classification scheme. It enables real-time experience capture and the externalization of design rationale so it can be shared with others. Cross-referencing experiences with contact information about people involved in design facilitates communication between the actual design team and the company's experts. So the experience folder is used to maintain competencies and to update the corporate design knowledge in an evolutive design memory.

KEY WORDS experience feedback, design rationale, corporate memory, competence management

1. BACKGROUND

Today, we experience the creation of the information society. Information is empowering people and organizations. A company in the information age needs a tremendous amount of data, information, and knowledge to be competitive on the world market. Intellectual resources as experiences and know-how become a decisive factor in business (Conklin 1996). But a company cannot store everything and if so, it would be nearly impossible to access problem relevant information afterwards. Thus, we have to make a choice in storing data, information, and knowledge[1]. Particularly in the iterative design of complex systems such as nuclear power plants or aircraft the need for an effective assistance in information management becomes obvious.

The aim of this research project is to improve product quality and performance and the underlying design

[1] we know about the differences of data, information, and knowledge according to different meaning and interpretation levels of a message (see Aamodt, 1995). But in this paper we use information as a generic term for all meaning and interpretation levels.

Human–Computer Interaction: INTERACT'97 S. Howard, J. Hammond & G. Lindgaard (editors)
Published by Chapman & Hall

process itself by better satisfaction of the designers' experience demands through the formalization and exploitation of experience feedback in design. This enables the capitalization of know-how, and the creation of a living design memory (Terveen, 1993) as part of an electronic corporate memory (ECM). It is utilized to represent and access design knowledge and design rationale (Gruber 1990; Steels 1993). This must not be a complex system. Already simple means can make the difference. Mark Ackerman showed in a field study with Answer Garden how experts by "just" answering questions contribute to the augmentation of the organizational memory within the habitual work frame (Ackerman 1994).

2. A MEMORY FOR DESIGN

Corporate memory is a generic concept to save, represent, and share essential knowledge and by this way to support cooperation in a multiple task and multiple user environment. The concept includes organizational, functional, and social aspects of the work, the worker and the workplace (CoMe 1994).

Today, we have the paradox that on one hand the designers claim information and on the other hand they cannot master the information overflow. Therefore ECM should rather inform the designer on his/her demand (Kidd 1994) and assist him/her in information access and retrieval (Boy 1995) than paralyze his/her decision creativity by presenting overwhelming amounts of information on the computer. ECM should not only be an information storage but a means for coordination and communication in problem-solving (Bannon 1996). The representation and measurement of the relevance of information is significant for the success of an ECM. Therefore consequent user feedback is needed (Boy 1991) and continuous update of the memory so that it can evolve with change in design.

We see two approaches of interaction for creating an ECM:

(1) *no limits approach* or « *just do it* ».

People are allowed to write down whatever they want and to exchange information with everybody without any restriction. Then we suppose the knowledge collection will be maximized. The problem is now to find a way how this knowledge collection can be organized and classified in order to be reusable in future problem-solving.

(2) *top-down approach* or « *do just this* ».

People have to follow rigid regulations. They have to write specific documents according to specific tasks and these documents then are approved in order to be distributed in a restricted way. We suppose that this approach which is very common in nowadays companies will generate a predefined classification structure but minimize the information flow.

In real world applications, designers of ECM must find a compromise between both approaches. In our research project we followed a collaborative system design approach where the designers and their interactions are in the center of interest.

2.1 Document management as problem-solving in design

We studied the design modification process, its procedures and the formal exchange of knowledge via documents. Therefore we observed and followed a group of designers in their everyday work. Our observation was accompanied by interviews. In particular, we focused on information needs and the use of design documents with respect to a specific design problem. Thus we paid attention on both, how the designers perceive the design process and influences of norms and regulations, and how they act in the real problem-solving process. This led us to the creation of a user and problem-oriented information flow model. We identified three main tasks in the designer's problem-solving process: (1) identification and observation of a problem, (2) analysis and interpretation of the problem, and (3) proposal and application of a valuable solution. Each task is related to specific types of documents like (1) incident report, technical follow up, (2) test result notification, technical specification, and (3) service bulletin. We recognized that the biggest part of design information is represented by these documents (see also Karsenty 1995). New documents arrive every day and one of the designer's biggest problems is how to dispose of all the documents on his/her desk without losing important information relevant to the actual problem. Nevertheless design rationale, the reasons why a solution was chosen, and the expert's know-how, the lessons learned from experience, mostly are not documented. In this situation it becomes very difficult to share knowledge and to anticipate problems. The designer has no time to think about and to decide whether or not an information might be of interest for a colleague in another department or for a future project. Here, document classification becomes the central issue. First we tried classification by chronological order according to the date of incoming documents. This was not sufficient with regard to information exchange and transfer. In fact, designers tend to classify documents according to specific types of problems. That is the reason why at least we elaborated the experience folder concept as a document classification scheme. The folder structure corresponds to the problem-solving process used by the designers.

2.2 Formalization of experience feedback

Our study showed that it is common for designers to reuse already validated and approved solutions of former similar design problem cases - if they are available! In this way, analogical and case-based reasoning is one of the basic techniques of design and in particular of the design-modification process. The exploitation of experience requires formal means for capture and exchange of information related to the prior case if we do not want to limit experience to the individual memory of the designer him/herself but allow experience exchange across departments and, eventually, across the whole company.

Herein we considered special events, abnormal situations, dysfunctionning, or incidents that occur while using a product. Then designers do not only assist in trouble-shooting but they also have to re-evaluate product quality, safety, and reliability. They have to elaborate a repair solution or eventually a design modification.

Incident reporting systems and formalized user feedback provide the information that is necessary to decide whether or not a design modification will be undertaken. The formalization of experience feedback by using experience folders provides the information that is necessary to find a valuable solution based on examples of prior cases. Furthermore the folder can be used to formulate the lessons learned from experience. Therefore the designers propose a design rule and/or recommendation which is validated by a committee of wise men before it is applied in the design process (see REAIMS project, Durstewitz 95). Keeping a link between rules and experience cases the original experience can assist the designer in problem-solving by illustrating valuable details about why and how to perform modifications while applying a rule and/or recommendation.

2.3 Real time experience capture

We continued our investigation with the question: how can the individual designer capture his/her design experience effectively (that means in respect of reuse), and how can he/she transfer this experience to the community of potentially concerned designers.

The problem of experience capture is related to the management of information and documents concerning design problems. We saw the need for a tool that enables the designer to structure and to classify documents according to the evolution of a specific design project, and which enables him/her to add important information, particularly design rationale and explanation to the considered document.

We introduced the experience folder as a means for simple (user oriented) and effective (use-oriented) project management and experience capture. An experience folder represents a structured and classified collection of documents[2] concerning one specific design problem or « case ». First, we created paper forms and then we implemented electronic experience folders linked to the company's design database. Documents are classified in chapters, sections, and subsections according to the steps in the resolution of a typical design problem. This enables the designer to capture experience in real-time, when it arises - and facilitates the later access to problem-relevant information.

The experience folder assists the designer in keeping track of the project status. He/she can organize and classify documents and his/her personal annotations, summaries, etc. in a problem-oriented way. We based the structure of the experience folder on the model corresponding to the designers' document-exchange procedure in a typical design modification process.

2.4 Active competence management

Problems are addressed to people, and people solve problems. In this way it is very important to have a connection between problems and people. To know who knows what becomes crucial. Therefore we investigated about the creation of the company's *white* and *yellow pages* as a means for competence management.

We proposed a structured problem and task-oriented personal competence page. It represents a kind of electronic CV of each designer. Then we only have to

[2] electronically each folder has its equivalent and each document can be represented by a file: text, illustration, image, sound, or video etc.

make link between problems and experts by adding a list of people involved in the design project to the experience folder. The list is attached to the different folder sections and refers to the personal competence page of each person involved in the specific task of the problem-solving process. Thus the folder can be used by the design team as a kind of project agenda and eases connections to competent experts.

3. INTERACTION WITH THE ECM

Up to now, we have implemented the folder structure models so that it can be coupled to a data-base. When a request for work or change arrives the designer consults the data base for similar problem cases. These can be used as examples in problem-solving. If no case was found or a former case cannot be applied without major changes then the designer creates a new experience folder. Therefore he/she fills in electronic forms (or paper forms the time the system is not completely deployed) by answering to standard questions like what has happened when and where, what is the probable cause of the problem, what do you intend to do to fix the problem and why, what are your recommendations. The system analyses the answer written in natural language style and proposes an indexation for the experience folder based on a predefined code lists. If a field keeps empty, the system will ask for more detail. At least the designer validates the proposed indexation or can change it using the code lists. If necessary the designer himself can extend the code list and add a new key word. The extra work of folder creation pays back in short term because it can be used as project protocol or agenda and avoids long search for documents or contacts.

The next steps are the validation and the deployment of an electronic experience folder system:

(1) computer supported update and upgrade of documentation.
(2) computer supported competence management introducing electronic *white- and yellow-pages*
(3) integration of electronic dictionaries and thesaurus, for example, definitions of profession specific terms
(4) automatic coherence check in documents, for example, in the use of abbreviations
(5) intranet deployment will offer the possibility of hyperlinks, for example, towards document references or expert contacts

4. CONCLUSION

Documents are the main information source and communication medium in design. Therefore designers need an effective assistance for document management. They reuse experience cases in design problem solving thus design rationale and the lessons learned from experience must be externalized and documented.

We elaborated by the systematic involvement of the designers a conceptual framework for experience feedback and competence management: the experience folder concept. It supports the acquisition, storage, and distribution of data, information, and knowledge. It is

⟨consequent integration of user feedback enables the measurement of the knowledge base quality and its improvement following the *law of supply and demand.*

⟨real time experience capture during the problem-solving process (in vivo) guarantees *up-to-date information* in the knowledge base.

⟨process- and problem-oriented *experience case collection* assists the designer in analogical reasoning by illustrating example solutions.

⟨direct links between the problem and the people involved in solving the design problem facilitates the contact with experts and enables the creation and management of *virtual project networks*.

The deployment of an information system is merely related to the company's organizational structure (Prinz, 1993) and social context. The efforts can only be estimated roughly because costs will depend on the technical state of the working environment as well as on social and human factors which have to be evaluated.

Information sharing will lead to unexpected and severe consequences in the companies' organization if we do not try to take into account seriously the close relation between technical, individual, and social aspects of work. For us it is a fact that any change on one of those elements will imply changes on the others (Israel, 1997).

Without a common effort and coordination of organizational changes, electronic document management initiatives, intelligent data base development, and intranet solutions we will not be able to create an *ECM*.

5. REFERENCES

Aamodt, A. and Nygaard, M. (1996) Different roles and mutual dependencies of data, information, and knowledge - an AI perspective on their integration, in *Data and Knowledge Engineering*, North-Holland

Ackerman, M. S. (1994) Augmenting the Organizational Memory: A Field Study of Answer Garden, in *CSCW'94*, New York, ACM Press

Bannon, L. and Kuutti, K. (1996) Shifting Perspectives on Organizational Memory: From Storage to Active Remembering, in *HICSS'96*, Hawaii

Boy, G. (1991) Computer Integrated Design, in *Sociomedia* (ed. E. Barrett), MIT Press, pp. 507-531

Boy, G. (1995) Design Rationale and Supportability: An Agent-Oriented Corporate Memory Approach, in *COOP'95*, Juan-Les-Pins, France

CoMe (1994) - in *Newsletter of the Corporate Memory Initiative* (Eurisco, IIG Universität Freiburg, IFIT at University of Trondheim, and TCD Dublin) ed. Durstewitz, M. D., Toulouse, France

Conklin, J. (1996) Designing Organizational Memory: Preserving Intellectual Assets in a Knowledge Economy, Memorandum, Corporate Memory Systems Inc., Austin, Texas

Durstewitz, M.D., Boy, G., Heckmann J.P. (1995) Experience-Based Aircraft Design, in *HMI-AI-AS '95*, Toulouse

Gruber, T.R. (1990) Design knowledge and design rationale: A framework for representing, capture, and use, KSL technical report, Stanford University

Israel, R., Durstewitz, M., and Hollender, M. (1997) Social Context in ECM, Eurisco Working paper, Toulouse, France

Karsenty, L., Attipoe, A., Durstewitz, M., and Lafrique, D. (1995) La communication via documents dans les projets de conception, in *01Design'95*, Autrans, France

Kidd, A. (1994) The Marks are on the Knowledge Worker, in proceedings of *CHI'94*, pp. 186-191, ACM Press, New York

Prinz, W. (1993) TOSCA - providing organizational information to CSCW applications, in *ECSCW'93*, Kluwer, pp. 139-154

Steels, L. (1993) Corporate Memory Management, AI-Memo 93-03, Vrije Universiteit Brussel, Belgium

Terveen, L.G., Selfridge, P.G., and Long, M.D. (1993) From "Folklore" to "Living Design Memory", in *INTERCHI'93*, pp 15-22, Amsterdam

111

Object-oriented Specification and Design of User-interfaces

Andrew Hussey

Software Verification Research Centre
School of Information Technology
The University of Queensland
Brisbane, Qld, 4072, Australia
email: ahussey@cs.uq.edu.au

ABSTRACT The specifier of a user-interface describes user-perceivable functions and information organisation in an implementation-independent way. The designer is concerned with both the presentation and software structure of the user-interface. The path from specification to software design can be assisted by design patterns. In this paper I examine techniques for specifying and designing both the presentation and software aspects of user-interfaces. I outline my research strategy for creating a specification and design framework for user-interface development.

KEYWORDS Human-computer interface, specification, design, object-orientation, formal methods.

1. Introduction

The user-interface of a system is the view of the system that is provided to users. So, the development of a user-interface is a specialised software engineering activity. Just as in other branches of software engineering, there is a need to describe user-interfaces both abstractly (specification) and at a more concrete implementation-dependent level (design). Formal methods have shown promise as a technique for specification and design in other branches of software engineering. In this thesis I address the question as to how they may be applied to user-interface specification and design.

I have conducted exploratory research projects on both specification and software design of user-interfaces. These exploratory projects have resulted in the selection of Object-Z as a formal specification and design language. Also as a result of my work on these projects, I have generated two specific aims:

- generate a specification and design framework based on the Object-Z language aimed at assisting the development of user-interfaces;
- produce guidelines (i.e., patterns) for designing the user-interface components of interactive systems, and the components of the functional core that directly communicate with the user-interface.

In Section 2, I describe my research plan to meet these objectives. Section 3 considers my view of user-interface specification, developed as a result of my research. Section 4 deals with my research results on design of user-interfaces and Section 5 describes my future work.

Human–Computer Interaction: INTERACT'97 S. Howard, J. Hammond & G. Lindgaard (editors)
Published by Chapman & Hall

2. Research Plan

I have produced specifications and designs for a variety of case studies. By taking a case-study approach, I hope to derive principles of broad applicability to user-interface specification and design. In addition, using case-studies has provided an opportunity to evaluate the strengths and weaknesses of Object-Z as a tool for interactive system modelling. To assess the suitability of the framework, I intend to conduct an experiment in which subjects are requested to construct an interactive system from either an informal or a formal Object-Z design description. Section 5 describes the experiment in more detail.

3. Specification

A specification describes the functions that a system provides to its users without detailing how those functions are implemented. Specification is the process of abstractly defining an entity from a certain perspective. The user-interface of a system can be defined as the view of a system that is provided to users. Therefore a user-interface specification is an abstract description of a system from the perspective of its users; such a specification is useful for developing user-interface designs.

A specification of an interactive system's user-interface indicates which functional aspects of the system (state and operations) are perceivable by the user and the logical organisation of information provided by the interface. Such a specification does not describe the presentation (e.g., visual/audio) aspects of the user-interface. The presentation aspects are design concerns (i.e., how the user-interface is implemented, rather than an abstract description of what is to be implemented). For this reason, a specification of a user-interface provides only part of the information needed to construct an implementation.

User-interfaces can be specified as a collection of interacting agents using an agent-based language (Abowd, 1991). Agents have state, operations upon that state and may respond to and initiate events (Abowd, 1991). In an interactive system, agents are presented to users. The agent and its presentation together define an *interactor* (Coutaz et al., 1995). An interactor has a presentation aspect which reflects the internal state of the application (Duke and Harrison, 1993) (i.e., as defined by the corresponding agent). Interactors can be combined to form larger (more complex) interactors. Each agent is a specification (i.e., state and operations) of a corresponding interactor (i.e., agent + presentation). The interactor specifications define the logical organisation of information presented by the user-interface and therefore provide a starting point for design of the presentation.

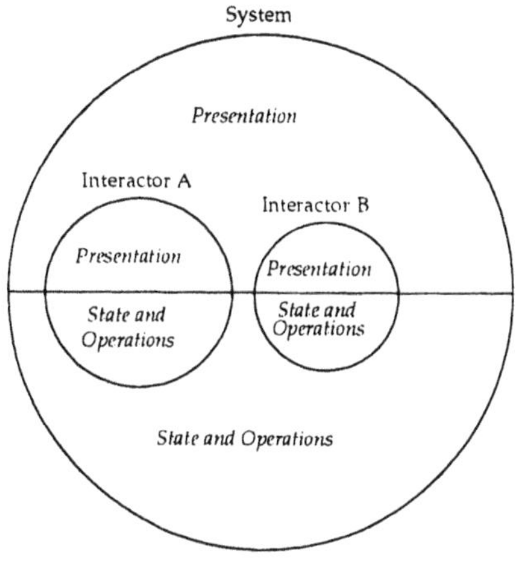

Figure 1: An interactor design

Object-Z (Duke et al., 1991), an object-oriented extension of Z (Spivey, 1992), can be used as a notation for interactor-based specification.

4. Designing User-Interfaces

The design of the presentation of a user-interface is distinct from and precedes the software design of the user-interface. Such a design defines how inputs and outputs of the system are presented. Presentation designs may be structured using interactors. An interactor framework may be constructed, using Object-Z, to support presentation design. The design case studies have generated an interactor-based "widget library" for describing the presentation of a user-interface in terms of common "widgets". A widget is a conceptually distinct sub-component of the presentation of a system. Widgets have characteristic appearance and behaviour. Common widgets include buttons and scrollbars. Figure 1 shows a presentation design that consists of several interactors. A widget-based design identifies the correspondence between interactors in a design and widgets in a widget library.

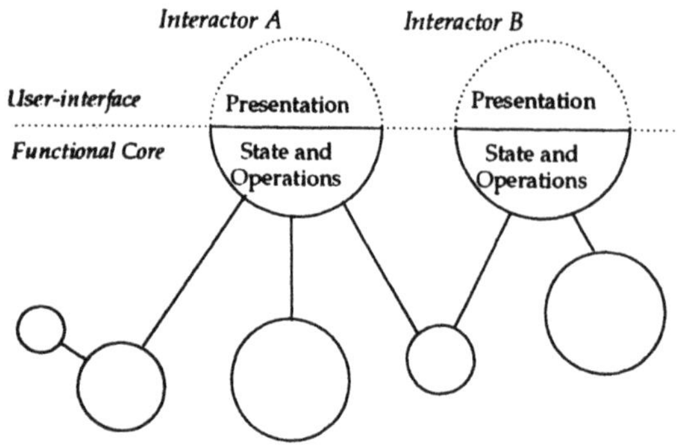

Figure 2: Interactor-based architecture

Software design requires the selection of an architecture which defines the system components and the communication between components. In an interactor-based architecture, the system is divided into interactors. Each interactor consists of a functional component and an interface component. The functional components are "sockets" which provide access to a functional-core. The functional core defines that part of an interactive system which is "invariant to change in the media used for interacting with the user" (Conference Working Group, 1990). Interactor specifications define the functional subcomponent of *one or more* design interactors and their interface to the presentation sub-component (see Figure 2). The specification defines a view of the functional-core – it does not necessarily define the entire functional-core of the system.

The path from specification to design can be assisted by design patterns. Patterns divide solutions into their elementary parts which can be later recombined and reused, providing a way of describing designs that communicates the reasons for design decisions (Gamma et al., 1994). Patterns can help designers recognise the appropriate software components required to implement each specification interactor. Such patterns can guide the designer in selecting both the appearance of the system and an architectural design suited to the requirements.

5. Future Work

In my future work I intend to analyse the extent to which my techniques are applicable to all the case studies and the extent to which they may be broadly applicable to all interactive systems. The results of this cross-study analysis may require some modification of the modelling techniques and design patterns.

I also intend to conduct an experimental study in which subjects construct a user-interface from a user-interface design. Subjects will be provided with either an informal presentation design (the "control" group) or a formal Object-Z presentation design and will be asked to construct the user-interface. Both experimental groups will use the same programming language; likewise, both designs will describe the same user-interface. Subjects will receive instruction in reading Object-Z designs and user-interface programming in a workshop format prior to the experiment. Subjects will be requested to note their activities during the course of constructing the user-interface. Subjects will be able to consult a tutor during the experiment and questions they ask will be noted.

My experiment will enable an assessment of the utility of my specification and design techniques. Assessment will be against effort expended by each group, questions asked and conformance to the intended design. Again, the results of the experiment may lead to modification of the modelling techniques and design patterns.

6. Conclusions

My thesis aims to find formal techniques for the specification and design of user-interfaces. The results of my research to date are summarised as follows. A user-interface specification indicates which functional aspects of a system are perceivable by the user and the logical organisation of information provided by the interface. User-interface specifications provide a basis for design of the presentation aspects of the user-interface. It provides a formalisation of the anticipated user model. A design defines the presentation and software structure of a system. Both specifications and designs can be structured using interactors. Patterns assist interactor-based software design.

My work makes several valuable contributions:

- formalising specification and design of user-interfaces provides developers with many of the benefits of formal methods (e.g., clarity, precision and conciseness).
- patterns for the transformation process from specification to software design, help streamline the development process, allowing more attention to be given to user-interface design.
- a specification and design framework helps developers ensure that the user-interfaces they develop meet the user's functional requirements.

References

Abowd, G. D. (1991). Formal descriptions of user interfaces. *Colloquium Digest*, 192:7/1–7/3.

Conference Working Group (1990). Concepts, Methods, Methodologies Working Group. In Duce, D. A., Gomes, M. R., Hopgood, F. R. A., and Lee, J. R., editors, *User Interface Management and Design: Proceedings of the Workshop on User Interface Management Systems and Environments*, pages 35–49. Springer-Verlag.

Coutaz, J., Nigay, L., and Salber, D. (1995). Agent-Based Architecture Modelling for Interactive Systems. Technical Report SM/WP53, LGI-IMAG, Grenoble. ESPRIT BRA 7040 Amodeus-2.

Duke, D. J. and Harrison, M. D. (1993). Abstract Interaction Objects. *Computer Graphics Forum Conference Issue*, 12(3):25–36.

Duke, R., King, P., Rose, G., and Smith, G. (1991). The Object-Z Specification Language Version 1. Software Verification Research Centre TR91-1, The University of Queensland.

Gamma, E., Helm, R., Johnson, R., and Vlissides, J. (1994). *Design Patterns: Elements of Reusable Object-Oriented Software*. Addison-Wesley.

Spivey, J. M. (1992). *The Z notation: a reference manual*. Prentice-Hall, 2nd edition.

112

Designing Virtual Environments for Usability

Kulwinder Kaur

Centre for HCI Design, City University, Northampton Square
London EC1V 0HB
UNITED KINGDOM
K.Kaur@soi.city.ac.uk

ABSTRACT The development of HCI guidelines for virtual environments, is reported, using interaction modelling.

KEYWORDS virtual reality, interaction models, interaction design

1. INTRODUCTION

Virtual Environments (VEs) are a novel interface type offering new possibilities for human-computer interaction. Notable features of VEs include their structure as 3D graphical models which the user navigates through and interacts with, typically using natural interaction styles, such as viewpoint control modelled on human head movements.

However, guidance on how to design usable VEs are hard to find, even though significant usability problems have been reported (e.g. Rushton and Wann 1993). The objective of this dissertation research is to develop guidelines for designing VEs from a usability perspective. The hypotheses are:

- **H1**: There is a need for interface design guidance specifically for VEs.
- **H2**: General patterns of interaction with VEs can be predicted.
- **H3**: Design properties required for interaction can be predicted using these general patterns (H2).
- **H4**: Interaction can be improved by implementing these design properties (H3).
- **H5**: The design properties (H3) can be presented in a usable form to support VE interface design and evaluation.

2. H1: NEED FOR VE DESIGN SUPPORT

To test hypothesis 1, two studies were carried out (see Kaur et al., 1996) to investigate the usability of VE interfaces and current design practice for VEs.

In the first study, usability was investigated through an evaluation of the Royal Navy's Virtual Submarine using observation of interaction sessions. Trainee submariners experienced major interaction problems, such as getting and maintaining a suitable viewing angle, navigating through tight areas, losing whereabouts after getting too close to objects (nose against the wall) and recognising interactive hot-spots in the environment (see figure 1).

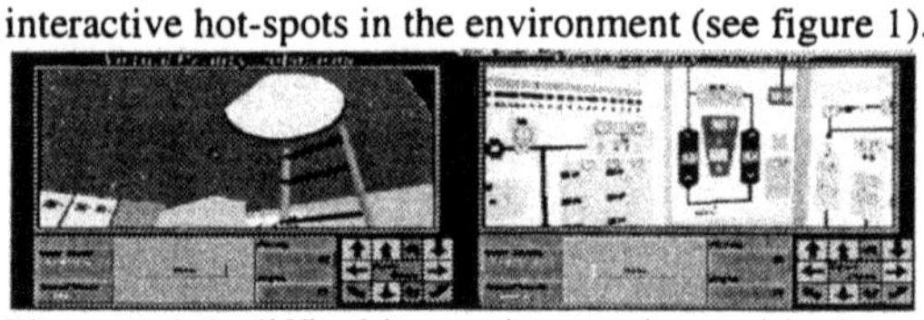

Figure 1: *left*: difficulties getting precise positioning to navigate through the hatch at the top of the ladder
right: only some dials/buttons on the switchboard are active but there is no clear indication which they are

Similar problems have been found in other evaluation studies of VEs, such as Miller (1994). Therefore, major interaction problems exist with current VEs and these

Human–Computer Interaction: INTERACT'97 S. Howard, J. Hammond & G. Lindgaard (editors)
Published by Chapman & Hall

problems appear to be very different to the typical problems found with conventional user interfaces (e.g. Sutcliffe and Springett 1992), thus supporting hypothesis 1.

In the second study, 10 VE designers participated in structured interviews, to gather information about their approaches to design and issues and problems encountered in design. Designers lacked a coherent approach to design, especially interaction design. They were preoccupied with technical difficulties and thought little about supporting user interaction. There was a lack of understanding of the concepts underlying VEs and conventional HCI methods/guidelines were not used.

Therefore, the designer study indicates there is a need to support the process of interface design with guidance specific to VEs, further supporting hypothesis 1.

3. A THEORY OF INTERACTION

To develop interface design guidance, an understanding of user interaction is required. Therefore, a theoretical model of interaction in VEs has been developed and is complete.

Previous work in interaction modelling has involved various approaches, such as the use of cognitive architectures (e.g. in the AMODEUS project, Barnard 1991), process models (e.g. Norman 1988) that describe interaction at a higher level of granularity, and models of user knowledge and its use (e.g. CCT, Kieras and Polson, 1985).

The approach here has been to begin with process modelling which describes interaction at a suitable level of granularity. Norman's generalised model of action was used and elaborated by adding further stages of activity to describe interactive behaviour in VEs. The elaboration of Norman's model was based on characteristics of VEs theorised to impact interaction behaviour.

Tasks in VEs are often loosely structured with exploration and opportunistic actions (Hayes-Roth and Hayes-Roth 1979). For example, in many simulation and tutorial applications, the user's task is to explore the environment so behaviour is primarily opportunistic following of cues. VEs are often active, with objects operating independently of the user's actions through system initiative (Bryson, 1995). Therefore, 3 inter-connected cycles have been used to model interaction:

Task/action cycle - describes purposeful, top-down behaviour in planning and carrying out specific actions as part of the user's task or goal, and then evaluating the success of actions.

Explore/navigate cycle - describes opportunistic and less goal directed behaviour when the user explores or searches for features of interest.

System initiative cycle - describes reactive behaviour to prompts and events, and to the system taking interaction control from the user (e.g. taking the user on a pre-set tour of the environment).

Figure 2 shows a section of the explore/navigate cycle. The user scans the environment with either an intention to explore or an intention to search for an object to carry out actions from the task/action cycle. The user then continually navigates and scans until target objects are found or features in the environment arouse interest, possibly prompting exploratory actions.

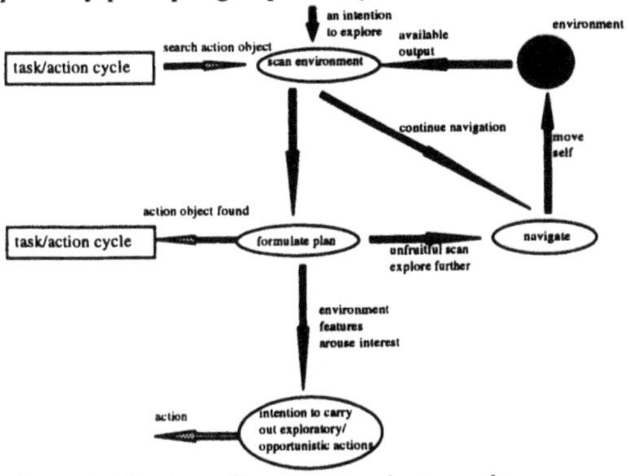

Figure 2: Section of explore/navigate cycle

Complementary to the interaction cycles, 6 knowledge sources are identified which together describe important information which is potentially available to the user during interaction. The sources are the part of the VE currently perceivable, the user's internal model of the VE, knowledge of the domain the VE is modelled on, knowledge of the user task, knowledge about real world phenomena (e.g. function/appearance of a door), and, standards and commonalities between VEs.

To summarise, a theory of interaction has been developed predicting general interaction behaviour and relevant sources of knowledge. To be useful, the theory must be accurate and representative of actual interaction behaviour and lead to usability principles for VEs.

4. REQUIRED DESIGN PROPERTIES

The interaction models provide a clear breakdown of interactive behaviour. The models have been used to systematically reason about what properties are required in a design to support the user during each identified stage in interaction, so that usability problems are avoided.

Forty-six design properties have been identified from analysis of the interaction models. The set of properties have been organised into more workable categories which are information about the user's task, spatial knowledge of the VE, the user's viewpoint and representation in the VE, objects in the vicinity, system initiative behaviour, available actions and action feedback. Table 1 lists a few of the design properties.

Objects	
distinguishable object/ object parts	Objects present in the immediate vicinity can be distinguished from the current environmental image.
identifiable object/ object parts	The object and its individual parts can be readily and reliably identified. If the object is copied from real world phenomena, then its representation is accurate and matches user expectations.
System initiative behaviour	
declared system control	It is clear when the system or an agent takes control of the interaction, and later when control is returned to the user.
Actions	
declared available action	It is clear to the user that the potential for action exists.
executable action	The action can be executed efficiently and without frequent obstacles/problems. The demand of manipulation precision and motor co-ordination is within usual human ability.

Table 1: Example desirable design properties.

The design properties have been linked to usability problems by identifying difficulties likely to occur if the properties are missing or inadequate, or if required user knowledge is lacking. Correspondence rules have been used to specify the conditions under which usability problems are likely to occur. For example, for the exploratory action stage in the explore/navigate cycle, the design needs to make clear what actions are available with objects or the user needs to have prior knowledge of available actions. Otherwise, a predicted problem is that the user will have difficulty determining what actions are available with features in the environment they wish to investigate, as the following rule states:

IF (*(opportunities for action)* NOT IN knowledge sources)
AND NOT design property*(declared available actions)*
THEN predicted problem*(difficulty detecting actions available with features of interest)*;

5. EVALUATING PREDICTIONS ABOUT INTERACTION - H2 & H3

Predictions about interaction detailed in sections 3 and 4 are being tested with ongoing experimental studies of users carrying out representative tasks with a VE developed in industry. Results will be available in July. Think aloud protocol analysis and analysis of video footage has been used to gather data on actual interaction behaviour and usability problems encountered. Observed patterns of mental and physical activity will be checked against the interaction models to test hypothesis 2.

The data on usability problems will be used to test predictions about desirable design properties, since the importance of the properties are linked to their avoiding usability problems. The test VE has been inspected and assessed for the presence of the design properties. Predictions for usability problems have been made from inspection of the correspondence rules using the assessments of the design and expectations about likely user knowledge. Observed critical incidents and interaction breakdowns will be checked with predictions made for usability problems. A good match will support the desirable design properties in hypothesis 3.

Results from the experiments will be used to refine the interaction models and improve predictions about required design properties.

6. H4: THE DESIGN PROPERTIES LEAD TO IMPROVED INTERACTION

Implementing the design properties in a VE is hypothesised to improve interaction by supporting the user during each stage of interaction and so avoiding usability problems. To test the impact of the design properties a controlled study has been planned. The study described in section 5 acts as the control condition. For the test condition, the same VE will be 'improved' by implementing missing design properties. A second set of users will then carry out the same task. Task performance is assessed for both groups with a post-study test. Improvements in interaction are defined as fewer usability problems, better task performance or lower task completion times. Hypothesis 4 will then be tested by comparing results for the 2 conditions. Results will be used to refine the set of design properties.

7. H5: DESIGN PROPERTIES CAN BE PRESENTED FOR VE DEVELOPMENT

The design properties are being used to develop design guidelines and checklist questionnaires to support the design and evaluation of VEs. This is ongoing work.

Concrete design guidelines are being developed from the properties by giving for each examples, a context of use, and explanation of the guidelines effect. A hypertext tool is planned for presenting the guidelines to designers. For example, the guideline and an example for the property 'declared available action' would be:

Salient cues, prompts and affordances should be provided for available actions. Active objects and active parts of objects should be highlighted.

Example: *On a switchboard, active buttons can be distinguished from inactive buttons because they protrude from the switchboard and are highlighted with an outline.*

For evaluating VEs, a cognitive walkthrough method (see Polson et al. 1992) is being developed, using the interaction models and design properties. A walkthrough analysis is applied for each interaction stage by expanding the correspondence rules into question checklists for the design properties and knowledge sources required for successful interaction. For example, at the scan stage in the explore/navigate cycle the question checklist would include:

When scanning the VE, can the users distinguish and recognise many/few/none of the objects? Does the object appearance match the users' expectations?

Future work involves testing hypothesis 5 by using expert evaluation and critiquing of the design guidelines to gain direct qualitative feedback on the usability of the guidelines and their potential impact on the design process. The walkthrough evaluation method will be tested through direct use providing quantitative data on usability problems identified and improvements suggested. Results will be used to improve the presentation of the design properties in the design guidelines and evaluation method.

8. CONCLUSION

An interaction modelling approach has been proposed for addressing problems of interaction design for VEs. The models lead to design properties for supporting important stages in interaction. The benefit gained from implementation of the design properties is assessed through user studies. The theoretical research can then be applied to the problem of interaction design by using it to develop design guidelines and evaluation methods.

ACKNOWLEDGMENTS

Kulwinder Kaur is funded by the EPSRC.

REFERENCES

Barnard P. (1991). Bridging between basic theories and artefacts of Human-Computer Interaction, in *Designing Interaction, Psychology at the Human Computer Interface,* Ed Carroll J.M. Cambridge University Press.

Bryson S. (1995). Approaches to the successful design and implementation of VR applications, in *Virtual Reality Applications,* Ed Earnshaw R.A., Vince J.A. and Jones H. London, Academic Press.

Hayes-Roth B. and Hayes-Roth F. (1979). A cognitive model of planning. *Cognitive Science* **3**, 275-310.

Kaur K., Maiden N. and Sutcliffe A. (1996). Design practice and usability problems with virtual environments, in: *Virtual Reality World '96 conference, Stuttgart.* Proceedings. IDG Conferences.

Kieras D. and Polson P.G. (1985). An approach to the formal analysis of user complexity. *International Journal of Man-Machine Studies,* **22,** 365-394.

Miller L.D. (1994). A usability evaluation of the Rolls-Royce virtual reality for aero engine maintenance system. Masters Thesis. University College London.

Norman D.A. (1988). *The psychology of everyday things.* New York, Basic Books Inc.

Polson P.G., Lewis C., Rieman J. and Wharton C. (1992). Cognitive walkthroughs: a method for theory-based evaluation of user interfaces. *International Journal of Man-Machine Studies,* **36,** 741-773.

Rushton S. and Wann J. (1993). Problems in perception and action in virtual worlds, in *Virtual Reality International 93, London.* Proceedings. London, Meckler, pp. 43-55.

Sutcliffe A.G. and Springett M.V. (1992). From user's problems to design errors: linking evaluation to improving design practice, in *People and Computers VII,* Ed Monk A.F. and Diaper D. and Harrison M.D. Cambridge University Press.

Specification-Based Testing of Interactive Systems

Ian MacColl *

Software Verification Research Centre
School of Information Technology
The University of Queensland, 4072
Australia
ianm@cs.uq.edu.au

ABSTRACT Achieving correct user interface software is difficult because such software is complex, highly interactive, modeless, concurrent, graphical, and has user-based real-time requirements. In this paper I propose developing a framework for applying formal methods to testing of user interface software. I survey relevant work in the areas of formal development of user interface software and specification-based testing. I then outline a case study based research plan to extend an existing specification-based testing framework to incorporate multiparadigm user interface specifications.

KEYWORDS Human-Computer Interface, HCI, user interface, UI, formal methods, testing

1. INTRODUCTION

A user interface (UI) is some boundary between a computer system, comprised of hardware and software, and a human user. UI software is a significant component of contemporary systems and graphical user interfaces (GUIs) are now almost universal.

Confidence in the correctness of UI software is usually achieved by prototyping or by testing. Software correctness is commonly described as validation ("Are we building the right software?") and verification ("Are we building the software right?"). Prototyping can be used for validation and to verify that the UI meets usability requirements. Testing can also be used for validation (acceptance test) and to evaluate usability. Traditional software testing (unit, integration and system test) is the major method for verifying the correctness of UI software. Testing UI software is difficult however, because such software is complex, highly interactive, modeless, concurrent, graphical and has user-based real-time requirements.

Industrial strength tools have been developed to automate UI testing. These tools provide facilities such as capture/playback for test development, bitmap- and widget-based test evaluation, and textual and point-and-click scripting. Little support is available, however, for generating test inputs or expected outputs (oracles).

Formal methods are also used to develop correct software, including UI software. Fully formal development is advocated for projects such as life-critical software, where the cost of failure is greater than the additional cost of formal development (although industrial experience indicates that additional costs are offset by other savings).

Formal methods have been combined with software testing to provide specification-based testing techniques that use a (formal) specification to support testing. Little use has been made of these techniques for UI testing to date.

*Ian MacColl is supported by an Australian Postrgraduate Award and a Telstra Research Laboratories Postgraduate Fellowship.

Human–Computer Interaction: INTERACT'97 S. Howard, J. Hammond & G. Lindgaard (editors)
Published by Chapman & Hall

This project aims to combine formal methods and software testing to develop specification-based testing techniques for UI software. Case studies will be used to extend an existing technique for specification-based testing to incorporate multi-paradigm UI specifications.

2. LITERATURE SURVEY

This section is a brief survey of work relevant to applying formal methods to testing of UI software, including using formal methods for UI development (§2.1) and for software testing (§2.2).

2.1 HCI and formal methods

Took identifies two paradigms for UI software: linguistic and agent-based (Took, 1990). The linguistic paradigm distinguishes lexical, syntactic and semantic aspects of UIs but formal linguistic notations, such as state-transition diagrams (Parnas, 1969), are not well suited to handling concurrency and attaching semantic information.

Agent-based architectures are an attempt to resolve the limitations of linguistic architectures as a basis for developing GUIs. The agent-based paradigm encapsulates data, functionality, and input and output within an 'agent' such as a button, a screen or an entire UI. The encapsulation is consistent with abstract data type and object-oriented (OO) software development.

In common with OO development, formal approaches to development of agent-based UIs must address both static and dynamic aspects of the system. Model- and property-based notations are well-suited to formalising static aspects whereas behaviour-based notations are preferable for dynamic aspects. Many formal, agent-based approaches use multiple notations of different styles, or extend an existing notation to encompass capabilities of a different style.

Behaviour-based notations, such as Petri Nets, are useful for modeling external behaviour but must be augmented to include static aspects of UIs. Palanque and Bastide, for example, use the Interactive Cooperative Objects (ICO) formalism to specify, verify and implement UIs (Palanque and Bastide, 1994). ICO provides an object-oriented framework for modeling static aspects of a system, and uses Petri Nets for modeling dynamic aspects.

Myers introduces a model for "highly interactive, direct manipulation, graphical user interfaces" that encapsulates interaction into interactor objects (Myers, 1990). The Esprit AMODEUS project has developed two formal models of interactors as encapsulations of a state, events to manipulate the state and a mechanism to present the state to users (Harrison and Duke, 1994). An interactor model developed at CNUCE in Pisa, Italy, uses the process algebra LOTOS, a property-based notation with behavioural capabilities. The CNUCE model is derived from work on graphics systems and input devices.

The second AMODEUS interactor model was developed at University of York, UK. The York model uses model-based notations such as Z and VDM augmented by CSP for behavioural aspects, and is a development of work extending Z to cover both static and dynamic aspects (Sufrin and He, 1990). The AMODEUS project has used interactor models for describing graphics systems and for analysing interactive systems. Current work includes integration of formal descriptions of users and systems in an interactive framework and investigation of scaling up formal development of UI implementations.

Much of the work applying formal methods to HCI emphasises reasoning and analysis rather than implementation. Hussey and Carrington use software patterns (Gamma et al., 1994) to informally transform interactor-based specifications, written in Object-Z (Duke et al., 1995), into widget-based designs (Hussey and Carrington, 1996a, Hussey and Carrington, 1996b). Object-Z enhances the model-based capabilities of Z with encapsulation constructs and includes operators for expressing dynamic aspects such as concurrency and communication between objects.

Partial specifications can be used to accommodate multiple views of a software specification, e.g., UI and functionality views. Jackson advocates partial specifications (in Z) as means to achieve clear and concise specifications with a modular structure to ease maintenance (Jackson, 1995). Zave and Jackson use augmented first order logic as a common representation for multiparadigm specifications (Zave and Jackson, 1996).

This section provided an overview of formal interactor models and object-oriented variants, and introduced partial and multiparadigm specification techniques. The next section is a survey of work on using formal methods to improve testing.

2.2 Formal methods and testing

Software testing is conventionally classified into behavioural and structural testing: behavioural testing emphasises testing against the functional requirements and structural testing emphasises testing based on the internal structure of the software.

The precise definition of behaviour provided by a formal specification is particularly useful for behavioural testing as a basis for deriving test inputs and as a means for determining the output expected from a particular test input.

The application of formal methods to testing, also called specification-based testing (SBT), is an active research topic. Gaudel, for example, summarises program testing based on algebraic specifications, describing methods for selecting a finite subset of an exhaustive test set (Gaudel, 1995). For model-based notations, Hörcher and Peleska show how Z specifications can be used to derive test input data and to automatically evaluate test results (Hörcher and Peleska, 1995), and Stepney reports on a method for deriving tests from Z specifications by a process of systematic abstraction (Stepney, 1995).

The Test Template Framework (TTF) is a formal, abstract model of testing, used to derive a hierarchy of test information, including test inputs and outputs, from a formal specification (Stocks and Carrington, 1996). The framework uses the Z notation and incorporates both traditional and new testing strategies.

It appears that only one group has applied formal methods to UI testing (Yip and Robson, 1991). Three notations are used to specify UI software: state-transition diagrams to express interaction sequences, a model-based notation similar to Z to define the state transitions and an algebraic notation for reasoning. Tests are derived from the state-transition diagrams, and the model-based specifications are used to determine expected outputs. The method for combining the notations appears informal and incomplete. Also, this work has not been updated to take account of subsequent developments in specification-based testing.

This section has outlined recent work on specification-based testing, including UI specification-based testing. The next section concludes this survey.

2.3 Conclusions

Formal methods have been applied to the development of UI software and to improve software testing. The Z notation (Z Base, 1995) is a common theme to much of the work surveyed above. Interactor-based formal specifications map to widget-based designs and implementations. Multiple paradigm and view-based specification techniques can be used to connect static and dynamic aspects of UI specifications and to connect UI and functionality specifications. The Test Template Framework (TTF) provides a framework for testing based on model-based specification notations but does not address sequencing issues such as UI behaviour. There is also no tool support for using the TTF, a requirement for automation of a potentially rapidly changing area such as UI testing.

Issues not addressed in this survey include: relationship of prototyping and specification; formal methods in an iterative, user-centred development context; dialogue separation, refinement and abstraction; and top-down and bottom-up approaches to writing specifications.

3. RESEARCH PLAN

My thesis project is development of a framework to support specification-based testing of UI software.

My work to date has involved a literature search to select this topic (alternatives were in the areas of formal methods, OO and functional programming, and software testing). I have also started a case study specifying the Parker Brothers game Boggle in Z.

I propose to conduct three case studies to extend the TTF to support multiparadigm UI specifications. This will require accommodating behaviour-based notations such as CSP and Statecharts, and identifying UI-specific testing strategies. I will then evaluate the extended TTF in a formal experiment comparing TTF-derived UI testing with non-TTF-derived UI testing.

References

Duke, R., Rose, G., and Smith, G. (1995). Object-Z: A specification language advocated for the description of standards. *Computer Standards & Interfaces*, 17:511–533.

Gamma, E., Helm, R., Johnson, R., and Vlissides, J. (1994). *Design Patterns: Elements of Reusable Object-Oriented Software*. Addison-Wesley.

Gaudel, M.-C. (1995). Testing can be formal, too. In *TAPSOFT '95: Sixth International Joint Conference on Theory and Practice of Software Development*, volume 915 of *Lecture Notes in Computer Science*, pages 82–96. Aarhus, Denmark.

Harrison, M. and Thimbleby, H., editors (1990). *Formal Methods in Human-Computer Interaction*. Cambridge University Press.

Harrison, M. D. and Duke, D. J. (1994). A review of formalisms for describing interactive behaviour. In Tayler, R. N. and Coutaz, J., editors, *Software Engineering and Human-Computer Interaction. ICSE '94 Workshop on SE-HCI: Joint Research Issues*, volume 896 of *Lecture Notes in Computer Science*, pages 49–75, Sorrento, Italy. Springer-Verlag.

Hörcher, H.-M. and Peleska, J. (1995). Using formal specifications to support software testing. *Software Quality Journal*, 4(4):309–327.

Hussey, A. and Carrington, D. (1996a). Using Object-Z to compare the MVC and PAC architectures. In Roast, C. R. and Siddiqi, J. I., editors, *Proceedings of BCS-FACS Workshop: Formal Aspects of the Human Computer Interface*, pages 45–60, Sheffield, UK.

Hussey, A. and Carrington, D. (1996b). Using Object-Z to specify a web browser interface. In Grundy, J. and Apperley, M., editors, *Proceedings OzCHI*, pages 236–243, Hamilton, New Zealand.

Jackson, D. (1995). Structuring Z specifications with views. *ACM Transactions on Software Engineering and Methodology*, 4(4):365–389.

Myers, B. A. (1990). A new model for handling input. *ACM Transactions on Information Systems*, 8(3):289–320.

Palanque, P. and Bastide, R. (1994). Petri Net based design of user-driven interfaces using the Interactive Cooperative Objects formalism. In Paterno, F., editor, *Eurographics Workshop on Design, Specification, and Verification of Interactive Systems*, pages 383–300, Bocca di Magra, Italy.

Parnas, D. L. (1969). On the use of transition diagrams in the design of a user interface. In *Proceedings of the 1969 National ACM Conference*, pages 739–743. Association for Computing Machinery.

Stepney, S. (1995). Testing as abstraction. In Bowen, J. P. and Hinchey, M. G., editors, *ZUM '95: The Z Formal Specification Notation*, volume 967 of *Lecture Notes in Computer Science*, pages 137–151, Limerick, Ireland. Springer-Verlag. Proceedings of the Ninth International Conference of Z Users.

Stocks, P. and Carrington, D. (1996). A framework for specification-based testing. *IEEE Transactions on Software Engineering*, 22(11):777–793.

Sufrin, B. and He, J. (1990). Specification, analysis and refinement of interactive processes. In (Harrison and Thimbleby, 1990), chapter 6, pages 153–200.

Took, R. (1990). Putting design into practice: Formal specification and the user interface. In (Harrison and Thimbleby, 1990), chapter 3, pages 63–96.

Yip, S. W. L. and Robson, D. J. (1991). Graphical user interfaces validation: A problem analysis and a strategy to solution. In Shriver, B. D., editor, *Proceedings of the Twenty-Fourth Annual Hawaii International Conference on System Sciences*, volume II, pages 91–101.

Z Base (1995). Z notation: Version 1.2. `ftp://ftp.comlab.ox.ac.uk/pub/Zforum/ZSTAN/versions/` (15 Jan 97).

Zave, P. and Jackson, M. (1996). Where do operations come from? A multiparadigm specification technique. *IEEE Transactions on Software Engineering*, 22(7):508–528.

Enhancing WWW Navigation

Chris Pilgrim

Swinburne Computer-Human Interaction Laboratory
Swinburne University of Technology
Hawthorn, Victoria, Australia
cpilgrim@swin.edu.au

ABSTRACT The overall goal of this research project is to investigate navigational issues relating to hypermedia information spaces such as the World Wide Web, particularly the problem of user orientation, in order to improve the general design principles of navigational interfaces by utilising visualisation techniques.

KEYWORDS World Wide Web, Hypertext, Navigation, Visualisation

1. Introduction

Despite its relative short history, the World Wide Web (WWW) is now emerging as a powerful resource which will have much impact on Internet users. The vast amount of information available on the WWW, coupled with its easy accessibility, has seen the exponential growth of users and WWW pages in recent months. However, the unprecedented success of the WWW has brought with it a number of problems which are constraining its usability.

One of the central problems relates to the vast amount of information that the web contains and the methods by which a user can access this information. It has been established that one of the usability problems associated with hypermedia information spaces such as the World Wide Web is the user's risk of disorientation whilst navigating (Nielsen, 1990; Jonassen & Mandl, 1990; Rivlin et al, 1994). Users, when presented with multiple paths to the same or different end points will quickly experience cognitive overloading as they struggle to maintain orientation (Hedberg & Harper, 1991). Whilst this problem has been recognised, there have been few usability studies to examine the nature and extent of the difficulties in web navigation (Cockburn & Jones, 1996).

Adequate help must be provided to maintain a user's sense of orientation and facilitate navigation within the context of the total information space. Hence there is a need for support for both the local navigation task of moving between pairs of specific nodes as well as the global navigation task which involves movements that spans many nodes (Kahn, 1995). Most browsers display a limited amount of orientation information consisting of document name and URL as well as the URLs of possible links from the current page. In addition, many browsers provide a history list of pages previously visited which enables the user to establish some notion of location and also provides the ability to backtrack. Whilst these orientation clues do provide adequate support for navigation at the local level, they lack the contextual overview required for global orientation.

The use of overview diagrams as an aid to navigating traditional hypertext structures have provided a solution to the problem of global orientation (Nielsen, 1990). An overview diagram is a graphical map of the structure of the hypermedia system showing all nodes and links. Such diagrams act as a two dimensional table of contents and are particularly suitable for providing a level of orientation in non-linear hypermedia information spaces. These diagrams support the user in generating an appropriate mental model of how the information space is structured. There is evidence to suggest that an appropriate mental model improves the users' ability to interact with the system (Rumelhart and Norman 1981).

A number of key issues have been identified as a result of the initial literature review. These issues relate to visualisation, generation and design of overview diagrams:

2.1 Visualisation

Although image map overviews are an excellent tool for orienting and navigating a hypermedia system such as the World Wide Web, there are some drawbacks when they are applied to large information spaces which involve many nodes and links (Mukherjea et al, 1994). Large image maps give rise to the need to use of scroll bars to enable the user to change views of the map and as the entire map cannot be display in its entirety. Researchers (Beard and Walker II, 1990) have provided empirical evidence to suggest that users perform sub-optimally with scroll bars in tasks which require navigating a large two-dimensional space.

The use of visualisation techniques to facilitate overview diagrams has been suggested by a number of

Human–Computer Interaction: INTERACT'97 S. Howard, J. Hammond & G. Lindgaard (editors)
Published by Chapman & Hall

researchers in order to provide users with both a local and global view of the information space (Lamping et al, 1995; Bederson & Hollan, 1994; Zizi & Beaudouin-Lafon, 1994). These techniques include the use of zooming, split screens, magnifying glasses, and distortion oriented displays such as fisheye lenses and bifocal displays. Generally these researchers agree that the solution to the navigation problems associated with hypermedia will result from the ability to visually represent the contents of the documents in the system and then to present these on a screen in such a way to provide the user with orientation and interactive navigation.

2.2 Generation

Overview diagrams may either be created manually or automatically. Manual methods are very time consuming and do not provide easy method of updating diagrams as systems grow and change. Automatic methods rely on computational techniques to generate maps dynamically as new documents are added to the system. One thread of research is examining methods by which a hypertext system may be automatically mapped into an overview diagram (Mukherjea et al, 1994; Masuda et al, 1994; Zizi & Beaudouin-Lafon, 1994). These methods are relatively primitive, produce highly complex structures and as yet have not been applied to the production of overview diagrams for the WWW. Other research (Cockburn & Jones, 1996; Mukherjea & Foley, 1995; Brown & Shiller, 1995) is concentrating on enhancing WWW browsers by providing a graphical history list and even a "possible links" list but is once again relatively primitive and have not been subjected to usability trials.

2.3 Design

A more general issue relates to the actual design and presentation of overview diagrams. Designing overview diagrams for complex systems is extremely difficult especially those that do not conform to regular hierarchies (Bernstein et al, 1991). There are few guidelines that have been developed for the production of overview diagrams (Zizi & Beaudouin-Lafon, 1994) and no evidence of usability studies to examine the features that make such diagrams effective. Furthermore, the use of metaphors is a powerful method for enhancing usability of systems. Many metaphorical tools such as footprints, compasses and magnifying glasses have been used in conjunction with overview diagrams but there is no evidence of usability studies within the context of the WWW to evaluate any perceived benefits.

3. Work to Date

Work on the project began mid-1996 with the development of a dynamic bifocal display for WWW overview maps (Pilgrim & Leung, 1996). The Bifocal Display was first proposed by Spence and Apperley (1982) to overcome the classical "window" problem associated with viewing large databases through the concurrent presentation of local detail with global context. The dynamic bifocal display was implemented as a Java applet and allows the user to establish overall orientation within the system in the 'out-of-focus' region and to then navigate through to the detail of the section of interest by dynamically controlling the focal area of the map by mouse movements. The central focal region , outlined by a white rectangle, is not distorted in any way. The area of the overview diagram outside of the central focus region is distorted in such a manner that the user can place the central focus region in the context of the whole map. The links between the nodes do not lose continuity over the boundary of the focal area thereby allowing the user to visually follow a path. A small toolbar allows the user to choose either the 'Focus Control' mode which allows the central focus region to be controlled, or the 'Page Navigation' mode which allows the user to select a specific node on the map with the mouse in order to jump to the corresponding URL.

It is postulated that the bifocal display technique is an effective way of presenting World Wide Web overview diagrams by concurrently providing the user with a detailed local view and global context to assist with navigation. Usability studies are required to determine whether the user will establish a more efficient mental model of the hypertext structure and subsequently improve navigational decisions.

The initial research has also examined the history of hypermedia navigation in order to survey and systematise the nature of the navigation problem. Research into visualisation techniques, the nature of mental models and technical advances in the WWW is currently proceeding. An investigation of how the problem of user disorientation in large information spaces has been addressed in other domains such as geographical information systems and complex databases has also been proposed.

4. References

Beard, D. & Walker, J. (1990) Navigational techniques to improve the display of large two-dimensional space, *Behaviour and Information Technology,* Vol 9, No 6.

Bederson, B. & Hollan, J. (1994) Pad++: A Zooming Graphical Interface for Exploring Alternate Interface Physics, *Proceedings of ACM Conference on User Interface Software and Technology.*

Bernstein, M., Garzotto, F., Paolini, P. & Schwabe, D. (1991) Tools for Designing Hyperdocuments, *Hypertext and Hypermedia Handbook*, McGraw Hill.

Brown, M. & Shillner, R. (1995) Deckscape: An Experimental Web Browser, *Proceedings of the Third International World Wide Web Conference*, Germany.

Cockburn A. & Jones S. (1996) Which Way Now? Analysing and Easing Inadequacies in WWW Navigation, (*to be published*).

Hedberg, J. & Harper, B. (1991) Creating Interface Metaphors for Interactive Multimedia, *Proceedings of the First International Interactive Multimedia Symposium*, Perth.
Jonassen D. & Mandl (eds) (1990) *Designing Hypermedia for Learning*. Springer-Verlag, Berlin.
Kahn, P. (1995) Visual Clues for Local and Global Coherence in the WWW, *Communications of the ACM*, 38(8).
Lamping J., Rao R. & Pirolli P. (1995) A Focus+Context Technique Based on Hyperbolic Geometry for Visualising Large Hirarchies, *Proceedings of CHI'95 Conference on Human Factors in Computer Systems*, Denver.
Masuda Y., Ishitobi Y. & Uedo M. (1994) Frame-Axis Model for Automatic Information Organizing and Spatial Navigation, *Proceedings of the ACM European Conference on Hypermedia Technology*, Edinburgh.
Mukherjea S., Foley J. & Hudson S. (1994) Interactive Clustering for Navigating in Hypermedia Systems, *Proceedings of the ACM European Conference on Hypermedia Technology*, Edinburgh.
Mukherjea S. & Foley J. (1995) Visualizing the World Wide Web with Navigational View Builder, *Proceedings of the Third International World Wide Web Conference*, Germany.
Nielsen, J. (1990) The Art of Navigating Through Hypertext. *Communications of the ACM*, 33(3).
Nielsen, J. (1993) *Usability Engineering*, Academic Press.
Pilgrim C. & Leung Y. (1996). Applying Bifocal Displays to Enhance WWW Navigation, *Proceedings of the Second Australian World Wide Web Conference*, Gold Coast, QLD.
Rivlin E., Botafogo R. & Schneiderman B. (1994) Navigating in Hyperspace: Designing a Structure Based Toolbox, *Communications of the ACM*, Vol 37 No 2.
Rumelhart, D. & Norman, D. (1981) Analogical processes in learning, In *J Anderson (ed) Cognitive Skills and Their Acquisition* , Hillsdale, NJ, Erlbaum.
Spence, R. and Apperley, M.D. (1982): Data base navigation: an office environment for the professional. *Behaviour and Information Technology*, Vol 1, No 1, 43-54.
Zizi M, & Beaudouin-Lafon M. (1994) Accessing Hyperdocuments through Interactive Dynamic Maps, *Proceedings of the ACM European Conference on Hypertext Technology*, Edinburgh.

115

Cross - National Decision Making in a Group Support Systems Environment

Nasrin Rahmati (Mrs.)

PhD Candidate
School of Information Systems
Faculty of Business and Management
University of South Australia
Email 9510372M@FBM.pcmail.levels.unisa.edu.au

ABSTRACT Group Support Systems were designed and developed with the aim of supporting groups in their decision making efforts. According to small group theories the important variables in groupwork were group size, task and environment (eg, McGrath, 1984). Psychologists believe that decision making entails two major phases: perception of the given situation, and selection of an option on the basis of what is perceived (Yates and Lee, 1996). The importance of the decision maker's perception in the decision making process suggests that in addition to age, sex, educational background and job experience of the decision maker his/her value system is also very important to be examined in GSS studies. The present study is an exploratory study using controlled laboratory experiments to examine the impact of the culture (value system) on decision making process in a Group Support Systems environment.

KEYWORDS: Group Support Systems , National Culture

Human–Computer Interaction: INTERACT'97 S. Howard, J. Hammond & G. Lindgaard (editors)
Published by Chapman & Hall

116

Redundancy in Multimedia Systems

Frank Vetere

Swinburne University of Technology
Swinburne Computer Human Interaction Laboratory
PO Box 218 Hawthorn Vic 3122 AUSTRALIA
fvetere@swin.edu.au

ABSTRACT New technologies permit complex combinations of media, sensory channels and interaction metaphors. These combinations introduce the likelihood of semantic and structural overlap over a temporal domain. This overlap, or redundancy, is often considered useful in complex and cognitively laden tasks. Redundancy has some history in human factors, but its nature is not well formulated. This research examines redundancy form an HCI perspective and attempts to apply it to multimedia systems.

KEYWORDS multimedia, media, mode, metaphor, language, redundancy

1. BACKGROUND

Multimedia systems are often described by their use of metaphors, modes, channels and media (Hutchins 1991, Alty 1991, Frohlich 1992). Hutchins, Hollan & Norman (1986) identifies two fundamental interaction metaphors, model world and conversation. Frohlich (1992) describes these two basic human activities (renamed action and language respectively) as interface modes. He also identifies the media which corresponds to these interface modes. The media for the language mode are speech, text and gesture. The media for the action mode are sound, image and motion.

Frohlich (1992) exemplifies the difference between the two modes by using the typical task of deleting a file within an operating system. This task might be achieved by the linguistic activity of typing 'Delete <filename>' or by the physical action of dragging an icon of the file over to a wastebasket icon and 'releasing it'. Therefore the combined use of the language mode and the action mode in human computer interaction is a description of the *redundancy* of user activity. That is, interface modes are states across which different user actions have the same outcome. Consequently multimodal interactions exploit some inherent redundancy.

The use of more than one mode (or media or channel) in a computer interface can create obvious semantic overlap and may allow for the possibility of redundancy in the interaction.

Human–Computer Interaction: INTERACT'97 S. Howard, J. Hammond & G. Lindgaard (editors)
Published by Chapman & Hall

A traditional approach to interface design suggests that this overlap generates unnecessary information which should be avoided; but many studies (Marmolin 1992, Alty 1994, Wickens 1984, Lang 1995) show that manipulating redundancy is an important component of improving human-machine interactions.

Marmolin (1992) states that interactions which involve complex information flow (especially multimodal and multimedia interaction) have mathematically redundant information, but he acknowledges that this mathematical redundancy bears a complex relationship with human perception and information processing.

One of the Alty's (1994) eight guidelines for multimedia interface design is 'the principle of apparent redundancy'. He states that people generally prefer too much rather than too little information. Unfortunately he does not reify this principle.

Edwards (1992) outlines the potential importance of redundancy for physically impaired users. Wickens (1984) says that interface redundancy gives users the flexibility to capitalise on a format that best suits their needs. Lang (1995) performed an extensive analysis of existing literature in an attempt to find whether audio/visual redundancy improves memory for television messages. A similar analysis has not been applied to improving human-computer interactions.

Many of these researchers (Hutchins 1991, Alty 1991, Frohlich 1992, Marmolin 1992, Lang 1995, Edwards 1992) agree that redundancy is a significant phenomenon in multimodal and multimedia interactions. This suggests that it is important to control interface redundancies in order to maximise usability of multimedia systems. Presently there is insufficient knowledge to help designers manipulate these redundancies to improve interactions.

2. UNDERSTANDING REDUNDANCY

Redundancy is the result of a synergistic phenomena. Redundancy can be considered to be the semantic overlap between two or more messages distributed over time or space or both. It typically refers to the repetition of some action or information and so is an indicator of the potentially acceptable loss in information (Wickens 1984), but it also refers to an increased 'dimensionality' of information (Lang 1995 quoting Garner).

Redundancy can occur in two ways. Within-channel redundancy (eg colour coding, illustrated text) occurs when information is presented in one sensory channel. Between-channel redundancy (eg a documentary video which shows an event and simultaneously uses speech to describe it) occurs when information is presented across two or more sensory channels. The two sensory channel are usually auditory and visual but could also include haptic.

Haptic acts are essentially nonverbal — where nonverbal is defined as any movement or position of the face and/or the body. In describing the occurrences of nonverbal acts, Ekman & Friesen (1969) outline the relationship between nonverbal and verbal behaviour. They identify a semantic relationship (the nonverbal act can repeat, augment, illustrate, accent, contradict or be unrelated to the words) and a temporal relationship (the nonverbal act can anticipate, coincide, substitute for or follow the verbal behaviour).

Basil (1994) recognises these categories as five forms of overlap between sensory channels: Redundancy (information in one channel *repeats* what is said in another channel), Substitution (information in one channel *replaces* something in another channel), Complement (information in one channel *adds* information to another channel), Contradictory (information in one channel is the *opposite* to some information in another channel), and Emphasis (information in one channel is used to *underscore* information in another channel)

Basil (1994) adds a sixth technique, Counterpoint, proposed by film theorists. Counterpoint occurs when channels are combined (according to rules) to achieve a desired effect (eg mood music and dim lighting in film). Lang (1995) defines four operational distinctions for redundancy; Single-channel, Multiple-channel Redundant, Multiple-channel Conflicting and Talking Heads.

These categorisation of redundancy are useful because they enable us to compare research and help to establish a deeper understanding of redundancy. However the categories are described in broad terms. There is a need for a common characteristic which allows a more detailed comparison between categories and perhaps place them on a continuum of redundancy.

The term *semantic fit* is introduced to give a measure of the 'relationship', 'match' or 'correspondence' (Lang 1995) between (or within) channels (or media or modes). Semantic fit spans from highly positive (repetition) to highly negative (contradiction). A semantic fit of zero refers to a set of information which is entirely unrelated.

It may then be possible to represent human-computer interactions which exploit redundancy on a Multimedia Interaction Space (MMIS) (Vetere, Howard & Leung, 1997). The semantic fit would be the metric and MMIS would be the diagrammatic notation for redundancy in multimodal interactions.

3. RESEARCH QUESTIONS AND OUTCOMES

This research aims to model redundancy in order to obtain generic guidelines and improve multimedia interactions. It is motivated by the following questions:

- What is the form and function of a theory of redundancy in computer-human interactions?
- What are the operating characteristics of a methodology for the development of redundancy when designing multimedia systems?
- How can multimedia systems successfully exploit redundancy to improve usability?

A framework has been established (Vetere et al. 1997) to model redundancy. This framework will help to formulate a theoretical base for the understanding of redundancy within HCI and to develop an interface design methodology (or component thereof) for the design of redundancy in multimedia systems.

4. REFERENCES

Alty, J. L. (1991) "Multimedia - What is it and how do we exploit it?" in Diaper, D. & Hammond, N. (Eds.) *People and Computers VI: Proceedings of the HCI '91 Conference* Cambridge University Press, Cambridge UK

Alty, J. L. (1994) "Multi-Media Interface Design: A tutorial for HCI '94" in Cockton, G., Draper, S. W. & Weir, G. R. S. (Eds.) *People and Computers IX: Proceedings of the HCI '94 Conference* Cambridge University Press, Cambridge UK

Basil, M. D. (1994) "Multiple Resource Theory I: Application to Television Viewing" *Communication Research* Vol 21, no. 2, 177-207

Edwards, A. D. N. (1992) "Redundancy and Adaptability" in Edwards, A. D. N. & Holland, S. (Eds.) *Multimedia Interface Design in Education.* Springer-Verlag, Berlin pp 145-155

Ekman, P. & Friesen, W. V. (1969) "The repertoire of nonverbal behavior: Categories, origins, usage and coding" *Semiotica*, 1, 49-98

Frohlich, D. M. (1992) "The Design Space of Interfaces" in Kjelldahl, L. (Ed.) *Multimedia: Systems, Interaction and Applications* Springer-Verlag, Berlin pp 53-69

Hutchins, E. (1991) "Metaphors for Interface Design" in Taylor, M. M., N_el, F. & Bouwhuis, D. G. (Eds.) *The Structure of Multimodal Dialogue* Elsevier Science, Amsterdam

Hutchins, E. L., Hollan, J. D. & Norman, D. A. (1986) "Direct Manipulation Interfaces" in Norman, D. A. & Draper, S. W. (Eds.) *User Centered System Design.* Lawrence Erlbaum, Hillside New Jersey pp 87-124

Lang, A. (1995) "Defining Audio/Video Redundancy from a Limited-Capacity Information Processing Perspective" *Communication Research* Vol 22, no. 1, 86-115

Marmolin, H. (1992) "Multimedia from the perspective of psychology" in Kjelldahl, L. (Ed.) *Multimedia: Systems, Interaction and Applications* Springer-Verlag, Berlin

Vetere, F., Howard, S. & Leung, Y. (1997) "A Multimedia Interaction Space" in Howard, S., Hammond, J & Lindgaard, G. (Eds.) *Human-Computer Interaction: INTERACT97* Champman & Hall. UK

Wickens, C. D. (1984) *Engineering Psychology and Human Performance* Charles E. Merrill, Columbus

PART SIX

Tutorials

Selling Usability to Organisations

Sarah Bloomer
The Hiser Group
P.O. Box 312
Prahran Vic 3181 Australia
+61 3 9521-3311
sarahb@mel.hiser.com.au

Rachel Croft
The Hiser Group
P.O. Box 312
Prahran Vic 3181 Australia
+61 3 9521-3311
rachelc@mel.hiser.com.au

ABSTRACT Usability is now practiced by a large number of software developers, but has yet to gain wide acceptance. In order to get usability off the ground in an organisation, its value must be communicated across multiple stakeholder groups, which requires speaking several "languages". This practical, hands-on tutorial will cover techniques for convincing management or potential clients of the value of usability, in terms each group understands. It will examine what is required to develop a usability strategy for a whole organisation, as well as how to find data to convince stakeholders of the value of a single usability activity.

Key Words Strategic usability, usability strategies, cost-justification, communicating usability data.

1. COURSE OVERVIEW

It is an ongoing source of frustration for usability professionals to continuously have to justify the value of their activities. Usability has yet to gain wide acceptance in software development practices.

Communicating the value of usability across multiple levels of an organisation requires speaking several "languages". IT departments, business areas and users each have different, often seemingly conflicting, agendas. They are measured differently, focus on different objectives and view the organisation from different perspectives. If they are to accept usability as having value, each area must be targeted and the benefits of usability clearly presented in terms they understand.

Usability is successfully integrated into an organisation when a strategy is developed which leads to key usability benefits and supports overall business objectives. Strategic usability looks at people, processes and tools across an organisation, analysing strategic needs, business objectives and culture. This information reveals barriers and opportunities which can hinder or facilitate usability acceptance. From this knowledge, an appropriate usability strategy can be determined.

A business objective may be to reduce overall costs, increase sales, or simply to provide better customer service. Taking a high level view, strategic usability aims to make software tools work for the whole business by assessing the usability of individual systems in the context of other systems, processes and people. It not only aligns usability goals to the needs of the users, but also to the needs of the IT department and the business through the development of a 'total business' strategy.

This tutorial will cover techniques for convincing management or potential clients of the value of usability. The key is to understand your organisation in terms of where usability can make a difference, and to present those opportunities in terms understood by each target audience. Using actual case studies and exercises, this

Human–Computer Interaction: INTERACT'97 S. Howard, J. Hammond & G. Lindgaard (editors)
Published by Chapman & Hall

tutorial will show how to identify key organisational opportunities, as well as barriers. We will look at where to collect data to support the usability initiative, such as benchmarking, leveraging other initiatives (such as total quality, reduced training costs etc.), cost-justification, and corporate strategies, to develop a strong message for communicating the value of usability specific to organisations.

This is an intermediate-level, full day tutorial.

2. AUDIENCE

Experienced usability professionals, user interface designers, developers and managers who are working to improve the acceptance of usability activities within their organisations, whether for in-house or commercial software development; consultants who wish to convince potential clients.

3. TUTORIAL METHOD

This tutorial takes a case study, hands-on approach. A variety of practical and achievable techniques will be presented, enabling participants to take away those appropriate to their own situation and company. A mock organisation, Red Rock Insurance, has been created and profiled to give participants an opportunity to analyse and identify potential barriers and opportunities which can hinder or support usability initiatives respectively.

Based on the barriers and opportunities found, the groups will examine and discuss ways to talk to management or developers in terms they understand. Using information form benchmarking, field studies and creating cost-justification analyses to build a case; identifying and interviewing stakeholders; developing a communications strategy and finding usability allies; developing the most effective tools and techniques for a specific organisation; cross-training for developers and users of other technology such as the intranet to convey usability information.

4. INSTRUCTORS

Rachel Croft is a usability consultant at The Hiser Group, responsible for defining strategic usability methodologies. With over 5 years experience in the field of HCI in Australia and the UK, Rachel brings experience in organisational analysis and change management to strategic usability. Rachel has developed two corporate usability strategies and supported several others.

Sarah Bloomer is co-founder and director of The Hiser Group. Sarah has 9 years experience consulting in user interface design and usability in both the USA and Australia. In addition to consulting in user interface design, usability training and style guide development, Sarah has been leading Hiser's strategic usability projects and initiatives since 1994.

5. REFERENCES

Bias, R and Rietmeyer, P.B. Usability Support Inside and Out. interactions (April 1995) ACM Press. 29-32

Billingsley, P. A. Starting from Scratch: Building a Usability Program at Union Pacific Railroad. interactions (October 1995). ACM Press. 27 - 30.

Comstock, E, and Duane, W.M. Embed User Values in System Architecture: The Declaration of System Usability. In Proceedings of CHI 1996. (Vancouver, Canada, April 1996), ACM Press, 420-427.

Dray, S. Usability Maturity: How to Know When Your Organisation Gets "There". Presented at the Usability Professionals' Association 4th Annual Conference, (Portland, ME, July 1995).

Kieboom, H and Howard, S. Communicating the Value of Usability Engineering through Cost-Benefit Analysis Techniques. In Proceedings of OZCHI95, (Wollongong, NSW, November 1995).

Lund, A. How Many Human Factors People are Enough? In Ergonomics in Design. January 1994.

Mayhew, Deborah and Bias, R. (eds.) Cost Justifying Usability. Boston: Academic Press, Inc 1994.

Meighan, F. The Usability Analyst Model: Using Minimum Resources to Gain Maximum Effect. In Proceedings of OZCHI95 (Wollongong, NSW November, 1995). 301-304.

Miller, A. Integrating Human Factors in Customer Support Systems Development Using a Multi-level Organisational Approach. In Proceedings of CHI 1996. (Vancouver, Canada, April 1996). ACM Press. 368 - 375.

Mrazek, D and Rafield, M. Integrating Human Factors on a Large Scale: Product Usability Champions. In Proceedings of CHI 1992. (Monterey, CA, May 1992) ACM Press. 1992. 570

Designing User Interfaces from Analyses of Users' Tasks

Peter Johnson, Stephanie Wilson and Hilary Johnson

HCI Laboratory, Department of Computer Science,
Queen Mary & Westfield College, University of London,
Mile End Road, London E1 4NS, U.K.
pete, steph, hilaryj@dcs.qmw.ac.uk

ABSTRACT This tutorial provides a detailed introduction to task analysis and task-based design. The focus of task analysis is the description of users' work tasks, while the focus of task-based design is designing from the perspective of users' work. Techniques from psychology, ethnomethodology and sociology are used to analyse and describe users' work tasks. A framework for modelling work tasks (Task Knowledge Structures) is used to represent relevant task information. Guidelines are provided to help envision how current tasks might be changed and improved through the design of interactive systems. Descriptions of envisioned tasks form the basis of interaction design, thus ensuring that designs are focused on the tasks they are intended to support.

KEYWORDS task analysis, task-based design, work-tasks, design guidelines, envisioning design

1. INTRODUCTION

Task analysis is concerned with understanding work. It is an important HCI technique that enables users to be involved in the design process and enables designers to understand users' work. Task-based design is concerned with developing interactive systems from the perspective of the users' work and usage of the designs. Task-based design provides work-tasks as the basis for the envisionment of new work and the design of new systems.

Task analysis can be used at multiple points in the design process, to identify and scope the situation of concern, to provide a well-grounded and detailed description of the current work situation, to identify scenarios of usage, to envision new ways of working and to provide benchmark tasks against which designs can be evaluated. Moreover, task analysis can be carried out at various levels of detail, ranging from gaining an overview of the range and type of tasks in a given organisation to providing a detailed description of how a complex activity is carried out. The aim of this tutorial is to provide HCI professionals with appropriate knowledge of how to carry out task analysis, how to envision potential changes to work tasks and how to design systems from the perspective of these tasks.

2. OBJECTIVES AND MOTIVATION

This is an intermediate level tutorial intended for HCI professionals including designers and developers of user interfaces, human factors practitioners and researchers. The overall objective of the tutorial is to teach the benefits and use of task analysis and task-based user interface design. There are three main aspects to this:

- To introduce the ideas of task analysis and task-based user interface design, and to consider some of the advantages and limitations of such approaches.
- To describe a selection of methods and guidelines for analysing tasks, modelling tasks and developing user interface designs.
- To provide practical experience in the application of these techniques.

A major motivation for the tutorial stems from recent studies of design practice which indicate poor take-up of task analysis and other HCI techniques, for reasons such as perceived cost and lack of expertise. With respect to

Human–Computer Interaction: INTERACT'97 S. Howard, J. Hammond & G. Lindgaard (editors)
Published by Chapman & Hall ©IFIP 1997

cost, it can be cost-effective to introduce HCI techniques such as task analysis and prototyping into the design process e.g. (Mantei and Teorey, 1988). Moreover, (Rossen et al, 1988) identified that designers consider obtaining information about users and tasks as a major contributor to the generation of design ideas. In surveying design practice, (Johnson and Johnson, 1989) found that designers believed task analysis could contribute significantly to interactive system design and the resulting usability of the designed systems. Knowledge about how users perform tasks enables designers to reason about what aspects of task should or should not be supported, how they could be supported and what changes to the task will come about as a result of a new design, i.e. an envisioned task will enable designers and users to consider and reason about how the user will interact with the new design.

3. CONTENT

This tutorial introduces participants to the concepts and methods of task analysis and task-based design. This includes understanding the TKS approach to task analysis and task modelling (Johnson and Johnson, 1991), and the ADEPT approach to task-based design (Johnson et al, 1995), (Wilson and Johnson, 1996). Participants are provided with practical experience of conducting a task analysis and producing a task model, and then using this as the basis for designing a user interface.

The tutorial lasts one full day and involves interactive presentations, demonstrations and small group exercises. The interactive presentations introduce the concepts and approaches of task-based user interface design. The demonstrations include video and real demonstrations of task-based design. The group work focuses on taking the participants through a task analysis and developing a user interface design. This involves participants constructing the various task and interaction models, and using design guidelines to develop a user interface. One design problem is used as a running example throughout the tutorial: designing a system to support querying of airline flight information and making a booking.

Introduction

The tutorial starts by providing participants with an overview of task-based design. The aims and motivations of task-based design and some of its advantages and limitations in relation to other design approaches are considered. A demonstration is given of a complete task-based design process, from the analysis of tasks to the design of a user interface.

Task analysis and task modelling

This part of the tutorial teaches participants the concepts of task modelling and the methods of task analysis and data collection. It introduces the Task Knowledge Structures framework for modelling and analysing tasks. Practical experience is given in choosing and using one or more methods to analyse the flight booking task.

Task-based design - envisioning future work tasks

In the third part of the tutorial, the students are taught principles and guidelines for envisioning and reasoning about changes to be made to current work tasks. Group exercises again give participants the opportunity to practice these techniques.

Task-based design - developing user interface designs

The final part of the tutorial provides students with methods and guidelines for developing a user interface design from an envisioned task model, and gives them practical experience in applying these to develop a prototype design for a user interface to the flight booking system. The tutorial closes with a plenary discussion and feedback session.

4. REFERENCES

Johnson, H. and Johnson, P. (1989) Integrating task analysis into system design: Surveying designers' needs, *Ergonomics*, 32(11), 1451-1467.

Johnson, H. and Johnson, P. (1991) Task knowledge structures: Psychological basis and integration into system design, *Acta Psychologica*, 78, 3-26..

Johnson, P. Johnson, H. and Wilson, S. (1995) Rapid prototyping of user interfaces driven by task models, in *Scenario Based Design*, (ed. J.M. Carroll), Wiley.

Mantei, M.M. and Teorey, T.J. (1988) Cost/benefit analysis for incorporating human factors in the software lifecycle. *Communications of the ACM*, 31, 428-443.

Rosson, M.B., Maass, S. and Kellogg, W.A. (1988) The designer as user: Building requirements for design tools from design practice. *Communications of the ACM*, 31, 1288-1298.

Wilson, S. and Johnson, P. (1996) Bridging the generation gap: From work tasks to user interface design, in *Computer-Aided Design of User Interfaces*, (ed. J. Vanderdonckt) Presses Universitaires de Namur, 44-55.

Planning and Implementing User-Centred Design Using ISO 13407

Nigel Bevan and Ian Curson

National Physical Laboratory, Usability Services
Teddington, Middlesex, TW11 0LW, UK
Nigel.Bevan@npl.co.uk, Ian.Curson@npl.co.uk

ABSTRACT The tutorial introduces participants to the forthcoming International Standard "Human centred design processes for interactive systems" (ISO CD 13407), and gives an overview of practical techniques which support the processes outlined in the standard. The INUSE consortium of usability practitioners has developed a set of core techniques to support the human-centred design process, selected on the basis of their applicability, maturity, stability, availability, and cost-effectiveness. The tutorial explains the basis for choosing appropriate techniques, and gives an overview of each method. The techniques are divided into three categories: Planning, Early Lifecycle and Late Lifecycle. The methods covered are: Planning – ISO 13407 checklist, usability context analysis, usability maturity assessment; Early lifecycle – guides and standards, rapid prototyping, usability inspection methods; Late lifecycle – performance measurement method, user satisfaction, adherence to guides and standards.

KEY WORDS: User-centred design, usability evaluation, standards, usability engineering, software engineering

OBJECTIVES

Many organisations now recognise the need for usability in interactive systems, and the benefits that usable systems deliver. But guidance about how to "do" usability tends to be technique-centred, concentrating on specific approaches for designing or evaluating systems. How can organisations at different levels of usability maturity, and with different criteria for usable systems, discover how to improve the usability of their systems?

ISO CD 13407 advocates a process-oriented approach to usability, whereby usable systems are achieved as the result of a human-centred design process. The standard provides a framework for applying human-centred design and evaluation techniques, and is intended to supplement existing lifecycle models.

Different organisations are at different levels of usability maturity – from not recognising usability as an issue, to having processes in place which ensure the development of consistently usable systems. Organisations can integrate the principles of ISO CD 13407 into their existing development process incrementally, to achieve an appropriate maturity level.

ISO CD 13407 specifies types of activity to be performed during the development of an interactive system, but does not demand nor recommend particular techniques or methods. The INUSE consortium of usability practitioners has developed a set of core techniques to support the human-centred design process, selected on the basis of their applicability, maturity, stability, availability, and cost-effectiveness.

Human–Computer Interaction: INTERACT'97 S. Howard, J. Hammond & G. Lindgaard (editors)
Published by Chapman & Hall

CONTENT

The tutorial gives an overview of the relevant standards, explains the basis for selecting appropriate techniques, and gives an overview of each method, including some practical exercises.

Standards

ISO CD 13407 Human centred design processes for interactive systems.

ISO 9241 Ergonomic requirements for office work with visual display terminals. Includes parts 10 to 17 on software ergonomics.

ISO DIS 14598-1 Evaluation of Software Products. Explains how software qualities (including usability) can be specified and measured during development, with the objective of achieving quality in use.

ISO WD 9126-1 Software quality characteristics and metrics. Defines six software quality characteristics (including usability) and quality in use, which is the combined result.

Planning methods

ISO 13407 gives an overall structure for user-centred design, and includes a checklist of activities required to adhere to the standard, in the following categories: planning, specification of context of use, specification of user and organisational requirements, production and testing of design solutions, and evaluation of designs against user requirements.

Usability Capability Maturity is a means of assessing the maturity of the organisation and identifying where improvements are required.

Usability Context Analysis is a structured method for eliciting and structuring information about the actual or intended Context of Use of an interactive system. The resulting specification of the characteristics of users, tasks, and environment can be used to inform design, and to specify valid and consistent evaluations. This method was originally developed as part of the MUSiC ESPRIT, and has since been developed and refined through commercial application.

Early development methods

Guides and standards: a method has been developed (by Lloyds Register) which uses the ISO 9241 parts 12-17 dialogue design guidelines as the basis for producing a style guide customised to specific organisational requirements.

Rapid prototyping is a collection of formal and informal techniques for developing, demonstrating and evaluating user interface designs quickly to support rapid iteration early in the design lifecycle. The techniques can be categorised depending on whether the prototypes are passive paper, animated paper or machine, and whether the user interaction with the prototype is naturalistic, prompted by the evaluator or participative design.

Usability inspection methods include inspection by human factors experts ("heuristic evaluation"), by designers, by users or by an appropriate combination. The choice of method depends on the skills available and the potential benefits of involving designers or users in each situation.

Late development methods

The Performance Measurement Method is a structured technique for delivering meaningful and objective metrics of the performance of the user-system combination in accordance with ISO DIS 9241. The metrics can be used for acceptance criteria, and to compare the performance of alternative designs and products. Originally developed in the MUSiC project, this method has been developed and refined through commercial application

User Satisfaction is a collection of methods for eliciting the subjective opinion of users of an interactive system. These include University College Cork questionnaires SUMI (for office systems), MUMMS (for multi-media) and WAMMI (for web evaluation), and the public-domain SUS, all of which measure user satisfaction as defined in ISO 9241-11.

Conformance to guides and standards including assessing adherence to ISO 9241 parts 13-17.

REFERENCES

Bevan N (1995) Human-computer interaction standards. In: Anzai & Ogawa (eds) Proc. 6th International Conference on HCI, July 1995. Elsevier.

Bevan, N (1996) Integrating usability into the development lifecycle. Proceedings of ICAE'96.

Bevan N and Azuma M (1997) Quality in use: Incorporating human factors into the software engineering lifecycle. In Proc. 1977 Internat. Soft–ware Engineering Standards Symposium (ISESS'97)

Bevan N, Macleod M (1994) Usability measurement in context. Behaviour and Information Technology, 13, 132-145.

Macleod M, Bowden R, Bevan N and Curson I. (1997) The MUSiC Performance Measurement Method. Behaviour and Information Technol., in publication.

Practical GUI Screen Design: Making It Usable

Cliff Wilding

PO Box 312
Prahran VIC 3181
AUSTRALIA
cliffw@mel.hiser.com.au

ABSTRACT There is much more to designing usable GUI screens than making them look good. The way a screen looks should tell the user how to interact with it, and what behaviour to expect. Screen design is about visual communication, the bridge between the look and the feel of the user interface. In this full day tutorial you will examine the principles of good screen design, including a detailed examination of screen layout, templates and metaphors.

The tutorial provides a clear understanding of how to take advantage of user knowledge when creating screen designs that work. Examine layout techniques, including colour, fonts and symbols, and learn the principles of creating easy-to-use software and interactive new media productions. The tutorial is very much hands-on with exercises – you will put the skills you learn into practice.

Learn valuable tips and techniques for the best ways to use icons, controls, text and graphics in user interfaces.

KEYWORDS user interface, design, screen design, interaction design, user-centred design

1. Overview

With the proliferation of graphical user interfaces (GUIs) many issues and problems have arisen regarding their design, in particular the design of GUI screens. In essence, screens enable the dialog to take place between the user and the system. Failure to communicate clearly results in an application that is difficult to use. This is primarily due to the plethora of widgets and objects that are now available. The variety of screen elements means that there is an infinite number of combinations possible and consequently many decisions to be made. Making the best decisions and trade-offs for a specific application and particular instance is often difficult and requires GUI design skills and knowledge. Adhering to standards adds to the complexity.

Screen design for GUIs not only encompasses the selection and layout of widgets and objects, but extends to the behaviour of those widgets and the way in which users interact with the interface. Screen design covers both the visual and behavioural aspects of a GUI; the design of both requires close attention to ensure usability. Practical GUI Screen Design is a one day tutorial that covers many aspects of GUI design pertinent to screen design.

The tutorial is highly visual, with many examples of both good and bad screen design. Each point is illustrated, described and discussed, giving the tutorial a "real world" feel. You will also learn valuable tips

Human–Computer Interaction: INTERACT'97 S. Howard, J. Hammond & G. Lindgaard (editors)
Published by Chapman & Hall

and techniques for the best ways to use icons, controls, text and graphics in user interfaces.

Your instructor is a User Interface Design Consultant, with several years experience designing user interfaces for corporate and home applications.

The tutorial is aimed at systems analysts and designers, business analysts, software developers, multimedia developers, visual design managers and computer-based training authors. It is an advantage if attendees are familiar with GUIs and/or GUI design.

2. Topics Covered In This Tutorial

- Introduction
  - User Interface Design
  - Basic GUI Concepts
- Anatomy of a Window
  - Windows
  - Templates
  - Metaphors
  - Screen Elements
  - Cursors
- Layout & Design
  - Visual Harmony
  - Clarity and Communication
  - Providing Functional Clues Visually
  - Colour
  - Graphical Elements
  - Typography
  - Language
- Wrap Up

3. Biography of the Presenter

Cliff Wilding is a User Interface Design Consultant with The Hiser Group, based in Melbourne, Australia.

Since joining The Hiser Group in 1994, Cliff has worked on numerous projects, performing analysis, design and usability testing tasks for organisations such as Telstra, BHP, Commonwealth Bank, Heath Insurance, the Royal Australian Air Force, Unisys, Woolworths and Wooden Eye Multimedia. These projects involved techniques such as contextual inquiry, user analysis, collaborative design, paper prototyping, usability testing, style-guide development and expert evaluation of user interfaces.

Cliff has extensive project management experience, and has also developed several electronic prototypes of user interface designs. He also teaches user interface design in The Hiser Group's course "User Interface Screen Design – Making it Usable", and has presented papers and workshops at OzCHI 96.

Following his graduation from the University of Melbourne, Cliff began his career with Disctronics Limited as a software engineer in the first team in Australia to produce a CD-ROM. Here he was responsible for designing and implementing successful CD-ROM information retrieval products.

Following his tenure at Disctronics, Cliff spent three years with INFO-ONE International, Australia's leading on-line and CD-ROM database developer and publisher. As Software Development Manager, he was responsible for designing and managing the implementation of information retrieval systems for clients including Dun & Bradstreet, Australian Stock Exchange, CSIRO, Department of Defence, NSW State Library, and NRMA.

Cliffs holds a degree in Computer Science (Hons. first class) from the University of Melbourne.

4. Timetable

Time	Length	Activity
9:10	40	1. Introduction
9:50	15	2. Anatomy of a Window (Windows)
10:10	25	2. Anatomy of a Window (Templates)
10:30	15	Morning Tea
11:00	20	2. Anatomy of a Window (Metaphor)
11:20	30	Detective Exercise
11:50	20	Detective Exercise Presentations
12:10	20	2. Anatomy of a Window (Elements)
12:30	60	Lunch
1:30	30	Sofa Touchscreen Exercise
2:00	30	Sofa Touchscreen Presentations
2:30	30	3. Layout and Design
3:00	15	Afternoon Tea
3:30	15	3. Layout and Design (cont.)
4:00	40	Elvis Activity
4:30	20	Elvis Activity Presentations
4:45	15	Video & Questions
5:00		Finish

CSCW, Groupware and Workflow: Experiences, State of Art, and Future Trends

Steven Poltrock

Boeing Information & Support Services
PO Box 3707 MS 7L-49
Seattle, WA 98124-2207
USA
steven.poltrock@boeing.com

Jonathan Grudin

Information and Computer Science Department
University of California at Irvine
Irvine, CA 92717
USA
grudin@ics.uci.edu

ABSTRACT Technology to support groups is rapidly coming into use and having an impact on us, our organizations, and society. This course addresses recent experiences, current possibilities, and future trends and shocks. Lecture and video illustrations are accompanied by discussions in which participants organize and present their collective experiences with groupware and workflow technologies, and CSCW issues and methods. The instructors summarize the current composition of the CSCW community and the state of the art in technology, and organize discussion of fundamental challenges that face us as users (and developers) of these technologies.

KEYWORDS Groupware, workflow, computer-supported cooperative work, coordination theory, organizational design, sociotechnical evolution

1. CSCW, GROUPWARE & WORKFLOW: DRAWING ON EXPERIENCE

Five years ago most experience in computer-supported cooperative work was confined to research laboratories. The situation has changed. Although relying primarily on lecture and video illustrations, this tutorial provides a framework for attendees to share and build on their diverse experiences with different types of groupware.

2. A MULTI-DISCIPLINARY CAST OF THOUSANDS

We will outline the major contributors to CSCW and groupware: researchers from diverse fields, developers working in varied contexts, and users in different cultures. By reviewing their backgrounds as technologists, behavioral and social scientists, customers, and users, we can see the opportunities to learn from people whose expertise or experience complements our own (see Grudin, 1994a).

3. THE STATE OF THE ART

Our survey of the state of the art serves two purposes: It provides information about research and development activity to tutorial participants whose experience or expertise is likely to be focused in one or two areas, and the framework for presenting the technologies serves to focus subgroup discussions of experiences with the

Human–Computer Interaction: INTERACT'97 S. Howard, J. Hammond & G. Lindgaard (editors)
Published by Chapman & Hall

technologies. We identify three categories of groupware: communication, cooperation, and coordination.

3.1 Communication Support

Electronic mail, desktop conferencing, and video conferencing are changing both personal and business communications. Businesses use email to accelerate the flow of information and reduce coordination costs [7]. Video conferencing is used for group communication within geographically distributed companies and between corporate partners. Desktop conferencing focuses communication on work products. Each type of communication groupware offers unique advantages, and new technologies can achieve all the advantages by integrating email and conferencing features.

3.2 Cooperation Support

Groupware supports cooperation by enabling interaction through a shared document or collection of documents. For example, document management systems help teams collaborate by providing access and version control, document search, and status tracking. Application development environments customize the structure and functionality of the system to the task. Meeting support technologies enable all participants to collaborate in the production of a shared document or documents. In a brainstorming session all users can enter as many ideas as they want anonymously.

3.3 Workflow: Support for Coordination

Businesses are attempting to increase quality and reduce cost by modeling and improving their internal processes. Coordination groupware can capture and coordinate these processes. Work flow management systems model the sequence of subtasks in a work process and the roles performed by each individual. When each subtask is completed, the work is automatically routed to the person responsible for the next subtask.

4. CHALLENGES IN DESIGN AND EVALUATION

Successfully overcoming technical hurdles has not guaranteed success. In this section of the tutorial we briefly review behavioral, social, and organizational phenomena that have been observed to undermine technically impressive applications (Grudin, 1994b). Some of these obstruct the development of useful and usable software, some hinder the acquisition of the systems, and many get in the way of successful use. Throughout the tutorial, participants will be invited to identify those challenges that they have encountered or anticipate as they set about acquiring, using, or developing groupware.

5. OVERCOMING THE CHALLENGES

The literature includes case studies of successful use of groupware technologies, including some recently conducted by the organizers (see Grudin & Palen, 1995). In this section, we will briefly review several promising, novel approaches to the successful design and introduction of groupware.

6. GROUPWARE AND THE FUTURE

Although we can point to trends and possibilities, we cannot predict which groupware or workflow products will emerge, which will succeed, or which will fail. Nevertheless, at a broader level, we can identify changes that are likely to raise fundamental questions for us as users as well as developers of these technologies. Members of society, informed or otherwise, will have to resolve how these technologies are used. We will conclude the tutorial by identifying a few global developments and invite the participants to identify others. One is the tension between liberating and constraining effects that often accompany technologies, including groupware. Another, perhaps the most fundamental, is the increased visibility of activity in the global village and our reaction to seeing much of that activity for the first time.

7. REFERENCES

Grudin, J. (1994a) CSCW: History and focus. *IEEE Computer, 27,* 5, 19-26.

Grudin, J. (1994b) Groupware and social dynamics: Eight challenges for developers. *Communications of the ACM, 37,* 1, 92-105.

Grudin, J. and Palen, L. (1995) Why groupware succeeds: Discretion or mandate? *Proceedings ECSCW'95 European Computer Supported Cooperative Work Conference.*

Object View and Interaction Design

Dave Roberts, Dick Berry, Scott Isensee

IBM United Kingdom Limited
PO Box 31, Birmingham Road
Warwick
England
Dave_Roberts@aussmtp.austin.ibm.com

ABSTRACT Several methods are already available for object oriented program design. These methods do not deal with user interface design. The tutorial teaches OVID, a systematic method for designing Object User Interfaces for use by product design teams. OVID is a major step in changing user interface design from art to science. It emphasizes the production of a complete, accurate model that can be used as input to program design methodologies.

KEYWORDS User Interface Design, Object Oriented, Task Analysis

1 INTRODUCTION

In this tutorial you will learn techniques for turning user requirements into design for an object-oriented user interface. The tools and techniques described will help to ensure accuracy and completeness of the model and will generate output that feeds into object-oriented code design methodologies such as OMT or Booch.

2 TUTORIAL CONTENT

The tutorial begins with a description of the software development life cycle to place OVID in context. It includes a definition of OUI and discussion of the users' and designer's models. These matters will not be discussed in depth. The bulk of the tutorial is devoted to the process of design.

OVID is an iterative method. It takes the output of task analysis and produces:

- a initial object model,
- views descriptions for the objects,
- new task descriptions using the objects and views,
- interactions within the views
- a more refined object model and so on.

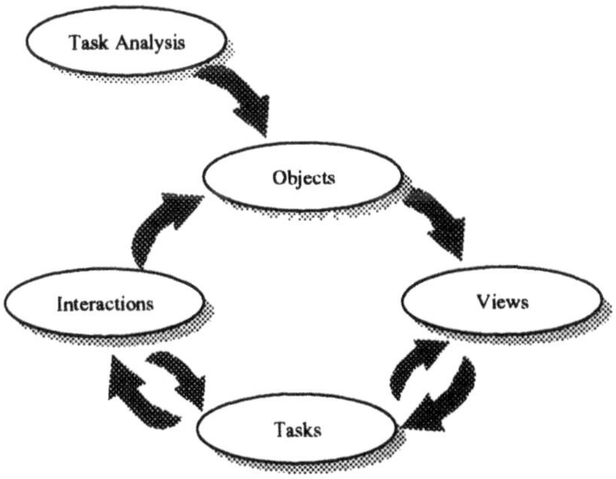

Figure 1: An outline of the OVID processes

Human–Computer Interaction: INTERACT'97 S. Howard, J. Hammond & G. Lindgaard (editors)
Published by Chapman & Hall ©IFIP 1997

2.1 Task Analysis

The tutorial does not teach task analysis. Instead, it concentrates on how the output of task analysis can be used as input to design and though out the design process.

2.2 Class Diagrams

The core of OVID is class diagrams showing the designer's model. To facilitate transfer of the output of OVID to code development these diagrams are best captured using a tool such as Rational Rose/C++. Examples shown during the tutorial will use Rational Rose/C++. However, exercises will be conducted using pencil and paper.

2.3 Objects

Stage 1 of the process is to find the objects that the user will deal with. Although several users' models may be found the objective is to consolidate to a single designer's model that is appropriate to all the users.

Analysis starts with the most frequent tasks. These are used to find the most concrete objects and the strongest relationships between them. As analysis proceeds the model is expanded to map the relationships for all tasks. In later iterations of the object model the design will express the most significant attributes as objects.

It often emerges that some users think of two classes as distinct when the designer thinks these are variants of the same object. The tutorial gives guidance on this and other modeling dilemmas such as how to represent *many-to-many* relationships.

2.4 Views

The next section deals with how to find the views of the objects that are needed . It also helps the designer decide which views can be treated as standard view types and which require special mechanisms. It goes on to discuss how represent the users as objects in the model can be useful both in the design and code phases of a project.

2.5 New Tasks

The next step in OVID is task synthesis. Tasks must be created that correspond to each of those described during the task analysis. These new tasks document how the users will work with the new system. The objects and views that have already been discovered are used to create the new tasks.

The synthesized tasks are recorded using the same Rose tool and will be used later by the code designers as test cases.

2.6 Detailed View Interactions

The final element within OVID is the use of state diagrams and state tables to provide detailed interaction descriptions for all of the objects and their views. Details are given of how other objects may be discovered during this process. This completes the designers arsenal of procedures used in the design.

2.7 Conclusion

To complete the tutorial a short session discusses: visual design, prototyping, usability evaluation and the transfer to code development.

3 INTENDED AUDIENCE

HCI professionals responsible for turning user requirements into object-oriented interface designs. Background in at least one (but not all) of the following areas is recommended: requirements gathering, user interface design, and object-oriented analysis. This tutorial is about object-oriented user interface design. It is not about object-oriented programming

4 BACKGROUND

The presenters are all members of IBM's User Interface Strategy team. They are currently engaged on development of next-generation user interfaces, style guidance for these interfaces and methods for their deployment.

The tutorial was presented at CHI 97 in March.

123

Techniques for the design of human error tolerant systems

Full day tutorial
P. Wright, B. Fields, A. Dearden, M. Harrison
Presented by: P. Wright & B. Fields

Human-Computer Interaction Group
Department of Computer Science
University of York
York YO1 5DD, UK.
Phone: +44 1904 432741 Fax: +44 1904 432767
Email: {pcw, bob}@minster.york.ac.uk

KEYWORDS: designing for error, human-error tolerance, human-reliability analysis, safety

INTRODUCTION

Interactive systems need to be robust to human error and provide for easy recovery. This tutorial describes techniques that can help designers to build human-error tolerance into their systems.

Have you ever set your VCR and returned only to find it missed your favourite program? Have you ever been frustrated when trying to set the time on a digital watch? Do any of the systems your company designs lead to similar frustrations for their users? What can you do to avoid these problems?

In safety-critical systems, such as power stations, chemical plants, or aircraft cockpits, the consequences of human error can be catastrophic rather than just frustrating. Methods for analysing designs to discover the potential for human error are critical in these fields.

TUTORIAL CONTENT

This tutorial will equip you with some simple techniques for tackling human error issues in design, provide a framework for thinking about error, and give pointers to where more information can be found. The areas covered are listed below.

Analysing the work context

One starting point for error analysis is to understand the tasks that the user intends to perform and the situation in which work is carried out. The tutorial discusses how tasks can be studied and represented, with a focus on one simple task description technique, Hierarchical Task Analysis. The importance of the situation or scenario, and ways of describing scenarios, will also be discussed.

Participants will be given an opportunity to try out these ideas by applying them to simple, everyday systems.

Analysing the system context

Understanding the work being carried out is an essential part of identifying potential error problems. The interactive systems and technology being used is another important contextual factor. This section of the tutorial introduces a collection of concepts and techniques that can help the analyst in isolating aspects of an interface design that could lead to errors (such as moding problems or display complexity).

Human–Computer Interaction: INTERACT'97 S. Howard, J. Hammond & G. Lindgaard (editors)
Published by Chapman & Hall

Identifying error and breakdown

Cognitive analysis of error

The tutorial will consider some of the accounts of error that are available from cognitive psychology, and how these can be used to identify and explain potential errors, using the contextual factors discussed earlier.

Behavioural analysis of error

A cognitive view of error causation may help to identify where problems might occur and how to design for them, but does not give the analyst a basis for deciding how serious errors will be. For this we need to look to a more detailed account of how errors are manifested in behaviour.

Given a description of a task, it is possible to generate some error scenarios by systematically applying a checklist of guide words to user actions.

Identifying significant errors

Not all errors are serious, and designers need to prioritise their work to ensure that the errors that have the greatest impact are the ones that are dealt with first. This part of the tutorial will discuss approaches that can be used to determine the most important errors. The emphasis will be on systematic ways of exploring the consequences of an error, and of determining the relative significance of different errors.

Participants will be given an opportunity to apply the knowledge of cognitive pre-cursors of error, and methods for exploring error consequences with a simple case study.

Designing to avoid error

The aim of error analysis is to develop designs that are resistant and tolerant to error. There are no automatic rules that will generate good designs, but this part of the tutorial discusses some ways in which a design can be made more or less tolerant of error. The tutorial covers 'localised' techniques such as confirmation dialogues and recovery mechanisms; ways of thinking about how information is presented to aid error detection and recovery; as well as approaches to conceptual design, i.e. the earliest stages of design.

The expanding context

The final part of the tutorial explores some of the most difficult problems in understanding error. Some events that lead to undesirable consequences are difficult to account for using only the tools of behavioural analysis and cognitive analysis. These events involve social, historical and cultural issues. The tutorial highlights some of these issues using examples of accidents and incidents in safety critical systems.

INTENDED AUDIENCE

The tutorial is intended for system designers and engineers involved in the design of user interfaces as well as human-computer interaction researchers. It is intended that the content of the tutorial be relevant not only to practitioners in the world of safety critical systems, but also to developers and systems where human error may cause problems. Examples used include everyday domestic items and high-volume products where usability is an important issue.

No prior experience will be assumed of task analysis, human reliability analysis or the psychology of human error.

ABOUT THE AUTHORS

Peter Wright, Bob Fields, Michael Harrison and Andy Dearden bring substantial academic and industrial experience of Human Computer Interaction and Human Reliability Analysis. Wright, Fields and Harrison, both software engineers, are members of the British Aerospace (BAe) Dependable Computing System Centre at the University of York. The centre was set up by BAe to carry out long-term research and focussing on safety and dependability in aerospace systems. Dearden is a member of the human-computer interaction group at York, and is investigating concepts of risk, impact and utility in human-machine interface design.

Between them they have conducted studies of human-error issues in several different domains, ranging from aircraft flight decks, to government agencies, and emergency services' control rooms.

Their research work is focussed on developing techniques to aid designers in building error tolerant and error resistant systems.

Modelling multimodal interaction: A theory-based technique for design analysis and support

Jon May

Department of Psychology
University of Sheffield
Western Bank
Sheffield UK –S10 2TN
jon.may@sheffield.ac.uk

Philip J. Barnard

MRC Applied Psychology Unit
15 Chaucer Road
Cambridge UK –CB2 2EF
philip.barnard@mrc-apu.cam.ac.uk

ABSTRACT: This tutorial introduces participants to a way of thinking about how users mentally represent different facets of their interactions with advanced interfaces involving multimodal information. The approach is theory-based. It assumes that human information processing deals with nine different types of mental representation. General rules of combination and decomposition of constituents, basic units and the superordinate organisation of all types of representation will be presented. The first part of the tutorial introduces the basic theoretical ideas. The second part links this basic theory into the domain of HCI and illustrates how core concepts can be used to analyse the course of interactions with static visual displays, dynamic visual displays and multimodal displays. In the final part a handbook will be introduced describing a simple technique and an associated notation for representing the static and dynamic properties of visual information, task structures and acoustic information.

KEYWORDS: Cognitive Models, Graphic Design, Multimedia, Usability Evaluation, User Models

1. AIM OF THE TUTORIAL

The aim of this tutorial is to introduce participants to a way of thinking about how users mentally represent different facets of their interactions with advanced interfaces involving static or dynamic visual displays and the integration of multimodal information.

The approach is theory-based. It assumes that the human information processing mechanism deals with information in terms of nine different types of mental representation.

Three of these representations are sensory in nature, two of them dealing with visual and auditory information and the third dealing with information about the state of the body - including proprioceptive information about the position of body parts and their state. Two further representations are assumed to mediate the control of physical actions in the world and verbal articulation. Four central representations complete the overall framework. Two of these deal with abstract structural descriptions of sounds and visual objects, whilst the final two representations capture meaning. These capture the underpinnings of our 'propositional' understanding of material and its more holistic or 'schematic' interpretation.

The different types of mental representation are all generated by specific processes and they are systematically related and constrained by a architecture governing information flow within the underlying mental mechanism. Although each type of representation is in a different 'code', they can each be described using a common notation. Within each type of representation, constituent element form basic units of representation and these basic units can themselves be combined into superordinate structuring of information.

Human–Computer Interaction: INTERACT'97 S. Howard, J. Hammond & G. Lindgaard (editors)
Published by Chapman & Hall

General rules of combination and decomposition of constituents, basic units and their superordinate organisation of all types of representation will be presented. These can be used to capture users mental representations of key features of relevance to the course of user system interactions. These include their ability to search complex graphical displays; their task representations and the ways in which information derived from different input modalities are combined.

The approach also supports an analysis of dynamic changes over time. As such it can capture how a user builds an overall schematic interpretation of moving images like animations or videoclips as well as supporting analyses of more traditional problems like the sequential conduct of a series of task steps. The involvement of body state information and higher level schematic meaning also supports a view of how interactions may relate to human affect and to the influences of environmental stress.

2. STRUCTURE OF THE TUTORIAL

The tutorial will progress through three parts. The first part will introduce the basic theoretical ideas. These will be presented via animations of the functioning of the human information processing mechanism.

The second part will link this basic theory through into the domain of HCI and illustrate how core concepts can be used to analyse the course of interactions with static visual displays, dynamic visual displays and multimodal displays. This will draw upon experimental evidence concerning interactions as well as example analyses of specific HCI design scenarios.

In the final part a specific handbook will be introduced describing a simple technique and an associated notation for representing the static and dynamic properties of visual information, task structures and acoustic information. The purpose of this section will be to provide participants with a sufficient understanding of the techniques so that they will be able to take them back to their own working environments with a view to shaping and extending them for their own applications.

3. TUTORIAL HANDBOOK

This handbook is intended to help people who design computer interfaces to use psychological principles to construct the appearance of computer interface objects, their arrangement on the display, their behaviour, and their relationship to the users' tasks.

There are many books that provide 'guidelines' for designing interfaces – some tell you how and when to use different colours and typefaces, how to format columns and tables, and how to make your designs aesthetically appealing. This handbook does not try to replicate one of those books.

Although they provide a valuable service, and sometimes also try to explain why they are providing the advice that they do, guidelines are intended to be prescriptive – telling you what you should do for each part of an interface.

You can follow all of the advice that they provide for every individual part of your interface, and still find that you produce a design that is not 'easy to use'. Guidelines cannot tell you how to decide for yourself whether an interface will be usable, nor how to identify the problematic parts of the design so that you can improve them. That is what this handbook tries to do.

The techniques this tutorial teaches will let participants decide how difficult it will be for people to group objects together, to tell objects apart, to search for objects, and to switch their attention from one part of the display to another. To do this, you will learn to distinguish different kinds of mental representation, and to use these ideas to understand why the same display can be perceived in different ways.

It will show you how to generalise these ideas to the structure of the tasks people carry out with interfaces, and how essential it is to make sure that the structure of the information presented by the interface matches the structure of the user's task.

The handbook is organised into several sections. Each section introduces some ideas about cognition, with some examples, and shows you how these ideas can be seen to affect the usability of interface designs. At several points in the handbook there are exercises, to check that you understand how the ideas can be used in practice.

The sections build on each other, introducing the simpler ideas first and the more complicated ideas later, and so the handbook isn't a book that you can 'dip into', like a collection of guidelines might be. You have to follow the handbook through section by section – but when you have done that, we hope that you'll have learnt enough to put your new skills into practice, without needing to keep the notes by your side.

125

Cognitive Factors in Design: Basic Phenomena in Human Memory and Problem Solving

Thomas T. Hewett
Department of Psychology, Sociology, and Anthropology
Drexel University
Philadelphia, PA 19104 USA
+01-215-895-2461, or 1313
hewett@duvm.ocs.drexel.edu

ABSTRACT
This tutorial provides a "hands-on" (actually, "minds-on") exploration of several basic processes and phenomena ofhuman memory, and problem solving. The emphasis is on developing both intuitiveand formal knowledge which can serve as background knowledge which will be useful in interpreting design guidelines and in making educateddesign judgments when design guidelines fail, conflict, or are nonexistent. Thedemonstrations used emphasize basic general phenomena with which any theory ofmemory or problem solving must deal. In addition, the tutorial suggests some ofthe implications of these phenomena for designing interactive computingsystems.

KEYWORDS: Memory, Problem Solving, Design,Models of the User

INTRODUCTION AND CAVEATS

The emphasis in this tutorial is on demonstrations and exercises which highlightsome of the quite remarkable things human beings do in interacting with, inlearning about, and in making sense out of the world around them. These thingsoften seem to be quite ordinary simply because we do them regularly, often without deliberation.Nonetheless, some of them are quite complex and not well understood. Many ofthe demonstrations replicate phenomena studied under controlled laboratoryconditions and some are drawn directly from research studies.

Since this tutorial emphasizes the development of anintuitive feel for the material, it is important to recognize that an intuitiveunderstanding must be informed and validated by research results. Ever sinceits founding, the findings of Experimental Psychology have taught us not to trust unsupportedpersonal hunches and intuitions about the reasons for human behavior. There area variety of ways in which ordinary day-to-day intuitions about behavior, bothour own and that of others, can lead one astray (some are illustrated in the tutorial). Mostof the demonstrations used in this tutorial are designed to replicate phenomenawhich have been studied or validated under controlled laboratory conditions. Infact, several of the demonstrations are drawn directly from research studies, although someprocedural license is taken for purposes of demonstration..

MEMORY

In one model of memory, short-term memory (STM) isdescribed (e.g., Solso, 1994) as having a limited storage capacity (seven plus or minus two chunks) for arelatively brief duration (estimates range from 12 to 30 seconds withoutrehearsal). Information can be maintained in STM for longer periods of timewith maintenance rehearsal (MR), although this simple repetition of material does not appear to be very efficient at transferring information intoLong Term Memory (LTM). Rather, elaborative rehearsal (ER) appears to be themost effective set of processes for the transfer of information into long-termstorage. Although the information in STM is usually thought to be represented by one of a relativelylimited number of codes, there are several reasons to believe that anyorganizational structure in LTM is accessible as a basis for forming the chunksthat are held in STM.

Human-Computer Interaction: INTERACT'97 S. Howard, J. Hammond & G. Lindgaard (editors)
Published by Chapman & Hall

LTM has a large capacity for storage of information for long periods of time.There is, however, no easy or obvious way to determine the limits of how muchcan be stored, or for how long it can be stored. Several types of informationare represented in LTM, including such things as facts and events, motor and perceptual skills,knowledge of physical laws and systems of mathematics, a spatial model of theworld around us, attitudes and beliefs about oneself and others, etc. Thisinformation is more or less well organized in a variety of ways and varies in its accessibility as afunction of several factors. The factors determining accessibility of theinformation in LTM include such things as the conditions which existed at thetime the information was stored, the recency of its last use, its degree of inter-relationship with otherknowledge, its degree of uniqueness relative to other information, etc. Mostdiscussions of failure to recall information from LTM focus on explanations suchas interference, the absence or inappropriateness of retrieval cues, or some type of organicdysfunction such as brain damage.

An alternative model of human memory holds that there is no need to postulate aSTM. Rather, there is a working memory which is part of the larger memorysystem and not a separate memory. Different degrees of persistence ofinformation in memory are thought to be a function of the elaborateness or the depth to which information hasbeen processed. The greater the degree of processing, the longer the retention period. In this model, chunks are organizational units in LTM andthe capacity limitation is on how much information can be actively scanned orheld in working memory at any time.

While the bulk of the evidence supports the model whichincludes working memory (Anderson, 1994), there are basic phenomena with which any theory of memory must deal. Forexample, regardless of whether one thinks of the seven plus or minus twocapacity limitation as the result of a limited capacity memory or as a resultof a limit on the amount of information which can be activated and maintained inan active state in working memory at any given time, it is clear that there is acapacity limitation. Similarly, regardless of whether one thinks that memoryrehearsal processes have different degrees of depth and elaboration or that there are twodifferent kinds of rehearsal processes, each associated with a different memorystore, it is clear that elaborative rehearsal is more effective than maintenancerehearsal in insuring that the information will be accessible in memory for a long period of time.

PROBLEM SOLVING

A major turning point in the literature on problem solvingoccurred with the work of Newell and Simon (1972). In their view, a problem can be analyzed by means of a "problem space"representing various states of knowledge of the problem solver, a series oftransformations between states, and a set of operators which produce thosetransformations. A problem exists when we have a gap between an initial state and a goal state. The means of solving the problem involves applying the appropriateset of operators required to complete a series of state transformations thatwill eliminate the gap. These transformations must be accomplished withoutviolating any of the conditions on the operators.

As a result of repeated experience with problems, solversbuild up an organized body of knowledge or information about the properties of aparticular type of problem and the operations or steps required to solve it.This organized body of information is usually referred to as a problem solving schema (e.g.,Norman, 1982). Humans develop a wide variety of familiar problem schemas(Hayes, 1981), and the typical individual has built up a wide stock of such schemas whichcome into play in solving problems problems with which one has prior experience.Some schemas are so familiar they are activated almost automatically and withoutmuch thought.

Typically, the effect of problem solving schemas is tohelp provide reasonably efficient methods of solving frequently encountered kinds of problems. Sometimes, however, a schema caninterfere with the problem solving process. Since it influences the problemsolver's early analysis of the problem and determines which schema, or schemas,will be brought to bear in solving a particular problem, the way in which that problem is represented canmake a vital difference in how easily the problem can be solved. When a problemis not solved as easily as expected. it is often quite fruitful to look to theadequacy of the representation of the problem, and to give thought to somehow modifying orchanging that representation.

SOME IMPLICATIONS FOR HUMAN-COMPUTER INTERACTION DESIGN

In considering the nature of human memory it is clear that designers need totake account of the fact that there are a limited number of "chunks" ofinformation with which a user can actively cope at any given time. While thesize of those chunks can be affected by the development of additional new knowledge structures, that growthof knowledge requires that the user be actively engaged in elaborating and assimilating that knowledge. Inaddition the demands upon human learning and memory can be reduced by providingappropriate mnemonic cues in the interface and the flow of interaction. Inconsidering the nature ofhuman problem solving it is clear that designers need to take account of thefact that users will bring to bear established problem solving strategies whichare developed from having solved problems encountered frequently in the past.While these established strategies can be used to facilitate usage they can also create processblockages which may only be solved by changing the way the problems ofinteraction are presented to the user or by creating a working environment inwhich the user has the flexibility to redefine, reconceptualize or re-represent the tasks or problems which thesoftware is being used to solve.

Among the more general implications of the phenomenadescribed above for human-computer interaction design, two stand out. The first, derived from consideration of the nature of long term memory and the processesgoverning storage and retrieval of information, is that humans interacting withcomputers can and do use existing memories and memory structures to assign aninterpretation to a wide variety of things, regardless of whether that meaningwas intended by the designers. The second major implication, derived fromconsideration of the nature of the way people solve problems is that, people,"...do not do what designers want them to do; instead they tend to get activelyinvolved and to think and plan and solve problems (Carroll & Mack,1985)."

REFERENCES

1. Anderson, J. R. *CognitivePsychology and Its Implications.* 4th ed. W. H. Freeman, New York,NY, 1994.

2. Carroll, J. M., and Mack, R. L.Metaphor, computing systems, and active learning. *Int. J. ofMan-Machine Studies, 22*, 1, (1985), 39-57.

3. Hayes, J. R. *The CompleteProblem Solver.* The Franklin Institute Press, Philadelphia, PA,1981.

4. Newell, A., and Simon, H. A.*Human Problem Solving.* Prentice-Hall, EnglewoodCliffs, NJ, 1972.

5. Norman, D. A. *Learning andMemory.* New York: W. H. Freeman, New York, NY, 1982.

6. Solso R. L. *CognitivePsychology.* 4th ed. Allyn and Bacon, Needham Heights, MA,1994.

126

Methods for Measuring Usability

Nigel Bevan and Ian Curson

National Physical Laboratory, Usability Services
Teddington, Middlesex, TW11 0LW, UK
Nigel.Bevan@npl.co.uk, Ian.Curson@npl.co.uk

ABSTRACT The tutorial explains the benefits of measuring usability as part of a user-centred design process, and introduces the participants to the methodology for usability measurement developed by the collaborative European ESPRIT MUSiC (Measurement of Usability in Context) project. The tutorial includes demonstration of the use of MUSiC tools, and class exercises to apply the methods to case studies.

KEY WORDS: Usability evaluation, metrics, usability engineering, video analysis

OBJECTIVES

In many organisations usability is ignored because there are no objective criteria for usability when developing and procuring products. The tutorial explains how usability can be operationalised as the prime quality goal: to provide quality in use (Bevan, 1995, 1996). Participants learn how to choose and apply appropriate cost-effective methods and tools in commercial projects at different stages of development, and how the methods relate to business goals. They gain experience in the use of tools for usability specification and measurement developed by the European MUSiC project (Bevan and Macleod, 1994), implementing the principles of ISO 9241-11.

The tutorial is intended for anyone who wishes to specify or measure usability as a quality objective during product development or to evaluate usability when purchasing. The emphasis is on explaining when it is beneficial to use evaluation procedures which provide usability measures in addition to design feedback.

Usability measurement provides benefits not available from qualitative evaluation methods. Measurement can be used to:

- predict, ensure and improve product quality
- control and improve the production processes
- decide on the acceptance of a software product
- select a product from among alternative products

CONTENT

The tutorial starts by introducing the benefits of setting and testing usability goals in design, and shows how usability goals can be derived by decomposing overall business goals for the product. In particular circumstances, the goals for usage in a particular context may be in terms of user performance, attitude or cognitive workload. The following topics are covered:

1. The benefits of usability measurement are related to evaluation procedures in ergonomics, software quality and quality management. Different approaches to usability are reviewed, and emphasis is given to the benefits of defining usability in terms of meeting the needs of users by providing quality of use.

2. The importance of specifying the context of use is explained, and using the Usability Context Analysis Guide (Macleod , 1994) the class carries out an exercise to specify the intended context of usage, the actual context of measurement and a measurement plan including specific usability goals.

3. Use of performance measures: including a description of the MUSiC Performance Measurement Method (Macleod et al 1997) and DRUM (Macleod and Rengger, 1993) which can be used to derive user performance metrics and diagnostic information from an analysis of a videotape of interaction.

Human–Computer Interaction: INTERACT'97 S. Howard, J. Hammond & G. Lindgaard (editors)
Published by Chapman & Hall

4. Use of attitude questionnaires: including a description of the validated SUMI scale which can be used to measure six components of attitude towards the interaction and identify problem areas of the interface.

5. Measurement of cognitive workload using questionnaires is explained.

6. Case studies: use of each of the tools is illustrated by case studies and class exercises which draw from the experience of the use of the methods in a wide variety of commercial applications.

Performance Measures (DRUM Tool)

The MUSiC User Performance Method is a technique for measuring the usability of a product by measuring the extent to which specific users of the product achieve specific goals in a specific environment.

The data on which the usability metrics are based is recorded from a variety of sources during evaluation sessions, in which subjects representative of the user community of the product being tested, carry out tasks that are typical of those the product's users undertake, in an environment similar to that in which the product is normally used. The typical characteristics of the product's users, the tasks they do, and the environment in which they do them are identified by following the guidance provided in the Usability Context Analysis Guide.

The analytical load on the analyst is reduced by firstly providing information, in a document called A Guide to Analysing Usability Sessions, that describes how an analyst can objectively identify particular user actions during the sessions, and secondly by providing a software tool, the Diagnostic Recorder for Usability Measurements, DRUM, that helps the analyst build a time-sequence log of the pre-defined user actions. From these logs of the sessions the DRUM can automatically calculate usability metrics for individual users and group the results of similar users together.

Attitude Measures: SUMI

The assessment of a computer system's usability should involve measuring not only aspects of users' performance, but also how users feel about the system they are using. The Software Usability Measurement Inventory (SUMI) has been designed specifically for this purpose. SUMI is designed to investigate users' perceptions of the quality of software systems. It is applicable to many sorts of applications. SUMI gives the investigator:

- A Global Usability measure
- Five Usability subscale measures
- A high level problem diagnosis.

SUMI offers the investigator norms based on large samples, and the possibility of comparing the system being tested either against generic usability profiles, or against the usability profile of another system.

Cognitive Workload Measures

Efficient use of the computer is intrinsic to usability. This means that in assessing the usability of software it is necessary to investigate both user performance and the effort a user invests in using the software. If a good performance can only be achieved at the expense of a high amount of invested effort, a system is not usable. MUSiC has objective and subjective measurement techniques suited for use in a wide variety of applications. Participants are introduced to the different measures of cognitive workload, and the situations in which the different measures can be used together or separately.

REFERENCES

Bevan N (1995) Usability is quality of use. In: Anzai & Ogawa (eds) Proc. 6th International Conference on Human Computer Interaction, July 1995. Elsevier.

Bevan N (1995) Measuring usability as quality of use. Journal of Software Quality, 4, 115-130.

Bevan N, Macleod M (1994) Usability measurement in context. Behaviour and Information Technology, 13, 132-145.

Macleod, M (1994) Usability in Context: Improving Quality of Use. In: G Bradley and HW Hendricks (eds.) Human Factors in Organizational Design and Management - IV - Proceedings of the International Ergonomics Association 4th International Symposium on Human Factors in Organizational Design and Management, (Stockholm, Sweden, May 29 - June 1 1994). Amsterdam, Elsevier.

Macleod M, Bowden R, Bevan N and Curson I. (1997) The MUSiC Performance Measurement Method. Behaviour and Information Technol., in publication

Macleod M and Rengger R. (1993) The Development of DRUM: A Software Tool for Video-assisted Usability Evaluation. In: People and Computers VIII, Proceedings of the HCI'93 Conference (Loughborough, UK, Sept 1993), CUP.

Cost-Justifying Your Usability Activities

Randolph G. Bias

BMC Software, Inc
10415 Morado Circle
Austin, Texas 78727
USA
rbias@bmc.com

Helen M. Kieboom

UCDESIGN Pty Ltd
PO Box 1297
St. Kilda South, Victoria 3182
Australia
hkieboom@ozemail.com.au

ABSTRACT Good product usability doesn't happen by accident. Good usability of human computer interfaces is not a luxury. Nor is it free. Usability engineering **IS**, however, typically well worth the time and money spent on it. Is it worth it in YOUR case ? This is exactly the question a product development manager is likely to ask. This tutorial arms participants with the tools needed to be able to answer that question meaningfully, and using a unit of measure (dollars) that everyone in the business community understands. The tutorial includes lecture on cost-justification methods, brainstorming about quantifiable costs and benefits, modeling of a formal cost-benefit analysis approach, an on-line usability engineering optimising tool, and a hands-on exercise involving implementing these concepts in the participant's own arena.

KEYWORDS usability, cost-benefit analysis, cost justification, discount usability methods

1. INTRODUCTION/JUSTIFICATION

Good product (or system, or process) usability doesn't happen by accident. Good usability of human computer interfaces is not a luxury. Especially in these competitive and economically constrained times, all contributors to any development effort must be able to justify their contributions or be prepared to suffer the budgeting axe. This is particularly true for human factors professionals, whose ultimate product, usability, has a history of being considered a luxury.

Good usability of human computer interfaces is not a luxury; customers are unequivocal in their call for more usable products. Nor is it free. Usability engineering **IS**, however, typically well worth the time and money spent on it. Is it worth it in YOUR case ?

This tutorial will arm participants with the tools to be able to answer this question meaningfully, and to employ a unit of measure with which all product development manangers are very familiar: dollars.

2. TARGET AUDIENCE

Our primary audience will be usability (or human factors) practitioners who have responsibility for driving usability into their products. This audience includes members of human factors/usability departments, lone practitioners integrated into software development teams, or independent human factors consultants (from within the company or from without). Others who will find this tutorial of value are software designers and developers, technical writers, software development managers, human factors researchers, and human factors educators.

3. GENERAL NOTES

Session 1 explicates the importance of the tutorial, and of a cost-benefit approach to usability engineering in general. It contrasts a cost-benefit approach with the

Human–Computer Interaction: INTERACT'97 S. Howard, J. Hammond & G. Lindgaard (editors)
Published by Chapman & Hall ©IFIP 1997

"old" approach, whereby the enthusiam of the usability engineer, and the product manager's inherent interest in usability, were the key variables in determining whether product development resources were earmarked for usability. Class discussion follows, on experiences with the old approach, any experiences with a cost-benefit approach, and successes and failures.

Session II focuses on the new business environment, and general pressures that usability customers face, which drive us toward this cost-justification approach. These business pressures include: Low profit margins; downsizing; shorter development cycles; the move toward smaller and ubiquitous computers; the move toward more powerful, and multi-media, interfaces; the fact of more casual computer users (encompassing web users); and the desire for quick delivery to market of technological innovation. A group discussion follows, to collect examples of quantifiable usability benefits and costs.

Session III begins with a lecture on formal versus informal cost-benefit analysis approaches. Tradeoffs are considered (e.g., formal approaches have a high cost in the usability practitioner's time, but are more likely to predict accurately the net present value of money spent on usability engineering support) and then an example of a formal analysis is presented as a model.

Session IV is a demonstration of an on-line tool, the Usability Decision Optimiser™. This tool takes as input project data (such as development schedule) plus data on usability engineering techniques, and makes recommendations regarding which usability engineering methods to employ.

Session V affords the tutorial participants with some hands-on experience with cost-benefit analysis planning. It is an exercise designed to start the participants thinking about how to cost-justify their own usability activities. First, participants in small groups complete their (individual) forms. The forms will steer participants toward identifying particular costs and benefits, and toward thinking about the appropriate time span over which to spread those costs and benefits. We will reconvene as a large group, and some individuals will be asked to share their skeleton cost-benefit analyses.

Session VI is a short summary of the day, with explicit attention to specific actions participants might take right away, by way of implementing the concepts learned in the tutorial.

4. SUMMARY

Usability – "The next competitive frontier" (Norman, 1990) -- is not just a "nice to have," it does not happen by accident, and it is not, typically, free. Usability engineering is, however, typically well worth the time and money spent on it. Is it worth it in YOUR case ? Armed with the tools – conceptual, textual (Bias and Mayhew, 1994), and on-line tool (Kieboom, 1996) – presented in this tutorial, the participant will be able to answer that question meaningfully, and using a unit of measure (dollars) that everyone in the business community understands.

5. REFERENCES

Bias, R. G., and Mayhew, D. J. (1994) *Cost-justifying usability*. Academic Press, Boston.

Kieboom, H. M. (1996) *Usability Decision Optimiser: A Product to Support Usability Practitioners Select the Most Cost-Effective Usability Engineering Technique for a Given Development Environment.* Unpublished manuscript, Swinburne University of Technology, Melbourne.

Norman, D. A. (1990) *The design of everyday things*. Doubleday-Currency, New York.

128

The MUSE Method for Usability Engineering

Kee Yong LIM

School of Mechanical & Production Engineering
Nanyang Technological University
Nanyang Avenue
SINGAPORE 639798
mkylim@ntuvax.ntu.ac.sg

John Brian LONG

Ergonomics Unit
University College London
26 Bedford Way, London WC1H OAP, UK.
j.long@ucl.ac.uk

ABSTRACT Human factors input to system development is often limited to evaluation following system implementation. Since design specifications are now 'frozen' and resistent to change, human factors recruitment at this stage would predispose its recommendations toward costly design modifications. Complete implementation of its design recommendations often become impossible. The human factors input is thus 'too-little' and 'too-late'.

One solution to the problem is to integrate structured human factors and software engineering methods. In this way, human factors inputs may be set appropriately against the system development context. To this end, a structured human factors method named MUSE (Method for USability Engineering), was developed in 1990. The objective of this tutorial is to provide participants a guided application of MUSE using design case-studies and exercises.

KEYWORDS System Development; User Interface Specification; Structured Analysis and Design Methods; Structured Human Factors Method; User Requirements and Task Analysis.

Human-Computer Interaction: INTERACT'97 S. Howard, J. Hammond & G. Lindgaard (editors)
Published by Chapman & Hall

1. OBJECTIVE OF TUTORIAL

This full-day tutorial will demonstrate how human factors design may be supported effectively using a structured human factors method named MUSE. Participants will be provided a guided application of MUSE in design case-studies and group exercises.

2. PARTICIPANTS TARGETED

This tutorial is intended for human factors designers interested in wider involvement in system development, and for software engineers who wish to understand human factors design. The tutorial is intermediate in level and is targeted at experienced participants.

3. OVERVIEW OF TUTORIAL

The tutorial will address the following: the case for wider human factors involvement in system development; the inadequacies of rapid prototyping for facilitating timely and efficient human factors input; the optimization of human factors input by integrating MUSE with similarly structured software engineering methods; a guided tour of MUSE covering requirements and task analysis to user interface specification. The MUSE method is presented and illustrated using case-study examples drawn from its development. Practical exercises will reinforce participants' learning of the design descriptions, procedures and notations of MUSE.

The tutorial is presented in eight units of approximately equal duration. The design concerns addressed comprise the following :

• The Case for Structured Human Factors Methods. This tutorial unit will inform participants on the advantages and disadvantages of structured methods. Contrasts with the rapid prototyping approach will be highlighted; including an account of why rapid prototyping alone is not sufficient for ensuring the development of usable human-computer systems.

• Overview of MUSE. Each stage of the method will be introduced generally and related to current practices of human factors design. In addition, relationships between MUSE and current software engineering design activities will be highlighted.

• Detailed Tour of MUSE Part I : User Requirements and Task Analysis. Participants will be shown how different classes of existing systems (both manual and computerised) may be analysed; and how task descriptions, generalised task models, and domain descriptions, may be derived to support user requirements specification and conceptual design. The human factors design products, processes and notations involved will be illustrated using case-studies.

• Group Exercise I. Participants will be guided on how a task description may be derived for a simple case-study system. Descriptions generated by participants will then be discussed as a group, to highlight how the descriptions could support human factors evaluation and the specification of user requirements.

• Detailed Tour of MUSE Part II : Conceptual and Detailed Task Design. This tutorial unit addresses how human factors products derived at earlier stages of the method, are used to support function allocation and interactive task design.

• Detailed Tour of MUSE Part III : User Interface Specification. A user-task approach for user interface specification will be introduced in this part of the presentation. Specifically, the human factors design products, processes and notations entailed by user interface specification (comprising screen actuations, screen composition and layout, screen object behaviours, etc.), are illustrated using case-studies.

• Group Exercises II and III. The first exercise will reinforce participants' understanding of how user interface specifications should be interpreted. The second exercise will allow participants to experience a 'hands-on' application of the method. Both exercises will involve a design case-study.

• Summary and Future Developments. The main concerns of the tutorial will be summarised, and future developments of the method reviewed, e.g. the development of computer-based tools based on MUSE; the extension of MUSE to support declarative human factors knowledge such as design guidelines; wider integration of MUSE with established structured Software Engineering methods; etc.

129

Intelligent Interface Technology

David Benyon

Professor David Benyon, Dept. Computer Studies, Napier University, 219 Colinton road, Edinburgh, EH14 1JD.

D.Benyon@dcs.napier.ac.uk

ABSTRACT Applying intelligent interface technology (IIT) will increasingly become an option for the interface designer. Although there have been many applications of IIT there are few general principles, guidelines or methods as to when designers could and should use IIT. This tutorial looks in detail at applications of IIT and at the techniques which it employs. It covers the construction of user, domain and interaction models and looks at how these have been applied in adaptive hypermedia systems, intelligent multi-media, agent-based interaction and other intelligent user interfaces. The tutorial follows on from the introductory tutorial and illustrates the methodology presented there. It also covers the enhanced methods of analysis and design which are needed in order to make effective use of IIT. Given a better understanding of both methods and structure, IIT not only becomes a solution to some usability problems, it opens up new horizons for a radical change in HCI through the use of interface agents and a more equitable sharing of domain knowledge.

KEYWORDS Intelligent user interfaces, Agent-based interaction, Adaptive systems

The Problem

A particularly stubborn problem in human-computer interaction (HCI) is that users change their knowledge and behaviour over time. Computer systems also have to deal with a diverse, heterogeneous user population. Thus any system which has a fixed interface will be more or less ill-adapted to interact with individual users at particular times. The fundamental nature of this problem prompted some early interest in adaptive systems (e.g. Edmonds, 1981, Benyon, 1984, Rich, 1979). Since then the idea of including intelligence at the interface has gained more acceptance as the publication of a number of books and journals can demonstrate (Chignell and Hancock, 1988; Sullivan and Tyler, 1991; Browne, Totterdell and Norman, 1990; Schneider-Hufschmidt, Kuhme and Malinowski, 1993; Gray, Heffley and Murray, 1993, AI Review, 1993, Knowledge-Based Systems, 1993, CACM, 1994). Researchers with backgrounds in artificial intelligence, expert systems, intelligent tutoring and human-computer interaction have begun to recognise some common ground (e.g. Kobsa and Wahlster, 1989). Although some HCI researchers criticise the idea of adaptive systems (e.g. Thimbleby, 1990) they have apparently been outpaced by recent developments. Agent-based interaction (e.g. Kay, 1990) and computer-supported co-operative working (e.g. Connoly and Edmonds, 1993) are demonstrating not just the feasibility and desirability of building intelligence into the interface, but also the necessity.

The Solution

This tutorial sets out to place the theory and practice of adaptive systems in an HCI context. It begins by accepting the existence of knowledge-based techniques and by recognising a fundamental problem for HCI; dealing with the variety and changeability of users. It argues that by employing knowledge-based techniques in HCI, that is by developing adaptive (or intelligent) systems, this problem can be effectively tackled. It concludes with an agenda for HCI research which arises from such an application of intelligence at the interface.

Human–Computer Interaction: INTERACT'97 S. Howard, J. Hammond & G. Lindgaard (editors)
Published by Chapman & Hall

There has, of course, been a large amount of research in artificial intelligence and knowledge-based techniques. Similarly there has been a lot of research in human-computer interaction. This tutorial does not seek to replicate any of this work. It takes as given the existence of various algorithms, heuristics and knowledge structures which may be used to implement intelligent or adaptive interfaces.

The contribution which the tutorial makes is to elucidate the what?, where? and when? questions surrounding the application of intelligence at the interface. The tutorial is rooted in the desire to improve human-computer interaction and in the contribution which knowledge-base techniques can make to that end. It seeks to identify where intelligent interface technology may be employed, what adaptive systems are like, when designers should consider using them and what types of analysis and design activities are required in order to construct them.

Any application of IIT must abstract aspects of the interaction by forming a dialogue record. It uses this, along with its internal representations, to make inferences about the user, to adapt aspects of the interaction and to evaluate its own operation. One of these representations is the user model. The structure and content of user models - particularly models of cognitive characteristics - is considered. The tutorial summarises the work on domain models and establishes a structure for these representations. Given this understanding of the structure and functions of adaptive systems, the tutorial looks at how intelligent interface technology can be used to improve the interaction and contribute to the usability of systems. In particular, the tutorial examines adaptive hypermedia and intelligent multi-media systems. Finally, the tutorial considers the wider impact which these developments may have on HCI and identifies a number of items which are now on the HCI research agenda.

References

AI Review (1993) *Special Issue on User Modelling*, McTear, M. (ed.) vol. 6 no.

Benyon, D.R. (1984) *Monitor: a self-adaptive user interface.* In: B. Shackel (Ed.), Proc. INTERACT '84, (Amsterdam: Elsevier Science Publishers B.V.).

Browne, D.P., Totterdell, P.A. and Norman, M.A. (1990) *Adaptive User Interfaces* : Academic Press, London

CACM (1994) *Special issue on Intelligent Agents*

Chignell, M.H. and Hancock, P.A. (1988) *Intelligent Interfaces* in M. Helander (Ed.) Handbook of Human-Computer Interaction (Amsterdam: Elsevier Science Publishers B.V.).

Connolly, J. H. and Edmonds, E.A . (eds.) (1993) *CSCW and AI Lawrence* Erlbaum, Brighton

Edmonds, E.A. (1981) Adaptive Man-Computer Dialogues. In Coombs, M. J. and Alty, J. L. *Computing Skills and the user Interface.* Academic Press, London

Gray, W., Heffley, W. and Murray, D. M. (eds.) (1993) *Proceedings of 1st international Workshop on Intelligent User Interfaces,* ACM Publications, New York

Kay, A. (1990) *User interface: A personal view*, B. Laurel (Ed.) *The Art of Human-Computer Interface Design*, Addison Wesley, Wokingham.

Knowledge-Based Systems, (1993) *Special Issue on Intelligent Interfaces*, Heffley, B. (ed.) vol. 6

Kobsa, A. and Wahlster, W. (1989) *User models in dialog systems* : Springer-Verlag, Berlin

Rich, E. (1979) User modelling via stereotypes, *Cognitive Science*, Vol. 3.

Schneider-Hufschmidt, M., Kuhme, T. and Malinowski, U. (eds.) (1993) *Adaptive User Interfaces - Results and Prospects,* Elsevier Science Publications, North-Holland, Amsterdam

Sullivan, J. W. and Tyler, S. W. (eds.) (1991) *Intelligent User Interfaces*, ACM Press, New York

Thimbleby, H. (1990) *User Interface Design* Addison Wesley, Wokingham

130

Scenario Based Requirements Generation Tools for Organisational Design

Ken Eason and Susan Harker

Department of Human Sciences
Loughborough University
Leics. LE11 3TU, UK.
E-mail: k.d.eason@lboro.ac.uk s.d.harker@lboro.ac.uk

ABSTRACT The tutorial provides participants with an understanding of the techniques available to assist with the development of options for organisational and technological change. The options provide a basis for evaluation and enable the specification of requirements for computer based systems. Experience of using of one of the techniques is applied to a case study based on the introduction of tele-medicine.

KEY WORDS Organisation, Users, Technological Change, Requirements

BACKGROUND

Modern information technology has the potential to transform the world of work. User organisations are faced with opportunities to exploit the capability of the technology to support virtual businesses, teleworking, electronic commerce, inter-organisational co-operation and many other things. Such developments offer the opportunity to become more competitive, to build new relationships with their suppliers and customers, to have staff work at home or in 'virtual settings', for example. Organisations contemplating such changes have little current experience of the relevant technology and therefore find it difficult to anticipate the effects it would have on their business or their staff. They may not appreciate that there are many different ways in which the technology may be applied nor that it may transform their ways of working in unanticipated ways. As a result, when they invest in new systems they often do so without a clear set of requirements or understanding of the issues that will be raised. These problems are manifest in the high rate of failure which occurs when organisational change accompanies technical innovation (Kearney 1994, LAS 1993).

THE OBJECTIVE

The objective of this tutorial is to provide participants with the opportunity to explore techniques which can be used to help people within organisations clarify their requirements when they are contemplating major change. These techniques seek to develop models of the future based on the user organisation and the technology. They provide the means for members of an organisation to evaluate the visions of the future embodied in the models in order that they can determine their requirements in relation to both the nature of the organisation and the form of information technology which is needed. One of these techniques is presented in depth in order to provide delegates with the opportunity to gain experience of how it works by applying it to a particular case study.

CONTENT

The techniques covered bring together a number of strands of work on requirements capture. They extend the concept of early prototyping of interfaces to the creation of prototypes with a broader socio-technical

Human–Computer Interaction: INTERACT'97 S. Howard, J. Hammond & G. Lindgaard (editors)
Published by Chapman & Hall

vision which include the future user roles and tasks as well as the technology. Another contribution comes from systems analysis techniques used to express organisational as well as technical requirements, including enterprise modelling (Martin and Dobson 1991), soft-systems analysis (Checkland 1981) and socio-technical systems analysis (Emery and Trist 1969). The way in which users need to be engaged with these techniques owes much to participative design techniques such as ETHICS (Mumford 1983) and to the forms of user participation practised in Search Conferences (Weisbord 1990)

The tutorial classifies the different approaches and assesses their strengths and weaknesses. The aim is to give attendees the opportunity to examine the issues associated with working with this kind of technique. The method presented in detail is ORDIT (Eason and Olphert 1996) (Organisational Requirements Definition for Information Technology Systems). This technique embodies the following features

(i) a method of modelling the socio-technical system which is based upon work roles, responsibilities and role relations which provides an integrating set of concepts linking the business process, the organisation and the technical system,

(ii) techniques for generating alternative models of future systems based upon early statements of user requirements,

(iii) ways of representing the alternative models in order that user participants can experience the essential elements of the future way of working and

(iv) evaluation techniques which enable users to assess a broad range of implications and as a result develop an informed set of requirements for the future system to be implemented.

The ORDIT approach is worked on using a case study in which a medical authority is planning to introduce tele-medicine linking local doctors (General Practitioners) and consultants in hospitals as a means of reducing the need for patients to travel for specialist attention. The tutorial includes presentations of two models of the future organisational framework in which tele-medicine is applied. One of these is offered as a scenario in which delegates can role play the users and undertake an evaluation of the impact on the different stakeholders and consider how this might affect the generation of requirements from an organisational perspective.

This experience provides tutorial participants with an opportunity to assess critical issues associated with these techniques, for example, the kind of requirements it leads to, the forms of model and representation needed and the processes needed for effective user engagement.

THE PRESENTERS

Ken Eason and Susan Harker are human factors specialists who have worked on the human and organisational aspects of developing and implementing IT systems in user organisations for over 20 years. They are currently working on methods of requirements capture and have created the ORDIT methodology as a comprehensive process for establishing the Organisational Requirements of future Information Technology Systems.

THE FORMAT OF THE TUTORIAL

The first half of the tutorial is devoted to a description of a number of requirements capture methods and an evaluation of their strengths and weaknesses. The second half of the tutorial will introduce the ORDIT methodology, and through the use of a case study, participants will undertake a scenario evaluation in a role play exercise.

REFERENCES

1. Checkland, P. (1981) 'Systems Thinking, Systems Practice', Wiley, Chichester.

2. Eason K.D. and Olphert, C.W. (1996) 'Early Evaluation of the Organisational Implications of CSCW Systems'. In: Thomas, P. (ed) 'CSCW Requirements and Evaluation', Springer-Verlag, London, pp 75-89.

3. Emery F. and Trist E. (1969) 'Socio-Technical Systems' In Emery (ed) 'Systems Thinking' Penguin, London.

4. Kearney J. (1994) 'The Cost of Implementing Information Technology' Scientific American, September.

5. L.A.S. (1993)' Report of the Enquiry into the London Ambulance Service' London Ambulance Service.

6. Martin, M. J. and Dobson, J. E. (1991) 'Enterprise modelling and security policies'. In Jajodia, S. and Landwehr, C. E. (eds), Database Security: Status and Prospects IV, North-Holland, Amsterdam. 117-150.

7. Mumford, E. (1983), 'Designing Human Systems'. Manchester Business School Publications, Manchester.

8. Weisbord, M.R. (1990) 'Productive Workplaces; Organising and Managing for Dignity, Meaning and Community'. Jossey-Bass, Oxford.

131

Activity Theory and HCI: Research and Practice

Helen Hasan, Edward Gould & Peter Hyland

Department of Business Systems
University of Wollongong
Wollongong 2522
AUSTRALIA
h.hasan@uow.edu.au

ABSTRACT The tutorial introduces attendees to Activity Theory, providing an overview of the theory as it applies to HCI and relating it to the use of information systems in organisations. An Activity Theory approach takes the whole activity as the core point of departure for any kind of human endeavour. The strengths of Activity Theory for HCI are its concept of tool mediation and its emphasis on activity in a social context.

KEY WORDS Activity Theory, Russian Psychology, Psychological Theory, Human-Computer Interaction

1. INTRODUCTION

In the development of the discipline of HCI, cognitive psychology has been a major influence on our current understanding of the characteristics and requirements of the human user of computer technology. This approach has led to rapid improvements in the usability of the technology by individuals but does not provide an appropriate conceptual basis for computer use in its wider social and organisational context. When cognitive psychology is applied, the HCI system is seen as being composed of two information processing units, the human being and the computer, so that the output of one unit is the input to the other. In this light, the role of the computer is seen as automating basic work practices by "replacing" the human. Many dynamic, interactive systems, such as decision support or management information systems, are not design to replace humans but rather as tools to support the higher-level decision making tasks which are not suitable for automation by existing technology. Such systems highlight the severe limitations of cognitive science as a theoretical basis to explain the interaction of people with the computer. A more holistic approach such as that provided by Activity Theory (AT) may be more helpful.

Activity Theory is a psychological theory developed by the Russian psychologists Vygotsky (1978), Leontjev (1981) and others during the first half of this century. The original foundation, as laid down by Vygotsky in the period 1920-30, revolves around the basic idea that human activity is mediated by cultural signs: words and tools, which cause changes in that activity, and thus its internal mental reflection. Vygotsky's work was continued by Leontjev who developed a conceptual framework for the theory of Activity.

An AT approach means that Activity is the core point of departure for any kind of human endeavour. AT is able to conceptualise humans in their context and positions tools, such as computerised information systems, as mediating work activities. An activity involves a **subject**, which can be a person or group, and an **object**, with a meaning beyond simple physical objects, but which includes social and cultural properties, more in the sense of the "object of the exercise". Activities are distinguished from each other

Human–Computer Interaction: INTERACT'97 S. Howard, J. Hammond & G. Lindgaard (editors)
Published by Chapman & Hall

according to their object, which motivates the activity transforming the object into its outcome. The strengths of AT are its concept of tool mediation and its emphasis on activity in social context. The holistic, centralised approach of AT to the use of technology is in stark contrast to that of cognitive science which, by virtue of its basic premise of the human as an information processor, has been forced into a piecemeal approach.

2. OBJECTIVES

The tutorial introduces attendees to AT, providing an overview of the theory as it applies to HCI and presenting a framework that relates to the use of information systems in organisations. We specifically show some examples of how this framework can provide a fresh perspective on certain extant problems in the fields of HCI. Participants should also become more aware of the nature and complexity of current controversies concerning the role of theory in HCI. As well as providing an introduction to the basic concepts of the theory, participants are given examples and a practical exercise illustrating how this general framework can be utilised in more specific settings. By the end of the tutorial, participants should be able to understand the basic principles of AT, and be able to describe their work activities in terms of this framework.

3. BACKGOUND

English translations of the original works of Vygotski (1978) and Leontjev 1981) are widely quoted by researchers in many fields. These are suggested reading for anyone wishing to come to terms with AT. However excellent companions to this tutorial would be the books by Bonnie Nardi (1996) and Susanne Boedker (1991), as well as publications of the presenters in this area .

4. CONTENT

The following topics are covered in the tutorial:

- Limitations of the cognitive science model of people as Information Processors
- The basic principles of AT
    - Activities as the objects of study
    - Object-orientedness
    - The Hierarchy of Activities
    - Internalisation / externalisation
    - Technical and Psychological Tools
    - Tool Meditation
    - The Dynamic Nature of Activity
- The Russian and Finnish Models of Activity
- Novice/expert differences and AT Hierarchies

5. PRESENTATION

As much of the information concerning AT may be new to participants the tutorial begins with an hour of substantial explanation and demonstration by the presenters. Following this the tutorial resembles more of a workshop format where participants are actively involved in applying AT concepts to real world problems. This leads to a discussion of the practical implications of what AT has to offer HCI.

The presenters have a background in Information Systems and Human-Computer Interaction. They were introduced to AT through the several East-West HCI conference held each year in Russia since 1991 and have formed cooperative reserach links with proponents of AT throughout the world.

6. REFERENCES

Aboulafia, A., Gould, E. and Spyrou, T., (1995) Activity Theory Vs Cognitive Science in the Study of Human-Computer Interaction, *IRIS 18*, Goeteborg, Sweden, 29-38.

Boedker, S., (1991) *Through the Interface - A Human Activity Approach to User Interface Design*, Lawrence Erlbaum.

Gould E.L. (1994) The Computer: A Brain or a Sophisticated Wheel? *Proceedings of the 38th Internation Conference for the Society for the Systems Sciences* California, 535-541.

Gould E and Hasan H (1995) An Activity Theory Approach to the HCI of Executive Information Systems *Proceedings of the East-West HCI Conference*, Moscow, 29-38.

Leontjev, A.N. (1981) *Problems of the Development of Mind* Moscow, Progress.

Nardi B. (1996) *Context and Consciousness: Activity Theory and Human-Computer Interaction* MIT Press.

Vygotsky, L.S. (1978) *Mind and Society*, Cambridge MA: Harvard University Press.

Adaptive Hypermedia: Systems, Efficient Techniques and Implementation on the World Wide Web

Peter Brusilovsky

School of Computer Science
Carnegie Mellon University
Pittsburgh 15213, USA
plb@cs.cmu.edu

ABSTRACT The aim of this 3-hour tutorial is to introduce the participants to *adaptive hypertext and hypermedia,* a new area of research in human-computer interaction, to present a number of recent efficient adaptive hypermedia technologies on a level of detail which will enable the use of these technologies in the attendees' own systems, and demonstrate the implementation of adaptive hypermedia on the WWW. The tutorial is oriented to an intermediate level audience: HCI researchers and practitioners interested in designing advanced hypermedia applications and advanced WWW applications, as well as researchers who work in, or who wish to learn more about, the field of adaptive and intelligent interfaces.

KEYWORDS adaptive hypermedia, navigation, WWW, electronic textbooks, user modeling

1. INTRODUCTION

Adaptive hypermedia (AH) is a new direction of research within the area of adaptive and user model-based interfaces. Adaptive hypermedia systems build a model of the individual user and apply it for adaptation to that user, for example, to adapt the content of a hypermedia page to the user's knowledge and goals, or to suggest the most relevant links to follow. AH systems are used now in several application areas where the hyperspace is reasonably large and where a hypermedia application is expected to be used by individuals with different goals, knowledge and backgrounds.

The goal of the tutorial is to present a practical introduction into adaptive hypermedia for an HCI-oriented audience. This introduction will cover the following issues: a brief review of adaptive hypermedia ideas and existing systems (including Web-based systems), a detailed description of several efficient and easy-to-implement adaptation techniques, and a step-by-step instruction in "how to implement your own adaptive hypermedia system on the WWW".

The first and second issues covered by the tutorial will be most interesting for HCI researchers who want to learn about adaptive hypermedia, adaptive interfaces, adaptive systems, and user modeling. The second and third issues will be most interesting for the practitioners who can benefit from making their Web-based systems adaptive. To support the practical level of presentation in the third part of the tutorial, some

Human–Computer Interaction: INTERACT'97 S. Howard, J. Hammond & G. Lindgaard (editors)
Published by Chapman & Hall

minimal prerequisite knowledge about WWW, HTML, and Common Gateway Interface is desirable.

2. OUTLINE OF THE CONTENT

1. Introduction: what is adaptive hypermedia (AH) and why it can be useful.

2. Where AH systems can be useful: review of existing application areas: educational hypermedia, information retrieval, on-line help and documentation systems, institutional hypermedia, personal information spaces

3. Adapting to what? Review of the most important features of the user which can be represented in the user model and used by adaptation techniques: knowledge on the subject, goals, background and experience, preferences.

4. What can be adapted in adaptive hypermedia. Introduction to general technologies of adaptation in AH: content adaptation, direct guidance, adaptive sorting of links, adaptive hiding of links, adaptive annotation of links, adaptive construction of hypermedia maps.

5. Methods and techniques of adaptation in AH systems. A review of existing techniques (about 20 existing techniques will be mentioned). Special attention will be paid to a detailed presentation of several selected techniques which proved to be efficient and can be relatively easy implemented: conditional explanations technique for content adaptation, adaptive annotation according the level of student knowledge, adaptive sorting of links according to their relevance, adaptive hiding of links to nodes "not-ready to be learned".

6. The role of user and the role of system in hypermedia adaptation. A review of different roles of user and system in the process of adaptation.

7. Efficacy of adaptive hypermedia. A brief review of known experimental studies of adaptive hypermedia. Experiments with content adaptation, adaptive sorting of links in IR hypermedia, adaptive annotation of links in educational hypermedia.

8. Lessons learned: a discussion on some requirements for creating effective adaptation techniques: transparency of adaptation, stepwise adaptation.

9. Implementation of AH techniques in Web based hypermedia systems. Examples. Implementation of adaptive annotation, hiding and sorting of links. Developing adaptive hypermedia with CGI scripts. Developing adaptive hypermedia MIT CL-HTTP second generation CL-HTTP server.

3.INSTRUCTOR

Peter Brusilovsky received his Ph.D. in Computer Science from the Moscow State University, 1987. His main research interests are Intelligent Tutoring Systems and Shells, Student and User Modeling, Adaptive Interfaces, and Adaptive Hypermedia Systems. He is an author of about 100 papers, editor of several conference proceedings, on the editorial panel for several journals, and member of program committees for a number of international and local conferences. In particular he is an author of recent review papers including reviews on adaptive hypermedia (Brusilovsky, 1996a; Brusilovsky, 1996b). He is an editor of several hypermedia-related books and a special issue of User Modeling and User-Adapted Interaction Journal (Kluwer) on adaptive hypermedia. He has been presenting his work at many international conferences, serving also as an invited speaker at several conferences including AI-ED'95. He has experience in presenting tutorials at several local and international conferences. The current adaptive hypermedia tutorial is an update of a popular tutorial presented at ED-MEDIA'96 conference in Boston.

REFERENCES

Brusilovsky, P. (1996a) Adaptive hypermedia, an attempt to analyze and generalize. In *Multimedia, Hypermedia, and Virtual Reality*, Lecture Notes in Computer Science, Vol. 1077, P. Brusilovsky, P. Kommers and N. Streitz (eds), Springer-Verlag, Berlin. pp. 288-304.

Brusilovsky, P. (1996b) Methods and techniques of adaptive hypermedia. *User Modeling and User-Adapted Interaction* **6** (2-3), 87-129.

PART SEVEN

Workshops

Relationships Between Work, Organisational Re–engineering and Information Systems

Patsy Segall

Union Research Centre on Organisation and Technology
171 La Trobe Street
Melbourne Australia 3000
zpatsy@minyos.its.rmit.edu.au

Andrew Clement

Faculty of Information Studies
University of Toronto
140 George Street
Toronto Canada M5S 1A1
clement@fis.utoronto.ca

Toni Robertson

School of Information Systems
University of New South Wales
Sydney Australia 2052
t.robertson@unsw.edu.au

ABSTRACT This workshop is sponsored by IFIP WG9.1 (Computers and Work), and the Union Research Centre on Organisation and Technology (URCOT). Increasingly organisations are under pressure to change their work practices and organisational structures. Typically these changes are supported by information and communication technologies that have major impacts on jobs, the workplace itself, and employment generally. Yet HCI research and practice have tended to focus on the interface between the individual user and the computer. This focus has excluded the relationships between the technology, the people who use it, the organisational environment and the work the technology is intended to support. The goal of the workshop is to clarify both the dynamics between organisational restructure and technological systems, as well as their implications for the work that is required to use the systems, how this is performed and under what conditions.

KEYWORDS Business process re–engineering, HCI in organisations, industrial democracy, management issues, user participation

1. PARTICIPANTS' PERSPECTIVES

Workshop participants will bring a range of perspectives to the issues under examination:

- experience in a particular kind of workplace, for example a teleservice centre;
- industry perspectives, for example the finance sector;
- specific areas under development for example electronic commerce;
- experience with a particular industrial agreement or dispute;
- analysis of relevant labour market and employment trends;
- case studies of organisational restructure and technological innovation.

Human–Computer Interaction: INTERACT'97 S. Howard, J. Hammond & G. Lindgaard (editors)
Published by Chapman & Hall

2. ISSUES IN ORGANISATIONAL CHANGE

There are pressures on organisations to restructure. Different types of organisational change have different implications and impacts. Examples include:

- business process re–engineering;
- multi-functional client–based teams;
- elimination of functions;
- downsizing;
- contracting of work, internally, externally;
- dispersal of work in space and time.

2.1 The Role of IT in Organisational Restructure

Requirements gathering for information systems involves multiple stakeholders, and is of great complexity.

The computer interface and systems can support intelligent, autonomous work (both individual and team) or enable 'plugging in' of operators to limited data entry or enquiry roles.

For systems developers there are specific issues:

- relationships with internal, external clients;
- responsibility for impact assessment;
- responsibility for user participation.

2.2 Employment and Quality of Work

For workers and their unions many issues arise:

- new kinds of work and employment relationships;
- hours and location of work;
- value of local knowledge and tailored customer service v. homogeneous service;
- if the technology is easy to use and requires little training, work can be moved off–shore relatively cheaply;
- worker participation in decision making and systems development;
- what should unions aim for in industrial agreements?
- relationships between unions in different countries.

3. ORGANISATION OF THE WORKSHOP

Participants will provide position papers for advance distribution. Formal group discussion of the papers will take place on 14 July, followed by optional participation in an additional half day's discussion to plan publication of material incorporating key aspects of papers and discussion.

HCI -- world wide

Lars Oestreicher[1], Matthias Rauterberg[2], Michael Tauber[3]

[1] Uppsala University
Department of Computing Science
P.O. Box 311, S-751 05 Uppsala
SWEDEN
larsoe@csd.uu.se

[2] Swiss Federal Institute of Technology (ETH)
Institute for Hygiene and Applied Physiology
Clausiusstr. 25, CH-8092 Zurich
SWITZERLAND
rauterberg@iha.bepr.ethz.ch

[3] University of Paderborn
Department of Mathematics
D-33095 Paderborn
GERMANY
tauber@uni-paderborn.de

ABSTRACT This workshop will be organized under the patronage of IFIP TC 13 "Human Computer Interaction" and establishes a platform to discuss international aspects of Human-Computer Interaction in different countries all over the world.

KEYWORDS international HCI, meta base, IFIP TC 13

1. OUTLINE OF THE THEME AND GOALS

The workshop is intended to address the status of Human-Computer Interaction (HCI) research and practise in different countries, with special attention paid to development countries. The outcome of the workshop should be an assessment of the HCI maturities and needs in different countries world wide, and the influence of their various cultures. One concrete outcome is a minimal definition/specification of an international resource database, ensuring that all participants will have the feeling that most of all relevant aspects are covered. This data-/meta-base will be accessable later on the World Wide Web under the patronage of IFIP TC 13.

Different cultures in different nations lead to different views on modern technology. These differences entail different needs and usage of technology. An overview and a comparison of these differences can help to get a better understanding of HCI activities world wide.

The main goal of the workshop is to broaden the knowledge assets to cover most relevant aspects of HCI on a truly international level, and to initiate a knowledge base that will cover international, rather than western/english aspects of HCI. This knowledge base will contain resources that can be of interest for international networking activities, and for local HCI communities, within single countries, cultures, too.

2. STATEMENTS OF HCI PEOPLE

World wide several HCI specialists were asked to describe their positions to the following three questions:

(1) Why is the topic "HCI world wide" interesting?
(2) What should be discussed at this WS?
(3) Who should participate, and/or be involved (organizations, people, nations)?

2.1 Africa

Edwin Blake is Professor and Head of Department of Computer Science (University of Cape Town, South Africa, edwin@cs.uct.ac.za). He wrote:

(ad 1): The global information society is upon us. A developing nation can exploit Information Technology (IT) to leapfrog into the new information age, or it can face new and debilitating forms of underdevelopment. Appropriate applications and content relevant to people's needs can only be developed via user centred design. The human aspects--usability, usefulness, empowerment, appropriateness, linguistic and cultural compatibility--are often more important to success or failure than the hardware and software. Currently, the majority of software applications originate in the developed world. Many are excellent, but sometimes the needs of the developing world are so different that completely new applications should be developed. For example, we have recently developed a pen based iconic interface that allows illiterate trackers to enter their field observations of endangered animals. The system is coupled to Satellite Positioning System (GPS) that records the location of the observations. Trackers have a very sophisticated understanding of their environment. As one of the trackers observed: "this machine makes me more intelligent", or rather, more effective. How IT is applied, and whose interests it serves, is central to whether this is an enabling technology, or a sophisticated way of keeping people and communities disempowered. The needs of the end users are paramount. One aim must be to break down the barrier between IT professionals and "ignorant users". People and nations have to understand and shape the applications rather than continually depend on external experts.

Human–Computer Interaction: INTERACT'97 S. Howard, J. Hammond & G. Lindgaard (editors)
Published by Chapman & Hall

(ad 2): User centred design for skilled but illiterate or semi-literate users. Effective tools for providing relevant content for multimedia and web based information.

(ad 3): The people who should attend the workshop should include both user interface specialists with an interest in the developing world and user centred system designers interested in the broader social functioning of computer and communications systems. A special effort should be made to attract user centred software developers from nations in the developing world.

Geoff Fairall lives in Zimbabwe (P O Box 2183, Harare, geoff@grf.icon.co.zw). He wrote:

(ad 1): Because it seems in so many developing countries that the HCI issues are being ignored with a potential for serious future consequences.

(ad 2): The most important aspect of HCI and Developing Countries (DCs) is the need to create awareness of the issues most likely to impact. I am not aware of any analysis of relevant issues to DCs that has been carried out but this would seem necessary. (I have recently been involved in computer operating environmental standards which were unheard of here and still a long way away from being enforced. More importantly to me is the role played for handicapped people and DCs do not have access to the services in industrialised countries - there ought to be a solution.)

2.2 Russia

Anna Leonova is Professor of Work and Engineering Psychology and Head of Laboratory for Human-Computer Interaction at Moscow State University (Russia, velich@psy1.psych.tu-dresden.de). She wrote:

(ad 1): The study of interaction between human and computers is relatively well-developed in Russia mostly from the perspective of Engeneering Psychology and Ergonomics. For a long period of time the use of computers was typical only for industrial jobs and broad distribution of the technology was limited. With the recent political changes also these artificial restriction have been abonded. Currently, there is a growing interest to the problems of HCI which is reflected in organization of several recent International East-West Conferences on CHI in Moscow and St.Petersburg. This development finds support from within the strong communities of software engineers and specialists in artificial intelligence. The main problem, at the moment, is the adaptation of international standards and methods of evaluation. The solurtion of this task can be achieved with concerted efforts of experts under auspiece of IFIP via WWW broadle accessible from the territory of former Soviet Union. The search for concrete solution of this problem should become the main topic of the WS.

2.3 Singapore

Kee Yong Lim is Senior Lecturer at the Nanyang Technological University (Singapore, mkylim@ntu-vax.ntu.ac.sg). Linda Herman is Managing Director and Principal Consultant of Ergonomics Design & Usability Consultants (Singapore, lindah@cyberway.com.sg). They wrote:

(ad 1): The focus of HCI has, in the past, followed closely developments in the IT industry. For instance, the initial focus of HCI was on supporting the development of personal applications, e.g. development of interaction models to support display design, etc. This initial focus was followed by wider consideration of organisational issues, e.g. when developing CSCW applications, etc. In this respect, socio-technical systems approaches and participative design techniques were developed to realise in full, the benefits of IT introduction. Now, with the emergence of a global market, the explosion of the WWW, and the advent of the information superhighway, the scope of HCI needs to be extended far beyond the user-centered design paradigm to span international and cross-cultural boundaries. This need should be investigated as it has been reported that HCI evaluation techniques developed in the West need to be tailored for application in the East, if reliable results are to be ensured. It is hoped that the workshop would help to highlight the HCI research agenda required to address political, sociological, economic and cross-cultural implications for design.

2.4 Sweden

Lars Oestreicher wrote:

(ad 1): One considerable problem concerning international HCI is the current dominance of Anglo-Saxon research. This has resulted in many unnecessary HCI problems, both large and small, such as the difficulty of sending an e-mail containing the word "Smörgåsbord" from one Swedish computer to another without it turning up as "Smlrg}sbord", or something even more unintelligible. Apparent is also the even greater ignorance about the special needs in HCI from the development countries. Through the gathering of researchers from a wide range of countries both these issues can be highlighted and combined into a first amendment of "international" HCI.

(ad 2): What can be done to remedy this situation? What are the international needs in HCI? An amendment of international HCI.

(ad 3): The participants should be selected so that they will represent the different continents as well as possible (Europe, North America, South America, Afrika, Australia and Asia).

Integrating software engineering and HCI

David Benyon, Alistair Kilgour and Bengt Sandblad

Napier University,
Dept. Computer Studies
219, Colinton road,
Edinburgh, EH9 2JU
d.benyon@dcs.napier.ac.uk

Heriot-Watt University,
Dept. Computer Science,
Riccarton,
Edinburgh
ack@cee.hw.ac.uk

Center for Human-Computer Studies,
Uppsala University,
S-752 37 Uppsala
bengt.sandblad@cmd.uu.se

Abstract: There can be little doubt that human-computer interaction has become a fundamental consideration in computer science. All but the most theoretical of computer science and computer studies courses in higher education now include HCI as a core subject and commercial methods for interactive systems development are increasingly paying attention to the needs of users. The purpose of this workshop is to bring together researchers and practitioners in order to explore further the issues of integrating HCI and SE.

Key Words: Software Engineering methods, HCI, SE/HCI

1. INTRODUCTION

There can be little doubt that human-computer interaction has become a fundamental consideration in computer science. All but the most theoretical of computer science and computer studies courses in higher education now include HCI as a core subject and commercial methods for interactive systems development are increasingly paying attention to the needs of users. Methods such as STUDIO (Browne, 1993) have recently been published aimed at making HCI approaches available to systems developers and conceptualisations of the development process such as MUSE (Lim and Long, 1994) aim to show where and how software engineering and HCI should come together and share knowledge of the design process. The popularity of scenario-based design (Carroll, 1995) and its relationship with object-oriented methods of systems development such as Objectory (Jacobson, *et al.*, 1995) represents another point of contact.

However, there remain many difficulties in producing a truly united approach to interactive systems development which deals adequately with both software engineering and human-computer interaction issues (e.g. Benyon and Palanque, 1996). Some of these are primarily practical, e.g. can we find a common language for software engineers and human factors experts to use? Others are more theoretical, e.g. are the concepts employed by the two disciplines compatible?

2. THE ROLE OF TASK ANALYSIS IN SYSTEMS DESIGN

One area of debate concerns the importance of the concept of a 'task' in HCI. This concept has dominated the ontology of HCI since the earliest days as the wealth of literature on task analysis techniques will demonstrate (e.g. Diaper, 1989). However, others (e.g. Fischer, 1989) argue for a communication model of HCI. This model recognises the existence of shared knowledge in a particular problem domain. Humans and computers possess different but complementary knowledge and skills and should cooperate in the problem-solving activity.

The debate about the role of task in systems development is unresolved (Benyon, 1992; Diaper and Addison, 1992). To what extent can the concept of task be introduced into software engineering methods and to what extent is the

Human–Computer Interaction: INTERACT'97 S. Howard, J. Hammond & G. Lindgaard (editors)
Published by Chapman & Hall

notion of task a useful and important concept in interactive systems design?

3. MODELS IN HCI/SE

A recent approach to user interface systems engineering is the 'model-based' approach (e.g. Sukaviriya, *et al.*, 1993). In this approach a domain, or application model is constructed which forms the basis for automated, semi-automated or manual systems design. The model-based approach promises to have many benefits, but one fundamental question which remains begging concerns the nature of the domain model; what should it be like, what should it focus upon?

A domain model for the purpose of software re-use may look very different from a domain model which has the purpose of automatically generating the human-computer interface. There are a number of candidate methods and formalisms which address both the conception and modelling of human-computer systems which focus on different aspects of HCI and SE (Sutcliffe, *et al.*, 1996). How can more recent approaches to HCI such as Activity Theory (Bødker, 1990) or Distributed Cognition (Hutchins, 1995) be reconciled with the needs and concepts of SE?.

4. DESIGN APPROACHES

Most attempts at providing an integrated framework for HCI/SE (e.g. Lim and Long, 1994) present the concerns of SE and HCI running in parallel rather than being cooperative and integrated. Participative approaches to systems design and cooperative design (e.g. Greenbaum and Kyng, 1991) appear to conflict with the need to fix requirements as demanded by an engineering approach. Alternative life cycles such as the Star or the spiral model need to be reconciled. How can designers include efficient interface design and development methods and techniques into an Object Oriented modelling and development environment?

5. CONCLUSIONS

The need to bring together and to integrate software engineering and HCI can only be addressed by discussion between the software engineering and human-computer interaction communities. This is as true from the perspective of systems developers as it is from the perspective of computer science educators. In the future do we expect our software engineers to be experts in HCI, or do we expect our HCI experts to be software engineers? This workshop will take an important step towards focusing the important issues and setting the agenda for future work in the area.

REFERENCES

Benyon, D.R. (1992) The Role of Task Analysis in Systems design in *Interacting with Computers* 4(1)

Benyon, D. R. and Palanque, P. (1996) (eds.) *Critical Issues in User Interface Systems Engineering* . Springer-Verlag; London

Bødker, S. (1990) *Through the Interface.* Lawrence Erlbaum; Hillsdale, NJ

Browne, D. (1993) *STUDIO* Prentice Hall

Carroll, J. (1995) *Scenario-based design* Wiley, New York

Diaper, D. (1989) (ed.) *Task Analysis for Human-Computer Interaction.* Ellis-Horwood,

Diaper, D. and Addison, M. (1992) Task Analysis and Systems Analysis for Software Development. In: *Interacting with Computers*.vol. 3(3) pp 124 - 139,

Fischer, G. (1989) Human-Computer Interaction Software: Lessons Learned, Challenges Ahead *IEEE Software,* (January) pp 44-52

Greenbaum, J. and Kyng, M. (eds.) (1991) *Design at Work: Cooperative Design of Computer Systems.* Lawrence Erlbaum Associates: Hillsdale, NJ

Hutchins, E. (1995) *Cognition in the Wild.* MIT press

Jacobson, J., Chistensen, M., Johnson, P. and Overgaard, G. (1993) *Object-Oriented Software Engineering*. Addison-Wesley

Lim, K. Y. and Long, J. (1994) *The MUSE method for usability engineering* Cambridge University Press

Sukaviriya, N., Foley, J. and Griffith (1993) A second generation user interface design environment. *Proceedings of interchi 93*, ACM publications, 375-382

Sutcliffe, A. G., Benyon, D. R. and Bubenko, J. (1996) (eds.) *Domain Knowledge for Interactive Systems Design.* Chapman and Hall; London

136

Workshop on "Guidelines for the design of HCI for people with disabilities"

Julio G. Abascal (1)
Monique Noirhomme-Fraiture (2)
Helen Petrie (3)
Floris Van Nes (4)

(1) Chairman of the IFIP WG 13.3
Laboratory of HCI for Special Needs. U. of the Basque Country (Spain)
(2) Institut d'Informatique, Facultés Univ. N.D. de la Paix. Namur (Belgium)
(3) University of Hertfordshire (UK)
(4) Institute for Perception Research. University of Eindhoven (NL).
(1) julio@si.ehu.es
(2) mnoirhomme@info.fundp.ac.be
(3) H.L.Petrie@herts.ac.uk
(4) flvannes@prl.philips.nl

Abstract This workshop, run by IFIP WG 13.3 Human Computer Interaction and Disability, aims to collect and discuss previously issued sets of guidelines, and to establish criteria to be able to develop a reviewed classification of guidelines. It is intended to make a contribution in helping designers world-wide find relevant guidelines to include the needs of elderly and disabled users.

Key words People with special needs, Design rationale, Standards and guidelines, Individual differences

Guidelines for the design of HCI for people with disabilities

"To make HCI designers aware of the needs of people with disabilities" and "To monitor the latest developments in the design of HCI and their impact on accessibility and usability" were two of the goals defined in the document proposing to the International Federation for Information Processing the creation of a

Human–Computer Interaction: INTERACT'97 S. Howard, J. Hammond & G. Lindgaard (editors)
Published by Chapman & Hall

Working Group on Human-Computer Interaction and Disability.

In its first meeting, held in Donostia-San Sebastián (Spain) on November/1993, the newly created working group, named IFIP WG 13.3, modified and extended its terms of reference. One of the most significant addition was this goal: **"To recommend guidelines for the design of HCI to facilitate the use of computers by people with disabilities"**.

It is felt that the WG can make a contribution in helping designers world-wide find relevant guidelines to include the needs of elderly and disabled users. WG 13.3 does not plan to develop a new set of guidelines, as much work has already been done in this area, e.g., by the TRACE CENTER[1], University of Madison, Wisconsin, USA, or the guidelines for software designers by the Sensory Disabilities Research Unit, University of Hertfordshire (Petrie, 95).

Thus, this workshop, run by WG 13.3, aims to collect and discuss previously issued sets of guidelines, and to establish criteria to be able to develop a reviewed classification of guidelines. To achieve previously mentioned goals two kind of interventions are foreseen:

- WG 13.3 will provide a list of keynote speakers to speak about criteria to analyse HCI guidelines.
- Authors are going to be asked to present papers about different sets of guidelines and other relevant material, (e.g. market figures to show implications for design and what industry will get out of it).

These guidelines and other materials will be considered according to their usability, user needs awareness, methodological aspects, evaluation procedures, etc., both from the point of view of users with disabilities and also the designers.

In this workshop discussions will also taken place as to how best to proceed to offer and disseminate the resulting conclusions through the IFIP media, for example whether designers would welcome a more concise paper document or a regularly updated WWW site.

References

(Petrie, 95) Helen Petrie "A Functional Classification of Disabilities: Implications for the Design of Accessible Technology" Proceedings of the European Conference on the Advancement of Rehabilitation Technology, ECART 3, October 10-13, 1995. Lisbon (P), pp. 250-252

[1] WWW address: trace.wisc.edu, under the menu items: Universal Access project and Project Info Curbcuts (General Information on the NII [the "Master Doc"],Project publications, Access to the NII by People with Disabilities or who are Aging.)

In and Out of the Box: Interaction Paradigms in Electronic Environments

Jacquelyn Martino and Lira Nikolovska
Philips Research, A division of Philips Electronics North America
345 Scarborough Road
Briarcliff, NY 10510 USA
tel: 914.945.6290
e-mail: iam@philabs.research.philips.com
L.Nikolovska@DESIGN.CORP.philips.com

ABSTRACT This two-day cross-disciplinary workshop is for those who have developed alternative interaction paradigms in electronic environments. The goal is to exchange information on issues surrounding the design and theory of electronic environments. The design of these environments stimulates innovative interaction paradigms while considering the boundaries that the physical computer may or may not present. Interaction designers, architects, artists, industrial designers, computer scientists, writers, cinematographers, media theorists, cognitive and perceptual psychologists, ergonomists and educators all look at the problem of engaging the user and creating solutions for users of electronic environments from different points of view. In this workshop we discuss the concepts and ideas that lead these innovators to designing alternative interaction paradigms.

KEYWORDS interaction design, immersive virtual environments, information spaces, input devices, interaction models

1. THEME OF THE WORKSHOP

This two-day workshop focuses on cross-disciplinary discussion of topics relevant to alternative user interaction paradigms that occur both inside and outside of the boundaries defined by the physical computer or "the box." In contrast to traditional interaction paradigms (e.g. windows, menus and icons accessed by mice and keyboards), approaches that challenge the physical or metaphorical boundaries of the computer lead to alternative interaction paradigms. Workshop themes are:

1. Alternative interaction paradigms that may include 3D graphics, 2D graphics and/or original hardware configurations,

2. Approaches to designing and theorizing electronic environment creation and interactions within these environments.

In preparing for the workshop, participants should consider the following questions:

1. Does the computer impose boundaries? How are the activities that occur inside and outside the edges of the computer monitor mitigated by the interaction paradigm?

2. What are the approaches and methodologies for designing electronic environments and alternative interaction paradigms?

3. How can traditional approaches and methodologies from disciplines such as architecture, industrial design, graphic design, fine arts, cinematography, psychology

Human–Computer Interaction: INTERACT'97 S. Howard, J. Hammond & G. Lindgaard (editors)
Published by Chapman & Hall

and education be translated to the design of electronic environments and alternative interaction paradigms?

4. How is traditional training transformed by the ability to design electronic environments and alternative interaction paradigms?

5. What knowledge from real world experiences can be applied to the design of electronic environments making human interaction natural and intuitive?

Although the specific discussions will be shaped by the participants' positions, the organizing topics are as follows:

1. Innovative interaction paradigms in
- art, education, training and entertainment
- information visualization
- cyber architecture
- immersive and non-immersive virtual environments

2. Interfaces and interaction paradigms in and out of the box, including
- intelligent objects and intelligent spaces
- computer-augmented environments and devices
- innovative input devices
- immersive and non-immersive virtual environments

3. Applied design concepts and methodologies

4. Theoretical and conceptual design frameworks

5. Spatial perception and cognition, including reflections on issues of relationship between physical and abstract information configuration and comprehension

6. Visions for future research

2. Goal of the Workshop

Many solutions exist to the problem of designing and theorizing electronic environments. Solutions may be immersive or non-immersive, require conscious participation or be transparent to the user. The common thread, however, remains that computer users live in a spatial world with functional understanding of interaction in day to day life. The goal of the workshop is to explore how diverse practitioners use this common understanding to manage electronic environment experiences through the development of their interaction paradigms. The issue at question is not if real world interaction is superior or inferior to electronic interaction, but to look critically into the potentials for designing and theorizing for the new electronic media that is already in use.

3. Participants

A maximum of sixteen workshop participants with demonstrable experience in developing and theorizing alternative interaction paradigms and who represent a wide variety of backgrounds will form three to four panels. The panels will be formed according to topics presented in position papers. Each panel will present to the remaining participants to foster interesting and provocative discussion.

4. Description of Workshop Activities

Day 1:

- General introduction position presentation by the organizers, with stress on the topics and goals of the workshop
- Position papers presented by individual workshop participants

Day 2:

- Topic-clustered panel sessions moderated by a pre-determined participant. Position papers of the panelists will serve as a framework for discussion. Panel moderators are responsible for developing a set of questions based on panelists' topic expertise. The goal is to tackle the topic from individual perspectives while engaging other workshop participants in active discussion.
- Closing statement by organizers, shaped by the discussions that took place during the workshop.

Summary of the INTERACT97 Workshop on the Next Generation of CSCW Systems

John Grundy

Department of Computer Science
University of Waikato
Private Bag 3105, Hamilton
NEW ZEALAND
jgrundy@cs.waikato.ac.nz

ABSTRACT The INTERACT'97 Workshop on the Next Generation of CSCW Systems focuses on new directions for CSCW. Participants are selected on the basis of short position papers which provide forward-looking insights into CSCW. Position papers cover diverse, yet related, topics ranging from new theoretical foundations for CSCW, design methodologies and HCI issues in groupware, architectures and infrastructure for groupware, evaluation of CSCW systems, and new applications for CSCW. All accepted position papers appear in the workshop proceedings, and it is intended to make this available electronically via the World Wide Web.

KEYWORDS CSCW, groupware, theory, design, infrastructure, evaluation, applications

1. WORKSHOP OVERVIEW

CSCW is a rapidly-expanding area of interest. Current research work in CSCW ranges from developing new theoretical models of how people can cooperatively work together using computer support (Fitzpatrick et al., 1995), investigating new design methodologies for CSCW systems (Reeves, 1996), developing new HCI techniques for use by groupware (Greenberg et al., 1996), developing new infrastructure for groupware (Patterson, 1995), conducting evaluations of CSCW systems (Twidale et al., 1994), and exploring ever-more diverse applications for CSCW technologies (Venable and Travis, 1996).

This workshop focuses on such next-generation issues in CSCW. General topics of the workshop include:

- new theoretical insights into CSCW
- new HCI issues in CSCW
- new design methodologies for groupware
- new infrastructure and architecture approaches
- new evaluation techniques or results of evaluations of CSCW systems
- new applications of CSCW

Participants are selected based on short position papers submitted for the workshop. Position papers are refereed by the workshop committee comprising of leading CSCW researchers and practitioners. All accepted position papers appear in the workshop proceedings. It is intended to make this accessible electronically via the WWW from:
http://www.cs.waikato.ac.nz/~jgrundy/interact_ws.html

2. WORKSHOP TOPICS

Topics for the workshop are grouped according to three key themes, as outlined below.

Human–Computer Interaction: INTERACT'97 S. Howard, J. Hammond & G. Lindgaard (editors)
Published by Chapman & Hall

2.1. Theoretical and Design Issues

Position papers focusing on this sub-theme present new insights into the nature of CSCW, how it effects collaborative work, and how a better understanding of the nature of CSCW can enble better groupware systems to be built and utilised.

Next-generation design issues include new methodologies for developing groupware systems, utilising new understandings of CSCW to influence the design process, and new HCI issues relevant to CSCW.

2.2. Infrastructure and Architecture Issues

This sub-theme is concerned with new infrastructure for support of groupware applications. Existing computer technologies do not sufficiently support the development of groupware as they focus on single-user applications and interfaces.

A related issue is next-generation software architectures for the construction of groupware. Such architectures may utilise component-based approaches, specialised architecture description languages, or new toolkits for groupware development.

2.3. Evaluation and New Applications

A crucial issue in the effective development and deployment of CSCW is identifying when different kinds of CSCW support is appropriate. Next-generation evaluation issues include methodologies for evaluating CSCW systems, results of evaluations of CSCW systems, and how evaluation results can be utilised to better understand CSCW and improve deployment of CSCW systems.

An ever-increasing number of applications are being developed which exhibit greater or lesser degrees of CSCW aspects. This sub-theme attempts to identify domains where CSCW can be effectively utilised, how CSCW systems can be deployed in these areas, and how the use of CSCW systems might affect how work is carried out within an organisation.

3. WORKSHOP ORGANISATION

This is a one-day workshop which comprises three sessions focusing on the sub-themes as outlined above, followed by a general discussion session. The sub-theme sessions enable participants to focus on theoretical and design issues which underlie CSCW, examine next-generation infrastructure and architectural issues which impact on the realisation of groupware, and examine how evaluations of CSCW systems can be utilised to improve our understanding and deployment of groupware in diverse situations.

A session leader will facilitate the discussion for each session, including summarising the position papers relevant to each session's sub-theme. The general discussion at the end of the workshop will provide an opportunity to relate and summarise issues raised in the preceding sessions.

4. SUMMARY

The INTERACT97 Workshop on the Next Generation of CSCW Systems is an informal gathering of researchers and practitioners to discuss forward-looking issues relevant to the CSCW field. It is hoped that during the course of this workshop a fruitful exchange of ideas between people working on disparate, yet related, aspects of CSCW will occur, and complementary research agendas may be facilitated.

4. REFERENCES

Fitzpatrick, G. Tolone, W.J., and Kaplan, S.M. (1995) Work, locales and distributed social wOrldS, in *Proceedings of the 4th European Conference on CSCW*, Kluwer Academic Publishers.

Greenberg, S., Gutwin, C. and Roseman, M. (1996) Semantic telepointers in groupware, in *Proceedings of OZCHI'96*, Hamilton, New Zealand, November 25-27, 1996, IEEE CS Press.

Patterson, J.F. (1995) A taxonomy of architectures for synchronous groupware applications, *SIGOIS Bulletin*, **15** (3), p. 27-29.

Reeves, S.V. (1996) Specifying and Reasoning about CSCW, in *Proceedings of DSV-IS'96*, Springer-Verlag.

Twidale, M., Randall, D., and Bently, R. (1994) Situated evaluation for Cooperative Systems, in *Proceedings of CSCW'94*, ACM Press.

Venable, J.R. and Travis, J. (1996) CSCW to Support Participative Systems Development, in *Proceedings of the OZCHI'96 Workshop on the Next Generation of CSCW Systems*, Hamilton, New Zealand, November 25, 1996, Department of Computer Science, University of Waikato.

Teaching HCI and Design of Interactive Systems

Peter Gorny
University of Oldenburg,
Oldenburg, Germany
Gorny@informatik.uni-oldenburg.de
http:=//www-cg-hci.informatik.uni-oldenburg.de

Thomas T. Hewett
Drexel University,
Philadelphia, PA, USA
HEWETT@duvm.ocs.drexel.edu
http://duvm.ocs.drexel.edu/~hewett/

IFIP Working Group 13.1 (Education in HCI and HCI Curriculum) continues discussion about how to organize the qualification process for HCI in Higher Education. In several workshops that have taken place at other conferences, and in a recent IFIP Workshop on Teaching Design of Interactive Systems, the aim has been to explore issues and enhance the integration of HCI education in the curricula of different disciplines such as Computer Science, Psychology, Graphics Design and, because of the growing use of embedded computer systems in all kinds of devices, Industrial Design.

In the conference workshop on Education in HCI: Transcending Disciplinary and National Boundaries held at INTERACT'90, the initial discussions quickly revealed that the structure of a university education in each of the countries represented at the workshop was different enough that discussing curricula within these structures was relatively difficult and that there was a strong need to establish a common terminology. The workshop participants also discovered that the different educational structures had a major impact on the ability to cross disciplinary boundaries, a necessity for the field of HCI. After the workshop participants had laid out the different structures of education, they identified the professional categories which students were being educated and trained to fill. These categories were: The Researcher, The Professionally Oriented Researcher, The Research Oriented Professional, and The Professional. In this workshop there was both strong and profound agreement on the categories, even though the academicpaths leading to them were different (Mantei, Hewett, Eason & Preece, 1991).

Human–Computer Interaction: INTERACT'97 S. Howard, J. Hammond & G. Lindgaard (editors)
Published by Chapman & Hall

In the conference workshop on Advances in Teaching the HCI Design Process, held over 2 days at INTERCHI 93, the emphasis was upon presentation of and practice with HCI design concepts, with four presentations by guest speakers articulating a variety of views. One of the important results of this workshop was a recognition on the part of many participants that tension and uncertainty are both a natural and a healthy part of teaching HCI design. Arising from different teaching approaches, different disciplines, different emphases on design product and design process, and different teaching philosophies, the underlying tensions and uncertainties in teaching HCI design can be used to improve the teaching-learning environment for both student and teacher (Gasen, Preece, Gorny, & Hewett, 1994).

In the IFIP Workshop on Teaching Design of Interactive Systems, held over 3 working days in Shaerding, Austria in May of 1997, the initial emphasis was on attempting to engage the participants in developing a common vision of the ideal way to teach design of interactive systems. The goal was to try to break free of the constraints imposed by different working environments, disciplines and organizational burdens to envision the future of teaching HCI Design. The follow up discussions were focused on attempting to use the common vision to derive recommendations for various educational settings. Preparation of a report on the position papers, the conclusions and recommendations, and the other results of this workshop is in progress.

In the conference workshop Teaching HCI and Design of Interactive Systems, held at INTERACT 97, the issue of integration of HCI education in the curricula of different countries and disciplines is revisited with participants from countries not represented in earlier workshops. The discussion is intended to focus in part on comparison of present approaches in different countries and subject areas. The expected result is a set of outlines for recommendations to serve as the basis for further development of HCI related education after the workshop.

References

Gasen, J. B., Preece, J., Gorny, P., & Hewett, T. (1994). Advances in Teaching the HCI Design Process. ACM SIGCHI Bulletin, 26 (1), 9-12.

Mantei, M., Hewett, T., Eason, K. & Preece, J. (1991). Report on the INTERACT '90 Workshop on Education in HCI: Transcending disciplinary and national boundaries. Interacting with Computers, 3, 232-240.

140

Dealing with Undo

Roberta Mancini*, Alan J. Dix+ and Stefano Levialdi*

* Dipartimento di Scienze dell'Informazione, Università degli Studi di Roma "La Sapienza", Via Salaria 113, 00198, Rome, Italy

+ School of Computing, Staffordshire University, PO Box 334, Beaconside, Stafford ST18 0DG, United Kingdom

e-mail address: roberta@dsi.uniroma1.it, A.J.Dix@soc.staffs.ac.uk, levialdi@dsi.uniroma1.it

ABSTRACT: In this paper we are going to take into account non-determinism in human-computer interaction. When a user is in control on the dialogue, that is he knows the system state and the system behaviour after any performed action, then the interaction is deterministic. Generally, an undo helps the user in *handling* non-determinism when he is employing such function as a navigational tool, and/or in reducing non-determinism when he is employing it as a recovery function. Unfortunately, not all functions at the application level may be undone; moreover, an undo may behave differently in different situations. As result, we have that the undo also adds risk along the interaction: the more powerful the system, the higher the risk!

KEYWORDS: HCI, undo, non-determinism, dialogue, granularity, PIE model.

1. Introduction

Predictions have always been very important to humans. This happened and happens because, in order to predict something, it is necessary to know the object of the prediction, and such a knowledge is, in some sense, a form of control, of power. For a human, a prediction about something is the expression of his power on that thing. It is possible to do very precise predictions in a closed world, accounted by mathematically expressed physical laws, because these are independent from the human behaviour (Barrow, 1988). But when humans are involved in something, it is not possible to do predictions any more. Human behaviour follows no physical law. Since humans play a role in HCI and they are unpredictable, the resulting interaction is non-deterministic. In this paper, we analyse non-determinism in interaction and we identify in the undo function a way to handle and reduce non-determinism.

2. Undo and non-determinism

While interacting with a computer, any user would like to feel in control on the dialogue. In order to do this, Cole, Lansdale and Christie (Cole 1985) suggested that any user should be able to answer the following questions: *Where am I? How did I get here? What can I do? Where can I go next?*

Analysing the answers of the four above questions we may note that, in order to really feel in control of his dialogue, the user basically needs to know the system state and the system behaviour after any one of his actions. When using interactive systems, the knowledge on system state and behaviour may be increased by employing the undo. In fact, not only undo allows the user to repair an error, if it occurs, by reaching a past state, but it also enables the user to handle and reduce non-determinism. More precisely, when a user is navigating through a system, exploiting the exploratory aspect, typical of interactive systems, he is enriching his knowledge about the system's behaviour. In this case he *handles* non-determinism. However, his knowledge is related to the external system behaviour, not to the internal system structure or status. Instead, if there is a mismatch between the user's and system's model, then an inexact matching between the interpretation of the user's action from the system's point of view and from the user's point of view occurs. In this case, the undo functions may provide more information on the internal system structure, so *reducing* non-determinism (Mancini 1996).

Often, undo is a very powerful tool, allowing the user to repair an error, but sometimes it may add confusion to the user while interacting. How many times have we tried to perform undo and, although present on the interface, such function was not allowable? Or how many times have we performed undo obtaining something different from what we expected? Such confusion is due to the fact undo is not as easy as it looks; in fact, it is a very complex function and we cannot simply say that it cancels the effect of the last performed action(s). The last action with respect to what? Last from the user's point of view, that is the last action in the interaction (the last user performed action), or from the computer's point of view, that is the last action in the computation, the last action which modified the result? For example, if working with a word processor a user types a word, then uses the scrollbar and then applies undo, which action will be cancelled? The typing, the scroll or both? The incomplete knowledge about what and how undo acts, makes its behaviour unpredictable, so adding non-determinism in interaction. An exhaustive discussion about different undo semantics is provided in (Yang 1988, Mancini 1996, Mancini 1997).

2. Undo and risky interaction

The undo function is useful to reduce the risk in interaction (Dix 1996). But what is this risk? The first kind of risk may be due to the presence of user's errors (slips) while interacting, so the undo can help the user in recovering from errors. Moreover, the other risk is due to the mismatch between the user's and system's point of view on the same action.

Anyway, not always the presence of undo assures a reliable interaction: in fact, it often can make a system more risky when, after performed an undo, the system behaves differently from the foreseen way. This means that the behaviour of this system function may add non-determinism in interaction when it is slightly inconsistent. But does it matter? For 99% of the time undo works, this is better than systems where undo was either absent or frequently did not work. Or is it? If undo works almost all the time, then users may become used to it. Indeed, one of the advantages of having undo is that users can take a more exploratory approach to their interaction, trying out possible courses of action, but then retracing their steps if negative results occur, i.e. their behaviour is more risky. But if they become more risky then they are more likely to do things that need undo, and if undo does not work uniformly then they will have problems which would never have occurred if they had been more careful. So although a 99% effective undo may be better than having no undo at all, there will be errors that occur when you have undo which would not have happened if you had never had undo at all!

8. Conclusions

In this paper issues related to non-determinism in interaction have been investigated. It has been stressed that undo function allows the user to feel more in control in his computer dialogue. In particular, such a function allows the user to handle and reduce non-determinism when it is used as navigational tool and recovery function respectively. Even if the undo allows the user to handle and reduce non-determinism, it is not always clear how and on which objects it acts. This incomplete knowledge on its behaviour adds, by itself, non-determinism to interaction, making it more risky.

9. References

[Barrow 1988] J.D. Barrow, *The world within the world*, Oxford University Press, 1988.

[Cole 1985] I. Cole, M.W. Lansdale and B. Christie, Dialogue Design Guidelines, in *Human Factors of Information Technology in the Office*, B. Christie ed., pp. 212-241, Wiley Inc.

[Dix 1996] A.J. Dix, R. Mancini and S. Levialdi, Alas I have undone- Reducing the risk of interaction?, in *Ancillary Proceedings of HCI'96*, A. Blandford and H. Thimbleby eds., pp. 51-56, The British HCI Group.

[Mancini 1996] R. Mancini, A. Dix and S. Levialdi, Formal and Informal Definitions of Undo, Research Report RR9611, School of Computing and Mathematics, University of Huddersfield, UK, 1996.

[Mancini 1997] Modelling Interactive Computing by exploiting the Undo, PhD thesis IX-97-5, Università degli Studi di Roma "La Sapienza", 1997.

[Yang 1988] Y. Yang, Undo support models, *International Journal of Man-Machine Studies*, N° 28, pp. 457-481, 1988.

INDEX OF CONTRIBUTORS

KEYWORD INDEX

GPSR Compliance
The European Union's (EU) General Product Safety Regulation (GPSR) is a set of rules that requires consumer products to be safe and our obligations to ensure this.

If you have any concerns about our products, you can contact us on

ProductSafety@springernature.com

In case Publisher is established outside the EU, the EU authorized representative is:

Springer Nature Customer Service Center GmbH
Europaplatz 3
69115 Heidelberg, Germany

www.ingramcontent.com/pod-product-compliance
Ingram Content Group UK Ltd.
Pitfield, Milton Keynes, MK11 3LW, UK
UKHW051455290926
15471UKWH00008B/1212
* 9 7 8 1 4 7 5 7 5 4 3 6 0 *